Themes and Writers Series

G. Robert Carlsen
General Editor

FOCUS *Themes in Literature*

PERCEPTION *Themes in Literature*

INSIGHTS *Themes in Literature*

ENCOUNTERS *Themes in Literature*

AMERICAN LITERATURE *Themes and Writers*

WESTERN LITERATURE *Themes and Writers*

About the Editors of the Themes and Writers Series

G. Robert Carlsen, Professor of English and Professor of Education at the University of Iowa, has taught English in the public schools of Minneapolis and at the universities of Minnesota, Colorado, Texas, Hawaii, and Iowa. He has served as consultant in curriculum revision to a number of school systems in Texas, Iowa, Colorado, California, Oklahoma, and Virginia. For many years he was book review editor of young people's books for the *English Journal* and was coauthor of an edition of *Books for You.* Dr. Carlsen is a past president of the National Council of Teachers of English. He has written some seventy articles for professional journals and is coauthor of *The Brown-Carlsen Test of Listening Comprehension* and of the National Council of Social Studies' publication entitled *Social Understanding Through Literature.* He is also an author of *Books and the Teen-Age Reader.*

Anthony Tovatt is Professor of English at Burris Laboratory School of Ball State University. Dr. Tovatt has been the director of an extended research study on the teaching of composition under the Program for English of the United States Office of Education. He has been cited by the National Council of Teachers of English and the Indiana Council of Teachers of English for outstanding contributions to the teaching of English in the secondary school. Since 1955 he has been a column editor of the *English Journal.* His articles have been published in many professional journals, and his poetry has appeared in magazines and newspapers.

Edgar H. Schuster, Assistant Professor of English at Beaver College, has taught in both urban and suburban high schools in the Philadelphia area, as well as at the college level. He has written articles for many professional journals, including *Educational Leadership* and the *English Journal.* Mr. Schuster is author of *Grammar, Usage, and Style,* a high school language text; is coauthor of McGraw-Hill's *American English Today,* a junior high and high school language and composition series; and is a contributing author of a new McGraw-Hill elementary language arts program.

Gabriele L. Rico, Instructor of English at the University of Santa Clara, has taught English and German at high schools, junior colleges, and colleges in California. At San Jose State College she was also a supervisor of student teachers and teaching interns. During the years that she taught at the high school level, she was instrumental in setting up the curriculum for the innovative Advanced Placement in English. She recently served as a consultant for McGraw-Hill's *Today: A Text-Workbook for English Language and Composition.*

Robert L. Donald, Assistant Professor of English at Oakland University, Rochester, Michigan, prepared the words study program for *Insights* and *Encounters.* He is a former John Hay Fellow at the University of California at Berkeley.

Don L. Wulffson, teacher of English at San Fernando High School in Los Angeles, prepared the words study program for *American Literature* and *Western Literature* and assisted in the preparation of resource guide material.

Themes and Writers Series

Second Edition

ENCOUNTERS

Themes in Literature

G. Robert Carlsen

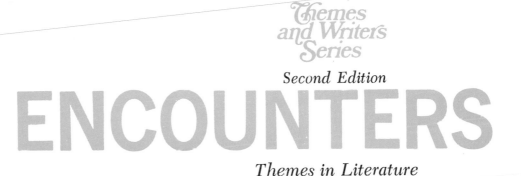

THE GULF STREAM
Winslow Homer
The Metropolitan Museum of Art,
Wolfe Fund, 1906

Webster Division, McGraw-Hill Book Company
New York, St. Louis, San Francisco, Dallas, Atlanta

Library of Congress Cataloging in Publication Data

Carlsen, G. Robert, 1921–   comp.
  Encounters: themes in literature.

  (Themes and writers series)
  SUMMARY: A thematically arranged anthology of poems, short stories, plays, and novellas for the tenth-grade reader.
  1. Literature—Collections. [1. Literature—Collections] I. Title.
[PN6014.C317 1973]   808.8   72–622
ISBN 0–07–009904–9

ISBN 07-009904-9

Editorial Development: Ron Osler; Editing and Styling: Julie Ziercher; Design: John Keithley; Production: Richard E. Shaw

Contents

DEMPSEY AND FIRPO
George Bellows
1924, Collection Whitney Museum
of American Art, New York

BRIEF ENCOUNTERS

The Parable of the Good Samaritan 1
St. Luke 10:30-37

Stopover in Querétaro 4
Jerrold Beim

Gallery of Fine Art 10

The Grains of Paradise 16
James Street

Techniques
Exposition, Conflict, Climax 27

Mateo Falcone 29
Prosper Mérimée

The Man He Killed 37
Thomas Hardy

Channing Way I 38
Rod McKuen

The Alarm Clock 39
Mari Evans

Corner 40
Ralph Pomeroy

Faces 43
Sara Teasdale

One Ordinary Day, With Peanuts 44
Shirley Jackson

The Enemy 52
Pearl Buck

Summing Up 65

HIS ENEMY, HIS FRIEND 66
John Tunis

Biographical Notes 128

CROSSCURRENTS

The Parable of the Prodigal Son   130
    ST. LUKE 15:11-24

The Stone Boy   133
    GINA BERRIAULT

Techniques
    Characterization, Plot   140

The Rocking-Horse Winner   141
    D. H. LAWRENCE

Mammon and the Archer   152
    O. HENRY

The Ambassador   157
    EDWARD NEWHOUSE

Souvenir de Londres   170
    STEPHEN SPENDER

The Whipping   171
    ROBERT HAYDEN

The Veldt   172
    RAY BRADBURY

Gallery of Fine Art   182

Summing Up   188

THE DIARY OF ANNE FRANK   189
    FRANCES GOODRICH and
    ALBERT HACKETT

Biographical Notes   245

FAMILY PICTURE   *Max Beckmann*
1920, Oil on canvas, 25⅝ x 39¾"
Collection, The Museum of Modern Art, New York
Gift of Abby Aldrich Rockefeller

PRIVATE MOODS

For Everything There Is a Season 247
ECCLESIASTES 3:1-8

RESTLESSNESS

Sympathy 250
PAUL LAURENCE DUNBAR

Spring 251
RICHARD HOVEY

Travel 251
EDNA ST. VINCENT MILLAY

Sea Fever 252
JOHN MASEFIELD

Ride a Wild Horse 252
HANNAH KAHN

Highway: Michigan 253
THEODORE ROETHKE

Death Is a Beautiful Car Parked Only 254
RICHARD BRAUTIGAN

Eldorado 255
EDGAR ALLAN POE

Techniques
Rhythm, Rhyme 255

FEAR

Country Night 258
SELMA ROBINSON

House Fear 259
ROBERT FROST

The Oft-Repeated Dream 259
ROBERT FROST

The Lady 259
ELIZABETH COATSWORTH

The Warning 260
ADELAIDE CRAPSEY

When I Have Fears That I May
Cease to Be 260
JOHN KEATS

The Panther Possible 261
WILLIAM D. BARNEY

Suicide Pond 262
KATHY McLAUGHLIN

Techniques
Simile 263

Gallery of Fine Art 264

ANGER AND HATRED

The Black Panther 270
JOHN HALL WHEELOCK

The Traveler's Curse After Misdirection 271
ROBERT GRAVES

Mood 271
COUNTÉE CULLEN

Does It Matter 272
SIEGFRIED SASSOON

Hate 272
JAMES STEPHENS

The White House 273
CLAUDE McKAY

Waves Against a Dog 274
TANER BAYBARS

A Poison Tree 275
WILLIAM BLAKE

Without a Cloak 275
PHYLLIS McGINLEY

The Heart 276
STEPHEN CRANE

Techniques
Metaphor 276

SORROW

My November Guest 278
ROBERT FROST

The Noise of Waters 279
JAMES JOYCE

Music I Heard 279
CONRAD AIKEN

The Widow 280
MILLER WILLIAMS

After Great Pain a Formal Feeling
Comes 281
EMILY DICKINSON

The Woodspurge 281
DANTE ROSSETTI

A Dirge 282
PERCY BYSSHE SHELLEY

Techniques
Rhythm and Sound Effects 282

NOSTALGIA

The House on the Hill 284
E. A. ROBINSON

The West Wind 285
JOHN MASEFIELD

Home Thoughts from Abroad 286
ROBERT BROWNING

Inland 286
EDNA ST. VINCENT MILLAY

My Lost Youth 287
HENRY WADSWORTH LONGFELLOW

Break, Break, Break 289
ALFRED, LORD TENNYSON

Those Winter Sundays 290
ROBERT HAYDEN

Techniques
Diction and Imagery 291

DELIGHT

Reveille 292
A. E. HOUSMAN

Afternoon on a Hill 293
EDNA ST. VINCENT MILLAY

Silver 293
WALTER DE LA MARE

Velvet Shoes 294
ELINOR WYLIE

in Just-spring 294
E. E. CUMMINGS

Wild Blackberries 295
FRANCES McCONNEL

Good Humor Man 296
PHYLLIS McGINLEY

A Vagabond Song 296
BLISS CARMAN

Miracles 297
WALT WHITMAN

Pied Beauty 298
GERARD MANLEY HOPKINS

Smells 298
CHRISTOPHER MORLEY

Precious Words 299
EMILY DICKINSON

Sonnet CVI 299
WILLIAM SHAKESPEARE

Fast Run in the Junkyard 300
JEANNETTE NICHOLS

Summing Up 302

Biographical Notes 304

THE DREAMS OF MEN

In A Glass of Cider   313
    ROBERT FROST

The Wooing of Ariadne   316
    HARRY MARK PETRAKIS

Techniques
    Irony, Organization   324

Dream Variation   327
    LANGSTON HUGHES

Daybreak in Alabama   328
    LANGSTON HUGHES

Youth   329
    LANGSTON HUGHES

The Dream Keeper   329
    LANGSTON HUGHES

Dreams   329
    LANGSTON HUGHES

I, Too   330
    LANGSTON HUGHES

As I Grew Older   331
    LANGSTON HUGHES

Let America Be America Again   332
    LANGSTON HUGHES

Dream Deferred   333
    LANGSTON HUGHES

Scars of Honor   335
    DOROTHY JOHNSON

Feels Like Spring   345
    MILTON KAPLAN

Project of Arriving at Moral Perfection   348
    BENJAMIN FRANKLIN

The Story of the Good Little Boy   355
    MARK TWAIN

Silent Snow, Secret Snow   359
    CONRAD AIKEN

Summing Up   371

Biographical Notes   371

Gallery of Fine Art   374

JULIUS CAESAR   382
    WILLIAM SHAKESPEARE

ALEXANDER THE GREAT

EIGHT BELLS
Winslow Homer

PEOPLE UNDER PRESSURE

Boots   469
RUDYARD KIPLING

The Open Window   472
SAKI

Techniques
Theme, Style, Identification   474

Going to Run All Night   476
HARRY SYLVESTER

Shooting an Elephant   484
GEORGE ORWELL

The Vertical Ladder   490
WILLIAM SANSOM

The Catbird Seat   498
JAMES THURBER

To Build a Fire   505
JACK LONDON

The Prisoner of Chillon   516
GEORGE GORDON, LORD BYRON

Paul's Case   523
WILLA CATHER

An Occurrence at Owl Creek Bridge   539
AMBROSE BIERCE

Miriam   547
TRUMAN CAPOTE

Gallery of Fine Art   556

A Summer Tragedy   562
ARNA BONTEMPS

Summing Up   569

THE PEARL   570
JOHN STEINBECK

Biographical Notes   610

LIFE'S IRONIES

We Real Cool 613
GWENDOLYN BROOKS

The Wrath of the Raped 616
MACKINLAY KANTOR

Techniques
Atmospherc, Suspense 619

The Ambitious Guest 621
NATHANIEL HAWTHORNE

The German Refugee 627
BERNARD MALAMUD

Suppressed Desires 636
SUSAN GLASPELL

The Cold, Cold Box 647
HOWARD FAST

Gallery of Fine Art 656

Prelude 662
ALBERT HALPER

The Sniper 669
LIAM O'FLAHERTY

The Pistol Shot 673
ALEXANDER PUSHKIN

The Blue Hotel 682
STEPHEN CRANE

Summing Up 698

THE MAN THAT CORRUPTED
HADLEYBURG 700
MARK TWAIN

Biographical Notes 728

Glossary 732

Literary Terms Index 752

Literary Types Index 752

Fine Art Index 753

General Index 754

Illustration Sources 755

E very man
who knows how to read
has it in his power to magnify himself,
to multiply the ways
in which he exists,
to make his life full, significant
and interesting.

ALDOUS HUXLEY

BRIEF ENCOUNTERS

The Parable
of the Good Samaritan

St. Luke 10:30–37

A certain man went down from Jerusalem to Jericho, and fell among thieves, who stripped him of his raiment, and wounded him, and departed, leaving him half dead.

And by chance there came down a certain priest that way: and when he saw him, he passed by on the other side.

And likewise a Levite, when he was at the place, came and looked on him, and passed by on the other side.

But a certain Samaritan, as he journeyed, came where he was: and when he saw him, he had compassion on him; and went to him, and bound up his wounds, pouring in oil and wine, and set him on his own beast, and brought him to an inn, and took care of him.

And on the morrow when he departed, he took out two pence, and gave them to the host, and said unto him, Take care of him; and whatsoever thou spendest more, when I come again, I will repay thee.

Which now of these three, thinkest thou, was neighbor unto him that fell among the thieves?

The Good Samaritan, *Vincent Van Gogh. Kröller-Müller Museum, Otterlo*
The great Dutch painter Van Gogh captures the climactic moment of this famous brief encounter.

For almost two thousand years, men have read and remembered the parable of the Good Samaritan. Its simplicity testifies to the power of a tale well told. Here in a few words is a varied gallery of unexpected meetings filled with open or hidden conflicts. The brief encounter with the robbers ends disastrously for the traveler; the meeting with the priest changes the fate of neither; but the encounter with the Samaritan is a rewarding one. Hence, this one short tale explores varieties of brief encounters.

Meetings between strangers are always interesting. When such meetings take place between extraordinary people or in extraordinary circumstances, they acquire the power to fascinate us. Out of these meetings develop dramatic changes in people's lives —some tragic, some comic, some lasting, and some fleeting.

Since the capable writer has an eye for change and for patterns in human existence, he is always interested in meetings that disrupt the calm, normal flow of life: the dramatic moment. Each meeting, no matter how casual, has some effect—good, bad, or callously indifferent—on the human character.

Theodore H. White in his book *The Mountain Road* gives an imaginative definition of this theme.

> You hold a block of metal in your hand. And it's solid. Yet within the metal there are molecules or atoms, all moving by laws of their own. Press a block of pure gold against a block of silver. When you separate them they seem unchanged. But a good physical chemist will show you that where they have been in contact invisible flecks of gold have wandered across the barrier of structure and buried themselves in the silver. And atoms of silver, somehow, in the structure of the gold.
>
> I think that when people are pressed close they act the same way. Part of you enters them, part of them enters you. Long after you forget the names and faces, they are still a part of you. Sometimes it is frightening to think that every person you have ever hated, or feared, or run away from is part of you. But so is every person you have ever learned from, every friend you ever had.

As you read the following selections, continually ask yourself questions about this theme. What meetings with others have changed your opinions or actions? What are the forces that set a man for one person but against another?

That the strangers who meet one another in the pages of this section meet only briefly and under extraordinary circumstances throws a strong light on their actions. Each reveals himself in attitudes that the ordinary routine of his life would normally conceal. For this reason, this theme is rich in sudden discoveries, surprising outcomes, dramatic choices.

If you were to ask a modern writer
to retell the parable of the Good Samaritan
in a modern setting, say, Mexico,
and to tell the story
from the victim's point of view, you might
get a story like "Stopover in Querétaro."
However, this personal narrative records
an actual experience. See whether the author
changes his attitude toward strangers
as he is forced into close contact
with people of a foreign land.

Stopover in Querétaro

JERROLD BEIM

Two years ago my family and I were driving to Mexico City on the Juarez highway.[1] We had a blowout and the car turned over. My wife, who was driving, and my daughter were killed instantly. One of my twin sons, Andy, suffered a severe concussion and had to be hospitalized in a town called Querétaro,[2] about ninety kilometers[3] from Mexico City. My other son, Seth, was uninjured but stunned by what had happened; and I had minor injuries and was in a state of shock.

Many people have said to me since: "Wasn't it awful that it had to happen in a strange country?" And I'll confess that at the time, staying at the hospital in Querétaro, I felt that I was at the end of the world, far from family or friends who could have been of help or comfort to me. But let me tell it as it happened.

Immediately after the accident we were surrounded by Mexicans, mostly country people in sombreros and *rebozos*,[4] and all, naturally, total strangers. But one man, in a business suit, was

leading Seth and me to his car. In excellent English he explained that he had been behind us and had seen our car turn over. It was he who had summoned the police and ambulance from Querétaro, and now he was driving Seth and me to the hospital. The ambulance had sped ahead with Andy. The man told me his name was Juan Martinez.[5] He asked if I knew any Spanish, and when I told him I spoke only a little he assured me that he would stay with me until he saw we were getting proper care.

Querétaro was a sizable town, but it seemed primitive, and I doubted that we could get adequate medical attention. The sight of the hospital did not ease my anxiety. It was run by a Dr. Francisco Alcozer Pozo,[6] and did not even look like a hospital. The nurse who greeted us explained that the doctor lived on one side of the patio, and his mother lived on the opposite side. To the rear was the hospital itself, a row of little rooms opening off the patio. Seth and I were taken into one of these rooms. The nurse explained too rapidly for me to understand (Juan Martinez interpreted) that the doctor was busy with Andy.

Juan took Seth out to the patio while the nurse cleaned and bandaged the cut on my head. I glanced about the room and noticed that the paint on the walls was scaling, the furnishings were antiquated. I was overwhelmed by what had happened to my wife and daughter, and certain that in this God-forsaken place Andy would not receive the medical care he would need to survive.

Soon Juan returned with Seth and a man in a white coat.

"This is the doctor," Juan said. "Doctor Pozo."

1. This is the highway south from Ciudad Juárez \'sē·ū ⁴thath ⁴hwa·rās\ the Mexican city across the Rio Grande from El Paso, Texas.
2. **Querétaro** \kā ⁴rā·ta·rō\ the capital of its state, has a population of about 35,000.
3. **kilometer** \kĭ ⁴lŏ·ma·tər\ 3,280.8 ft., about three-fifths of a mile.
4. **rebozo** \rā ⁴bō·sō\ a long colorful scarf or drape worn by Mexican women.
5. **Juan Martinez** \hwan mar ⁴tē·nās\
6. **Francisco Alcozer Pozo** \fran ⁴sēs·kō al·kō ⁴sār ⁴pō·sō\

My spirit rallied slightly when I saw the doctor. He was tall and thin, and he had an intelligent face. In slow and not very good English he expressed his deep sympathy for all that had happened. He said he doubted that any of Andy's bones were broken—he'd have to wait for the X rays—but he was sure Andy had a severe concussion. The boy was still unconscious.

I wanted to send to Mexico City for a specialist at once. Doctor Pozo said he would do whatever I desired but he thought we should see the X rays first. He looked at the cut on my head, my finger, and then he examined Seth, who was sitting on the foot of the bed.

Suddenly from outside I heard voices that made my heart leap. They were definitely American!

"It must be *Señor* and *Señora*[7] MacKenzie," Doctor Pozo explained. "They are Americans who live here."

Americans here! They came in, an attractive man and woman, who apparently knew the doctor well. Doctor Pozo left me alone with them.

The MacKenzies had heard of the accident and had come at once to offer help. They said they were the only Americans in Querétaro, Mr. MacKenzie being the manager of a local gabardine factory. They assured me that Doctor Pozo was a very competent physician; but I felt that they would have to say that, under the circumstances.

Seth, apparently still stunned, sat silent on the bed.

"Let us take Seth home for the time being," Mrs. MacKenzie suggested. "We have a five-year-old boy who would love his company. At least, you won't have to worry about him."

Even though these people were complete strangers, Seth readily went with them. I think he was glad to get away from all the horrors of the past few hours.

There were scores of things I had to do. My family and my wife's family had to be notified, and the MacKenzies helped get them on the telephone which was just outside the room. My wife and I had always approved of cremation, and the MacKenzies offered to make all the arrangements. When they finally left they promised to bring Seth back for a visit the next day.

It wasn't until they were gone that I realized Juan Martinez had disappeared. I rang for the nurse and made her understand that I was looking for the man who had brought me here. She said he had left the hospital. And I hadn't even had a chance to thank him for all he had done.

Later Doctor Pozo returned. Andy was still unconscious, and it was clearly evident that he had a severe concussion. I repeated that I wanted to call in a brain specialist from Mexico City, and Doctor Pozo put in the call. The specialist said that Andy could not be moved for weeks, and he didn't feel there was any point in his coming to Querétaro. It was obvious to him that Andy's progress depended on time and he said that Doctor Pozo could handle the situation as well as he. He suggested, however, that we keep him informed by telephone. I still wasn't satisfied. If Andy pulled through, I felt it would be only a matter of luck.

Doctor Pozo now turned to setting my dislocated finger. I remember fading from consciousness while it was being done and dreaming we were in the car again, on our way to Mexico City. Then I would come to and realize what had happened. Only heavy sedatives put me to sleep that night.

Another nurse was on duty in the morning. This one spoke a bit of English, and told me there was no change in Andy, but that a man was waiting to see me.

It was Juan Martinez. I greeted him like an old friend. Where had he disappeared to yesterday?

He had seen me with the Americans, and knew they would take care of me. But he had stayed overnight in Querétaro wanting to be of further help and hoping that maybe the little boy would be better. Now he had to get on to Mexico City.

---

7. **Señor**\sän ▲yōr\ mister. **Señora**\sän ▲yō•ra\ mistress.

I didn't know how to express my gratitude for all he had done. We exchanged addresses. I would look him up in Nogales.[8] We would be sure to see each other again.

I was lonelier than ever after Juan Martinez left. Only the telephone kept me bolstered through the day. Family and friends called, offering all kinds of help. It was decided that I should send Seth to his grandmother's while I remained with Andy.

Mrs. MacKenzie visited me during the day, too, bringing Seth, along with her own boy. The children had had a wonderful time together. Arrangements were made for Seth to be driven to Mexico City, then to go on to the United States by plane.

While Mrs. MacKenzie was there Doctor Pozo summoned me. Andy had regained consciousness. He stared at me with recognition, though not a sound came from his lips. Doctor Pozo said it might be weeks before he spoke.

Bidding good-by to Seth was hard. Though I knew the separation was only temporary, it emphasized how broken my family had become.

---

8. **Nogales**\sp. pron. nō ▲ga·läs\ evidently the Mexican town of about 14,000 across the border from the Arizona town of Nogales.

Late in the afternoon an unexpected call came through from my brother. He lived in San Francisco, but he had flown to Mexico City and was leaving for Querétaro in a few minutes.

His first words as he came in were, "We must have you removed to Mexico City at once!"

I explained why that couldn't be done. But it was wonderful having him with me. He spent the night in the hospital, and we sat up talking for hours.

For the next few days Andy's condition scarcely changed. Doctor Pozo drained fluid from the boy's spine and hinted that an operation might be necessary if he didn't begin to talk soon.

Doctor Pozo had suggested to my brother that I should leave Andy's bedside for a while, and explore the town. So one sunny morning we ventured outdoors. The hospital was located on a narrow, cobblestoned street and at the very next corner was a small-town Mexican market place, swarming with flies and filled with unappetizing food. My brother had come through this market on his arrival in Querétaro —that was why he had been so shocked. We walked until we reached the plaza, with its inevitable bandstand, and we sat on one of the benches under large shade trees. I felt myself being eyed by everyone who walked past.

"This town is off the usual tourist beat," I told my brother. "They're not accustomed to seeing Americans."

An old woman in a dark-blue shawl approached us.

"I guess she wants money," my brother said, digging into his pocket. But her hand wasn't out, and she was speaking to me. After she had repeated her words, I understood, and I fought to keep back the tears.

"She knows that I am the American who was in the accident," I told my brother, "and that my little boy is very sick. She is praying—for the souls of my wife and daughter—and for the recovery of my boy."

One afternoon just before my brother had to leave, I was sunning in the patio while he sat with Andy. Suddenly he came running toward me.

"I showed him a book and asked if he'd like me to read it to him—and he spoke. Just one word—'*Yes*'—but he spoke!"

We found the doctor and went to Andy's bedside. Yes—he spoke—just a word at a time, slowly, with effort, and only when asked something—but he spoke!

As I returned to the hospital after seeing my brother off, a cluster of ragged urchins was around the door. They looked at me and grinned.

"*El niño está hablando!*"[9] one of them said. They had heard the good news already. And one of the children held out a toy, a little horse carved of balsa wood and painted colorfully. "*Por el niño!*"[10]

One afternoon I ventured into a local hotel for lunch; I had waited until Andy had fallen asleep, and had left word where I would be. Soon after I was seated the waiter told me I was wanted on the telephone. I became alarmed, and as I lifted the phone it was a vast relief to hear the voice of an American—a man:

"You don't know me, sir, but I'm here with a group of American doctors visiting hospitals and clinics all over Mexico. I met Doctor Pozo this morning and he told me about your accident. I saw him perform an operation this morning, and I thought you would be interested in knowing that I consider him a very fine doctor and an excellent surgeon. Your son is in very good hands."

I apologized to Doctor Pozo for my lack of confidence. He said that it was only natural for a father to be anxious, especially one who had gone through all I had.

As the days went by Andy got constantly better. He was talking more and soon he was able to sit up in the sunny patio.

One afternoon Doctor Pozo said Andy could travel at the end of the week, if we would like

---

9. **El niño está hablando**\ĕl ⁴nēn·yō ĕs ⁴ta 'ha ⁴blan-dō\ The boy is talking.
10. **Por el niño**\pōr ĕl ⁴nēn·yō\ For the boy.

to move to Mexico City. Andy would have to be hospitalized for a while longer, but Doctor Pozo thought we would be more comfortable there.

I had a job to do before I left, one that I had put off for days. I had to decide what to do with my wife's and daughter's clothes. I spoke to Doctor Pozo and he suggested that I give the adult clothes to the clinic where they would be distributed to needy people, and the child's things to the orphanage. Doctor Pozo would take the things for the clinic, but he thought it would be nice if I went to the orphanage myself. It was in a building that once had been a private residence, and Doctor Pozo said it was an example of pure colonial architecture[11] that I ought to see.

It wasn't an easy mission, sorting my little girl's clothes and then carrying them to the orphanage. All the buildings along the street looked very much alike, with crumbling pink, blue or white walls; but the convent was easily distinguishable by its sturdy architecture and by the cross over the doorway. I rang the bell and managed to say to the old man who let me in, "Clothes for the children."

He led me into the most beautiful patio I have ever seen. A fountain played in an expanse of green lawn, and arches curved on the three walls of the house that enclosed it. The Mother Superior[12] in her long black robes came toward me. We conversed for a few moments, and then I started to leave.

"The children wish to thank you," she said, and motioned me into one of the interior rooms.

It was an immense, beautiful room, with shiny tile floors and a high, carved ceiling. It was sparsely furnished, but what there was looked like precious Spanish antiques. The Mother Superior disappeared for a moment, then returned leading a line of small girls in neat blue pinafores.

My daughter had been blue-eyed and flaxen-haired. These little girls were black-haired, with dark, shining eyes. I had been deprived of my daughter and these were children without fathers or mothers. I wanted to take every

one in my arms. They thanked me for the clothes, in clear, piping voices, and then I left.

I remember being unable to go right back to the hospital. I sat in the plaza, getting control of myself, so that I could return to Andy. Then I noticed a tall, nice-looking man about my age, walking hesitantly toward me.

He sat down beside me. Was I the gentleman staying at the hospital with the little boy who had been hurt?

Yes, I was.

He owned that dry-goods store on the corner, he told me, nodding proudly toward it. I tried to convey that I thought it a fine-looking store. I couldn't bring myself to say that I wanted to be alone.

And then he explained why he had ventured to intrude on my privacy. He had seen me sitting here in the plaza and had wanted to talk to me many times. Because he felt a deep sympathy for me. A few years ago he and his family had started for Mexico City. His wife's parents lived there, and he used to take his wife and their three children to visit them once or twice a year. On that last trip, his car had been in an accident, too— a speeder had crashed into it. His wife and two of his children had been killed. And since then life for him had been an agony.

"Only now it is a little better. It is such an old proverb and it must sound foolish to you now, but time does help things. And time will help you, even though you still have much pain to live through."

I couldn't answer him. But suddenly I wasn't alone and I knew that really I had never been a stranger in Querétaro, nor was this such a foreign land. I was sitting beside someone who had been through the same ordeal. There were benches like this and people like us in every country of the world.

---

11. **colonial architecture,** the style of architecture in vogue when the American states and Mexico were colonies of Great Britain and Spain, respectively. It often blended sturdy strength with pleasant simplicity and graceful adornment.
12. **Mother Superior,** the title of the woman in charge of a convent.

It was about two days later that I left by hired car for Mexico City. Andy was settled comfortably in the back seat and I was beside the driver.

Doctor Pozo, the MacKenzies, the nurses, the servants—all had said good-by to us from the hospital door. Word had got around that we were leaving, and people of the town—men in sombreros, women in shawls, a man in the doorway of a dry-goods store—waved to us as we left Querétaro.

I

TRACING A CHANGE OF ATTITUDE

Although a stopover is ordinarily a casual and unimportant interruption of a trip, this stopover is neither casual nor unimportant, for the lives of the Beim family are terribly and finally changed by the automobile accident. As Beim recovers from the shock of his loss, an equally profound change takes place in the mind of the writer. It is brought about directly by his encounters with the people of Querétaro. Here are some quotations from the story. What feelings and attitudes on the writer's part do they reveal? Trace a developing pattern from the first through the last.

1. " 'Wasn't it awful that it had to happen in a strange country?' "

2. "Americans here!"

3. "And I hadn't even had a chance to thank him for all he had done."

4. "An old woman . . . approached us. . . . She was 'praying—for the souls of my wife and daughter—and for the recovery of my boy.' "

5. "I apologized to Dr. Pozo for my lack of confidence. He said that it was only natural for a father to be anxious. . . ."

6. ". . . I wasn't alone and I knew that really I never had been a stranger in Querétaro, nor was this such a foreign land."

II

IMPLICATIONS

Reading should always be a pleasure. Whether a story is light or serious, a reader's enjoyment of it will be greater and his understanding more last-ing if he lets it stimulate his own thinking. After most of the selections in this anthology, you will find general statements like the ones that follow. Their purpose is to ask you to evaluate what you have read in your own terms. They may be used as the basis of class discussions, of debates, or of brief written essays. And while they help you clarify and organize your reactions to the story, they will also sharpen your ability to express your own opinions more accurately.

1. Something inside us seems to make us distrust foreigners.

2. Tragedy tends to remove the barriers between strangers.

3. Although Jerrold Beim lost a great deal through the accident, he also gained something valuable through his encounters with the people of Querétaro.

III

TECHNIQUES

"Stopover in Querétaro" is an informal essay, a short piece of prose written in everyday conversational language about one subject and its effects upon the writer. There are many kinds of essays, ranging, for instance, from a highly impersonal report of scientific research to such deeply personal accounts as this one. In an informal essay, the writer reveals much about his own personality, as he describes his experiences.

1. What would you say are the most important character traits the author reveals in this essay? Compare your opinions with those of the rest of the class.

2. If this account had been written in the third person instead of the first person, what differences would it have made in your reactions to it?

3. From each of the following pairs of adjectives, choose the one that better describes the quality of this essay.

a.	down to earth	high-flown
b.	difficult	easy
c.	objective	subjective
d.	straightforward	devious
e.	emotional	unemotional
f.	restrained	unrestrained
g.	quiet	brassy

Do the seven adjectives you have selected completely describe the style of the essay? What others would you add?

Gallery

BRIEF
ENCOUNTERS

The unpredictable drama of the brief encounter,
like every theme of the human experience, has intrigued the artist
as well as the writer for countless ages.
Battle scenes, moments of conquest, brief, tense struggles
between individuals are all common in the art of every land.
Also richly pictured are those prized moments when individuals
meet on other ground and offer a helping hand,
or rejoice together, or drown their sorrows, or even when there is a
second of mutual awareness as lonely people pass in the night.
    This gallery gives a brief glimpse of the wide range
of paintings that tell in their own terms of line and color
the excitement and emotional stir created
by the theme of brief encounters.

The giant Goliath, in the well-known Bible story
of David's victory with a slingshot, expected his encounter
with the stripling shepherd boy to be brief and victorious.
Sheer contrast of the unexpected outcome and the overturning
of expected odds have made this brief encounter
a treasured story for thousands of years.
From the conquests of Charlemagne comes the ancient French
epic of *The Song of Roland*. It tells of the return
of Charlemagne's legions from Spain and of the heroic deeds
and death of the knight Roland. The original epic gave rise
to other tales, among them Ariosto's *Orlando Furioso*,
in which Roland fights with Rodomonte the Saracen King
of Algiers in an attempt to cross his bridge. Examine the details.
    Notice the contrast between the serenity of the landscape
and the brief turbulence of the struggling men in the foreground.

DAVID
WITH THE HEAD
OF GOLIATH
Guido Reni

THE COMBAT
BETWEEN ROLAND
AND RODOMONTE
Dosso Dossi
Wadsworth Atheneum,
Hartford, Connecticut

In 354 A.D., Martin was a young
and reluctant soldier
whose principles had already
led him to give away
everything he owned.
When he came upon a poor
shivering beggar, he had little
to contribute so he divided
the cloak he was wearing
and gave the beggar the
sheepskin lining.
Later, according to the legends
of St. Martin, Bishop of Tours,
he received a vision of Christ
wearing this lining
and blessing Martin
for his noble gesture.
Pondering the meaning
of this brief encounter
led Martin to seek baptism
in the early Christian church
and to dedicate his life
to its causes.

ST. MARTIN
AND THE BEGGAR
El Greco
National Gallery of Art,
Washington, D.C.,
Widener Collection

Like so many of
Winslow Homer's paintings,
this brief facing of soldiers
from the Union
and the Confederacy
is full of the stuff
of storytellers.
The characters are presented
in detail, caught in an
instant of awareness
—a "moment of truth."

PRISONERS
FROM THE FRONT
Winslow Homer

This brief encounter occurred on September 14, 1923,
and is a matter of newspaper record and boxing history.
Firpo was KO'd in two rounds!

DEMPSEY AND FIRPO
George Bellows
1924, Oil, Collection
of the Whitney
Museum of
American Art, New York

Also a matter of history is the topic of the paintings of Montezuma
and Cortes marching to meet each other as the Spanish conqueror entered
Mexico on November 8, 1519. Within a few months, Montezuma was dead
and Cortes was master of much of what is now Mexico.

CORTÉS (left) and
MONTEZUMA (right)

FIGHT FOR THE
WATERHOLE
*Frederic
Remington*

Water was precious in the desert areas of the far West, as the frontier painter
Remington tells us vividly. This encounter could not be brief enough
for the embattled men. Note how the pale but intense colors give a sense
of the great dry heat of the desert bowl.

After lonely stretches of months or even years at sea,
the returning captains made the most of their brief encounters with their fellow
seamen. Judging from the events the self-taught American painter recorded
with fascination in the Dutch Guinea port of Surinam,
for many the merriment should have been much more brief.

SEA CAPTAINS
CAROUSING IN SURINAM
John Greenwood
The St. Louis Art Museum

**NIGHT
HAWKS**
Edward Hopper

In startling contrast to the roistering sea captains,
the city painter Edward Hopper has painted a stark
and touching scene: four people, not really meeting, in an
all-night cafe. As in Homer's paintings, we are conscious
of the tension of an untold story.

〰 Contests of courage and endurance
often produce strange results: respect, fear,
hate, admiration. In such contests,
winning or losing may well be a secondary issue.
What are the results of the meeting
between strangers in "The Grains of Paradise"?
Is it ever true that from defeat comes victory?

The Grains of Paradise

JAMES STREET

I do not like stories that suggest one thing and mean another and so, right off, I want you to know that the grains of paradise are the seeds of little hot peppers, very hot; and that this is a story about some fiery little peppers and some people in the village of Feliz,[1] which is down in Mexico's state of Tabasco and nine hundred miles from nowhere.

The hotel was on a corner when I was there years ago, and across the way was a church which was surrounded by a gray wall, and the wall was shared by bougainvillaea, buzzards and unmeasured time. It was mid-afternoon when I got out of the bus at the hotel. The bus was painted purple and yellow, and bore the name of Rosaura, painted in red. I am sure it was the name of the driver's sweetheart. In Feliz, everything was personalized.[2]

An Indian was sleeping by the doorway. And his ox team was sleeping, hitched to a two wheeled cart, and two or three dogs. Everything was sleeping. Nothing stirred in the high-mountain solitude of Feliz. The hotel was cool inside, and shadowy, and the clerk opened his eyes when he heard my steps and greeted me

sleepily in Spanish. I replied in Spanish, my very best, and that's pretty bad.

Quickly he was alert and spoke to me in English. His English was no better than my Spanish. He was smaller than I am, considerably smaller, and I am about average. His clothes were mussy, but his little black mustache was trim.

I signed the register, and he studied my signature and then he spoke it aloud, "Mr. Cordell Hoyle, Lystra, North Carolina."

For a second he hesitated, and looked up at me and down at my name, and I had the feeling he was going to ask me a question or make some comment, some pleasantry about the weather or the trip or maybe about American visitors. But he didn't. He asked me if I'd had lunch, and when I told him I hadn't, he said that the kitchen was closed, but that he'd arrange for me to have a snack after I'd washed up. Then he hissed, "Psst, psst," and a barefooted Indian came out of the shadows. The clerk told him to take my bags to Room No. 3.

It was a bowl-and-pitcher room[3] and was on the corner and had two windows. Out of one I could see the plaza of Feliz, empty at that hour and its trees drooping their somnolence. Out of the other I could see the church—the Church of the Tears of the Blessed Virgin—and beyond the church were the mountains, hovering high in desperate grandeur, heavy green for miles, then hazy blue into the sky.

It was these mountains that had brought me to Southern Mexico, down almost to where the country joins Guatemala. In those days I worked for the University of North Carolina's College of Agriculture and for months I had been in Tabasco and in the adjacent state of Chiapas,[4] looking for a certain variety of corn

---

1. **Feliz**\\'fā ˈlēs\ Tabasco\tə ˈbăs·kō\ is in southern Mexico, southeast of Vera Cruz.
2. **personalize**\ˈpər·sə·nə ˈlaiz\ to endow with a personality, to give a name to and treat as a person.
3. **bowl-and-pitcher room**, one equipped with a wash basin and a water pitcher. The room (and perhaps the whole hotel) lacked modern plumbing.
4. **Chiapas**\ˈchya ˈpas\ a state south of Tabasco and north and west of Guatemala.

16

to be used for experimental purposes. I had come to Feliz to rest a day or two before pulling out for home.

I washed the dust from my face and hands, and changed my shirt and went back to the lobby. The owner of the hotel was there. He was a paunchy man, glistening sweat, and his clothes were as disheveled as the clerk's, and his mustache was just as trim.

None of the Indians had mustaches, but the owner and the clerk were Ladinos[5] and their mustaches were evidence of this classification, which is economic and not racial. A Ladino is a townsman, an owner of property, a Christian who follows Latin ways. He wears shoes, and never sandals, and always the mustache. He may be part Indian, a mestizo,[6] but he is never all Indian.

The Indians profess Christianity, in a way, but really cling to their Mayan[7] faith. Some own property in town, but not many. There is a caste barrier between the Ladinos and the Indians, and, again, this is economic and not racial.

The clerk introduced me to the owner, whose name I do not remember, and he said that my lunch would be ready in a few minutes, and walked away. I leaned against the desk and lit a cigarette, and then I remembered my manners and offered one to the clerk. He accepted it gravely and with thanks.

"I have been in the United States," he said.

"Is that so? Where?"

"I went to school in the United States. For a year."

"Yes? Where?"

He looked at the ash of his cigarette and tapped it off. "In Mississippi." He glanced at me quickly, almost defiantly, as though he expected me to challenge him or laugh, or something.

"The university?" I asked. "Or Mississippi State?"

"No." He was not quite sure of himself, even timid, and I wondered what the to-do was about and why the hesitation, and then he said, "At a place you never heard of, I'm sure. At

Hattiesburg,[8] Mississippi. There's a college there."

I laughed. "Hattiesburg! Well, now, whatta you know."

He drew back. "It is amusing?"

"No. Just cockeyed. Funny peculiar, not funny laughing. I married in Hattiesburg."

"You say." He was very serious.

"Yes, I say. My wife's from Hattiesburg. So you went to Mississippi Southern, huh?"

Have you ever seen gratitude and good will ooze from a man? No, "flow" is a better word. Have you ever seen a man so pleased that he just sort of melts, and grins? That's what this fellow did. He flipped away his cigarette, a sassy, cocky little flip, and propped his elbow on the register. "You went to Mississippi Southern?"

"No. But I know about it."

"Where is it?"

"In Hattiesburg. Like you said." I wasn't peeved, but maybe a little bit short because I couldn't figure out what he was getting at.

"Where in Hattiesburg?"

"Now look, mister. I don't follow you. Mississippi Southern is a college in the little city of Hattiesburg, and Hattiesburg is in Southern Mississippi. You go down—yes, you go down West Pine Street, past the post office, and make a bend to the right. That'll be Hardy Street. Then out Hardy Street, past a cemetery, and on out to the college. What's it all about?"

His smile was so bright and so warm that I began grinning, and then I laughed again, and so did he.

"I tell you." He reached out his hand and we shook. "My name is Tio Felipe Ignacio de Fuestes. The people here call me Tio."

---

5. **Ladinos**\lə ˈdē·nōs\
6. **mestizo**\mĕsˈtē·zō\ a half-breed, a person of mixed blood.
7. **Mayan**\ˈma·yən *or* ˈmai·yən\ The Maya Indians of Central America showed a relatively high civilization when Columbus visited America.
8. **Hattiesburg** is in southeastern Mississippi between Laurel and Gulfport. The name of the college has been changed from Mississippi Southern to Southern Mississippi.

"Yes?" I knew I mustn't hurry him.

"This is not my village. I am of Mérida,[9] in Yucatán."

"Mérida, huh?"

"I was a tourist guide. To the ruins and places. I met a professor from Mississippi Southern and he got me in and helped me. He was Professor Johnson. You know him maybe—Professor Johnson?"

I said I didn't, and looked in toward the dining room, where an Indian girl was putting my lunch on a table. She wore a brightly colored blouse and her hand-woven skirt was tight around her thighs. She was barefooted and as graceful as a cat, and as noiseless.

The clerk came out from behind the desk and stood between me and the girl, and touched my arm to get my attention. "The people in this village will not believe I went to school in the United States."

"The devil you say. What's so strange about going to school in the United States? Lots of Mexicans do."

He shrugged that mean-anything gesture of Latins, the hands out and the shoulders rising. "Not to Hattiesburg, Mississippi, Mr. Hoyle. If I had told them New Orleans or Texas. Or Florida or California. But Hattiesburg, Mississippi ____" He shrugged again.

I knew exactly what he meant—exactly. Hattiesburg, Mississippi, just doesn't sound like a place where a man would go to college from a long ways off. Boston, yes. Chicago, New York, Atlanta—a dozen places, a hundred. But not Mississippi Southern in Hattiesburg. So I knew he was telling the truth. There was no reason for him to kid me and, besides, a four-flusher[10] never would have picked out Hattiesburg.

"The Ladinos think I have lied. To show off," he explained.

"Making like a big shot. I follow you now."

"The Indians don't care, or matter. But the Ladinos think I am a big mouth."

"And you want me to tell them that you really have been to school in the United States. O.K. I'll tell them."

"Only a few North Americans ever come to

Feliz. From Los Angeles, New York—places like that. They have never heard of my college. Or of Hattiesburg. I ask them and they look at me and shake their heads, and the Ladinos laugh."

The Indian waitress had stepped back from my table and my lunch was ready, and so I told the fellow to send the scoffers to me and that I'd put them right, and I went into the dining room. A couple of greasy meat patties were on my plate, and some canned corn and shriveled tomatoes. In a land that dripped exotic fruits, a land of fine peppers and black beans, here I was getting lunch-wagon hamburgers. Anyway, the coffee was good.

I was thinking of enchiladas and avocados, of thin tortillas[11] spread with black-bean paste or mountain honey, and then the owner came in and pulled up a chair. He "Psst-psst'd" at the Indian girl and she brought him a cup of coffee. He sipped his brew noisily and wiped his mustache with his fingers.

"Tio ____" He nodded toward the lobby. "Tio in there tells me you have been in Mississippi."

"That's right. In Hattiesburg. I know about the college where he went."

He was not impressed and took another sip of coffee. "There is a hotel in this place?"

"Two or three, last time I was there." I was having fun, sort of like playing a quiz game. "The largest one was the Forrest Hotel."

Now he was impressed, but tried not to show it. Even so, he was persistent, "Tio says there is a railroad in this place."

"Three, last time I was there." I didn't like the owner particularly, and thought it was about time to dress him down. I figured him for a flabby little tyrant who probably had given

---

9. **Mérida**\sp. pron. ▲mä·rē·tha\ a city of about 100,000, is the capital of Yucatán. Yucatán\'yū·kə ▲tan\ is northeast of Tabasco.

10. **four-flusher**\'fŏr ▲flə·shər\ a bluffer or impostor.

11. **enchilada**\'ĕn·chĭ ▲la·da\ a roll of thin fried dough with a chopped meat filling. **avocado**\'a·və ▲ka·dō\ a pulpy green tropical vegetable eaten raw and often used in salads. **tortilla**\'tŏr ▲tē·ya\ a very thin round, crisp, fried cake.

Tio a hard time. "Tell you something, mister." I pushed my empty cup away and lit a cigarette. "Your clerk says he has been to college in Hattiesburg, Mississippi. He has. I've got a hundred pesos to ten pesos that he has."

I have never seen a Latin American who wouldn't cover a bet if he had the slightest outside chance of winning.

"A hundred to ten," I repeated, and loud enough for the Indian waitress to hear.

The owner drained his cup and got up. "I never bet with strangers. Have some more coffee, Mr. Hoyle, but you will excuse me, please."

He left me and walked out into the afternoon, and I knew to spread the news that Tio really had been to college, like he said, and that he was willing to bet that it was so, and that he had a gringo[12] to back it up.

Tio waited until the boss was safely away, and came to my table and sat down, and the waitress brought him coffee without being told to do so. She smiled at him, a quick, sly little smile of triumph shared. "You have done me a gracious service, Mr. Hoyle." He offered me one of his own cigarettes and lit one for himself.

"That's more than you've done for me." I nodded toward the food that I hadn't touched. "Is this the sort of stuff you eat?"

Tio was surprised. "I thought you would approve. I told them about the hamburgers. In Hattiesburg—hamburgers. Day and night, hamburgers."

"In Mexico I like Mexican food. Good hot Mexican food, red-hot."

"Oh?" Tio was delighted and proud. "You say?"

"Sure, I say. Have you got any tortillas back there? And bean paste? And some hot peppers?"

Tio clapped his hands like a proprietor, and the waitress came running, and he spoke to her so rapidly that I caught none of it, and she, too, was proud and hurried back to the kitchen. Tio leaned back in his chair and blew smoke toward the ceiling, like a man suddenly sure of himself, like a bantam cockerel[13] that had found his

way around the barnyard. "It is the food of the land, my friend."

The tortillas were thin and the bean paste was spicy and without lumps. And there was a bottle of beer with a red rooster on the label. The peppers, however, weren't much. No authority. Long red peppers that had been dried so long that their kick was gone. I recognized them immediately as Ashanti, the dried fruit of *Piper clusii*.[14] I picked up one and tasted it, and to me it was almost bland.

"Be careful," Tio cautioned me. "They are hot."

"Hot? Those things?" I tossed the pepper back into the dish and took a long swallow of beer. "They are for children. For nursing children."

"They do not burn?" Tio's cigarette was almost to his fingers and he seemed not to notice it. "There is no sweat? No fire in the belly?"

"Listen, my friend." I picked up another of the peppers and tore it open and tasted the seeds, and they were mild. That is, to me they were mild. "I'm a hot-pepper man, Tio. And when I say hot-pepper man, I mean *hot*-pepper man."

"But they do not eat hot peppers in the United States. Here and there, yes. But hot peppers there are weak peppers here."

"I'm from here and there." I spread a tortilla thick with bean paste and smacked my delight. "I used to live in Louisiana and they have hot peppers in Louisiana. Little red devils with fire in their skin and hell in their seeds."

Tio clapped his hands again and spoke to the Indian girl, and she quickly was back with a little bowl of *furias*. Nice and fat and sort of a greenish yellow. They had been steeped in vinegar, though, and much of the sting was out. Still, they had some authority, unless you happen to be a hot-pepper man like me. I took two

---

12. **gringo**\▲grĭŋ•gō\ a foreigner to Mexico or Central America, especially an American.

13. **bantam**\▲băn•təm\ **cockerel**\▲kŏ•kə•rəl\ a miniature rooster, often having a bold disposition.

14. **Ashanti**\a ▲shan•tē\ **Piper clusii** is the scientific botanical designation.

of them in one bite, and the waitress actually gaped at me, and turned and ran back to the kitchen.

Tio was fascinated. "You do not sweat. Or grab for the beer. You do not even blow your breath out hard. This is a thing, my friend. Those are *furias*."

"For growing boys," I said.

The Indian girl had come back to the doorway of the dining room, and three or four other Indians were with her, and they were watching me. Tio waved his hand and she ran and fetched a bottle of beer for him.

"Bring two more," he said. "And one for Manuel in the kitchen, and one for Ricardo in the garden. For Pablo and Pedro." The boss was gone and he really was big-wheeling. "One over to Father Francisco. To little Father Diego and big Father Diego. A Rooster beer for all."

The hotel was as gay as a *cantina*.[15] The Indians beamed and the chef gave the waitress a pat when she passed by him. Tio went to the desk and took two cigars from the owner's private box, and we lit up.

Then he said, "So you like Mexican food. And hot peppers. You will come with me. I take you to the place of Hilario Villareal."

I was warm inside from the beer and peppers, and felt chipper for the first time in weeks, and he told one of the Indians to look after things and we went forth. The village was waking up and some of our hotel Indians were shooting off firecrackers over by the church gate.

"To arouse the saints from their siesta," Tio explained. "They think the saints should be up and about their jobs."

We crossed over to the plaza and walked around it twice. He was puffing his cigar and talking up a storm and making sure that everybody in the plaza saw us together. He led the way into a *cantina* and ordered two more beers. A radio was limping a scratchy melody, and Tio spoke up so all could hear, "In Feliz, not so much as a movie. In Hattiesburg, Mississippi —in Hattiesburg, where I went to college, talking pictures every night. And the baseball."

"You tell 'em, brother," I said. "In Hattiesburg, the football also. And hamburgers."

"You tell 'em, brother," he said.

We made another round of the plaza, in case somebody had missed us, and Tio was silent for a spell, a mighty short one. Then he glanced up at me and away, and said, "In Hattiesburg, my friends called me Chili. I didn't mind. In Mexico, chili is a pepper. In Hattiesburg, it is meat and beans and pepper powder. But they called me Chili. You know how it is up there. Always the nickname."

"Chili, huh? O.K., Chili. My friends call me Pete." I started laughing, "Goes back to when I was so high. Just a kid. Little boy." I don't know why I told him, just wanted to tell him. "Used to run around playing like I was a biddy,[16] a little chicken. Going 'Peep, peep.' My sister got to calling me Peep, and it got to be Pete. You know how it is."

He took off his hat and leaned against a tree and laughed. "O.K., Pete. Now we go to the place of Hilario Villareal. Me and you."

We walked on, and again he was silent, this time for several minutes. The beer was wearing off and I noticed that he was frowning.

At last he said, "About me going to college in the United States. I told you the Indians do not care, and do not matter. Well, Hilario Villareal is an Indian. He matters."

I knew that something was eating him and that he would tell me at his own time. Sure enough, we had walked almost another block and he picked up his story. "Hilario Villareal is the best pepper man in Feliz. He eats *furias* for breakfast. With beer."

"They'll wake you up all right," I said. "And put fire in your blood."

Tio's cigar was soggy and frayed and he threw it away. The exhilaration had gone out of him. "Hilario Villareal grows his own peppers and has a secret. He wet-rots[17] leaves for

---

15. **cantina**\ˈkan ᴧtē·na\ a small restaurant, often one with entertainment for evening trade.
16. **biddy,** a small hen.
17. **wet-rot,** to induce rotting under very moist conditions.

his plants and grows them on a south slope that is sheltered on three sides. And in the dry season he waters them from a bucket. I tell you to have respect for his peppers. His soil is very sour and his peppers are very hot."

It meant only that the Indian understood prevailing winds, that he used acid soil, humus[18] and controlled moisture. I was looking forward to a session at his table, to a bait of *tacos* and *tortas compuestas,* maybe with some real Capsicums, fresh from the bush and oozing their pungent piperine.[19]

"Hilario Villareal is very proud. He does not like Ladinos. Particularly, he does not like me. He thinks I am a big mouth."

"About Hattiesburg, huh?"

"Yes. He thinks I am a man of guile."

"What do you care?"

"Hilario Villareal has a daughter. Her name is Nena.[20]"

So that was it: A Ladino, an Indian girl and her father, who didn't like Ladinos. There was nothing for me to say, and besides, I was hungry. And then we were at Villareal's place. Like the hotel, it was on a corner and several Indians were loafing around the door, and we made our way inside, and there was Hilario Villareal, Indian-faced and grave and with all the dignity of the Mayan, the unchanged. And there was Nena. She and her father saw us come in, and her father glanced her way and she walked out, across the patio to the family's quarters. I didn't get a good look at her, but what I got was good.

Tio stepped to the counter and bought a little black cigar that was strong enough to do push-ups. I went over and sat at a table, and Tio said to the proprietor, "He is my friend. He has been to Hattiesburg, Mississippi, where I went to school, as you know."

Hilario did not even give him the courtesy of a reply. He was a heavy man, very heavy for an Indian, and although standing, he folded his hands across his stomach and looked disdainfully away from Tio. Several Indians drifted in and stood around, looking at me and at Tio, but mostly at me.

Then Hilario came over to my table, and I said, "My friend Tio tells me you have the best food in Feliz. And peppers."

"You like Mexican food?"

"Only if it is good."

He walked toward the kitchen, and I looked over at Tio and grinned, and then I looked around the place: the old calendars, a poster about a bullfight in Mexico City, and the clock that advertised an American soft drink.

Hilario was back much sooner than I expected, and I had an idea he wanted me to be through and both of us out of there. He had *tacos* and tortillas and honey. Also a little bowl of long peppers. They were *Pipers officinarum.* Tasty, but with about as much kick as ginger ale. The tacos were marvelous, however, and the tortillas were as thin as paper and the best I had ever eaten. I reached over and picked up one of the peppers and spoke slowly to Tio, so that they all could make out my words, "In Hattiesburg—in Hattiesburg, Mississippi, where you went to college, we eat these for dessert, eh, Chili?"

"Only children," he said, and tilted his cigar. "Sometimes old women who are sick, but always children."

"With sugar and cream." I tossed the pepper back into the bowl.

Hilario came to my table again and ate one of the peppers, smacking his lips in approval. Then he spoke to me, but did not look at me, "You like peppers?"

"Only if they are good."

It was Tio's cue, and he took it. He walked slowly, proudly, to my side and felt in his pocket and pulled out seventeen pesos. It wasn't much—only about $3.40—but I knew that it was all he had, and he put it on the table

18. **humus**\ʌhyū·məs\ recently decayed leaf and other vegetable material in soil.
19. **tacos**\ʌta·kōs\ tortilla rolls with meat filling. **tortas compuestas**\ʌtōr·tas ˈkŏm·pu ʌěs·tas\ tarts of thin fried dough with a filling, often of fruit. **Capsicum**\ʌkăp·sĭ·kəm\ a typical pepper fruit. **piperine**\ʌpĭ·pə ˈrēn\ the chemical alkaloid that is the main component of pepper.
20. **Nena**\ʌnā·na\

"The Inn," Rene d'Harnoncourt. Courtesy of the artist.

and said, "My friend, Pete, is the best pepper man in Feliz."

Hilario glanced scornfully at the money, and with all the contempt of a dueling master who has been challenged by an insolent cove.[21] For a second, I thought he was going to ignore Tio's challenge. That could have led to trouble, and so I took out my wallet and counted out a hundred pesos and slipped them under Tio's wager.

"For a cushion," I said. "The confidence of my friend is worthy of a cushion."

The spectators, all Indians, looked from one to the other, and then hard at Hilario, and he turned his back to me and walked behind his counter and picked up a cigar box and counted the money that was in it. Apparently it wasn't

---

21. **cove**\kōv\ a slang expression more English than American to mean "fellow; chap."

enough, because he left us and, without haste, crossed his patio to the family quarters. Soon he was back, and with Nena.

She never looked up lest she meet the gaze of Tio, but went behind the counter and waited. Hilario put a hundred and seventeen pesos on the table and said, "My daughter will serve us."

I nodded and he sat down and Tio moved closer behind me. The Indians moved over behind Hilario. I pushed the tacos aside, but kept the tortillas in front of me.

"You must have bread with peppers?" Hilario asked.

"Never yet have I seen peppers so hot that I must reach for the bread."

"You sweat?" Hilario was laying down the rules.

"In the sun, yes. But never from peppers. With me, the peppers warm my blood, not my skin."

"You blow hard the breath?"

"No."

"Then you sip?"

"No. I nibble."

"I sip."

"That is fair."

I moved the tortillas closer to me, and Nena brought him a bottle of beer, and the rules were set. He could sip and I could nibble. But he must wait a full minute between pepper and beer, and I must wait a full minute between pepper and bread.

Nena brought out some spiced meat and two bowls of ground pepper. One of plain black pepper which is the dried fruit of *Piper nigrum*, picked green. This is the pepper of antiquity, of Malabar and Travancore.[22] This is the pepper that sent men venturing in the days of Solomon and Sheba.[23] Rome paid ransom to Alaric[24] in *Piper nigrum*. It is romantic, but tame. The other bowl contained white pepper, which is *Piper nigrum* prepared from the ripe fruits.

Hilario dipped a bit of meat into the black pepper and another into the white pepper and ate them. I crossed my arms and leaned back in my chair as though I had been given offense.

"No?" Hilario was surprised, and tried not to show it.

"No. Does the hospitality of Feliz offer pap[25] to a stranger?" I took fifty more pesos out of my wallet. "This is for the white pepper and the black pepper. I will not tease my tongue."

Hilario stared at me and some of the hauteur went out of him, and I felt a possibility of understanding between us, of friendship a far way off, but moving toward us. Slowly he reached into his pocket and took out more money and matched my ante.

Then he turned to Nena and said, "The cayennes.[26] Only the cayennes. We have here a man of mettle."

The girl ran across the patio and more Indians came into the place and ranged themselves alongside the counter and behind Hilario. Then Ladinos came in and stood by Tio and behind me. I don't know how the word got around so fast, but there they were: the mustached Ladinos and the Indians, each backing his own kind, for I had become associated with the Ladinos. The hotel owner was there, and he whispered to Tio and stepped to the table and counted out a hundred pesos and put them in front of me, and stepped back.

Hilario reached into his pocket again, but one of the Indians touched his arm. Then all the Indians gave money to the one and he matched the hotel owner's bet.

Nena came back in and she had a tray of peppers, each kind in little piles. Only cayennes,

22. **Malabar**\\ᵃmă·lə 'bar\\ a district in the southwest coast of India. **Travancore**\\ᵃtră·van 'kōr\\ a state in the western part of extreme south India.
23. **Solomon,** a Hebrew king, important in the Old Testament, noted for his wisdom and for his building the great temple of Jerusalem. **Sheba**\\ᵃshē·bə\\ the Queen of Sheba, hearing of the temple and Solomon's fame, paid him a famous state call.
24. **Alaric**\\ᵃa·lə·rĭk\\ the Visigoth who conquered and occupied Rome in A.D. 410. For a huge ransom he withdrew his armies from it.
25. **pap**\\păp\\ baby food.
26. **cayenne**\\ᵃkai·ĕn\\ a strong, long, twisted red pepper.

the burning Capsicums. There are about thirty species of this delicacy, and she had six. There were green infernos and green terrors, yellow-jackets and yellow furies, red torrids and red frenzies.

Hilario selected one of the red frenzies and held it up for all to see. It was wrinkled near the stem; then fat and tapering to a point. He put the whole pepper in his mouth and chewed slowly. The Indian nodded solemnly, and as he chewed we both watched the clock, and when a minute had passed he reached for his beer and took a sip.

I pulled the tray close to me and fingered through the frenzies until I found two that suited me, both wrinkling their ripeness and then swelling fat into juice and skin and seeds. I held them up for Tio to approve and put both of them into my mouth. My lips stung and the lining of my mouth was hot quick and then prickling stings. I watched the clock through my minute of grace and took my nibble of tortilla.

The Ladinos crowded around Tio and patted him on the back; not me at all, but my sponsor. Then the hotel owner went among them and they gave him money and he receipted it and laid it on the table. The Indians matched it, digging deep this time because they did not have so much money as the Ladinos.

There was a quizzical look in Hilario's eyes. Maybe it was doubt. But, then, maybe it was admiration because I had taken two red frenzies, and without sweat, without the hard blowing of the breath.

We both took torrids, and this time I took only one. My lips had hardened to the sting, but my mouth was ridging inside. I puckered fast to draw saliva. Then the tingle was in my throat and deep down, but not yet to the belly. The tortilla helped some.

The bets were anted[27] again and the hotel owner called out that he was offering odds on me. "Seven to five," he called out. "On Mr. Hoyle. He is the friend of Tio, and Tio is my employee, and as all of you know"—he waved his arm in a broad gesture—"my employee

went to the school, to the college, in the United States. And Mr. Hoyle, who is my guest, knows the place. This is a truth, and I say seven to five."

There were no takers from among the Indians. They were shamefaced because they had no more money, and the Ladinos snickered. One of the Indians took off his jacket, a hand-woven garment of blue, embroidered with sacred pagan symbols. It was his most valued possession, and he walked to the table to put it there, but Hilario held out his hand and stopped him and shook his head.

Then Hilario spoke to me, ignoring the hotel owner and all the other Ladinos, "You have made your bets, Mr. Hoyle?"

"I have made my bets, Mr. Villareal."

He called his daughter, and she raised her eyes as she walked to him and seemed to be looking at him, but she was looking at Tio. The father spoke low to her, and I did not hear his words, but she nodded understanding and ran across the patio and returned with a little hide-covered box. Hilario counted out five hundred pesos—about a hundred dollars. A lot of money anywhere, a fortune in Feliz. "I take no odds," he said. "Cover the wager, gentlemen."

The Ladinos hesitated and Tio was embarrassed for them and jerked off his ring and threw it on the table. It was a gold band and worn and obviously old. Hilario picked it up and felt it and looked at it a long time, and handed it back to Tio. "I will not take a man's ring. It has memories. So have I. And now I have a new memory, the honor of knowing a man who has faith in a stranger."

The hotel owner motioned his friends into a huddle and they emptied their pockets and the owner counted out five hundred pesos and covered the bet. He held the rest of the money in his hand. Hilario pushed his box to the side of the table. I don't know if he had more money in there or not. I just knew they were not going to

---

27. **ante**\ˈăn·tē\ a poker stake put up before the deal to build the pot. Here, more bets were placed before the next round of the contest began.

bluff that fellow. If there was no more money, then there was his cantina and his house, and his land and the land of his friends.

Everything was set again and we chose our peppers—this time the yellow ones—greenish yellow, and hotter than the reds. I got by my first one and was on a yellow fury when I felt the sweat ooze out on the back of my neck, down under my collar. They couldn't see it. I was hurting, the numbing burn of piperine, which is a crystalline alkaloid that tightens the tissues like wet rawhide. Each minute got longer, and the tortillas didn't help much.

Next Hilario reached for the green ones—the busters. So did I, and the heat seared down to my belly, and I straightened quickly to stave off a cramp.

I made it through the terrors and the infernos, but Hilario was in visible agony. He was blowing hard the breath, and sweat was rolling from under his chin and down his neck. There was consternation among the Indians and jubilation among the Ladinos. Hilario spread his hands on the table, his fingers wide, and blinked at me and the tears flowed.

He managed to smile. "They are hot, sir."

"They are hot." I smiled too.

We had gone through the cayennes and I was hoping that the thing was over, and was willing, even anxious, to settle for a draw.

Hilario, though, took a deep gulp of beer and wiped his eyes and nodded to Nena. She hurried across the patio and came back with a little bowl, and in it were two little peppers. The Ladinos began jabbering excitedly and the Indians moved closer. Nena put the peppers on the table and I got a good look at them.

Amomum melegueta! I had never seen a whole one before. The spice trade calls them Guinea peppers. Such little nuggets launched armadas in the old days, sails from Spain and Portugal. Men died for those peppers as for gold and glory. They are the hottest things that grow and their seeds are praised as the grains of paradise.

Hilario studied me for my reaction, and then he said, "You have seen such before?"

"No. Only the seeds."

"They are the grains of paradise. I raise them."

"They are hot."

"You say. And I tell you, for I will be fair with you, I never before have eaten a whole one. At one time. Only the nibble."

"This will end it," I said.

"This will end it. I will wait two minutes for the sip."

"And I will wait two minutes for the bread."

We rested a spell, relaxing in an armistice, and I glanced over my shoulder to catch Tio's eye and to reassure him, but he was looking at Nena. Hilario loosened his collar and pulled his shirt wide open and reached out and picked up one of the peppers. I took the other. We put them in our mouths at the same time and began chewing. The heat jolted me. The roof of my mouth corroded and the tissues inside my cheeks contracted like burning cellophane. But I knew I was going to make it—I just knew it.

But Hilario was in contorted misery. His mouth was pinched and he was blowing hard, and then the sweat popped out of his forehead and the tears rolled out of his eyes. He was breathing deeply, like a man who had run a long race. I had him.

I heard the Ladinos muttering their boasts, their vaunts of triumph. I saw the Indians and the stricken looks on their faces. They had been beaten again. The mighty had crushed the humble. The meek must remain the downtrodden.

Then I did a crazy thing. I still don't know why, and don't ask me why. I had a minute to go and the heat inside me was wearing off. But I reached over and grabbed a tortilla. The Ladinos yelled out their astonishment and spluttered their wrath. The Indians looked from one to the other, and they could not believe they had won. Hilario was staring at me, probing deep for an explanation. Then he snatched his bottle of beer and drained it and swished the beer around in his mouth and spat and spat.

The Ladinos turned on Tio and berated him, and he seemed not to mind at all, only looking down at me and across the room at Nena and at the Indians. Then the Ladinos stomped out and left much of their money behind and much of their pride.

"It was too hot," I said to Tio.

"But it was almost over and he was blowing hard the breath."

"I was burning up inside, Chili. Maybe it didn't show, but I was burning up."

He said no more; only shrugged.

Hilario pushed back his chair. "There will be drinks. Beer for all and brandy for those who want it." He walked behind his counter and stood by Nena. "I will drink first, and to my daughter and to my daughter's man, Tio Felipe Ignacio de Fuestes. Only a good man is worthy of the friendship of such a man as Mr. Hoyle."

The Indians nodded their acceptance of the pronouncement and their approval of Tio. He walked from behind me and over to the counter and near Nena, and she raised her eyes from the floor and looked up at him and then down again. He helped Hilario open the beer. Some of the Indians took brandy and we all drank, and then Hilario said, "And now to Mr. Hoyle, who is not a stranger among us. If there is a favor we can do, we do it."

It came to me then. I don't care what has been written or what has been told before, it came to me for the first time, right then. Acid soil. Controlled moisture. A sheltered south slope and the grains of paradise. I had been offered a favor and I asked it: a few of the peppers to remember this day. Hilario was glad to give them to me. He put the *Amomum melegueta* in a paper bag, and I hung around only long enough for another round of drinks, and then I hurried to the hotel and packed. A bus left at twilight and I was on it, heading home.

The first year I planted them in a hothouse and nursed them through. The green nuggets and their seeds of gold. Then I had enough seed for a patch, and then enough seed for several acres. That's the way it started, and now I know of no place where you cannot buy my peppers or spices from the Hoyle Spice Company. I even ship peppers back to Tabasco, even to

Feliz, for there is money in coals to Newcastle[28] if you do it right. I have never been back to Feliz or to Hattiesburg. I have never heard from Tio or from any of them.

Sometimes it bothers me that I let the Ladinos down. We were talking about it just the other day, sitting around my swimming pool. I told this story, and we got to talking about whether I'd done right or wrong. My wife said I'd done right because I'd got Tio and Nena together. Some of the others said I'd been downright noble because I'd sided with the Indians, who had been pushed around so much. A few said that my successful business was proof that I was right, that I was sharp, that I was clever.

However, three of my friends—the three I like best—said I'd done a lowdown thing, that I had patronized the humble and had thrown down those who had trusted me. The least I could do, they said, was to go back to Feliz and give them a clinic or a movie house, or something. Someday I might do it. I know such gifts are not deductible,[29] but all the same, I might do it. I just might.

I

BREAKING DOWN BARRIERS

People may be pitched together in a brief encounter and yet have no meeting of minds because a wall exists between them—a wall of prejudice, fear, hatred, distaste, or ignorance. A brief encounter has significance, especially if the wall is broken down. In "Stopover in Querétaro" the love and kindness of the Mexicans overcame the author's distrust. In this story it is the American who changes the attitudes of the Mexicans. What do you think are the qualities that destroy the barrier

---

28. **Newcastle,** a coal mining center on the northeast coast of England. "To carry coals to Newcastle" is to take a commodity to a place where it is already plentiful.
29. The author means that such gifts would not be deductible on a United States income tax return.

of distrust between the following characters: Pete and Tio, Pete and Hilario, Tio and Hilario?

In the following quotations who is the speaker? Who is the person spoken to or spoken about? What does each quotation tell you about the feelings between the two persons?

1. "His clothes were mussy, but his little black mustache was trim."

2. "Have you ever seen gratitude and good will ooze from a man?"

3. "I felt a possibility of understanding between us, of friendship a far way off, but moving toward us."

4. "'. . . And now I have a new memory, the honor of knowing a man who has faith in a stranger.'"

II

IMPLICATIONS

Which of the two judgments expressed in the following passage do you agree with? State your reasons. If you agree with neither and have a third interpretation, be sure to back up your opinion with evidence from the story.

"Some . . . said I'd been downright noble because I'd sided with the Indians, who had been pushed around so much. . . . Three of my friends . . . said I'd done a lowdown thing, that I had patronized the humble and thrown down those who had trusted me."

III

TECHNIQUES

In a sense, any story written exists in two places at the same time—on the printed page and in the reader's mind. On the printed page, the writer has ordered and arranged his insights and impressions of people, places, and events into a meaningful pattern. The reader must first make an honest effort to grasp the writer's meaning and then test the insights and the pattern given by the writer against what he knows about life. Each reader must find in the story the meaning it has for him.

Throughout this book, you will study the various elements that experienced readers look for in different kinds of literature. As your skill in recognizing these elements increases, so will your ability to read, to appreciate, and to enjoy good literature. Three of the basic elements in every story are exposition, conflict, and climax. These are the elements which you will examine in the short stories in BRIEF ENCOUNTERS.

Exposition

When a reader begins a short story, he instinctively looks for the answers to four questions: Who are the people? Where are they? When is the story taking place? What is the basic situation, or starting point of the story? It is the writer's task to supply answers to these questions as quickly and naturally as possible. This material is called the *exposition* of the story. It does not necessarily all come in one block at the beginning. Sometimes clues are given through the dialogue, sometimes through the careful use of a single sentence here and there or even a single adjective or clause. In most nineteenth-century short stories, the writer often seemed to stop and say, "Now, reader, here are the things you need to know before getting into this story." In contemporary writing, the author usually tries to provide this information so quickly and casually that the reader is not conscious of it.

The first sentence of "The Grains of Paradise" gives you a clear idea of what kind of man the narrator is. By *not* giving you any information about dates or time, the author lets you know that the time could be either the past or the present. Time, therefore, is not a crucial element in the story.

Skim the first part of "The Grains of Paradise" and locate the passages where the author answers the following questions: Who are the characters? Where is the story taking place? What is the basic situation?

Conflict

Stories are built around a conflict, a struggle between two or more opposing forces. The writer establishes this conflict in such a way that the reader's curiosity is aroused and he reads on to find out how the conflict will come out. In some stories, the conflict exists between people—one person is pitted against another. In others, the conflict may develop between a person and a set of circumstances that threaten his security or a force of nature that threatens his life. And often, in the finest writing, the conflict is an inner one between two or more instincts, emotions, or values in one person. There is usually more than one conflict in a story, as in "The Grains of Paradise," but there is always one major conflict to which the others contribute.

There are at least three conflicts at work in "The Grains of Paradise." Two are between individuals, and one is between opposing groups. Name the persons involved in each conflict. Which, in your opinion, is the main conflict? Why?

Climax

Whatever the nature of the major conflict in a story, the two opposing forces inevitably progress to a point in the action when one must win and the other lose. This point at which the reader feels certain that the story must turn one way or another is the climax. It is the moment when "something's got to give" . . . when the conflict turns toward a solution.

This resolution is not necessarily the end of the story. A concluding section often explains the resolution and tells some of the effects it had or will have on the characters.

All three of the conflicts in "The Grains of Paradise" are brought together in the pepper-eating contest. What is the moment of climax in this contest, and how is each conflict resolved by the outcome of the contest? Would you say that the author made the resolution seem plausible? What reasons can you find for the decision that the narrator made? How did the decision lead to the resolution?

IV

WORDS

A. Context frequently supplies clues which permit you to infer the general meaning of an unfamiliar word. You probably can guess the general meaning of *antiquated* in the following sentence: "I glanced about the room and noticed that the paint on the walls was scaling, the furnishings *antiquated*." If you do not know what *antiquated* means, the fact of paint scaling tells you that it has something to do with the poor condition of the room. Look up *antiquated* in your dictionary. What special effect did the author achieve through the use of the word? In the following phrases and clauses, determine first from context the meaning of the italicized words and then check your meaning in the dictionary:

1. Only heavy *sedatives* put me to sleep that night.

2. A *cluster* of ragged *urchins* was around the door. One of the children held out a toy. . . .

3. . . . explained why he had ventured to *intrude* on my privacy.

4. . . . someone who had been through the same *ordeal.*

5. . . . made some comment, some *pleasantry* about the weather.

6. He was a paunchy man glistening sweat and his clothes were as *disheveled* as the clerk's, and his mustache was just as trim.

7. I could see the plaza, empty at that hour, and its trees drooping their *somnolence.*

8. At one point a character in "Grains of Paradise" "looked *disdainfully* away" and later he "glanced *scornfully* at the money." What is the difference in meaning between *disdain* and *scorn*?

B. In English words of two or more syllables are likely to be composed of either affixes and roots or of compound roots. An affix is a prefix like the *in-* in *inclose,* and *dis-* in *distrust,* or a suffix like the *-y* in *lucky,* the *-ish* in *bookish.* The part of a word to which a prefix or suffix is attached is called a root. Sometimes the root is an independent word—*close, trust, luck,* and *book* in the illustrations above. But sometimes the root has no independent existence without affixes, like the *-clude* of *conclude,* the *-flect* of *reflect,* the *-dict* of *diction,* the *-junct* of *juncture.*

Three very common roots, all of them from Latin, are *-fin,* meaning "limit, term, end" as in *define, final, infinite; -port-,* meaning "bear, carry" as in *transport, import,* and *porter;* and *-junct-,* meaning "join" as in *juncture, adjunct,* and *conjunction.* Watch for these and other roots in your reading. Use your dictionary to analyze the roots in the following words from "Stopover in Querétaro" and from "Grains of Paradise": *concussion, confess, adequate, opposite, sympathy, dislocated, intrude, solitude, profess, proprietor, pungent, confidence, spectator, associated, admiration, corrode, contract, contort.*

C. Though *tortilla* is a Spanish word, it is fairly familiar to speakers of American English. The reason for its familiarity is that it is a word that was borrowed from Spanish settlers during the early history of America. Other loan-words traceable to the Spanish colonists include: *mustang, corral, stampede, bronco, tamale, bonanza, desperado, vigilante, cafeteria, chaparral, rodeo, chili con carne, taco.*

Corsica is an island noted for its warm climate
and its hot-tempered people. They are a people
who live according to an ancient
and primitive code. One mellow autumn day,
two people are thrust together
under circumstances that test this code.

Mateo Falcone

PROSPER MÉRIMÉE

On leaving Porto-Vecchio[1] from the north-west and directing his steps towards the interior of the island, the traveler will notice that the land rises rapidly, and after three hours' walking over tortuous paths obstructed by great masses of rock and sometimes cut by ravines, he will find himself on the border of a great maquis.[2] The maquis is the domain of the Corsican shepherds and of those who are at variance with justice. It must be known that, in order to save himself the trouble of manuring his field, the Corsican husbandman sets fire to a piece of woodland. If the flame spread farther than is necessary, so much the worse! In any case he is certain of a good crop from the land fertilized by the ashes of the trees which grow upon it. He gathers only the heads of his grain, leaving the straw, which it would be unnecessary labor to cut. In the following spring the roots that have remained in the earth without being destroyed send up their tufts of sprouts, which in a few years reach a height of seven or eight feet. It is this kind of tangled thicket that is called a maquis. They are made up of different kinds of trees and shrubs, so crowded and mingled together at the caprice of nature that only with an ax in hand can a man open a passage through them, and maquis are frequently seen so thick and bushy that the wild sheep themselves cannot penetrate them.

If you have killed a man, go into the maquis of Porto-Vecchio. With a good gun and plenty of powder and balls, you can live there in safety. Do not forget a brown cloak furnished with a hood, which will serve you for both cover and mattress. The shepherds will give you chestnuts, milk and cheese, and you will have nothing to fear from justice nor the relatives of the dead except when it is necessary for you to descend to the city to replenish your ammunition.

When I was in Corsica, Mateo Falcone had his house half a league from this maquis. He was rich enough for that country, living in noble style—that is to say, doing nothing—on the income from his flocks, which the shepherds, who are a kind of nomads, lead to pasture here and there on the mountains. When I saw him, two years after the event that I am about to relate, he appeared to me to be about fifty years old or more. Picture to yourself a man, small but robust, with curly hair, black as jet, an aquiline nose, thin lips, large, restless eyes, and a complexion the color of tanned leather. His skill as a marksman was considered extraordinary even in his country, where good shots are so common. For example, Mateo would never fire at a sheep with buckshot; but at a hundred and twenty paces, he would drop it with a ball in the head or shoulder, as he chose. He used his arms as easily at night as during the day. I was told this feat of his skill, which will, perhaps seem impossible to those who have not traveled in Corsica. A lighted candle was placed at eighty paces, behind a paper transparency about the size of a plate. He would take aim, then the candle would be extinguished, and, at the end of a moment, in the most complete darkness, he would fire and hit the paper three times out of four.

With such a transcendent accomplishment, Mateo Falcone had acquired a great reputation. He was said to be as good a friend as he

---

1. **Porto-Vecchio**\ˈpȯr·tō ˈvĕk·yō\ a seaport town in southeastern Corsica.
2. **maquis**\ˈma ˈkē\ a thick underbrush.

A general view of Corte, isolated in the rugged mountains of central Corsica.

was a dangerous enemy; accommodating and charitable, he lived at peace with all the world in the district of Porto-Vecchio. But it is said of him that in Corte,[3] where he had married his wife, he had disembarrassed himself very vigorously of a rival who was considered as redoubtable in war as in love; at least, a certain gun-shot which surprised this rival as he was shaving before a little mirror hung in his window was attributed to Mateo. The affair was smoothed over and Mateo was married. His wife Giuseppa had given him at first three daughters (which infuriated him), and finally a son, whom he named Fortunato, and who became the hope of his family, the inheritor of the name. The daughters were well married: their father could count at need on the poniards and carbines of his sons-in-law. The son was only ten years old, but he already gave promise of fine attributes.

On a certain day in autumn, Mateo set out at an early hour with his wife to visit one of his flocks in a clearing of the maquis. The little Fortunato wanted to go with them, but the clearing was too far away; moreover, it was necessary someone should stay to watch the house; therefore the father refused; it will be seen whether or not he had reason to repent.

He had been gone some hours, and the little Fortunato was tranquilly stretched out in the sun, looking at the blue mountains, and thinking that the next Sunday he was going to dine in the city with his uncle, the Caporal,[4] when he was suddenly interrupted in his meditations by the firing of a musket. He got up and turned to that side of the plain whence the noise came.

---

3. **Corte**\\▲kōr·tā\ a town in central Corsica.
4. **Caporal**\\▲kā·pə 'ral\ foreman.

Other shots followed, fired at irregular intervals, and each time nearer; at last, in the path which led from the plain to Mateo's house, appeared a man wearing the pointed hat of the mountaineers, bearded, covered with rags, and dragging himself along with difficulty by the support of his gun. He had just received a wound in his thigh.

This man was an outlaw, who, having gone to the town by night to buy powder, had fallen on the way into an ambuscade of Corsican light-infantry. After a vigorous defense he was fortunate in making his retreat, closely followed and firing from rock to rock. But he was only a little in advance of the soldiers, and his wound prevented him from gaining the maquis before being overtaken.

He approached Fortunato and said: "You are the son of Mateo Falcone?"—"Yes."

"I am Gianetto Saupiero. I am followed by the yellow-collars.[5] Hide me, for I can go no farther."

"And what will my father say if I hide you without his permission?"

"He will say that you have done well."

"How do you know?"

"Hide me quickly; they are coming."

"Wait till my father gets back."

"How can I wait? Malediction! They will be here in five minutes. Come, hide me, or I will kill you."

Fortunato answered him with the utmost coolness:

"Your gun is empty, and there are no more cartridges in your belt."

"I have my stiletto."

"But can you run as fast as I can?"

He gave a leap and put himself out of reach.

"You are not the son of Mateo Falcone! Will you then let me be captured before your house?"

The child appeared moved.

"What will you give me if I hide you?" said he, coming nearer.

The outlaw felt in a leather pocket that hung from his belt, and took out a five-franc piece, which he had doubtless saved to buy ammunition with. Fortunato smiled at the sight of the silver piece; he snatched it, and said to Gianetto:

"Fear nothing."

Immediately he made a great hole in a pile of hay that was near the house. Gianetto crouched down in it and the child covered him in such a way that he could breathe without it being possible to suspect that the hay concealed a man. He bethought himself further, and, with the subtlety of a tolerably ingenious savage, placed a cat and her kittens on the pile, that it might not appear to have been recently disturbed. Then, noticing the traces of blood on the path near the house, he covered them carefully with dust, and, that done, he again stretched himself out in the sun with the greatest tranquillity.

A few moments afterwards, six men in brown uniforms with yellow collars, and commanded by an Adjutant, were before Mateo's door. This Adjutant was a distant relative of Falcone's. (In Corsica the degrees of relationship are followed much further than elsewhere.) His name was Tiodoro Gamba; he was an active man, much dreaded by the outlaws, several of whom he had already entrapped.

"Good day, little cousin," said he, approaching Fortunato; "how tall you have grown. Have you seen a man go past here just now?"

"Oh! I am not yet so tall as you, my cousin," replied the child with a simple air.

"You soon will be. But haven't you seen a man go by here, tell me?"

"If I have seen a man go by?"

"Yes, a man with a pointed hat of black velvet, and a vest embroidered with red and yellow."

"A man with a pointed hat, and a vest embroidered with red and yellow?"

"Yes, answer quickly, and don't repeat my questions!"

"This morning the curé[6] passed before our

---

5. **yellow-collars**, regular Corsican soldiery.
6. **curé**\ᴬkyū 'rā\ a parish priest.

door on his horse, Piero. He asked me how papa was, and I answered him—"

"Ah, you little scoundrel, you are playing sly! Tell me quickly which way Gianetto went? We are looking for him, and I am sure he took this path."

"Who knows?"

"Who knows? It is I who know that you have seen him."

"Can any one see who passes when they are asleep?"

"You were not asleep, rascal; the shooting woke you up."

"Then you believe, cousin, that your guns make so much noise? My father's carbine has the advantage of them."

"The devil take you, you cursed little scapegrace. I am certain that you have seen Gianetto. Perhaps, even, you have hidden him. Come, comrades, go into the house and see if our man is there. He could only go on one foot, and the knave has too much good sense to try to reach the maquis limping like that. Moreover, the bloody tracks stop here."

"And what will papa say?" asked Fortunato with a sneer. "What will he say if he knows that his house has been entered while he was away?"

"You rascal," said the Adjutant, taking him by the ear, "do you know that it only remains for me to make you change your tone? Perhaps you will speak differently after I have given you twenty blows with the flat of my sword."

Fortunato continued to sneer.

"My father is Mateo Falcone," said he with emphasis.

"You little scamp, you know very well that I can carry you off to Corte or to Bastia. I will make you lie in a dungeon, on straw, with your feet in shackles, and I will have you guillotined if you don't tell me where Gianetto is."

The child burst out laughing at this ridiculous menace. He repeated:

"My father is Mateo Falcone."

"Adjutant," said one of the soldiers in a low voice, "let us have no quarrels with Mateo."

Gamba appeared evidently embarrassed. He spoke in an undertone with the soldiers who had already visited the house. This was not a very long operation, for the cabin of a Corsican consists only of a single square room, furnished with a table, some benches, chests, housekeeping utensils and those of the chase. In the meantime, little Fortunato petted his cat and seemed to take a wicked enjoyment in the confusion of the soldiers and of his cousin.

One of the men approached the pile of hay. He saw the cat, and gave the pile a careless thrust with his bayonet, shrugging his shoulders as if he felt that his precaution was ridiculous. Nothing moved; the boy's face betrayed not the slightest emotion.

The Adjutant and his troop were cursing their luck. Already they were looking in the direction of the plain, as if disposed to return by the way they had come, when their chief, convinced that menaces would produce no impression on Falcone's son, determined to make a last effort, and try the effect of caresses and presents.

"My little cousin," said he, "you are a very wide-awake little fellow. You will get along. But you are playing a naughty game with me; and if I wasn't afraid of making trouble for my cousin, Mateo, the devil take me, but I would carry you off with me."

"Bah!"

"But when my cousin comes back I shall tell him about this, and he will whip you till the blood comes for having told such lies."

"You don't say so!"

"You will see. But hold on!—be a good boy and I will give you something."

"Cousin, let me give you some advice: if you wait much longer Gianetto will be in the maquis and it will take a smarter man than you to follow him."

The Adjutant took from his pocket a silver watch worth about ten crowns, and noticing that Fortunato's eyes sparkled at the sight of it, said, holding the watch by the end of its steel chain:

"Rascal! you would like to have such a watch as that hung around your neck, wouldn't you, and to walk in the streets of Porto-Vecchio proud as a peacock? People would ask you what time it was, and you would say: 'Look at my watch.'"

"When I am grown up, my uncle, the Caporal, will give me a watch."

"Yes; but your uncle's little boy has one already; not so fine as this either. But then, he is younger than you."

The child sighed.

"Well! Would you like this watch, little cousin?"

Fortunato, casting sidelong glances at the watch, resembled a cat that has been given a whole chicken. It feels that it is being made sport of, and does not dare to use its claws; from time to time it turns its eyes away so as not to be tempted, licking its jaws all the while, and has the appearance of saying to its master, "How cruel your joke is!"

However, the Adjutant seemed in earnest in offering his watch. Fortunato did not reach out his hand for it, but said with a bitter smile:

"Why do you make fun of me?"

"By heaven! I am not making fun of you. Only tell me where Gianetto is and the watch is yours."

Fortunato smiled incredulously, and fixing his black eyes on those of the Adjutant tried to read there the faith he ought to have had in his words.

"May I lose my epaulettes," cried the Adjutant, "if I do not give you the watch on this condition. These comrades are witnesses; I cannot deny it."

While speaking he gradually held the watch nearer till it almost touched the child's pale face, which plainly showed the struggle that was going on in his soul between covetousness and respect for hospitality. His breast swelled with emotion; he seemed about to suffocate. Meanwhile the watch was slowly swaying and turning, sometimes brushing against his cheek. Finally, his right hand was gradually stretched toward it; the ends of his fingers touched it; then its whole weight was in his hand, the Adjutant still keeping hold of the chain. The face

was light blue; the cases newly burnished. In the sunlight it seemed to be all on fire. The temptation was too great. Fortunato raised his left hand and pointed over his shoulder with his thumb at the hay against which he was reclining. The Adjutant understood him at once. He dropped the end of the chain and Fortunato felt himself the sole possessor of the watch. He sprang up with the agility of a deer and stood ten feet from the pile, which the soldiers began at once to overturn.

There was a movement in the hay, and a bloody man with a poniard in his hand appeared. He tried to rise to his feet, but his stiffened leg would not permit it and he fell. The Adjutant at once grappled with him and took away his stiletto. He was immediately secured, notwithstanding his resistance.

Gianetto, lying on the earth and bound like a fagot, turned his head towards Fortunato, who had approached.

"Son of—!" said he, with more contempt than anger.

The child threw him the silver piece which he had received, feeling that he no longer deserved it; but the outlaw paid no attention to the movement, and with great coolness said to the Adjutant:

"My dear Gamba, I cannot walk; you will be obliged to carry me to the city."

"Just now you could run faster than a buck," answered the cruel captor; "but be at rest. I am so pleased to have you that I would carry you a league on my back without fatigue. Besides, comrade, we are going to make a litter for you with your cloak and some branches, and at the Crespoli farm we shall find horses."

"Good," said the prisoner. "You will also put a little straw on your litter that I may be more comfortable."

While some of the soldiers were occupied in making a kind of stretcher out of some chestnut boughs and the rest were dressing Gianetto's wound, Mateo Falcone and his wife suddenly appeared at a turn in the path that led to the maquis. The woman was staggering under the weight of an enormous sack of chestnuts, while her husband was sauntering along, carrying one gun in his hands, while another was slung across his shoulders, for it is unworthy of a man to carry other burdens than his arms.

At the sight of the soldiers Mateo's first thought was that they had come to arrest him. But why this thought? Had he then some quarrels with justice? No. He enjoyed a good reputation. He was said to have a particularly good name, but he was a Corsican and a highlander, and there are few Corsican highlanders who, in scrutinizing their memory, cannot find some peccadillo, such as a gun-shot, dagger-thrust, or similar trifles. Mateo more than others had a clear conscience; for more than ten years he had not pointed his carbine at a man, but he was always prudent, and put himself into a position to make a good defense if necessary. "Wife," said he to Giuseppa, "put down the sack and hold yourself ready."

She obeyed at once. He gave her the gun that was slung across his shoulders, which would have bothered him, and, cocking the one he held in his hands, advanced slowly towards the house, walking among the trees that bordered the road, ready at the least hostile demonstration, to hide behind the largest, whence he could fire from under cover. His wife followed closely behind, holding his reserve weapon and his cartridge-box. The duty of a good housekeeper, in case of a fight, is to load her husband's carbines.

On the other side the Adjutant was greatly troubled to see Mateo advance in this manner, with cautious steps, his carbine raised, and his finger on the trigger.

"If by chance," thought he, "Mateo should be related to Gianetto, or if he should be his friend and wish to defend him, the contents of his two guns would arrive amongst us as certainly as a letter in the post; and if he should see me, notwithstanding the relationship!"

In this perplexity he took a bold step. It was to advance alone towards Mateo and tell him of the affair while accosting him as an old acquaintance, but the short space that separated him from Mateo seemed terribly long.

"Hello! old comrade," cried he. "How do you do, my good fellow? It is I, Gamba, your cousin."

Without answering a word, Mateo stopped, and in proportion as the other spoke, slowly raised the muzzle of his gun so that it was pointing upward when the Adjutant joined him.

"Good-day, brother," said the Adjutant, holding out his hand. "It is a long time since I have seen you."

"Good-day, brother."

"I stopped while passing, to say good-day to you and to cousin Pepa here. We have had a long journey to-day, but have no reason to complain, for we have captured a famous prize. We have just seized Gianetto Saupiero."

"God be praised!" cried Giuseppa. "He stole a milch goat from us last week."

These words reassured Gamba.

"Poor devil!" said Mateo, "He was hungry."

"The villain fought like a lion," continued the Adjutant, a little mortified. "He killed one of my soldiers, and not content with that, broke Caporal Chardon's arm; but that matters little, he is only a Frenchman. Then, too, he was so well hidden that the devil couldn't have found him. Without my little cousin, Fortunato, I should never have discovered him."

"Fortunato!" cried Mateo.

"Fortunato!" repeated Giuseppa.

"Yes, Gianetto was hidden under the haypile yonder, but my little cousin showed me the trick. I shall tell his uncle, the Caporal, that he may send him a fine present for his trouble. Both his name and yours will be in the report that I shall send to the Attorney-general."

"Malediction!" said Mateo in a low voice.

They had rejoined the detachment. Gianetto was already lying on the litter ready to set out. When he saw Mateo and Gamba in company he smiled a strange smile, then, turning his head towards the door of the house, he spat on the sill, saying:

"House of a traitor."

Only a man determined to die would dare pronounce the word traitor to Falcone. A good blow with the stiletto, which there would be no need of repeating, would have immediately paid the insult. However, Mateo made no other movement than to place his hand on his forehead like a man who is dazed.

Fortunato had gone into the house when his father arrived, but now he reappeared with a bowl of milk which he handed with downcast eyes to Gianetto.

"Get away from me!" cried the outlaw, in a loud voice. Then, turning to one of the soldiers, he said:

"Comrade, give me a drink."

The soldier placed his gourd in his hands, and the prisoner drank the water handed to him by a man with whom he had just exchanged bullets. He then asked them to tie his hands across his breast instead of behind his back.

"I like," said he, "to lie at my ease."

They hastened to satisfy him; then the Adjutant gave the signal to start, said adieu to Mateo, who did not respond, and descended with rapid steps towards the plain.

Nearly ten minutes elapsed before Mateo spoke. The child looked with restless eyes, now at his mother, now at his father, who was leaning on his gun and gazing at him with an expression of concentrated rage.

"You begin well," said Mateo at last with a calm voice, but frightful to one who knew the man.

"Oh, father," cried the boy, bursting into tears, and making a forward movement as if to throw himself on his knees. But Mateo cried, "Away from me!"

The little fellow stopped and sobbed, immovable, a few feet from his father.

Giuseppa drew near. She had just discovered the watch-chain, the end of which was hanging out of Fortunato's jacket.

"Who gave you that watch?" demanded she in a severe tone.

"My cousin, the Adjutant."

Falcone seized the watch and smashed it in a thousand pieces against a rock.

"Wife," said he, "is this my child?"

Giuseppa's cheeks turned a brick-red.

"What are you saying, Mateo? Do you know to whom you speak?"

"Very well, this child is the first of his race to commit treason."

Fortunato's sobs and gasps redoubled as Falcone kept his lynx-eyes upon him. Then he struck the earth with his gunstock, shouldered the weapon, and turned in the direction of the maquis, calling to Fortunato to follow. The boy obeyed. Giuseppa hastened after Mateo and seized his arm.

"He is your son," said she with a trembling voice, fastening her black eyes on those of her husband to read what was going on in his heart.

"Leave me alone," said Mateo. "I am his father."

Giuseppa embraced her son, and bursting into tears entered the house. She threw herself on her knees before an image of the Virgin and prayed ardently. In the meanwhile Falcone walked some two hundred paces along the path and only stopped when he reached a little ravine which he descended. He tried the earth with the butt-end of his carbine, and found it soft and easy to dig. The place seemed to be convenient for his design.

"Fortunato, go close to that big rock there."

The child did as he was commanded, then he kneeled.

"Say your prayers."

"Oh, father, father, do not kill me!"

"Say your prayers!" repeated Mateo in a terrible voice.

The boy, stammering and sobbing, recited the Pater and the Credo.[7] At the end of each prayer the father loudly answered, "Amen!"

"Are those all the prayers you know?"

"Oh! father, I know the Ave Maria[8] and the litany that my aunt taught me."

"It is very long, but no matter."

---

7. **Pater**\ˈpä·tär\ the Lord's Prayer. **Credo**\ˈkrē·dō\ an official profession of faith.

8. **Ave Maria**\ˈä·vä ma ˈrē·a\ a salutation and prayer to the Virgin Mary.

The child finished the litany in a scarcely audible tone.

"Are you finished?"

"Oh! my father, have mercy! Pardon me! I will never do so again. I will beg my cousin, the Caporal, to pardon Gianetto."

He was still speaking. Mateo raised his gun, and, taking aim, said:

"May God pardon you!"

The boy made a desperate effort to rise and grasp his father's knees, but there was not time. Mateo fired and Fortunato fell dead.

Without casting a glance on the body, Mateo returned to the house for a spade with which to bury his son. He had gone but a few steps when he met Giuseppa, who, alarmed by the shot, was hastening hither.

"What have you done?" cried she.

"Justice."

"Where is he?"

"In the ravine. I am going to bury him. He died a Christian. I shall have a mass said for him. Have my son-in-law, Tiodoro Bianchi, sent for to come and live with us."

I

AN ANCIENT CODE OF HONOR

The reader is left with a sense of shock when he finishes "Mateo Falcone." This reaction occurs because he brings his own feelings and his own code of a more civilized and stable society to the situation. Only upon reflection does he come to see that given all the circumstances that the writer has carefully presented, the devastating outcome is inevitable. The brief encounter that begins as a meeting between a man and a boy on a lazy autumn day changes forever the lives of all the people involved in it.

II

IMPLICATIONS

Consider and discuss this story in terms of the following questions:

1. What is the code that Mateo Falcone has set for his life?

2. Is this code the result of the conditions under which he lives or the result of the kind of person he is?

3. In what ways does Fortunato indicate that he is learning the ways of his father?

4. Is it an impulse of the moment that makes Mateo kill his son?

5. Actually, Mateo Falcone appears very briefly in the story; far more space is given to the other characters. Why then is the story called "Mateo Falcone"?

III

TECHNIQUES

"Mateo Falcone" has been referred to as a masterpiece. As Poe turned the short work of fiction into a distinctive literary form in America, so Mérimée, through this story, made the short story a polished work of art in France. He holds himself to a concise, objective portrayal of the actions of a small group of people. But the compressed record hits the reader's mind with great force.

Exposition

"Mateo Falcone" illustrates the handling of exposition as it was typically done a hundred years ago. How would you describe this method? Why is it effective for this story?

The setting which is part of the exposition is of particular importance in "Mateo Falcone." Imagine the story taking place in a city, and you will quickly see that such a setting would have been inappropriate. What effect does the kind of country they live in have on the lives of the characters? What qualities of the landscape are reflected in the characteristics of those who live there?

Conflict

The conflict in "Mateo Falcone" is an inner one occurring in both Fortunato's and Mateo's decisions. Both make a choice between their personal feelings and their adherence to the code of the maquis. Why does Fortunato decide the way he does? Why does Mateo decide he must kill his son?

Climax

At what point in the story does Mateo Falcone seem to determine what he must do? Does the reader suspect his decision at the time he makes it? Why?

Sometimes people we do not know may influence our feelings,
our thoughts, and our lives. In the following poems, five poets probe the effects
of brief encounters between strangers.

◇ *The Man He Killed*

Had he and I but met
By some old ancient inn,
We should have sat us down to wet
Right many a nipperkin![1]

But ranged[2] as infantry,   5
And staring face to face,
I shot at him as he at me,
And killed him in his place.

I shot him dead because—
Because he was my foe,   10
Just so: my foe of course he was;
That's clear enough; although

He thought he'd 'list,[3] perhaps,
Offhand like—just as I—
Was out of work—had sold his traps[4]—   15
No other reason why.

Yes; quaint and curious war is!
You shoot a fellow down
You'd treat if met where any bar is,
Or help to half-a-crown.[5]   20

THOMAS HARDY

---

1. **nipperkin**\ˈnĭ·pər ˈkĭn\ a cup or glass containing about half a cup.
2. **ranged**, arranged, ordered in ranks.
3. **'list**, enlist.
4. his **traps**, tools, equipment, whatever he used in his trade.
5. **half-a-crown** or half-crown, a British coin worth two shillings and six-pence, about $0.35 in U.S. currency.

HOW STRANGE
AND CURIOUS WAR IS

Using the voice of a soldier, Hardy presents the troubled thoughts of one who has killed a stranger for no personal reason at all. The rambling, conversational tone of the poem makes the speaker seem warmly human and, in the process, underlines the inhumanity of his act. What were the man's feelings at the moment he met the enemy soldier? What disturbs him later about the encounter?

The third stanza of this poem does a masterful job of fitting the poetic form to the meaning. In the first line, as the soldier gropes for an explanation of his action, his inability to find a satisfactory answer is underscored when the rhythm and meaning are left hanging on "because—." The futility of his search is further emphasized in the second line by his hollow repetition of "because" followed hurriedly by the obvious, empty answer expressed in simple, single-syllable words. Then, pausing to reassure himself, the rush of repetition in the third line shows his relief at having found *an* answer. But the last word of the stanza breaks the established stanza pattern, indicating the doubt that has crept into his mind. Find other places in this poem where the form of the lines fits the meaning of the lines.

◇ *Channing Way I*

It's always the strangers that do the most damage.
The ones you never get to know.
      Seen in passing cars
               mirrored in windows
and remembered.   5

               And the others—
the ones who promise everything, then go away.

Sometimes I think people were meant to be strangers.
Not to get to know one another,
not to get close enough to damage the heart   10
made older by each new encounter.

But then,
someone comes along
and changes all that.
For a while anyway.   15

Still, as the years go by
it's easier to remember
the streets where it happened
               than the names
and who was the one on Channing Way.   20

ROD McKUEN

**PEOPLE WERE MEANT
TO BE STRANGERS**
In the middle of the poem, Rod McKuen says that people are not meant to know one another. What might have happened that leads him to this conclusion? Does he seem to change his opinion?

◈ *The Alarm Clock*

Alarm clock
sure sound
loud
this mornin' . . .
remind me of the time   5
I sat down
in a drug store
with my
mind
away far off . . .   10
until the girl
and she was small
it seems to me
with yellow hair
a hangin'   15
smiled up and said
"I'm sorry but
we don't serve

you people
here"   20
and I woke up
quick
like I did this mornin'
when the
alarm   25
went off . . .
It don't do
to wake up
quick . . .

MARI EVANS

I AM A BLACK WOMAN,
publ. Wm. Morrow & Company 1970, by permission of
the author.

STRANGE ASSOCIATIONS

We all know the feeling of waking up suddenly, whether by the ring of an alarm clock or the terror of a bad dream. We react with a whole medley of feelings: shame, irritation, confusion. The day is off to a bad start. But there are sudden awakenings other than those from a sound sleep. What are some of these? What do you know about the speaker of this poem? Why did the alarm clock remind her of a brief encounter she had with a blonde girl? Did the encounter have any impact on the blonde girl?

We generally think that poetry uses more pattern in language than does prose. Pattern is achieved by the organized use of repetitions. It may be repeated beats (rhythm); repeated word sounds (rhyme); or repeated phrases. Contemporary poetry tends to discard the older kinds of repetition, but it still uses a pattern to hold it together and make it different from prose. Its repetitions are more like the irregular pounding of waves on the shore than the steady beat of a machine. Can you detect any repeated elements in "The Alarm Clock"?

◇ *Corner*

The cop slumps alertly on his motorcycle,
Supported by one leg like a leather stork.
His glance accuses me of loitering.
I can see his eyes moving like a fish
In the green depths of his green goggles.   5

His ease is fake. I can tell.
My ease is fake. And he can tell.
The fingers armored by his gloves
Splay and clench, itching to change something.
As if he were my enemy or my death,   10
I just standing there watching.

I spit out my gum which has gone stale.
I knock out a new cigarette—
Which is my bravery.
It is all imperceptible: 15
The way I shift my weight,
The way he creaks in his saddle.

The traffic is specific though constant.
The sun surrounds me, divides the street between us.
His crash helmet is whiter in the shade.   20
It is like a bull ring as they say it is just before the fighting.

I cannot back down. I am there.

Everything holds me back.
I am in danger of disappearing into the sunny dust.
My levis bake and my T shirt sweats.   25

My cigarette makes my eyes burn.
But I don't dare drop it.

Who made him my enemy?
Prince of coolness. King of fear.
Why do I lean here waiting?   30
Why does he lounge there watching?

I am becoming sunlight.
My hair is on fire. My boots run like tar.
I am hung-up by the bright air.

Something breaks through all of a sudden,   35
And he blasts off, quick as a craver,
Smug in his power; watching me watch.

RALPH POMEROY

Reprinted with permission of The Macmillan Company
from IN THE FINANCIAL DISTRICT by Ralph
Pomeroy. Copyright © by Ralph Pomeroy, 1961.

WHO MADE HIM MY ENEMY?

The stand-off in this poem is classic. Two people, separated by age, levels of authority, differing attitudes, and fear of the other meet in a brief encounter where nothing happens but everything does.

From the stacatto style of the short lines ("His ease is fake. I can tell. / My ease is fake. And he can tell.") we immediately sense the tension between the two men. Find other lines that either heighten or describe the tension. Can you describe the policeman? The narrator? How can a person be a "Prince of coolness. King of fear"? Can you answer the narrator's question, "Who made him my enemy?" Are your answers any more satisfactory than the simple one of the soldier's found in Hardy's poem?

41

Faces

People that I meet and pass
   In the city's broken roar,
Faces that I lose so soon
   And have never found before,

Do you know how much you tell   5
   In the meeting of our eyes,
How ashamed I am, and sad
   To have pierced your poor disguise?

Secrets rushing without sound
   Crying from your hiding places—   10
Let me go, I cannot bear
   The sorrow of the passing faces.

—People in the restless street,
   Can it be, oh can it be
In the meeting of our eyes   15
   That you know as much of me?

SARA TEASDALE

DO WE ALL WEAR DISGUISES?

Sara Teasdale suggests that we all wear disguises, even when we feel, as in a crowded street, that nobody could be watching us. According to this poem, what is it that people try to hide from one another? What understanding does she gain of herself?

IMPLICATIONS

Look at the following statements and see if the poems you have just read support or negate the idea presented.

1. People tend to wear masks no matter where they may be.

2. Each encounter leaves its own mark on those involved.

3. Not all wars are fought on the battlefield with live ammunition.

4. Both young and old people are vulnerable and easy to hurt in a brief encounter.

Is there something in human
nature that makes one distrust strangers?

One Ordinary Day, With Peanuts

SHIRLEY JACKSON

Mr. John Philip Johnson shut his front
door behind him and came down his front
steps into the bright morning with a feeling
that all was well with the world on this best
of all days, and wasn't the sun warm and
good, and didn't his shoes feel comfortable
after the resoling, and he knew that he had
undoubtedly chosen the precise very tie which
belonged with the day and the sun and his
comfortable feet, and, after all, wasn't the
world just a wonderful place? In spite of the
fact that he was a small man, and the tie was
perhaps a shade vivid, Mr. Johnson irradiated
this feeling of well-being as he came down the
steps and onto the dirty sidewalk, and he
smiled at people who passed him, and some of
them even smiled back. He stopped at the
newsstand on the corner and bought his paper,
saying "*Good* morning" with real conviction
to the man who sold him the paper and the
two or three other people who were lucky
enough to be buying papers when Mr. Johnson skipped up. He remembered to fill his
pockets with candy and peanuts, and then he
set out to get himself uptown. He stopped in
a flower shop and bought a carnation for his
buttonhole, and stopped almost immediately
afterward to give the carnation to a small

child in a carriage, who looked at him dumbly
and smiled, and Mr. Johnson smiled, and the
child's mother looked at Mr. Johnson for a
minute and then smiled too.

When he had gone several blocks uptown,
Mr. Johnson cut across the avenue and went
along a side street, chosen at random; he did
not follow the same route every morning, but
preferred to pursue his eventful way in wide
detours, more like a puppy than a man intent
upon business. It happened this morning that
halfway down the block a moving van was
parked, and the furniture from an upstairs
apartment stood half on the sidewalk, half on
the steps, while an amused group of people
loitered, examining the scratches on the tables
and the worn spots on the chairs, and a
harassed woman, trying to watch a young
child and the movers and the furniture all at
the same time, gave the clear impression of en-
deavoring to shelter her private life from the
people staring at her belongings. Mr. Johnson
stopped, and for a moment joined the crowd,
and then he came forward and, touching his
hat civilly, said, "Perhaps I can keep an eye
on your little boy for you?"

The woman turned and glared at him distrustfully, and Mr. Johnson added hastily,
"We'll sit right here on the steps." He beckoned to the little boy, who hesitated and then
responded agreeably to Mr. Johnson's genial
smile. Mr. Johnson brought out a handful of
peanuts from his pocket and sat on the steps
with the boy, who at first refused the peanuts
on the grounds that his mother did not allow
him to accept food from strangers; Mr. Johnson said that probably his mother had not
intended peanuts to be included, since elephants at the circus ate them, and the boy
considered, and then agreed solemnly. They
sat on the steps cracking peanuts in a com-
radely fashion, and Mr. Johnson said, "So
you're moving?"

"Yep," said the boy.

"Where you going?"

"Vermont."

"Nice place. Plenty of snow there. Maple

sugar too; you like maple sugar?"

"Sure."

"Plenty of maple sugar in Vermont. You going to live on a farm?"

"Going to live with Grandpa."

"Grandpa like peanuts?"

"Sure."

"Ought to take him some," said Mr. Johnson, reaching smoothly into his pocket. "Just you and Mommy going?"

"Yep."

"Tell you what," Mr. Johnson said. "You take some peanuts to eat on the train."

The boy's mother, after glancing at them frequently, had seemingly decided that Mr. Johnson was trustworthy, because she had devoted herself wholeheartedly to seeing that the movers did not—what movers rarely do, but every housewife believes they will—crack a leg from her good table, or set a kitchen chair down on a lamp. Most of the furniture was loaded by now, and she was deep in that nervous stage when she knew there was something she had forgotten to pack—hidden away in the back of a closet somewhere, or left at a neighbor's and forgotten, or on the clothesline—and was trying to remember under stress what it was.

"This all, lady?" the chief mover said, completing her dismay.

Uncertainly, she nodded.

"Want to go on the truck with the furniture, sonny?" the mover asked the boy, and laughed. The boy laughed too and said to Mr. Johnson, "I guess I'll have a good time at Vermont."

"Fine time," said Mr. Johnson, and stood up. "Have one more peanut before you go," he said to the boy.

The boy's mother said to Mr. Johnson, "Thank you so much; it was a great help to me."

"Nothing at all," said Mr. Johnson gallantly. "Where in Vermont are you going?"

The mother looked at the little boy accusingly, as though he had given away a secret of some importance, and said unwillingly, "Greenwich."

"Lovely town," said Mr. Johnson. He took out a card, and wrote a name on the back. "Very good friend of mine lives in Greenwich," he said. "Call on him for anything you need. His wife makes the best doughnuts in town," he added soberly to the little boy.

"Swell," said the little boy.

"Good-bye," said Mr. Johnson.

He went on, stepping happily with his new-shod feet, feeling the warm sun on his back and on the top of his head. Halfway down the block he met a stray dog and fed him a peanut.

At the corner, where another wide avenue faced him, Mr. Johnson decided to go on uptown again. Moving with comparative laziness, he was passed on either side by people hurrying and frowning, and people brushed past him going the other way, clattering along to get somewhere quickly. Mr. Johnson stopped on every corner and waited patiently for the light to change, and he stepped out of the way of anyone who seemed to be in any particular hurry, but one young lady came too fast for him, and crashed wildly into him when he stopped to pat a kitten which had run out onto the sidewalk from an apartment house and was now unable to get back through the rushing feet.

"Excuse me," said the young lady, trying frantically to pick up Mr. Johnson and hurry on at the same time. "Terribly sorry."

The kitten, regardless now of danger, raced back to its home. "Perfectly all right," said Mr. Johnson, adjusting himself carefully. "You seem to be in a hurry."

"Of course I'm in a hurry," said the young lady. "I'm late."

She was extremely cross and the frown between her eyes seemed well on its way to becoming permanent. She had obviously awakened late, because she had not spent any extra time in making herself look pretty, and her dress was plain and unadorned with collar or brooch, and her lipstick was noticeably crooked. She tried to brush past Mr. Johnson, but, risking her suspicious displeasure, he took her arm and said, "Please wait."

"Look," she said ominously, "I ran into you and your lawyer can see my lawyer and I will gladly pay all damages and all inconveniences suffered therefrom but please this minute let me go because I am late."

"Late for what?" said Mr. Johnson; he tried his winning smile on her but it did no more than keep her, he suspected, from knocking him down again.

"Late for work," she said between her teeth. "Late for my employment. I have a job and if I am late I lose exactly so much an hour and I cannot really afford what your pleasant conversation is costing me, be it ever so pleasant."

"I'll pay for it," said Mr. Johnson. Now these were magic words, not necessarily because they were true, or because she seriously expected Mr. Johnson to pay for anything, but because Mr. Johnson's flat statement, obviously innocent of irony, could not be, coming from

Mr. Johnson, anything but the statement of a responsible and truthful and respectable man.

"What do you mean?" she asked.

"I said that since I am obviously responsible for your being late I shall certainly pay for it."

"Don't be silly," she said, and for the first time the frown disappeared. "I wouldn't expect you to pay anything—a few minutes ago I was offering to pay you. Anyway," she added, almost smiling, "it was my fault."

"What happens if you don't go to work?"

She stared. "I don't get paid."

"Precisely," said Mr. Johnson.

"What do you mean, precisely? If I don't show up at the office exactly twenty minutes ago I lose a dollar and eighty cents an hour, or three cents a minute or . . . ." She thought. ". . . About a dime for the time I've spent talking to you."

Mr. Johnson laughed, and finally she laughed, too. "You're late already," he pointed out. "Will you give me another six cents worth?"

"I don't understand why."

"You'll see," Mr. Johnson promised. He led her over to the side of the walk, next to the buildings, and said, "Stand here," and went out into the rush of people going both ways. Selecting and considering, as one who must make a choice involving perhaps whole years of lives, he estimated the people going by. Once he almost moved, and then at the last minute thought better of it and drew back. Finally, from half a block away, he saw what he wanted, and moved out into the center of the traffic to intercept a young man, who was hurrying, and dressed as though he had awakened late, and frowning.

"Oof," said the young man, because Mr. Johnson had thought of no better way to intercept anyone than the one the young woman had unwittingly used upon him. "Where do you think you're going?" the young man demanded from the sidewalk.

"I want to speak to you," said Mr. Johnson ominously.

The young man got up nervously, dusting himself and eyeing Mr. Johnson. "What for?" he said. "What'd I do?"

"That's what bothers me most about people nowadays," Mr. Johnson complained broadly to the people passing. "No matter whether they've done anything or not, they always figure someone's after them. About what you're going to do," he told the young man.

"Listen," said the young man, trying to brush past him, "I'm late, and I don't have any time to listen. Here's a dime, now get going."

"Thank you," said Mr. Johnson, pocketing the dime. "Look," he said, "what happens if you stop running?"

"I'm late," said the young man, still trying to get past Mr. Johnson, who was unexpectedly clinging.

"How much do you make an hour?" Mr. Johnson demanded.

"A Communist, are you?" said the young man. "Now will you please let me—"

"No," said Mr. Johnson insistently, "how much?"

"Two fifty," said the young man. "And now will you—"

"You like adventure?"

The young man stared, and, staring, found himself caught and held by Mr. Johnson's genial smile; he almost smiled back and then repressed it and made an effort to tear away. "I got to hurry," he said.

"Mystery? Like surprises? Unusual and exciting events?"

"You selling something?"

"Sure," said Mr. Johnson. "You want to take a chance?"

The young man hesitated, looked longingly up the avenue toward what might have been his destination and then, when Mr. Johnson said "I'll pay for it" with his own peculiar convincing emphasis, turned and said, "Well, okay. But I got to see it first, what I'm buying."

Mr. Johnson, breathing hard, led the young man over to the side where the girl was standing; she had been watching with interest Mr. Johnson's capture of the young man and now, smiling timidly, she looked at Mr. Johnson as though prepared to be surprised at nothing.

Mr. Johnson reached into his pocket and took out his wallet. "Here," he said, and handed two bills to the girl. "This about equals your day's pay."

"But no," she said, surprised in spite of herself. "I mean, I couldn't."

"Please do not interrupt," Mr. Johnson told her. "And here," he said to the young man, "this will take care of you." The young man accepted the money dazedly, but said, "Probably counterfeit" to the young woman out of the side of his mouth. "Now," Mr. Johnson went on, disregarding the young man, "what is your name, miss?"

"Kent," she said helplessly. "Mildred Kent."

"Fine," said Mr. Johnson. "And you, sir?"

"Arthur Adams," said the young man stiffly.

"Splendid," said Mr. Johnson. "Now, Miss Kent, I would like you to meet Mr. Adams. Mr. Adams, Miss Kent."

Miss Kent stared, wet her lips nervously, made a gesture as though she might run, and said, "How do you do?"

Mr. Adams straightened his shoulders, scowled at Mr. Johnson, made a gesture as though he might run, and said, "How do you do?"

"Now this," said Mr. Johnson, taking several bills from his wallet, "should be enough for the day for both of you. I would suggest perhaps, Coney Island—although I personally am not fond of the place—or perhaps a nice lunch somewhere, and dancing, or a matinee, or even a movie, although take care to choose a really good one; there are so many bad movies these days. You might," he said, struck with an inspiration, "visit the Bronx Zoo, or the Planetarium. Anywhere, as a matter of fact," he concluded, "that you would like to go. Have a nice time."

As he started to move away, Arthur Adams, breaking from his dumbfounded stare, said, "But look here, mister, you can't do this. Why —how do you know—I mean, we don't even know—I mean, how do you know we won't just take the money and not do what you said?"

"You've taken the money," Mr. Johnson said. "You don't have to follow any of my suggestions. You may know something you prefer to do—perhaps a museum, or something."

"But suppose I just run away with it and leave her here?"

"I know you won't," said Mr. Johnson gently, "because you remembered to ask me that. Good-bye," he added, and went on.

As he stepped up the street, conscious of the sun on his head and his good shoes, he heard from somewhere behind him the young man saying, "Look, you know you don't have to if you don't want to," and the girl saying, "But unless you don't want to . . ." Mr. Johnson smiled to himself and then thought that he better hurry along; when he wanted to he could move very quickly, and before the young woman had gotten around to saying, "Well, I will if you will," Mr. Johnson was several blocks away and had already stopped twice, once to help a lady lift several large packages into a taxi and once to hand a peanut to a sea gull. By this time he was in an area of large stores and many more people and he was buffeted constantly from either side by people hurrying and cross and late and sullen. Once he offered a peanut to a man who asked him for a dime, and once he offered a peanut to a bus driver who had stopped his bus at an intersection and had opened the window next to his seat and put out his head as though longing for fresh air and the comparative quiet of the traffic. The man wanting a dime took the peanut because Mr. Johnson had wrapped a dollar bill around it, but the bus driver took the peanut and asked ironically, "You want a transfer, Jack?"

On a busy corner Mr. Johnson encountered two young people—for one minute he thought they might be Mildred Kent and Arthur Adams—who were eagerly scanning a newspaper, their backs pressed against a storefront to avoid the people passing, their heads bent together. Mr. Johnson, whose curiosity was insatiable, leaned onto the storefront next to them and peeked over the man's shoulder; they were scanning the "Apartments Vacant" columns.

Mr. Johnson remembered the street where the woman and her little boy were going to Vermont and he tapped the man on the shoulder and said amiably, "Try down on West Seventeen. About the middle of the block, people moved out this morning."

"Say, what do you—" said the man, and then, seeing Mr. Johnson clearly, "Well, thanks. Where did you say?"

"West Seventeen," said Mr. Johnson. "About the middle of the block." He smiled again and said, "Good luck."

"Thanks," said the man.

"Thanks," said the girl, as they moved off.

"Good-bye," said Mr. Johnson.

He lunched alone in a pleasant restaurant, where the food was rich, and only Mr. Johnson's excellent digestion could encompass two whipped-cream-and-chocolate-and-rum-cake pastries for dessert. He had three cups of coffee, tipped the waiter largely, and went out into the street again into the wonderful sunlight, his shoes still comfortable and fresh on his feet. Outside he found a beggar staring into the windows of the restaurant he had left and, carefully looking through the money in his pocket, Mr. Johnson approached the beggar and pressed some coins and a couple of bills into his hand. "It's the price of the veal cutlet lunch plus tip," said Mr. Johnson. "Good-bye."

After his lunch he rested; he walked into the nearest park and fed peanuts to the pigeons. It was late afternoon by the time he was ready to start back downtown, and he had refereed two checker games and watched a small boy and girl whose mother had fallen asleep and awakened with surprise and fear which turned to amusement when she saw Mr. Johnson. He had given alway almost all of his candy, and had fed all the rest of his peanuts to the pigeons, and it was time to go home. Although the late afternoon sun was pleasant, and his shoes were still entirely com-

fortable, he decided to take a taxi downtown.

He had a difficult time catching a taxi, because he gave up the first three or four empty ones to people who seemed to need them more; finally, however, he stood alone on the corner and—almost like netting a frisky fish—he hailed desperately until he succeeded in catching a cab which had been proceeding with haste uptown and seemed to draw in toward Mr. Johnson against its own will.

"Mister," the cab driver said as Mr. Johnson climbed in, "I figured you was an omen, like. I wasn't going to pick you up at all."

"Kind of you," said Mr. Johnson ambiguously.

"If I'd of let you go it would of cost me ten bucks," said the driver.

"Really?"

"Yeah," said the driver. "Guy just got out of the cab, he turned around and give me ten bucks, said take this and bet it in a hurry on a horse named Vulcan, right away."

"Vulcan?" said Mr. Johnson, horrified. "A fire sign on a Wednesday?"

"What?" said the driver. "Anyway, I said to myself if I got no fare between here and there I'd bet the ten, but if anyone looked like they needed the cab I'd take it as a omen and I'd take the ten home to the wife."

"You were very right," said Mr. Johnson heartily. "This is Wednesday, you would have lost your money. Monday, yes, or even Saturday. But never never never a fire sign on a Wednesday. Sunday would have been good, now."

"Vulcan don't run on Sunday," said the driver.

"You wait till another day," said Mr. Johnson. "Down this street, please, driver. I'll get off on the next corner."

"He TOLD me Vulcan, though," said the driver.

"I'll tell you," said Mr. Johnson, hesitating with the door of the cab half open. "You take that ten dollars and I'll give you another ten dollars to go with it, and you go right ahead and bet that money on any Thursday on any horse that has a name indicating . . . let me see, Thursday . . . well, grain. Or any growing food."

"Grain?" said the driver. "You mean a horse named, like, Wheat or something?"

"Certainly," said Mr. Johnson. "Or, as a matter of fact, to make it even easier, any horse whose name includes the letters C, R, L. Perfectly simple."

"Tall corn?" said the driver, a light in his eye. "You mean a horse named, like, Tall Corn?"

"Absolutely," said Mr. Johnson. "Here's your money."

"Tall Corn," said the driver. "Thank *you*, mister."

"Good-bye," said Mr. Johnson.

He was on his own corner and went straight up to his apartment. He let himself in and called "Hello?" and Mrs. Johnson answered from the kitchen, "Hello, dear, aren't you early?"

"Took a taxi home," Mr. Johnson said. "I remembered the cheesecake too. What's for dinner?"

Mrs. Johnson came out of the kitchen and kissed him; she was a comfortable woman, and smiling as Mr. Johnson smiled. "Hard day?" she asked.

"Not very," said Mr. Johnson, hanging his coat in the closet. "How about you?"

"So-so," she said. She stood in the kitchen doorway while he settled into his easy chair and took off his good shoes and took out the paper he had bought that morning. "Here and there," she said.

"I didn't do so badly," Mr. Johnson said. "Couple young people."

"Fine," she said. "I had a little nap this afternoon, took it easy most of the day. Went into a department store this morning and accused the woman next to me of shoplifting, and had the store detective pick her up. Sent three dogs to the pound—*you* know, the usual thing. Oh, and listen," she added, remembering.

"What?" asked Mr. Johnson.

"Well," she said, "I got onto a bus and asked the driver for a transfer, and when he helped someone else first I said that he was impertinent, and quarreled with him. And then I said why wasn't he in the army, and I said it loud enough for everyone to hear, and I took his number and I turned in a complaint. Probably got him fired."

"Fine," said Mr. Johnson. "But you do look tired. Want to change over tomorrow?"

"I *would* like to," she said. "I could do with a change."

"Right," said Mr. Johnson. "What's for dinner?"

"Veal cutlet."

"Had it for lunch," said Mr. Johnson.

I

PLAYING A GAME

The skeptical reader probably cannot quite believe that Mr. Johnson is as good as he appears to be at the beginning of the story. Still, his actions are eccentric enough in themselves to keep the reader's interest. It comes as a shock to discover at the story's end that the Johnsons are playing a deliberate game which includes taking turns at the "good" and the "evil" role. Pretending to be what we are not is a deep desire in human beings: children play at being adults or pirates or cowboys and Indians. As adults we continue to play roles, but not quite so obviously or necessarily consciously.

II

IMPLICATIONS

How do you react to the following statements? Are they true, false or something in between?

1. People have desires to help and desires to hurt. The Johnsons have found a way to balance their positive and negative desires.

2. Most people are instantly suspicious of strangers in a brief encounter.

3. Deliberately playing this game of "brief encounters" as the Johnsons do is morally wrong.

III

TECHNIQUES

Exposition

As this story proceeds, the reader continues to be mystified by Mr. Johnson's actions and keeps looking for that important part of the exposition that will explain things. Where does this material come in the story? How did you react to this technique of retaining significant information about characters until the end of the story? If most short stories were written this way, would the impact be the same?

Conflict and Climax

There can be conflict between characters, within a character, or between a character and the environment. Are any of these present in "One Ordinary Day, With Peanuts"? What holds the interest of the reader? What question does he have in his mind? Where is this resolved? Try skimming back through the story now that you know the outcome. Do the events take on more significance, or less?

IV

WORDS

1. Having given Mildred and Arthur some money, Mr. Johnson suggests they take in a matinee or some other entertainment. Like a number of other English words, *matinee*, meaning "a dramatic or musical performance given usually in the afternoon," was borrowed from the French. Another word of French origin, *marquee* (from *marquise*) refers to the signboard over the entrance to the building where shows, including matinees, are given.

Borrowing words from the French language has a long history; it began, in fact, with the Norman victory over the English in 1066. After their victory the Normans (who were Frenchmen) made French the official language of the upper classes in England, while the lower classes maintained their native language. Many French words came into the English language at this time. In early America, the English-speaking colonists came into contact with French explorers and French settlements, and naturally there was mutual borrowing of words. And this borrowing of words continues to this day, although not at such a great rate as before.

Test your knowledge of the following French loan-words, and look up the meaning of those that you do not know: *connoisseur, picayune, bayou, cache, communique, bouillon, chaise longue, camouflage.*

2. When Mrs. Johnson said, "I had a little nap this afternoon, took it easy most of the day," no native speaker of English would have trouble understanding what she meant. But a foreigner just learning the language might be mystified by the expression "took it easy," for Mrs. Johnson was not literally "taking" anything. She was resting. This expression, which doesn't mean what the actual words say, is said to be *idiomatic.*

Idiomatic expressions are plentiful in English. Upon meeting someone, we say, "How do you do?" Here we clearly are not asking the person how to perform some act, but we are politely greeting him. And when a girl says that she and Johnny are "going together," she obviously doesn't mean that they are taking a trip; she is saying that they date on a more or less steady basis.

Can you explain why each of the following expressions is idiomatic: catch a cold; catch on (understand); foot the bill; look out!; make a date; look up a buddy; catch fire; strike up a conversation; wait on tables (in a restaurant); gave himself away (revealed his secret).

3. What was the color, would you imagine, of the carnation that Mr. Johnson bought for his buttonhole? It could have been red or pink or white. However, the carnation was originally thought of as being pink, or flesh colored; in fact, it gets its name from the Latin stem *carn-,* meaning "flesh."

It seems incredible that a delicate, beautiful flower like the carnation could be related to a repulsive term like *carnage*—but it is. During a holiday period, we bemoan the carnage on our highways; that is, we grieve because of the mass slaughter of human flesh in car accidents.

See whether you can answer these questions involving words derived from the *carn-* stem: How does a *carnivorous* animal differ from a *herbivorous* one? Why is the period (several weeks long) before Lent referred to as *carnival* season in New Orleans? What is meant by *reincarnation*?

The United States entered the Second World War
when the Japanese bombed Pearl Harbor
on December 7, 1941. Immediately the two nations
that had been allies in the First World War,
only twenty-five years earlier, became enemies.
Suddenly habits of friendship were to be uprooted
and replaced by enmity. What happens in a brief
encounter between members of two nations
that have experienced such an abrupt change
in national attitude? Pearl Buck, who possesses
a unique understanding of Eastern peoples
from having lived among them for many years,
examines such a case in this story.
As you read it, ask yourself this question:
Are there human values or instincts
that are stronger even than loyalty
or the conviction that one's country is right?

The Enemy

PEARL BUCK

Dr. Sadao Hoki's house was built on a spot of the Japanese coast where as a little boy he had often played. The low square stone house was set upon rocks well above a narrow beach that was outlined with bent pines. As a boy Sadao had climbed the pines, supporting himself on his bare feet, as he had seen men do in the South Seas when they climbed for coconuts. His father had taken him often to the islands of those seas, and never had he failed to say to the little grave boy at his side, "Those islands yonder, they are the stepping stones to the future for Japan."

"Where shall we step from them?" Sadao had asked seriously.

"Who knows?" his father had answered. "Who can limit our future? It depends on what we make it."

Sadao had taken this into his mind as he did everything his father said, his father who never joked or played with him but who spent infinite pains upon him who was his only son. Sadao knew that his education was his father's chief concern. For this reason he had been sent at twenty-two to America to learn all that could be learned of surgery and medicine. He had come back at thirty and before his father died he had seen Sadao become famous not only as a surgeon but as a scientist. Because he was now perfecting a discovery which would render wounds entirely clean, he had not been sent abroad with the troops. Also, he knew, there was some slight danger that the old General might need an operation for a condition for which he was now being treated medically, and for this possibility Sadao was being kept in Japan.

Clouds were rising from the ocean now. The unexpected warmth of the past few days had at night drawn heavy fog from the cold waves. Sadao watched mists hide outlines of a little island near the shore and then come creeping up the beach below the house, wreathing around the pines. In a few minutes fog would be wrapped about the house too. Then he would go into the room where Hana, his wife, would be waiting for him with the two children.

But at this moment the door opened and she looked out, a dark-blue woolen haori[1] over her kimono. She came to him affectionately and put her arm through his as he stood, smiled and said nothing. He had met Hana in America, but he had waited to fall in love with her until he was sure she was Japanese. His father would never have received her unless she had been pure in her race. He wondered often whom he would have married if he had not met Hana, and by what luck he had found her in the most casual way, by chance literally, at an American professor's house. The professor and his wife had been kind people, anxious to do something for their few foreign students, and the students,

1. **haori**\'ha ▲u·rē\ a long, loose, light coat.

though bored, had accepted this kindness. Sadao had often told Hana how nearly he had not gone to Professor Harley's house that night —the rooms were so small, the food so bad, the professor's wife so voluble. But he had gone and there he had found Hana, a new student, and had felt he would love her if it were at all possible.

Now he felt her hand on his arm and was aware of the pleasure it gave him, even though they had been married years enough to have the two children. For they had not married heedlessly in America. They had finished their work at school and had come home to Japan, and when his father had seen her the marriage had been arranged in the old Japanese way, although Sadao and Hana had talked everything over beforehand. They were perfectly happy. She laid her cheek against his arm.

It was at this moment that both of them saw something black come out of the mists. It was a man. He was flung up out of the ocean—flung, it seemed, to his feet by a breaker. He staggered a few steps, his body outlined against the mist, his arms above his head. Then the curled mists hid him again.

"Who is that?" Hana cried. She dropped Sadao's arm and they both leaned over the railing of the veranda. Now they saw him again. The man was on his hands and knees crawling. Then they saw him fall on his face and lie there.

"A fisherman perhaps," Sadao said, "washed from his boat." He ran quickly down the steps and behind him Hana came, her wide sleeves flying. A mile or two away on either side there were fishing villages, but here was only the bare and lonely coast, dangerous with rocks. The surf beyond the beach was spiked with rocks. Somehow the man had managed to come through them—he must be badly torn.

They saw when they came toward him that indeed it was so. The sand on one side of him had already a stain of red soaking through.

"He is wounded," Sadao exclaimed. He made haste to the man, who lay motionless, his face in the sand. An old cap stuck to his head soaked with sea water. He was in wet rags of garments. Sadao stooped, Hana at his side, and turned the man's head. They saw the face.

"A white man!" Hana whispered.

Yes, it was a white man. The wet cap fell away and there was his wet yellow hair, long, as though for many weeks it had not been cut, and upon his young and tortured face was a rough yellow beard. He was unconscious and knew nothing that they did to him.

Now Sadao remembered the wound, and with his expert fingers he began to search for it. Blood flowed freshly at his touch. On the right side of his lower back Sadao saw that a gun wound had been reopened. The flesh was blackened with powder. Sometime, not many days ago, the man had been shot and had not been tended. It was bad chance that the rock had struck the wound.

"Oh, how he is bleeding!" Hana whispered again in a solemn voice. The mists screened them now completely, and at this time of day no one came by. The fishermen had gone home and even the chance beachcombers would have considered the day at an end.

"What shall we do with this man?" Sadao muttered. But his trained hands seemed of their own will to be doing what they could to stanch the fearful bleeding. He packed the wound with the sea moss that strewed the beach. The man moaned with pain in his stupor but he did not awaken.

"The best thing that we could do would be to put him back in the sea," Sadao said, answering himself.

Now that the bleeding was stopped for the moment he stood up and dusted the sand from his hands.

"Yes, undoubtedly that would be best," Hana said steadily. But she continued to stare down at the motionless man.

"If we sheltered a white man in our house we should be arrested and if we turned him over as a prisoner, he would certainly die," Sadao said.

"The kindest thing would be to put him back into the sea," Hana said. But neither of them moved. They were staring with a curious repulsion upon the inert figure.

"What is he?" Hana whispered.

"There is something about him that looks American," Sadao said. He took up the battered cap. Yes, there, almost gone was the faint lettering. "A sailor," he said, "from an American warship." He spelled it out: "U. S. Navy." The man was a prisoner of war!

"He has escaped," Hana cried softly, "and that is why he is wounded."

"In the back," Sadao agreed.

They hesitated, looking at each other. Then Hana said with resolution:

"Come, are we able to put him back into the sea?"

"If I am able, are you?" Sadao asked.

"No," Hana said. "But if you can do it alone. . . ."

Sadao hesitated again. "The strange thing is," he said, "that if the man were whole I could turn him over to the police without difficulty. I care nothing for him. He is my enemy. All Americans are my enemy. And he is only a common fellow. You see how foolish his face is. But since he is wounded. . . ."

"You also cannot throw him back to the sea," Hana said. "Then there is only one thing to do. We must carry him into the house."

"But the servants?" Sadao inquired.

"We must simply tell them that we intend to give him to the police—as indeed we must, Sadao. We must think of the children and your position. It would endanger all of us if we did not give this man over as a prisoner of war."

"Certainly," Sadao agreed. "I would not think of doing anything else."

Thus agreed, together they lifted the man. He was very light, like a fowl that has been half-starved for a long time until it is only feathers and skeleton. So, his arms hanging, they carried him up the steps and into the side door of the house. This door opened into a passage and down the passage they carried the man toward an empty bedroom. It had been the bedroom of Sadao's father and since his

death it had not been used. They laid the man on the deeply matted floor. Everything here had been Japanese to please the old man, who would never in his own home sit on a chair or sleep in a foreign bed. Hana went to the wall cupboards and slid back a door and took out a soft quilt. She hesitated. The quilt was covered with flowered silk and the lining was pure white silk.

"He is so dirty," she murmured in distress.

"Yes, he had better be washed," Sadao agreed. "If you will fetch hot water I will wash him."

"I cannot bear for you to touch him," she said. "We shall have to tell the servants he is here. I will tell Yumi now. She can leave the children for a few minutes and she can wash him."

Sadao considered a moment. "Let it be so," he agreed. "You tell Yumi and I will tell the others."

But the utter pallor of the man's unconscious face moved him first to stoop and feel his pulse. It was faint but it was there. He put his hand against the man's cold breast. The heart too was yet alive.

"He will die unless he is operated on," Sadao said, considering. "The question is whether he will not die anyway."

Hana cried out in fear. "Don't try to save him! What if he should live?"

"What if he should die?" Sadao replied. He stood gazing down on the motionless man. This man must have extraordinary vitality or he would have been dead by now. But then he was very young—perhaps not yet twenty-five.

"You mean die from the operation?" Hana asked.

"Yes," Sadao said.

Hana considered this doubtfully, and when she did not answer Sadao turned away. "At any rate something must be done with him," he said, "and first he must be washed." He went quickly out of the room and Hana came behind him. She did not wish to be left alone with the white man. He was the first she had seen since she left America and now he seemed to have nothing to do with those whom she had known there. Here he was her enemy, a menace, living or dead.

She turned to the nursery and called, "Yumi!"

But the children heard her voice and she had to go in for a moment and smile at them and play with the baby boy, now nearly three months old.

Over the baby's soft black hair she motioned with her mouth, "Yumi—come with me."

"I will put the baby to bed," Yumi replied. "He is ready."

She went with Yumi into the bedroom next to the nursery and stood with the boy in her arms while Yumi spread the sleeping quilts on the floor and laid the baby between them.

Then Hana led the way quickly and softly to the kitchen. The two servants were frightened at what their master had just told them. The old gardener who was also a house servant pulled the few hairs on his upper lip.

"The master ought not to heal the wound of this white man," he said bluntly to Hana. "The white man ought to die. First he was shot. Then the sea caught him and wounded him with her rocks. If the master heals what the gun did and what the sea did they will take revenge on us."

"I will tell him what you say," Hana replied courteously. But she herself was also frightened, although she was not superstitious as the old man was. Could it ever be well to help an enemy? Nevertheless she told Yumi to fetch the hot water and bring it to the room where the white man was.

She went ahead and slid back the partitions. Sadao was not yet there. Yumi, following, put down her wooden bucket. Then she went over to the white man. When she saw him her thick lips folded themselves into stubbornness. "I have never washed a white man," she said, "and I will not wash so dirty a one now."

Hana cried at her severely, "You will do what your master commands you!"

"My master ought not to command me to wash the enemy," Yumi said stubbornly.

There was so fierce a look of resistance upon Yumi's round dull face that Hana felt unreasonably afraid. After all, if the servants should report something that was not as it happened?

"Very well," she said with dignity. "You understand we only want to bring him to his senses so that we can turn him over as a prisoner?"

"I will have nothing to do with it," Yumi said. "I am a poor person and it is not my business."

"Then please," Hana said gently, "return to your own work."

At once Yumi left the room. But this left Hana with the white man alone. She might have been too afraid to stay had not her anger at Yumi's stubbornness now sustained her.

"Stupid Yumi," she muttered fiercely. "Is this anything but a man? And a wounded helpless man!"

In the conviction of her own superiority she bent impulsively and untied the knotted rags that kept the white man covered. When she had his breast bare she dipped the small clean towel that Yumi had brought into the steaming hot water and washed his face carefully. The man's skin, though rough with exposure, was of a fine texture and must have been very blond when he was a child.

While she was thinking these thoughts, though not really liking the man better now that he was no longer a child, she kept on washing him until his upper body was quite clean. But she dared not turn him over. Where was Sadao? Now her anger was ebbing and she was anxious again and she rose, wiping her hands on the wrung towel. Then lest the man be chilled she put the quilt over him.

"Sadao!" she called softly.

He had been about to come in when she called. His hand had been on the door and now he opened it. She saw that he had brought his surgeon's emergency bag and that he wore his surgeon's coat.

"You have decided to operate!" she cried.

"Yes," he said shortly. He turned his back to her and unfolded a sterilized towel upon the floor of the *tokonoma*[2] alcove, and put his instruments out upon it.

---

2. **tokonoma** \'tō·kō ᵃnō·ma\ flower niche.

"Fetch towels," he said.

She went obediently, but how anxious now, to the linen shelves and took out the towels. There ought also to be old pieces of matting so that the blood would not ruin the fine floor covering. She went out to the back veranda where the gardener kept strips of matting with which to protect delicate shrubs on cold nights and took an armful of them.

But when she went back into the room, she saw this was useless. The blood had already soaked through the packing in the man's wound and had ruined the mat under him.

"Oh, the mat!" she cried.

"Yes, it is ruined," Sadao replied, as though he did not care. "Help me to turn him," he commanded her.

She obeyed him without a word, and he began to wash the man's back carefully.

"Yumi would not wash him," she said.

"Did you wash him then?" Sadao asked, not stopping for a moment his swift concise movements.

"Yes," she said.

He did not seem to hear her. But she was used to his absorption when he was at work. She wondered for a moment if it mattered to him what was the body upon which he worked so long as it was for the work he did so excellently.

"You will have to give the anesthetic if he needs it," he said.

"I?" she repeated blankly. "But never have I!"

"It is easy enough," he said impatiently.

He was taking out the packing now and the blood began to flow more quickly. He peered into the wound with the bright surgeon's light fastened on his forehead. "The bullet is still there," he said with cool interest. "Now I wonder how deep this rock wound is. If it is not too deep it may be that I can get the bullet. But the bleeding is not superficial. He has lost much blood."

At this moment Hana choked. He looked up and saw her face the color of sulphur.

"Don't faint," he said sharply. He did not put down his exploring instrument. "If I stop now the man will surely die." She clapped her hands to her mouth and leaped up and ran out of the room. Outside in the garden he heard her retching. But he went on with his work.

"It will be better for her to empty her stomach," he thought. He had forgotten that of course she had never seen an operation. But her distress and his inability to go to her at once made him impatient and irritable with this man who lay like dead under his knife.

"This man," he thought, "there is no reason under heaven why he should live."

Unconsciously this thought made him ruthless and he proceeded swiftly. In his dream the man moaned, but Sadao paid no heed except to mutter at him.

"Groan," he muttered, "groan if you like. I am not doing this for my own pleasure. In fact, I do not know why I am doing it."

The door opened and there was Hana again. She had not stopped even to smooth back her hair.

"Where is the anesthetic?" she asked in a clear voice.

Sadao motioned with his chin. "It is as well that you came back," he said. "This fellow is beginning to stir."

She had the bottle and some cotton in her hand.

"But how shall I do it?" she asked.

"Simply saturate the cotton and hold it near his nostrils," Sadao replied without delaying for one moment the intricate detail of his work. "When he breathes badly move it away a little."

She crouched close to the sleeping face of the young American. It was a piteously thin face, she thought, and the lips were twisted. The man was suffering whether he knew it or not. Watching him, she wondered if the stories they heard sometimes of the sufferings of prisoners were true. They came like flickers of rumor, told by word of mouth and always contradicted. In the newspapers the reports were always that wherever the Japanese armies went the people received them gladly, with cries of joy at their liberation. But sometimes she remembered such men as General Takima, who at home beat his wife cruelly, though no one mentioned it now that he had fought so victorious a battle in Manchuria.[3] If a man like that could be so cruel to a woman in his power, would he not be cruel to one like this for instance?

She hoped anxiously that this young man had not been tortured. It was at this moment that she observed deep red scars on his neck, just under the ear. "Those scars," she murmured, lifting her eyes to Sadao.

But he did not answer. At this moment he felt the tip of his instrument strike against something hard, dangerously near the kidney. All thought left him. He felt only the purest pleasure. He probed with his fingers, delicately, familiar with every atom of this human body. His old American professor of anatomy had seen to that knowledge. "Ignorance of the human body is the surgeon's cardinal sin, sirs!" he had thundered at his classes year after year. "To operate without as complete knowledge of the body as if you had made it—anything less than that is murder."

"It is not quite at the kidney, my friend," Sadao murmured. It was his habit to murmur to the patient when he forgot himself in an operation. "My friend," he always called his patients and so now he did, forgetting that this was his enemy.

Then quickly, with the cleanest and most precise of incisions, the bullet was out. The man quivered but he was still unconscious. Nevertheless he muttered a few English words.

"Guts," he muttered, choking. "They got . . . my guts. . . ."

"Sadao!" Hana cried sharply.

"Hush," Sadao said.

The man sank again into silence so profound that Sadao took up his wrist, hating the touch of it. Yes, there was still a pulse so faint, so feeble, but enough, if he wanted the man to live, to give hope.

"But certainly I do not want this man to live," he thought.

"No more anesthetic," he told Hana.

He turned as swiftly as though he had never paused and from his medicines he chose a small vial and from it filled a hypodermic and thrust it into the patient's left arm. Then, putting down the needle, he took the man's wrist again. The pulse under his fingers fluttered once or twice and then grew stronger.

"This man will live in spite of all," he said to Hana and sighed.

The young man woke, so weak, his blue eyes so terrified when he perceived where he was, that Hana felt compelled to apology. She served him herself, for none of the servants would enter the room.

When she came in the first time she saw him summon his strength to be prepared for some fearful thing.

"Don't be afraid," she begged him softly.

"How come . . . you speak English?" he gasped.

"I was a long time in America," she replied.

She saw that he wanted to reply to that but he could not, and so she knelt and fed him gently from the porcelain spoon. He ate unwillingly, but still he ate.

"Now you will soon be strong," she said, not liking him and yet moved to comfort him.

He did not answer.

When Sadao came in the third day after the operation he found the young man sitting up, his face bloodless with the effort.

"Lie down," Sadao cried. "Do you want to die?"

He forced the man down gently and strongly and examined the wound. "You may kill yourself if you do this sort of thing," he scolded.

"What are you going to do with me?" the boy muttered. He looked just now barely seventeen. "Are you going to hand me over?"

For a moment Sadao did not answer. He finished his examination and then pulled the silk quilt over the man.

---

3. **Manchuria,** the territory north of China proper and of Korea. Japanese troops fought in this area first against the Chinese and later, in the last days of World War II, against the Russians.

"I do not know myself what I shall do with you," he said. "I ought of course to give you to the police. You are a prisoner of war—no, do not tell me anything." He put up his hand as he saw the young man about to speak. "Do not even tell me your name unless I ask it."

They looked at each other for a moment, and then the young man closed his eyes and turned his face to the wall.

"Okay," he whispered, his mouth a bitter line.

Outside the door Hana was waiting for Sadao. He saw at once that she was in trouble.

"Sadao, Yumi tells me the servants feel they cannot stay if we hide this man here any more," she said. "She tells me that they are saying that you and I were so long in America that we have forgotten to think of our own country first. They think we like Americans."

"It is not true," Sadao said harshly, "Americans are our enemies. But I have been trained not to let a man die if I can help it."

"The servants cannot understand that," she said anxiously.

"No," he agreed.

Neither seemed able to say more, and somehow the household dragged on. The servants grew daily more watchful. Their courtesy was as careful as ever, but their eyes were cold upon the pair to whom they were hired.

"It is clear what our master ought to do," the old gardener said one morning. He had worked with flowers all his life, and had been a specialist too in moss. For Sadao's father he had made one of the finest moss gardens in Japan, sweeping the bright green carpet constantly so that not a leaf or a pine needle marred the velvet of its surface. "My old master's son knows very well what he ought to do," he now said, pinching a bud from a bush as he spoke. "When the man was so near death why did he not let him bleed?"

"That young master is so proud of his skill to save life that he saves any life," the cook said contemptuously. She split a fowl's neck skillfully and held the fluttering bird and let its blood flow into the roots of a wistaria vine.

Blood is the best of fertilizers, and the old gardener would not let her waste a drop of it.

"It is the children of whom we must think," Yumi said sadly. "What will be their fate if their father is condemned as a traitor?"

They did not try to hide what they said from the ears of Hana as she stood arranging the day's flowers in the veranda near by, and she knew they spoke on purpose that she might hear. That they were right she knew too in most of her being. But there was another part of her which she herself could not understand. It was not sentimental liking of the prisoner. She had come to think of him as a prisoner. She had not liked him even yesterday when he had said in his impulsive way, "Anyway, let me tell you that my name is Tom." She had only bowed her little distant bow. She saw hurt in his eyes but she did not wish to assuage it. Indeed, he was a great trouble in this house.

As for Sadao, every day he examined the wound carefully. The last stitches had been pulled out this morning, and the young man would in a fortnight be nearly as well as ever. Sadao went back to his office and carefully typed a letter to the chief of police reporting the whole matter. "On the twenty-first day of February an escaped prisoner was washed up on the shore in front of my house." So far he typed and then he opened a secret drawer of his desk and put the unfinished report into it.

On the seventh day after that two things happened. In the morning the servants left together, their belongings tied in large square cotton kerchiefs. When Hana got up in the morning nothing was done, the house not cleaned and the food not prepared, and she knew what it meant. She was dismayed and even terrified, but her pride as a mistress would not allow her to show it. Instead, she inclined her head gracefully when they appeared before her in the kitchen, and she paid them off and thanked them for all they had done for her. They were crying, but she did not cry. The cook and the gardener had served Sadao since he was a little boy in his father's house, and

Yumi cried because of the children. She was so grieving that after she had gone she ran back to Hana.

"If the baby misses me too much tonight send for me. I am going to my own house and you know where it is."

"Thank you," Hana said smiling. But she told herself she would not send for Yumi however the baby cried.

She made the breakfast and Sadao helped with the children. Neither of them spoke of the servants beyond the fact that they were gone. But after Hana had taken morning food to the prisoner she came back to Sadao.

"Why is it we cannot see clearly what we ought to do?" she asked him. "Even the servants see more clearly than we do. Why are we different from other Japanese?"

Sadao did not answer. But a little later he went into the room where the prisoner was and said brusquely, "Today you may get up on your feet. I want you to stay up only five minutes at a time. Tomorrow you may try it twice as long. It would be well that you get back your strength as quickly as possible."

He saw the flicker of terror on the young face that was still very pale.

"Okay," the boy murmured. Evidently he was determined to say more. "I feel I ought to thank you, doctor, for having saved my life."

"Don't thank me too early," Sadao said coldly. He saw the flicker of terror again in the boy's eyes—terror as unmistakable as an animal's. The scars on the neck were crimson for a moment. Those scars! What were they? Sadao did not ask.

In the afternoon the second thing happened. Hana, working hard on unaccustomed labor, saw a messenger come to the door in official uniform. Her hands went weak and she could not draw her breath. The servants must have told already. She ran to Sadao, gasping, unable to utter a word. But by then the messenger had simply followed her through the garden and there he stood. She pointed at him helplessly.

Sadao looked up from his book. He was in his office, the outer partition of which was thrown open to the garden for the southern sunshine.

"What is it?" he asked the messenger and then he rose, seeing the man's uniform.

"You are to come to the palace," the man said, "the old General is in pain again."

"Oh," Hana breathed, "is that all?"

"All?" the messenger exclaimed. "Is it not enough?"

"Indeed it is," she replied. "I am very sorry."

When Sadao came to say good-by she was in the kitchen, but doing nothing. The children were asleep and she sat merely resting for a moment, more exhausted from her fright than from work.

"I thought they had come to arrest you," she said.

He gazed down into her anxious eyes. "I must get rid of this man for your sake," he said in distress. "Somehow I must get rid of him."

"Of course," the General said weakly, "I understand fully. But that is because I once took a degree in Princeton. So few Japanese have."

"I care nothing for the man, Excellency," Sadao said, "but having operated on him with such success . . ."

"Yes, yes," the General said. "It only makes me feel you more indispensable to me. Evidently you think I can stand one more such attack as I have had today?"

"Not more than one," Sadao said.

"Then certainly I can allow nothing to happen to you," the General said with anxiety. His long pale Japanese face became expressionless, which meant that he was in deep thought. "You cannot be arrested," the General said, closing his eyes. "Suppose you were condemned to death and the next day I had to have my operation?"

"There are other surgeons, Excellency," Sadao suggested.

"None I trust," the General replied. "The best ones have been trained by Germans and would consider the operation successful even if I died. I do not care for their point of view." He sighed. "It seems a pity that we cannot better combine the German ruthlessness with the American sentimentality. Then you could turn your prisoner over to execution and yet I could be sure you would not murder me while I was unconscious." The General laughed. He had an unusual sense of humor. "As a Japanese, could you not combine these two foreign elements?" he asked.

Sadao smiled. "I am not quite sure," he said, "but for your sake I would be willing to try, Excellency."

The General shook his head. "I had rather not be the test case," he said. He felt suddenly weak and overwhelmed with the cares of his life as an official in times such as these when repeated victory brought great responsibilities all over the South Pacific. "It is very unfortunate that this man should have washed up on your doorstep," he said irritably.

"I feel it so myself," Sadao said gently.

"It would be best if he could be quietly killed," the General said. "Not by you, but by someone who does not know him. I have my own private assassins. Suppose I send two of them to your house tonight—or better, any night. You need know nothing about it. It is now warm—what would be more natural than that you should leave the outer partition of the white man's room open to the garden while he sleeps?"

"Certainly it would be very natural," Sadao agreed. "In fact, it is so left open every night."

"Good," the General said, yawning. "They are very capable assassins—they make no noise and they know the trick of inward bleeding. If you like I can even have them remove the body."

Sadao considered. "That perhaps would be best, Excellency," he agreed, thinking of Hana.

He left the General's presence then and went home, thinking over the plan. In this way the whole thing would be taken out of his hands. He would tell Hana nothing, since she would be timid at the idea of assassins in the house, and yet certainly such persons were essential in an absolute state such as Japan was. How

else could rulers deal with those who opposed them?

He refused to allow anything but reason to be the atmosphere of his mind as he went into the room where the American was in bed. But as he opened the door, to his surprise he found the young man out of bed, and preparing to go into the garden.

"What is this!" he exclaimed. "Who gave you permission to leave your room?"

"I'm not used to waiting for permission," Tom said gaily. "Gosh, I feel pretty good again! But will the muscles on this side always feel stiff?"

"Is it so?" Sadao inquired surprised. He forgot all else. "Now I thought I had provided against that," he murmured. He lifted the edge of the man's shirt and gazed at the healing scar. "Massage may do it," he said, "if exercise does not."

"It won't bother me much," the young man said. His young face was gaunt under the stubbly blond beard. "Say, doctor, I've got something I want to say to you. If I hadn't met a Jap like you—well, I wouldn't be alive today. I know that."

Sadao bowed but he could not speak.

"Sure, I know that," Tom went on warmly. His big thin hands gripping a chair were white at the knuckles. "I guess if all the Japs were like you there wouldn't have been a war."

"Perhaps," Sadao said with difficulty. "And now I think you had better go back to bed."

He helped the boy back into bed and then bowed. "Good night," he said.

Sadao slept badly that night. Time and time again he woke, thinking he heard the rustling of footsteps, the sound of a twig broken or a stone displaced in the garden—a noise such as men might make who carried a burden.

The next morning he made the excuse to go first into the guest room. If the American were gone he then could simply tell Hana that so the General had directed. But when he opened the door he saw at once that it was not last night. There on the pillow was the shaggy blond head.

He could hear the peaceful breathing of sleep and he closed the door again quietly.

"He is asleep," he told Hana. "He is almost well to sleep like that."

"What shall we do with him?" Hana whispered her old refrain.

Sadao shook his head. "I must decide in a day or two," he promised.

But certainly, he thought, the second night must be the night. There rose a wind that night, and he listened to the sounds of bending boughs and whistling partitions.

Hana woke too. "Ought we not to go and close the sick man's partition?" she asked.

"No," Sadao said. "He is able now to do it for himself."

But the next morning the American was still there.

Then the third night of course must be the night. The wind changed to quiet rain and the garden was full of the sound of dripping eaves and running springs. Sadao slept a little better, but he woke at the sound of a crash and leaped to his feet.

"What was that?" Hana cried. The baby woke at her voice and began to wail. "I must go and see."

But he held her and would not let her move.

"Sadao," she cried, "what is the matter with you?"

"Don't go," he muttered, "don't go!"

His terror infected her and she stood breathless, waiting. There was only silence. Together they crept back into the bed, the baby between them.

Yet when he opened the door of the guest room in the morning there was the young man. He was very gay and had already washed and was now on his feet. He had asked for a razor yesterday and had shaved himself and today there was a faint color in his cheeks.

"I am well," he said joyously.

Sadao drew his kimono round his weary body. He could not, he decided suddenly, go through another night. It was not that he cared for this young man's life. No, simply it was not worth the strain.

"You are well," Sadao agreed. He lowered his voice. "You are so well that I think if I put my boat on the shore tonight, with food and extra clothing in it, you might be able to row to that little island not far from the coast. It is so near the coast that it has not been worth fortifying. Nobody lives on it because in storm it is submerged. But this is not the season of storm. You could live there until you saw a Korean[4] fishing boat pass by. They pass quite near the island because the water is many fathoms deep there."

The young man stared at him, slowly comprehending. "Do I have to?" he asked.

"I think so," Sadao said gently. "You understand—it is not hidden that you are here."

The young man nodded in perfect comprehension. "Okay," he said simply.

Sadao did not see him again until evening. As soon as it was dark he had dragged the stout boat down to the shore and in it he put food and bottled water that he had bought secretly during the day, as well as two quilts he had bought at a pawnshop. The boat he tied to a post in the water, for the tide was high. There was no moon and he worked without a flashlight.

When he came to the house he entered as though he were just back from his work, and so Hana knew nothing. "Yumi was here today," she said as she served his supper. Though she was so modern, still she did not eat with him. "Yumi cried over the baby," she went on with a sigh. "She misses him so."

"The servants will come back as soon as the foreigner is gone," Sadao said.

He went into the guest room that night before he went to bed and himself checked carefully the American's temperature, the state of the wound, and his heart and pulse. The pulse was irregular but that was perhaps because of excitement. The young man's pale lips were pressed together and his eyes burned. Only the scars on his neck were red.

---

4. The **Koreans** were neutral in World War II and presumably would not harm the American.

"I realize you are saving my life again," he told Sadao.

"Not at all," Sadao said. "It is only inconvenient to have you here any longer."

He had hesitated a good deal about giving the man a flashlight. But he had decided to give it to him after all. It was a small one, his own, which he used at night when he was called.

"If your food runs out before you catch a boat," he said, "signal me two flashes at the same instant the sun drops over the horizon. Do not signal in darkness, for it will be seen. If you are all right but still there, signal me once. You will find fish easy to catch but you must eat them raw. A fire would be seen."

"Okay," the young man breathed.

He was dressed now in the Japanese clothes which Sadao had given him, and at the last moment Sadao wrapped a black cloth about his blond head.

"Now," Sadao said.

The young American without a word shook Sadao's hand warmly, and then walked quite well across the floor and down the step into the darkness of the garden. Once—twice—Sadao saw his light flash to find his way. But that would not be suspected. He waited until from the shore there was one more flash. Then he closed the partition. That night he slept.

"You say the man escaped?" the General asked faintly. He had been operated upon a week before, an emergency operation to which Sadao had been called in the night. For twelve hours Sadao had not been sure the General would live. The gall bladder was much involved. Then the old man had begun to breathe deeply again and to demand food. Sadao had not been able to ask about the assassins. So far as he knew they had never come. The servants had returned and Yumi had cleaned the guest room thoroughly and had burned sulphur in it to get the white man's smell out of it. Nobody said anything. Only the gardener was cross because he had got behind with his chrysanthemums.

But after a week Sadao felt the General was well enough to be spoken to about the prisoner.

"Yes, Excellency, he escaped," Sadao now said. He coughed, signifying that he had not said all he might have said, but was unwilling to disturb the General farther. But the old man opened his eyes suddenly.

"That prisoner," he said with some energy, "did I not promise you I would kill him for you?"

"You did, Excellency," Sadao said.

"Well, well!" the old man said in a tone of amazement, "so I did. But you see, I was suffering a good deal. The truth is, I thought of nothing but myself. In short, I forgot my promise to you."

"I wondered, Your Excellency," Sadao murmured.

"It was certainly very careless of me," the General said. "But you understand it was not lack of patriotism or dereliction of duty." He looked anxiously at his doctor. "If the matter should come out you would understand that, wouldn't you?"

"Certainly, Your Excellency," Sadao said. He suddenly comprehended that the General was in the palm of his hand and that as a consequence he himself was perfectly safe. "I can swear to your loyalty, Excellency," he said to the old General, "and to your zeal against the enemy."

"You are a good man," the General murmured and closed his eyes. "You will be rewarded."

But Sadao, searching the spot of black in the twilighted sea that night, had his reward. There was no prick of light in the dusk. No one was on the island. His prisoner was gone—safe, doubtless, for he had warned him to wait only for a Korean fishing boat.

He stood for a moment on the veranda, gazing out to the sea from whence the young man had come that other night. And into his mind, although without reason, there came other white faces he had known—the professor at whose house he had met Hana, a dull man, and his wife had been a silly talkative woman, in spite of her wish to be kind. He remembered his old teacher of anatomy, who had been so insistent on mercy with the knife, and then he remembered the face of his fat and slatternly landlady. He had had great difficulty in finding a place to live in America because he was a Japanese. The Americans were full of prejudice and it had been bitter to live in it, knowing himself their superior. How he had despised the ignorant and dirty old woman who had at last consented to house him in her miserable home! He had once tried to be grateful to her because she had in his last year nursed him through influenza, but it was difficult, for she was no less repulsive to him in her kindness. But then, white people were repulsive of course. It was a relief to be openly at war with them at last. Now he remembered the youthful, haggard face of his prisoner—white and repulsive.

"Strange," he thought, "I wonder why I could not kill him?"

I

A DILEMMA OF CONSCIENCE

Wars have always presented men with problems of conscience. Despite a conviction that his country's cause is just, a man may be deeply troubled by the inhuman acts that war calls on him to perform. You have already examined one treatment of the theme in "The Man He Killed" by Thomas Hardy on page 37. As Pearl Buck shows in this story, a loyal Japanese in the Second World War may discover that he has loyalties to other things than his country. When an unexpected encounter brings the terms of war down to a choice of letting an enemy live or die, Sadao finds his conscience will not let him take an easy way out. Miss Buck explores his problem from many sides. The servants have no doubts about what should be done. The old general lets his anxiety about his own life compromise his patriotic duty. Tom has no understanding at all of Sadao's dilemma; all he can see is that

someone has saved his life. As these various attitudes bring their pressure to bear on Hana and Sadao's minds, they must decide what to do. But even at the end, Sadao is not sure why he could not kill Tom or even turn him over to the authorities.

II

IMPLICATIONS

In the light of your understanding of the story, discuss the following quotations. What feelings or motivations on the part of the persons speaking or spoken about do they reveal?

1. "But his trained hands seemed of their own will to be doing what they could to stanch the fearful bleeding."

2. " 'Now you will soon be strong,' she said, not liking him and yet moved to comfort him."

3. "That they [the servants] were right she knew too in most of her being. But there was another part of her which she herself could not understand. It was not sentimental liking of the prisoner."

4. "Those scars! What were they? Sadao did not ask."

5. " 'I realize you are saving my life again,' he told Sadao."

" 'Not at all,' Sadao said. 'It is only inconvenient to have you here any longer.' "

III

TECHNIQUES

Conflict

The main conflict in "The Enemy" is not between any two characters or sets of characters. Although Japan and America are at war, Sadao and Tom are not soldiers in combat. Rather, the conflict exists within the characters; both Sadao and Hana are at war with themselves. What are the conflicting forces within each? How are they different? How are they the same?

Climax

For Hana, the conflict is resolved by obedience to her husband. You will notice that, near the end, she drops entirely out of the story. For Sadao, it is a different matter. Although he acts to resolve the situation and thus brings the story to its climax, the conflict in his mind is never resolved. Of the two questions raised—What will Sadao do about Tom? Why does he save his life?—only one is answered.

What effect does it have on the reader to leave the other question unanswered?

Exposition

Although the exposition in this story is quite straightforward—it comes in one piece at the beginning—even this material contributes to the conflicts. Consider, for example, Sadao and Hana's training in America. In what ways do these experiences affect their internal conflicts?

IV

WORDS

A. Context clues have limited value. Which of the following examples contain a clue that is helpful? What is the clue? Check your answers in a good dictionary.

1. . . . mingled together at the *caprice* of nature that only with an ax in hand can a man open a passage.

2. . . . descend to the city to *replenish* your ammunition.

3. . . . with the *subtlety* of a tolerably *ingenious* savage, placed a cat and her kittens on the pile . . .

4. . . . stretched himself out in the sun with the greatest *tranquillity.*

5. Fortunato smiled *incredulously,* and fixing his black eyes on those of the Adjutant tried to read there the faith he ought to have had in his words.

6. . . . child's pale face . . . plainly showed the struggle that was going on in his soul between *covetousness* and respect for hospitality.

7. . . . he took a bold step. It was to advance alone towards Mateo and tell him of the affair while *accosting* him as an old acquaintance . . .

8. She threw herself on her knees before an image of the Virgin and prayed *ardently.*

9. . . . who never joked or played with him but who spent *infinite* pains upon him who was his only son.

10. The man moaned with pain in his *stupor* but he did not awaken.

B. 1. As time passes, words sometimes change their original meaning and, as it were, slide downhill (although they may also go uphill). For instance, the word *politician,* while respectable in British English, has a negative connotation in American English which it has not always had. Another example of downgrading is the word *notorious*: now meaning "infamous," it once simply meant "well known." And *boor* originally meant "a peasant," not "a rude person" as it does today.

2. The two words *reduce* and *reduction* are obviously related. They have a common prefix, *re-,* but what is the root? Is it *-duc-, -duce-* (which will not fit with *reduction*), or *-duct-* (which will not fit with *reduce*)? We have a similar problem in many sets of words: what can we say about such common forms as *drink* and *drank,* or *strong* and *strength?* Differences in these forms show that in English many roots have more than one form. The following list contains some which have more than one form: *-clud-* and *-clus-,* meaning "close, shut," as in *conclude* and *conclusion, -dic-* and *-dict-,* meaning "say, speak, word," as in *indicate, diction,* and *-frag-* and *-fract-,* meaning "break," as in *fragment* and *fraction.*

3. For the following words used in the selections that you have just read, use your dictionary to find the roots: *solitary, plaintive, tortuous, obstruct, transparency, reputation, interrupt, irregular, permission, ridiculous, convince, incredulous, enormous, separate, audible, complexion, translation, innocent, depend, voluble, repulsion, vitality, exposure, concise, contradict, impulsive, oppose, submerge, prejudice.*

4. Sometimes a word may be composed of two roots. Notice the word *malediction* that Mateo Falcone uses. It is composed of two roots, *-mal-,* meaning "bad, evil," and *-dict-,* meaning "word, say," along with a suffix, *-ion.* By using your dictionary find the meanings of the roots in *uniform, automobile,* and *melancholy.* Note how the last has changed its meaning.

Brief Encounters

THEME

I think that when people are pressed close they act the same way. Part of you enters them, part of them enters you. Long after you forget the names and faces, they are still a part of you. Sometimes it is frightening to think that every person you have ever hated, or feared, or run away from is part of you. But so is every person you have ever learned from, every friend you ever had."

—Theodore H. White

In daily life, people are thrown together in innumerable accidental situations. These meetings are neither planned nor permanent. The people involved separate and go their different ways. But in the momentary coming together something happens. The effects may be great or small, for good or bad, but whether it is recognized by the participants or not, an effect is there. Their lives have been changed.

IMPLICATIONS

Now, before reading the novel *His Enemy, His Friend,* pull together your impressions of the short selections in BRIEF ENCOUNTERS by evaluating the following set of propositions. Consider as many of the selections as you think the propositions apply to, before you form an opinion. The more evidence you can cite, the sounder your opinion will be.

1. Brief encounters seem to be accidents, but it is possible that they are part of a plan that we, as human beings, do not understand.

2. Beneath superficial differences, most people are alike in basic human traits and characteristics.

3. Whether a person is a friend or an enemy sometimes depends on circumstances outside one's own control.

4. Brief encounters may change the direction of one's life.

5. A person with a strong personal code of conduct is never at a loss in an unusual encounter. He never has any doubts about what his reactions should be.

6. In all of us, there lie hidden qualities that brief encounters may surprisingly bring out.

TECHNIQUES

Exposition

As you have seen in the five short stories in BRIEF ENCOUNTERS, exposition may be presented in different ways. Describe the kinds of exposition that you find in each of the stories. How was each method appropriate or inappropriate to the nature of the story?

Conflict

There are also many different kinds of conflict, as many as you may find in life itself. Between whom or within whom does the conflict exist in each of the selections? In which stories is neither side all right or all wrong? In which stories is the conflict a matter of choice and in which is it forced on the characters? According to your own taste, what kind of conflict makes the most gripping story? Why?

Climax

Find the moment that provides the climax in each story. You may disagree with others in the class, so be prepared to back your own opinion with a sound interpretation of the story. Supposing the story had stopped at the climax, what questions would have remained in your mind? Are these questions always answered before the end? If not, why do you think they are left hanging?

Poetry

The five poems you have read cover a variety of poetic styles. In a few words, characterize the style of each poem. Is it lofty, conversational, polished, rough? Show how each style is appropriate or inappropriate to the poem's subject matter. What experiences are similar to those in the prose selections? Which are different? How? What does poetry accomplish that prose does not?

Essay

"Stopover in Querétaro" is an essay rather than a short story. However, as an essay that recounts a personal experience, it is in many ways similar to a story. How do exposition, conflict, and climax function in this essay?

Introduction to
His Enemy, His Friend

Thomas Hardy's poem, "The Man He Killed," speculates about the strange quirk of fate in which the relationship between two people is determined by the circumstances under which they meet. *His Enemy, His Friend* is a further exploration of this quality of human life. How does a person become your enemy? How does another become your friend? Do you control the relationship or does it come about simply by the accident of being thrown together in a neighborhood or classroom? Is friendship determined by qualities you like or dislike in another person or is it perhaps a matter of psychological chemistry? Or are one's reactions determined by forces in the culture: the accident of your being born in a given country, a member of a given race, into a given religion? We all like to think that we are the masters of our fates, as a familiar English poem states. But are we? Do we really have control over who becomes our enemy and who becomes our friend?

John Tunis says that this story of his is about the conscience of a man. Conscience is the faculty of recognizing right from wrong in regard to one's own conduct. So conscience is a very personal thing. Individuals may recognize certain actions as right and have no sense of guilt in performing them. Other actions are considered wrong, and, though a person may go ahead and do them, he is uneasy or uncomfortable in the act. People who have no such guide for their actions, who act purely on the basis of a pain or pleasure scale, are deficient as human beings. Conscience may be a quality that is learned or imposed by one's culture. But in its finest sense it is a system of values that an individual has fought through and determined for himself. It comes from an ability to get inside the skin of another person and walk around in it so that the world can be seen through that person's eyes, feeling his needs and understanding his rights. It comes from a realization of how one's own actions set up ripples that affect other people.

One of the continuing problems of human existence occurs when the individual's conscience conflicts with the demands of his culture. This is the theme of much great literature: of *Antigone*, one of the greatest of the ancient Greek plays, of *Hamlet*, perhaps the greatest play written in the English language. It is the problem of the conscientious objector in modern America and of many young adults who see some aspects of contemporary society as hypocritical.

This story of conscience you are about to read is laid in France during the German occupation of that country during World War II. The map is important to help you locate places and movements of characters. During the 1930s Hitler made his spectacular rise to power in Germany and for awhile lifted the Germans out of the hopelessness they had felt since World War I. France and Germany had a long, traditional history of enmity. When Germany was suddenly reinvigorated, France put all of its efforts into fortifying its common border with Germany. Much to France's surprise, Germany swept through Belgium around the end of the fortified defenses and overwhelmed the defenders. For the next four years France was governed by a puppet government of Frenchmen who were willing to collaborate with Germany, but the Germans continued to occupy the country. It was a time of great deprivation. Most young male Frenchmen were shipped east to Germany to serve almost as slave labor in the German war effort. The French Jews were systematically eliminated by being sent to German concentration camps. However, there was a strong underground organization of Frenchmen who resisted the conquerors. There were frequent incidents against the Germans.

As the war dragged along and the allied forces gained increasing strength, Hitler knew that the invasion of France would probably

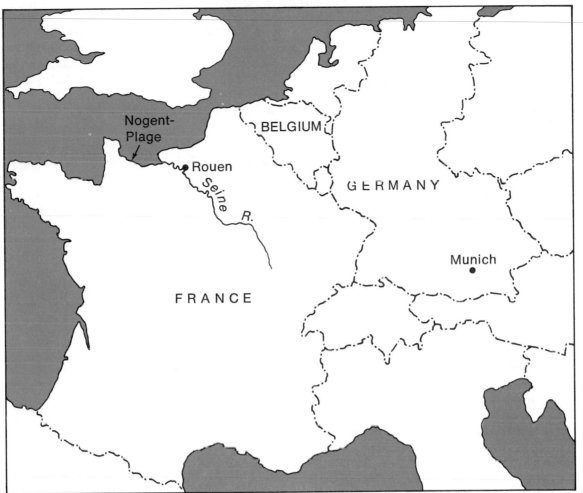

come from England. He therefore built a strong system of defenses along the French coast, actually extending them all the way to Norway. Natives in the coast villages lived in both great expectancy and dread of the coming assault. The invasion would throw out the hated Germans, but it would also probably bring devastation to the towns. The actual invasion began on June 6, 1944, at a spot on the Normandy coast called by the code name of Omaha Beach. From the details of geography given in the story, you must conclude that the setting of *His Enemy, His Friend* is a village on the French coast of the English Channel, north of the actual invasion area.

Before you start, it is also important to read the author's note about the story. Tunis writes:

. . . sport plays an important part in these pages. The sport dealt with is the game that Europeans call football. When played in the United States, it is association football, or soccer. Since my story is set abroad, I have used the term "football" throughout.

Unlike American football, which is half football and half basketball and neither the one nor the other, the European sport is based upon kicking and passing along the ground. No player save the goalkeeper may touch the ball with his hands. The game is played by eleven men on each side. No substitutions are permitted. There are two halves of forty-five minutes each, and the ball used is round, not oval as in American football. It is a game enormously popular with the young, and draws immense crowds all over the world.

HIS ENEMY, HIS FRIEND

JOHN TUNIS

Part I

Eve of Battle
June, 1944

1

The black-haired sergeant, in the gray-green uniform of the army of Adolf Hitler's Third Reich,[1] sat smoking his pipe on the stone steps of the house. Beside him was a boy of eight or nine in a faded polo shirt, a ragged pair of dark blue shorts, and sneakers so frayed that both his big toes stuck out of them.

The sergeant and the boy were discussing a subject that each considered important and their serious faces reflected this.

"Was that the time, Feldwebel[2] Hans, when you scored the only goal for Hamburg against Stuttgart?" asked the boy.

"Noooo . . ." responded the young soldier. "No, as I remember now," he went on in excellent French, "that was the year . . . ."

"I know, I know. Don't tell me," the boy cried, excitement in his voice. "I have an account in my scrapbook. Can I show you my scrapbook sometime, Feldwebel Hans? I can? I know; it was the year Hamburg was tied by the Racing Club of Paris, thanks to Bonvallet's last-minute goal. Am I right?"

"Right! Only actually I didn't play in that particular match. A bad knee. And bad luck, too. It was the spring before the war and that

knee kept me out of service for thirteen months. Psst . . . come here . . . here . . . ."

He snapped his fingers and held out one hand. A dog was coming toward them, a white and black, short-haired distant relative of a fox terrier. He was a kind of Grande Rue[3] dog, an animal born in the street, heaven knows where and when, a dog of most uncertain heritage. He approached with caution as the big man took the square pipe from his mouth and leaned forward encouragingly.

The dog edged nearer. One glance told you it was a long while since anyone had stroked him, given him a good meal, said a kind word to him. The sergeant reached out and kneaded the back of the animal's neck. Immediately the dog responded by coming in closer. Then he sat on his haunches, seemingly content, for once befriended.

Finally the German rose, knocked his pipe on the stone steps, and stretched. "Yes, of course you can show me your scrapbook. I'd be interested. Bring it along anytime in the afternoon. Well, we must get the morning report from the blockhouse. It hasn't come yet and the *Herr Hauptmann*[4] will be annoyed."

Together they walked down the Grande Rue, the main and only street of the village of Nogent-Plage,[5] the tawny-haired boy in the ragged shorts and the tall *Feldwebel*. The dog walked between them, his tail wagging.

Since it was a lovely morning in early June, the street was full of people. It seemed as though everyone they met greeted the sergeant. Old ladies in black carrying half-empty shopping bags, housewives with long loaves of grayish bread under their arms, children, espe-

1. **Reich**\raihk\ literally, empire. The Third Reich refers to the German government under Hitler from 1933–1945.
2. **Feldwebel**\⁀fĕlt 'vä·bĕl\ sergeant.
3. **Grande Rue**\⁀grand ⁀rū\ Grand Street, as common as our Main Street; Grande Rue dog, a stray dog.
4. **Herr Hauptmann**\⁀hĕr ⁀haupt 'man\ (Mr.) Captain. The German language uses *Herr* before such titles.
5. **Nogent-Plage**\nō 'zhɔnt ⁀plazh\ Nogent Beach, the name of the town.

cially the boys who invariably appeared when the *Feldwebel* was around, all wished him good day, addressing him as Colonel and speaking in German.

"*Guten Tag,*[6] *Herr Oberst.*[7] *Guten Tag . . . .*"

Although he had told them all a hundred times that he was not an *Oberst*, a colonel, but a *Feldwebel*, a sergeant, and a supply sergeant at that, he responded to their words with an old-fashioned courtesy, speaking in French as a rule, touching one finger to the brim of his stained forage cap in a most unsoldierly gesture, and wishing them good day in return.

"*Eh . . . bonjour,*[8] Madame Dupont. *Bonjour.*"

The old lady in the faded black dress bobbed and ducked her head. "*Guten Tag, Herr Oberst. Guten Tag . . . .*"

There it was once again! How often he had spelled it out for them, sometimes severely.

"*Nein, nein, bitte. Ich bin ein Feldwebel, ein Unteroffizier, nicht ein Oberst . . . .*"[9]

The people of the village simply smiled and went on addressing him as *Herr Oberst*.

At first he felt this was intentional. After all, with these tricky French one could never tell. Perhaps it was their cynical way of sneering at the fact that the son of a baron, from an old army family, should be merely a sergeant. Occasionally at night when he could not sleep due to the roar of the guns along the coast spattering antiaircraft fire into the heavens, he wondered whether the French were stubborn, stupid, or insolent. As time went on, however, he realized that to the people in Nogent-Plage he represented authority. For them he was a person to whom they could protest, appeal, with whom they could discuss their grievances. It was the *Feldwebel* who listened to their objections to what they felt were unfair regulations of the German High Command along the coast.

Occasionally these regulations were changed. More often they were just ignored by the sergeant and his superiors. It was easier that way. Hence he accepted the greetings of the vil-

lagers, and although the military rank they conferred upon him amused his men and not infrequently annoyed his commanding officer, there was little anyone could do with the stubborn French.

The only person who did not call him *Herr Oberst* was the boy in the ragged blue shorts. He felt immediately that the sergeant disliked this and always addressed him as Feldwebel Hans. Perhaps this was how the big German first noticed him. It drew them together; their passion for football cemented the bond.

That day, the fourteen hundredth and fifth day of the occupation of the village of Nogent-Plage by the Germans, a day that was to explode in such violence and change forever the lives of the boy, the *Feldwebel*, and everyone in town, began in calm and quiet. During the long months of the occupation, people in the village had passed and repassed the same troops for days without end. Often even their first names were known to the townsfolk—harsh sounding Teutonic[10] names such as Helmut, Gottfried, and Gerhardt. Over the years, many regiments had visited this hamlet by the sea, the men sunning themselves along the waterfront, or playing football under the direction of the *Feldwebel* on the hard, sandy beach below the cliff. Never was anyone else accorded recognition by the villagers. In fact, they often made fun of the other Germans, not infrequently to their faces. Of all the soldiers, only the Feldwebel Hans was a friend.

He was a friend above all to the boys of the village, because he was a former football player, and especially to young Jean-Paul Varin.[11] Wherever the sergeant went the boy attached himself, following from place to place, often with his pal, René Le Gallec,[12]

---

6. **Guten Tag**\\'gü·tən ᴧtagk\\ Good day.
7. **Oberst**\\ᴧō 'bĕrst\\ Colonel.
8. **bonjour**\\bōn 'zhur\\ Good day.
9. No, no, please. I am a sergeant, a non-commissioned officer, not a colonel.
10. **Teutonic**\\tü ᴧtän·ək\\ Germanic.
11. **Jean-Paul Varin**\\ᴧzha(n)ᴧpōl·və ᴧrä(n)\\
12. **René Le Gallec**\\rə ᴧnä·lə·gal ᴧlĕk\\

slightly older and also a *fervent*[13] of football. When the German sergeant played or coached his men, the two boys could not take their eyes off him. The younger, especially, watched with a furious intentness. Unconsciously even his body moved, swung, stopped short, riposted[14] as the big German athlete's did. In vain his mother rang the bell for dinner. You spoke to him and he did not hear. The boy watched, listened to the football talk, played and practiced, went so far as to learn German so that he would fully understand the soldiers talking. Football was his life, his passion, his existence. And the Feldwebel Hans was his god.

2

Not only Jean-Paul Varin but all the good people of Nogent-Plage had definite feelings about the Feldwebel Hans. If one had to be occupied by the Germans, the villagers all agreed, it was better that he should be in town.

"Why, the *Herr Oberst* is the son of a baron, if his brother is killed in the Luftwaffe[1] he too will be a baron. Ah, say what you like, *monsieur*,[2] blood does tell. He's part of that old Schleswig-Holstein[3] aristocracy. You know what those people are like."

"How true, *madame*, how true! Besides, he is a man of the world, not merely an ace of the football. He plays the cello and appreciates the good wine of Bordeaux[4]—and the Normandy[5] cider too, yes indeed. Well, his mother was French, you know, from Sedan.[6] To my way of thinking, he might just as well have been French. *Yes*, I agree . . . ."

"*Eh bien*,[7] his mother was a De Mezière from Sedan. For me he is no militarist, but really a civilized type. He loves the children in town and they love him. Why, *monsieur*, he is their hero. That Varin boy follows him everywhere. You know the *Herr Oberst* was the great defensive back for Bayern of Munich. Once before the war he played for Germany, at the age of nineteen, too!"

"Yes indeed, the boys and girls love him. If I call my René, and he doesn't answer, I know he is watching the *Herr Oberst* coaching football."

"To be sure," interjected a fat woman. "I, for one, shan't forget either when the partisans[8] burned the bridge at Verville and that *Hauptmann* tried to take my husband off to Germany, last year. Ah, no, I told the *Herr Oberst*. Look, my husband was beside me in bed that awful night. He believed me. He even convinced the High Command. He has connections, you know."

Now the villagers were all talking at once.

"Ah, yes, only he could have done it. Why not? A supply sergeant, perhaps, but he understands and respects French culture and French civilization. Naturally, his mother was French. But yet after all, he is German . . . ."

"Yes, *monsieur*, most of these barbarians know neither France nor the French. Well, this man is no stony-faced Prussian[9] such as some we've had stationed in this town since 1940."

"Indeed, *madame*, I recall when the town had to be evacuated, remember, at the time of the big raid on Dieppe.[10] The *Herr Oberst* interceded for us with the *Kommandant*[11] at Caen,[12] you recall? Those who really lived here were permitted to stay. Oh, I am entirely in accord with you. We are truly fortunate to have him here in Nogent-Plage. Truly . . . ."

---

13. **fervent**\fər 'va(n)\ enthusiastic fan.
14. **riposted**\rĭ ˄pōs•təd\ quickly returned a thrust—a fencing term.

---

1. **Luftwaffe**\˄luft 'vaf•ə\ air force.
2. **monsieur**\mə 'syə\ Sir or Mister.
3. **Schleswig-Holstein**, a state in west Germany.
4. **Bordeaux**, a city and port in southwest France.
5. **Normandy**, region in northwest France.
6. **Sedan**, a city in northeast France.
7. **Eh bien**\ĕ 'byĕ(n)\ Oh, well.
8. **partisans**, a guerrilla band; here, the Underground.
9. **Prussian**, a despotic and ruthless individual.
10. **Dieppe**\dē 'ĕp\ port of northern France.
11. **Kommandant**\'kō•man ˄dant\ Commander.
12. **Caen**\ka(n)\ city in northwest France.

"Fortunate to have him," that was how the villagers felt about the Feldwebel Hans Joachim Wolfgang von und zu Kleinschrodt,[13] to give him his full name. And he was the one German soldier who seemed to be permanently stationed at Nogent-Plage, which after a while became a rest camp for troops from the Russian front. Usually a regiment or a battalion stayed only a few weeks or a month in this village on the Normandy coast. Then one wet, foggy morning the siren would blow. That piercing noise meant the end of peace and repose for those Germans. From work, from relaxation, from the football game on the beach coached by the *Feldwebel*, they hustled back to their billets,[14] fear in every heart. Early on in the war when Hitler's forces were winning from Crete to Norway and each month a different nation was gobbled up by the Greater Reich, the troops had left for the East singing and cheering.

Then the war was a glorious romp. But two winters in the snow outside Moscow changed this. Now they hardly spoke as they packed and made ready to depart. Sullenly they collected the regimental baggage, silently loaded the transport wagons. When the short, sharp whistle of the *Ober-Feldwebel*[15] rang out, they would line up along the Grande Rue dismally waiting inspection and the command to move off.

"*Achtung!*[16] Right face! Forward . . . hup . . . hup . . . ."

So, off in columns of four down the coastal road to entrain[17] for the East. Nowadays the villagers of Nogent-Plage made an event of this. They lined the streets, watching not without pleasure the grim faces of the soldiers, making sardonic[18] remarks the Germans could not understand.

"*Hein!*[19] They don't seem quite so happy to say good-by, do they?"

"Would you, my friend, with the Russian bear breathing down your neck?"

"Ah, but remember, they used to have nothing but motorized equipment. And all that new English matériel captured at Dunkerque.[20]

Remember, *madame*? That has worn out now. Look at those poor old horses. And the wagons falling apart . . . ."

No, the war was no longer glorious for the Germans. Troops of different regiments came and went, only the *Herr Oberst* remained. It was a corps decision to leave him at Nogent-Plage. He was valuable there because he had a quality few of his countrymen possessed. The villagers hated the occupying forces with a fierce Norman hatred, looking and longing for only one thing—the Allied invasion and freedom from German domination. The *Herr Oberst* knew this quite as well as anyone. Yet, thanks largely to him, order prevailed in the village. There were no shootings, no terrorist attacks, no raids as in other towns along the coast. So far as the Germans could tell, the villagers never tried to signal planes or ships. Never had a *Gauleiter*[21] been summoned from Berlin to restore order. In fact, the High Command at Caen had such a good opinion of Nogent-Plage that it considered awarding the town a medal for its correct attitude toward German troops.

Certainly nobody ever called the *Feldwebel* a keen soldier. He obeyed orders and did his duty. That was all. In private life he was a von und zu Kleinschrodt, younger son of an ancient Baltic military family famous in the history of his country. His father had been a Colonel of Uhlans[22] in the First World War. Brought up in the army tradition, he had, perhaps, had too much of it. Not only did the

---

13. **Hans Joachim Wolfgang von und zu Kleinschrodt** \hans 'yō·ə ▲hkĭm ▲vōlf·gaŋ·fōn·undt·tzū ▲klĭn 'shrōdt\
14. **billets**\▲bil·ətz\ quarters assigned to soldiers.
15. **Ober-Feldwebel,** sergeant-major, warrant officer class.
16. **Achtung**\ahk ▲tūŋ\ Attention!
17. **entrain,** take a train.
18. **sardonic**\sar ▲dan·ĭk\ bitter, mocking.
19. **Hein!** Ha!
20. **Dunkerque**\▲dən 'kərk\ seaport of northern France. It was the scene of the rescue under German fire of some 300,000 British soldiers by volunteer civilian boats.
21. **Gauleiter**\▲gau·lai·tər\ chief official of a political district under Nazi control.
22. **Uhlans**\▲ū·lənz\ Prussian light cavalry.

big, seemingly awkward young man look out of place in uniform beside his brisk, competent, Heil Hitlering[23] comrades, but the way he saluted, even his reports, left much to be desired. Many a commanding officer at Nogent-Plage had tried to reform him and given up the attempt. Because of his family and his connections he was no laughing stock —in fact, quite the reverse. Yet he was not entirely in favor with the High Command at Caen.

What attracted the people of Nogent-Plage to the *Feldwebel* was not merely his fame as an athlete, but his agreeable manner, so different from that of many of the Germans. Also there was his love of music. As he was an indifferent soldier, he was an indifferent musician and played the cello, to tell the truth, rather badly. However, he enjoyed playing with Georges Varin, the local schoolmaster and father of young Jean-Paul. Monsieur Varin was an equally bad violinist, but often, when the priest came to accompany them of an evening on the sadly inadequate piano, the three sat immersed in Bach and Beethoven until long after curfew. As a consequence, on those nights, the padre[24] was forced to stay with the schoolmaster until morning.

In the single *café* in town, the Bleu Marin, the German soldiers, playing the harmonica and singing as they drank their beer, were ignored by the French natives. But whenever the tiny bell on the door tinkled ever so slightly and the *Herr Oberst* entered, the fishermen at their *belote* game glanced up and nodded pleasantly. When the curfew sounded they picked up their cards, avoided the gaze of the harmonica players, and left, bidding the *Feldwebel* good night on the way out.

"*Guten Nacht,*[25] *Herr Oberst,*" they said to him.

"*Eh . . . bon soir,*[26] *bon soir, messieurs,*"[27] he replied.

3

Nogent-Plage was like a sheltered spot in a storm. Yet during four long years, though the villagers were never in danger, they heard sounds all day and night that brought the war inside them. One was the endless clack-clack, clack-clack of hobnailed boots on concrete. You heard it in daylight, late at night after curfew, early in the black hours before dawn when the patrols stomped down the Grande Rue. You heard it and soon hated it more than anything else, because it brought the presence of German troops into your home and your heart.

Another familiar sound was the thromb-thromb of the motorized fishing vessels, indistinctly heard, indistinctly seen through the fog which so often covered the coast. Nogent-Plage was a fishing village, and the Germans permitted certain selected fishermen to go out three kilometers—no more—on Mondays and Thursdays. People in town could tell the day of the week by this sound. Naturally, when the vessels returned to the shingled beach below the cliff, a platoon of Germans was waiting to requisition (meaning grab off) their share of the catch. This share was anything up to sixty or seventy-five percent.

If you stood at a certain point on the cliff outside the village, or if you watched from a second-story window of Madame Dupont's house, you could make out the coastal road winding into the distance like a long black ribbon. To use it a Frenchman had to have a special permit, or *Ausweiss,*[1] from the German High Command in Caen.

The road, Route Nationale Number 40, twisted and turned, dipped and rose, as it followed the coast. From Nogent-Plage you could see it stretching for miles, empty of

---

23. **Heil Hitlering,** *Hail Hitler* was the salute and greeting used during the Nazi regime. *Heil Hitlering* in this context refers to soldiers who greeted other soldiers properly at all times.
24. **padre,** father; priest.
25. **Guten Nacht**\\'gū·tən ▲nahkt\\ good night (German).
26. **bon soir**\\bōn 'swȯir\\ good evening (French).
27. **messieurs**\\mē 'syə\\ gentlemen; plural of *monsieur.*

---

1. **Ausweiss**\\▲aus 'vais\\ permit.

traffic save for a few German army trucks. To travel upon it was, as the French said, "to make the *gymnastique*."[2] Indeed, it resembled an obstacle course, what with the sand from the dunes that had blown over it in places and the holes that had not been filled in since the start of the war four years before.

The whole region was bare and barren, especially in winter, and the winds harsh, cold, strong. They blew so fiercely that few trees survived, and on clear days one had an unobstructed view up and down the coast. The first thing you noticed was the big blockhouse just below the top of the cliff on which the village rested, then other blockhouses at intervals of a mile or so along the shore. They were all size, large and small, of gray concrete, which the Germans had forced the French to construct and pay for. These fortifications and others around the *Haupt Kämpflinie*,[3] the great warline, were Hitler's main defense against invasion from the sea.

Here and there along the coastal road were sentry boxes, six feet tall, with conical roofs. Each was large enough for two men and two machine guns. You could see their barrels sticking through the slits on each side. They served to check on traffic and also acted as lookouts over the ocean. Behind the road, away from the water, the dunes stretched for miles, bristling with stakes against parachutists and seeded with mines and booby traps.

To the pilots of the R.A.F. planes Nogent-Plage was a landmark: the first glimpse of enemy-held territory, the first sight of occupied France, the first shriek and whistle of antiaircraft fire, and, if it was night, the first tracer bullets rushing up in the dark. By day the surf crashing on the beach was the first thing they saw below as they roared in out of the mist. Then the rocky cliff above the sand, the village with its single street, and the black ribbon of road stretching away to left and right.

Nogent-Plage itself consisted of only a handful of brick and stone houses, with a gap here and there where a field of fire had been cleared for the guns of the blockhouse. Beyond, in back, was nothing save those endless dunes stretching away to the horizon.

The sand had been there when William the Conqueror set off in his small boats in 1066 to invade England, when Napoleon in 1803 stood on the cliff and looked across to the shores of Sussex, when Hitler on the same cliff in 1940 shook his fist at Britain, the endlessly moving sand was still there. At times the wind blew so fiercely it made one feel that the sand would eventually smother the tiny settlement on its rock jutting into the English Channel.

The German soldiers who garrisoned Nogent-Plage at the start of the war were giant six-footers who had awed the villagers. That had changed. Now the German troops were usually a dismal-looking lot. They were farmers' boys from Thuringia, stunted adolescents or weary old men. But this June morning the people of the town felt uneasy. For some weeks a new breed of German soldiers, a tough battery of Silesians, had been stationed in town. They were a motorized flak[4] unit, highly trained, efficient, equipped with light and heavy machine guns and antiaircraft weapons, continually marching up and down the single street in tight formation. They were shock troops and wanted everyone to know it. They appeared invincible. Their smartness, their discipline, even the way they saluted and their officers returned salutes were impressive.

Above everything, accompanying all comings and goings, was noise—the pound-pound of a hundred pairs of hobnailed boots in unison, the shouts of their noncoms,[5] the raucous calls on the loudspeakers.

Machen Sie schnell,[6] *schnell, schnell,* hup, hup . . . .

These men seemed forever on their toes, ready for anything, not war-weary troops rest-

---

2. **make the gymnastique,** perform athletic stunts.
3. **Haupt Kämpflinie**\haʊpt ᴧkĕmp 'flĭn·ē\ main line of battle.
4. **flak,** antiaircraft fire.
5. **noncoms,** noncommissioned officers.
6. **Machen Sie schnell**\'mahk·ən·zē ᴧshnĕl\ hurry.

ing after months on the icy plains of Russia. They were stationed in Nogent-Plage to kill and be killed. Quite evidently.

Uneasiness hung over the village that day. For one thing there was organized movement in the Bloch villa. This house had been taken by the occupying forces early in the war, because it belonged to a family of Jews long since dead, deported, or forgotten. It made an excellent headquarters in the center of town. Dispatch riders coated with dust dashed up, black leather briefcases under one arm. Engineers worked on the radio aerial on the roof. From the blockhouse came a sudden burst of fire.

Could all this mean, the villagers speculated, that the invasion was coming? That long-promised, long-awaited, long-hoped-for invasion, so often hinted at in the B.B.C.[7] broadcasts from London called by the natives, "The *Bibbice*." Against all regulations, those Normans, proud, unbending in their attitude toward the occupiers, listened every day to the *Bibbice*. Once Monsieur Varin, the teacher who lived next door to the Bloch villa, had switched his radio on to the B.B.C. wavelength and sat waiting to turn the volume down before the news from London began. Unfortunately he fell asleep. Those first words woke him with a start.

"*Ici Londres* . . . ."[8]

With a bound he leaped across the room and shut the set off. But the Germans billeted in the next house, almost in the next room, must surely have heard it and reported it. He went to bed in a sweat of anguish, lying awake all night waiting for the hammering on the door that meant a German prison camp—or worse.

Nothing happened. The night patrols passed as usual. He heard the low, mechanical beat of their metal heels on the concrete, clack-clack, clack-clack. But no thunderous pounding on his door. The *Herr Oberst*, he guessed, knew what had happened and had arranged things so the German headquarters at Caen did not.

DISCUSSION FOR UNDERSTANDING

1. Who is Feldwebel Hans? Where is he stationed? What is his personal background?

2. What do the villagers think of the *Feldwebel*?

3. What are the reactions of his fellow officers toward him?

4. How does the young Jean-Paul Varin show his admiration for the *Feldwebel*?

5. How do the German soldiers now stationed in Nogent-Plage differ from the ones stationed there earlier?

6. Describe Nogent-Plage and the surrounding area.

7. What has made the townspeople uneasy on this day?

8. Jean-Paul Varin is still a child, yet how have his encounters with the *Feldwebel* had an effect on him?

4

The Feldwebel Hans, as the boy called him, sat on the stone steps of his billet in the pleasant spring sunshine. He rose and yawned. If the glorious *Reichswehr*,[1] the German army, didn't think much of him as a soldier, he, in turn, didn't think much of the *Reichswehr*. He was hardly passionate about roll calls, drilling, medals, uniforms, saluting, family tradition, army tradition, national tradition—all this seemed to mean little to him. He could easily have obtained a commission through his connections, but the officer corps with its caste feeling nauseated him. Once you get to be an officer, even a lieutenant, he always said, everyone below you suspects you.

Now, with the thin dog near him and the boy as usual at his side, he picked up a clipboard with papers attached, stuck his empty pipe in his pocket, and walked down the Grande Rue and past the sign *Juden Ver-*

---

7. **B.B.C.,** British Broadcasting Company.
8. **Ici Londres**\ē 'sē ▲lōnd(rə)\ London here, or, London calling (French).

---

1. **Reichswehr**\▲raihks·vär\

boten,[2] with the name of the general command officer underneath. The boy did not notice it. That sign banishing Jews had been there four years, which was forever to Jean-Paul Varin. It dated back so far he could not remember when it hadn't been there. His father, he well knew, hated it, but there it was, part of the town like the Grande Rue and the cliff on which the town stood and the ocean below.

Down the street they walked, the French boy and the German supply sergeant. Since they were invariably together, nobody took this as strange. The *Herr Oberst* this morning was hardly Hitler's ideal of a soldier of the Greater Reich. He wore a rather grubby tunic[3] and an ancient garrison cap.[4] If his bearing and general attitude did not express contentment, neither did he appear dissatisfied with his job. The boy beside him, he simply walked along greeting those who greeted him.

Clack-clack-clack-clack, his heels sounded on the concrete pavement. Not clack-clack, clack-clack, short, sharp, brutal, as those of most soldiers sounded, but leisurely, in a slow cadence. At the end of the village the sergeant and the boy reached the vacant lot beside the small church. The thin, lonely dog had scampered ahead and now was in the middle of the road, sitting and waiting. As often at this time of day, the Père Clement,[5] the village priest, was coaching René Le Gallec with a football, or *ballon*, as the French called it. The Feldwebel Hans liked the padre, who had been retired to this backwater when the Occupation submerged everyone. Still active at seventy, he especially enjoyed coaching the football players, for he had been a great athlete himself in his youth.

This morning Père Clement's soutane[6] was tied up around his waist with a coarse rope so he could run. This arrangement disclosed thick cotton underdrawers, heavy black-wool stockings reaching to his knees, and rough peasant boots, badly scuffed and scarred. The padre in his time at Nogent-Plage had developed many young football stars, and the Le Gallec boy

with whom he was practicing was the best of all. The *Herr Oberst* stood watching, sucking on his empty pipe, throwing in an occasional suggestion or word of advice. Finally he could no longer resist getting into it himself. Glancing up the street to make sure the new, fire-eating *Hauptmann* commanding the battery was engaged in his office, he yanked off his tunic, snapping a button in the process. The button bounced and rolled. He let it go, intending to pick it up later, placed his tunic on the grass, laid the clipboard beside it, and stepped forward.

Immediately something inside changed. Now he was in his world, in his element, master of himself. His big frame loose and coordinated, he controlled that round ball with his feet almost delicately, pushing a short stab over to the padre, taking it back, turning it across to the boy with an insolent accuracy beautiful to watch.

A spurt past the old man, a short step to the right to dodge the boy, then to the left to catch the pair off balance. All the time he was babying the ball until he had René and the Père Clement so confused that they were ducking first one way, then the other, totally unsure of themselves.

The boy in the blue shorts stood transfixed, his body moving as the *Feldwebel* moved, twisted, stopped, and ran. Two young women going past watched, fascinated.

"Ahhhh, ahhh . . ." they said in admiration. At Nogent-Plage, whenever the Feldwebel Hans played football with the boys a crowd gathered. If he was on the beach coaching the regimental team, a gang of the local lads always sat on the sea wall, commenting.

So this morning half a dozen younger boys

<hr>

2. **Juden Verboten**\ˈyü·dən·fĕr ˈbō·tən\ Jews not allowed.
3. **tunic,** a long close-fitting jacket worn as part of a uniform.
4. **garrison cap,** wedge-shaped cap worn as part of a uniform.
5. **Père Clement**\ˈpār ˈklə ˈma(n)\
6. **soutane**\sü ˈtan\ cassock with buttons down the front.

suddenly appeared from nowhere the second he began to play. Now he was concentrating upon René's moves.

"No, no, not with the right foot, the left . . . . You must learn to pass equally well with either foot . . . . Don't shoot too soon . . . . Take your time, you have time . . . . Watch that ball . . . and keep your head down. Just watch the ball. Try to remember your teammates are all watching you. They will get it if your pass is a good one. Be careful, don't lift your head. That's better . . . lifting the head is always fatal."

He was no longer the casual *Feldwebel*. Now he had become a wonderful, moving, vibrant force, the great athlete, the virtuoso of ball control, master of himself and his well-coordinated body. When he took the ball to explain what he meant with a cross or a kick, he seemed almost to caress it.

One of the young women watching glanced up the street as she heard a door slam. She saw the new commanding officer step out of the Bloch villa, heard a clicking of heels that resounded down the Grande Rue, observed the sentries presenting arms. *"Herr Oberst,"* she said. *"Herr Oberst! Der Hauptmann kommt."* The captain is coming.

The athlete stopped instantly, picked up his tunic, hastily put it on, and, reaching to the ground for his pipe and the clipboard, again became the nondescript *Feldwebel*. His garrison cap on one side of his head, he sauntered off toward the blockhouse for the morning report—now an hour overdue.

The dog rose and followed him. At that moment the *Feldwebel* noticed the little Deschamps girl in the middle of the road, about fifteen yards ahead. Evidently the child had strayed from home. There she stood, a target for passing military vehicles. He got down on one knee and called to her.

"Hier Liebling."[7] Come here.

The child turned to look. She was adorable in her faded pink dress, the tiny skirt so short and shrunken from constant washings that it flared out from her thin legs. The big man held out his arms. It was not precisely the typical picture of a German soldier in France in the fifth year of the Occupation.

Instantly the child responded, toddling toward the *Feldwebel,* her arms also outstretched. Then the door of a house banged open, and the girl's mother rushed up to the *Feldwebel.* Knowing she did not understand German, he said in French, "She was in the middle of the street."

The woman took the child from him and began to scold her. Frightened, the little girl started to cry. Together they went into the house, leaving the Feldwebel Hans in the road, the stray dog at his side.

He walked briskly down the street toward the blockhouse, and as he did the dog again rose and followed along.

5

By noon a wind had arisen, bringing a chill from the water. The fog was burning off as it so frequently did at this time of the year. Superficially it was like every day in Nogent-Plage, but there were signs of things to come. Formations of large planes passed over the village all morning, roaring off into the interior. What did they portend? Were they the usual attacks on bridges, railroad yards, and airfields around Paris? Who could tell?

Georges Varin, the teacher, sat alone at a small iron table on the pavement before the Bleu Marin, chatting with Monsieur Lavigne[1] the proprietor, a heavy-set man of forty-five with a dirty white apron around his waist. On the table was a cup of bitter coffee made of acorns and heaven-knows-what, the result of wartime shortages.

"Another cup, Monsieur the Professor?" asked the *patron.*[2] Monsieur Varin was no more a professor than the Feldwebel Hans was a colonel, being only the village school-

---

7. **Hier, Liebling**\ˈhēr ˈlēb·lĭŋ\ Come here, honey.

---

1. **Lavigne**\la ˈvēn(yə)\

2. **patron**\pa ˈtrō(n)\ proprietor.

master. However, everyone called him professor since he had studied two years in Paris and was an educated man, one to be treated with respect in the village. He was useful in various ways. For instance, he helped the farmers across the dunes who could neither read nor write by penning letters for them, in a script full of flourishes, to their sons in German prison camps.

Dark, small, stocky, and articulate, he used to wear glasses, for he was nearsighted. Unfortunately they had broken and as no new ones were obtainable, even in Caen or Rouen, he carried a pocket magnifying glass to read the communiques in the daily papers. Whenever he read his forehead wrinkled and his eyebrows rose.

Though accepted by everybody, Monsieur Varin was not popular with the right-thinking, church-going part of Nogent-Plage. He was a Marxist and regularly voted the Communist ticket, a fact he never concealed from anyone. Yet even those who disliked him and distrusted his political convictions respected him as a good Frenchman. Had he not fought three years in the First World War, been wounded and returned to combat? Again he had been called to the colors and served through the whole campaign of 1940 as a noncommissioned officer in a frontline unit.

All his life Georges Varin and his family had lived in Nogent-Plage. Early in the Occupation he became acquainted with the Feldwebel Hans. They respected each other and had a love of music in common. Slowly over the years they became friends. In times of trouble there had been instances when only the teacher through the Feldwebel Hans had managed to get German headquarters in Caen to listen to the protests of the villagers. Once Marcel Deschamps, the fisherman, had lost his bearings in a dense fog and against regulations did not reach shore until the next morning. Ordinarily he would have been imprisoned for this offense, but the Feldwebel Hans saved him so that he received a warning only.

Few villagers felt there was anything wrong between the schoolmaster and the German sergeant, or considered Monsieur Varin a collaborator and friend of the Nazis. Not only did he despise collaborators, he invariably spoke of Marshal Pétain, head of the French collaborationist regime, as "that old donkey." So Monsieur Varin, though not entirely popular, found his friendship with the *Feldwebel* accepted because it helped the town. In much the same way the *Feldwebel* was accepted by his superiors.

Because of his background and army connections, the *Feldwebel* talked freely and frankly to an old family friend, Major Kessler, Adjutant at Headquarters of the Northern Command. Usually Major Kessler was accessible to the *Feldwebel* on the telephone in a tight moment. The officer in charge of the garrison at Nogent-Plage knew this and obtained favors for himself through his subordinate, the sergeant. On the staff at Headquarters in Caen, they regarded von Kleinschrodt with amusement and indulgence.

"Yes, a strange chap, that von Kleinschrodt. Prefers to remain a *Feldwebel* when he could, of course, have a commission. I remember his father well at Verdun in 1917—a brave man. But this lad is different. Ah well, he saves us a lot of headaches by his knowledge of the people and the region. Nobody knows them better."

Thus each side and all concerned had something to gain by the arrangement, and the Germans officially ignored the sergeant's friendship with the schoolmaster, something irregular between enemies in time of war.

This morning while Monsieur Varin was sitting on the terrace of the Bleu Marin waiting for the arrival of the Feldwebel Hans, the widow Dupont passed by. Her late husband had actually fought in the Franco-Prussian War of 1870, and she was a little dried-up apple of a woman, weighing perhaps eighty pounds, bent and shrunk with age. She always nodded good morning to everyone she met as she proceeded along the Grande Rue. Her black string bag contained four carrots, a turnip, and an onion for her usual midday meal of soup, even now starting to simmer on the back of her stove at home. The moment she saw Monsieur Varin she stood still and beckoned to him.

Reluctantly he rose to meet her. The widow Dupont was celebrated in the village for buttonholing people, usually grasping the men by the lapel of their jackets. Also for her bad breath, a compound of garlic and red wine consumed twice a day for eighty years. Hence the teacher did not regard her approach with anticipation.

As ever, she came close to him, far too close, and seized the lapel of his jacket as if to keep him from edging off.

"Monsieur Varin," she said, "would you perhaps care to do a favor for me?"

"Willingly, *madame*," he replied, trying to disengage himself from her grasp. "Always a pleasure to be of use to you."

"*Ah, bon.*[3] One can always count upon you, Monsieur Varin. I wish I could say the same for others in this town. I mention no names— oh no, no names—but doubtless you are aware to whom I refer. Well, it is about my grandson. You may remember he was sent off to work in Germany when he became seventeen by the Fritz[4] in their forced-labor organization, the Todt[5] organization they called it. He worked in an airplane factory. Such a nice lad, too, respectful and honest, and a good Catholic besides, I assure you . . ."

"Yes, yes, *madame*." Impossible to bring her to the point, but at least he managed to move back slightly. He was awaiting not only the arrival of the Feldwebel Hans, but who knows perhaps a glass of that good German beer. "Yes, I remember Michel, a fine boy. What happened, Madame Dupont?"

She drew herself up. "*Ah, justement* nothing! You see each month he wrote me faithfully. I'm all he has left. Now for over two months—almost three, Monsieur Varin—nothing. You see he was working in that airplane factory at Altona, near Hamburg, I believe. The British have been bombing it now for

several weeks. So I wonder . . . would it be possible . . . do you think you could get me news of him?"

The teacher took out a worn black notebook with a small pencil attached. He wrote: "Dupont, Michel. Aged 17."

"Do you know his number?"

"Six . . . four . . . nine . . . three . . . one . . . zero."

He wrote it down. "Good, count upon me to do whatever is possible. Although I warn you it won't be easy with these fire-eaters that have come to town, these Silesians. But I'll talk to the Feldwebel Hans; he's always helpful. You know his brother is on Goering's staff. I'll try; I'll do my best."

Her aged, wrinkled face beamed. "Thank you, Monsieur Varin, thank you infinitely. I knew I could count upon your help. Ah, what would Nogent-Plage ever do without you? *Au 'voir!*"[6] And she weaved off downstreet, ducking and bobbing to everyone she met.

✿ 6

The schoolmaster replaced the black notebook in his pocket and resumed his seat at the iron table. Here we are, coming to a crisis in the war, and she wants news of her greatgrandson, one of God knows how many foreigners forced to work for the Germans. Well, I suppose he is all she has.

At this moment the Feldwebel Hans, clipboard in his hand, strolled up. In warm weather the two often met at noon and the sergeant usually offered the teacher a glass of German beer, which was reserved by the *patron* of the *café* for the German soldiers who had to sign for it. The *Feldwebel*, wiping his face, sat down. The stray dog, still accompanying him, also sat down, panting.

"Hot, very hot," remarked the German. Then to the proprietor, "Two beers, please."

3. **bon**\bō(n)\ good.
4. **Fritz**, nickname for the Germans.
5. **Todt**\tōt\ Death.
6. **Au 'voir**, shortened form of *au revoir*\ō•rə ▲vwar\ good-bye.

Monsieur Lavigne wiped a corner of the table with his dirty white apron.

"*Merci*,"[1] said the teacher. "*Eh bien,* what's new today? Are we ready for the invasion?" At times he enjoyed needling the young German. "Your compatriots act as though they expected it this afternoon at the latest."

"*Ach,* these frontline furiosos,[2] they are impossible. Always drilling, shouting at each other, saluting. Frankly, my friend, I am skeptical about your invasion. Perhaps, yes . . . it is possible. But look at that blockhouse over there. Nothing can wreck it, nothing. You saw it built yourself. There are ten meters of solid concrete over those guns. Tell me, what shells could penetrate such a depth?" He took a large swallow of the beer.

Enjoying his own beer as a guest of the *Reichswehr* and one not permitted by German army regulations to drink it, Monsieur Varin did not care to contradict his host. But he did not hesitate to voice his doubt.

"*Ah, oui,* you may be right. But after all, my friend, things haven't been going too well for you people lately. One has only to look at the maps. They tell the story of what's happening over there on the Eastern front."

The *Feldwebel* did not wish to betray a lack of confidence before a Frenchman, so he said, "Ha-ha, ho-ho, let the English come. We are ready for them."

The teacher nodded, but he wondered. Daily he read between the lines of the censored Paris press and followed the maps with attention. As he often told the Père Clement when they were alone, those maps indicated plainly the extent of the impending disaster for the Germans.

It's coming, he told himself. I only want to be here to see it. And surely, he thought, it must come before long or it will be too late. After four years of occupation, of hardships and privation, tempers in the village were rising. That little girl who choked to death last month because no doctor could get through the coastal road. The thin legs of the boys and girls on the street. When you see your children go to bed hungry night after night, well, a man will do anything.

And those strange warships spotted off the coast when the fog lifted suddenly one afternoon. What were they doing? Those massive flights of planes on their daily bombing runs from England. Were they pounding the enemy's lines of communications in preparation for an imminent invasion? Certainly the Germans were on the alert. Signs of crisis abounded. Nogent-Plage was obviously no longer a kind of convalescent area for battered troops. It had been transformed, by orders from Berlin, of course, into a frontline garrison, a pivotal point of the main coastal defense. That was plain. And the battalion of Silesians was here for one purpose. To repel an invasion on the beaches. Somehow the invasion must succeed.

"It must," said the teacher out loud.

7

The Hauptmann Seeler, new commanding officer of the garrison, sat at his desk in the Bloch villa. The windows overlooking the sea were boarded up and his only company was à photograph of Hitler. A thin sheet of paper was before him. It was typewritten, marked at the top: *Geheim.*[1] Secret. Below was a heading *Oberkommando Des Heeres.* From the Army High Command.

This document was about the invasion, which the *Abwehr,* Intelligence Department of the German General Staff, felt to be imminent. It outlined the steps being taken to repel the assault and detailed the disposition of troops and reserves in the neighborhood of Nogent-Plage. The Hauptmann Seeler was on the telephone. His voice was crisp, soldierly.

"*Ja,* Major Kessler, *ja. Jawohl . . . .*"[2]

"In an hour or more, *Hauptmann,* you will

---

1. **Merci**\mār ᵃsē\ Thanks.
2. **furiosos**\ᵃfyʊr•e ᵃō•sōz\ enthusiasts.

---

1. **Geheim**\gĕ ᵃhaim\
2. **Jawohl**\ya ᵃvōl\ yes indeed.

x

receive *Alarmstruppe*[3] II. Do you understand?"

"*Ja, ja*, Major Kessler." Of course he understood. *Alarmstruppe* II was the order for the highest state of readiness against an invasion. The *Major* continued, "We know nothing for certain, *Hauptmann,* but there is a rumor well substantiated that the invasion fleet is at sea. Perhaps, who knows . . . ."

"I understand, *Major*."

"Remember, Nogent-Plage is a pivotal position in the defense of the coast."

"*Jawohl, Herr Major*. We are ready; my troops are veterans. We won't be caught asleep."

"Good. *Heil* Hitler!" The *Major* rang off.

But the *Hauptmann* was perturbed. He rose and stalked the room. A former *Feldwebel*, promoted to commissioned rank on the field of battle in North Africa, he was a fussy, myopic little man with thick glasses, a strict disciplinarian who strutted with authority. He was also a brave officer, as the decorations from his campaigns in the desert showed.

The month before he had been sent in with his Silesians to take over and reorganize the defense of Nogent-Plage, but the situation he had found was worse than he had imagined. Until he arrived, nobody seemed alert and discipline was indifferent. Then there was that *Feldwebel*. The invasion imminent, the Fatherland in the very greatest peril, and what was he doing? Playing football with the boys, greeting civilians in the street. True, the town was quiet for the moment. Yet with all the terrorists about, one could never tell.

The *Hauptmann* trusted nobody and experience told him this was a wise attitude in war. Although his men all said the *Feldwebel* was a great football star, this nonsense must end. The captain, whose fattish body and thick glasses betrayed the fact that he could not run across the street or see a football unless it hit him in the face, was determined to maintain the discipline so essential in this moment of crisis.

Furiously he shuffled the papers on his desk. Paperwork was his soul, his goal, his be-all and end-all. As a sergeant he had been celebrated for his impeccable reports, always forwarded through channels, always on time. Large forms, legible, correctly indented, and sent along to a superior were in his belief the mark of a professional officer. Paperwork, he often told his men, was the other, seldom seen side of discipline.

As for that lazy *Feldwebel*, it made no difference if he was the greatest centre forward Germany ever had. We're at war. I'm in charge here and the troops and the townspeople had better realize it! The more he reflected about the *Feldwebel*, the more annoyed he became. That sloppy soldier's popularity with the troops and, worse still, the townsfolk was a cause of concern for the *Hauptmann*. Why, he thought, everyone knows that but for his family connections he would have been reduced to the ranks long ago.

In any event, it is my duty as his superior officer to report his inefficiency to the *Oberkommando* at Caen. Let them do as they wish. And they will have to do something after they hear from me. I shall make a point of telephoning this morning. But first I must have it out with him, Count *von und zu* Whatshisname. Utter nonsense, that title business. Four years now he has been enjoying himself in the safety of this charming seaside resort while I was up to my neck in sandstorms, fighting with Rommel[4] in North Africa. And promoted from the ranks by the General Bayerlein himself!

He seized the telephone and called the blockhouse beyond the village. "*Unteroffizier Kleinschrodt,*" he said curtly.

The soldier at the other end of the line feeling tenseness in the voice of his commanding officer, informed him that the *Feldwebel* had left some minutes ago with the morning report.

"Which should have been on my desk when

---

3. **Alarmstruppe**\a ˈlarm ˈstrū·pə\ readiness signal.
4. **Rommel,** German field marshal, commander of the German forces in North Africa in World War II.

I came to this office at seven o'clock today," said the *Hauptmann*. "Punctuality is the first duty of the soldier."

Knowing the officer's passion for paperwork, the soldier at the blockhouse quickly agreed. The *Hauptmann* slammed down the phone without bothering to reply. He took the papers from his desk, put them into his safe, tried the handle to be sure it was locked, and rose. Straightening his tunic with a sharp tug, adjusting the angle of his cap, locking the door behind him, buttoning the key into the upper pocket of his blouse, he left the office and went out into the street.

The two sentries whirled to attention in unison, presenting arms. The *Hauptmann* flicked a glove carelessly to the visor of his cap in his best imitation of General Rommel. After the dimly lit office the sunlight from the sea dazzled him a moment. His first sight was the *café* almost opposite. What he observed enraged him.

There sat the lazy *Feldwebel*, smugly smoking his pipe and talking to a French civilian. Worse, as the *Hauptmann* noticed on approaching, the Frenchman was drinking beer against all army regulations. Obviously it was German beer. The *Hauptmann* also recognized the man, a teacher in town. He had been pointed out as a possible partisan, perhaps even someone who would transmit intelligence to the British.

The *Hauptmann* stalked across the street, anger flushing his face. The clack-clack of his heels had an ominous sound. Suddenly spotting his commanding officer approaching, the *Feldwebel* rose hastily, too hastily, stepping back squarely onto the dog's front paw. The animal yelped twice and skittered away and the *Feldwebel* lost his balance. He reached out and caught at the table, which overturned, and the two half-empty glasses of beer and the two beer bottles fell to the stone sidewalk. Then, retrieving his balance, he stood stiffly at attention, waiting for the storm to break. It broke with a thunderclap.

"*Was haben Sie*, Kleinschrodt?"[5] asked the *Hauptmann*, ice in his voice. The Iron Cross (First Class) and the Knight's Cross (with a golden oak leaf) trembled on his chest as he spoke. To have to stand here with this lout, he thought. Me, with my decorations and four wound stripes on my sleeve!

But he stood there, saying nothing now, simply looking the *Feldwebel* up and down. As he did so his eye caught one of the bottles of beer on the ground, label up.

"Reserved for the *Wehrmacht*,"[6] it said.

The *Hauptmann* looked the *Feldwebel* over angrily. An ancient garrison cap with stained visor was on the back of his head, not over his eyes as regulations stipulated. His tunic was dirty. One button was missing. His shoes were unshined, no doubt from that stupid football he played with the village boys. As the *Hauptmann* stood contemplating this sorry figure of a noncommissioned officer in the army of our glorious *Führer*,[7] he reflected suddenly on those deadly battles in North Africa, where for over two years he had risked his life.

The injustice infuriated the *Hauptmann* and his dislike of the *Feldwebel* was so intense that he completely lost control of his temper. For the first time his voice rose.

"What's the matter with you?" he cried, reaching out and grabbing the *Feldwebel's* tunic where the button was missing. He gave it a strong yank and the other three buttons spattered onto the pavement. The tunic fell open and hung grotesquely from the broad shoulders of the younger man.

There he stood, a ridiculous-looking soldier, while the little *Hauptmann*, baring his teeth, spewed out a torrent of guttural abuse. Like all former noncommissioned officers, the *Hauptmann* was an expert in flaying the lower ranks. He did not raise his voice again, or shout, but his words were plain.

---

5. Literally, "What have you, Kleinschrodt?" He means, "What's the matter?"
6. **Wehrmacht**\ˈvär ˈmäkt\ German armed forces in World War II.
7. **Führer**\ˈfyu̇·rər\ literally, leader; the title applied to Hitler.

"You'll put away childish things, *Feldwebel. Kein Fussball. Verstehen Sie?*" No football. Understand?

And he had only begun. For a fact, this *Feldwebel* really did not know what war was, and the *Hauptmann* took pains to tell him so. Monsieur Varin, who had also risen, wanted intensely to leave, but this meant getting round the overturned table and attracting the attention of the *Hauptmann*. So he stood there while the abuse continued. Scornfully the little officer pointed down at the bottles, the glasses, and the spilled beer, now a wet spot on the pavement.

Sweat appeared on the *Feldwebel's* forehead. A drop rolled off his nose. Still the tirade continued, every syllable distinct. Monsieur Varin had served in two wars under officers of every social class, all grades and temperaments. Never had he listened to such humiliation of a fellow soldier. A nasty piece of work indeed, this *Hauptmann*, thought Monsieur Varin, listening. It was quite obvious, as the officer pointed to the overturned table, what was being said. Do this again and you will be reduced to the ranks.

"You call yourself a soldier, Kleinschrodt?" said the *Hauptmann*, utter contempt in his tone. It was a question needing no answer. "*Verstehen Sie? Verstehen Sie?*"

"*Ja, mein Hauptmann, jawohl.*"

The abuse went on for several minutes more, and then without warning the officer half turned and held out his hand across the upset table.

"*Papieren!*"[8]

It was a command. The teacher fumbled in his coat pocket and yanked out the *Ausweiss* that everyone in the Zone of the Armies was required to carry at all times.

The officer looked at it attentively, then inspected Monsieur Varin up and down. "*Schulmeister, nicht?*"[9]

The Frenchman nodded. Yes, a schoolmaster. He was tense and frightened, not knowing what was coming, but sure it would be unpleasant. Did it mean he would be arrested?

"*Kommunist, nicht wahr?*[10] In France all schoolmasters are Communists."

A sweeping accusation. But in France many teachers were indeed Leftists and quite a few were Communists. Monsieur Varin stood silently before the German officer, so youthful to him yet so old in battle years. For a few seconds the silence persisted. The teacher could have denied the accusation. What real proof was there? No, even though his life depended upon it, he could not forgo his deep beliefs. So he nodded.

"*Ja, Herr Hauptmann.* I am a Communist."

There he stood, expecting immediate arrest. Now the sweat appeared on the forehead of the Frenchman. Men had been sent to prison for less. But apparently, with this career soldier who obviously knew France, truth was best. The next question would be harder still, because he could never betray his heritage. The officer would ask him if he was a Jew, and one grandfather on his mother's side had been Jewish. As long as France was France and a nation, he was a Frenchman, but to the Germans, if they knew of that grandfather, he would be a Jew.

Surely the *Feldwebel*, with access to the records in the little town hall, knew all about his background, yet had never reported him. Nobody else in Nogent-Plage was aware of his ancestry, for his grandfather had long since died in Lyon.

The teacher stood waiting for the obvious question, but the bespectacled little officer kept silent. He turned, slapped his gloves in a gesture of contempt, and without bothering to return the salute of the *Feldwebel*, stalked down the street. Activity among the soldiers visibly increased as he passed.

Monsieur Varin discovered his legs were weak. He was trembling. Strange, he thought, feeling his heart bump, how the heat grows at noon on a spring day in Nogent-Plage.

---

8. **Papieren!**\pä ˄pē•rən\ Your identification papers!
9. Schoolmaster, aren't you?
10. Communist, isn't that true?

DISCUSSION FOR UNDERSTANDING

1. What do you learn about Père Clement?

2. What sort of man is Georges Varin, the schoolteacher?

3. What kind of relationship does the *Feldwebel* have with the schoolteacher?

4. Why does the Hauptmann Seeler dislike the *Feldwebel*?

5. Describe the scene and action when the *Hauptmann* comes upon the *Feldwebel* at the inn.

6. What is the effect of this *brief encounter* on the schoolteacher; the *Hauptmann*; the *Feldwebel*?

8

It was afternoon. The farmer Marquet[1] sat on the plank seat of his old-fashioned cart, with wooden slats sloping outward at the top, filled with thick, oozy seaweed—fertilizer for his land. Years of harsh work had made him seem older than he was. But his horse, although thin like every living thing after four years of occupation, had a cared-for look.

The farmer's home was an ancient stone house in a hamlet called La Roye, beyond the dunes in back of town. His wife was long since dead, one son had been killed in the campaign of 1940, another, Pierre, was a prisoner of war in Germany. He lived alone and the people of Nogent-Plage considered him slightly mad, because he had a habit of talking to himself. Twice each year he took the long road around the dunes to the coast for fertilizer.

His only companion was his horse whose name was Sebastian. Why Sebastian? Nobody ever found out. But between them was a bond of affection. The animal seemed to understand his lonely master's needs. And the farmer cared more for the horse, perhaps, than anything save his land, for which he had the fierce possessiveness of the peasant. Between them they would manage to keep the soil nourished and the fields cultivated until the day when his boy would return from Germany.

Slowly the horse pulled the heavy load, up the hill, past the blockhouse, and into the village. Half a dozen young soldiers, stripped to the waist, torsos tanned, towels over their shoulders, picked their way down the cliff to the sea, carefully avoiding the mines and barbed wire. The old man watched with a passionate hatred. How much longer, he wondered, shall we have to look on these well-fed barbarians?

As the cart entered the village, the door of a house at which two sentries were stationed opened and a bespectacled officer stepped out. On his breast was a double row of campaign medals and the Iron Cross. His boots, which reached to his knees, shone in the sun. He walked briskly, shoulders back, every inch of his small frame an officer of the *Wehrmacht*. From the cart, the old man observed that his gaze went from right to left along the street—he missed nothing. On he moved, the Grande Rue now empty save for a few soldiers at the far end.

As the farmer watched he heard a sudden report, like a shot from a hunting rifle, not loud like an army weapon, being fired. At first he was not sure what had happened. To his amazement, one moment the officer was striding down the street, then he was stretched out on the pavement. As he crumpled, one arm fell behind in a peculiar gesture.

A siren went off. Soldiers rushed from a house, rifles at the ready. A tall, black-haired sergeant ran into the street as the siren kept screaming.

All around, soldiers appeared. By this time the farmer Marquet was near enough to see blood on the spotless tunic of the officer who lay, legs outstretched, on the pavement. Two medical corpsmen opened his blouse and listened to his heart.

The tall, black-haired man in charge was exploding orders, pointing first to one side of the street, then the other. A group of soldiers began working the left side. If the door of a

---

1. **Marquet**\mar ˈkā\

house was locked, they pounded it in with rifle butts. From windows on the second floor, shutters opened and frightened faces of women appeared. The same words echoed back and forth.

"*Pas possible!*"[2]

"*Pas possible!*"

Who could have done such a thing? "Impossible! And here in Nogent-Plage!"

Suddenly the farmer Marquet's horse was stopped, and he was yanked roughly to the ground. Two helmeted young soldiers gripped him, two others searched him, but to his surprise did not ask for his *Ausweiss*. They merely hustled him across the road.

He tried to protest. "*Voila*,[3] I only happened to be in town for the moment. I came in from my farm at La Roye for a load of seaweed for fertilizer. *M'ssieurs* . . . for my land. I live . . . over there . . . back of the dunes . . . ."

Not understanding what he was saying and not caring, they pushed him along. Quite plainly they were taking him someplace. A strange and terrible fear seized him, not for himself but for his horse. The horse was being left behind, his only friend, all he had. The beast realized his master was leaving him and whinnied loudly. Then the farmer heard that familiar clop-clop as the horse attempted to follow.

"Sebastian! Sebastian!" he shouted, twisting halfway around in the grip of the soldiers.

The horse, pulling the heavy cart, fell farther and farther behind, the reins dragging on the pavement.

"Sebastian!" shrieked the farmer, realizing what was happening and where, in all probability, he was being taken. In utter despair he cried out, "Ah, who will take care of Sebastian when I am gone?"

9

The *Feldwebel* sank into the chair of the murdered officer. His cap was on the desk before him. He reflected grimly that he had rushed into the street at the sound of the shot without a cap, something the *Hauptmann* had never done in all his army life. Before the *Feldwebel* were the neat piles of orders— orders from field headquarters in Bayeux, orders from Division Headquarters in Caen, orders from the High Command in Berlin. Each pile was carefully clipped and filed chronologically, according to regulations.

He took up the telephone. "Major Kessler at Division Headquarters," he said to the operator in the blockhouse.

Replacing the phone he sank forward with his head in his hands. What idiot could have done this? So great was the misery of the Feldwebel Hans, so keen his understanding of what had happened and, more important, of what lay ahead, that a cry of agony burst from him there in the empty room: "*Ach, du Lieber Gott.*"[1]

The telephone rang. Immediately he straightened up, controlled himself. "This is the Feldwebel von Kleinschrodt."

"Good. Major Kessler here. Have your men been alerted, *Feldwebel?*"

"Indeed yes, *Major*. But I have bad news to report. The Hauptmann Seeler has just been shot by a terrorist."

"Shot? Impossible! I talked to him an hour ago . . . ."

"Yes, *Major*, it just happened. He was dead in the middle of the street when the men reached him."

"Have you found the assassin?"

"No, *Major*, not yet, but the men have sealed up the village and are making a house-to-house search. They will surely turn him up."

"He must be found, *must* be found, and made an example of. Execute him publicly. Let me talk to the Oberleutnant Schmidt."

"*Herr Major*, he is at the Defense School at Ostend."

---

2. **Pas possible!**\ˢpa ˈpɔ ˢsēb(l)\ Not possible!
3. **Voilà**\vwa ˈla\ Look; see here.

---

1. **Ach, du Lieber Gott**\ˢahk·dū ˢlē·bər·gɔt\ Oh, dear God.

"Well then, the *Leutnant*—what's his name?
—Wirtig, isn't it?"

"Sir, he is on leave in Bremen."

"All leaves were cancelled as of yesterday.
He should be back this afternoon. For the
moment you are the senior officer there. To be
sure, we will get another officer to you immediately, for with these terrorist raids up
and down the coast Schmidt and Wirtig may
have trouble returning. Let me see, perhaps
the Leutnant Brandt from Blockhouse 242 . . . .
No, that won't do, we need him for those big
guns; he is a specialist. Let me see now. *Ach*,
what a time for this to happen! That Polish
chap, that Silesian in Blockhouse H98. No, he
is a meteorologist and needed where he is.
Well, we'll get someone to you as soon as possible. In the meantime, *Feldwebel*, until the
criminal is found, six hostages should be taken
into custody. Here"—he turned to someone in
his office—"get me that folder on Nogent-
Plage, Beckenbauer. We were discussing it
with the Hauptmann Seeler a short while
ago . . . . No, you didn't put it back. Ah, this
is indeed a bad moment for a thing of this sort,
and with two officers away . . . . Now, here it
is. According to this, you have a teacher there
named Martin. No, V-Varin, have you not?
Right. Do you know the man?"

The *Feldwebel* froze. Faced with what lay
ahead, he could not speak. The *Major* continued.

"Are you there, *Feldwebel?* Do you hear
me? Those damned terrorists have been cutting wires all along the coast today. I say, are
you there? Do you know this man? I can't
hear you. Do you know him? It appears he is
a Communist . . . ."

Finally the *Feldwebel* found his voice. "Yes,
you are right, *Major*. I believe he is a Communist. But never active to my belief. I've
known him three or four years now and—"

The other broke in. "They're all alike, all of
them, these darned Communists. I've had a
lot of experience with them; they don't care a
bit for the land where they were born and
raised. Moreover, this one is Jewish."

For a few seconds the *Feldwebel* was
stunned. How, he wondered, had this ever
reached Caen? "No one ever said he was
Jewish, *Herr Major*," he suggested tentatively.

"The records show it. I cannot understand
how he was ever permitted to remain in that
sensitive area all these years. Someone has
blundered badly, and I intend to discover who
it was. At any rate, get him now. Then there
is another chap, man by the name of Lavigne.
Runs the *café* on the Grande Rue." He read
from a paper. " 'A hangout for dubious characters.' So the report states. Here it is. 'To be
watched. Owner was mixed up with terrorists
at the time of the Dieppe raid in '42.' We suspect him also. Is there a priest in the village?"

This was too much. In the mind of the
Feldwebel rose the picture of old Père Clement with his soutane tied up around his waist
and those thick cotton underdrawers. "Why
yes, *Major*, there is, but actually the local
padre is old and inoffensive. Not at all the
kind of person to give us any trouble . . . ."

"*Feldwebel*, we are making examples of
these men. Was anyone taken at the time of
the murder?"

"No, *Major*, that is . . . only an old farmer
from the back country. He merely happened
to be passing in his cart at the time. He knows
nothing whatever . . . ."

"Yes, yes," interrupted the officer impatiently. "You miss the point. Get him. Or did
he escape? Did you pick him up?"

"Yes, *Major*, we have him. Only, if you
would permit, sir, I'd like to suggest . . . ."

"No comments necessary, *Feldwebel*. Just
obey orders. We want six—the teacher, the
café proprietor, the old farmer, the priest, a
fisherman, a boy perhaps. Give them one hour
in which to confess. If the culprit is not found
and none of them confesses, make an example
of them. Have them shot. As a warning, you
understand, to other terrorists."

"Yes, *Major*, I quite understand."

"Good. Now for your personal information
as you are in charge at Nogent-Plage temporarily. Terrorists have been at work up and

down the coast since dawn. This line may be cut any minute. We have patrols out, but the bridge at Varengeville has been blown up and the highway below Dampart completely destroyed. Hence, as far as reinforcements are concerned, you are isolated for the time being. In fact, we are all isolated. Fécamp is isolated. So is Étretat. We are on our own, *Feldwebel.* Is that quite clear?"

"*Jawohl, Herr Major.*" It was only too clear. For the first time in his long years at Nogent-Plage the Feldwebel Hans felt the isolation and the loneliness and the danger. They were Germans in a hostile land, about to be attacked from the front and perhaps the rear. The *Major* went on.

"Meanwhile, do not forget. The defense rests in your hands. You are responsible."

"We are ready, sir," he replied resolutely. After all, perhaps a way out could be found. Perhaps, he thought, the invasion will intervene; perhaps they won't be shot.

The *Major* lowered his voice. "For your information, *Feldwebel,* we are advised that the invasion fleet is now in mid-Channel, making about six knots. Most likely they are planning an early-morning assault, hoping to be covered by this fog. It is thick here at present. And at such a moment! *Feldwebel,* only one thing counts. The Fatherland. Our country is in peril. The Greater Reich faces its most critical hour. Your first duty is to round up the six hostages. Unless the assassin of the Hauptmann Seeler is found within the hour, have a firing squad shoot them. Report to me as soon as you have them in custody. Remember, this is not a football game . . . ."

The *Feldwebel* started to say something, but the *Major* cut him short. "I repeat, Feldwebel von Kleinschrodt, this is not a football game. Understand? *Heil* Hitler."

He rang off. The *Feldwebel* rose from the desk. There was tragedy ahead. And he was in the middle of it. To shoot, to kill a friend. In a way, they were all friends. But they were also enemies of his country, and he was in charge at Nogent-Plage. He represented the Third Reich for the moment. What choice did he have? He was responsible for the safety of his men. There were the orders.

"Corporal Eicke," he called out, yanking down his tunic with the same gesture the Hauptmann Seeler had used at the same desk just a little while ago.

First, of course, comes one's country.

10

The farmer Marquet half fell, half stumbled down the badly lit stairs. He picked himself up and looked around. He was in the cellar of the Bloch villa.

Opposite was a narrow, oblong, barred window through which came a dampness from the sea. He noticed a fog was collecting, for the wind had died away. On the other side of the stairs another small window gave onto a vacant lot where, he knew, the boys of the village practiced football. There was no glass in either window.

The earth floor of the cellar was moist. The place was filled with odds and ends left behind by the Jewish Bloch family when the war had burst upon them, driving them from Nogent-Plage. Where were they now? What woman had used that rusty sewing machine? What child had played with that faceless doll? Who had sat on that old wooden bench or those chairs without backs?

He slumped down on the bench. The thought of Sebastian with the load of seaweed standing patiently in the street above struck him with such a stabbing pain that he groaned aloud.

"Ah, Sebastian," he cried. "And my poor Pierre in Germany. He will never know what happened to his old father."

The door at the top of the cellar opened and light penetrated the gloom. He glanced up from his misery as Lavigne, in his dirty white apron, was shoved roughly downstairs. The *café* owner, a stout man, picked himself up, rubbing his hip.

"But," he shouted, "I tell you I had nothing

whatever to do with it. I was inside washing dishes. I was inside when the shot was fired. I had nothing to do with it." Then realizing that nobody was listening, he saw the futility of his protestations and shook his fist at the door above. "Ah, those *Fridolins,* those barbarians!"

The door opened again, and a German voice said, "*Unter . . . .*"[1]

Monsieur Varin, the teacher, was pushed down. Next came the Père Clement and young René Le Gallec, with whom he had been practicing football. The priest picked himself up as the door slammed and shouted, "But I had nothing to do with the shooting of the *Hauptmann.* I was playing football beside my church with this boy. The *Herr Oberst* knows I could have had nothing to do with it. He passed by, himself, but a short while before. He played with us. Ask the *Herr Oberst . . . .*"

The door opened once more and Marcel Deschamps, the fisherman, was hurled down. Then a helmeted soldier with a submachine gun stomped downstairs, followed by a corporal. The corporal went over to the teacher, sitting on the bench and rubbing the knee he had scraped during his tumble into the cellar.

"*Sprechen Sie Deutsch?*"[2] he asked.

"*Ja. Ich kann Deutsch sprechen.*"[3]

Then followed a torrent of guttural words, so fast that the teacher had trouble making them out. But he understood enough to put the sense of the remarks into French.

"This village is surrounded," he translated. "Every exit is guarded. Every house in town is being searched. But we have orders from Headquarters that if the murderer of the Hauptmann Seeler is not found—or none of you confesses to the murder—you will all be shot within one hour. These orders are from our *Kommandateur* at Caen."

The German corporal spun around and went up the stairs, followed at a respectful distance by the soldier. The door opened, then slammed shut. A key turned in the lock. Darkness and silence fell over the cellar.

Their eyes gradually became accustomed to the gloom. The farmer Marquet wept tears of despair. Monsieur Lavigne stalked in a rage up and down the dirt floor. The priest, hands extended, asked, "But who could have done such a thing? Surely it must have been somebody from outside the town."

"Yes, certainly, it must have been a stranger. Someone from Évreux, no doubt."

"They will find him soon, and we shall all be released, I am sure," said the Père Clement.

Only Monsieur Varin was thinking clearly enough at the moment to fit the pieces together. It took no genius to guess what had happened—and also what lay ahead. The Silesian shock troops sent in as a garrison, the cutting of bridges along the coast, the soldiers in battle dress—everything told him the invasion was imminent. Some young hothead must have felt this was a chance not to be missed, a chance to throw the garrison into confusion by killing its commanding officer and so to hurt the outfit at this critical instant in the war. To a rifleman firing through the blinds of a second-story window the Hauptmann Seeler was an easy target.

Ah, thought the teacher, those crazy young people, acting as young people so often do, without thinking of others, with no regard for what might happen to those of us left here in the village. Naturally the Germans would avenge the death of the *Hauptmann.* Anyone could have foretold that.

And what difference who the assassin was. If the slayer escapes, we six will be executed. He rose from the bench.

"Come, my friends, the *Feldwebel* is now in command here. He has helped us before, but even if he has authority we mustn't depend on him. He may know we are innocent, he will do all he can at Headquarters, but we must help ourselves. We must organize . . . ."

"Organize!" snorted Monsieur Lavigne.

---

1. **Unter,** Down; Get down there.
2. Do you speak German?
3. Yes, I can speak German.

"How can we organize locked in this cellar, with fifty minutes of life left?"

The teacher ignored his outburst. "Look, I have friends up the coast. Things have been happening, things that are the signal I anticipated. And see that fog coming in? What better weather for an invasion fleet to approach the coast? They plan these things, you know; they leave nothing to chance."

Suddenly René Le Gallec, who had been watching from the narrow window, shouted, "They're coming! I hear them! Listen!"

A rumble came from the sea. It grew louder, louder. Soon it turned into a massive roar. Together the men rushed to the window. There in the haze above the low-lying fogbank were planes, planes, more planes than they had ever seen before, so many that they seemed to blacken the sky.

The five men and the boy shouted, yelled, screamed, waved white handkerchiefs through the narrow, barred window, turned and embraced each other. Rescue! Deliverance! Release! Unquestionably those planes were headed straight for the Bloch villa. Already the antiaircraft batteries down the coast were sputtering, then the blockhouse just outside the town joined in. But the planes roared majestically on. Their sound was that of a thousand express trains, a thousand thunderstorms, drowning out the guns.

The invasion at last! Long-awaited, long-hoped-for! They were saved!

Now the planes were directly above, passing overhead, continuing on. None detached themselves to descend on Nogent-Plage. Whatever it meant, wherever they were going, it was no attack upon the garrison of the town. Soon the planes vanished from sight. The noise died away. The antiaircraft fire from the blockhouse stuttered and stopped. One by one, the men left the window. The Père Clement stood staring into space. The farmer sank back again on the bench. Young René Le Gallec crumpled to the floor as if hit by a blow.

The hostages heard the voice of the *Herr Oberst* up above, giving a harsh, crisp command. It seemed somehow out of character. It had an ominous sound. Then came the stomping of boots. Evidently they were reinforcing the guard outside the front door of the Bloch villa.

Below, in the cellar, five men and a boy faced death in forty-eight minutes.

11

When the Hauptmann Seeler had come to Nogent-Plage in the spring that year, he, like everyone else, was immediately attracted to the Feldwebel von Kleinschrodt. Old army family. Nobility. Celebrated German athlete. The *Hauptmann* was impressed. But not for long. He soon had the young man sized up and perceived that he lacked real soldierly qualities. He then tried his best to reform him as other commanding officers in Nogent-Plage had done, to help him live up to the great traditions of his heritage.

Often he used to stand the *Feldwebel* at attention and lecture him. "Kleinschrodt, your trouble is you are like the Americans. I know well the Americans. For nine years I was head porter at the Schweitzerhof in Dresden and met many of them. Americans want to be liked. They are almost pathetic in this childish desire to be liked. Actually, this is an infantile trait. Americans are children, young and old. It is why they do not make good soldiers. In North Africa we had no trouble with them at Kasserine. We have nothing to fear from them, nothing. They wish to be liked. That is agreeable, yes; it is better to be liked than disliked. Best of all is for a man to be respected. Respect is the basis for discipline—at home, in business, in the Army. Now you are greatly admired by the troops here and liked by the people of the village. But you are not respected. Never forget that soldiers, too, are children. They will never obey you unless they respect you."

These words the *Feldwebel* remembered, for he was finding the *Hauptmann* right about obedience and respect. As he sat at the desk which an hour before had belonged to the murdered man, as he checked the deployment of the troops—his troops for the moment—around the village, as he listened to the telephoned report of a sentry a mile from town, he was amazed at himself. He had assumed responsibility. He had become the senior officer of the garrison at Nogent-Plage.

No time to waste words. His voice was quite as crisp and curt over the phone, his tunic as spotless, as carefully hooked under the chin as that of the late *Hauptmann*. The invasion was at hand. It might come anywhere, any moment, surely by morning. Maybe right now advance elements were trying to land up the coast under cover of the fog. His duty was to his men, to his country, to the Third Reich. He felt attuned to it without thinking.

And the men? There was a change in their bearing toward him, a surprising deference as they knocked on the door or addressed him. A certain respect that was new had crept into everyone's voice. They seemed to be turning to him, leaning on him, trustfully, hopefully. That was as natural as it was for him to assume the duties and the responsibilities of command.

And yet, all this solved nothing. It is not easy to obey order when the orders are to have your friends shot; it is hard to issue orders when those orders mean a firing squad for your friends. Hanging over him was the thought of what lay ahead. When his mind was busy with other things it was all right. But the moment he stopped to think about it, revulsion took possession of him. Those men were his friends. That boy he had played football with. Obviously the teacher had Marxist leanings. Certainly, we had discussed them together. But brave. Loyal. A good Frenchman. How on earth can I kill a man like him? A veteran of two wars, already decorated upon the field of battle. For I'm the one who has to give the orders to fire. To watch them fall. To certify to their deaths. How can I do this? And that boy! A child really. My God . . . .

He rose and walked up and down the silent, empty room. The Le Gallec boy haunted him, devastated him, destroyed him. How could he? But he must obey orders.

A short, sharp knock at the door and the corporal entered to hand him a radio dispatch from Headquarters. It merely confirmed what the *Major* had told him, alerting all officers commanding troops that a landing, either a feint or the real thing, was expected along the Normandy coast late tonight or early tomorrow morning. He filed it carefully with the other orders.

The telephone rang, and the operator said, "The Major Kessler, *Herr Feldwebel*."

"Von Kleinschrodt? Is that you?" The anxious tone in the *Major's* voice was meaningful. Now the *Feldwebel* began to feel and appreciate the terrible responsibility of command. The *Major* was obviously full of the imminent crisis, obviously worried.

"*Ja*, Major Kessler."

"You were to report to me as soon as you secured those hostages. Have you done so?"

"Yes sir, I was about to call you. They have been apprehended as you ordered." In the back of the *Feldwebel's* mind the same question kept rising. How can I save them? Surely some way must be found.

"And have you discovered the murderer of the Hauptmann Seeler?"

"No, *Major,* not yet, but we are still . . . ."

"Good grief, man, how can he escape from a small village? Was the place surrounded? It was? Did you post sentries at all exits? Have you searched the houses thoroughly? Thoroughly, *Feldwebel?*" His tone was packed with exasperation. Plainly he was edgy. "Get him. It's important to teach these partisans a lesson. When they kill, Frenchmen must be killed. No nonsense about it."

"Quite, *Major*. My Silesians here are first-class troops. They have been through many partisan attacks in Poland and Russia. I have three search parties out under the most experienced noncoms. They will dig up the man. Just a question of time, I assure you."

"Good. If not, you understand, those six

French must be executed. You understand, do you not, *Feldwebel?*"

"Perfectly, sir. I only wondered . . . I only meant . . . . I do happen to know these six hostages. I can guarantee myself that none of them had a thing to do with the murder of the *Hauptmann*."

The voice of the older man rose irritably. "*Hier haben Sie nicht mitzureden.*" That's none of your business. "*Feldwebel*, listen to me carefully. These men are an example to the populace. A warning, you might say. If they are all innocent, so much the better. The villagers along the coast must be impressed with the seriousness of the situation and know what measures we shall take if there is trouble. We have shot sixteen terrorists at Abbeville and are rounding up a dozen at Yvetot."

A pause, then the *Major* went on. "You may recall, *Feldwebel*, that in March a band of Italian partisans killed thirty-three of our SS men outside Rome?"

"Yes, *Herr Major*."

"Then you also remember that we were forced to execute three hundred and thirty-five Italians, that is, slightly over ten Italians for every German. At Nogent-Plage we are moderate, only six for one German and an officer at that. We are being lenient, really. Are you there, *Feldwebel?*"

The annoyed voice at the other end persisted. "These lines are being cut constantly now. Did you get that Jewish fellow? What's his name? Are you still on the line? Do you hear me?"

"Yes, *Herr Major*, we got him. His name is Varin."

"And the priest, as I suggested?"

"The Père Clement. But truly, *Major*, he had nothing whatever to do with the killing of the Hauptmann Seeler. Actually he is almost eighty. That I would vouch for myself."

The *Major* paid no attention to the *Feldwebel's* comments. "And the *café* owner, probably a Communist also."

"His place is closed up. We have him."

"His name? I had it before, I think. We must have his name. Remember, you are to post a notice after the execution listing these Frenchmen by name and stating that any further sabotage or interference with German forces carrying out their duties will mean that twenty-five more hostages will be selected and dealt with in the same manner. Is that quite clear? Now the man's name . . . . Are you there, *Feldwebel?* Or are you perhaps dreaming of football? This is not a game. You are a soldier of the Greater Reich."

"Yes, *Major*, I am still on the line. The man's name is Charles Lavigne."

"Good! You realize, of course, that the situation is critical. Perhaps *the* most critical moment of the war. The Herr Generalfeldmarschall Rommel, under whom I had the honor of serving two years in North Africa, sent around a secret bulletin last week before he was wounded. He anticipated an attempt at a landing by the English and Americans about this period, with the moon full and the tide high. He urged us all in the strictest terms, *Feldwebel*, not to forget that we must defeat the invaders here, on the beaches. We cannot permit them to get a foothold inland where their superiority in the air will count. We must throw them back at all costs, von Kleinschrodt. You understand?"

"Yes, *Major*, I understand."

"You are in a key position. Your responsibility is therefore great. From that rock—I inspected it myself with the *Herr Generalfeldmarschall*—one can sweep the coast for several miles in each direction. We depend upon you. The Fatherland is in peril tonight; the invasion may burst on us any moment. Germany counts on all her sons, *Feldwebel*, especially those from an old and famous army family such as yours. Remember your father, who died gloriously on the field of battle, and your grandfather, the General von Kleinschrodt. Be worthy of them! Obey orders implicitly. Do not fail. Do you hear me?"

"Yes, *Major* . . . ."

"Good. Now if we cannot get an officer to you, then you must carry out the execution and post the proclamation. As soon as the assassin of the Hauptmann Seeler is found or the hostages shot, notify me at once by telephone. Yes, of course, if you find the partisan who committed the crime, you may release the hostages with a warning. But be sure to take pains to frighten them. I gave you one hour. How much time is left?"

The Feldwebel Hans looked carefully at his watch. "Thirty-nine minutes, *Major.*"

"Right! Let me have a report. And *Heil Hitler!*"

The Feldwebel Hans replaced the telephone and sat staring into the empty room. The face of every person in the cellar rose before him: Varin, Lavigne, the Père Clement, Marquet, Deschamps, and the boy. He couldn't even bear to say the boy's name to himself.

At least this much he could do. He pressed the buzzer on the desk. A corporal knocked and entered immediately, alert, attentive, keyed up. And deferential. Amazing how the man's whole bearing and attitude had changed in one hour.

He met the gaze of the soldier steadily.

"Here, Grossman. Take pencils and paper down to those people in the cellar. For messages . . . ." His voice shook ever so slightly, as he said, "They will understand."

Only too well, he thought. They will now realize that their friend the *Herr Oberst* has failed them. They are about to be shot. How could he? they will ask each other. Ah, all Germans are alike, each one will say. Underneath they are all Boches.[1] He is like all the rest; they are all the same, they will say.

The corporal took the pads and pencils, clicked his heels, and went out, shutting the door carefully. The *Feldwebel* put his head down on the desk and wept. He wept for the affection that was gone, the friendships that had failed, the trust that was no more. He cried for those six hostages, but most of all he cried for himself. Because for the first time in his life he saw so plainly and so well that there was no health in him.

Monsieur Lavigne, the *café* owner, and Monsieur Varin, the teacher, were quietly talking beside the small cellar window that gave onto the vacant lot adjoining the Bloch villa. Despite the commotion caused by the killing of the Hauptmann Seeler, half a dozen boys were playing football there as usual. One was Jean-Paul, the teacher's young son. Occasionally the ball bounced back off the brick wall of the Bloch villa.

The teacher, a shortish man, took a small wooden box and found he could see plainly through the window. A helmeted sentry with a fixed bayonet stalked back and forth before the house. Monsieur Varin looked at his watch. It was an old-fashioned timepiece, a thick, gold affair that once had belonged to his father and his grandfather. He treasured it and wore it attached to his trouser pocket by a worn leather strap. He soon discovered that the sentry walking back and forth in front of the house was out of sight of the cellar window for about twenty-one or twenty-two seconds, eleven going and eleven returning.

"Pssst . . . pssst . . . psst . . . Jean-Paul . . . Jean-Paul!"

The boy hearing his name, yet not sure where the sound of his father's voice came from, stood perplexed with the ball under one arm. Then he saw that face framed by the little cellar window.

"Papa . . . ."

"Sssh . . . don't look this way," cautioned the teacher. "Wait until the *Fridolin* gets past. Play! Kick that ball!"

The boy instantly obeyed. As soon as the sentry vanished from sight, he kicked the round balloon almost up to the window and leaned down.

"Papa!"

"Sssh, a message. I'm giving you a message

---

1. **Boches**\bosh\ German soldiers, a term of disparagement.

for Madame Borel, out on the road to Varenge-ville. Understand?"

The boy understood. He gulped. "*Ouai, ouai.*[1] I understand," he panted, now frightened at the sight of his father behind the barred window. He took the ball, whirled, kicked it high into the air and raced after it.

The sentry turned, stomped his heels, and went into his act. Except for the little cellar window which the man had failed to notice, all the windows of the Bloch villa giving onto the empty lot had been bricked up. Hence he paid little attention to the band of boys at play. As soon as he disappeared, Jean-Paul grabbed the ball, kicked it toward the window, ran after it, and knelt down to hear his father's instructions.

"Listen carefully. Go get your bicycle. And your fishing pole. Go to the end of town and tell the sentry if he stops you that you are going fishing. Then get to Madame Borel's house as soon as you can, and explain what has happened. That we have been taken by the Fritz."

The lad rushed away as Monsieur Varin stepped down from the wooden box. His face was wet with anxiety. Would the boy get through? Could Madame Borel summon help in time? Is the old truck available?

"Whoof! At least there is a chance. If they get here before the hour is up. How much left?"

"Thirty-six minutes."

"*Eh, juste!* If they get that old Berleit truck they used to derail the train at Montford. The sides are armored. This will take time. Also men and guns to tackle these Silesians. But boldness must pay off. With the old truck they can make it here in fifteen, eighteen minutes. Unless they run into a German patrol."

Everyone listened with attention. Nobody in that cellar had suspected that Monsieur Varin was so close to the Resistance, yet no one was greatly surprised. He seemed to assume leadership.

At this point the door above opened and a helmeted soldier entered, followed by another who stood at the top of the stairs watching with a gun. The first man handed each of the hostages a pencil and a pad of paper. No words were spoken. Nor were any necessary. Each one turned the pad over, examining it. The pads were blocks of old German army orders, blank on the back.

The soldiers left, relocking the cellar door, leaving the six looking down at those ominous squares of paper. Still nobody said a word. Nothing the *Herr Oberst* could have done would have been so utterly final.

"Ah—" A kind of sob came from young René Le Gallec, curled up on the dirt floor. "*Ah, mon père,*" he addressed the priest. "Once you said that someday I would be good enough to play for France. You should know; you played for France long ago. Now I shall never, never . . ." he cried.

"*Chut!*"[2] The priest leaned down and placed his hand on the shoulder of the boy. "Come, René, we are not lost yet. We are alive. They may send us to Germany, but we shall return. The *Fridolins* are beaten; they know it themselves. See, the *Herr Oberst* is now commanding the garrison. They cannot find an officer to relieve him!"

In a little while everyone except the farmer Marquet was writing. The teacher, crouched against the wall, had his pad on his knees. He wrote clumsily with the aid of his magnifying glass, forehead wrinkled, eyebrows raised in the air.

By ancestry I am at least partly a Jew, although not by religion, for in all honesty I have never attended any synagogue or professed any creed. Yet I feel neither pride nor shame in my origins; indeed I never think about them save in the presence of an anti-Semite, of whom there appear to be many in my beloved France today. First of all, I am a Frenchman. Second, a teacher of French youth. Third, a Marxist, something that, like my origin I have never attempted to conceal.

---

1. **Ouai**\wĕ\ yes.
2. **Chut!**\sh̄ut\ Hush!

Why should I? My great great grandfather served as a soldier of Napoleon at Austerlitz. My grandfather was wounded in the Franco-Prussian War of 1870. I, myself, was twice wounded in the battles along the Somme in the campaigns of 1917 and 1918. I fought through the disaster of 1940. Because of this or because of my decorations—for the Germans like the French have a military tradition and a respect for soldiers, even their enemies —I have not been sent away from my home here in Nogent-Plage. Hence this France, from which today some of my compatriots would like to exile me, remains the land where my emotions are fixed, my being is centered. I have drunk her culture. I have done my best to defend her honor with my body, to help train her youth. I breathe fully only when in her climate. Next to my wife whom I adore, and my dear son Jean-Paul who is my pride and joy, I count my country as my nearest and dearest.

Adieu La France,
Georges Varin

Across the room, Marcel Deschamps the fisherman was kneeling before the priest. René Le Gallec waited his turn. The farmer Marquet, his head between his hands, sat motionless on the bench. He had written nothing and was muttering to himself.

For how can you write a letter of farewell to a horse named Sebastian?

13

René had made his confession, yet his blond head remained bowed. At last he looked up, still on his knees before the padre. There were tears in his eyes.

"My parents don't even know where I am. They think I went swimming. I told them I was going swimming with Michel." Then he voiced the thought of everyone in that cellar. "Why doesn't the *Herr Oberst* do something? Only this morning he told me I should use the left foot more. You remember, don't you, Père? He said I had an excellent left foot. Why doesn't he do something? Now he must be in

command here. He has always been good to the people of Nogent-Plage, always . . . ."

He broke down, sobbing, staggered by the brutal injustice of what had happened. Half an hour before he had been free, outside in the sunshine kicking his precious football, the one the *Herr Oberst* had obtained for him. Now he was locked up in the cellar of the Bloch villa, soon to be sentenced to a German prison camp for life. Or something worse, though he could not quite bring himself to believe the Germans would really shoot six innocent people.

Except for the farmer, the men stood talking in knots, Monsieur Lavigne and the teacher leaning against an iron stanchion, the fisherman saying something softly, all shaking a little. All thinking much the same thing. It simply can't be. Things aren't like this. We've never had anything like this before in Nogent-Plage, never. The *Herr Oberst* knows us all. He has worked miracles before. He got us out of trouble so often these past years. Surely he will today.

Their faith in the Feldwebel Hans was touching. Only the teacher was dubious. "You'll get out of this mess," he remarked to the *café* owner. "It will be all right for you, not for me. To the Germans, I am a Jew." He held out his hands in a little Gallic gesture of despair.

At this point they were interrupted by sudden noises overhead. A whistle blew shrilly. The boots of running soldiers above thudded on the floor. They heard the voice of the *Herr Oberst* shouting orders in that guttural German. His voice had changed. Now it was the tone of all the many officers who had garrisoned Nogent-Plage during those long years of occupation.

Far down the street a machine gun gave a stuttering bark, fell silent, barked once more. Monsieur Varin quickly reached the top of the wooden box beside the window. Jean-Paul and the other football players had scattered. Peering out, he could see about fifty feet of the Grande Rue.

The door at the top of the cellar stairs opened with a crash. A soldier stood there pointing a gun at the hostages below. *"Nicht bewegen! Nicht bewegen!"* he shouted. Don't move.

Nobody moved. Nobody had any intention of moving. All were far too frightened to move.

The teacher knew immediately what was happening. The Underground was mounting an attack on the Bloch villa in a desperate attempt to free the six prisoners. Unfortunately, the Germans directed by the Feldwebel Hans were ready. Upstairs they began firing out of the windows facing the street. A heavy truck roared past on the Grande Rue, firing in turn.

Below another machine gun went into action. Bullets bit into the walls of the Bloch villa, sending stone splinters flying. Windowpanes shattered, showering glass onto the pavement. Then came bursts of firing the teacher assumed to be from the rescue truck. Finally he heard it racing off in the direction of Varengeville.

The soldier at the head of the cellar stairs lowered his gun as the noise died away in the distance. The sound of the door closing and the key turning in the lock was painfully definitive. The teacher leaned as far as the little window allowed. He saw German troops moving up the street with the body of a French civilian on a stretcher, the arms of the dead man hanging over the sides. Soon two more bodies went by, then a badly wounded German limping along and assisted by two comrades.

The young football players, not entirely unaccustomed to the sound of machine guns in recent years, returned to the lot and stood watching the activity on the Grande Rue. There was too much commotion in the street for the Germans to pay any attention to them.

"Jean-Paul!"

The boy turned, startled. He grabbed the football from a comrade and kicked it toward the low cellar window, then trotted after it casually. Meanwhile, Monsieur Varin hastily untied the worn leather strap of his watch from his belt and, taking it out of his pocket, tossed it through the barred window on the ground before his son. The boy leaning over for the football scooped up the watch in one deft movement and kicked the ball hard against the house, letting it rebound. His father stood admiring the quickness and ease of the boy's movement, so utterly free and natural, so unconscious, and watched him stuff the watch into his trouser pocket of the ragged blue shorts.

Pray God nobody was looking. Nobody was. The boy raced off home, down the street. At least he was safe. Monsieur Varin stepped down from the box.

"Ahhhh," he said, shaking his head.

That futile rescue attempt had cost three lives and completely failed. *"Ahhhh!"* he exclaimed in despair. He leaned down and picked up the block of paper, with his small, precise writing, and slumped to the bench.

The farmer Marquet, his head in his hands, still sat motionless. Still he had written nothing.

14

The Chateau de Varennes on the outskirts of Normandy was a busy place that June day. As Headquarters of the Northern Command, it was the nerve center of the defense of the entire region. From a peak of the roof of the Chateau hung dozens of telephone wires that went off in every direction. Camouflaged Mercedes[1] deposited staff officers carrying black briefcases under one arm. Dispatch riders roared up on olive-drab motorcycles. Inside, in a larger corner apartment on the second floor that had once been an upstairs sitting room, two staff officers were in earnest consultation.

Behind a desk in this office sat the Baron General von Wenig, chief of staff of the North-

---

1. **Mercedes**\mər ⁴sā·dēz\ a make of car.

ern Command. He was a strong, stocky man with close-cropped hair and a stretched-out mouth used to giving orders and having them instantly obeyed. He looked out through French windows at a cherry tree in blossom and the park beyond, where the grass was green in the spring sunshine.

"Ah, I see. You could do nothing with him."

"Nothing," answered the other man, also a general, tall, tanned, stalking the carpeted room. "Absolutely nothing. He seems to me to exist in a world of his own. However, as you know, it is difficult to talk on the telephone in times such as these. One doesn't dare speak openly with so many listening in. But he seems determined."

"He seems to me determined to die. I've heard medical men talk of a death wish. Now I begin to understand. Doesn't he realize, Klaus, that it is far better to die for one's country under English gunfire than to die from the bullets of a firing squad?"

The tall officer walking up and down nodded. He had a fine, intelligent face, sensitive yet strong. His hair was neatly brushed back from his forehead and this gave him a spare, well-groomed appearance. When he spoke, his eyes had a kind of irony in them, as though he had seen everything.

"Yes, naturally, he knows. He understands the army viewpoint. He must realize this has been done numberless times in the last war. But he cannot bring himself to shoot those six French."

"But Klaus, he knows the necessity for firmness in dealing with *franc-tireurs*.[2] They are enemies of his country. In short, they are murderers."

"True, but he claims they are simply men of the village."

"Makes no difference. They must be made an example of. Otherwise he is a traitor to the Army. Doesn't he see that? If we didn't take measures, we should have riots throughout our rear, with those British and Americans firing at us from the sea. This is the overriding consideration. He is disobeying the orders of a superior. There is only one thing to do." The seated man slammed his fist down on the desk.

"Heinrich, permit me. It isn't as easy as all that. This young man believes he is right."

"He believes what? What is right? Does he believe in a duty to the land of his birth? His father died for the Fatherland here in France. Does he believe in tradition? In family obligations? Does he, Klaus? His brother risks his life daily in the *Luftwaffe,* and this young man sits comfortably in a seaside village discussing right and wrong. Let us not waste time on the matter. You and I know that were it not for his connections at home, he would be behind bars right now. Tell me, who is replacing him at Nogent-Plage?"

"A certain Leutnant Rancke from Blockhouse 262B, about five miles east."

The man behind the desk half rose. "Not Rancke. R-A-N-C-K-E?" He broke into an agonized scream. "That fellow was attached to my division at Anzio last year. He is worthless, absolutely worthless! Quite incapable of making a decision on anything, even the smallest matter. What is the *Wehrmacht* coming to? Surely we are down to the dregs if we have to depend on the likes of Rancke! We cannot entrust even a small garrison such as Nogent-Plage to this idiot. Until that *Oberleutnant* gets back tomorrow from Ostend, we must find a replacement. Not Rancke. Meanwhile, as I see it, there is only one thing to do. You are taking over Wissant tomorrow from Straub, right? Then you must leave immediately, stop off and see von Kleinschrodt yourself, persuade him . . . ."

"*Jawohl, Herr General.*"

"At once. You are an older man, a career soldier, not only his family friend, but someone he trusts and respects. He knows you and takes your advice. I shall cancel the order for Rancke and get that man back from Ostend. You take over Nogent-Plage until he arrives."

"But suppose the boy refuses to carry out orders. Suppose he refuses to execute those Frenchmen."

---

2. **franc-tireurs**\\'fra(n)·tē 'rěr\\ snipers.

"Then of course you must do it. He should be made to attend as a witness. Everything done strictly according to regulations, *General*. Leave him in command until his lieutenant returns. Then we must court-martial him, as soon that is, as we have repelled the invasion."

The General Froelicher, speeding along in the Mercedes on Route Nationale Number 40 glanced through the haze out to sea. It made him recall the big estate on the Baltic, and the Colonel von Kleinschrodt who had been his dearest friend and a comrade for three years in World War I. He did not like his mission in the least as he thought about the boy. A strange, quiet youth, different from the others, except that he liked football and, I must admit, always played it excellently. I remember once on a wild boar hunt on the family place, he was then about ten or twelve. By mistake somebody shot a stag. The animal dropped, but did not die. I recall he writhed on the ground until one of the beaters went up and killed him. As the blood poured from the stag's head, the boy took one look and fainted. Just like that . . . he fell to the ground . . . .

All the way to Nogent-Plage he thought and worried about the interview to come. Finally they drew up before the Bloch villa in Nogent-Plage. Outside in the Grande Rue, Madame Dupont was hobbling along, nodding and bobbing her head to the other women, the inevitable black string bag in her hand. Observing a vehicle approaching in a cloud of dust, she hastily stepped onto the sidewalk. With these young army drivers one was never safe.

The car stopped with a screaming of brakes. It was covered with a film of sand that could not obscure its high polish. A soldier jumped out and smartly held the rear door open, clicking his heels together. And an officer stepped onto the pavement.

He was tall, well-tanned, with fine features. There was a row of ribbons on his tunic. She recognized the Ritterkreuz and the Order Pour Le Merité, one of the highest combat decorations of the German Army. Somehow the aristocratic-looking officer and his whirlwind arrival reminded her of the white horses, the plumes and the gleaming breastplates of the Garde Republicaine of her youth.

Ah, she thought, what smartness, what discipline! No wonder we French could not withstand these people. Surely there is no Army like this. We had only ineffectual troops like Monsieur Varin and young Pierre Marquet, the farmer's son. A nice man, Monsieur Varin, to be sure, certainly, but careless in his dress. And actually, a Communist. He doesn't even conceal it, either.

The smart officer returned the salute of the soldier at the door of the car, saluted again with a glove in his hand as the sentries before the Bloch villa came to attention, and went inside.

In the office of the Hauptmann Seeler, the *Feldwebel* sat by himself where he had been sitting alone for over an hour. The clock on the wall of the silent room showed more than sixty minutes past time for the execution. The *Feldwebel* was more lonely than he had ever been in his life. This loneliness hurt. There was nobody to help, to talk with him, to advise or even disagree with him. The decision was all his. He, too, had heard the big car arriving. Since a car was an event in Nogent-Plage at the moment, it could mean only one thing. Someone from Headquarters had come to place him under arrest, perhaps bringing a replacement to command the garrison. They waste no time in the Army, he thought, as he caught the slamming of the car doors, the sound of the front door opening, the crisp clicking of the sentry's heels. An officer of importance, no doubt the Major Kessler himself. He was ready. The terrible uncertainty was over, the doubts and hesitations finished. The *Feldwebel* felt glad. Standing straight, he put on his cap, yanked down his tunic, and waited for whatever was to come.

A stomping of feet in the corridor. Then the orderly knocked and simultaneously threw open the office door. The *Feldwebel* felt the pride in his subordinate's tone as he announced the visitor. Not every *Feldwebel* was called upon by a staff officer. Let alone a general.

"The General Froelicher," affirmed the soldier, saluting and holding the door open stiffly, then quickly closing it.

The *Feldwebel* had expected anything but this. He was astonished, bewildered, but he, too, clicked his heels and saluted. The visitor came toward him, arms outstretched.

"My poor boy, my poor boy . . . ." He embraced the younger man. Suddenly a little of the aching and loneliness ceased. Someone cared.

"My boy, my boy . . . ." The visitor stepped back, holding him tightly by the forearm, looking into his eyes.

"Yes, my *General*." He was not far from tears, and the older man realized it and broke in.

"*General! General* indeed! I am still your godfather, am I not? I am still old Uncle Klaus. I had to see you, Hans. This is all so terrible."

He moved away, sat down, crossed his legs, showing an expensive pair of leather boots burnished with age and constant polishing. He took out a cigarette case of gold and extended it. "Have one. They are Turkish. Very good."

The *Feldwebel* refused politely. To have accepted would have been a kind of surrender at the start. However, he pushed a small china ashtray across the desk to his godfather. "You know, you cannot imagine what it means to see you at this moment, Uncle Klaus."

The general, elegant, poised, lit his cigarette with a gold lighter. "Of course. You need help. That is what godfathers are for, my boy. Now tell me. What is this all about? Frankly, I don't understand."

The *Feldwebel* started to talk. He desperately needed and indeed wanted to tell the whole story to this man he loved and respected, who knew him so well, who had been part of his existence since childhood. But it was difficult to begin. Although the Froelichers

were old family friends and neighbors back home along the Baltic Sea, they were traditional army people. How could the general be expected to understand? It would make no sense to him.

"You see, Uncle Klaus . . . . I don't quite know how to put it. I have been ordered to do something I cannot bring myself to do."

"Hans, my boy, I didn't come here this afternoon when we are all in such danger to deliver platitudes or preach a sermon. The situation we face is much too serious. I came to save you from yourself."

The younger man nodded. He looked at his godfather, using an old expression of his mother's. "*Um Gottes Willen.*"[3]

"All right. Now tell me everything. I know you have been ordered to execute six hostages. I realize you do not want to do it. But what makes you feel you are more important than the German Reich? Isn't that a bit egotistical?"

The face of the *Feldwebel* flushed. "I don't feel that way at all, Uncle Klaus, and you must know it. I am merely a noncommissioned officer who has never seen battle, the only soldier in Nogent-Plage who doesn't wear a row of combat ribbons on his chest. The *only one*. I am unimportant. I realize this. But, Uncle Klaus, I am me. What I am asked to do betrays myself."

"Hans, my boy, you know you are in the wrong, don't you now? To set your own opinion against that of your country at war? You must see that. You are not in contact with realities, my boy. These people are our enemies. We have occupied them with firmness, but correctly, and with politeness. We have even been lenient with them at times. Yet they still resist. They do not want us here. They hate us, Hans. Many good German soldiers in France and in Italy and Russia, too, have carried out equally distasteful orders. This is accepted military practice."

"I am well aware of that, Uncle Klaus. But

---

3. **Um Gottes Willen**\um ˈgɔtəs ˈvĭ·lən\ God willing.

once again, I am me. They are other people. I am Hans Joachim Wolfgang von und zu Kleinschrodt. This disobedience of orders is the most difficult thing I ever did in all my life, believe me."

"Of course. Your gesture is a fine one. I respect it. I am a liberal. I can see your side as perhaps some of my colleagues would not. It does you great credit, Hans. But do you appreciate the consequences? You will most certainly be court-martialed for refusing to carry out a direct command. Nogent-Plage is in the front lines now. You cannot have an Army which obeys some orders and doesn't obey others. We obey all orders, the orders of our superiors, the orders of the *Führer*. If you go through with this, nothing I can do will save you. Nobody can save you. And you are one of the young Germans who should lead the Fatherland of tomorrow. Hans, my boy, we look to you to carry out our hopes for the future, to help govern Europe unified by the Greater Reich."

Suddenly his voice became weary. Now the general was no longer a trim, alert staff officer, but an aging, tired man who had carried the burden long years and was appealing to the next generation. The spark had left him. His eyes grew black with fatigue.

Feldwebel Hans moved his head as if in acquiescence. His eyes caught the clock on the wall. It was an hour and a half beyond the time set for the execution, and those six hostages still waited in the cellar.

"Let me say just one thing, my boy. In life, you will find that the things we long for beyond all others, the things we really desire most, are the things we cannot have. Life is that way, full of disappointments for us all. Believe me, nobody escapes this."

Again the young man seemed to acknowledge the words, to accept them, but he did not speak. Finally he looked at his godfather. "My uncle, I hardly know . . . I am not sure . . . . I am not conceited enough to be certain, but in my deep heart I feel it is wrong to kill these six men. It is worse than wrong; it is

evil. José Marti said once: 'He who witnesses a crime and does not protest, commits it himself.' "

Now the general was taken aback. "Who on earth is José Marti?"

"He was a Cuban."

"A Cuban!" A lesser breed, the scorn in the tone of the general plainly indicated.

"Yes, a Cuban revolutionary, a great patriot. He is a hero even today throughout South America. I believe he was killed by the Spaniards, I am not sure. Anyhow, he was telling us a truth, Uncle Klaus. By the way, have you ever read Rilke?"[4]

"No." The general felt slightly uncomfortable. He suddenly realized that his godson was in some ways older than himself. Truly this boy had matured. There was a new firmness about the mouth. It was not unimpressive. Here was a twenty-year-old standing up against the authority of the *Wehrmacht*. For a few seconds the general was caught up in admiration of his godson. Why, I was like him as a young man, he thought. I had faith. Whatever happened to me? Why did I never take a stand against Adolf Hitler? Or at least have the guts to resign my commission. Why did I sit back and accept it all as my friends and colleagues did, until we discovered he owned us entirely, and it was too late? Why?

Reluctantly he returned to the somber situation at hand. He pulled a paper from his pocket and took out glasses.

"Hans, my boy, this is a brutal thing we are doing. I agree. But war is brutal. Only by being brutal can we save the lives of the good German soldiers under your command. Sometimes, like yourself, I have doubts. Then I always come back to this, an activity report which I cut out and kept. It is Herr Himmler, then Gauleiter of Poland, speaking: 'If the local population from the Nazi point of view is hostile, racially inferior, or composed of criminal elements who attack German troops in the act of carrying out their duties, all those

---

4. **Rilke**\ˈrĭl·kə\ German poet, born in Prague.

suspected of supporting these terrorists are to be shot and the women and children deported.' Now we did this in the First World War to protect our troops; we did it here in France at Oradour, we did it at Lidice[5] in Czechoslovakia, and we did it many times in Poland. In Nogent-Plage I consider we have really been most lenient."

"But Uncle Klaus . . . ."

"Wait! Listen to me. It is past midafternoon. We may well have the invasion any minute, at any place along the coast. I speak to you, Hans, in the name of your father whom I so deeply loved. Think! Reflect! Obey your superiors."

"But don't you see. I cannot excuse myself by depositing my conscience with my superiors. Sometimes disobedience is not wrong. Believe me, Uncle Klaus, there are times when it is not wrong. To disobey when your whole being tells you to is obeying your conscience."

"Nonsense, my boy, nonsense! Suppose everyone did that? What kind of an Army would we have? Would we be here? Would we be on the Vistula? Would we hold everything from Narvik to Rome? What would happen to us if everyone acted as you are doing?"

"What everyone does is their concern. What I do is mine."

"Hans! For the last time, I beg you, no matter what you feel, no matter the rights and wrongs and your inner struggle which I respect, obey the orders of your superior officer. Were you not a von und zu Kleinschrodt, do you know what would happen to you?

"We would tie you to the rear of an army truck and invite you to run until you were so badly cut up you would collapse and give in. That is what we would do. You are betraying your family and your class."

The young man sat motionless behind the desk in misery. Although he loved his godfather and trusted him, although he was so close to him that he felt his presence deeply, he was still terribly alone. But he gave no sign of yielding. A tiny spiral of smoke rose from the ashtray as the cigarette burned out. There was a sad, heavy silence. Neither man spoke.

Then the general rose, his chair scraping the floor. He pressed the buzzer on the desk. The orderly entered immediately, standing at attention before the general.

"Where are the six prisoners?"

"Downstairs, sir. In the cellar."

"Bring them up."

15

"Are you certain that your watch is at the hour?"

"No. But if it is wrong, the church clock is wrong also."

The only remaining watch belonged to the padre. There were twelve minutes left, then ten minutes, then five. At last the hour was up. The cellar door did not slam open with a crash. No helmeted soldiers came for them. What did it mean? The six looked at each other more easily.

"I feel sure the *Herr Oberst* has persuaded them to do nothing. He knows none of us played any part in the killing. I felt certain, I said so, remember? I said he would get us out . . . ."

Only the teacher was less sure. True, it was not like the Germans to be late, especially where death was concerned. Perhaps they had caught the murderer. If so, nobody would bother to tell them.

Half an hour passed. An hour. A little more than an hour. Above, telephones rang. Long discussions followed in German. After a while a car screamed to a stop on the Grande Rue outside. How strange, thought Monsieur Varin, that one's hearing becomes so acute at moments like this. He could hear men walking on the hard floor above and distinguish footsteps, the slow pacing of the *Feldwebel*, the quick, brisk steps of the orderlies. Clack-clack, clack-clack, clack - clack . . . clack - clack - clack - clack . . . . Then silence.

They waited, tired now, weary from fatigue

5. **Lidice**\ˈlĭ·dyĭ·tsē\ a village in Czechoslovakia destroyed by the Nazis in 1942 in reprisal for the assassination of a high Nazi official.

and anxiety and tension, drooping a little, all of them. They sat on the hard dirt floor, back against the stone wall, heads nodding.

At last the key turned in the lock and the cellar door flew open. At the top of the stairs stood a soldier with the usual submachine gun in his hands.

"*Hinaus!*"[1] He beckoned them up. Horrible sound, thought the teacher. A horrible sound and a horrible language. I always disliked it and I always will.

The hostages rose clumsily to their feet. They'll probably release us now. They have no evidence against us. The *Herr Oberst* knows we had nothing to do with the killing of the Hauptmann Seeler. Silently, meekly, they went up the stairs one by one. Just outside the cellar door stood the *Feldwebel* with a tall German officer, elegant in shiny boots, his chest covered with campaign ribbons and combat decorations. The hostages stared at them dully, drained now of all emotion.

The *Feldwebel* signaled a squad of soldiers and turned quickly away, unable to stand the look on those French faces, feeling their faith vanish as he gave the silent orders. The troops formed about them, half leading, half pushing the five men and the boy into the Grande Rue.

When the farmer Marquet, the first in line, was thrust outside, a wild shrieking arose. The prisoners stood for a few seconds blinking in the unaccustomed sunlight. All the women of Nogent-Plage, old and young, surrounded the steps of the Bloch villa in a semicircle. They were being held off by helmeted soldiers with bayonets attached to their rifles.

The women also were armed. They had brought brooms, shovels, pitchforks, and rakes. They brandished them before the soldiers, screaming as the hostages stepped hesitantly into the street.

"Marcel! Marcel! *Mon bien-aimé* . . . ."[2]

"Georges! Georges! *Suis ici . . . ici . . . .*"[3]

The wife of the fisherman tried to break through to her husband. A German soldier seized her and tossed her roughly to the pavement.

At this, like a kind of signal, the women attacked *en masse*. With their shovels and pitchforks, their rakes and brooms, they tried to break through the soldiers and reach the men and the boy. It was impossible for the *Feldwebel* standing on the steps of the Bloch villa to give the order to fire into the melee. To have done so would have meant the massacre of both townspeople and troops. For long seconds the street was in utter confusion.

Run! Run! Run! Run, you idiots, thought the *Feldwebel*, half hoping that the six would burst away in all directions. Surely a few would escape. But they were dazed so they did nothing. The *Feldwebel* blew a short blast on the whistle he had removed from his upper breast pocket, shouted crisp commands, and slowly the women were overpowered and forced back. Pitchforks were seized and tossed aside. The troops formed quickly about the prisoners and the column moved down the street. Only two, the Catholic and the Communist went with heads erect.

My God, thought the *Feldwebel*, I'm marching them to death. Just what I said I'd never do. How did I get here?

From the pleading women who stumbled along beside the column came sobs and screams. Impossible to think coherently, to act intelligently in that emotion. He glanced around.

The General Froelicher was bringing up the rear, there to see the sentence was carried out. He gave no orders, although the soldiers needed no orders. They had done it many times in other, distant lands.

"Charles! Charles!" shrieked the wife of the *café* owner. "Charles! *Regarde-moi.*"[4]

"*Ah, mon fils,*"[5] cried the teacher, seeing his wife with the boy at her side. Jean-Paul had the white football under his arm. He was

---

1. **Hinaus!**\hĭn ▴aus\ Out!
2. **Mon bien-aimé**\mō(n)▴byĕn·ā 'mā\ My best beloved.
3. **Suis ici . . . ici**\swē·ē ▴sē·ē ▴sē\ Here I am . . . here.
4. **Regarde-moi**\rə ▴gard 'mwa\ Look at me.
5. **mon fils**\'mō(n) ▴fēs\ my son.

101

sobbing bitterly, tears on his face. *"Adieu, Jean-Paul. Adieu. Et toi, chérie . . . ."*[6]

No man, no woman was shouting to the farmer Marquet. Nor, indeed, did he expect anyone to. But the moment he had come out on the steps of the Bloch villa, his eyes searched the Grande Rue anxiously. What had become of Sebastian? Only a mangy dog trotting along beside the weeping women was now visible. The farmer knew what had happened. The villagers had led Sebastian away. No meat had been available in Nogent-Plage for a long time. They would shoot Sebastian at once.

The soldiers marched in cadence, their boots striking the concrete with that harsh sound. Suddenly Jean-Paul Varin burst away from his mother's arm and rushed up to the *Feldwebel* at the head of the column.

"Jean-Paul!" cried Madame Varin. "Jean-Paul."

Now he was attacking the big German, hitting him with clenched fists, kicking at his legs, weeping and shouting.

Instantly his mother was beside him, dragging him back to the sidewalk. Kneeling down, she held him tightly to her. He buried his head in her shoulder.

Quickly the column reached the end of the Grande Rue—and the low wall with its machine guns. A raging tide of women surrounded the troops, held back only by their bayonets.

Each hostage was blindfolded. They knew no hope at last. All illusions were gone. A quiet descended so deep you could hear the half slap, half crunch of the waves on the pebbly beach below. And the sobs of Jean-Paul tearing his body as he clung to the arms of his mother.

René Le Gallec next to the teacher reached out, groping for the hand of the older man. His anguished voice was plainly audible. "Will it hurt, Monsieur the Professor, will it hurt?"

And the reply of the man, distinct above the weeping that now swept the circle of waiting women. *"Non, mon petit,* it won't hurt. You

won't feel it." Then the teacher threw back his head and shouted with all his strength.

"Vive La France."[7]

The *Feldwebel* could stand it no longer. Then from behind came the voice of his godfather, composed, clear, crisp. *"Schiessen!"*[8]

"Vive La . . . ."

The rifles sounded in unison. They made a queer echo in the fog now approaching from the sea. Startled, the thin dog raced down the road, past the six crumpled figures on the sea wall, toward St.-Valéry in the distance.

DISCUSSION FOR UNDERSTANDING

1. How do the following react to the killing of the *Hauptmann*? the villagers; the soldiers; the *Feldwebel*; the *Major* at division headquarters?

2. How are the hostages selected? How long does the *Feldwebel* have to find the assassin?

3. Why is the German command so set on this sudden, swift judgment?

4. What is Feldwebel Hans' dilemma?

5. What happens to the Underground's rescue attempt?

6. How do the hostages react to their imprisonment?

7. Why do the hostages not break and make a run for it when the women attack?

8. What is the effect of the General's brief encounter with the *Feldwebel*?

----

6. **Adieu. Et toi, chérie**\a ˄dyə·ā ˄twa·shā 'rē\ Goodbye. And you too, dear.
7. **Vive La France**\ˇvēv·la ˄fra(n)s\ Long live France.
8. **Schiessen!**\ˇshē-sən\ Fire!

Part II

Judgment at Rouen
1948

For most Americans, World War II did not begin until December 7, 1941, at Pearl Harbor. For the French it really began in early May, 1940, with the invasion of France, and the fighting was over in six weeks—almost as soon as it started. Then followed more than four years of occupation by a foreign army, of living under enemy rule.

After the end of the war came trials of various war criminals. Especially remembered are those at Nuremberg, which sentenced to death the most notorious of the Nazi leaders who had not emulated Hitler by taking their own lives: Frank, Frick, Streicher, von Ribbentrop, and others. Here for the first time was established the principal that made not states but individuals answerable to law for acts committed in war.

Less celebrated than the trials at Nuremberg were smaller trials in various lands where the people had suffered at the hands of Gestapo men, Storm Troopers, and even some German army officers. One of them, perhaps the most discussed all over France, was the trial of the Baron Hans Joachim Wolfgang von und zu Kleinschrodt.

It was held in Rouen, the city where Joan of Arc was burned to death by English troops in 1431. In 1499 a building was begun to house the Parliament of Normandy. Later it was turned over to the Law Courts and became the Palais de Justice.[1] Here, several years after the war, the baron was brought to justice for the shooting of six innocent French civilians on the afternoon of June 5, 1944, only hours before Nogent-Plage was stormed under cover of the guns of the British fleet and the *Feldwebel* with almost a hundred of his soldiers was taken prisoner by Canadian troops.

When his case was called he was offered either French or German counsel or, if he so desired, both. He asked for neither. His defense was that he had not shot the hostages or given the order to do so. The order was given by a superior officer, the General Klaus Froelicher, who had been in Nogent-Plage at the time.

Obviously the court found this hard to accept. The General Froelicher had later been killed leading an encircled division at the Battle of St.-Lô. Germans, everyone knew, were not in the habit of disobeying commands, and it was established that Headquarters had commanded the Feldwebel von Kleinschrodt to have the six hostages shot. Moreover, his signature was at the bottom of the proclamation issued to the townspeople after the execution.

The trial attracted attention in all of Europe because the defendant was a prominent athlete, celebrated for his football exploits. The proceedings were short and passionate. Witnesses, mostly inhabitants of Nogent-Plage, including several widows of the men who had been killed, testified against him. Their quiet bitterness was impressive. It was shown that a Hauptmann Seeler commanding the garrison at Nogent-Plage had been shot to death in the street on June 5, 1944, the day before the invasion of Normandy. The baron, then an ordinary *Feldwebel*, or noncommissioned officer, assumed command and was ordered to seize six hostages and confine them. This he did. Unless the murderer was discovered, he was to shoot the six within the hour.

Was there a superior officer present at the execution? One had come to town, yes. Madame Dupont and others had seen him arrive at the Bloch villa in a big Mercedes. But was he actually present when the six hostages were shot? Nobody was sure. After all, there had been all that swirling, screaming confusion when the women had attacked the German troops with pitchforks and rakes. And later, during the execution itself, all eyes had

---

1. **Palais de Justice**\pă ▲lä·də·z̄hūs ▲tēs\ Hall of Justice.

been on the condemned six. So if he was there, nobody could recall seeing him. And anyway it was the *Feldwebel,* at the head of the column, who had marched the men down with the firing squad, and presumably he had given the order for their death.

Because of the fame of the accused, public interest in the trial was great. Foreign as well as French journalists were present. One American correspondent, perhaps more imaginative than his colleagues, sent on to New York a vivid description of the baron as the Butcher of Nogent-Plage. The title stuck. So that was how all the witnesses and spectators in the high-vaulted fifteenth-century courtroom of the Palais de Justice at Rouen came to think of him.

A *hussier,* or bailiff, in knee breeches, stood up with a document in his hands. He read rapidly.

"Whereasontheafternoonof Junefifth nineteenhundredandfortyfourtheaforesaid defendantcausedtodieatthehandsofafiring squadthefollowinginnocentFrenchcivilians RenéLeGallecGeorgesVarinCharlesLavigne LouisMarquetMarcelDeschampsandthePère Clementthereforeyou HansJoachimWolfgang vonundzuKleinschrodthavebeenconvictedof themurderoftheabovenamedsixFrenchmen. Thedefendantwillcomeforwardtobe sentenced."

The spectators half rose to watch the black-haired man stand and, with shoulders squared, step into the box. He was in civilian clothes, wearing a sports jacket with leather patches on the elbows that told of happier times. It fitted his muscular frame tightly because of its age, but still it became him. The witnesses, especially those women in black wearing black veils, watched with icy anger. Nothing could bring back their men.

The bearded judge with the little red-and-white cap upon his brow leaned forward.

"Has the defendant anything to say?"

The courtroom was quiet. Since the baron had hardly spoken in his defense except to deny his guilt, it hardly seemed likely that he would talk now. But after a moment he nodded.

Arms folded, he said, *"Hauptrichter,*[2] I have only this to say. I am not guilty of the charges. I did not pronounce the order to have the six hostages shot. In fact, I disobeyed that order. Had Germany won the war, I should have been court-martialed by my own countrymen and faced a firing squad myself."

A murmur ran through the courtroom. The bearded judge gavelled sharply for silence. The defendant resumed.

"No, I did not kill the hostages. I did not kill them because the order to do so offended my conscience. And when conscience and the state conflict, the conscience of a man must take precedence.

"But if I did not obey this order, I perhaps obeyed others I should not have obeyed. As my chiefs were wrong to obey the orders of a madman. We were all guilty, *nous étions tous des assassins.*[3] Hence we must pay the price. I am ready. But first, I wish to say this. Someday you French and"—here he looked at the row of correspondents—"you Americans, even you Americans who were victorious and therefore think such a thing is impossible, someday you may also murder, torture, drop bombs, and kill innocent people in the name of some cause or in the belief that you are somehow defending your country while fighting in a foreign land, as we did."

Once again the gavel sounded. The judge said, "The defendant will now be sentenced. Hans Joachim Wolfgang von und zu Kleinschrodt, acting for the Court of Cassation, I sentence you to ten years at hard labor. Sentence to begin immediately.

"The case is now ended. The court is dismissed."

---

2. **Hauptrichter**\ˈhaupt·rĭhk·tər\ Judge.
3. **nous étions tous des assassins**\ˈnū·zā 'tyō(n) ▲tū·dā·za·sa ▲să(n)\ we were all murderers.

Part III
Soldier from the Wars Returning
June, 1964

1

Germany came to a full stop that day. France also ground to a standstill. So did Scandinavia, the Low Countries, and lands far more distant from the ancient city of Rouen, where the contest was to be held.

Saturday afternoon is a busy time in Europe. Not that day. Factories everywhere shut long before the kickoff. Stores, shops, offices closed. Theaters emptied. Traffic subsided. Each metropolis suspended its normal activities.

The only crowded places were bars, *cafés, bistros, hierstubes, trattorie.*[1] People poured into them to watch the game on television. Twelve countries had requested the match live for their national networks. All Europe was aroused.

Why this excitement over a game of football? First, because it was more than a game. This contest pitted the Stade Rouennais, champions of France, against Bayern-Munich, champions of Germany. Hence it was a French-German contest, the first time since the end of the war that a team from across the Rhine was to play in a country which had suffered more than four years of occupation, deportation, and even starvation.

Everyone who knew football realized there would be a twelfth man on the field for France: the French crowd in the stands.

But chiefly the match was important because of two outstanding players. Who in all France could forget that the greatest of German goalkeepers was the man who had shot French hostages during the war and been tried in the very city of Rouen? And if the Munich team was led and inspired by its veteran captain and goalkeeper, the French also had their star. He was a young, nervous, magnificent forward named Jean-Paul Varin.

Everywhere in France he was called the *"comingman français."*

In cities, towns, and villages throughout the land, thousands of boys addressed a football the way Jean-Paul did. Young men of every age tried to run like him, shoot like him, pass like him. He was far better known than any politician or movie star. When you saw men with their heads together in a *café* or a train, they were not necessarily talking about business or politics. More likely they were discussing Jean-Paul Varin.

Now he would come up against the great German veteran. After the Feldwebel von Kleinschrodt had gotten out of prison, serving six years of his ten-year term, he had felt lost. His brother had been killed in action in the last week of the war. Many friends were also gone. Some were still in Russian prisoner-of-war camps. His mother was dead. His family vanished. The great estate on the Baltic was in ruins, devastated by the Russians, then occupied by the British. Finally one night the main house and other buildings caught fire and burned to the ground.

Where could he go? What could he do? He did the thing that came naturally, the thing he liked best of all—he turned to football. It was a poorish living, coaching junior teams in and around Hamburg. For several years he practiced continually, running to get his legs back. At first it was difficult for him to keep up with his boys when refereeing one of their matches. Gradually his legs returned. So did his form. Often he played goal. As goalie he could see the entire field, watch all the boys in action, coach them as they ran and passed. With a whistle around his neck he would blow twice to stop play and race out to correct their mistakes.

The boys learned. They liked the challenge of the man in the goal before them. They improved. Before long his teams began to win. They were noticed, and he became known as

---

1. English, French, German, and Italian words for bars and eating places.

the animator[2] of football among the youth of Germany.

After several years in which he kept attracting attention, the manager of Werder of Berlin had the idea of asking him to try out for the team. He did, playing superbly. As a goalkeeper his age—he was then thirty-eight— mattered less. True, he had slowed down, but in goal he was magnificent. He knew all the techniques of the attacker. His reflexes were still keen, his coordination perfect, and he could outlast anybody on the field. When he stepped in for Werder-Berlin the team won nineteen straight games.

Next he transferred to Bayern-Munich and helped them win a title with his superb play in goal. He soon became mentor and team leader. Within a few years he had twelve caps —that is, he had played twelve times for his native land in international competition. Once he traveled to London, where his defensive play won a game against West Ham, the English champions. By this time he was God the father of German sport.

Now, with his team, he was returning for the first time to France. The small stadium at Rouen was, of course, sold out. It normally held fewer than 20,000 people, and although 10,000 extra wooden seats had been added, hordes had to be turned away. A makeshift press box had been constructed for the dozens of sportswriters and radio and television reporters. They came from as far away as Oslo in the north and Rome in the south. Suddenly this sleepy city on the Seine had become the sporting capital of the entire continent. Dozens of commentators speaking every language in Europe appeared, all concentrating on that afternoon of football.

So wherever you happened to be that day you heard their rapid-fire commentary—across the street, from the *café* on the corner, from every open window and every open door.

In France and Germany middle-aged men stared at television screens, dreaming dreams of their youth. Young men and boys saw themselves on other fields for other teams: Rotweiss

of Essen, Real of Madrid, Benficia of Lisbon. No other single event in the history of sport had ever before united so many millions in so many disparate lands.

Yet who could forget one salient fact? Certainly nobody present at the game, no one watching in France, was unaware that the father of young Jean-Paul Varin had been murdered by the Feldwebel von Kleinschrodt in a small Normandy village twenty years ago. Everyone knew that as a boy of seven or eight he had witnessed the killing of his father. There it was. There it remained in the hearts and minds of French men and women. Try as they would, and many honestly did try, they could not expunge the bitter memories of that June day. The story of the shooting had been brought out in the trial. It had burned into them all. You might try to thrust it aside, you might say it was ancient history, an incident of two decades ago, best forgotten. You might make an effort to ignore it.

The fact, however, was that the greatest goalkeeper in the history of German football was the hated symbol of French defeat. He was the Butcher of Nogent-Plage.

2

The German team arrived several days prior to the game and put up at a small hotel on the Seine nearly six miles from Rouen. Each morning before practice they went for a five-mile walk across country.

"Stamina, that's what football is all about," the baron said to them. "The team that is the freshest in the last five minutes usually wins. We took the league because we outlasted better teams. Look at me. I'm over forty, but I believe I could outlast some of you young chaps because I've still got my legs. You fellows with your Porsches and Karmann Ghias will lose the use of your legs someday."

They realized he was right. Had they not seen him run in a practice match when occa-

---

2. **animator,** promoter.

sionally he came forward on the field to coach the offense?

The afternoon before the day of the game he took each man out alone for a stroll in the countryside, discussing the tactics to be used, the makeup of the French team, how they should handle their adversaries, and especially what to do about Varin.

"We should allow Varin and the French to do the running. Let them play their game and hold them. Nothing is more discouraging than to play your best and not score. Then every few minutes you boys turn it on. When the opportunity arises, go. You can score goals, Sepp. Turn it on, suddenly, unexpectedly. These boys are dangerous here in Rouen before their own crowd, but they can be beaten."

Never did he mention his notoriety as the Butcher of Nogent-Plage, which would make the match so bitterly fought. He did not need to. His teammates were as aware of it as he was.

Early that evening, before dinner, a press conference was arranged in the dining room of the hotel. Television cameras pointed directly at the baron. On a table before him a dozen microphones had been placed to pick up his words. The journalists and commentators kept after him from every corner of the room, talking in four or five languages, some needling, others more understanding and less insistent. He replied evenly to each man, pausing a few seconds to think before responding, never permitting himself to be ruffled by the most hostile remarks. Even when a blond Dane asked whether he was pleased to be back in France again.

Those queries he did not care to answer he turned aside tactfully, discussing only matters pertinent to the game. His adroitness at handling this rather unfriendly group of newsmen made you appreciate his qualities. You could understand why he had been chosen to assume responsibility and lead his team into action. How, he was asked, would Germany defend against the marvelous French offense, which nobody to date had stopped?

He thought a moment and then replied slowly, "France is a nation of individualists. You would expect the French players to be a great team, of course they are. To win in their league they had to be. I saw them play last year at Dusseldorf—they are magnificent attackers, finely trained, skillful, never letting up. But, nevertheless, though they are a team of champions, they are also and primarily a team of individualists. By that I mean they sometimes ask a man to do it on his own. Now our tactics are somewhat different."

As he spoke, the room grew unnaturally quiet. Here was a football captain talking frankly, freely, and yet modestly about his opponents and the tactics he would use against them the following afternoon. His cool confidence was contagious. Reporters bent forward to catch every word. All present knew of whom he was thinking: Jean-Paul Varin, the greatest centre forward ever produced in France.

Then a small dark Italian spoke. His German was excellent, his tone unpleasant. "Do you fear Varin?"

A collective sigh, a sort of "aaahhh" rose. One reporter stopped midway in the act of lighting a cigarette. Another, who had stood up to rush away and file copy to meet an early deadline, quietly sat down again.

Surely this was too much. This was pushing him too far. This was unfair. The tall figure behind the table did not stir. But watching closely, you could see his right hand tighten around the stem of a microphone.

The newsmen waited for his answer. Would he explode in anger? Would he suggest that he had been tried, convicted, and imprisoned by the French for a crime he had not committed. Or would he ignore the question entirely?

For endless seconds he stood motionless. Then his mouth opened and in flawless Italian he replied. "We Germans greatly respect the French team and all their players. We do not fear anyone."

3

The football played abroad is a sport in which there is less violence than the football played in the United States. Names are taken by the referee, players are cautioned, but only occasionally is a man sent off the field for deliberate roughness. Since there is no substitution in European football, the loss of a player is a severe penalty because then a team must play with only ten men against eleven. To lose a goalkeeper or an important forward can be disastrous.

But if there is usually no great amount of violence on the field in games between top-class teams, violence persists in the stands. In Spain and Italy especially, the fans go crazy, and football riots are front-page news everywhere.

Recently a French sporting newspaper published an advertisement which read: "Monsieur Collet, the referee of the football match last Sunday between the Racing Club de Calais and the Stade Roubaisienne, wishes to thank the members of the Calais team for saving his life after the match." A joke? No, it happened. Football abroad is a serious affair. Many teams keep a car under the stadium during their games. The engine is running and a chauffeur sits at the wheel to rush the referee to safety if the home team loses.

Sometimes riots get out of hand. Fixtures in the stands are uprooted, rocks, bricks, and even seats have been torn loose and hurled onto the field. Players have been shot at during a contest. In the coalfields of Yorkshire in the North of England, they throw what is called a Barnsley snowball. This is a lump of coal covered with snow and hurled at an offending referee.

The day of the game at Rouen, a great broad river of people flowed through the turnstiles of the stadium. Young people, old people, poor people, rich people, people of all kinds and classes. Men in expensive Alpine hats, men in cloth caps and work clothes. Thousands of women and girls were there, for the game had breached the sex barrier be-

cause of the attraction of the young football genius on the French side. Speculators were getting fifty dollars a ticket outside, and selling all they could obtain.

Many Germans carried huge banners of greeting from across the Rhine. *München Grüsst Frankreich. Berlin Grüsst Frankreich. Bremen Grüsst Frankreich.*[1]

Then outside the stadium came an explosion. A car had caught fire. Two men leaped from it and were lost in the crowd. Successive blasts rocked the car as one bunch of firecrackers after another went off. The fire was put out by the Rouen Fire Department—luckily on hand and waiting—and policemen, who then searched the parked vehicles. Many were filled with fireworks and other explosives, guns, even small cannon to celebrate the victory or perhaps menace the winners. These cars were seized and put under guard.

Inside, the chanting, cheering, and sometimes jeering crowd roared at everything. Hawkers passed through the stands selling programs, beer, and souvenirs, from T-shirts to ties and blazers with France or Germany embroidered on the pockets. At last the German team trotted single file onto the field. Thousands of horns blew triumphantly, thousands of Germans waved red-black-and-gold banners with drill-hall precision, left-right, left-right, left-right, all in unison.

"Hoi, hoi, hoi," they shouted. This was their team, the one that had shut out Torpedo Moscow for the first time. The noise from the stands beat down on the field like heavy surf pounding on sand or shale.

The Germans wore blue shorts and white jerseys. Then the French appeared in dark red jerseys and white shorts. Immediately thousands of tricolored flags sprang up on the opposite side, fluttering in a kind of irreverent pattern of color in the afternoon sunshine. All over the stands strangers addressed each other.

"There! That's Jules Garnier, Number four."

"That's Bonnet . . . ."

---

1. Munich (Berlin, Bremen) greets France.

"That's Laffont, six. With the bandage around his left knee. He was hurt against Lille, you know. They said he might not play."

"Which is Varin?"

"Varin! You've never seen Varin! He's Number two. That's him, the tall boy who looks like an angel."

"Ah, so that's Varin. We only saw him once on television. We're from Marseille."

"We've come all the way from Bordeaux. Ah, there's Rudy now."

The referee, in blue shorts, high blue stockings and a blue jersey, appeared below. He was Rudolph Stampfli, a former fullback for Zurich and once a Swiss international who spoke four languages. He was known as the best referee in all Europe, firm, decisive, noted for his quick decisions, and possessing a vast knowledge of the game.

The two captains conferred with him, the tall baron twitching the brim of his gray cap, that lucky cap he had saved since before the war and wore only in an international match. Garnier, the captain of France and the massive outside right who had competed fifteen times for his country, shook the hands of the Munich goalkeeper.

On the sidelines the two teams waited. The tension built up and up. The players longed for the game to start. After the opening rush downfield they would forget everything—the crowds, the shouts, the whistles—everything save that round balloon at their feet.

It'll be all right, each man told himself. I'll be fine as soon as play begins.

4

But it did not start. The band played "The Watch on the Rhine," the German national anthem. Then the "Marseillaise." Still the game did not start. Time passed. Seconds were minutes, minutes seemed as long as a day. The athletes did what athletes the world over do in such circumstances. They leaped high in the air, squatted and squatted again. They kicked their feet out and up. They bent over, twisting

at the waist, to touch the ground on either side. Some walked around nervously, unable to stand still.

Nothing happened. From above, the French stands whistled and shouted. The delay was torture for everyone. The captains standing beside the stocky referee straightened up. But the ball stayed under the arm of Rudy Stampfli. The crowd all over now yelled for action.

"*Commencez!*"[1]

"*Anfangen!*"[2]

"Why don't they begin?"

"*Commencez! Commencez! COMMENCEZ!*"

It appeared that the jam at the entrance gates had been so great, the confusion in the stands so widespread, that many spectators had not yet found their seats and were blocking the aisles. Hence the kickoff was delayed. The wait seemed forever.

The referee looked at his watch. Six, seven minutes had passed. Eight. Nine. Ten.

His arm went up. He snapped his outpointed hand toward the small circle at midfield. The whole stadium roared as the teams rushed out, eager for action. One Frenchman crossed himself as he stood poised for action, not for victory, no, but to acquit himself well that day.

Suddenly the whistle sounded. The start proved that this was no match for weak hearts. France kicked off and pushed the ball gently to Bonnet, a wing, who kicked it far ahead to the right, a pass beautifully spotted. Varin set off at full speed as though the ball were already there. Sepp Obermeyer, Uncle Sepp, the German veteran who had been assigned to mark Varin, was caught flat-footed by that amazing and effortless burst of speed. You had to play against the boy to appreciate him.

Here it was, the very first minute of the game and the famous French attack built around their young star centre forward, around ball control, around pace and more pace was taking over.

---

1. **Commencez!**\kɔ•ma(n) 'sā\ Begin! (French).
2. **Anfangen!**\ˈan•fang•gĕn\ Begin! (German).

"VarIN . . . Var . . . IN . . . Var . . . IN . . . Var . . . IN . . . ."

The cheers rose, burst into an unearthly roar as the tall Number 2, taking the ball back on the pass, snaked his way through the German defense, stopped short, twisted, curled the ball around his feet, raced ahead, evading the defensive backs. A dart, a dash, a stop, a pivot, a turn, a twist, and he was nearing the goal.

"*Regardez!* Look at that! *Allez, Jean-Paul, Allez!*[3] *ALLEZ FRANCEFRANCEFRANCE* . . . ."

In millions of homes all over the nation millions of men and women were screaming the same refrain. "*Allez! Allez,* Jean-Paul . . . ."

The crowd on the French side of the stadium went wild. They were in a frenzy as that red-shirted Number 2 bore down on the goal.

The huge knot of photographers behind the left goalpost steadied themselves, feet wide apart, straining forward, cameras at their eyes. Before the goal the tall German veteran waited coolly. He tugged at his cap, watching the French boy pass the ball to a teammate and receive it back. The baron was wise and knowledgeable. Better than anyone he knew the importance of his slightest move. He had to guess and guess correctly. Waiting just long enough, he raced out, bent low, and scooped the ball away as the Frenchman slammed into him and went flying over his shoulder to land with a crash on the turf. The shock of their collision could be heard all over the field.

The German was older, more solid, more inured to blows of this sort. Besides, anticipating the shock he had braced for the boy's onrush. Yet even he staggered from the impact before he could rise, straighten out, and kick the ball far down the field. The French player who had tumbled as though shot from the sky lay unconscious upon the turf. The whistle blew loudly.

For a moment there was silence in the stadium, a silence more violent than the roaring that had preceded it. Then a screaming chant

---

3. **Allez!**\a 'lā\ Come on! Go! (French).

rose from the French side. What had been in the back of their minds all afternoon now came out in a torrent of sound. It wasn't that the French—both present in the stadium and elsewhere watching—lived in the past. But that the past lived in them.

"Le Boucher! Le Boucher! Le Boucher!"[4]

5

The French stood and chanted. Now a shrill, derogatory whistling could be heard, too, mixed with boos. A brick arched up from the crowd and landed on the field. Another entangled itself in the nets of the goal, then another and another. Immediately armed policemen with riot guns appeared. They fanned out, facing the stands and scanning them from the edge of the field. They were tough cops in boots and helmets, ready to toss out anyone who disturbed play.

No more bricks were hurled, but the chanting and whistling continued. "Le Boucher! Le Boucher!"

Nothing more fell onto the field, but the shouting and whistling continued.

Players frequently know nothing and hear nothing the moment play begins. Often the baron had to be told which opponents had scored a goal on him. But this time it was hard for him not to recognize the name they were calling him. Every Frenchman and Frenchwoman in the stadium or watching on TV was sure that the baron had injured Varin on purpose.

"*Ah, quel sale type, quel salot!*"[1]

But then, everyone agreed, what would you expect? Those Germans just have to win at any cost, at any cost.

The long legs of the boy stretched out on the ground stirred ever so slightly, the first sign of returning consciousness. The baron walked over to see how he was, but the French players who had formed a circle around Jean-Paul, refused to step aside for him. Now the boy sat up, his head in his hands. Yves Robin, the French trainer, and

Garnier bent over him, slopping water on his face. They helped him up and he walked a few steps, plainly dizzy. There was a cut on the right side of his forehead. Blood ran down his cheek.

The crowd noticed it immediately. "Aaaahhh . . ." they cried. But what would you expect from the Butcher of Nogent-Plage?

The trainer gave the boy something from a bottle to drink and wound a bandage around his head. Jean-Paul raised his hands in protest, but the trainer, paying no attention, taped the bandage securely.

The baron leaned against a goalpost. He had in his time survived many on-field collisions, but this one had shaken him up, too. His body ached. He bent over, panting, then straightened up. The French stands jeered. However, he went to Varin and patted his shoulder. Jean-Paul nodded. He was all right.

His fans shrieked for a penalty kick. Even the captain of the French team stood protesting. But the referee shook his head. Varin jogged up and down to cheers from the stands. Finally he indicated that he was ready.

The referee placed the ball near midfield, and the game got under way again. For a while the play was negative, nervous, and uncertain. Because of the injury to their star the French momentarily lost their poise. The Germans at once seized their chance. Quick, direct, with passes short and sure, their game well coordinated and neat, they broke dangerously into French territory. Schroeder, their centre forward, shook loose, and after a series of passes had a great opportunity to the left of the goal, and young Helmut Herberger, the punch of the German team, crossed over, reached the ball, and drove it with all the force of his instep toward the goalie. Bosquier, the Frenchman, made a magnificent save at point-blank range. The ball, however, spun from his grasp.

---

4. **Le Boucher!**\lə·bü 'shā\ The Butcher.

---

1. Oh, what a rotten guy!

Big Schwartz, following up, kicked it again. Again Bosquier saved, diving at the ball just in time. The French stands were ecstatic.

Two great teams, two superb goalies.

As play progressed, Varin slowly regained his top form, and as he did the French side came to life, now attacking without mercy, using long, articulated passes. So perfect was their position play that a teammate was invariably reaching the ball on those passes at the exact moment. Their surge downfield was a joy to watch.

Even the Germans were impressed. So were the sportscasters. High on top of the stands a wooden platform had been constructed over supporting uprights—a precarious perch for cameramen and commentators. The little Italian television man from Milan who had been so rough with the baron at the press conference was speaking what seemed a thousand words a minute into his microphone. As Varin, taking and passing the balloon, bore down on the German goal, he screamed, *Ah, il furia francese . . . ."*[2]

The French attack, especially that of Varin and the wingbacks, was built on speed and more speed and tinged with that Frenchiness of the French, containing all their national characteristics—dash, drive, cerebration. Whereas the Germans felt that ball control was vital at all times, the French took risks and brought them off. When the Germans obtained the balloon, they kept it until it could safely be passed to a teammate. Their passes were short, accurate. Yet, watching, one felt that there was power in their game, that they were a team that could explode at any time.

Of the two, France was seductive, artful; Germany stronger and more brutal. Never again did Obermeyer allow Varin to get loose. He kept continually at the heels of the French star, for he also was fast. And although France always seemed to be attacking, forever banging away at the German goal, the Germans' defense was so tight that after that first sortie it looked as if the home team was never going to score. The crowd watched, cheered, groaned as two national temperaments, two styles of play, unfolded below them. Millions all over Europe sat transfixed by their TV sets.

His youthful, dynamic energy fully regained, Varin dominated the field, perhaps even more noticeably because of the white bandage around his head, a kind of helmet of Navarre. If you don't learn football by the time you are ten years old, you never will. Jean-Paul Varin, the French centre forward, had learned it truly and well as a boy from the Père Clement, once an international competitor for France. He had learned it also by listening to and playing with the *Herr Oberst* or, as he called him, the Feldwebel Hans, now calmly awaiting his onslaught in the German goal.

6

Nobody can play truly inspired football in an empty arena. It was the roaring mass of the crowd that brought out the greatness of the teams and their stars. There were twenty-two players on the field, but the concentration of the stands was on two: the baron and Jean-Paul.

The struggle became a duel not between France and Germany, but between the veteran and the youngster. Often when the German had blocked a sudden thrust or caught a stinging kick, he would tease Varin by holding out the ball, then dodging a few steps, bouncing it a few times in the penalty box as he ran forward. Then would come a sly roll-out to a forward at one side or that great zooming kick, high, far back into French territory.

Thousands of local fans who had no tickets, but had come to the stadium hoping to pick up one at the last minute, stood patiently outside in the sunshine, willing merely to listen to the noise from within.

They could tell with exactitude whenever Jean-Paul was off and running by that surge of sound from the French stands, that rising roar: *"Allez*, Jean-Paul! *Allez! Allez! Allez!"*

---

2. Ah, the avenging Frenchman (Italian).

112

It would reach a frenzied pitch, a crescendo, as the boy neared the German goal, then subside into a vast, collective groan as the baron made another acrobatic catch, another desperate save, and the German stands cheered.

The two defenses were equally effective, but the French side had a diversity that their opponents lacked. They kept the home crowd up by the fluidity of their play. On the attack they pressed forward constantly, always assaulting the enemy goal. On the defense they contracted smoothly. The amazing accuracy of their passing was such that each man seemed to have eyes in the back of his head. They could send and receive a ground pass at full speed. Suddenly, without warning, would come that quick cross to a teammate, perhaps with his back to the German goal, who instantly whirled and shot.

But if the French were the more thrustful, tearing holes in the German defense at thirty yards out, still they could not score. That big panther in the goal, leaping from side to side, blocked everything.

He deftly deflected a stray shot over the crossbar, coolly punched another ball around the corner post, then dived to prevent a score on a low kick from Bonnet, the French winger. The Germans were technically superb. They were the epitome of controlled power. Yet over all was the baron, completely in command, vigilant, watching each man, calling crisply to his teammates as the play fluctuated up and down. He was the soul of the German side, the great tactician, the Rommel of football.

A truly magnificent player, even the French spectators agreed. But for him France would have scored and scored again as the forwards pressed the attack. In the sense that they were in German territory most of the time, the French were winning. They held the upper hand. But what good is it to dominate a game if you cannot score?

With a top-notch goalkeeper, even second-rate teams find it easy to defend—if, that is, they do nothing else. But the tactics of the Germans were by no means solely defensive. Strong, intelligent, they waited until the precise moment to strike—then struck hard. Their team had no offensive genius like Varin. But they had perfect ball control with short, accurate passes, unspectacular but impossible to intercept. It was football that demanded much of a man: patience, skill, and fitness. Especially fitness.

On the home team was that great centre forward of France, that boy with the white bandage around his head. Centre forward is one of the most important positions on a team. Rarely is it given to a youngster. But Jean-Paul Varin had an old football head on his young shoulders. He could move either way, pass with either foot. His control was so perfect that he was always able to do the unexpected: kick to the goal the instant an opportunity presented itself or pass to an unmarked teammate. Moreover, he had a peculiar trick of moving the ball up to an adversary, showing it to him, and then slipping away, almost magically, with the balloon still at his feet. There was an electric quality about his moves that communicated to his teammates and the crowd alike.

He was indeed *"guele d'ange,"* angel face, as the French called him.

There was a studied elegance, a kind of joy in his bearing on the field. Despite the injury he had suffered, he kept smiling. On the white bandage was a spreading reddish stain. He had a French fineness of feature that was seductive. Tall, frank, outrageously spoiled by nature, he was the boy that everyone wanted for a brother, that every woman would have liked for a husband or a son.

His character, too, made itself felt. You were attracted to him despite yourself. If you had never seen him play, you came to the field determined not to enthuse over Varin. In five minutes you were on your feet, shouting like everyone else: *"Allez,* Jean-Paul! *Allez! Allez!"*

Even the Germans applauded his skills, his moves on the field so marvelously thought out in advance.

"Ein fussballwunderkind,"[1] they said to each other.

"Ja, ja, ein fussballwunderkind . . . ja, ja . . . ."

The interchanging forward line of France, whirling, twisting, shifting, moving in a pattern to the exact spot on the field, kept passing the ball from one teammate to another. Sepp Obermeyer, who had been so completely fooled in the opening sequences of the game, now stuck to Varin unerringly.

As one German in the stands remarked to a friend, "Sepp stays with that Frenchman so closely he'll end up in their dressing room at half time."

Varin's function was to set up the goal, to create the opening for others as well as score himself. Sometimes he was the decoy forward, quite as important as the man with the ball. Then next time, with everyone expecting a pass, he would turn suddenly and strike himself. Often the Germans knew exactly what he was going to do—only they didn't know when.

On the field the referee blew his whistle for a German tripping and gave France a free kick from thirty yards out. His manner was firm and decisive. You could see he was a no-nonsense kind of referee.

The ball was beyond the penalty box. A wall of huge Germans stood before Garnier, the French captain, as he went back to kick. He tried hard to curve the ball around them and did so, but Borkowski, the big blond Silesian, knocked it away and the baron had no trouble reaching and holding it. That penalty could have been costly, he thought, as he rolled the balloon out to Otto Schoen, his winger at the left.

Play continued, chiefly about the German defensive zone. Suddenly the referee's whistle sounded again. It was half time. The game came to a halt. Neither side had scored. The players, shoulders hunched with fatigue and strain, bodies consumed by the fierce intensity of the struggle, slumped off to their dressing rooms.

The first forty-five minutes of the match had seemed to last forever. In another way, it seemed that only a few minutes ago they had all filed out onto the field, waiting for play to begin.

DISCUSSION FOR UNDERSTANDING

1. How did von Kleinschrodt come to be the goalie on the championship Bayern-Munich football team?

2. How does the European game of football differ from the American version?

3. What indications are there that the situation at the game between the champions of Germany and France is tense—before the game? during play?

4. What is the difference in playing style between the French and German teams?

 7

Not much was said in the German dressing room between the halves. What was there to say? The players were too weary to talk. They sat on the benches, heads bowed, panting, speechless. Only the baron moved from one to the other, praising a stop made, a pass executed, a kick here, a thrust there, warning someone about a single careless moment of play. The men listened to their captain. Otto Schoen was the man who spoke up. The veteran winger raised his head. He saw the lines in the goalkeeper's face, recognized the tremendous responsibility that was on him. Rising, he put his arms around the baron.

"Hans, if you keeping playing like this, we can beat that team."

Time to resume play. They clattered across the wooden floor of the dressing room, down the long concrete corridor, and onto the field. Their appearance brought the German stands up. An ecstatic display of red-gold-and-black flags greeted them.

---

1. A football wonder child, superstar.

The second half began. The French pressure, sharp, incisive, continued. The baron's goalkeeping was still amazing. He was a cross between an acrobat and an octopus. Unerringly he sized up each play coming toward him, guessed where the ball was going to go even before it was kicked. His arms, his big hands, his long fingers seemed to attract every shot to his grasp. Now a hard one was knocked over the crossbar, now a cannonball drive at his ankles was cleanly stopped and held. Often the kick was going away from him, but he reached and saved them all.

In that saturated bombardment of the German goal it looked so easy. But that was his trademark, making those stops look easy.

Why, you said to yourself, watching from the stands, I could have held that one. I could have stopped that kick, held that ball. You forgot, unless you knew the game, his experience and that knack of anticipating each play. Above all you ignored his amazing reflexes, which contributed so much to his skill and to keeping Germany even with France as the second half moved along without a score.

Equally steady on the high ones just under the crossbar, the short, quick stabs from in close, or those long, hard kicks beyond the penalty box, he contained them all. The ball would come at him out of a melee of arms, legs, and feet, so hard it stung his hands. But he held it. Gradually the sportswriters, the television commentators in the makeshift press box, their field glasses to their eyes, began to realize the German goalie was extracting the poison from the French attack.

Still the waves of attackers in red jerseys bore down on the baron. Each time he held them off, cleared the goal, saved Germany. Each time the dagger of France was blunted. Once Robert Laffont, the French inside left, made a superb thrust. From a mix-up in the penalty box he cleared a kick low, hard to the corner. The French stands went wild for it seemed a sure score. Somehow the baron got across, stopped the balloon with outstretched hands, an impossible stab. It got away from him and dribbled along the ground. Two French players were on the ball but he reached it first, quick as only the great player can be. Diving for it, he rolled over and over on the turf, the ball cradled in his stomach. Both sides cheered his great preventive football.

To make such a save is the mark of genius. A little while before the French were calling him a butcher. Now they applauded along with the exultant Germans. The French are like the rest of us. They wanted terribly to win that match. But, like the rest of us, they were not insensitive to talent when they saw it. What they were watching was football genius, and every French spectator knew it.

After a corner kick for France from which nothing resulted, Germany now moved to the attack alertly. France fell back, regrouped, ready, anxiously watching. For a moment the baron stood panting, weary, one arm outstretched against a goalpost. However, the swing of fortune was shortlived, the respite soon over. Following some infighting around the French goal, Varin stole the ball and was off, moving with those long, effortless strides across midfield and into enemy territory.

There it was, that quick, accurate flick to Bonnet, the burst of speed into open country ahead for the return. The young centre forward took a cross back, and the moment he stopped the ball made a sudden, unexpected flip to Carpentier, the inside right, just behind him. Again that roar rose: "France . . . France . . . France . . . ." Once more they threatened.

Carpentier charged in. Before the goal, Borkowski of Germany, one of the stoppers of the Munich defense, a great oak of a man, made a slashing slide tackle which jarred the ball loose. But in the full momentum of his drive the Frenchman was a truck with the brakes gone. What happened was partly, perhaps, resentment over the blow to Varin, but mostly explosive exasperation at the so-near-and-yet-so-far game that France had played all afternoon. Carpentier leaped into the air and collided with the baron.

When the French go in they go in hard. Away flew the gray cap the baron wore. He fell to the ground as the referee raced over, blowing his whistle and pointing to Carpentier.

First a hush. Then a half moan swept the German stands as they stared at their man stretched out on the ground. Without that goalie Germany would be helpless. Everyone knew it.

Each spectator seemed to have felt the shock of that collision. Along the German side of the stadium they watched anxiously. The unvoiced thought hung in the air: if he is finished, we're finished. We're through if the baron has to leave the game. Every eye focused upon the knot of men around the figure at the goal line. The baron writhed on the turf as the trainer bent over him. He twisted and turned. His knees came up slowly. You could see the agony on his face.

The men watched him solicitously. After a while they helped him up. He leaned over, straightened his body, staggered a little, shaken from his second blow of the afternoon. Cheers came from all over the stadium. He walked around unaided. The whole crowd burst into applause.

Once or twice he half stumbled as he took his place, jogging back and forth along the goal line. Then he washed his neck and face with cold water, toweled himself, picked up his cap, and went back into the goal. The German banners waved triumphantly.

This time the ball went to the far end with Germany getting a free kick. Otto Schoen stood ready. A free kick from close up is dangerous for the defense. Will it be a soft, lofted ball or a hard, swift kick? He kicked. The ball just cleared the crossbar above the goal. No score. A tremendous roar of joy exploded from French throats, an enormous groan from the German spectators.

Aching all over, holding on to one goalpost, the baron watched a play developing at the far end. He saw no crowd, heard nothing, felt nothing but the danger ahead. Every instant

his eyes under the old gray cap were fixed on that white balloon moving toward him in a kind of inexorable pattern.

France was coming on the attack with Varin upon the ball. For a second he lost it in a welter of legs and feet at midfield. Then once again that graceful, moving athlete came up with the ball.

"Look out, Sepp! Watch that winger, Horst! Watch him! Watch him, WATCH HIM . . . ."

Now it's over to Varin . . . to Bonnet . . . stop him, Fritz, stop him . . . back to Varin . . . a cross to Garnier almost intercepted . . . no! Back to Varin, who is breaking through . . . .

The kick was low, hard, into the far corner of the goal. The baron jumped for it with all his great strength, his body parallel to the ground, touched the ball, missed it, and lay prone on the turf.

Pandemonium! Horns. Cheers. Red-white-and-blue flags aflame in the sunshine. Cheers. Shouts. Yells. France! France! France!

Jean-Paul turned and raced away, both arms high in the air. Skip-skip, leap-leap. He somersaulted on the grass in joy; as he came back he was surrounded by several teammates who hugged and kissed him. Others rushed up to embrace him. It was all his. After the shots missed, the kicks blocked, after those endless and hopeless assaults it was his own, his first goal in his first international match for France.

Can happiness be greater?

All the while the big German goalie lay flat on his stomach, pounding the turf in anguish with his bruised fists and knuckles. Helmut Herberger, the winger, young in years yet somehow old with insight and understanding, recognized the agony inside his captain. He raced over, knelt beside him, bent over and caressed the man's shoulders.

Finally the baron rose. The whistle of the referee sounded. Germany kicked off, a little push to the right. The game was practically over now, for only three minutes remained. The stadium was a cockpit of noise, nerves, passion. The thousands in the stands lived and died a hundred deaths. The delirious French shouted and screamed with joy. They even joined in as the baron coolly repulsed another thrust.

"Ah, let's admit it. He is a *brave type*, strong, stubborn. *Un maître*, a master. *Un vrai*[1] champion."

But up in the press box the old hands all said, "Watch out, France. The game isn't finished. Be careful. Any team that scores first and camps on a one-goal lead may find itself in trouble if it merely tries to defend."

8

France! France! France! France! A great, lusty, full-throated roar. The French felt victory ahead. It was over, done, almost through. Triumph was there for the taking.

Jules Garnier, the captain and winger, and every man on the French team knew, however, that the Germans were still dangerous. Perhaps they knew it even better than those experts shaking their heads from side to side in the press box. Because they had lived through many games won and lost in the final minutes. They had often felt the inconsequence of fate dealing them an unexpected blow or turning disaster into sudden victory.

Keep moving! Keep up the pressure, they urged each other. Whatever happens, don't let down now.

The soccer player needs the stamina of the long-distance runner, the reflexes of a boxer, and the concentration of a golfer. But it wasn't so easy after ninety minutes of attacking football. France had been setting the pace; now legs ached, feet were leaden. To run required an effort of will, to race down the field was torture. Every French forward had lost a little drive, a tiny part of his reflexes. But they did not give in or let up. Those red jerseys still pressed forward around the German goal.

As ever, the baron controlled the ball with that fluid beauty which was his alone. He seemed to wait until the last possible second before flinging his big frame at the white sphere. But he needed every inch of his height and every ounce of his power to reach those kicks, those punches from the feet and heads of the French forwards. Now it was a shot diverted to one side, now a ball that ricocheted off his chest. The French gave him no respite. They realized to a man that another goal would put the game on ice. Yet they could not hammer through.

The contest was a football match no longer. It was war. It was nation against nation. It was those two eternal rivals, France and Germany. It was life and death in the afternoon. Play grew rougher as the seconds passed. Rough tactics begot rough tactics. Only one thing counted—victory before the final whistle blew.

"France! France! France!" chanted the French spectators in unison. Only a minute and a half to go now. The Germans, backs against the wall, still fought stubbornly and savagely. They could not match the consummate artistry of Jean-Paul Varin. They simply had no forward in his class. But they were still a team and team play counts. They remained solid players, unshaken by misfortune, refusing to accept defeat until the whistle blew.

A slow ball, a bobbler from thirty feet out, came bouncing irregularly toward the baron. He knew how often a mistimed shot can catch a goalie off balance. Carefully and deliberately he went down on one knee, watched the French forwards rushing toward him, then rose, stepped calmly aside, and booted the ball high in the air and far downfield.

There was a mix-up before the French goal. Bosquier cleared the ball, but it rolled over the line and Germany received a corner kick. Nobody scores anymore on corner kicks, and the French defense loomed high and powerful.

Schroeder's kick went up, came down. As it did, Otto Schoen, the German winger, crashed in like an American tackle blocking a punt. Short, square, Otto was the retriever, the uninspired but ever dependable man of the German team. He threw his compact frame into that wall of French defenders, squeezed through, and headed the ball at the goal.

---

1. **vrai**\vrā\ true.

117

A French back headed it away. A German headed it back in. A Frenchman leaped up, a German hit it with his forehead. Ping . . . ping . . . ping . . . ping . . . the ball never touched the ground.

Then Borkowski, the halfback, tall and powerful, leaped high in the air above everyone and caught it squarely on his blond, flat head. But the shot struck the crossbar, bounced back, bobbled dangerously along the ground before the goal. Three men were on it, but Sepp Obermeyer, following it up like a cat, was first. With one quick blow of his foot he hammered it home. The score was tied.

Pandemonium shook the German stands, a kind of collective madness. Thousands of red-black-and-gold flags gyrated in the sunshine. Thousands of Bavarian hunting horns echoed in the air. Thousands of voices roared out his name.

"Sepp . . . Sepp . . . Sepp . . . ."

Yes, and Otto, too, who started it, the man you never noticed on the field, the player you always took for granted, Otto, steady, unspectacular, always taking the weight off his teammates by his tackles and pass interceptions. Sepp had scored the goal, but it had been invented by Otto.

Sepp. Otto. The Germans in the stands cheered them, jumped up and down in jubilation, and their teammates embraced the two men.

The French stood silent. Less than a minute left in the final half. Now for the first time France felt the pressure. Big Garnier leaned over in exhaustion, utterly spent, shaking his head in agonized disappointment. Even young Varin felt like a coasting car, moving without the motor running. He was still dangerous, but worn down by his efforts all afternoon.

Here the soundness of the baron's tactics told. Now Germany, elated at having tied the score, began to control play with an insolent competence. The halfbacks, the bombers, sure-footed and disciplined, rolled into action, their passes accurate, their position play perfect, despite the chewed-up turf. Now the Germans were the ones who seemed to have eyes in the back of their heads, often sending the ball to a spot they could not see, knowing a teammate would be there at the exact moment to receive it.

The unbearable tension increased. The stands were in an absolute frenzy. Each second was charged with electricity. The game was a fraction of a minute from the end.

It all began so innocuously, so innocently. Horst Heppner came downfield with the ball and threaded a pass to Schwartz. Speed told, for the entire French defense was caught on the hop. A tiny mistake, a failure of anticipation or lack of concentration due to over-fatigue, a defender two feet behind instead of two feet ahead, and Germany was off.

Schwartz made a short, crisp pass to Heppner and received the ball back. Then, with the ball at his feet, he raced in a wide arc around two weary defenders. His speed was dazzling. Now he was in open territory and within twenty-five yards of the French net.

He sighted the goal and let go with his left foot. The ball was moving away from Bosquier, who made a desperate stab, rolling over and over on the ground as it shot past him.

An instant later the whistle blew. The game was over. Germany had won.

9

Down on the field one man stood out for everyone to see.

Big Jules Garnier, the French captain, never shaved before an important match. Now his face was black with beard. Sweat poured from his forehead. His red jersey was filthy and torn. Panting, exhausted, he rushed up to Rudy Stampfli, still immaculate in his blue shorts, pointing at Heppner and arguing with what breath he had left.

The French stands, silent, horror-struck after that unexpected goal, understood immediately. Suddenly everyone took up the refrain. *"Faute! Faute! FAUTE!"*[1]

---

1. **Faute!**\fōt\ Foul!

Obviously Garnier was claiming offside on the last play. The Frenchman towered over the stocky little Swiss. Two, three, four French players, all equally positive and vehement, surrounded the referee as he stood with the ball under one arm.

There he remained, listening impassively, holding his ground, feet apart. Finally he moved away, shaking his head firmly. Then someone caught his free arm and spun him around. He was face to face with Bosquier, the goalkeeper, a hot-headed Marseillais.

"*Nein . . . nein . . . nein . . . .*" Even from the press box you could see Rudy Stampfli's expression and the set of his jaw.

"*NEIN!*" There it was. The goal was good. No, there was no German offside on the play. The score stands. The game is over, done, lost, and won.

By this time French troops had swarmed all over the field and were encircling the German players to protect them from an ugly, menacing crowd that had poured down from the stands.

The enraged French fans, milling around on the turf shouted at the Germans and the referee. Good sense, fair play were not at the moment in them. To a man they honestly believed that France had been cheated.

Look, they cried to one another, what can you expect? Rudy is from Zurich. I don't trust the German-Swiss. Had he been from Geneva, from the Suisse Romande, things would have been different. You know, everyone claims he was a friend of the baron's family, that he knew the von Kleinschrodts before the war. Besides he often played against him. It's unfair. The referee should have been Dutch or English or Spanish or Portuguese or even a Macaroni.

Why anyone could see that German halfback was plainly offside on that pass. Otherwise Jules would have caught him and cut him down. France was robbed by that second goal.

Still Stampfli shook his head, pushing away the French players. Still the angry fans howled at the Germans and hurled imprecations at the referee. Soldiers formed a tight ring around Stampfli and the victorious team and forced a passage through the mob. So into a tunnel under the stands they went, past the back of the stadium where in improvised cubbyholes sportswriters were dictating copy to Berlin, Madrid, or Rome.

"*Ne coupez pas, mademoiselle, ne coupez pas!*"[2] screamed an agonized voice.

"*Und dann . . . Varin . . . nein, nein. Varin . . . V-A-R-I-N.*"

"Final score: Germany two, France one. Yes, that's the final. Germany scored in the last second of the game."

The hot, sweaty, exhausted players and the Swiss referee, as emotionally drained as any of them, rushed by these reporters hard at work and were hustled over to a German bus that was standing and waiting, its engine running, a driver at the wheel.

Beside the bus was a row of police cars and army jeeps. Helmeted soldiers sat in each jeep, cradling tommy guns on their knees. The players' clothes, bags, and personal belongings had already been loaded, and one by one with Stampfli they filed aboard and sank into a seat. Soon the bus filled up. Behind it was a smaller vehicle, a Volkswagen minibus. Into it piled five players who could not get into the larger bus: the baron, Otto Schoen, Sepp Obermeyer, Helmut Herberger, and young Schroeder, the centre forward.

The troops formed a cordon around the two buses, letting nobody near. In three minutes they were off. All traffic was held up to let them get away. The buses swung out with their armed escort ahead and behind, crossed the Seine, and went down a long, straight avenue lined with poplar trees. For twenty minutes they rolled along at a good speed, the jeeps leading the way with honking horns, the police cars following. About fifteen miles from the city and well out into the countryside, they turned into a long driveway leading to a large

---

2. **Ne coupez pas!**\nə·kū·pā ᵃpa\ Don't cut me off!

hotel. Everybody climbed out. Clothes and bags were unloaded, and they all filed into the hotel where the manager passed out keys to rooms with baths on the upper floors.

An hour later they piled back into the buses and the caravan set out again. They had been told to avoid the main roads and take the coastal highway to the frontier. So they rode for an hour through the radiant spring countryside, and when they reached the sea the jeeps and police car honked several times, pulled over, turned around, and left.

Now the two buses went on alone, headed for Munich and its streets packed with thousands upon thousands of celebrating football fans.

❦ 10

The point of playing a game is to win. To fight hard, to play fairly, but to win. Otherwise, what on earth is the use? Defeat kills a great athlete. Defeat is numbing. It silences a dressing room after a game, renders everyone speechless. Defeat is humbling, obscene.

But victory is sweet. When you also play well in a game it is sweeter. Every man in that minibus from young Helmut Herberger to the veteran Otto Schoen had played a part in the triumph. Each one was elated. Each one had given his best. Had they not beaten a better team, stopped young Varin and held him to a single goal?

Inter of Milan couldn't do that! Nor Real of Madrid, either!

How quickly, when one wins, the aches and pains, the bone weariness, the bruises, and the hurts are forgotten. They sat there, not singing and cheering as their teammates were doing ahead in the larger bus, which was now almost lost on the horizon, but suffused in happiness. Each man savored the moments, remembering that pass, that stop, that last final team rush downfield. Yes, they were a team; they had played as a team, won as a team. As they had done all year in Germany against the rest of the league, as they had done against Torpedo Dynamo of Moscow and Chelsea Bridge of London. The world was warm. The world always is when you want badly to win and finally do.

They rode in silence: dependable Otto, Sepp Obermeyer, with a bruise across his forehead, Helmut Herberger, Schroeder, the centre forward, his blond hair standing straight up after the shower he had taken in the hotel, and the baron, exhausted, slumped in his seat. They were happy, relaxed, anxious only to get out of France and reach home. The straight road led along the coast as far as they could see, winding up and along the dunes and cliffs and headlands in the distance. The larger bus by this time was so far ahead it had vanished. They were alone.

Soon they passed concrete blockhouses that once, long ago, had been part of Rommel's famous Atlantic wall. Some were now tilted upward at weird angles, their guns pointing harmlessly at the sky. Others were mounds of rubble. Still others were untouched, remaining exactly as they were when their garrisons filed out with hands behind heads in surrender twenty years before.

The players watched them slip past uneasily. This was a defeat they preferred to ignore.

They went up a hill. The sea was smooth and calm in the evening light of June. Then the minibus rolled into a village of one street, the children parting in the road to watch it go by. All at once the bus slowed, groaned, stopped dead.

The driver shook his head in exasperation. "Ah, that darn magneto again."

He opened the door, got down, and raised the hood in the rear. Immediately a crowd of youngsters gathered to watch. Behind the driver the players rose, stretched, and filed slowly into the street. The last man out was the baron. You could tell how stiff and sore he was by the careful way he left the bus, how he held the door handle as he descended.

Ernst, the driver, was now underneath the vehicle, and Sepp, who knew engines, was leaning down and talking to him. Just ahead, beside a low seawall, was a monument. The baron walked over and looked at it.

Nothing ornate, nothing overdone, the monument was neither elaborate nor expensive. It consisted of a slab of roughly hewn granite topped by a granite arm and fist rising into space. High above the water, it must have been visible far out at sea. Silhouetted against the sky, the stone fist held a sword broken just above the hilt.

On the slab was a metal plaque. Twenty years of moisture-laden fogs had weathered it so badly that it was barely legible. The baron bent down. With difficulty he made out names of those who had been his enemies, his friends.

Mort pour la France
June 5, 1944

Georges Varin, *Instituteur*
Le Père Clement, *Prêtre*
Charles Lavigne, *Gérant*
Louis Marquet, *Agriculteur*
Marcel Deschamps, *Pécheur*
René Le Gallec, *quinze ans, Étudiant*[1]

My God, thought the baron, this is Nogent Plage! We're on the Grande Rue and it is the fifth of June!

11

Young Schroeder and Herberger joined him before the monument, leaning over to read the lettering on the plaque. What could it possibly mean to these boys? the baron wondered. They were but a few years old when it all happened, twenty years ago to the day.

The children of the village, openly curious, surrounded the strangers from the stranded bus. Once again the baron reflected, as he had so often in the past, on how appealing were the French youngsters. The boys wore shorts and striped jerseys, the girls checked dresses and wide-brimmed straw hats.

Like everyone else in the home town of Jean-Paul Varin, these children had spent the afternoon watching the game. Therefore, the face of Otto Schoen, the crewcut of Sepp Obermeyer, above all the lined, handsome features of the baron were familiar to them.

One boy, bolder than the others, edged toward the big man and with up-turned face asked, "Are you Monsieur the Baron von Kleinschrodt?"

For a minute the man almost shook his head. Then looking down at the child, he realized the boy could have been the son of René Le Gallec, had René Le Gallec lived and played for France. The denial died away in his throat. At least he owed the truth to those six whose names were on the simple monument. So he nodded.

Elated, the boy shrieked, jumping up and down, "Laurent! Kiki! Jules! *Viens vite! Le Baron est à* Nogent-Plage."[1]

They came from nowhere, they scrambled up the cliff, they swarmed about him, thrusting bits of paper and grubby pencils at him. Others rushed from their houses to join the group. He stood there signing his name, hearing as he did that familiar half slap, half crunch of the waves on the pebbly beach below. It took him back to that distant June afternoon, that day which began in such calm and quiet and ended in such disaster for everyone concerned. Suddenly he felt a jab in his sore ribs. It was the more painful side, where he had fallen and perhaps injured himself. It hurt. He looked up angrily.

Before his face were the eyes of a madman. It was more than mere madness; there was ferocity in those eyes, a kind of animal savagery. The man had quite obviously not shaved for a week. His hair was long and matted. In his hands was a hunting rifle. It felt most uncomfortable against the baron's ribs.

The children immediately explained. "Ah, it's only Pierre. Crazy Pierre, Monsieur the Baron, don't take any notice of him."

---

1. The identifications are as follows: schoolmaster, priest, tavern keeper, farmer, fisherman, fifteen-year-old student.

---

1. Come quickly! The Baron is in Nogent-Beach.

"It's only Pierre Marquet. Don't worry . . . ."

"He was in prison camp five years. He's touched in the head . . . ."

So the demented son of old Louis Marquet stood there, holding a deadly weapon, and incredibly, as if the madman simply did not exist, the boys kept after the baron for his autograph. The baron was a famous football player, the same as Jean-Paul. They had heard their elders talk about him many times in connection with the killing of six hostages from the village during the war. But to the children, the hostages were merely names on a monument, whereas the baron was a living legend, someone everybody had watched that afternoon on TV, the incredible German goalkeeper.

Suddenly Crazy Pierre was joined by a biggish man, also with an insane look in his eyes. He, too, had a weapon, a tommy gun cradled in his arm.

The boys spoke up. "It's the Racleur. The fiddler. He was at Dachau[2] five years. He's mad, too."

Vaguely the baron remembered a village youth who had assaulted a German officer when he was picked up in a labor sweep at Verville. That was all. How strange he should remember.

A big, wild-faced woman joined the growing circle. Her straggly hair blew about in the wind. The baron had recognized her coming down the street. She carried a small pistol which once belonged to some German officer.

Her voice was grating, menacing. "So, you have returned! You have dared to come back!" She next addressed herself to what was now a sizable crowd of villagers, young and old, crying out that the *Herr Oberst* had pretended to be a friend and then butchered her only son, René. Her rapid French was much too fast for any of the Germans but the baron to follow. She was taking over and the crowd was with her, stirring uneasily at her words.

"Monsieur Le Boucher," she suddenly screamed. She motioned the baron ahead with her pistol. Crazy Pierre and the Racleur aped

her gesture with their weapons. He moved along with his teammates and the minibus driver beside him.

On both sides of the street the wooden shutters of second-story windows flew open with that whanging sound he recalled so well. Women leaned out to watch. *"Herr Oberst,"* they said, pointing at him. *"Herr Oberst."* They did not say it in a polite, pleasant fashion as they used to long ago. Now they mouthed the old familiar name in a brutal, savage way. The strange procession moved up the Grande Rue, followed by every child in town.

That house there was the home of the widow Dupont. She must be dead by now. She had a small white fox terrier, which stood outside yapping at everyone who passed. He never yapped at me; he knew I liked dogs. That's where the Bleu Marin used to be. I see they call it the Café des Mariniers now. The awning is yellow and the chairs outside are different. I always liked those old iron ones.

Schroeder, Herberger, Obermeyer, Schoen, and the driver looked at him. What's up? Where are they taking us? He had no idea, save that it was ridiculous. They must all be mad.

They paused before an unoccupied stone house. It was the Bloch villa.

Someone kicked roughly at the front door. It crashed open. They were all pushed inside by the insane French with their guns. The room on the right, he could dimly see, had been his headquarters. They were shoved down a flight of steps into the cellar, dark and dank, a dirty floor underfoot. This, he recalled, had been where those six hostages had huddled while he sat upstairs in the office so tormented and alone.

The five other Germans surrounded him, asking questions. What does it all mean? Who are these crazy people with guns? Did the end of the game upset them this much? Did

---

2. **Dachau**\ˆda·hkau\ a notorious Nazi concentration camp.

they take football that seriously? What's the matter with them? The baron's teammates knew, of course, that he was the so-called Butcher of Nogent-Plage. What they did not know was that this was Nogent-Plage. So what's going on, Herr Hans?

Footsteps echoed overhead. Then Madame Le Gallec's voice could be heard giving orders. She was obviously in command. But what was happening? The minutes seemed eternal. Just so, thought the baron, they must have seemed to those five Frenchmen and a boy in this same cellar twenty years before.

12

The little red Renault rolled along the back roads, following almost exactly the same course the two German buses had taken half an hour before. The packed crowd around the French dressing room had given Jean-Paul a tremendous ovation when he appeared, and the police had to wedge a path to his parked car. Now, out in the country, with his mother beside him, the bitterness of defeat still hung over his heart.

She knew how desperately he had wanted victory in that match and how badly he felt. So she said little at first. Then, as they spun along toward Nogent-Plage, as they drew farther and farther from the stadium, from the crowd and the noise and the scarred turf, above all from the black depression which had pervaded the dressing room, he began to answer briefly.

"Yes, to play well is satisfying. I did my best. But I was playing today for France. I was part of a team."

"The whole team played well. You deserved to win."

"Both teams played well; both deserved to win." There was a hardness, a bleakness about his voice. Unfortunately he was right. Both teams deserved to win and fate had not smiled upon France.

She tried to change the subject. "You know the thing that amazed me about him?" No need to explain to whom she referred. "He

seems so little changed. Prison and all the years since the war haven't greatly altered him. How did he look close up?"

"Like Gibraltar. Like the world's best goalie. Put him on our side, and we would have won by six to ten points. Not that Georges Bosquier isn't a good goalkeeper; he is, the best in France. But the baron today . . . well, I've never seen anything like it and nobody else has either."

She was silent for several miles. He was right; nobody had ever seen such a goalie in action before.

"You know, Jean-Paul, I've always felt all my life that there was something different about the Germans, even about the *Herr Oberst*, even before that day . . . . He . . . you see . . . they've been our enemies . . . ."

The young man shrugged his shoulders. "Oh, *Maman,* they are no different from ourselves. They want to win; they would always give anything to beat us. We too wanted to win; we gave everything to beat them and failed. As a boy I felt we would never do the things the Germans did to us during the war. Then came our colonial wars, in Vietnam and in Algeria. Oh, especially in Algeria. Tortures. Massacres. Cruelty. Dropping bombs on innocent villages. You see the point is that everyone loses control in a war. Sometimes in sport, too."

They were coming to the sea now, and it was calm in the June evening. Madame Varin started to protest. Surely this was going a bit far. She pointed out that the Algerian war was not the same as a World War.

"You must realize, Jean-Paul, Algeria was a *département*[1] of France. It had been so ever since 1830 . . . a long time, my boy."

He was tired, ravaged by defeat when victory had been so close he could taste it. Although he loved his mother and tried to be patient, he burst out. "Yes, of course I know. Did I not hear this repeated a hundred times in school, in books, in the newspapers! I know

---

1. **département,** province.

it all. I can say it by heart, like every French schoolboy. I learned about the army that landed at Sidi-Ferraud on June 14, 1830. About the Insurrection of 1871 and the creation of the new *département* of Algeria. I know it all. But what is the fact? The fact is that we invaded North Africa and colonized it. We subjugated the people . . . ."

"But Jean-Paul, surely Algeria is different. It had been French for over a hundred years. Even the Moslems were French citizens."

"Yes, they were French citizens, and they were allowed to serve in our armed forces and die for France. What other rights did they have? Algeria had been settled by French *colons*[2] for a hundred years . . . ."

"My boy, you forget the Marêchal Lyautey.[3] And how the Moslems prayed for him in their mosques during the war with the Riff and how they sobbed openly in the streets at his death. Ah, you are far too young to remember these things."

"*Maman, chère Maman,* I know about the *marêchal.* He built Morocco into a fruitful consumer for French products."

How stubborn he was, she thought, how exactly like his father with these strange ideas of Marxism and equality. "Jean-Paul, you forget that we poured money, French money, into North Africa, and lives too, thousands of them, some of our noblest and best, men who had the interests of the North Africans at heart."

"Spare me, *Maman,*" he said, fatigue in his voice. "True, we poured money into North Africa, but we took millions more from it. We . . . ."

His mother interrupted. "Look! What's that? Ahead, off to the right. It looks like a glow on the horizon. A fire, perhaps. Could it be in Nogent-Plage?"

He looked ahead. There was a slight glow in the distance over the cliffs. "Well, it could be. But most likely it is Varengeville. They're forever having fires there. We'll be able to tell when we get around the next headland."

He increased the little car's speed. They

zipped along the empty coastal road toward the glow in the distance. Soon it became larger. Yes, it could be Nogent-Plage.

13

The whole town was in the Grande Rue as he pulled up with his mother in the red Renault. They almost dragged him from behind the wheel, raised him to their shoulders, carried him up the street past the smoldering ruin of the Volkswagen minibus, twisted and charred.

"Var . . . IN! Var . . . IN! Var . . . IN!"

He's ours. Ours, you understand, ours from Nogent-Plage. Win or lose, the greatest centre forward in all Europe, the best France has ever produced. Born right here in this village, too.

"Var . . . IN! Var . . . IN! Var . . . IN!"

At first the noise and excitement and the faces of the crowd confused Jean-Paul. What was it? What was happening? There was a smell of smoke in the air. In agitated tones a half-dozen voices shouted the explanation.

"They burned the bus, Jean-Paul. The bus that was carrying the Fritz back to Germany. The Germans cheated this afternoon at Rouen. They cheated . . . ."

"Crazy Pierre started it . . . ."

"He has the Germans locked up in the cellar of the Bloch villa, Jean-Paul . . . ."

Now he began to understand. Something evil was happening. The evil could be seen in those faces. Immediately he forced his way down from their shoulders as they crowded about, yelling and cheering, echoing the same cry that had resounded over the Stade Rouennais that afternoon.

"Var . . . IN! Var . . . IN! Var . . . IN!"

"But attention! Listen to me! Those German players . . . ."

"Oh they're under lock and key in that cellar. And their baron, too. Ah, let me tell you

---

2. **colons,** colonists.
3. **Lyautey**\\'lyō ▲tā\\ French marshal who was resident general of Morocco 1912–1916, 1917–1925.

the Feldwebel Hans is locked up in the cellar for a change. *Et comment!* We have him. Let him fry with the others."

"Jean-Paul, Madame Le Gallec and Pierre are going to burn the place to the ground . . . ."

"But you can't do that!"

"We will. We are doing it already. We are burning that foul building where such harm was done in Nogent-Plage. And the baron shot your father, didn't he? Didn't he? He murdered six people from this town. Then this afternoon the Germans cheated; that's why they won. France was the better team. Everyone knew it, everyone could see it . . . ."

Jean-Paul shoved, pushed, worked his way out of the embraces, the back slapping, toward the Bloch villa. Crazy Pierre was carrying hay on a pitchfork, evidently to supplement the fire that he and Madame Le Gallec had started, that now was beginning to blaze up in earnest. The boy knew the madman was capable of anything.

He fought through the crowd and stood facing them on the steps of the villa. It was easy to see the fever in their eyes. This was a mob, led in whole or in part by Crazy Pierre, and the mob was momentarily insane. He raised his hand and shouted at the top of his lungs, "Listen to me! Listen to me!"

Behind him he heard the crackle of old paint. He could smell the ancient wainscoting burning.

"Friends, neighbors, we must stop this insanity. We cannot . . . ."

"Jean-Paul, he killed your father," a woman screamed. "He murdered six of us."

"He shot my boy, René," Madame Le Gallec cried. "He shot your father, too."

For a second Jean-Paul realized this sickness was the same malady which had swept the French stands in Rouen that afternoon. "Look, my friends. Today I was hurt. I was sore, bruised, inside and out . . . ." Hurry, hurry, he thought to himself, in a few minutes it will be too late. "I also felt bitter towards those Germans. But we cannot take human lives. What would my father say, I ask you? He was a humanist; he would have told us we cannot continue to cherish grudges. If we keep feeding on these hatreds handed down to us by our ancestors, our grandfathers and great grandfathers, where are we? Friends, what good are wars? Who ever won a war? Who ever profited from them in the end?"

Slowly the madness that hung over the mob seemed to diminish and even the anger in the faces lessened. He could feel the decent people on the far edges of the crowd asserting themselves. Why, Jean-Paul is right. We cannot murder these men. We must not let them die in the cellar.

"Friends! Marcel! Pierre! Yves, you knew my father. You, Madame Bonnet, you also knew him. Reflect! There were six French in that cellar twenty years ago. Now, in the same cellar, we have six Germans. Shall we do to them what they did to us? If so, how are we different from those who murdered my father? If we kill them, we are guilty of the same crime. Somehow, somewhere, we must break this evil chain and look on each other as human beings."

He seized the moment of their hesitation, turned abruptly, rushed at the door. Crazy Pierre barred the way. Jean-Paul gave him a body block, tore the rifle from his grasp, and threw it to the street. He rushed into the hallway. One thrust of his powerful right leg knocked a cellar door panel loose. There was sufficient space for the Germans to squeeze through.

"Quick! Quick, or the building will fall in on us all!"

"Here, Sepp, give me your hand."

Then he pulled Otto through and young Herberger, frightened and babbling something to him. Someone was beside him now, attacking the door with an axe. It cracked, splintered, burst apart. Another panting German stepped out and another. Last of all came the baron.

Through the smoke in the light of the blaze, the German recognized Varin and threw his arms around him.

"Jean-Paul, believe me! I did not give the order to fire. I did not kill your father."

He held the younger man tight. Varin in turn clasped him. He nodded. *"Oui, je sais, je sais,"* he said. I know. I know.

Once outside in the crisp sea air the Germans staggered about, limp and dazed, some trembling. But the dementia of the moment seemed to have passed. That evil atmosphere seemed to have vanished. Villagers were helping the German athletes and the minibus driver, supporting them, leading them away from the fire. A woman brought them water from a bucket.

Now, except for Crazy Pierre and the widow Le Gallec, who was still screaming about the Butcher of Nogent-Plage, everybody was quiet, chastened, frightened as they perceived how narrowly a tragedy had been averted. Inside the Bloch villa the flames hissed and roared, but hoses were now playing into the windows. The danger was past.

Jean-Paul and the baron had appeared on the steps with their arms around each other's shoulders. Now they stood across the street from the burning building, still with their arms around each other's shoulders. It was difficult to tell who was supporting whom.

Then quick, explicit, unmistakable came the sound of the shot. The baron's hand went up, clutching his temple. He spun around and tumbled to the pavement at Varin's feet.

"Ah . . ." a collective groan came from them all as Crazy Pierre raced down the Grande Rue, waving his rifle in the air.

There lay the man. Jean-Paul looked at the red puncture on his forehead from which the blood was pouring. He slipped down beside him weeping, beside the dead body of his enemy, his friend.

SOMEHOW, SOMEWHERE, WE MUST BREAK THIS EVIL CHAIN AND LOOK ON EACH OTHER AS HUMAN BEINGS!

So says Jean-Paul Varin as he stands on the steps of the burning villa and tries to reason with the townspeople who are intent on incinerating the six Germans in the cellar. His words, standing alone, express the moral of this story. The incidents have been carefully constructed to move toward this point. Great numbers of people have been thrown together in accidental encounters that have led to this moment. Their relationships have been colored, as the young man says, by hatreds handed down from grandfathers and great-grandfathers. Jean-Paul and Hans almost succeed in meeting on the basis of fellow human beings. But their relationship is frustrated by forces outside themselves: by barriers of nationality (even though Hans is half-French); by the assassination of the *Hauptmann* for which neither is responsible and the execution of the six hostages which neither can prevent. The continuing, inherited enmity that colors their relations is further illustrated by the football game. As the game nears its end, the players lose control of their feelings and seek brutal body contacts with their opponents. When the game ends, the French cannot accept the score as simply the whim of fate or the result of a supreme moment of endurance on the part of the rival athletes. Instead they insist that the Germans have cheated. So encounters throughout the book have shown evidence of inherited prejudices. Meeting people openly and frankly as fellow human beings is never quite possible . . . unless the chain can be broken. As a reader, could you accept these characters as people like yourself, or were your reactions colored by your inherited prejudices?

II

IMPLICATIONS

Consider the following quotations from the story. What do you think the story implies by the statement? How do you react from your own experiences?

1. "First, of course, comes one's country." (p. 87)

2. "Americans want to be liked. They are almost pathetic in this childish desire to be liked . . . . It is why they do not make good soldiers." (p. 89)

3. "Best of all is for a man to be respected. Respect is the basis for discipline—at home, in business, in the Army." (p. 89)

4. "He who witnesses a crime and does not protest, commits it himself." (p. 99)

5. "I cannot excuse myself by depositing my conscience with my superiors . . . . What everyone does is their concern. What I do is mine." (p. 100)

6. "When conscience and the state conflict, the conscience of a man must take precedence." (p. 104)

7. "You cannot have an Army which obeys some orders and doesn't obey others. We obey all orders . . . ." (p. 99)

8. "Nobody can play truly inspired football in an empty arena." (p. 112)

9. "You see the point is that everyone loses control in a war. Sometimes in sport, too." (p. 123)

10. "The point of playing a game is to win. To fight hard, to play fairly, but to win. Otherwise, what on earth is the use?" (p. 120)

11. "Victory is sweet. When you also play well in a game it is sweeter." (p. 120)

III
TECHNIQUES

Exposition

Throughout this unit you have examined the way writers provide necessary background information to a story. This is called *exposition*. In general, the more naturally and unobtrusively this is done, the greater the literary craftsmanship of the writer. In older literature, writers were inclined almost to say, "Dear Reader, here are a few things you ought to know." So casually is the exposition inserted into *His Enemy, His Friend* that it may surprise you to look back on the story and see how much space it actually occupies. The first real incident of the book is the shooting of the German officer.

1. What things did you have to be told as background to that incident?

2. In which chapter does the shooting take place?

3. Is there anything in the chapters preceding the assassination that is not exposition?

Conflict

The conflict of the story is summed up in the title: *His Enemy, His Friend*.

A.1. How does the title define the problem of the *Feldwebel*?

2. How does the title define Jean-Paul's problem?

B. In addition to the central conflicts involving the two major characters in the story, there are several minor ones involving other people.

1. What is the conflict the teacher faces?

2. What is the conflict troubling Hans' godfather?

3. What is the *Hauptmann's* problem?

Climax

Each of the main conflicts has its own resolution or climax.

1. Where does Hans resolve his conflict?

2. Where does Jean-Paul resolve his conflict?

IV
WORDS

A. Like other national groups, Germans have contributed to American English. As early as 1683, there were German settlements in Pennsylvania, and by the middle of the nineteenth century German communities had sprung up in such cities as Detroit, New York, Cleveland, and Milwaukee. To these Germans and their descendants American English is indebted, in one way or another, for the following words: *stein, kindergarten, rathskeller, ouch, pretzel, pinochle, liverwurst, sauerkraut, delicatessen, pumpernickel, poker,* and *frankfurter*. Can you think of others?

B. In *His Enemy, His Friend*, the highly trained shock troops are referred to as a *motorized flak unit*. The word *flak* is derived from *Fliegerabwehrkanone*, which is German for "aircraft defense cannon." A word formed, as *flak* was, by combining the first letter or letters from several longer words, is called an *acronym*. Other examples of acronyms are *radar* (radio detection and ranging), *gestapo* (*Geheime Staats Polizei*, meaning "secret state police"), *laser* (light amplification by stimulated emission of radiation), and *sonar* (sound navigation ranging). From what words is each of the following acronyms formed: *scuba, AWOL, jeep, posh, loran, NASA,* and *quasars*?

C. Using contextual clues as well as your word analysis skills, see whether you can figure out the meaning of the italicized word in the following sentences from *His Enemy, His Friend:*

1. "Above everything, accompanying all comings and goings, was noise . . . the *raucous* calls on the loudspeakers."

2. "Stores, shops, offices closed. Theaters emptied. Traffic *subsided.*"

3. "The soldiers marched in *cadence,* their boots striking the concrete with that harsh sound."

BIOGRAPHICAL NOTES

Jerrold Beim

Jerrold Beim (1910–1957) was an author of children's stories, essays, and short stories. When he was in the fourth grade, his teacher read aloud his story "The Life of a Christmas Seal" and then said, "Jerry, you ought to be a writer." He took her seriously. Unable to afford college, he worked in a bank and then as advertising manager for a department store while he wrote on the side. Later he quit advertising because he wanted to write full time. After a period of little success, he began selling his work. In 1935, he married and after selling a story to *Cosmopolitan* he and his wife spent the proceeds on a car and took off for Mexico, staying two years. During this time, he wrote *The Burro That Had a Name,* a story for children; this started him on his career in the children's field. Strangely enough, the boy who survived the Mexican crash was later killed in an auto accident in the United States.

James Street

James Street (1903–1954), Mississippi-born, was a reporter at age fifteen. At seventeen, he attended a seminary and served as a Baptist minister from 1923 to 1926 before returning to the newspaper field. In 1933, he moved to New York City and worked as a reporter for two New York papers. In 1937, he decided to try to earn his living by free-lance writing and produced novels, news and feature stories for newspapers, articles and short stories for magazines. He was a regular contributor to *Holiday* with his travel articles. Many of his novels concerned the South and its people. He died in Chapel Hill, North Carolina.

Prosper Mérimée

Prosper Mérimée (1803–1870) achieved renown as a French novelist, archaeologist, and essayist, but his full power and mind is best demonstrated in a score of tales which he wrote over a period of 40 years. They range in length from the 150 pages of *Colomba* to a mere 12 in *L'Enlèvement de la Redoute.* As a group they are considered to be "novellas" ("little novels"). *Carmen,* which probed the character of gypsies, was later used as the libretto for an opera by Bizet; *Mateo Falcone* explored the subject of Corsican honor; *La Venus d'Ille* and *Lokis* were built on some grisly superstitions. Many critics consider his novellas as the finest nineteenth-century examples of their kind.

Thomas Hardy

Thomas Hardy (1840–1928) had three careers in his lifetime. Born in Dorsetshire, England, he was educated at King's College, London. At sixteen he went to work for a church architect and even won a prize for one of his designs. When he was twenty-three, he began writing poems, though he continued his work as an architect for five more years. His next career was as a novelist. In general, he set these works in a section of England called Wessex and explored, through his characters' actions, the theme of the helplessness of man caught by fate. *Far from the Madding Crowd, The Return of the Native, The Mayor of Casterbridge, Tess of the D'Urbervilles* were highly successful novels that are still popular with readers today. *Jude, the Obscure,* published in 1896, was severely attacked by critics; the attacks so angered Hardy that he swore he would never write another novel. He turned then to poetry and achieved great recognition with his long poem, *The Dynasts,* an epic-drama chronicling England's struggle against Napoleon. He began to publish lyric poetry when he was seventy years old.

Rod McKuen

Rod McKuen (1933–   ), with the publishing of *Stanyan Street and Other Sorrows* (1966) and *Listen to the Warm* (1967), became the best-selling contemporary poet in the United States. Born in Oakland, California, he has worked as a laborer, movie star, stunt man, radio disc jockey, newspaper columnist, and as a psychological-warfare script writer during the Korean War.

More recently, he has moved on to writing poetry and stories, composing music for his poems and for the backgrounds of two movies (*The Prime of Miss Jean Brodie* and *Joanna*), and appearing as an entertainer. Interestingly, more than fifty million records of his compositions performed by artists other than himself have been sold.

Mari Evans

Mari Evans, a native of Toledo, Ohio, was a John Hay Whitney Fellow, 1965–66, and a consultant for the National Endowment of the Arts. Her poetry has been used extensively in textbooks and anthologies. Producer/Director of a weekly half-hour television series "The Black Experience," she is Writer-in-Residence and Assistant Professor in Black Literature at Indiana University, Bloomington. Her poetry volume *I Am A Black Woman* was published in 1970.

Ralph Pomeroy

Ralph Pomeroy (1926–   ), was educated at the Art Institute of Chicago, the University of Illinois, and at the University of Chicago. His varied career has included work as a magazine editor, art gallery director, stage manager, and bartender. His most recent collection of poems, *In the Financial District*, was published in 1968.

Sara Teasdale

Sara Teasdale (1884–1933) was a Missouri-born poet who was educated by tutors and in a private school. While still quite young, she toured Europe and the Near East and at one time was enthusiastically courted by the poet, Vachel Lindsay, whose overwhelming exuberance fascinated and frightened her. In 1914 she married Ernst Filsinger and moved to New York City. But she was essentially a lone spirit and the marriage ended in divorce. During her lifetime she published seven books of poetry, of which *Love Songs* (1917) won a special Pulitzer Prize. Her poetry, direct and almost barren of imagery and metaphor, strives to communicate a mood rather than to state universal truths. Her last years were spent in seclusion . . . almost friendless. She drowned in her bath in a New York apartment.

Shirley Jackson

Shirley Jackson (1919–1965), novelist and short story writer, graduated from Syracuse University in 1940. One of her short stories, "The Lottery," which appeared in *The New Yorker*, established her as the master of the Gothic horror tale. Her works center on two types of writing: the humorous, in which the delights and turmoils of ordinary home life are made hilarious, and the horror story, in which abnormal behavior is made perilously ordinary. *Raising Demons* (1957) and *Life Among the Savages* (1953) represent the first type, and *We Have Always Lived in the Castle* (1962) is an example of the second. She once said she wrote because "it's the only chance I get to sit down," and that writing "gives me an excuse not to clean out closets."

Pearl Buck

Pearl Buck (1892–   ) was born in Hillsboro, West Virginia, but spent most of her youth in Chen-chian, China, with her missionary parents. Her early education took place in Shanghai, but she was graduated from Randolph-Macon Woman's College in Lynchburg, Virginia, in 1914. She then returned to Nanking, China, as a teacher. Her first articles and stories about Chinese life appeared in 1923, but it was not until *The Good Earth* was published in 1931 that she became widely known. In 1938, she received the Nobel prize in literature. Since 1935, she has lived in the United States and has written many serious novels, her autobiography, and short stories, most of which have Oriental settings. She has also written popular magazine stories under the pseudonym of Sedgewich.

John Tunis

John Tunis (1889–   ) was born in Cambridge, Massachusetts, and graduated from Harvard University. He served in World War I in overseas service and later turned to sports writing for the *New York Evening Post*. His articles and stories have appeared in most popular American magazines in recent years, and he has authored nearly two dozen books for the teen-age reader, most of them with a sports-oriented theme. He is one of the most popular writers of this type of story in the country. Some of his works are: *Silence Over Dunkerque, Buddy and the Old Pro, The Kid Comes Back, Schoolboy Johnson, All-American,* and *Iron Duke*. He now lives in Connecticut.

The Parable
of the Prodigal Son

St. Luke 15:11–24

There was a man who had two sons; and the younger of them said to his father, "Father, give me the share of property that falls to me." And he divided his living between them. Not many days later, the younger son gathered all he had and took his journey into a far country, and there he squandered his property in loose living. And when he had spent everything, a great famine arose in that country, and he began to be in want. So he went and joined himself to one of the citizens of that country, who sent him into his fields to feed swine. And he would gladly have fed on the pods that the swine ate; and no one gave him anything. But when he came to himself he said, "How many of my father's hired servants have bread enough and to spare, but I perish here with hunger! I will arise and go to my father, and I will say to him, Father I have sinned against heaven and before you; I am no longer worthy to be called your son; treat me as one of your hired servants."

And he arose and came to his father. But while he was yet at a distance, his father saw him and had compassion, and ran and embraced him and kissed him. And the son said to him, "Father, I have sinned against heaven and before you; I am no longer worthy to be called your son." But the father said to his servants, "Bring quickly the best robe and put it on him; and put a ring on his hand, and shoes on his feet; and bring the fatted calf and make merry; for this my son was dead, and is alive again; he was lost, and is found." And they began to make merry.

Now his elder son was in the field; and as he came and drew near to the house, he heard music and dancing. And he called one of the servants and asked what this meant. And he said to him, "Your brother has come, and your father has killed the fatted calf, because he has received him safe and sound." But he was angry and refused to go in. His father came out and entreated him, but he answered his father, "Lo, these many years I have served you, and I never disobeyed your command, yet you never gave me a kid, that I might make merry with my friends. But when this one of yours came, who has devoured your living with harlots, you killed for him the fatted calf!" And he said to him, "Son, you are always with me, and all that is mine is yours. It was fitting to make merry and be glad, for this your brother was dead, and is alive; he was lost, and is found."

Return of the Prodigal Son, *Rembrandt, National Gallery of Art, Washington, D.C.*
Rembrandt made many remarkable etchings of Bible stories. Here
he suggests the crosscurrents present in this memorable moment of reunion.

Conflicts are a writer's raw material. Because the ties that hold a family together are those of need and those of love, conflicts are nowhere more dramatic than within the family circle. The parable of the Prodigal Son suggests that family problems have not changed much in their basic patterns over the last 2,000 years. The son's departure with his inheritance is typical of a young man's desire to leave his family and strike out on his own. Once out in the world and on his own, he squanders his money on riotous living. Finally, he turns homeward. There he is welcomed by his father with a lavish feast and an outpouring of love. Naturally, the reliable, hard-working older brother feels cheated and bitter.

Crosscurrents in family life is one of the oldest themes in literature. An ancient Egyptian tale relates the problems arising in a family from the presence of a mother-in-law. The *Ramayana* of India is an epic of family jealousy. Even such folk tales as "Cinderella," "Snow White," and "The Ugly Duckling" point up family conflicts. Similarly, all the stories that follow will explore this theme. You will see such conflicts leading to tragedy, as in D. H. Lawrence's "The Rocking-Horse Winner," and to happy and humorous outcomes, as in O. Henry's "Mammon and the Archer." Ray Bradbury's "The Veldt" uses the eerie techniques of science fiction to expose the age-old conflict between children and their parents.

In spite of the selfless love which should ideally guide the members of a family, each person grows up with his own personal desires, private sets of feelings and reactions, and individual goals. The conflicts that result when these individual desires, feelings, and goals collide are the writer's raw material in the following selections. Events that might seem trivial or harmless to a stranger may acquire, when passed through the magnifying glass of family relationships, the power to hurt deeply. But not all family crises are tragic ones, by any means. The exaggerated explosions that occur in families are matter as much for comedy as they are for grief.

Just what humor is, or why we are amused by certain things, has been the subject of much serious thought. One of the most inclusive explanations is that humor lies in the deviation from the expected or normal pattern of behavior. The mind expects one action and an unexpected action occurs. Such twists of the normal highlight the incongruous in life, the unsuitable, inappropriate, illogical.

In the stories that follow, you will have the opportunity to examine, from both the serious and the humorous viewpoint, situations that reflect the crosscurrents in life.

◆A tragic accident! . . . Family members
freeze in shock . . . crosscurrents springing
from need and guilt emerge.

The Stone Boy

GINA BERRIAULT

Arnold drew his overalls and raveling gray sweater over his naked body. In the other narrow bed his brother Eugene went on sleeping, undisturbed by the alarm clock's rusty ring. Arnold, watching his brother sleeping, felt a peculiar dismay; he was nine, six years younger than Eugie, and in their waking hours it was he who was subordinate. To dispel emphatically his uneasy advantage over his sleeping brother, he threw himself on the hump of Eugie's body.

"Get up! Get up!" he cried.

Arnold felt his brother twist away and saw the blankets lifted in a great wing, and, all in an instant, he was lying on his back under the covers with only his face showing, like a baby, and Eugie was sprawled on top of him.

"Whassa matter with you?" asked Eugie in sleepy anger, his face hanging close.

"Get up," Arnold repeated. "You said you'd pick peas with me."

Stupidly, Eugie gazed around the room as if to see if morning had come into it yet. Arnold began to laugh derisively, making soft snorting noises, and was thrown off the bed. He got up from the floor and went down the stairs, the laughter continuing, like hiccups, against his will. But when he opened the staircase door and entered the parlor, he hunched up his shoulders and was quiet because his parents slept in the bedroom downstairs.

THE STONE BOY by Gina Berriault. First published in *Mademoiselle*. Copyright 1957 by Gina Berriault. By permission of Toni Strassman, Agent.

Arnold lifted his .22-caliber rifle from the rack on the kitchen wall. It was an old lever-action Winchester that his father had given him because nobody else used it any more. On their way down to the garden he and Eugie would go by the lake, and if there were any ducks on it, he'd take a shot at them. Standing on the stool before the cupboard, he searched on the top shelf in the confusion of medicines and ointments for man and beast and found a small yellow box of .22 cartridges. Then he sat down on the stool and began to load his gun.

It was cold in the kitchen so early, but later in the day when his mother canned the peas, the heat from the wood stove would be almost unbearable. Yesterday she had finished preserving the huckleberries that the family had picked along the mountain, and before that she had canned all the cherries his father had brought from the warehouse in Corinth. Sometimes on these summer days Arnold would deliberately come out from the shade where he was playing and make himself as uncomfortable as his mother was in the kitchen by standing in the sun until the sweat ran down his body.

Eugie came clomping down the stairs and into the kitchen, his head drooping with sleepiness. From his perch on the stool Arnold watched Eugie slip on his green knit cap. Eugie didn't really need a cap; he hadn't had a haircut in a long time and his brown curls grew thick and matted, close around his ears and down his neck, tapering there to a small whorl. Eugie passed his left hand through his hair before he set his cap down with his right. The very way he slipped his cap on was an announcement of his status; almost everything he did was a reminder that he was eldest— first he, then Nora, then Arnold—and called attention to how tall he was (almost as tall as his father), how long his legs were, how small he was in the hips, and what a neat dip above his buttocks his thick-soled logger's boots gave him. Arnold never tired of watching Eugie offer silent praise unto himself. He wondered, as he sat enthralled, if when he got to be Eugie's age, he would still be undersized and his hair still straight.

Eugie eyed the gun. "Don't you know this ain't duck season?" he asked gruffly, as if he were the sheriff.

"No, I don't know," Arnold said with a snigger.

Eugie picked up the tin washtub for the peas, unbolted the door with his free hand, and kicked it open. Then, lifting the tub to his head, he went clomping down the back steps. Arnold followed, closing the door behind him.

The sky was faintly gray, almost white. The mountains behind the farm made the sun climb a long way to show itself. Several miles to the south, where the range opened up, hung an orange mist, but the valley in which the farm lay was still cold and colorless.

Eugie opened the gate to the yard, and the boys passed between the barn and the row of chicken houses, their feet stirring up the carpet of brown feathers dropped by the molting chickens. They paused before going down the slope to the lake. A fluky morning wind ran among the shocks of wheat that covered the slope. It sent a shimmer northward across the lake, gently moving the rushes that formed an island in the center. Killdeer, their white markings flashing, skimmed the water, crying their shrill sweet cry. And there at the south end of the lake were four wild ducks swimming out from the willows into open water.

Arnold followed Eugie down the slope, stealing, as his brother did, from one shock of wheat to another. Eugie paused before climbing through the wire fence that divided the wheat field from the marshy pasture around the lake. They were screened from the ducks by the willows along the lake's edge.

"If you hit your duck, you want me to go in after it?" Eugie said.

"If you want," Arnold said.

Eugie lowered his eyelids, leaving slits of mocking blue. You'd drown 'fore you got to it, them legs of yours are so puny," he said.

He shoved the tub under the fence and,

pressing down the center wire, climbed through into the pasture.

Arnold pressed down the bottom wire, thrust a leg through, and leaned forward to bring the other leg after. His rifle caught on the wire and he jerked at it. The air was rocked by the sound of the shot. Feeling foolish, he lifted his face, baring it to an expected shower of derision from his brother. But Eugie did not turn around. Instead, from his crouching position, he fell to his knees and then pitched forward onto his face. The ducks rose up crying from the lake, cleared the mountain background, and beat away northward across the pale sky.

Arnold squatted beside his brother. Eugie seemed to be climbing the earth, as if the earth ran up and down, and when he found he couldn't scale it, he lay still.

"Eugie?"

Then Arnold saw it, under the tendril of hair at the nape of the neck—a slow rising of bright blood. It had an obnoxious movement, like that of a parasite.

"Hey, Eugie," he said again. He was feeling the same discomfort he had felt when he had watched Eugie sleeping; his brother didn't know that he was lying face down in the pasture.

Again he said, "Hey, Eugie," an anxious nudge in his voice. But Eugie was as still as the morning about them.

Arnold set his rifle on the ground and stood up. He picked up the tub and, dragging it behind him, walked along by the willows to the garden fence and climbed through. He went down on his knees among the tangled vines. The pods were cold with the night, but his hands were strange to him, and not until some time had passed did he realize that the pods were numbing his fingers. He picked from the top of the vine first, then lifted the vine to look underneath for pods and then moved on to the next.

It was a warmth on his back, like a large hand laid firmly there, that made him raise his

134

head. Way up on the slope, the gray farmhouse was struck by the sun. While his head had been bent the land had grown bright around him.

When he got up, his legs were so stiff that he had to go down on his knees again to ease the pain. Then, walking sideways, he dragged the tub, half full of peas, up the slope.

The kitchen was warm now; a fire was roaring in the stove with a closed-up rushing sound. His mother was spooning eggs from a pot of boiling water and putting them into a bowl. Her short brown hair was uncombed and fell forward across her eyes as she bent her head. Nora was lifting a frying pan full of trout from the stove, holding the handle with a dish towel. His father had just come in from bringing the cows from the north pasture to the barn and was sitting on the stool, unbuttoning his red-plaid mackinaw.

"Did you boys fill the tub?" his mother asked.

"They ought of by now," his father said. "They went out of the house an hour ago. Eugie woke me up comin' downstairs. I heard you shootin'—did you get a duck?"

"No," Arnold said. They would want to know why Eugie wasn't coming in for breakfast, he thought. "Eugie's dead," he told them.

They stared at him. The pitch crackled in the stove.

"You kids playin' a joke?" his father asked.

"Where's Eugene?" his mother asked scoldingly. She wanted, Arnold knew, to see his eyes, and when he had glanced at her, she put the bowl and spoon down on the stove and walked past him. His father stood up and went out the door after her. Nora followed them with little skipping steps, as if afraid to be left alone.

Arnold went into the barn, down along the foddering passage past the cows waiting to be milked, and climbed into the loft. After a few minutes he heard a terrifying sound coming toward the house. His parents and Nora were returning from the willows, and sounds sharp

as knives were rising from his mother's breast and carrying over the sloping fields. In a short while he heard his father go down the back steps, slam the car door, and drive away.

Arnold lay still as a fugitive, listening to the cows eating close by. If his parents never called him, he thought, he would stay up in the loft forever, out of the way. In the night he would sneak down for a drink of water from the faucet over the trough and for whatever food they left for him by the barn.

The rattle of his father's car as it turned down the lane recalled him to the present. He heard voices of his Uncle Andy and Aunt Alice as they and his father went past the barn to the lake. He could feel the morning growing heavier with sun. Someone, probably Nora, had let the chickens out of their coops, and they were cackling in the yard.

After a while another car turned down the road off the highway. The car drew to a stop and he heard the voices of strange men. The men also went past the barn and down to the lake. The undertakers, whom his father must have phoned from Uncle Andy's house, had arrived from Corinth. Then he heard everybody come back and heard the car turn around and leave.

"Arnold!" It was his father calling from the yard.

He climbed down the ladder and went out into the sun, picking wisps of hay from his overalls.

Corinth, nine miles away, was the county seat. Arnold sat in the front seat of the old Ford between his father, who was driving, and Uncle Andy; no one spoke. Uncle Andy was his mother's brother, and he had been fond of Eugie because Eugie had resembled him. Andy had taken Eugie hunting and had given him a knife and a lot of things, and now Andy, his eyes narrowed, sat tall and still beside Arnold.

Arnold's father parked the car before the courthouse. It was a two-story brick building with a lamp on each side of the bottom step.

135

They went up the wide stone steps, Arnold and his father going first, and entered the darkly paneled hallway. The shirt-sleeved man in the sheriff's office said that the sheriff was at Carlson's Parlor examining the Curwing boy.

Andy went off to get the sheriff while Arnold and his father waited on a bench in the corridor. Arnold felt his father watching him, and he lifted his eyes with painful casualness to the announcement, on the opposite wall, of the Corinth County Annual Rodeo and then to the clock with its loudly clucking pendulum. After he had come down from the loft, his father and Uncle Andy had stood in the yard with him and asked him to tell them everything, and he had explained to them how the gun had caught on the wire. But when they had asked him why he hadn't run back to the house to tell his parents, he had had no answer —all he could say was that he had gone down into the garden to pick the peas. His father had stared at him in a pale, puzzled way, and it was then that he had felt his father and the others set their cold turbulent silence against him. Arnold shifted on the bench, his only feeling a small one of compunction imposed by his father's eyes.

At a quarter past nine Andy and the sheriff came in. They all went into the sheriff's private office, and Arnold was sent forward to sit in the chair by the sheriff's desk; his father and Andy sat down on the bench against the wall.

The sheriff lumped down into his swivel chair and swung toward Arnold. He was an old man with white hair like wheat stubble. His restless green eyes made him seem not to be in his office but to be hurrying and bobbing around somewhere else.

"What did you say your name was?" the sheriff asked.

"Arnold," he replied, but he could not remember telling the sheriff his name before.

"Curwing?"

"Yes."

"What were you doing with a .22, Arnold?"

"It's mine," he said.

"Okay. What were you going to shoot?"

"Some ducks," he replied.

"Out of season?"

He nodded.

"That's bad," said the sheriff. "Were you and your brother good friends?"

What did he mean—good friends? Eugie was his brother. That was different from a friend, Arnold thought. A best friend was your own age, but Eugie was almost a man. Eugie had had a way of looking at him, slyly and mockingly and yet confidentially, that had summed up how they both felt about being brothers. Arnold had wanted to be with Eugie more than with anybody else, but he couldn't say they had been good friends.

"Did they ever quarrel?" the sheriff asked his father.

"Not that I know," his father replied. "It seemed to me that Arnold cared a lot for Eugie."

"Did you?" the sheriff asked Arnold.

If it seemed so to his father, then it was so. Arnold nodded.

"Were you mad at him this morning?"

"No."

"How did you happen to shoot him?"

"We was crawlin' through the fence."

"Yes?"

"An' the gun got caught on the wire."

"Seems the hammer must of caught," his father put in.

"All right, that's what happened," said the sheriff. "But what I want you to tell me is this, why didn't you go back to the house and tell your father right away? Why did you go and pick peas for an hour?"

Arnold gazed over his shoulder at his father, expecting his father to have an answer for this also. But his father's eyes, larger and even lighter blue than usual, were fixed upon him curiously. Arnold picked at a callus in his right palm. It seemed odd now that he had not run back to the house and wakened his father, but he could not remember why he had not. They were all waiting for him to answer.

"I come down to pick peas," he said.

"Didn't you think," asked the sheriff, stepping carefully from word to word, "that it was more important for you to go tell your parents what had happened?"

"The sun was gonna come up," Arnold said.

"What's that got to do with it?"

"It's better to pick peas while they're cool."

The sheriff swung away from him, laid both hands flat on his desk. "Well, all I can say is," he said across to Arnold's father and Uncle Andy, "he's either a moron or he's so reasonable that he's way ahead of us." He gave a challenging snort. "It's come to my notice that the most reasonable guys are mean ones. They don't feel nothing."

For a moment the three men sat still. Then the sheriff lifted his hand like a man taking an oath. "Take him home," he said.

Andy uncrossed his legs. "You don't want him?"

"Not now," replied the sheriff. "Maybe in a few years."

Arnold's father stood up. He held his hat against his chest. "The gun ain't his no more," he said wanly.

Arnold went first through the hallway, hearing behind him the heels of his father and Uncle Andy striking the floorboards. He went down the steps ahead of them and climbed into the back seat of the car. Andy paused as he was getting into the front seat and gazed back at Arnold, and Arnold saw that his uncle's eyes had absorbed the knowingness from the sheriff's eyes. Andy and his father and the sheriff had discovered what made him go down into the garden. It was because he was cruel, the sheriff had said, and didn't care about his brother. Was that the reason? Arnold lowered his eyelids meekly against his uncle's stare.

The rest of the day he did his tasks around the farm, keeping apart from the family. At evening when he saw his father stomp tiredly into the house, Arnold did not put down his hammer and leave the chicken coop he was

repairing. He was afraid that they did not want him to eat supper with them. But in a few minutes another fear that they would go to the trouble of calling him and that he would be made conspicuous by his tardiness made him follow his father into the house. As he went through the kitchen he saw the jars of peas standing in rows on the workbench, a reproach to him.

No one spoke at supper, and his mother, who sat next to him, leaned her head in her hand all through the meal, curving her fingers over her eyes so as not to see him. They were finishing their small, silent supper when the visitors began to arrive, knocking hard on the back door. The men were coming from their farms now that it was growing dark and they could not work any more.

Old Man Matthews, gray and stocky, came first, with his two sons, Orion, the elder, and Clint, who was Eugie's age. As the callers entered the parlor, where the family ate, Arnold sat down in a rocking chair. Even as he had been undecided before supper whether to remain outside or take his place at the table, he now thought that he should go upstairs, and yet he stayed to avoid being conspicuous by his absence. If he stayed, he thought, as he always stayed and listened when visitors came, they would see that he was only Arnold and not the person the sheriff thought he was. He sat with his arms crossed and his hands tucked into his armpits and did not lift his eyes.

The Matthews men had hardly settled down around the table, after Arnold's mother and Nora had cleared away the dishes, when another car rattled down the road and someone else rapped on the back door. This time it was Sullivan, a spare and sandy man, so nimble of gesture and expression that Arnold had never been able to catch more than a few of his meanings. Sullivan, in dusty jeans, sat down in the other rocker, shot out his skinny legs, and began to talk in his fast way, recalling everything that Eugene had ever said to him. The other men interrupted to tell of occasions they remembered, and after a time Clint's young voice, hoarse like Eugene's had been, broke in to tell about the time Eugene had beat him in a wrestling match.

Out in the kitchen the voices of Orion's wife and of Mrs. Sullivan mingled with Nora's voice but not, Arnold noticed, his mother's. Then dry little Mr. Cram came, leaving large Mrs. Cram in the kitchen, and there was no chair left for Mr. Cram to sit in. No one asked Arnold to get up, and he was unable to rise. He knew that the story had got around to them during the day about how he had gone and picked peas after he had shot his brother, and he knew that although they were talking only about Eugie, they were thinking about him, and if he got up, if he moved even his foot, they would all be alerted. Then Uncle Andy arrived and leaned his tall lanky body against the doorjamb, and there were two men standing.

Presently Arnold was aware that the talk had stopped. He knew without looking up that the men were watching him.

"Not a tear in his eye," said Andy, and Arnold knew that it was his uncle who had gestured the men to attention.

"He don't give a hoot, is that how it goes?" asked Sullivan, trippingly.

"He's a reasonable fellow," Andy explained. "That's what the sheriff said. It's us who ain't reasonable. If we'd of shot our brother, we'd of come runnin' back to the house, cryin' like a baby. Well, we'd of been unreasonable. What would of been the use of actin' like that? If your brother is shot dead, he's shot dead. What's the use of gettin' emotional about it? The thing to do is go down to the garden and pick peas. Am I right?"

The men around the room shifted their heavy, satisfying weight of unreasonableness.

Matthews' son Orion said: "If I'd of done what he done, Pa would've hung my pelt by the side of that big coyote's in the barn."

Arnold sat in the rocker until the last man had filed out. While his family was out in the kitchen, bidding the callers good night, and

the cars were driving away down the dirt lane to the highway, he picked up one of the kerosene lamps and slipped quickly up the stairs. In his room he undressed by lamplight, although he and Eugie had always undressed in the dark, and not until he was lying in his bed did he blow out the flame. He felt nothing, not any grief. There was only the same immense silence and crawling inside of him; it was the way the house and fields felt under a merciless sun.

He awoke suddenly. He knew that his father was out in the yard, closing the doors of the chicken houses so that the chickens could not roam out too early and fall prey to the coyotes that came down from the mountains at daybreak. The sound that had wakened him was the step of his father as he got up from the rocker and went down the back steps. And he knew that his mother was awake in her bed.

Throwing off the covers, he rose swiftly, went down the stairs and across the dark parlor to his parents' room. He rapped on the door.

"Mother?"

From the closed room her voice rose to him, a seeking and retreating voice. "Yes?"

"Mother?" he asked insistently. He had expected her to realize that he wanted to go down on his knees by her bed and tell her that Eugie was dead. She did not know it yet—nobody knew it—and yet she was sitting up in bed, waiting to be told, waiting for him to confirm her dread. He had expected her to tell him to come in, to allow him to dig his head into her blankets and tell her about the terror he had felt when he had knelt beside Eugie. He had come to clasp her in his arms and, in his terror, to pommel her breasts with his head. He put his hand upon the knob.

"Go back to bed, Arnold," she called sharply.

But he waited.

"Go back! Is night when you get afraid?"

At first he did not understand. Then, silently, he left the door and for a stricken moment stood by the rocker. Outside, everything was still. The fences, the shocks of wheat seen through the window before him were so still it was as if they moved and breathed in the daytime and had fallen silent with the lateness of the hour. It was a silence that seemed to observe his father, a figure moving alone around the yard, his lantern casting a circle of light by his feet. In a few minutes his father would enter the dark house, the lantern still lighting his way.

Arnold was suddenly aware that he was naked. He had thrown off his blankets and come down the stairs to tell his mother how he felt about Eugie, but she had refused to listen to him, and his nakedness had become unpardonable. At once he went back up the stairs, fleeing from his father's lantern.

At breakfast he kept his eyelids lowered as if to deny the humiliating night. Nora, sitting at his left, did not pass the pitcher of milk to him, and he did not ask for it. He would never again, he vowed, ask them for anything, and he ate his fried eggs and potatoes only because everybody ate meals—the cattle ate, and the cats; it was customary for everybody to eat.

"Nora, you gonna keep that pitcher for yourself?" his father asked.

Nora lowered her head unsurely.

"Pass it on to Arnold," his father said.

Nora put her hands in her lap.

His father picked up the metal pitcher and set it down at Arnold's plate.

Arnold, pretending to be deaf to the discord, did not glance up, but relief rained over his shoulders at the thought that his parents recognized him again. They must have lain awake after his father had come in from the yard: had they realized together why he had come down the stairs and knocked at their door?

"Bessie's missin' this morning," his father called out to his mother, who had gone into the kitchen. "She went up the mountain last night and had her calf, most likely. Some-

body's got to go up and find her 'fore the coyotes get the calf."

That had been Eugie's job, Arnold thought. Eugie would climb the cattle trails in search of a newborn calf and come down the mountain, carrying the calf across his back, with the cow running down along behind him, mooing in alarm.

Arnold ate the few more forkfuls of his breakfast, put his hands on the edge of the table, and pushed back his chair. If he went for the calf, he'd be away from the farm all morning. He could switch the cow down the mountain slowly, and the calf would run along at its mother's side.

When he passed through the kitchen, his mother was setting a kettle of water on the stove. "Where you going?" she asked awkwardly.

"Up to get the calf," he replied, averting his face.

"Arnold?"

At the door he paused reluctantly, his back to her, knowing that she was seeking him out, as his father was doing, and he called upon his pride to protect him from them.

"Was you knocking at my door last night?"

He looked over his shoulder at her, his eyes narrow and dry.

"What'd you want?" she asked humbly.

"I didn't want nothing," he said flatly.

Then he went out the door and down the back steps, his legs trembling from the fright his answer gave him.

I
HOW UNFATHOMABLE IS HUMAN NATURE?

The reader in this story knows what is happening only through Arnold's view of the things people say and do. The boy cannot really explain why he does what he does. Neither can the reader, although he may have known a similar iciness in his own family under somewhat less drastic circumstances. Arnold is beset by complex reactions, both understanding and not understanding what he has done. He is not a monster, just a small boy who knows of no way to change the horrible situation and bring Eugie back to life. Neither can he find a way to rid himself of the blackness that has settled on him. Fumblingly, he tries many things: hiding in the hay loft, stubbornly sitting in the living room, leaving the lamp on while he undresses, going to his mother's room, refusing to ask that food be passed to him, setting out to find the cow. Why is it that human behavior and emotions are so incomprehensible, even in the family, where those involved should know one another best?

II
IMPLICATIONS

Consider the following statements and discuss them in the light of your reactions to the story and your own personal experiences. None of them is necessarily true or false.

1. The family would have treated Arnold differently if he had run back immediately and told his parents about the accident.

2. The story indicates that Arnold is jealous of Eugie.

3. Most children try to ignore accidents for which they are responsible.

4. It is normal for a family to be insensitive to the wrongdoer's inner agony.

5. Adults tend to treat children as if they were deaf and dumb, saying things about them and to them that are needlessly cruel.

6. It is the nature of people to want the wrongdoer to demonstrate his guilt and his regret for his actions.

7. Arnold's picking the peas is a more rational action than reporting the accident.

III
TECHNIQUES

In BRIEF ENCOUNTERS, attention was focused on the writer's use of exposition, conflict, and climax. CROSSCURRENTS will consider characterization and plot.

Characterization

Characterization refers to the writer's ability to picture an imaginary person so vividly that the reader feels the character is a real, live human being. Characterization may include a detailed physical description of a character; but, more important, it should build a feeling about the personality of the character so that the reader knows how that character reacts and feels and thinks. Human beings are not simple but complicated; hence, the writer has the job of suggesting in a few deft strokes the inconsistencies, the desires, the longings, and the values that his characters possess. He may do this through direct statement, conversation, description of action, and by the reaction of one character to another.

In "The Stone Boy" everything is told from Arnold's point of view. Thus there is little direct reference to the kind of person he is. Yet the reader probably has the feeling that he knows him intimately. What do you learn about him from the following:

1. His way of treating Eugie when he gets up in the morning.

2. His reaction to the fact that this is not duck hunting season.

3. His response when his father calls him down from the loft.

4. His sitting in the living room when the neighbors call.

5. His knocking on his mother's door at night.

6. His response the next day when his mother asks him if he knocked at her door in the night.

Plot

Plot is the sequence of related actions in a story. Just as a highway engineer plots a road from one city to the next, so an author must lay out his incidents leading from the beginning to the end of his story. As a blueprint of a road may be either richly detailed or the barest of outlines, so too a plot may be loaded with incidents or starkly limited to a few. A plot may go directly by the shortest route to the story's destination or it may go off on a detour.

A good writer makes events in a story occur plausibly. The action should flow naturally from the characters. If the author forces the characters into unlikely behavior in order to advance the plot, the story will seem artificial.

What events lead up to each of the following:

1. Arnold's killing of Eugie.

2. The family's actions on finding Eugie's body.

3. The neighbors' discussion of the accident.

❖

Sometimes a story is so told
that the characters and the actions
seem real, yet the reader feels
that the author is driving at something
different from the surface meaning. The events
become symbols of a deeper significance.
"The Rocking-Horse Winner" is such a story,
for the actions on the surface,
interesting as they are, are really the means
to point up the irreconcilable crosscurrents
in a family's life.

The Rocking-Horse Winner

D. H. LAWRENCE

There was a woman who was beautiful, who started with all the advantages, yet she had no luck. She married for love, and the love turned to dust. She had bonny children, yet she felt they had been thrust upon her, and she could not love them. They looked at her coldly, as if they were finding fault with her. And hurriedly she felt she must cover up some fault in herself. Yet what it was that she must cover up she never knew. Nevertheless, when her children were present, she always felt the centre of her heart go hard. This troubled her, and in her manner she was all the more gentle and anxious for her children, as if she loved them very much. Only she herself knew that at the centre of her heart was a hard little place that could not feel love, no, not for anybody. Everybody else said of her: "She is such a good mother.

She adores her children." Only she herself, and her children themselves, knew it was not so. They read it in each other's eyes.

There were a boy and two little girls. They lived in a pleasant house, with a garden, and they had discreet servants and felt themselves superior to any one in the neighbourhood.

Although they lived in style, they felt always an anxiety in the house. There was never enough money. The mother had a small income, and the father had a small income, but not nearly enough for the social position which they had to keep up. The father went into town to some office. But though he had good prospects, these prospects never materialized. There was always the grinding sense of the shortage of money, though the style was always kept up.

At last the mother said: "I will see if I can't make something." But she did not know where to begin. She racked her brains, and tried this thing and the other, but could not find anything successful. The failure made deep lines come into her face. Her children were growing up, they would have to go to school. There must be more money, there must be more money. The father, who was always very handsome and expensive in his tastes, seemed as if he never would be able to do anything worth doing. And the mother, who had a great belief in herself, did not succeed any better, and her tastes were just as expensive.

And so the house came to be haunted by the unspoken phrase: *There must be more money! There must be more money!* The children could hear it all the time, though nobody said it aloud. They heard it at Christmas, when the expensive and splendid toys filled the nursery. Behind the shining modern rocking-horse, behind the smart doll's-house, a voice would start whispering: "There *must* be more money! There *must* be more money!" And the children would stop playing, to listen for a moment. They would look into each other's eyes, to see if they had all heard. And each one saw in the eyes of the other two that they too had heard. "There *must* be more money! There *must* be more money!"

It came whispering from the springs of the still-swaying rocking-horse, and even the horse, bending his wooden champing head, heard it. The big doll, sitting so pink and smirking in her new pram,[1] could hear it quite plainly, and seemed to be smirking all the more self-consciously because of it. The foolish puppy, too, that took the place of the teddy-bear, he was looking so extraordinarily foolish for no other reason but that he heard the secret whisper all over the house: "There *must* be more money!"

Yet nobody ever said it aloud. The whisper was everywhere, and therefore no one spoke it. Just as no one ever says: "We are breathing!" in spite of the fact that breath is coming and going all the time.

"Mother," said the boy Paul one day, "why don't we keep a car of our own? Why do we always use uncle's, or else a taxi?"

"Because we're the poor members of the family," said the mother.

"But why are we, mother?"

"Well—I suppose," she said slowly, and bitterly, "it's because your father has no luck."

The boy was silent for some time.

"Is luck money, mother?" he asked, rather timidly.

"No, Paul. Not quite. It's what causes you to have money."

"Oh!" said Paul vaguely. "I thought when Uncle Oscar said *filthy lucker,* it meant money."

"*Filthy lucre* does mean money," said the mother. "But it's lucre, not luck."

"Oh!" said the boy. "Then what *is* luck, mother?"

"It's what causes you to have money. If you're lucky you have money. That's why it's better to be born lucky than rich. If you're rich, you may lose your money. But if you're lucky, you will always get more money."

"Oh! Will you? And is father not lucky?"

"Very unlucky, I should say," she said bitterly.

The boy watched her with unsure eyes.

"Why?" he asked.

"I don't know. Nobody ever knows why one person is lucky and another unlucky."

"Don't they? Nobody at all? Does *nobody* know?"

"Perhaps God. But He never tells."

"He ought to, then. And aren't you lucky either, mother?"

"I can't be, if I married an unlucky husband."

"But by yourself, aren't you?"

"I used to think I was, before I married. Now I think I am very unlucky indeed."

"Why?"

"Well—never mind! Perhaps I'm not really," she said.

The child looked at her, to see if she meant it. But he saw by the lines of her mouth that she was only trying to hide something from him.

"Well, anyhow," he said stoutly, "I'm a lucky person."

"Why?" said his mother, with a sudden laugh.

He stared at her. He didn't even know why he had said it.

"God told me," he asserted, brazening it out.

"I hope He did, dear!" she said, again with a laugh, but rather bitter.

"He did, mother!"

"Excellent!" said the mother, using one of her husband's exclamations.

The boy saw she did not believe him; or, rather, that she paid no attention to his assertion. This angered him somewhat, and made him want to compel her attention.

He went off by himself, vaguely, in a childish way, seeking for the clue to "luck." Absorbed, taking no heed of other people, he went about with a sort of stealth, seeking inwardly for luck. He wanted luck, he wanted it, he wanted it. When the two girls were playing dolls in the nursery, he would sit on his big rocking-horse, charging madly into space, with a frenzy that made the little girls peer at him uneasily. Wildly the horse careered, the waving dark hair of the boy tossed, his eyes had a strange glare in them. The little girls dared not speak to him.

When he had ridden to the end of his mad little journey, he climbed down and stood in

---

1. **pram**\prăm\ a baby carriage or perambulator. (The word is mostly British rather than American.)

front of his rocking-horse, staring fixedly into its lowered face. Its red mouth was slightly open, its big eye was wide and glassy-bright.

"Now!" he would silently command the snorting steed. "Now, take me to where there is luck! Now take me!"

And he would slash the horse on the neck with the little whip he had asked Uncle Oscar for. He knew the horse could take him to where there was luck, if only he forced it. So he would mount again, and start on his furious ride, hoping at last to get there. He knew he could get there.

"You'll break your horse, Paul!" said the nurse.

"He's always riding like that! I wish he'd leave off!" said his elder sister Joan.

But he only glared down on them in silence. Nurse gave him up. She could make nothing of him. Anyhow he was growing beyond her.

One day his mother and his Uncle Oscar came in when he was on one of his furious rides. He did not speak to them.

"Hallo, you young jockey! Riding a winner?" said his uncle.

"Aren't you growing too big for a rocking-horse? You're not a very little boy any longer, you know," said his mother.

But Paul only gave a blue glare from his big, rather close-set eyes. He would speak to nobody when he was in full tilt. His mother watched him with an anxious expression on her face.

At last he suddenly stopped forcing his horse into the mechanical gallop, and slid down.

"Well, I got there!" he announced fiercely, his blue eyes still flaring, and his sturdy long legs straddling apart.

"Where did you get to?" asked his mother.

"Where I wanted to go," he flared back at her.

"That's right, son!" said Uncle Oscar. "Don't you stop till you get there. What's the horse's name?"

"He doesn't have a name," said the boy.

"Gets on without all right?" said the uncle.

"Well, he has different names. He was called Sansovino last week."

"Sansovino, eh? Won the Ascot.[2] How did you know his name?"

"He always talks about horse-races with Bassett," said Joan.

The uncle was delighted to find that his small nephew was posted with all the racing news. Bassett, the young gardener, who had been wounded in the left foot in the war and had got his present job through Oscar Cresswell, whose batman he had been, was a perfect blade[3] of the "turf." He lived in the racing events, and the small boy lived with him.

Oscar Cresswell got it all from Bassett.

"Master Paul comes and asks me, so I can't do more than tell him, sir," said Bassett, his face terribly serious, as if he were speaking of religious matters.

"And does he ever put anything on a horse he fancies?"

"Well—I don't want to give him away—he's a young sport, a fine sport, sir. Would you mind asking him yourself? He sort of takes a pleasure in it, and perhaps he'd feel I was giving him away, sir, if you don't mind."

Bassett was serious as a church.

The uncle went back to his nephew, and took him off for a ride in the car.

"Say, Paul, old man, do you ever put anything on a horse?" the uncle asked.

The boy watched the handsome man closely.

"Why, do you think I oughtn't to?" he parried.

"Not a bit of it! I thought perhaps you might give me a tip for the Lincoln."

The car sped on into the country, going down to Uncle Oscar's place in Hampshire.[4]

"Honour bright?" said the nephew.

"Honour bright, son!" said the uncle.

"Well, then, Daffodil."

---

2. **Ascot** \ˈăs ˈkŏt\ a famous English horse race. Later this story mentions other famous English races, the **Lincoln,** the **Leger,** the **Grand National,** and the **Derby** \ˈdar•bē\.
3. **batman,** a British army officer's personal orderly and servant. **blade,** English and informal, means "lively young fellow, often a fan or devotee of something."
4. **Hampshire** \ˈhămp•shər\ a south-central shire, or county, in England.

Bassett: "Master Paul would get me talking about racing events, spinning yarns."

"Daffodil! I doubt it, sonny. What about Mirza?"

"I only know the winner," said the boy. "That's Daffodil."

"Daffodil, eh?"

There was a pause. Daffodil was an obscure horse comparatively.

"Uncle!"

"Yes, son?"

"You won't let it go any further, will you? I promised Bassett."

"Bassett be hanged, old man! What's he got to do with it?"

"We're partners. We've been partners from the first. Uncle, he lent me my first five shillings, which I lost. I promised him, honour bright, it was only between me and him; only you gave me that ten-shilling note I started winning with, so I thought you were lucky. You won't let it go further, will you?"

The boy gazed at his uncle from those big, hot, blue eyes, set rather close together. The uncle stirred and laughed uneasily.

"Right you are, son! I'll keep your tip private.

Daffodil, eh? How much are you putting on him?"

"All except twenty pounds," said the boy. "I keep that in reserve."

The uncle thought it a good joke.

"You keep twenty pounds in reserve, do you, you young romancer? What are you betting, then?"

"I'm betting three hundred," said the boy gravely. "But it's between you and me, Uncle Oscar! Honour bright?"

The uncle burst into a roar of laughter.

"It's between you and me all right, you young Nat Gould," he said, laughing. "But where's your three hundred?"

"Bassett keeps it for me. We're partners."

"You are, are you! And what is Bassett putting on Daffodil?"

"He won't go quite as high as I do, I expect. Perhaps he'll go a hundred and fifty."

"What, pennies?" laughed the uncle.

"Pounds," said the child, with a surprised look at his uncle. "Bassett keeps a bigger reserve than I do."

Between wonder and amusement Uncle Oscar was silent. He pursued the matter no further, but he determined to take his nephew with him to the Lincoln races.

"Now, son," he said, "I am putting twenty on Mirza, and I'll put five for you on any horse you fancy. What's your pick?"

"Daffodil, uncle."

"No, not the fiver[5] on Daffodil!"

"I should if it was my own fiver," said the child.

"Good! Good! Right you are! A fiver for me and a fiver for you on Daffodil."

The child had never been to a race-meeting before, and his eyes were blue fire. He pursed his mouth tight, and watched. A Frenchman just in front had put his money on Lancelot. Wild with excitement, he flayed his arms up and down, yelling *Lancelot! Lancelot!* in his French accent.

Daffodil came in first, Lancelot second, Mirza third. The child, flushed and with eyes blazing, was curiously serene. His uncle brought him four five-pound notes, four to one.

"What am I to do with these?" he cried, waving them before the boy's eyes.

"I suppose we'll talk to Bassett," said the boy. "I expect I have fifteen hundred now; and twenty in reserve; and this twenty."

His uncle studied him for some moments.

"Look here, son!" he said. "You're not serious about Bassett and that fifteen hundred, are you?"

"Yes, I am. But it's between you and me, uncle. Honour bright!"

"Honour bright all right, son! But I must talk to Bassett."

"If you'd like to be a partner, uncle, with Bassett and me, we could all be partners. Only, you'd have to promise, honour bright, uncle, not to let it go beyond us three. Bassett and I are lucky, and you must be lucky, because it was your ten shillings I started winning with. . . ."

Uncle Oscar took both Bassett and Paul into Richmond Park for an afternoon, and there they talked.

"It's like this, you see, sir," Bassett said. "Master Paul would get me talking about racing events, spinning yarns, you know, sir. And he was always keen on knowing if I'd made or if I'd lost. It's about a year since, now, that I put five shillings on Blush of Dawn for him— and we lost. Then the luck turned, with that ten shillings he had from you that we put on Singhalese. And since that time, it's been pretty steady, all things considering. What do you say, Master Paul?"

"We're all right when we're sure," said Paul. "It's when we're not quite sure that we go down."

"Oh, but we're careful then," said Bassett.

"But when are you sure?" smiled Uncle Oscar.

"It's Master Paul, sir," said Bassett, in a secret, religious voice. "It's as if he had it from

---

5. fiver\ˈfai·vər\ English slang, a five-pound note.

heaven. Like Daffodil, now, for the Lincoln. That was as sure as eggs."

"Did you put anything on Daffodil?" asked Oscar Cresswell.

"Yes, sir. I made my bit."

"And my nephew?"

Bassett was obstinately silent, looking at Paul.

"I made twelve hundred, didn't I, Bassett? I told uncle I was putting three hundred on Daffodil."

"That's right," said Bassett, nodding.

"But where's the money?" asked the uncle.

"I keep it safe locked up, sir. Master Paul he can have it any minute he likes to ask for it."

"What, fifteen hundred pounds?"

"And twenty! And forty, that is, with the twenty he made on the course."

"It's amazing!" said the uncle.

"If Master Paul offers you to be partners, sir, I would, if I were you; if you'll excuse me," said Bassett.

Oscar Cresswell thought about it.

"I'll see the money," he said.

They drove home again, and sure enough, Bassett came round to the garden-house with fifteen hundred pounds in notes. The twenty pounds reserve was left with Joe Glee, in the Turf Commission deposit.

"You see, it's all right, uncle, when I'm *sure!* Then we go strong, for all we're worth. Don't we, Bassett?"

"We do that, Master Paul."

"And when are you sure?" said the uncle, laughing.

"Oh, well, sometimes I'm *absolutely* sure, like about Daffodil," said the boy; "and sometimes I have an idea; and sometimes I haven't even an idea, have I, Bassett? Then we're careful, because we mostly go down."

"You do, do you! And when you're sure, like about Daffodil, what makes you sure, sonny?"

"Oh, well, I don't know," said the boy uneasily. "I'm sure, you know, uncle; that's all."

"It's as if he had it from heaven, sir," Bassett reiterated.

"I should say so!" said the uncle.

But he became a partner. And when the Leger was coming on, Paul was "sure" about Lively Spark, which was a quite inconsiderable horse. The boy insisted on putting a thousand on the horse, Bassett went for five hundred, and Oscar Cresswell two hundred. Lively Spark came in first, and the betting had been ten to one against him. Paul had made ten thousand.

"You see," he said, "I was absolutely sure of him."

Even Oscar Cresswell had cleared two thousand.

"Look here, son," he said, "this sort of thing makes me nervous."

"It needn't, uncle! Perhaps I shan't be sure again for a long time."

"But what are you going to do with your money?" asked the uncle.

"Of course," said the boy, "I started it for mother. She said she had no luck, because father is unlucky, so I thought if I was lucky, it might stop whispering."

"What might stop whispering?"

"Our house. I *hate* our house for whispering."

"What does it whisper?"

"Why—why"—the boy fidgeted—"why, I don't know. But it's always short of money, you know, uncle."

"I know it, son, I know it."

"You know people send mother writs,[6] don't you, uncle?"

"I'm afraid I do," said the uncle.

"And then the house whispers, like people laughing at you behind your back. It's awful, that is! I thought if I was lucky . . ."

"You might stop it," added the uncle.

The boy watched him with big blue eyes that had an uncanny cold fire in them, and he said never a word.

"Well, then!" said the uncle. "What are we doing?"

"I shouldn't like mother to know I was lucky," said the boy.

"Why not, son?"

"She'd stop me."

---

6. **writ**\rĭt\ a court order to pay one's bills.

"I don't think she would."

"Oh!"—and the boy writhed in an odd way—"I don't want her to know, uncle."

"All right, son! We'll manage it without her knowing."

They managed it very easily. Paul, at the other's suggestion, handed over five thousand pounds to his uncle, who deposited it with the family lawyer, who was then to inform Paul's mother that a relative had put five thousand pounds into his hands, which sum was to be paid out a thousand pounds at a time, on the mother's birthday, for the next five years.

"So she'll have a birthday present of a thousand pounds for five successive years," said Uncle Oscar. "I hope it won't make it all the harder for her later."

Paul's mother had her birthday in November. The house had been "whispering" worse than ever lately, and, even in spite of his luck, Paul could not bear up against it. He was very anxious to see the effect of the birthday letter, telling his mother about the thousand pounds.

When there were no visitors, Paul now took his meals with his parents, as he was beyond the nursery control. His mother went into town nearly every day. She had discovered that she had an odd knack of sketching furs and dress materials, so she worked secretly in the studio of a friend who was the chief "artist" for the leading drapers.[7] She drew the figures of ladies in furs and ladies in silk and sequins for the newspaper advertisements. This young woman artist earned several thousand pounds a year, but Paul's mother only made several hundreds, and she was again dissatisfied. She so wanted to be first in something, and she did not succeed, even in making sketches for drapery advertisements.

She was down to breakfast on the morning of her birthday. Paul watched her face as she read her letters. He knew the lawyer's letter. As his mother read it, her face hardened and became more expressionless. Then a cold determined look came on her mouth. She hid the letter under the pile of others, and said not a word about it.

"Didn't you have anything nice in the post for your birthday, mother?" said Paul.

"Quite moderately nice," she said, her voice cold and absent.

She went away to town without saying more.

But in the afternoon Uncle Oscar appeared. He said Paul's mother had had a long interview with the lawyer, asking if the whole five thousand could be advanced at once, as she was in debt.

"What do you think, uncle?" said the boy.

"I leave it to you, son."

"Oh, let her have it, then! We can get some more with the other," said the boy.

"A bird in the hand is worth two in the bush, laddie!" said Uncle Oscar.

"But I'm sure to know for the Grand National; or the Lincolnshire; or else the Derby. I'm sure to know for one of them," said Paul.

So Uncle Oscar signed the agreement, and Paul's mother touched the whole five thousand. Then something very curious happened. The voices in the house suddenly went mad, like a chorus of frogs on a spring evening. There were certain new furnishings, and Paul had a tutor. He was really going to Eton,[8] his father's school, in the following autumn. There were flowers in the winter, and a blossoming of the luxury Paul's mother had been used to. And yet the voices in the house, behind the sprays of mimosa and almond blossoms, and from under the piles of iridescent cushions, simply trilled and screamed in a sort of ecstasy: "There must be more money! Oh-h-h, there must be more money. Oh, now now-w! Now-w-w-w—there must be more money!—more than ever! More than ever!"

It frightened Paul terribly. He studied away at his Latin and Greek with his tutors. But his intense hours were spent with Basset. The Grand National had gone by: he had not "known," and had lost a hundred pounds. Summer was at hand. He was in agony for the Lin-

---

7. **draper**\ˈdrā·pər\ chiefly British, a seller of clothes and dry goods.

8. **Eton**\ˈē·tən\ a very famous boys' school in England.

coln. But even for the Lincoln he didn't "know" and he lost fifty pounds. He became wild-eyed and strange, as if something were going to explode in him.

"Let it alone, son! Don't you bother about it!" urged Uncle Oscar. But it was as if the boy couldn't really hear what his uncle was saying.

"I've got to know for the Derby! I've got to know for the Derby!" the child reiterated, his big blue eyes blazing with a sort of madness.

His mother noticed how overwrought he was.

"You'd better go to the seaside. Wouldn't you like to go now to the seaside, instead of waiting? I think you'd better," she said, looking down at him anxiously, her heart curiously heavy because of him.

But the child lifted his uncanny blue eyes.

"I couldn't possibly go before the Derby, mother!" he said. "I couldn't possibly!"

"Why not?" she said, her voice becoming heavy when she was opposed. "Why not? You can still go from the seaside to see the Derby with your Uncle Oscar, if that's what you wish. No need for you to wait here. Besides, I think you care too much about these races. It's a bad sign. My family has been a gambling family, and you won't know till you grow up how much damage it has done. But it has done damage. I shall have to send Bassett away, and ask Uncle Oscar not to talk racing to you, unless you promise to be reasonable about it; go away to the seaside and forget it. You're all nerves!"

"I'll do what you like, mother, so long as you don't send me away till after the Derby," the boy said.

"Send you away from where? Just from this house?"

"Yes," he said, gazing at her.

"Why, you curious child, what makes you care about this house so much, suddenly? I never knew you loved it."

He gazed at her without speaking. He had a secret within a secret, something he had not divulged, even to Bassett or to his Uncle Oscar.

But his mother, after standing undecided and a little bit sullen for some moments, said:

"Very well, then! Don't go to the seaside till after the Derby, if you don't wish it. But promise me you won't let your nerves go to pieces. Promise you won't think so much about horse-racing and *events*, as you call them!"

"Oh, no," said the boy casually. "I won't think much about them, mother. You needn't worry. I wouldn't worry, mother, if I were you."

"If you were me and I were you," said his mother, "I wonder what we *should* do!"

"But you know you needn't worry, mother, don't you?" the boy repeated.

"I should be awfully glad to know it," she said wearily.

"Oh, well, you *can*, you know. I mean, you ought to know you needn't worry," he insisted.

"Ought I? Then I'll see about it," she said.

Paul's secret of secrets was his wooden horse, that which had no name. Since he was emancipated from a nurse and a nursery-governess, he had had his rocking-horse removed to his own bedroom at the top of the house.

"Surely, you're too big for a rocking-horse!" his mother had remonstrated.

"Well, you see, mother, till I can have a real horse, I like to have some sort of animal about," had been his quaint answer.

"Do you feel he keeps you company?" she laughed.

"Oh, yes! He's very good, he always keeps me company, when I'm there," said Paul.

So the horse, rather shabby, stood in an arrested prance in the boy's bedroom.

The Derby was drawing near, and the boy grew more and more tense. He hardly heard what was spoken to him, he was very frail, and his eyes were really uncanny. His mother had sudden seizures of uneasiness about him. Sometimes, for half-an-hour, she would feel a sudden anxiety about him that was almost anguish. She wanted to rush to him at once, and know he was safe.

Two nights before the Derby, she was at a big party in town, when one of her rushes of anxiety about her boy, her first-born, gripped her heart till she could hardly speak. She fought with the feeling, might and main, for she believed in common sense. But it was too strong. She had to leave the dance and go downstairs to telephone to the country. The children's nursery-governess was terribly surprised and startled at being rung up in the night.

"Are the children all right, Miss Wilmot?"

"Oh yes, they are quite all right."

"Master Paul? Is he all right?"

"He went to bed as right as a trivet.[9] Shall I run up and look at him?"

"No," said Paul's mother reluctantly. "No! Don't trouble. It's all right. Don't sit up. We shall be home fairly soon." She did not want her son's privacy intruded upon.

"Very good," said the governess.

It was about one o'clock when Paul's mother and father drove up to their house. All was still. Paul's mother went to her room and slipped off her white fur cloak. She had told her maid not to wait up for her. She heard her husband downstairs, mixing a whiskey-and-soda.

And then, because of the strange anxiety at her heart, she stole upstairs to her son's room. Noiselessly she went along the upper corridor. Was there a faint noise? What was it?

She stood, with arrested muscles, outside his door, listening. There was a strange, heavy, and yet not loud noise. Her heart stood still. It was a soundless noise, yet rushing and powerful. Something huge, in violent, hushed motion. What was it? What in God's name was it? She ought to know. She felt that she knew the noise. She knew what it was.

Yet she could not place it. She couldn't say what it was. And on and on it went, like a madness.

Softly, frozen with anxiety and fear, she turned the doorhandle.

The room was dark. Yet in the space near the window, she heard and saw something plunging to and fro. She gazed in fear and amazement.

Then suddenly she switched on the light, and saw her son, in his green pajamas, madly surging on the rocking-horse. The blaze of light suddenly lit him up, as he urged the wooden horse, and lit her up, as she stood, blonde, in her dress of pale green and crystal, in the doorway.

"Paul!" she cried. "Whatever are you doing?"

"It's Malabar!" he screamed, in a powerful, strange voice. "It's Malabar."

His eyes blazed at her for one strange and senseless second, as he ceased urging his wooden horse. Then he fell with a crash to the ground, and she, all her tormented motherhood flooding upon her, rushed to gather him up.

But he was unconscious, and unconscious he remained, with some brain-fever. He talked and tossed, and his mother sat stonily by his side.

"Malabar! It's Malabar! Bassett, Bassett, I know! It's Malabar!"

So the child cried, trying to get up and urge the rocking-horse that gave him his inspiration.

"What does he mean by Malabar?" asked the heart-frozen mother.

"I don't know," said the father stonily.

"What does he mean by Malabar?" she asked her brother Oscar.

"It's one of the horses running for the Derby," was the answer.

And, in spite of himself, Oscar Cresswell spoke to Bassett, and himself put a thousand on Malabar: at fourteen to one.

The third day of the illness was critical: they were waiting for a change. The boy, with his rather long, curly hair, was tossing ceaselessly on the pillow. He neither slept nor regained consciousness, and his eyes were like blue stones. His mother sat, feeling her heart had gone, turned actually into a stone.

In the evening, Oscar Cresswell did not come, but Bassett sent a message, saying could he come up for one moment, just one moment? Paul's mother was very angry at the intrusion, but on second thought she agreed. The boy was the same. Perhaps Bassett might bring him to consciousness.

The gardener, a shortish fellow with a little brown mustache, and sharp little brown eyes,

---

9. **trivet**\trĭ·vət\ a tripod, but here used idiomatically to mean "entirely all right."

tiptoed into the room, touched his imaginary cap to Paul's mother, and stole to the bedside, staring with glittering, smallish eyes, at the tossing, dying child.

"Master Paul!" he whispered. "Master Paul! Malabar come in first all right, a clean win. I did as you told me. You've made over seventy thousand pounds, you have; you've got over eighty thousand. Malabar came in all right, Master Paul."

"Malabar! Malabar! Did I say Malabar, mother? Did I say Malabar? Do you think I'm lucky, mother? I knew Malabar, didn't I? Over eighty thousand pounds! I call that lucky, don't you, mother? Over eighty thousand pounds! I knew, didn't I know I knew? Malabar came in all right. If I ride my horse till I'm sure, then I tell you, Bassett, you can go as high as you like. Did you go for all you were worth, Bassett?"

"I went a thousand on it, Master Paul."

"I never told you, mother, that if I can ride my horse, and *get there,* then I'm absolutely sure—oh, absolutely! Mother, did I ever tell you? I *am* lucky."

"No, you never did," said the mother.

But the boy died in the night.

And even as he lay dead, his mother heard her brother's voice saying to her: "Actually, Hester, you're eighty-odd thousand to the good and a poor devil of a son to the bad. But, poor devil, poor devil, he's best gone out of a life where he rides his rocking-horse to find a winner."

I
IS LUCK ENOUGH?

In this story, Lawrence takes a bitter woman, incapable of any real depth of feeling, and shows how her dissatisfaction and unhappiness permeate her family, represented here by Paul. She has faith in only one thing—luck. But even that is a bitter faith, for she believes that she herself has none. Although Paul's extraordinary luck at the races brings her a fortune, he really can do nothing to satisfy her. She and the family are on a rocking-horse riding harder and harder to nowhere.

II
IMPLICATIONS

"The Rocking-Horse Winner" is a story exceptionally rich in implications. The statements that follow touch on some of them. Remember that the purpose of these discussions is not that everyone should agree but that each should bring his own experience and thinking clearly to bear on the questions that are raised.

1. The mother communicates her anxieties to the children although she never mentions them directly.

2. Paul's desperate eagerness to help his mother is not natural.

3. Paul's mother is a person who is incapable of love, even of loving her own children.

4. In every society there are drones and workers . . . the mother represents the one segment and Paul the other.

5. Paul is "best gone out of a life where he rides his rocking-horse to find a winner."

III
TECHNIQUES

Characterization

Two methods of characterization are used in "The Rocking-Horse Winner." Reread the first four paragraphs. What details are given to establish the picture of the mother? Reread the first conversation between Paul and his mother and Paul's treatment of the rocking-horse immediately afterwards. How many impressions do you gather of Paul from what he says and from the way he treats his horse, even though no direct statements are made about him?

Plot

In modern short stories, writers are increasingly concerned with the relationship between character and incident. What happens is dependent on the kind of people that are involved. In what ways does the personality of the following characters determine what happens?

a. The mother
b. Bassett
c. Uncle Oscar

IV

WORDS

A. 1. A writer often adds force to his work through the use of carefully selected adverbs of manner, those that express the manner in which something is done as in these expressions: a curve which projected *giddily,* staring *fixedly,* grinned *inanely.* Find other expressive adverbs of manner in the selections you have read. Observe how the exact adverbs add conciseness. Instead of "it seems to me" a writer may use "seemingly" to express doubt; or instead of "it was obvious" he uses _____; instead of "with great speed" he may use _____.

2. A good writer, however, depends more upon vivid verbs; for many active, vivid verbs suggest manner as well as action. Compare: he went away with great speed; he went away speedily; he sped away. What general action is indicated by the italicized verbs below? What additional information is concentrated in the verb?

The light *glinted* merrily upon his horn-rimmed spectacles.

He *pitched* forward upon his face.

Arnold felt his brother *twist* away.

He *pursed* his mouth tight.

The boy *writhed* in an odd way.

His face *hardened* and became more expressionless.

He was *emancipated* from a nurse and a nursery-governess.

Paul's mother *slipped* off her white fur coat.

The gardener *tiptoed* into the room.

B. From context determine the meanings of the italicized words. Then check the meanings in your dictionary.

1. "They had *discreet* servants and felt themselves superior to everyone in the neighborhood."

2. "Wildly the rocking-horse *careened.*"

3. "He would speak to nobody when he was in full *tilt.*"

4. "He had a secret within a secret, something he had not *divulged.*"

C. 1. Often forms of roots may vary because English has sometimes used one form of a Latin word for one series of English words, another form for another. In taking roots from Latin verbs, for instance, English has sometimes used present tense forms and sometimes past participle forms. Notice the following sets of roots: *-pend-, -pens-,* meaning "to hang," as in *suspend* and *suspense; -pon-, -pos-,* meaning "to place," as in *postpone* and *compose; -scrib-, -script-,* meaning "to write," as in *describe* and *description;* and *-string-, -strict-,* meaning "to pull or bind tight," as in *stringent* and *stricture.* In these roots the first form is from the present tense of the Latin verb, the second form the past participle. Analyze the following words into affixes and roots, with the aid of your dictionary: *recognize, defiant, vibration, solicitude, terrify, immense, tentative, inspect, perfect, intervene, appreciably, sufficient, annihilation, accumulation, illusion, commendable, protrude, unison, reject, prospect, assertion, obscure, inspiration.*

2. Find out from the etymologies in your dictionary whether the following pairs of words contain the same root: *convince, evince; terrify, terrestrial; protect, detect; definite, finally; complete, replete; immense, commensurate; museum, amuse; fervor, fervid; impulse, propulsion; recite, citation; exclamation, reclamation.*

Mammon is a Biblical symbol for money
and the archer in this title is Cupid,
the Roman god of love. Do money and love mix?
Only O. Henry could serve up
such a delightful comedy as he explores
the crosscurrents between a father's
and a son's different attitudes
toward these subjects.

Mammon and the Archer

O. HENRY

Old Anthony Rockwall, retired manufacturer and proprietor of Rockwall's Eureka[1] Soap, looked out the library window of his Fifth Avenue mansion and grinned. His neighbor to the right—the aristocratic clubman, G. Van Schuylight Suffolk-Jones—came out to his waiting motor-car, wrinkling a contumelious nostril, as usual, at the Italian renaissance sculpture of the soap palace's front elevation.[2]

"Stuck-up old statuette of nothing doing!" commented the ex-Soap King. "The Eden Musée'll get that old frozen Nesselrode[3] yet if he don't watch out. I'll have this house painted red, white, and blue next summer and see if that'll make his Dutch nose turn up any higher."

And then Anthony Rockwall, who never cared for bells, went to the door of his library and shouted "Mike!" in the same voice that had once chipped off pieces of the welkin[4] on the Kansas prairies.

"Tell my son," said Anthony to the answering menial, "to come in here before he leaves the house."

When young Rockwall entered the library the old man laid aside his newspaper, looked at him with a kindly grimness on his big, smooth, ruddy countenance, rumpled his mop of white hair with one hand and rattled the keys in his pocket with the other.

"Richard," said Anthony Rockwall, "what do you pay for the soap that you use?"

Richard, only six months home from college, was startled a little. He had not yet taken the measure of this sire of his, who was as full of unexpectednesses as a girl at her first party.

"Six dollars a dozen, I think, dad."

"And your clothes?"

"I suppose about sixty dollars, as a rule."

"You're a gentleman," said Anthony, decidedly. "I've heard of these young bloods[5] spending $24 a dozen for soap, and going over the hundred mark for clothes. You've got as much money to waste as any of 'em and yet you stick to what's decent and moderate. Now I use the old Eureka—not only for sentiment, but it's the purest soap made. Whenever you pay more than 10 cents a cake for soap you buy bad perfumes and labels. But 50 cents is doing very well for a young man in your generation, position and condition. As I said, you're a gentleman. They say it takes three generations to make one. They're off. Money'll do it as slick as soap grease. It's made you one. By hokey! it's almost made one of me. I'm nearly as impolite and disagreeable and ill-mannered as these two old Knickerbocker[6] gents on each side of me that can't sleep of nights because I bought in between 'em."

"There are some things that money can't accomplish," remarked young Rockwall, rather gloomily.

"Now, don't say that," said old Anthony, shocked. "I bet my money on money every time. I've been through the encyclopedia down to Y

---

1. **Eureka**\yʊ ˄rē·kə\.
2. The aristocratic clubman is displeased by the ornate sculptures of Mr. Rockwall's house.
3. **Eden Musée**\˄myū·zē\ an art collection. **Nesselrode** \˄nĕ·səl ˈrōd\ a frozen pudding with very rich ingredients.
4. **welkin**\˄wĕl·kĭn\ sky.
5. **blood**, a fashionable young man given to social life, recreation, and night life.
6. **Knickerbocker**\˄nĭ·kər ˄bŏ·kər\ a descendent of the early Dutch settlers of New York and hence members of high society.

looking for something you can't buy with it; and I expect to have to take up the appendix next week. I'm for money against the field. Tell me something money won't buy."

"For one thing," answered Richard, rankling a little, "it won't buy one into the exclusive circles of society."

"Oho! won't it?" thundered the champion of the root of evil. "You tell me where your exclusive circles would be if the first Astor hadn't had the money to pay for his steerage[7] passage over?"

Richard sighed.

"And that's what I was coming to," said the old man, less boisterously. "That's why I asked you to come in. There's something going wrong with you, boy. I've been noticing it for two weeks. Out with it. I guess I could lay my hands on eleven millions within twenty-four hours, besides the real estate. If it's your liver, there's the *Rambler* down in the bay, coaled, and ready to steam down to the Bahamas[8] in two days."

"Not a bad guess, Dad; you haven't missed it far."

"Ah," said Anthony, keenly; "what's her name?"

Richard began to walk up and down the library floor. There was enough comradeship and sympathy in this crude old father of his to draw his confidence.

"Why don't you ask her?" demanded old Anthony. "She'll jump at you. You've got the money and the looks, and you're a decent boy. Your hands are clean. You've got no Eureka soap on 'em. You've been to college, but she'll overlook that."

"I haven't had a chance," said Richard.

"Make one," said Anthony. "Take her for a walk in the park, or a straw ride, or walk home with her from church. Chance! Pshaw!"

"You don't know the social mill, dad. She's part of the stream that turns it. Every hour and minute of her time is arranged for days in advance. I must have that girl, Dad, or this town is a black-jack[9] swamp forevermore. And I can't write it—I can't do that."

"Tut!" said the old man. "Do you mean to tell me that with all the money I've got you can't get an hour or two of a girl's time for yourself?"

"I've put it off too late. She's going to sail for Europe at noon day after tomorrow for a two years' stay. I'm to see her alone tomorrow evening for a few minutes. She's at Larchmont[10] now at her aunt's. I can't go there. But I'm allowed to meet her with a cab at the Grand Central Station[11] tomorrow evening at the 8:30 train. We drive down Broadway to Wallack's[12] at a gallop, where her mother and a box party[13] will be waiting for us in the lobby. Do you think she would listen to a declaration from me during that six or eight minutes under those circumstances? No. And what chance would I have in the theater or afterwards? None. No, dad, this is one tangle that your money can't unravel. We can't buy one minute of time with cash; if we could, rich people would live longer. There's no hope of getting a talk with Miss Lantry before she sails."

"All right, Richard, my boy," said old Anthony, cheerfully. "You may run along down to your club now. I'm glad it ain't your liver. But don't forget to burn a few punk sticks in the joss house to the great god Mazuma from time to time.[14] You say money won't buy time? Well, of course, you can't order eternity

---

7. The **Astor** family rose from poor beginnings to great wealth. **Steerage**\ˈstē·rəj\ that part of a passenger ship with the least comfortable and cheapest quarters.
8. **Rambler**, the Rockwall yacht. **Bahamas**\bə ˈha-məz\ West Indies islands east of Cuba.
9. **black-jack**, a scrubby oak tree common to poor ground in southeastern and southern U.S. Richard means that the city will have no appeal or value to him.
10. **Larchmont**\ˈlarch·mŏnt\ a wealthy suburb north of New York City.
11. **Grand Central Station** is on 42nd Street several blocks east of Broadway.
12. **Wallack's**, a theater on the west side below 33rd Street.
13. **box party**, a group that would occupy a box in the theater.
14. **punk stick**, a stick of incense. **joss**\jŏs\ **house,** a Chinese temple. **Mazuma**\mə ˈzū·mə\ money. His father is telling Richard not to underestimate what money can accomplish.

New York City, at the turn of the century. A sudden turn and a locked wheel could result in a tangle of horses and carriages.

wrapped up and delivered at your residence for a price, but I've seen Father Time get pretty bad stone bruises on his heels when he walked through the gold diggings."

That night came Aunt Ellen, gentle, sentimental, wrinkled, sighing, oppressed by wealth, in to brother Anthony at his evening paper, and began discourse on the subject of lovers' woes.

"He told me all about it," said brother Anthony, yawning. "I told him my bank account was at his service. And then he began to knock money. Said money couldn't help. Said the rules of society couldn't be bucked for a yard by a team of ten-millionaires."

"Oh, Anthony," sighed Aunt Ellen, "I wish you would not think so much of money. Wealth is nothing where a true affection is concerned. Love is all-powerful. If he only had spoken earlier! She could not have refused our Richard. But now I fear it is too late. He will have no opportunity to address her. All your gold cannot bring happiness to your son."

At eight o'clock the next evening Aunt Ellen took a quaint old gold ring from a moth-eaten case and gave it to Richard.

"Wear it tonight, nephew," she begged. "Your mother gave it to me. Good luck in love she said it brought. She asked me to give it to you when you had found the one you loved."

Young Rockwall took the ring reverently and tried it on his smallest finger. It slipped as far as the second joint and stopped. He took it off and stuffed it into his vest pocket, after the manner of man. And then he 'phoned for his cab.

At the station he captured Miss Lantry out of the gadding mob at eight thirty-two.

"We mustn't keep mamma and the others waiting," said she.

"To Wallack's Theater as fast as you can drive!" said Richard loyally.

They whirled up Forty-second to Broadway, and then down the white-starred lane that leads from the soft meadows of sunset to the rocky hills of morning.

At Thirty-fourth Street young Richard quickly thrust up the trap and ordered the cabman to stop.

"I've dropped a ring," he apologized, as he climbed out. "It was my mother's, and I'd hate to lose it. I won't detain you a minute—I saw where it fell."

In less than a minute he was back in the cab with the ring.

But within that minute a crosstown car had stopped directly in front of the cab. The cabman tried to pass to the left, but a heavy express wagon cut him off. He tried the right, and had to back away from a furniture van that had no business to be there. He tried to back out, but dropped his reins and swore dutifully. He was blockaded in a tangled mess of vehicles and horses.

One of those street blockades had occurred that sometimes tie up commerce and movement quite suddenly in the big city.[15]

"Why don't you drive on?" said Miss Lantry, impatiently. "We'll be late."

Richard stood up in the cab and looked around. He saw a congested flood of wagons, trucks, cabs, vans and street cars filling the vast space where Broadway, Sixth Avenue and Thirty-fourth street cross one another[16] as a twenty-six inch maiden fills her twenty-two inch girdle. And still from all the cross streets they were hurrying and rattling toward the converging point at full speed, and hurling themselves into the struggling mass, locking wheels and adding their drivers' imprecations to the clamor. The entire traffic of Manhattan seemed to have jammed itself around them. The oldest New Yorker among the thousands of spectators that lined the sidewalks had not witnessed a street blockade of the proportions of this one.

"I'm very sorry," said Richard, as he resumed his seat, "but it looks as if we are stuck. They won't get this jumble loosened up in an hour. It was my fault. If I hadn't dropped the ring we—"

"Let me see the ring," said Miss Lantry. "Now that it can't be helped, I don't care. I think theaters are stupid, anyway."

At 11 o'clock that night somebody tapped lightly on Anthony Rockwall's door.

"Come in," shouted Anthony, who was in a red dressing-gown, reading a book of piratical adventures.

Somebody was Aunt Ellen, looking like a gray-haired angel that had been left on earth by mistake.

"They're engaged, Anthony," she said, softly. "She has promised to marry our Richard. On their way to the theater there was a street blockade, and it was two hours before their cab could get out of it.

"And oh, brother Anthony, don't ever boast of the power of money again. A little emblem of true love—a little ring that symbolized unending and unmercenary affection—was the cause of our Richard finding his happiness. He dropped it in the street, and got out to recover it. And before they could continue the blockade occurred. He spoke to his love and won her there while the cab was hemmed in. Money is dross compared with true love, Anthony."

"All right," said old Anthony. "I'm glad the boy has got what he wanted. I told him I wouldn't spare any expense in the matter if—"

"But, brother Anthony, what good could your money have done?"

"Sister," said Anthony Rockwall. "I've got my pirate in a devil of a scrape. His ship has just been scuttled, and he's too good a judge of the value of money to let drown. I wish you would let me go on with this chapter."

The story should end here. I wish it would as heartily as you who read it wish it did. But we must go to the bottom of the well for truth.

The next day a person with red hands and a blue polka-dot necktie, who called himself Kelly, called at Anthony Rockwall's house, and was at once received in the library.

"Well," said Anthony, reaching for his checkbook, "it was a good bilin' of soap.[17] Let's see— you had $5,000 in cash."

"I paid out $300 more of my own," said Kelly. "I had to go a little above the estimate. I got the express wagons and cabs mostly for $5; but the trucks and two-horse teams mostly raised me to $10. The motormen wanted $10, and some of

---

15. Such traffic jams were not uncommon in the days before modern methods of directing traffic.
16. The Herald Square Section some nine blocks south of Times Square.
17. **a good bilin' of soap,** a good performance.

the loaded teams $20. The cops struck me hardest—$50 I paid two, and the rest $20 and $25. But didn't it work beautiful, Mr. Rockwall? I'm glad William A. Brady[18] wasn't onto that little outdoor vehicle mob scene. I wouldn't want William to break his heart with jealousy. And never a rehearsal, either! The boys was on time to the fraction of a second. It was two hours before a snake could get below Greeley's statue."[19]

"Thirteen hundred—there you are, Kelly," said Anthony, tearing off a check. "Your thousand, and the $300 you were out. You don't despise money, do you, Kelly?"

"Me?" said Kelly. "I can lick the man that invented poverty."

Anthony called Kelly when he was at the door.

"You didn't notice," said he, "anywhere in the tie-up, a kind of a fat boy[20] without any clothes on shooting arrows around with a bow, did you?"

"Why, no," said Kelly, mystified. "I didn't. If he was like you say, maybe the cops pinched him before I got there."

"I thought the little rascal wouldn't be on hand," chuckled Anthony. "Good-by, Kelly."

I
FAMILY CONTRASTS

The great-hearted gruffness of Anthony Rockwall, who frankly enjoys being the way he is, delights the reader. Because many of us hide what we really are and are also painfully aware of the pretenses of others, we enjoy the unshakable self-confidence of a man like Rockwall. His son, on the other hand, lives largely according to the standards of polite society. His views are the conventional, or common, ones in that society.

II
IMPLICATIONS

What are your reactions to the following statements?

1. If money is spent wisely, it can buy happiness.

2. True love is a state of mind which cannot be altered by money or the lack of it.

3. Everybody has his price for which he can be bought.

4. It is unusual for a father to be unconventional and his son conventional.

III
TECHNIQUES
Characterization

O. Henry wrote for magazines, and his methods of storytelling are still the pattern for many of today's magazine writers. In this type of writing, characters are quickly drawn with a few bold strokes and little shading or complication. This technique has been criticized for making the characters seem flat and oversimplified and unlike real people. Take Anthony Rockwall, Richard, Aunt Ellen, and Miss Lantry and see what information O. Henry gives about them. Which of them seem well-rounded, full-blooded people?

Plot

O. Henry is famous for his skill in developing plots. How do the following elements in the story create situations that move the plot ahead?

1. Richard's disbelief in the powers of money.

2. The shortness of time that Richard has with Miss Lantry and the fact that they must spend it in a cab.

3. Aunt Ellen's giving Richard his mother's ring.

---

18. **William A. Brady,** a theatrical producer whose productions sometimes had very large casts and very large audiences. He was also manager for some world's champion heavyweights. In both roles he was familiar with mob scenes.
19. **Horace Greeley** (1811–1872), journalist and political leader, at Herald Square.
20. The reference is to Cupid.

Differences between generations have long been a source of crosscurrents among men, but they are not the only source. In "The Ambassador" two different life styles, one growing out of a concentration camp and one out of America's middle class, provide the basis for conflict.

The Ambassador

EDWARD NEWHOUSE

Henry Applegate liked familiar objects. Although his view of shaving was no different from that of most men, once he got down to it he rather enjoyed the process of working up lather in the meerschaum mug that had served two generations of Applegates before him. With time out for wars and minor trips, the mug had been in constant use since Grant's first year in the White House. It had accompanied Grandfather Applegate through the decades of his lackluster service as a diplomat, and Henry's father had had it even longer. When the boys' turn came— But Mark and Ben, neither of whom was old enough to shave, had already announced that they would use electric razors. The mug, if it remained intact, would then attain the status of an heirloom. Henry liked the feel of it.

He had not got around to shaving until it was almost time for lunch. Gwen must have known how late he had turned in, and she had let him sleep through most of the morning. Nice of Gwen. Nice also of Gwen to have left him alone with Lucy so soon after dinner last night. As always she had sensed when Lucy wanted to talk. It was not that Lucy talked any less freely to her mother; she had just grown used to trying things out on her father, to begin with. The boys did it the other way around.

Home on her first Easter vacation from college, Lucy had had a lot to say. Her French teacher had a beard, exactly the kind that Frenchmen are supposed to have. The Dean of Women was a sweetie pie. Ancient History was all right, but no more than that—much too superficial. There were saddle horses to be had not too far from campus, but the rates were absolutely criminal. She had been to Boston only four times since Christmas. You were simply strapped without a car. She was in love. The real thing, this time. He was a senior at Harvard, and his parents didn't understand why he should be studying to become an art critic—but Henry would. In fact, Henry would give him a job at the museum next year—yes? Alan was a wonderful-*looking* boy, though he could use an inch or two more in height. Make that three. She wished he'd learn to ride a horse. Didn't Henry think that criticism could be *creative?*

They had spent half the night talking in front of the open fire. Later in the day, Henry thought, he would have to get the boys out of the house and give Gwen a chance to be alone with Lucy, too. He would take the boys down to the old quarry and let them use the .22. They would like that. He dried the meerschaum mug and put it back in the cabinet.

Gwen came in, a little breathless, and handed him a shirt. "Quick, put it on," she said. "Anton's here. Out in the driveway with Lucy and the boys."

"Darn. I thought he'd crossed us off his list for good," Henry said. "How long has it been? Two years? Two and a half? I don't want this kind of shirt. I'm not going anywhere."

"*He's* dressed to the teeth. Including the teeth, in fact. Brand-new set—all white. Brand-new suit—tropical worsted. Brand-new Cadillac—robin's-egg blue. And all paid for. In cash. It was one of the first things he told us. Henry, where would Anton get that kind of money? Something crooked?"

"Not necessarily."

"Smuggling? You remember all those postcards from South America? Smuggling people across the border, you think? I'm sure it's something crooked."

"Not necessarily," Henry said. "If we give him a good enough lunch, perhaps he'll tell us."

"I wish he'd phone ahead before he shows up at mealtime. I asked him to, once, years ago. He said I'd only go to a lot of trouble and prepare something elaborate. I couldn't tell him it's more trouble this way."

"You could have. It wouldn't have made much of an impression."

He went to the bedroom to get a different shirt. Gwen followed him. Through the window they could see the driveway.

"My, that is a car," he said. "Is that what they call robin's-egg blue?"

"Henry, if he's involved in something crooked— Are you still in some way responsible for him?"

"I was never responsible for his morals. All I signed was a document affirming that he would not become a public charge. And even that's run out by now, I think. Does that car look as though he were on the point of becoming a public charge? *Your* cousins may all become public charges. Not mine. Why, at this rate he'll be running around in a Continental soon. Do you remember the times he walked here from the bus stop? Let's go down before the boys take his car apart."

The boys were playing with the knobs and buttons on the dashboard.

"Lucy thinks he's in some kind of awful racket," Gwen said. "She told me so downstairs."

"And she, of course, would know."

"Oh, I'd just hoped he'd never come again."

"So had I," said Henry. "But he's here."

As a child, Henry had loved to hear his grandmother tell stories about Prague,[1] where she had been born and, to some extent, bred. Even then, he had been vaguely aware that the stories did not always hold up (his grandfather had been third, not first, secretary at the American Consulate), but that did not make them any less absorbing. A mettlesome Czech patriot who shared her countrymen's traditional view of their neighbors to the south, she had been the first person Henry heard say, "If you have a Magyar[2] for a friend, you don't need an enemy." After her death, there had been no one who wanted to keep up a correspondence with the brother she had left in Prague, let alone with his issue through the generations. Henry had not known he had a second cousin until a social worker named Mrs. Platt came to see him at his office in the museum. That was a couple of years after the war.

Anton was then in a displaced persons' camp somewhere in the American Zone of Germany. He had left Prague after the Communists took over, and he wanted to come to the United States. Mrs. Platt felt that he was an exceptionally deserving case. For one thing, he had spent most of the war years in German concentration camps. That he had survived at all was due to his skill as a goldsmith and watchmaker; the camp officials had kept him alive and busy, repairing watches and working on gold taken from Jews. It was to his credit, too, that he could not get along under the current regime in Czechoslovakia.

Mrs. Platt's agency had power to act only if Mr. Applegate or some other American citizen was willing to provide a guarantee that Anton would not become a public charge. Just a formality, she said. Red tape. The agency would assume full responsibility. Through its connections, it would have no trouble at all in finding work for a skilled goldsmith and watchmaker. Anton spoke good English; he had been studying it from the time he was a small boy, always with the idea of one day coming to America. It was a matter of giving a man, a young man still under thirty, a chance to start life over again.

Henry sent his affidavit the following day, and received acknowledgment of it at once.

---

1. **Prague**\prag\ capital and largest city of Czechoslovakia.
2. **Magyar**\ᵔmag 'yar\ a member of the principal ethnic group in Hungary.

Then he heard nothing until, two years later, Mrs. Platt telephoned him at his office. The young man was on Ellis Island, she said. The red tape had all been attended to. There was a job for him with a reputable jewelry firm, one of whose senior partners, a German Jew, had himself lived under Hitler. A furnished room with a fine Czech family, in Yorkville, had been secured, and the rent paid for a month in advance. Mrs. Platt was going out to the Island now. She thought she'd bring Anton back to her office late in the afternoon. Would Mr. Applegate like to meet him there?

Henry said he would indeed. Since it was Friday, he thought it might be pleasant if he drove Anton out to his place for the weekend. Anton could take possession of the furnished room on Monday.

"That would be fine," she said. "That might be just the thing."

When Henry arrived at her office, shortly after five, she came out to meet him in the waiting room. "He's in there," she said. "I wanted a word with you first. He's—not what you'd call communicative. Maybe I haven't found the right approach. He does speak English. He— Good heavens, he looks like you! You could pass for brothers. Twins, if he weren't younger. And you're only cousins."

"Second cousins."

"Remarkable. Well, he's in there. He seems eager to start working. He wants to change his name from Havranek to Byron. Anthony Byron. I guess it's all right. Anybody who's spent four years in places like Neuengamme and Buchenwald is entitled to any name he likes."

"Did he tell you why they put him in a camp in the first place?" Henry asked.

"We haven't talked about it," she said. "Let me see, now. The original arrest was made in Hamburg. Anton—Anthony—was representing his Czech firm there. I think he was accused of arranging to help a Jew escape. Then, once they had him, that was it. They found him useful. He made trinkets for the S.S. men,[3] worked on watches. Maybe you'll find him

more willing to talk. Please don't press him."

"I wasn't going to."

"Oh, I'm sorry. You wouldn't, of course. I was just doing my professional duty. Would you like to meet him now?"

They went in. Mrs. Platt had not exaggerated. Anton could easily have passed for Henry's brother. His eyes were on the same level, and for Henry it was like looking into a mirror that made him appear ten or twelve years younger. Somebody, he thought—the great-grandfather they shared, or somebody—must have spawned the mightiest genes on either bank of the Moldau. For all he knew, it gave Anton a turn to catch a glimpse of himself as a man of forty. The resemblance diminished, though, when Anton opened his mouth. He had a full set of teeth made of a dull metal alloy. He wore an ill-fitting, unpressed suit of a material that had begun to fade in irregular patches. Everything he owned was in a cardboard valise not much larger than a briefcase. He would not let Henry carry it.

Downstairs, the combined effect of that suit and that valise made Henry a bit self-conscious about his car, which was an Oldsmobile less than two weeks old. It had never been rained on. Henry still had that Oldsmobile the morning, three years later, when Anton showed up in the blue Cadillac. By then, it had run many thousands of miles and its fenders bore the marks of Lucy's course in driving, but it was in showroom condition the day Anton first saw it, and he took a long look before he got in. He asked, "Are you rich?"

"I'm afraid not," Henry said.

"In Europe, if you owned nothing only this car, you would be."

His accent was just slightly reminiscent of what Henry remembered of his grandmother's. Besides the Czech, there seemed to be a little German in it, and some British. There was no "th" sounds and no w's. And he had a number

---

3. **SS men,** the *Schutzstaffel* (protection staff), a special police force of the Nazi party under Hitler.

of expressions that he might have picked up from the Americans who supervised the D.P. camp; "rakeoff" was one.

Driving up Fifth Avenue, Henry made a few attempts to call his cousin's attention to a notable building, a landmark, a store window. Anton barely glanced at each. He did not crane his neck at the Empire State. He uttered a faintly nasal "Mmm" as they passed Radio City. Somewhere Henry had read of the emotional torpor that often settles permanently over people who have spent many years in concentration camps. The writer had compared it to accidie, the sloth that loomed in some monastic theologies as not only the deadliest of the seven deadly sins but the source of all the others. Henry thought of it that afternoon as the possible cause of Anton's apparently total lack of interest in the City of New York. Later, it seemed more as though Anton were making it a point of honor not to let Henry see he was impressed. "Mmm," he said in response to a comment about the Metropolitan Museum.

Farther uptown, he did incline his head a little as they drove by the museum of which Henry was curator. He even asked what the duties of a curator might be. Henry told him, and, in a burst of relief at this first sign of mild interest, went on to describe how the staff had gone about establishing the authenticity of a Tiepolo etching—rather an involved process. Anton said, "So I suppose part of your income is the rakeoff from the dealers."

Henry turned his head to look at him. Anton was not smiling.

"No," Henry said.

"No?"

"No."

"You bought this car out from the salary they pay you?"

"Yes."

"Mmm," said Anton.

To reach the Applegates' house, which was in a village called Brandy Point, in the Highlands of the Hudson, they had to cross the river. Henry wondered whether it would be more interesting for his guest to go over by ferry or across the bridge. From the ferry Anton might have got a more leisurely view of Manhattan, but Friday-evening traffic on the George Washington can be something of an experience, too. They took the bridge. Anton did not consider the traffic worthy of remark, but he did ask how much Henry had paid at the tollgate. Then he wanted to know when the bridge had been built and what it had cost. Henry gave him the approximate date and made an estimate in the tens of millions.

"But this means the bridge have been paid for already," Anton said.

"Maybe several times over. I don't know. There's maintenance, of course."

"So where goes all the money?"

Henry gave him a moderately well-informed account of the workings of the Port of New York Authority.

"I mean who gets rich from all the half dollars?" Anton asked.

"Why, I don't believe anyone does, really."

"No?"

"No."

"No rakeoff, you don't think?"

"No."

"Mmm."

Some miles north, on the Palisades across from Yonkers, Henry stopped to give Anton a view of the river, and offered to put a dime into one of the telescopes mounted there, but Anton declined. "How far you live from the city?" he asked.

"A little over twenty miles."

Anton transposed miles into kilometers in half the time it would have taken Henry. "And you are sure that is safe from atom bomb?" he asked.

"No, I'm not sure. I like to think so—hope so, let's say."

"Wind could bring the radioactive up the river between hills."

"Wind could also blow it out to sea. That's what I'm counting on."

"You do not worry?"

"Not often."

"Mmm. You were in the war?"

"Yes."

"Army?"

"Navy."

"You have been bombed?"

"Just once. Off Okinawa."

"Did it hit?"

"No."

"You were on a big ship?"

"Aircraft carrier. Pretty big."

"Those ships are nice and clean," said Anton. "That is the way to fight in the war. You live to tell."

He doesn't feel like staring across at Yonkers any more, Henry thought. And I don't feel like telling him about the *Lexington* and the *Wasp*. All right. I had an easy time in the war. Let it go at that.

They were both quiet during the rest of the drive to Brandy Point. Henry wondered whether that nasal "Mmm" was a noncommittal sound or one of active disbelief.

As they pulled into the Applegates' garage, Anton looked at the station wagon in the other space. "Yours?" he asked.

Henry nodded.

"You do trucking?"

Before Henry could begin explaining the uses of a station wagon, Anton's eyes were fixed on the house. It was a white frame house, well built by Henry's father shortly after Henry's birth. Set on top of a hill that sloped down to the river, it received its shelter from a remarkable group of trees, which enjoyed great local celebrity by reason of size and age. Because of the trees, there was just one other house visible from any of the windows, and only part of its roof, at that. A family of raccoons lived in the large elm behind the garage. The flagstones in the terrace probably had some salt content, because Henry had seen as many as five deer licking them at once. The squirrels and the chipmunks liked them, too.

"In Europe," said Anton, "a man who owned two cars would have a house made from stone. Or brick."

Gwen and Lucy met them at the door. The boys were down in the basement, Gwen said, with a snapping turtle they had caught beside the pond. Lucy offered to take Anton's valise, but he would not hand it over. Lucy was fifteen that year—a tall, slender, awkward, lovely child. She played the piano a lot and wrote poetry. Henry doubted whether any one of the poems could be described as good, but each had a line or two that surprised and delighted him.

At dinner, Anton wanted to know why, in a house supplied with electric lights, candles were used to eat by. Somewhat to Henry's surprise, he accepted Gwen's answer without making the nasal sound. In fact, he made it again only when they settled down to coffee in front of the fire. He said it was foolish to waste wood in a house with central heating.

"He's right," said Lucy, though usually it was she who insisted on having a fire. (She could not take her eyes off Anton. She and Henry had been talking about him only a few weeks before; afterward she had found a book about German concentration camps and had spent an afternoon reading every word of it. Images based on the nightmare photographs had cropped up in two of her poems.) "Now he's going to write his people in Czechoslovakia and tell them how foolish we are."

"I have no people in Czechoslovakia," Anton said.

"No parents?" She had been told not to question him, but the words slipped out.

Anton did not appear to mind. He said, "My father died when I was little boy. My mother was killed when the Russians cannoned the village."

"Oh, I'm sorry," Lucy said.

"Is all right. I did not like her very much."

"You must have," she said. "Everybody does. Most everybody."

"Not most everybody," Anton said. He seemed to be amused. His smile showed the upper row of the dull metal teeth. "Do you remember the Ten Commandments? He tells you must honor your father and your mother.

He tells nothing about you must honor your son and your daughter. Why? Because people honor their children without somebody tells they must. To like your father and your mother, this must be Commandment. If most everybody liked his father and his mother, it would not have to be Commandment. You understand?"

"I suppose it's one thing to honor them and another to like them," Lucy said. She kept winding her watch, rather nervously.

"Don't do that, dear," her mother said. "You'll break it."

"Then I will fix," Anton said.

He stared into the fire, and talked a little about how he happened to learn watchmaking. As a trained goldsmith, he had at first been put to work at his own trade in the Neuengamme camp. For the most part, his job consisted of making rings and other negotiable jewelry out of gold taken from the mouths of inmates, dead or alive. This was a private, local enterprise, and Anton remained for a time under the protection of the S.S. man in charge of it. But then the government placed the camp on a sounder bookkeeping basis, and there was a steady fall in the supply of gold that could be held out for local use. So Anton and another young man in the shop decided to learn watch-repair work under an old Jew, whom they kept alive out of their scanty food rations. In due course, Anton and his friend, Otto Pflaum, were transferred to Buchenwald as expert watchmakers. There were thousands of watches to repair at Buchenwald, though their owners no longer had use for them.

"He did a bad thing there, my friend," said Anton. "You see, he was the messenger. He carried the watches from our shop to the office of the *Untersturmführer*.[4] And when he was not sure he had did good job, he changed the tickets. And that put the responsible to somebody else, and so two watchmakers got hanged for sabotage. Fifty with the strap and then hanged."

"Hanged?" Lucy repeated.

"Yes. With rope. And almost I was third, but they let me go with the fifty and some other things. Very trickful man, Herr Otto Pflaum. From all the people I knowed, the first to go to America. Rich now, I hear. Someday I will meet with him."

"What will you say?" Lucy asked.

"To Otto? I will say good morning, how are you, glad to see. Show me how to get rich, I will say."

"That's all? To *him*?"

"What else? What you think, Miss? I am the Graf[5] Monte Cristo? Revenge? No, no. If I responsible Otto, then why not the *Untersturmführer*? Why shall I not responsible the *Hauptsturmführer*?[6] Or the *Obersturmbannführer*?[7] No, no. I live. Otto lives. He has mark like this on his arm, but he lives. So I say him good morning, how are you, glad to see. Show me how to get rich." He pushed his sleeve up, and on his forearm there was a tattooed number so large that it reached from his wrist halfway to his elbow. It was a number in the millions, Henry thought, or at least in the hundreds of thousands. The first two figures were in red, the rest in blue. Henry's eyes turned to Lucy. Her fingernails were dug deep into the flesh of her thin arm. He tried to think of something to say, but Gwen was quicker. In her subject-changing voice, she said, "How could he have got rich in so short a time? With taxes as they are."

"Anybody can make money in this country," Anton said. "What is rich? A million dollar? I will have that."

"That'll be nice," Gwen said.

And so the rest of the talk, that first evening, was devoted mostly to the tax structure. Henry could answer some of Anton's questions easily enough, but many were well beyond a layman's competence. Lucy went upstairs, and after a while Gwen suggested that the adults go, too. Anton was taken to his room and

---

4. Untersturmführer\ˈən·tər·stürm ˈfyū·rər\ Lieutenant.
5. Graf\graf\ Count.
6. Hauptsturmführer\ˈHaupt·sturm ˈfyū·rər\ Colonel.
7. Obersturmbannführer\ˈō·bər·sturm·bən ˈfyū·rər\ Lieutenant-Colonel.

shown where things were. He stopped as he passed the window. "You left the bicycles out," he said.

"It's all right," Gwen said. "It isn't going to rain."

"Will they not be stealed?"

"No."

"That is what I meaned," he said. "One million dollar. Anybody can get rich in this country. You are a country of innocent."

Henry was in his pajamas before he remembered to say good night to Lucy. She was lying awake in bed.

"He looks so much like you," she said. "All those things could have happened to you."

"But they didn't. Go to sleep, girl. It's late."

"Why are his teeth made of metal?" she asked.

"I don't know," he said. "Go to sleep. He'll be all right now. We'll help him."

In the morning, Anton said he wanted to go back to New York. He would not say why, and he insisted. Henry offered to drive him there, but he refused, with finality. All he would accept was a ride to the bus stop. There he took the Applegates' address and phone number. "Soon," he said, "I will give signal of myself."

When Henry got home, Gwen said, "The thing that frightens me about him is that he practically never changes his expression. Did you notice that? He's all twisted up, poor fellow."

"So would I be," Lucy said, almost harshly. "So would you, if you'd been through all that."

"Yes, darling. Yes, of course." Gwen turned to Henry. "Please call him next week and see that he's all right, won't you?"

Henry promised he would call.

On Monday, he got the telephone number from Mrs. Platt, and in the evening he rang up the Czech family in Yorkville. But Anton had already moved away. He had given no reason, the man who answered said, and had left no forwarding address.

On Tuesday morning, Henry called Mrs. Platt.

"Yes, I know," she said. "I just talked to him at the jewelry place. Apparently, he wants to be on his own. I didn't press him for his address, but I told him the immigration people would have to know. He said he would notify them at once. I guess we can always reach him at Wright & Schindler's, where he works. But I think I'd leave him be for a while—wait till he gets his bearings. Funny boy."

Just how much Anton wanted to be on his own, the Applegates found out the following week, when they got his first letter:

Dear Henry:

Here is ten dollar. It will I believe pay for my automobil ride to Brandy Point and for my room and for the meals. It is out from my first salary. So you see I pay my way so I will not be a public charge or your charge. Thank you for lending me this money. I consider it a lending. Mr. Schindler says he likes my work. I will see you in the future.

With highest regards I remain,
ANTHONY BYRON

About a month later, just before lunch on a Sunday, Anton showed up in Brandy Point. He had walked the two miles from the nearest bus stop. He had acquired a new pair of shoes and all sorts of other new clothing. He would not hear of taking his ten dollars back. As a matter of fact, he had brought Lucy a box of candy, as payment, he said, for the lunch he knew the Applegates would want him to eat. Again, all he would accept was a ride back to the bus stop.

These unannounced visits of Anton's, always on Sunday, continued for something less than a year. He never failed to bring a small gift in exchange for his lunch, and he never appeared when the Applegates had guests. Gwen thought he reconnoitered the terrain first and, when he saw a strange car in front of the garage, simply took the bus back to New York. From time to time, she professed to see an improvement in what she called his general attitude. Gwen, who came from Indiana, had great faith, not always shared by Henry, in the healing powers of life in the United States.

She was jubilant when Anton turned up on the day before Christmas and put in several hours helping the children with the tree. After the tree had been trimmed, and the presents (among them were two, originally intended for Henry, that now carried Anton's name) heaped under it, she succeeded in persuading him to spend the night. The gifts were to be opened on Christmas day after dinner.

The next morning, Henry came down late. Everyone else had had breakfast, and Gwen had started to prepare a turkey for the oven. When Henry had finished eating, she said, "I'm glad you slept well last night. We had trouble. Lucy. I guess you didn't know they stayed up after we turned in."

"Who stayed up?"

"Lucy and Anton. They were up till half past one. About half past three, I thought I heard her crying in bed, and I went in there, and sure enough. She still hadn't had a wink of sleep. He'd been talking about the camps again."

"I've told him not to," Henry said. "I've told him what it does to her."

"This time, he must have gone on and on. He told her about a boy who was forced to watch while his father— Oh, you can imagine the sort of thing. And he showed her his back. She says it's just a mass of scars from that whipping. She felt them. All rough, up and down his whole back. I had to stay with her most of the night. If he'd only talk to you, instead. Or me. Or even the boys. They've heard him talk, and it doesn't seem to affect them much. They like him. He did a beautiful job of fixing the brakes on Mark's bicycle."

"They're not Lucy. And they haven't read that book or seen those photographs. Is he with her now?"

"They're all down in the basement," Gwen said.

"One of these days, I'll have to tell him where to go."

"No, don't," Gwen said. "But I wish he'd do his talking to you or me. Lucy isn't equipped to handle it—not yet. Last night, it just broke

her down. She kept wanting to know if anything like that could happen here. To you, mostly. She kept saying how much he looks like you. It was starting to get light when I finally got her off to sleep."

Henry went down to the basement. The boys were playing ping-pong, and Anton was sitting with Lucy on the old porch swing that Henry had rigged up near the hot-water tank. ". . . like a sandwich," Anton was saying. "First the bodies, then the mix of lime, and then more bodies . . . ."

"Lucy, your mother wants you up in the kitchen," Henry said. "She thinks it's about time you learned how to stuff a turkey."

"Right this minute?"

"Yes."

She looked at him and saw that he meant it. He waited till she was gone, and then he said, "Anton, remember my asking you not to talk to her about the camps?"

"I remember. I do not understand why not."

"I explained it to you then. She takes it hard. Much too hard, harder than you'd think. She was up most of the night. She cried. She's very fond of you, you know. She imagines all those things being done to you and it's almost more than she can stand. If the—"

"All those things are true. They happened. I saw."

"Of course they're true. And Gwen wants to hear about them, and so do I. But—"

"You want Lucy should live in fairyland? Lucy is not child."

"In some ways she is," Henry said. "In others she's a remarkably intelligent young lady and you can talk to her about anything you like. If you'll just leave the camps out of it. Gwen and I—"

Anton broke in again. "You mean she is young lady, young gentle-lady, and too high" —he stopped for a moment in search of a word —"too high and too good to hear the bad things I say. So. Is easy. I stop talking."

He walked past Henry and up the stairs. Henry followed him slowly part of the way. He heard Anton's voice in the kitchen, and the voices of Lucy and Gwen. They were all casual, even gay; they were discussing the turkey. Fine, Henry thought. We'll wait till after dinner and then soothe such hurt feelings as may show.

The boys called after Henry, begging him to play ping-pong. He went back down, and played for the best part of an hour.

When Henry and the boys went upstairs, Anton was gone. He had taken off without his dinner and without having said goodbye to anyone in the house. Gwen and Lucy had assumed he had returned to the basement.

Henry and Mark drove to the bus stop on the chance of catching him there, but the bus had passed ten minutes before.

"What a goofy thing to do," Mark said.

Several times during the next few days, Gwen asked Henry to call Anton at Wright & Schindler's; they still did not know his home address. Henry decided not to. The truth was, he looked forward to a whole series of Sundays without Anton. And when he got them, he enjoyed them. It took three months for his conscience to catch up with him. Then he called Wright & Schindler's only to find that Anton no longer worked there.

He tried Mrs. Platt.

"I thought you knew," she said. "I'm afraid he lost that job."

"I didn't know."

"Well, it was quite some time ago. Mr. Schindler rated him pretty high, and felt sorry it had to end that way. But it seems the other workers got together and said if your cousin didn't leave, they would, in a body. They threatened to take it to the union. Personally, I don't see what they could have based charges on. All they'd say to Mr. Schindler was they didn't want to work in the same room with him. They said he was surly, wouldn't answer them, made the place unpleasant. That isn't anything for a union to act on. Mr. Schindler tried to tell them about the awful things in Germany, but it didn't help. Did you find him as unpleasant as all that?"

"He's not the jolliest of companions," Henry said.

"So, practically overnight and entirely on his own, he found another job that paid much better," Mrs. Platt said. "But he quit that one, and now he's in business for himself. Just what it is, I don't know. He's on the road a lot. Maybe that's why he hasn't been going to see you. He checks in with the immigration people all right. I wouldn't be too concerned. He seems well able to look after himself."

Whether or not Anton was able to look after himself, he did spend a lot of time on the road. A month or two after the conversation with Mrs. Platt, the Applegates got a card postmarked Rio de Janeiro. It was a view of Sugar Loaf Mountain, and on the back Anton had written, "Grietings, A. Byron." After that, there were cards from Mexico City, Los Angeles, Cleveland, Havana, and Des Moines, always with the same words: "Grietings, A. Byron." The only time Anton varied the formula was when he sent one from Buenos Aires. That one said, "This city is not so inosent. Not enough Americans, too many from Europe. Respectfully yours, A. Byron."

Between the time the card came from Havana and the time the one came from Des Moines, a fat man named Stephen Osička called on Henry at his office. Mr. Osička said he had gone to school with Anton in Prague. Someone, writing from Prague, had mentioned that Anton had finally got to this country, and Mr. Osička was eager to see the boy for old times' sake. He had traced Henry through Mrs. Platt's agency. She no longer worked there, but the other people had given him Henry's address. He was disappointed to find that Henry could not give him Anton's. Henry advised him to try the Bureau of Immigration and Naturalization.

Instead of taking his leave at that point, Mr. Osička leaned back in his chair and lighted up a pipe. "I will do that," he said. "And if they won't tell me, I will hear some other way. Anton is the kind of man you're bound to hear about, don't you think? Now that he's here, I lay money he's going to make good in a big way. He's going to be a big man, like all his teachers said. A big, important man. Mr. Applegate, do you know who wrote the best piece of music about America? A Czech. Anton Dvořák. Do you know the name of the man who could teach you more about the American Indians than anybody? Aleš Hrdlička. A Czech. Anton is going to do something big like that. That's the kind of man he is. Don't you agree?"

"Perhaps," Henry said.

"When we were Sixth Class—that's like maybe second-year high school here—Anton started a club. The Five, he called it. There were only five of us in it, so that was the name. The Five. We were supposed to help poor boys who needed a certain book or a pair of soccer shoes—even a suit of clothes. It was all in secret. The boys never found out where those things came from. Don't you think that's fine? It was all Anton's idea. He did the organizing, too, all of it. The rest of us just went along."

"Did he really do that?" Henry asked.

"He did more. Anton didn't give only things. He gave from himself. Of himself. Which is correct?"

"Of himself."

"Examination time, he stayed up nights after nights to help us through," Mr. Osička said. "Examination is a much more serious thing in Czechoslovakia than it is over here. I can tell. I watch my nephews. In Czechoslovakia, now they have doctors, lawyers, scientists whom Anton helped. He would be one of these, too, if his mother could have sent him to the university. Well. The main thing is, he's here. He'll make good. Don't you agree?"

"Yes," Henry said.

Mr. Osička presented his business card, which identified him as part owner of a printing establishment in Queens. Henry understood him to say that the plant was run by Old World craftsmen, and was equipped to meet the museum's most exacting requirements.

"My sainted grandmother once puzzled me

by defining a Magyar as a person who enters a revolving door after you but manages somehow to come out in front," Henry said to Gwen that night. "If that's so, and I doubt it, Mr. Osička must be at least part Magyar. Granted that he had a business reason for wanting to butter me up, how much of what he said about Anton would you say was true?"

"I think it was all true," she said.

"The secret club? The examinations?"

"Yes."

"I wonder if Lucy saw all that. God knows I didn't. Did you?"

"Glimmerings of it, every now and then," she said. "Once, he told me about an old blind teacher he used to visit as a boy. But when I remarked how thoughtful that had been of him, he quickly explained that the man's sister served marvelous pastry. I'm not sure he would have thought it necessary to make that explanation to Lucy. I wish I could have helped him more."

"You tried. We all tried, one way or another."

"My way wasn't good enough," Gwen said. "Nothing would satisfy him but the kind of response he could always get from Lucy. He seemed to find a species of fulfillment in reducing her to tears. I guess I'm not a crying woman, Henry. He probably put it down to callousness. Should we have let him go on talking to her?"

"No."

"Money was the only other thing I've known to give him satisfaction. He used to produce his bankbook the way some men take out snapshots of their first-born. Not that he ever opened it for inspection. Do you think he's really going to make a lot of money?"

"No," Henry said. "How could he?"

"I wish we'd been able to help him more," she said.

Now, at Easter, as Henry and Gwen went out to meet Anton in the driveway, Henry remembered her having said that. She no longer feels so protective, he thought. Gwen had never minded before when someone stopped in just before a meal. She loved unexpected guests. But now, by turning up in this preposterous robin's-egg-blue Cadillac, Anton had proved that, at least financially, he could look after himself. He had parked his car in the dog-leg of the driveway, right alongside the aging Oldsmobile. "Hello, Anton," Henry said. "Good to see you again. Mark! Ben! Hop out of that car before it runs away with you."

Anton wore a chocolate-colored suit, impeccably pressed. He smiled with his new white teeth. "Let them play," he said. "Ben, please give me the small package from the glove place."

That would be his present, in payment for the lunch to come, Henry thought. But Anton did not hand it over at once, as he used to. He carried it into the house and put it on the mantelpiece.

Lunch was uneventful. They talked about air travel, the Spanish language, hotel accommodations. Anton's English had become somewhat more idiomatic, but his accent remained much the same. There was no mention of his running off two Christmases before. They had their coffee around the fireplace, and he took the occasion to present his gift. It was a gold cigarette box, beautifully made.

"No," Henry said, "it's much too—"

"Is all right. I made it," Anton said.

"Still, I wish you—"

"Is all right. Please. It is very little to give for your affidavit. It is nothing."

Then, ostensibly as an afterthought, he pulled a couple of wristwatches out of his pocket and gave them to the boys.

"No, Anton," Henry said. "You can't do that."

"Please. They are not good watches. In two, three months, they stop running. Can't be fixed. That is truth. When they stop running, the boys can take them in parts, see what made them go. Only toys. Is my guarantee they will stop in two, three months."

"Will they really?" Henry asked.

"I guarantee. That is my business. I import those watches."

"From where?" Lucy asked.

"Not from Switzerland." Anton laughed.

Lucy said, "But if they're really no good, who buys them?"

"Americans," he said, and laughed again. "Americans buys anything. Good watches, bad watches—anything. Long time ago, I tell you you are a country of innocent."

"I'm no innocent." She was eighteen and high up on the Dean's List, and she did not wish to be called an innocent. As Anton continued to laugh, she said, "What's so innocent about buying a watch in good faith? That could happen anywhere. I should think you'd want to import decent watches while you were at it." Then she recalled that she was a hostess, and added, "You know, I've never seen you laugh so much before. Your teeth look very nice, much nicer than those metal ones."

"They look like my own teeth before they get knocked out," he said.

"*Knocked* out?" Lucy said.

"At Buchenwald, when they thought I was sabotage. I did not tell you?"

"No," Lucy said. "Not about that."

"It did not hurt so bad after the first three, because the conscious stopped. So I was without mind for hours. It hurt more the next week, when they put cotton in my ear and lighted it with candle." He smiled at her.

"You never told me that, either," she said.

Henry knew that voice. As a child of five, she had broken her thumb, and the way Henry learned of it, she had walked into his study just after her fall and said, in that same tight voice, "Look, Dad, there's something wrong with my finger."

Anton's laugh was hearty and resonant. "See?" he said. "Little red mark here? Some of it under the hair. That was very painful, more worse than the teeth. I tried to make the conscious stop and I could not. I thought of such many funny things. Someday I will tell, if your father will let. I think is all right, Henry, yes? Lucy is big college girl now. No innocent, she says. Lucy is smart now—smart Yankee. I sell undecent watches to the smart, decent

Yankees, like Lucy, and they sell them at higher price to the stupids in Peru, Nicaragua. Everybody happy."

"I didn't mean to hurt your feelings about the watches," Lucy began. Her voice had not changed.

Abruptly, Gwen began to clear the dishes. She made Lucy help her. The boys had gone off with their watches. Anton smiled again. He *is* happy, Henry thought; for the moment, he *is* happy, the conqueror left in possession of the field. I've got to get him out of this house, away from Lucy. "I'm going to take a walk," he said. "Want to come along?"

"Yes," said Anton. "Is nice out."

The chocolate suit would not have stood up in the woods, so Henry took him out on the road. They turned north. Anton said he had never been that way before. Henry said nothing. They had walked about half a mile when Anton stopped to look at a house.

"Who lives there?" he asked.

"Old lady. Miss Holbrook. Her father made hairpins."

"Now, that is a house. Big. Stone. That is what you should build."

"I like mine."

"You are angry," Anton said. "You are angry because I tell bad things to Lucy. You wish to keep her still living in fairyland. You wish to keep her sweet young lady—innocent. But you make mistake. I do not do the harm to her. You do the harm. You do the bad harm to Lucy."

"What bad harm have I done Lucy?"

"You try to keep her sweet young lady, very high. Must not sell undecent watches to nice American people. Is all right to know the life, but only from the books. From museums. Do not listen to the crazy man tell truth."

"Put it any way you like," said Henry. "I've asked you twice before not to talk to her about the camps, and now I'm asking you once more."

"I talk to anybody about anything I want."

"Not to her, you don't."

They turned to face each other.

"You fool!" said Anton. "You know what happened in my country to the sweet young ladies? When the Russians come, the smart girls know what to do. They cut their hair crooked. They dirty up their face. They go to bed, put typhus sign on door. Not the sweet young ladies. They wait. They put hands in their sweet young lap and wait. Pretty soon—"

"Shut up now," Henry said. He took hold of the chocolate lapels and dug his knuckles into his cousin's chest. "Shut up!" he said again. And he thought, Let him hit me first, and then . . . But Anton made no move. Impassive, he waited until Henry let go of the lapels. Then he turned and, at his normal pace, walked back toward the house.

He was out of sight around the bend of the road before Henry started back, too. Henry tried hard to imagine what would be said or done when he got home. He could not. By the time he reached the next-door driveway, all his anger was gone. He could not imagine what Gwen would say, or Lucy. He wondered what to do about the gold cigarette box. At the foot of his own driveway, he was nearly struck by the blue Cadillac as it made a sharp turn south and bolted down the road to New York.

I

IN THE LAND OF THE INNOCENT WHO WILL SURVIVE?

Anton has learned from his experiences in the concentration camps that man has a bestial side. His determination to reveal his experiences to Lucy sets up crosscurrents that ruffle the calm of the family. Why does he persist in revealing the grim horrors of his life at Neuengamme and Buchenwald?

II

IMPLICATIONS

Consider the following quotations. What crosscurrent is set in motion by the words? What is the speaker implying? Do you agree with him?

1. "Henry, if he's involved in something crooked . . . are you still in some way responsible for him?" (Gwen speaking)

2. "If most everybody liked his father and his mother, it would not have to be Commandment." (Anton speaking)

3. "No, no. I live. Otto lives. He has mark like this on his arm, but he lives. So I say him good morning, how are you, glad to see. Show me how to get rich." (Anton speaking)

4. "Anybody can make money in this country . . . You are a country of innocent." (Anton speaking)

5. "In Europe," said Anton, "a man who had two cars would have a house made from stone. Or brick."

6. "I wish we'd been able to help him more." (Gwen speaking)

7. "You try to keep her sweet young lady, very high. Must not sell undecent watches to nice American people. Is all right to know the life, but only from the books. From museums. Do not listen to the crazy man tell truth."

III

TECHNIQUES

Characterization

1. How did you gain a picture of Anton from what he said? from what Henry and Gwen said?

2. How did his past contribute to what he has become?

3. How would you describe his character? Was he devil or saint or something in between?

Plot

Do the actions in the plot move in a direct or indirect line? How does this affect the movement of the story? Does the action flow naturally from the characters? Is the ending plausible and expected?

IV

WORDS

A. In "The Ambassador," proud and self-reliant Anton is an *immigrant* to the United States. From the point of view of his native Czechoslovakia, however, he was an *emigrant*. An immigrant is one who enters and settles in a new country, whereas an emigrant is one who leaves his native country to settle elsewhere. Both *immigrant* and *emigrant* are derived from the Latin root -*migr*-, meaning "to move from one country or region to another." The prefix *e*-, a variant form of *ex*-, means "from," "away from," or "out of," and the prefix *im*-, a variant form of *in*-, means "in" or "into." *Im*- is used before the sounds represented by the letters *p*, *m*, and *b*. With what you know about the meaning of -*migr*-, try to answer these questions: What is a migratory bird? Why would some means of transportation be especially important to a migrant worker? What difference, if any, is there between *emigrate* and *migrate*?

B. Proper names often have interesting histories. Take, for instance, *Yankee, American,* and *Easter,* all of which are mentioned in "The Ambassador." The origin of *Yankee* is uncertain, but the word probably comes from *Jan Kees,* meaning in Dutch "John Cheese." In the eighteenth century, *Jan Kees* was a disapproving nickname applied by the colonial Dutch in New York to the English settlers in Connecticut. *American* is traceable to the Italian navigator Amerigo Vespucci, who explored the New World coastline from 1499–1502. Vespucci, the story goes, wrote an account of his voyages for his patrons. Impressed by Vespucci's narration, which he was translating, a German mapmaker labeled the New World *America.* Later mapmakers simply picked up the name and used it on maps of the New World. Understandably, the Spanish, who sent Columbus, became angry and until the eighteenth century refused to use the name. *Easter* is derived from the name of the old Germanic goddess of the dawn and spring. Dawn comes up, of course, in the east. The festival associated with the goddess was held in the spring fairly close to the time Easter is celebrated. Through confusion, the pagan name was attached to the Christian holy day. What fascinating stories lie behind *January, Halloween,* and *Valentine's Day?*

C. Anton was a *goldsmith*; that is, an artisan who fashioned objects of gold. The word *smith* means "a worker in metal." It is used mostly in combination: *silversmith, gunsmith,* and *blacksmith.* Also used mainly in combination is the word *wright,* meaning "one who constructs something." Examples are *playwright, shipwright,* and *wheelwright.* Both words have given rise to common English surnames—*Smith* and *Wright.*

Divisive crosscurrents
between parents and their children
provide the dramatic base in the
next two poems.

Souvenir de Londres

My parents quarrel in the neighbour room:—
"How did you sleep last night?" "I woke at four
To hear the wind that sulks along the floor
Blowing up dust like ashes from the tomb."

"I was awake at three." "I heard the moth   5
Breed perilous worms." "I wept
All night, watching you rest." "I never slept
Nor sleep at all." Thus ghastly they speak, both.

How can these sleep who eat upon their fear
And watch their dreadful love fade as it grows?   10
Their life flowers like an antique lover's rose
Set puff'd and spreading in the chemist's jar.

I am your son, and from bad dreams arise.
My sight is fixed with horror, as I pass
Before the transitory[1] glass   15
And watch the fungus cover up my eyes.

STEPHEN SPENDER

---

1. **transitory**\\'trăn(t)s•ə ˣtōr•ē\\ of brief duration.

A NIGHT EVALUATION OF PARENTS
The title of the poem you just read means "Memory of London." And it also uses an experience common to most young people—that of overhearing their parents quarreling at night. The reaction of the speaker is one of horror. "How can these sleep?" he asks. What does he feel about his parents' relationship? What figure of speech is used to describe their life? Do you expect your marriage to be different?

The Whipping

The old woman across the way
    is whipping the boy again
and shouting to the neighborhood
    her goodness and his wrongs.

Wildly he crashes through elephant ears,   5
    pleads in dusty zinnias,
while she in spite of crippling fat
    pursues and corners him.

She strikes and strikes the shrilly circling
    boy till the stick breaks   10
in her hand. His tears are rainy weather
    to woundlike memories:

My head gripped in bony vise
    of knees, the writhing struggle
to wrench free, the blows, the fear   15
    worse than blows that hateful

Words could bring, the face that I
    no longer knew or loved . . .
Well, it is over now, it is over,
    and the boy sobs in his room,   20

And the woman leans muttering against
    a tree, exhausted, purged—
avenged in part for lifelong hidings
    she has had to bear.

ROBERT HAYDEN

NEW UNDERSTANDINGS

The writer in this poem has taken an experience common to most of us and has transformed it so that it gains a meaning we may not have seen before. Why is the woman really punishing the boy? Is the punishment of children usually motivated by such needs? Notice that the speaker says that the boy's tears start the flow of his own memories. What are these memories?

Two thousand years ago
the story of "The Prodigal Son"
told of conflicts between parents and children
that are still present in families today.
Is there any reason to assume that they will be
any different in families of the future?
Will more gadgets, more creature comforts,
more scientific "miracles" relieve the tensions
in a family? Ray Bradbury turns his ingenious
and imaginative mind to this problem
in "The Veldt." Though the reader
may be horrified and want to reject the events
in this tale, he is persuaded to believe them
by Bradbury's skill as a storyteller.

The Veldt

RAY BRADBURY

George, I wish you'd look at the nursery."

"What's wrong with it?"

"I don't know."

"Well, then."

"I just want you to look at it, is all, or call a psychologist in to look at it."

"What would a psychologist want with a nursery?"

"You know very well what he'd want." His wife paused in the middle of the kitchen and watched the stove busy humming to itself, making supper for four.

"It's just that the nursery is different now than it was."

"All right, let's have a look."

They walked down the hall of their sound-proofed, Happylife Home, which had cost them thirty thousand dollars installed, this house which clothed and fed and rocked them to sleep and played and sang and was good to them. Their approach sensitized a switch some-

where and the nursery light flicked on when they came within ten feet of it. Similarly, behind them, in the halls, lights went on and off as they left them behind, with a soft automaticity.

"Well," said George Hadley.

They stood on the thatched floor of the nursery. It was forty feet across by forty feet long and thirty feet high; it had cost half again as much as the rest of the house. "But nothing's too good for our children," George had said.

The nursery was silent. It was empty as a jungle glade at hot high noon. The walls were blank and two dimensional. Now, as George and Lydia Hadley stood in the center of the room, the walls began to purr and recede into crystalline distance, it seemed, and presently an African veldt appeared, in three dimensions, on all sides, in color, reproduced to the final pebble and bit of straw. The ceiling above them became a deep sky with a hot yellow sun.

George Hadley felt the perspiration start on his brow.

"Let's get out of this sun," he said. "This is a little too real. But I don't see anything wrong."

"Wait a moment, you'll see," said his wife.

Now the odorophonics[1] were beginning to blow a wind of odor at the two people in the middle of the baked veldtland. The hot straw smell of lion grass, the cool green smell of the hidden water hole, the great rusty smell of animals, the smell of dust like a red paprika in the hot air. And now the sounds: the thump of distant antelope feet on grassy sod, the papery rustling of vultures. A shadow passed through the sky. The shadow flickered on George Hadley's upturned, sweating face.

"Filthy creatures," he heard his wife say.

"The vultures."

"You see, there are the lions, far over, that way. Now they're on their way to the water hole. They've just been eating," said Lydia. "I don't know what."

1. This story is of course a fantasy of the future. To make the future seem true the author has invented some new words like odorophonics\'ō·də·rə ▴fŏ·nĭks\. This word would suggest devices intended to send out appropriate odors and sounds together.

"Some animal." George Hadley put his hand up to shield off the burning light from his squinted eyes. "A zebra or a baby giraffe, maybe."

"Are you sure?" His wife sounded peculiarly tense.

"No, it's a little late to be sure," he said, amused. "Nothing over there I can see but cleaned bone, and the vultures dropping for what's left."

"Did you hear that scream?" she asked.

"No."

"About a minute ago?"

"Sorry, no."

The lions were coming. And again George Hadley was filled with admiration for the mechanical genius who had conceived this room. A miracle of efficiency selling for an absurdly low price. Every home should have one. Oh, occasionally they frightened you with their clinical accuracy, they startled you, gave you a twinge, but most of the time what fun for everyone, not only your own son and daughter, but for yourself when you felt like a quick jaunt to a foreign land, a quick change of scenery. Well, here it was!

And here were the lions now, fifteen feet away, so real, so feverishly and startlingly real that you could feel the prickling fur on your hand, and your mouth was stuffed with the dusty upholstery smell of their heated pelts, and the yellow of them was in your eyes like the yellow of an exquisite French tapestry, the yellows of lions and summer grass, and the sound of the matted lion lungs exhaling on the silent noontide, and the smell of meat from the panting, dripping mouths.

The lions stood looking at George and Lydia Hadley with terrible green-yellow eyes.

"Watch out!" screamed Lydia.

The lions came running at them.

Lydia bolted and ran. Instinctively, George sprang after her. Outside, in the hall, with the door slammed, he was laughing and she was crying, and they both stood appalled at the other's reaction.

"George!"

"Lydia! Oh, my dear poor sweet Lydia!"

"They almost got us!"

"Walls, Lydia, remember; crystal walls, that's all they are. Oh, they look real, I must admit— Africa in your parlor—but it's all dimensional superreactionary, supersensitive color film and mental tape film behind glass screens. It's all odorophonics and sonics, Lydia. Here's my handkerchief."

"I'm afraid." She came to him and put her body against him and cried steadily. "Did you see? Did you feel? It's too real."

"Now, Lydia . . ."

"You've got to tell Wendy and Peter[2] not to read any more on Africa."

"Of course—of course." He patted her.

"Promise?"

"Sure."

"And lock the nursery for a few days until I get my nerves settled."

"You know how difficult Peter is about that. When I punished him a month ago by locking the nursery for even a few hours—the tantrum he threw! And Wendy too. They *live* for the nursery."

"It's got to be locked, that's all there is to it."

"All right." Reluctantly he locked the huge door. "You've been working too hard. You need a rest."

"I don't know—I don't know," she said, blowing her nose, sitting down in a chair that immediately began to rock and comfort her. "Maybe I don't have enough to do. Maybe I have time to think too much. Why don't we shut the whole house off for a few days and take a vacation?"

"You mean you want to fry my eggs for me?"

"Yes," she nodded.

"And darn my socks?"

"Yes." A frantic, watery-eyed nodding.

"And sweep the house?"

"Yes, yes—oh, yes!"

"But I thought that's why we bought this house, so we wouldn't have to do anything?"

---

2. There is irony in the choice of **Peter** and **Wendy** as the children's names. Children named Peter and Wendy are prominent in J. M. Barrie's *Peter Pan*, a totally different kind of story.

"That's just it. I feel like I don't belong here. The house is wife and mother now and nurse-maid. Can I compete with an African veldt? Can I give a bath and scrub the children as efficiently or quickly as the automatic scrub bath can? I cannot. And it isn't just me. It's you. You've been awfully nervous lately."

"I suppose I have been smoking too much."

"You look as if you didn't know what to do with yourself in this house, either. You smoke a little more every morning and drink a little more every afternoon and need a little more sedative every night. You're beginning to feel unnecessary too."

"Am I?" He paused and tried to feel into himself to see what was really there.

"Oh, George!" She looked beyond him, at the nursery door. "Those lions can't get out of there, can they?"

He looked at the door and saw it tremble as if something had jumped against it from the other side.

"Of course not," he said.

At dinner they ate alone, for Wendy and Peter were at a special plastic carnival across town and had televised home to say they'd be late, to go ahead eating. So George Hadley, bemused, sat watching the dining-room table produce warm dishes of food from its mechanical interior.

"We forgot the ketchup," he said.

"Sorry," said a small voice within the table, and ketchup appeared.

As for the nursery, thought George Hadley, it won't hurt for the children to be locked out of it awhile. Too much of anything isn't good for anyone. And it was clearly indicated that the children had been spending a little too much time on Africa. That *sun*. He could feel it on his neck, still, like a hot paw. And the *lions*. And the smell of blood. Remarkable how the nursery caught the telepathic emanations of the children's minds and created life to fill their every desire. The children thought lions, and there were lions. The children thought zebras, and there were zebras. Sun—sun. Giraffes—giraffes. Death and death.

That *last*. He chewed tastelessly on the meat that the table had cut for him. Death thoughts. They were awfully young, Wendy and Peter, for death thoughts. Or, no, you were never too young, really. Long before you knew what death was you were wishing it on someone else. When you were two years old you were shooting people with cap pistols.

But this—the long, hot African veldt—the awful death in the jaws of a lion. And repeated again and again.

"Where are you going?"

He didn't answer Lydia. Preoccupied, he let the lights glow softly on ahead of him, extinguish behind him as he padded to the nursery door. He listened against it. Far away, a lion roared.

He unlocked the door and opened it. Just before he stepped inside, he heard a faraway scream. And then another roar from the lions, which subsided quickly.

He stepped into Africa. How many times in the last year had he opened this door and found Wonderland, Alice, the Mock Turtle, or Aladdin and his Magical Lamp, or Jack Pumpkinhead of Oz, or Dr. Doolittle, or the cow jumping over a very real-appearing moon—all the delightful contraptions of a make-believe world.[3] How often had he seen Pegasus[4] flying in the sky ceiling, or seen fountains of red fireworks, or heard angel voices singing. But now, this yellow hot Africa, this bake oven with murder in the heat. Perhaps Lydia was right. Perhaps they needed a little vacation from the fantasy which was growing a bit too real for ten-year-old children. It was all right to exercise one's mind with gymnastic fantasies, but when the lively child mind settled on one pattern . . .? It seemed that, at a distance, for the past month, he had heard lions roaring, and smelled their strong odor seeping as far away as his study door. But, being busy, he had paid it no attention.

George Hadley stood on the African grassland alone. The lions looked up from their feeding, watching him. The only flaw to the illusion was the open door through which he could see his wife, far down the dark hall, like a framed picture, eating her dinner abstractedly.

"Go away," he said to the lions.

They did not go.

He knew the principle of the room exactly. You sent out your thoughts. Whatever you thought would appear.

"Let's have Aladdin and his lamp," he snapped.

The veldtland remained; the lions remained.

"Come on, room! I demand Aladdin!" he said.

Nothing happened. The lions mumbled in their baked pelts.

"Aladdin!"

He went back to dinner. "The fool room's out of order," he said. "It won't respond."

"Or—"

"Or what?"

---

3. **Wonderland,** the background for the adventures of Alice in *Alice in Wonderland,* in which the **Mock Turtle** appears. **Aladdin and his Magical Lamp** figure in one of the well-known stories from the *Arabian Nights.* **Jack Pumpkinhead of Oz**\ŏz\ is a character in the Oz books by Frank Baum. **Dr. Doolittle** is another character in stories that children might be expected to enjoy.

4. **Pegasus**\ᵃpĕ·gə·səs\ a winged horse that figures in the adventures of Bellerophon \bĕ ᵃlā·rə·fən\ a Greek legendary hero.

"Or it can't respond," said Lydia, "because the children have thought about Africa and lions and killing so many days that the room's in a rut."

"Could be."

"Or Peter's set it to remain that way."

"Set it?"

"He may have got into the machinery and fixed something."

"Peter doesn't know machinery."

"He's a wise one for ten. That I.Q. of his—"

"Nevertheless—"

"Hello, Mom. Hello, Dad."

The Hadleys turned. Wendy and Peter were coming in the front door, cheeks like peppermint candy, eyes like bright blue agate marbles, a smell of ozone on their jumpers from their trip in the helicopter.[5]

"You're just in time for supper," said both parents.

"We're full of strawberry ice cream and hot dogs," said the children, holding hands. "But we'll sit and watch."

"Yes, come tell us about the nursery," said George Hadley.

The brother and sister blinked at him and then at each other. "Nursery?"

"All about Africa and everything," said the father with false joviality.

"I don't understand," said Peter.

"Your mother and I were just traveling through Africa with rod and reel; Tom Swift[6] and his Electric Lion," said George Hadley.

"There's no Africa in the nursery," said Peter simply.

"Oh, come now, Peter. We know better."

"I don't remember any Africa," said Peter to Wendy. "Do you?"

"No."

"Run see and come tell."

She obeyed.

"Wendy, come back here!" said George Hadley, but she was gone. The house lights followed her like a flock of fireflies. Too late, he realized he had forgotten to lock the nursery door after his last inspection.

"Wendy'll look and come tell us," said Peter.

"She doesn't have to tell *me*. I've seen it."

"I'm sure you're mistaken, Father."

"I'm not, Peter. Come along now."

But Wendy was back. "It's not Africa," she said breathlessly.

"We'll see about this," said George Hadley, and they all walked down the hall together and opened the nursery door.

There was a green, lovely forest, a lovely river, a purple mountain, high voices singing, and Rima,[7] lovely and mysterious, lurking in the trees with colorful flights of butterflies, like animated bouquets, lingering in her long hair. The African veldtland was gone. The lions were gone. Only Rima was here now, singing a song so beautiful that it brought tears to your eyes.

George Hadley looked in at the changed scene. "Go to bed," he said to the children.

They opened their mouths.

"You heard me," he said.

They went off to the air closet, where a wind sucked them like brown leaves up the flue to their slumber rooms.

George Hadley walked through the singing glade and picked up something that lay in the corner near where the lions had been. He walked slowly back to his wife.

"What is that?" she asked.

"An old wallet of mine," he said.

He showed it to her. The smell of hot grass was on it and the smell of a lion. There were drops of saliva on it, it had been chewed, and there were blood smears on both sides.

He closed the nursery door and locked it, tight.

In the middle of the night he was still awake and he knew his wife was awake. "Do you

---

5. **Agate**\\ˈă·gət\\ the material from which colored marbles are often made. **Ozone**\\ˈō'zōn\\ a form of oxygen especially associated with fresh and bracing air.

6. **Tom Swift,** the hero of a long series of boys' books during the early decades of this century. Often his adventures were fantastic.

7. **Rima**\\ˈrē·mə\\ the forest heroine of *Green Mansions,* a romance by W. H. Hudson placed in Argentina.

think Wendy changed it?" she said at last, in the dark room.

"Of course."

"Made it from a veldt into a forest and put Rima there instead of lions?"

"Yes."

"Why?"

"I don't know. But it's staying locked until I find out."

"How did your wallet get there?"

"I don't know anything," he said, "except that I'm beginning to be sorry we bought that room for the children. If children are neurotic at all, a room like that—"

"It's supposed to help them work off their neuroses in a healthful way."

"I'm starting to wonder." He stared at the ceiling.

"We've given the children everything they ever wanted. Is this our reward—secrecy, disobedience?"

"Who was it said, 'Children are carpets, they should be stepped on occasionally'? We've never lifted a hand. They're insufferable—let's admit it. They come and go when they like; they treat us as if we were offspring. They're spoiled and we're spoiled."

"They've been acting funny ever since you forbade them to take the rocket to New York a few months ago."

"They're not old enough to do that alone, I explained."

"Nevertheless, I've noticed they've been decidedly cool toward us since."

"I think I'll have David McClean come tomorrow morning to have a look at Africa."

"But it's not Africa now, it's Green Mansions country and Rima."

"I have a feeling it'll be Africa again before then."

A moment later they heard the screams.

Two screams. Two people screaming from downstairs. And then a roar of lions.

"Wendy and Peter aren't in their rooms," said his wife.

He lay in his bed with his beating heart.

"No," he said. "They've broken into the nursery."

"Those screams—they sound familiar."

"Do they?"

"Yes, awfully."

And although their beds tried very hard, the two adults couldn't be rocked to sleep for another hour. A smell of cats was in the night air.

"Father?" said Peter.

"Yes."

Peter looked at his shoes. He never looked at his father any more, nor at his mother. "You aren't going to lock up the nursery for good, are you?"

"That all depends."

"On what?" snapped Peter.

"On you and your sister. If you intersperse this Africa with a little variety—oh, Sweden perhaps, or Denmark or China—"

"I thought we were free to play as we wished."

"You are, within reasonable bounds."

"What's wrong with Africa, Father?"

"Oh, so now you admit you have been conjuring up Africa, do you?"

"I wouldn't want the nursery locked up," said Peter coldly. "Ever."

"Matter of fact, we're thinking of turning the whole house off for about a month. Live sort of a carefree one-for-all existence."

"That sounds dreadful! Would I have to tie my own shoes instead of letting the shoe tier do it? And brush my own teeth and comb my hair and give myself a bath?"

"It would be fun for a change, don't you think?"

"No, it would be horrid. I didn't like it when you took out the picture painter last month."

"That's because I wanted you to learn to paint all by yourself, son."

"I don't want to do anything but look and listen and smell; what else *is* there to do?"

"All right, go play in Africa."

"Will you shut off the house sometime soon?"

"We're considering it."

"I don't think you'd better consider it any more, Father."

"I won't have any threats from my son!"

"Very well." And Peter strolled off to the nursery.

"Am I on time?" said David McClean.

"Breakfast?" asked George Hadley.

"Thanks, had some. What's the trouble?"

"David, you're a psychologist."

"I should hope so."

"Well, then, have a look at our nursery. You saw it a year ago when you dropped by; did you notice anything peculiar about it then?"

"Can't say I did; the usual violences, a tendency toward a slight paranoia here or there, usual in children because they feel persecuted by parents constantly, but, oh, really nothing."

They walked down the hall. "I locked the nursery up," explained the father, "and the children broke back into it during the night. I let them stay so they could form the patterns for you to see."

There was a terrible screaming from the nursery.

"There it is," said George Hadley. "See what you make of it."

They walked in on the children without rapping.

The screams had faded. The lions were feeding.

"Run outside a moment, children," said George Hadley. "No, don't change the mental combination. Leave the walls as they are. Get!"

With the children gone, the two men stood studying the lions clustered at a distance, eating with great relish whatever it was they had caught.

"I wish I knew what it was," said George Hadley. "Sometimes I can almost see. Do you think if I brought high-powered binoculars here and—"

David McClean laughed dryly. "Hardly." He turned to study all four walls. "How long has this been going on?"

"A little over a month."

"It certainly doesn't *feel* good."

"I want facts, not feelings."

"My dear George, a psychologist never saw a fact in his life. He only hears about feelings; vague things. This doesn't feel good, I tell you Trust my hunches and my instincts. I have a nose for something bad. This is very bad. My advice to you is to have the whole damn room torn down and your children brought to me every day during the next year for treatment."

"Is it that bad?"

"I'm afraid so. One of the original uses of these nurseries was so that we could study the patterns left on the walls by the child's mind, study at our leisure, and help the child. In this case, however, the room has become a channel toward—destructive thoughts, instead of a release away from them."

"Didn't you sense this before?"

"I sensed only that you had spoiled your children more than most. And now you're letting them down in some way. What way?"

"I wouldn't let them go to New York."

"What else?"

"I've taken a few machines from the house and threatened them, a month ago, with closing up the nursery unless they did their homework. I did close it for a few days to show I meant business."

"Ah, ha!"

"Does that mean anything?"

"Everything. Where before they had a Santa Claus now they have a Scrooge.[8] Children prefer Santas. You've let this room and this house replace you and your wife in your children's affections. This room is their mother and father, far more important in their lives than their real parents. And now you come along and want to shut it off. No wonder there's hatred here. You can feel it coming out of the sky. Feel that sun. George, you'll have to change your life. Like too many others, you've built it around creature comforts. Why, you'd

---

8. **Scrooge**\skrūj\ a character in Dickens' *Christmas Carol* who refused to feel the joy of the Christmas Season.

starve tomorrow if something went wrong in your kitchen. You wouldn't know how to tap an egg. Nevertheless, turn everything off. Start new. It'll take time. But we'll make good children out of bad in a year, wait and see."

"But won't the shock be too much for the children, shutting the room up abruptly, for good?"

"I don't want them going any deeper into this, that's all."

The lions were finished with their red feast.

The lions were standing on the edge of the clearing watching the two men.

"Now *I'm* feeling persecuted," said McClean. "Let's get out of here. I never have cared for these rooms. Make me nervous."

"The lions look real, don't they?" said George Hadley. "I don't suppose there's any way—"

"What?"

"—that they could *become* real?"

"Not that I know."

"Some flaw in the machinery, a tampering or something?"

"No."

They went to the door.

"I don't imagine the room will like being turned off," said the father.

"Nothing ever likes to die—even a room."

"I wonder if it hates me for wanting to switch it off?"

"Paranoia is thick around here today," said David McClean. "You can follow it like a spoor. Hello." He bent and picked up a bloody scarf. "This yours?"

"No," George Hadley's face was rigid. "It belongs to Lydia."

They went to the fuse box together and threw the switch that killed the nursery.

The two children were in hysterics. They screamed and pranced and threw things. They yelled and sobbed and swore and jumped at the furniture.

"You can't do that to the nursery, you can't!"

"Now, children."

The children flung themselves onto a couch, weeping.

"George," said Lydia Hadley, "turn on the nursery, just for a few moments. You can't be so abrupt."

"No."

"You can't be so cruel."

"Lydia, it's off, and it stays off. And the whole damn house dies as of here and now. The more I see of the mess we've put ourselves in, the more it sickens me. We've been contemplating our mechanical, electronic navels for too long. How we need a breath of honest air!"

And he marched about the house turning off the voice clocks, the stoves, the heaters, the shoe shiners, the shoe lacers, the body scrubbers and swabbers and massagers, and every other machine he could put his hand to.

The house was full of dead bodies, it seemed. It felt like a mechanical cemetery. So silent. None of the humming hidden energy of machines waiting to function at the tap of a button.

"Don't let them do it!" wailed Peter at the ceiling, as if he was talking to the house, the nursery. "Don't let Father kill everything." He turned to his father. "Oh, I hate you!"

"Insults won't get you anywhere."

"I wish you were dead!"

"We were, for a long while. Now we're going to really start living. Instead of being handled and massaged, we're going to *live*."

Wendy was still crying and Peter joined her again. "Just a moment, just one moment, just another moment of nursery," they wailed.

"Oh, George," said the wife, "it can't hurt."

"All right—all right, if they'll only just shut up. One minute, mind you, and then off forever."

"Daddy, Daddy, Daddy!" sang the children, smiling with wet faces.

"And then we're going on a vacation. David McClean is coming back in half an hour to help us move out and get to the airport. I'm going to dress. You turn the nursery on for a minute, Lydia, just a minute, mind you."

And the three of them went babbling off while he let himself be vacuumed upstairs through the air flue and set about dressing himself. A minute later Lydia appeared.

"I'll be glad when we get away," she sighed.

"Did you leave them in the nursery?"

"I wanted to dress, too. Oh, that horrid Africa. What can they see in it?"

"Well, in five minutes we'll be on our way to Iowa. Lord, how did we ever get in this house? What prompted us to buy a nightmare?"

"Pride, money, foolishness."

"I think we'd better get downstairs before those kids get engrossed with those damned beasts again."

Just then they heard the children calling, "Daddy, Mommy, come quick—quick!"

They went downstairs in the air flue and ran down the hall. The children were nowhere in sight. "Wendy? Peter!"

They ran into the nursery. The veldtland was empty save for the lions waiting, looking at them. "Peter, Wendy?"

The door slammed.

"Wendy, Peter!"

George Hadley and his wife whirled and ran back to the door.

"Open the door!" cried George Hadley, trying the knob. "Why, they've locked it from the outside! Peter!" He beat at the door. "Open up!"

He heard Peter's voice outside, against the door.

"Don't let them switch off the nursery and the house," he was saying.

Mr. and Mrs. George Hadley beat at the door. "Now, don't be ridiculous, children. It's time to go. Mr. McClean'll be here in a minute and . . ."

And then they heard the sounds.

The lions on three sides of them, in the yellow veldt grass, padding through the dry straw, rumbling and roaring in their throats.

The lions.

Mr. Hadley looked at his wife and they turned and looked back at the beasts edging slowly forward, crouching, tails stiff.

Mr. and Mrs. Hadley screamed.

And suddenly they realized why those other screams had sounded familiar.

"Well, here I am," said David McClean in the nursery doorway. "Oh, hello." He stared at the two children seated in the center of the open glade eating a little picnic lunch. Beyond them was the water hole and the yellow veldtland; above was the hot sun. He began to perspire. "Where are your father and mother?"

The children looked up and smiled. "Oh, they'll be here directly."

"Good, we must get going." At a distance Mr. McClean saw the lions fighting and clawing and then quieting down to feed in silence under the shady trees.

He squinted at the lions with his hand up to his eyes.

Now the lions were done feeding. They moved to the water hole to drink.

A shadow flicked over Mr. McClean's hot face. Many shadows flickered. The vultures were dropping down the blazing sky.

"A cup of tea?" asked Wendy in the silence.

I

MAKING THE IMAGINARY REAL

One problem in writing of the unknown is to make it seem possible and even ordinary to the reader. Bradbury uses many devices to accomplish this task. Principally, he writes as if you, the reader, already knew about the age with which he is dealing. He comments casually about the automatic shoe lacers, the lighting system, the air closet, and the playroom. But he combines enough familiar details with the strange so that the reader accepts the strange the same way he accepts the familiar.

II

IMPLICATIONS

1. Consider the following quotations from the story. Who is speaking in each? How do the attitudes expressed reveal the conflicts in the story?

a. "But nothing's too good for our children."

b. "They *live* for the nursery."

c. "I don't remember any Africa . . . do you?"

d. "I don't want to do anything but look and listen and smell, what else *is* there to do?"

e. "We've given the children everything they ever wanted. Is this our reward . . . secrecy, disobedience?"

f. "Too much of anything isn't good for anyone."

g. "Children are like carpets, they should be stepped on occasionally."

2. How do such statements serve as a bridge between the world of today and the world of the story?

3. What do you believe to be the cause of the violent crosscurrents between these children and their parents? Would the vacation have lessened their conflicts?

III
TECHNIQUES

Characterization

This story is almost devoid of characterization. The reader knows that he is dealing with parents and their two children, but this is basically all the information that is given. Why isn't it necessary to know these four people better?

Plot

Why did Bradbury find it necessary to have the children off at the plastic carnival as the story opened? Later, why must he introduce the psychologist into the story? Notice that this story is divided into sections. What happens or what is said in the last three or four lines of each section that makes the reader aware of the deepening of the conflict?

IV
WORDS

A. A good writer uses exact adjectives which add sharpness to the word being modified. Explain how the modifier adds sharpness in these clusters from "The Ambassador": nasal sound, noncommittal sound, nightmare photographs, negotiable jewelry, lackluster service, reputable jewelry firm, leisurely view, moderately well-informed account, active disbelief.

B. From context determine the meaning of the italicized words:

1. "So George Hadley, *bemused*, sat watching the dining-room table produce warm dishes of food from its mechanical interior."

2. "Remarkable how the nursery caught the telepathic *emanations* of the children's minds."

3. "*Preoccupied*, he let the lights glow softly on ahead of him, extinguish behind him as he padded to the nursery door."

4. "The lions looked up from their feeding, watching him. The only flaw in the *illusion* was the open door through which he could see his wife . . . ."

5. "Oh, so you admit you have been *conjuring* up Africa, do you?"

6. ". . . a slight *paranoia*, usual in children because they feel persecuted by parents constantly."

C. 1. More very common roots include *-vert-*, *-vers-*, meaning "turn"; and *-vid-*, *-vis-*, meaning "to see, sight"; as in the words *convert* and *conversion*, *evident* and *vision*. Sometimes a common Latin root may appear in not only two but even three different forms. The root *-ced-*, as in *precede*, or *-ceed-*, as in *proceed*, or *-cess-*, as in *recession* or *procession*, is a good illustration. You can probably conclude that it may mean "go, pass" (although it has other uses, as in *cede* and *cession*, in which it means "to pass over or yield"). A Latin root meaning "to run, a running, a course" appears as *-cur-*, in *concur* or *occur*; *-curr-*, in *current* or *concurrent*; and *-curs-* in *cursory* or *precursor*.

2. Some common prefixes are *ab-* (or *a-* or *abs-*), meaning "off, away," and *ad* (or *ac-*, *af-*, *ag-*, *al-*, *an-*, *ap-*, *ar-*, *as-*, *at-*, depending on the following consonant), meaning "to, toward." How many words can you make up by joining these prefixes to the common roots that you have studied so far?

CROSSCURRENTS

As soon as one person is joined by another,
crosscurrents of needs, ambitions, and purposes begin.
Writers have dramatized this aspect of the human condition
within their own medium of words. The painter
and the engraver visualize the same area of personal tension
within the confines of their canvases or their drawing boards.
Notice how the pictures in this gallery overlap in content
and then begin to set up crosscurrents of their own.

MY PARENTS
Henry Koerner

The old people on their lonely, separate roads in the autumn forest
very obviously speak of the divided channels of crosscurrents.
But it is interesting to learn that to the artist the picture, MY PARENTS,
was an attempt to reunite his beloved family,
which had been separated by death and the concentration camps
of World War II. The old people are his devoted parents,
forced apart in lonely old age but together now in the eye of the beholder.
The locket hanging from the tree in the foreground
pictures their children and completes the family group so irretrievably
washed apart by the crosscurrents of life in time of war.

PEASANTS INTERIOR
Louis LeNain

IN THE PARLOR
Honoré Sharrer

Family groups inevitably
contain crosscurrents, and through
the sensitive eye of the painter
these differing moods become
more obvious to the rest of us.

Look closely at the individuals
in the peasants group
from seventeenth-century France.
Who seems resentful?
Who full of hope?
Who may be in despair
and who appears determined?
Can you imagine something of
their lives from what you see here?

In the parlor there are
rather ordinary twentieth-century
Americans. The artist
is commenting on the quality
of life today. What do you
suppose her comment is?

FAMILY PICTURE *Max Beckmann*
1920, Oil on canvas, 25⅝ x 39¾"
Collection, The Museum of Modern Art, New York
Gift of Abby Aldrich Rockefeller

Max Beckman, like Koerner,
suffered deeply from the disasters
of World War II and his view of life
became harsh and painful.
His picture of a family
uses the exaggerations
of a very modern style
as well as differing activities
and brooding expressions
to make his point
about the crosscurrents that may
exist within a single family.
What currents can you pick out
from this complex picture?

THE SICK CHILD
Edvard Munch

The pale but determined head
of the sick child
sets up a crosscurrent washing
over the fatigue and despair
of the mother. The emotional paths
of even the closest people
may not run a parallel course.

Saltimbanques are entertainers somewhat like the circus performers
you have seen in America. Picasso painted this picture
during his lovely rose and blue periods and the crosscurrents within it
may not be the first thing you see. But if you look closely
and with imagination you will pick up the same threads
that were woven into each of the other family pictures in this gallery.

185

SAMSON THREATENS
HIS FATHER-IN-LAW
Rembrandt Van Rijn

Most of what you need to know
to guess at the nature
of the crosscurrents
in this sentimental
but once popular picture
is contained in the title,
PAST AND PRESENT.
Whatever has gone before
in this story-rich picture
looks different to each person,
"present" and "past."

Rembrandt uses an incident
from the ancient Bible story
of the boisterous hero
Samson as a means
of portraying the crosscurrents
between a man
who feels himself ill-used
and his adversary.
The actual Bible story is
from episodes told
of Samson's early life.

Not all crosscurrents
are troubled ones.
The serene South Sea island people
pictured by Gauguin are,
in their separate ways,
setting up very gentle crosscurrents.

THE BIG TREE
Paul Gauguin

Crosscurrents

Unlike friendships, families are not of our own choosing; each person inherits his family when he is born. It is inevitable that people bound so closely together should be subject to controversies and conflicts as they express their feelings, hopes, ambitions, and beliefs. Because of the universality of the family experience, it is one of the most natural subjects for literature. And because the very essence of storytelling lies in problems and conflicts, family disputes have always been raw material for stories. As you have seen, writers sometimes treat such material with grim seriousness and sometimes with humor.

In the preceding group of selections, you have viewed several different kinds of problems typical of family living. Some were caused by the lust for money or status. One was created by the overprotectiveness of the parents. But most of the conflicts came about because of a difference in point of view between child and parents. In all of them, however, the conflicts were heightened and the reactions of the people were sharpened because the participants were members of a family, not merely friends or chance acquaintances.

IMPLICATIONS

1. Disturbances in families may spring from many causes. In which of the stories do you find evidence of conflicts or problems arising from the following:

a. Indifference of one member of the family for another.

b. A difference in the goals or desires among the family members.

2. What are some of the basic emotions that you found involved in these stories about families?

3. To outsiders, the family unit may seem to have a definite personality which is different from the personalities of the individuals who make up the family. In a sentence or two, describe the families in the following stories.

a. "The Rocking-Horse Winner"

b. "The Veldt"

Characterization

1. Think back through the stories in this section. Which characters are the most memorable? Are the most memorable characters for you the ones you would like best if you actually knew them? How do you explain your reaction?

2. What are the principal devices that writers use to characterize the people they create? Which writer made the most skillful use of these devices?

3. Is it possible to have a good story without fully developed characters?

Plot

1. What kind of problems does a writer face in plotting a story?

2. Name some of the characteristics of a satisfying plot.

3. Cite examples of plots in these stories that are closely tied to characterization.

Humor

1. How are Anton's ideas in "The Ambassador" a deviation from the expected pattern of behavior? Were you amused?

2. How is the mother's treatment of Arnold in "The Stone Boy" and the children's treatment of their parents in "The Veldt" unexpected? Did you find this amusing?

3. It has been said that there is a fine line between humor and tragedy. Do your findings in the questions above support this statement or not?

The Diary
of
Anne Frank

Introduction

ANN BIRSTEIN
and
ALFRED KAZIN

In March 1945, a young girl died in Bergen-Belsen,[1] unaware that she was leaving behind her a work that shed the first tiny human light on an episode in history that was unspeakably inhuman. She was a lovely girl, not quite sixteen when she died, with enormous dark gray eyes, a pretty little mouth, and a very brave heart. But like any awkward and self-conscious adolescent, she was weighed down by a sense of her shortcomings. She worried about her looks; she thought of herself as a coward, so often full of fear that she never realized how heroically she overcame it. Certainly, it would have been beyond her to imagine that the diary she kept for two years would have an impact on the entire world; how could it when the events of her lifetime were so enormous she could only seem puny by comparison? Her only real certainty was that she meant to be a writer anyway, and that her subject would have to be the world in which she found herself alive, no matter how terrible or even how unaccountably lovely her experiences in it might seem. For two years before her arrest she wrote all the time. She wrote while she was in hiding from the Nazis and could not take one step outdoors or in the daytime speak above a whisper. She wrote although the bombs came down so heavily at night that she fled for comfort into her father's bed. She wrote so steadily that by the time she was fifteen she had finished the equivalent of two books, one the *Diary*, the other a collection of short stories, essays, and reminiscences. As she said, with amazement at her own daring, she wrote because, "I want to go on living even after my death!" She has—reminding us that each of those millions who died in agony and despair, each of those victims whom the Nazis "exterminated" was, like Anne Frank, a separate and precious human spirit.

Of Anne Frank's actual life, as apart from her work, there is very little to tell; she did not live to see her sixteenth birthday. But because she had a great capacity for happiness, her life all in all was quite a happy one. She was born in Frankfurt, Germany, on June 12, 1929, to fairly wealthy Jewish parents, and she was lucky in her family, for although no one in her lifetime considered her unusual or profound, she was always able to count on a great deal of love and mutual respect in her home. She had a grandmother whom she adored and whom she refers to both in her diary and her stories as a "guardian angel," and an older sister, Margot, who was by everyone's account both beautiful and kind. With her mother she got on less well, though her complaints are largely just the usual ones of any growing girl. Actually, her mother taught Anne a great deal, especially lessons in charity. "No one ever becomes poor from giving," Mrs. Frank used to say, and Anne herself repeats this in her little essay called "Give." But it was her father Anne loved best, and with reason. He was and is a cultured man of great personal nobility and quiet courage, exactly the kind of father an adolescent girl could always turn to.

In 1933, when Hitler came to power, the Franks moved to Amsterdam, and though life soon closed in on them—the Franks, no longer wealthy, had to take in boarders; Holland was

1. **Bergen-Belsen,** a notorious Nazi concentration camp in southern Germany.

The large house in the middle is the rear of the Anne Frank house. The fourth floor window was for two years Anne's only access to the outside world.

invaded and capitulated to Germany; the Nazis issued strict anti-Jewish decrees; Anne had to leave the Montessori School, which she had loved, and go to the Jewish Lyceum—Anne remained the same humorous child she had always been. Lies Goosens, an old school friend in Amsterdam, who later saw Anne in Belsen, remembers her being considered a "problem child, very talkative"; by Mr. Frank's own tender confession, she never in life seemed so "deep" as she appeared in her diary. She was a vivid girl, but definitely not a prodigy. Ironically enough, the very vividness and intensity of the adolescent self-confrontation that was to make the *Diary* famous perhaps made Anne seem more conventional than she really was. The headmistress of the Montessori School in Amsterdam (now the Anne Frank School) remembers that Anne did not show any early promise, and that many of her pupils wrote with more imagination and feeling than did Anne.

When we read the accounts of those who had known Anne, we can see that although she had always been very distinct to them and often arresting, she had been seen only as a very young girl, and externally very much a girl of her own age. She had a passion for movie stars, whose pictures she collected, and for royalty— one of her main preoccupations was the difficulty of finding suitable husbands for Princess Elizabeth and Princess Margaret of Great Britain. She was a great talker, often an incessant one, as her family and teachers knew only too well, and her fondness for make-believe was such that she would bring a suitcase along even when she was just visiting for an hour next door. Anne giggled with her girl friends, was saucy and flirtatious with boys, played a lot of ping-pong, and consumed great quantities of ice cream afterward. She had a lovely thirteenth birthday with a party, home movies, flowers, and many presents, among them a small clothbound diary which Anne decided at once was "possibly the nicest of all." Then, a month after this birthday, life closed in on the Franks for good. On a hot July morning in 1942 they went into hiding, walking across Amsterdam in the pouring rain to a small group of rooms behind Mr. Frank's former offices. Here they and four others were to stay cooped up for more than two years, until the Dutch Green Police routed them out on August 4, 1944; and here Anne's diary, that nice present, was to grow and grow until, like all truly remarkable books, it finally outgrew its own author.

In a certain sense, however, it isn't fair to call the *Diary of a Young Girl* a diary at all, since from the very first it was more to her than a purely personal record of triumphs and defeats. Always she had toward her own experience the marvelous ambivalence of the born novelist, and immediately after claiming that "neither I—nor for that matter anyone else— will be interested in the unbosomings of a thirteen-year-old schoolgirl," on the very same page of her journal she has already chosen a literary form—the entries will be in the shape of letters to an imaginary girl named Kitty—

and embarked on a concise sketch, not only of her own life, but of general conditions in Holland. This same uncanny sense of an unseen audience, actually of posterity, prevails throughout her work. Scared out of her wits as she must have been when she went into hiding, one of the first things she writes about it is a detailed description of the hiding place and the bits and pieces of furnishings that went into it. When new people arrive, first the Van Daans and then Dussel, the dentist, she has them down on paper practically the minute they are through the door. With a writer's eye for how much is implied in the ordinary events of an ordinary day, she describes a typical morning, afternoon, and evening in the annexe; how they went to the toilet; where they slept; what they talked about while they peeled potatoes and shelled peas and stuffed sausages. She fell in love with the boy upstairs, yearned desperately for her first kiss, and in the breathless moment before it finally came broke into tears—which she described meticulously: "I sat pressed closely against him and felt a wave of emotion come over me, tears sprang into my eyes, the left one trickled onto his dungarees, the right one ran down my nose and also fell onto his dungarees. Did he notice? He made no move or sign to show that he did. . . . At half past eight I stood up and went to the window, where we always say good-by. . . . He came toward me, I flung my arms around his neck and gave him a kiss on his left cheek, and was about to kiss the other cheek, when my lips met his and we pressed them together."

To everything that happened to her, to everything that she felt, Anne gave a kind of permanence by transcribing it, and day after day she went on adding still another segment to the world she was creating. In the stories, where she chose her subjects, this world is not so real. But in her diary, where her subject chose her, its vividness and poignance are overwhelming. We can see them all: Mrs. Frank, always a little in the shadows, defending the upbringing of her children, or discussing with Mrs. Van Daan the best way to address servants; Mrs.

Behind this bookcase are the stairs leading to the hideout. Through this passage Miep and Mr. Kraler funneled all the food, clothing, medicine, and news.

Van Daan taking time out for a little flirtation with Dussel, the pompous old dentist, or else picking a fight with Mr. Van Daan ("But Putti . . . Mr. Frank always answers his wife, doesn't he?"); young, shy Peter Van Daan lying listlessly in his cluttered boy's room upstairs; Margot, always composed and gentle; Mr. Frank putting aside his beloved Dickens to settle a quarrel and put things right again; their Dutch protectors coming upstairs with their thoughtful little presents and their tantalizing whiffs of the outside world; and Anne, working out her genealogical tables, pasting up her pictures of movie stars, talking so much that everyone has to tell her to shut up—and then transforming herself into the ninth member, the one who retired to the little table so hard won from Mr. Dussel to bring the others to life.

What makes her achievement really amazing is how little, aside from her own natural gifts of observation and her sense of humor, she had to work with. Other people have countrysides and multitudes. For Anne, the one boy upstairs was

191

love; a single chestnut tree seen from her window, nature; a patch of blue sky—heaven. No wonder that soon she began to think of her diary and some of her sketches as the basis for a book after the war. *Het Achterhuis* (The House Behind) she meant to call it—a perfect title for the first book of a young girl, suggesting mystery and suspense and excitement; she even had a list of pseudonyms for the people in it.

The fourth floor window (shown on page 190) from the inside. To Anne the branches of the chestnut tree and the patch of sky became "nature" and "heaven."

When life in "the house behind" finally came to an end with the raid of the Green Police, it is ironic that in their search for loot the Police overlooked the precious diary. But Dutch friends who had sustained the Franks during the two-year confinement found Anne's notebooks and hid them until she should return. Only the father returned—to learn that he alone was left and to be given his daughter's notebooks by Miep and Elli. The little books

must have seemed pathetic enough to Otto Frank when, after his own slow recovery to health, he returned to Amsterdam to learn, after agonizing inquiries, that his wife and two children were dead.

At first Mr. Frank had copies of the *Diary* privately circulated as a memorial to his family. It was a Dutch university professor who urged formal publication of the book, and with only very slight excisions by Mr. Frank, *Het Achterhuis* was published in Amsterdam by Contact Publishers, in June 1947. The book soon went through several editions. In 1950, it was published in Germany by the Heidelberg firm of Lambert Schneider. The first printing was 4,500 copies, and many booksellers were actually afraid to show it in their windows; but the book caught on rapidly, and the sales of the pocket edition, published by S. Fischer Verlag, total more than half a million. In 1950 it was published in France; in 1952, in England and the United States. By now the book has been translated into twenty-two languages, has been published in twenty countries, and has sold more than two and a half million copies. In the United States it had an enormous success in the Pocket Book edition and later was circulated by the Teen Age Book Club, the Book Find Club, and republished in the Modern Library. The book was serialized by an American newspaper syndicate, with a calculated audience of ten million readers, and millions more read it when it was condensed in *Omnibook* and *Compact* magazines. A German translation of the book has been used in the United States as a school reader.

The book had a second life when it was dramatized by Frances Goodrich and Albert Hackett and became one of the most successful enterprises of the contemporary theater. In the United States the play won all the principal theater awards, and has since been produced in over twenty countries; it has now been made into a film, and soon the story of Anne Frank will have become perhaps the most celebrated document of a single human being's ordeal during World War II.

THE

DIARY

OF

ANNE FRANK

Dramatized
by

FRANCES GOODRICH
and
ALBERT HACKETT

Based upon the book,
Anne Frank: Diary of a Young Girl

Characters
(in order of appearance)

MR. FRANK
MIEP
MRS. VAN DAAN
MR. VAN DAAN
PETER VAN DAAN
MRS. FRANK
MARGOT FRANK
ANNE FRANK
MR. KRALER
MR. DUSSEL

The time: During the years of World War II and immediately thereafter.

The place: Amsterdam.

There are two acts.

Act One

SCENE I

*T*he scene remains the same throughout the play. It is the top floor of a warehouse and office building in Amsterdam, Holland. The sharply peaked roof of the building is outlined against a sea of other rooftops, stretching away into the distance. Nearby is the belfry of a church tower, the Westertoren, whose carillon rings out the hours. Occasionally faint sounds float up from below: the voices of children playing in the street, the tramp of marching feet, a boat whistle from the canal.

The three rooms of the top floor and a small attic space above are exposed to our view. The largest of the rooms is in the center, with two small rooms, slightly raised, on either side. On the right is a bathroom, out of sight. A narrow steep flight of stairs at the back leads up to the attic. The rooms are sparsely furnished with a few chairs, cots, a table or two. The windows are painted over, or covered with makeshift blackout curtains.[1] In the main room there is a sink, a gas ring for cooking and a wood-burning stove for warmth.

The room on the left is hardly more than a closet. There is a skylight in the sloping ceiling. Directly under this room is a small steep stairwell, with steps leading down to a door. This is the only entrance from the building below. When the door is opened we see that it has been concealed on the outer side by a bookcase attached to it.

The curtain rises on a empty stage. It is late afternoon November, 1945.

The rooms are dusty, the curtains in rags. Chairs and tables are overturned.

The door at the foot of the small stairwell swings open. MR. FRANK *comes up the steps*

---

1. **Blackout curtain,** a heavy dark curtain to prevent light from within from being seen.

into view. He is a gentle, cultured European in his middle years. There is still a trace of a German accent in his speech.

He stands looking slowly around, making a supreme effort at self-control. He is weak, ill. His clothes are threadbare.

After a second he drops his rucksack on the couch and moves slowly about. He opens the door to one of the smaller rooms, and then abruptly closes it again, turning away. He goes to the window at the back, looking off at the Westertoren as its carillon strikes the hour of six, then he moves restlessly on.

From the street below we hear the sound of a barrel organ and children's voices at play. There is a many-colored scarf hanging from a nail. MR. FRANK *takes it, putting it around his neck. As he starts back for his rucksack, his eye is caught by something lying on the floor. It is a woman's white glove. He holds it in his hand and suddenly all of his self-control is gone. He breaks down, crying.*

We hear footsteps on the stairs. MIEP[2] GIES *comes up, looking for* MR. FRANK. MIEP *is a Dutch girl of about twenty-two. She wears a coat and hat, ready to go home. She is pregnant. Her attitude toward* MR. FRANK *is protective, compassionate.*

MIEP. Are you all right, Mr. Frank?

MR. FRANK. (*Quickly controlling himself*) Yes, Miep, yes.

MIEP. Everyone in the office has gone home . . . It's after six. (*Then pleading*) Don't stay up here, Mr. Frank. What's the use of torturing yourself like this?

MR. FRANK. I've come to say good-bye . . . I'm leaving here, Miep.

MIEP. What do you mean? Where are you going? Where?

MR. FRANK. I don't know yet. I haven't decided.

MIEP. Mr. Frank, you can't leave here! This is your home! Amsterdam is your home. Your business is here, waiting for you . . . You're needed here . . . Now that the war is over, there are things that . . .

MR. FRANK. I can't stay in Amsterdam, Miep. It

has too many memories for me. Everywhere there's something . . . the house we lived in . . . the school . . . that street organ playing out there . . . I'm not the person you used to know, Miep. I'm a bitter old man. (*Breaking off*) Forgive me. I shouldn't speak to you like this . . . after all that you did for us . . . the suffering . . .

MIEP. No. No. It wasn't suffering. You can't say we suffered.

(*As she speaks, she straightens a chair which is overturned.*)

MR. FRANK. I know what you went through, you and Mr. Kraler. I'll remember it as long as I live. (*He gives one last look around*) Come, Miep.

(*He starts for the steps, then remembers his rucksack, going back to get it.*)

MIEP. (*Hurrying up to a cupboard*) Mr. Frank, did you see? There are some of your papers here. (*She brings a bundle of papers to him*) We found them in a heap of rubbish on the floor after . . . after you left.

MR. FRANK. Burn them.

(*He opens his rucksack to put the glove in it.*)

MIEP. But, Mr. Frank, there are letters, notes . . .

MR. FRANK. Burn them. All of them.

MIEP. Burn *this?*

(*She hands him a paperbound notebook.*)

MR. FRANK. (*Quietly*) Anne's diary. (*He opens the diary and begins to read*) "Monday, the sixth of July, nineteen forty-two." (*To* MIEP) Nineteen forty-two. Is it possible, Miep? . . . Only three years ago. (*As he continues his reading, he sits down on the couch*) "Dear Diary, since you and I are going to be great friends, I will start by telling you about myself. My name is Anne Frank. I am thirteen years old. I was born in Germany the twelfth of June, nineteen twenty-nine. As my family

---

2. **Miep**\mēp\.

194

is Jewish, we emigrated to Holland when Hitler came to power."

(*As* MR. FRANK *reads on, another voice joins his, as if coming from the air. It is* ANNE'S *voice.*)

MR. FRANK AND ANNE. "My father started a business, importing spice and herbs. Things went well for us until nineteen forty. Then the war came, and the Dutch capitulation, followed by the arrival of the Germans. Then things got very bad for the Jews."

(MR. FRANK'S *voice dies out.* ANNE'S *voice continues alone. The lights dim slowly to darkness. The curtain falls on the scene.*)

ANNE'S VOICE. You could not do this and you could not do that. They forced Father out of his business. We had to wear yellow stars. I had to turn in my bike. I couldn't go to a Dutch school any more. I couldn't go to the movies, or ride in an automobile, or even on a streetcar, and a million other things. But somehow we children still managed to have fun. Yesterday Father told me we were going into hiding. Where, he wouldn't say. At five o'clock this morning Mother woke me and told me to hurry and get dressed. I was to put on as many clothes as I could. It would look too suspicious if we walked along carrying suitcases. It wasn't until we were on our way that I learned where we were going. Our hiding place was to be upstairs in the building where Father used to have his business. Three other people were coming in *with* us . . . The Van Daans and their son Peter . . . *Father* knew the Van Daans but we had never met them . . .

(*During the last lines the curtain rises on the scene. The lights dim on.* ANNE'S *voice fades out.*)

SCENE II

It is early morning, July, 1942. The rooms are bare, as before, but they are now clean and orderly.

MR. VAN DAAN, *a tall, portly man in his late forties, is in the main room, pacing up and down, nervously smoking a cigarette. His clothes and overcoat are expensive and well cut.*

MRS. VAN DAAN *sits on the couch, clutching her possessions, a hatbox, bags, etc. She is a pretty woman in her early forties. She wears a fur coat over her other clothes.*

PETER VAN DAAN *is standing at the window of the room on the right, looking down at the street below. He is a shy, awkward boy of sixteen. He wears a cap, a raincoat, and long Dutch trousers like "plus fours."*[1] *At his feet is a black case, a carrier for his cat.*

The yellow Star of David[2] *is conspicuous on all of their clothes.*

MRS. VAN DAAN. (*Rising, nervous, excited*) Something's happened to them! I know it!

MR. VAN DAAN. Now, Kerli!

MRS. VAN DAAN. Mr. Frank said they'd be here at seven o'clock. He said . . .

MR. VAN DAAN. They have two miles to walk. You can't expect . . .

MRS. VAN DAAN. They've been picked up. That's what's happened. They've been taken . . .

(MR. VAN DAAN *indicates that he hears someone coming.*)

MR. VAN DAAN. You see?

(PETER *takes up his carrier and his school-bag, etc., and goes into the main room as* MR. FRANK *comes up the stairwell from below.* MR. FRANK *looks much younger now. His movements are brisk, his manner confident. He wears an overcoat and carries his hat and a small cardboard box. He crosses to the* VAN DAANS, *shaking hands with each of them.*)

MR. FRANK. Mrs. Van Daan, Mr. Van Daan, Peter. (*Then, in explanation of their late-*

---

1. **plus fours,** baggy, loose, knee breeches.
2. **Star of David,** a six-pointed star formed by two intersecting equilateral triangles. It is often a symbol of Judaism, and Jews under Hitler were forced to wear it.

ness) There were too many of the Green Police[3] on the streets . . . we had to take the long way around.

(*Up the steps come* MARGOT FRANK, MRS. FRANK, MIEP (*not pregnant now*) *and* MR. KRALER. *All of them carry bags, packages, and so forth. The Star of David is conspicuous on all of the* FRANKS' *clothing.* MARGOT *is eighteen, beautiful, quiet, shy.* MRS. FRANK *is a young mother, gently bred, reserved. She, like* MR. FRANK, *has a slight German accent.* MR. KRALER *is a Dutchman, dependable, kindly.*

As MR. KRALER *and* MIEP *go upstage to put down their parcels,* MRS. FRANK *turns back to call* ANNE.)

MRS. FRANK. Anne?

(ANNE *comes running up the stairs. She is thirteen, quick in her movements, interested in everything, mercurial in her emotions. She wears a cape, long wool socks and carries a schoolbag.*)

MR. FRANK. (*Introducing them*) My wife, Edith. Mr. and Mrs. Van Daan (MRS. FRANK *hurries over, shaking hands with them*) . . . their son, Peter . . . my daughters, Margot and Anne.

(ANNE *gives a polite little curtsy as she shakes* MR. VAN DAAN's *hand. Then she immediately starts off on a tour of investigation of her new home, going upstairs to the attic room.*

MIEP *and* MR. KRALER *are putting the various things they have brought on the shelves.*)

MR. KRALER. I'm sorry there is still so much confusion.

MR. FRANK. Please. Don't think of it. After all, we'll have plenty of leisure to arrange everything ourselves.

MIEP. (*To* MRS. FRANK) We put the stores of food you sent in here. Your drugs are here . . . soap, linen here.

MRS. FRANK. Thank you, Miep.

MIEP. I made up the beds . . . the way Mr. Frank

and Mr. Kraler said. (*She starts out*) Forgive me. I have to hurry. I've got to go to the other side of town to get some ration books for you.

MRS. VAN DAAN. Ration books? If they see our names on ration books, they'll know we're here.

MR. KRALER. There isn't anything . . . ⎱

MIEP. Don't worry. Your names won't be on them. (*As she hurries out*) I'll be up later. ⎰ *Together*

MR. FRANK. Thank you, Miep.

MRS. FRANK. (*To* MR. KRALER) It's illegal, then, the ration books? We've never done anything illegal.

MR. FRANK. We won't be living here exactly according to regulations.

(*As* MR. KRALER *reassures* MRS. FRANK, *he takes various small things, such as matches, soap, etc., from his pockets, handing them to her.*)

MR. KRALER. This isn't the black market,[4] Mrs. Frank. This is what we call the white market . . . helping all of the hundreds and hundreds who are hiding out in Amsterdam.

(*The carillon is heard playing the quarter-hour before eight.* MR. KRALER *looks at his watch.* ANNE *stops at the window as she comes down the stairs.*)

ANNE. It's the Westertoren!

MR. KRALER. I must go. I must be out of here and downstairs in the office before the workmen get here. (*He starts for the stairs leading out*) Miep, or I, or both of us, will be up each day to bring you food and news and find out what your needs are. Tomorrow I'll get you a better bolt for the door at the foot of the stairs. It needs a bolt that you can throw yourself and open only at our signal. (*To* MR. FRANK) Oh . . . You'll tell them about the noise?

---

3. **Green Police,** an auxiliary Dutch police force created to aid Nazi occupation forces.
4. **A black market** deals in illegal commodities or makes sales under illegal conditions.

MR. FRANK. I'll tell them.

MR. KRALER. Good-bye then for the moment. I'll come up again, after the workmen leave.

MR. FRANK. Good-bye, Mr. Kraler.

MRS. FRANK. (*Shaking his hand*) How can we thank you?

(*The others murmur their good-byes.*)

MR. KRALER. I never thought I'd live to see the day when a man like Mr. Frank would have to go into hiding. When you think—

(*He breaks off, going out. MR. FRANK follows him down the steps, bolting the door after him. In the interval before he returns, PETER goes over to MARGOT, shaking hands with her. As MR. FRANK comes back up the steps, MRS. FRANK questions him anxiously.*)

The Franks and Van Daans have just arrived and are removing their extra clothes. They are in the common room in the center of the stage. The attic space is above.

MRS. FRANK. What did he mean, about the noise?

MR. FRANK. First let us take off some of these clothes.

(*They all start to take off garment after garment. On each of their coats, sweaters, blouses, suits, dresses, is another yellow Star of David. MR. and MRS. FRANK are underdressed quite simply. The others wear several things, sweaters, extra dresses, bathrobes, aprons, nightgowns, etc.*)

MR. VAN DAAN. It's a wonder we weren't arrested, walking along the streets . . . Petronella with a fur coat in July . . . and that cat of Peter's crying all the way.

ANNE. (*As she is removing a pair of panties*) A cat?

MRS. FRANK. (*Shocked*) Anne, please!

ANNE. It's all right. I've got on three more.

(*She pulls off two more. Finally, as they have all removed their surplus clothes, they look to* MR. FRANK, *waiting for him to speak.*)

MR. FRANK. Now. About the noise. While the men are in the building below, we must have complete quiet. Every sound can be heard down there, not only in the workrooms, but in the offices too. The men come at about eight-thirty, and leave at about five-thirty. So, to be perfectly safe, from eight in the morning until six in the evening we must move only when it is necessary, and then in stockinged feet. We must not speak above a whisper. We must not run any water. We cannot use the sink, or even, forgive me, the W.C. The pipes go down through the workrooms. It would be heard. No trash . . . (MR. FRANK *stops abruptly as he hears the sound of marching feet from the street below. Everyone is motionless, paralyzed with fear.* MR. FRANK *goes quietly into the room on the right to look down out of the window.* ANNE *runs after him, peering out with him. The tramping feet pass without stopping. The tension is relieved.* MR. FRANK, *followed by* ANNE, *returns to the main room and resumes his instructions to the group*) . . . No trash must ever be thrown out which might reveal that someone is living up here . . . not even a potato paring. We must burn everything in the stove at night. This is the way we must live until it is over, if we are to survive.

(*There is silence for a second.*)

MRS. FRANK. Until it is over.

MR. FRANK. (*Reassuringly*) After six we can move about . . . we can talk and laugh and have our supper and read and play games . . . just as we would at home. (*He looks at his watch*) And now I think it would be wise if we all went to our rooms, and were settled before eight o'clock. Mrs. Van Daan, you and your husband will be upstairs. I regret that there's no place up there for Peter. But he will be here, near us. This will be our common room, where we'll meet to talk and eat and read, like one family.

MR. VAN DAAN. And where do you and Mrs. Frank sleep?

MR. FRANK. This room is also our bedroom.

MRS. VAN DAAN. That isn't right. We'll sleep here and you take the room upstairs. ⎱ *Together*

MR. VAN DAAN. It's your place. ⎰

MR. FRANK. Please. I've thought this out for weeks. It's the best arrangement. The only arrangement.

MRS. VAN DAAN. (*To* MR. FRANK) Never, never can we thank you. (*Then to* MRS. FRANK) I don't know what would have happened to us, if it hadn't been for Mr. Frank.

MR. FRANK. You don't know how your husband helped me when I came to this country . . . knowing no one . . . not able to speak the language. I can never repay him for that. (*Going to* VAN DAAN) May I help you with your things?

MR. VAN DAAN. No. No. (*To* MRS. VAN DAAN) Come along, *liefje.*[5]

MRS. VAN DAAN. You'll be all right, Peter? You're not afraid?

PETER. (*Embarrassed*) Please, Mother.

(*They start up the stairs to the attic room above.* MR. FRANK *turns to* MRS. FRANK.)

MR. FRANK. You too must have some rest, Edith. You didn't close your eyes last night. Nor you, Margot.

ANNE. I slept, Father. Wasn't that funny? I knew it was the last night in my own bed, and yet I slept soundly.

MR. FRANK. I'm glad, Anne. Now you'll be able to help me straighten things in here. (*To* MRS. FRANK *and* MARGOT) Come with me . . . You and Margot rest in this room for the time being.

---

5. liefje\ᵃlēf·yə\ dear.

(*He picks up their clothes, starting for the room on the right.*)

MRS. FRANK. You're sure . . . ? I could help . . . And Anne hasn't had her milk . . .

MR. FRANK. I'll give it to her. (*To* ANNE *and* PETER) Anne, Peter . . . it's best that you take off your shoes now, before you forget.

(*He leads the way to the room, followed by* MARGOT.)

MRS. FRANK. You're sure you're not tired, Anne?

ANNE. I feel fine. I'm going to help Father.

MRS. FRANK. Peter, I'm glad you are to be with us.

PETER. Yes, Mrs. Frank.

(MRS. FRANK *goes to join* MR. FRANK *and* MARGOT.)

(*During the following scene* MR. FRANK *helps* MARGOT *and* MRS. FRANK *to hang up their clothes. Then he persuades them both to lie down and rest. The* VAN DAANS *in their room above settle themselves. In the main room* ANNE *and* PETER *remove their shoes.* PETER *takes his cat out of the carrier.*)

ANNE. What's your cat's name?

PETER. Mouschi.

ANNE. Mouschi! Mouschi! Mouschi! (*She picks up the cat, walking away with it. To* PETER) I love cats. I have one . . . a darling little cat. But they made me leave her behind. I left some food and a note for the neighbors to take care of her . . . I'm going to miss her terribly. What is yours? A him or a her?

PETER. He's a tom. He doesn't like strangers.

(*He takes the cat from her, putting it back in its carrier.*)

ANNE. (*Unabashed*) Then I'll have to stop being a stranger, won't I? Is he fixed?

PETER. (*Startled*) Huh?

ANNE. Did you have him fixed?

PETER. No.

ANNE. Oh, you ought to have him fixed—to keep him from—you know, fighting. Where did you go to school?

PETER. Jewish Secondary.

ANNE. But that's where Margot and I go! I never saw you around.

PETER. I used to see you . . . sometimes . . .

ANNE. You did?

PETER. . . . in the school yard. You were always in the middle of a bunch of kids.

(*He takes a penknife from his pocket.*)

ANNE. Why didn't you ever come over?

PETER. I'm sort of a lone wolf.

(*He starts to rip off his Star of David.*)

ANNE. What are you doing?

PETER. Taking it off.

ANNE. But you can't do that. They'll arrest you if you go out without your star.

(*He tosses his knife on the table.*)

PETER. Who's going out?

ANNE. Why, of course! You're right! Of course we don't need them any more. (*She picks up his knife and starts to take her star off*) I wonder what our friends will think when we don't show up today?

PETER. I didn't have any dates with anyone.

ANNE. Oh, I did. I had a date with Jopie to go and play ping-pong at her house. Do you know Jopie de Waal?

PETER. No.

ANNE. Jopie's my best friend. I wonder what she'll think when she telephones and there's no answer? . . . Probably she'll go over to the house . . . I wonder what she'll think . . . we left everything as if we'd suddenly been called away . . . breakfast dishes in the sink . . . beds not made . . . (*As she pulls off her star, the cloth underneath shows clearly the color and form of the star*) Look! It's still there! (PETER *goes over to the stove with his star*) What're you going to do with yours?

PETER. Burn it.

ANNE. (*She starts to throw hers in, and cannot*) It's funny, I can't throw mine away. I don't know why.

PETER. You can't throw . . . ? Something they branded you with . . . ? That they made you wear so they could spit on you?

ANNE. I know. I know. But after all, it *is* the Star of David, isn't it?

(*In the bedroom, right,* MARGOT *and* MRS. FRANK *are lying down.* MR. FRANK *starts quietly out.*)

PETER. Maybe it's different for a girl.

(MR. FRANK *comes into the main room.*)

MR. FRANK. Forgive me, Peter. Now let me see. We must find a bed for your cat. (*He goes to a cupboard*) I'm glad you brought your cat. Anne was feeling so badly about hers. (*Getting a used small washtub*) Here we are. Will it be comfortable in that?

PETER. (*Gathering up his things*) Thanks.

MR. FRANK. (*Opening the door of the room on the left*) And here is your room. But I warn you, Peter, you can't grow any more. Not an inch, or you'll have to sleep with your feet out of the skylight. Are you hungry?

PETER. No.

MR. FRANK. We have some bread and butter.

PETER. No, thank you.

MR. FRANK. You can have it for luncheon then. And tonight we will have a real supper . . . our first supper together.

PETER. Thanks. Thanks.

(*He goes into his room. During the following scene he arranges his possessions in his new room.*)

MR. FRANK. That's a nice boy, Peter.

ANNE. He's awfully shy, isn't he?

MR. FRANK. You'll like him, I know.

ANNE. I certainly hope so, since he's the only boy I'm likely to see for months and months.

(MR. FRANK *sits down, taking off his shoes.*)

MR. FRANK. Anneke,[6] there's a box there. Will you open it?

(*He indicates a carton on the couch.* ANNE *brings it to the center table. In the street below there is the sound of children playing.*)

ANNE. (*As she opens the carton*) You know the way I'm going to think of it here? I'm going to think of it as a boarding house. A very peculiar summer boarding house, like the one that we—(*She breaks off as she pulls out some photographs*) Father! My movie stars! I was wondering where they were! I was looking for them this morning . . . and Queen Wilhelmina![7] How wonderful!

MR. FRANK. There's something more. Go on. Look further.

(*He goes over to the sink, pouring a glass of milk from a thermos bottle.*)

ANNE. (*Pulling out a pasteboard-bound book*) A diary! (*She throws her arms around her father*) I've never had a diary. And I've always longed for one. (*She looks around the room*) Pencil, pencil, pencil, pencil. (*She starts down the stairs*) I'm going down to the office to get a pencil.

MR. FRANK. Anne! No!

(*He goes after her, catching her by the arm and pulling her back.*)

ANNE. (*Startled*) But there's no one in the building now.

MR. FRANK. It doesn't matter. I don't want you ever to go beyond that door.

ANNE. (*Sobered*) Never . . . ? Not even at night-time, when everyone is gone? Or on Sundays? Can't I go down to listen to the radio?

MR. FRANK. Never. I am sorry, Anneke. It isn't safe. No, you must never go beyond that door.

(*For the first time* ANNE *realizes what "going into hiding" means.*)

ANNE. I see.

MR. FRANK. It'll be hard, I know. But always remember this, Anneke. There are no walls, there are no bolts, no locks that anyone can put on your mind. Miep will bring us books. We will read history, poetry, mythology. (*He gives her the glass of milk*) Here's your milk. (*With his arm about her, they go over to the*

---

6. **Anneke**\ˈa·nə·kə\ little Anne.
7. **Wilhelmina**\ˈwil·hĕl ˈmē·na\ (1880–1962), Queen of the Netherlands from 1890 to 1948.

couch, sitting down side by side) As a matter of fact, between us, Anne, being here has certain advantages for you. For instance, you remember the battle you had with your mother the other day on the subject of overshoes? You said you'd rather die than wear overshoes? But in the end you had to wear them? Well now, you see, for as long as we are here you will never have to wear overshoes! Isn't that good? And the coat that you inherited from Margot, you won't have to wear that any more. And the piano! You won't have to practice on the piano. I tell you, this is going to be a fine life for you!

(ANNE's *panic is gone.* PETER *appears in the doorway of his room, with a saucer in his hand. He is carrying his cat.*)

PETER. I . . . I . . . I thought I'd better get some water for Mouschi before . . .

MR. FRANK. Of course.

(*As he starts toward the sink the carillon begins to chime the hour of eight. He tiptoes to the window at the back and looks down at the street below. He turns to* PETER, *indicating in pantomime that it is too late.* PETER *starts back for his room. He steps on a creaking board. The three of them are frozen for a minute in fear. As* PETER *starts away again,* ANNE *tiptoes over to him and pours some of the milk from her glass into the saucer for the cat.* PETER *squats on the floor, putting the milk before the cat.* MR. FRANK *gives* ANNE *his fountain pen, and then goes into the room at the right. For a second* ANNE *watches the cat, then she goes over to the center table, and opens her diary.*

In the room at the right, MRS. FRANK *has sat up quickly at the sound of the carillon.* MR. FRANK *comes in and sits down beside her on the settee, his arm comfortingly around her.*

Upstairs, in the attic room, MR. *and* MRS. VAN DAAN *have hung their clothes in the closet and are now seated on the iron bed.*

Mr. Frank: "But always remember this, Anne. There are no walls, there are no bolts, no locks that anyone can put on your mind."

MRS. VAN DAAN *leans back exhausted.* MR. VAN DAAN *fans her with a newspaper.*

ANNE *starts to write in her diary. The lights dim out, the curtain falls.*

In the darkness ANNE's *voice comes to us again, faintly at first, and then with growing strength.*)

ANNE'S VOICE. I expect I should be describing what it feels like to go into hiding. But I really don't know yet myself. I only know it's funny never to be able to go outdoors . . .

never to breathe fresh air . . . never to run and shout and jump. It's the silence in the nights that frightens me most. Every time I hear a creak in the house, or a step on the street outside, I'm sure they're coming for us. The days aren't so bad. At least we know that Miep and Mr. Kraler are down there below us in the office. Our protectors, we call them. I asked Father what would happen to them if the Nazis found out they were hiding us. Pim said that they would suffer the same fate that we would . . . Imagine! They know this, and yet when they come up here, they're always cheerful and gay as if there were nothing in the world to bother them . . . Friday, the twenty-first of August, nineteen forty-two. Today I'm going to tell you our general news. Mother is unbearable. She insists on treating me like a baby, which I loathe. Otherwise things are going better. The weather is . . .

(*As* ANNE's *voice is fading out, the curtain rises on the scene.*)

SCENE III

It is little after six o'clock in the evening, two months later.

MARGOT *is in the bedroom at the right, studying.* MR. VAN DAAN *is lying down in the attic room above.*

The rest of the "family" is in the main room. ANNE *and* PETER *sit opposite each other at the center table, where they have been doing their lessons.* MRS. FRANK *is on the couch.* MRS. VAN DAAN *is seated with her fur coat, on which she has been sewing, in her lap. None of them are wearing their shoes.*

Their eyes are on MR. FRANK, *waiting for him to give them the signal which will release them from their day-long quiet.* MR. FRANK, *his shoes in his hand, stands looking down out of the window at the back, watching to be sure that all of the workmen have left the building below.*

After a few seconds of motionless silence, MR. FRANK *turns from the window.*

MR. FRANK. (*Quietly, to the group*) It's safe now. The last workman has left.

(*There is an immediate stir of relief.*)

ANNE. (*Her pent-up energy explodes*) WHEE!
MRS. FRANK. (*Startled, amused*) Anne!
MRS. VAN DAAN. I'm first for the w.c.

(*She hurries off to the bathroom.* MRS. FRANK *puts on her shoes and starts up to the sink to prepare supper.* ANNE *sneaks* PETER's *shoes from under the table and hides them behind her back.* MR. FRANK *goes in to* MARGOT's *room.*)

MR. FRANK. (*To* MARGOT) Six o'clock. School's over.

(MARGOT *gets up, stretching.* MR. FRANK *sits down to put on his shoes. In the main room* PETER *tries to find his.*)

PETER. (*To* ANNE) Have you seen my shoes?
ANNE. (*Innocently*) Your shoes?
PETER. You've taken them, haven't you?
ANNE. I don't know what you're talking about.
PETER. You're going to be sorry!
ANNE. Am I?

(PETER *goes after her.* ANNE, *with his shoes in her hand, runs from him, dodging behind her mother.*)

MRS. FRANK. (*Protesting*) Anne, dear!
PETER. Wait till I get you!
ANNE. I'm waiting! (PETER *makes a lunge for her. They both fall to the floor.* PETER *pins her down, wrestling with her to get the shoes*) Don't! Don't! Peter, stop it. Ouch!
MRS. FRANK. Anne! . . . Peter!

(*Suddenly* PETER *becomes self-conscious. He grabs his shoes roughly and starts for his room.*)

ANNE. (*Following him*) Peter, where are you going? Come dance with me.
PETER. I tell you I don't know how.
ANNE. I'll teach you.
PETER. I'm going to give Mouschi his dinner.

ANNE. Can I watch?

PETER. He doesn't like people around while he eats.

ANNE. Peter, please.

PETER. No!

(*He goes into his room.* ANNE *slams his door after him.*)

MRS. FRANK. Anne, dear, I think you shouldn't play like that with Peter. It's not dignified.

ANNE. Who cares if it's dignified? I don't want to be dignified.

(MR. FRANK *and* MARGOT *come from the room on the right.* MARGOT *goes to help her mother.* MR. FRANK *starts for the center table to correct* MARGOT's *school papers.*)

MRS. FRANK. (*To* ANNE) You complain that I don't treat you like a grownup. But when I do, you resent it.

ANNE. I only want some fun . . . someone to laugh and clown with . . . After you've sat still all day and hardly moved, you've got to have some fun. I don't know what's the matter with that boy.

MR. FRANK. He isn't used to girls. Give him a little time.

ANNE. Time? Isn't two months time? I could cry. (*Catching hold of* MARGOT) Come on, Margot . . . dance with me. Come on, please.

MARGOT. I have to help with supper.

ANNE. You know we're going to forget how to dance . . . When we get out we won't remember a thing.

(*She starts to sing and dance by herself.* MR. FRANK *takes her in his arms, waltzing with her.* MRS. VAN DAAN *comes in from the bathroom.*)

MRS. VAN DAAN. Next? (*She looks around as she starts putting on her shoes*) Where's Peter?

ANNE. (*As they are dancing*) Where would he be!

MRS. VAN DAAN. He hasn't finished his lessons, has he? His father'll kill him if he catches him in there with that cat and his work not done. (MR. FRANK *and* ANNE *finish their dance. They bow to each other with extravagant*

formality) Anne, get him out of there, will you?

ANNE. (*At* PETER's *door*) Peter? Peter?

PETER. (*Opening the door a crack*) What is it?

ANNE. Your mother says to come out.

PETER. I'm giving Mouschi his dinner.

MRS. VAN DAAN. You know what your father says.

(*She sits on the couch, sewing on the lining of her fur coat.*)

PETER. For heaven's sake, I haven't even looked at him since lunch.

MRS. VAN DAAN. I'm just telling you, that's all.

ANNE. I'll feed him.

PETER. I don't want you in there.

MRS. VAN DAAN. Peter!

PETER. (*To* ANNE) Then give him his dinner and come right out, you hear?

(*He comes back to the table.* ANNE *shuts the door of* PETER's *room after her and disappears behind the curtain covering his closet.*)

MRS. VAN DAAN. (*To* PETER) Now is that any way to talk to your little girl friend?

PETER. Mother . . . for heaven's sake . . . will you please stop saying that?

MRS. VAN DAAN. Look at him blush! Look at him!

PETER. Please! I'm not . . . anyway . . . let me alone, will you?

MRS. VAN DAAN. He acts like it was something to be ashamed of. It's nothing to be ashamed of, to have a little girl friend.

PETER. You're crazy. She's only thirteen.

MRS. VAN DAAN. So what? And you're sixteen. Just perfect. Your father's ten years older than I am. (*To* MR. FRANK) I warn you, Mr. Frank, if this war lasts much longer, we're going to be related and then . . .

MR. FRANK. *Mazeltov!*[1]

MRS. FRANK. (*Deliberately changing the conversation*) I wonder where Miep is. She's usually so prompt.

(*Suddenly everything else is forgotten as*

---

1. **mazeltov**\⌃ma·zəl 'tav\ congratulations.

they hear the sound of an automobile coming to a screeching stop in the street below. They are tense, motionless in their terror. The car starts away. A wave of relief sweeps over them. They pick up their occupations again. ANNE *flings open the door of* PETER's *room, making a dramatic entrance. She is dressed in* PETER's *clothes.* PETER *looks at her in fury. The others are amused.*)

ANNE. Good evening, everyone. Forgive me if I don't stay. (*She jumps up on a chair*) I have a friend waiting for me in there. My friend Tom. Tom Cat. Some people say that we look alike. But Tom has the most beautiful whiskers, and I have only a little fuzz. I am hoping . . . in time . . .

PETER. All right, Mrs. Quack Quack!

ANNE. (*Outraged—jumping down*) Peter!

PETER. I heard about you . . . How you talked so much in class they called you Mrs. Quack Quack. How Mr. Smitter made you write a composition . . . " 'Quack, quack,' said Mrs. Quack Quack."

ANNE. Well, go on. Tell them the rest. How it was so good he read it out loud to the class and then read it to all his other classes!

PETER. Quack! Quack! Quack . . . Quack . . . Quack . . .

(ANNE *pulls off the coat and trousers*)

ANNE. You are the most intolerable, insufferable boy I've ever met!

(*She throws the clothes down the stairwell.* PETER *goes down after them.*)

PETER. Quack, quack, quack!

MRS. VAN DAAN. (*To* ANNE) That's right, Anneke! Give it to him!

ANNE. With all the boys in the world . . . Why I had to get locked up with one like you! . . .

PETER. Quack, quack, quack, and from now on stay out of my room!

(*As* PETER *passes her,* ANNE *puts out her foot, tripping him. He picks himself up, and goes on into his room.*)

MRS. FRANK. (*Quietly*) Anne, dear . . . your hair. (*She feels* ANNE's *forehead*) You're warm. Are you feeling all right?

ANNE. Please, Mother.

(*She goes over to the center table, slipping into her shoes.*)

MRS. FRANK. (*Following her*) You haven't a fever, have you?

ANNE. (*Pulling away*) No. No.

MRS. FRANK. You know we can't call a doctor here, ever. There's only one thing to do . . . watch carefully. Prevent an illness before it comes. Let me see your tongue.

ANNE. Mother, this is perfectly absurd.

MRS. FRANK. Anne, dear, don't be such a baby. Let me see your tongue.

(*As* ANNE *refuses,* MRS. FRANK *appeals to* MR. FRANK) Otto . . .?

MR. FRANK. You hear your mother, Anne.

(ANNE *flicks out her tongue for a second, then turns away.*)

MRS. FRANK. Come on—open up! (*As* ANNE *opens her mouth very wide*) You seem all right . . . but perhaps an aspirin . . .

MRS. VAN DAAN. For heaven's sake, don't give that child any pills. I waited for fifteen minutes this morning for her to come out of the w.c.

ANNE. I was washing my hair!

MR. FRANK. I think there's nothing the matter with our Anne that a ride on her bike, or a visit with her friend Jopie de Waal wouldn't cure. Isn't that so, Anne?

(MR. VAN DAAN *comes down into the room. From outside we hear faint sounds of bombers going over and a burst of ack-ack.[2]*)

MR. VAN DAAN. Miep not come yet?

MRS. VAN DAAN. The workmen just left, a little while ago.

MR. VAN DAAN. What's for dinner tonight?

MRS. VAN DAAN. Beans.

---

2. **ack-ack** \'ăk'ăk\ antiaircraft fire.

MR. VAN DAAN. Not again!

MRS. VAN DAAN. Poor Putti! I know. But what can we do? That's all that Miep brought us.

(MR. VAN DAAN *starts to pace, his hands behind his back.* ANNE *follows behind him, imitating him.*)

ANNE. We are now in what is known as the "bean cycle." Beans boiled, beans en casserole, beans with strings, beans without strings . . .

(PETER *has come out of his room. He slides into his place at the table, becoming immediately absorbed in his studies.*)

MR. VAN DAAN. (*To* PETER) I saw you . . . in there, playing with your cat.

MRS. VAN DAAN. He just went in for a second, putting his coat away. He's been out here all the time, doing his lessons.

MR. FRANK. (*Looking up from the papers*) Anne, you got an excellent in your history paper today . . . and very good in Latin.

ANNE. (*Sitting beside him*) How about algebra?

MR. FRANK. I'll have to make a confession. Up until now I've managed to stay ahead of you in algebra. Today you caught up with me. We'll leave it to Margot to correct.

ANNE. Isn't algebra *vile*, Pim!

MR. FRANK. Vile!

MARGOT. (*To* MR. FRANK) How did I do?

ANNE. (*Getting up*) Excellent, excellent, excellent, excellent!

MR. FRANK. (*To* MARGOT) You should have used the subjunctive here . . .

MARGOT. Should I? . . . I thought . . . look here . . . I didn't use it here . . .

(*The two become absorbed in the papers.*)

ANNE. Mrs. Van Daan, may I try on your coat?

MRS. FRANK. No, Anne.

MRS. VAN DAAN. (*Giving it to* ANNE) It's all right . . . but careful with it. (ANNE *puts it on and struts with it*) My father gave me that the year before he died. He always bought the best that money could buy.

ANNE. Mrs. Van Daan, did you have a lot of boy friends before you were married?

MRS. FRANK. Anne, that's a personal question. It's not courteous to ask personal questions.

MRS. VAN DAAN. Oh I don't mind. (*To* ANNE) Our house was always swarming with boys. When I was a girl we had . . .

MR. VAN DAAN. Not again!

MRS. VAN DAAN. (*Good-humored*) Shut up! (*Without a pause, to* ANNE. MR. VAN DAAN *mimics* MRS. VAN DAAN, *speaking the first few words in unison with her*) One summer we had a big house in Hilversum. The boys came buzzing round like bees around a jam pot. And when I was sixteen! . . . We were wearing our skirts very short those days and I had good-looking legs. (*She pulls up her skirt, going to* MR. FRANK) I still have 'em. I may not be as pretty as I used to be, but I still have my legs. How about it, Mr. Frank?

MR. VAN DAAN. All right. All right. We see them.

MRS. VAN DAAN. I'm not asking you. I'm asking Mr. Frank.

PETER. Mother, for heaven's sake.

MRS. VAN DAAN. Oh, I embarrass you, do I? Well, I just hope the girl you marry has as good. (*Then to* ANNE) My father used to worry about me, with so many boys hanging round. He told me, if any of them gets fresh, you say to him . . . "Remember, Mr. So-and-So, remember I'm a lady."

ANNE. "Remember, Mr. So-and-So, remember I'm a lady."

(*She gives* MRS. VAN DAAN *her coat.*)

MR. VAN DAAN. Look at you, talking that way in front of her! Don't you know she puts it all down in that diary?

MRS. VAN DAAN. So, if she does? I'm only telling the truth!

(ANNE *stretches out, putting her ear to the floor, listening to what is going on below. The sound of the bombers fades away.*)

MRS. FRANK. (*Setting the table*) Would you mind, Peter, if I moved you over to the couch?

ANNE. (*Listening*) Miep must have the radio on.

(PETER *picks up his papers, going over to the couch beside* MRS. VAN DAAN.)

MR. VAN DAAN. (*Accusingly, to* PETER) Haven't you finished yet?

PETER. No.

MR. VAN DAAN. You ought to be ashamed of yourself.

PETER. All right. All right. I'm a dunce. I'm a hopeless case. Why do I go on?

MRS. VAN DAAN. You're not hopeless. Don't talk that way. It's just that you haven't anyone to help you, like the girls have. (*To* MR. FRANK) Maybe you could help him, Mr. Frank?

MR. FRANK. I'm sure that his father . . . ?

MR. VAN DAAN. Not me. I can't do anything with him. He won't listen to me. You go ahead . . . if you want.

MR. FRANK. (*Going to* PETER) What about it, Peter? Shall we make our school coeducational?

MRS. VAN DAAN. (*Kissing* MR. FRANK) You're an angel, Mr. Frank. An angel. I don't know why I didn't meet you before I met that one there. Here, sit down, Mr. Frank . . . (*She forces him down on the couch beside* PETER) Now, Peter, you listen to Mr. Frank.

MR. FRANK. It might be better for us to go into Peter's room.

(PETER *jumps up eagerly, leading the way.*)

MRS. VAN DAAN. That's right. You go in there, Peter. You listen to Mr. Frank. Mr. Frank is a highly educated man.

(*As* MR. FRANK *is about to follow* PETER *into his room,* MRS. FRANK *stops him and wipes the lipstick from his lips. Then she closes the door after them.*)

ANNE. (*On the floor, listening*) Shh! I can hear a man's voice talking.

MR. VAN DAAN. (*To* ANNE) Isn't it bad enough here without your sprawling all over the place?

(ANNE *sits up.*)

MRS. VAN DAAN. (*To* MR. VAN DAAN) If you didn't smoke so much, you wouldn't be so bad-tempered.

MR. VAN DAAN. Am I smoking? Do you see me smoking?

MRS. VAN DAAN. Don't tell me you've used up all those cigarettes.

MR. VAN DAAN. One package. Miep only brought me one package.

MRS. VAN DAAN. It's a filthy habit anyway. It's a good time to break yourself.

MR. VAN DAAN. Oh, stop it, please.

MRS. VAN DAAN. You're smoking up all our money. You know that, don't you?

MR. VAN DAAN. Will you shut up? (*During this,* MRS. FRANK *and* MARGOT *have studiously kept their eyes down. But* ANNE, *seated on the floor, has been following the discussion interestedly.* MR. VAN DAAN *turns to see her staring up at him*) And what are you staring at?

ANNE. I never heard grownups quarrel before. I thought only children quarreled.

MR. VAN DAAN. This isn't a quarrel! It's a discussion. And I never heard children so rude before.

ANNE. (*Rising, indignantly*) I, rude!

MR. VAN DAAN. Yes!

MRS. FRANK. (*Quickly*) Anne, will you get me my knitting? (ANNE *goes to get it*) I must remember, when Miep comes, to ask her to bring me some more wool.

MARGOT. (*Going to her room*) I need some hairpins and some soap. I made a list.

(*She goes into her bedroom to get the list.*)

MRS. FRANK. (*To* ANNE) Have you some library books for Miep when she comes?

ANNE. It's a wonder that Miep has a life of her own, the way we make her run errands for us. Please, Miep, get me some starch. Please take my hair out and have it cut. Tell me all the latest news, Miep. (*She goes over, kneeling on the couch beside* MRS. VAN DAAN) Did you know she was engaged? His name is Dirk, and Miep's afraid the Nazis will ship him off to Germany to work in one of their war plants. That's what they're doing with some of the young Dutchmen . . . they pick them up off the streets—

MR. VAN DAAN. (*Interrupting*) Don't you ever get tired of talking? Suppose you try keeping still for five minutes. Just five minutes.

(*He starts to pace again. Again* ANNE *follows him, mimicking him.* MRS. FRANK *jumps up and takes her by the arm up to the sink, and gives her a glass of milk.*)

MRS. FRANK. Come here, Anne. It's time for your glass of milk.

MR. VAN DAAN. Talk, talk, talk. I never heard such a child. Where is my . . . Every evening it's the same, talk, talk, talk. (*He looks around*) Where is my . . . ?

MRS. VAN DAAN. What're you looking for?

MR. VAN DAAN. My pipe. Have you seen my pipe?

MRS. VAN DAAN. What good's a pipe? You haven't got any tobacco.

MR. VAN DAAN. At least I'll have something to hold in my mouth! (*Opening* MARGOT's *bedroom door*) Margot, have you seen my pipe?

MARGOT. It was on the table last night.

(ANNE *puts her glass of milk on the table and picks up his pipe, hiding it behind her back.*)

MR. VAN DAAN. I know. I know. Anne, did you see my pipe? . . . Anne!

MRS. FRANK. Anne, Mr. Van Daan is speaking to you.

ANNE. Am I allowed to talk now?

MR. VAN DAAN. You're the most aggravating . . . The trouble with you is, you've been spoiled. What you need is a good old-fashioned spanking.

ANNE. (*Mimicking* MRS. VAN DAAN) "Remember, Mr. So-and-So, remember I'm a lady."

(*She thrusts the pipe into his mouth, then picks up her glass of milk.*)

MR. VAN DAAN. (*Restraining himself with difficulty*) Why aren't you nice and quiet like your sister Margot? Why do you have to show off all the time? Let me give you a little advice, young lady. Men don't like that kind of

thing in a girl. You know that? A man likes a girl who'll listen to him once in a while . . . a domestic girl, who'll keep her house shining for her husband . . . who loves to cook and sew and . . .

ANNE. I'd cut my throat first! I'd open my veins! I'm going to be remarkable! I'm going to Paris . . .

MR. VAN DAAN. (*Scoffingly*) Paris!

ANNE. . . . to study music and art.

MR. VAN DAAN. Yeah! Yeah!

ANNE. I'm going to be a famous dancer or singer . . . or something wonderful.

(*She makes a wide gesture, spilling the glass of milk on the fur coat in* MRS. VAN DAAN's *lap.* MARGOT *rushes quickly over with a towel.* ANNE *tries to brush the milk off with her skirt.*)

MRS. VAN DAAN. Now look what you've done . . . you clumsy little fool! My beautiful fur coat my father gave me . . .

ANNE. I'm so sorry.

MRS. VAN DAAN. What do you care? It isn't yours . . . So go on, ruin it! Do you know what that coat cost? Do you? And now look at it! Look at it!

ANNE. I'm very, very sorry.

MRS. VAN DAAN. I could kill you for this. I could just kill you!

(MRS. VAN DAAN *goes up the stairs, clutching the coat.* MR. VAN DAAN *starts after her.*)

MR. VAN DAAN. Petronella . . . *liefje! Liefje!* . . . Come back . . . the supper . . . come back!

MRS. FRANK. Anne, you must not behave in that way.

ANNE. It was an accident. Anyone can have an accident.

MRS. FRANK. I don't mean that. I mean the answering back. You must not answer back. They are our guests. We must always show the greatest courtesy to them. We're all living under terrible tension. (*She stops as* MARGOT *indicates that* VAN DAAN *can hear. When he is gone, she continues*) That's why we must control ourselves . . . You don't hear Margot getting into arguments with them, do you? Watch Margot. She's always courteous with them. Never familiar. She keeps her distance. And they respect her for it. Try to be like Margot.

ANNE. And have them walk all over me, the way they do her? No, thanks!

MRS. FRANK. I'm not afraid that anyone is going to walk all over you, Anne. I'm afraid for other people, that you'll walk on them. I don't know what happens to you, Anne. You are wild, self-willed. If I had ever talked to my mother as you talk to me . . .

ANNE. Things have changed. People aren't like that any more. "Yes, Mother." "No, Mother." "Anything you say, Mother." I've got to fight things out for myself! Make something of myself!

MRS. FRANK. It isn't necessary to fight to do it. Margot doesn't fight, and isn't she . . . ?

ANNE. (*Violently rebellious*) Margot! Margot! Margot! That's all I hear from everyone . . . how wonderful Margot is . . . "Why aren't you like Margot?"

MARGOT. (*Protesting*) Oh, come on, Anne, don't be so . . .

ANNE. (*Paying no attention*) Everything she does is right, and everything I do is wrong! I'm the goat around here! . . . You're all against me! . . . And you worst of all!

(*She rushes off into her room and throws herself down on the settee, stifling her sobs.* MRS. FRANK *sighs and starts toward the stove.*)

MRS. FRANK. (*To* MARGOT) Let's put the soup on the stove . . . if there's anyone who cares to eat. Margot, will you take the bread out? (MARGOT *gets the bread from the cupboard*) I don't know how we can go on living this way . . . I can't say a word to Anne . . . she flies at me . . .

MARGOT. You know Anne. In half an hour she'll be out here, laughing and joking.

MRS. FRANK. And . . . (*She makes a motion upwards, indicating the* VAN DAANS) . . . I told your father it wouldn't work . . . but no . . .

no . . . he had to ask them, he said . . . he owed it to him, he said. Well, he knows now that I was right! These quarrels! . . . This bickering!

MARGOT. (*With a warning look*) Shush. Shush.

(*The buzzer for the door sounds.* MRS. FRANK *gasps, startled.*)

MRS. FRANK. Every time I hear that sound, my heart stops!

MARGOT. (*Starting for* PETER's *door*) It's Miep. (*She knocks at the door*) Father?

(MR. FRANK *comes quickly from* PETER's *room.*)

MR. FRANK. Thank you, Margot. (*As he goes down the steps to open the outer door*) Has everyone his list?

MARGOT. I'll get my books. (*Giving her mother a list*) Here's your list. (MARGOT *goes into her and* ANNE's *bedroom on the right.* ANNE *sits up, hiding her tears, as* MARGOT *comes in*) Miep's here.

(MARGOT *picks up her books and goes back.* ANNE *hurries over to the mirror, smoothing her hair.*)

MR. VAN DAAN. (*Coming down the stairs*) Is it Miep?

MARGOT. Yes. Father's gone down to let her in.

MR. VAN DAAN. At last I'll have some cigarettes!

MRS. FRANK. (*To* MR. VAN DAAN) I can't tell you how unhappy I am about Mrs. Van Daan's coat. Anne should never have touched it.

MR. VAN DAAN. She'll be all right.

MRS. FRANK. Is there anything I can do?

MR. VAN DAAN. Don't worry.

(*He turns to meet* MIEP. *But it is not* MIEP *who comes up the steps. It is* MR. KRALER, *followed by* MR. FRANK. *Their faces are grave.* ANNE *comes from the bedroom.* PETER *comes from his room.*)

MRS. FRANK. Mr. Kraler!

MR. VAN DAAN. How are you, Mr. Kraler?

MARGOT. This is a surprise.

MRS. FRANK. When Mr. Kraler comes, the sun begins to shine.

MR. VAN DAAN. Miep is coming?

MR. KRALER. Not tonight.

> (KRALER *goes to* MARGOT *and* MRS. FRANK *and* ANNE, *shaking hands with them.*)

MRS. FRANK. Wouldn't you like a cup of coffee? . . . Or, better still, will you have supper with us?

MR. FRANK. Mr. Kraler has something to talk over with us. Something has happened, he says, which demands an immediate decision.

MRS. FRANK. (*Fearful*) What is it?

> (MR. KRALER *sits down on the couch. As he talks he takes bread, cabbages, milk, etc., from his briefcase, giving them to* MARGOT *and* ANNE *to put away.*)

MR. KRALER. Usually, when I come up here, I I try to bring you some bit of good news. What's the use of telling you the bad news when there's nothing that you can do about it? But today something has happened . . . Dirk . . . Miep's Dirk, you know, came to me just now. He tells me that he has a Jewish friend living near him. A dentist. He says he's in trouble. He begged me, could I do anything for this man? Could I find him a hiding place? . . . So I've come to you . . . I know it's a terrible thing to ask of you, living as you are, but would you take him in with you?

MR. FRANK. Of course we will.

MR. KRALER. (*Rising*) It'll be just for a night or two . . . until I find some other place. This happened so suddenly that I didn't know where to turn.

MR. FRANK. Where is he?

MR. KRALER. Downstairs in the office.

MR. FRANK. Good. Bring him up.

MR. KRALER. His name is Dussel . . . Jan Dussel.

MR. FRANK. Dussel . . . I think I know him.

MR. KRALER. I'll get him.

> (*He goes quickly down the steps and out.* MR. FRANK *suddenly becomes conscious of the others.*)

MR. FRANK. Forgive me. I spoke without consulting you. But I knew you'd feel as I do.

MR. VAN DAAN. There's no reason for you to consult anyone. This is your place. You have a right to do exactly as you please. The only thing I feel . . . there's so little food as it is . . . and to take in another person . . .

> (PETER *turns away, ashamed of his father.*)

MR. FRANK. We can stretch the food a little. It's only for a few days.

MR. VAN DAAN. You want to make a bet?

MRS. FRANK. I think it's fine to have him. But, Otto, where are you going to put him? Where?

PETER. He can have my bed. I can sleep on the floor. I wouldn't mind.

MR. FRANK. That's good of you, Peter. But your room's too small . . . even for *you*.

ANNE. I have a much better idea. I'll come in here with you and Mother, and Margot can take Peter's room and Peter can go in our room with Mr. Dussel.

MARGOT. That's right. We could do that.

MR. FRANK. No, Margot. You mustn't sleep in that room . . . neither you nor Anne. Mouschi has caught some rats in there. Peter's brave. He doesn't mind.

ANNE. Then how about *this?* I'll come in here with you and Mother, and Mr. Dussel can have my bed.

MRS. FRANK. No. No. *No!* Margot will come in here with us and he can have her bed. It's the only way. Margot, bring your things in here. Help her, Anne.

> (MARGOT *hurries into her room to get her things.*)

ANNE. (*To her mother*) Why Margot? Why can't I come in here?

MRS. FRANK. Because it wouldn't be proper for Margot to sleep with a . . . Please, Anne. Don't argue. Please.

> (ANNE *starts slowly away.*)

MR. FRANK. (*To* ANNE) You don't mind sharing your room with Mr. Dussel, do you, Anne?

ANNE. No. No, of course not.

MR. FRANK. Good. (ANNE *goes off into her bedroom, helping* MARGOT. MR. FRANK *starts to search in the cupboards*) Where's the cognac?

MRS. FRANK. It's there. But, Otto, I was saving it in case of illness.

MR. FRANK. I think we couldn't find a better time to use it. Peter, will you get five glasses for me?

(PETER *goes for the glasses.* MARGOT *comes out of her bedroom, carrying her possessions, which she hangs behind a curtain in the main room.* MR. FRANK *finds the cognac and pours it into the five glasses that* PETER *brings him.* MR. VAN DAAN *stands looking on sourly.* MRS. VAN DAAN *comes downstairs and looks around at all the bustle.*)

MRS. VAN DAAN. What's happening? What's going on?

MR. VAN DAAN. Someone's moving in with us.

MRS. VAN DAAN. In here? You're joking.

MARGOT. It's only for a night or two . . . until Mr. Kraler finds him another place.

MR. VAN DAAN. Yeah! Yeah!

(MR. FRANK *hurries over as* MR. KRALER *and* DUSSEL *come up.* DUSSEL *is a man in his late fifties, meticulous, finicky . . . bewildered now. He wears a raincoat. He carries a briefcase, stuffed full, and a small medicine case.*)

MR. FRANK. Come in, Mr. Dussel.

MR. KRALER. This is Mr. Frank.

DUSSEL. Mr. Otto Frank?

MR. FRANK. Yes. Let me take your things. (*He takes the hat and briefcase, but* DUSSEL *clings to his medicine case*) This is my wife Edith . . . Mr. and Mrs. Van Daan . . . their son, Peter . . . and my daughters, Margot and Anne.

(DUSSEL *shakes hands with everyone.*)

MR. KRALER. Thank you, Mr. Frank. Thank you all. Mr. Dussel, I leave you in good hands. Oh . . . Dirk's coat.

(DUSSEL *hurriedly takes off the raincoat, giving it to* MR. KRALER. *Underneath is his white dentist's jacket, with a yellow Star of David on it.*)

DUSSEL. (*To* MR. KRALER) What can I say to thank you . . . ?

MRS. FRANK. (*To* DUSSEL) Mr. Kraler and Miep . . . They're our life line. Without them we couldn't live.

MR. KRALER. Please. Please. You make us seem very heroic. It isn't that at all. We simply don't like the Nazis. (*To* MR. FRANK, *who offers him a drink*) No, thanks. (*Then going on*) We don't like their methods. We don't like . . .

MR. FRANK. (*Smiling*) I know. I know. "No one's going to tell us Dutchmen what to do with our damn Jews!"

MR. KRALER. (*To* DUSSEL) Pay no attention to Mr. Frank. I'll be up tomorrow to see that they're treating you right. (*To* MR. FRANK) Don't trouble to come down again. Peter will bolt the door after me, won't you, Peter?

PETER. Yes, sir.

MR. FRANK. Thank you, Peter. I'll do it.

MR. KRALER. Good night. Good night.

GROUP. Good night, Mr. Kraler.
We'll see you tomorrow, etc., etc.

(MR. KRALER *goes out with* MR. FRANK. MRS. FRANK *gives each one of the "grownups" a glass of cognac.*)

MRS. FRANK. Please, Mr. Dussel, sit down.

(MR. DUSSEL *sinks into a chair.* MRS. FRANK *gives him a glass of cognac.*)

DUSSEL. I'm dreaming. I know it. I can't believe my eyes. Mr. Otto Frank here! (*To* MRS. FRANK) You're not in Switzerland then? A woman told me . . . She said she'd gone to your house . . . the door was open, everything was in disorder, dishes in the sink. She said she found a piece of paper in the wastebasket with an address scribbled on it . . . an address in Zurich.[3] She said you must have escaped to Zurich.

ANNE. Father put that there purposely . . . just so people would think that very thing!

DUSSEL. And you've been *here* all the time?

---

3. **Zurich**\ˈzu̇•rĭk\ a city in Switzerland (which the Nazis did not control).

MRS. FRANK. All the time . . . ever since July.

(ANNE *speaks to her father as he comes back.*)

ANNE. It worked, Pim . . . the address you left! Mr. Dussel says that people believe we escaped to Switzerland.

MR. FRANK. I'm glad. . . . And now let's have a little drink to welcome Mr. Dussel. (*Before they can drink,* MR. DUSSEL *bolts his drink.* MR. FRANK *smiles and raises his glass*) To Mr. Dussel. Welcome. We're very honored to have you with us.

MRS. FRANK. To Mr. Dussel, welcome.

(*The* VAN DAANS *murmur a welcome. The "grownups" drink.*)

MRS. VAN DAAN. Um. That was good.

MR. VAN DAAN. Did Mr. Kraler warn you that you won't get much to eat here? You can imagine . . . three ration books among the seven of us . . . and now you make eight.

(PETER *walks away, humiliated. Outside a street organ is heard dimly.*)

DUSSEL. (*Rising*) Mr. Van Daan, you don't realize what is happening outside that you should warn me of a thing like that. You don't realize what's going on . . . (*As* MR. VAN DAAN *starts his characteristic pacing,* DUSSEL *turns to speak to the others*) Right here in Amsterdam every day hundreds of Jews disappear . . . They surround a block and search house by house. Children come home from school to find their parents gone. Hundreds are being deported . . . people that you and I know . . . the Hallensteins . . . the Wessels . . .

MRS. FRANK. (*In tears*) Oh, no. No!

DUSSEL. They get their call-up notice . . . come to the Jewish theatre on such and such a day and hour . . . bring only what you can carry in a rucksack. And if you refuse the call-up notice, then they come and drag you from your home and ship you off to Mauthausen.[4] The death camp!

MRS. FRANK. We didn't know that things had got so much worse.

DUSSEL. Forgive me for speaking so.

ANNE. (*Coming to* DUSSEL) Do you know the de Waals? . . . What's become of them? Their daughter Jopie and I are in the same class. Jopie's my best friend.

DUSSEL. They are gone.

ANNE. Gone?

DUSSEL. With all the others.

ANNE. Oh, no. Not Jopie!

(*She turns away, in tears.* MRS. FRANK *motions to* MARGOT *to comfort her.* MARGOT *goes to* ANNE, *putting her arms comfortingly around her.*)

MRS. VAN DAAN. There were some people called Wagner. They lived near us . . . ?

MR. FRANK. (*Interrupting, with a glance at* ANNE) I think we should put this off until later. We all have many questions we want to ask . . . But I'm sure that Mr. Dussel would like to get settled before supper.

DUSSEL. Thank you. I would. I brought very little with me.

MR. FRANK. (*Giving him his hat and briefcase*) I'm sorry we can't give you a room alone. But I hope you won't be too uncomfortable. We've had to make strict rules here . . . a schedule of hours . . . We'll tell you after supper. Anne, would you like to take Mr. Dussel to his room?

ANNE. (*Controlling her tears*) If you'll come with me, Mr. Dussel?

(*She starts for her room.*)

DUSSEL. (*Shaking hands with each in turn*) Forgive me if I haven't really expressed my gratitude to all of you. This has been such a shock to me. I'd always thought of myself as Dutch. I was born in Holland. My father was born in Holland, and my grandfather. And now . . . after all these years . . . (*He breaks off*) If you'll excuse me.

(DUSSEL *gives a little bow and hurries off after* ANNE. MR. FRANK *and the others are subdued.*)

---

4. **Mauthausen**\ˈmaut ˈhau·zən\ a Danube village in upper Austria, where a concentration camp was located.

ANNE. (*Turning on the light*) Well, here we are.

(DUSSEL *looks around the room. In the main room* MARGOT *speaks to her mother.*)

MARGOT. The news sounds pretty bad, doesn't it? It's so different from what Mr. Kraler tells us. Mr. Kraler says things are improving.

MR. VAN DAAN. I like it better the way Kraler tells it.

(*They resume their occupations, quietly.* PETER *goes off into his room. In* ANNE'S *room,* ANNE *turns to* DUSSEL.)

ANNE. You're going to share the room with me.

DUSSEL. I'm a man who's always lived alone. I haven't had to adjust myself to others. I hope you'll bear with me until I learn.

ANNE. Let me help you. (*She takes his briefcase*) Do you always live all alone? Have you no family at all?

DUSSEL. No one.

(*He opens his medicine case and spreads his bottles on the dressing table.*)

ANNE. How dreadful. You must be terribly lonely.

DUSSEL. I'm used to it.

ANNE. I don't think I could ever get used to it. Didn't you even have a pet? A cat, or a dog?

DUSSEL. I have an allergy for fur-bearing animals. They give me asthma.

ANNE. Oh, dear. Peter has a cat.

DUSSEL. Here? He has it here?

ANNE. Yes. But we hardly ever see it. He keeps it in his room all the time. I'm sure it will be all right.

DUSSEL. Let us hope so.

(*He takes some pills to fortify himself.*)

ANNE. That's Margot's bed, where you're going to sleep. I sleep on the sofa there. (*Indicating the clothes hooks on the wall*) We cleared these off for your things. (*She goes over to the window*) The best part about this room . . . you can look down and see a bit of the street and the canal. There's a houseboat . . . you can see the end of it . . . a bargeman lives there with his family . . . They have a

baby and he's just beginning to walk and I'm so afraid he's going to fall into the canal some day. I watch him. . . .

DUSSEL. (*Interrupting*) Your father spoke of a schedule.

ANNE. (*Coming away from the window*) Oh, yes. It's mostly about the times we have to be quiet. And times for the w.c. You can use it now if you like.

DUSSEL. (*Stiffly*) No, thank you.

ANNE. I suppose you think it's awful, my talking about a thing like that. But you don't know how important it can get to be, especially when you're frightened . . . About this room, the way Margot and I did . . . she had it to herself in the afternoons for studying, reading . . . lessons, you know . . . and I took the mornings. Would that be all right with you?

DUSSEL. I'm not at my best in the morning.

ANNE. You stay here in the mornings then. I'll take the room in the afternoons.

DUSSEL. Tell me, when you're in here, what happens to me? Where am I spending my time? In there, with all the people?

ANNE. Yes.

DUSSEL. I see. I see.

ANNE. We have supper at half past six.

DUSSEL. (*Going over to the sofa*) Then, if you don't mind . . . I like to lie down quietly for ten minutes before eating. I find it helps the digestion.

ANNE. Of course. I hope I'm not going to be too much of a bother to you. I seem to be able to get everyone's back up.

(DUSSEL *lies down on the sofa, curled up, his back to her.*)

DUSSEL. I always get along very well with children. My patients all bring their children to me, because they know I get on well with them. So don't you worry about that.

(ANNE *leans over him, taking his hand and shaking it gratefully.*)

ANNE. Thank you. Thank you, Mr. Dussel.

(*The lights dim to darkness. The curtain falls on the scene.* ANNE'S *voice comes to us faintly at first, and then with increasing power.*)

ANNE'S VOICE. . . . And yesterday I finished Cissy Van Marxvelt's latest book. I think she is a first-class writer. I shall definitely let my children read her. Monday the twenty-first of September, nineteen forty-two. Mr. Dussel and I had another battle yesterday. Yes, Mr. Dussel! According to him, nothing, I repeat . . . nothing, is right about me . . . my appearance, my character, my manners. While he was going on at me I thought . . . sometime I'll give you such a smack that you'll fly right up to the ceiling! Why is it that every grownup thinks he knows the way to bring up children? Particularly the grownups that never had any. I keep wishing that Peter was a girl instead of a boy. Then I would have someone to talk to. Margot's a darling, but she takes everything too seriously. To pause for a moment on the subject of Mrs. Van Daan. I must tell you that her attempts to flirt with father are getting her nowhere. Pim, thank goodness, won't play.

(*As she is saying the last lines, the curtain rises on the darkened scene.* ANNE's *voice fades out.*)

SCENE IV

It is the middle of the night, several months later. The stage is dark except for a little light which comes through the skylight in PETER'S *room.*

Everyone is in bed. MR. *and* MRS. FRANK *lie on the couch in the main room, which has been pulled out to serve as a make-shift double bed.*

MARGOT *is sleeping on a mattress on the floor in the main room, behind a curtain stretched across for privacy. The others are all in their accustomed rooms.*

From outside we hear two drunken soldiers singing "Lili Marlene."[1] *A girl's high giggle*

is heard. The sound of running feet is heard coming closer and then fading in the distance. Throughout the scene there is the distant sound of airplanes passing overhead.

A match suddenly flares up in the attic. We dimly see MR. VAN DAAN. *He is getting his bearings. He comes quickly down the stairs, and goes to the cupboard where the food is stored. Again the match flares up, and is as quickly blown out. The dim figure is seen to steal back up the stairs.*

There is quiet for a second or two, broken only by the sound of airplanes, and running feet on the street below.

Suddenly, out of the silence and the dark, we hear ANNE *scream.*

ANNE. (*Screaming*) No! No! Don't . . . don't take me!

(*She moans, tossing and crying in her sleep. The other people wake, terrified.* DUSSEL *sits up in bed, furious.*)

DUSSEL. Shush! Anne! Anne, for God's sake, shush!

ANNE. (*Still in her nightmare*) Save me! Save me!

(*She screams and screams.* DUSSEL *gets out of bed, going over to her, trying to wake her.*)

DUSSEL. For God's sake! Quiet! Quiet! You want someone to hear?

(*In the main room* MRS. FRANK *grabs a shawl and pulls it around her. She rushes in to* ANNE, *taking her in her arms.* MR. FRANK *hurriedly gets up, putting on his overcoat.* MARGOT *sits up, terrified.* PETER'S *light goes on in his room.*)

MRS. FRANK. (*To* ANNE, *in her room*) Hush, darling, hush. It's all right. It's all right. (*Over her shoulder to* DUSSEL) Will you be kind enough to turn on the light, Mr. Dussel? (*Back to* ANNE) It's nothing, my darling. It was just a dream.

1. **"Lili Marlene"**\ˈlē·lĭ ˈmär ˈlān\ a very popular song among German soldiers in World War II.

(DUSSEL *turns on the light in the bedroom.* MRS. FRANK *holds* ANNE *in her arms. Gradually* ANNE *comes out of her nightmare, still trembling with horror.* MR. FRANK *comes into the room, and goes quickly to the window, looking out to be sure that no one outside has heard* ANNE's *screams.* MRS. FRANK *holds* ANNE, *talking softly to her. In the main room* MARGOT *stands on a chair, turning on the center hanging lamp. A light goes on in the* VAN DAANS' *room overhead.* PETER *puts his robe on, coming out of his room.*)

DUSSEL. (*To* MRS. FRANK, *blowing his nose*) Something must be done about that child, Mrs. Frank. Yelling like that! Who knows but there's somebody on the streets? She's endangering all our lives.

MRS. FRANK. Anne, darling.

DUSSEL. Every night she twists and turns. I don't sleep. I spend half my night shushing her. And now it's nightmares!

(MARGOT *comes to the door of* ANNE's *room, followed by* PETER. MR. FRANK *goes to them, indicating that everything is all right.* PETER *takes* MARGOT *back.*)

MRS. FRANK. (*To* ANNE) You're here, safe, you see? Nothing has happened. (*To* DUSSEL) Please, Mr. Dussel, go back to bed. She'll be herself in a minute or two. Won't you, Anne?

DUSSEL. (*Picking up a book and a pillow*) Thank you, but I'm going to the w.c. The one place where there's peace!

(*He stalks out.* MR. VAN DAAN, *in underwear and trousers, comes down the stairs.*)

MR. VAN DAAN. (*To* DUSSEL) What is it? What happened?

DUSSEL. A nightmare. She was having a nightmare!

MR. VAN DAAN. I thought someone was murdering her.

DUSSEL. Unfortunately, no.

(*He goes into the bathroom.* MR. VAN DAAN *goes back up the stairs.* MR. FRANK, *in the*

main room, sends PETER *back to his own bedroom.*)

MR. FRANK. Thank you, Peter. Go back to bed.

(PETER *goes back to his room.* MR. FRANK *follows him, turning out the light and looking out the window. Then he goes back to the main room, and gets up on a chair, turning out the center hanging lamp.*)

MRS. FRANK. (*To* ANNE) Would you like some water? (ANNE *shakes her head*) Was it a very bad dream? Perhaps if you told me . . . ?

ANNE. I'd rather not talk about it.

MRS. FRANK. Poor darling. Try to sleep then. I'll sit right here beside you until you fall asleep.

(*She brings a stool over, sitting there.*)

ANNE. You don't have to.

MRS. FRANK. But I'd like to stay with you . . . very much. Really.

ANNE. I'd rather you didn't.

MRS. FRANK. Good night, then. (*She leans down to kiss* ANNE. ANNE *throws her arm up over her face, turning away.* MRS. FRANK, *hiding her hurt, kisses* ANNE's *arm*) You'll be all right? There's nothing that you want?

ANNE. Will you please ask Father to come.

MRS. FRANK. (*After a second*) Of course, Anne dear. (*She hurries out into the other room.* MR. FRANK *comes to her as she comes in*) *Sie verlangt nach Dir!*

MR. FRANK. (*Sensing her hurt*) Edith, *Liebe, schau . . .*

MRS. FRANK. *Es macht nichts! Ich danke dem lieben Herrgott, dass sie sich wenigstens an Dich wendet, wenn sie Trost braucht! Geh hinein, Otto, sie ist ganz hysterisch vor Angst.* (*As* MR. FRANK *hesitates*) *Geh zu ihr.*[2] (*He looks at her for a second and then goes to get a cup of water for* ANNE. MRS. FRANK *sinks down on the bed, her face in her hands, trying to keep from sobbing aloud.* MARGOT

---

2. The German may be translated as follows: "She is asking for you." "Edith, dear one, look." "It does not matter. I thank the dear Lord that she at least thought of you if she was in doubt. Go in, Otto; she is entirely hysterical from anxiety. Go to her."

comes over to her, putting her arms around her) She wants nothing of me. She pulled away when I leaned down to kiss her.

MARGOT. It's a phase . . . You heard Father . . . Most girls go through it . . . they turn to their fathers at this age . . . they give all their love to their fathers.

MRS. FRANK. You weren't like this. You didn't shut me out.

MARGOT. She'll get over it . . .

(She smooths the bed for MRS. FRANK and sits beside her a moment as MRS. FRANK lies down. In ANNE's room MR. FRANK comes in, sitting down by ANNE. ANNE flings her arms around him, clinging to him. In the distance we hear the sound of ack-ack.)

ANNE. Oh, Pim. I dreamed that they came to get us! The Green Police! They broke down the door and grabbed me and started to drag me out the way they did Jopie.

MR. FRANK. I want you to take this pill.

ANNE. What is it?

MR. FRANK. Something to quiet you.

(She takes it and drinks the water. In the main room MARGOT turns out the light and goes back to her bed.)

MR. FRANK. *(To ANNE)* Do you want me to read to you for a while?

ANNE. No. Just sit with me for a minute. Was I awful? Did I yell terribly loud? Do you think anyone outside could have heard?

MR. FRANK. No. No. Lie quietly now. Try to sleep.

ANNE. I'm a terrible coward. I'm so disappointed in myself. I think I've conquered my fear . . . I think I'm really grown-up . . . and then something happens . . . and I run to you like a baby . . . I love you, Father. I don't love anyone but you.

MR. FRANK. *(Reproachfully)* Anneke!

ANNE. It's true. I've been thinking about it for a long time. You're the only one I love.

MR. FRANK. It's fine to hear you tell me that you love me. But I'd be happier if you said you

loved your mother as well . . . She needs your help so much . . . your love . . .

ANNE. We have nothing in common. She doesn't understand me. Whenever I try to explain my views on life to her she asks me if I'm constipated.

MR. FRANK. You hurt her very much just now. She's crying. She's in there crying.

ANNE. I can't help it. I only told the truth. I didn't want her here . . . *(Then, with sudden change)* Oh, Pim, I was horrible, wasn't I? And the worst of it is, I can stand off and look at myself doing it and know it's cruel and yet I can't stop doing it. What's the matter with me? Tell me. Don't say it's just a phase! Help me.

MR. FRANK. There is so little that we parents can do to help our children. We can only try to set a good example . . . point the way. The rest you must do yourself. You must build your own character.

ANNE. I'm trying. Really I am. Every night I think back over all of the things I did that day that were wrong . . . like putting the wet mop in Mr. Dussel's bed . . . and this thing now with Mother. I say to myself, that was wrong. I make up my mind, I'm never going to do that again. Never! Of course I may do something worse . . . but at least I'll never do *that* again! . . . I have a nicer side, Father . . . a sweeter, nicer side. But I'm scared to show it. I'm afraid that people are going to laugh at me if I'm serious. So the mean Anne comes to the outside and the good Anne stays on the inside, and I keep on trying to switch them around and have the good Anne outside and the bad Anne inside and be what I'd like to be . . . and might be . . . if only . . . only . . .

(She is asleep. MR. FRANK watches her for a moment and then turns off the light, and starts out. The lights dim out. The curtain falls on the scene. ANNE's voice is heard dimly at first, and then with growing strength.)

ANNE'S VOICE. . . . The air raids are getting worse. They come over day and night. The noise is terrifying. Pim says it should be music to our ears. The more planes, the sooner will come the end of the war. Mrs. Van Daan pretends to be a fatalist. What will be, will be. But when the planes come over, who is the most frightened? No one else but Petronella! . . . Monday, the ninth of November, nineteen forty-two. Wonderful news! The Allies have landed in Africa. Pim says that we can look for an early finish to the war. Just for fun he asked each of us what was the first thing we wanted to do when we got out of here. Mrs. Van Daan longs to be home with her own things, her needle-point chairs, the Beckstein piano her father gave her . . . the best that money could buy. Peter would like to go to a movie. Mr. Dussel wants to get back to his dentist's drill. He's afraid he is losing his touch. For myself, there are so many things . . . to ride a bike again . . . to laugh till my belly aches . . . to have new clothes from the skin out . . . to have a hot tub filled to overflowing and wallow in it for hours . . . to be back in school with my friends . . .

(*As the last lines are being said, the curtain rises on the scene. The lights dim on as* ANNE's *voice fades away.*)

SCENE V

It is the first night of the Hanukkah[1] celebration. MR. FRANK *is standing at the head of the table on which is the Menorah. He lights the Shamos, or servant candle, and holds it as he says the blessing. Seated listening is all of the "family," dressed in their best. The men wear hats,* PETER *wears his cap.*

MR. FRANK. (*Reading from a prayer book*) "Praised be Thou, oh Lord our God, Ruler of the universe, who has sanctified us with Thy commandments and bidden us kindle the Hanukkah lights. Praised be Thou, oh Lord our God, Ruler of the universe, who has wrought wondrous deliverances for our fathers in days of old. Praised be Thou, oh Lord our God, Ruler of the universe, that

Thou has given us life and sustenance and brought us to this happy season." (MR. FRANK *lights the one candle of the Menorah as he continues*) "We kindle this Hanukkah light to celebrate the great and wonderful deeds wrought through the zeal with which God filled the hearts of the heroic Maccabees,[2] two thousand years ago. They fought against indifference, against tyranny and oppression, and they restored our Temple to us. May these lights remind us that we should ever look to God, whence cometh our help." Amen. [Pronounced *O-mayn.*]

ALL. Amen.

(MR. FRANK *hands* MRS. FRANK *the prayer book.*)

MRS. FRANK. (*Reading*) "I lift up mine eyes unto the mountains, from whence cometh my help. My help cometh from the Lord who made heaven and earth. He will not suffer thy foot to be moved. He that keepeth thee will not slumber. He that keepeth Israel doth neither slumber nor sleep. The Lord is thy keeper. The Lord is thy shade upon thy right hand. The sun shall not smite thee by day, nor the moon by night. The Lord shall keep thee from all evil. He shall keep thy soul. The Lord shall guard thy going out and thy coming in, from this time forth and forevermore." Amen.

ALL. Amen.

(MRS. FRANK *puts down the prayer book and goes to get the food and wine.* MARGOT *helps her.* MR. FRANK *takes the men's hats and puts them aside.*)

DUSSEL. (*Rising*) That was very moving.

ANNE. (*Pulling him back*) It isn't over yet!

---

1. **Hanukkah**\ˈha·nə·kə\ an eight-day Jewish festival in remembrance of victories of the Maccabees. **Menorah**\mə ˈnō·rə\ a candlestick used in Hebrew Services, often with holders for seven candles. The **Shamos**\ˈsha·məs\ candle, one used to light the others. Men keep their hats on at many Jewish ceremonials.
2. **Maccabees**\ˈmă·kə·bēz\ Jewish patriots of the second and first centuries B.C.

MRS. VAN DAAN. Sit down! Sit down!

ANNE. There's a lot more, songs and presents.

DUSSEL. Presents?

MRS. FRANK. Not this year, unfortunately.

MRS. VAN DAAN. But always on Hanukkah everyone gives presents . . . everyone!

DUSSEL. Like our St. Nicholas' Day.

(*There is a chorus of "no's" from the group.*)

MRS. VAN DAAN. No! Not like St. Nicholas! What kind of a Jew are you that you don't know Hanukkah?

MRS. FRANK. (*As she brings the food*) I remember particularly the candles . . . First one, as we have tonight. Then the second night you light two candles, the next night three . . . and so on until you have eight candles burning. When there are eight candles it is truly beautiful.

MRS. VAN DAAN. And the potato pancakes.

MR. VAN DAAN. Don't talk about them!

MRS. VAN DAAN. I make the best *latkes*[3] you ever tasted!

MRS. FRANK. Invite us all next year . . . in your own home.

MR. FRANK. God willing!

MRS. VAN DAAN. God willing.

MARGOT. What I remember best is the presents we used to get when we were little . . . eight days of presents . . . and each day they got better and better.

MRS. FRANK. (*Sitting down*) We are all here, alive. That is present enough.

ANNE. No, it isn't. I've got something . . .

(*She rushes into her room, hurriedly puts on a little hat improvised from the lamp shade, grabs a satchel bulging with parcels and comes running back.*)

MRS. FRANK. What is it?

ANNE. Presents!

MRS. VAN DAAN. Presents!

DUSSEL. Look!

MR. VAN DAAN. What's she got on her head?

PETER. A lamp shade!

ANNE. (*She picks out one at random*) This is for

Margot. (*She hands it to* MARGOT, *pulling her to her feet*) Read it out loud.

MARGOT. (*Reading*)
"You have never lost your temper.
You never will, I fear,
You are so good.
But if you should,
Put all your cross words here."

(*She tears open the package*)

A new crossword puzzle book! Where did you get it?

ANNE. It isn't new. It's one that you've done. But I rubbed it all out, and if you wait a little and forget, you can do it all over again.

MARGOT. (*Sitting*) It's wonderful, Anne. Thank you. You'd never know it wasn't new.

(*From outside we hear the sound of a streetcar passing.*)

ANNE. (*With another gift*) Mrs. Van Daan.

MRS. VAN DAAN. (*Taking it*) This is awful . . . I haven't anything for anyone . . . I never thought . . .

MR. FRANK. This is all Anne's idea.

MRS. VAN DAAN. (*Holding up a bottle*) What is it?

ANNE. It's hair shampoo. I took all the odds and ends of soap and mixed them with the last of my toilet water.

MRS. VAN DAAN. Oh, Anneke!

ANNE. I wanted to write a poem for all of them, but I didn't have time. (*Offering a large box to* MR. VAN DAAN) Yours, Mr. Van Daan, is *really* something . . . something you want more than anything. (*As she waits for him to open it*) Look! Cigarettes!

MR. VAN DAAN. Cigarettes!

ANNE. Two of them! Pim found some old pipe tobacco in the pocket lining of his coat . . . and we made them . . . or rather, Pim did.

MRS. VAN DAAN. Let me see . . . Well, look at that! Light it, Putti! Light it.

(MR. VAN DAAN *hesitates.*)

---

3. **latke**\ˈlät·kə\ a griddle cake, usually made of potatoes.

ANNE. It's tobacco, really it is! There's a little fluff in it, but not much.

(*Everyone watches intently as* MR. VAN DAAN *cautiously lights it. The cigarette flares up. Everyone laughs.*)

PETER. It works!

MRS. VAN DAAN. Look at him.

MR. VAN DAAN. (*Spluttering*) Thank you, Anne. Thank you.

(ANNE *rushes back to her satchel for another present.*)

ANNE. (*Handing her mother a piece of paper*) For Mother, Hanukkah greeting.

(*She pulls her mother to her feet.*)

MRS. FRANK. (*She reads*)
"Here's an I.O.U. that I promise to pay.
 Ten hours of doing whatever you say.
 Signed, Anne Frank."

(MRS. FRANK, *touched, takes* ANNE *in her arms, holding her close.*)

DUSSEL. (*To* ANNE) Ten hours of doing what you're told? *Anything* you're told?

ANNE. That's right.

DUSSEL. You wouldn't want to sell that, Mrs. Frank?

MRS. FRANK. Never! This is the most precious gift I've ever had!

(*She sits, showing her present to the others.* ANNE *hurries back to the satchel and pulls out a scarf, the scarf that* MR. FRANK *found in the first scene.*)

ANNE. (*Offering it to her father*) For Pim.

MR. FRANK. Anneke . . . I wasn't supposed to have a present!

(*He takes it, unfolding it and showing it to the others.*)

ANNE. It's a muffler . . . to put around your neck . . . like an ascot, you know. I made it myself out of odds and ends . . . I knitted it in the dark each night, after I'd gone to bed. I'm afraid it looks better in the dark!

MR. FRANK. (*Putting it on*) It's fine. It fits me perfectly. Thank you, Anneke.

(ANNE *hands* PETER *a ball of paper, with a string attached to it.*)

ANNE. That's for Mouschi.

PETER. (*Rising to bow*) On behalf of Mouschi, I thank you.

ANNE. (*Hesitant, handing him a gift*) And . . . this is yours . . . from Mrs. Quack Quack. (*As he holds it gingerly in his hands*) Well . . . open it . . . Aren't you going to open it?

PETER. I'm scared to. I know something's going to jump out and hit me.

ANNE. No. It's nothing like that, really.

MRS. VAN DAAN. (*As he is opening it*) What is it, Peter? Go on. Show it.

ANNE. (*Excitedly*) It's a safety razor!

DUSSEL. A what?

ANNE. A razor!

MRS. VAN DAAN. (*Looking at it*) You didn't make that out of odds and ends.

ANNE. (*To* PETER) Miep got it for me. It's not new. It's second-hand. But you really do need a razor now.

DUSSEL. For what?

ANNE. Look on his upper lip . . . you can see the beginning of a mustache.

DUSSEL. He wants to get rid of that? Put a little milk on it and let the cat lick it off.

PETER. (*Starting for his room*) Think you're funny, don't you.

DUSSEL. Look! He can't wait! He's going in to try it!

PETER. I'm going to give Mouschi his present!

(*He goes into his room, slamming the door behind him.*)

MR. VAN DAAN. (*Disgustedly*) Mouschi, Mouschi, Mouschi.

(*In the distance we hear a dog persistently barking.* ANNE *brings a gift to* DUSSEL.)

ANNE. And last but never least, my roommate, Mr. Dussel.

DUSSEL. For me? You have something for me?

(*He opens the small box she gives him.*)

ANNE. I made them myself.

DUSSEL. (*Puzzled*) Capsules! Two capsules!

ANNE. They're ear-plugs!

DUSSEL. Ear-plugs?

ANNE. To put in your ears so you won't hear me when I thrash around at night. I saw them advertised in a magazine. They're not real ones . . . I made them out of cotton and candle wax. Try them . . . See if they don't work . . . see if you can hear me talk . . .

DUSSEL. (*Putting them in his ears*) Wait now until I get them in . . . so.

ANNE. Are you ready?

DUSSEL. Huh?

ANNE. Are you ready?

DUSSEL. Good God! They've gone inside! I can't get them out! (*They laugh as MR. DUSSEL jumps about, trying to shake the plugs out of his ears. Finally he gets them out. Putting them away*) Thank you, Anne! Thank you!

MR. VAN DAAN. A real Hanukkah!

MRS. VAN DAAN. Wasn't it cute of her?

MRS. FRANK. I don't know when she did it.

MARGOT. I love my present.

⎫
⎬ *Together*
⎭

ANNE. (*Sitting at the table*) And now let's have the song, Father . . . please . . . (*To DUSSEL*) Have you heard the Hanukkah song, Mr. Dussel? The song is the whole thing! (*She sings*) "Oh, Hanukkah! Oh, Hanukkah! The sweet celebration . . ."

MR. FRANK. (*Quieting her*) I'm afraid, Anne, we shouldn't sing that song tonight. (*To DUSSEL*) It's a song of jubilation, of rejoicing. One is apt to become too enthusiastic.

ANNE. Oh, please, please. Let's sing the song. I promise not to shout!

MR. FRANK. Very well. But quietly now . . . I'll keep an eye on you and when . . .

(*As ANNE starts to sing, she is interrupted by DUSSEL, who is snorting and wheezing.*)

DUSSEL. (*Pointing to PETER*) You . . . You! (*PETER is coming from his bedroom, ostentatiously holding a bulge in his coat as if he were holding his cat, and dangling ANNE's present be-* fore it) How many times . . . I told you . . . Out! Out!

MR. VAN DAAN. (*Going to PETER*) What's the matter with you? Haven't you any sense? Get that cat out of here.

PETER. (*Innocently*) Cat?

MR. VAN DAAN. You heard me. Get it out of here!

PETER. I have no cat.

(*Delighted with his joke, he opens his coat and pulls out a bath towel. The group at the table laugh, enjoying the joke.*)

DUSSEL. (*Still wheezing*) It doesn't need to be the cat . . . his clothes are enough . . . when he comes out of that room . . .

MR. VAN DAAN. Don't worry. You won't be bothered any more. We're getting rid of it.

DUSSEL. At last you listen to me.

(*He goes off into his bedroom.*)

MR. VAN DAAN. (*Calling after him*) I'm not doing it for you. That's all in your mind . . . all of it! (*He starts back to his place at the table*) I'm doing it because I'm sick of seeing that cat eat all our food.

PETER. That's not true! I only give him bones . . . scraps . . .

MR. VAN DAAN. Don't tell me! He gets fatter every day! Damn cat looks better than any of us. Out he goes tonight!

PETER. No! No!

ANNE. Mr. Van Daan, you can't do that! That's Peter's cat. Peter loves that cat.

MRS. FRANK. (*Quietly*) Anne.

PETER. (*To MR. VAN DAAN*) If he goes, I go.

MR. VAN DAAN. Go! Go!

MRS. VAN DAAN. You're not going and the cat's not going! Now please . . . this is Hanukkah . . . Hanukkah . . . this is the time to celebrate . . . What's the matter with all of you? Come on, Anne. Let's have the song.

ANNE. (*Singing*)
"Oh, Hanukkah! Oh, Hanukkah!
The sweet celebration."

MR. FRANK. (*Rising*) I think we should first blow out the candle . . . then we'll have something for tomorrow night.

MARGOT. But, Father, you're supposed to let it burn itself out.

MR. FRANK. I'm sure that God understands shortages. (*Before blowing it out*) "Praised be Thou, oh Lord our God, who has sustained us and permitted us to celebrate this joyous festival."

(*He is about to blow out the candle when suddenly there is a crash of something falling below. They all freeze in horror, motionless. For a few seconds there is complete silence.* MR. FRANK *slips off his shoes. The others noiselessly follow his example.* MR. FRANK *turns out a light near him. He motions to* PETER *to turn off the center lamp.* PETER *tries to reach it, realizes he cannot and gets up on a chair. Just as he is touching the lamp he loses his balance. The chair goes out from under him. He falls. The iron lamp shade crashes to the floor. There is a sound of feet below, running down the stairs.*)

MR. VAN DAAN. (*Under his breath*) God Almighty! (*The only light left comes from the Hanukkah candle.* DUSSEL *comes from his room.* MR. FRANK *creeps over to the stairwell and stands listening. The dog is heard barking excitedly*) Do you hear anything?

MR. FRANK. (*In a whisper*) No. I think they've gone.

MRS. VAN DAAN. It's the Green Police. They've found us.

MR. FRANK. If they had, they wouldn't have left. They'd be up here by now.

MRS. VAN DAAN. I know it's the Green Police. They've gone to get help. That's all. They'll be back!

MR. VAN DAAN. Or it may have been the Gestapo,[4] looking for papers . . .

MR. FRANK. (*Interrupting*) Or a thief, looking for money.

MRS. VAN DAAN. We've got to do something . . . Quick! Quick! Before they come back.

MR. VAN DAAN. There isn't anything to do. Just wait.

(MR. FRANK *holds up his hand for them to be quiet. He is listening intently. There is complete silence as they all strain to hear any sound from below. Suddenly* ANNE *begins to sway. With a low cry she falls to the floor in a faint.* MRS. FRANK *goes to her quickly, sitting beside her on the floor and taking her in her arms.*)

MRS. FRANK. Get some water, please! Get some water!

(MARGOT *starts for the sink.*)

MR. VAN DAAN. (*Grabbing* MARGOT) No! No! No one's going to run water!

MR. FRANK. If they've found us, they've found us. Get the water. (MARGOT *starts again for the sink.* MR. FRANK, *getting a flashlight*) I'm going down.

(MARGOT *rushes to him, clinging to him.* ANNE *struggles to consciousness.*)

MARGOT. No, Father, no! There may be someone there, waiting . . . It may be a trap!

MR. FRANK. This is Saturday. There is no way for us to know what has happened until Miep or Mr. Kraler comes on Monday morning. We cannot live with this uncertainty.

MARGOT. Don't go, Father!

MRS. FRANK. Hush, darling, hush. (MR. FRANK *slips quietly out, down the steps and out through the door below*) Margot! Stay close to me.

(MARGOT *goes to her mother.*)

MR. VAN DAAN. Shush! Shush!

(MRS. FRANK *whispers to* MARGOT *to get the water.* MARGOT *goes for it.*)

MRS. VAN DAAN. Putti, where's our money? Get our money. I hear you can buy the Green Police off, so much a head. Go upstairs quick! Get the money!

MR. VAN DAAN. Keep still!

MRS. VAN DAAN. (*Kneeling before him, pleading*) Do you want to be dragged off to a concentration camp? Are you going to stand

---

4. **Gestapo**\\'gĕs ᴬta·pō\\ the dreaded Nazi secret police.

there and wait for them to come up and get you? Do something, I tell you!

MR. VAN DAAN. (*Pushing her aside*) Will you keep still!

(*He goes over to the stairwell to listen. PETER goes to his mother, helping her up onto the sofa. There is a second of silence, then ANNE can stand it no longer.*)

ANNE. Someone go after Father! Make Father come back!

PETER. (*Starting for the door*) I'll go.

MR. VAN DAAN. Haven't you done enough?

(*He pushes PETER roughly away. In his anger against his father PETER grabs a chair as if to hit him with it, then puts it down, burying his face in his hands. MRS. FRANK begins to pray softly.*)

ANNE. Please, please, Mr. Van Daan. Get Father.

MR. VAN DAAN. Quiet! Quiet!

(*ANNE is shocked into silence. MRS. FRANK pulls her closer, holding her protectively in her arms.*)

MRS. FRANK. (*Softly, praying*) "I lift up mine eyes unto the mountains, from whence cometh my help. My help cometh from the Lord who made heaven and earth. He will not suffer thy foot to be moved . . . He that keepeth thee will not slumber . . ."

(*She stops as she hears someone coming. They all watch the door tensely. MR. FRANK comes quietly in. ANNE rushes to him, holding him tight.*)

MR. FRANK. It was a thief. That noise must have scared him away.

MRS. VAN DAAN. Thank God.

MR. FRANK. He took the cash box. And the radio. He ran away in such a hurry that he didn't stop to shut the street door. It was swinging wide open. (*A breath of relief sweeps over them*) I think it would be good to have some light.

MARGOT. Are you sure it's all right?

MR. FRANK. The danger has passed. (*MARGOT goes to light the small lamp*) Don't be so terrified, Anne. We're safe.

DUSSEL. Who says the danger has passed? Don't you realize we are in greater danger than ever?

MR. FRANK. Mr. Dussel, will you be still!

(*MR. FRANK takes ANNE back to the table, making her sit down with him, trying to calm her.*)

DUSSEL. (*Pointing to PETER*) Thanks to this clumsy fool, there's someone now who knows we're up here! Someone now knows we're up here, hiding!

MRS. VAN DAAN. (*Going to DUSSEL*) Someone knows we're here, yes. But who is the someone? A thief! A thief! You think a thief is going to go to the Green Police and say . . . I was robbing a place the other night and I heard a noise up over my head? You think a thief is going to do that?

DUSSEL. Yes. I think he will.

MRS. VAN DAAN. (*Hysterically*) You're crazy!

(*She stumbles back to her seat at the table. PETER follows protectively, pushing DUSSEL aside.*)

DUSSEL. I think some day he'll be caught and then he'll make a bargain with the Green Police . . . if they'll let him off, he'll tell them where some Jews are hiding!

(*He goes off into the bedroom. There is a second of appalled silence.*)

MR. VAN DAAN. He's right.

ANNE. Father, let's get out of here! We can't stay here now . . . Let's go . . .

MR. VAN DAAN. Go! Where?

MRS. FRANK. (*Sinking into her chair at the table*) Yes. Where?

MR. FRANK. (*Rising, to them all*) Have we lost all faith? All courage? A moment ago we thought that they'd come for us. We were sure it was the end. But it wasn't the end. We're alive, safe. (*MR. VAN DAAN goes to the table and sits. MR. FRANK prays*) "We thank Thee, oh Lord our God, that in Thy infinite mercy Thou hast again seen fit to spare us."

(*He blows out the candle, then turns to* ANNE) Come on, Anne. The song! Let's have the song! (*He starts to sing.* ANNE *finally starts falteringly to sing, as* MR. FRANK *urges her on. Her voice is hardly audible at first.*)

ANNE. (*Singing*)
"Oh, Hanukkah! Oh, Hanukkah!
The sweet . . . celebration . . ."

(*As she goes on singing, the others gradually join in, their voices still shaking with fear.* MRS. VAN DAAN *sobs as she sings.*)

GROUP.
"Around the feast . . . we . . . gather
In complete . . . jubilation . . .
Happiest of sea . . . sons
Now is here.
Many are the reasons for good cheer."

(DUSSEL *comes from the bedroom. He comes over to the table, standing beside* MARGOT, *listening to them as they sing.*)

"Together
We'll weather
Whatever tomorrow may bring."

(*As they sing on with growing courage, the lights start to dim*)

"So hear us rejoicing
And merrily voicing
The Hanukkah song that we sing.
Hoy!"

(*The lights are out. The curtain starts slowly to fall*)

"Hear us rejoicing
And merrily voicing
The Hanukkah song that we sing."

(*They are still singing, as the curtain falls.*)

Curtain

Act Two

SCENE I

In the darkness we hear ANNE's *voice, again reading from the diary.*

ANNE'S VOICE. Saturday, the first of January, nineteen forty-four. Another new year has begun and we find ourselves still in our hiding place. We have been here now for one year, five months and twenty-five days. It seems that our life is at a standstill.

The curtain rises on the scene. It is late afternoon. Everyone is bundled up against the cold. In the main room MRS. FRANK *is taking down the laundry which is hung across the back.* MR. FRANK *sits in the chair down left, reading.* MARGOT *is lying on the couch with a blanket over her and the many-colored knitted scarf around her throat.* ANNE *is seated at the center table, writing in her diary.* PETER, MR. *and* MRS. VAN DAAN *and* DUSSEL *are all in their own rooms, reading or lying down.*

As the lights dim on, ANNE's *voice continues, without a break.*

ANNE'S VOICE. We are all a little thinner. The Van Daans' "discussions" are as violent as ever. Mother still does not understand me. But then I don't understand her either. There is one great change, however. A change in myself. I read somewhere that girls of my age don't feel quite certain of themselves. That they become quiet within and begin to think of the miracle that is taking place in their bodies. I think that what is happening to me is so wonderful . . . not only what can be seen, but what is taking place inside. Each time it has happened I have a feeling that I have a sweet secret. (*We hear the chimes and then a hymn being played on the carillon outside*) And in spite of any pain, I long for the time when I shall feel that secret within me again.

(*The buzzer of the door below suddenly*

sounds. Everyone is startled, MR. FRANK *tiptoes cautiously to the top of the steps and listens. Again the buzzer sounds, in* MIEP's *V-for-Victory[1] signal.*)

MR. FRANK. It's Miep!

(*He goes quickly down the steps to unbolt the door.* MRS. FRANK *calls upstairs to the* VAN DAANS *and then to* PETER.)

MRS. FRANK. Wake up, everyone! Miep is here! (ANNE *quickly puts her diary away.* MARGOT *sits up, pulling the blanket around her shoulders.* MR. DUSSEL *sits on the edge of his bed, listening, disgruntled.* MIEP *comes up the steps, followed by* MR. KRALER. *They bring flowers, books, newspapers, etc.* ANNE *rushes to* MIEP, *throwing her arms affectionately around her*) Miep . . . and Mr. Kraler . . . What a delightful surprise!

MR. KRALER. We came to bring you New Year's greetings.

MRS. FRANK. You shouldn't . . . you should have at least one day to yourselves.

(*She goes quickly to the stove and brings down teacups and tea for all of them.*)

ANNE. Don't say that, it's so wonderful to see them! (*Sniffing at* MIEP's *coat*) I can smell the wind and the cold on your clothes.

MIEP. (*Giving her the flowers*) There you are. (*Then to* MARGOT, *feeling her forehead*) How are you, Margot? . . . Feeling any better?

MARGOT. I'm all right.

ANNE. We filled her full of every kind of pill so she won't cough and make a noise.

(*She runs into her room to put the flowers in water.* MR. *and* MRS. VAN DAAN *come from upstairs. Outside there is the sound of a band playing.*)

MRS. VAN DAAN. Well, hello, Miep. Mr. Kraler.

MR. KRALER. (*Giving a bouquet of flowers to* MRS. VAN DAAN) With my hope for peace in the New Year.

PETER. (*Anxiously*) Miep, have you seen Mouschi? Have you seen him anywhere around?

MIEP. I'm sorry, Peter. I asked everyone in the neighborhood had they seen a gray cat. But they said no.

(MRS. FRANK *gives* MIEP *a cup of tea.* MR. FRANK *comes up the steps, carrying a small cake on a plate.*)

MR. FRANK. Look what Miep's brought for us!

MRS. FRANK. (*Taking it*) A cake!

MR. VAN DAAN. A cake! (*He pinches* MIEP's *cheeks gaily and hurries up to the cupboard*) I'll get some plates.

(DUSSEL, *in his room, hastily puts a coat on and starts out to join the others.*)

MRS. FRANK. Thank you, Miepia. You shouldn't have done it. You must have used all of your sugar ration for weeks. (*Giving it to* MRS. VAN DAAN) It's beautiful, isn't it?

MRS. VAN DAAN. It's been ages since I even saw a cake. Not since you brought us one last year. (*Without looking at the cake, to* MIEP) Remember? Don't you remember, you gave us one on New Year's Day? Just this time last year? I'll never forget it because you had "Peace in nineteen forty-three" on it. (*She looks at the cake and reads*) "Peace in nineteen forty-four!"

MIEP. Well, it has to come sometime, you know. (*As* DUSSEL *comes from his room*) Hello, Mr. Dussel.

MR. KRALER. How are you?

MR. VAN DAAN. (*Bringing plates and a knife*) Here's the knife, *liefje*. Now, how many of us are there?

MIEP. None for me, thank you.

MR. FRANK. Oh, please. You must.

MIEP. I couldn't.

MR. VAN DAAN. Good! That leaves one . . . two . . . three . . . seven of us.

DUSSEL. Eight! Eight! It's the same number as it always is!

---

1. **V-for-Victory** signal, made often by the Allies and their European supporters in World War II, consists of three short notes and one long, the Morse code for the letter *V*. The first four notes of Beethoven's Fifth Symphony were sometimes used.

MR. VAN DAAN. I left Margot out. I take it for granted Margot won't eat any.

ANNE. Why wouldn't she!

MRS. FRANK. I think it won't harm her.

MR. VAN DAAN. All right! All right! I just didn't want her to start coughing again, that's all.

DUSSEL. And please, Mrs. Frank should cut the cake.

MR. VAN DAAN. What's the difference?

MRS. VAN DAAN. It's not Mrs. Frank's cake, is it, Miep? It's for all of us.

Together

DUSSEL. Mrs. Frank divides things better.

MRS. VAN DAAN. (*Going to* DUSSEL) What are you trying to say?

MR. VAN DAAN. Oh, come on! Stop wasting time!

Together

MRS. VAN DAAN. (*To* DUSSEL) Don't I always give everybody exactly the same? Don't I?

MR. VAN DAAN. Forget it, Kerli.

MRS. VAN DAAN. No. I want an answer! Don't I?

DUSSEL. Yes. Yes. Everybody gets exactly the same . . . except Mr. Van Daan always gets a little bit more.

(VAN DAAN *advances on* DUSSEL, *the knife still in his hand.*)

MR. VAN DAAN. That's a lie!

(DUSSEL *retreats before the onslaught of the* VAN DAANS.)

MR. FRANK. Please, please! (*Then to* MIEP) You see what a little sugar cake does to us? It goes right to our heads!

MR. VAN DAAN. (*Handing* MRS. FRANK *the knife*) Here you are, Mrs. Frank.

MRS. FRANK. Thank you. (*Then to* MIEP *as she goes to the table to cut the cake*) Are you sure you won't have some?

MIEP. (*Drinking her tea*) No, really, I have to go in a minute.

(*The sound of the band fades out in the distance.*)

PETER. (*To* MIEP) Maybe Mouschi went back to our house . . . they say that cats . . . Do you ever get over there . . . ? I mean . . . do you suppose you could . . . ?

MIEP. I'll try, Peter. The first minute I get I'll try. But I'm afraid, with him gone a week . . .

DUSSEL. Make up your mind, already someone has had a nice big dinner from that cat!

(PETER *is furious, inarticulate. He starts toward* DUSSEL *as if to hit him.* MR. FRANK *stops him.* MRS. FRANK *speaks quickly to ease the situation.*)

MRS. FRANK. (*To* MIEP) This is delicious, Miep!

MRS. VAN DAAN. (*Eating hers*) Delicious!

MR. VAN DAAN. (*Finishing it in one gulp*) Dirk's in luck to get a girl who can bake like this!

MIEP. (*Putting down her empty teacup*) I have to run. Dirk's taking me to a party tonight.

ANNE. How heavenly! Remember now what everyone is wearing, and what you have to eat and everything, so you can tell us tomorrow.

MIEP. I'll give you a full report! Good-bye, everyone!

MR. VAN DAAN. (*To* MIEP) Just a minute. There's something I'd like you to do for me.

(*He hurries off up the stairs to his room.*)

MRS. VAN DAAN. (*Sharply*) Putti, where are you going? (*She rushes up the stairs after him, calling hysterically*) What do you want? Putti, what are you going to do?

MIEP. (*To* PETER) What's wrong?

PETER. (*His sympathy is with his mother*) Father says he's going to sell her fur coat. She's crazy about that old fur coat.

DUSSEL. Is it possible? Is it possible that anyone is so silly as to worry about a fur coat in times like this?

PETER. It's none of your darn business . . . and if you say one more thing . . . I'll, I'll take you and I'll . . . I mean it . . . I'll . . .

(*There is a piercing scream from* MRS. VAN DAAN *above. She grabs at the fur coat as* MR. VAN DAAN *is starting downstairs with it.*)

MRS. VAN DAAN. No! No! No! Don't you dare take that! You hear? It's mine! (*Downstairs

PETER *turns away, embarrassed, miserable*)
My father gave me that! You didn't give it to
me. You have no right. Let go of it . . . you
hear?

(MR. VAN DAAN *pulls the coat from her
hands and hurries downstairs.* MRS. VAN
DAAN *sinks to the floor, sobbing. As* MR.
VAN DAAN *comes into the main room the
others look away, embarrassed for him.*)

MR. VAN DAAN. (*To* MR. KRALER) Just a little
—discussion over the advisability of selling
this coat. As I have often reminded Mrs. Van
Daan, it's very selfish of her to keep it when
people outside are in such desperate need of
clothing . . . (*He gives the coat to* MIEP) So
if you will please to sell it for us? It should
fetch a good price. And by the way, will you
get me cigarettes. I don't care what kind they
are . . . get all you can.

MIEP. It's terribly difficult to get them, Mr. Van
Daan. But I'll try. Good-bye.

(*She goes.* MR. FRANK *follows her down the
steps to bolt the door after her.* MRS. FRANK
gives MR. KRALER *a cup of tea.*)

MRS. FRANK. Are you sure you won't have some
cake, Mr. Kraler?

MR. KRALER. I'd better not.

MR. VAN DAAN. You're still feeling badly? What
does your doctor say?

MR. KRALER. I haven't been to him.

MRS. FRANK. Now, Mr. Kraler! . . .

MR. KRALER. (*Sitting at the table*) Oh, I tried.
But you can't get near a doctor these days
. . . they're so busy. After weeks I finally managed to get one on the telephone. I told him
I'd like an appointment . . . I wasn't feeling
very well. You know what he answers . . . over
the telephone . . . Stick out your tongue!
(*They laugh. He turns to* MR. FRANK *as* MR.
FRANK *comes back*) I have some contracts
here . . . I wonder if you'd look over them
with me . . .

MR. FRANK. (*Putting out his hand*) Of course.

MR. KRALER. (*He rises*) If we could go downstairs . . . (MR. FRANK *starts ahead,* MR. KRALER
speaks to the others) Will you forgive us? I
won't keep him but a minute.

(*He starts to follow* MR. FRANK *down the
steps.*)

MARGOT. (*With sudden foreboding*) What's
happened? Something's happened! Hasn't it,
Mr. Kraler?

(MR. KRALER *stops and comes back, trying
to reassure* MARGOT *with a pretense of
casualness.*)

MR. KRALER. No, really. I want your father's
advice . . .

MARGOT. Something's gone wrong! I know it!

MR. FRANK. (*Coming back, to* MR. KRALER) If
it's something that concerns us here, it's better that we all hear it.

MR. KRALER. (*Turning to him, quietly*) But . . .
the children . . . ?

MR. FRANK. What they'd imagine would be
worse than any reality.

(*As* MR. KRALER *speaks, they all listen with
intense apprehension.* MRS. VAN DAAN
*comes down the stairs and sits on the bot-
tom step.*)

MR. KRALER. It's a man in the storeroom . . . I
don't know whether or not you remember
him . . . Carl, about fifty, heavy-set, near-
sighted . . . He came with us just before you
left.

MR. FRANK. He was from Utrecht?

MR. KRALER. That's the man. A couple of weeks
ago, when I was in the storeroom, he closed
the door and asked me . . . how's Mr. Frank?
What do you hear from Mr. Frank? I told
him I only knew there was a rumor that you
were in Switzerland. He said he'd heard that
rumor too, but he thought I might know
something more. I didn't pay any attention
to it . . . but then a thing happened yesterday
. . . He'd brought some invoices to the office
for me to sign. As I was going through them,
I looked up. He was standing staring at the
bookcase . . . your bookcase. He said he
thought he remembered a door there . . .
Wasn't there a door there that used to go up

to the loft? Then he told me he wanted more money. Twenty guilders[2] more a week.

MR. VAN DAAN. Blackmail!

MR. FRANK. Twenty guilders? Very modest blackmail.

MR. VAN DAAN. That's just the beginning.

DUSSEL. (*Coming to* MR. FRANK) You know what I think? He was the thief who was down there that night. That's how he knows we're here.

MR. FRANK. (*To* MR. KRALER) How was it left? What did you tell him?

MR. KRALER. I said I had to think about it. What shall I do? Pay him the money? . . . Take a chance on firing him . . . or what? I don't know.

DUSSEL. (*Frantic*) Don't fire him! Pay him what he asks . . . keep him here where you can have your eye on him.

MR. FRANK. Is it so much that he's asking? What are they paying nowadays?

MR. KRALER. He could get it in a war plant. But this isn't a war plant. Mind you, I don't know if he really knows . . . or if he doesn't know.

MR. FRANK. Offer him half. Then we'll soon find out if it's blackmail or not.

DUSSEL. And if it is? We've got to pay it, haven't we? Anything he asks we've got to pay!

MR. FRANK. Let's decide that when the time comes.

MR. KRALER. This may be all my imagination. You get to a point, these days, where you suspect everyone and everything. Again and again . . . on some simple look or word, I've found myself . . .

(*The telephone rings in the office below.*)

MRS. VAN DAAN. (*Hurrying to* MR. KRALER) There's the telephone! What does that mean, the telephone ringing on a holiday?

MR. KRALER. That's my wife. I told her I had to go over some papers in my office . . . to call me there when she got out of church. (*He starts out*) I'll offer him half then. Good-bye . . . we'll hope for the best!

(*The group call their good-bye's half heartedly.* MR. FRANK *follows* MR. KRALER,

to bolt the door below. During the following scene, MR. FRANK comes back up and stands listening, disturbed.*)

DUSSEL. (*To* MR. VAN DAAN) You can thank your son for this . . . smashing the light! I tell you, it's just a question of time now.

(*He goes to the window at the back and stands looking out.*)

MARGOT. Sometimes I wish the end would come . . . whatever it is.

MRS. FRANK (*Shocked*) Margot!

(ANNE *goes to* MARGOT, *sitting beside her on the couch with her arms around her.*)

MARGOT. Then at least we'd know where we were.

MRS. FRANK. You should be ashamed of yourself! Talking that way! Think how lucky we are! Think of the thousands dying in the war, every day. Think of the people in concentration camps.

ANNE. (*Interrupting*) What's the good of that? What's the good of thinking of misery when you're already miserable? That's stupid!

MRS. FRANK. Anne!

(*As* ANNE *goes on raging at her mother,* MRS. FRANK *tries to break in, in an effort to quiet her.*)

ANNE. We're young, Margot and Peter and I! You grownups have had your chance! But look at us . . . If we begin thinking of all the horror in the world, we're lost! We're trying to hold onto some kind of ideals . . . when everything . . . ideals, hopes . . . everything, are being destroyed! It isn't our fault that the world is in such a mess! We weren't around when all this started! So don't try to take it out on us!

(*She rushes off to her room, slamming the door after her. She picks up a brush from the chest and hurls it to the floor. Then she*

---

2. **guilder**\ˈgil·dər\ a unit of currency in the Netherlands, worth approximately twenty-six cents.

sits on the settee, trying to control her anger.)

MR. VAN DAAN. She talks as if we started the war! Did we start the war?

(*He spots* ANNE's *cake. As he starts to take it,* PETER *anticipates him.*)

PETER. She left her cake. (*He starts for* ANNE's *room with the cake. There is silence in the main room.* MRS. VAN DAAN *goes up to her room, followed by* VAN DAAN. DUSSEL *stays looking out the window.* MR. FRANK *brings* MRS. FRANK *her cake. She eats it slowly, without relish.* MR. FRANK *takes his cake to* MARGOT *and sits quietly on the sofa beside her.* PETER *stands in the doorway of* ANNE's *darkened room, looking at her, then makes a little movement to let her know he is there.* ANNE *sits up, quickly, trying to hide the signs of her tears.* PETER *holds out the cake to her.*) You left this.

ANNE. (*Dully*) Thanks.

(PETER *starts to go out, then comes back.*)

PETER. I thought you were fine just now. You know just how to talk to them. You know just how to say it. I'm no good . . . I never can think . . . especially when I'm mad . . . That Dussel . . . when he said that about Mouschi . . . someone eating him . . . all I could think is . . . I wanted to hit him. I wanted to give him such a . . . a . . . that he'd . . . That's what I used to do when there was an argument at school . . . That's the way I . . . but here . . . And an old man like that . . . it wouldn't be so good.

ANNE. You're making a big mistake about me. I do it all wrong. I say too much. I go too far. I hurt people's feelings . . .

(DUSSEL *leaves the window, going to his room.*)

PETER. I think you're just fine . . . What I want to say . . . if it wasn't for you around here, I don't know. What I mean . . .

(PETER *is interrupted by* DUSSEL's *turning on the light.* DUSSEL *stands in the doorway,*

startled to see PETER. PETER *advances toward him forbiddingly.* DUSSEL *backs out of the room.* PETER *closes the door on him.*)

ANNE. Do you mean it, Peter? Do you really mean it?

PETER. I said it, didn't I?

ANNE. Thank you, Peter!

(*In the main room* MR. *and* MRS. FRANK *collect the dishes and take them to the sink, washing them.* MARGOT *lies down again on the couch.* DUSSEL, *lost, wanders into* PETER's *room and takes up a book, starting to read.*)

PETER. (*Looking at the photographs on the wall*) You've got quite a collection.

ANNE. Wouldn't you like some in your room? I could give you some. Heaven knows you spend enough time in there . . . doing heaven knows what . . .

PETER. It's easier. A fight starts, or an argument . . . I duck in there.

ANNE. You're lucky, having a room to go to. His lordship is always here . . . I hardly ever get a minute alone. When they start in on me, I can't duck away. I have to stand there and take it.

PETER. You gave some of it back just now.

ANNE. I get so mad. They've formed their opinions . . . about everything . . . but we . . . we're still trying to find out . . . We have problems here that no other people our age have ever had. And just as you think you've solved them, something comes along and bang! You have to start all over again.

PETER. At least you've got someone you can talk to.

ANNE. Not really. Mother . . . I never discuss anything serious with her. She doesn't understand. Father's all right. We can talk about everything . . . everything but one thing. Mother. He simply won't talk about her. I don't think you can be really intimate with anyone if he holds something back, do you?

PETER. I think your father's fine.

ANNE. Oh, he is, Peter! He is! He's the only one who's ever given me the feeling that I have any sense. But anyway, nothing can take the place of school and play and friends of your own age . . . or near your age . . . can it?

PETER. I suppose you miss your friends and all.

ANNE. It isn't just . . . (*She breaks off, staring up at him for a second*) Isn't it funny, you and I? Here we've been seeing each other every minute for almost a year and a half, and this is the first time we've ever really talked. It helps a lot to have someone to talk to, don't you think? It helps you to let off steam.

PETER. (*Going to the door*) Well, any time you want to let off steam, you can come into my room.

ANNE. (*Following him*) I can get up an awful lot of steam. You'll have to be careful how you say that.

PETER. It's all right with me.

ANNE. Do you mean it?

PETER. I said it, didn't I?

(*He goes out. ANNE stands in her doorway looking after him. As PETER gets to his door he stands for a minute looking back at her. Then he goes into his room. DUSSEL rises as he comes in, and quickly passes him, going out. He starts across for his room. ANNE sees him coming, and pulls her door shut. DUSSEL turns back toward PETER's room. PETER pulls his door shut. DUSSEL stands there, bewildered, forlorn.*

The scene slowly dims out. The curtain falls on the scene. ANNE's voice comes over in the darkness . . . faintly at first, and then with growing strength.)

ANNE'S VOICE. We've had bad news. The people from whom Miep got our ration books have been arrested. So we have had to cut down on our food. Our stomachs are so empty that they rumble and make strange noises, all in different keys. Mr. Van Daan's is deep and low, like a bass fiddle. Mine is high, whistling like a flute. As we all sit around waiting for supper, it's like an orchestra tuning up. It only needs Toscanini to raise his baton and we'd be off in the Ride of the Valkyries.[3] Monday, the sixth of March, nineteen forty-

four. Mr. Kraler is in the hospital. It seems he has ulcers. Pim says we are his ulcers. Miep has to run the business and us too. The Americans have landed on the southern tip of Italy. Father looks for a quick finish to the war. Mr. Dussel is waiting every day for the warehouse man to demand more money. Have I been skipping too much from one subject to another? I can't help it. I feel that spring is coming. I feel it in my whole body and soul. I feel utterly confused. I am longing . . . so longing . . . for everything . . . for friends . . . for someone to talk to . . . someone who understands . . . someone young, who feels as I do . . .

(*As these last lines are being said, the curtain rises on the scene. The lights dim on. ANNE's voice fades out.*)

SCENE II

It is evening, after supper. From outside we hear the sound of children playing. The "grownups," with the exception of MR. VAN DAAN, are all in the main room. MRS. FRANK is doing some mending, MRS. VAN DAAN is reading a fashion magazine. MR. FRANK is going over business accounts. DUSSEL, in his dentist's jacket, is pacing up and down, impatient to get into his bedroom. MR. VAN DAAN is upstairs working on a piece of embroidery in an embroidery frame.

In his room PETER is sitting before the mirror, smoothing his hair. As the scene goes on, he puts on his tie, brushes his coat and puts it on, preparing himself meticulously for a visit from ANNE. On his wall are now hung some of ANNE's motion picture stars.

In her room ANNE too is getting dressed. She stands before the mirror in her slip, trying various ways of dressing her hair. MARGOT

---

3. Arturo **Toscanini**\tŏs·kə ▲nē·nē\ (1867–1957), a famous conductor. "**The Ride of the Valkyries**," a composition, both fast and loud, from Wagner's *Die Walküre.*

is seated on the sofa, hemming a skirt for ANNE *to wear.*

In the main room DUSSEL *can stand it no longer. He comes over, rapping sharply on the door of his and* ANNE's *bedroom.*

ANNE. (*Calling to him*) No, no, Mr. Dussel! I am not dressed yet. (DUSSEL *walks away, furious, sitting down and burying his head in his hands.* ANNE *turns to* MARGOT) How is that? How does that look?

MARGOT. (*Glancing at her briefly*) Fine.

ANNE. You didn't even look.

MARGOT. Of course I did. It's fine.

ANNE. Margot, tell me, am I terribly ugly?

MARGOT. Oh, stop fishing.

ANNE. No. No. Tell me.

MARGOT. Of course you're not. You've got nice eyes . . . and a lot of animation, and . . .

ANNE. A little vague, aren't you?

(*She reaches over and takes a brassière out of* MARGOT's *sewing basket. She holds it up to herself, studying the effect in the mirror. Outside,* MRS. FRANK, *feeling sorry for* DUSSEL, *comes over, knocking at the girls' door.*)

MRS. FRANK. (*Outside*) May I come in?

MARGOT. Come in, Mother.

MRS. FRANK. (*Shutting the door behind her*) Mr. Dussel's impatient to get in here.

ANNE. (*Still with the brassière*) Heavens, he takes the room for himself the entire day.

MRS. FRANK. (*Gently*) Anne, dear, you're not going in again tonight to see Peter?

ANNE. (*Dignified*) That is my intention.

MRS. FRANK. But you've already spent a great deal of time in there today.

ANNE. I was in there exactly twice. Once to get the dictionary, and then three-quarters of an hour before supper.

MRS. FRANK. Aren't you afraid you're disturbing him?

ANNE. Mother, I have some intuition.

MRS. FRANK. Then may I ask you this much, Anne. Please don't shut the door when you go in.

ANNE. You sound like Mrs. Van Daan!

(*She throws the brassière back in* MARGOT's *sewing basket and picks up her blouse, putting it on.*)

MRS. FRANK. No. No. I don't mean to suggest anything wrong. I only wish that you wouldn't expose yourself to criticism . . . that you wouldn't give Mrs. Van Daan the opportunity to be unpleasant.

ANNE. Mrs. Van Daan doesn't need an opportunity to be unpleasant!

MRS. FRANK. Everyone's on edge, worried about Mr. Kraler. This is one more thing . . .

ANNE. I'm sorry, Mother. I'm going to Peter's room. I'm not going to let Petronella Van Daan spoil our friendship.

(MRS. FRANK *hesitates for a second, then goes out, closing the door after her. She gets a pack of playing cards and sits at the center table, playing solitaire. In* ANNE's *room* MARGOT *hands the finished skirt to* ANNE. *As* ANNE *is putting it on,* MARGOT *takes off her high-heeled shoes and stuffs paper in the toes so that* ANNE *can wear them.*)

MARGOT (*To* ANNE) Why don't you two talk in the main room? It'd save a lot of trouble. It's hard on Mother, having to listen to those remarks from Mrs. Van Daan and not say a word.

ANNE. Why doesn't she say a word? I think it's ridiculous to take it and take it.

MARGOT. You don't understand Mother at all, do you? She can't talk back. She's not like you. It's just not in her nature to fight back.

ANNE. Anyway . . . the only one I worry about is you. I feel awfully guilty about you.

(*She sits on the stool near* MARGOT, *putting on* MARGOT's *high-heeled shoes.*)

MARGOT. What about?

ANNE. I mean, every time I go into Peter's room, I have a feeling I may be hurting you. (MARGOT *shakes her head*) I know if it were me, I'd be wild. I'd be desperately jealous, if it were me.

MARGOT. Well, I'm not.

ANNE. You don't feel badly? Really? Truly? You're not jealous?

MARGOT. Of course I'm jealous . . . jealous that you've got something to get up in the morning for . . . But jealous of you and Peter? No.

(ANNE *goes back to the mirror.*)

ANNE. Maybe there's nothing to be jealous of. Maybe he doesn't really like me. Maybe I'm just taking the place of his cat . . . (*She picks up a pair of short white gloves, putting them on*) Wouldn't you like to come in with us?

MARGOT. I have a book.

(*The sound of the children playing outside fades out. In the main room* DUSSEL *can stand it no longer. He jumps up, going to the bedroom door and knocking sharply.*)

DUSSEL. Will you please let me in my room!

ANNE. Just a minute, dear, dear Mr. Dussel. (*She picks up her Mother's pink stole and adjusts it elegantly over her shoulders, then gives a last look in the mirror*) Well, here I go . . . to run the gauntlet.

(*She starts out, followed by* MARGOT.)

DUSSEL. (*As she appears—sarcastic*) Thank you so much.

(DUSSEL *goes into his room.* ANNE *goes toward* PETER's *room, passing* MRS. VAN DAAN *and her parents at the center table.*)

MRS. VAN DAAN. Look at her! (ANNE *pays no attention. She knocks at* PETER's *door*) I don't know what good it is to have a son. I never see him. He wouldn't care if I killed myself. (PETER *opens the door and stands aside for* ANNE *to come in*) Just a minute, Anne. (*She goes to them at the door*) I'd like to say a few words to my son. Do you mind? (PETER *and* ANNE *stand waiting*) Peter, I don't want you staying up till all hours tonight. You've got to have your sleep. You're a growing boy. You hear?

MRS. FRANK. Anne won't stay late. She's going to bed promptly at nine. Aren't you, Anne?

ANNE. Yes, Mother . . . (*To* MRS. VAN DAAN) May we go now?

MRS. VAN DAAN. Are you asking me? I didn't know I had anything to say about it.

MRS. FRANK. Listen for the chimes, Anne dear.

(*The two young people go off into* PETER's *room, shutting the door after them.*)

MRS. VAN DAAN. (*To* MRS. FRANK) In my day it was the boys who called on the girls. Not the girls on the boys.

MRS. FRANK. You know how young people like to feel that they have secrets. Peter's room is the only place where they can talk.

MRS. VAN DAAN. Talk! That's not what they called it when I was young.

(MRS. VAN DAAN *goes off to the bathroom.* MARGOT *settles down to read her book.* MR. FRANK *puts his papers away and brings a chess game to the center table. He and* MRS. FRANK *start to play. In* PETER's *room,* ANNE *speaks to* PETER, *indignant, humiliated.*)

ANNE. Aren't they awful? Aren't they impossible? Treating us as if we were still in the nursery.

(*She sits on the cot.* PETER *gets a bottle of pop and two glasses.*)

PETER. Don't let it bother you. It doesn't bother me.

ANNE. I suppose you can't really blame them . . . they think back to what *they* were like at our age. They don't realize how much more advanced we are . . . When you think what wonderful discussions we've had! . . . Oh, I forgot. I was going to bring you some more pictures.

PETER. Oh, these are fine, thanks.

ANNE. Don't you want some more? Miep just brought me some new ones.

PETER. Maybe later.

(*He gives her a glass of pop and, taking some for himself, sits down facing her.*)

ANNE. (*Looking up at one of the photographs*) I remember when I got that . . . I won it. I bet Jopie that I could eat five ice-cream cones. We'd all been playing ping-pong . . . We used to have heavenly times . . . we'd finish up with

Peter and Anne visiting in Peter's room. With crosscurrents among the inmates of the hideout intensified by the unnatural confinement, Peter and Anne found much needed understanding in each other.

ice cream at the Delphi, or the Oasis, where Jews were allowed . . . there'd always be a lot of boys . . . we'd laugh and joke . . . I'd like to go back to it for a few days or a week. But after that I know I'd be bored to death. I think more seriously about life now. I want to be a journalist . . . or something. I love to write. What do you want to do?

PETER. I thought I might go off some place . . . work on a farm or something . . . some job that doesn't take much brains.

ANNE. You shouldn't talk that way. You've got the most awful inferiority complex.

PETER. I know I'm not smart.

ANNE. That isn't true. You're much better than I am in dozens of things . . . arithmetic and algebra and . . . well, you're a million times better than I am in algebra. (*With sudden di-*

rectness) You like Margot, don't you? Right from the start you liked her, liked her much better than me.

PETER. (*Uncomfortably*) Oh, I don't know.

(*In the main room* MRS. VAN DAAN *comes from the bathroom and goes over to the sink, polishing a coffee pot.*)

ANNE. It's all right. Everyone feels that way. Margot's so good. She's sweet and bright and beautiful and I'm not.

PETER. I wouldn't say that.

ANNE. Oh, no, I'm not. I know that. I know quite well that I'm not a beauty. I never have been and never shall be.

231

PETER. I don't agree at all. I think you're pretty.

ANNE. That's not true!

PETER. And another thing. You've changed . . . from at first, I mean.

ANNE. I have?

PETER. I used to think you were awful noisy.

ANNE. And what do you think now, Peter? How have I changed?

PETER. Well . . . er . . . you're . . . quieter.

(*In his room* DUSSEL *takes his pajamas and toilet articles and goes into the bathroom to change.*)

ANNE. I'm glad you don't just hate me.

PETER. I never said that.

ANNE. I bet when you get out of here you'll never think of me again.

PETER. That's crazy.

ANNE. When you get back with all of your friends, you're going to say . . . now what did I ever see in that Mrs. Quack Quack.

PETER. I haven't got any friends.

ANNE. Oh, Peter, of course you have. Everyone has friends.

PETER. Not me. I don't want any. I get along all right without them.

ANNE. Does that mean you can get along without me? I think of myself as your friend.

PETER. No. If they were all like you, it'd be different.

(*He takes the glasses and the bottle and puts them away. There is a second's silence and then* ANNE *speaks, hesitantly, shyly.*)

ANNE. Peter, did you ever kiss a girl?

PETER. Yes. Once.

ANNE. (*To cover her feelings*) That picture's crooked. (PETER *goes over, straightening the photograph*) Was she pretty?

PETER. Huh?

ANNE. The girl that you kissed.

PETER. I don't know. I was blindfolded. (*He comes back and sits down again*) It was at a party. One of those kissing games.

ANNE. (*Relieved*) Oh. I don't suppose that really counts, does it?

PETER. It didn't with me.

ANNE. I've been kissed twice. Once a man I'd never seen before kissed me on the cheek when he picked me up off the ice and I was crying. And the other was Mr. Koophuis, a friend of Father's who kissed my hand. You wouldn't say those counted would you?

PETER. I wouldn't say so.

ANNE. I know almost for certain that Margot would never kiss anyone unless she was engaged to them. And I'm sure too that Mother never touched a man before Pim. But I don't know . . . things are so different now . . . What do you think? Do you think a girl shouldn't kiss anyone except if she's engaged or something? It's so hard to try to think what to do, when here we are with the whole world falling around our ears and you think . . . well . . . you don't know what's going to happen tomorrow and . . . What do you think?

PETER. I suppose it'd depend on the girl. Some girls, anything they do's wrong. But others . . . well . . . it wouldn't necessarily be wrong with them. (*The carillon starts to strike nine o'clock*) I've always thought that when two people . . .

ANNE. Nine o'clock. I have to go.

PETER. That's right.

ANNE (*Without moving*) Good night.

(*There is a second's pause, then* PETER *gets up and moves toward the door.*)

PETER. You won't let them stop you coming?

ANNE. No. (*She rises and starts for the door*) Sometime I might bring my diary. There are so many things in it that I want to talk over with you. There's a lot about you.

PETER. What kind of things?

ANNE. I wouldn't want you to see some of it. I thought you were a nothing, just the way you thought about me.

PETER. Did you change your mind, the way I changed my mind about you?

ANNE. Well . . . You'll see . . .

(*For a second* ANNE *stands looking up at* PETER, *longing for him to kiss her. As he makes no move she turns away. Then suddenly* PETER *grabs her awkwardly in his arms, kissing her on the cheek.* ANNE *walks out dazed. She stands for a minute, her back to the people in the main room. As she regains her poise she goes to her mother and father and* MARGOT, *silently kissing them. They murmur their good nights to her. As she is about to open her bedroom door, she catches sight of* MRS. VAN DAAN. *She goes quickly to her, taking her face in her hands and kissing her first on one cheek and then on the other. Then she hurries off into her room.* MRS. VAN DAAN *looks after her, and then looks over at* PETER'S *room. Her suspicions are confirmed.*)

MRS. VAN DAAN. (*She knows*) Ah hah!

(*The lights dim out. The curtain falls on the scene. In the darkness* ANNE'S *voice comes faintly at first and then with growing strength.*)

ANNE'S VOICE. By this time we all know each other so well that if anyone starts to tell a story, the rest can finish it for him. We're having to cut down still further on our meals. What makes it worse, the rats have been at work again. They've carried off some of our precious food. Even Mr. Dussel wishes now that Mouschi was here. Thursday, the twentieth of April, nineteen forty-four. Invasion fever is mounting every day. Miep tells us that people outside talk of nothing else. For myself, life has become much more pleasant. I often go to Peter's room after supper. Oh, don't think I'm in love, because I'm not. But it does make life more bearable to have someone with whom you can exchange views. No more tonight. P.S. . . . I must be honest. I must confess that I actually live for the next meeting. Is there anything lovelier than to sit under the skylight and feel the sun on your cheeks and have a darling boy in your arms? I admit now that I'm glad the Van Daans had a son and not a daughter. I've outgrown another dress. That's the third. I'm having to wear Margot's clothes after all. I'm working hard on my French and am now reading *La Belle Nivernaise.*

(*As she is saying the last lines—the curtain rises on the scene. The lights dim on, as* ANNE'S *voice fades out.*)

SCENE III

It is night, a few weeks later. Everyone is in bed. There is complete quiet. In the VAN DAANS' *room a match flares up for a moment and then is quickly put out.* MR. VAN DAAN, *in bare feet, dressed in underwear and trousers, is dimly seen coming stealthily down the stairs and into the main room, where* MR. *and* MRS. FRANK *and* MARGOT *are sleeping. He goes to the food safe and again lights a match. Then he cautiously opens the safe, taking out a half-loaf of bread. As he closes the safe, it creaks. He stands rigid.* MRS. FRANK *sits up in bed. She sees him.*

MRS. FRANK. (*Screaming*) Otto! Otto! *Komme schnell!*

(*The rest of the people wake, hurriedly getting up.*)

MR. FRANK. *Was ist los? Was ist passiert?*

(DUSSEL, *followed by* ANNE, *comes from his room.*)

MRS. FRANK. (*As she rushes over to* MR. VAN DAAN) *Er stiehlt das Essen!*[1]

DUSSEL. (*Grabbing* MR. VAN DAAN) You! You! Give me that.

MRS. VAN DAAN. (*Coming down the stairs*) Putti . . . Putti . . . what is it?

DUSSEL. (*His hands on* VAN DAAN'S *neck*) You dirty thief . . . stealing food . . . you good-for-nothing . . .

MR. FRANK. Mr. Dussel! In the name of heaven! Help me, Peter!

(PETER *comes over, trying, with* MR. FRANK, *to separate the two struggling men.*)

PETER. Let him go! Let go!

---

1. The German may be translated as follows: "Otto! Otto! Come right away." "What's up? What is happening?" "He is stealing the food!"

(DUSSEL *drops* MR. VAN DAAN, *pushing him away. He shows them the end of a loaf of bread that he has taken from* VAN DAAN.)

DUSSEL. You greedy, selfish . . . !

(MARGOT *turns on the lights.*)

MRS. VAN DAAN. Putti . . . what is it?

(*All of* MRS. FRANK'S *gentleness, her self-control, is gone. She is outraged, in a frenzy of indignation.*)

MRS. FRANK. The bread! He was stealing the bread!

DUSSEL. It was you, and all the time we thought it was the rats!

MR. FRANK. Mr. Van Daan, how could you!

MR. VAN DAAN. I'm hungry.

MRS. FRANK. We're all of us hungry! I see the children getting thinner and thinner. Your own son Peter . . . I've heard him moan in his sleep, he's so hungry. And you come in the night and steal food that should go to them . . . to the children!

MRS. VAN DAAN. (*Going to* MR. VAN DAAN *protectively*) He needs more food than the rest of us. He's used to more. He's a big man.

(MR. VAN DAAN *breaks away, going over and sitting on the couch.*)

MRS. FRANK. (*Turning on* MRS. VAN DAAN) And you . . . you're worse than he is! You're a mother, and yet you sacrifice your child to this man . . . this . . . this . . .

MR. FRANK. Edith! Edith!

(MARGOT *picks up the pink woolen stole, putting it over her mother's shoulders.*)

MRS. FRANK. (*Paying no attention, going on to* MRS. VAN DAAN) Don't think I haven't seen you! Always saving the choicest bits for him! I've watched you day after day and I've held my tongue. But not any longer! Not after this! Now I want him to go! I want him to get out of here!

MR. FRANK. Edith!

MR. VAN DAAN. Get out of here? } *Together*

MRS. VAN DAAN. What do you mean?

MRS. FRANK. Just that! Take your things and get out!

MR. FRANK. (*To* MRS. FRANK) You're speaking in anger. You cannot mean what you are saying.

MRS. FRANK. I mean exactly that!

(MRS. VAN DAAN *takes a cover from the* FRANKS' *bed, pulling it about her.*)

MR. FRANK. For two long years we have lived here, side by side. We have respected each other's rights . . . we have managed to live in peace. Are we now going to throw it all away? I know this will never happen again, will it, Mr. Van Daan?

MR. VAN DAAN. No. No.

MRS. FRANK. He steals once! He'll steal again!

(MR. VAN DAAN, *holding his stomach, starts for the bathroom.* ANNE *puts her arms around him, helping him up the step.*)

MR. FRANK. Edith, please. Let us be calm. We'll all go to our rooms . . . and afterwards we'll sit down quietly and talk this out . . . we'll find some way . . .

MRS. FRANK. No! No! No more talk! I want them to leave!

MRS. VAN DAAN. You'd put us out, on the streets?

MRS. FRANK. There are other hiding places.

MRS. VAN DAAN. A cellar . . . a closet. I know. And we have no money left even to pay for that.

MRS. FRANK. I'll give you money. Out of my own pocket I'll give it gladly.

(*She gets her purse from a shelf and comes back with it.*)

MRS. VAN DAAN. Mr. Frank, you told Putti you'd never forget what he'd done for you when you came to Amsterdam. You said you could never repay him, that you . . .

MRS. FRANK. (*Counting out money*) If my husband had any obligation to you, he's paid it, over and over.

MR. FRANK. Edith, I've never seen you like this before. I don't know you.

MRS. FRANK. I should have spoken out long ago.

DUSSEL. You can't be nice to some people.

234

MRS. VAN DAAN. (*Turning on* DUSSEL) There would have been plenty for all of us, if *you* hadn't come in here!

MR. FRANK. We don't need the Nazis to destroy us. We're destroying ourselves.

(*He sits down, with his head in his hands.* MRS. FRANK *goes to* MRS. VAN DAAN.)

MRS. FRANK. (*Giving* MRS. VAN DAAN *some money*) Give this to Miep. She'll find you a place.

ANNE. Mother, you're not putting *Peter* out. Peter hasn't done anything.

MRS. FRANK. He'll stay, of course. When I say I must protect the children, I mean Peter too.

(PETER *rises from the steps where he has been sitting.*)

PETER. I'd have to go if Father goes.

(MR. VAN DAAN *comes from the bathroom.* MRS. VAN DAAN *hurries to him and takes him to the couch. Then she gets water from the sink to bathe his face.*)

MRS. FRANK. (*While this is going on*) He's no father to you . . . that man! He doesn't know what it is to be a father!

PETER (*Starting for his room*) I wouldn't feel right. I couldn't stay.

MRS. FRANK. Very well, then. I'm sorry.

ANNE. (*Rushing over to* PETER) No, Peter! No! (PETER *goes into his room, closing the door after him.* ANNE *turns back to her mother, crying*) I don't care about the food. They can have mine! I don't want it! Only don't send them away. It'll be daylight soon. They'll be caught . . .

MARGOT. (*Putting her arms comfortingly around* ANNE) Please, Mother!

MRS. FRANK. They're not going now. They'll stay here until Miep finds them a place. (*To* MRS. VAN DAAN) But one thing I insist on! He must never come down here again! He must never come to this room where the food is stored! We'll divide what we have . . . an equal share for each! (DUSSEL *hurries over to get a sack of potatoes from the food safe.* MRS.

FRANK *goes on, to* MRS. VAN DAAN) You can cook it here and take it up to him.

(DUSSEL *brings the sack of potatoes back to the center table.*)

MARGOT. Oh, no. No. We haven't sunk so far that we're going to fight over a handful of rotten potatoes.

DUSSEL. (*Dividing the potatoes into piles*) Mrs. Frank, Mr. Frank, Margot, Anne, Peter, Mrs. Van Daan, Mr. Van Daan, myself . . . Mrs. Frank . . .

(*The buzzer sounds in* MIEP'*s signal.*)

MR. FRANK. It's Miep.

(*He hurries over, getting his overcoat and putting it on.*)

MARGOT. At this hour?

MRS. FRANK. It is trouble.

MR. FRANK. (*As he starts down to unbolt the door*) I beg you, don't let her see a thing like this!

MR. DUSSEL (*Counting without stopping*) . . . Anne, Peter, Mrs. Van Daan, Mr. Van Daan, myself . . .

MARGOT (*To* DUSSEL) Stop it! Stop it!

DUSSEL. . . . Mr. Frank, Margot, Anne, Peter, Mrs. Van Daan, Mr. Van Daan, myself, Mrs. Frank . . .

MRS. VAN DAAN. You're keeping the big ones for yourself! All the big ones . . . Look at the size of that! . . . And that! . . .

(DUSSEL *continues on with his dividing.* PETER, *with his shirt and trousers on, comes from his room.*)

MARGOT. Stop it! Stop it!

(*We hear* MIEP'*s excited voice speaking to* MR. FRANK *below.*)

MIEP. Mr. Frank . . . the most wonderful news! . . . The invasion has begun!

MR. FRANK. Go on, tell them! Tell them!

(MIEP *comes running up the steps, ahead of* MR. FRANK. *She has a man's raincoat on over her nightclothes and a bunch of orange-colored flowers in her hand.*)

MIEP. Did you hear that, everybody? Did you hear what I said? The invasion has begun! The invasion!

(*They all stare at* MIEP, *unable to grasp what she is telling them.* PETER *is the first to recover his wits.*)

PETER. Where?

MRS. VAN DAAN. When? When, Miep?

MIEP. It began early this morning . . .

(*As she talks on, the realization of what she has said begins to dawn on them. Everyone goes crazy. A wild demonstration takes place.* MRS. FRANK *hugs* MR. VAN DAAN.)

MRS. FRANK. Oh, Mr. Van Daan, did you hear that?

(DUSSEL *embraces* MRS. VAN DAAN. PETER *grabs a frying pan and parades around the room, beating on it, singing the Dutch National Anthem.* ANNE *and* MARGOT *follow him, singing, weaving in and out among the excited grown-ups.* MARGOT *breaks away to take the flowers from* MIEP *and distribute them to everyone. While this pandemonium is going on* MRS. FRANK *tries to make herself heard above the excitement.*)

MRS. FRANK. (*To* MIEP) How do you know?

MIEP. The radio . . . The B.B.C.![2] They said they landed on the coast of Normandy!

PETER. The British?

MIEP. British, Americans, French, Dutch, Poles, Norwegians . . . all of them. More than four thousand ships! Churchill spoke, and General Eisenhower![3] D-Day they call it!

MR. FRANK. Thank God, it's come!

MRS. VAN DAAN. At last!

MIEP. (*Starting out*) I'm going to tell Mr. Kraler. This'll be better than any blood transfusion.

MR. FRANK. (*Stopping her*) What part of Normandy did they land, did they say?

MIEP. Normandy . . . that's all I know now . . . I'll be up the minute I hear some more!

(*She goes hurriedly out.*)

MR. FRANK. (*To* MRS. FRANK) What did I tell you? What did I tell you?

(MRS. FRANK *indicates that he has forgotten to bolt the door after* MIEP. *He hurries down the steps.* MR. VAN DAAN, *sitting on the couch, suddenly breaks into a convulsive sob. Everybody looks at him, bewildered.*)

MRS. VAN DAAN. (*Hurrying to him*) Putti! Putti! What is it? What happened?

MR. VAN DAAN. Please. I'm so ashamed.

(MR. FRANK *comes back up the steps.*)

DUSSEL. Oh, for God's sake!

MRS. VAN DAAN. Don't, Putti.

MARGOT. It doesn't matter now!

MR. FRANK. (*Going to* MR. VAN DAAN) Didn't you hear what Miep said? The invasion has come! We're going to be liberated! This is a time to celebrate!

(*He embraces* MRS. FRANK *and then hurries to the cupboard and gets the cognac and a glass.*)

MR. VAN DAAN. To steal bread from children!

MRS. FRANK. We've all done things that we're ashamed of.

ANNE. Look at me, the way I've treated Mother . . . so mean and horrid to her.

MRS. FRANK. No, Anneke, no.

(ANNE *runs to her mother, putting her arms around her.*)

ANNE. Oh, Mother, I was. I was awful.

MR. VAN DAAN. Not like me. No one is as bad as me!

DUSSEL. (*To* MR. VAN DAAN) Stop it now! Let's be happy!

MR. FRANK. (*Giving* MR. VAN DAAN *a glass of cognac*) Here! Here! *Schnapps!*[4] *Locheim!*

(VAN DAAN *takes the cognac. They all watch him. He gives them a feeble smile.* ANNE

---

2. **B.B.C.,** the British Broadcasting Corporation.
3. Sir Winston **Churchill,** Prime Minister of Britain. General Dwight D. **Eisenhower,** commander of Allied Forces.
4. **Schnapps** \sh̶naps\ German brandy.

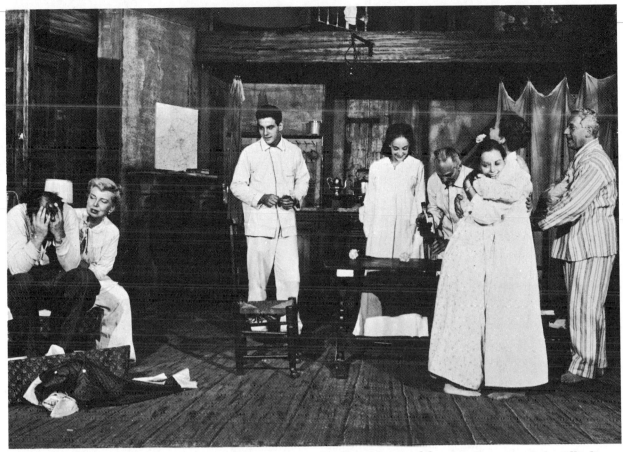

puts up her fingers in a V-for-Victory sign. As VAN DAAN *gives an answering V-sign, they are startled to hear a loud sob from behind them. It is* MRS. FRANK, *stricken with remorse. She is sitting on the other side of the room.*)

MRS. FRANK. (*Through her sobs*) When I think of the terrible things I said . . .

(MR. FRANK, ANNE *and* MARGOT *hurry to her, trying to comfort her.* MR. VAN DAAN *brings her his glass of cognac.*)

MR. VAN DAAN. No! No! You were right!

MRS. FRANK. That I should speak that way to you! . . . Our friends! . . . Our guests!

(*She starts to cry again.*)

DUSSEL. Stop it, you're spoiling the whole invasion!

In the midst of celebrating the news of the Allied invasion, Mr. Van Daan (left) weeps at betraying the Frank's trust; Anne "makes up" with her mother.

(*As they are comforting her, the lights dim out. The curtain falls.*)

ANNE'S VOICE. (*Faintly at first and then with growing strength*) We're all in much better spirits these days. There's still excellent news of the invasion. The best part about it is that I have a feeling that friends are coming. Who knows? Maybe I'll be back in school by fall. Ha, ha! The joke is on us! The warehouse man doesn't know a thing and we are paying him all that money! . . . Wednesday, the second of July, nineteen forty-four. The invasion seems temporarily to be bogged down. Mr. Kraler has to have an operation, which looks bad. The Gestapo have found the radio that

237

was stolen. Mr. Dussel says they'll trace it back and back to the thief, and then, it's just a matter of time till they get to us. Everyone is low. Even poor Pim can't raise their spirits. I have often been downcast myself . . . but never in despair. I can shake off everything if I write. But . . . and that is the great question . . . will I ever be able to write well? I want to so much. I want to go on living even after my death. Another birthday has gone by, so now I am fifteen. Already I know what I want. I have a goal, an opinion.

(*As this is being said—the curtain rises on the scene, the lights dim on, and* ANNE'S *voice fades out.*)

SCENE IV

It is an afternoon a few weeks later . . . Everyone but MARGOT *is in the main room. There is a sense of great tension.*

Both MRS. FRANK *and* MR. VAN DAAN *are nervously pacing back and forth,* DUSSEL *is standing at the window, looking down fixedly at the street below.* PETER *is at the center table, trying to do his lessons.* ANNE *sits opposite him, writing in her diary.* MRS. VAN DAAN *is seated on the couch, her eyes on* MR. FRANK *as he sits reading.*

The sound of a telephone ringing comes from the office below. They all are rigid, listening tensely. MR. DUSSEL *rushes down to* MR. FRANK.

DUSSEL. There it goes again, the telephone! Mr. Frank, do you hear?

MR. FRANK. (*Quietly*) Yes. I hear.

DUSSEL. (*Pleading, insistent*) But this is the third time, Mr. Frank! The third time in quick succession! It's a signal! I tell you it's Miep, trying to get us! For some reason she can't come to us and she's trying to warn us of something!

MR. FRANK. Please. Please.

MR. VAN DAAN. (*To* DUSSEL) You're wasting your breath.

DUSSEL. Something has happened, Mr. Frank. For three days now Miep hasn't been to see us! And today not a man has come to work. There hasn't been a sound in the building!

MRS. FRANK. Perhaps it's Sunday. We may have lost track of the days.

MR. VAN DAAN. (*To* ANNE) You with the diary there. What day is it?

DUSSEL. (*Going to* MRS. FRANK) I don't lose track of the days! I know exactly what day it is! It's Friday, the fourth of August. Friday, and not a man at work. (*He rushes back to* MR. FRANK, *pleading with him, almost in tears*) I tell you Mr. Kraler's dead. That's the only explanation. He's dead and they've closed down the building, and Miep's trying to tell us!

MR. FRANK. She'd never telephone us.

DUSSEL. (*Frantic*) Mr. Frank, answer that! I beg you, answer it!

MR. FRANK. No.

MR. VAN DAAN. Just pick it up and listen. You don't have to speak. Just listen and see if it's Miep.

DUSSEL. (*Speaking at the same time*) For God's sake . . . I ask you.

MR. FRANK. No. I've told you, no. I'll do nothing that might let anyone know we're in the building.

PETER. Mr. Frank's right.

MR. VAN DAAN. There's no need to tell us what side you're on.

MR. FRANK. If we wait patiently, quietly, I believe that help will come.

(*There is silence for a minute as they all listen to the telephone ringing.*)

DUSSEL. I'm going down. (*He rushes down the steps.* MR. FRANK *tries ineffectually to hold him.* DUSSEL *runs to the lower door, unbolting it. The telephone stops ringing.* DUSSEL *bolts the door and comes slowly back up the steps.*) Too late. (MR. FRANK *goes to* MARGOT *in* ANNE'S *bedroom.*)

MR. VAN DAAN. So we just wait here until we die.

MRS. VAN DAAN. (*Hysterically*) I can't stand it! I'll kill myself! I'll kill myself!

MR. VAN DAAN. For God's sake, stop it!

(*In the distance, a German military band is heard playing a Viennese waltz.*)

MRS. VAN DAAN. I think you'd be glad if I did! I think you want me to die!

MR. VAN DAAN. Whose fault is it we're here? (MRS. VAN DAAN *starts for her room. He follows, talking at her*) We could've been safe somewhere . . . in America or Switzerland. But no! No! You wouldn't leave when I wanted to. You couldn't leave your things. You couldn't leave your precious furniture.

MRS. VAN DAAN. Don't touch me!

(*She hurries up the stairs, followed by* MR. VAN DAAN. PETER, *unable to bear it, goes to his room.* ANNE *looks after him, deeply concerned.* DUSSEL *returns to his post at the window.* MR. FRANK *comes back into the main room and takes a book, trying to read.* MRS. FRANK *sits near the sink, starting to peel some potatoes.* ANNE *quietly goes to* PETER'S *room, closing the door after her.* PETER *is lying face down on the cot.* ANNE *leans over him, holding him in her arms, trying to bring him out of his despair.*)

ANNE. Look, Peter, the sky. (*She looks up through the skylight*) What a lovely, lovely day! Aren't the clouds beautiful? You know what I do when it seems as if I couldn't stand being cooped up for one more minute? I *think* myself out. I think myself on a walk in the park where I used to go with Pim. Where the jonquils and the crocus and the violets grow down the slopes. You know the most wonderful part about *thinking* yourself out? You can have it any way you like. You can have roses and violets and chrysanthemums all blooming at the same time . . . It's funny . . . I used to take it all for granted . . . and now I've gone crazy about everything to do with nature. Haven't you?

PETER. I've just gone crazy. I think if something doesn't happen soon . . . if we don't get out of here . . . I can't stand much more of it!

ANNE. (*Softly*) I wish you had a religion, Peter.

PETER. No, thanks! Not me!

ANNE. Oh, I don't mean you have to be Orthodox . . . or believe in heaven and hell and purgatory and things . . . I just mean some religion . . . it doesn't matter what. Just to believe in something! When I think of all that's out there . . . the trees . . . and flowers . . . and seagulls . . . when I think of the dearness of you, Peter . . . and the goodness of the people we know . . . Mr. Kraler, Miep, Dirk, the vegetable man, all risking their lives for us every day . . . When I think of these good things, I'm not afraid any more . . . I find myself, and God, and I . . .

(PETER *interrupts, getting up and walking away.*)

PETER. That's fine! But when I begin to think, I get mad! Look at us, hiding out for two years. Not able to move! Caught here like . . . waiting for them to come and get us . . . and all for what?

ANNE. We're not the only people that've had to suffer. There've always been people that've had to . . . sometimes one race . . . sometimes another . . . and yet . . .

PETER. That doesn't make me feel any better!

ANNE. (*Going to him*) I know it's terrible, trying to have any faith . . . when people are doing such horrible . . . But you know what I sometimes think? I think the world may be going through a phase, the way I was with Mother. It'll pass, maybe not for hundreds of years, but some day . . . I still believe, in spite of everything, that people are really good at heart.

PETER. I want to see something now . . . Not a thousand years from now!

(*He goes over, sitting down again on the cot.*)

ANNE. But, Peter, if you'd only look at it as part of a great pattern . . . that we're just a little minute in the life . . . (*She breaks off*) Listen to us, going at each other like a couple of stupid grownups! Look at the sky now. Isn't it lovely? (*She holds out her hand to him.*

Anne: "In spite of everything, I still believe that people are really good at heart."

PETER *takes it and rises, standing with her at the window looking out, his arms around her*) Some day, when we're outside again, I'm going to . . .

(*She breaks off as she hears the sound of a car, its brakes squealing as it comes to a sudden stop. The people in the other rooms also become aware of the sound. They listen tensely. Another car roars up to a screeching stop.* ANNE *and* PETER *come from* PETER'S *room.* MR. *and* MRS. VAN DAAN *creep down the stairs.* DUSSEL *comes out*

from his room. Everyone is listening, hardly breathing. A doorbell clangs again and again in the building below. MR. FRANK *starts quietly down the steps to the door.* DUSSEL *and* PETER *follow him. The others stand rigid, waiting, terrified.*

In a few seconds DUSSEL *comes stumbling back up the steps. He shakes off* PETER'S *help and goes to his room.* MR. FRANK *bolts the door below, and comes slowly back up the steps. Their eyes are all on him as he stands there for a minute. They realize that what they feared has happened.* MRS. VAN DAAN *starts to whimper.* MR. VAN DAAN *puts her gently in a chair, and then hurries off up the stairs to their room to collect their things.* PETER *goes to comfort his mother. There is a sound of violent pounding on a door below.*)

MR. FRANK. (*Quietly*) For the past two years we have lived in fear. Now we can live in hope.

(*The pounding below becomes more insistent. There are muffled sounds of voices, shouting commands.*)

MEN'S VOICES. *Auf machen! Da drinnen! Auf machen! Schnell! Schnell! Schnell! etc., etc.*[1]

(*The street door below is forced open. We hear the heavy tread of footsteps coming up.* MR. FRANK *gets two school bags from the shelves, and gives one to* ANNE, *and the other to* MARGOT. *He goes to get a bag for* MRS. FRANK. *The sound of feet coming up grows louder.* PETER *comes to* ANNE, *kissing her good-bye, then he goes to his room to collect his things. The buzzer of their door starts to ring.* MR. FRANK *brings* MRS. FRANK *a bag. They stand together, waiting. We hear the thud of gun butts on the door, trying to break it down.*)

ANNE *stands, holding her school satchel,*

---

1. The German may be translated as "Open up, you there inside! Open up! Fast! Fast! Fast!" Use of German indicates that this is a Gestapo raid.

looking over at her father and mother with a soft, reassuring smile. She is no longer a child, but a woman with courage to meet whatever lies ahead.

The lights dim out. The curtain falls on the scene. We hear a mighty crash as the door is shattered. After a second ANNE'S *voice is heard.*)

ANNE'S VOICE. And so it seems our stay here is over. They are waiting for us now. They've allowed us five minutes to get our things. We can each take a bag and whatever it will hold of clothing. Nothing else. So, dear Diary, that means I must leave you behind. Good-bye for a while. P.S. Please, please, Miep, or Mr. Kraler, or anyone else. If you should find this diary, will you please keep it safe for me, because some day I hope . . .

(*Her voice stops abruptly. There is silence. After a second the curtain rises.*)

SCENE V

It is again the afternoon in November, 1945. The rooms are as we saw them in the first scene. MR. KRALER *has joined* MIEP *and* MR. FRANK. *There are coffee cups on the table. We see a great change in* MR. FRANK. *He is calm now. His bitterness is gone. He slowly turns a few pages of the diary. They are blank.*

MR. FRANK. No more.

(*He closes the diary and puts it down on the couch beside him.*)

MIEP. I'd gone to the country to find food. When I got back the block was surrounded by police . . .

MR. KRALER. We made it our business to learn how they knew. It was the thief . . . the thief who told them.

(MIEP *goes up to the gas burner, bringing back a pot of coffee.*)

MR. FRANK. (*After a pause*) It seems strange to say this, that anyone could be happy in a concentration camp. But Anne was happy in the camp in Holland where they first took us. After two years of being shut up in these rooms, she could be out . . . out in the sunshine and the fresh air that she loved.

MIEP. (*Offering the coffee to* MR. FRANK) A little more?

MR. FRANK. (*Holding out his cup to her*) The news of the war was good. The British and Americans were sweeping through France. We felt sure that they would get to us in time. In September we were told that we were to be shipped to Poland . . . The men to one camp. The women to another. I was sent to Auschwitz. They went to Belsen. In January we were freed, the few of us who were left. The war wasn't yet over, so it took us a long time to get home. We'd be sent here and there behind the lines where we'd be safe. Each time our train would stop . . . at a siding, or a crossing . . . we'd all get out and go from group to group . . . Where were you? Were you at Belsen? At Buchenwald? At Mauthausen?[1] Is it possible that you knew my wife? Did you ever see my husband? My son? My daughter? That's how I found out about my wife's death . . . of Margot, the Van Daans . . . Dussel. But Anne . . . I still hoped . . . Yesterday I went to Rotterdam. I'd heard of a woman there . . . She'd been in Belsen with Anne . . . I know now.

(*He picks up the diary again, and turns the pages back to find a certain passage. As he finds it we hear* ANNE'S *voice.*)

ANNE'S VOICE. In spite of everything, I still believe that people are really good at heart.

(MR. FRANK *slowly closes the diary.*)

MR. FRANK. She puts me to shame.

(*They are silent.*)

The Curtain Falls

---

1. The places named are notorious concentration camps at which Jews were killed: **Auschwitz**\ˈaush-vĭts\ in southern Poland; **Belsen**\ˈbĕl·sən\ in southern Germany; **Buchenwald**\ˈbū·kən 'vald\ in central Germany; **Mauthausen**\ˈmaut 'hau·zən\ in Austria.

I

THE AFTERMATH

From Mr. Frank's words, we know that only he survived the horror of the concentration camp. Slowly the stories of the others came to light. Mrs. Frank gradually lost her mind, and near the end often hid bits of bread under her blanket to give to her husband. She died in January, 1945. Margot became increasingly frail, slipped into a coma, and in February died by falling out of bed. Anne became ill with typhus and died peacefully soon after Margot. Even at the end she felt that nothing bad was happening to her. Mr. Van Daan was gassed and his wife also died, though no details are known of her death. Peter was marched away by Hitler's troups as they fled before the Russian invasion and was never heard of again. Mr. Dussel died in another camp. And Mr. Frank survived because, just by chance, he was in the hospital when Auschwitz was captured by the Russians.

After the book was put into play form by Frances Goodrich and Albert Hackett, it was translated into German and opened simultaneously in seven German theaters. The impact on the German audience is described by Kenneth Tynan, a British theater critic:

"And at the Schlosspark last Monday I survived the most drastic emotional experience the theatre has ever given me. It had little to do with art, for the play was not a great one; yet its effect, in Berlin, at that moment of history, transcended anything that art has yet learned to achieve. It invaded the privacy of the whole audience: I tried hard to stay detached, but the general catharsis engulfed me. Like all great theatrical occasions, this was not only a theatrical occasion: it involved the world outside. The first page of the programme prepared one: a short, stark essay on collective guilt. Turn over for the title: *The Diary of Anne Frank*, directed by Boleslaw Barlog, *premiere* performance. It is not a vengeful dramatization. Quietly, often gaily, it re-creates the daily life of eight Jews who hid for two years in an Amsterdam attic before the Gestapo broke in. Otto Frank was the sole survivor: Anne was killed in Belsen.

"When I saw the play in New York, it vaguely perturbed me. There seemed no *need* to do it: it smacked of exploitation. The Berlin actors (especially Johanna von Koczian and Walter Franck) were better, on the whole, and devouter than the Americans, but I do not think that was why the play seemed so much more urgent and necessary on Monday night. After the interval the man in front of me put his head in his hands and did not afterwards look at the stage. He was not, I believe, Jewish. It was not until the end that one fully appreciated Barlog's wisdom and valour in using an entirely non-Jewish cast. Having read the last lines of the diary, which affirm, movingly and irrationally, Anne Frank's unshattered trust in human goodness, Otto Frank closes the book and says, very slowly: 'She puts me to shame.'

"Thus the play ended. The house-lights went up on an audience that sat drained and ashen, some staring straight ahead, others staring at the ground, for a full half-minute. Then, as if awakening from a nightmare, they rose and filed out in total silence, not looking at each other, avoiding even the customary nods of recognition with which friend greets friend. There was no applause, and there were no curtain-calls.

"All of this, I am well aware, is not drama criticism. In the shadow of an event so desperate and traumatic, criticism would be an irrelevance. I can only record an emotion that I felt, would not have missed, and pray never to feel again."

II

IMPLICATIONS

A. Look at the second scene where the group is coming together for the first time. Also look at the end of scene three where Mr. Dussel first arrives. At these moments, what is the attitude of one person toward another? What are their intentions toward one another? How do these intentions change in subsequent actions? What are the things over which they argue? Are they important or unimportant?

B. Read the following quotations carefully. Try and put in your own words the attitude of young people toward their parents which is expressed in each of the remarks. How typical are they of family life and your own reactions?

1. "Mother is unbearable. She insists on treating me like a baby which I loathe." (I,2, p. 202)

From "Curtains" by Kenneth Tynan. Copyright © 1961 by Kenneth Tynan. Reprinted by permission of Atheneum Publishers.

2. MR. VAN DAAN. "Haven't you finished yet?"
PETER. "No."
MR. VAN DAAN. "You ought to be ashamed of yourself."
PETER. "All right. All right. I'm a dunce. I'm a hopeless case. Why do I go on?"
(I,3, p. 206)

3. "Now, Peter, you listen to Mr. Frank."
(I,3, p. 206)

4. "Margot! Margot! Margot! That's all I hear from everyone . . . how wonderful Margot is . . . 'Why aren't you like Margot?' " (I,3, p. 208)

5. "Everything I do is wrong! I'm the goat around here!" . . . (I,3, p. 208)

6. "Whenever I try to explain my views on life to her she asks me if I'm constipated." (I,4, p. 215)

7. "You grownups have had your chance! But look at us. . . . It isn't our fault that the world is in such a mess! We weren't around when all this started! So don't try to take it out on us!" (II,1, p. 226)

8. "I suppose you can't really blame them . . . they think back to what they were like at our age. They don't realize how much more advanced we are. . . ." (II,2, p. 230)

C. Now read the following lines and decide what points of view the parents hold about their children. Once again try to express the parents' reactions in your own words. Do you think your own parents may share some of these feelings toward you?

1. "You complain that I don't treat you like a grownup. But when I do, you resent it." (I,3, p. 203)

2. "Don't you ever get tired of talking? Suppose you try keeping still for five minutes. Just five minutes." (I,3, p. 207)

3. "The trouble with you is, you've been spoiled." (I,3, p. 207)

4. "Watch Margot. She's always courteous with them. Never familiar. She keeps her distance. And they respect her for it. Try to be like Margot." (I,3, p. 208)

5. "She wants nothing of me. She pulled away when I leaned down to kiss her." (I,4, p. 215)

6. "There is so little that we parents can do to help our children. We can only try to set a good example . . . point the way. The rest you must do yourself." (I,4, p. 215)

7. "I only wish that you wouldn't expose yourself to criticism." (II,2, p. 229)

8. "I don't know what good it is to have a son. I never see him." (II,2, p. 230)

D. The remarks that characters make in a play often cause the reader to think about himself and his own values. Thus, lines may do two jobs: They help the progress of the immediate action on the stage; they force the reader to do some thinking on his own.

Select one of the following quotations and be prepared to present your opinion of the ideas presented in the lines. You may agree or disagree.

1. "There are no walls, there are no bolts, no locks that anyone can put on your mind." (I,2, p. 200)

2. "I can stand off and look at myself doing it and know it's cruel and yet I can't stop doing it. What's the matter with me?" (I,4, p. 215)

3. "If we begin thinking of all the horror in the world, we're lost! We're trying to hold onto some kind of ideals." (II,1, p. 226)

4. "It's easier. A fight starts, or an argument . . . I duck in here." (II,1, p. 227)

5. "We don't need the Nazis to destroy us. We're destroying ourselves." (II,3, p. 235)

6. "I think the world may be going through a phase, the way I was with Mother. It'll pass, maybe not for hundreds of years, but some day. . . ." (II,4, p. 239)

7. "In spite of everything, I still believe that people are really good at heart." (II,5, p. 241)

III
TECHNIQUES

Characterization

A. You have learned that characters are revealed to the reader through what they do, what they say, and what others say about them. What specific lines or incidents show the following traits about the characters:

1. That Mrs. Van Daan is vain.
   That she is shallow.
   That she is selfish.

2. Anne:
   That she is talkative.
   That she is sentimental
   That she is bright.
   That she is sensitive.

That she is a tease.

That she is enthusiastic.

3. Peter:

That he is unsocial.

That he is easily embarrassed.

That he is an average student.

That he is lonely.

B. If you were to rate the general strength of character of Mr. Frank, Mrs. Frank, Mr. Van Daan, Mrs. Van Daan, and Dussel, how would you rank them? What is the evidence for your ranking?

C. If you were to judge the relative intelligence of the three children, Peter, Anne, and Margot, how would you rank them? What in the play did you use as the basis for your judgment?

D. In real life, Mrs. Frank became insane after being sent to the concentration camp. Are there any indications in the play that this could happen to her? In actual life, Margot became increasingly frail and sickly. She died falling out of bed. What details in the play indicate this possibility?

Plot

A. Discuss whether you feel the first and last scenes are basically necessary to the impact of the play on the audience.

B. What devices are used to let the audience know the passage of time in the play? How effective would it have been if the dates of the scenes had simply been printed in the programs as is done in most dramas?

C. This play consists mainly of isolated happenings that occur over a period of two years. What is the thread that holds these isolated incidents together like beads of a necklace? In other words, how has the author made a plot out of a series of incidents?

D. Louis Kronenberger's review of the play said that it was a "weird blend of the brightly ordinary, the hideously abnormal, of comic fault finding, and heroic adjustment." Take these four aspects and list under each one the incidents that illustrate it.

Symbol

A. Sometimes an object may be a very personal symbol to an individual; that is, it takes on a greater significance than it normally merits. What does:

1. The fur coat mean to Mrs. Van Daan?

2. The cat mean to Peter?

3. The diary mean to Anne?

B. A whole work of literature may stand as a symbol of a truth in human life. This is particularly true with *The Diary of Anne Frank*. You have read of the impact it had on the German audience. What do you think the play symbolized to the Germans sitting in the theater that night? In what way might it have meant something different to an American audience?

IV

WORDS

A. The environment of a word, what is said before and after an unfamiliar word, helps to suggest a general meaning. Grammatical construction—coordination, subordination, parallelism, apposition—further aids in determining meaning. Word analysis is yet another tool. Determine as much as you can of the meaning of the following words. Which clue helped the most: connection of the word to the context, grammatical construction, modifiers, word analysis?

carillon (p. 193), *compassionate* (p. 194), *capitulation* (p. 195), *conspicuous* (p. 195), *unabashed* (p. 199), *intolerable* (p. 204), *subjunctive* (p. 205), *meticulous* (p. 210), *humiliated* (p. 211), *fatalist* (p. 216), *improvised* (p. 217), *jubilation* (p. 219), *appalled silence* (p. 221), *foreboding* (p. 225), *intuition* (p. 229), *indignant* (p. 230), *pandemonium* (p. 236), *convulsive* (p. 236).

B. 1. Three-form roots also include *-leg-*, as in *legible* or *legend; -lig-*, as in *eligible* or *negligent;* and *-lect-*, as in *select* or *elect*. This root means "choose, choose to read, read." Similar is the three-form root *-reg-*, as in *regent* or *regal; -rig-*, as in *incorrigible;* and *-rect-*, as in *correct* or *rectangle*. It means "to rule," "to rule rightly," "right, straight, correct." The root meaning "to look, view, see" also appears in English in three forms: *-spec-*, as in *specimen; -spic-*, as in *conspicuous* ("compelling one to look at"); and *-spect-*, as in *inspect* or *suspect*.

2. There is no fixed number of forms a given Latin root may eventually show in English. There are two important Latin roots showing four forms in English. One is the Latin root meaning "to make, accomplish, perform, or do," which we sometimes have as *-fac-*, as in *facile; -fact-*, as in *factory* or *manufacture; -fect-,* as in *effective* or *defective;* and *-fic-,* as in *deficient* or *efficiency.* A great many English words employ this root. Make a list of as many as you can find. Another root with four forms in English is one meaning "to take, seize, capture": *-cap-,* as in *capacity; -capt-,* as in *captive; -cept-,* as in *reception;* and *-cip-,* as in *recipient.* Like the root for "to make or do," this root yields a great many words in English. Make up a list of as many as you can think of.

BIOGRAPHICAL NOTES

Gina Berriault

Gina Berriault has published several novels, among them *The Son, The Descent* (1960), and *Conference of Victims* (1962). Her stories have won the Aga Khan Fiction Award and three O'Henry Awards. They have appeared in periodicals such as *Esquire, Harper's Bazaar, Saturday Evening Post* and *Contact.* Married, she now lives in California.

D. H. Lawrence

D. H. Lawrence (1885–1930) is considered by some critics as one of the most powerful of modern English novelists. He was born in Nottinghamshire and educated at both the high school and the University of Nottingham. He published his first book in 1911. His writing is sometimes classified as psychological, but he showed spiritual insight and great artistic power in his descriptions, both of scenery and people. *Sons and Lovers* and *Lady Chatterly's Lover* are two of his best known works.

O. Henry

O. Henry (William Sidney Porter) (1862–1910) was an American short-story writer who developed the device of the "surprise ending." Born in North Carolina, he went to Texas in his youth where he worked as ranch hand, bank clerk, and newspaper reporter. Indicted and convicted of embezzling bank funds, he served three years in prison. He was given a job as night druggist in the prison hospital so that he could write short stories to support his daughter Margaret. He emerged from

prison as O. Henry, a pseudonym he may have taken from the name of a guard in the penitentiary. He then went to New York, and often roamed about the streets looking for material. He wrote about a story a week and his unexpected endings, his good humor, and the plainness and simpleness of his characters and plots made his work popular.

Edward Newhouse

Edward Newhouse (1911–), born in Budapest, is an author of both novels and short stories. *You Can't Sleep Here* (1934) and *The Hollow of the Wave* (1949) are two of his novels. A collection of his short stories, *Anything Can Happen,* was published in 1941, and another, *Many Are Called,* was brought out in 1951. The latter collection consisted of forty-two stories, thirty-nine of which first appeared in *The New Yorker.* One reviewer commented that Newhouse has a talent for portraiture and story telling and that his stories clearly and completely represent what has been termed *The New Yorker* story. That type of story is usually filled with local color and deals generally with urban or suburban characters and settings.

Stephen Spender

Stephen Spender (1909–), born in London, England, supported himself in his teens by printing labels on his hand press, later going on to print entire books for friends. While attending Oxford University from 1928–30, Spender, along with W. H. Auden, Louis MacNeice, and C. Day Lewis, formed the Oxford Group which had a tremendous influence on poetry and poetics. Spender was probably the most romantic and lyrical of the group. Supporting himself by editing, teaching, and lecturing, Spender wrote not only poems, but autobiographies, dramas, and critical essays. He recently told an American audience that American poetry today is more interesting than contemporary British poetry.

Robert Hayden

Robert Hayden (1913–), rejecting the label "Negro poet," attempts in his poetry, through his direct observations and responses, to capture common human experiences, not necessarily only the black experience. But his works cannot escape the history and folklore of his race which filter through his works. Born in Detroit, Michigan, Hayden graduated from Wayne State University and then went on to the University of Michigan, where he received an M.A. and taught from 1944–46. Since then he has been a Professor of English at Fisk University and has not only won honors and awards for his poetry, but has also written plays and radio scripts.

Ray Bradbury

Ray Bradbury (1920–   ), born in Waukegan, Illinois, moved with his family to California when he was in his early teens. While still in high school he wrote science-fiction stories for his own magazine, *Futuria Fantasia,* which ran for four issues. One of his favorite subjects is the clash between society and the individual in an overdeveloped civilization. Bradbury states that "Science fiction is really sociological studies of the future; things that the writer believes are going to happen by putting two and two together. Fantasy fiction is the improbable. If you had a leprechaun or a dinosaur appearing in the streets of New York—that's highly improbable. But science fiction is a logical mathematical projection of reality." Since 1947, he has written almost two dozen books. Some of his most popular works are: *Martian Chronicles* (1950), *Fahrenheit 451* (1953), *Switch on the Night* (1955), *A Medicine for Melancholy* (1959), *Something Wicked This Way Comes* (1962).

PRIVATE MOODS

For everything there is a season, and a time for everything under heaven:
> a time to be born, and a time to die;
> a time to plant, and a time to pluck up what is planted;
> a time to kill, and a time to bear;
> a time to break down, and a time to build up;
> a time to weep, and a time to laugh;
> a time to mourn, and a time to dance;
> a time to cast away stones, and a time to gather stones together;
> a time to embrace, and a time to refrain from embracing;
> a time to seek, and a time to lose;
> a time to keep, and a time to cast away;
> a time to rend, and a time to sew;
> a time to keep silence, and a time to speak;
> a time to love, and a time to hate;
> a time for war, and a time for peace.
> ECCLESIASTES 3:1–8 (Revised Standard Version of the Bible)

An ancient Hebrew writer saw the diversity of experiences and the complexity of feelings that all men undergo. He saw that life is not only a matter of actions, but it is also a matter of feelings that no man can escape. Sorrow and delight, hatred and love, desire and regret—each in its own time sweeps over man.

Private and personal because they are experienced inwardly, moods are like transparent color flooding the mind. They color the picture of the world that the senses transmit. Sometimes they may last for a long time; sometimes they are momentary flashes; but they are never long absent. The poetry in this unit examines and evokes many of man's most characteristic moods.

Of all the kinds of writing, lyric poetry is especially concerned with a man's personal emotions—his private moods. Like all people, the poet experiences the sights, sounds, smells, tastes, and touches common to all—train whistles, waves slapping the shore, houses at night, oak trees, freshly ground coffee, sharp winds, the ping of an ice cream vendor's bell. But unlike most people, his reactions to such common experiences are extraordinary, often profound, always intense. He sees far deeper and his experiences mean far more to him than similar experiences mean to most people.

Through vivid language the lyric poet attempts to recreate his personal experience. He crystallizes little bits of life that are exciting, beautiful, or memorable. The reader, by sharing these moments of the poet, adds to his own fund of experiences and broadens his sense of life. In his peculiar way the poet reminds us of things we know but did not realize we knew. He makes us say, "Yes, I have felt that way, but I did not understand the meaning or depth of that feeling." Or, "I have seen that, but now I really understand what I saw." In this way poetry adds to the richness of our own private moods.

To begin to grasp even a portion of this richness, you must read more intently than when skimming a newspaper or studying a textbook. For the poet compresses his experience into a unique fusion of words, images, and rhythms. In order to share the experience the reader must follow closely the meaning of the words, hear their sounds, imagine the sensations and comparisons, and feel the rhythm of the lines. The study notes in PRIVATE MOODS help you take up these important considerations systematically. These aids, if followed, give you a method of reading that will increase your understanding and hence your enjoyment of private moods.

The Cry
Edvard Munch.
National Gallery of Art,
Washington, D.C.,
Rosenwald Collection.
The emotional impact of
The Cry *vividly states the*
power of private moods.

RESTLESSNESS No one is ever quite content. The worlds beyond the horizons always seem to promise something strange, new, exotic. Jet streams across the sky lead the imagination. Magazine pictures of foreign countries suggest a more exciting life than one knows. Even maps lure the mind and make one discontent with his present state. Restlessness is a confusing, cloudy emotion that one is never really without.

Have you ever yearned to be free
from cares, duties, and social restrictions
and yet could not follow the restless urgings of your heart?
If you have, perhaps you too know
"what the caged bird feels."

Sympathy

I know what the caged bird feels, alas!
   When the sun is bright on the upland slopes;
When the wind stirs soft through the springing grass,
And the river flows like a stream of glass;
   When the first bird sings and the first bud opes,   5
And the faint perfume from its chalice steals—
I know what the caged bird feels!

I know why the caged bird beats his wing
   Till its blood is red on the cruel bars;
For he must fly back to his perch and cling   10
When he fain would be on the bough a-swing;
   And a pain still throbs in the old, old scars
And they pulse again with a keener sting—
I know why he beats his wing!

I know why the caged bird sings, ah me,   15
   When his wing is bruised and his bosom sore,—
When he beats his bars and he would be free;
It is not a carol of joy or glee,
   But a prayer that he sends from his heart's deep core,
But a plea, that upward to Heaven he flings—   20
I know why the caged bird sings!

PAUL LAURENCE DUNBAR

Reprinted by permission of Dodd, Mead & Company from *The Complete Poems of Paul Laurence Dunbar.*

Restlessness begins with a sickness of the heart,
   a yearning to break with the old patterns.

Spring

I said in my heart, "I am sick of four walls and a ceiling.
I have need of the sky.
I have business with the grass.
I will up and get me away where the hawk is wheeling,
Lone and high,
And the slow clouds go by . . ."

RICHARD HOVEY

The restless heart often turns to travel
   as the best means for easing its discontent.

Travel

The railroad track is miles away,
   And the day is loud with voices speaking,
Yet there isn't a train goes by all day
   But I hear its whistle shrieking.

All night there isn't a train goes by,   5
   Though the night is still for sleep and dreaming,
But I see its cinders red on the sky,
   And hear its engine steaming.[1]

My heart is warm with the friends I make,
   And better friends I'll not be knowing,   10
Yet there isn't a train I wouldn't take,
   No matter where it's going.

EDNA ST. VINCENT MILLAY

Reprinted by permission of Dodd, Mead & Company from *Poems* by Richard Hovey.

Copyright 1917, 1921, 1945, 1948 by Edna St. Vincent Millay. Reprinted by permission of Norma Millay Ellis.

1. The reference is to the old coal-burning, steam-driven locomotive.

For centuries the sea has called many men.
In Masefield's "Sea Fever"
the longing for the sea is tinged with melancholy
and loneliness.

Sea Fever

I must go down to the seas again, to the lonely sea and the sky,
And all I ask is a tall ship and a star to steer her by,
And the wheel's kick and the wind's song and the white sail's shaking,
And a gray mist on the sea's face and a gray dawn breaking.

I must down to the seas again, for the call of the running tide   5
Is a wild call and a clear call that may not be denied;
And all I ask is a windy day with the white clouds flying,
And the flung spray and the blown spume,[1] and the seagulls crying.

I must down to the seas again to the vagrant gypsy life.
To the gull's way and the whale's way where the wind's like a whetted[2] knife: 10
And all I ask is a merry yarn from a laughing fellow rover,
And quiet sleep and a sweet dream when the long trick's[3] over.

JOHN MASEFIELD

Should one fight against
the inner restlessness
that makes one dissatisfied?

Ride
a Wild Horse

Ride a wild horse
with purple wings
striped yellow and black
except his head
which must be red.   5

Ride a wild horse
against the sky—
hold tight to his wings

before you die
whatever else you leave undone—   10
once ride a wild horse
into the sun.

HANNAH KAHN

1. **spume**\spyūm\ ocean foam or spray.
2. **whet**\wĕt\ sharpen.
3. **trick**, tour of duty.

When you are caught in heavy traffic there is little you can do to speed your way home. Yet what is the need that compels you to fight this situation?

Highway: Michigan

Here from the field's edge we survey
The progress of the jaded. Mile
On mile of traffic from the town
Rides by, for at the end of day
The time of workers is their own.   5

They jockey for position on
The strip reserved for passing only.
The drivers from production lines
Hold to advantage dearly won.
They toy with death and traffic fines.   10

Acceleration is their need:
A mania keeps them on the move
Until the toughest nerves are frayed.
They are the prisoners of speed
Who flee in what their hands have made.   15

The pavement smokes when two cars meet
And steel rips through conflicting steel.
We shiver at the siren's blast.
One driver, pinned beneath the seat,
Escapes from the machine at last.   20

THEODORE ROETHKE

Feeling restless, with a need to be doing something?
A parked car can be an invitation to excitement and
the ultimate in danger.

Death Is a Beautiful
Car Parked Only

For Emmett

Death is a beautiful car parked only
to be stolen on a street lined with trees
whose branches are like the intestines
   of an emerald.

You hotwire death, get in, and drive away   5
like a flag made from a thousand burning
   funeral parlors.

You have stolen death because you're bored.
There's nothing good playing at the movies
   in San Francisco.   10

You joyride around for a while listening
to the radio, and then abandon death, walk
away, and leave death for the police
   to find.

RICHARD BRAUTIGAN

There are many dreams that lure man
from the beaten track. All of them have been given
the generalized name of "Eldorado," a city or country
which is beautiful and elusive.

Eldorado

Gaily bedight,[1]
A gallant knight,
In sunshine and in shadow,
Had journeyed long,
Singing a song,   5
In search of Eldorado.[2]

But he grew old—
This knight so bold—
And o'er his heart a shadow
Fell as he found   10
No spot of ground
That looked like Eldorado.

And, as his strength
Failed him at length,
He met a pilgrim shadow—   15
"Shadow," said he,
"Where can it be—
This land of Eldorado?"

"Over the Mountains
Of the Moon,   20
Down the Valley of the Shadow,
Ride, boldly, ride,"
The Shade replied—
"If you seek for Eldorado!"

EDGAR ALLAN POE

1. **bedight**\bē ᴬdait\ costumed and equipped.
2. **Eldorado** may be translated as "the golden land."
In other uses, the pronunciation \'ĕl·də ᴬrā·dō\ may be
found, but Poe's rhyme calls for \'ĕl·də ᴬrā·dō\.

UNDERSTANDING POETRY

Titles Are Important

A well-chosen title is often an important key to understanding a piece of writing, and it is especially useful for reading poetry. A title usually tells the reader what the poem is about by naming the poem's subject. This John Masefield does with the title "Sea Fever." His title tells that the poem is about a kind of sickness, an abnormal state, caused by or somehow related to the sea. Often, too, a title suggests the poem's theme, or meaning. In the title "Eldorado," Poe not only tells the reader that, in some fashion, his poem deals with the subject of impossible dreams but at the same time partly suggests the theme or meaning of the poem: the attitude that, in spite of the futility of chasing "pipe dreams," man cannot resist the hopeless pursuit.

Titles are so obvious that one often overlooks them. Always ask yourself how the title is related to the subject matter and theme of the poem.

TECHNIQUES

Rhythm

In normal English speech, some words and syllables are stressed and some are not (to-mór-row). This fact makes it possible to establish a beat with the sounds of words. As in music, recurrent beat forms a rhythm (tomórrow and tomórrow and tomórrow). In poetry the basic rhythms (measures, or meters) result from the repetition of regular patterns of accented and unaccented syllables.

Rhythm is not something artificially imposed upon a poem; it grows out of the ideas and feelings expressed in the poem and, ideally, complements them perfectly. Indeed, rhythm is one of the poet's chief means for intensifying a mood and reinforcing the reader's emotions. And just as the background music of a movie or a TV play changes as the action shifts from a gun battle to a love scene, so the rhythm of a poem fits the mood: now slow and sad, now fast and gay, now strong and triumphant.

The most natural and hence most frequently used rhythmic pattern in English poetry is the iambic. An iambic *foot* (a foot is the single unit of the stress pattern which when repeated forms a pattern—the rhythm) is composed of an unaccented followed by an accented syllable (de-light). Of the poems included in this section of the unit, "Travel" and "Ride a Wild Horse" are basically iambic. But a quick reading of these poems reveals that even within a single poem a poet rarely uses just one type of foot. Frequently, he substitutes other feet for the sake of variety, emphasis, or feeling. A most common substitution is the trochaic foot—an accented syllable followed by an unaccented (ox en). Note that Hanna Kahn's trochee which opens "Ride a Wild Horse" emphasizes the forceful call to action. Used by itself, the trochaic rhythm suits light, gay poems and songs. When used to excess, however, its strong rocking rhythm becomes "singsong" and hence more appropriate for nursery rhymes than for serious poetry. The spondee and the pyrrhic are two other substitutes for the iambic, although unlike the trochee, neither is often sustained for more than a few syllables. The spondee is composed of two accented syllables (great hall). It tends to be slow and heavy and therefore gives greater force, importance or solemnity to the rhythm. The pyrrhic, on the other hand, is composed of two unaccented syllables (and a) and hence is quick and light. In an unusual piling up of alternating pyrrhics and spondees, John Masefield reproduces the relentless, forceful surging of wave on wave.

And the / wheel's kick / and the / wind's song /
  and the / white sail's / shak ing,
And a / gray mist / on the / sea's face / and the
  / gray dawn / break ing

Two other basic feet are the anapest and the dactyl. Although both may be used alone (like the iambic and the trochaic), they occur infrequently in English poetry. The anapest (two unaccented, one accented—"to the hills") gives swiftness and emphasizes the last word in the line.

Like a child / from the womb, / like a ghost /
  from the tomb,
I arise / and unbuild / it again.
                              "The Cloud" . . . Shelley

The dactyl (one accented, two unaccented) has a stately, even grand, movement but is seldom consistently written because it becomes monotonous.

Ye who be/lieve in af/fection that / hopes, and
  en/dures, and is / patient,
Ye who be/lieve in the / beauty and / strength
  of / woman's de/votion.
                              "Evangeline" . . . Longfellow

The quantity, or length, of a line is also an important factor in determining the rhythm of a poem. The line is measured by the number of feet it contains. A line with one foot is called *monometer;* two feet, *dimeter;* three feet, *trimeter;* four feet, *tetrameter;* five feet, *pentameter;* six feet, *hexameter.* The basic rhythm of a poem is described in terms of the predominant foot and the number of feet per line.

To discover the rhythm of a poem, read the poem aloud several times. Let your ear rather than your eye determine the pattern.

In this section, what kind of basic rhythm does each poem have? Can you explain why poems about restlessness should frequently employ unusual rhythms?

Rhyme

A poet may use many devices to vary his basic rhythm. The one most people associate exclusively with poetry is rhyme: the patterned repetition and variation of similar sounds. Rhyme serves two purposes: it delights the ear and it emphasizes the rhythm of a stanza. In this way rhyme identifies and sets off individual stanzas as separate sound and thought units.

Masculine rhymes are those that rhyme the final accented syllable of two or more lines, as "sky" and "by" in lines 1 and 2 of "Sea Fever." Feminine rhymes are those in which the last two syllables of two or more lines rhyme; the first syllable is accented and the second is unaccented, as "shrieking" and "squeaking." Masculine rhymes end a line with force, giving a feeling of completeness. Feminine rhymes leave the rhythm "hanging," wanting to move on, and give a feeling of incompleteness. How many of the poems in this section use feminine rhymes? Can you show why poems about restlessness should use such rhymes?

Sympathy

1. What specific experiences awaken the bird's restlessness? Why should they be so provocative?

2. Why does the caged bird sing? What perhaps has the poet experienced to give him such sympathy for the bird?

Spring

1. What does the title "Spring" have to do with the poet's sickness?

2. Why are the lines so uneven in length?

3. Why does the pace of the poem slow down in the last two lines?

Travel

1. What is the progression of restlessness that the poet develops in each stanza?

2. What aspect of the train is suggested by the use of feminine rhymes such as *squeaking* and *shrieking*?

3. Does the poet ever reveal the source of her discontent?

Sea Fever

1. What unpleasant memories do the details of sea life suggest? What pleasant memories? Can people long for things physically difficult and unpleasant?

2. What quality of sound do the long line and the use of many long vowel sounds give the poem?

3. To what effect does the poet use masculine and feminine rhymes?

Ride a Wild Horse

1. Here the poet has used a symbol to suggest her meaning. She is thinking of Pegasus, the winged horse of mythology, that has long represented man's flight of fancy. Why does she color him so startlingly?

2. What does she imply man's reactions should be to his inner desires?

Highway: Michigan

1. Do you agree with Roethke that the riders in the cars are jaded . . . that they jockey for position on the highway . . . that they toy with death . . . that speed satisfies a need?

2. Describe the incident in the last stanza.

Death Is a Beautiful Car Parked Only

1. What does the title mean to you?

2. Why is the car stolen? Is this a usual reason for this act?

3. Contemporary poetry often startles the reader by strange combinations of ideas. Pick out one such combination from the poem.

Eldorado

1. Does the poet consider the search for Eldorado rewarding or futile?

2. What does the rhythm and the haunting repetition of the word *Eldorado* suggest?

IMPLICATIONS

A. In terms of the different ideas presented about human restlessness in this group of poems, what is your reaction to the following statements:

1. No man is ever completely content with his own present situation.

2. Without restlessness, man would never progress.

3. When men feel restless they never really know exactly what it is that would satisfy their longing.

B. Skim back over the group of poems and answer the following questions:

1. What kinds of experiences are mentioned that bring on restlessness?

2. What seems to be the attitude toward giving in to restlessness and following a whim? Do you agree or disagree?

3. Do the poems suggest that man ever finds the thing he seeks?

4. Which poems suggest and how do they suggest that the search is almost more important than the goal?

FEAR Men hide some emotions in secret places, ashamed to admit that they possess them. Fear is such a black sheep. Still, fear is often basic to life itself, clueing one to retreat from danger; yet, at other times, fear is foolish . . . the result of ignorance and superstition. The baby is afraid of loud noises and of falling. The child may fear water, snakes, strangers, the dark. The adolescent may fear being alone, being different, or being ridiculed. And the adult may fear marrying unhappily, bungling his job, losing his youth.

The sensations of fear, ill-founded, come slowly and mount in intensity.

Country Night

She lived in terror of the country night;
As soon as afternoon began to fade
She went about the house, lit every light,
Bolted the doors, and drew every window-shade.

The house was like a ship that slowly listed,[1]   5
The night was water, and it seemed to her
It rose relentlessly and unresisted,
Inevitable, black, and sinister.

The little liquid noises that she heard
Were friendly and familiar things by day: 10
Tree and insect, flower and grass and bird,
Nothing at all to frighten her this way—
But still the night rose higher, till it found
Her tense and quivering and almost drowned.

SELMA ROBINSON

1. **list,** to lean to one side.

Reprinted by permission; Copr. © 1931, 1959 The New Yorker Magazine, Inc.

Often there is nothing reasonable about fear.
What one does to escape it
is usually ridiculous and irrational.

House Fear

Always—I tell you this they learned—
Always at night when they returned
To the lonely house from far away,
To lamps unlighted and fire gone gray,
They learned to rattle the lock and key   5
To give whatever might chance to be,
Warning and time to be off in flight:
And preferring the out- to the indoor night,
They learned to leave the house door wide
Until they had lit the lamp inside.   10

ROBERT FROST

Sometimes the openness of the out-of-doors
seems to offer escape . . . a feeling
that makes indoor darkness even more terrifying.
And sometimes the indoors seems a haven
into which mysterious and frightening things
try to force their way.

The Oft-Repeated Dream

She had no saying dark enough
For the dark pine that kept
Forever trying the window-latch
Of the room where they slept.

The tireless but ineffectual hands   5
That with every futile pass
Made the great tree seem as a little bird
Before the mystery of glass!

It never had been inside the room,
And only one of the two   10
Was afraid in an oft-repeated dream
Of what the tree might do.

ROBERT FROST

What are the defenses against fear?
When it finally pushes one into a corner,
when it has to be faced, how does one react?

The Lady

The candle is out,
it has crashed to the floor,
she follows the wall
to find the door.

Her petticoats hiss   5
with a hiss of fear,
a path of sound
for a sensitive ear.

When she puts out her hand,
her breath gives a catch,   10
fingers are there
instead of a latch!

When she reaches back
lest she should fall,
a body is there   15
instead of a wall!

What use to scream
so sole alone,
what use to struggle
against the unknown?   20

"Very well," she said
imperiously,
"Pray light the sconces[1]
so we may see.

"Here are my pearls,   25
And here are my rings.
And take off your hats,
you filthy things!"

ELIZABETH COATSWORTH

1. **sconce**\skŏns\ a candle holder, a candle in its holder.

The compression of poetry makes it possible to suggest more than is actually said. A few words, well selected and arranged, can produce a sudden, inexplicable shudder of fear.

The Warning

Just now,
Out of the strange
Still dusk . . . as strange, as still . . .
A white moth flew. Why am I grown
So cold?

ADELAIDE CRAPSEY

When I Have Fears That I May Cease To Be

Fear may be a more diffuse emotion as well, not just a sudden physical response to an immediate situation. It may be a haunting, continuing thing.

When I have fears that I may cease to be
Before my pen has gleaned my teeming brain,
Before high-pilèd books, in charact'ry,[1]
Hold like rich garners the full-ripened grain;
When I behold, upon the night's starred face,   5
Huge cloudy symbols of a high romance,
And think that I may never live to trace
Their shadows, with the magic hand of chance;
And when I feel, fair creature of an hour!
That I shall never look upon thee more   10
Never have relish in the faery[2] power
Of unreflecting love—then on the shore
Of the wide world I stand alone, and think,
Till Love and Fame to nothingness do sink.

JOHN KEATS

1. **charact'ry**\ˈkă·rək·trē\ **charactery,** writing, written characters.
2. **faery**\ˈfā·rē\ a by-form of **fairy,** but the word here as in other older writing is stronger than its modern meanings. It may be interpreted as meaning "showing awesome supernatural strength."

When imagined fear runs out of control . . .

The Panther Possible

The old man's words (Something has skittered the cattle
    or else it's to rain hard—storm—tonight)
That, and the tale of someone coming upon
    a Mexican lion that didn't take fright
but looked up from the calf it ate   5
    and made a horrible rosin-rub
        of sound in its throat, laid its ears flat,
        and walked off stiffly in the scrub.

And the man who got his tractor to see what that was
    of heavy shape and sound in the prickly pear—   10
who found huge prints and suffered the white fangs
    of a hidden explodable stare—
who hurried back to mount
    the tractor, found it wouldn't start,
        and had to walk five miles in dark   15
        with padding steps timed to his heart—

Was it a wonder the boy heard the panther scream
    in the chaparral[1] (how do you tell for certain?)
a wonder his nose began to itch and his right eye water
    (it always did when he was scared)? What's the hurt in 20
achieving a fear of panthers, pure
    or imaginary? Wasn't his nose
        made itchable? What's a dry eye worth
        compared with one that, stricken, glows?

WILLIAM D. BARNEY

---

1. **chaparral**\ᵃchăp·ə·răl\ a dense thicket of shrubs or dwarf trees.

By permission of August Derleth.

It almost seems that people enjoy having their fears stimulated by strange, eerie places.

Suicide Pond

It lay, dark in the corner of the field,
Deep and unclouded, like a devil's well,
The dank fern gathered round it in great clumps;
All the wild air was heavy with the smell
Of tansy;[1] and it had the awful look   5
Of hidden and forbidden water. When
The seasons changed and winter dropped its cloud,
It did not dream in silver, but this fen
Remained a black hole gaping in the snow.
No stream led out of it, no stream led in;   10
No stars reflected in it; rumor said
Men plunged into its cold and took their sin,
Downing it with clenched hands and blinded eyes,
Far down the pitted water; and, alone
And trembling, we, when young, looked down and saw 15
Grim suicides in bottom-rock and stone.

KATHY McLAUGHLIN

---

1. **tansy**\ˈtăn·zē\ an herb with an aromatic odor and a bitter taste.

UNDERSTANDING POETRY

Locating the Subject

The meaning of a poem often hinges upon the accurate perception of the poem's subject matter. As noted previously, titles usually help to define what a poet is talking about. Still, there are times when the title simply names the thing, person, memory, or idea which caused the poet to ponder some deeper subject. In the set of poems here, what is the real subject of Keats' poem? Is it really about fear, or is fear only part of the universal problem concerning the conflict between man's desire for fulfillment and permanence, and the world's frustration and brevity?

TECHNIQUES

Simile, the Stated Comparison

In the second stanza of "Country Night," Selma Robinson states, "The house was like a ship that slowly listed." Through this comparison the reader can share the woman's fear-caused sensations. The house takes on the qualities of a ship on a rolling sea. The woman is so upset mentally and physically that the house seems to rock beneath her just as a ship at sea rises and falls with each swell. Poets often make statements and convey ideas and sensations through comparison. Stated comparisons indicated by *like* or *as* are called "similes." They are essential to poetry, for through them the poet is able to convey what is unfamiliar to the reader in terms of something familiar. The study questions (below) call your attention to several more similes.

Country Night

1. What precautions did the woman take against the night? Explain why they were rational or irrational.

2. How does the simile in the second stanza show the extent and nature of her fear?

House Fear

1. Is Frost's poem humorous or serious?

2. Are the actions described familiar or strange?

The Oft-Repeated Dream

1. How is the title related to the subject and meaning of the poem?

2. How does the simile in the second stanza point up the foolishness of her fear?

The Lady

1. In what ways does the poem show the woman to be "a lady"?

2. What effect is achieved by the short lines?

The Warning

1. The poem is a "cinquain," a name for a five-line poem. Notice that the first line has one stress; the second, two; the third, three; the fourth, four; and the last line, one. What effect does this rhythm have on the reader?

2. What reaction to fear is suggested in these few lines?

When I Have Fears That I May Cease To Be

1. How are Keats' fears similar to those that most people have about life?

2. Explain the simile in line four; how does it make his fears more urgent?

The Panther Possible

1. What are the stories told about the mountain lion?

2. Is the panther that frightens the boy real or imagined?

Suicide Pond

1. How important is the title to the poem?

2. What qualities about the pond make it seem a fearful place?

IMPLICATIONS

The following statements are matters of opinion. Think back over the poems that present man and his fears. What then are your reactions to the following propositions:

1. The earlier poems in this section deal with the unreasoning, panicky fear triggered by a moment. Keats is speaking of a fear that comes from unsureness of life in general. The second kind of fear is less dramatic but a more devastating fear to have.

2. Each person fears his "unknown." The things with which he is familiar hold no fears.

3. The real roots of fear lie deep in each person's insecurities.

4. Fear is an emotion that eventually kills the adventurous spirit.

PRIVATE MOODS

To explore the depths of our deepest emotions and to understand their intensity are the unfailing challenges accepted by storyteller and poet, theologian and psychologist, sculptor and painter. The painter, like the writer, makes his statements about the mysteries of private moods in several ways: he may record every detail he can to hold the mood in place for you to see it too; he may put down only those details which contribute to a particular view so that you see through his eyes some quality that might otherwise be overlooked; or he may speak in a kind of cryptograph, putting together bits and pieces that seem very unrelated so that you must work with him in solving the problem of a highly individual view of life.

In this gallery there is a wide range of private moods and artists' statements about them. The notes will guide you somewhat, but the real work of understanding is a private matter you must do alone.

Van Gogh knew much about despair, and this painting is edged with the strong line of his intense sympathy.

DESPAIR
Vincent Van Gogh

THE FOLLY OF FEAR
Francisco Goya
National Gallery of Art, Washington, D.C.,
Rosenwald Collection

The magnificent Spanish printmaker
Goya explored many human emotions,
both public and private,
and was often disgusted
with what he saw. In his prints
the cruelty, the pettiness,
the utter stupidity of mankind
is thoroughly exposed.
Notice the small face at the end
of the specter's arm. Could it suggest
the unreality of the great figure
which has terrified the foolish men?

The modern painter Vickrey
deals in symbols. What private mood
is indicated by a child's game played
over a tension-filled pattern
on an empty road leading nowhere?

HOPSCOTCH   *Robert Vickrey*

THE SUBWAY *George Tooker*
1950, Egg Tempera on composition
board, Collection of the Whitney
Museum of American Art, New York

The cold efficiency of a city subway disturbs many observers.
But few have made as pointed a statement about it
as the painter Tooker. His is a lonely crowd
with completely uncommunicating private moods.

This view of the moon
over harbor waters
not only tells its own story
but records the romantic
ideas about moods enjoyed
by the nineteenth century.

PAST AND PRESENT, NO. 3
Augustus Egg
Reproduced by courtesy
of The Tate Gallery, London

One of the most serene occupations of the civilized world
is that of watching fish swim in an aquarium. The fine modern French
painter Henri Matisse has caught this private mood in depth.

WOMAN BEFORE AN AQUARIUM
Henri Matisse

AN APRIL MOOD
Charles Burchfield
1946/55, Watercolor,
Collection of the Whitney Museum
of American Art, New York,
gift of Mr. and Mrs. Lawrence A. Fleischman

What is the mood of April?
For Burchfield it is life awakening
out of winter bareness
and the restlessness of spring.
The coming storm will nourish
new life and new dreams.

A rare and lovely private mood
has been captured by Chapin
as he shows Ruby Green singing.
The contentment and poise
of the figure
contrast with the surging spirit
of the young singer's
uplifted head.

RUBY GREEN SINGING
James Chapin

CHAMBERED NAUTILUS
Andrew Wyeth

Quietness and morning, contentment serenely contained
within the canopied bed; the artist compares the moment
to the perfection of the sea's chambered nautilus,
with its graceful spiral.

ANGER AND HATRED

ANGER AND HATRED Anger is probably the most vivid and easily recognized of the emotions. It may burst suddenly, blocking out love, understanding, and reason. Or like a long-burning coal it may steadily burn and slowly consume the individual's soul.

What is the nature of anger?
What can it do to body and soul?
If anger became incarnate,
what would it be?

The Black Panther

There is a panther caged within my breast;
But what his name, there is no breast shall know
Save mine, nor what it is that drives him so,
Backward and forward, in relentless quest—
That silent rage, baffled but unsuppressed,   5
The soft pad of those stealthy feet that go
Over my body's prison to and fro,
Trying the walls forever without rest.
All day I feed him with my living heart;
But when the night puts forth her dreams and stars   10
The inexorable Frenzy reawakes:
His wrath is hurled upon the trembling bars,
The eternal passion stretches me apart,
And I lie silent—but my body shakes.

JOHN HALL WHEELOCK
as printed in *Home Book of Modern Verse*

🔔 Not many people can keep anger shut up within themselves. Anger calls
for action. What do you wish to happen to those who have upset you?

The Traveler's Curse After Misdirection

May they wander stage by stage
On the same vain pilgrimage,
Stumbling on, age after age,
Night and day, mile after mile,
At each and every step, a stile;[1]   5
At each and every stile, withal,
May they catch their feet and fall;
At each and every fall they take,
May a bone within them break;
And may the bones that break within   10
Not be, for variation's sake,
Now rib, now thigh, now arm, now shin,
But always, without fail, THE NECK.

ROBERT GRAVES
from the Welsh

From *Collected Poems* by Robert Graves.
Published by Doubleday & Company, Inc.
and Cassell & Company, Ltd. Reprinted by
permission of A. P. Watt & Son and International Authors N. V.

1. **stile**\stail\ a set of steps for crossing over a fence.

🔔 Anger may explode so suddenly and violently
that it shatters momentarily one's deepest principles. Here the poet fears
what one day may happen if he loses control of his feelings.

Mood

I think an impulse stronger than my mind
May some day grasp a knife, unloose a vial,
Or with a little leaden ball unbind
The cords that tie me to the rank and file.
My hands grow quarrelsome with bitterness,   5
And darkly bent upon the final fray;
Night with its stars upon a grave seems less
Indecent than the too complacent day.

God knows I would be kind, let live, speak fair,
Requite an honest debt with more than just,   10
And love for Christ's dear sake these shapes that wear
A pride that had its genesis in dust,—
The meek are promised much in a book I know
But one grows weary turning cheek to blow.

COUNTÉE CULLEN

From *On These I Stand* by Countée Cullen.
Copyright 1929 by Harper & Brothers, renewed 1957 by Ida M. Cullen. Reprinted
by permission of Harper & Row, Publishers.

Poets deal not only with the anatomy of anger, but they also show the depths of submerged anger, the kind man feels toward unexplained evil and suffering.

Does It Matter

Does it matter?—losing your leg? . . .
For people will always be kind;
And you need not show that you mind
When the others come in after hunting
To gobble their muffins and eggs.   5

Does it matter?—losing your sight? . . .
There's such splendid work for the blind;
And people will always be kind,
As you sit on the terrace remembering
And turning your face to the light.   10

Do they matter?—those dreams from the pit? . . .
You can drink and forget and be glad;
And people won't say that you're mad;
For they know that you've fought for your country,
And no one will worry a bit!   15

SIEGFRIED SASSOON

Anger is, of course,
the soil in which the seed of hatred grows.

Hate

My enemy came nigh,
And I
Stared fiercely in his face.
My lips went writhing back in a grimace,
And stern I watched him with a narrow eye.   5
Then, as I turned away, my enemy,
That bitter heart and savage, said to me:
"Some day, when this is past,
When all the arrows that we have are cast,
We may ask one another why we hate,   10
And fail to find a story to relate.
It may seem to us then a mystery
That we could hate each other."

            Thus said he,
And did not turn away,   15
Waiting to hear what I might have to say.
But I fled quickly, fearing if I stayed
I might have kissed him as I would a maid.

JAMES STEPHENS

What is it like to be a black man in a "white" world?

The White House

Your door is shut against my tightened face,
And I am sharp as steel with discontent;
But I possess the courage and the grace
To bear my anger proudly and unbent.
The pavement slabs burn loose beneath my feet,   5
A chafing savage, down the decent street;
And passion rends my vitals as I pass,
Where boldly shines your shuttered door of glass.
Oh, I must search for wisdom every hour,
Deep in my wrathful bosom sore and raw,   10
And find in it the superhuman power
To hold me to the letter of your law!
Oh, I must keep my heart inviolate[1]
Against the potent poison of your hate.

CLAUDE MCKAY

---

1. **inviolate**\ĭn ˈvai·ə·lat\ untouched; undisturbed.

THE WHITE HOUSE from SELECTED POEMS OF CLAUDE McKAY, Copyright 1953 by Bookman Associates, Inc. Reprinted by permission of Twayne Publishers, Inc. and Bookman Associates, Inc.

A frustrating experience—striking out in anger at things about you and connecting only with air.

Waves Against a Dog

Had I had the power I would have stretched
that wave on this rock and bitten it. But now
I have to thrust a jaw at this foam. Salting
my teeth, adultering[1] my saliva. And my teeth
get hold of just nothing, just whiteness and sun.   5

Afraid? Not I. Not of this salty anger. I have
killed a lot in my life. Not frightened. Not I.
But nothing to my teeth, just touch and goes
this big blue wave. Afraid of me. Circles my feet.
Vanishes. Must catch before it breaks on the rock. 10

Dive. What strength! I'm hurled back to the rock,
whirling round, looking at the hill, not the sea.
Dive again. A large blue tongue shows me
the pattern of the rocks, puts me on my feet,
there. Soaked. If only I had teeth. If only.   15

To bite this blueness to pieces, to pierce this
blue big belly, take my revenge, bite—If.
But now I cannot even touch: the salt teases me.
I look around: always the white foam. And I bark.
I bark while the rock ducks under another wave.   20

TANER BAYBARS

---

1. **adultering**\ə ᴬdəl·tər·iŋ\ shortened from *adulterating;*
making impure by adding a foreign or inferior substance.

Even in anger's rich soil, hatred will wither.
It must be watered and nourished faithfully.

A Poison Tree

I was angry with my friend:
I told my wrath, my wrath did end.
I was angry with my foe:
I told it not, my wrath did grow.

And I watered it in fears   5
Night and morning with my tears,
And I sunned it with smiles
And with soft deceitful wiles.

And it grew both day and night,
Till it bore an apple bright,   10
And my foe beheld it shine,
And he knew that it was mine.

And into my garden stole
When the night had veiled the pole;
In the morning, glad I see   15
My foe outstretched beneath the tree.

WILLIAM BLAKE

What price hatred?
The hater, clothed in self-righteousness,
    isolates himself from other people.
Is hatred worth it?

Without a Cloak

Hate has a fashionable cut.
    It is the garment man agrees on,
Snug, colorful, the proper weight
    For comfort in an icy season.

And it is weatherproof, they say—   5
    Becoming, also, to the spirit.
I fetched Hate homeward yesterday,
    But there it hangs. I cannot wear it.

It is a dress that suits me ill,
    However much the mode sustains me   10
At once too ample and too small,
    It trips, bewilders, and confines me.

And in my blood do fevers flow,
    Corruptive, where the fabric presses,
Till I must pluck it off as though   15
    It were the burning shirt of Nessus.[1]

Proud walk the people folded warm
    In Hate. They need not pray for spring.
But threadbare do I face the storm
    Or hug my hearthstone, shivering.   20

PHYLLIS MC GINLEY

---

1. Putting on a magic shirt soaked in the blood of
the centaur **Nessus**\ˈnĕ·səs\, the Greek hero Hercules
was burned to death by it. Hence, a "shirt of Nessus"
is a garment that might produce a similar result.

The Heart

In the desert
I saw a creature, naked, bestial,
Who, squatting upon the ground,
Held his heart in his hands,
And ate of it.   5
I said, "Is it good, friend?"
"It is bitter—bitter," he answered;
"But I like it
Because it is bitter,
And because it is my heart."   10

STEPHEN CRANE

UNDERSTANDING POETRY

Finding the Theme

The lyric poet not only recreates his experience, but he also tells or implies what the experience means to him. Wheelock, for example, does not merely recreate the experience of being greatly angered; he tells, in a general way, that his unexpressed anger torments him mentally and physically . . .

The eternal passion stretches me apart,
And I lie silent—but my body shakes.

Here is an example of a poet explicitly stating his *theme, the idea or attitude expressed in a poem.* But the poet does not always state his theme openly. Sometimes it is implied in the key words, images—similes and metaphors, and rhythm of the poem. Find one other poem in this section in which the theme seems to be definitely stated by a phrase or line in the poem.

TECHNIQUES

Metaphor, the Implied Comparison

Specific poems in this section compare anger and hatred to a black panther, a poison tree, and a very modish coat. These comparisons differ from similes primarily in that they are not announced by *like* or *as.* In each case they imply that the two objects compared are identical with each other. The poet *implies* that anger and hatred share some action(s) or quality(ies), or both in common with a panther,

a tree, a coat. Such implied comparisons are called "metaphors." Metaphor is the only way we have of expressing inner reactions for which we have no meaningful words. They demand that the reader take his knowledge of familiar things and apply it to his understanding of unfamiliar things.

Discuss some of the metaphors you find vivid and appropriate.

The Black Panther

1. Why is the title a good one? Does it define the true subject?

2. What details about the panther are mentioned in the poem? How do they make the nature of anger clearer?

The Traveler's Curse After Misdirection

1. How important is the poem's title to the meaning?

2. Why does Graves withhold the full extent of his anger until the last line?

3. Why is the accelerating pace of the rhythm, line by line, appropriate to the meaning of the lines?

Mood

1. What two forces does the poet feel in conflict within himself? Point out and explain the lines in which he makes this tension clear.

2. What does he mean when he says "a little leaden ball" may "unbind the cords that tie me to the rank and file"?

Does It Matter

1. How does the poet answer the question in his title? Why does he repeat it three times?

2. What actually happened to him?

3. Why aren't the people's kindnesses enough?

4. What is the poet implying about war?

Hate

1. Contrast the picture the poet gives of himself in the first seven lines with the calm, good reason of his enemy in the next six lines.

2. What strange thing does Stephens observe about hatred? Can you state it in one sentence?

The White House

1. How does the interpretation of the poem change if you know that the poet is a black American?

2. What is the speaker afraid that his anger may do to him?

Waves Against a Dog

1. Who is the speaker? What is he describing?

2. What situations in human life are comparable to this one?

A Poison Tree

1. Explain the contrast in the first stanza.

2. Why is the metaphor announced in the title a good one for the quality of hatred Blake is portraying?

3. Blake starts seven lines with *and;* what quality does this repetition give the poem?

4. What kind of rhythm is Blake using? What is its effect?

Without a Cloak

1. Compare the two subjects of the central metaphor as they progress point by point throughout the poem.

2. What reasons does the poet give for rejecting the cloak?

3. In several stanzas, the second and the fourth lines do not rhyme precisely. Such rhymes are called *slant* rhymes. What quality do they give the poem?

The Heart

1. What does the title tell about the subject matter and theme of the poem?

2. What is Crane saying about human nature?

IMPLICATIONS

Consider the poems you have just read on anger. Would you agree or disagree with the following statements in light of what the poets have presented?

1. Anger is an emotion that wells up inside a person until he feels he must spew it out.

2. Anger tends to make a person irrational in what he says and does.

3. People enjoy being angry and tend to want to nourish their hatred rather than overcome it.

4. Anger may be constructive as well as destructive.

5. Anger serves no useful purpose in human life, destroying the person who harbors it.

6. Poetry portraying anger makes the reader see his own moments of anger in a new light.

WORDS

All nouns may be classified either as *abstract* nouns—things that cannot be touched, smelled, tasted, heard, or seen; or as *concrete* nouns—words that label things observable through the senses. The moods of *restlessness, fear, anger,* and *hatred* are abstractions, and the words which label them are abstract nouns. The words *wheel, wind, sea, train* are concrete nouns which refer to something tangible. When a writer uses such words as *sea* and *wind,* he depends upon the reader to see, feel, and hear the sea and wind.

Concrete nouns, then, because they label something observable, evoke an image. Part of the value of the image is the associations the reader makes. Look up the word *sea* in the dictionary. A dictionary definition generally gives first the specific, or denotative, meaning of a word. What is the denotative meaning of *sea?* But the word *sea* also suggests, or connotes, travel, vastness, freedom, the unknown. The specific meaning, literal meaning, is the *denotation* of a word. The additional associations, the emotional colorings, are the *connotations* of a word. Although words have generally the same denotative meanings for most people, words may not produce the same connotations. From the group of poems you have just read, make a list of nouns which suggest restlessness, fear, anger, and hatred. What connotations does each word produce?

SORROW Pain, disillusionment, and death are ever with man. Living is tinged with sorrow. Even in moments of greatest happiness it is not far away, but lies like an undercurrent ready to break forth. Much of man's greatest music, painting, and poetry is shot through with sorrow for the sufferings of mankind. Some of the great music of the world, such as Tchaikovsky's *Pathétique Symphony*, throbs darkly, mournfully. The Renaissance painters turned to the intimate, frequent incidents of sorrowing people found in the Bible stories. And much of the world's greatest poetry evokes beauty through man's sorrow.

Sorrow and beauty
are inevitably mixed,
as Frost shows.

My November Guest

My Sorrow, when she's here with me,
　　Thinks these dark days of autumn rain
Are beautiful as days can be;
She loves the bare, the withered tree;
　　She walks the sodden[1] pasture lane.　　　5

Her pleasure will not let me stay.
　　She talks and I am fain to list:[2]
She's glad the birds are gone away,
She's glad her simple worsted grey
　　Is silver now with clinging mist.　　　10

The desolate, deserted trees,
　　The faded earth, the heavy sky,
The beauties she so truly sees,
She thinks I have no eye for these,
　　And vexes me for reason why.　　　15

Not yesterday I learned to know
　　The love of bare November days
Before the coming of the snow,
But it were vain to tell her so,
　　And they are better for her praise.　　　20

ROBERT FROST

1. **sodden**\ˈsŏ·dən\ rain-soaked and muddy.
2. **fain**\fān\ pleased and eager. **list**, listen.

The sea has many faces, many moods.
The sounds of wind and wave in never-ending ebb and flow
chill Joyce with sadness.

The Noise of Waters

All day I hear the noise of waters
    Making moan,
Sad as the sea-bird is, when, going
    Forth alone,
He hears the winds cry to the waters'   5
    Monotone.

The grey winds, the cold winds are blowing
    Where I go.
I hear the noise of many waters
    Far below.   10
All day, all night, I hear them flowing
    To and fro.

JAMES JOYCE

From *Collected Poems* by James Joyce. Copyright 1918 by B. W. Huebsch, 1946 by Nora Joyce. Reprinted by permission of The Viking Press, Inc.

The loss of loved ones through death
has long been a sorrow explored in poetry.

Music I Heard

Music I heard with you was more than music,
And bread I broke with you was more than bread.
Now that I am without you, all is desolate,
All that was once so beautiful is dead.

Your hands once touched this table and this silver,   5
And I have seen your fingers hold this glass.
These things do not remember you, beloved:
And yet your touch upon them will not pass.

For it was in my heart you moved among them,
And blessed them with your hands and with your eyes. 10
And in my heart they will remember always:
They knew you once, O beautiful and wise!

CONRAD AIKEN

From *Collected Poems* by Conrad Aiken. Copyright 1953 by Conrad Aiken. Reprinted by permission of Oxford University Press, Inc.

*Coarse imagery in the following poem provides
a jarring impression of the funeral ritual.*

The Widow

The Hammond Organ lubricates the air.
The kind mortician conducts her to her place
of honor. A man with a painted puppet's face
they say is her husband's face is obviously there

in front of her. She would have the casket   5
closed, but his sister would not. The minister cries
how gloriously the man is dead who lies
before him daily with a face like plastic,

prays that God who took him out of order
will keep his soul from torment, will adorn him   10
with a crown of stars, will hold with those that mourn him.
It is not hard, she thinks, but it will be harder.

The wail of the Hammond weakens, her mind goes black,
turning quickly out of the moment meanders
on curious ways. She looks at his nose. She wonders   15
if they went and slit the good blue suit in the back

and if his shoes are tied, if he has on
the socks they didn't ask for but she sent,
if they still use pennies, decides of course they don't,
hopes they will have their fill and be done with him soon.   20

It would not be fair to say she is not grieving.
She did not want to come, but she is aware
how there will be silence, there will be pleasures to bear
in silence, and dark creatures unbehaving.

She did not want to come. She will not be taken   25
to tears. But she is aware some moment will crush
the brain suddenly, that she will go home and wish
burglars had come there and the blind windows were broken.

MILLER WILLIAMS

From SO LONG AT THE FAIR by Miller Williams. Copyright © 1968, 1967,
1966, 1965, 1964, 1963, 1960, 1958 by Miller Williams. Published by E. P.
Dutton & Co., Inc. and reprinted with their permission.

The mind will absorb just so much sorrow, and then something must happen. The next two poems tell something about the effect of deep grief on a person.

After Great Pain a Formal Feeling Comes

After great pain a formal feeling comes—
The nerves sit ceremonious like tombs;
The stiff heart questions—was it He that bore?
And yesterday—or centuries before?

The feet mechanical   5
Go round a wooden way
Of ground or air or Ought, regardless grown,
A quartz contentment like a stone.

This is the hour of lead
Remembered if outlived,   10
As freezing persons recollect the snow—
First chill, then stupor, then the letting go.

EMILY DICKINSON

The Woodspurge

The wind flapped loose, the wind was still,
Shaken out dead from tree and hill:
I had walked on at the wind's will,
I sat now, for the wind was still.

Between my knees my forehead was,—   5
My lips, drawn in, said not Alas!
My hair was over in the grass,
My naked ears heard the day pass.

My eyes, wide open, had the run
Of some ten weeds to fix upon;   10
Among those few, out of the sun,
The woodspurge[1] flowered, three cups in one.

From perfect grief there need not be
Wisdom or even memory:
One thing that learnt remains to me,—   15
The woodspurge has a cup of three.

DANTE ROSSETTI

1. woodspurge\ˈwʊd ˌspərj\ a European plant with greenish-yellow flowers in clusters of three.

At times all of nature
seems to mirror man's grief.
To Shelley, sorrow is stark and violent.

A Dirge

Rough wind, that moanest loud
　　Grief too sad for song;
Wild wind, when sullen cloud
　　Knells[1] all the night long;
Sad storm, whose tears are vain,
　　Bare woods, whose branches strain,
Deep caves and dreary main,[2]—
　　Wail, for the world's wrong!

PERCY BYSSHE SHELLEY

---

1. **knell**\nĕl\ to sound a death bell to make
a similar mournful sound or sign.
2. **main,** sea or ocean.

---

sometimes *if*) each stanza contributed to the meaning you have found.

UNDERSTANDING POETRY
Structure

The structure of a poem is the way its topics, scenes, statements, and ideas are arranged. To see how these parts are related to form one dominant impression and meaning adds greatly to one's enjoyment of poetry. Most poems are composed of stanzas which are easily recognized because of their fixed pattern of lines and rhymes. In many poems the stanzas also show the thought divisions of the poem, each stanza developing some different aspect of the poet's subject and theme.

An awareness of structure can help you in two ways. On the one hand, if you are not sure of a poem's subject and theme after several readings, examine each part or stanza individually, because it is sometimes much easier to work up from a knowledge of the parts to a grasp of the whole. On the other hand, if you believe that you grasp the meaning of the poem after a reading or two, you may test your belief by asking yourself how (and

TECHNIQUES
Rhythm and Sound Effects

As noted earlier, the poet varies the basic rhythm of a poem by substituting other *feet* and by using rhyme, principally *end-rhyme*. But poets often make use of other devices, such as alliteration, assonance, and consonance, in place of actual rhyme within poems. These devices not only may delight the ear but also may add interesting sub-rhythms to highlight an action, emotion, or key word. Alliteration may be defined as the repetition of similar initial consonant sounds ("*M*aking *m*oan"); assonance as the repetition of identical vowel sounds ("M*o*n*o*t*o*ne"); consonance as the repetition of the same consonants but not the same vowels, such as "*try*" and "*tree*."

Find examples of alliteration in "The Noise of Waters," "The Dirge," "After Great Pain a Formal Feeling Comes," and "The Woodspurge." Find examples of assonance in "The Noise of Waters."

My November Guest

1. What does the title have to do with the poem?

2. What reward does sorrow bring to Frost?

3. What images carry the feeling of November?

The Noise of Waters

1. What kind of "seascape" is Joyce describing?

2. What is the basic sound quality of the rhyming words in the poem?

3. How does the rhythm affect the mood? Especially what is the rhythmic effect of the short lines?

Music I Heard

1. What are the intimate details that the poet remembers which bring to him an awareness of his loss?

2. Is the language conversational or elevated, natural or unnatural, strained or easy?

The Widow

1. How does the tone of this poem compare with the tone of "Music I Heard"?

2. What details give the reader a concrete impression of the funeral service and of the widow's thoughts?

After Great Pain a Formal Feeling Comes

1. According to the poem, what effects do sorrow and pain have upon one's mind? upon one's actions? How do the similes in lines 2 and 8 help or hinder the meaning?

2. Pick out examples of Dickinson's use of slant rhymes, assonance, and consonance in the poem.

The Woodspurge

1. What does the mind do when it is overwhelmed with grief?

2. What is the memory that is left from grief?

A Dirge

1. What does the title mean in relation to the poem?

2. What kind of night is Shelley describing?

3. What particular sounds are emphasized in the poem? What effect do they have?

4. Why does Shelley use so many spondees?

IMPLICATIONS

In light of the poems you have just read, consider your reactions to the following statements. Do you accept them or reject them?

1. Sorrow can be transmitted through a series of sound qualities and images of nature without the poet's directly mentioning it.

2. Sorrow, in spite of its unpleasantness, has the ability to make the individual see beauty where he could not see it before.

3. Sorrow makes a person seek certain kinds of sights and sounds to harmonize with his mood.

4. After a certain amount of sorrow the human mind rebels and refuses to react.

5. Intense sorrow may intensify one's reactions to seemingly trivial things around one.

6. In moods of depression or melancholy, we tend to remind ourselves of all the defects we have and all the unpleasant things that have happened to us.

NOSTALGIA Man is able to compare and to contrast the "here and now" with the "there and then." He can think back to childhood, remember the places he has been, recall the people he used to know. When man's memories cause him to yearn wistfully to return to the past, he is moved by a mixture of joy and sadness called nostalgia. Nostalgia is perhaps composed of regret, desire, and sorrow at the realization of the inevitability of change. Poets have delighted in summoning it, perhaps because poetry itself so often grows out of the vision of "what might be" against the background of "what is."

Did you ever see an old house and wonder about the people who lived and loved and worked and died there?

The House on the Hill

They are all gone away,
　The House is shut and still,
There is nothing more to say.

Through broken walls and gray
　The winds blow bleak and shrill;　5
They are all gone away.

Nor is there only one today
　To speak them good or ill:
There is nothing more to say.

Why is it then we stray　　　　10
　Around that sunken sill?
They are all gone away,

And our poor fancy-play
　For them is wasted skill:
There is nothing more to say.　　15

There is ruin and decay
　In the House on the Hill:
They are all gone away,
There is nothing more to say.

E. A. ROBINSON

They Are All Gone Away *by Stanford W. Williamson.*
He was inspired by the poem "The House on the Hill."

The quality of a particular kind of day
can make one long for a way of life
that he formerly knew.

The West Wind

It's a warm wind, the west wind, full of birds' cries;
I never hear the west wind but tears are in my eyes.
For it comes from the west lands, the old brown hills,
And April's in the west wind, and daffodils.

It's a fine land, the west land, for hearts as tired as mine,   5
Apple orchards blossom there, and the air's like wine.
There is cool green grass there, where men may lie at rest,
And the thrushes are in song there, fluting[1] from the nest.

"Will ye not come home brother: Ye have been long away,
It's April, and blossom time, and white is the May;   10
And bright is the sun, brother, and warm is the rain—
Will ye not come home, brother, home to us again?

"The young corn is green, brother, where the rabbits run,
It's blue sky, and white clouds, and warm rain and sun,
It's song to a man's soul, brother, fire to a man's brain,   15
To hear the wild bees and see the merry spring again.

"Larks are singing in the west, brother, above the green wheat,
So will ye not come home, brother, and rest your tired feet?
I've balm for bruised hearts, brother, sleep for aching eyes,"
Says the warm wind, the west wind, full of birds' cries.   20

It's the white road westwards is the road I must tread
To the green grass, the cool grass, and rest for heart and head,
To violets and the brown brooks and the thrushes' song,
In the fine land, the west land, the land where I belong.

JOHN MASEFIELD

---

1. **flute**\flūt\ to sing with an effect like the sound of a flute.

Reprinted with permission of the publisher from *Collected Poems* by John Masefield. Copyright 1912 by The Macmillan Company, Renewed 1940 by John Masefield.

In spring, Browning's thoughts turn from Italy
where he is to memories of spring in England.

Home Thoughts from Abroad

Oh, to be in England now that April's there,
And whoever wakes in England sees, some morning, unaware,
That the lowest boughs and the brushwood sheaf
Round the elm-tree bole[1] are in tiny leaf,
While the chaffinch[2] sings on the orchard bough   5
In England—now!

And after April, when May follows,
And the white throat[3] builds, and all the swallows!
Hark, where my blossomed pear-tree in the hedge
Leans to the fields and scatters on the clover   10
Blossoms and dewdrops—at the bent-spray's[4] edge—
That's the wise thrush; he sings each song twice over,
Lest you should think he never could recapture
The first fine careless rapture!
And, though the fields look rough with hoary[5] dew,   15
All will be gay when noontide wakes anew
The buttercups, the little children's dower,[6]
—Far brighter than this gaudy melon-flower!

ROBERT BROWNING

1. **bole**\bōl\ a tree trunk.
2. **chaffinch**\ˈchă·finch\ a colorful European finch
with a pleasing song.
3. **white throat**, a European gray and blue warbler.
4. **bent-spray**, grass clump or cluster.
5. **hoary**\ˈhō·rē\ white, gray
6. **dower**\dau̇r\ gift given by nature.

Edna St. Vincent Millay never outgrew her passion for the seacoast of New England
where she grew up. In this poem she succeeds in communicating that deep, almost unbearable anguish
that nostalgia can become when something one desires desperately is unobtainable.

Inland

People that build their houses inland,
  People that buy a plot of ground
Shaped like a house, and build a house there,
  Far from the sea-board, far from the sound

Of water sucking the hollow ledges,   5
  Tons of water striking the shore,—
What do they long for, as I long for
  One salt smell of the sea once more?

People the waves have not awakened,
  Spanking the boats at the harbour's head,   10

What do they long for, as I long for,
  Starting up in my inland bed,

Beating the narrow walls, and finding
  Neither a window nor a door,
Screaming to God for death by drowning,—   15
  One salt taste of the sea once more?

EDNA ST. VINCENT MILLAY

From COLLECTED POEMS, Harper & Row. Copyright
1917, 1921, 1934, 1945, 1948, 1962, by Edna St. Vincent
Millay and Norma Millay Ellis.

When a child, man looks forward to maturity.
When mature, he often looks back wistfully, remembering the youthful times
that are past. This kind of nostalgia is well expressed
by one of America's favorite nineteenth-century poets.

My Lost Youth

Often I think of the beautiful town
  That is seated by the sea;
Often in thought go up and down
The pleasant streets of that dear old town,
  And my youth comes back to me.   5
    And a verse of a Lapland[1] song
    Is haunting my memory still:
    "A boy's will is the wind's will,
And the thoughts of youth are long, long thoughts."

I can see the shadowy lines of its trees,   10
  And catch, in sudden gleams,
The sheen of the far-surrounding seas,
And islands that were the Hesperides[2]
  Of all my boyish dreams.
    And the burden of that old song,   15
    It murmurs and whispers still:
    "A boy's will is the wind's will,
And the thoughts of youth are long, long thoughts."

I remember the black wharves and the slips,
  And the sea tides tossing free;   20
And Spanish sailors with bearded lips,
And the beauty and mystery of the ships,
  And the magic of the sea.
    And the voice of that wayward song
    Is singing and saying still: 25
    "A boy's will is the wind's will,
And the thoughts of youth are long, long thoughts."

I remember the bulwarks by the shore,
  And the fort upon the hill;
The sunrise gun, with its hollow roar,   30
The drumbeat repeated o'er and o'er,
  And the bugle wild and shrill.

---

1. **Lapland**\ˈlăp·lănd\ the region of the Scandinavian
peninsula above the Arctic Circle.
2. **Hesperides**\hĕsˈpā·rĭ ˈdēz\ the mythical blessed
islands far to the west in early Greek and Latin story.

And the music of that old song
  Throbs in my memory still:
  "A boy's will is the wind's will,   35
And the thoughts of youth are long, long thoughts."

I remember the sea fight far away,
  How it thundered o'er the tide!
And the dead captains, as they lay
In their graves, o'erlooking the tranquil bay   40
  Where they in battle died.
    And the sound of that mournful song
    Goes through me with a thrill:
    "A boy's will is the wind's will,
And the thoughts of youth are long, long thoughts."   45

I can see the breezy dome of groves,
  The shadows of Deering's Woods;[3]
And the friendships old and the early loves
Come back with a Sabbath sound, as of doves
  In quiet neighborhoods.   50
    And the verse of that sweet old song,
    It flutters and murmurs still:
    "A boy's will is the wind's will,
And the thoughts of youth are long, long thoughts."

I remember the gleams and glooms that dart   55
  Across the schoolboy's brain;
The song and the silence in the heart,
That in part are prophecies, and in part
  Are longings wild and vain.
    And the voice of that fitful song   60
    Sings on, and is never still:
    "A boy's will is the wind's will,
And the thoughts of youth are long, long thoughts."

There are things of which I may not speak;
  There are dreams that cannot die;   65
There are thoughts that make the strong heart weak,
And bring a pallor into the cheek,
  And a mist before the eye.
    And the words of that fatal song
    Come over me like a chill: 70
    "A boy's will is the wind's will,
And the thoughts of youth are long, long thoughts."

Strange to me now are the forms I meet
  When I visit the dear old town;

---

3. **Deering's Woods,** a woods near Portland, Maine.

But the native air is pure and sweet, 75
And the trees that o'ershadow each well-known street,
   As they balance up and down,
     Are singing the beautiful song,
     Are sighing and whispering still:
     "A boy's will is the wind's will, 80
And the thoughts of youth are long, long thoughts."

And Deering's Woods are fresh and fair,
   And with joy that is almost pain
My heart goes back to wander there,
And among the dreams of the days that were, 85
   I find my lost youth again.
     And the strange and beautiful song,
     The groves are repeating it still:
     "A boy's will is the wind's will,
And the thoughts of youth are long, long thoughts." 90

HENRY WADSWORTH LONGFELLOW

Similar in theme,
but not quite so gentle as "My Lost Youth,"
is Tennyson's "Break, Break, Break."

Break, Break, Break

Break, break, break
   On thy cold gray stones, O Sea!
And I would that my tongue could utter
   The thoughts that arise in me.

O well for the fisherman's boy, 5
   That he shouts with his sister at play!
O well for the sailor lad,
   That he sings in his boat on the bay!

And the stately ships go on
   To their haven under the hill; 10
But O for the touch of a vanished hand,
   And the sound of a voice that is still!

Break, break, break,
   At the foot of thy crags, O Sea!
But the tender grace of a day that is dead 15
   Will never come back to me.

ALFRED, LORD TENNYSON

Sometimes the significance of certain acts is
understood only in retrospect.

Those Winter Sundays

Sundays too my father got up early
and put his clothes on in the blueblack cold,
then with cracked hands that ached
from labor in the weekday weather made
banked fires blaze. No one ever thanked him.   5

I'd wake and hear the cold splintering, breaking.
When the rooms were warm, he'd call,
and slowly I would rise and dress,
fearing the chronic[1] angers of that house,

Speaking indifferently to him,   10
who had driven out the cold
and polished my good shoes as well.
What did I know, what did I know
of love's austere[2] and lonely offices?[3]

ROBERT HAYDEN

————————

1. **chronic**\ˈkrŏn·ĭk\ ever present; always continuing.
2. **austere**\ŏˈstē(ə)r\ forbidding.
3. **offices**, duties.

————————

UNDERSTANDING POETRY

Tone

One of the oldest complaints in the world is,
"It's not what he said; it's the way he said it." Such
statements attest to an important truth verified
every day: the tone of voice is an important ingredient in shaping human communication. But
when language is written, the audible voice of the
writer disappears. Does "no" on the printed page
signify delight, dismay, resoluteness, anger, insolence, or ignorance? One no longer has the inflec-
tions and volume of the voice, facial expressions,
and body gestures to help. The reader must depend upon the clues in the printed context in order
to grasp the writer's tone—*his emotional attitude
toward his subject.*

Even though these poems deal with nostalgia in
general, each has its own unique attitude and emotional intensity. Sometimes the poet will say that
he is "gay" or "sad"; but more often he embodies
his tone in the rhythm (see page 171), choice of
words, and images in the poem. Be alert to catch
these clues as you read these poems and answer
the study questions. (The term—tone—is also used
to mean the poet's attitude toward his audience.)

TECHNIQUES

Diction and Imagery

Poetry, because it is so compressed, demands that the poet choose his diction (his words) most carefully. Sometimes words strike the reader because they summon up vivid sense impressions: "Bleak and shrill," "brown hills . . . cool green grass . . . white clouds, and warm rain and sun," "chaffinch sings on the orchard bough," "water sucking the hollow ledges . . . one salt smell," "black wharves," "cold gray stones." Sometimes the poet surprises the reader by using precise language in unusual ways: "waves . . . spanking the boats" . . . "peace comes dropping slow" . . . "and noon a purple glow." Such words and phrases that appeal to the senses and the imagination are called imagery. (Because similes and metaphors appeal to the senses and imagination they are images, too.) The poet who wishes to share scenes and actions and feelings with the reader uses imagery that is sharp and definite. He selects the right noun, adjective, verb, or adverb for the precise impression he desires.

The House on the Hill

1. What effect does Robinson achieve by weaving the two melancholy refrains back and forth?

2. Why are so few rhymes used?

3. What specific images are especially appropriate for the mood?

The West Wind

1. The poet suggests a whole series of pictures. Which are most picturesque and haunting? Which appeal to sight and which to sound?

2. How do the rhythm and the rhyme scheme affect the tone? What use does Masefield make of alliteration? assonance?

Home Thoughts from Abroad

1. One memory seems to ignite another as the poet rushes onward to get them all down. What images call up specific sights and sounds? Are they pleasant or unpleasant?

2. What is the rhyme scheme? What variation in it makes it somewhat irregular?

Inland

1. How does the title fit the poem?

2. What is the tone? Is nostalgia a pleasant or an unpleasant emotion in this poem? How many sentences are there and what is the dominant sound in the last line of each? What qualities of the sea are suggested?

My Lost Youth

1. What are the sensations and thoughts that the poet remembers?

2. Does Longfellow state his theme? How? Where?

3. How does the tone of this poem differ from "Inland"?

4. Longfellow clearly illustrates the combination of repetition with variation which is so essential to keeping poetry from becoming monotonous. Lines 6–9 form a refrain. Why isn't it always the same?

Break, Break, Break

1. What relation does the title have to the poem?

2. What pleasant things are mentioned?

3. What unpleasant images does Tennyson use and how do they affect the tone? What harsh sounds does he use and how do they affect the tone?

Those Winter Sundays

1. As he thinks back to Sunday mornings, what does the speaker now understand about his father that he did not understand as a child?

2. What kind of feeling comes to your mind from the words "blueblack cold"?

IMPLICATIONS

Reflect on the truth or falsity of the following statements in terms of the group of poems you have read in this mood.

1. Nostalgia is an enjoyable emotion.

2. Nostalgia is different from homesickness.

3. Nostalgia is usually a mood of older people. It seldom affects the young.

4. Without experiencing nostalgia occasionally, most people would be somewhat hard.

5. Things out of sight tend to be remembered in an idealized way.

DELIGHT is a sudden intensification of a sensation, an experience, or a relationship. A sniff of frying bacon, a crisp May morning, a loved one may unexpectedly evoke the feeling of delight. In expressing his delight, the poet depends upon rich imagery and the lilting quality of sounds and rhythm. Poets often find their delight in a particular time of day. The first three poems are expressions of delight in different times of the day.

With fresh images, Housman exhorts the reader to share the delight of the morning.

Reveille

Wake: the silver dusk returning
 Up the beach of darkness brims,
And the ship of sunrise burning
 Strands upon the eastern rims.[1]

Wake: the vaulted shadow shatters,   5
 Trampled to the floor it spanned,
And the tent of night in tatters
 Straws the sky-pavillioned land.

Up, lad, up, 'tis late for lying:
 Hear the drums of morning play;   10
Hark, the empty highways crying
 "Who'll beyond the hills away?"

Towns and countries woo together,
 Forelands beacon, belfries call;
Never lad that trod on leather   15
 Lived to feast his heart with all.

Up, lad, thews that lie and cumber[2]
 Sunlit pallets[3] never thrive;
Morns abed and daylight slumber
 Were not meant for man alive.   20

Clay lies still, but blood's a rover;
 Breath's a ware that will not keep.
Up, lad: when the journey's over
 There'll be time enough to sleep.

A. E. HOUSMAN

1. The ship of sunrise appears as though stranded.
2. **thews**\thūz\ muscles, sinews. **cumber**\ˈkəm·bər\ clutter.
3. **pallet**\ˈpă·lət\ a thin straw mattress.

Like afternoon itself,
there is the slightest suggestion of drowsiness
about Millay's delight.

Afternoon on a Hill

I will be the gladdest thing
    Under the sun!
I will touch a hundred flowers
    And not pick one.

I will look at cliffs and clouds   5
    With quiet eyes,
Watch the wind blow down the grass,
    And the grass rise.

And when lights begin to show
    Up from the town,   10
I will mark which must be mine,
    And then start down.

EDNA ST. VINCENT MILLAY

In folklore and literature
the magic of the moon and its light
has long been celebrated
more than any other aspect of the night.

Silver

Slowly, silently, now the moon
Walks the night in her silver shoon;[1]
This way, and that, she peers and sees
Silver fruit upon silver trees;
One by one the casements catch   5
Her beams beneath the silvery thatch;
Couched in his kennel, like a log,
With paws of silver sleeps the dog;
From their shadowy cote the white breasts peep
Of doves in silver-feathered sleep   10
A harvest mouse goes scampering by,
With silver claws and a silver eye;
And moveless fish in the water gleam,
By silver reeds in a silver stream.

WALTER DE LA MARE

1. shoon\shūn\ shoes.

Not only does each time of day have its particular joys, but each season of the year also brings a special delight if one has the vision to see it. Here follow five poems of delight, each praising a season.

The utter softness of "Velvet Shoes" has caught the essence of the poet's delight in a snowstorm.

Velvet Shoes

Let us walk in the white snow
   In a soundless space;
With footsteps quiet and slow,
At a tranquil pace,
Under veils of white lace.   5

I shall go shod in silk,
   And you in wool,
White as a white cow's milk,
   More beautiful
Than the breast of a gull.   10

We shall walk through the still town
   In a windless peace;
We shall step upon white down,
   Upon silver fleece,
   Upon softer than these.   15

We shall walk in velvet shoes:
   Wherever we go
Silence will fall like dews
   On white silence below.
   We shall walk in the snow.   20

ELINOR WYLIE

A modern poet suggests the joy of spring through unusual phrases and words and through the unexpected arrangement and length of lines.

in Just-spring

in Just-
spring   when the world is mud-
luscious the little
lame balloonman

whistles   far   and wee   5

and eddieandbill come
running for marbles and
piracies and it's
spring

when the world is puddle-wonderful   10

the queer
old balloonman whistles
far   and   wee
and bettyandisbel come dancing

from hopscotch and jump-rope and   15

it's
spring
and
   the

      goat-footed   20

balloonMan   whistles
far
and
wee

E. E. CUMMINGS

Wild Blackberries

Summer in the country?
For the city dweller its joys may be remote,
but Frances McConnel helps us share her delight
through an unusual symbol for summer.

We dressed for December then,
When the heat crawled on our skin:
Not an inch open to the thorns
Except our mouths, necessary to tongue
The berries from our bruised fingers.   5
My father put socks on our hands
And with old strong hat pulled to his ears
He led us into the thickest thorns.

That bright July heart above us
Beat its anguish to our heavy bones.   10
Our juices fermented from the pores
Became blood with the berries' smears.
Yet we plucked the fruit lightly;
Stifled in our protection while
Thorns clawed at our hair   15
But fell away. Gladly the hot berries,
July berries, melted our quick tongues.

There were creatures at odds with us.
Chiggers so sly and small
The pungent oil filtered none away.   20
If there were a way to revoke them
My father would have known it.
Even fat ticks are known
To bury in the picker's skin:
Our harehound pup came home   25
Dalmatiated with the black bulbs.

Also the yellow-banded bees,
The ones that bumble into your legs,
Attack your sneakered feet,
Defied our protection.   30
Those bees nest near the briars,
Under the lame grass we trampled,
Are easily shaken to erupt
From the earth in lava bubbles.

And so then, run home   35
To the scrubbed kitchen; wash
The green spiders from the harvest;
Husk your hot bodies;
Shower away the afternoon;
And in white dress and shirt   40
Taste the blackberry, absorbed
Summer in fragrant cream, black suns
Dancing in the white, white summer sky.

Reprinted by permission of Frances McConnel.

FRANCES MCCONNEL

What is summer in the city?
Phyllis McGinley shows her joy in summer through a completely contemporary symbol.

Good Humor Man

Listen! It is the summer's self that ambles
    Through the green lanes with such a coaxing tongue.
Not birds or daisy fields were ever symbols
    More proper to the time than this bell rung
    With casual insistence—no, not swallow   5
    Circling the roof or bee in hollyhock.
His is the season's voice, and children follow,
    Panting, from every doorway down the block.

So, long ago, in some such shrill procession
    Perhaps the Hamelin[1] children gave pursuit   10
To one who wore a red-and-yellow fashion
    Instead of white, but made upon his flute
The self-same promise plain to every comer:
Unending sweets, imperishable summer.

PHYLLIS MC GINLEY

From *Times Three* by Phyllis McGinley. Copyright 1947 by Phyllis McGinley. Originally appeared in *The New Yorker*. Reprinted by permission of The Viking Press, Inc.

1. The author is referring to the story of the Pied Piper of **Hamelin,** who played such bewitching music with his pipes that all the children of the town followed him.

Gone are the youthful songs of spring
and the languid airs of summer. But autumn, too, has its delights.

A Vagabond Song

There is something in the Autumn that is native to my blood,
Touch of manner, hint of mood;
And my heart is like a rhyme,
With the yellow and the purple and the crimson keeping time.

The scarlet of the maples can shake me like a cry   5
Of bugles going by.
And my lonely spirit thrills
To see the frosty asters like smoke upon the hills.

There is something in October sets the gypsy blood astir;
We must rise and follow her,   10
When from every hill a flame
She calls and calls each vagabond by name.

BLISS CARMAN

Reprinted by permission of Dodd, Mead & Company from *Bliss Carman's Poems*. Copyright, 1929, by Bliss Carman.

All manner of things may bring delight to a person: sights ... sounds ... smells ... objects. The next group of poems deals with delights inspired by these kinds of things.

Whitman's great, gusty enthusiasm for life often flows out in catalogs, listing item after item.

Miracles

Why, who makes much of a miracle?
As to me I know of nothing else but miracles,
Whether I walk the streets of Manhattan,
Or dart my sight over the roofs of houses toward the sky,
Or wade with naked feet along the beach just in the edge of the water,   5
Or stand under trees in the woods,
Or talk by day with any one I love,
Or sit at table at dinner with the rest,
Or look at strangers opposite me riding in the car,
Or watch honey-bees busy around the hive of a summer forenoon,   10
Or animals feeding in the fields,
Or birds, or the wonderfulness of insects in the air,
Or the wonderfulness of the sundown, or of stars shining so quiet and bright,
Or the exquisite delicate thin curve of the new moon in spring;
These with the rest, one and all, are to me miracles,   15
The whole referring, yet each distinct and in its place.
To me every hour of the light and dark is a miracle,
Every cubic inch of space is a miracle,
Every square yard of the surface of the earth is spread with the same,
Every foot of the interior swarms with the same.   20

To me the sea is a continual miracle,
The fishes that swim—the rocks—the motion of the waves—the ships
    with men in them,
What stranger miracles are there?

WALT WHITMAN

This poem is also a catalog, one of delight in *pied* things, that is,
in things having two or more colors in blotches. To many people such objects may seem imperfect,
indeed blemished, but Hopkins finds them both beautiful and charged with meaning.

Pied Beauty

Glory be to God for dappled[1] things—
   For skies of couple-color as a brinded[2] cow;
     For rose-moles[3] all in stipple upon trout that swim;
Fresh-firecoal chestnut-falls; finches' wings;
   Landscapes plotted and pieced—fold, fallow, and plow;[4]   5
     And all trades, their gear and tackle and trim.
All things counter, original, spare, strange;
   Whatever is fickle,[5] freckled (who knows how?)
     With swift, slow; sweet, sour; adazzle, dim;
He fathers-forth whose beauty is past change: 10
     Praise him.

GERARD MANLEY HOPKINS

---

1. **dappled**\ˈdă·pəld\ marked or variegated with small spots.
2. **brinded** (or **brindled**)\ˈbrĭn·dəld\ marked with dark streaks or spots.
3. **rose-mole**\ˈrōz 'mōl\ a distinctive spot on a fish.
4. **fold**, an enclosed pasture. **fallow**\ˈfă·lō\ land left uncultivated for a time. **plow**, plowed land.
5. **fickle**\ˈfĭ·kəl\ readily changeable and showing much variety.

How seldom we examine smells
or even become conscious of their effect on our moods.
Morley gives a whole catalog of them
for us to consider.

Smells

Why is it that the poets tell
So little of the sense of smell?
These are the odors I love well:

The smell of coffee freshly ground;
Or rich plum pudding, holly-crowned;   5
Or onions fried and deeply browned.

The fragrance of a fumy pipe;
The smell of apples, newly ripe
And printers' ink on leaden type.

Woods by moonlight in September   10
Breathe most sweet; and I remember
Many a smoky camp-fire ember.

Camphor, turpentine, and tea,
The balsam[1] of a Christmas tree,
These are whiffs of gramarye[2] ...   15
A ship smells best of all to me!

CHRISTOPHER MORLEY

---

1. **balsam**\ˈbȯl·səm\ an aromatic resin.
2. **gramarye**\ˈgră·mə 'rē\ magic, enchantment. (This word comes from the old French word *grammaire*, and so does the word *grammar*.)

From the book POEMS by Christopher Morley. Copyright, 1929, ©, 1957 by Christopher Morley. Reprinted by permission of J. B. Lippincott Company.

Emily Dickinson takes a simple thing,
joy in books, and tells of her delight.

Precious Words

He ate and drank the precious words.
His spirit grew robust;
He knew no more that he was poor,
Nor that his frame was dust.
He danced along the dingy days,
And this bequest[1] of wings
Was but a book. What liberty
A loosened spirit brings!

EMILY DICKINSON

1. **bequest**\'hē ▴kwĕst\ a legacy, something willed and to be inherited.

Shakespeare's sonnets often deal with the praise of his loved one or a friend.
Here is a famous one that shows his utter joy in the beauty of his beloved.

Sonnet CVI

When in the chronicle of wasted time
I see descriptions of the fairest wights,[1]
And beauty making beautiful old rhyme,
In praise of ladies dead and lovely knights,
Then, in the blazon[2] of sweet beauty's best,   5
Of hand, of foot, of lip, of eye, of brow,
I see their antique pen would have express'd
Even such a beauty as you master now.
So all their praises are but prophecies
Of this our time, all you prefiguring,   10
And, for they look'd but with divining eyes,
They had not still enough your worth to sing:
    For we, which now behold these present days,
    Have eyes to wonder, but lack tongues to praise.

WILLIAM SHAKESPEARE

1. **wight**\wait\ creature, person.
2. **blazon**\▴blā·zən\ flowery description or display.

Fast Run in the Junkyard

That junkyard fell down the side of the hill
like a river: baby buggy, black leather
cracked car back seat, sofa wind-siphoned
by a clutch of tangled wire hangers hanging on
like spiders. We stood and fell as momentum told us   5
toward somebody's sodden Sealey[1] dying of galloping miasma,[2]
jumped on bedsprings sprung to pogos, and leaped
for king-of-the-mountain where boxes and cans fountained
up the hill's other side. Sailing saucers, we rode
back down, flinging hat racks, burlap sacks, chairs cropped   10
of backs and flotsam crockery,[3] breezed in league boots[4]
back out of everybody's past hazards, up to the road
to break tar bubbles all-the-way-home where things
were wearing out as fast as we were growing up.

JEANNETTE NICHOLS

---

1. **sodden Sealey,** a thoroughly soaked Sealy mattress.
2. **miasma**\mē·ˈaz·mə\ a vapor formerly believed to cause disease.
3. **flotsam crockery,** discarded earthenware such as pots, jars, dishes, made of baked clay.
4. **league boots,** making giant strides.

From MOSTLY PEOPLE, Jeannette Nichols, Rutgers University Press, New Brunswick, New Jersey, 1966.

UNDERSTANDING POETRY
The Whole Poem—Experience and Meaning

One of the finest shortcuts for widening and deepening one's experience of life and the world is lyric poetry. No other type of literature offers more intense and compressed expressions of truths about human life. The lyric poet widens his reader's vision by revealing to him experiences he has never had before. He takes the landlubber to surfs and seas, the city dweller to the forlorn farmhouse lost in deep night, or to the blackberry patch under a July sun; the Midwesterner to New England in November and to England "when April's there"; he takes his readers swiftly to strange streets, hills, skies, moonlight nights . . . foreign shores . . . other centuries. But more than this, he may lead the reader beneath the surface of the reader's own everyday experiences—to give new meaning to familiar feelings, ideas, and thoughts.

The mature, experienced reader may grasp, almost spontaneously, the full impact of the poet's broad, deep vision the first time he reads a poem. But because the poet's experience is so intense and because he usually sees more than the reader is accustomed to seeing on his own, most readers must *reach* a little. Consequently, if one sincerely wishes to share and to enjoy the poet's vision, he should consciously develop what has become natural and even subconscious to the good reader. That is, he should cultivate the habit of asking himself the few simple questions about the title, subject matter, theme, tone, structure, rhythm, imagery, and diction taken up throughout PRIVATE MOODS. These elements are not important in themselves but only as they contribute to the total effect of the poem. They should never be studied as ends in themselves but as parts of a whole. It is by coming to know each part better that the reader climbs toward a deeper, more enjoyable realization of the experience and meaning communicated in the whole poem. In this way, the reader tests his own emotions and thoughts against those of the poet, and he discovers that what he thought was purely personal is a universal experience.

Reveille

1. What is the theme? Where and how is it stated?

2. What is the tone? How do the imagery and rhythm affect it?

3. What are the vivid metaphors Housman uses in the first three stanzas?

Afternoon on a Hill

1. What do Millay's proposed actions reveal about her?

2. What things are contrasted in the poem?

3. What is the effect of the alternating long and short lines?

Silver

1. How many things are "besilvered" in the poem?

2. The first two words, "Slowly, silently," state the movement and sound quality carried out in the rest of the poem. Show how the poet, through the imagery and rhythm, maintains the almost motionless silence.

Velvet Shoes

1. How is the title related to the poem?

2. What images are especially appropriate for suggesting softness, slowness, quietness?

3. The poet uses many *l*'s, *m*'s, *n*'s, *s*'s, *w*'s, and *wh*'s. What effect do they have on the sound in the poem?

in Just-spring

1. What does the title mean?

2. What elements of spring delight the poet?

3. What is the significance of the balloonman?

4. What words characterize the tone of the poem?

Wild Blackberries

1. What elements of the July afternoon are "at odds" with the pickers? What is the poet's attitude toward these elements?

2. To which sense does the poet appeal most often?

3. Select four images that are vivid and unusual.

Good Humor Man

1. What are the images of a country summer? Why is the Good Humor man a more fitting symbol for the city? What other symbols might represent summer to the city dweller?

2. What kind of sonnet has the poet used?

A Vagabond Song

1. What is the quality of autumn that the poet communicates: its somberness? its quiet? its melancholy? its brilliance?

2. What specific delights compose autumn's song?

Miracles

1. Classify Whitman's miracles: are they predominantly sights, sounds, places, actions, people, ideas?

2. Some people claim that while Whitman's lines are uneven in length, they are intended to be equal in ideas and to be read with an equal amount of time. Therefore, a long line is to be read relatively fast and a short line slowly, so that each is given the same duration of time. Try reading "Miracles" aloud, and see if you think this contention is a valid one.

Pied Beauty

1. What is Hopkins' theme? How and where does he state it?

2. Make a list of the things he praises. What is unusual about the images he uses to describe each?

3. How does the poem move—quickly or slowly? How does Hopkins control his rhythm? What use does he make of alliteration?

Smells

Notice the mixture of pleasant and unpleasant, sweet and acrid smells. If only one kind had been used, would the poem have had the same appeal?

Precious Words

1. The idea of the poem is fairly trite. State it in a single sentence.

2. What are the elements about the poem that have made it fresh and alive?

Sonnet CVI

1. How does each quatrain advance Shakespeare's theme?

2. What is the basic comparison he uses throughout the sonnet to praise his loved one? Is this fresh or trite?

Fast Run in the Junkyard

1. Why do children like junkyards?

2. How is a sense of speed conveyed in the poem?

IMPLICATIONS

Poets try to transmit their feelings of delight more frequently than any other single mood. What you have read is a sampling of the art they have made from it. Consider your own reactions to the following statements:

1. Delight takes a special set of circumstances to set it in motion.

2. Delight comes from inside a person rather than from the external world.

3. Delight is a mood whose depths are increased by being expressed.

4. Delight is usually tinged with a shadow of melancholy.

5. Delight is a momentary thing that quickly fades.

Private Moods

Moods are reflections of strange and wonderful emotions flooding a person's consciousness. If experiences are the framework on which life is structured, moods give the color and texture and depth to that framework. When one is caught in the meshes of a mood, life becomes more intense.

Take spring, when restlessness seizes your soul and you yearn to be off to a far place. Then your everyday world takes on different dimensions, a different meaning. Or if fear strikes, you are caught by a dark mood that almost strangles your initiative. Once filled with anger or hatred, your mood becomes one of violent and blinding action that may disrupt your pattern of living momentarily or forever. And the dark, agonizing mood of sorrow can almost drown you in its depths and leaves a melancholy thread of color dimming the vividness of today. Nostalgia is a gentle mood, seldom bitter, leading to dreams and memories. But delight heightens joy in the essence of the moment and sends one dancing toward tomorrow.

Poets have written of many subjects, many themes, but nowhere have they found a more satisfying subject than that of private moods: violent or quiet, sad or happy, dreamy or full of action, a mood lends itself to the poetic arts. Like mustard and hot dogs, a boy and a dog, a teacher and a book, poetry and moods go together. Happy indeed is the reader who can respond to these lyric poems and thus increase his own understanding and enjoyment.

IMPLICATIONS

A. Consider the following statements in relation to the poetry you have just read. Would you agree with the propositions?

1. Though many of the moods dealt with are unpleasant, they nevertheless become deeply moving as experiences when described in poetry.

2. The poetry in this group of selections explores the world inside the individual's mind, a world that it is difficult to talk about.

3. Often poems such as these help you to understand things about yourself that you didn't completely understand before.

4. Part of the satisfaction in reading poetry such as this is the revelation that other people have the same feelings and reactions that you do.

5. Beauty is created only out of beautiful things. The dark and ugly moods proved unsuitable for poetry.

6. An individual's deepest and most meaningful moods should never be revealed to another. For a poet to describe his deep emotions is embarrassing and often dull.

7. The only positive mood studied in PRIVATE MOODS was delight. The rest are negative or destructive moods, indicating that poets are negative in their approach to life.

8. It is necessary to be a moody person if one is to be a poet.

9. The poets are not urging people to steep themselves in moods. Instead they have almost a scientific approach of carefully examining a mood, probing its full meaning, and then moving on to something else.

B. In the light of the poems you have read, evaluate the following well-known definitions of poetry:

1. "Poetry is the silence and speech between a wet struggling root of a flower and a sunlit blossom of that flower."—Sandburg

2. "Poetry is the imaginative expression of strong feeling, usually rhythmical . . . the spontaneous overflow of powerful feelings . . . recollected in tranquillity."—Wordsworth

3. "By poetry we mean the art of employing words in such a manner as to produce an illusion of the imagination, the art of doing by means of words what the painter does by means of colors."—Macaulay

4. "Poetry, therefore, we will call musical thought."—Carlyle

5. "Poetry is the record of the best and happiest moments of the happiest and best minds."—Shelley

6. "Poetry is language that tells us, through a more or less emotional reaction, something that cannot be said. All poetry, great or small, does this."—Robinson

TECHNIQUES

A. Poets use different devices to express different moods. Look back at the different sections. In which mood poems were:

1. Images stressed?

2. Catalogs a favorite device?

3. Rhythm important to convey the mood?

4. Sound quality of words used to increase mood?

5. Rhyme patterns important for the mood?

B. Agree or disagree with the following statements regarding literary devices:

1. The images (including figures of speech) that poets use to describe the moods are fantastically accurate in expressing an emotion exactly. Cite examples that you felt were either good or bad.

2. Rhythm seems to have little importance in mood poetry.

3. The way a word sounds can convey as much toward the description of a mood as the meaning of the word itself.

4. Rhyme has less and less importance in poetry because it makes it so trite and singsongy. This is why modern poets have abandoned rhyme.

5. Shakespeare is one of the greatest of poets because he can combine rhythm, sound, and rhyme and produce new understandings or catch a familiar meaning.

6. The real skill of a poet is mirrored by his ability to take familiar words and combine them in new patterns that catch the essence of a mood or image . . . "puddle-wonderful," "couple-color," "a quartz contentment." Can you find examples that appealed to you or repelled you?

WORDS

A. *Personification,* a subclass of metaphor, is the figure of speech which endows ideas, nature, animals, inanimate objects with human qualities. Words which label ideas are generally abstract nouns, but nouns referring to animals and inanimate objects are generally concrete nouns. Concrete nouns may be further divided into *animate,* things endowed with life and the ability to reproduce; and *inanimate,* things which occupy space but are lifeless, such as water, pastures. Animate nouns may be divided again into those which refer to people and those which refer to nonhumans, animals or plants. Frequently we attribute to abstract nouns human emotions, human form, human characters. Expressions such as "night's starred face," "magic hand of chance," and "the sea's face" are examples of personification. What other examples of personification do you find in the poems you have just read?

B. In the poem "Music I Heard" the poet writes "And bread I broke with you." The word *bread* stands for a whole, all things edible. The figure of speech in which a basic part stands for the whole is called *synecdoche* \sĭˈnĕk·də ˈkē\. In the poem "Spring" the poet says "I have need of the *sky*." The word *sky* has been substituted for another word which it suggests *space*. *Metonymy* \məˈtŏ·nə ˈmē\ is the substitution of one word for another which it suggests. An expression like "I have read Shakespeare" is a metonymy since what you probably read was the poem by Shakespeare. Metonymy and synecdoche, because a comparison is implied, are subclasses of metaphor.

C.1. Joyce writes of "the waters' monotone." What does *monotone* mean and what are its roots?

2. Aiken says "all is desolate"; what is the relationship between *desolate, sole,* and *solitaire*?

3. In "My November Guest," Frost writes of the "sodden pasture lane." What connection is there between *pasture* and *pastor*?

4. Dickinson asks a question about "centuries before" in "After Great Pain a Formal Feeling Comes." What is the connection between *cent, century,* and *percentage*?

5. In "Home Thoughts from Abroad," Browning talks of "the first fine careless rapture." Is there a relationship between *rapture* and *rapacious*?

6. Shakespeare's "Sonnet CVI" refers to "the chronicle of wasted time." What is the connection between *chronicle* and *chronic*, as in "a chronic disease"?

BIOGRAPHICAL NOTES

Paul Laurence Dunbar

Paul Laurence Dunbar (1872–1906), American poet, was born in Dayton, Ohio, the son of an escaped Negro slave. He gained a reputation with *Lyrics* (1896), a collection of poems, many of which were in dialect. His complete poems appeared posthumously in 1913.

Richard Hovey

Richard Hovey (1864–1900), a dark and bearded, romantic-looking American poet, was born in Normal, Illinois. He began to write poetry early, publishing his first small volume when only sixteen. After graduating from Dartmouth, he became in succession an art student, theological student, journalist, actor, and lecturer. His early writing attempts were poetic dramas and an elegy, *Seaward*. Collaborating with Bliss Carman, he produced *Songs of Vagabondia* (1884, 1896, 1901), celebrating the joys of the open road, youth, and companionship.

Edna St. Vincent Millay

Edna St. Vincent Millay, American poet, was born in Rockland, Maine, 1892. The most popular poet of her time, Miss Millay was still a student when her first major published poem, "Renascence," appeared in *The Lyric Year* in 1912. While at Vassar, she won the Intercollegiate Poetry Prize; and, in 1917, she published her first volume of poetry. In 1923, she received the Pulitzer Prize for "The Harp-Weaver." She died in 1950.

John Masefield

John Masefield (1878–   ), the Poet Laureate of England, went to sea as a cabin boy when he was fourteen, and his wanderings continued for several years. In 1895, he worked as third assistant barkeeper in a saloon in New York City. He returned to England in 1897, where he lived for a while with the Irish poet and playwright, Synge. He attributes his decision to become a poet to his reading of Chaucer's *The Parlement of Foules*. In his early works, based on his wanderings, Masefield's poetry tended to overemphasize passion and brutality, but he managed to capture a feeling of reality. When he turned to narrative verse his poetry seemed to bloom, though some critics said they were somewhat overwhelmed by his blending the rough physical with the exalted spiritual. He was made Poet Laureate in 1930.

Hannah Kahn

Hannah Kahn (1911–   ) was born in New York City, the daughter of David and Sarah Abrahams. She married Frank Kahn in 1941 and had three children. Her poems have been published in national magazines and she has won many prizes, including an award by the Poetry Society of Great

The Bibliography

Early in your research you will begin developing a working bibliography, which is a list of reference sources you use when gathering information about your subject. You will write a bibliography card for every source you use. This bibliographical data will be recorded on an individual 3x5 index card. Each card should include the following:

1. Author's name, followed by a period. Invert the order; that is, put the last name first and provide the name in the fullest form available. Don't use initials if the name is spelled out.

2. Title of the work, followed by a period, if the source is a book. If the source is a periodical (magazine, newspaper, journal), the name of the article, in quotation marks, comes before the title of the work. The title of the work, whether a book or periodical, is underlined.

Note: Fill each line completely before beginning a new one. Start the first line at the left margin; indent all other lines about 3 spaces.

3. Publication information. For a book: the place, followed by a colon; the publisher, followed by a comma; the date, followed by a period. For a periodical, you would have only the issue date, except in the rare occasions when a volume is included, and all inclusive page numbers.

4. Library call number placed in the extreme upper right-hand corner.

Sample entries

Book: Wellman, Carl. Morals and Ethics. Glenview, IL: Scott, Inc., 1975.

Magazine: Sontag, Susan. "Baby." Playboy, Feb. 1974, pp. 52-59.
(monthly)

Magazine: McDavid, Raven. "Sense and Nonsense." Time, 16 Dec. 1974,
(weekly)   pp. 10-15, 25.

Journal: Mangan, Doreen. "Harry Cogell." American Artist, 38
                   (Dec. 1974), 39-43.

Encyclopedia: "Research Papers." World Book. Vol. 12, 1980.

Note: If the article in a periodical has no known author, you begin
       the entry with the name of the article.

       If a book has no publishing date, use the notation n. d.

       If a source has two authors, invert only the name of the first
       one; e.g. Allison, Lee G. and Melton Ellerbe.

       If a source has many authors (3 or more), use only the name of
       the first one listed and substitute the phrase et al; e.g.
       Allison, Lee G. et al. "Bowman's Discipline." Bearcat Beat,
       Oct. 1981, pp. 3, 7.

Britain and the American Parsons' Sonnet Award, both in 1957. In 1958 she became the poetry review editor for the *Miami* (Florida) *Herald.*

Theodore Roethke

Theodore Roethke (1908–1963), born in Saginaw, Michigan, was both an educator and a poet. He taught at the University of Washington's English department from 1947 until his death. His first book of verse was *Open House* (1941). A volume of his collected poems was brought out in 1958.

Richard Brautigan

Richard Brautigan (1935–   ) was born in Tacoma, Washington. He now lives in San Francisco where he writes haunting, very contemporary, mind-jolting poems and novels. A book of verse, *The Pill vs. the Springhill Mine Disaster,* presented a collection of his poems written between 1957 and 1968. His three novels *In Watermelon Sugar* (1969), *A Confederate General from Big Sur* (1967), and *Trout Fishing in America* (1967) have had an enthusiastic reception by college students.

Edgar Allan Poe

Edgar Allan Poe (1809–1849) led a tragic life, which has made him a romantic figure in American literary history. He felt himself set apart from the spring of ordinary joys and sorrows and so became what he thought he was: "haunted, self-doomed, a weary wayworn traveler." Raised by foster parents, he entered the University of Virginia where he drank too much, ran into debt, and left after a year. He quarreled with his foster-father, tried the army for two years, took a stab at West Point, drifted in and out of editorships. His life was marked by brief successes and dreary, long defeats. He considered the death of a beautiful woman as the most poetic of all subjects and it seems but a natural step to his specializing in horror tales. In addition to horror tales, he wrote many "mystery" stories which have since set the standard for the modern detective story.

Selma Robinson

Selma Robinson (1902–   ), a Brooklyn-born writer, was educated in public schools and trained in New York University's School of Journalism. She married Howard Markel but continued her writing for *Harper's, New Yorker, Harper's Bazaar, McCalls, Colliers,* and has even tried her hand at television plays. She has also served as staff feature writer for several New York newspapers.

Robert Frost

Robert Frost (1874–1963), though born in California, is most often called the poet of New England. He went to Massachusetts when he was 10 years old because his mother honored her husband's request to be buried in the family plot in the East. With no money for the return trip, Mrs. Frost settled down in New Hampshire and supported the family by teaching. Frost himself later tried teaching, then farming and journalism, but he really wanted to write poetry. He kept writing poetry even though no one would buy his work. In 20 years of writing he averaged only $10 a year from his poetry. Feeling rejected by America, he moved his family to England and there published his first two volumes of poetry, *A Boy's Will* (1913) and *North of Boston* (1914). The English readers applauded his ability to use common, almost conversational, language in the established forms of poetry. When his two books were published in the United States, Frost returned (1915). His poetry has a regional locale, but its meaning is universal. Frost himself said that poetry must begin in delight and end in wisdom. In 1960, when he was eighty-six years old, he was asked by John F. Kennedy to read a poem at Kennedy's inauguration . . . the first time any poet was thus honored in America.

Elizabeth Coatsworth

Elizabeth Coatsworth (1893–   ) began her writing career as a poet. Although she has written some 50 children's books and several novels, she still prefers to express herself in poetry rather than in prose. She was born in Buffalo, New York, but since her marriage to Henry Beston in 1929 has made her home in New England. Educated at Vassar College and at Columbia University, she traveled widely for many years in the Orient, North Africa, and Europe. "Sometimes," she says, "in my books I return to these memories. But, in general, I have written about New England, and for everyone from children four or five years old through the late teens into the adult field."

Adelaide Crapsey

Adelaide Crapsey (1878–1914) was the author of a slender volume of verse written in the last year of her life and published in 1915, a year after her death. Of her refined, sensitive verse, her *cinquains* are best known. The *cinquain,* a plain, almost stark, five-line stanza, was her own invention.

John Keats

John Keats (1795–1821) one of the finest of the English romantic poets, wrote for only a few years before dying of tuberculosis. Son of a London stablekeeper, he was short and stocky, enjoying athletics and fighting as a boy. Orphaned in his teens, Keats was apprenticed as a surgeon; but when he was twenty-one he shocked his guardian by announcing he did not wish to follow this profession and intended to write instead. His first book of poems was published in 1817. It was at this time he wrote, "I find I cannot exist without poetry. Half the day will not do . . . the whole of it." Many critics feel that Keats' skill in transmitting the experiences of the senses is unsurpassed in English poetry. His great odes, "On a Grecian Urn," "To a Nightingale," "To Autumn," and "On Melancholy" are among the greatest lyrics in the English Language. Like his mother and brother before him, he contracted tuberculosis. He died in Rome, barely twenty-five.

John Hall Wheelock

John Hall Wheelock (1886–   ) was born at Far Rockaway, Long Island. He graduated from Harvard, studied in Germany, and returned to New York City to become a publisher. His early poetry (1911–1912) was distinguished by its exuberance. His later verse is less vigorous, reflecting his shift from athletic to philosophical poetry. His poetry had now gained greater dignity and his philosophy might be expressed by one of his own lines—"Life, the dreadful, the magnificent."

Robert Graves

Robert Graves (1895–   ) is an English poet, the son of an Irish songwriter. He was educated at Charterhouse School and St. John's College, Cambridge. He was severely wounded while serving with the Welsh fusiliers in World War I. Since 1922 he has lived in Majorca, Spain. Despite his statement that "I decided to be a poet at the age of fifteen and have since denied priority to all my other activities," he has produced an astonishing amount of literature in addition to his poetry: two dozen historical novels (1925–1957), more than thirty nonfiction books (1922–1962), thirty volumes of poetry (1916–1963), and ten translations (1937–1959). In his poetry he says that he strives for the pure, the unpretentious, the essential, the vigorous, and the "nonliterary." In his novels and other prose works, he displays a lucid style and far-ranging scholarship.

Countée Cullen

Countée Cullen (1903–1946), American Negro poet, was born in New York City and educated at New York University and Harvard. He began his literary career with *Color* (1925), a book of poems in which classical models such as the sonnet are used with considerable effect. He published several volumes of verse and a novel, *One Way to Heaven* (1932); he also collaborated with Arna Bontemps in the play *St. Louis Woman* (1946).

Siegfried Sassoon

Siegfried Sassoon (1886–1967), an English poet, descended from Persian Jews on his father's side and traditional English country people on his mother's side. Hence, he spent his boyhood alternating between rugged activities like fox-hunting and literary endeavors like rhyme-making. When Sassoon published a book of poems in 1917 called *The Old Huntsman,* he was called a "brilliant rising star" by some critics. Some of these poems were violent protests against the glorification of war. *Counter-Attack* (1918) and *Picture Show* (1920), with the first book, form a devastating record of men in World War I. Sassoon once said: "Were there even anything to say for it [war], it should not be said; for its spiritual disasters far outweigh any of its advantages . . . war is hell." *Memoirs of a Fox-Hunting Man* (1928), published anonymously, won the two most coveted literary prizes in England for that year.

James Stephens

James Stephens (1882–1950) was an Irish poet and storyteller whose fairy tales set in the Dublin slums and his gentle poems about animals reveal his philosophy that nature and God are one. *The Crock of Gold,* with its Celtic theme, established his reputation in 1912. Actively working in the Irish nationalist movement, he moved to London in 1940 and there discovered he had a natural talent for broadcasting, a medium in which he worked until his death.

Claude McKay

Claude McKay (1891–1948) was born the son of a farmer on the island of Jamaica. He was already known as "the Bobby Burns of Jamaica" when he came to the United States in 1912 to study at Tuskegee Institute and at Kansas State University. Moving to Harlem, McKay supported himself with menial jobs while he wrote poetry. In 1919 he moved to Europe and while living in London published *Spring in New Hampshire* (1920), a collection of his poems. Returning to New York in 1921, he became editor of two radical publications and the next year published what is often considered his finest collection of verse, *Harlem Shadows. Home to Harlem* (1928) was his first novel and the most popular of the three he wrote. This work, along with a collection of short stories, an autobiography, and a sociological study, indicate McKay's writing versatility. But he is best known for his poetry, especially his sonnets. McKay's militancy may be explained by a legend in his family which claimed that his ancestors, brought from Madagascar in chains, avoided having their family separated by vowing publicly that they would kill themselves if sold to separate owners.

Taner Baybars

Taner Baybars (1936–   ) was born in Nicosia, Cyprus, and was first educated privately and then at the Turkish Lycea, Nicosia. But he feels that his chief educational influences were "life itself and many ordinary people." He has lived in London since 1955 and now works for the British Council in their Books Division. His publications include *To Catch a Falling Man* (1963), *A Trap for the Burglar* (1965), and *Plucked in a Far-off Land* (1970). He has also translated and edited three collections of poems from Turkish.

William Blake

William Blake (1757–1827) was born in London, England, the second son of a hosiery merchant. He demonstrated visionary leanings at the age of four, when he screamed because God put his forehead against the window pane. In later years he commented that Heaven pressed close—he could touch it with his walking stick. Recognizing his artistic abilities, his father (unusual for his time) sent him to drawing school at age ten, and when he was twelve apprenticed him to an engraver. His achievement as an artist was remarkable, but equally remarkable were his efforts as a poet. His first poems, created before he was fourteen, are astonishing, for they show a child's delight in his visible world and yet somehow manage to imply far more than they say. This symbolism, suggested in his early works, dominates his later writing, as Blake sought to show his own spiritual struggle.

Phyllis McGinley

Phyllis McGinley (1905–   ) is a suburban wife and mother who has become well known for her light, satirical verse and her children's books. In 1960 she received the Pulitzer Prize for her volume of poems, *Times Three*. Born in Ontario, Oregon, she reports that the nearest town, six miles away, looked like a scene from a TV Western. Her father died when she was twelve and her mother took the family to her native Ogden, Utah. Phyllis McGinley began selling poetry to national publications while still at the University of Utah. She spent a year teaching, then went to New York. After the *New Yorker* began publishing her poems, she moved to Manhattan, married, and began writing regularly, until by 1960 she had published 20 volumes of prose and verse. Many feel Miss McGinley has helped break down the line between light verse and serious poetry. She has been characterized as both kitten and tiger—she uses language laced with wit to point out men's foibles, the amazing fluctuation in emotional fashions, the humor in the commonplace.

Stephen Crane

Stephen Crane (1871–1900) was the last of 14 children born to a Methodist minister. He spent two uninspired semesters in college, but during this time he wrote the first draft of *Maggie, a Girl of the Streets,* a book that was to influence greatly the naturalistic writers of the twentieth century. Crane's first popular success was *The Red Badge of Courage,* a story of the Civil War, which he wrote without ever having been in battle. Later, a tour of the Far West and Mexico inspired some of his finest stories, such as "The Blue Hotel" and

"The Bride Comes to Yellow Sky." Then, while covering the gunrunning activities of the men supplying equipment to the rebels in Cuba, he was shipwrecked. From this experience he wrote a classic story, "The Open Boat." He moved to England to escape the criticism of the press, which gave the impression that he was as bizarre in character as Poe and Byron. From there he wrote his brother: "Your little brother . . . knows that he is going on steadily to make his simple little place and he can't be stopped, he can't even be retarded. He is coming." But just three years later, when he was only twenty-nine, he died of tuberculosis.

James Joyce

James Joyce (1882–1941), an Irish writer, spent most of his adult life in France, though he used Dublin as the setting for his works. He was a gifted tenor with a fantastic knowledge of music. At various times in his life, he began the study of medicine, considered beginning a great Irish daily newspaper, ran a motion-picture theater in Dublin, and took part in the legitimate theater in Zurich. Perhaps this very extraordinary range of interests and abilities led to his experimentation in his writings. In his novel, *Ulysses* (the record of one day), and in *Finnegan's Wake* (the record of one night), he tried to show the stream of thoughts and impressions moving through his characters' minds. Some readers find his work tremendously difficult to understand for he piles one meaning on another until, like a prism, one can find so many interpretations that confusion results. Hence, some call him the master of "extreme obscurity." Yet the poet T. S. Eliot says Joyce is the greatest master of the English language since Milton.

Conrad Aiken

Conrad Aiken (1889–   ) was born in 1889 in Savannah, Georgia, and was orphaned at ten when his father killed Conrad's mother and then himself. A great-great-aunt took the boy to Massachusetts, where, except for residence abroad, he has lived ever since. After being educated at Harvard he turned to writing. His first three books of poetry tended to be imitative, but his next publications were "symphonies of poetry," in which he tried to write lyrics that resembled music. Though Aiken's prose has never received the same acclaim as his

poetry, certain short stories such as "Silent Snow, Secret Snow" and "Mr. Arcularis" have been widely reprinted. His *Collected Poems,* representing some 18 previously printed books of poetry, received the National Book Award in 1953. In 1958, he received the Gold Medal for Poetry from the Institute of Arts and Letters.

Miller Williams

Miller Williams was born in Arkansas and received a B.S. in biology from Arkansas State College and an M.S. in zoology from the University of Arkansas. His first book of verse, *A Circle of Stone* (1964), received good reviews from the critics and was followed by *Recital* and *So Long at the Fair* (1968), from which the selection in this unit was taken. At present, he teaches at Loyola University in New Orleans and continues to write poetry, critical articles, translations, and short stories for journals in both North and South America.

Emily Dickinson

Emily Dickinson (1830–1886) lived her entire life in Amherst, Massachusetts. She spent only intermittent periods in formal schooling, and attended Mt. Holyoke Female Seminary for one year in 1847. Apparently she began writing poetry soon after her return from Mt. Holyoke. In 1862, she sent some poems to a critic for comment and his verdict was that her obscurity and fractured grammar stood in the way of public approval. Since she refused to change her methods of expression, she never consented to have her poetry published while she lived. Only three poems were published in her lifetime out of a total of 1,775. Upon Miss Dickinson's death, her sister, Lavinia, was amazed to find hundreds of poems, neatly placed in packets in a locked box. Lavinia persuaded a friend to help her select and publish a group of them. The critics were hostile, but the public demanded more. Emily Dickinson tried always to find new ways of handling words for, she said, "the old words are numb."

Dante Gabriel Rossetti

Dante Gabriel Rossetti (1828–1882) was a tortured, haunted poet born into an Italian family that had fled to England. Rossetti was also a painter and the acknowledged leader of his talented family, consisting of one brother—who became an art critic, biographer, and editor of *The Germ*—and two sisters: the older, Maria Francesca, became a nun; the younger, Christina, became a lyricist of note. The Rossetti family had a great impact upon the arts and letters of Victorian England. Trying in his poetry to capture the sensuous imagery of Keats, Rossetti's work often has an unbodied, almost unearthly, quality. When his wife Elizabeth died, he ordered all his unpublished love poems placed in her casket and 9 years later had the body exhumed to retrieve his manuscript. He wrote "The Blessed Damozel" as a companion piece to Poe's "The Raven." Poe had shown the grief of a lover on earth; Rossetti showed the yearnings of the dead woman in heaven. His dependence on drugs led to his increased melancholy and ultimately to his death, which occurred as his finest book, *Ballads and Sonnets,* was being printed.

Percy Bysshe Shelley

Percy Bysshe Shelley (1792–1822), one of the best-known English romantic poets, was a political, ideological, and moral rebel of his day. At Oxford University, he published *The Necessity of Atheism,* which resulted in his being expelled. His elopement with Harriet Westbrook, the fifteen-year-old daughter of a tavernkeeper, almost brought his father to disinherit him. Later, as he traveled about Europe with Mary Godwin, his deserted wife drowned herself when she was just twenty. When he went to court to gain control of his two children by Harriet, the court awarded the children to Harriet's sister. Plagued by a lung ailment, Mary and he, now legally married, went to Italy, where Clara and William, their two children died. Shelley's poetry efforts were received with the same public reactions that greeted his social life. "Queen Mab" was used in court to prevent his getting the control of his children. "Prometheus Unbound," "Adonais," and "Ode to the West Wind" had cold receptions. In his works some say there are two Shelleys . . . the thinker and the pure poet. His reputation has gone from complete rejection to near sanctification. Most would agree that Shelley can catch in words . . . a sheer, "Unbodied joy." He was drowned in a boating accident off Italy and his ashes were buried in Rome.

E. A. Robinson

E. A. Robinson (1869–1935), the son of a grain merchant in Gardiner, Maine, entered Harvard determined to write, but his poems were rejected by the *Harvard Monthly* and he left after two years when the family fortune vanished. He kept writing and sending his work out and it kept coming back unpublished. A now famous poem, "The House on the Hill," was printed in a little quarterly with no payment. At twenty-eight he left home for New York without money and without influential friends, determined to live by poetry alone. When Theodore Roosevelt befriended him by getting him a job with the New York custom house, Robinson confided to a friend that he could now not only write poetry but own two pairs of shoes at one time. Three times he won the Pulitzer Prize for poetry. One of his special abilities was the skill to catch, in light verse, the character of the failure, the discarded, the defeated.

Robert Browning

Robert Browning (1812–1889) was a famous English poet whose life spanned a period of tremendous change in politics and poetry. Browning had little formal education, but he read broadly in his father's library of 6,000 volumes and was encouraged to follow a literary career. His first book of poetry, *Pauline,* much influenced by the great Romantic poet Shelley, appeared when Browning was twenty-one. He had little interest in nature, as did many of the poets of his time, but instead used men and women as the subject of his writing. He tried his hand at drama and finally turned to dramatic monologues in which he condensed a whole life into a few telling stanzas. He married the poetess Elizabeth Barrett after a romance as exciting as anything to be found in fiction. Her reputation far outstripped his during their lifetime, but in the twentieth century Browning has been recognized as one of the great poets of the English language.

Henry Wadsworth Longfellow

Henry Wadsworth Longfellow (1807–1882) achieved great popularity during his life both as a poet and a respected professor of Modern European Literature at Harvard. His home was the famous Craigie House, which George Washington used as his headquarters in 1775. His first poem, published when he was thirteen, showed no great promise but did indicate his early eagerness to write. At fourteen he entered Bowdoin College and after graduation was invited by Bowdoin to fill a chair especially created for him, a chair in modern languages and literature. He was only nineteen and felt the need to prepare for this position, so he went abroad where he remained for almost four years. Though he claimed that he never liked teaching, he taught for 24 years. When he was twenty-seven, he became professor of languages and belles-lettres at Harvard. In 1854, he retired to devote full time to his writing. Longfellow's poetry is direct, easy to read, filled with a lilting melody and appealing ideas. At his best he is a fascinating teller of tales. At his worst he is banal and dull. Revered and applauded during his lifetime, Longfellow has been underrated ever since.

Alfred, Lord Tennyson

Alfred, Lord Tennyson (1809–1892), one of the greatest of the Victorian poets, was for his age at once a living embodiment of Victorian virtues and the perfect "bard." He was born at Somersby Rectory, Lincolnshire. His father was a melancholy man forced into the ministry against his wishes. In 1828, Tennyson entered Cambridge but left without achieving a degree, joined the Spanish insurgents, and when he was twenty-four published a volume of poetry. His efforts were so derided by critics that Tennyson published nothing more for nine years. Having fallen in love with Emily Sellwood, he was rejected by her family because he lacked money to support a wife. Fourteen years later, when he was forty-one and successful, he and Emily were married. Added joys of this year were the enthusiastic public reception of *In Memoriam* and his appointment as Poet Laureate of England. *Idylls of the King*, a collection of verse stories about King Arthur and his knights of the round table, is one of his best-known works. Tennyson was the most popular poet of his time. Almost everyone in England, from professional men to farmers, read and recited his best-loved poems which went through edition after edition and were often illustrated and set to music. Many of his lyrics are unsurpassed in English poetry.

Robert Hayden

For a biography of Robert Hayden, see page 245.

A. E. Housman

A. E. Housman (1859–1936) was both a scholar and a poet. For years he was a professor of Latin. In this scholarly post, he was noted not only for his knowledge but for his vigor in critical controversies. As a poet he was best known for his book, *A Shropshire Lad* (1896). The title led many to believe that Housman was born in Shropshire, when in truth he was born in another area and only used the hilly Shropshire country as a background . . . a kind of symbolic setting for his childhood fantasies. As a child, Housman was so small and so very quiet that he was nicknamed "mousie." Both literary critics and the less sophisticated admire Housman's poetry for its use of simple language, the flowing melody, the easily understood ideas, and his flawless execution.

Walter de la Mare

Walter de la Mare (1879–1956) was a clerk in the English branch of the Standard Oil Co. for 20 years; he escaped the monotony of his job by writing imaginative adventures. It has been said that de la Mare longed to dwell in an enchanted past rather than in the ugly present and his poetry is filled with nostalgic, misty memories. Seemingly, he loved all that was "little and lost." He felt that nature was like a veil over some "further" reality of which one could find evidence only in visionary moments. Hence, his writing lies in these visionary moments when he moves into that area that is just slightly removed from reality. Eventually he was awarded an annual grant from the privy purse, so that he was able to give up his office work and write. Outwardly his life remained uneventful . . . his adventures continued to be on paper.

Elinor Wylie

Elinor Wylie (1885–1928) spent most of her childhood in Washington, D.C. Her first volume of verse was published anonymously in England in 1912. Upon her return to America she wrote four novels and several collections of poetry: *Nets to Catch the Wind, Black Armour, Trivial Breath*, and *Angels and Earthly Creatures*. When she married William Rose Benét, she joined a family of poets and novelists and a stimulating literary group in New York. After her death in 1928, Benét edited her *Collected Poems* and *Collected Prose*.

e. e. cummings

e. e. cummings (1894–1962) had the reputation of being the "bad boy" of American letters because of his habit of playing clown, critic, lyricist, and satirist almost in the same breath. He is especially noted for his experiments with typography, punctuation, and verse form. Massachusetts-born, he volunteered for service in World War I upon his graduation from Harvard and spent three months in a French concentration camp on an unfounded charge of treasonable correspondence. From this experience came his first novel, *The Enormous Room* (1922). Shortly thereafter he published his first of several volumes of poetry, *Tulips and Chimneys* (1923).

Frances McConnel

Frances Ruhlen McConnel (1941–   ) was born in Providence, Rhode Island. She moved with her family to Oak Ridge, Tennessee, at the age of four, and again to Anchorage, Alaska, when she was twelve. At fifteen she published her first poem in *American Girl* magazine. In 1960, with her husband, she moved to Seattle, Washington, where she attended the University of Washington. Her poems have been published in *Atlantic Monthly, Poetry Northwest*, and several university magazines.

Bliss Carman

Bliss Carman (1861–1929) was a Canadian poet whose family descended from English loyalists who fled to Canada during the American Revolution. For professions he prepared for law, then teaching, and finally civil engineering; but abandoned them all as careers. Poetry had always been his love, especially nature poetry. In 1885, he cut loose from his ties and went to Harvard where he met Richard Hovey. Deciding to devote themselves to writing poetry, they went to New York. Poetry as a career was an invitation to starvation, so Carman kept the two of them going by doing editorial work. The poems he wrote with Hovey (who died in 1900) were light, romantic verse. Carman's real talent lay, however, in vigorous nature poems. Fame and a settled income reduced the color and flamboyancy of his poetry, though technically it improved. In 1928, the Canadian Parliament awarded him the Poet Laureate's medal.

Walt Whitman

Walt Whitman (1819–1892) is an American poet whose book, *Leaves of Grass,* is considered by many as a landmark in American literature. He was born of simple farm people on Long Island; his father took up carpentry and moved the family to Brooklyn while Walt was still a small child. Here the country boy grew to know the city sounds, to enjoy the warm smells of his father's carpentry work and the excitement of the city streets. He left school when he was eleven, working first as an errand boy and then as a "printer's devil." This led him toward journalism and writing. Losing his job on the *Brooklyn Eagle* after two years as a writer (he was then twenty-nine), he accepted a job in New Orleans as a special writer on the daily *Crescent*. Some biographers feel that this city taught him to slow his tempo and opened to him a whole new world of sights and sounds. At thirty-one, back in New York, he gave up his fashionable clothes to wear those of a common workman and let his beard grow long and loose-flowing. *Leaves of Grass* (1855) was hailed by Ralph Waldo Emerson in these words . . . "I greet you at the beginning of a great career." Whitman continued to publish editions (nine in his own lifetime) of this work and increased the number of poems from the original 12 to the almost 400 that have been reprinted many times in this century. In 1864, friends got him a job in the Indian Bureau which he lost almost instantly because his superior thought his poems immoral. A stroke in 1873 almost incapacitated him. He once said of his poetry: "I depart as air . . . If you want me again, look for me under your boot-soles."

Gerard Manley Hopkins

Gerard Manley Hopkins (1844–1889) was an English poet who graduated from Balliol College in Oxford when he was nineteen. He was much influenced in his undergraduate years by Matthew Arnold and Walter Pater and became such a good friend of Robert Bridges that when Hopkins lay dying, he entrusted his poetry to Bridges. At twenty-one, seeking answers to the religious problems that troubled him, he was converted to Catholicism and in 1877 was ordained a priest. A superior suggested he write a poem about the sinking of the German steamer, *Deutschland,* in which five exiled Franciscan nuns died. This attempt seemed to open the floodgates of Hopkins' creativity, and he began to write poetry. His work is distinguished by the manner in which he unites the sublime with the seemingly ridiculous and by his use of unusual rhythms, striking images, as well as obscure words. Like Emily Dickinson, Hopkins' poetry was not published until after his death. The first publication of his poems, edited by Robert Bridges, came almost 30 years after Hopkins had died from typhoid fever.

Christopher Morley

Christopher Morley (1890–1957) was an American writer best known for his novels such as *Kitty Foyle, Where the Blue Begins,* and *Parnassus on Wheels* and for his light-hearted verse and essays.

He was born two years after his parents came from England to the United States. His father was a professor of mathematics at Haverford College in Pennsylvania and Morley graduated from there with honors in 1910. He spent the next years at Oxford University in England as a Rhodes scholar and while abroad published his first book of verse. On his return in 1913, he worked for Doubleday, Page and Company, a publishing house, and later wrote a column for the *New York Evening Post.* He then became a contributing editor to the *Saturday Review of Literature.*

William Shakespeare

For a biography of Shakespeare, see page 467.

THE DREAMS
OF MEN

In a Glass
of Cider

It seemed I was a mite of sediment
That waited for the bottom to ferment
So I could catch a bubble in ascent.
I rode up on one till the bubble burst
And when that left me to sink back reversed
I was no worse off than I was at first.
I'd catch another bubble if I waited.
The thing was to get now and then elated.

ROBERT FROST

The Architect's Dream, *Thomas Cole.*
The Toledo Museum of Art, Toledo, Ohio.
Gift of Florence Scott Libbey.
Pyramids and pillars, arches, domes, and
spires crystallize the dreams of the
past. The architect, contemplating the
glories of the past, dreams of his and
man's future achievements.

Robert Frost, through a common, homely observation from daily life, says something universal about man's experience on this earth. Watching the bubbles rise in a glass of cider, he imagines himself an infinitesimal speck of sediment that is carried occasionally by a bubble up toward the top of the glass. When the bubble explodes, he sinks; but he knows he will find another bubble and rise again.

The bubbles are men's dreams of what they want their lives to become. A dream carries one along until it bursts, but man being what he is will construct another dream and another and another. For to be alive and to be human is to imagine a better world, a better way of living, a better personality than we now know. The dreams a man has, even though farfetched, determine the direction in which he will try to move.

Every man lives his life in the world of nature which surrounds him. But he also lives in the world that he has rearranged to suit himself. This is the world of fenced fields, of roads, of buildings, and of machines. In addition, he lives in the world of his own imagination, the shadowy world of what he would like to have or become. He has the ability to live a kind of double life in which he is physically in one world and mentally in another. This ability to dream makes it possible for man to hope, to plan, to change. From it comes his willingness to struggle, to undergo hardship, to delay immediate rewards.

The literature in THE DREAMS OF MEN examines the interaction between people's physical lives and the dreams they dream for themselves. These works show how dreams grow out of people's basic desires: the desire for social status, for material wealth, for security in a family, for moral betterment, the desire for artistic achievement, for better government, or for gaining power over other people.

Not all dreams are pleasant, nor are all dreams admirable. Some are too big or intangible for a person ever to achieve. Some must necessarily lead to disappointment and frustration, but all are deeply human.

Without examining dreams and their impact on life, no one can understand the nature of man.

A modern Greek courts a contemporary
Grecian maiden in a heroic fashion.
But the dream of romance, which he actively
sets out to achieve,
meets with an unusual reception.

The Wooing of Ariadne

HARRY MARK PETRAKIS

I knew from the beginning she must accept
my love—put aside foolish female protestations. It is the distinction of the male to be the
aggressor and the cloak of the female to lend
grace to the pursuit. Aha! I am wise to these
wiles.

I first saw Ariadne at a dance given by the
Spartan brotherhood in the Legion Hall on
Laramie Street. The usual assemblage of
prune-faced and banana-bodied women smelling of virtuous anemia. They were an outrage
to a man such as myself.

Then I saw her! A tall stately woman, perhaps in her early thirties. She had firm and
slender arms bare to the shoulders and a
graceful neck. Her hair was black and thick
and piled in a great bun at the back of her
head. That grand abundance of hair attracted
me at once. This modern aberration women
have of chopping their hair close to the scalp
and leaving it in fantastic disarray I find re-
volting.

I went at once to my friend Vasili, the
baker, and asked him who she was.

"Ariadne Langos," he said. "Her father is
Janco Langos, the grocer."

"Is she engaged or married?"

"No," he said slyly. "They say she frightens
off the young men. They say she is very
spirited."

"Excellent," I said and marveled at my good
fortune in finding her unpledged. "Introduce
me at once."

"Marko," Vasili said with some apprehension. "Do not commit anything rash."

I pushed the little man forward. "Do not
worry, little friend," I said. "I am a man suddenly possessed by a vision. I must meet her
at once."

We walked together across the dance floor
to where my beloved stood. The closer we
came the more impressive was the majestic
swell of her breasts and the fine great sweep
of her thighs. She towered over the insignifi-
cant apple-core women around her. Her eyes,
dark and thoughtful, seemed to be restlessly
searching the room.

Be patient, my dove! Marko is coming.

"Miss Ariadne," Vasili said. "This is Mr.
Marko Palamas. He desires to have the honor
of your acquaintance."

She looked at me for a long and piercing
moment. I imagined her gauging my mighty
strength by the width of my shoulders and the
circumference of my arms. I felt the tips of my
mustache bristle with pleasure. Finally she
nodded with the barest minimum of courtesy.
I was not discouraged.

"Miss Ariadne," I said, "may I have the
pleasure of this dance?"

She stared at me again with her fiery eyes. I
could imagine more timid men shriveling before her fierce gaze. My heart flamed at the
passion her rigid exterior concealed.

"I think not," she said.

"Don't you dance?"

Vasili gasped beside me. An old prune-face
standing nearby clucked her toothless gums.

"Yes, I dance," Ariadne said coolly. "I do
not wish to dance with you."

"Why?" I asked courteously.

"I do not think you heard me," she said. "I do not wish to dance with you."

Oh, the sly and lovely darling. Her subterfuge so apparent. Trying to conceal her pleasure at my interest.

"Why?" I asked again.

"I am not sure," she said. "It could be your appearance, which bears considerable resemblance to a gorilla, or your manner, which would suggest closer alliance to a pig."

317

"Now that you have met my family," I said engagingly, "let us dance."

"Not now," she said, and her voice rose. "Not this dance or the one after. Not tonight or tomorrow night or next month or next year. Is that clear?"

Sweet, sweet Ariadne. Ancient and eternal game of retreat and pursuit. My pulse beat more quickly.

Vasili pulled at my sleeve. He was my friend, but without the courage of a goat. I shook him off and spoke to Ariadne.

"There is a joy like fire that consumes a man's heart when he first sets eyes on his beloved," I said. "This I felt when I first saw you." My voice trembled under a mighty passion. "I swear before God from this moment that I love you."

She stared shocked out of her deep dark eyes and, beside her, old prune-face staggered as if she had been kicked. Then my beloved did something which proved indisputably that her passion was as intense as mine.

She doubled up her fist and struck me in the eye. A stout blow for a woman that brought a haze to my vision, but I shook my head and moved a step closer.

"I would not care," I said, "if you struck out both my eyes. I would cherish the memory of your beauty forever."

By this time the music had stopped, and the dancers formed a circle of idiot faces about us. I paid them no attention and ignored Vasili, who kept whining and pulling at my sleeve.

"You are crazy!" she said. "You must be mad! Remove yourself from my presence or I will tear out both your eyes and your tongue besides!"

You see! Another woman would have cried, or been frightened into silence. But my Ariadne, worthy and venerable, hurled her spirit into my teeth.

"I would like to call on your father tomorrow," I said. From the assembled dancers who watched there rose a few vagrant whispers and some rude laughter. I stared at them care-

fully and they hushed at once. My temper and strength of arm were well known.

Ariadne did not speak again, but in a magnificent spirit stamped from the floor. The music began, and men and women began again to dance. I permitted Vasili to pull me to a corner.

"You are insane!" he said. He wrung his withered fingers in anguish. "You assaulted her like a Turk! Her relatives will cut out your heart!"

"My intentions were honorable," I said. "I saw her and loved her and told her so." At this point I struck my fist against my chest. Poor Vasili jumped.

"But you do not court a woman that way," he said.

"*You* don't, my anemic friend," I said. "Nor do the rest of these sheep. But I court a woman that way!"

He looked to heaven and helplessly shook his head. I waved good-by and started for my hat and coat.

"Where are you going?" he asked.

"To prepare for tomorrow," I said. "In the morning I will speak to her father."

I left the hall and in the street felt the night wind cold on my flushed cheeks. My blood was inflamed. The memory of her loveliness fed fuel to the fire. For the first time I understood with a terrible clarity the driven heroes of the past performing mighty deeds in love. Paris stealing Helen in passion, and Menelaus pursuing with a great fleet.[1] In that moment if I knew the whole world would be plunged into conflict I would have followed Ariadne to Hades.

I went to my rooms above my tavern. I could not sleep. All night I tossed in restless frenzy. I touched my eye that she had struck with her spirited hand.

---

1. **Paris stealing Helen . . . fleet.** Paris, the son of Priam, king of Troy, abducted Helen, the wife of Menelaus, brother of Agamemnon. This incident set off the Trojan War, a ten-year war waged by the confederated Greeks under King Agamemnon against the Trojans.

Ariadne! Ariadne! my soul cried out.

In the morning I bathed and dressed carefully. I confirmed the address of Langos, the grocer, and started to his store. It was a bright cold November morning, but I walked with spring in my step.

When I opened the door of the Langos grocery, a tiny bell rang shrilly. I stepped into the store piled with fruits and vegetables and smelling of cabbages and greens.

A stooped little old man with white bushy hair and owlish eyes came toward me. He looked as if his veins contained vegetable juice instead of blood, and if he were, in truth, the father of my beloved I marveled at how he could have produced such a paragon of women.

"Are you Mr. Langos?"

"I am," he said and he came closer. "I am."

"I met your daughter last night," I said. "Did she mention I was going to call?"

He shook his head somberly.

"My daughter mentioned you," he said. "In thirty years I have never seen her in such a state of agitation. She was possessed."

"The effect on me was the same," I said. "We met for the first time last night, and I fell passionately in love."

"Incredible," the old man said.

"You wish to know something about me," I said. "My name is Marko Palamas. I am a Spartan[2] emigrated to this country eleven years ago. I am forty-one years old. I have been a wrestler and a sailor and fought with the resistance movement in Greece in the war. For this service I was decorated by the king. I own a small but profitable tavern on Dart Street. I attend church regularly. I love your daughter."

As I finished he stepped back and bumped a rack of fruit. An orange rolled off to the floor. I bent and retrieved it to hand it to him, and he cringed as if he thought I might bounce it off his old head.

"She is a bad-tempered girl," he said. "Stubborn, impatient and spoiled. She has been the cause of considerable concern to me. All the eligible young men have been driven away by her temper and disposition."

"Poor girl," I said. "Subjected to the courting of calves and goats."

The old man blinked his owlish eyes. The front door opened and a battleship of a woman sailed in.

"Three pounds of tomatoes, Mr. Langos," she said. "I am in a hurry. Please to give me good ones. Last week two spoiled before I had a chance to put them into Demetri's salad."

"I am very sorry," Mr. Langos said. He turned to me. "Excuse me, Mr. Poulmas."

"Palamas," I said. "Marko Palamas."

He nodded nervously. He went to wait on the battleship, and I spent a moment examining the store. Neat and small. I would not imagine he did more than hold his own. In the rear of the store there were stairs leading to what appeared to be an apartment above. My heart beat faster.

When he had bagged the tomatoes and given change, he returned to me and said, "She is also a terrible cook. She cannot fry an egg without burning it." His voice shook with woe. "She cannot make pilaf or lamb with squash." He paused. "You like pilaf and lamb with squash?"

"Certainly."

"You see?" he said in triumph. "She is useless in the kitchen. She is thirty years old, and I am resigned she will remain an old maid. In a way I am glad because I know she would drive some poor man to drink."

"Do not deride her to discourage me," I said. "You need have no fear that I will mistreat her or cause her unhappiness. When she is married to me she will cease being a problem to you." I paused. "It is true that I am not pretty by the foppish standards that prevail today. But I am a man. I wrestled Zahundos and pinned him two straight falls in Baltimore. A giant of a man. Afterward he con-

---

2. **Spartan,** suggesting Spartan characteristics—brave, undaunted.

ceded he had met his master. This from Zahundos was a mighty compliment."

"I am sure," the old man said without enthusiasm. "I am sure."

He looked toward the front door as if hoping for another customer.

"Is your daughter upstairs?"

He looked startled and tugged at his apron. "Yes," he said. "I don't know. Maybe she has gone out."

"May I speak to her? Would you kindly tell her I wish to speak with her."

"You are making a mistake," the old man said. "A terrible mistake."

"No mistake," I said firmly.

The old man shuffled toward the stairs. He climbed them slowly. At the top he paused and turned the knob of the door. He rattled it again.

"It is locked," he called down. "It has never been locked before. She has locked the door."

"Knock," I said. "Knock to let her know I am here."

"I think she knows," the old man said. "I think she knows."

He knocked gently.

"Knock harder," I suggested. "Perhaps she does not hear."

"I think she hears," the old man said. "I think she hears."

"Knock again," I said. "Shall I come up and knock for you?"

"No, no," the old man said quickly. He gave the door a sound kick. Then he groaned as if he might have hurt his foot.

"She does not answer," he said in a quavering voice. "I am very sorry she does not answer."

"The coy darling," I said and laughed. "If that is her game." I started for the front door of the store.

I went out and stood on the sidewalk before the store. Above the grocery were the front windows of their apartment. I cupped my hands about my mouth.

"Ariadne!" I shouted. "Ariadne!"

The old man came out the door running disjointedly. He looked frantically down the street.

"Are you mad?" he asked shrilly. "You will cause a riot. The police will come. You must be mad!"

"Ariadne!" I shouted. "Beloved!"

A window slammed open, and the face of Ariadne appeared above me. Her dark hair tumbled about her ears.

"Go away!" she shrieked. "Will you go away!"

"Ariadne," I said loudly. "I have come as I promised. I have spoken to your father. I wish to call on you."

"Go away!" she shrieked. "Madman! Imbecile! Go away!"

By this time a small group of people had assembled around the store and were watching curiously. The old man stood wringing his hands and uttering what sounded like small groans.

"Ariadne," I said. "I wish to call on you. Stop this nonsense and let me in."

She pushed farther out the window and showed me her teeth.

"Be careful, beloved," I said. "You might fall."

She drew her head in quickly, and I turned then to the assembled crowd.

"A misunderstanding," I said. "Please move on."

Suddenly old Mr. Langos shrieked. A moment later something broke on the sidewalk a foot from where I stood. A vase or a plate. I looked up, and Ariadne was preparing to hurl what appeared to be a water pitcher.

"Ariadne!" I shouted. "Stop that!"

The water pitcher landed closer than the vase, and fragments of glass struck my shoes. The crowd scattered, and the old man raised his hands and wailed to heaven.

Ariadne slammed down the window.

The crowd moved in again a little closer, and somewhere among them I heard laughter. I fixed them with a cold stare and waited for some one of them to say something offensive.

I would have tossed him around like sardines, but they slowly dispersed and moved on. In another moment the old man and I were alone.

I followed him into the store. He walked an awkward dance of agitation. He shut the door and peered out through the glass.

"A disgrace," he wailed. "A disgrace. The whole street will know by nightfall. A disgrace."

"A girl of heroic spirit," I said. "Will you speak to her for me? Assure her of the sincerity of my feelings. Tell her I pledge eternal love and devotion."

The old man sat down on an orange crate and weakly made his cross.

"I had hoped to see her myself," I said. "But if you promise to speak to her, I will return this evening."

"That soon?" the old man said.

"If I stayed now," I said, "it would be sooner."

"This evening," the old man said and shook his head in resignation. "This evening."

I went to my tavern for a while and set up the glasses for the evening trade. I made arrangements for Pavlakis to tend bar in my place. Afterward I sat alone in my apartment and read a little of majestic Pindar[3] to ease the agitation of my heart.

Once in the mountains of Greece when I fought with the guerrillas in the last year of the great war, I suffered a wound from which it seemed I would die. For days high fever raged in my body. My friends brought a priest at night secretly from one of the captive villages to read the last rites. I accepted the coming of death and was grateful for many things. For the gentleness and wisdom of my old grandfather, the loyalty of my companions in war, the years I sailed between the wild ports of the seven seas, and the strength that flowed to me from the Spartan earth. For one thing only did I weep when it seemed I would leave life, that I had never set ablaze the world with a burning song of passion for one woman. Women I had known, pockets of pleasure that I tumbled for quick joy, but I had been denied

mighty love for one woman. For that I wept.

In Ariadne I swore before God I had found my woman. I knew by the storm-lashed hurricane that swept within my body. A woman whose majesty was in harmony with the earth, who would be faithful and beloved to me as Penelope had been to Ulysses.[4]

That evening near seven I returned to the grocery. Deep twilight had fallen across the street, and the lights in the window of the store had been dimmed. The apples and oranges and pears had been covered with brown paper for the night.

I tried the door and found it locked. I knocked on the glass, and a moment later the old man came shuffling out of the shadows and let me in.

"Good evening, Mr. Langos."

He muttered some greeting in answer. "Ariadne is not here," he said. "She is at the church. Father Marlas wishes to speak with you."

"A fine young priest," I said. "Let us go at once."

I waited on the sidewalk while the old man locked the store. We started the short walk to the church.

"A clear and ringing night," I said. "Does it not make you feel the wonder and glory of being alive?"

The old man uttered what sounded like a groan, but a truck passed on the street at that moment and I could not be sure.

At the church we entered by a side door leading to the office of Father Marlas. I knocked on the door, and when he called to us to enter we walked in.

Young Father Marlas was sitting at his desk in his black cassock and with his black goatee

---

3. **Pindar,** a Greek poet.
4. **Penelope . . . Ulysses,** Penelope, wife of Ulysses, remained faithful and devoted to her husband while waiting twenty years for him to fight in and return from the Trojan War. Homer's *Odyssey* records Ulysses' experiences while returning home.

trim and imposing beneath his clean-shaven cheeks. Beside the desk, in a dark blue dress sat Ariadne, looking somber and beautiful. A bald-headed, big-nosed old man with flint and fire in his eyes sat in a chair beside her.

"Good evening, Marko," Father Marlas said and smiled.

"Good evening, Father," I said.

"Mr. Langos and his daughter you have met," he said and he cleared his throat. "This is Uncle Paul Langos."

"Good evening, Uncle Paul," I said. He glared at me and did not answer. I smiled warmly at Ariadne in greeting, but she was watching the priest.

"Sit down," Father Marlas said.

I sat down across from Ariadne, and old Mr. Langos took a chair beside Uncle Paul. In this way we were arrayed in battle order as if we were opposing armies.

A long silence prevailed during which Father Marlas cleared his throat several times. I observed Ariadne closely. There were grace and poise even in the way her slim-fingered hands rested in her lap. She was a dark and lovely flower, and my pulse beat more quickly at her nearness.

"Marko," Father Marlas said finally. "Marko, I have known you well for the three years since I assumed duties in this parish. You are most regular in your devotions and very generous at the time of the Christmas and Easter offerings. Therefore, I find it hard to believe this complaint against you."

"My family are not liars!" Uncle Paul said, and he had a voice like hunks of dry hard cheese being grated.

"Of course not," Father Marlas said quickly. He smiled benevolently at Ariadne. "I only mean to say——"

"Tell him to stay away from my niece," Uncle Paul burst out.

"Excuse me, Uncle Paul," I said very politely. "Will you kindly keep out of what is not your business."

Uncle Paul looked shocked. "Not my business?" He looked from Ariadne to Father Marlas and then to his brother. "Not my business?"

"This matter concerns Ariadne and me," I said. "With outside interference it becomes more difficult."

"Not my business!" Uncle Paul said. He couldn't seem to get that through his head.

"Marko," Father Marlas said, and his composure was slightly shaken. "The family feels you are forcing your attention upon this girl. They are concerned."

"I understand, Father," I said. "It is natural for them to be concerned. I respect their concern. It is also natural for me to speak of love to a woman I have chosen for my wife."

"Not my business!" Uncle Paul said again, and shook his head violently.

"My daughter does not wish to become your wife," Mr. Langos said in a squeaky voice.

"That is for your daughter to say," I said courteously.

Ariadne made a sound in her throat, and we all looked at her. Her eyes were deep and cold, and she spoke slowly and carefully as if weighing each word on a scale in her father's grocery.

"I would not marry this madman if he were one of the Twelve Apostles," she said.

"See!" Mr. Langos said in triumph.

"Not my business!" Uncle Paul snarled.

"Marko," Father Marlas said. "Try to understand."

"We will call the police!" Uncle Paul raised his voice. "Put this hoodlum under a bond!"

"Please!" Father Marlas said. "Please!"

"Today he stood on the street outside the store," Mr. Langos said excitedly. "He made me a laughingstock."

"If I were a younger man," Uncle Paul growled, "I would settle this without the police. Zi-ip!" He drew a callused finger violently across his throat.

"Please," Father Marlas said.

"A disgrace!" Mr. Langos said.

"An outrage!" Uncle Paul said.

"He must leave Ariadne alone!" Mr. Langos said.

"We will call the police!" Uncle Paul said.

"Silence!" Father Marlas said loudly.

With everything suddenly quiet he turned to me. His tone softened.

"Marko," he said and he seemed to be pleading a little. "Marko, you must understand."

Suddenly a great bitterness assailed me, and anger at myself, and a terrible sadness that flowed like night through my body because I could not make them understand.

"Father," I said quietly, "I am not a fool. I am Marko Palamas and once I pinned the mighty Zahundos in Baltimore. But this battle, more important to me by far, I have lost. That which has not the grace of God is far better in silence."

I turned to leave and it would have ended there.

"Hoodlum!" Uncle Paul said. "It is time you were silent!"

I swear in that moment if he had been a younger man I would have flung him to the dome of the church. Instead I turned and spoke to them all in fire and fury.

"Listen," I said. "I feel no shame for the violence of my feelings. I am a man bred of the Spartan earth and my emotions are violent. Let those who squeak of life feel shame. Nor do I feel shame because I saw this flower and loved her. Or because I spoke at once of my love."

No one moved or made a sound.

"We live in a dark age," I said. "An age where men say one thing and mean another. A time of dwarfs afraid of life. The days are gone when mighty Pindar sang his radiant blossoms of song. When the noble passions of men set ablaze cities, and the heroic deeds of men rang like thunder to every corner of the earth."

I spoke my final words to Ariadne. "I saw you and loved you," I said gently. "I told you of my love. This is my way—the only way I know. If this way has proved offensive to you I apologize to you alone. But understand clearly that for none of this do I feel shame."

I turned then and started to the door. I felt my heart weeping as if waves were breaking within my body.

"Marko Palamas," Ariadne said. I turned slowly. I looked at her. For the first time the warmth I was sure dwelt in her body radiated within the circles of her face. For the first time she did not look at me with her eyes like glaciers.

"Marko Palamas," she said and there was a strange moving softness in the way she spoke my name. "You may call on me tomorrow."

Uncle Paul shot out of his chair. "She is mad too!" he shouted. "He has bewitched her!"

"A disgrace!" Mr. Langos said.

"Call the police!" Uncle Paul shouted. "I'll show him if it's my business!"

"My poor daughter!" Mr. Langos wailed.

"Turk!" Uncle Paul shouted. "Robber!"

"Please!" Father Marlas said. "Please!"

I ignored them all. In that winged and zestful moment I had eyes only for my beloved, for Ariadne, blossom of my heart and black-eyed flower of my soul!

I
OLD STORIES RETOLD

Literature abounds in story patterns, many of which are found in different cultures. Similar stories may be found in ancient Greek myths, the Bible, children's fairy tales, and American folklore. Often, these old stories carry the accumulated feelings of the common people about the nature of life. In the selection you have just read, there are three familiar patterns: the "sleeping" heroine waiting to be awakened; the ugly duckling that turns into a swan; and the shrew who needs to be tamed. Looking back at the selection, you can see how old patterns can be blended into a thoroughly modern story.

324

II
IMPLICATIONS

Consider the following statements. Do you agree or disagree with the implication suggested?

1. "It is the distinction of the male to be the aggressor and the cloak of the female to lend grace to the pursuit."

2. Ariadne is basically bad-tempered, stubborn, and spoiled.

3. Marko's relationships with people are amusing in a story, but he would be unpleasant to know personally.

4. Marko has a dream of a perfect wife which he attempts to superimpose on Ariadne's personality.

III
TECHNIQUES

Irony

Irony always involves incongruity: incongruity between what one says and what one is understood to say; between what one wants and what one gets; between what one professes and what one actually does; and sometimes between what the reader knows and what the characters know. An example of the first category follows. See if you can explain the irony created in this dialogue between Marko and Ariadne's father.

"My daughter mentioned you," he said. "In thirty years I have never seen her in such a state of agitation. She was possessed."

"The effect on me was the same," I said. "We met for the first time last night and I fell passionately in love."

"Incredible," the old man said.

Sometimes irony is used with humorous effect, as in "The Wooing of Ariadne." Sometimes it creates deeply troubling, disturbing reactions. In both cases, however, irony increases the emotional impact of the story on the reader.

Organization

Organization is the writer's patterning of the elements of his story. Suppose that you had a handful of sticks cut to three different lengths. You could organize them in a number of patterns: in known geometrical shapes; from big to little, from little to big; in a contrasting pattern—one size vertically; another, horizontally; the third, diagonally. The writer working with characters, emotions, and events may also move these aspects of a story about to create a variety of patterns and effects.

One of the common patterns of storytelling is the arrangement of a series of trials for a character to meet, often three or four in number. The last is usually successful or somehow significantly different from those leading up to it. This is the pattern in many children's stories, as well as in jokes. For instance, each of the three Billy Goats Gruff tries to cross the river. The first two fail, but the third one makes it across the bridge. The "Three Bears" uses a similar but more complicated pattern, for it is a three times three pattern. There are *three* objects in each of the *three* trials: the testing of the chairs, the tasting of the porridge, and the selection of the bed. Furthermore, there are *three* bears who have *three* different reactions as they confront the obvious results of the *three* trials.

"The Wooing of Ariadne" is built on this old, old pattern. How many trials are there? What makes the early trials alike? How is the last one different?

IV

WORDS

A. In "The Wooing of Ariadne," there are references to characters in Greek mythology such as Menelaus, Penelope, Helen, and Ulysses. The name *Ariadne* itself has a mythic background. Greek mythology has been a wellspring of words and phrases that are now a familiar part of our language. When a person is called a *Cassandra*, it means that he or she is a prophet of calamity. In the Greek myth, Cassandra was given the gift of prophecy by Apollo, who loved her. However, she did not return his love as she had promised. Angered, Apollo decreed that no one would believe her prophecies though she spoke the truth. In ancient Greek literature, Cassandra was a prophet of doom. Thus, anyone who predicts disaster—whether it is believed or not—is called a *Cassandra.*

Also from a mythic origin comes the phrase *Achilles' heel,* referring to a person's weak spot. As an infant, Achilles was dipped in the River Styx by his mother to make him immune to wounds or death in later battles. Unfortunately, she held him by the heel, and that was the one part of his body not covered by the magical water. As fate would have it, Achilles was eventually killed in battle by a poison arrow shot by Paris into his heel. Therefore, a person's "Achilles' heel" is a weakness which makes him vulnerable.

Yet another contribution from Greek mythology is *Pandora's box.* According to the myth, Pandora was entrusted with a box containing all the evils that could plague mankind. She was instructed never to open the box, but she did so out of curiosity, letting loose all the ills that afflict man. *Pandora's box,* then, as it is used today, is a source of potential evil.

Now that you know the story behind each of the above mythological references, you may wish to find out more about Ariadne. She is a famous character in Greek mythology. See if you can explain the similarities between the Ariadne of the myth and the one in the story.

B. If one source of words in our language is Greek mythology, another source is from idiomatic compounds. These are constructions made up of two or more smaller words. The meaning of the idiomatic compound is not the sum of the two words that make it up, and the meaning cannot be taken literally. *Brainwash,* for instance, does not actually refer to cleansing of the brain; it means the intensive indoctrination of someone. Similarly, the *iron curtain* spoken of in world affairs is not really a curtain of iron; it refers to the political barrier between Western Europe and the Soviet bloc after World War II. And *horseplay* involves no horses, but it does involve rough, noisy play of the kind children engage in. What do the following idiomatic compounds mean: *Molotov cocktail, fourth estate, pen name,* and *red tape?*

DREAM POEMS

LANGSTON HUGHES

Although for some forty-five years of writing, Langston Hughes' main purpose
was "to explain and illuminate the Negro condition in America," he came back
again and again to the subject of dreams and their impact on life. The collection
which follows is arranged to show something of the evolution of
his thought on this subject.

Dream Variation

To fling my arms wide
In some place of the sun,
To whirl and to dance
Till the white day is done.
Then rest at cool evening   5
Beneath a tall tree
While night comes on gently,
   Dark like me—
That is my dream!

To fling my arms wide   10
In the face of the sun,
Dance! Whirl! Whirl!
Till the quick day is done.
Rest at pale evening . . . .
A tall, slim tree   15
Night coming tenderly
   Black like me.

Daybreak in Alabama

When I get to be a composer
I'm gonna write me some music about
Daybreak in Alabama
And I'm gonna put the purtiest songs in it
Rising out of the ground like a swamp mist   5
And falling out of heaven like soft dew.
I'm gonna put some tall tall trees in it
And the scent of pine needles
And the smell of red clay after rain
And long red necks   10
And poppy colored faces
And big brown arms
And the field daisy eyes
Of black and white black white black people.
And I'm gonna put white hands   15
And black hands and brown and yellow hands
And red clay earth hands in it
Touching everybody with kind fingers
And touching each other natural as dew
In that dawn of music when I   20
Get to be a composer
And write about daybreak
In Alabama.

Youth

We have tomorrow
Bright before us
Like a flame.

Yesterday
A night-gone thing,   5
A sun-down name.

And dawn-today
Broad arch above the road we came.

We march!

The Dream Keeper

Bring me all of your dreams,
You dreamers,
Bring me all of your
Heart melodies
That I may wrap them   5
In a blue cloud-cloth
Away from the too-rough fingers
Of the world.

Dreams

Hold fast to dreams
For if dreams die
Life is a broken-winged bird
That cannot fly.

Hold fast to dreams   5
For when dreams go
Life is a barren field
Frozen with snow.

I, Too

I, too, sing America.

I am the darker brother.
They send me to eat in the kitchen
When company comes,
But I laugh,   5
And eat well,
And grow strong.

Tomorrow,
I'll sit at the table
When company comes.   10
Nobody'll dare
Say to me,
"Eat in the kitchen,"
Then.

Besides,   15
They'll see how beautiful I am
And be ashamed—

I, too, am America.

As I Grew Older

It was a long time ago.
I have almost forgotten my dream.
But it was there then,
In front of me,
Bright like a sun—   5
My dream.

And then the wall rose,
Rose slowly,
Slowly,
Between me and my dream.   10
Rose slowly, slowly,
Dimming,
Hiding,
The light of my dream.
Rose until it touched the sky—   15
The wall.

Shadow.
I am black.

I lie down in the shadow.
No longer the light of my dream before me,   20
Above me.
Only the thick wall.
Only the shadow.

My hands!
My dark hands!   25
Break through the wall!
Find my dream!
Help me to shatter this darkness,
To smash this night,
To break this shadow   30
Into a thousand lights of sun,
Into a thousand whirling dreams
Of sun!

Let America Be America Again

Let America be America again.
Let it be the dream it used to be.
Let it be the pioneer on the plain
Seeking a home where he himself is free.

(America never was America to me.)

Let America be the dream the dreamers dreamed—
Let it be that great strong land of love
Where never kings connive nor tyrants scheme
That any man be crushed by one above.

(It never was America to me.)

O, let my land be a land where Liberty
Is crowned with no false patriotic wreath,
But opportunity is real, and life is free,
Equality is in the air we breathe.

(There's never been equality for me,
Nor freedom in this "homeland of the free.")

Say who are you that mumbles in the dark?
And who are you that draws your veil across the stars?

I am the poor white, fooled and pushed apart,
I am the red man driven from the land.
I am the refugee clutching the hope I seek—
But finding only the same old stupid plan
Of dog eat dog, of mighty crush the weak.
I am the Negro, "problem" to you all.
I am the people, humble, hungry, mean—
Hungry yet today despite the dream.
Beaten yet today—O, Pioneers!
I am the man who never got ahead,
The poorest worker bartered through the years.

Yet I'm the one who dreamt our basic dream
In that Old World while still a serf of kings,
Who dreamt a dream so strong, so brave, so true,
That even yet its mighty daring sings
In every brick and stone, in every furrow turned
That's made America the land it has become.
O, I'm the man who sailed those early seas
In search of what I meant to be my home—
For I'm the one who left dark Ireland's shore,
And Poland's plain, and England's grassy lea,
And torn from Black Africa's strand I came
To build a "homeland of the free."

The free?
Who said the free? Not me?
Surely not me? The millions on relief today?
The millions who have nothing for our pay
For all the dreams we've dreamed
And all the songs we've sung
And all the hopes we've held
And all the flags we've hung,
The millions who have nothing for our pay—
Except the dream we keep alive today.

O, let America be America again—
The land that never has been yet—
And yet must be—the land where *every* man is free.
The land that's mine—the poor man's, Indian's, Negro's, ME—
Who made America,
Whose sweat and blood, whose faith and pain,
Whose hand at the foundry, whose plow in the rain,
Must bring back our mighty dream again.

O, yes,
I say it plain,
America never was America to me,
And yet I swear this oath—
America will be!

Dream Deferred

What happens to a dream deferred?

Does it dry up
like a raisin in the sun?
Or fester like a sore—
And then run?
Does it stink like rotten meat?
Or crust and sugar over—
like a syrupy sweet?

Maybe it just sags
like a heavy load.

Or does it explode?

I
THE DREAM DEFERRED

The right blending of words with an idea has always had the power to stir men's souls. Pericles in the days of ancient Greece, Lincoln during the Civil War, Roosevelt and Churchill in World War II, and John F. Kennedy—all caught the public's imagination in the web of a phrase. And this is what poetry is really all about. Consider Langston Hughes' phrase "a dream deferred." Why is this ordering of the words so much more effective than "a deferred dream" or "a put-off dream"? Why should the common words "a raisin in the sun" have taken such a hold of Lorraine Hansberry's imagination that she wrote one of the great plays of contemporary black life in America using Hughes' phrase as her title?

II
IMPLICATIONS

Hughes, by the way he combines word sounds, movement, and pattern, creates for the reader feelings, perceptions, and intimations about dreams that go far beyond the face value of the individual words used. Reread the group of poems several times until they seem familiar to you. Then respond to the following statements.

Dream Variation

1. The speaker seems to associate himself with night. This means that day is somehow less congenial to him.
2. The title of the poem has little significance.

Daybreak in Alabama

1. The poem has a breathless quality like a child imagining one thing after another.
2. There is a vein of bitterness underlying the poem's seemingly joyful mood.

Youth

The poem is out of keeping with today's mood among young people.

The Dream Keeper

Speculate about possible definitions of "heart melodies" and the "blue cloud-cloth." Do you agree or disagree that such concepts are important in life, though at a casual glance they seem vague abstractions?

Dreams

1. To live fully and deeply, one must dream.
2. Every person has some dream.

I, Too

There is a change in the poem expressed in the difference in the choice of words between the first line, "I . . . sing America," and the last line, "I . . . am America."

As I Grew Older

This poem expresses anguish? bitterness? despair? hope? frustration?

Let America Be America Again

1. Who is the speaker of the poem?
2. Why are two lines in italics?
3. Why are some lines in parentheses?
4. Explain the apparent inconsistency between the first lines

Let America be America again.
Let it be the dream it used to be.

and the lines in the next-to-last stanza beginning

O, let America be America again—
The land that never has been yet—
And yet must be—the land where *every* man is free.

Is the poem bitter or hopeful?

Dream Deferred

A dream too long unrealized injures the dreamer.

III
TECHNIQUES

When you studied the poems in the first unit of this book, you looked at the way rhythm is achieved through repetition of certain elements. Reread this material on pages 37 and 39 if you have forgotten it. Choose one of Langston Hughes' poems and be prepared to explain how elements are repeated to make the pattern.

Choose the poem you liked the best in this group of selections. Point out phrases, word arrangements, or word choices that seem unusually apt.

There was a time when it was a good thing to be an Indian, and old. But Charley was cheated—almost—of his honors, because he lived at the wrong time.

Scars of Honor

DOROTHY JOHNSON

Charley Lockjaw died last summer on the reservation. He was very old—a hundred years, he had claimed. He still wore his hair in braids, as only the older men do in his tribe, and the braids were thin and white. His fierce old face was like a withered apple. He was bent and frail and trembling, and his voice was like a wailing of the wind across the prairie grass.

Old Charley died in his sleep in the canvas-covered tepee where he lived in warm weather. In the winter he was crowded with the younger ones among his descendants in a two-room log cabin, but in summer they pitched the tepee. Sometimes they left him alone there, and sometimes his great-grandchildren scrambled in with him like a bunch of puppies.

His death was no surprise to anyone. What startled the Indian agent and some of Charley's own people, and the white ranchers when they heard about it, was the fact that some of the young men of the tribe sacrificed a horse on his grave. Charley wasn't buried on holy ground; he never went near the mission. He was buried in a grove of cottonwoods down by the creek that is named for a dead chief. His lame great-grandson, Joe Walking Wolf, and

three other young Indians took this horse out there and shot it. It was a fine sorrel gelding, only seven years old, broke fairly gentle and nothing wrong with it. Young Joe had been offered eighty dollars for that horse.

The mission priest was disturbed about the killing of the horse, justifiably suspecting some dark pagan significance, and he tried to find out the reason the young men killed it. He urged Joe's mother, Mary, to find out, but she never did—or if she did, she never told. Joe only said, with a shrug, "It was my horse."

The white ranchers chuckled indulgently, a little shocked about the horse, but never too much upset about anything Indians did. The rancher who told the story oftenest and with most interest was the one who had made the eighty-dollar offer to Joe Walking Wolf. Joe had said to him, "Ain't my horse." But Joe was the one who shot it on old Charley's grave, and it didn't belong to anyone else.

But the Indian agent guessed what had been going on. He knew more about Indians than the Federal Government required him to know. The horse was not government property nor the tribe's common property; everybody knew it belonged to Joe. The agent did not investigate, figuring it was none of his business.

That was last summer, when old Charley died and the young men took the horse out to where he was buried.

The story about the killing of the horse begins, though, in 1941, before that horse was ever born. The young men were being drafted then, and the agent explained it all, over and over again, through an interpreter, so nobody would have an excuse for not understanding. In the agent's experience, even an Indian who had been clear through high school could fail completely to understand English if he didn't happen to want to.

Some of the white ranchers explained it, too. Some of them were expecting to go, or to have their sons or hired cowboys go, and the draft was a thing they mentioned casually to the Indians who worked for them at two or three dollars a day, digging irrigation ditches or hoe-ing in the kitchen garden or working in the hay fields. So the Indians understood the draft all right, with everybody talking about it.

The agent kept telling them, "In the World War you were not citizens, so you did not have to go in the Army." (He meant the First World War, of course. The United States hadn't got into the second one yet; there was only the draft.) "Many of your fathers enlisted in the Army anyway and they were good fighters. They did not have to go, but they wanted to. Now you are citizens, you can vote, and some of you will have to go in the Army. When the letters come for you, we will talk about it again."

Well, some of the young men didn't want to wait until the letters came. Fighting was part of their tradition. It was in the old men's stories, and the names of their long-dead war-riors were in history books, as well as in the stories the old men told around the cabin stoves when snow was deep outside and the cabins were crowded with many people and the air foul with much breathing and not much bathing. (Long ago, before any of these young men were born, their forefathers had bathed every morning in rivers or creeks, even if they had to break the ice, but that custom had passed with their glory.)

The middle-aged men of the tribe remem-bered the white man's war they had fought in, and some of them still had parts of their old uniforms put away. But the stories they told were of places too distant for understanding, foreign places with no meaning except for the men who had been there. The stories the grandfathers told were better. They were about the stealthy approach through the grass after the men had prayed and painted, the quick, sharp action on riverbanks that were familiar still or in tepee camps where white men now live in brick houses.

The grandfathers' stories were of warriors who never marched or drilled but walked softly in moccasins or rode naked on fleet war ponies. They had no uniforms; they wore mys-tic painted symbols on face and body. In those battles there was the proud waving of eagle-feathered war bonnets and the strong courage of warriors who dared to carry a sacred buffalo shield, although a man who carried one was pledged not to retreat. They were battles with-out artillery, but with muzzle-loading rifles and iron-tipped lances and the long feathered arrows hissing out from a horn bow. Killing was not paramount in those old battles; more important was proof of a man's courage in the face of death, and the bravest were those few who dared to carry no weapon at all, but only a whip, for counting coup[1] on a living, unhurt enemy. Nobody was drafted for those battles, and death was often the price of glory.

Only two or three of the old men remem-bered so far back. One of them was Charley Lockjaw. He was suddenly important. If he had not lived two generations too late, he would have been important simply because he was old. His people would have taken it for granted that he was wise, because his medicine had protected him for so long against death. They would have listened respectfully when he spoke. There was a time when it was a good thing to be an Indian, and old. But Charley was cheated—almost—of his honors, because he lived at the wrong time.

Suddenly he was needed. He was sitting in front of his summer tepee, nodding in the sun, with the good warmth seeping into his joints, when four young men came to him. They were modern Indians, with white men's haircuts. They wore torn blue jeans and faded shirts and white men's boots, because they were all cowboys, even the lame one, his great-grandson, Joe.

Charley looked up, ready to be angry, ex-pecting some disrespectful, hurried greeting, like "Hey, grampa, look here."

They did not say anything for a while. Em-barrassed, they shuffled their boots in the dust. Joe Walking Wolf took off his broad-brimmed

---

1. **counting coup**, to touch an enemy in battle, con-sidered the most dangerous test of bravery.

hat, and the other three took their hats off, too, and laid them on the ground.

Joe cleared his throat and said in Cheyenne, "Greetings, my grandfather." It was the way a young man talked to a wise old one in the buffalo years that were gone.

Old Charley blinked and saw that Joe was carrying, with awkward care, an ancient ceremonial pipe of red stone.

Joe asked gravely, "Will you smoke with us, my grandfather?"

Charley was at first indignant, thinking they meant to tease him, because they were atheists who did not believe in the old religion or any of the new ones. He railed at them in English. But they did not go away; they stood there respectfully with their heads bent, accepting what he said and, in the old, courteous way, not interrupting.

He looked at their sober faces and their steady eyes, and he was ashamed for his own lack of courtesy. When he understood that they were sincere, he would have done anything for them, anything they asked. There was not much he could do any more, and nobody had asked him to do anything for a long time.

If he took the pipe and smoked, that said, "I will do whatever you ask." He did not know what they were going to ask, but he would have let them cut him into pieces if that was what they wanted, because his heart was full at being approached in the remembered, ceremonial way, clumsy as these modern Indians were about it. He answered in his reedy voice, "I will smoke with you."

They were going to do it all wrong. One of the young men brought out a sack of tobacco, and that was all right if there was none that had been raised with the right prayers said over it. But Joe pulled out a pocket lighter a white man had given him and another young man brought out some kitchen matches and old Charley could not endure such innovations.

He made them build a fire in the center of his summer tepee, under the fire hole in the peak, and he sat down with a groan of stiffness at the back, in the honor seat, the place of the lodge owner. The young men were patient. They sat where he told them to, on the old ragged carpet his granddaughter had put on the earth floor.

He filled the pipe with pinches of tobacco without touching the bowl and lighted it with a coal from the fire. With slow, remembered ceremony he offered the pipestem to Heammawihic, the Wise One Above, to Ahktunowihic, the power of the earth below, and to the spirits of the four directions—where the sun comes up, where the cold wind goes to, where the sun comes over and where the cold wind comes from.

He spoke reverently to each of these. Then he himself took four puffs and passed the pipe, slowly, carefully, holding the stem upright, to young Yellowbird, who was on his left.

Yellowbird smoked, though awkwardly, in the sacred manner and passed the pipe to Joe Walking Wolf. When Joe had finished, he stood up to take the pipe to the two young men on the other side of Charley, but the old man corrected him patiently. The pipe must not cross the doorway of the lodge; it must be passed back from hand to hand, first to Robert Stands in Water and then on to Tom Little Hand.

The young men were humble when he corrected them. They thanked him when he told them how to do things right.

When he signified that the time had come for them to talk, young Joe, the lame one, said formally in Cheyenne, "My grandfather has told of the old times long ago, and we have listened. He has told how the warriors used to go on a hilltop with a wise old man and stay there and dream before they went on the warpath."

Old Charley said, "I told you those things and they were true. I dreamed on a hilltop when I was young."

Joe Walking Wolf said, "We want to dream that way, my grandfather, because we are going to war."

The old man did not have to promise to help them. He had promised when he took the pipe. He sat for a while with his eyes closed, his head bowed, trying to remember what his instructors had said to him the three times he had gone through the *wu-wun,* the starving. How would anyone know the right way if the old men had forgotten? But he was able to remember, because he remembered his youth better than yesterday.

He remembered the chanted prayers and the hunger and thirst and the long waiting for mystery to be revealed. He remembered the grave warnings, the sympathetic teaching of the wise old men seventy years before.

"It is a hard thing to do," he told the young men. "Some men cannot do it. Alone on a high place for four days and four nights, without food or water. Some men dream good medicine, and some dream bad medicine, and some have no dream. It is good to finish this hard thing, but it is no disgrace not to finish."

"A man lies on a bed of white sage," he told them, "and he is alone after his teacher, his grandfather, has taught him what to do. After four days, his grandfather goes up the hill and gets him—if he has not come back before that time."

Charley Lockjaw remembered something else that was important and added firmly, "The young men bring the grandfather a gift."

And so they went through the *wu-wun,* each of them alone on a high hill, hungering and thirsting for four days and nights. First they brought Charley gifts: four silver dollars from one, new moccasins from another, and two bottles of whiskey. (After the ordeals were over, he spent the four silver dollars for whiskey, too, getting it with difficulty through a man who was going off the reservation and who did not look like an Indian, so he could buy it, though it was against the law. An Indian could vote and be drafted, but he could not buy whiskey.)

The whole thing was secret, so that no one would complain to anybody who might want to interfere. Charley Lockjaw had been inter-

fered with so much that he was suspicious. All his long life, white men had been interfering with him and, he thought, his own grand-daughter might go to the priest if she knew what was going on, or the other young men's families might make trouble. No good would come of telling what went on.

Because of the secrecy, the old man had to ride horseback several times. Usually he had to be helped into a saddle because his joints were stiff and his legs hurt, so that if he did not stop himself and remember that now he could be proud again, he might groan.

He took each young man out separately to a hill chosen because of its height, its loneliness and its location. It had to be south or west of a river—that had always been the rule. He had never known the reason, and neither did anyone else. It was one of the things that was right, that was all, and he was very anxious to do everything right.

At the foot of the hill, he and the young man left the horses hobbled. The young man helped Charley up the hill, respectfully and with great patience. He made a bed of white sage, and Charley sang his prayers to the Spirit above.

He added a humble plea that had not been in the ritual when he was young. "If I make a mistake," he cried to the blue sky, "it is be-cause I am old. Do not blame the young man. He wants to do right. If he does wrong, it is my fault. Give him good medicine."

Then he stumbled down the hill and got on the borrowed horse by himself and rode home. If the young man should give up before his time had passed, he could catch up the horse that was left.

None of them gave up, and none of them cheated. Each of them lay alone on the sage bed on the hill, singing the songs Charley Lockjaw had taught him, sometimes watching the sky (and seeing airplanes more often than wheeling eagles) and three times a day smok-ing the sacred pipe.

The first was Joe Walking Wolf. Charley was proud of him when he toiled up the hill with a canteen of water and a chunk of dry bread. He was proud when the boy first splashed water on his face and then drank, unhurriedly, from the canteen.

When Joe's tongue was moistened enough so he could talk, he said briefly, "I dreamed a horse was kicking me."

"I do not know what that means," Charley told him. "Maybe you will know after you think about it."

He was afraid, though, that the dream was bad. The reason Joe limped was that a horse had kicked him when he was three years old.

The second man was Yellowbird. He was impatient. He was standing up, watching, when Charley Lockjaw came in sight on his old bag-of-bones borrowed horse, and he came down the hill to gulp the water the old man had brought. But he had endured the whole four days.

He said in English, "I dreamed I was dead and gone to hell." Then he said it in Cheyenne, except "hell," and Charley knew what that word was. There was no hell for Cheyennes after they were dead, according to the old religion.

Charley said, "That may be good medicine. I do not know."

The third man was Robert Stands in Water. He was sick and he vomited the first water he drank, but he got better in a little while and they went home. He didn't say what his dream was.

The fourth and last was Tom Little Hand, a laughing young man except when there were white people around. He was a proud rider and a dandy; he wore green sunglasses when he went outdoors, and tight shirts like the white cowboys. When Charley brought the water, he was no dandy any more. Naked to the waist, he lay flat on the sage bed, and the old man had to help him sit up so he could drink and eat.

"There was a bright light," he said when he felt like talking. "It floated in the air and I tried to catch it."

Charley didn't know what kind of medicine

that was, but he said Tom Little Hand would probably be able to understand it after a while.

Anyway, they had all done the best they could, the right thing, and they were ready to be warriors. They had endured in the old fashion.

When they got back to the cabin settlement beside the creek that is named for a dead chief, old Charley dug up his whiskey and went into his lodge and drank, and slept, and drank some more. A teacher is worthy of his hire, and Charley Lockjaw was tired out from all that riding and climbing of high hills. For all that time, four days for four men, sixteen days altogether, he had not slept very much. He had been singing in his lodge or in front of it, in his reedy voice like the wailing of the wind across the prairie. The little boys had not bothered him by crowding in to tumble around like puppies. They were afraid of him.

While Charley was having his drunk, the four young men went down to town to enlist in the Army. He did not know that. When he was sober again, two of them had come back —his grandson Joe and Tom Little Hand, the dandy.

Tom said, "They don't want me. I don't see so good."

Joe Walking Wolf didn't say anything. He went around with his bad limp and got a job for a few days on a white man's ranch, sawing branches off some trees in the yard. The cook gave him his meals separate from the white hired hands, but he heard them talking about the draft and joking with each other about being 4F. Some were 4F because cowboys get stove up by bad horses. Joe felt better, knowing he was not the only one.

In the winter the war clouds broke with lightning and thunder, and the Army decided Tom Little Hand could see plenty well enough to go to war. The Army began to take some married men, too, and almost all the single ones except lame Joe Walking Wolf, and a couple who had an eye disease, and six who had tuberculosis and one who was stone-deaf.

Then for a couple of years old Charley Lockjaw wasn't important any more. The people who were important were those who could read the letters that came to the cabin settlement, and those who could write the answers.

Some of the young men came back on furlough, hitchhiking eighty miles from the railroad. In wartime people would pick up a soldier, even if he was an Indian. They strolled around the settlement and rode over to the agency in their uniforms and went to the white men's store, and some of the white ranchers went out of their way to shake hands with them and say, "Well, boy, how goes it?" They were important, the fledgling warriors.

Old Charley, sitting in front of his peaked lodge in the summer, saw them strut, saw the shawl-wrapped, laughing girls hang around them. He saw them walk down the road after dark, and he felt bad about some of the girls. When he was a young man, the Cheyennes took pride in the virtue of their women. His first wife had worn the rope of chastity until he removed it himself, the fourth night after her father had accepted his gift of captured horses.

He was ashamed of the Cheyenne girls, but not of the young warriors. He pitied them a little, remembering the proud nodding eagle-feathered war bonnets and the tall, straight men who wore them. He remembered his own courting; for five years it had gone on. There were many other gallants who had stood in front of the girl's lodge, blanket-wrapped, waiting for her to come out.

One of the letters that came to the reservation had bad news in it. It was in a yellow envelope, and the agent brought it over himself and explained it to the mother of Tom Little Hand.

Tom had been wounded, it said, and was in a hospital.

The next morning Joe Walking Wolf, the lame one, made a ceremonial visit to old Charley, carrying the old stone pipe. He was not embarrassed this time, because he knew how to smoke in the sacred way.

Charley drew in a breath sharply and was ashamed because he trembled.

"The gift for that, to the grandfather," he cautioned, "must be a big gift, because it is a hard ceremony."

"The gift is outside with the pole," Joe said humbly.

And outside was picketed Joe's good sorrel colt.

There was a time when the Cheyennes, the Cut Arm people, could be lordly in their generosity with gifts of captured horses, sometimes bought with their blood. They could be splendid in their charity, giving buffalo meat to the needy and fine robes to the poor. But that time was when Charley Lockjaw was young. He had not owned a horse of his own for thirty years. And this was the only horse his great-grandson had, for the old mare this colt belonged to had died.

Charley blinked at the horse, a beautiful colt without a blemish. He walked over to stroke its neck, and the colt threw its head back and tried to get away. Charley spoke to it sharply, with approval. The colt was no stable pet, but used to running across the prairie with its mane flying in the wind and the snow. It would throw a rider before it was broke, Charley thought.

He nodded and said, "The gift is enough."

When he was a young man, he had paid many fine horses to the old one who taught him the ceremony for swinging at the pole and whose hard, gentle hands had supported him when he fainted. But he had had many horses to give, and plenty of them left. This was a finer present than he had given, because it was all Joe had.

"We will have to wait," Charley said. "We cannot do this thing today. We will wait four days."

He chose four because it was the sacred number and because he needed time to remember. He had been a pupil for this sacrifice, but never a teacher.

"Come back in four days," he said.

In the time while he was remembering and

praying for a return, in some part, of his old strength and steadiness, he fasted for one whole day. His granddaughter fretted and murmured, coming out to the lodge to bring soup because he said he was sick and could not eat.

"I will send one of the children to tell the nurse at the agency," she decided, but he waved her away, promising, "I will be well tomorrow."

He was afraid, not only because he might forget something important or his hand might slip, but because someone might find out and try to stop him. Somebody was always interfering. For years the old religion had been outlawed by the government in Washington. For years no one dared even to make the Medicine Lodge when the grass was tall in summer, so those years passed without the old, careful ceremony of prayer and paint and reverence that brought new life to the tribe and honor to the Lodge Maker.

This was no longer true by the time of the Second World War, though. Every year now the Medicine Lodge was made by some man who could afford it and wanted to give thanks for something. Perhaps his child had been sick and was well again. A man who made the Lodge, who learned the ritual, could teach another man. So that was not lost, though some of it had changed and some was forgotten, and it was very hard to find a buffalo skull to use in the ceremony.

The white ranchers and their guests came to the reservation in July to watch the making of the Lodge and see the prayer cloths waving from the Thunderbird's nest, and Charley took part in those ceremonies. The white people vaguely approved of the Indians keeping their quaint old customs.

But the Medicine Lodge, the Sun Dance, was a public ceremony. Swinging at the pole, as Joe Walking Wolf wanted to do it, was private suffering.

It was a long time since a young man had wished to swing at the pole. There was no one left in the tribe, except Charley Lockjaw, who could instruct a pupil in the ceremony. No one could teach it except a man who had himself endured it. And only Charley had on his withered breast the knotted scars of that ordeal.

Now that Joe was going to do it, Charley could not keep this great thing to himself. A man who suffered at the pole gained honor—but how could he be credited if no one knew what he had done?

At sunrise on the fourth day, Joe and Charley rode far out to a safe place among the sandstone cliffs.

Then Charley was shaken by terror. He denied his gods. He said, "Do not be too sure about this thing. Maybe the spirits will not hear my voice or yours. Maybe they are all dead and will never hear anything any more. Maybe they starved to death."

Joe Walking Wolf said, "I will do it anyway. Tom Little Hand has a bad wound, and he is my friend. I will make this sacrifice because maybe it will help him get well. Anyway, I will know what it is to be wounded. I did not go to war."

Charley dug a hole to set the pole in. He told Joe how to set up the pole and fasten a lariat to it, and all the time he was thinking about long ago. He could not remember the pain any more. He remembered his strong voice crying out prayers as he jerked against the thong. He had not flinched when the knife cut or when the thong jerked the skewers in the bloody flesh.

He said, "I did this to pay a pledge. My wife, Laughing Woman—my first wife—she was very sick, and I pledged this sacrifice. The baby died, because it was winter and the white soldiers chased our people through the snow in the bitter cold. Lots of people died. But Laughing Woman lived, and in the spring I paid what I had promised."

He had Joe make a bed of white sage. When everything was ready, Joe said, "Fasten it to my back. I don't want to see it."

Charley said, "Kneel on the sage bed."

He made his gnarled hands as steady as he

could and pinched up the skin on Joe's right shoulder. He tunneled through the pinched part with a sharp knife, and the bright blood sprang to the dark skin. Through the tunnel he thrust a wooden skewer three inches long. Joe did not move or murmur. Kneeling on the sage bed, with his head bowed, he was silent as a stone.

Charley put another skewer under the skin on the left shoulder, and over each skewer he put a loop of rawhide, which he tied to the lariat that hung from the pole. The skewers would never be pulled out as they had been put in.

He lifted Joe to his feet and made him lean forward to see that the rope was tight and the pull even. Joe walked a quarter of a circle to the right four times, and back, sagging forward hard on the lariat's pull, trying to tear the skewers through. Then he walked four times to the left, with his blood running down his back.

Charley left the red stone pipe where he could reach it and said, "Three times before the sun goes down, stop and smoke for a little while."

His heart was full of Joe's pain. He ached with tenderness and pride.

"Break away if you can," he urged, "but if you cannot, there is no wrong thing done. If you cannot break away, I will cut you free when the sun goes down.. Nobody can take away the honor."

Joe said, "I am not doing it to get honor. I am doing it to make Tom Little Hand get well again."

He kept walking with his bad limp and pulling mightily, but he could not break through the tough flesh that stretched like rubber.

"I will come back when the sun goes down," Charley Lockjaw said.

Back in the settlement he went around and told a few safe, religious men what was happening in the sandstone cliffs. They said their hearts were with Joe, and Charley knew that Joe would have his honor among his people.

When he went back to the pole at sunset, Joe was still walking, still pulling.

Charley asked, "Did you have a dream?"

Joe said, "I saw Tom Little Hand riding a horse."

"What a man dreams when he swings at the pole," Charley told him, "is sure to come true. I saw myself with thin, white braids, and I have lived to be old instead of being killed in battle." He got out his knife and said, "Kneel down."

He cut out a small piece of skin from the right shoulder and the left, freeing the skewers, and laid the bits of bloody skin on the ground as an offering.

He touched Joe's arm and said gently, "It is ended."

Joe stood up, not even giving a deep breath to show he was glad the suffering was over.

Charley did something new then. He bandaged the wounds as well as he could, with clean gauze and tape from the white man's store. These were new things, not part of the ceremony, but he saw that some new things were good as long as there were young men strong enough to keep to the old ones.

"Tonight," he said, "you sleep in my lodge and nobody will bother you." In the sagging bed in the cabin where Joe slept, there were also two or three children who might hurt those wounds.

"Now," Charley said, "I am going to give you something."

He brought from a hiding place, behind a rock, a pint whiskey bottle, still half full, and said, "I am sorry there is not more here."

He told Joe, "Now you can teach the ritual of swinging at the pole. Two men can teach it, you and I, if anyone wants to learn. It will not be forgotten when my shadow walks the Hanging Road across the stars."

The spirits may be dead, he thought, but the strong hearts of the Cheyenne people still beat with courage like the steady sound of drums.

Charley never rode his sorrel horse, but when it was three years old, Joe broke it. The horse threw him two or three times, and the old man cackled, admiring its spirit, while Joe picked himself up from the dust, swearing. Joe used the horse, but he never put a saddle on that sorrel without first asking Charley's permission.

Some of the short-haired young men never did come back from the Army, but Joe's three friends came back, wearing their uniforms and their medals. Tom Little Hand walked on crutches the first time he came home, with a cane the second time, but when he came home to stay he needed only a brace on the leg that had been wounded, and a special shoe on that foot.

The three soldiers went to the agency to show off a little, and to the white man's store off the reservation, to buy tobacco and stand around. The white ranchers, coming in for the mail, shook hands with them and called each one by name and said, "Glad to see you back, boy! Sure glad to see you back!"

The Indian soldiers smiled a little and said, "Yeah."

The ranchers never thought of shaking hands with Joe Walking Wolf. He had been around all the time, and the marks of his honor were not in any medals but in the angry scars under his faded shirt.

After all the girls had had a chance to admire the uniforms, the young men took off their medals, to be put away with the broken-feathered war bonnets and the ancient, unstrung bows. They wore parts of their uniforms to work in, as the white veterans did, and they went back to raising cattle or doing whatever work they could get.

Tom Little Hand, that proud rider, never wore his old cowboy boots again because of the brace on his leg. He could not even wear moccasins, but always the special shoe. But he walked and he rode, and pretty soon he married Joe's sister, Jennie, whose Cheyenne name was Laughing Woman, the same as her great-grandmother's.

That's all there is to the story, except that last summer Charley Lockjaw died. He had thought he was a hundred years old, but his granddaughter told the Indian agent that he had always said he was born the year a certain treaty was made with the white chiefs. The agent knew what year that treaty was, and he figured out that Charley must have been ninety when he died.

The agent was interested in history, and so he asked, "Was Charley in the fight with Yellow Hair at the Little Big Horn?" Charley's granddaughter said she didn't know.

Her son, Joe Walking Wolf, knew but did not say so. Charley Lockjaw had been there, a warrior seventeen years old, and had counted coup five times on blue-coated soldiers of the Seventh Cavalry that June day when General Custer and his men died in the great victory of the Cheyennes and the Sioux. But Joe did not tell everything Charley Lockjaw had told him.

When Charley died, he left his horse to Joe. So Joe wasn't lying when, after he shot the beautiful eighty-dollar sorrel on Charley's grave, he simply said, "It was my horse."

The three other young men were there when Joe killed it. That was the right thing to do, they agreed soberly, because in the old days when a warrior died, his best horse was sacrificed for him. Then he would have it to ride as he went along the Hanging Road to the place where the shadows of the Cheyenne people go. The place is neither heaven nor hell, but just like earth, with plenty of fighting and buffalo and horses, and tall peaked lodges to live in, and everybody there who has gone before. It is just like earth, as Charley Lockjaw remembered earth from his young days.

When Joe had shot the horse, the young men took the sharp knives they had brought along and peeled the hide off. They butchered the carcass and took the great hunks of horse meat home to their families.

Because the buffalo are gone from earth now, and in the dirt-roofed cabins of the Cheyennes, the conquered people, there is not often enough food to get ready a feast.

DREAMS ARE DIFFERENT THINGS
TO DIFFERENT PEOPLE

Dreams in this story are of two different kinds. Each of the young Indians, as he experiences the ceremony of a warrior fasting on a hill before setting out for war, hopes for a prophetic dream, one to point to the direction of his future. A dream here is being used as a tool . . . a voice from the gods. The four young men find interpreting their dreams baffling, confusing, indefinite. Charley Lockjaw knows a different dreaming . . . a yearning in his heart to pass on the old ways and the old ceremonies to the young. He fulfills his dream. But is either kind of dreaming relevant in today's society?

II

IMPLICATIONS

A. In this story, many of the white people's attitudes toward the Indians are included. What do the quotations below imply? How valid do you think each idea is?

1. "The white ranchers chuckled indulgently, a little shocked about the horse, but never too much upset about anything Indians did."

2. "In the agent's experience, even an Indian who had been clear through high school could fail completely to understand English if he didn't happen to want to."

3. ". . . some of the young men didn't want to wait until the letters [draft notices] came. Fighting was part of their tradition."

4. "An Indian could vote and be drafted, but he could not buy whiskey."

5. "In wartime people would pick up a soldier, even if he was an Indian."

6. "The white people vaguely approved of the Indians keeping their quaint old customs."

B. What do the following quotations imply about the Indians' feelings about themselves and the white world?

1. "Killing was not paramount in those old battles; more important was proof of a man's courage in the face of death."

2. "How would anyone know the right way if the old men had forgotten?"

3. "Charley Lockjaw had been interfered with so much that he was suspicious."

4. "These were new things, not part of the ceremony, but he saw that some new things were good as long as there were young men strong enough to keep to the old ones."

5. ". . . . the buffalo are gone from earth now, and in the dirt-roofed cabins of the Cheyennes, the conquered people, there is not often enough food to get ready a feast."

6. "But Joe did not tell everything Charley Lockjaw had told him."

TECHNIQUES

Irony

A. This story is filled with ironic touches, not only in the relationships between the old man and the four boys, but between the tribe and the whites. Some of the ironic scenes follow. Explain what the characters expected and what actually happened.

1. Charley Lockjaw's first encounter with Joe Walking Wolf and his friends.

2. The dreams the four boys report and the old man's interpretation of each.

3. Joe and Tom Little Hand's experience with the draft.

B. Look over the first group of quotations in IMPLICATIONS. What is ironic in some of the remarks?

Organization

The author begins this short story in the present, but quickly shifts the setting back in time to take the reader through the events that lead up to the present. What advantage do you see in this pattern? How does it emphasize the fulfillment of Charley Lockjaw's dream?

I'm afraid she'll get sore and move away
if she catches me at it, and then I won't
have anyone, because she's my only
real friend, even if she doesn't know it.

Feels Like Spring

MILTON KAPLAN

I stop at the corner drugstore for a breakfast of doughnuts and coffee. I eat fast because I'm a little late, and then I race to the subway station and gallop down the steps to catch my usual train. I hold on to the strap and make believe I'm reading my newspaper, but I keep glancing at the people crowded in around me. They're the same ones I see every day. They know me and I know them, but we don't smile. We're strangers thrown together accidentally.

I listen to them talk about their troubles and their friends, and I wish I had someone to talk to, someone to break the monotony of the long subway ride.

As we approach the 175th Street station, I begin to get tense again. She usually gets into the train at this station. She slips in gracefully, not pushing or shoving like the rest, and she squeezes into a little space, clinging to the pole and holding on to an office envelope that probably contains her lunch. She never carries a newspaper or a book; I guess there isn't much sense in trying to read when you're mashed like that.

There's a fresh outdoor look about her, and I figure she must live in New Jersey. The Jersey crowd gets in at that stop. She has a sweet face with that scrubbed look that doesn't need powder or rouge. She never wears make-

up except for lipstick. And her wavy hair is natural, just a nice light brown, like the color of poplar leaves when they turn in the fall. And all she does is hold on to the pole and think her own thoughts, her eyes clear blue and warm.

I always like to watch her, but I have to be careful; I'm afraid she'll get sore and move away if she catches me at it, and then I won't have anyone, because she's my only real friend, even if she doesn't know it. I'm all alone in New York City, and I guess I'm kind of shy and don't make friends easily. The fellows in the bank are all right, but they have their own lives to lead. Besides, I can't ask anyone to come up to a furnished room; so they go their way and I go mine.

The city is getting me. It's too big, and noisy —too many people for a fellow who's all by himself. I can't seem to get used to it. I'm used to the quiet of a small New Hampshire farm, but there isn't any future on a New Hampshire farm any more; so after I was discharged from the Navy, I applied for this position in the bank and got it. I suppose it's a good break, but I'm kind of lonesome.

As I ride along, swaying to the motion of the car, I like to imagine that I'm friends with her. Sometimes I'm even tempted to smile at her, not in a fresh way, but just friendlylike, and say something like "Nice morning, isn't it?" But I'm scared. She might think I'm one of those wise guys and she'd freeze up and look right through me as if I didn't exist, and then the next morning she wouldn't be there any more and I'd have no one to think about. I keep dreaming that maybe someday I'll get to know her. You know, in a casual way.

Like maybe she'd be coming through the door and someone would push her and she'd brush against me and she'd say quickly. "Oh, I beg your pardon," and I'd lift my hat politely and answer, "That's perfectly all right," and I'd smile to show her that I meant it. Then she'd smile back at me and say, "Nice day, isn't it?" and I'd say, "Feels like spring." And we wouldn't say anything more, but when she'd be ready to get off at 34th Street, she'd wave her finger a little at me and say, "Goodbye," and I'd tip my hat again.

The next morning when she'd come in, she'd see me and say, "Hello," or maybe "Good morning," and I'd answer and add something like "Violets ought to be coming up soon"—something like that to show her I really knew a little about spring. No wisecracks, because I wouldn't want her to think that I was one of those smooth-talking guys who pick up girls in the subway.

And, after a while, we'd get a little friendlier and start talking about things like the weather or the news, and one day she'd say, "Isn't it funny? Here we are talking every day and we don't even know each other's names." And I'd stand up straight and tip my hat and say, "I'd like you to meet Mr. Thomas Pearse," and she'd say very seriously, "How do you do, Mr. Pearse. I want you to meet Miss Elizabeth Altemose." She'd be wearing those clean white gloves girls wear in the spring, and the other people around us would smile because people in the subway are so close to you that they just can't help sharing a little of your life.

"Thomas," she'd say, as if she were trying out the sound of it.

"What?" I'd ask.

"I can't possibly call you Thomas," she'd say. "It's so formal."

"My friends call me Tommy," I'd tell her.

"And mine call me Betty."

And that's the way it would be. Maybe after a while I'd mention the name of a good movie that was playing at the Music Hall and suggest if she weren't doing anything in particular—

And she would come right out with "Oh, I'd love it." I'd knock off a little earlier and meet her where she worked, and we would go out to dinner somewhere. I'd ask some of the men at the bank for the name of a good restaurant. And I would talk to her and tell her about New Hampshire and maybe mention how lonesome I got, and if it's a really nice place and it's quiet and cozy, maybe I'd tell her how

shy I was, and she'd be listening with shining eyes and she'd clasp her hands and lean over the table until I could smell the fragrance of her hair and she'd whisper, "I'm shy, too." Then we'd both lean back and smile secretly, and we'd eat without saying much because, after all, what's there to say after that?

We'd go to the Music Hall and I'd get reserved seats and we'd sit there, relaxed, enjoying the movie. Some time during the picture, in an exciting part, maybe her hand would brush against mine, or maybe I'd be shifting my position and my hand would touch hers accidentally, but she wouldn't take it away and I'd hold it, and there I'd be in the middle of eight million people, but I wouldn't be alone any more; I'd be out with my girl.

And afterwards I'd take her home. She wouldn't want me to travel all the way out. "I live in New Jersey," she'd say. "It's very nice of you to offer to take me home but I couldn't ask you to make a long trip like that. Don't worry, I'll be all right." But I'd take her arm and say, "Come on. I want to take you home. I like New Jersey." And we'd take the bus across the George Washington Bridge with the Hudson River flowing dark and mysterious below us, and then we'd be in New Jersey and we'd see the lights of small homes and we'd stop in one of those little towns, Englewood, Leonia, Ridgewood—I looked them up on a map, wondering which one was hers—and she'd invite me in but I'd say it was too late and then she'd turn to me and say, "Then you must promise to come for dinner this Sunday," and I'd promise and then—

The train is slowing down and the people are bracing themselves automatically for the stop. It's the 175th Street station. There's a big crowd waiting to get in. I look out anxiously for her, but I don't see her anywhere and my heart sinks, and just then I catch a glimpse of her, way over at the side. She's wearing a new hat with little flowers on it. The door opens and the people start pushing in. She's caught in the rush and there's nothing she can do about it. She bangs into me and she grabs the strap I'm holding and hangs on to it for her life.

"I beg your pardon," she gasps.

My hand is pinned down and I can't tip my hat, but I answer politely, "That's all right."

The doors close and the train begins to move. She has to hold on to my strap; there isn't any other place for her.

"Nice day, isn't it?" she says.

The train swings around a turn and the wheels squealing on the rails sound like the birds singing in New Hampshire. My heart is pounding like mad.

"Feels like spring," I say.

Organization

The basic elements of the story are:

1. A lonely young man regularly rides the subway to work.

2. At 175th Street a young woman usually gets on and rides to work.

3. One morning, she is shoved and apologizes for bumping him.

4. He has daydreamed about how he might meet her.

How are these elements arranged so that the story has an interesting twist to it?

I

DAYDREAMS

Everyone indulges in daydreams. The narrator is a quiet, shy kind of person, and his dream is one that fits his personality. Notice that his own behavior is a real factor in his dream. He is imagining how he will act. He wants to be bold and worldly, but he has been taught to be a gentleman and so wants to be sure that the girl does not think him forward or cheap. Do your daydreams tell as much about you?

II

IMPLICATIONS

Find support for your opinion about the following statements both in the story and from your own experiences.

1. Lonely people tend to be dreamers.

2. Mental telepathy made this dream come true.

3. The reality is never as good as the dream.

4. Though this story may seem like fantasy, dreams like Tommy's can come true.

III

TECHNIQUES

Irony

What change could be made in the ending of the story to make it deeply ironic?

In the history
of the world, there are few people
who have made more dreams come true
than Ben Franklin, inventor, engineer,
city planner, writer, politician, statesman.
In his long life he saw many of his dreams
for a better world realized, and not
by accident. He planned his dreams carefully.
In his *Autobiography* he tells of his dream
of perfecting himself morally. But even he found
that human nature couldn't be mastered
as much as he had hoped.

Project of Arriving at Moral Perfection

BENJAMIN FRANKLIN

It was about this time I conceiv'd the bold and arduous project of arriving at moral perfection. I wish'd to live without committing any fault at any time; I would conquer all that either natural inclination, custom, or company might lead me into. As I knew, or thought I knew, what was right and wrong, I did not see why I might not always do the one and avoid the other. But I soon found I had undertaken a task of more difficulty than I had imagined. While my care was employ'd in guarding against one fault, I was often surprised by another: habit took the advantage of inattention; inclination was sometimes too strong for reason. I concluded, at length, that the mere speculative conviction[1] that it was our interest to be completely virtuous, was not sufficient to prevent our slipping; and that the contrary habits

---

1. **speculative**\ˈspĕ·kyə·lə·tĭv\ **conviction,** a conviction reached by meditating or pondering upon a subject.

From *The Autobiography of Benjamin Franklin* by John Bigelow. Copyright 1905 by J. B. Lippincott Company. Reprinted by permission of G. P. Putnam's Sons.

must be broken, and good ones acquired and established, before we can have any dependence on a steady, uniform rectitude of conduct. For this purpose I therefore contrived the following method.

In the various enumerations of the moral virtues I had met with in my reading, I found the catalogue more or less numerous, as different writers included more or fewer ideas under the same name. Temperance, for example, was by some confined to eating and drinking, while by others it was extended to mean the moderating of every other pleasure, appetite, inclination, or passion, bodily or mental, even to our avarice and ambition. I propos'd to myself, for the sake of clearness, to use rather more names, with fewer ideas annex'd to each, than a few names with more ideas; and I included under thirteen names of virtues all that at that time occurr'd to me as necessary or desirable, and annexed to each a short precept, which fully express'd the extent I gave to its meaning.

These names of virtues, with their precepts, were:

1. *Temperance*

Eat not to dullness; drink not to elevation.

2. *Silence*

Speak not but what may benefit others or yourself; avoid trifling conversation.

3. *Order*

Let all your things have their places; let each part of your business have its time.

4. *Resolution*

Resolve to perform what you ought; perform without fail what you resolve.

5. *Frugality*

Make no expense but to do good to others or yourself; *i.e.*, waste nothing.

6. *Industry*

Lose no time; be always employ'd in something useful; cut off all unnecessary actions.

7. *Sincerity*

Use no hurtful deceit; think innocently and justly; and, if you speak, speak accordingly.

8. *Justice*

Wrong none by doing injuries, or omitting the benefits that are your duty.

9. *Moderation*

Avoid extreams;[2] forbear resenting injuries so much as you think they deserve.

10. *Cleanliness*

Tolerate no uncleanliness in body, cloaths, or habitation.

11. *Tranquillity*

Be not disturbed at trifles, or at accidents common or unavoidable.

12. *Chastity*

Rarely use venery[3] but for health or offspring, never to dullness, weakness, or the injury of your own or another's peace or reputation.

13. *Humility*

Imitate Jesus and Socrates.[4]

My intention being to acquire the *habitude* of all these virtues, I judg'd it would be well not to distract my attention by attempting the whole at once, but to fix it on one of them at a time; and, when I should be master of that, then proceed to another, and so on till I had gone thro' the thirteen; and, as the previous acquisition of some might facilitate the acquisition of certain others, I arrang'd them with that view, as they stand above. Temperance first, as it tends to procure that coolness and clearness of head, which is so necessary where constant vigilance was to be kept up, and guard maintained against the unremitting attraction of ancient habits, and the force of perpetual temptations. This being acquir'd and establish'd, Silence would be more easy; and my desire being to gain knowledge at the same time that I improv'd in virtue, and considering that in conversation it was obtain'd rather by the use of the ears than of the tongue, and therefore wishing to break a habit I was getting into of prattling, punning, and joking, which only made me acceptable to trifling company, I gave *Silence* the second place. This and the next, *Order*, I expected would allow me more time for attending to my project and my studies. *Resolution*, once become habitual, would

Advice from Franklin, as it appears in
Poor Richard's Almanac.

IT IS FOOLISH TO LAY OUT MONEY IN A PURCHASE OF REPENTANCE.

BUY WHAT THOU HAST NO NEED OF, AND ERE LONG THOU SHALT SELL THY NECESSARIES.

---

2. **extreams,** eighteenth-century spelling of our word, *extremes.*
3. **venery**\\ˈvĕ·nə·rē\\ *archaic:* yielding to sexual desires.
4. **Socrates**\\ˈsä·krə·tēz\\ Greek philosopher of Athens (469–399 B.C.) who dedicated himself to the task of arousing a love of truth and virtue in the young men of Athens.

keep me firm in my endeavours to obtain all the subsequent virtues; *Frugality* and Industry freeing me from my remaining debt, and producing affluence and independence, would make more easy the practice of Sincerity and Justice, etc., etc. Conceiving, then, that, agreeably to the advice of Pythagoras[5] in his *Golden Verses,* daily examination would be necessary, I contrived the following method for conducting that examination.

I made a little book, in which I allotted a page for each of the virtues. I rul'd each page with red ink, so as to have seven columns, one for each day of the week, marking each column with a letter for the day. I cross'd these columns with thirteen red lines, marking the beginning of each line with the first letter of one of the virtues, on which line, and in its proper column, I might mark, by a little black spot, every fault I found upon examination to have been committed respecting that virtue upon that day.

I determined to give a week's strict attention to each of the virtues successively. Thus, in the first week, my great guard was to avoid every the least offence against *Temperance,* leaving the other virtues to their ordinary chance, only marking every evening the faults of the day. Thus, if in the first week I could keep my first line, marked T, clear of spots, I suppos'd the habit of that virtue so much strengthen'd, and its opposite weaken'd, that I might venture extending my attention to include the next, and for the following week keep both lines clear of spots. Proceeding thus to the last, I could go thro' a course compleat in thirteen weeks, and four courses in a year. And like him who, having a garden to weed, does not attempt to eradicate all the bad herbs at once, which would exceed his reach and his strength, but works on one of the beds at a time, and, having accomplish'd the first, proceeds to a second, so I should have, I hoped, the encouraging pleasure of seeing on my pages the progress I made in virtue, by clearing successively my lines of their spots, till in the end, by a number of courses, I should be happy in viewing a clean book, after a thirteen weeks' daily examination.

Form of the Pages

TEMPERANCE.

EAT NOT TO DULLNESS;
DRINK NOT TO ELEVATION.

	S.	M.	T.	W.	T.	F.	S.
T.							
S.	❋	❋		❋		❋	
O.	❋ ❋	❋	❋		❋	❋	❋
R.			❋			❋	
F.		❋			❋		
I.			❋				
S.							
J.							
M.							
C.							
T.							
C.							
H.							

This my little book had for its motto these lines from Addison's *Cato:*

Here will I hold. If there's a power above us
(And that there is, all nature cries aloud
Thro' all her works), He must delight in virtue;
And that which He delights in must be happy.

Another from Cicero,

O vitæ Philosophia dux! O virtutum indagatrix expultrixque vitiorum! Unus dies, bene et ex præceptis tuis actus, peccanti immortalitati est anteponendus.[6]

---

5. **Pythagoras**\pə ᵇthă·gə·ras\ Greek philosopher of the sixth century B.C. who believed that the essence of all things was number. He and his brotherhood discovered the numerical relationship of tones in music and some of the principles of geometry.

6. "Oh, Philosophy, the director of life. Oh, Philosophy, you seek virtue and reject vice. One day of life is better if you have acted well and according to right principles than an immortality full of sin."

Another from the Proverbs of Solomon, speaking of wisdom or virtue:

Length of days is in her right hand, and in her left hand riches and honour. Her ways are ways of pleasantness, and all her paths are peace.
—iii. 16, 17.

And conceiving God to be the fountain of wisdom, I thought it right and necessary to solicit his assistance for obtaining it; to this end I formed the following little prayer, which was prefix'd to my tables of examination, for daily use.

O powerful Goodness! bountiful Father! merciful Guide! Increase in me that wisdom which discovers my truest interest. Strengthen my resolutions to perform what that wisdom dictates.

Accept my kind offices to thy other children as the only return in my power for thy continual favours to me.

I used also sometimes a little prayer which I took from Thomson's *Poems*, viz.:

Father of light and life, thou Good Supreme!
O teach me what is good; teach me Thyself!
Save me from folly, vanity, and vice,
From every low pursuit; and fill my soul
With knowledge, conscious peace, and virtue
    pure;
Sacred, substantial, never-fading bliss!

The precept of *Order* requiring that *every part of my business should have its allotted time,* one page in my little book contain'd the following scheme of employment for the twenty-four hours of a natural day.

THE MORNING. *Question.* What good shall I do this day?	5 6 7	Rise, wash, and address *Powerful Goodness!* Contrive day's business, and take the resolution of the day; prosecute the present study, and breakfast.
	8 9 10 11	Work.
NOON.	12 1	Read, or overlook my accounts, and dine.
	2 3 4 5	Work.
EVENING. *Question.* What good have I done to-day?	6 7 8 9	Put things in their places. Supper. Music or diversion, or conversation. Examination of the day.
NIGHT.	10 11 12 1 2 3 4	Sleep.

I enter'd upon the execution of this plan for self-examination, and continu'd it with occasional intermissions for some time. I was surpris'd to find myself so much fuller of faults than I had imagined; but I had the satisfaction of seeing them diminish. To avoid the trouble of renewing now and then my little book, which, by scraping out the marks on the paper of old faults to make room for new ones in a new course, became full of holes, I transferr'd my tables and precepts to the ivory leaves of a memorandum book, on which the lines were drawn with red ink, that made a durable stain, and on those lines I mark'd my faults with a black-lead pencil, which marks I could easily wipe out with a wet sponge. After a while I went thro' one course only in a year, and afterward only one in several years, till at length I omitted them entirely, being employ'd in voyages and business abroad, with a multiplicity of affairs that interfered; but I always carried my little book with me.

My scheme of ORDER gave me the most trouble; and I found that, tho' it might be practicable where a man's business was such as to leave him the disposition of his time, that of a journeyman printer, for instance, it was not possible to be exactly observed by a master

351

who must mix with the world and often receive people of business at their own hours. *Order,* too, with regard to places for things, papers, etc., I found extreamly difficult to acquire. I had not been early accustomed to it, and, having an exceeding good memory, I was not so sensible of the inconvenience attending want of method. This article, therefore cost me so much painful attention and my faults in it vexed me so much, and I made so little progress in amendment, and had such frequent relapses that I was almost ready to give up the attempt, and content myself with a faulty character in that respect, like the man who, in buying an ax of a smith, my neighbour, desired to have the whole of its surface as bright as the edge. The smith consented to grind it bright for him if he would turn the wheel; he turn'd while the smith press'd the broad face of the ax hard and heavily on the stone which made the turning of it very fatiguing. The man came every now and then from the wheel to see how the work went on and at length would take his ax as it was, without farther grinding. "No," said the smith, "turn on, turn on; we shall have it bright by and by; as yet, it is only speckled." "Yes," says the man, *"but I think I like a speckled ax best."* And I believe this may have been the case with many who, having, for want of some such means as I employ'd, found the difficulty of obtaining good and breaking bad habits in other points of vice and virtue, have given up the struggle, and concluded that *"a speckled ax was best"*; for something, that pretended to be reason, was every now and then suggesting to me that such extream nicety[7] as I exacted of myself might be a kind of foppery[8] in morals, which, if it were known, would make me ridiculous; that a perfect character might be attended with the inconvenience of being envied and hated; and that a benevolent man should allow a few faults in himself, to keep his friends in countenance.

In truth, I found myself incorrigible with respect to Order; and now I am grown old and my memory bad, I feel very sensibly the want[9] of it. But, on the whole, tho' I never arrived at the perfection I had been so ambitious of obtaining, but fell far short of it, yet I was, by the endeavour, a better and a happier man than I otherwise should have been if I had not attempted it; as those who aim at perfect writing by imitating the engraved copies, tho' they never reach the wish'd-for excellence of those copies, their hand is mended by the endeavour, and is tolerable while it continues fair and legible.

It may be well my posterity should be informed that to this little artifice,[10] with the blessing of God, their ancestor ow'd the constant felicity of his life, down to his 79th year, in which this is written. What reverses may attend the remainder is in the hand of Providence; but, if they arrive, the reflection on past happiness enjoy'd ought to help his bearing them with more resignation. To Temperance he ascribes his long-continued health, and what is still left to him of a good constitution; to Industry and Frugality, the early easiness of his circumstances and acquisition of his fortune, with all that knowledge that enabled him to be a useful citizen, and obtained for him some degree of reputation among the learned; to Sincerity and Justice, the confidence of his country, and the honorable employs it conferred upon him; and to the joint influence of the whole mass of virtues, even in the imperfect state he was able to acquire them, all that evenness of temper, and that cheerfulness in conversation, which makes his company still sought for and agreeable even to his younger acquaintances. I hope, therefore, that some of my descendants may follow the example and reap the benefit.

It will be remark'd that, tho' my scheme was not wholly without religion, there was in it no

---

7. **nicety**\\ˈnai·sə·tē\\ exactness.

8. **foppery**\\ˈfä·prē\\ folly, silly vanity.

9. **want**, lack.

10. **posterity**\\pŏˈstĕr·ə·tē\\ all future generations; Franklin wrote his autobiography for his grandchildren. **artifice**\\ˈar·tə·fəs\\ a device, a clever trick; here, Franklin's little book with its record of his progress in the habits of right living.

mark of any of the distinguishing tenets of any particular sect.[11] I had purposely avoided them; for, being fully persuaded of the utility and excellence of my method, and that it might be serviceable to people in all religions, and intending some time or other to publish it, I would not have any thing in it that should prejudice any one, of any sect, against it. I purposed writing a little comment on each virtue, in which I would have shown the advantages of possessing it, and the mischiefs attending its opposite vice; and I should have called my book THE ART OF VIRTUE, because it would have shown the means and manner of obtaining virtue, which would have distinguished it from the mere exhortation to be good, that does not instruct and indicate the means, but is like the apostle's man of verbal charity, who only, without showing to the naked and hungry how or where they might get clothes or victuals, exhorted them to be fed and clothed.—James ii. 15, 16.

But it so happened that my intention of writing and publishing this comment was never fulfilled. I did, indeed, from time to time, put down short hints of the sentiments, reasonings, etc., to be made use of in it, some of which I have still by me; but the necessary close attention to private business in the earlier part of my life, and public business since, have occasioned my postponing it; for, it being connected in my mind with *a great and extensive project* that required the whole man to execute, and which an unforeseen succession of employs prevented my attending to, it has hitherto remain'd unfinish'd.

In this piece it was my design to explain and enforce this doctrine, that vicious actions are not hurtful because they are forbidden, but forbidden because they are hurtful, the nature of man alone considered; that it was, therefore, every one's interest to be virtuous who wish'd to be happy even in this world; and I should, from this circumstance (there being always in the world a number of rich merchants, nobility, states, and princes, who have need of honest instruments for the management of their af-fairs, and such being rare), have endeavoured to convince young persons that no qualities were so likely to make a poor man's fortune as those of probity and integrity.[12]

My list of virtues contain'd at first but twelve; but a Quaker friend having kindly informed me that I was generally thought proud; that my pride show'd itself frequently in conversation; that I was not content with being in the right when discussing any point, but was overbearing, and rather insolent, of which he convinc'd me by mentioning several instances; I determined endeavouring to cure myself, if I could, of this vice or folly among the rest, and I added *Humility* to my list, giving an extensive meaning to the word.

I cannot boast of much success in acquiring the *reality* of this virtue, but I had a good deal with regard to the *appearance* of it. I made it a rule to forbear all direct contradiction to the sentiments of others, and all positive assertion of my own. I even forbid myself, agreeably to the old laws of our Junto,[13] the use of every word or expression in the language that imported a fix'd opinion, such as *certainly, undoubtedly*, etc., and I adopted, instead of them, *I conceive, I apprehend*, or *I imagine* a thing to be so or so; or it *so appears to me at present.* When another asserted something that I thought an error, I deny'd myself the pleasure of contradicting him abruptly, and of showing immediately some absurdity in his proposition; and in answering I began by observing that in certain cases or circumstances his opinion would be right, but in the present case there *appear'd* or *seem'd* to me some difference, etc. I soon found the advantage of this change in my manner; the conversations I engag'd in went on more pleasantly. The modest way in

---

11. **tenets of any particular sect,** the teaching of any denomination.
12. **probity**\ᵃprō·bə·tē\ and **integrity**\ĭn ᵃtĕ·grə·tē\ proven honesty and complete trustworthiness.
13. **Junto**\ᵃjən̊t·ō\ a group of persons joined for a common purpose. This was the name of the club which Franklin formed when he was a young man. The members shared their books and practiced public speaking.

which I propos'd my opinions procur'd them a readier reception and less contradiction; I had less mortification when I was found to be in the wrong, and I more easily prevail'd with others to give up their mistakes and join with me when I happened to be in the right.

And this mode, which I at first put on with some violence to natural inclination, became at length so easy, and so habitual to me, that perhaps for these fifty years past no one has ever heard a dogmatical[14] expression escape me. And to this habit (after my character of integrity) I think it principally owing that I had early so much weight with my fellow-citizens when I proposed new institutions, or alterations in the old, and so much influence in public councils when I became a member; for I was but a bad speaker, never eloquent, subject to much hesitation in my choice of words, hardly correct in language, and yet I generally carried my points.

In reality, there is, perhaps, no one of our natural passions so hard to subdue as *pride*. Disguise it, struggle with it, beat it down, stifle it, mortify it as much as one pleases, it is still alive, and will every now and then peep out and show itself; you will see it, perhaps, often in this history; for, even if I could conceive that I had compleatly overcome it, I should probably be proud of my humility.

I
THE ARDUOUS PURSUIT

Probably most people want to improve themselves, whether it is by developing a better personality, new skills, or a more pleasing physical appearance. And most people have probably resolved along with Ben Franklin to set up a systematic program to achieve their dream. As a consequence most readers respond to Franklin because he is dealing with something familiar. They may have varied reactions: They may find the formality of Franklin's program something to copy, or they may be reassured when they discover that

---

14. **dogmatical**\dȯg ▲mă·tĭ·kəl\ **expression,** an authoritative statement based on insufficient grounds.

Franklin is also a backslider who can't hold himself to his course.

II
IMPLICATIONS

A. What is Franklin saying about man, his dreams, and the achievement of moral perfection in the following quotations?

1. As I knew, or thought I knew, what was right and wrong, I did not see why I might not always do the one and avoid the other.

2. . . . inclination was sometimes too strong for reason.

3. . . . I judg'd it would be well not to distract my attention by attempting the whole at once, but to fix it on one of them at a time; and, when I should be master of that, then proceed to another, and so on. . . .

4. After a while I went thro' one course only in a year, and afterward only one in several years, till at length I omitted them entirely, being employ'd in voyages and business abroad, with a multiplicity of affairs that interfered; but I always carried my little book with me.

5. . . . I was, by the endeavour, a better and a happier man than I otherwise should have been if I had not attempted it. . . .

B. Statements to discuss: After reading this essay would you agree or disagree?

1. It is better to try for a dream and fail than never to try.

2. The thirteen virtues Franklin sets out to attain would make a good pattern for the average person to pursue today.

3. Men today are generally satisfied to settle for the "speckled ax."

4. Franklin indicates that his striving for moral perfection was an actual asset in his life.

5. In striving for a dream it is necessary to follow a certain order.

6. If one waited to conquer each virtue in turn, he'd never get beyond the first one.

III
TECHNIQUES

Irony

1. For almost a hundred years after Franklin's death it was fashionable to magnify the virtues and ignore the faults of our nation's heroes. Thus, men like George Washington, Thomas Jefferson, and particularly Benjamin Franklin were made to seem like austere giants, much better in every way than ordinary people. It was not until the twentieth century that a careful reexamination of Franklin turned him up to be a human being—an extremely brilliant and effective one, but like us with his share of human faults. He loved the ladies more than he should; he was unable to manage money; he could connive with rascals on occasions; he liked a good rousing party. Knowing this, how would you perhaps reinterpret what Franklin says about his dream of moral perfection?

2. Reexamine the statements given you under Implications. Do any of these imply an ironic tone: Do they mean something different from what they seem to be saying?

3. What is ironic about Franklin's constantly pointing out that when he becomes busy with affairs, he does not have the time for cultivating his virtues?

Organization

Franklin's writing is illustrative of a tightly knit system more usual years ago than it is today. Skim through a half dozen paragraphs, paying particular attention to the first sentence of each. What do you discover about the relationship between the first sentence and the remainder of the paragraph? Test your generalization by looking at a few more of his paragraphs. What is your reaction to writing that is so organized?

IV
WORDS

From context determine the meaning of the italicized words. Then consult a good dictionary to check your meaning. What clues helped you unlock the meaning of each?

1. People drooped and *shambled,* but the girls carried themselves tall and walked a straight line. . . .

2. . . . they bumped against each other, without notice or apology, and *caromed* away again.

3. . . . it offended him that the links should lie in enforced *fallowness,* haunted by ragged sparrows for the long season.

4. But he had received a strong emotional shock, and his *perturbation* required a violent and immediate outlet.

The distance between dream
and reality is sometimes insurmountable.
Even a most practical dreamer,
such as Ben Franklin, sometimes forgets
to take into account things as they really are.
Being too literal about a dream can be absurd,
or so Mark Twain suggests.

The Story
of the
Good Little Boy

MARK TWAIN

Once there was a good little boy by the name of Jacob Blivens. He always obeyed his parents, no matter how absurd and unreasonable their demands were; and he always learned his book, and never was late at Sabbath school. He would not play hookey, even when his sober judgment told him it was the most profitable thing he could do. None of the other boys could ever make that boy out, he acted so strangely. He wouldn't lie, no matter how convenient it was. He just said it was wrong to lie, and that was sufficient for him. And he was so honest that he was simply ridiculous. The curious ways that that Jacob had, surpassed everything. He wouldn't play marbles on Sunday, he wouldn't rob birds' nests, he wouldn't give hot pennies to organ-grinders' monkeys; he didn't seem to take any interest in any kind of rational amusement. So the other boys used to try to reason it out and come to an understanding of him, but they couldn't arrive at any satisfactory conclusion. As I said before, they could only figure out a sort of vague idea that he was "afflicted," and so they took him under their protection, and never allowed any harm to come to him.

This good little boy read all the Sunday-school books; they were his greatest delight. This was the whole secret of it. He believed in the good little boys they put in the Sunday-school books; he had every confidence in them. He longed to come across one of them alive once; but he never did. They all died before his time, maybe. Whenever he read about a particularly good one he turned over quickly to the end to see what became of him, because he wanted to travel thousands of miles and gaze on him; but it wasn't any use; that good little boy always died in the last chapter, and there was a picture of the funeral, with all his relations and the Sunday-school children standing around the grave in pantaloons[1] that were too short, and bonnets that were too large, and everybody crying into handkerchiefs that had as much as a yard and a half of stuff in them. He was always headed off in this way. He never could see one of those good little boys on account of his always dying in the last chapter.

Jacob had a noble ambition to be put in a Sunday-school book. He wanted to be put in, with pictures representing him gloriously declining to lie to his mother, and her weeping for joy about it; and pictures representing him standing on the doorstep giving a penny to a poor beggar-woman with six children, and telling her to spend it freely, but not to be extravagant, because extravagance is a sin; and pictures of him magnanimously refusing to tell on the bad boy who always lay in wait for him around the corner as he came from school, and welted him over the head with a lath, and then chased him home, saying, "Hi! hi!" as he proceeded. That was the ambition of young Jacob Blivens. He wished to be put in a Sunday-school book. It made him feel a little uncomfortable sometimes when he reflected that the good little boys always died. He loved to live, you know, and this was the most unpleasant feature about being a Sunday-school-book boy. He knew it was not healthy to be good. He knew it was more fatal than consumption to be so supernaturally good as the boys in the books were; he knew that none of them had ever been

able to stand it long, and it pained him to think that if they put him in a book he wouldn't ever see it, or even if they did get the book out before he died it wouldn't be popular without any picture of his funeral in the back part of it. It couldn't be much of a Sunday-school book that couldn't tell about the advice he gave to the community when he was dying. So at last, of course, he had to make up his mind to do the best he could under the circumstances— to live right, and hang on as long as he could, and have his dying speech all ready when his time came.

But somehow nothing ever went right with this good little boy; nothing ever turned out with him the way it turned out with the good little boys in the books. They always had a good time, and the bad boys had the broken legs; but in his case there was a screw loose somewhere, and it all happened just the other way. When he found Jim Blake stealing apples, and went under the tree to read to him about the bad little boy who fell out of a neighbor's apple tree and broke his arm, Jim fell out of the tree, too, but he fell on *him* and broke *his* arm, and Jim wasn't hurt at all. Jacob couldn't understand that. There wasn't anything in the books like it.

And once, when some bad boys pushed a blind man over in the mud, and Jacob ran to help him up and receive his blessing, the blind man did not give him any blessing at all, but whacked him over the head with his stick and said he would like to catch him shoving *him* again, and then pretending to help him up. This was not in accordance with any of the books. Jacob looked them all over to see.

One thing that Jacob wanted to do was to find a lame dog that hadn't any place to stay, and was hungry and persecuted, and bring him home and pet him and have that dog's imperishable gratitude. And at last he found one and was happy; and he brought him home and fed him, but when he was going to pet him the dog flew at him and tore all the clothes off him ex-

1. **pantaloons**\păn·tə ᴬlūnz\ trousers.

cept those that were in front, and made a spectacle of him that was astonishing. He examined authorities, but he could not understand the matter. It was of the same breed of dogs that was in the books, but it acted very differently. Whatever this boy did he got into trouble. The very things the boys in the books got rewarded for turned out to be about the most unprofitable things he could invest in.

Once, when he was on his way to Sunday-school, he saw some bad boys starting off pleasuring in a sailboat. He was filled with consternation, because he knew from his reading that boys who went sailing on Sunday invariably got drowned. So he ran out on a raft to warn them, but a log turned with him and slid him into the river. A man got him out pretty soon, and the doctor pumped the water out of him, and gave him a fresh start with his bellows, but he caught cold and lay sick abed nine weeks. But the most unaccountable thing about it was that the bad boys in the boat had a good time all day, and then reached home alive and well in the most surprising manner. Jacob Blivens said there was nothing like these things in the books. He was perfectly dumfounded.

When he got well he was a little discouraged, but he resolved to keep on trying anyhow. He knew that so far his experiences wouldn't do to go in a book, but he hadn't yet reached the allotted term of life for good little boys, and he hoped to be able to make a record yet if he could hold on till his time was fully up. If everything else failed he had his dying speech to fall back on.

He examined his authorities, and found that it was now time for him to go to sea as a cabin-boy. He called on a ship-captain and made his application, and when the captain asked for his recommendations he proudly drew out a tract[2] and pointed to the word, "To Jacob Blivens, from his affectionate teacher." But the captain was a coarse, vulgar man, and he said, "Oh, that be blowed! *that* wasn't any proof that he knew how to wash dishes or handle a slush-bucket,[3] and he guessed he didn't want him." This was altogether the most extraordinary

thing that ever happened to Jacob in all his life. A compliment from a teacher, on a tract, had never failed to move the tenderest emotions of ship-captains, and open the way to all offices of honor and profit in their gift—it never had in any book that ever *he* had read. He could hardly believe his senses.

This boy always had a hard time of it. Nothing ever came out according to the authorities with him. At last, one day, when he was around hunting up bad little boys to admonish,[4] he found a lot of them in the old iron-foundry fixing up a little joke on fourteen or fifteen dogs, which they had tied together in long procession, and were going to ornament with empty nitroglycerin cans made fast to their tails. Jacob's heart was touched. He sat down on one of those cans (for he never minded grease when duty was before him), and he took hold of the foremost dog by the collar, and turned his reproving eye upon wicked Tom Jones. But just at that moment Alderman Mc-Welter, full of wrath, stepped in. All the bad boys ran away, but Jacob Blivens rose in conscious innocence and began one of those stately little Sunday-school-book speeches which always commence with "Oh, sir!" in dead opposition to the fact that no boy, good or bad, ever starts a remark with "Oh, sir." But the alderman never waited to hear the rest. He took Jacob Blivens by the ear and turned him around, and hit him a whack in the rear with the flat of his hand; and in an instant that good little boy shot out through the roof and soared away toward the sun, with the fragments of those fifteen dogs stringing after him like the tail of a kite. And there wasn't a sign of that alderman or that old iron-foundry left on the face of the earth; and, as for young Jacob Blivens, he never got a chance to make his last dying speech after all his trouble fixing it up,

---

2. **tract**\trăkt\ a booklet or leaflet on some moral or religious subject.
3. **slush-bucket,** a bucket used in washing the decks of a ship.
4. **to admonish**\ăd ᴧmŏ·nĭsh\ to warn, to advise.

unless he made it to the birds; because, although the bulk of him came down all right in a tree-top in an adjoining county, the rest of him was apportioned[5] around among four townships, and so they had to hold five inquests[6] on him to find out whether he was dead or not, and how it occurred. You never saw a boy scattered so.

Thus perished the good little boy who did the best he could, but didn't come out according to the books. Every boy who ever did as he did prospered except him. His case is truly remarkable. It will probably never be accounted for.

I
TONGUE IN CHEEK

The reader knows almost immediately that Twain meant his picture to be ridiculous. Certainly by the end of the first paragraph a reader is sure that Twain is pulling his leg. But how does he know it? For every sentence by itself is perfectly straightforward: The words seem to mean exactly what they say. But subtly Twain somehow suggests an interpretation different from the apparent one. Skim through paragraph one and see if you can discover any particular words and techniques that tell you Twain has his "tongue in his cheek."

II
IMPLICATIONS

Answer the following questions.

1. What reward does Jacob Blivens expect for being a good little boy?

2. How does Jacob Blivens' dream of moral perfection differ from Franklin's?

---

5. **apportioned**\ə ⁴pōr·shənd\ distributed in proper shares.
6. **inquests**\⁴ĭn·kwĕsts\ investigations by a coroner and a coroner's jury of any death not clearly due to natural causes.

3. What is your reaction to Twain's suggestion that it is more fun to be bad than good?

4. Why is Twain's picture of the good little boy amusing?

III
TECHNIQUES
Irony

The contrast between appearance and reality is obvious in this sketch. For the most part Twain makes use of what is called dramatic irony—events turn out differently from what is expected or intended. Sometimes the writer lets the reader see what the outcome will be while the character(s) are in ignorance of the real outcome until the dramatic moment when the surprise or shock at the outcome will be greatest.

1. What examples of dramatic irony are there in this sketch?

2. Does Twain let the reader know what the outcome will be while he keeps Jacob Blivens in the dark? Always? If so, how does he do it?

Organization

The organizing principle of this sketch is very similar to a principle commonly used in expository essays. Twain uses the principle of *illustration* (or *multiple examples,* as it is sometimes called). According to this principle, the writer states his thesis, then explains what it means, and then "proves" it by a series of examples often ending with a climactic (or clincher) one which demonstrates the thesis beyond a doubt. Taking as Twain's thesis statement, "nothing ever went right for this good little boy; nothing ever turned out with him the way it turned out with the good little boys in the books," what are the examples used to prove the point?

IV
WORDS

Analyze the following words into affixes and roots, giving the general meanings of the latter. In each case determine how the original meaning of the root is related to the current meaning of the word: *arrogant, lethargically, hazard, elation, preposterous, precarious, eccentricity, transcend, affluence, proposition.*

Ha'penny's dream world
and the real world became one
shortly before his death. Suppose, however,
his imaginary world had become so powerful
that it completely overshadowed reality.
In the following story, Conrad Aiken explores
what can happen when a person abandons
the physical world for the mental.

Silent Snow, Secret Snow

CONRAD AIKEN

I

Just why it should have happened, or why it should have happened just when it did, he could not, of course, possibly have said; nor perhaps would it even have occurred to him to ask. The thing was above all a secret, something to be preciously concealed from Mother and Father; and to that very fact it owed an enormous part of its deliciousness. It was like a peculiarly beautiful trinket to be carried unmentioned in one's trouser-pocket—a rare stamp, an old coin, a few tiny gold links found trodden out of shape on the path in the park, a pebble of carnelian,[1] a seashell distinguishable from all others by an unusual spot or stripe—and, as if it were any one of these, he carried around with him everywhere a warm and persistent and increasingly beautiful sense of possession. Nor was it only a sense of possession—it was also a sense of protection. It was as if, in some delightful way, his secret gave him a fortress, a wall behind which he could retreat into heavenly

seclusion. This was almost the first thing he had noticed about it—apart from the oddness of the thing itself—and it was this that now again, for the fiftieth time, occurred to him, as he sat in the little schoolroom. It was the half-hour for geography. Miss Buell was revolving with one finger, slowly, a huge terrestrial globe which had been placed on her desk. The green and yellow continents passed and repassed, questions were asked and answered, and now the little girl in front of him, Deirdre, who had a funny little constellation of freckles on the back of her neck, exactly like the Big Dipper, was standing up and telling Miss Buell that the equator was the line that ran round the middle.

Miss Buell's face, which was old and grayish and kindly, with gray stiff curls beside the cheeks, and eyes that swam very brightly, like little minnows, behind thick glasses, wrinkled itself into a complication of amusements.

"Ah! I see. The earth is wearing a belt, or a sash. Or some one drew a line round it!"

"Oh no—not that—I mean——"

In the general laughter, he did not share, or only a very little. He was thinking about the Arctic and Antarctic regions, which of course, on the globe, were white. Miss Buell was now telling them about the tropics, the jungles, the steamy heat of equatorial swamps, where the birds and butterflies, and even the snakes, were like living jewels. As he listened to these things, he was already, with a pleasant sense of half-effort, putting his secret between himself and the words. Was it really an effort at all? For effort implied something voluntary, and perhaps even something one did not especially want; whereas this was distinctly pleasant, and came almost of its own accord. All he needed to do was to think of that morning, the first one, and then of all the others——

But it was all so absurdly simple! It had amounted to so little. It was nothing, just an idea—and just why it should have become so wonderful, so permanent, was a mystery—a

1. **carnelian**\kŏr ᴬnē·lyən\ a semiprecious stone of red or reddish color.

very pleasant one, to be sure, but also, in an amusing way, foolish. However, without ceasing to listen to Miss Buell, who had now moved up to the north temperate zones, he deliberately invited his memory of the first morning. It was only a moment or two after he had waked up—or perhaps the moment itself. But was there, to be exact, an exact moment? Was one awake all at once? or was it gradual? Anyway, it was after he had stretched a lazy hand up toward the headrail, and yawned, and then relaxed again among his warm covers, all the more grateful on a December morning, that the thing had happened. Suddenly, for no reason, he had thought of the postman, he remembered the postman. Perhaps there was nothing so odd in that. After all, he heard the postman almost every morning in his life—his heavy boots could be heard clumping round the corner at the top of the little cobbled hill-street, and then, progressively nearer, progressively louder, the double knock at each door, the crossings and re-crossings of the street, till finally the clumsy steps came stumbling across to the very door, and the tremendous knock came which shook the house itself.

(Miss Buell was saying "Vast wheat-growing areas in North America and Siberia."

Deirdre had for the moment placed her left hand across the back of her neck.)

But on this particular morning, the first morning, as he lay there with his eyes closed, he had for some reason *waited* for the postman. He wanted to hear him come round the corner. And that was precisely the joke—he never did. He never came. He never had come—*round the corner*—again. For when at last the steps *were* heard, they had already, he was quite sure, come a little down the hill, to the first house; and even so, the steps were curiously different —they were softer, they had a new secrecy about them, they were muffled and indistinct; and while the rhythm of them was the same, it now said a new thing—it said peace, it said remoteness, it said cold, it said sleep. And he had understood the situation at once—nothing

could have seemed simpler—there had been snow in the night, such as all winter he had been longing for; and it was this which had rendered the postman's first footsteps inaudible, and the later ones faint. Of course! How lovely! And even now it must be snowing—it was going to be a snowy day—the long white ragged lines were drifting and sifting across the street, across the faces of the old houses, whispering and hushing, making little triangles of white in the corners between cobblestones, seething a little when the wind blew them over the ground to a drifted corner; and so it would be all day, getting deeper and deeper and silenter and silenter.

(Miss Buell was saying "Land of perpetual snow.")

All this time, of course (while he lay in bed), he had kept his eyes closed, listening to the nearer progress of the postman, the muffled footsteps thumping and slipping on the snow-sheathed cobbles; and all the other sounds— the double knocks, a frosty far-off voice or two, a bell ringing thinly and softly as if under a sheet of ice—had the same slightly abstracted quality, as if removed by one degree from actuality—as if everything in the world had been insulated by snow. But when at last, pleased, he opened his eyes, and turned them toward the window, to see for himself this long-desired and now so clearly imagined miracle—what he saw instead was brilliant sunlight on a roof; and when, astonished, he jumped out of bed and stared down into the street, expecting to see the cobbles obliterated by the snow, he saw nothing but the bare bright cobbles themselves.

Queer, the effect this extraordinary surprise had had upon him—all the following morning he had kept with him a sense as of snow falling about him, a secret screen of new snow between himself and the world. If he had not dreamed such a thing—and how could he have dreamed it while awake?—how else could one explain it? In any case, the delusion had been so vivid as to affect his entire behavior. He could not now remember whether it was on the first or the second morning—or was it even the third?—that his mother had drawn attention to some oddness in his manner.

"But my darling—" she had said at the breakfast table—"what has come over you? You don't seem to be listening. . . ."

And how often that very thing had happened since!

(Miss Buell was now asking if any one knew the difference between the North Pole and the Magnetic Pole. Deirdre was holding up her flickering brown hand, and he could see the four white dimples that marked the knuckles.)

Perhaps it hadn't been either the second or third morning—or even the fourth or fifth. How could he be sure? How could he be sure just when the delicious *progress* had become clear? Just when it had really *begun?* The intervals weren't very precise. . . . All he now knew was, that at some point or other—perhaps the second day, perhaps the sixth—he had noticed that the presence of the snow was a little more insistent, the sound of it clearer; and, conversely, the sound of the postman's footsteps more indistinct. Not only could he not hear the steps come round the corner, he could not even hear them at the first house. It was below the first house that he heard them; and then, a few days later, it was below the second house that he heard them; and a few days later again, below the third. Gradually, gradually, the snow was becoming heavier, the sound of its seething louder, the cobblestones more and more muffled. When he found, each morning, on going to the window, after the ritual of listening, that the roofs and cobbles were as bare as ever, it made no difference. This was, after all, only what he had expected. It was even what pleased him, what rewarded him: the thing was his own, belonged to no one else. No one else knew about it, not even his mother and father. There, outside, were the bare cobbles; and here, inside, was the snow. Snow growing heavier each day, muffling the world, hiding the ugly, and deadening increasingly—above all—the steps of the postman.

"But my darling—" she had said at the luncheon table—"what has come over you? You don't seem to listen when people speak to you. That's the third time I've asked you to pass your plate. . . ."

How was one to explain this to Mother? or to Father? There was, of course, nothing to be done about it: nothing. All one could do was to laugh embarrassedly, pretend to be a little ashamed, apologize, and take a sudden and somewhat disingenuous interest in what was being done or said. The cat had stayed out all night. He had a curious swelling on his left cheek—perhaps somebody had kicked him, or a stone had struck him. Mrs. Kempton was or was not coming to tea. The house was going to be housecleaned, or "turned out," on Wednesday instead of Friday. A new lamp was provided for his evening work—perhaps it was eyestrain which accounted for this new and so peculiar vagueness of his—Mother was looking at him with amusement as she said this, but with something else as well. A new lamp? A new lamp. Yes, Mother, No, Mother, Yes, Mother. School is going very well. The geometry is very easy. The history is very dull. The geography is very interesting—particularly when it takes one to the North Pole. Why the North Pole? Oh, well, it would be fun to be an explorer. Another Peary or Scott or Shackleton. And then abruptly he found his interest in the talk at an end, stared at the pudding on his plate, listened, waited, and began once more—ah, how heavenly, too, the first beginnings—to hear or feel—for could he actually hear it?—the silent snow, the secret snow.

(Miss Buell was telling them about the search for the Northwest Passage, about Hendrik Hudson, the *Half Moon*.)

This had been, indeed, the only distressing feature of the new experience; the fact that it so increasingly had brought him into a kind of mute misunderstanding, or even conflict, with his father and mother. It was as if he were trying to lead a double life. On the one hand, he had to be Paul Hasleman, and keep up the appearance of being that person—dress, wash,

"Something white! something cold! something sleepy! something of cease, of peace, and the long, bright curve of space."

quite separate existence, one which could not easily (if at all) be spoken of—how was one to manage? How was one to explain? Would it be safe to explain? Would it be absurd? Would it merely mean that he would get into some obscure kind of trouble?

These thoughts came and went, came and went, as softly and secretly as the snow; they were not precisely a disturbance, perhaps they were even a pleasure; he liked to have them; their presence was something almost palpable,[2] something he could stroke with his hand, without closing his eyes, and without ceasing to see Miss Buell and the schoolroom and the globe and the freckles on Deirdre's neck; nevertheless he did in a sense cease to see, or to see the obvious external world, and substituted for this vision the vision of snow, the sound of snow, and the slow, almost soundless, approach of the postman. Yesterday, it had been only at the sixth house that the postman had become audible; the snow was much deeper now, it was falling more swiftly and heavily, the sound of its seething was more distinct, more soothing, more persistent. And this morning, it had been —as nearly as he could figure—just above the seventh house—perhaps only a step or two above: at most, he had heard two or three footsteps before the knock had sounded. . . . And with each such narrowing of the sphere, each nearer approach of the limit at which the postman was first audible, it was odd how sharply was increased the amount of illusion which had to be carried into the ordinary business of daily life. Each day, it was harder to get out of bed, to go to the window, to look out at the—as always—perfectly empty and snowless street. Each day it was more difficult to go through the perfunctory[3] motions of greeting Mother and Father at breakfast, to reply to their questions, to put his books together and go to school. And

and answer intelligently when spoken to—; on the other, he had to explore this new world which had been opened to him. Nor could there be the slightest doubt—not the slightest—that the new world was the profounder and more wonderful of the two. It was irresistible. It was miraculous. Its beauty was simply beyond anything—beyond speech as beyond thought—utterly incommunicable. But how then, between the two worlds, of which he was thus constantly aware, was he to keep a balance? One must get up, one must go to breakfast, one must talk with Mother, go to school, do one's lessons— and, in all this, try not to appear too much of a fool. But if all the while one was also trying to extract the full deliciousness of another and

2. **palpable**\ˈpăl·pə·bəl\ something that could be perceived by touch.
3. **perfunctory**\pər ˈfəŋk·tə·rē\ uninteresting and routine.

at school, how extraordinarily hard to conduct with success simultaneously the public life and the life that was secret! There were times when he longed—positively ached—to tell every one about it—to burst out with it—only to be checked almost at once by a far-off feeling as of some faint absurdity which was inherent in it—but *was* it absurd?—and more importantly by a sense of mysterious power in his very secrecy. Yes: it must be kept secret. That, more and more, became clear. At whatever cost to himself, whatever pain to others——

(Miss Buell looked straight at him, smiling, and said, "Perhaps we'll ask Paul. I'm sure Paul will come out of his daydream long enough to be able to tell us. Won't you, Paul." He rose slowly from his chair, resting one hand on the brightly varnished desk, and deliberately stared through the snow toward the blackboard. It was an effort, but it was amusing to make it. "Yes," he said slowly, "it was what we now call the Hudson River. This he thought to be the Northwest Passage. He was disappointed." He sat down again, and as he did so Deirdre half turned in her chair and gave him a shy smile, of approval and admiration.)

At whatever pain to others.

This part of it was very puzzling, very puzzling. Mother was very nice, and so was Father. Yes, that was all true enough. He wanted to be nice to them, to tell them everything—and yet, was it really wrong of him to want to have a secret place of his own?

At bed-time, the night before, Mother had said, "If this goes on, my lad, we'll have to see a doctor, we will! We can't have our boy—" But what was it she had said? "Live in another world"? "Live so far away"? The word "far" had been in it, he was sure, and then Mother had taken up a magazine again and laughed a little, but with an expression which wasn't mirthful. He had felt sorry for her. . . .

The bell rang for dismissal. The sound came to him through long curved parallels of falling snow. He saw Deirdre rise, and had himself risen almost as soon—but not quite as soon—as she.

II

On the walk homeward, which was timeless, it pleased him to see through the accompaniment, or counterpoint,[4] of snow, the items of mere externality on his way. There were many kinds of brick in the sidewalks, and laid in many kinds of pattern. The garden walls too were various, some of wooden palings, some of plaster, some of stone. Twigs of bushes leaned over the walls: the little hard green winter-buds of lilac, on gray stems, sheathed and fat; other branches very thin and fine and black and desiccated. Dirty sparrows huddled in the bushes, as dull in color as dead fruit left in leafless trees. A single starling creaked on a weather vane. In the gutter, beside a drain, was a scrap of torn and dirty newspaper, caught in a little delta of filth: the word ECZEMA appeared in large capitals, and below it was a letter from Mrs. Amelia D. Cravath, 2100 Pine Street, Fort Worth, Texas, to the effect that after being a sufferer for years she had been cured by Caley's Ointment. In the little delta, beside the fan-shaped and deeply runnelled continent of brown mud, were lost twigs, descended from their parent trees, dead matches, a rusty horse-chestnut burr, a small concentration of eggshell, a streak of yellow sawdust which had been wet and now was dry and congealed, a brown pebble, and a broken feather. Farther on was a cement sidewalk, ruled into geometrical parallelograms, with a brass inlay at one end commemorating the contractors who had laid it, and, halfway across, an irregular and random series of dog-tracks, immortalized in synthetic stone. He knew these well, and always stepped on them; to cover the little hollows with his own foot had always been a queer pleasure; to-day he did it once more, but perfunctorily and detachedly, all the while thinking of something else. That was a

---

4. **counterpoint**\\ˈkaun·tər·pɔint\\ *music:* A melody composed to be combined with another melody. Here, Paul's advancing deafness creates the illusion of the hushed music of falling snow heard against the cruder harmony and discord of the real world.

dog, a long time ago, who had made a mistake and walked on the cement while it was still wet. He had probably wagged his tail, but that hadn't been recorded. Now, Paul Hasleman, aged twelve, on his way home from school, crossed the same river, which in the meantime had frozen into rock. Homeward through the snow, the snow falling in bright sunshine. Homeward?

Then came the gateway with the two posts surmounted by egg-shaped stones which had been cunningly balanced on their ends, as if by Columbus, and mortared in the very act of balance: a source of perpetual wonder. On the brick wall just beyond, the letter H had been stenciled, presumably for some purpose. H? H.

The green hydrant, with a little green-painted chain attached to the brass screw-cap.

The elm tree, with the great gray wound in the bark, kidney-shaped, into which he always put his hand—to feel the cold but living wood. The injury, he had been sure, was due to the gnawings of a tethered horse. But now it deserved only a passing palm, a merely tolerant eye. There were more important things. Miracles. Beyond the thoughts of trees, mere elms. Beyond the thoughts of sidewalks, mere stone, mere brick, mere cement. Beyond the thoughts even of his own shoes, which trod these sidewalks obediently, bearing a burden—far above —of elaborate mystery. He watched them. They were not very well polished; he had neglected them, for a very good reason: they were one of the many parts of the increasing difficulty of the daily return to daily life, the morning struggle. To get up, having at last opened one's eyes, to go to the window, and discover no snow, to wash, to dress, to descend the curving stairs to breakfast——

At whatever pain to others, nevertheless, one must persevere in severance,[5] since the incommunicability of the experience demanded it. It was desirable of course to be kind to Mother and Father, especially as they seemed to be worried, but it was also desirable to be resolute. If they should decide—as appeared likely— to consult the doctor, Doctor Howells, and have

Paul inspected, his heart listened to through a kind of dictaphone, his lungs, his stomach— well, that was all right. He would go through with it. He would give them answer for question, too—perhaps such answers as they hadn't expected? No. That would never do. For the secret world must, at all costs, be preserved.

The bird-house in the apple tree was empty —it was the wrong time of year for wrens. The little round black door had lost its pleasure. The wrens were enjoying other houses, other nests, remoter trees. But this too was a notion which he only vaguely and grazingly entertained—as if, for the moment, he merely touched an edge of it; there was something further on, which was already assuming a sharper importance; something which already teased at the corners of his eyes, teasing also at the corner of his mind. It was funny to think that he so wanted this, so awaited it—and yet found himself enjoying this momentary dalliance[6] with the bird-house, as if for a quite deliberate postponement and enhancement of the approaching pleasure. He was aware of his delay, of his smiling and detached and now almost uncomprehending gaze at the little bird-house; he knew what he was going to look at next: it was his own little cobbled hill-street, his own house, the little river at the bottom of the hill, the grocer's shop with the cardboard man in the window—and now, thinking of all this, he turned his head, still smiling, and looked quickly right and left through the snow-laden sunlight.

And the mist of snow, as he had foreseen, was still on it—a ghost of snow falling in the bright sunlight, softly and steadily floating and turning and pausing, soundlessly meeting the snow that covered, as with a transparent mirage, the bare bright cobbles. He loved it—he stood still and loved it. Its beauty was paralyzing—beyond all words, all experience, all dream. No fairy-story he had ever read could be compared

---

5. **severance**\ˈsĕ·və·rəns\ a breaking off of relations with others.
6. **dalliance**\ˈdă·lē·əns\ wasting of time, dawdling.

with it—none had ever given him this extraordinary combination of ethereal[7] loveliness with a something else, unnameable, which was just faintly and deliciously terrifying. What was this thing? As he thought of it, he looked upward toward his own bedroom window, which was open—and it was as if he looked straight into the room and saw himself lying half awake in his bed. There he was—at this very instant he was still perhaps actually there—more truly there than standing here at the edge of the cobbled hill-street, with one hand lifted to shade his eyes against the snow-sun. Had he indeed ever left his room, in all this time? since that very first morning? Was the whole progress still being enacted there, was it still the same morning, and himself not yet wholly awake? And even now, had the postman not yet come round the corner? . . .

This idea amused him, and automatically, as he thought of it, he turned his head and looked toward the top of the hill. There was, of course, nothing there—nothing and no one. The street was empty and quiet. And all the more because of its emptiness it occurred to him to count the houses—a thing which, oddly enough, he hadn't before thought of doing. Of course, he had known there weren't many—many, that is, on his own side of the street, which were the ones that figured in the postman's progress—but nevertheless it came as something of a shock to find that there were precisely *six*, above his own house—his own house was the seventh.

Six!

Astonished, he looked at his own house—looked at the door, on which was the number thirteen—and then realized that the whole thing was exactly and logically and absurdly what he ought to have known. Just the same, the realization gave him abruptly, and even a little frightening, a sense of hurry. He was being hurried—he was being rushed. For—he knit his brows—he couldn't be mistaken—it was just above the *seventh* house, his *own* house, that the postman had first been audible this very morning. But in that case—in that case—did it mean that to-morrow he would hear nothing? The knock he had heard must have been the knock of their own door. Did it mean—and this was an idea which gave him a really extraordinary feeling of surprise—that he would never hear the postman again?—that to-morrow morning the postman would already have passed the house, in a snow so deep as to render his footsteps completely inaudible? That he would have made his approach down the snow-filled street so soundlessly, so secretly, that he, Paul Hasleman, there lying in bed, would not have waked in time, or waking, would have heard nothing?

But how could that be? Unless even the knocker should be muffled in the snow—frozen tight perhaps? . . . But in that case——

A vague feeling of disappointment came over him; a vague sadness as if he felt himself deprived of something which he had long looked forward to, something much prized. After all this, all this beautiful progress, the slow delicious advance of the postman through the silent and secret snow, the knock creeping closer each day, and the footsteps nearer, the audible compass of the world thus daily narrowed, narrowed, narrowed, as the snow soothingly and beautifully encroached and deepened, after all this, was he to be defrauded of the one thing he had so wanted—to be able to count, as it were, the last two or three solemn footsteps, as they finally approached his own door? Was it all going to happen, at the end, so suddenly? or indeed, had it already happened? with no slow and subtle gradations of menace, in which he could luxuriate?[8]

He gazed upward again, toward his own window which flashed in the sun: and this time almost with a feeling that it would be better if he *were* still in bed, in that room; for in that case this must still be the first morning, and there would be six more mornings to come—or,

---

7. **ethereal**\ē ᵃthē·rē·əl\ extremely delicate and refined.
8. **luxuriate**\ləg ᵃzhū·rē·āt\ to take great delight in, to revel in.

for that matter, seven or eight or nine—how could he be sure?—or even more.

III

After supper, the inquisition[9] began. He stood before the doctor, under the lamp, and submitted silently to the usual thumpings and tappings.

"Now will you please say 'Ah!'?"

"Ah!"

"Now again please, if you don't mind."

"Ah."

"Say it slowly, and hold it if you can——"

"Ah-h-h-h-h-h——"

"Good."

How silly all this was. As if it had anything to do with his throat! Or his heart or lungs!

Relaxing his mouth, of which the corners, after all this absurd stretching, felt uncomfortable, he avoided the doctor's eyes, and stared toward the fireplace, past his mother's feet (in gray slippers) which projected from the green chair, and his father's feet (in brown slippers) which stood neatly side by side on the hearth rug.

"Hm. There is certainly nothing wrong there . . . ?"

He felt the doctor's eyes fixed upon him, and, as if merely to be polite, returned the look, but with a feeling of justifiable evasiveness.

"Now, young man, tell me—do you feel all right?"

"Yes, sir, quite all right."

"No headaches? no dizziness?"

"No, I don't think so."

"Let me see. Let's get a book, if you don't —mind—yes, thank you, that will do splendidly —and now, Paul, if you'll just read it, holding it as you would normally hold it——"

He took the book and read:

"And another praise have I to tell for this the city our mother, the gift of a great god, a glory of the land most high; the might of horses, the might of young horses, the might of the sea. . . . For thou, son of Cronus, our lord Poseidon,

hath throned herein this pride, since in these roads first thou didst show forth the curb that cures the rage of steeds. And the shapely oar, apt to men's hands, hath a wondrous speed on the brine, following the hundred-footed Nereids. . . . O land that art praised above all lands, now is it for thee to make those bright praises seen in deeds."

He stopped, tentatively, and lowered the heavy book.

"No—as I thought—there is certainly no superficial sign of eyestrain."

Silence thronged the room, and he was aware of the focussed scrutiny of the three people who confronted him. . . .

"We could have his eyes examined—but I believe it is something else."

"What could it be?" That was his father's voice.

"It's only this curious absent-mindedness—" This was his mother's voice.

In the presence of the doctor, they both seemed irritatingly apologetic.

"I believe it is something else. Now Paul—I would like very much to ask you a question or two. You will answer them, won't you—you know I'm an old, old friend of yours, eh? That's right! . . ."

His back was thumped twice by the doctor's fat fist—then the doctor was grinning at him with false amiability, while with one fingernail he was scratching the top button of his waistcoat. Beyond the doctor's shoulder was the fire, the fingers of flame making light prestidigitation[10] against the sooty fireback, the soft sound of their random flutter the only sound.

"I would like to know—is there anything that worries you?"

The doctor was again smiling, his eyelids low against the little black pupils, in each of which was a tiny white bead of light. Why answer

---

9. **inquisition**\ĭn·kwə ▲zĭ·shən\ an investigation, a searching into a matter by questioning.
10. **prestidigitation**\'prĕ·stə 'dĭ·jə ▲tā·shən\ sleight of hand, magic.

him? why answer him at all? "At whatever pain to others"—but it was all a nuisance, this necessity for resistance, this necessity for attention: it was as if one had been stood up on a brilliantly lighted stage, under a great round blaze of spotlight; as if one were merely a trained seal, or a performing dog, or a fish, dipped out of an aquarium and held up by the tail. It would serve them right if he were merely to bark or growl. And meanwhile, to miss these last few precious hours, these hours of which each minute was more beautiful than the last, more menacing—! He still looked, as if from a great distance, at the beads of light in the doctor's eyes, at the fixed false smile, and then, beyond, once more at his mother's slippers, his father's slippers, the soft flutter of the fire. Even here, even amongst these hostile presences, and in this arranged light, he could see the snow, he could hear it—it was in the corners of the room, where the shadow was deepest, under the sofa, behind the half-opened door which led to the dining room. It was gentler here, softer, its seethe the quietest of whispers, as if, in deference to a drawing-room, it had quite deliberately put on its "manners"; it kept itself out of sight, obliterated itself, but distinctly with an air of saying, "Ah, but just wait! Wait till we are alone together! Then I will begin to tell you something new! Something white! something cold! something sleepy! something of cease, and peace, and the long bright curve of space! Tell them to go away. Banish them. Refuse to speak. Leave them, go upstairs to your room, turn out the light and get into bed—I will go with you, I will be waiting for you, I will tell you a better story than Little Kay of the Skates, or The Snow Ghost—I will surround your bed, I will close the windows, pile a deep drift against the door, so that none will ever again be able to enter. Speak to them! . . ." It seemed as if the little hissing voice came from a slow white spiral of falling flakes in the corner by the front window—but he could not be sure. He felt himself smiling, then, and said to the doctor, but without looking at him, looking beyond him still——

"Oh no, I think not——"

"But are you sure, my boy?"

His father's voice came softly, and coldly then—the familiar voice of silken warning.

"You needn't answer at once, Paul—remember we're trying to help you—think it over and be quite sure, won't you?"

He felt himself smiling again, at the notion of being quite sure. What a joke! As if he weren't so sure that reassurance was no longer necessary, and all this cross-examination a ridiculous farce, a grotesque parody![11] What could they know about it? these gross intelligences, these humdrum minds so bound to the usual, the ordinary? Impossible to tell them about it! Why, even now, even now, with the proof so abundant, so formidable, so imminent, so appallingly present here in this very room, could they believe it?—could even his mother believe it? No—it was only too plain that if anything were said about it, the merest hint given, they would be incredulous—they would laugh—they would say "Absurd!"—think things about him which weren't true. . . .

"Why no, I'm not worried—why should I be?"

He looked then straight at the doctor's low lidded eyes, looked from one of them to the other, from one bead of light to the other, and gave a little laugh.

The doctor seemed to be disconcerted by this. He drew back in his chair, resting a fat white hand on either knee. The smile faded slowly from his face.

"Well, Paul!" he said, and paused gravely, "I'm afraid you don't take this quite seriously enough. I think you perhaps don't quite realize —don't quite realize—" He took a deep quick breath, and turned, as if helplessly, at a loss for words, to the others. But Mother and Father were both silent—no help was forthcoming.

"You must surely know, be aware, that you have not been quite yourself, of late? don't you know that? . . ."

---

11. **grotesque**\grō ᴬtĕsk\ **parody**\ᴬpă·rə·dē\ an absurd imitation.

It was amusing to watch the doctor's renewed attempt at a smile, a queer disorganized look, as of confidential embarrassment.

"I feel all right, sir," he said, and again gave the little laugh.

"And we're trying to help you." The doctor's tone sharpened.

"Yes sir, I know. But why? I'm all right. I'm just *thinking*, that's all."

His mother made a quick movement forward, resting a hand on the back of the doctor's chair.

"Thinking?" she said. "But my dear, about what?"

This was a direct challenge—and would have to be directly met. But before he met it, he looked again into the corner by the door, as if for reassurance. He smiled again at what he saw, at what he heard. The little spiral was still there, still softly whirling, like the ghost of a white kitten chasing the ghost of a white tail, and making as it did so the faintest of whispers. It was all right! If only he could remain firm, everything was going to be all right.

"Oh, about anything, about nothing—*you* know the way you do!"

"You mean—daydreaming?"

"Oh, no—thinking!"

"But thinking about *what*?"

"Anything."

He laughed a third time—but this time, happening to glance upward toward his mother's face, he was appalled at the effect his laughter seemed to have upon her. Her mouth had opened in an expression of horror. . . . This was too bad! Unfortunate! He had known it would cause pain, of course—but he hadn't expected it to be quite so bad as this. Perhaps—perhaps if he just gave them a tiny gleaming hint——?

"About the snow," he said.

"What on earth!" This was his father's voice. The brown slippers came a step nearer on the hearth-rug.

"But my dear, what do you mean?" This was his mother's voice.

The doctor merely stared.

"Just *snow*, that's all. I like to think about it."

"Tell us about it, my boy."

"But that's all it is. There's nothing to tell. *You* know what snow is?"

This he said almost angrily, for he felt that they were trying to corner him. He turned sideways so as no longer to face the doctor, and the better to see the inch of blackness between the window-sill and the lowered curtain—the cold inch of beckoning and delicious night. At once he felt better, more assured.

"Mother—can I go to bed, now, please? I've got a headache."

"But I thought you said——"

"It's just come. It's all these questions—! Can I, mother?"

"You can go as soon as the doctor has finished."

"Don't you think this thing ought to be gone into thoroughly, and *now*?" This was Father's voice. The brown slippers again came a step nearer, the voice was the well-known "punishment" voice, resonant and cruel.

"Oh, what's the use, Norman——"

Quite suddenly, every one was silent. And without precisely facing them, nevertheless he was aware that all three of them were watching him with an extraordinary intensity—staring hard at him—as if he had done something monstrous, or was himself some kind of monster. He could hear the soft irregular flutter of the flames; the cluck-click-cluck-click of the clock; far and faint, two sudden spurts of laughter from the kitchen, as quickly cut off as begun; a murmur of water in the pipes; and then, the silence seemed to deepen, to spread out, to become world-long and world-wide, to become timeless and shapeless, and to center inevitably and rightly, with a slow and sleepy but enormous concentration of all power, on the beginning of a new sound. What this new sound was going to be, he knew perfectly well. It might begin with a hiss, but it would end with a roar —there was no time to lose—he must escape. It mustn't happen here——

Without another word, he turned and ran up the stairs.

IV

Not a moment too soon. The darkness was coming in long white waves. A prolonged sibilance[12] filled the night—a great seamless seethe of wild influence went abruptly across it—a cold low humming shook the windows. He shut the door and flung off his clothes in the dark. The bare black floor was like a little raft tossed in waves of snow, almost overwhelmed, washed under whitely, up again, smothered in curled billows of feather. The snow was laughing: it spoke from all sides at once: it pressed closer to him as he ran and jumped exulting into his bed.

"Listen to us!" it said. "Listen! We have come to tell you the story we told you about. You remember? Lie down. Shut your eyes, now—you will no longer see much—in this white darkness who could see, or want to see? We will take the place of everything. . . . Listen——"

A beautiful varying dance of snow began at the front of the room, came forward and then retreated, flattened out toward the floor, then rose fountain-like to the ceiling, swayed, recruited itself from a new stream of flakes which poured laughing in through the humming window, advanced again, lifted long white arms. It said peace, it said remoteness, it said cold—it said——

But then a gash of horrible light fell brutally across the room from the opening door—the snow drew back hissing—something alien had come into the room—something hostile. This thing rushed at him, clutched at him, shook him —and he was not merely horrified, he was filled with such a loathing as he had never known. What was this? this cruel disturbance? this act of anger and hate? It was as if he had to reach up a hand toward another world for any understanding of it—an effort of which he was only barely capable. But of that other world he still remembered just enough to know the exorcising words. They tore themselves from his other life suddenly——

"Mother! Mother! Go away! I hate you!"

And with that effort, everything was solved, everything became all right: the seamless hiss advanced once more, the long white wavering lines rose and fell like enormous whispering seawaves, the whisper becoming louder, the laughter more numerous.

"Listen!" it said. "We'll tell you the last, the most beautiful and secret story—shut your eyes —it is a very small story—a story that gets smaller and smaller—it comes inward instead of opening like a flower—it is a flower becoming a seed—a little cold seed—do you hear? we are leaning closer to you——"

The hiss was now becoming a roar—the whole world was a vast moving screen of snow —but even now it said peace, it said remoteness, it said cold, it said sleep.

I

LIVING IN TWO WORLDS

The introduction to THE DREAMS OF MEN stated that men live double lives. One is the physical life, the other is the dream life of their imaginations. There is little doubt that Paul is living in two worlds, but he seems to be progressively moving away from one and into the other. As readers we are appalled as he turns his back on the physical world more and more completely. But it might be interesting to speculate on whether it is equally terrifying for a person to live completely in the physical world and to turn his back completely on dreams.

II

IMPLICATIONS

1. What is significant about each of the following passages in understanding Paul and what is happening to him?

a. . . . and all the other sounds—the double knocks, a frosty far-off voice or two, a bell ringing thinly and softly as if under a sheet of ice—had the same slightly abstracted quality, as if removed by one degree from actuality—as if everything in the world had been insulated by snow.

---

12. **sibilance**\ˈsĭ·bə·ləns\ a hissing sound.

b. It was even what pleased him, what rewarded him: the thing was his own, belonged to no one else. No one else knew about it, not even his mother and father.

c. Yes, Mother, No, Mother, Yes, Mother. School is going very well. The geometry is very easy. The history is very dull. The geography is very interesting. . . .

d. On the one hand, he had to be Paul Hasleman, and keep up the appearance of being that person—dress, wash, and answer intelligently when spoken to—; on the other, he had to explore this new world which had been opened to him.

e. . . . Mother had taken up a magazine again and laughed a little, but with an expression which wasn't mirthful.

f. . . . they were one of the many parts of the increasing difficulty of the daily return to daily life, the morning struggle. To get up, having at last opened one's eyes, to go to the window, and discover no snow, to wash, to dress, to descend the curving stairs to breakfast——

g. He loved it—he stood still and loved it. Its beauty was paralyzing—beyond all words, all experience, all dream. No fairy-story he had ever read could be compared with it—none had ever given him this extraordinary combination of ethereal loveliness with a something else, unnameable, which was just faintly and deliciously terrifying.

h. "Mother! Mother! Go away! I hate you!"

2. What are the characteristics of the snow that Paul dwells upon in his dream of it?

3. What possible pressures of his physical life is Paul trying to escape through his dream?

III
TECHNIQUES

Irony

What irony, if any, is in the following situations:

1. The teacher's lesson on the parts of the world.

2. The conversation Paul has with his mother.

3. The doctor's examination of Paul.

Organization

1. The story is divided neatly into four parts. What is the setting of each of the parts? What is the probable time that each is happening? In each scene the dream world remains the same, but the real world is symbolized by something different. What are the representatives of the real world in each?

2. How does Aiken use the postman to emphasize the progression of the story?

IV
WORDS

1. Cousins writes of Schweitzer's "unorthodox religious views." How are the words *orthodox* and *orthopedics* related? He also uses the phrase, "the incalculable advantages which this new wealth gives us." How are the roots of *calculate* and *calcium* related?

2. Hawthorne says of the stranger, "His face at first wore the melancholy expression, almost despondency, of one who travels a wild and bleak road. . . ." Does the root of *despondency* help you understand its present meaning? At another point he says, "and the proud, contemplative, yet kindly soul." Is the root of *contemplative* related to *contempt? contest?*

3. In "The Piazza" the narrator says that he has had a "panoramic piazza" built. What is the meaning of the root *pan?* the root *oramic?* How does the former help you understand the meaning of the word *Pan-American?* Is the latter in the word *oracle?*

4. In "Time for Learning" a character remarks, "There's a concoction ought to be mighty sweet." Is *concoction* related to *concord?* to *coquette?*

5. In "Silent Snow, Secret Snow" Paul believes, "At whatever pain to others, one must persevere in severance. . . ." Do *persevere* and *severance* come from the same root?

The Dreams of Men

Lord Byron, a famous English poet, epitomized the impact of dreams on men's lives in the following lines. Read them as you recall the individual stories you have read in this section:

And dreams in their development have breath,
And tears, and tortures, and the touch of joy;
They leave a weight upon our waking toils,
They do divide our being; they become
A portion of ourselves as of our time,
And look like heralds of eternity;
They pass like spirits of the past,—they speak
Like sibyls of the future; they have power—
The tyranny of pleasure and of pain:
They make us what we were not—what they will,
And shake us with the vision that is gone by,
The dread of vanished shadows—are they so?
Is not the past all shadow?—What are they?
Creations of the mind?—The mind can make
Substance, and people planets of its own
With beings brighter than have been, and give
A breath to forms which can outlive all flesh. . . .

—from *Dreams*

IMPLICATIONS

1. Open your book to the table of contents for this unit, THE DREAMS OF MEN. Looking at the titles, think back over the stories. Then select one story that illustrates each of the following statements from Byron's poem "Dreams."

   a. Dreams bring tears and tortures.
   b. Dreams bring a touch of joy.
   c. Dreams divide our being.
   d. Dreams are heralds of eternity.
   e. Dreams make us what we were not.
   f. Dreams can create forms that outlive flesh.

2. In each of the selections the basic conflict is between the dream a person has and the real world in which he lives. With this in mind, examine the selections in the unit. In which of the stories does the individual manage to make his dream come true? In which does the real world seem to win out and crush the dream? In what ways are the people whose dreams were crushed still richer for having had the dream?

Irony

Review the discussion of irony on page 324 and then test your understanding by answering the following questions.

1. Why do stories in which the conflict is between the dreams of men and the reality of the world they live in almost inevitably involve irony?

2. Which of the works in THE DREAMS OF MEN seemed the most ironic? Back up your choice by pinpointing the ironic aspects of the story.

3. What emotional reactions does irony produce in the reader?

4. Think of one example of irony from your own experiences.

Organization

An author takes the elements of a story and arranges them to achieve a definite purpose. He may slow down the action to increase suspense; use contrasting details to emphasize a particular point; or tie his incident to the natural movement of time such as a day, a month, or a year. Consider the stories in this unit, THE DREAMS OF MEN. Select one story that illustrates each of the methods of organization given above.

BIOGRAPHICAL NOTES

Robert Frost

For a biography of Robert Frost, see page 305.

Harry Mark Petrakis

Harry Mark Petrakis (1923–   ), son of Greek immigrants, was born in St. Louis, Missouri. He attended the University of Illinois for two years before working as a steelworker, real estate salesman, and speech writer to support himself while writing short stories. In 1957 Petrakis won two awards for his short stories and in 1959 a novel, *Lion at My Heart*, was published. A collection of short stories, *Pericles on 31st Street*, from which the selection in this unit was taken, was one of the final nominees in 1965 for the National Book Award. Recently, another novel, *A Dream of Kings*, was made into a movie. Writing mostly about Greeks, Petrakis credits Nikos Kazantzakis, the creator of *Zorba, the Greek,* as having had the greatest influence on his writing. Readers may indeed see that Marko Palamas shares with Zorba a zest for living that creates an appealing kind of charm.

Langston Hughes

Langston Hughes (1902–1967), whose parents separated early in his life, had, by the age of twelve, lived in Buffalo; Cleveland; Lawrence and Topeka, Kansas; Colorado Springs; Mexico City; and Lincoln, Illinois. In 1921 Hughes began his publishing career when his famous poem, "The Negro Speaks of Rivers," was published. Abandoning college after an uncongenial year at Columbia University, Hughes held various jobs, finally sailing as a mess boy on a ship touching African ports. When the entire crew was fired, he found a job on a Holland-bound freighter, and during 1924 worked his way about Europe. His experience with the blues as played by top black musicians in Paris nightclubs had a special impact on him. Returning to Harlem, he published several books of poetry in the next few years while supporting himself at odd jobs. At the time of his death in 1967, Hughes had probably written more and longer than any other Negro author, producing thirty-nine volumes of his own, five collaborative adult books, four full-length translated works, and hundreds of uncollected selections of all types. During his forty-five years as a writer, Hughes said that his central purpose was "to explain and illuminate the Negro condition in America."

Dorothy Johnson

Dorothy Johnson (1905–   ), short story writer and novelist, was born in McGregor, Iowa. After receiving her B.A. from Montana State University, she worked as editor of a magazine in New York. Later she returned to Montana to work as editor of the *Whitefish Pilot.* After this she worked for two years as the secretary and manager of the Montana State Press Association and then became an Assistant Professor of Journalism at Montana State University. Many of Mrs. Johnson's writings center on Indians, and she is now an honorary member of the Blackfoot tribe of Montana, having been given the name of Kills-Both-Places. Several movies have been made from her stories: *The Hanging Tree, The Man Who Shot Liberty Valence,* and *A Man Called Horse.*

Benjamin Franklin

Son of a Boston tallow chandler and soapmaker, Benjamin Franklin (1706–1790) went to work for his father at the age of ten after only two years of formal schooling. As a young man he went to Philadelphia as a printer and, while in his early twenties, began the *Pennsylvania Gazette,* which soon became the most successful weekly newspaper in America. At twenty-six he wrote and published his first annual *Poor Richard's Almanac;* for the next twenty-six years it was the most popular book of its kind. He soon had his finger in many business, scientific, and civic enterprises. He helped initiate a city police force, an improved fire company, improved street lights, and the paving of the streets. He established the first circulating library in America, and later founded the college which was to become the University of Pennsylvania. In 1748 he had enough wealth to retire and pursue scientific experiments. But the political turmoil in the colonies demanded his attention. In the years before the American Revolution, he went to England to represent the colonists. His writings and speeches in Parliament gave him the status of the unofficial ambassador from the New World. He worked constantly for reconciliation of the colonies with England until 1775, when he accepted the inevitability of separation. He became a member of the Second Continental Congress and was made Postmaster General to the new nation. In 1776 he was sent to France to negotiate a treaty and remained for nine years. Returning to America at eighty, Franklin plunged into new work as President of the executive council for three years. His *Autoboigraphy,* begun in 1771, covered his life up to 1757. It was never finished, yet it has been called by many the first American book of literature.

Mark Twain

Mark Twain (Samuel Langhorne Clemens, 1835–1910) was born in Florida, Missouri, the son of a lawyer who traded in land. A few years later the family moved to Hannibal, Missouri, a Mississippi river town which Twain used as a setting for some of his most famous novels: *Tom Sawyer* (1876), *The Adventures of Huckleberry Finn* (1884), and *Pudd'nhead Wilson* (1894). His father died when Twain was 12 and the boy became a printer's apprentice. He worked on the *Hannibal Courier* for two years and then joined his older brother Orion on *The Journal.* In 1857 he apprenticed himself to a riverboat pilot and, once licensed, spent two and a half years at the trade. When the Civil War ended his career as a pilot, he went West to Nevada and became a reporter on the Virginia City paper. Here he began using the pen name "Mark Twain," a river term meaning water two fathoms—twelve feet—in depth (which was safe water for the river steamboats). After returning from a junket to Hawaii, Twain decided to go on the lecture trail and became such a famous platform speaker that the *Alta California* financed a trip to Europe. Publication of *Innocents Abroad* (1869) established Twain as a humorist and made it possible for him to marry Olivia Langdon, a New York girl. His later life seemed dogged by financial and domestic tragedies: several business ventures ended in bankruptcy, his only son died in infancy; his daughter Susie died while he was abroad lecturing; his wife died in 1905 and his daughter Jean, in 1909. Only Clara, the third daughter, survived Twain, who died as he prophesied when Halley's comet returned in 1910.

Conrad Aiken

For a biography of Conrad Aiken, see page 308.

William Shakespeare

For a biography of William Shakespeare, see page 467.

Gallery | THE DREAMS OF MEN

Throughout recorded history individual men have altered
the course of civilization with their dreams of reform, conquest,
power. In Caesar you will meet a man who for a time
was the most powerful political figure in the world,
a man whose ambitions altered Rome's and, consequently,
Western civilization's future permanently. This gallery pictures
dramatic moments from the lives of other powerful men whose
dreams have affected the political history of the Western World.

After conquering Greece
from his northern kingdom of Macedon,
Alexander the Great continued south
into Asia Minor where at Issus,
in 334 B.C., he defeated
the Persian ruler Darius III
and went on to conquer
the Middle East.
Alexander created a new empire,
spreading into Asia the influence
of Greek thought and culture.

THE BATTLE OF ISSUS
Albrecht Altdorfer

ALEXANDER THE GREAT
a sculptured portrait

ALEXANDER MDARIVM VLT SVPERAT
CASIS SIMVL PERSAR PEDIT X M EQVIT
VLT CX M IN TERFECTIS MATRE QVOQVE
CONIVGE LIBERIS DARII REG CVM MILIA D
AMPLIVS EQVITIB FVGA DILAPSI CAPTIS

THE DEATH OF MAXENTIUS
Peter Paul Rubens

At the twilight of the Roman Empire,
the emperor Maxentius was defeated at the Tiber River
on October 28, A.D. 312. The victor was
Constantine the Great who moved the seat of the Roman Empire
to the East. At the ancient Greek city, Byzantium,
he created the renowned capital Constantinople,
center of the Byzantine Empire which survived the fall of Rome
by seven hundred years. Here the culture of the West
blended again with the East during centuries
in which chaos and turmoil covered Europe.

Here are two modern counterparts of ancient enemies. On the right Hitler,
like an ancient Roman emperor, returns the salutes of the mob. On the left
is Hitler's great adversary, a modern champion of freedom, Winston Churchill.

Roughly a hundred years
after Alexander's marches,
the powerful
North African city of Carthage
ruled the Mediterranean.
But on the boot of Italy,
Rome was unifying
into a competing power.
Soon the two began
a long struggle
known as the Punic Wars.
During the second
of these wars
there emerged
a remarkable military leader,
Hannibal of Carthage,
who, crossing into Europe
at Spain, marched north
and moved his army
over the Alps and into Italy
where he began defeating
the Romans on their own soil.
For fifteen years
he successfully made great
inroads toward Rome, but
his support slowly weakened.
During Hannibal's absence
a Roman general attacked
Carthage, and finally Hannibal
had to retreat from Italy
in order to defend his own
homeland. The picture shows
the searing turning point
of Hannibal's fortunes.
His brother Hasdrubal
had been leading reinforcement
troops from Spain
when he was defeated
by a Roman legion.
His severed head
was thrown to Hannibal
in mockery
of his hopes.

**HANNIBAL WITH THE HEAD
OF HIS BROTHER HASDRUBAL**
Giovanni Domenico Tiepolo

Charles the Great, the Frankish king Charlemagne,
united and ruled Western Europe from 768 until 814.
A unique organizer, Charles himself planned
his military expeditions with such remarkable skill
that his tactics were studied by a later conqueror, Napoleon.
The picture commemorates
the Christmas Day in A.D. 800 when Pope Leo III crowned
Charlemagne, Emperor of the Holy Roman Empire.

Below are two photographs of *Il Duce,* Benito Mussolini,
Italian Fascist premier from 1922 to 1945,
haranguing the crowd in a manner reminiscent of scenes
from Shakespeare's *Julius Caesar.*

Toward the end of the Napoleonic campaigns
a particularly bloody two-day battle was fought
around the Prussian town of Eylau in February, 1807.
Though the outcome was undecisive,
some 33,000 men were killed and Napoleon himself was often
in danger. By summer of that year,
the French had been more successful,
and Prussia lost half of her territory to France
under the treaty of Tilsit. Prussia's ally,
Czar Alexander of Russia,
established a closed European-Russian commerce
with Napoleon which was designed
to force the submission of Britain.

Lenin (left) and his cruel successor Stalin (hand raised),
leaders of the Communist world, have shaken
the twentieth century with their dreams
of world revolution and power. Although their
political theories may belong to modern times,
their purges, executions, thought control and other tyrannical
tactics were borrowed, with a few modern twists,
from the power politicians of the past.

BATAILLE D'EYLAU
Jean Baron Gros

JULIUS CAESAR

Introduction

The dreams you have met so far in THE DREAMS OF MEN have, for the most part, concentrated on the conflict between the dream of an individual and the reality of the world. Sometimes, however, when the dreams of one individual come in conflict with those of others, people find themselves locked in a struggle, each trying to impose his particular vision of the world upon the others. When such a struggle takes place among powerful men in the state, it affects masses of people and even whole civilizations. William Shakespeare found the rudiments of such a struggle in Plutarch's account of the assassination of Julius Caesar. Using the bare outline of the events as they happened, he fills in the dreams which the participants must have had and recreates the murder and its effects in terms of the conflicts between dreams of power, dreams of freedom, dreams of revenge.

Pompey, the great general crushed by Caesar.

Shakespeare's Audience

To understand fully the background of this grisly murder and its chain of terrible consequences, we need to grasp some of the information and assumptions that were common to Shakespeare's audience. This is not surprising, for during the three and a half centuries that have elapsed since his time, language and customs have changed as radically as clothing and transportation. Shakespeare wrote for his own time and people. He could count on their reactions to certain situations just as today's playwright knows the impact that such references as lynching, teen-age gangs, and communism have on the modern audience. Let's consider, then, how an Elizabethan audience would differ from one today.

An audience in Shakespeare's day would be familiar with the words and expressions he used. Though the basic English sentence patterns are the same, some words have changed in spelling, meaning, or usage. Just as an adult may be confused today by teen-age slang, so the reader may be confused by Shakespeare's language. The sound is familiar but the meaning sometimes is lost. Footnotes interpret the strange meaning of familiar words, but they also tend to slow down the impact of the dramatic action. Although you may miss some of the details, your first reading should be for the main story; you can return later for careful study of details.

Shakespeare's audience also held a different body of beliefs from today's audience. During

Julius Caesar. His dreams of reform, conquest, and power altered the course of history.

Sha⸍ ... ⸍en
Elizabe⸍ ... ⸍lute
monarchs w⸍ ... been
chosen by God a⸍ ... to ordinary men. In additio⸍ ... was held
to be the source of orde⸍ ... ⸍ility in the
state, just as God is the sourc⸍ ... ⸍aw and order
in the universe. Therefore, to murder a king
was not just murder, but a great crime against
the order of the universe and consequently
against the will of God Himself. In order to
feel the full horror of such an act the reader
must accept the Elizabethan viewpoint.

The audience also firmly believed in ghosts
and took them very seriously. Whether a good
or a bad spirit, an apparition was an awesome
and terrifying creature. Obviously, the same
reaction is not felt by today's audience. The
Elizabethans also felt that the moods of nature
corresponded to the moods of men. When horrible acts were put in motion by men, then nature responded with darkness, strange sounds,
terrible storms, and unnatural events. Although
we mentally reject such a theory, we still respond to movies and television shows which
heighten a dark, dramatic moment with the
eerie sounds of wind and storm.

The Elizabethan audience also differed from
today's in their expectations. They expected to
be completely familiar with the story of the
play, so the plot unfolding on the stage held
no surprises for them. What they came to see
was the handling of characters and to hear
language of great beauty.

Caesar and Rome

Shakespeare expected his audience to know the history of Rome and the story of Caesar's rise and fall. Even when Caesar was born in approximately 100 B.C., Rome was an old city tracing its history back to 753 B.C. when the legendary Romulus supposedly founded the city and became its first king. About two hundred and fifty years later, in 509 B.C., the last of the cruel and unscrupulous kings of the Tarquin family was expelled from Rome under the leadership of a noble man and great patriot, Lucius Junius Brutus, ancestor of the Brutus you are about to meet in Shakespeare's *Julius Caesar*.

The Tarquins had made the name of king so hated that the nobles (patricians) and the common people (plebeians) enacted a law that anyone expressing a desire for the return of the monarchy should be put to death. Instead, they formed a republic in which, theoretically at least, both the patricians and the plebeians had a share in the government. Over the next four hundred years (more than double the age of our own republic), both factions worked out a balance of power which helped to form the basis of Rome's strength, a strength which made her the leading nation of the Mediterranean world.

By the first century B.C., however, the republic had begun to crumble. Uneasy balances of power exploded sporadically into civil wars in which Rome vacillated between a monarchy, a republic, and a dictatorship. It was in such a world of great political unrest that Caesar rose to power.

Julius Caesar was born of a patrician family but early in his career cast his lot with the common people. As a representative of the popular party he climbed rapidly from one office to another. His eloquence, lavish games, and entertainments for the people, as well as political accomplishments for them, won him a large following in Rome. In 60 B.C., Caesar formed a triumvirate to rule Rome with the wealthy patrician Crassus and a well-known general, Pompey. Two years later Caesar was made governor of Gaul and by brilliant generalship went on to conquer all of Gaul, almost doubling the empire. For almost ten years he served in Gaul, winning the admiration of his legions and the support of the commoners at home. After Crassus was killed in battle, Caesar's growing popularity so frightened the Senators and Pompey that they issued the order for Caesar to disperse his troops and return to Rome.

Caesar took up this challenge to his authority, and in full battle splendor, leading his legions, he crossed the Rubicon, the river separating Gaul from Italy. Pompey fled in fear to Greece. Before pursuing him, Caesar subdued Italy within sixty days . . . then defeated two of Pompey's officers in Spain . . . and then on returning to Rome was elected consul in 48 B.C. Finally turning to Greece, Caesar swiftly crushed Pompey. Three years later he defeated the remnants of Pompey's faction in Spain. During this period of wars, Caesar had been delegated tremendous powers, first being made dictator (customarily a one-year appointment or for the duration of a crisis) in 48 B.C., then dictator for ten years in 46 B.C., and finally dictator for life in 45 B.C. In the full glory of his honors at home and his successes in Spain, Caesar returned to Rome. This is the moment at which Shakespeare begins his drama, *Julius Caesar*.

Preparing to Read

Watch carefully from the very beginning for the conflicts that will lead to the climax and its repercussions. Note, too, how they are embodied in specific characters whom Shakespeare masterfully reveals through what they say and do, and what others say about them. Watch carefully, too, for Shakespeare's handling of the necessary background details. For just as there is exposition in a short story, so there must be exposition in a drama. It is difficult to make this necessary material seem a part of the action, but Shakespeare does it very

Marcus Brutus

Marc Antony

Julius Cæsar

Cast of Characters

JULIUS CÆSAR.
OCTAVIUS CAESAR, } *triumvirs*
MARCUS ANTONIUS, } *after the death*
M. ÆMILIUS LEPIDUS, } *of Julius Cæsar.*
CICERO,
PUBLIUS, } *senators.*
POPILIUS LENA,
MARCUS BRUTUS,
CASSIUS,
CASCA, } *conspirators*
TREBONIUS, } *against*
LIGARIUS, } *Julius Cæsar.*
DECIUS BRUTUS,
METELLUS CIMBER,
CINNA,
FLAVIUS AND MARULLUS, *tribunes.*
ARTEMIDORUS of Cnidos,
  a teacher of Rhetoric.
A Soothsayer.
CINNA, *a poet.* Another Poet.
LUCILIUS,
TITINIUS, } *friends*
MESSALA, } *to Brutus*
Young CATO, } *and Cassius.*
VOLUMNIUS,
VARRO,
CLITUS,
CLAUDIUS, } *servants to Brutus.*
STRATO,
LUCIUS,
DARDANIUS,
PINDARUS, *servant to Cassius.*

CALPURNIA, *wife to Cæsar.*
PORTIA, *wife to Brutus.*

Senators, Citizens, Guards, Attendants, &c.

Scene:
Rome: the neighbourhood of Sardis:
the neighbourhood of Philippi.

cleverly. Notice in the first scenes how carefully he works together the little bits of information that you need for background.

As nearly as scholars can determine, the Elizabethan plays were originally given in two parts. The action played continuously for an hour or so and was interrupted by an intermission which was followed by another period of action. The division of the play into five acts was made at a later date when the plays were printed. *Julius Caesar* breaks neatly into two parts: the first moves through the death of Caesar; the second deals with the results of the murder. If you can, read steadily until you reach the end of the murder scene before going back for a more detailed study of the play. Then start with the funeral oration and read through to the end.

Note that Shakespeare has written most of the play in blank verse. Blank verse is a line of iambic pentameter verse (see page 256). It has five stresses per line, each usually occurring on the second, fourth, sixth, eighth, and tenth syllables of the line. Blank verse has no end rhyme and its rhythm is particularly suited to drama because it so closely resembles the rhythm of normal English speech. In reading blank verse aloud, as you should to sense its grace and power, read it according to the sense of the passage rather than according to the length of individual lines.

JULIUS CAESAR

Act I

SCENE 1

A street in Rome. The news of CAESAR's *military victory over the sons of* POMPEY *has spread excitement among the people. A group of tradesmen have quit their shops and have made* CAESAR's *triumph occasion for a holiday. Led by a burly and loud-laughing* COBBLER, *they shout and cheer down the cobbled street and decorate* CAESAR's *statue with garlands of flowers. The tribunes[1]* FLAVIUS *and* MARULLUS *arrive and angrily confront the celebrating tradesmen.*

FLAVIUS. Hence! Home, you idle creatures, get you home!
　Is this a holiday? What! know you not,
　Being mechanical,[2] you ought not walk
　Upon a laboring day[3] without the sign
　Of your profession?[4] (*Points to a man in the group.*)
　　Speak, what trade art thou?　　　　　　　　　　5

CARPENTER. Why, sir, a carpenter.

MARULLUS. Where is thy leather apron and thy rule?
　What dost thou with thy best apparel on?
　(*Singling out the* COBBLER.) You, sir, what trade are
　　you?

COBBLER. Truly, sir, in respect of a fine workman, I am but,　10
　as you would say, a cobbler.[5]

MARULLUS. (*Impatiently.*) But what trade art thou? Answer me directly.[6]

COBBLER. (*Smirking and winking at his friends.*) A trade,
　sir, that I hope I may use with a safe conscience; which
　is, indeed, sir, a mender of bad soles.[7]　　　　　15

MARULLUS. What trade, thou knave? thou naughty knave,
　what trade?

COBBLER. Nay, I beseech you, sir, be not out with me;[8]
　yet if you be out, sir, I can mend you.

MARULLUS. (*Indignant.*) What mean'st thou by that?
　Mend me, thou saucy fellow!

COBBLER. Why, sir, cobble you.　　　　　　　　　　20

1. **tribune**\ᴧtrĭ·byūn\ a magistrate originally intended to protect the plebians from oppression by the aristocracy.

2. **mechanical**, artisan, skilled worker.

3. **laboring day**, work day.

4. **without . . . profession**, in Shakespeare's time English craftsmen were required to wear their work clothes and carry the tools of their trade on working days.

5. **cobbler**, (1) a clumsy workman, (2) a mender of shoes. Here Shakespeare uses the word in both senses; such a use of a word in a double sense is called *punning*, a very popular form of word play in Shakespeare's time.
6. **directly**, at once.
7. **soles**, another pun.

8. **be not out**, "do not be angry" in one sense, but in another, he is punning. What is the pun?

FLAVIUS. (*Stepping forward to settle the confusion.*) Thou
    art a cobbler, art thou?
COBBLER. Truly, sir, all that I live by is with the awl.[9] I
    meddle with no tradesman's matters, nor women's mat-
    ters, but with all. I am, indeed, sir, a surgeon to old
    shoes; when they are in great danger, I recover them.   25
    As proper men as ever trod upon neat's[10] leather have
    gone upon my handiwork.
FLAVIUS. But wherefore art not in thy shop today?
    Why dost thou lead these men about the streets?
COBBLER. Truly, sir, to wear out their shoes, to get myself   30
    into more work. But, indeed, sir, we make holiday, to
    see Caesar and to rejoice in his triumph.
MARULLUS. (*Swelling with anger.*) Wherefore rejoice?
    What conquests brings he home?
    What tributaries[11] follow him to Rome
    To grace in bonds his chariot-wheels?   35
    You blocks, you stones, you worse than senseless things!
    O you hard hearts, you cruel men of Rome,
    Knew you not Pompey? Many a time and oft
    Have you climbed up to walls and battlements,
    To towers and windows, yea, to chimney-tops,   40
    Your infants in your arms, and there have sat
    The live-long day, with patient expectation,
    To see great Pompey pass the streets of Rome;
    And when you saw his chariot but appear
    Have you not made a universal shout,   45
    That Tiber[12] trembled underneath her banks
    To hear the replications[13] of your sounds
    Made on her concave shores?
    And do you now put on your best attire?
    And do you now cull out a holiday?   50
    And do you now strew flowers in his way
    That comes in triumph over Pompey's blood?[14]
    Be gone!
    Run to your houses, fall upon your knees,
    Pray to the gods to intermit[15] the plague   55
    That needs must light on this ingratitude.
FLAVIUS. Go, go, good countrymen, and, for this fault,
    Assemble all the poor men of your sort;
    Draw them to Tiber's banks, and weep your tears
    Into the channel, till the lowest stream   60
    Do kiss the most exalted shores of all.

[*Hesitant and with lowered heads the tradesmen
leave.*]

See, whether their basest metal be not moved;

9. **awl,** shoemaker's tool. The cobbler is
punning.

10. **neat**\nēt\ cow.

11. **tributaries,** conquered leaders forced
into slavery or, if wealthy, sometimes required to pay for their release.

12. **Tiber**\ˈtai·bər\ the river that runs
through Rome.
13. **replications**\ˈrĕ·plĭˈkā·shəns\ rever-
berations.

14. **over Pompey's blood,** over the sons
of Pompey.

15. **intermit,** withhold.

They vanish tongue-tied in their guiltiness.
Go you down that way towards the Capitol;
This way will I. Disrobe the images   65
If you do find them decked with ceremonies.[16]
MARULLUS. May we do so?
    You know it is the feast of Lupercal.[17]
FLAVIUS. It is no matter; let no images
    Be hung with Caesar's trophies. I'll about   70
And drive away the vulgar from the streets.
So do you too, where you perceive them thick.
These growing feathers plucked from Caesar's wing
Will make him fly an ordinary pitch,[18]
Who else would soar above the view of men   75
And keep us all in servile fearfulness.

[*They hurry off in opposite directions.*]

SCENE 2

*Later the same day in a public square prepared for the ritual
of honoring the god Pan.*[1] CAESAR *enters, attended by* AN-
TONY, *who is dressed for competition in the athletic games.*
DECIUS,[2] CICERO, BRUTUS, CASSIUS, *and* CASCA *follow.* CAL-
PURNIA, *the wife of* CAESAR, *and* PORTIA, *wife of* BRUTUS,
are in the group with their husbands. A crowd follows
CAESAR'S *train toward the festival to celebrate the Lupercal. A* SOOTHSAYER *in the crowd struggles to attract* CAESAR'S
attention.

CAESAR. Calpurnia!
CASCA. (*Waving his arms.*)   Peace, ho! Caesar speaks.
CAESAR. Calpurnia!
CALPURNIA.   Here, my lord.
CAESAR. Stand you directly in Antonius' way
    When he doth run his course. Antonius!
ANTONY. Caesar, my lord?   5

16. **Disrobe . . . ceremonies,** take the
decorations (**ceremonies**) from the statues (**images**) of Caesar.

17. **Lupercal****lū·pər 'kal**\\ a general
celebration (held annually on February
15) conducted by priests to insure fer-
tility and easy childbirth among women.
The priests, young noblemen, ran a
course through the streets on the Palatine Hill. As they ran they struck people
in their way with a goatskin whip.
Childless women so struck were thought
to be cured of their barrenness.

18. **These growing . . . pitch,** Caesar is
compared to a falcon whose wings must
be clipped to keep it from flying too
high (**pitch**) and out of the Falconer's
control. In other words, Flavius is saying that by depriving Caesar of his popular support now, his lofty political ambitions will be checked in spite of Caesar's wishes.

1. **Pan****păn**\\ the classical god of flocks
and pastures honored in the Lupercal.

2. **Decius****dē·shəs**\\. **Cicero****sĭ·sə 'rō**\\
(106–43 B.C.) a statesman and orator.
Brutus**brū·təs**\\. **Cassius****kă·shəs**\\.
Casca**kăs·kə**\\. **Calpurnia****kăl 'pər-
nē·ə**\\. **Portia****pōr·shə**\\.

CAESAR. Forget not, in your speed, Antonius,
  To touch Calpurnia; for our elders say,
  The barren, touched in this holy chase,[3]
  Shake off their sterile curse.
ANTONY.   I shall remember:
  When Caesar says, "Do this," it is performed.   10
CAESAR. Set on; and leave no ceremony out.

[*Trumpets announce the start of the games.* ANTONY
  leaves.]

SOOTHSAYER. (*Crying out from the crowd.*) Caesar!
CAESAR. Ha! Who calls?
CASCA. Bid every noise be still; peace yet again!
CAESAR. Who is it in the press[4] that calls on me?   15
  I hear a tongue shriller than all the music,
  Cry "Caesar!" Speak! Caesar is turned to hear.
SOOTHSAYER. Beware the ides of March.[5]
CAESAR. (*Gazing around to see who has spoken.*) What
  man is that?
BRUTUS. A soothsayer bids you beware the ides of March.
CAESAR. Set him before me! Let me see his face.   20
CASSIUS. Fellow, come from the throng; look upon Caesar.
CAESAR. What say'st thou to me now? Speak once again.
SOOTHSAYER. Beware the ides of March.
CAESAR. He is a dreamer; let us leave him. Pass.

[*Trumpets sound again. The procession and crowd
  move on.* BRUTUS *and* CASSIUS *lag behind.*]

CASSIUS. Will you go see the order of the course?[6]   25
BRUTUS. Not I.
CASSIUS. I pray[7] you, do.
BRUTUS. I am not gamesome;[8] I do lack some part
  Of that quick[9] spirit that is in Antony.
  Let me not hinder, Cassius, your desires.   30
  I'll leave you.
CASSIUS. Brutus, I do observe you now of late;
  I have not from your eyes that gentleness
  And show of love as I was wont[10] to have.
  You bear too stubborn and too strange a hand   35
  Over your friend that loves you.
BRUTUS.   Cassius,
  Be not deceived; if I have veiled my look,
  I turn the trouble of my countenance
  Merely upon myself.[11] Vexed as I am
  Of late with passions of some difference,   40
  Conceptions only proper to myself,
  Which give some soil[12] perhaps to my behaviors;

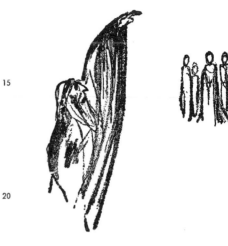

3. **this holy chase**, this race being run in honor of Pan. **Barren** and **sterile**, unable to bear children; Caesar and Calpurnia were childless.

4. **press**, crowd.

5. **ides** \aidz\ March 15.

6. **see . . . course**, see what happens in the race.

7. **pray**, beg, entreat.

8. **gamesome**, given to play.

9. **quick**, lively.

10. **wont**, accustomed.

11. **I turn . . . myself**. That is, I am turning inwardly, only against myself, whatever troubles, griefs, and worries my countenance seems to show.
12. **soil**, ground or basis and also nurturing element.

389

But let not therefore my good friends be grieved—
Among which number, Cassius, be you one—
Nor construe any further my neglect, 45
Than that poor Brutus, with himself at war,
Forgets the shows of love[13] to other men.

CASSIUS. Then, Brutus, I have much mistook your passion;
By means whereof this breast of mine hath buried
Thoughts of great value, worthy cogitations. (*Pauses*) 50
Tell me, good Brutus, can you see your face?

BRUTUS. No, Cassius, for the eye sees not itself
But by reflection, by some other things.

CASSIUS. 'Tis just;
And it is very much lamented, Brutus, 55
That you have no such mirrors as will turn
Your hidden worthiness into your eye
That you might see your shadow. I have heard
Where many of the best respect in Rome,
Except immortal Caesar, speaking of Brutus 60
And groaning underneath this age's yoke,
Have wished that noble Brutus had his eyes.

BRUTUS. Into what dangers would you lead me, Cassius,
That you would have me seek into myself
For that which is not in me? 65

CASSIUS. Therefore, good Brutus, be prepared to hear;
And since you know you cannot see yourself
So well as by reflection, I, your glass,
Will modestly discover to yourself
That of yourself which you yet know not of. 70
And be not jealous[14] on me, gentle Brutus.
Were I a common laugher,[15] or did use
To stale with ordinary oaths my love
To every new protester;[16] if you know
That I do fawn on men and hug them hard 75
And after scandal them, or if you know
That I profess myself in banqueting
To all the rout,[17] then hold me dangerous.

[*Trumpets flourish in the distance, followed by a wave
of cheers.*]

BRUTUS. (*Startled and anxious.*) What means this shouting? I do fear, the people
Choose Caesar for their king.

CASSIUS.   Ay, do you fear it? 80
Then must I think you would not have it so.

BRUTUS. I would not, Cassius, yet I love him well.
But wherefore do you hold me here so long?
What is it that you would impart to me?

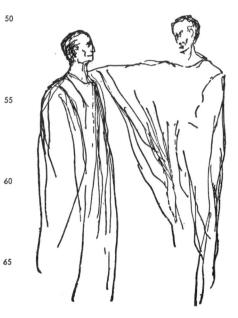

13. **shows of love,** ordinary signs of friendship.

14. **jealous,** suspicious.

15. **laugher,** jester, clown.

16. **protester,** one who professes friendship.

17. **rout,** rabble, worthless crowd.

390

If it be aught toward the general good, 85
Set honor in one eye and death i' th' other,
And I will look on both indifferently;
For let the gods so speed me as I love
The name of honor more than I fear death.
CASSIUS. I know that virtue to be in you, Brutus, 90
As well as I do know your outward favor.[18]
Well, honor is the subject of my story.
I cannot tell what you and other men
Think of this life; but, for my single self,
I had as lief not be as live to be 95
In awe of such a thing as I myself.
I was born free as Caesar; so were you.
We both have fed as well, and we can both
Endure the winter's cold as well as he;
For once, upon a raw and gusty day, 100
The troubled Tiber chafing with her shores,
Caesar said to me, "Dar'st thou, Cassius, now
Leap in with me into this angry flood
And swim to yonder point?" Upon the word,
Accoutred[19] as I was, I plunged in 105
And bade him follow; so indeed he did.
The torrent roared, and we did buffet it
With lusty sinews, throwing it aside
And stemming it with hearts of controversy;[20]
But ere we could arrive the point proposed, 110
Caesar cried, "Help me, Cassius, or I sink!"
I, as Aeneas,[21] our great ancestor,
Did from the flames of Troy upon his shoulder
The old Anchises bear, so from the waves of Tiber
Did I the tired Caesar. And this man 115
Is now become a god, and Cassius is
A wretched creature, and must bend his body
If Caesar carelessly but nod on him.
He had a fever when he was in Spain,
And when the fit was on him, I did mark 120
How he did shake. 'Tis true, this god did shake.
His coward lips did from their color fly,
And that same eye whose bend[22] doth awe the world
Did lose his luster; I did hear him groan.
Ay, and that tongue of his that bade the Romans 125
Mark him and write his speeches in their books,
Alas, it cried, "Give me some drink, Titinius,"
As a sick girl! Ye gods, it doth amaze me
A man of such a feeble temper should
So get the start[23] of the majestic world 130
And bear the palm[24] alone.

18. **outward favor,** outward appearance.

19. **accoutred**\ə▲kū·tərd\ dressed. Cassius was fully dressed.

20. **and stemming . . . controversy,** overcoming the waves with hearts determined and resolute for the struggle.

21. **Aeneas**\ə ▲nē·əs\ a Trojan leader in the Trojan War, the war between Trojans and Greeks in early Greek history. When the device of the Trojan Horse was successful and the Greeks captured Troy at night, Aeneas, leading his son and taking his elderly father **Anchises** \'ăn ▲kai·sēz\ on his shoulders, escaped from the city. Cassius carried Caesar in the same manner from the Tiber. Virgil tells the story of Aeneas in his **Aeneid** \ə ▲nē·ĭd\. After wandering homeless about the Mediterranean for many years, Aeneas and his Trojan refugees eventually established Rome. This is what Cassius means by calling Aeneas "our great ancestor."

22. **bend,** glance.

23. **get the start,** become leader or commander.
24. **palm,** a token of victory given in athletic contests.

391

[More trumpet flourishes in the distance, followed by general shouting.]

BRUTUS. *(Distracted by the noise.)* Another general shout!
    I do believe that these applauses are
    For some new honors that are heaped on Caesar.
CASSIUS. Why, man, he doth bestride the narrow world   135
    Like a Colossus,[25] and we petty men
    Walk under his huge legs, and peep about
    To find ourselves dishonorable graves.
    Men at some time are masters of their fates;
    The fault, dear Brutus, is not in our stars,   140
    But in ourselves, that we are underlings.
    Brutus and Caesar: what should be in that "Caesar"?
    Why should that name be sounded more than yours?
    Write them together; yours is as fair a name.
    Sound them; it doth become the mouth as well.   145
    Weigh them; it is as heavy; conjure[26] with them;
    "Brutus" will start a spirit as soon as "Caesar."
    Now, in the names of all the gods at once,
    Upon what meat doth this our Caesar feed
    That he is grown so great? Age, thou art shamed!   150
    Rome, thou hast lost the breed of noble bloods!
    When went there by an age, since the great flood,
    But it was famed with more than with one man?
    When could they say, till now, that talked of Rome,
    That her wide walls encompassed but one man?   155
    Now is it Rome indeed and room[27] enough,
    When there is in it but one only man.
    O, you and I have heard our fathers say
    There was a Brutus once that would have brooked[28]
    The eternal devil to keep his state in Rome   160
    As easily as a king.
BRUTUS. That you do love me, I am nothing jealous.
    What you would work me to, I have some aim.
    How I have thought of this and of these times,
    I shall recount hereafter; for this present,   165
    I would not, so with love I might entreat you,
    Be any further moved. What you have said
    I will consider; what you have to say
    I will with patience hear, and find a time
    Both meet[29] to hear and answer such high things.   170
    Till then, my noble friend, chew[30] upon this—
    Brutus had rather be a villager
    Than to repute himself a son of Rome
    Under these hard conditions as this time
    Is like to lay upon us.

25. **Colossus**\kə ˈlŏ·səs\ the huge statue of Rhodes, made in honor of the god Apollo in the third century B.C. It supposedly straddled the harbor entrance and ships passed between its legs.

26. **conjure**\kŏn ˈjūr (note the stress)\ to raise spirits of the dead by charms and incantations.

27. In Elizabethan English the words **Rome** and **room** were pronounced similarly. Cassius is punning.

28. **brooked,** endured, permitted. This is a reference to the revolt of Junius Brutus (see Introduction) against the early Tarquin Kings of Rome.

29. **meet,** proper.
30. **chew,** think.

CASSIUS.   I am glad   175
That my weak words have struck but thus much show
Of fire from Brutus.

[*Caesar and his train approach.*]

BRUTUS. The games are done and Caesar is returning.
CASSIUS. (*Whispering.*) As they pass by, pluck Casca by
    the sleeve;
And he will, after his sour fashion, tell you   180
What hath proceeded worthy note today.
BRUTUS. I will do so. But, look you, Cassius,
The angry spot doth glow on Caesar's brow,
And all the rest look like a chidden[31] train.   31. **chidden,** scolded, rebuked.
Calpurnia's cheek is pale, and Cicero   185
Looks with such ferret and such fiery eyes[32]   32. **ferret . . . eyes,** with eyes red and
As we have seen him in the Capitol,   angry like those of a ferret, a small ani-
Being crossed in conference by some senators.   mal like a weasel.
CASSIUS. Casca will tell us what the matter is.
CAESAR. (*Leaning toward* ANTONY *and glancing in*
    CASSIUS' *direction.*) Antonius.   190
ANTONY. Caesar?
CAESAR. Let me have men about me that are fat,
Sleek-headed men and such as sleep o' nights.
Yond Cassius has a lean and hungry look.
He thinks too much; such men are dangerous.   195
ANTONY. Fear him not, Caesar; he's not dangerous.
He is a noble Roman and well given.
CAESAR. Would he were fatter! But I fear him not.
Yet if my name were liable to fear,
I do not know the man I should avoid   200
So soon as that spare Cassius. He reads much,
He is a great observer, and he looks
Quite through[33] the deeds of men. He loves no plays 33. **looks/Quite through,** examines
As thou dost, Antony; he hears no music;   closely, scrutinizes.
Seldom he smiles, and smiles in such a sort   205
As if he mocked himself and scorned his spirit
That could be moved to smile at anything.
Such men as he be never at heart's ease
Whiles they behold a greater than themselves,
And therefore are they very dangerous.   210
I rather tell thee what is to be feared
Than what I fear; for always I am Caesar.
Come on my right hand, for this ear is deaf,
And tell me truly what thou think'st of him.

[CAESAR *and* ANTONY *walk away talking quietly to-*
gether. The train follows. BRUTUS *gently pulls at* CASCA'S

sleeve as he passes. CASCA *draws aside and speaks to* BRUTUS.]

CASCA. You pulled me by the cloak. Would you speak
    with me?   215

BRUTUS. Ay, Casca; tell us what hath chanced today
    That Caesar looks so sad.

CASCA. Why, you were with him, were you not?

BRUTUS. I should not then ask Casca what had chanced.

CASCA. Why, there was a crown offered him; and being 220
    offered him, he put it by with the back of his hand, thus;
    and then the people fell a-shouting.

BRUTUS. What was the second noise for?

CASCA. Why, for that too.

CASSIUS. They shouted thrice; what was the last cry for? 225

CASCA. Why, for that too.

BRUTUS. Was the crown offered him thrice?

CASCA. Ay, marry,[34] was't, and he put it by thrice, every
    time gentler than other; and at every putting-by mine
    honest neighbors shouted.   230

CASSIUS. Who offered him the crown?

CASCA. Why, Antony.

BRUTUS. Tell us the manner of it, gentle Casca.

CASCA. I can as well be hanged as tell the manner of it. It
    was mere foolery; I did not mark it. I saw Mark Antony 235
    offer him a crown—yet 'twas not a crown neither, 'twas
    one of these coronets[35]—and, as I told you, he put it by
    once; but for all that, to my thinking, he would fain
    have had it. Then he offered it to him again; then
    he put it by again, but, to my thinking, he was very 240
    loath to lay his fingers off it. And then he offered it the
    third time; he put it the third time by; and still as he
    refused it, the rabblement hooted and clapped their
    chapped hands and threw up their sweaty night-caps
    and uttered such a deal of stinking breath because 245
    Caesar refused the crown, that it had almost choked
    Caesar, for he swounded[36] and fell down at it; and for
    mine own part, I durst not laugh for fear of opening my
    lips and receiving the bad air.

CASSIUS. But, soft, I pray you. What, did Caesar swound? 250

CASCA. He fell down in the market-place, and foamed at
    the mouth, and was speechless.

BRUTUS. 'Tis very like; he hath the falling sickness.[37]

CASSIUS. No, Caesar hath it not; but you and I
    And honest Casca, we have the falling sickness. 255

CASCA. I know not what you mean by that, but I am sure
    Caesar fell down. If the tag-rag people did not clap him

34. **marry,** a light oath in Elizabethan times. Originally "by Mary," that is, the mother of Christ (an anachronism here).

35. **coronet**\\'kŏ·rə ▲nĕt\\ a small crown, for one with a rank lower than a king's.

36. **swounded**\\▲swūn·dəd\\ fainted.

37. **falling sickness,** epilepsy. It is not certain historically whether or not Caesar had this affliction.

and hiss him, according as he pleased and displeased them, as they use to do the players in the theater, I am no true man. 260

BRUTUS. What said he when he came unto himself?

CASCA. Marry, before he fell down, when he perceived the common herd was glad he refused the crown, he plucked me ope his doublet[38] and offered them his throat to cut. An[39] I had been a man of any occupa- 265 tion,[40] if I would not have taken him at a word, I would I might go to hell among the rogues. And so he fell. When he came to himself again, he said, if he had done or said anything amiss, he desired their worships to think it was his infirmity. Three or four wenches, where 270 I stood, cried, "Alas, good soul!" and forgave him with all their hearts. But there's no heed to be taken of them. If Caesar had stabbed their mothers, they would have done no less.

BRUTUS. And after that he came, thus sad, away? 275

CASCA. Ay.

CASSIUS. Did Cicero say anything?

CASCA. Ay, he spoke Greek.

CASSIUS. To what effect?

CASCA. Nay, an I tell you that, I'll ne'er look you i' th' face 280 again. But those that understood him smiled at one another and shook their heads; but for mine own part, it was Greek to me. I could tell you more news too. Marullus and Flavius, for pulling scarfs off Caesar's images are put to silence.[41] Fare you well. There was 285 more foolery yet, if I could remember it.

CASSIUS. Will you sup[42] with me tonight, Casca?

CASCA. No, I am promised forth.

CASSIUS. Will you dine with me tomorrow?

CASCA. Ay, if I be alive and your mind hold and your 290 dinner be worth the eating.

CASSIUS. Good! I will expect you.

CASCA. Do so. Farewell, both.

[CASCA *leaves.*]

BRUTUS. What a blunt fellow is this grown to be! He was quick[43] mettle when he went to school. 295

CASSIUS. So is he now in execution
Of any bold or noble enterprise,
However he puts on this tardy form.[44]
This rudeness is a sauce to his good wit,
Which gives men stomach to digest his words 300
With better appetite.

BRUTUS. And so it is. For this time I will leave you.

38. **doublet**, a tight, colorful jacket worn in Shakespeare's time.
39. **an**, if.
40. **occupation**, self-possession.

41. **put to silence**, either exiled and banished or put to death.

42. **sup**, have dinner.

43. **quick**, lively.

44. **he puts . . . form**, he puts on this appearance of slowness and inactivity.

Tomorrow, if you please to speak with me,
I will come home to you; or, if you will,
Come home to me, and I will wait for you.   305
CASSIUS. I will do so. Till then, think of the world.

[BRUTUS *turns and leaves.*]

(CASSIUS *watches* BRUTUS *depart and muses to himself.*)
    Well, Brutus, thou art noble; yet, I see,
Thy honorable metal may be wrought
From that it is disposed;[45] therefore 'tis meet
That noble minds keep ever with their likes;   310
For who so firm that cannot be seduced?
Caesar doth bear me hard,[46] but he loves Brutus.
If I were Brutus now and he were Cassius,
He should not humor me. I will this night,
In several hands,[47] in at his windows throw,   315
As if they came from several citizens,
Writings all tending to the great opinion
That Rome holds of his name; wherein obscurely
Caesar's ambition shall be glanced[48] at.
And after this let Caesar seat him sure,   320
For we will shake him, or worse days endure.

[CASSIUS *leaves slowly.*]

45. yet, I see, . . . disposed, despite your fundamentally honorable nature, which would cause you to take one course, you may be swayed to another. **46. bear me hard,** dislike and suspect me.

47. In several hands, in different kinds of handwriting, as though written by many different people.

48. glanced at, mentioned.

scene 3

A street at night. A violent thunderstorm flashes and roars.
The flickering light reveals the blank white walls of houses
and the dark, staring windows. There is no sign of life.
CASCA *and* CICERO *enter from opposite sides.* CASCA *has*
drawn his sword and moves along warily.

CICERO. Good even,[1] Casca. Brought you Caesar home?
  Why are you breathless? And why stare you so?
CASCA. Are you not moved, when all the sway of earth
  Shakes like a thing unfirm? O Cicero,
  I have seen tempests when the scolding winds   5
  Have rived[2] the knotty oaks, and I have seen
  The ambitious ocean swell and rage and foam
  To be exalted with the threat'ning clouds;
  But never till tonight, never till now,
  Did I go through a tempest dropping fire.   10
  Either there is a civil strife in heaven,
  Or else the world, too saucy[3] with the gods,
  Incenses them to send destruction.
CICERO. Why, saw you anything more wonderful?

1. even, evening.

2. rived\raivd split.

3. saucy, impudent.

396

CASCA. A common slave—you know him well by sight— 15
    Held up his left hand, which did flame and burn
    Like twenty torches joined, and yet his hand,
    Not sensible of fire, remained unscorched.
    Besides—I have not since put up my sword—
    Against[4] the Capitol I met a lion,   20
    Who glared upon me, and went surly by
    Without annoying me. And there were drawn
    Upon a heap a hundred ghastly women,
    Transformed with their fear, who swore they saw
    Men all in fire walk up and down the streets.   25
    And yesterday the bird of night[5] did sit
    Even at noonday upon the market-place,
    Hooting and shrieking. When these prodigies
    Do so conjointly meet, let not men say,
    "These are their reasons; they are natural";   30
    For, I believe, they are portentous things
    Unto the climate that they point upon.[6]
CICERO. Indeed, it is a strange-disposed time;
    But men may construe things after their fashion[7]
    Clean from the purpose of the things themselves.   35
    Comes Caesar to the Capitol tomorrow?
CASCA. He doth; for he did bid Antonius
    Send word to you he would be there tomorrow.
CICERO. Goodnight then, Casca. This disturbed sky
    Is not to walk in.
CASCA.   Farewell, Cicero.   40

[*As* CICERO *leaves,* CASSIUS *enters from another direction
and is startled by* CASCA, *who stands in the shadows.*]

CASSIUS. Who's there?
CASCA.   A Roman.
CASSIUS.   Casca, by your voice.
CASCA. Your ear is good. Cassius, what night is this!
CASSIUS. A very pleasing night to honest men.
CASCA. Who ever knew the heavens menace so?
CASSIUS. Those that have known the earth so full of faults.   45
    For my part, I have walked about the streets,
    Submitting me unto the perilous night,
    And, thus unbraced,[8] Casca, as you see,
    Have bared my bosom to the thunder-stone.[9]
    And when the cross blue lightning seemed to open   50
    The breast of heaven, I did present myself
    Even in the aim and very flash of it.
CASCA. But wherefore did you so much tempt the heavens?
    It is the part of men to fear and tremble
    When the most mighty gods by tokens send   55

4. **against,** by.

5. **bird of night,** owl.

6. **For, I believe . . . point upon.** Casca believes that the unnatural events are omens of impending disaster for Rome.
7. **their fashion,** their (the men) own opinion.

8. **unbraced,** not armored or otherwise protected by heavy clothing.
9. **thunder-stone,** thunder bolt.

Such dreadful heralds to astonish us.

CASSIUS. You are dull, Casca, and those sparks of life
  That should be in a Roman you do want,
  Or else you use not. You look pale and gaze
  And put on fear and cast yourself in wonder   60
  To see the strange impatience of the heavens.
  But if you would consider the true cause
  Why all these fires, why all these gliding ghosts,
  Why birds and beasts from quality and kind,[10]
  Why old men, fools, and children calculate,   65
  Why all these things change from their ordinance
  Their natures and pre-formed faculties[11]
  To monstrous quality, why, you shall find
  That heaven hath infused them with these spirits,[12]
  To make them instruments of fear and warning   70
  Unto some monstrous state.
  Now could I, Casca, name to thee a man
  Most like this dreadful night,
  That thunders, lightens, opens graves, and roars
  As doth the lion in the Capitol,   75
  A man no mightier than thyself or me
  In personal action, yet prodigious grown
  And fearful, as these strange eruptions are.

CASCA. 'Tis Caesar that you mean; is it not, Cassius?

CASSIUS. Let it be who it is; for Romans now   80
  Have thews[13] and limbs like to their ancestors.
  But woe the while! our fathers' minds are dead,
  And we are governed with our mothers' spirits.
  Our yoke and sufferance[14] show us womanish.

CASCA. Indeed, they say the senators tomorrow   85
  Mean to establish Caesar as a king;
  And he shall wear his crown by sea and land,
  In every place, save here in Italy.[15]

CASSIUS. I know where I will wear this dagger then;
  Cassius from bondage will deliver Cassius.[16]   90
  Therein, ye gods, you make the weak most strong;
  Therein, ye gods, you tyrants do defeat.
  Nor stony tower, nor walls of beaten brass,
  Nor airless dungeon, nor strong links of iron,
  Can be retentive to the strength of spirit;   95
  But life, being weary of these worldly bars,
  Never lacks power to dismiss itself.
  If I know this, know all the world besides,
  That part of tyranny that I do bear
  I can shake off at pleasure.

[*Claps of thunder roar in the sky.*]

398

10. **from quality and kind,** against their true quality or nature.

11. **pre-formed faculties,** natural powers and functions.

12. **these spirits,** unnatural tendencies.

13. **thews,** sinews.

14. **yoke and sufferance,** our acceptance of oppression.

15. The feelings against a Kingship were stronger in the Italian peninsula than in other parts of the Roman Empire.
16. **Cassius . . . Cassius,** that is, he will commit suicide.

CASCA. (*Inspired by* CASSIUS' *bold statement of rebellion.*) So can I!   100
So every bondman in his own hand bears
The power to cancel his captivity.
CASSIUS. And why should Caesar be a tyrant then?
Poor man! I know he would not be a wolf,
But that he sees the Romans are but sheep;   105
He were no lion, were not Romans hinds.[17]
Those that with haste will make a mighty fire
Begin it with weak straws. What trash is Rome,
What rubbish and what offal, when it serves
For the base matter to illuminate   110
So vile a thing as Caesar! But, O grief,
Where has thou led me? I perhaps speak this
Before a willing bondman.[18] Then I know
My answer must be made. But I am armed,
And dangers are to me indifferent.   115
CASCA. You speak to Casca, and to such a man
That is no fleering tell-tale.[19] Hold, my hand.
Be factious[20] for redress of all these griefs,
And I will set this foot of mine as far
As who goes farthest.
CASSIUS.   There's a bargain made.   120
Now you know, Casca, I have moved already
Some certain of the noblest-minded Romans
To undergo with me an enterprise
Of honorable-dangerous consequence.
And I do know, by this they stay[21] for me   125
In Pompey's Porch;[22] for now, this fearful night,
There is no stir or walking in the streets.
And the complexion of the element
In favor's[23] like the work we have in hand,
Most bloody, fiery, and most terrible.   130

[CINNA *approaches, hurrying along the street.*]

CASCA. (*Softly to* CASSIUS.) Stand close awhile, for here
    comes one in haste.
CASSIUS. 'Tis Cinna. I do know him by his gait;
    He is a friend. (*Calling out.*) Cinna, where haste you
        so?
CINNA. To find out you. (*Peering at* CASCA.) Who's that?
    Metellus Cimber?[24]
CASSIUS. No, it is Casca: one incorporate[25]   135
    To our attempts. Am I not stayed for, Cinna?
CINNA. I am glad on't. What a fearful night is this!
    There's two or three of us have seen strange sights.
CASSIUS. Am I not stayed for? Tell me.

17. **hinds,** deer.

18. **a willing bondman,** a person willing to be a bondman or slave of Caesar and who might report to him.

19. **fleering tell-tale,** mocking or insincere informer.
20. **be factious,** get together a party, faction, or conspiracy.

21. **stay,** wait.

22. **Pompey's Porch,** the vestibule or entrance to the theater of Pompey.

23. **favor,** appearance.

24. **Metellus Cimber**\mə ˈtĕ·ləs ˈsĭm-bər\.
25. **one incorporate,** one who has joined.

A.   Yes, you are.

    O Cassius, if you could   140
    But win the noble Brutus to our party—

CASSIUS. Be you content. Good Cinna, take this paper,
    And look you lay it on the praetor's[26] chair,
    Where Brutus may but find it; and throw this
    In at his window; set this up with wax   145
    Upon old Brutus' statue. All this done,
    Repair to Pompey's Porch, where you shall find us.
    Is Decius Brutus and Trebonius[27] there?

CINNA. All but Metellus Cimber, and he's gone
    To seek you at your house. Well, I will hie   150
    And so bestow these papers as you bade me.

CASSIUS. That done, repair to Pompey's theater.
    [CINNA *hurries off.*]
    Come, Casca, you and I will yet ere day
    See Brutus at his house. Three parts of him
    Is ours already, and the man entire   155
    Upon the next encounter yields him ours.

CASCA. O, he sits high in all the people's hearts;
    And that which would appear offense in us,
    His countenance, like richest alchemy,[28]
    Will change to virtue and to worthiness.   160

CASSIUS. Him and his worth and our great need of him
    You have right well conceited.[29] Let us go,
    For it is after midnight; and ere day
    We will awake him and be sure of him.

    [CASSIUS *and* CASCA *set off together.*]

26. **praetor**\ˈprē ′tōr\ a high-ranking official with judicial duties.

27. **Trebonius**\trĕ ˈbō·nē·əs\ formerly a lieutenant of Caesar in Britain.

28. **alchemy,** an alchemist could allegedly change baser materials into gold.

29. **conceited,** understood.

Act II

SCENE 1

Rome. BRUTUS' *garden, a graceful arrangement of trees and shrubbery, fountains and white marble statuary. To the side a gate that leads to the street. It is March 15, shortly before dawn. The dark sky still convulses with periodic flashes of lightning.* BRUTUS *paces nervously. He looks suddenly toward the house, and calls:*

BRUTUS. What, Lucius,[1] ho!
  I cannot by the progress of the stars
  Give guess how near to day. Lucius, I say!
  I would[2] it were my fault to sleep so soundly.
  When, Lucius, when? Awake, I say! What, Lucius!   5
LUCIUS. (*Entering, rubbing his eyes.*) Called you, my
    lord?
BRUTUS. Get me a taper in my study, Lucius.
  When it is lighted, come and call me here.
LUCIUS. (*Leaving, speaking through a yawn.*) I will,
    my lord.
BRUTUS. (*Musing to himself.*) It must be by his death;
    and for my part   10
  I know no personal cause to spurn at him
  But for the general.[3] He would be crowned:
  How that might change his nature; there's the question.
  It is the bright day that brings forth the adder,[4]
  And that craves wary walking. Crown him? That—   15
  And then, I grant, we put a sting in him
  That at his will he may do danger with.
  The abuse of greatness is when it disjoins
  Remorse from power. And, to speak truth of Caesar,
  I have not known when his affections swayed   20
  More than his reason.[5] But 'tis a common proof
  That lowliness is young ambition's ladder,
  Whereto the climber-upward turns his face;
  But when he once attains the utmost rung,
  He then unto the ladder turns his back,   25
  Looks in the clouds, scorning the base degrees
  By which he did ascend. So Caesar may.
  Then, lest he may, prevent.[6] And, since the quarrel
  Will bear no color for the thing he is,
  Fashion it thus—that what he is, augmented,   30
  Would run to these and these extremities;
  And therefore think him as a serpent's egg

1. **Lucius**\ᴧlū·shəs *or* ᴧlū·shi·əs\ Brutus' servant.

2. **I would,** I wish.

3. Brutus knows of no personal reason to object to Caesar, as though kicking at him, but he is concerned about the general good of the Roman state and people.
4. **adder,** snake.

5. He has not known Caesar to be ruled by his emotions and passions rather than his reason.

6. **Then, . . . prevent,** lest Caesar do so, let us anticipate and prevent him.

Which, hatched, would, as his kind, grow mischievous,[7]
And kill him in the shell.

LUCIUS. (*Reentering, a folded paper in his hand.*)
   The taper burneth in your closet,[8] sir.   35
Searching the window for a flint, I found
This paper,[9] thus sealed up. And I am sure
It did not lie there when I went to bed.

BRUTUS. (*Taking the letter.*) Get you to bed again.
   It is not day.
Is not tomorrow, boy, the ides of March?   40

LUCIUS. I know not, sir.

BRUTUS. Look in the calendar, and bring me word.

LUCIUS. (*Leaving.*) I will, sir.

BRUTUS. The exhalations[10] whizzing in the air
Give so much light that I may read by them.   45

[*Opening the letter and peering close to read.*]

"Brutus, thou sleep'st. Awake, and see thyself!
Shall Rome, etc. Speak, strike, redress!"

(*Looking up from the letter, frowning.*) "Brutus,
   thou sleep'st. Awake!"
Such instigations have been often dropped
Where I have took them up.   50
"Shall Rome, etc." Thus must I piece it out:
Shall Rome stand under one man's awe? What, Rome?
My ancestors did from the streets of Rome
The Tarquin drive when he was called a king.
"Speak, strike, redress!" Am I entreated   55
To speak and strike? O Rome, I make thee promise—
If the redress will follow, thou receivest
Thy full petition[11] at the hand of Brutus!

LUCIUS. (*Reentering.*) Sir, March is wasted fifteen days.

[*A knocking comes from the gate.*]

BRUTUS. 'Tis good. Go to the gate. Somebody knocks.   60

[LUCIUS *leaves.*]

Since Cassius first did whet[12] me against Caesar,
I have not slept.
Between the acting of a dreadful thing
And the first motion,[13] all the interim is
Like a phantasma or a hideous dream.   65
The Genius and the mortal instruments[14]
Are then in council; and the state of man,
Like to a little kingdom, suffers then
The nature of an insurrection.

[LUCIUS *reenters.*]

---

7. **mischievous,** injurious, harmful. The word had a stronger meaning in Shakespeare's day than now.

8. **closet,** study.

9. Cinna has been obeying orders. See Act I, Scene 3.

10. **exhalations,** fiery vapors; flashing meteoric lights.

11. **Thy full petition,** all that you ask.

12. **whet,** incite.

13. **the first motion,** the first suggestion.

14. **The Genius and the mortal instruments,** the guiding spirit (personality, soul) of a man and his body (the means for carrying out the deadly purpose of his "Genius").

402

LUCIUS. Sir, 'tis your brother[15] Cassius at the door,   70
  Who doth desire to see you.

BRUTUS.   Is he alone?

LUCIUS. No, sir. There are more with him.

BRUTUS.   Do you know
  them?

LUCIUS. No, sir. Their hats are plucked about their ears,
  And half their faces buried in their cloaks,
  That by no means I may discover them   75
  By any mark of favor.

BRUTUS.   Let 'em enter.

[LUCIUS *exits toward the gate.*]

They are the faction. O conspiracy,
Shamest thou to show thy dangerous brow by night,
When evils are most free? O, then by day
Where wilt thou find a cavern dark enough   80
To mask thy monstrous visage? Seek none, conspiracy!
Hide it in smiles and affability;
For if thou path, thy native semblance on,
Not Erebus itself were dim enough
To hide thee from prevention.[16]   85

[*The conspirators gather quietly. They are:* CASSIUS,
CASCA, DECIUS, CINNA, METELLUS CIMBER, *and* TRE-
BONIUS. CASSIUS *moves to* BRUTUS' *side. The others stand
back.*]

CASSIUS. I think we are too bold upon your rest.
  Good morrow, Brutus. Do we trouble you?

BRUTUS. I have been up this hour, awake all night.
  Know I these men that come along with you?

CASSIUS. Yes, every man of them, and no man here   90
  But honors you; and every one doth wish
  You had but that opinion of yourself
  Which every noble Roman bears of you.
  This is Trebonius.

[*One by one the conspirators step forward and reveal
themselves to Brutus.*]

BRUTUS.   He is welcome hither.

CASSIUS. This, Decius Brutus.

BRUTUS.   He is welcome too.   95

CASSIUS. This, Casca. This, Cinna. And this, Metellus
  Cimber.

BRUTUS. They are all welcome.
  What watchful cares do interpose themselves
  Betwixt your eyes and night?

CASSIUS. Shall I entreat a word?   100

15. **brother,** brother-in-law, Cassius had married Junia, Brutus' sister.

16. **For if thou . . . prevention. path,** walk about openly, without disguise. **thy native semblance on,** in their true or natural character. **Erebus**\ˈā·rə ˈbəs\ in Roman mythology, the gloomy space through which souls passed to hell. **prevention,** detection, anticipating, and forestalling. If they went about openly indicating their true character, the passageway to hell itself would not be dark enough to prevent their being detected and guarded against.

[*Leads* BRUTUS *aside, and they whisper.*]

DECIUS. Here lies the east. Doth not the day break here?

CASCA. No.

CINNA. O, pardon, sir, it doth. And yon gray lines
  That fret[17] the clouds are messengers of day.

CASCA. You shall confess that you are both deceived.
  Here, as I point my sword, the sun arises,
  Which is a great way growing on the south,
  Weighing[18] the youthful season of the year.
  Some two months hence up higher toward the north
  He first presents his fire, and the high east
  Stands, as the Capitol, directly here.

[BRUTUS *and* CASSIUS *approach the others.*]

BRUTUS. Give me your hands, all over, one by one.

CASSIUS. And let us swear our resolution.

BRUTUS. No, not an oath! If not the face of men,
  The sufferance of our souls, the time's abuse,—
  If these by motives weak, break off betimes,
  And every man hence to his idle bed;
  So let high-sighted tyranny range on,
  Till each man drop by lottery.[19] But if these,
  As I am sure they do, bear fire enough
  To kindle cowards and to steel with valor
  The melting spirits of women, then, countrymen,
  What need we any spur but our own cause
  To prick us to redress? what other bond
  Than secret Romans, that have spoke the word
  And will not palter?[20] and what other oath
  Than honesty to honesty engaged
  That this shall be, or we will fall for it?
  Swear priests and cowards and men cautelous,[21]
  Old feeble carrions[22] and such suffering souls
  That welcome wrongs. Unto bad causes swear
  Such creatures as men doubt; but do not stain
  The even virtue of our enterprise,
  Nor the insuppressive[23] mettle of our spirits,
  To think that or[24] our cause or our performance
  Did need an oath; when every drop of blood
  That every Roman bears, and nobly bears,
  Is guilty of a several bastardy,[25]
  If he do break the smallest particle
  Of any promise that hath passed from him.

CASSIUS. But what of Cicero? Shall we sound him?
  I think he will stand very strong with us.

CASCA. Let us not leave him out.

CINNA.   No, by no means.

---

17. **fret,** break up, wear away or consume.

18. **weighing,** taking into consideration. In late winter the sun rises somewhat south of east.

19. **If not the face . . . by lottery. face,** honor or renown; **sufferance,** suffering; **betimes,** at once; **idle,** useless. If honor itself, the suffering our souls undergo, and the abuses of the present times are weak motives for acting, let us break off at once and every one retire uselessly to bed, permitting the arrogant tyrant to continue until every good man is killed at the whim of the tyrant.

20. **palter,** play false.

21. **cautelous,** overcautious.

22. **carrions,** feeble men.

23. **insuppressive,** not to be suppressed.

24. **or,** either.

25. **Is guilty . . . bastardy,** is obviously illegitimate (as unfaithful to his noble ancestors) many times over.

METELLUS. O, let us have him, for his silver hairs
   Will purchase us a good opinion————————   145
   And buy men's voices to commend our deeds.
   It shall be said his judgment ruled our hands.
   Our youths and wildness shall no whit appear,
   But all be buried in his gravity.
BRUTUS. O, name him not. Let us not break with him,²⁶   150
   For he will never follow anything
   That other men begin.
CASSIUS.   Then leave him out.
CASCA. Indeed he is not fit.
DECIUS. Shall no man else be touched but only Caesar?
CASSIUS. Decius, well urged. I think it is not meet,   155
   Mark Antony, so well beloved of Caesar,
   Should outlive Caesar. We shall find of him
   A shrewd contriver. And, you know, his means,
   If he improve them, may well stretch so far
   As to annoy us all; which to prevent,   160
   Let Antony and Caesar fall together.
BRUTUS. Our course will seem too bloody, Caius Cassius,
   To cut the head off and then hack the limbs,
   Like wrath in death and envy afterwards;
   For Antony is but a limb of Caesar.   165
   Let's be sacrificers, but not butchers, Caius.
   We all stand up against the spirit of Caesar,
   And in the spirit of men there is no blood.
   O, that we then could come by Caesar's spirit,
   And not dismember Caesar! But, alas,   170
   Caesar must bleed for it! And, gentle friends,
   Let's kill him boldly, but not wrathfully.
   Let's carve him as a dish fit for the gods,
   Not hew him as a carcass fit for hounds;
   And let our hearts, as subtle masters do,   175
   Stir up their servants to an act of rage,
   And after seem to chide them. This shall make
   Our purpose necessary and not envious;²⁷
   Which so appearing to the common eyes,
   We shall be called purgers,²⁸ not murderers.   180
   And for Mark Antony, think not of him;
   For he can do no more than Caesar's arm
   When Caesar's head is off.
CASSIUS.   Yet I do fear him;
   For in the ingrafted²⁹ love he bears to Caesar—
BRUTUS. Alas, good Cassius, do not think of him.   185
   If he love Caesar, all that he can do
   Is to himself—take thought and die for Caesar;³⁰
   And that were much he should, for he is given

26. **break with him,** tell him the plans under way.

27. **This shall . . . envious,** this procedure will make us seem driven by political necessity but not by hateful envy.

28. **purgers,** persons who purge or clean out an evil from the state.

29. **ingrafted,** grown to be a part of him.

30. **take thought . . . Caesar,** become despondent about Caesar and commit suicide because of his death.

To sports, to wildness, and much company.[31]

TREBONIUS. There is no fear in him.[32] Let him not die;   190
For he will live and laugh at this hereafter.

[*A clock strikes faintly from within the house.*]

BRUTUS. Peace! Count the clock.

CASSIUS.   The clock hath stricken three.

TREBONIUS. 'Tis time to part.

CASSIUS.   But it is doubtful yet
Whether Caesar will come forth today or no;
For he is superstitious grown of late,   195
Quite from the main opinion he held once
Of fantasy, of dreams, and ceremonies.
It may be these apparent prodigies,
The unaccustomed terror of this night,
And the persuasion of his augurers[33]   200
May hold him from the Capitol today.

DECIUS. Never fear that. If he be so resolved,
I can o'ersway him; for he loves to hear
That unicorns may be betrayed with trees,
And bears with glasses, elephants with holes,   205
Lions with toils,[34] and men with flatterers.
But when I tell him he hates flatterers,
He says he does, being then most flattered.
Let me work;
For I can give his humor the true bent,[35]   210
And I will bring him to the Capitol.

CASSIUS. Nay, we will all of us be there to fetch him.

BRUTUS. By the eighth hour; is that the uttermost?

CINNA. Be that the uttermost, and fail not then.

METELLUS. Caius Ligarius[36] doth bear Caesar hard,   215
Who rated him for speaking well of Pompey.
I wonder none of you have thought of him.

BRUTUS. Now, good Metellus, go along by him.
He loves me well, and I have given him reasons.
Send him but hither, and I'll fashion[37] him.   220

CASSIUS. The morning comes upon us. We'll leave you,
    Brutus,
And, friends, disperse yourselves; but all remember
What you have said, and show yourselves true Romans.

BRUTUS. Good gentlemen, look fresh and merrily.
Let not our looks put on[38] our purposes,   225
But bear it as our Roman actors do,
With untired spirits and formal constancy.
And so good morrow to you every one.

[*The conspirators slip quietly out through the gate,
leaving* BRUTUS *alone in the garden.*]

31. Brutus believes that "playboys" like Antony are incapable of serious, purposeful actions.
32. **There is . . . him,** there is nothing to be feared about him.

33. **augurers,** augurs—religious officials —who predicted the future by interpreting omens.

34. **That unicorns . . . toils,** according to the belief, the unicorn might be captured by luring it into driving its horn into a tree and bears might be trapped by luring them on with mirrors. Elephants were trapped in pits and lions by snares or nets (toils).
35. **I can give . . . bent,** I can humor and persuade him in the right way.

36. **Caius**\ᴧkā·əs\ **Ligarius**\lĭ ᴧgā·rĭ·əs\.

37. **fashion,** mold (to our will).

38. **put on,** show, betray.

Boy! Lucius! Fast asleep? It is no matter.
Enjoy the honey-heavy dew of slumber. 230
Thou hast no figures nor no fantasies
Which busy care draws in the brains of men;
Therefore thou sleepest so sound.

[BRUTUS' *wife* PORTIA *enters the garden as
he speaks.*]

PORTIA.   Brutus, my lord!
BRUTUS. Portia, what mean you? Wherefore rise you now?
It is not for your health thus to commit 235
Your weak condition to the raw cold morning.
PORTIA. Nor for yours neither. You've ungently, Brutus,
Stole from my bed; and yesternight at supper
You suddenly arose and walked about,
Musing and sighing, with your arms across. 240
And when I asked you what the matter was,
You stared upon me with ungentle looks.
I urged you further. Then you scratched your head
And too impatiently stamped with your foot.
Yet I insisted; yet you answered not. 245
But with an angry wafture[39] of your hand
Gave sign for me to leave you. So I did,
Fearing to strengthen that impatience
Which seemed too much enkindled, and withal
Hoping it was but an effect of humor,[40] 250
Which sometime hath its hour with every man.
It will not let you eat, nor talk, nor sleep,
And could it work so much upon your shape
As it hath much prevailed on your condition,
I should not know you, Brutus. Dear my lord, 255
Make me acquainted with your cause of grief.
BRUTUS. I am not well in health, and that is all.
PORTIA. Brutus is wise, and, were he not in health,
He would embrace the means to come by it.
BRUTUS. Why, so I do. Good Portia, go to bed. 260
PORTIA. Is Brutus sick? and is it physical
To walk unbraced and suck up the humors
Of the dank morning? What, is Brutus sick,
And will he steal out of his wholesome bed
To dare the vile contagion of the night, 265
And tempt the rheumy and unpurged air[41]
To add unto his sickness? No, my Brutus;
You have some sick offense within your mind,
Which, by the right and virtue of my place,
I ought to know of; and upon my knees 270
I charm you, by my once commended beauty,

39. **wafture,** wave.

40. **humor,** a passing mood.

41. **the rheumy . . . air,** risk the moist
air not yet purified by the sun.

407

By all your vows of love, and that great vow
Which did incorporate and make us one,
That you unfold to me, yourself, your half,
Why you are heavy,[42] and what men tonight   275   42. **heavy,** sad.
Have had resort to you; for here have been
Some six or seven who did hide their faces
Even from darkness.

BRUTUS.   Kneel not, gentle Portia.

PORTIA. I should not need, if you were gentle Brutus.
　Within the bond of marriage, tell me, Brutus,   280
　Is it excepted I should know no secrets
　That appertain to you? Am I yourself
　But, as it were, in sort or limitation,
　To keep with you at meals, comfort your bed,
　And talk to you sometimes? Dwell I but in the suburbs 285
　Of your good pleasure? If it be no more,
　Portia is Brutus' harlot, not his wife.

BRUTUS. You are my true and honorable wife,
　As dear to me as are the ruddy drops
　That visit my sad heart.   290

PORTIA. If this were true, then should I know this secret.
　I grant I am a woman; but withal[43]   43. **withal,** nevertheless.
　A woman that Lord Brutus took to wife.
　I grant I am a woman; but withal
　A woman well-reputed, Cato's daughter.   295
　Think you I am no stronger than my sex,
　Being so fathered[44] and so husbanded?   44. **fathered,** her father, Cato the
　Tell me your counsels; I will not disclose them.   younger, had killed himself (46 B.C.)
　I have made strong proof of my constancy,   rather than submit to Caesar. He was
　Giving myself a voluntary wound   300   considered a martyr to the cause of
　Here, in the thigh. Can I bear that with patience,   Roman liberty by Caesar's opponents.
　And not my husband's secrets?

BRUTUS.   O ye gods!
　Render me worthy of this noble wife!

[*A knock comes from the garden gate.* BRUTUS *leads*
PORTIA *toward the house.*]

Hark, hark! One knocks. Portia, go in awhile,
And by and by thy bosom shall partake   305
The secrets of my heart.
All my engagements I will construe[45] to thee;   45. **construe,** explain fully.
All the charactery of my sad brows.
Leave me with haste.

[PORTIA *enters the house.* BRUTUS *turns anxiously*
toward the gate, calling for LUCIUS.]

　　　　　　　Lucius, who's that knocks?

[*Lucius comes from the garden gate, leading* LIGARIUS, *whose head is bandaged with a handkerchief.*]

LUCIUS. Here is a sick man that would speak with you. 310
BRUTUS. Caius Ligarius, that Metellus spake of.
　Boy, stand aside. Caius Ligarius! How?
LIGARIUS. Vouchsafe good morrow from a feeble tongue.
BRUTUS. O, what a time have you chose out, brave Caius,
　To wear a kerchief![46] Would you were not sick! 315

LIGARIUS. I am not sick, if Brutus have in hand
　Any exploit worthy the name of honor.
BRUTUS. Such an exploit have I in hand, Ligarius,
　Had you a healthful ear to hear of it.
LIGARIUS. By all the gods that Romans bow before, 320
　I here discard my sickness! Soul of Rome!
　Brave son derived from honorable loins!
　Thou, like an exorcist, hast conjured up
　My mortified[47] spirit. Now bid me run,
　And I will strive with things impossible; 325
　Yea, get the better of them. What's to do?
BRUTUS. A piece of work that will make sick men whole.
LIGARIUS. But are not some whole that we must make sick?
BRUTUS. That must we also. What it is, my Caius,
　I shall unfold to thee as we are going 330
　To whom it must be done.
LIGARIUS. 　　　　　　　　Set on your foot,
　And with a heart new-fired I follow you,
　To do I know not what; but it sufficeth
　That Brutus leads me on.
BRUTUS. 　　　　　　　　Follow me, then.

[*Thunder rumbles in the distance as they leave.*]

46. **To wear a kerchief,** in Shakespeare's day, if one became sick he wrapped his head in a woman's headcloth for protection against drafts.

47. **mortified,** deadened.

SCENE 2

Rome. CAESAR's *house, spacious and decorated with royal magnificence. Outside, thunder rumbles and lightning flickers. The time is shortly before 8 o'clock the same morning.* CAESAR *enters.*

CAESAR. Nor heaven nor earth have been at peace tonight.
　Thrice hath Calpurnia in her sleep cried out,
　"Help! ho! They murder Caesar!" (*Turns quickly.*)
　　Who's within?

[*Servant enters.*]

SERVANT. My lord?

CAESAR. Go bid the priests do present[1] sacrifice
  And bring me their opinions of success.
SERVANT. I will, my lord.

[SERVANT *leaves.* CALPURNIA *enters and anxiously approaches* CAESAR.]

CALPURNIA. What mean you, Caesar? Think you to walk
    forth?
  You shall not stir out of your house today.
CAESAR. Caesar shall forth. The things that threatened me 10
  Ne'er looked but on my back; when they shall see
  The face of Caesar, they are vanished.
CALPURNIA. Caesar, I never stood on ceremonies,[2]
  Yet now they fright me. There is one within,
  Besides the things that we have heard and seen,
  Recounts most horrid sights seen by the watch.[3] 15
  A lioness hath whelped in the streets,
  And graves have yawned and yielded up their dead!
  Fierce fiery warriors fought upon the clouds
  In ranks and squadrons and right form of war,
  Which drizzled blood upon the Capitol; 20
  The noise of battle hurtled in the air;
  Horses did neigh, and dying men did groan,
  And ghosts did shriek and squeal about the streets.
  O Caesar! these things are beyond all use,[4] 25
  And I do fear them.
CAESAR.   What can be avoided
  Whose end is purposed by the mighty gods?
  Yet Caesar shall go forth; for these predictions
  Are to the world in general[5] as to Caesar.

1. **present,** immediate.

2. **stood on ceremonies,** paid attention to auguries and predictions.

3. **watch,** watchmen.

4. **use,** ordinary experience.

5. **in general,** they apply as much to the world in general as to Caesar in particular.

410

CALPURNIA. When beggars die there are no comets seen.   30
    The heavens themselves blaze forth the death of
      princes.
CAESAR. Cowards die many times before their death;
    The valiant never taste of death but once.
    Of all the wonders that I yet have heard,
    It seems to me most strange that men should fear,   35
    Seeing that death, a necessary end,
    Will come when it will come.

[*Servant returns from the priests.*]

                          What say the augurers?
SERVANT. They would not have you to stir forth today.
    Plucking the entrails of an offering forth,
    They could not find a heart within the beast.   40
CAESAR. The gods do this in shame of cowardice!
    Caesar should be a beast without a heart
    If he should stay at home today for fear.
    No, Caesar shall not! Danger knows full well
    That Caesar is more dangerous than he.   45
    We are two lions littered in one day,
    And I the elder and more terrible.
    And Caesar shall go forth!
CALPURNIA.   Alas, my lord,
    Your wisdom is consumed in confidence.
    Do not go forth today. Call it my fear   50
    That keeps you in the house, and not your own.
    We'll send Mark Antony to the Senate House,
    And he shall say you are not well today.
    Let me, upon my knee, prevail in this.
CAESAR. Mark Antony shall say I am not well;   55
    And, for thy humor,[6] I will stay at home.

[DECIUS BRUTUS *enters.*]

    Here's Decius Brutus; he shall tell them so.
DECIUS. Caesar, all hail! Good morrow, worthy Caesar.
    I come to fetch you to the Senate House.
CAESAR. And you are come in very happy time   60
    To bear my greetings to the Senators
    And tell them that I will not come today.
    Cannot is false, and that I dare not, falser.
    I will not come today. Tell them so, Decius.
CALPURNIA. Say he is sick.
CAESAR.   Shall Caesar send a lie?   65
    Have I in conquest stretched mine arm so far
    To be afraid to tell graybeards the truth?
    Decius, go tell them Caesar will not come.

6. **humor,** disposition at the moment, whim.

411

DECIUS. Most mighty Caesar, let me know some cause,
Lest I be laughed at when I tell them so.   70
CAESAR. The cause is in my will—I will not come.
That is enough to satisfy the Senate.
But for your private satisfaction,
Because I love you, I will let you know:
Calpurnia here, my wife, stays me at home.   75
She dreamt tonight she saw my statue
Which, like a fountain with a hundred spouts,
Did run pure blood; and many lusty Romans
Came smiling and did bathe their hands in it.
And these does she apply for warnings and portents   80
And evils imminent, and on her knee
Hath begged that I will stay at home today.
DECIUS. This dream is all amiss interpreted!
It was a vision fair and fortunate.
Your statue spouting blood in many pipes,   85
In which so many smiling Romans bathed,
Signifies that from you great Rome shall suck
Reviving blood, and that great men shall press
For tinctures, stains, relics, and cognizance.
This by Calpurnia's dream is signified.   90
CAESAR. And this way have you well expounded it.
DECIUS. I have, when you have heard what I can say;
And know it now. The Senate have concluded
To give this day a crown to mighty Caesar.
If you shall send them word you will not come,   95
Their minds may change. Besides, it were a mock
Apt⁷ to be rendered, for someone to say,
"Break up the Senate till another time,
When Caesar's wife shall meet with better dreams."
If Caesar hide himself, shall they not whisper,   100
"Lo, Caesar is afraid"?
Pardon me, Caesar, for my dear dear love
To your proceeding bids me tell you this;
And reason to my love is liable.
CAESAR. How foolish do your fears seem now, Calpurnia! 105
I am ashamed that I did yield to them.
Give me my robe, for I will go.

[*Enter* PUBLIUS, *a stately, elderly Senator, followed
by the conspirators,* BRUTUS, LAGARIUS, METELLUS,
CASCA, TREBONIUS, *and* CINNA. *They approach*
CAESAR.]

And look where Publius is come to fetch me.
PUBLIUS. Good morrow, Caesar.
CAESAR.   Welcome, Publius.

7. **apt,** ready.

412

What, Brutus, are you stirred so early too?　　　110
Good morrow, Casca, Caius Ligarius;
Caesar was ne'er so much your enemy[8]
As that same ague which has made you lean.
What is't o'clock?

BRUTUS.　　　　　　　　Caesar, 'tis strucken eight.

CAESAR. I thank you for your pains and courtesy.　　115

[*Antony enters.*]

See! Antony, that revels long o' nights,
Is notwithstanding up. Good morrow, Antony.

ANTONY. So to most noble Caesar.

CAESAR.　　　　　　　　　Bid them prepare within;
I am to blame to be thus waited for.
Now, Cinna; now, Metellus. What, Trebonius!　　120
I have an hour's talk in store for you.
Remember that you call on me today;
Be near me, that I may remember you.

TREBONIUS. Caesar, I will. (*To himself.*) And so near will
　　I be,
That your best friends shall wish I had been further.　　125

CAESAR. Good friends, go in, and taste some wine with me;
And we, like friends, will straightway go together.

BRUTUS. (*To himself.*) That every like is not the same,
　　O Caesar,
The heart of Brutus yearns to think upon![9]

[*Talking quietly together, they all leave.*]

SCENE 3

Rome. An empty street near the Capitol. Enter ARTEMIDORUS,
*a teacher of rhetoric. He strolls hesitantly, preoccupied by
the paper in his hand from which he reads.*

ARTEMIDORUS. (*Reading aloud.*) *Caesar, beware of
Brutus; take heed of Cassius; come not near Casca;
have an eye to Cinna; trust not Trebonius; mark well
Metellus Cimber; Decius Brutus loves thee not; thou
hast wronged Caius Ligarius. There is but one mind in*　　5
*all these men, and it is bent against Caesar. If thou be
not immortal, look about you. Security gives way to conspiracy. The mighty gods defend thee!*
　　　　　　　　　　　Thy lover,[1]
　　　　　　　　　ARTEMIDORUS　　10

[*Clutching the paper to him and looking anxiously up
and down the street.*]

Here will I stand till Caesar pass along,
And as a suitor will I give him this.

8. **your enemy,** Ligarius, recently restored to civil rights, had fought on Pompey's side in the civil war.

9. **That every . . . upon,** Brutus regrets to think that everything is not as it appears, that everyone who seems to be a friend is not a true friend.

1. **lover,** devoted friend.

413

My heart laments that virtue cannot live
Out of the teeth of emulation.[2]
If thou read this, O Caesar, thou mayst live.   15
If not, the fates with traitors do contrive.

[*He leaves slowly.*]

2. **that virtue . . . emulation,** that a virtuous man cannot live safe from the teeth (or weapons) of emulation, of envious rivalry.

SCENE 4

Rome. The same street in front of BRUTUS' *house.* PORTIA *and* LUCIUS *enter through the gate.* PORTIA *stares in the direction of the Capitol.*

PORTIA. I prithee, boy, run to the Senate House!
Stay not to answer me, but get thee gone.
Why dost thou stay?

LUCIUS.   To know my errand, madam.

PORTIA. I would have had thee there and here again
Ere I can tell thee what thou should do there.   5
O constancy,[1] be strong upon my side;
Set a huge mountain 'tween my heart and tongue!
I have a man's mind, but a woman's might.
How hard it is for women to keep counsel!
(*Sharply to Lucius.*) Art thou here yet?

LUCIUS.   Madam, what should I do?   10
Run to the Capitol and nothing else?
And so return to you, and nothing else?

PORTIA. Yes, bring me word, boy, if thy lord look well,
For he went sickly forth. And take good note
What Caesar doth, what suitors press to him.   15
Hark, boy! What noise is that?

LUCIUS. I hear none, madam.

PORTIA.   Prithee, listen well!
I heard a bustling rumor, like a fray,
And the wind brings it from the Capitol.

LUCIUS. Sooth,[2] madam, I hear nothing.   20

[*The* SOOTHSAYER *who had warned* CAESAR *to beware the ides of March shuffles by slowly in the direction of the Capitol.*]

PORTIA. Come hither, fellow. Which way hast thou been?

SOOTHSAYER. At mine own house, good lady.

PORTIA. What is it o'clock?

SOOTHSAYER.   About the ninth hour, lady.

PORTIA. Is Caesar yet gone to the Capitol?

SOOTHSAYER. Madam, not yet. I go to take my stand   25
To see him pass on to the Capitol.

PORTIA. Thou hast some suit to[3] Caesar, hast thou not?

1. **constancy,** self-control.

2. **sooth,** truth—in truth or indeed.

3. **suit to,** request for.

SOOTHSAYER. That I have, lady. If it will please Caesar
  To be so good to Caesar as to hear me,
  I shall beseech him to befriend himself. 30
PORTIA. Why, know'st thou any harm's intended toward
    him?
SOOTHSAYER. None that I know will be; much that I fear
    may chance.
  Good morrow to you. Here the street is narrow.
  The throng that follows Caesar at the heels,
  Of senators, of praetors, common suitors, 35
  Will crowd a feeble man almost to death.
  I'll get me to a place more void,[4] and there
  Speak to great Caesar as he comes along.

  [*Moves painfully off.*]

PORTIA. (*Speaking aloud to herself.*) I must go in. Ay me,
    how weak a thing
  The heart of woman is! O Brutus, 40
  The heavens speed[5] thee in thine enterprise!
  (*Startled by her revealing words, she glances warily at*
  LUCIUS.) Sure, the boy heard me. (*Addressing* LUCIUS.)
    Brutus hath a suit
  That Caesar will not grant. O, I grow faint!
  Run, Lucius, and commend me to my lord;
  Say I am merry. Come to me again 45
  And bring me word what he doth say to thee.

  [LUCIUS *races off toward the Capitol.* PORTIA *slowly*
  passes through the gate to the house.]

4. **more void,** more nearly vacant, less crowded.

5. **speed,** prosper.

Act III

Rome. The Capitol. Before the entrance to the Senate Chamber, a large room in the shape of an amphitheater, where tiers of wooden senatorial benches curve before the statue of Pompey. A group of anxious petitioners press close to the marble steps leading up to the chamber. ARTEMIDORUS *and the* SOOTHSAYER *struggle to take front positions. There is a flourish of trumpets, and* CAESAR *arrives, attended by* BRUTUS, CASSIUS, CASCA, DECIUS, METELLUS, TREBONIUS, CINNA, MARK ANTONY, LEPIDUS, POPILIUS, PUBLIUS, *and others.*

CAESAR. (*Noticing the* SOOTHSAYER *as he mounts the steps.*) The ides of March are come.

SOOTHSAYER. Ay, Caesar, but not gone.

ARTEMIDORUS. (*Waving his message of warning.*) Hail, Caesar! Read this schedule![1]

DECIUS. (*Crowding* ARTEMIDORUS *aside.*) Trebonius doth desire you to o'er-read,

At your best leisure, this his humble suit.   5

ARTEMIDORUS. O Caesar, read mine first, for mine's a suit That touches Caesar nearer. Read it, great Caesar!

CAESAR. What touches us ourself shall be last served.

ARTEMIDORUS. Delay not, Caesar! Read it instantly!

CAESAR. What, is the fellow mad?

PUBLIUS. (*Roughly forcing* ARTEMIDORUS *back.*) Sirrah, give place!   10

CASSIUS. (*Annoyed and impatient.*) What, urge you your petitions in the street?

Come to the Capitol.

[*He mounts the steps to the Senate Chamber. The others follow.* POPILIUS *casually separates himself from* CAESAR'S *train and lingers at* CASSIUS' *side.*]

POPILIUS. (*Softly.*) I wish your enterprise today may thrive.

CASSIUS. What enterprise, Popilius?

POPILIUS. (*Winking and smiling.*) Fare you well.

[*Brutus approaches* CASSIUS *with a troubled look on his face.*]

BRUTUS. What said Popilius Lena?[2]   15

CASSIUS. He wished our enterprise might thrive.

I fear our enterprise is discovered!

BRUTUS. Look, how he makes to Caesar. Mark him.

1. **schedule,** a document, especially one containing a list.

2. **Popilius Lena**\pō ᐱpĭ·lĭ·əs ᐱLē·nə\.

CASSIUS. (*Over his shoulder to* CASCA.) Casca, be sudden,
    for we fear prevention.
  Brutus, what shall be done? If this be known,   20
  Cassius or Caesar never shall turn back,
  For I will slay myself.

BRUTUS. (*In stern anger*). Cassius, be constant!
  Popilius Lena speaks not of our purposes,
  For, look! He smiles, and Caesar doth not change.

CASSIUS. Trebonius knows his time; for, look you, Brutus.   25
  He draws Mark Antony out of the way.

[ANTONY *and* TREBONIUS *talk quietly together and stroll
out of the Senate Chamber.* DECIUS BRUTUS *slips urgently
over to where* BRUTUS *and* CASSIUS *stand talking.*]

DECIUS. Where is Metellus Cimber? Let him go
  And presently prefer his suit to Caesar.

BRUTUS. (*Nodding toward where* METELLUS *speaks to*
  CAESAR.) He is addressed.[3] Press near and second him.   **3. addressed,** ready.

CINNA. (*Whispering.*) Casca, you are the first that rears
  his hand.   30

[*The conspirators encircle* CAESAR'S *chair at the foot of
Pompey's statue. The Senate grows quiet as* CAESAR *begins the session. The senators lean forward on their
benches to listen.*]

CAESAR. Are we all ready? What is now amiss
  That Caesar and his senate must redress?

[METELLUS CIMBER *comes forward and kneels before*
CAESAR.]

METELLUS. Most high, most mighty, and most puissant
    Caesar,
  Metellus Cimber throws before thy seat
  An humble heart—

CAESAR.   I must prevent thee, Cimber.   35
  These couchings[4] and these lowly courtesies   **4. couchings,** bending down, bowing.
  Might fire the blood of ordinary men,
  And turn pre-ordinance and first decree[5]   **5. pre-ordinance and first decree,** established laws and decisions already made.
  Into the law of children. Be not fond[6]   **6. fond,** foolish.
  To think that Caesar bears such rebel blood   40
  That will be thawed from the true quality
  With that which melteth fools. I mean, sweet words,
  Low-crooked[7] curtsies and base spaniel-fawning.   **7. Low-crooked,** bent low.
  Thy brother[8] by decree is banished!   **8. Thy brother,** Publius Cimber.
  If thou dost bend and pray and fawn for him,   45
  I spurn thee like a cur out of my way.
  Know, Caesar doth not wrong, nor without cause
  Will he be satisfied.

METELLUS. Is there no voice more worthy than my own,
To sound more sweetly in great Caesar's ear   50
For the repealing of my banished brother?

[BRUTUS *steps forward and bows.*]

BRUTUS. I kiss thy hand, but not in flattery, Caesar,
Desiring thee that Publius Cimber may
Have an immediate freedom of repeal.

CAESAR. What, Brutus!

CASSIUS. (*On his knees.*) Pardon, Caesar! Caesar, pardon!   55
As low as to thy foot doth Cassius fall
To beg enfranchisement[9] for Publius Cimber.

CAESAR. I could be well moved if I were as you;
If I could pray to move, prayers would move me.
But I am constant as the northern star,   60
Of whose true-fixed and resting[10] quality
There is no fellow in the firmament.
The skies are painted with unnumbered sparks;
They are all fire and every one doth shine.
But there's but one in all doth hold his place.   65
So in the world; 'tis furnished well with men,
And men are flesh and blood, and apprehensive.[11]
Yet in the number, I do know but one
That unassailable holds on his rank,
Unshaked of motion: and that I am he,   70
Let me a little show it, even in this—
That I was constant Cimber should be banished,
And constant do remain to keep him so.

[*The conspirators begin to edge closer to* CAESAR, *and
he draws back suspiciously.*]

CINNA. O Caesar—

CAESAR. (*Angered by their persistence.*) Hence! Wilt thou
   lift up Olympus?

DECIUS. Great Caesar—

CAESAR.   Doth not Brutus bootless[12] kneel? 75

CASCA. (*From a position just behind and to the side of*
   CAESAR, *where he has slipped unnoticed.*) Speak, hands,
   for me!

[*He draws his dagger from the folds of his toga and
strikes at* CAESAR's *back. The conspirators lunge forward, their weapons flashing. They gather about their
victim and drive their daggers into his flesh. There are
cries and shouts, and smears of blood appear on white
togas.* CAESAR, *weaving and faint, sees* BRUTUS' *dagger
poised.*]

CAESAR. *Et tu, Brute!*[13] Then fall, Caesar!

9. **enfranchisement,** the right of citizenship. Here, Cassius begs Caesar to re-
new Cimber's rights as a Roman citizen.

10. **resting,** unchanging.

11. **apprehensive,** perceptive and likely
to be influenced (especially by emotions).

12. **bootless,** without avail, in vain.

13. **Et tu, Brute!**\ĕt tū ᴀbrū·tĕ\ And you
too, Brutus!

418

[*He collapses at the foot of Pompey's statue and dies.
A moment of terrified silence follows as the conspirators
stare at their deed. Panic spreads throughout the Senate
Chamber, and the senators murmur in disbelief and
start for the doors.*]

CINNA. Liberty! Freedom! Tyranny is dead!
  Run hence, proclaim. Cry it about the streets!
CASSIUS. Some to the common pulpits,[14] and cry out: 80
  "Liberty, freedom, and enfranchisement!"
BRUTUS. (*To the escaping senators.*) People and senators,
    be not affrighted.
  Fly not; stand still—ambition's debt is paid.
CASCA. Go to the pulpit, Brutus.
DECIUS.   And Cassius too.
BRUTUS. Where's Publius? 85
CINNA. Here, quite confounded with this mutiny.
METELLUS. Stand fast together, lest some friends of
    Caesar's
  Should chance—
BRUTUS. Talk not of standing. Publius, good cheer.
  There is no harm intended to your person, 90
  Nor to no Roman else. So tell them, Publius.
CASSIUS. And leave us, Publius, lest that the people,
  Rushing on us, should do your age some mischief.
BRUTUS. Do so, and let no man abide[15] this deed,
  But we the doers.

  [*Dazed with horror and disbelief,* PUBLIUS *leaves, just
  as* TREBONIUS *rushes in among the conspirators to learn
  of their success.*]

14. **pulpits,** raised places in the Forum
used for public speeches and debates.

15. **abide,** suffer the consequences of.

CASSIUS.   Where is Antony?   95
TREBONIUS. Fled to his house amazed.
  Men, wives, and children stare, cry out, and run,
  As it were doomsday.[16]

16. **doomsday,** literally, judgment day. (An anachronism.)

BRUTUS.   Fates, we will know your
    pleasures.
  That we shall die, we know. 'Tis but the time
  And drawing days out, that men stand upon.[17]   100

17. **stand upon,** make a point of.

CASSIUS. Why, he that cuts off twenty years of life
  Cuts off so many years of fearing death.
BRUTUS. Grant that, and then is death a benefit.
  So are we Caesar's friends that have abridged
  His time of fearing death. Stoop, Romans, stoop,   105
  And let us bathe our hands in Caesar's blood
  Up to the elbows, and besmear our swords.
  Then walk we forth, even to the market-place,
  And, waving our red weapons o'er our heads,
  Let's all cry: "Peace, freedom, and liberty!"   110
CASSIUS. Stoop, then, and wash. How many ages hence
  Shall this our lofty scene be acted over
  In states unborn and accents yet unknown!

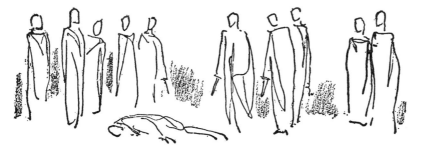

BRUTUS. How many times shall Caesar bleed in sport,[18]
  That now on Pompey's basis lies along   115
  No worthier than the dust!

18. **sport,** plays.

CASSIUS.   So oft as that shall be,
  So often shall the knot of us be called
  The men that gave their country liberty.
DECIUS. What, shall we forth?
CASSIUS.   Ay, every man away!
  Brutus shall lead, and we will grace his heels[19]   120
  With the most boldest and best hearts of Rome.

19. **grace his heels,** honor him by following.

[ANTONY'S SERVANT *arrives and stands in terror at the doorway watching the conspirators.*]

BRUTUS. Soft! Who comes here? A friend of Antony's?
SERVANT. (*Approaching fearfully.*) Thus, Brutus, did my
    master bid me kneel;

Thus did Mark Antony bid me fall down.
And, being prostrate, thus he bade me say: — 125
Brutus is noble, wise, valiant, and honest;
Caesar was mighty, bold, royal, and loving;
Say I love Brutus, and I honor him;
Say I feared Caesar, honored him, and loved him.
If Brutus will vouchsafe that Antony 130
May safely come to him, and be resolved[20]
How Caesar hath deserved to lie in death,
Mark Antony shall not love Caesar dead
So well as Brutus living; but will follow
The fortunes and affairs of noble Brutus 135
Through all the hazards of this untrod state[21]
With all true faith. So says my master Antony.

BRUTUS. Thy master is a wise and valiant Roman.
I never thought him worse.
Tell him, so please him come unto this place, 140
He shall be satisfied; and, by my honor,
Depart untouched.

SERVANT.   I'll fetch him presently.

[*Backs off slowly and then races to* ANTONY *to deliver*
BRUTUS' *message.*]

BRUTUS. I know that we shall have him well to friend.[22]

CASSIUS. I wish we may; but yet have I a mind
That fears him much, and my misgiving still 145
Falls shrewdly to the purpose.[23]

[ANTONY *enters, his stare fixed on the body of fallen*
CAESAR.]

BRUTUS. But here comes Antony! Welcome, Mark Antony!

[ANTONY *approaches until he stands directly over*
CAESAR.]

ANTONY. O mighty Caesar! Dost thou lie so low?
Are all thy conquests, glories, triumphs, spoils,
Shrunk to this little measure? Fare thee well! 150
(*He looks at each conspirator in turn.*) I know not,
    gentlemen, what you intend;
Who else must be let blood; who else is rank.[24]
If I myself, there is no hour so fit
As Caesar's death hour, nor no instrument 155
Of half that worth as those your swords, made rich
With the most noble blood of all this world.
I do beseech ye, if you bear me hard,
Now, whilst your purpled hands do reek and smoke,
Fulfill your pleasure! Live a thousand years,
I shall not find myself so apt[25] to die. 160

20. **be resolved,** have his questions answered and his doubts dispelled.

21. **untrod state,** new situation.

22. **to friend,** as a friend.

23. **my misgiving . . . purpose,** my doubts always show themselves to be confoundedly near the truth.

24. **rank,** overgrown in power. Hence, to be killed.

25. **apt,** ready.

421

No place will please me so, no means of death,
As here by Caesar, and by you cut off,
The choice and master spirits of this age.

BRUTUS. O Antony, beg not your death of us.
Though now we must appear bloody and cruel,   165
As by our hands and this our present act
You see we do; yet see you but our hands
And this the bleeding business they have done.
Our hearts you see not; they are pitiful.
And pity to the general wrong of Rome—   170
As fire drives out fire, so pity pity[26]—
Hath done this deed on Caesar. For your part,
To you our swords have leaden points, Mark Antony.
Our arms, in strength of malice, and our hearts
Of brothers' temper, do receive you in   175
With all kind love, good thoughts, and reverence.

CASSIUS. Your voice shall be as strong as any man's
In the disposing of new dignities.

BRUTUS. Only be patient till we have appeased
The multitude, beside themselves with fear.   180
And then we will deliver you the cause
Why I, that did love Caesar when I struck him,
Have thus proceeded.

ANTONY.   I doubt not of your wisdom.
Let each man render me his bloody hand.
First, Marcus Brutus, will I shake with you;   185
Next, Caius Cassius, do I take your hand;
Now, Decius Brutus, yours; now yours, Metellus;
Yours, Cinna; and, my valiant Casca, yours;
Though last, not least in love, yours, good Trebonius.
Gentlemen all! Alas, what shall I say?   190
My credit now stands on such slippery ground
That one or two bad ways you must conceit me,[27]
Either a coward or a flatterer.
(*Addressing the body of* CAESAR.) That I did love thee,
    Caesar, O, 'tis true!
If then thy spirit look upon us now,   195
Shall it not grieve thee dearer[28] than thy death
To see thy Antony making his peace,
Shaking the bloody fingers of thy foes,
Most noble! in the presence of thy corpse?
Had I as many eyes as thou hast wounds,   200
Weeping as fast as they stream forth thy blood,
It would become me better than to close
In terms of friendship with thine enemies.
Pardon me, Julius! Here wast thou bayed, brave hart.[29]
Here didst thou fall; and here thy hunters stand,   205

26. **pity pity,** pity for "the general wrong of Rome" "drives out" pity for Caesar's death.

27. **conceit me,** regard me.

28. **dearer,** more intensely.

29. **bayed, brave hart,** brought to bay, brave stag.

Signed in thy spoil, and crimsoned in thy lethe.[30]
O world, thou wast the forest to this hart;
And this, indeed, O world, the heart of thee.
How like a deer, strucken by many princes,
Dost thou here lie!   210

CASSIUS. (*Showing anger and impatience at* ANTONY's
    bold show of allegiance.) Mark Antony—
ANTONY.   Pardon me, Caius Cassius!
    The enemies of Caesar shall say this;
    Then, in a friend, it is cold modesty.[31]
CASSIUS. I blame you not for praising Caesar so;
    But what compact mean you to have with us?   215
    Will you be pricked in number of our friends,[32]
    Or shall we on, and not depend on you?
ANTONY. Therefore I took your hands, but was, indeed,
    Swayed from the point by looking down on Caesar.
    Friends as I am with you all, and love you all,   220
    Upon this hope: that you shall give me reasons
    Why and wherein Caesar was dangerous.
BRUTUS. Or else were this a savage spectacle.
    Our reasons are so full of good regard[33]
    That were you, Antony, the son of Caesar,   225
    You should be satisfied.
ANTONY.   That's all I seek;
    And am, moreover, suitor that I may
    Produce his body to the market-place
    And in the pulpit, as becomes a friend,
    Speak in the order of his funeral.   230
BRUTUS. You shall, Mark Antony.
CASSIUS. (*Frowning, urgently pulling* BRUTUS *aside.*)
    Brutus, a word with you!
    (*Whispering.*) You know not what you do. Do not
    consent
    That Antony speak in his funeral.

31. **cold modesty,** moderate.

32. **Will you . . . friends,** will your name be counted as among our friends?

33. **regard,** consideration, thought.

Know you how much the people may be moved
By that which he will utter?
BRUTUS.   By your pardon.   235
    I will myself into the pulpit first
    And show the reason of our Caesar's death.
    What Antony shall speak, I will protest[34]
    He speaks by leave and by permission,
    And that we are contented Caesar shall   240
    Have all true rites and lawful ceremonies.
    It shall advantage more than do us wrong.
CASSIUS. I know not what may fall. I like it not!
BRUTUS. (*Turning to* ANTONY.) Mark Antony, here, take
        you Caesar's body.
    You shall not in your funeral speech blame us,   245
    But speak all good you can devise of Caesar,
    And say you do it by our permission;
    Else shall you not have any hand at all
    About his funeral. And you shall speak
    In the same pulpit whereto I am going,   250
    After my speech is ended.
ANTONY.   Be it so.
    I do desire no more.
BRUTUS. Prepare the body then, and follow us.

[*The conspirators file out of The Senate Chamber after*
BRUTUS, *leaving* ANTONY *alone beside* CAESAR's *body.*]

ANTONY. (*Kneeling.*) O, pardon me, thou bleeding piece
        of earth,
    That I am meek and gentle with these butchers!   255
    Thou art the ruins of the noblest man
    That ever lived in the tide of times.
    Woe to the hand that shed this costly blood!
    Over thy wounds now do I prophesy,
    Which, like dumb mouths, do ope their ruby lips   260
    To beg the voice and utterance of my tongue:
    A curse shall light upon the limbs of men;
    Domestic fury and fierce civil strife
    Shall cumber all the parts of Italy;
    Blood and destruction shall be so in use   265
    And dreadful objects so familiar
    That mothers shall but smile when they behold
    Their infants quartered with the hands of war;
    All pity choked with custom of fell deeds;
    And Caesar's spirit ranging for revenge,   270
    With Ate[35] by his side, come hot from hell,
    Shall in these confines with a monarch's voice
    Cry "Havoc!"[36] and let slip the dogs of war,[37]

34. **protest,** assert.

35. **Ate**\ᴬā·tē\ a classical goddess of revenge.
36. **"Havoc"**\ᴬhă·vək\ a direction to take no prisoners but to kill indiscriminately.
37. **dogs of war,** famine, sword, and fire.

That this foul deed shall smell above the earth
With carrion men, groaning for burial.   275

[OCTAVIUS' SERVANT *enters.* ANTONY *turns.*]

You serve Octavius Caesar,[38] do you not?
SERVANT. I do, Mark Antony.
ANTONY. Caesar did write for him to come to Rome.
SERVANT. He did receive his letters, and is coming;
  And bid me say to you by word of mouth—   280
  (*Recognizes the body of* CAESAR.) O Caesar!—
ANTONY. Thy heart is big. Get thee apart and weep.
  Passion,[39] I see, is catching; for mine eyes,
  Seeing those beads of sorrow stand in thine,
  Began to water. Is thy master coming?   285
SERVANT. He lies tonight within seven leagues of Rome.
ANTONY. Post back with speed and tell him what hath
    chanced.
  Here is a mourning Rome, a dangerous Rome,
  No Rome of safety for Octavius yet.
  Hie[40] hence and tell him so. Yet, stay awhile.   290
  Thou shalt not back till I have borne this corpse
  Into the market-place. There shall I try,
  In my oration, how the people take
  The cruel issue of these bloody men;
  According to the which thou shalt discourse   295
  To young Octavius of the state of things.
  (*Arranging* CAESAR's *mantle around the body.*) Lend
    me your hand.

[*Together they carry* CAESAR *out of the Senate
Chamber.*]

38. **Octavius**\ŏk ᴬtā·vē·əs\ **Caesar**, Caesar's adopted heir, his grand nephew, who later became the emperor Augustus Caesar.

39. **Passion**, suffering, sorrow.

40. **Hie**\hai\ hurry.

CHARACTERIZATION

Shakespeare develops his characters by what others say about them, what they say about themselves, and by their reactions to various situations. Consider and discuss what Shakespeare implies about each of the following characters through the quotations from the characters themselves or from others.

BRUTUS

Brutus, Act I, scene 2
Into what dangers would you lead me, Cassius,
That you would have me seek into myself
For that which is not in me?

Brutus, Act I, scene 2
For let the gods so speed me as I love
The name of honor more than I fear death.

Cassius, Act I, scene 2
Well, Brutus, thou art noble; yet, I see,
Thy honorable metal may be wrought
From that it is disposed; . . .

Casca, Act I, scene 3
O, he sits high in all the people's hearts;
And that which would appear offense in us,
His countenance, like richest alchemy,
Will change to virtue and to worthiness.

Portia, Act II, scene 1
Brutus is wise, and, were he not in health,
He would embrace the means to come by it.

Ligarius, Act II, scene 1
I am not sick, if Brutus have in hand
Any exploit worthy the name of honor.

Caesar, Act III, scene 1
Et tu, Brute! Then fall, Caesar!

Antony through servant, Act III, scene 1
Brutus is noble, wise, valiant, and honest; . . .

CAESAR

Cassius, Act I, scene 2
I, as Aeneas, our great ancestor,
Did from the flames of Troy upon his shoulder
The old Anchises bear, so from the waves of Tiber
Did I the tired Caesar.

Cassius, Act I, scene 2
Why, man, he doth bestride the narrow world
Like a Colossus, . . .

Caesar, Act I, scene 2
I rather tell thee what is to be feared
Than what I fear; for always I am Caesar.

Casca, Act I, scene 2
He fell down in the market-place, and foamed at the mouth, and was speechless.

Brutus, Act II, scene 1
And, to speak truth of Caesar,
I have not known when his affections swayed
More than his reason.

Decius, Act II, scene 1
Never fear that. If he be so resolved,
I can o'ersway him; . . .

Caesar, Act II, scene 2
What can be avoided
Whose end is purposed by the mighty gods?

Caesar, Act II, scene 2
The valiant never taste of death but once.

Caesar, Act II, scene 2
Decius, go tell them Caesar will not come.

Caesar, Act III, scene 1
What touches us ourself shall be last served.

Caesar, Act III, scene 1
Know, Caesar doth not wrong, . . .

Antony through servant, Act III, scene 1
Caesar was mighty, bold, royal, and loving; . . .
Say I feared Caesar, honored him, and loved him.

Antony, Act III, scene 1
Thou art the ruins of the noblest man
That ever lived in the tide of times.

CASSIUS

Cassius, Act I, scene 2
I was born free as Caesar; so were you.
We both have fed as well, and we can both
Endure the winter's cold as well as he; . . .

Caesar, Act I, scene 2
Yond Cassius has a lean and hungry look.
He thinks too much; such men are dangerous.

Caesar, Act I, scene 2
Yet if my name were liable to fear,
I do not know the man I should avoid
So soon as that spare Cassius. He reads much,
He is a great observer, and he looks
Quite through the deeds of men.

Cassius, Act I, scene 2
If I were Brutus now and he were Cassius,
He should not humor me.

ANTONY

Brutus, Act I, scene 2
I am not gamesome; I do lack some part
Of that quick spirit that is in Antony.

Cassius, Act II, scene 1
We shall find of him
A shrewd contriver; and, you know, his means,
If he improve them, may well stretch so far
As to annoy us all; . . .

Brutus, Act II, scene 1
For Antony is but a limb of Caesar.

Brutus, Act II, scene 1
For he is given
To sports, to wildness, and much company.

Caesar, Act II, scene 2
See! Antony, that revels long o' nights,
Is notwithstanding up.

Brutus, Act III, scene 1
Thy master is a wise and valiant Roman.
I never thought him worse.

Cassius (whispering), Act III, scene 1
Brutus, a word with you!
You know not what you do. Do not consent
That Antony speak in his funeral.
Know you how much the people may be moved
By that which he will utter?

IMPLICATIONS

Would you agree or disagree with the following statements? Remember to find support for your opinion in the lines of the play.

1. Shakespeare gives characteristics to Caesar which make him obviously a man to be king.

2. Caesar was not ambitious.

3. Brutus is a stoic, an individual who solves all things by his intellect and rules out emotion in his decisions.

4. A good man, like Brutus, is defenseless before evil.

5. Portia senses disaster because a woman is sensitive to people instead of events.

6. It is not characteristic of Cassius to let Brutus make two fatal decisions: (1) To let Antony live; (2) To let Antony speak at the funeral.

7. Caesar is involved in a series of brief encounters in the first part of the play. His handling of them changed his life.

WORDS

A. What do the italicized words mean in the following phrases and clauses: (1) there is no fellow in the *firmament*, (2) till we have *appeased* the multitude, (3) all true *rites* and lawful ceremonies, (4) and none so poor to do him *reverence*, (5) *bequeathing* it as a rich *legacy*, (6) *ingratitude*, more strong than traitors' arms, quite *vanquished* him, (7) *contaminate* our fingers with base bribes, (8) with *meditating* that she must die once, (9) that shapes this monstrous *apparition*, (10) to stay the *providence* of some high powers, (11) alas, thou hast *misconstrued* everything.

B. What is the relationship between the following pairs of words: *defer-prefer* ("And presently prefer his suit to Caesar"); *ordinary* ("Might fire the blood of ordinary men")-*pre-ordinance* ("And turn pre-ordinance . . . Into the law of children"); *belligerent-rebel* ("that Caesar bears such rebel blood"); *comprehensive-apprehensive* ("And men are flesh and blood, and apprehensive"); *consistent-persistence* (stage direction—angered by their persistence); *elapse-collapse* (stage direction—He collapses at the foot of Pompey's statue); *acclaim-proclaim* ("Proclaim! Cry it about in the streets!"); *malady-malice* ("in strength of malice"); *suspend-depend* ("or shall we on, and not depend on you?"); *contest-protest* ("I will protest"); *terrestrial-interred* ("The good is oft interred with their bones"); *repel-compel* ("You will compel me, then to read the will?").

427

*The Roman forum today
as viewed from the
Palatine Hill.*

SCENE 2

*Rome. The Forum, the great public square of the city. It is
the occasion of* CAESAR's *funeral, and a noisy mob waits
nervously near a speaker's platform.*

CROWD. (*Chanting.*) We will be satisfied! Let us be satisfied.

[BRUTUS *and* CASSIUS *appear, followed by a train of
anxious citizens.*]

BRUTUS. (*Calling out over the roar.*) Then follow me and
give me audience, friends!
(*To* CASSIUS *at his side.*) Cassius, go you into the other
street,
And part the numbers.[1]
(*Crying out to the milling crowd.*) Those that will hear   5
me speak, let 'em stay here!

1. **part the numbers,** divide the crowds.

428

Those that will follow Cassius, go with him,
And public reasons shall be rendered
Of Caesar's death.

FIRST CITIZEN. I will hear Brutus speak.

SECOND CITIZEN. I will hear Cassius, and compare their
    reasons
When severally we hear them rendered. 10

[CASSIUS *strides off, followed by those in the crowd who
have chosen to hear him.* BRUTUS *climbs the steps to the
platform and looks out over his eager audience.*]

THIRD CITIZEN. The noble Brutus is ascended! Silence!

BRUTUS. Be patient till the last.
Romans, countrymen, and lovers! Hear me for my cause,
and be silent that you may hear. Believe me for mine
honor, and have respect to mine honor that you may be- 15
lieve. Censure me in your wisdom, and awake your
senses that you may the better judge. If there be any in
this assembly, any dear friend of Caesar's, to him I say,
that Brutus' love to Caesar was no less than his. If then
that friend demand why Brutus rose against Caesar, 20
this is my answer—Not that I loved Caesar less, but
that I loved Rome more. Had you rather Caesar were
living and die all slaves, than that Caesar were dead, to
live all free men? As Caesar loved me, I weep for him;
as he was fortunate, I rejoice at it; as he was valiant, I 25
honor him; but, as he was ambitious, I slew him. There
is tears for his love; joy for his fortune; honor for his
valor; and death for his ambition. Who is here so base
that would be a bondman? If any, speak; for him I have
offended. Who is here so rude that would not be a 30
Roman? If any, speak; for him have I offended. Who
is here so vile that will not love his country? If any,
speak; for him have I offended. I pause for a reply.

CROWD. (*Roaring enthusiastically.*) None, Brutus, none!

BRUTUS. Then none have I offended. I have done no more 35
to Caesar than you shall do to Brutus. The question of
his death is enrolled[2] in the Capitol; his glory not extenuated,[3] wherein he was worthy, nor his offenses enforced,[4] for which he suffered death.

[ANTONY *appears, solemnly following bearers who carry*
CAESAR's *body on their shoulders.*]

Here comes his body, mourned by Mark Antony; who, 40
though he had no hand in his death, shall receive the
benefit of his dying, a place in the commonwealth; as
which of you shall not? With this I depart, that, as I

2. **The question . . . enrolled,** the matter
of Caesar's death is on record.
3. **his glory not extenuated,** his glory is
not diminished or disparaged.
4. **enforced,** exaggerated.

slew my best lover for the good of Rome, I have the
same dagger for myself, when it shall please my country 45
to need my death.

CROWD. Live, Brutus! Live, live!

FIRST CITIZEN. Bring him with triumph home unto his
    house!

SECOND CITIZEN. Give him a statue with his ancestors!

THIRD CITIZEN. Let him be Caesar!

FOURTH CITIZEN.   Caesar's better parts   50
    Shall be crowned in Brutus!

FIRST CITIZEN. We'll bring him to his house with shouts
    and clamors!

BRUTUS. My countrymen—

SECOND CITIZEN.   Peace, silence! Brutus speaks!

FIRST CITIZEN. Peace, ho!

BRUTUS. Good countrymen, let me depart alone,   55
    And, for my sake, stay here with Antony.
    Do grace to Caesar's corpse, and grace his speech
    Tending to Caesar's glories; which Mark Antony,
    By our permission, is allowed to make.
    I do entreat you, not a man depart   60
    Save I alone, till Antony have spoke.

[BRUTUS *descends from the speaking platform, while
the bearers place* CAESAR's *body at the base.* BRUTUS
leaves amid cheers. ANTONY *waits.*]

FIRST CITIZEN. Stay, ho! and let us hear Mark Antony.

THIRD CITIZEN. Let him go up into the public chair.
    We'll hear him. Noble Antony, go up!

[*Antony climbs the steps of the platform.*]

ANTONY. For Brutus' sake, I am beholding[5] to you.   65   **5. beholding,** obliged.

FOURTH CITIZEN. (*Threateningly.*) What does he say of
    Brutus?

THIRD CITIZEN.   He says, for Brutus' sake
    He finds himself beholding to us all.

FOURTH CITIZEN. 'Twere best he speak no harm of Brutus
    here.
FIRST CITIZEN. This Caesar was a tyrant.
THIRD CITIZEN.   Nay, that's certain.
   We are blest that Rome is rid of him.   70
SECOND CITIZEN. Peace! Let us hear what Antony can say.
ANTONY. You gentle Romans—
CROWD.   Peace, ho! Let us hear him.
ANTONY. Friends, Romans, countrymen, lend me your
    ears!
   I come to bury Caesar, not to praise him.
   The evil that men do lives after them;   75
   The good is oft interred with their bones.
   So let it be with Caesar. The noble Brutus
   Hath told you Caesar was ambitious.
   If it were so, it was a grievous fault,
   And grievously hath Caesar answered it.   80
   Here, under leave of Brutus and the rest—
   For Brutus is an honorable man;
   So are they all, all honorable men—
   Come I to speak in Caesar's funeral.
   He was my friend, faithful and just to me;   85
   But Brutus says he was ambitious,
   And Brutus is an honorable man.
   He hath brought many captives home to Rome,
   Whose ransoms did the general coffers[6] fill.
   Did this in Caesar seem ambitious?   90
   When that the poor have cried, Caesar hath wept;
   Ambition should be made of sterner stuff.
   Yet Brutus says he was ambitious,
   And Brutus is an honorable man.
   You all did see that on the Lupercal   95
   I thrice presented him a kingly crown,
   Which he did thrice refuse. Was this ambition?
   Yet Brutus says he was ambitious,
   And, sure, he is an honorable man.
   I speak not to disprove what Brutus spoke,   100
   But here I am to speak what I do know.
   You all did love him once, and not without cause;
   What cause withholds you then to mourn for him?
   O judgment! thou art fled to brutish beasts,
   And men have lost their reason. Bear with me. 105
   My heart is in the coffin there with Caesar,
   And I must pause till it come back to me.
FIRST CITIZEN. Methinks there is much reason in his
    sayings.
SECOND CITIZEN. If thou consider rightly of the matter,

6. general coffers\ˈkŏ·fərz\ the public
treasury.

Caesar has had great wrong.

THIRD CITIZEN.   Has he, masters?   110
I fear there will a worse come in his place.

FOURTH CITIZEN. Marked ye his words? He would not take
the crown.
Therefore 'tis certain he was not ambitious.

FIRST CITIZEN. If it be found so, some will dear abide[7] it.

SECOND CITIZEN. Poor soul! His eyes are red as fire with
weeping.   115

THIRD CITIZEN. There's not a nobler man in Rome than
Antony.

FOURTH CITIZEN. Now mark him! He begins again to
speak.

ANTONY. But yesterday the word of Caesar might
Have stood against the world. Now lies he there,
And none so poor to do him reverence.   120
O masters, if I were disposed to stir
Your hearts and minds to mutiny and rage,
I should do Brutus wrong, and Cassius wrong,
Who, you all know, are honorable men.
I will not do them wrong. I rather choose   125
To wrong the dead, to wrong myself and you,
Than I will wrong such honorable men.
But here's a parchment with the seal of Caesar;
I found it in his closet. 'Tis his will.
Let but the commons hear this testament—   130
Which, pardon me, I do not mean to read—
And they would go and kiss dead Caesar's wounds
And dip their napkins[8] in his sacred blood;
Yea, beg a hair of him for memory,
And, dying, mention it within their wills,   135
Bequeathing it as a rich legacy
Unto their issue.

FOURTH CITIZEN. We'll hear the will! Read it, Mark
Antony!

CROWD. The will, the will! We will hear Caesar's will!

ANTONY. Have patience, gentle friends. I must not read it.   140
It is not meet[9] you know how Caesar loved you.
You are not wood; you are not stones, but men;
And, being men, hearing the will of Caesar,
It will inflame you. It will make you mad.
'Tis good you know not that you were his heirs;   145
For, if you should, O, what would come of it!

FOURTH CITIZEN. Read the will! We'll hear it, Antony.
You shall read the will, Caesar's will!

ANTONY. Will you be patient? Will you stay awhile?
I have o'ershot myself to tell you of it.   150

7. **abide**, pay for, atone for.

8. **napkins**, handkerchiefs.

9. **meet**, suitable.

I fear I wrong the honorable men
Whose daggers have stabbed Caesar. I do fear it.
FOURTH CITIZEN. They were traitors! (*Contemptuously.*)
    Honorable men.
CROWD. The will! The testament!
SECOND CITIZEN. They were villains, murderers! The will!
    Read the will!   155
ANTONY. You will compel me, then, to read the will?
    Then make a ring about the corpse of Caesar,
    And let me show you him that made the will.
    Shall I descend? And will you give me leave?
CROWD. Come down!   160
SECOND CITIZEN. Descend!
THIRD CITIZEN. You shall have leave!

[ANTONY *descends from the platform. The crowd
surges forward and encircles him and the body of
CAESAR. They are excited and press close.*]

FOURTH CITIZEN. A ring! Stand round!
FIRST CITIZEN. Stand from the hearse![10] Stand from the
    body!
SECOND CITIZEN. Room for Antony, most noble Antony!   165
ANTONY. Nay, press not so upon me. Stand far off.
CROWD. Stand back! Room! Bear back!
ANTONY. If you have tears, prepare to shed them now.
    (*Lifting CAESAR's bloodstained robe.*) You all do know
        this mantle. I remember
    The first time ever Caesar put it on.   170
    'Twas on a summer's evening, in his tent,
    That day he overcame the Nervii.[11]
    Look, in this place ran Cassius' dagger through!
    See what a rent the envious Casca made!
    Through this the well-beloved Brutus stabbed,   175
    And as he plucked his cursed steel away,
    Mark how the blood of Caesar followed it,
    As rushing out of doors to be resolved
    If Brutus so unkindly knocked or no;
    For Brutus, as you know, was Caesar's angel.[12]   180
    Judge, O you gods, how dearly Caesar loved him!
    This was the most unkindest[13] cut of all;
    For when the noble Caesar saw him stab,
    Ingratitude, more strong than traitors' arms,
    Quite vanquished him. Then burst his mighty heart!   185
    And, in his mantle muffling up his face,
    Even at the base of Pompey's statue,
    Which all the while ran blood, great Caesar fell.
    O, what a fall was there, my countrymen!

10. **hearse,** here the stand or platform that supports the body.

11. **Nervii**\ˈnər·vē·ı\ a Celtic tribe in Gaul, conquered by Caesar.

12. **angel,** dearest friend.

13. **unkindest,** unnatural. (This suggestion is also present in unkindly, line 179.)

Then I, and you, and all of us fell down,   190
Whilst bloody treason flourished over us.
O, now you weep, and I perceive you feel
The dint of pity. These are gracious drops.
Kind souls, what, weep you when you but behold
Our Caesar's vesture wounded? (*Pulling aside* CAESAR's
    mantle, exposing the body.) Look you here!   195
Here is himself, marred, as you see, with traitors!

FIRST CITIZEN. O piteous spectacle!

SECOND CITIZEN. O noble Caesar!

THIRD CITIZEN. O woeful day!

FOURTH CITIZEN. O traitors, villains!   200

FIRST CITIZEN. O most bloody sight!

SECOND CITIZEN. We will be revenged!

CROWD. Revenge! About! Seek! Burn! Fire! Kill! Slay!
    Let not a traitor live!

ANTONY. Stay, countrymen!   205

FIRST CITIZEN. Peace there! Hear the noble Antony!

SECOND CITIZEN. We'll hear him! We'll follow him! We'll
    die with him!

ANTONY. Good friends, sweet friends! Let me not stir
    you up
To such a sudden flood of mutiny.
They that have done this deed are honorable.   210
What private griefs they have, alas, I know not,
That made them do it. They are wise and honorable
And will, no doubt, with reasons answer you.
I come not, friends, to steal away your hearts.
I am no orator, as Brutus is.   215
But, as you know me all, a plain blunt man
That love my friend; and that they know full well
That gave me public leave to speak of him;
For I have neither wit, nor words, nor worth,
Action, nor utterance, nor the power of speech   220
To stir men's blood. I only speak right on.
I tell you that which you yourselves do know;
Show you sweet Caesar's wounds—poor, poor, dumb
    mouths—
And bid them speak for me. But if I were Brutus,
And Brutus Antony, there were an Antony   225
Would ruffle up your spirits, and put a tongue
In every wound of Caesar that should move
The stones of Rome to rise and mutiny.

CROWD. We'll mutiny!

FIRST CITIZEN. We'll burn the house of Brutus!   230

THIRD CITIZEN. Away, then! Come seek the conspirators!

ANTONY. Yet hear me, countrymen! Yet hear me speak!

434

CROWD. Peace, ho! Hear Antony, most noble Antony!

ANTONY. Why, friends, you go to do you know not what.
    Wherein hath Caesar thus deserved your loves?   235
    Alas, you know not. I must tell you, then.
    You have forgot the will I told you of.

CROWD. Most true! The will! Let's stay and hear the will!

ANTONY. (*Holding up the parchment.*) Here is the will,
    and under Caesar's seal:
    (*Reads.*) To every Roman citizen he gives,   240
    To every several[14] man, seventy-five drachmas.[15]

SECOND CITIZEN. Most noble Caesar! We'll revenge his
    death!

THIRD CITIZEN. O royal Caesar!

ANTONY. Hear me with patience!

CROWD. Peace, ho!   245

ANTONY. Moreover, he hath left you all his walks,
    His private arbors and new-planted orchards,
    On this side[16] Tiber. He hath left them you
    And to your heirs forever, common pleasures,
    To walk abroad and recreate yourselves.   250
    Here was a Caesar! When comes such another?

FIRST CITIZEN. Never, never! Come away, away!
    We'll burn his body in the holy place,
    And with the brands fire the traitors' houses.
    Take up the body!   255

SECOND CITIZEN. Go fetch fire!

THIRD CITIZEN. Pluck down benches!

FOURTH CITIZEN. Pluck down forms, windows, anything!

[*Screaming threats of violence, the aroused mob storms
out of the Forum along streets that lead outward in all
directions. They light torches and stampede away in
search of the conspirators. One group bears off the
body of* CAESAR.]

ANTONY. (*Grimly to himself.*) Now, let it work. Mis-
    chief,[17] thou art afoot;
    Take thou what course thou wilt!

14. **several,** individual.

15. **drachma**\ˈdrăk·mə\ a silver coin, originally Greek. It is usually rated at about nineteen cents, but its real value was considerable since the purchasing power of money in ancient times was great.

16. **side,** side of the

17. **Mischief,** strife, commotion. The meaning of the word was much stronger in Shakespeare's day than now.

[OCTAVIUS' SERVANT *arrives, breathless from running.*]

How now, fellow?   260

SERVANT. Sir, Octavius is already come to Rome.

ANTONY. Where is he?

SERVANT. He and Lepidus are at Caesar's house.

ANTONY. And thither will I straight to visit him.
  He comes upon a wish. Fortune is merry,
  And in this mood will give us anything.   265

SERVANT. I heard him say: Brutus and Cassius
  Are rid like madmen through the gates of Rome.

ANTONY. Belike[18] they had some notice of the people,   18. **Belike,** most likely, probably.
  How I had moved them. Bring me to Octavius.   270

[*They hurry off together.*]

SCENE 3

*Rome. A street near the Forum. In the distance shouts of
alarm and noises of rioting. Along the narrow, quiet,
cobbled street, the poet* CINNA *strolls, musing to himself.*

CINNA. I dreamt tonight that I did feast with Caesar,
  And things unluckily charge[1] my fantasy.   1. **charge,** load, weigh down.
  I have no will to wander forth of doors,
  Yet something leads me forth.

[*A group of enraged citizens swarm down the street
and surround* CINNA. *They are armed with torches and
clubs.*]

FIRST CITIZEN. What is your name?   5

SECOND CITIZEN. Whither are you going?

THIRD CITIZEN. Where do you dwell?

FOURTH CITIZEN. Are you a married man or a bachelor?

SECOND CITIZEN. Answer every man directly.

FIRST CITIZEN. Ay, and briefly.   10

FOURTH CITIZEN. Ay, and wisely.

THIRD CITIZEN. Ay, and truly, you were best.[2]   2. **ay . . . best,** and you would be best advised to do so truly.

CINNA. (*Confused and frightened.*) What is my name?
  Whither am I going? Where do I dwell? Am I a married
  man or a bachelor? Then, to answer every man directly   15
  and briefly, wisely and truly: wisely I say, I am a
  bachelor.

SECOND CITIZEN. That's as much as to say: they are fools
  that marry. You'll bear me a bang[3] for that, I fear. Pro-   3. **bear . . . bang,** get a knock from me.
  ceed; directly.   20

CINNA. Directly, I am going to Caesar's funeral.

FIRST CITIZEN. As a friend or an enemy?

CINNA. As a friend.

SECOND CITIZEN. That matter is answered directly.

FOURTH CITIZEN. For your dwelling—briefly. 25

CINNA. Briefly, I dwell by the Capitol.

THIRD CITIZEN. Your name, sir, truly.

CINNA. Truly, my name is Cinna.

[*The crowd closes in on* CINNA, *their weapons raised.*]

FIRST CITIZEN. Tear him to pieces! He's a conspirator!

CINNA. (*Screaming.*) I am Cinna the poet! I am Cinna 30
the poet!

FOURTH CITIZEN. Tear him for his bad verses! Tear him for
his bad verses!

CINNA. I am not Cinna the conspirator!

FOURTH CITIZEN. It is no matter, his name's Cinna. Pluck 35
but his name out of his heart, and turn him going!

[*They leap upon* CINNA *and club him brutally.*]

THIRD CITIZEN. Tear him! Tear him! Come, brands ho! Fire
brands! To Brutus'! To Cassius'! Burn all! Some to
Decius' house, and some to Casca's! Some to Ligarius'! Away, go! 40

[*The crowd runs off shouting, leaving* CINNA's *mangled
body alone on the street.*]

Act IV

Rome. The interior of ANTONY's *house. By flickering lamplight* ANTONY, OCTAVIUS, *and* LEPIDUS, *the young ruling Triumvirate[1] since the flight of the conspirators, sit at a table. They study a parchment listing the names of political enemies. It has been some time since the death of* CAESAR, *and Rome has undergone political turmoil. The conspirators have long since fled beyond Italy.*

ANTONY. These many, then, shall die. Their names are
    pricked.[2]
OCTAVIUS. Your brother too must die. Consent you,
    Lepidus?[3]
LEPIDUS. I do consent—
OCTAVIUS.   Prick him down, Antony.
LEPIDUS. Upon condition Publius shall not live,
  Who is your sister's son, Mark Antony.   5
ANTONY. He shall not live. Look, with a spot I damn[4] him!
  But, Lepidus, go you to Caesar's house;
  Fetch the will hither, and we shall determine
  How to cut off some charge[5] in legacies.
LEPIDUS. What, shall I find you here?   10
OCTAVIUS. Or here, or at the Capitol.

[ANTONY *watches carefully to make sure that* LEPIDUS
has left before he speaks.]

ANTONY. This is a slight unmeritable man,
  Meet to be sent on errands. Is it fit,
  The threefold world divided,[6] he should stand
  One of the three to share it?
OCTAVIUS.   So you thought him; 15
  And took his voice who should be pricked to die,
  In our black sentence and proscription.[7]
ANTONY. Octavius, I have seen more days than you;
  And though we lay these honors on this man
  To ease ourselves of divers sland'rous loads,[8]   20
  He shall but bear them as the ass bears gold—
  To groan and sweat under the business,
  Either led or driven, as we point the way;
  And having brought our treasure where we will,
  Then take we down his load, and turn him off,   25
  Like to the empty ass, to shake his ears
  And graze in commons.[9]

1. **Triumvirate**\'trai **ə**m·və·rət\ a governing coalition of three leaders.

2. **pricked,** marked (on the death list).

3. **Lepidus****lĕ·pĭ·dəs\.

4. **damn,** condemn.

5. **cut off some charge,** reduce in significance. The Triumvirate wishes to decrease the legacies in Caesar's will (which Antony read to the crowd in the preceding scene).

6. **The threefold world divided,** with the world divided into three spheres of power.

7. **proscription,** list of those condemned.

8. **divers sland'rous loads,** various burdens of shame.

9. **commons,** the public pasture land held by a town or a village. (An anachronism.)

OCTAVIUS. You may do your will;
But he's a tried and valiant soldier.

ANTONY. (*With contempt.*) So is my horse, Octavius, and
for that
I do appoint him store of provender. 30
It is a creature that I teach to fight,
To wind, to stop, to run directly on;
His corporal[10] motion governed by my spirit.
And, in some taste,[11] is Lepidus but so—
He must be taught and trained and bid go forth; 35
A barren-spirited fellow, one that feeds
On objects, orts,[12] and imitations,
Which, out of use and staled by other men,
Begin his fashion.[13] Do not talk of him
But as a property. And now, Octavius, 40
Listen great things—Brutus and Cassius
Are levying powers.[14] We must straight make head.[15]
Therefore let our alliance be combined,
Our best friends made, and our best means stretched
out;
And let us presently go sit in council 45
How covert matters may be best disclosed
And open perils surest answered.[16]

OCTAVIUS. Let us do so, for we are at the stake
And bayed about[17] with many enemies;
And some that smile have in their hearts, I fear, 50
Millions of mischiefs.

[*They leave.*]

10. **corporal**, bodily.

11. **taste**, degree.

12. **objects**, things discarded; **orts**, scraps, bits of refuse.

13. **which . . . fashion**, which, now discarded by others and in fact made stale, are the fashions he takes up as new.

14. **levying powers**, raising armies.
15. **make head**, make headway, proceed (in raising an army).

16. **How covert . . . answered**, how concealed dangers may be discovered and known dangers met.
17. **for we are . . . about**, we are tied to the stake at bay before many enemies. The wording comes from bear-baiting, a recreation in Shakespeare's time in which a bear was tied to a stake and tormented with dogs.

SCENE 2

*Sardis (an ancient city in Asia Minor, capital of
Lydia). A military camp on the outskirts of the city.
It is night. Sentries stand in the shadows. A single light
from inside Brutus' tent dimly illuminates the area. A
roll of drums.* BRUTUS *emerges from the tent with* LU-
CIUS. LUCILIUS, *an officer, approaches with* CASSIUS'
servant, PINDARUS.

BRUTUS. Stand, ho!

LUCILIUS. Give the word,[1] ho! and stand.

BRUTUS. What now, Lucilius? Is Cassius near?

LUCILIUS. He is at hand, and Pindarus is come
To do you salutation from his master. 5

BRUTUS. He greets me well. Your master, Pindarus,
In his own change, or by ill officers,[2]
Hath given me some worthy cause to wish

1. **The word**, the password.

2. **In his own . . . officers**, by some change in his nature or through untrustworthy officers.

Things done undone. But, if he be at hand,
I shall be satisfied.

PINDARUS.   I do not doubt   10
But that my noble master will appear
Such as he is, full of regard and honor.[3]
BRUTUS. He is not doubted. (*Taking* LUCILIUS' *elbow and
    leading him off.*) A word, Lucilius—
How he received you let me be resolved.[4]
LUCILIUS. With courtesy and respect enough;   15
But not with such familiar instances,[5]
Nor with such free and friendly conference
As he hath used of old.
BRUTUS.   Thou hast described
A hot friend cooling. Ever note, Lucilius,
When love begins to sicken and decay   20
It uses an enforced ceremony.
There are no tricks in plain and simple faith;
But hollow men, like horses hot at hand,[6]
Make gallant show and promise of their mettle.
But when they should endure the bloody spur,   25
They fall their crests, and, like deceitful jades,[7]
Sink in the trial.[8]

[*The confused sounds of marching soldiers and shouted
orders come from the distance.*]

            Comes his army on?

3. **full of regard and honor,** that is, for
Brutus.

4. **resolved,** informed.

5. **instances,** marks of friendship.

6. **hot at hand,** spirited when held in.

7. **jades,** plugs, nags.

8. **Sink in the trial,** fail when tried.

440

LUCILIUS. They mean this night in Sardis to be quartered.
    The greater part, the horse[9] in general,
    Are come with Cassius.

9. **the horse,** the cavalry.

BRUTUS.   Hark! He is arrived.   30
    March gently on to meet him.

[LUCILIUS *salutes and turns to leave.* CASSIUS, *flanked by his lieutenants, strides out of the shadows toward* BRUTUS.]

CASSIUS. Stand, ho!

BRUTUS. Stand, ho! Speak the word along.

[CASSIUS' *lieutenants shout, each echoing the other.*]

FIRST LIEUTENANT. Stand!

SECOND LIEUTENANT. Stand!   35

THIRD LIEUTENANT. Stand!

[CASSIUS *approaches* BRUTUS *with his arms outstretched.*]

CASSIUS. Most noble brother, you have done me wrong.

BRUTUS. (*Severely.*) Judge me, you gods! Wrong I my
    enemies?
    And, if not so, how should I wrong a brother?

CASSIUS. Brutus, this sober form[10] of yours hides wrongs;   40
    And when you do them—

10. **sober form,** serious appearance and manner.

BRUTUS. (*Sharply.*)   Cassius, be content!
    Speak your griefs softly. I do know you well.
    Before the eyes of both our armies here,
    Which should perceive nothing but love from us,
    Let us not wrangle. Bid them move away.   45
    Then, in my tent, Cassius, enlarge your griefs,
    And I will give you audience.

CASSIUS. (*Turning away from* BRUTUS.) Pindarus!
    Bid our commanders lead their charges off
    A little from this ground.

BRUTUS. Lucilius! Do you the like, and let no man   50
    Come to our tent till we have done our conference.
    Lucius and Titinius! Guard our door.

[BRUTUS *pulls aside the tent flap for* CASSIUS, *and follows him inside.* LUCIUS *and* TITINIUS *take up their positions as sentries.*]

SCENE 3

The same. Inside BRUTUS' *tent. Armor and weapons are piled in the corner. A single lamp on a map-strewn table makes flickering shadows in the dark interior.* CASSIUS *paces.* BRUTUS *stands watching him.*

CASSIUS. That you have wronged me does appear in this—
  You have condemned and noted[1] Lucius Pella
  For taking bribes here of the Sardinians;
  Wherein my letters, praying on his side,
  Because I knew the man, were slighted off.   5
BRUTUS. (*His arms folded, looking steadily at* CASSIUS.)
  You wronged yourself to write in such a case.
CASSIUS. In such a time as this it is not meet
  That every nice[2] offense should bear his comment.
BRUTUS. Let me tell you, Cassius, you yourself
  Are much condemned to have an itching palm,   10
  To sell and mart your offices for gold
  To undeservers.
CASSIUS.   I! An itching palm?
  You know that you are Brutus that speaks this,
  Or, by the gods, this speech were else your last.
BRUTUS. The name of Cassius honors this corruption,   15
  And chastisement does therefore hide his head.[3]
CASSIUS. Chastisement!
BRUTUS. Remember March? The ides of March? Remember?
  Did not great Julius bleed for justice' sake?
  What villain touched his body, that did stab   20
  And not for justice? What, shall one of us,
  That struck the foremost man of all this world
  But for supporting robbers, shall we now
  Contaminate our fingers with base bribes,
  And sell the mighty space of our large honors   25
  For so much trash as may be grasped thus?
  I had rather be a dog, and bay[4] the moon,
  Than such a Roman.
CASSIUS.   Brutus, bait[5] not me!
  I'll not endure it! You forget yourself
  To hedge me in. I am a soldier; I,   30
  Older in practice, abler than yourself
  To make conditions.[6]
BRUTUS.   Go to! You are not, Cassius.
CASSIUS. I am!
BRUTUS. I say you are not!
CASSIUS. Urge me no more! I shall forget myself!   35
  Have mind upon your health. Tempt me no farther!
BRUTUS. Away, slight man.
CASSIUS. Is it possible?
BRUTUS.   Hear me, for I will speak.
  Must I give way and room to your rash choler?[7]
  Shall I be frighted when a madman stares?   40
CASSIUS. O ye gods! Ye gods! Must I endure all this?

1. **noted,** marked for disgrace or banishment.

2. **nice,** minor.

3. **The name . . . head,** the great name of Cassius makes corruption respectable with the result that wrongdoing goes unpunished.

4. **bay,** bay at.

5. **bait,** torment, as a bull or bear was tormented in Elizabethan entertainments.

6. **conditions,** statements of policy or procedure, decisions.

7. **choler**\ˈkŏ·lər\ here, anger.

BRUTUS. All this! Ay, more. Fret till your proud heart
    break.
    Go show your slaves how choleric you are,
    And make your bondmen tremble. Must I budge?
    Must I observe you? Must I stand and crouch   45
    Under your testy humor?[8] By the gods,
    You shall digest the venom of your spleen,[9]
    Though it do split you; for, from this day forth,
    I'll use you for my mirth. Yea, for my laughter,
    When you are waspish.
CASSIUS. (*Staring in disbelief.*) Is it come to this? 50
BRUTUS. You say you are a better soldier.
    Let it appear so. Make your vaunting true,
    And it shall please me well. For my own part,
    I shall be glad to learn of noble men.
CASSIUS. You wrong me every way. You wrong me,
    Brutus.   55
    I said an elder soldier, not a better.
    Did I say "better"?
BRUTUS.   If you did, I care not.
CASSIUS. When Caesar lived, he durst not thus have moved
    me.
BRUTUS. Peace, peace! You durst not so have tempted him.
CASSIUS. I durst not!   60
BRUTUS. No!
CASSIUS. What? Durst not tempt him!
BRUTUS.   For your life you durst not.
CASSIUS. Do not presume too much upon my love.
    I may do that I shall be sorry for.   65
BRUTUS. You have done that you should be sorry for.
    There is no terror, Cassius, in your threats,
    For I am armed so strong in honesty
    That they pass by me as the idle wind,
    Which I respect not. I did send to you
    For certain sums of gold, which you denied me; 70
    For I can raise no money by vile means.
    (By heaven! I had rather coin my heart
    And drop my blood for drachmas than to wring
    From the hard hands of peasants their vile trash
    By any indirection.[10]) I did send   75
    To you for gold to pay my legions,
    Which you denied me. Was that done like Cassius?
    Should I have answered Caius Cassius so?
    When Marcus Brutus grows so covetous
    To lock such rascal counters[11] from his friends, 80
    Be ready, gods, with all your thunderbolts!
    Dash him to pieces!

8. **testy humor,** irritable disposition.

9. **You shall . . . spleen,** you shall swallow your anger; you shall control your bad temper. The **spleen** was thought to be the bodily source of anger and jealousy.

10. **indirection,** dishonest means.

11. **rascal counters,** worthless coins.

CASSIUS. I denied you not!

BRUTUS. You did!

CASSIUS. I did not! He was but a fool that brought
My answer back. Brutus has rived[12] my heart.
A friend should bear his friend's infirmities,
But Brutus makes mine greater than they are.

BRUTUS. I do not, till you practice them on me.

CASSIUS. You love me not.

BRUTUS. I do not like your faults.

CASSIUS. A friendly eye could never see such faults.

BRUTUS. A flatterer's would not, though they do appear
As huge as high Olympus.[13]

CASSIUS. (*Throwing up his arms in despair.*) Come,
Antony, and young Octavius! Come,
Revenge yourselves alone on Cassius,
For Cassius is aweary of the world!
Hated by one he loves; braved by his brother;
Checked like a bondman;[14] all his faults observed,
Set in a notebook, learned and conned by rote[15]
To cast into my teeth. O, I could weep
My spirit from my eyes! (*Offering his knife to* BRUTUS.)
There is my dagger,
And here my naked breast; within, a heart
Dearer than Pluto's mine,[16] richer than gold.
If that thou be'st a Roman, take it forth.
I, that denied thee gold, will give my heart!
Strike, as thou did'st at Caesar; for I know
When thou did'st hate him worst, thou lovedst him
better
Than ever thou lovedst Cassius.

BRUTUS. Sheathe your dagger.
Be angry when you will, it shall have scope.
Do what you will, dishonor shall be humor.[17]
O Cassius, you are yoked with a lamb
That carries anger as the flint bears fire:
Who, much enforced,[18] shows a hasty spark,
And straight is cold again.

CASSIUS. Hath Cassius lived
To be but mirth and laughter to his Brutus,
When grief and blood ill-tempered vexes him?

BRUTUS. When I spoke that, I was ill-tempered too.

CASSIUS. (*Putting his knife away.*) Do you confess so
much? Give me your hand.

BRUTUS. (*Warmly clasping* CASSIUS' *hand.*) And my heart
too.

CASSIUS. O Brutus!

BRUTUS. What's the matter?

85

90

95

100

105

110

115

12. **rived**\raivd\ broken.

13. **Olympus**\ō ᴬlĭm·pəs\ a mountain in Greece, the legendary home of the gods of classical mythology.

14. **Checked like a bondman,** scolded like a slave.
15. **learned and conned by rote,** memorized by heart.

16. **Pluto's**\ᴬplū·tō\ the god of the underworld and hence lord of all mines of precious metals and gems.

17. **humor,** here, a whim or temporary inclination. I will excuse your insults merely as effects of your irritable disposition.
18. **enforced,** provoked.

CASSIUS. Have not you love enough to bear with me,
  When that rash humor which my mother gave me   120
  Makes me forgetful?
BRUTUS.   Yes, Cassius; and from henceforth,
  When you are over-earnest with your Brutus,
  He'll think your mother chides, and leave you so.

[*A violent outburst of angry voices comes from the door of the tent. An elderly* POET *has tried to force his way past* LUCIUS *and* TITINIUS *for an audience with* BRUTUS *and* CASSIUS. LUCILIUS *arrives to assist* LUCIUS *and* TITINIUS *in restraining the* POET.]

POET. (*From outside the tent.*) Let me go in to see the
  generals!
There is some grudge between them. 'Tis not meet   125
They be alone.
LUCILIUS.   You shall not come to them!
POET. Nothing but death shall stay me!

[*The* POET *bursts into the tent.* LUCIUS *and* TITINIUS *seize his arms.* LUCILIUS, *his sword drawn, follows.*]

CASSIUS. How now! What's the matter?
POET. For shame, you generals! What do you mean?
  Love, and be friends, as two such men should be;   130
  For I have seen more years, I'm sure, than ye.
CASSIUS. Ha, ha! How vilely doth this cynic rhyme!
BRUTUS. Get you hence, sirrah! Saucy[19] fellow, hence!
CASSIUS. Bear with him, Brutus. 'Tis his fashion.
BRUTUS. I'll know his humor, when he knows his time.   135
  What should the wars do with these jigging fools?
  Companion,[20] hence!
CASSIUS.   Away, away! Be gone!

[*Soldiers arrive to drag the* POET *from the tent. He leaves struggling and protesting.*]

BRUTUS. Lucilius and Titinius, bid the commanders
  Prepare to lodge their companies tonight.
CASSIUS. And come yourselves, and bring Messala with
  you   140
  Immediately to us.

[LUCILIUS *and* TITINIUS *salute and leave.*]

BRUTUS.   Lucius, a bowl of wine!

[LUCIUS *bows and leaves.*]

CASSIUS. I did not think you could have been so angry.
BRUTUS. O Cassius, I am sick of many griefs!
CASSIUS. Of your philosophy[21] you make no use
  If you give place to accidental evils.   145

19. **Saucy,** impudent. The word was much stronger in Elizabethan times than now.

20. **Companion,** fellow (used contemptuously).

21. **philosophy,** Stoicism. Stoics held that the ideal man directed his life by reason. Hence, he kept his emotions in check and was indifferent to life's sorrows and misfortunes.

445

BRUTUS. No man bears sorrow better. Portia is dead.

CASSIUS. (*Stiffening with surprise.*) Ha! Portia?

BRUTUS. She is dead.

CASSIUS. How 'scaped I killing when I crossed you so?　　150
　　O insupportable and touching loss!
　　Upon what sickness?

BRUTUS. 　　　　　　　　Impatient of my absence,
　　And grief that young Octavius with Mark Antony
　　Have made themselves so strong—for with her death
　　That tiding came—with this she fell distract,
　　And, her attendants absent, swallowed fire.[22]　　155

CASSIUS. And died so?

BRUTUS. 　　　　　　　Even so.

CASSIUS. 　　　　　　　　　　　O ye immortal gods!

[LUCIUS *reenters bearing a bowl of wine and cups.*]

BRUTUS. Speak no more of her. (*To* LUCIUS.) Give me a
　　bowl of wine.
　　(*He holds up his cup toward* CASSIUS.) In this I bury all
　　unkindness, Cassius.

[*Drinks.*]

CASSIUS. My heart is thirsty for that noble pledge.
　　Fill, Lucius, till the wine o'erswell the cup;　　160
　　(*He takes the wine offered him by* LUCIUS.) I cannot
　　drink too much of Brutus' love.

[*As he drinks,* TITINIUS *enters the tent and stands near
the door. Beside him stands* MESSALA *in battle dress.*
LUCIUS *quietly slips by the two and out of the tent.*]

BRUTUS. Come in, Titinius! Welcome, good Messala![23]
　　Now sit we close about this taper here,
　　And call in question our necessities.[24]

CASSIUS. Portia, art thou gone?

BRUTUS. (*To* CASSIUS.) 　　　　No more, I pray you.　　165
　　(*Separating papers on the table.*) Messala, I have here
　　received letters
　　That young Octavius and Mark Antony
　　Come down upon us with a mighty power,
　　Bending their expedition toward Philippi.[25]

MESSALA. Myself have letters of the self-same tenor.[26]　　170

BRUTUS. With what addition?

MESSALA. That by proscription and bills of outlawry,[27]
　　Octavius, Antony, and Lepidus
　　Have put to death a hundred senators.

BRUTUS. Therein our letters do not well agree.　　175
　　Mine speak of seventy senators that died
　　By their proscriptions, Cicero[28] being one.

22. **fire,** Plutarch says that Portia committed suicide by swallowing glowing coals.

23. **Messala**\mĕ ˄sā·lə\.

24. **question our necessities,** discuss our problems.

25. **Bending . . . Philippi,** directing their forces toward Philippi\fĭ ˄lĭ·pai\, a city in northern Greece.
26. **tenor,** significance.
27. **bills of outlawry,** proscription lists which put certain citizens thereon outside the protection of the law. It was not only legal to kill such citizens but rewards were offered for their deaths.

28. **Cicero,** killed by Antony's orders in 43 B.C.

CASSIUS. Cicero one?

MESSALA.   Cicero is dead,

And by that order of proscription.

Had you your letters from your wife, my lord?   180

BRUTUS. No, Messala.

MESSALA. Nor nothing in your letters writ of her?

BRUTUS. Nothing, Messala.

MESSALA.   That, methinks, is strange.

BRUTUS. Why ask you? Heard you aught of her in yours?

MESSALA. (*Confused. Hesitating before he speaks.*) No,

my lord.   185

BRUTUS. Now, as you are a Roman, tell me true!

MESSALA. Then like a Roman bear the truth I tell—

For certain she is dead, and by strange manner.

BRUTUS. Why, farewell, Portia. We must die, Messala.

With meditating that she must die once,   190

I have the patience to endure it now.

MESSALA. Even so great men great losses should endure.

CASSIUS. I have as much of this in art[29] as you,

But yet my nature could not bear it so.

BRUTUS. (*Spreading out a map on the table.*) Well, to our

work alive![30] What do you think   195

Of marching to Philippi presently?[31]

CASSIUS. I do not think it good.

BRUTUS.   Your reason?

CASSIUS.   This is it—

'Tis better that the enemy seek us.

So shall he waste his means, weary his soldiers,

Doing himself offense; whilst we, lying still,   200

Are full of rest, defense, and nimbleness.

BRUTUS. Good reasons must, of force, give place to better.

The people 'twixt Philippi and this ground

Do stand but in a forced affection,

For they have grudged us contributions.   205

The enemy, marching along by them,

By them shall make a fuller number up,

Come on refreshed, new-added, and encouraged;

From which advantage shall we cut him off

If at Philippi we do face him there,   210

These people at our back.

CASSIUS.   Hear me, good brother.

BRUTUS. Under your pardon. You must note beside

That we have tried the utmost of our friends.

Our legions are brimful; our cause is ripe.

The enemy increases every day;   215

We, at the height, are ready to decline.

There is a tide in the affairs of men

29. **in art,** in theory. Cassius means that he knows the Stoic philosophy regarding fortitude, yet he could not control his emotions as Brutus does.

30. **to our work alive,** let us take up the work which we living men have to do.

31. **presently,** at once.

Which, taken at the flood, leads on to fortune;
Omitted, all the voyage of their life
Is bound in shallows and in miseries.   220
On such a full sea are we now afloat,
And we must take the current when it serves,
Or lose our ventures.
CASSIUS.   Then, with your will, go on.
  We'll along ourselves, and meet them at Philippi.
BRUTUS. The deep of night is crept upon our talk   225
  And nature must obey necessity,
  Which we will niggard with a little rest.[32]
  There is no more to say?
CASSIUS.   No more. Good night.
  Early tomorrow will we rise and hence.
BRUTUS. (*Calling out.*) Lucius!

  [LUCIUS *appears at the door of the tent.*]

                        My gown.
  [LUCIUS *goes to the rear of the tent and opens a trunk.*]

                        Farewell,
    good Messala;   230
  Good night. Noble, noble Cassius,
  Good night, and good repose.
CASSIUS.   O my dear brother!
  This was an ill beginning of the night.
  Never come such division 'tween our souls!
  Let it not, Brutus.
BRUTUS.   Everything is well.   235
CASSIUS. Good night, my lord.
BRUTUS.   Good night, good brother.
MESSALA. Good night, Lord Brutus.
BRUTUS.   Farewell, everyone.

  [CASSIUS *and* MESSALA *leave.* LUCIUS *stands holding*
  BRUTUS' *gown.*]

  Give me the gown. (*Stands lost in thought for a mo-
    ment.*) Where is thy instrument?[33]
LUCIUS. (*Yawning.*) Here in the tent.
BRUTUS. (*Gently.*)   What, thou speakest drowsily?
  Poor knave, I blame thee not; thou art overwatched.[34] 240
  Call Claudius and some other of my men.
  I'll have them sleep on cushions in my tent.
LUCIUS. (*Calling out.*) Varro and Claudius!

  [VARRO *and* CLAUDIUS *enter.*]

VARRO. Calls my lord?
BRUTUS. I pray you, sirs, lie in my tent and sleep;   245
  It may be I shall raise you by and by

32. **which we . . . rest,** which (the antecedent is "nature") however, we will slight with only a little rest.

33. **instrument,** lute.

34. **overwatched,** tired out from watching too long.

448

On business to my brother Cassius.

VARRO. So please you, we will stand and watch your
    pleasure.[35]

BRUTUS. I will not have it so. Lie down, good sirs.
    It may be I shall otherwise bethink me: 250

[VARRO *and* CLAUDIUS *arrange cushions on the floor and
lie down, covering themselves with their cloaks.* BRUTUS
takes his gown from LUCIUS. *He reaches into a pocket.*]

    Look, Lucius! Here's the book I sought for so.
    I put it in the pocket of my gown.

LUCIUS. I was sure your lordship did not give it me.

BRUTUS. Bear with me, good boy. I am much forgetful.
    Canst thou hold up thy heavy eyes awhile,   255
    And touch thy instrument a strain or two?

LUCIUS. Ay, my lord, an't[36] please you.

BRUTUS.   It does, my boy.
    I trouble thee too much, but thou art willing.

LUCIUS. It is my duty, sir.

BRUTUS. I should not urge thy duty past thy might.   260
    I know young bloods look for a time of rest.

[LUCIUS *sits cross-legged on a floor cushion, and readies
his lute.*]

LUCIUS. I have slept, my lord, already.

BRUTUS. It was well done, and thou shalt sleep again.
    I will not hold thee long. If I do live,
    I will be good to thee.   265

[LUCIUS *strums his lute and sings softly.*]

    This is a sleepy tune.

[LUCIUS' *head nods forward; his hands slide across
the strings of his lute, and he sleeps.*]

               O murderous slumber,
    Lay'st thou thy leaden mace[37] upon my boy
    That plays thee music? Gentle knave, good night.
    I will not do thee so much wrong to wake thee.
    If thou dost nod, thou break'st thy instrument.   270
    (*Slides the lute out from* LUCIUS' *hands and lays it
        aside.*) I'll take it from thee; and, good boy, good
        night.
    (*Taking his book to the light on the table.*) Let me see.
        Let me see. Is not the leaf turned down
    Where I left reading? Here it is, I think.

[*As he speaks, the glowing ghost of* CAESAR *moves
stealthily out from the shadows and stands watching
in the flickering lamplight.*]

---

35. **Watch your pleasure,** watch out for
whatever wish you may have.

36. **an't,** if it.

37. **mace,** here, a staff used by a sheriff's
officer to touch on the shoulder of a
person as a sign that the person is
placed under arrest.

How ill this taper burns! (*Looks up suddenly.*) Ha!
  Who comes here?
I think it is the weakness of my eyes   275
That shapes this monstrous apparition.
It comes upon me! Art thou anything?
Art thou some god, some angel, or some devil,
That makes my blood cold and my hair to stand?
Speak to me what thou art!   280
GHOST. Thy evil spirit, Brutus.
BRUTUS.   Why com'st thou?
GHOST. To tell thee thou shall see me at Philippi.
BRUTUS. Well, then I shall see thee again?
GHOST. Ay, at Philippi.
BRUTUS. Why, I will see thee at Philippi, then.   285

[*The ghost backs toward the shadows in the tent and
fades out of sight.* BRUTUS *advances cautiously, peering
anxiously into the darkness.*]

Now I have taken heart thou vanishest!
Ill spirit, I would hold more talk with thee.
(*Shouting.*) Boy! Lucius! Varro! Claudius! Sirs, awake!
  Claudius!
LUCIUS. The strings, my lord, are false.   290
BRUTUS. He thinks he still is at his instrument.
  Lucius, awake!
LUCIUS. My lord?
BRUTUS. Did'st thou dream, Lucius, that thou so cried
  out?
LUCIUS. My lord, I do not know that I did cry.   295
BRUTUS. Yes, that thou did'st. Did'st thou see anything?
LUCIUS. Nothing, my lord.
BRUTUS. Sleep again, Lucius. Sirrah, Claudius! Fellow,
  thou! awake!
VARRO. My lord?
CLAUDIUS. My lord?   300
BRUTUS. Why did you so cry out, sirs, in your sleep?
VARRO, CLAUDIUS. Did we, my lord?
BRUTUS.   Ay! Saw you anything?
VARRO. No, my lord. I saw nothing.
CLAUDIUS.   Nor I, my lord.
BRUTUS. Go and commend me to my brother Cassius.
  Bid him set on his powers betimes before,[38]   305
  And we will follow.
VARRO, CLAUDIUS.   It shall be done, my lord.

[*They leave.* BRUTUS *sits at the table and rests his head
on his arms.*]

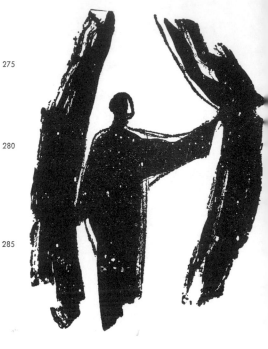

38. **Bid him . . . before,** order him to
start his forces marching in advance at
once.

Act V

SCENE 1

Philippi, a city of ancient Macedon,[1] named after Phillip, father of Alexander the Great. In 168 B.C., the city fell under the power of conquering Romans. On the great plains outside Philippi, the armies of BRUTUS *and* CASSIUS *have formed to meet the legions of* ANTONY *and* OCTAVIUS. *Amid the dust and confusion of cavalry and infantry units hurrying to their positions,* ANTONY *and* OCTAVIUS *stand together looking toward the distant ranks of the enemy. They are dressed for battle. From behind come the sounds of drums and excited barks of command.*

OCTAVIUS. Now, Antony, our hopes are answered.
You said the enemy would not come down,
But keep[2] the hills and upper regions.
It proves not so. Their battles[3] are at hand.
They mean to warn us at Philippi here,   5
Answering before we do demand of them.
ANTONY. Tut! I am in their bosoms,[4] and I know
Wherefore they do it. They could be content
To visit other places, and come down
With fearful bravery, thinking by this face[5]   10
To fasten in our thoughts that they have courage.
But 'tis not so.

[*A* MESSENGER *runs up to* ANTONY *and* OCTAVIUS.
He salutes.]

MESSENGER.   Prepare you, Generals!
The enemy comes on in gallant show.
Their bloody sign of battle[6] is hung out,
And something to be done immediately.   15
ANTONY. (*Looking toward the horizon and pointing.*)
Octavius, lead your battle softly on
Upon the left hand of the even field.
OCTAVIUS. (*Stiffening at* ANTONY's *assumption of total command.*) Upon the right hand I! Keep thou the left.
ANTONY. Why do you cross me in this exigent?[7]
OCTAVIUS. I do not cross you, but I will do so.   20

[*They walk off toward their separate commands.*

At the head of the conspirators' armies BRUTUS *and* CASSIUS *enter, attended by* LUCILIUS, TITINIUS, MESSALA, *and other officers.*]

1. **Macedon**\ˈmă·sə·dən\ an ancient kingdom, including northeastern Greece and adjacent areas.

2. **keep,** keep to.
3. **battles,** battalions, forces.

4. **I am in their bosoms,** I understand them.

5. **face,** outward show.

6. **sign of battle,** a red flag displayed outside the general's tent was the battle sign.

7. **Why do . . . exigent,** why do you oppose me in this urgent occasion?

451

*The famous Appian Way, a portion of it as it appears
today. Over similar roads throughout the empire,
Rome moved her troops and commerce.*

BRUTUS. They stand and would have parley.
CASSIUS. Stand fast, Titinius! We must out and talk.

   [OCTAVIUS *from his position on the field sees* BRUTUS *and*
   CASSIUS *walking forth. He calls to* ANTONY.]

OCTAVIUS. Mark Antony! Shall we give sign of battle?
ANTONY. No, Caesar. We will answer on their charge.[8]
   Make forth! The generals would have some words.   25
OCTAVIUS. (*To his officers.*) Stir not until the signal.

   [BRUTUS *approaches* OCTAVIUS *and* ANTONY, *who now
   stand together.*]

BRUTUS. Words before blows. Is it so, countrymen?
OCTAVIUS. Not that we love words better, as you do.
BRUTUS. Good words are better than bad strokes, Octavius.

8. **charge**, a message indicating bidding
or request.

452

ANTONY. In[9] your bad strokes, Brutus, you give good
    words.   30
    Witness the hole you made in Caesar's heart,
    Crying, "Long live! Hail, Caesar!"

CASSIUS.   Antony,
    The posture[10] of your blows are yet unknown!
    But for your words, they rob the Hybla[11] bees,
    And leave them honeyless.

ANTONY.   Not stingless too?   35

BRUTUS. O, yes, and soundless too,
    For you have stolen their buzzing, Antony;
    And very wisely threat before you sting.

ANTONY. Villains! You did not so when your vile
    daggers
    Hacked one another in the sides of Caesar!   40
    You showed your teeth like apes, and fawned like
    hounds,
    And bowed like bondmen, kissing Caesar's feet;
    Whilst damned Casca, like a cur, behind
    Struck Caesar on the neck. O you flatterers!

CASSIUS. Flatterers! Now, Brutus, thank yourself.   45
    This tongue had not offended so today
    If Cassius might have ruled.

OCTAVIUS. Come, come! The cause?[12] If arguing make us
    sweat,
    The proof of it will turn to redder drops.
    Look!   50
    I draw a sword against conspirators!
    When think you that the sword goes up again?
    Never! till Caesar's three and thirty wounds
    Be well avenged; or till another Caesar[13]
    Have added slaughter to the sword of traitors!   55

BRUTUS. Caesar, thou canst not die by traitors' hands
    Unless thou bring'st them with thee.

OCTAVIUS.   So I hope!
    I was not born to die on Brutus' sword.

BRUTUS. O, if thou wert the noblest of thy strain,
    Young man, thou could'st not die more honorable.   60

CASSIUS. A peevish schoolboy, worthless of such honor,
    Joined with a masker and a reveller!

ANTONY. (*Gripping the hilt of his sword.*) Old Cassius,
    still!

OCTAVIUS. (*Restraining him.*)   Come, Antony, away!
    Defiance, traitors, hurl we in your teeth!
    If you dare fight today, come to the field;   65
    If not, when you have stomachs.

9. **In,** with.

10. **posture,** condition, fashion.

11. **Hybla** \ˈhaiˑblə\ a town in Sicily famous for its bees and honey.

12. **come, . . . cause,** come to the point of this meeting.

13. **another Caesar,** Octavius likewise bore the name Caesar.

[ANTONY *and* OCTAVIUS *turn and stride back toward their armies.*]

CASSIUS. Why, now, blow wind, swell billow, and swim bark!
The storm is up, and all is on the hazard.[14]

BRUTUS. (*Calling back.*) Ho, Lucilius! Hark, a word with you.

[LUCILIUS *races from his battle position to* BRUTUS' *side.*]

LUCILIUS. My lord?

[BRUTUS *takes his arm and guides him off to the side, and they talk softly, their heads together, facing away from* CASSIUS.]

CASSIUS. Messala!

[MESSALA *approaches* CASSIUS.]

MESSALA.   What says my General?
CASSIUS.   Messala,   70
This is my birthday; as this very day
Was Cassius born. Give me thy hand, Messala.
Be thou my witness that against my will,
As Pompey was, I am compelled to set
Upon one battle all our liberties.   75
You know that I held Epicurus strong
And his opinion.[15] Now I change my mind,
And partly credit things that do presage.
Coming from Sardis, on our former[16] ensign
Two mighty eagles fell, and there they perched,   80
Gorging and feeding from our soldier's hands,
Who to Philippi here consorted[17] us.
This morning are they fled away and gone;
And in their steads do ravens, crows, and kites
Fly o'er our heads and downward look on us,   85
As we were sickly prey. Their shadows seem
A canopy[18] most fatal, under which
Our army lies, ready to give up the ghost.
MESSALA. Believe not so!
CASSIUS.   I but believe it partly;
For I am fresh of spirit, and resolved   90
To meet all perils very constantly.

[BRUTUS *and* LUCILIUS *finish their private talk and return to* CASSIUS.]

BRUTUS. Even so, Lucilius.
CASSIUS.   Now, most noble Brutus,
The gods today stand friendly, that we may,

14. **all is on the hazard,** everything is hazarded; everything depends on dangerous chances.

15. **You know . . . opinion,** you know that I was a strong believer in the opinions of Epicurus (\'ĕ·pĭ ᴧkyū·rəs\ a Greek philosopher of the Fourth and Third Centuries B.C., who disbelieved in omens).
16. **former,** foremost.
17. **consorted,** accompanied.

18. **canopy,** a tapestry hung overhead.

Lovers in peace, lead on our days to age![19]
But since the affairs of men rest still uncertain, 95
Let's reason[20] with the worst that may befall:
If we do lose this battle, then is this
The very last time we shall speak together.
What are you then determined to do?

BRUTUS. Even by the rule of that philosophy 100
By which I did blame Cato[21] for the death
Which he did give himself—I know not how,
But I do find it cowardly and vile,
For fear of what might fall, so to prevent
The time of life[22]—arming myself with patience 105
To stay[23] the providence of some high powers
That govern us below.

CASSIUS.   Then, if we lose this battle,
You are contented to be led in triumph
Through the streets of Rome?

BRUTUS. No, Cassius, no! Think not, thou noble Roman, 110
That ever Brutus will go bound to Rome.
He bears too great a mind. But this same day
Must end that work the ides of March begun;
And whether we shall meet again I know not;
Therefore our everlasting farewell take. 115
Forever, and forever, farewell, Cassius!
If we do meet again, why, we shall smile.
If not, why then, this parting was well made.

CASSIUS. Forever, and forever, farewell, Brutus!
If we do meet again, we'll smile indeed. 120
If not, 'tis true this parting was well made.

BRUTUS. Why, then, lead on! O that a man might know
The end of this day's business ere it come!
But it sufficeth that the day will end,
And then the end is known. Come, ho! Away! 125

[*They walk back toward their waiting legions.*]

SCENE 2

The plains beyond Philippi. The battle has begun. BRUTUS'
forces hurl themselves on the enemy. BRUTUS *himself,*
flushed by the fever of combat, enters with MESSALA.

BRUTUS. Ride, ride, Messala! Ride, and give these bills[1]
Unto the legions on the other side!
(*Pointing with his sword.*) Let them set on at once,
    for I perceive
But cold demeanor in Octavius' wing,

---

19. **lead on . . . age,** live to old age.

20. **reason,** consider.

21. **The younger Cato**\ ˈkā·tō\ (95–46
B.C.) the father-in-law of Brutus com-
mitted suicide rather than submit to
Caesar.

22. **to prevent . . . life,** to cut short
one's full term of life, to commit suicide.
23. **to stay,** to await.

1. **bills,** written orders.

And sudden push gives them the overthrow.   5
Ride, ride, Messala! Let them all come down!

[MESSALA *runs for his horse.* BRUTUS *heads back toward the fighting.*]

SCENE 3

The part of the field where CASSIUS' *forces fall back in disorganized retreat from the powerful thrusts of* ANTONY'S *disciplined legions.* CASSIUS, *furious at the failure of his men, tries to rally them to resist more fiercely. With one hand gripping the staff of his ensign and the other clenching the hilt of his sword, he watches the gathering defeat from the slope of a small hill.* TITINIUS *stands at his side.*

CASSIUS. (*In despair.*) O, look, Titinius, look! The villains
    fly!
Myself have to mine own turned enemy.[1]
This ensign here of mine was turning back.
I slew the coward, and did take it from him.
TITINIUS. O Cassius, Brutus gave the word too early;   5
Who, having some advantage on Octavius,
Took it too eagerly. His soldiers fell to spoil,[2]
Whilst we by Antony are all enclosed.

[PINDARUS *arrives, torn and battered from the fighting.*]

PINDARUS. Fly further off, my lord! Fly further off!
Mark Antony is in your tents, my lord.   10
Fly, therefore, noble Cassius! Fly far off!
CASSIUS. This hill is far enough. Look, look, Titinius!
Are those my tents where I perceive the fire?
TITINIUS. They are, my lord.
CASSIUS.   Titinius, if thou lovest me,
Mount thou my horse, and hide thy spurs in him   15
Till he have brought thee up to yonder troops
And here again; that I may rest assured
Whether yon troops are friend or enemy.
TITINIUS. I will be here again, even with a thought.

[*He mounts* CASSIUS' *horse and dashes off.*]

CASSIUS. Go, Pindarus, get higher on that hill.   20
My sight was ever thick.[3] Regard Titinius,
And tell me what thou not'st about the field.

[PINDARUS *turns to climb to the crest of the hill.*]

This day I breathed first. Time is come around,
And where I did begin, there shall I end.
My life has run his compass. (*Calling up to* PINDARUS.)
    Sirrah, what news?   25

1. **Myself . . . enemy,** I have turned to fighting against my own men (who were deserting).

2. **fell to spoil,** turned to looting and pillaging.

3. **thick,** bad, indistinct.

456

PINDARUS. (*From above.*) O, my lord!

CASSIUS. (*Anxiously.*) What news!

PINDARUS. Titinius is enclosed round about
With horsemen, that make to him on the spur;
Yet he spurs on. Now, they are almost on him.   30
Now, Titinius! Now some light. O, he lights too!
He's ta'en!

[*A faint volley of shouts from the distance.*]

        And, hark! They shout for joy.

CASSIUS. Come down. Behold no more.
O, coward that I am, to live so long
To see my best friend ta'en before my face!   35

[PINDARUS *climbs down from his lookout position on the
hill and stands waiting at his master's side.*]

(*After a long moment lost in thought.*) Come hither,
   sirrah.
In Parthia[4] did I take thee prisoner,
And then I swore thee, saving of thy life,[5]
That whatsoever I did bid thee do,
Thou should'st attempt it. (*Drawing his sword and
   handing it hilt first to* PINDARUS.) Come now! Keep
   thine oath.   40
Now be a freeman, and with this good sword
That ran through Caesar's bowels, search this bosom.

[PINDARUS *backs away and holds up his hand in
protest.*]

Stand not to answer! Here, take thou the hilt,
And, when my face is covered, as 'tis now,
Guide thou the sword.

[PINDARUS *stands staring at the sword in his hands, as
if he does not know what to do with it.* CASSIUS, *defeated but proudly erect, waits, his face covered with
his cloak.* PINDARUS *grips the sword in both hands and
plunges it into his master.* CASSIUS *staggers backward
from the thrust.*]

        Caesar, thou art revenged,   45
Even with the sword that killed thee.

[*He falls and dies.*]

PINDARUS. (*Looking down at the sword in his hands.*)
So, I am free; yet would not so have been,
Durst I have done my will. O Cassius!
Far from this country Pindarus shall run,
Where never Romans shall take note of him.   50

4. Parthia\\▲par·thē·ə\\ Persia.

5. **And then . . . life,** and then I made
you swear, in return for saving your life.

[*He drops the sword beside* CASSIUS' *body and runs off.* TITINIUS *arrives with* MESSALA *at the hill where* CASSIUS *lies dead.* TITINIUS *looks around anxiously.*]

MESSALA. It is but change,[6] Titinius, for Octavius   6. **change,** an exchange.
  Is overthrown by noble Brutus' power,
  As Cassius' legions are by Antony.
TITINIUS. (*Frowning as he looks about.*) These tidings
    will well comfort Cassius.
MESSALA. Where did you leave him?
TITINIUS.   All disconsolate,   55
  With Pindarus his bondman, on this hill.
MESSALA. Is not that he that lies upon the ground?
TITINIUS. He lies not like the living. O my heart!
MESSALA. Is not that he?
TITINIUS. (*Kneeling beside* CASSIUS' *body.*) No, this was
    he, Messala,
  But Cassius is no more. O setting sun,   60
  As in thy red rays thou dost sink tonight,
  So in his red blood Cassius' day is set.
  The sun of Rome is set! Our day is gone!
  Clouds, dews, and dangers come; our deeds are done!
  Mistrust of my success hath done this deed.   65
MESSALA. Mistrust of good success hath done this deed.
  O hateful error, Melancholy's child,
  Why dost thou show to the apt[7] thoughts of men   7. **apt,** ready.
  The things that are not? O error, soon conceived,
  Thou never com'st unto a happy birth,   70
  But kill'st the mother that engendered[8] thee!   8. **engendered,** bore.
TITINIUS. (*Standing over* CASSIUS *and looking from side
    to side.*) What, Pindarus! Where art thou, Pindarus?
MESSALA. Seek him, Titinius, whilst I go to meet
  The noble Brutus, thrusting this report
  Into his ears. I may say "thrusting" it,   75
  For piercing steel and darts envenomed
  Shall be as welcome to the ears of Brutus
  As tidings of this sight.
TITINIUS.   Hie[9] you, Messala,   9. **hie,** hurry.
  And I will seek for Pindarus the while.

[MESSALA *hurries off to find* BRUTUS. TITINIUS *lifts* CASSIUS' *sword and stares at the bloodstained blade.*]

(*To himself.*) Why did'st thou send me forth, brave
    Cassius?   80
  Did I not meet thy friends? And did not they
  Put on my brows this wreath of victory
  And bid me give it thee? Did'st thou not hear their
    shouts?

Alas, thou hast misconstrued everything!

[TITINIUS *bends over and puts the laurel wreath on* CASSIUS' *head.*]

But, hold thee, take this garland on thy brow.   85
Thy Brutus bid me give it thee, and I
Will do his bidding. Brutus, come apace[10]
And see how I regarded Caius Cassius.
(*Holding up the sword.*) By your leave, gods! This is
    a Roman's part.
Come, Cassius' sword, and find Titinius' heart!   90

[*He drives the sword into his breast and falls.* MESSALA
returns, leading BRUTUS, *young* CATO, STRATO,[11] VO-
LUMNIUS,[12] LUCILIUS, *and other officers.*]

BRUTUS. Where, where, Messala, doth his body lie?
MESSALA. Lo, yonder, and Titinius mourning it.
BRUTUS. Titinius' face is upward.
CATO.   He is slain!
BRUTUS. O Julius Caesar, thou art mighty yet!
    Thy spirit walks abroad, and turns our swords   95
    In our own proper entrails.

[*From the distance, shouts and sounds of renewed
battle.*]

CATO.   Brave Titinius!
    Look, whether he have not crowned dead Cassius!
BRUTUS. Are yet two Romans living such as these?
    The last of all the Romans, fare thee well!
    It is impossible that ever Rome   100
    Should breed thy fellow.[13] Friends, I owe more tears
    To this dead man than you shall see me pay.
    I shall find time, Cassius! I shall find time.
    Come, therefore, and to Thasos[14] send his body;
    His funerals shall not be in our camp,   105
    Lest it discomfort[15] us. Lucilius, come;
    And come, young Cato; let us to the field.
    Labeo and Flavius set our battles on.
    'Tis three o'clock; and, Romans, yet ere night
    We shall try fortune in a second fight.   110

[*With drawn swords, they set off toward the noise of
fighting.*]

SCENE 4

The field of battle. ANTONY'S *forces have begun to overwhelm*
BRUTUS' *army. The fighting has broken up into scattered
engagements.* BRUTUS *tries desperately to re-form his dis-*

10. **apace,** at once.

11. **Strato**\▲strā·tō\.
12. **Volumnius**\və ▲lyŭm 'nē·əs\.

13. **follow,** equal, match.

14. **Thasos**\▲thā 'sōs\ an island in the northern Aegean Sea.

15. **discomfort,** discourage.

persed men for an organized attack. He enters, accompanied by MESSALA, *young* CATO, LUCILIUS, *and* FLAVIUS.

BRUTUS. Yet, countrymen! O, yet hold up your heads!

CATO. What bastard doth not? (*Flourishing his sword.*)
　　Who will go with me?
　　I will proclaim my name about the field.
　　I am the son of Marcus Cato, ho!
　　A foe to tyrants, and my country's friend.　　　　　5
　　I am the son of Marcus Cato, ho!

[*He hurls himself at a roving group of* ANTONY's *soldiers.*]

BRUTUS. (*Holding his sword aloft and shouting.*) And I
　　am Brutus! Marcus Brutus, I!

[*He heads for the fighting in another part of the field.*
CATO *falls back from his struggle mortally wounded.*]

LUCILIUS. (*Hurrying over to support* CATO's *lifeless body.*)
　　O young and noble Cato, art thou down?
　　Why, now thou diest as bravely as Titinius,
　　And may'st be honored, being Cato's son.　　　　　10

[ANTONY's *soldiers surround* LUCILIUS *and threaten him
with their swords.*]

FIRST SOLDIER. Yield, or thou diest!

LUCILIUS.　　　　　　　　　Only I yield to die.
　　(*He offers money.*) There is so much that thou wilt
　　　kill me straight.[1]　　　　　　　　　　　　　　　　　1. **straight,** straightway.
　　Kill Brutus, and be honored in his death.

FIRST SOLDIER. (*Stepping forward to protect* LUCILIUS.)
　　We must not. (*Shouting.*) A noble prisoner!

[ANTONY *withdraws from the fighting and approaches.*]

SECOND SOLDIER. Room, ho! Tell Antony Brutus is ta'en.　15

FIRST SOLDIER. I'll tell the news. Here comes the general.
　　Brutus is ta'en! Brutus is ta'en, my lord!

ANTONY. Where is he?

LUCILIUS. (*Laughing bitterly.*) Safe, Antony. Brutus is
　　safe enough.
　　I dare assure thee that no enemy　　　　　　　　　20
　　Shall ever take alive the noble Brutus.
　　The gods defend him from so great a shame!
　　When you do find him, or[2] alive or dead,　　　　　2. **or,** either.
　　He will be found like Brutus, like himself.

ANTONY. (*To the* FIRST SOLDIER.) This is not Brutus,
　　friend; but, I assure you,　　　　　　　　　　　　25
　　A prize no less in worth. Keep this man safe.
　　Give him all kindness; I had rather have

Such men as friends than enemies. Go on,
And see if Brutus be alive or dead;
And bring us word unto Octavius' tent 30
How everything is chanced.[3]

[*He returns to the fighting.*]

3. **is chanced**, has happened.

SCENE 5

The field of battle. Night has fallen. BRUTUS, *weary and hope-less, stands near a cluster of huge boulders. With him are* DARDANIUS,[1] CLITUS, STRATO, *and* VOLUMNIUS.

1. **Dardanius**\'dar ▲dā·nē·əs\.

BRUTUS. Come, poor remains of friends. Rest on this rock.
CLITUS. Statilius[2] showed the torchlight, but, my lord,
  He came not back. He is or ta'en, or slain.
BRUTUS. Sit thee down, Clitus. Slaying is the word.
  It is a deed in fashion. Hark thee, Clitus. 5

2. **Statilius**\stə ▲tĭ·lē·əs\ a scout who was to signal with his torch if all was well.

[*He leans over and whipers into* CLITUS' *ear.*]

CLITUS. What, I, my lord? No, not for all the world!
BRUTUS. Peace, then! No words.
CLITUS.   I'll rather kill myself.
BRUTUS. (*Turning to where* DARDANIUS *sits.*) Hark thee,
  Dardanius.

[*He whispers.*]

DARDANIUS.   Shall I do such a deed?
CLITUS. O Dardanius!
DARDANIUS. O Clitus! 10
CLITUS. What ill request did Brutus make to thee?
DARDANIUS. To kill him, Clitus. Look, he meditates.
CLITUS. Now is that noble vessel full of grief,
  That it runs over even at his eyes.
BRUTUS. Come hither, good Volumnius; list a word.[3] 15
VOLUMNIUS. What says my lord?
BRUTUS.   Why, this, Volumnius—
  The ghost of Caesar hath appeared to me
  Two several[4] times by night; at Sardis once,
  And, this last night, here in Philippi fields.
  I know my hour has come.
VOLUMNIUS.   Not so, my lord. 20
BRUTUS. Nay, I am sure it is, Volumnius.
  Thou see'st the world, Volumnius, how it goes;
  Our enemies have beat us to the pit.[5]

[*The sounds of scattered fighting come from the darkness.*]

It is more worthy to leap in ourselves

3. **list a word**, listen to a word or so.

4. **several**, separate.

5. **Our enemies . . . pit**, our enemies have driven us, like encircled animals, backward into a pit (in which we will be taken).

461

Than tarry till they push us. Good Volumnius,   25
Thou know'st that we two went to school together;
Even for that our love of old, I prithee,
Hold thou my sword-hilt, whilst I run on it.
VOLUMNIUS. That's not an office for a friend, my lord.

[*From nearby the shouts and cries of approaching
enemy troops.*]

CLITUS. Fly, fly, my lord! There is no tarrying here!   30
BRUTUS. Farewell to you, and you, and you, Volumnius.
Strato, thou has been all this while asleep;
Farewell to thee, Strato. Countrymen,
My heart doth joy that yet in all my life
I found no man but he was true to me.   35
I shall have glory by this losing day
More than Octavius and Mark Antony
By this vile conquest shall attain unto.
So fare you well at once, for Brutus' tongue
Hath almost ended his life's history.   40
Night hangs upon mine eyes. My bones would rest,
That have but labored to attain this hour.

[*Voices and the excited commands of the searching
enemy.*]

CLITUS. Fly, my lord! Fly!
BRUTUS.   Hence! I will follow.

[CLITUS, DARDANIUS, *and* VOLUMNIUS *slip away into the
shadows.* BRUTUS *grips* STRATO's *arm as he attempts to
follow.*]

I prithee, Strato, stay thou by thy lord.
Thou art a fellow of a good respect.[6]   45
Thy life hath had some smatch[7] of honor in it.
Hold then my sword, and turn away thy face,
While I do run upon it. Wilt thou, Strato?

[STRATO *turns away in a momentary gesture of refusal.
Then he faces* BRUTUS *and grips his hand firmly.*]

STRATO. Give me your hand first. Fare you well, my lord.
BRUTUS. Farewell, good Strato.

[*He grips* STRATO's *shoulders and pulls himself upon
the blade.*]

                         Caesar, now be still;   50
I killed not thee with half so good a will.

[BRUTUS *falls.* OCTAVIUS *and* ANTONY *and their troops
appear out of the darkness. The captives,* MESSALA *and*
LUCILIUS, *are with them.* OCTAVIUS *points to* STRATO,
who stands beside BRUTUS' *body.*]

Octavius (Augustus) Caesar

6. **respect,** reputation.
7. **smatch,** hint, suggestion.

OCTAVIUS. What man is that?

MESSALA. My master's man. Strato, where is thy master?

STRATO. Free from the bondage you are in, Messala.
    The conquerors can but make a fire of him,   55
    For Brutus only overcame himself,
    And no man else hath honor by his death.

LUCILIUS. So Brutus should be found. I thank thee, Brutus,
    That thou hast proved Lucilius' saying true.

OCTAVIUS. All that served Brutus, I will entertain[8] them. 60
    Fellow, wilt thou bestow[9] thy time with me?

STRATO. Ay, if Messala will prefer[10] me to you.

OCTAVIUS. Do so, good Messala.

MESSALA. How died my master, Strato?

STRATO. I held the sword, and he did run on it.   65

MESSALA. Octavius, then take him to follow thee,
    That did the latest service to my master.

ANTONY. (*Walking slowly until he stands over the body
    of* BRUTUS.) This was the noblest Roman of them all.
    All the conspirators, save only he,
    Did that they did in envy of great Caesar.   70
    He only, in a general honest thought
    And common good to all, made one of them.
    His life was gentle, and the elements
    So mixed in him that Nature might stand up
    And say to all the world, "This was a man!"   75

OCTAVIUS. According to his virtue let us use him,
    With all respect and rites of burial.
    Within my tent his bones tonight shall lie,
    Most like a soldier, ordered honorably.
    So call the field to rest, and let's away   80
    To part[11] the glories of this happy day.

[*They leave, bearing away the body of* BRUTUS.]

8. **entertain,** receive and maintain without hostility.
9. **bestow,** employ.
10. **prefer,** recommend.

11. **part,** divide.

CHARACTERIZATION
How many ages hence
Shall this our lofty scene be acted over
In states unborn and accents yet unknown

As a study of politics and political maneuvering among men, *Julius Caesar* is probably the greatest play ever written. Except for Brutus, all the major characters in the play are politicians. The decisions they make are primarily political decisions. It is interesting to note that *Julius Caesar* has been popular during certain periods of history and forgotten during others. It has been extremely popular in the last thirty years in the United States which may indicate the state of political unrest in the world. Of course, political power resides in flesh and blood human beings whose moods, motives, and aspirations are similar to our own. Shakespeare brings his characters alive, vividly and warmly.

1. Shakespeare adds new dimensions to the characters in the last half of the play. Study the following quotations. What do they reveal about these men?

BRUTUS

Brutus, Act IV, scene 2
There are no tricks in plain and simple faith; . . .

Cassius, Act IV, scene 3
When Caesar lived, he durst not thus have moved me.

Brutus, Act IV, scene 3
There is no terror, Cassius, in your threats
For I am armed so strong in honesty
That they pass by me as the idle wind,
Which I respect not.

Cassius, Act IV, scene 3
A friendly eye could never see such faults.

Brutus, Act IV, scene 3
O Cassius, I am sick of many griefs!

Brutus, Act IV, scene 3
Bear with me, good boy. I am much forgetful.

Brutus, Act V, scene 5
Caesar, now be still;
I killed thee not with half so good a will.

Antony, Act V, scene 5
This was the noblest Roman of them all.
All the conspirators, save only he,

Did that they did in envy of great Caesar.
He only, in a general honest thought
And common good to all, made one of them.
His life was gentle, and the elements
So mixed in him that Nature might stand up
And say to all the world, "This was a man!"

CASSIUS

Brutus, Act IV, scene 2
Your master, Pindarus,
In his own change, or by ill officers,
Hath given me some worthy cause to wish
Things done undone.

Brutus, Act IV, scene 3
Let me tell you, Cassius, you yourself
Are much condemned to have an itching palm, . . .

Cassius, Act IV, scene 3
Brutus, bait not me!
I'll not endure it!

Cassius, Act IV, scene 3
I am a soldier; I,
Older in practice, abler than yourself
To make conditions.

Brutus, Act IV, scene 3
Away, slight man.

Brutus, Act IV, scene 3
Must I give way and room to your rash choler?
Shall I be frighted when a madman stares?

Cassius, Act IV, scene 3
For Cassius is aweary of the world!
Hated by one he loves; braved by his brother;
Checked like a bondman; all his faults observed,
Set in a notebook, learned and conned by rote
To cast into my teeth.

Cassius, Act V, scene 3
Caesar, thou art revenged
Even with the sword that killed thee.

Brutus, Act V, scene 3
The last of all the Romans, fare thee well!

ANTONY

Antony, Act III, scene 2
But, as you know me all, a plain blunt man
That love my friend; and that they know full well
That gave me public leave to speak of him;
For I have neither wit, nor words, nor worth,

Action, nor utterance, nor the power of speech
To stir men's blood.

2. Great tragedy is often built around an individual in high position who is basically an admirable person, but who has a flaw in his character which eventually leads to downfall or death. If you think back through the play, you will realize that Brutus is the one character for whom all the others feel respect, love and affection. But his chief flaw is that he thinks those about him are motivated by the same love of honor that he himself holds. He lets himself be led into a terrible murder and yet in the final act he wins the sympathy of the audience as he stumblingly tries to retrieve his honor.

In addition to Brutus, Cassius and Caesar die and apparently fall in the course of the play. What is Cassius' major flaw? What is Caesar's? Are both tragic figures in the full sense described above?

IMPLICATIONS

1. Does Shakespeare in *Julius Caesar* support or deny the following statements?

a. No good can come from an evil beginning.

b. Antony's funeral oration is a masterpiece of propaganda.

c. When a strong man dies many factions spring into being throwing a nation into chaos.

d. An idealist is seldom a practical man.

e. Fate plays a bigger part in an individual's life than does a man's character.

f. Caesar, Cassius and Mark Antony are all politicians.

2. Following are some larger implications of the play . . . the meaning goes beyond the lines. What is your opinion?

a. What can happen to a country if one person has total power?

b. Hitler and Mussolini had much in common with Caesar.

c. What are the dangers when a person lets his ideals run away with his reason?

d. What are some of the things that can happen to a person if he lets jealousy rule his life?

e. Can a person be a dictator and still be a wise, competent leader?

f. It has been said that power corrupts and absolute power corrupts absolutely. Do you agree?

g. Offering a crown to Caesar would be as repulsive to most Romans of that day as offering a crown to the President of the United States would be to most Americans today.

TECHNIQUES

Irony

Julius Caesar is a play that is built largely around the irony of a situation. In addition, it has many examples of irony in specific scenes and speeches.

1. What does Brutus hope to accomplish by joining the conspirators? What does he accomplish and why is it ironic?

2. When the conspirators are planning the murder, Brutus argues Cassius out of killing Antony along with Caesar. Why is this ironic?

3. After the murder Brutus says:

"And let us bathe our hands in Caesar's blood
Up to the elbows, and besmear our swords.
Then walk we forth, even to the market-place,
And waving our red weapons o'er our heads,
Let's all cry: 'Peace, freedom, and liberty!' "

What is ironic about the idea expressed? Why is it particularly ironic that Brutus should suggest such actions?

4. Antony's funeral oration speech is one of the greatest examples of the use of irony that has ever been written. Examine it closely to see how Antony makes his words mean almost exactly the opposite of what they seem to be saying.

5. What is ironic about Antony's final appraisal of Brutus?
"This was the noblest Roman of them all. . . ."

Organization

Julius Caesar has often seemed disorganized to people who read it for the first time. It seems to involve two stories instead of one. The murder of Caesar appears to form one neat unit, but the fourth and fifth acts may seem confused and less interesting. Is the play disorganized or has the reader misread Shakespeare's intentions? Think through the answers to the following:

1. The Elizabethan audience probably saw the play in two parts. Part one ended with the murder of Caesar. Part two began with the funeral oration.

Shakespeare's audience would, of course, be familiar with the stage of that period. This stage had evolved from the days when plays were presented in the courtyards of inns. A wagon was moved against one side of the yard to support the platform on which the players presented the drama. The audience watched either from the balconies if they could afford it or stood on the ground if they wanted a cheaper point of observation. Shakespeare's theater, the Globe, had departed from the rectangular shape of the inn yard and was built instead in a circle, but still there were balconies around the open space which seated the well to do and an open space on the floor where the groundlings stood. At one end a platform with a partial roof jutted out. On either side of this platform, near the back, a door opened to the actors' dressing rooms. Between these was a small room called the back stage which was the only section to have a curtain. Here scenes in caves, bedrooms, tombs, and the like were played. Above this room a gallery or balcony served for scenes involving high places such as battlements or upper windows. All plays were put on in the afternoon when there was plenty of daylight to illuminate the stage. A flag flying from the tower of the theater indicated that a play would be performed that day.

Supposing you were asked to give a title to each of the two parts separately. What would you entitle them? Do your two titles show a kind of organizational structure?

2. Who is the hero, or leading character, of the play? Most works of literature that use the name of a character as the title are named for the major character. Is this true in *Julius Caesar*? If you feel that Caesar is the central character, how is his character important even in the last two acts?

3. At the end of the second and fourth acts of his plays, Shakespeare has a habit of causing something to happen or a character to say something

which sets up the action for the following acts. What is said and/or what happens at the end of Act II which leads to the action in Acts III and IV? Likewise, what is said and/or what happens at the end of Act IV which brings about the action in Act V?

WORDS

A. What do the italicized words mean in the following phrases and clauses: (1) with thy best *apparel* on, (2) in her *concave* shores, (3) thoughts of great value, worthy *cognitations,* (4) he doth *bestride* the narrow world, (5) her side walls *encompassed* but one man, (6) to *repute* himself a son of Rome, (7) the nature of an *insurrection,* (8) To mask thy monstrous *visage,* (9) Hide it in smiles and *affability,* (10) A shrewd *contriver,* (11) To dare the vile *contagion* of the night, (12) Any *exploit* worthy the name of honor, (13) for warnings and portents, And evils *imminent?*

B. In the three hundred and fifty years since Shakespeare's day, some words have changed their meaning. Most obvious illustrations of semantic change have been pointed out in the notes. A number of other words, however, that have not changed so radically are interesting. Examine the denotation and the connotation of the italicized words in the following phrases. How have they changed their meaning somewhat? (1) without the sign of your *profession,* (2) what *trade,* thou knave? (3) thou *saucy* fellow, (4) to rejoice in his *triumph,* (5) for this *fault* assemble all the poor men, (6) who is it in the *press* that calls on me? (7) that *quick* spirit that is in Antony, (8) vexed I am of late with *passions,* (9) will modestly *discover* to yourself, (10) to keep his *state* in Rome.

C. 1. Following are a number of words from Act I of *Julius Caesar.* In these words the roots are italicized, and the general meanings of the roots are given in quotes. Indicate what specific sense of the general meaning is used in the play: re*spect* "look, see," 1, 10; di*rect*ly "straight, correct," 1, 12; con*fus*ion "pour, pour out," 1, 21; con*quest* "seek, search, ask," 1, 33; inter*mit* "send," 1, 55; *hes*itant "stick, cling," 1, 62; *vulg*ar "common," 1, 71; per*form* "form," 2, 10, pro*cess*ion "go, move," 2, 24; con*cept*ion "take, seize, catch," 2, 41; pro*pose* "put, place," 2, 110; dis*tract* "draw," 2, 132; con*jure* "swear," 2, 146; *senat*or "old," 2, 188; in*firm*ity "strong," 2, 270; di*gest* "eat, take in," 2, 300; se*duc*ed "lead," 2, 311; e*rupt*ion "break," 3, 78; *fact*ious "make, do," 3, 118.

2. Analyze the following italicized words from Act II into affixes and roots. Does the general meaning given for the root always agree with the meaning Shakespeare intended for the word? Then, lest he may, *prevent* 1, 28; what watchful cares do *interpose* themselves 1, 98; giving myself a *voluntary* wound 1, 300; decorated with royal

magnificence 2, stage direction; for these *predictions* are to the world as to Caesar 2, 28; your wisdom is consumed in *confidence* 2, 49; from you great Rome shall suck *reviving* blood 2, 88; the Senate have *concluded* 2, 93; Why, know'st thou any harm's *intended* towards him? 4, 31.

Shakespeare— the Artist and the Man

The Artist

In *Julius Caesar,* Shakespeare demonstrates the many facets of the playwright's craft in which he excelled. You have already examined his minute and intricate development of characters. Even without careful study you were aware of the moving story he unfolds. Short scenes prepare for the long dramatic moments or add emphasis to a scene just past. The change of pace keeps the audience alert, tense, eager. Shakespeare also had a way with language. Not only could he catch an idea with a few telling words and images but he could put ideas into the flowing rhythm of powerful blank verse.

But the quality that has made Shakespeare survive through the ages is his ability to capture in words and actions the great problems that have always tormented men. Look about you in your school, your town, your state and you will find people exactly like Brutus and Cassius, Caesar and Antony. They are not just government officials. You can find them in your clubs, your school, your sports. Our stumbling efforts to find our way in life may be reflected by Brutus or Cassius. Perhaps you find comfort in the fact that a strong man like Caesar is also superstitious or worry that you may feel as ruthless as Antony. But each individual in the audience can find in this play some interpretation of life that makes his own more meaningful.

Other great writers have sometimes succeeded in doing one or two of these things with excellence, but no one else since his time has been able to turn out play after play, year after year with the high degree of excellence that is Shakespeare's. Who then was this man, Shakespeare?

The Man (1564–1616)

For several hundred years scholars have probed dusty old records, dug through crumbling papers and books trying to find the answer to who Shakespeare was. Lawyers insist that he must have been a lawyer . . . he seems to know so much about the law. Sailors are equally sure that he must have gone to sea, for his knowledge of the sea is so astute. And so it goes. The truth is that no one tried to collect any information about Shakespeare until a hundred years after his death and by that time most of the records had disappeared or been destroyed.

He was born at an agricultural trading center, Stratford-on-Avon, about 90 miles from London. Here his mother and father were both people of some prominence, and it is supposed that he was sent to school. At eighteen he married Anne Hathaway, a girl eight years older than himself. They had a daughter, and two years later, twins, a boy and a girl. For the next eight years there is no tangible record of his activities, but in 1592 he turned up in London, acting and writing plays.

At this time it was common for groups of actors to join together and form a company to produce plays and split the profits. Shakespeare soon became a member of such a group, both writing plays and acting in them. His company was unusually successful and eventually bought its own theater, the Globe. It later became officially connected with the court and was known as The King's Company. During the long middle period of his life, Shakespeare was a rising businessman as well as a writer; and his worldly success can be traced through various pieces of property he purchased at this time. He bought a large tract of land near Stratford and later two large houses, one in Stratford and one in London. With a 10 percent interest in the Globe and a 14 percent interest in the Blackfriar's Theater his financial situation was a secure one.

After 1612 he seems to have retired to Stratford where he supposedly died on his birthday in 1616. Thus the pattern of his life was a kind of circle. He grew up in a small rural town, went to the city where he made a dramatic splash, and returned to the small town to live quietly and die.

PEOPLE UNDER PRESSURE

Boots

We're foot—slog—slog—slog—sloggin' over Africa
Foot—foot—foot—foot—sloggin' over Africa—
(Boots—boots—boots—boots—movin' up an' down again!)
  There's no discharge in the war!

Seven—six—eleven—five—nine an'-twenty miles today—
Four—eleven—seventeen—thirty-two the day before—
(Boots—boots—boots—boots—movin' up an' down again!)
  There's no discharge in the war!

Don't—don't—don't—don't—look at what's in front of you.
(Boots—boots—boots—boots—movin' up an' down again!)
Men—men—men—men—men go mad with watchin' 'em,
  An' there's no discharge in the war!

Try—try—try—try—to think o' something different—
Oh—my—God—keep—men from goin' lunatic!
(Boots—boots—boots—boots—movin' up an' down again!)
  There's no discharge in the war!

Count—count—count—count—the bullets in the bandoliers.[1]
If—your—eyes—drop—they will get atop o' you!
(Boots—boots—boots—boots—movin' up an' down again!)
  There's no discharge in the war!

Reprinted by permission of Doubleday & Company, Inc.

---

1. **bandolier**\ˈbănˑdəˈlēr\ belts worn over the shoulder and across the chest, used for carrying cartridges.

We—can—stick—out—'unger, thirst, an' weariness,
But—not—not—not—not the chronic sight of 'em—
(Boots—boots—boots—boots—movin' up an' down again!)
  An' there's no discharge in the war!

'Tain't—so—bad—by—day because o' company,
But—night—brings—long—strings—o' forty thousand million
(Boots—boots—boots—boots—movin' up an' down again!)
  There's no discharge in the war!

I—'ave—marched—six—weeks in 'ell an' certify
It—is—not—fire—devils, dark, or anything,
But boots—boots—boots—boots—movin' up an' down again,
  An' there's no discharge in the war!

RUDYARD KIPLING

The Gulf Stream
Winslow Homer
The Metropolitan Museum of Art
Wolfe Fund, 1906

*The fisherman fights a lonely
struggle against the perils
of the sea.*

Life is lived in the midst of many kinds of pressures. The pressure of environment, the pressure of nature, the pressure of other people, the pressure of our own emotions: all of these come to bear on each of us. In turn, we seek ways to adjust and to establish a balance between these pressures and ourselves. There is a thrust and counterthrust.

In Kipling's "Boots," the soldiers, under the pressure of great physical strain, are driven close to madness. Their minds become numb, their perceptions distorted, until the only real thing in their world is the endless tramping of their own boots. The only refuge for their sanity is to define their suffering and, by defining it, to save themselves from destruction.

Writers, as you know, take the elements of actual life as their raw material and put these elements together in meaningful patterns. Through the process of recording and arranging their experience, writers not only produce satisfying artistic creations, but also help the reader deepen his understanding of himself and of the life around him. By examining the brief encounters between people, the emotional states of individuals, and the tensions of family life, skillful writers have led you to discover and to interpret experiences which would take many lifetimes to gather by yourself. It is natural that writers should also be fascinated with the moments in living when severe pressures are brought to bear on individuals.

Some of the selections that follow show people under momentary tensions; others show them living for long periods under steady strains. Some of the characters actively fight back, others do not. Some react to seemingly trivial matters, while others require catastrophic events to make them struggle against the oppressive force.

Working with the pressures that bear on human lives, the writers represented in this group of selections have created different kinds of literary experiences. Sometimes they amuse the reader with the absurdity of a situation. Sometimes they evoke the despair of hopeless frustration. Sometimes they stir our pride in the dignity of man's ability to fight back. But whatever the mood, each selection will carry the reader toward a better understanding of man pushed to the breaking point.

Early in John Milton's great epic,
Paradise Lost, Satan claims that the mind
can make a heaven of hell
or a hell of heaven. Can the mind be pressured
into seeing perfectly ordinary events
as something horrifying? Saki, an English writer
of bizarre tales, has one answer.
When "The Open Window" begins,
the reader is thrust into the center
of the action and must, from the rush of events,
figure out the situation for himself.

The Open Window

SAKI

My aunt will be down presently, Mr. Nuttel," said a very self-possessed young lady of fifteen. "In the meantime you must try and put up with me."

Framton Nuttel endeavoured to say the correct something which should duly flatter the niece of the moment without unduly discounting the aunt that was to come. Privately he doubted more than ever whether these formal visits on a succession of total strangers would do much towards helping the nerve cure which he was supposed to be undergoing.

"I know how it will be," his sister had said when he was preparing to migrate to this rural retreat; "You will bury yourself down there and not speak to a living soul, and your nerves will be worse than ever from moping. I shall just give you letters of introduction to all the people I know there. Some of them, as far as I can remember, were quite nice."

Framton wondered whether Mrs. Sappleton, the lady to whom he was presenting one of the letters of introduction, came into the nice division.

"Do you know many of the people round here?" asked the niece, when she judged that they had had sufficient silent communion.

"Hardly a soul," said Framton. "My sister was staying here, at the rectory,[1] you know, some four years ago, and she gave me letters of introduction to some of the people here."

He made the last statement in a tone of distinct regret.

"Then you know practically nothing about my aunt?" pursued the self-possessed young lady.

"Only her name and address," admitted the caller. He was wondering whether Mrs. Sappleton was in the married or widowed state. An undefinable something about the room seemed to suggest masculine habitation.

"Her great tragedy happened just three years ago," said the child; "that would be since your sister's time."

"Her tragedy?" asked Framton. Somehow in this restful country spot tragedies seemed out of place.

"You may wonder why we keep that window wide open on an October afternoon," said the niece, indicating a large French window[2] that opened on to a lawn.

"It is quite warm for the time of the year," said Framton; "but has that window got anything to do with the tragedy?"

"Out through that window, three years ago to a day, her husband and her two young brothers went off for their day's shooting. They never came back. In crossing the moor to their favourite snipe-shooting ground they were all three engulfed in a treacherous piece of bog. It had been that dreadful wet summer, you know, and places that were safe in other years gave way suddenly without warning. Their bodies were never recovered. That was the dreadful part of it." Here the child's voice lost its self-possessed note and became falteringly human. "Poor aunt always thinks that they will

1. **rectory**\▲rĕk·tə·rē\ the residence of a parish clergyman.
2. **French window,** a casement window reaching to the floor.

come back some day, they and the little brown spaniel that was lost with them, and walk in at that window just as they used to do. That is why the window is kept open every evening till it is quite dusk. Poor dear aunt, she has often told me how they went out, her husband with his white waterproof coat over his arm, and Ronnie, her youngest brother, singing, 'Bertie, why do you bound?' as he always did to tease her, because she said it got on her nerves. Do you know, sometimes on still, quiet evenings like this, I almost get a creepy feeling that they will all walk in through that window—"

She broke off with a little shudder. It was a relief to Framton when the aunt bustled into the room with a whirl of apologies for being late in making her appearance.

"I hope Vera has been amusing you?" she said.

"She has been very interesting," said Framton.

"I hope you don't mind the open window," said Mrs. Sappleton briskly. "My husband and brothers will be home directly from shooting, and they always come in this way. They've been out for snipe in the marshes today, so they'll make a fine mess over my poor carpets. So like you menfolk, isn't it?"

She rattled on cheerfully about the shooting and the scarcity of birds, and the prospects for duck in the winter. To Framton it was all purely horrible. He made a desperate but only partially successful effort to turn the talk on to a less ghastly topic. He was conscious that his hostess was giving him only a fragment of her attention, and her eyes were constantly straying past him to the open window and the lawn beyond. It was certainly an unfortunate coincidence that he should have paid his visit on this tragic anniversary.

"The doctors agree in ordering me complete rest, and absence of mental excitement, and avoidance of anything in the nature of violent physical exercise," announced Framton, who laboured under the tolerably widespread delusion that total strangers and chance acquaintances are hungry for the least detail of one's ailments and infirmities, their cause and cure. "On the matter of diet they are not so much in agreement," he continued.

"No?" said Mrs. Sappleton, in a voice which only replaced a yawn at the last moment. Then she suddenly brightened into alert attention— but not to what Framton was saying.

"Here they are at last!" she cried. "Just in time for tea, and don't they look as if they were muddy up to the eyes!"

Framton shivered slightly and turned towards the niece with a look intended to convey sympathetic comprehension. The child was staring out through the open window with dazed horror in her eyes. In a chill shock of nameless fear Framton swung round in his seat and looked in the same direction.

In the deepening twilight three figures were walking across the lawn towards the window. They all carried guns under their arms, and one of them was additionally burdened with a white coat hung over his shoulders. A tired brown spaniel kept close at their heels. Noiselessly they neared the house, and then a hoarse young voice chanted out of the dusk: "I said, Bertie, why do you bound?"

Framton grabbed wildly at his stick and hat. The hall-door, the gravel-drive, and the front gate were dimly noted stages in his headlong retreat. A cyclist[3] coming along the road had to run into the hedge to avoid imminent collision.

"Here we are, my dear," said the bearer of the white mackintosh,[4] coming in through the window; "fairly muddy, but most of it's dry. Who was that who bolted out as we came up?"

"A most extraordinary man, a Mr. Nuttel," said Mrs. Sappleton; "could only talk about his illness, and dashed off without a word of good-by or apology when you arrived. One would think he had seen a ghost."

---

3. **cyclist**\ˈsaɪ·klɪst\ a bicycle rider.
4. **mackintosh**\ˈmă·kən ˈtŏsh\ chiefly British: a light raincoat.

"I expect it was the spaniel," said the niece calmly. "He told me he had a horror of dogs. He was once hunted into a cemetery somewhere on the banks of the Ganges by a pack of pariah[5] dogs, and had to spend the night in a newly-dug grave with the creatures snarling and grinning and foaming just above him. Enough to make any one lose their nerve."

Romance at short notice was her specialty.

I
CALLING ON THE READER'S IMAGINATION

Part of the charm of "The Open Window" lies in so much story being packed into so little space. Much of the reader's pleasure comes from his active participation in the story. He must make connections between the characters and supply a final explanation of the story from his own imagination.

II
IMPLICATIONS

You have probably used your imagination more than you realize while reading this story. When you have answered the following questions, you will see how skillfully Saki has stimulated and made use of his readers' private responses.

1. What must have been the secret reactions of the following characters to each other? (a) Vera to Mr. Nuttel; (b) Mr. Nuttel to Vera; (c) Mr. Nuttel to Mrs. Sappleton; (d) Mrs. Sappleton to Mr. Nuttel.

2. What pressures were operating on Mr. Nuttel? How did he react to them?

3. Do you think Saki means you to feel sorry for Mr. Nuttel? If not, what evidence is there in the story that Mr. Nuttel at least partly deserves what happens to him?

4. What details of setting, time, and place, add to the pressures on Mr. Nuttel?

III
TECHNIQUES

In the creation of a story, a writer must, as you know, solve the problems of exposition, conflict, climax, characterization, plot, and symbol. In these selections you will examine three more elements of the story: theme, style, and identification.

---

5. **pariah**\ˈpă·rē·ə *or* pəˈrai·ə\ outcast, wild. **Ganges** \ˈgăn ˈjēz\ the great river of northern India.

Theme

There are two ways of considering themes in literature. The first is best illustrated by the organization of this book. Each group of selections in this anthology is built around a particular theme, that is, an underlying motif or idea. The ten selections which follow, for instance, deal with the behavior of people under pressure. Thus, PEOPLE UNDER PRESSURE is the general theme. There are many other such general themes in literature. "The Struggle for Justice," "Man Looks at the Future," "Young Love" might be cited as random examples.

The other way of looking at themes is more particular. The theme, in this sense, is what a story itself is about. It is the meaning embodied in interplay of setting, plot, and characters in a story. Note that it is not a summary of its plot or a capsule description of its characters. Thus, the theme of "The Open Window" is not "a nervous man frightened by an imaginative young girl." You must look below the surface events of the story to discover the real theme. The surface actions, however, have been carefully arranged by the author to reveal what lies beneath them. If you have read "The Open Window" carefully, you will doubtless agree that the theme of this story is actually the power of suggestion. It is the pressure exerted by the young girl's story on Mr. Nuttel's nervous mind that makes him believe her version of the open window, rather than her aunt's more sensible and realistic explanation.

The particular themes of all the selections that follow will be related to the general theme of the group in a similar way. They will serve as variations on the general theme and will show you instances of specific kinds of pressure on different kinds of people.

Style

Style is that special handling of language that makes one piece of writing distinct from another. Style is to writing what personality is to the human being—the distinctive, individual quality. A famous French critic once said "Style is the man himself." All writers of talent and originality develop a particular way of writing. It shows in the kinds of words they choose, the figures of speech they invent, and even in the grammatical structure of their sentences.

Some writers pay closer attention than others to the kind of language they use. Searching for exactly the right word or phrase to express their meaning, they try to give their writing the elegance, roughness, or naturalness that they consider appropriate to their story. But in the deepest sense of the word, all good writing reveals a concern with style. Although a distinctive style of writing is as natural to a good writer as a distinctive way of throwing a baseball is to a good pitcher or a way of sewing to a good dressmaker, it has usually been acquired only after years of hard work and diligent practice.

Reread the first few paragraphs of "The Open Window," and decide which adjective in the following pairs best describes Saki's style.

1. restrained   emotional
2. rambling   precise
3. cloudy   sparkling
4. light   heavy
5. informal   formal

In what way would you say the kind of story he is telling influences the kind of language he uses?

Identification

As a friend recounts to you something that has happened to him, you automatically put yourself in his place and live through his experience with him. Much the same thing happens when you read a story. But there is this difference: A friend can count on your sympathy, a writer cannot. A writer must win a reader's sympathy for his characters. He does this by leading the reader to identify himself with them. By giving a character personality traits that are familiar, by placing him in exciting situations, and, most of all, by giving him hopes, fears, and other feelings that the reader recognizes, a writer skillfully draws the reader into the character's life. The reader soon finds himself sharing the character's experience and emotions. Identification is the means by which a writer persuades his readers to take as deep an interest in the story and in its people as he himself has done.

In "The Open Window," with which character did you identify yourself most strongly? In whose shoes did you put yourself while reading? Name some of the personality traits of this character which you found familiar.

On certain extraordinary occasions,
as in this story, the mind and the body
seem to operate independently of one another.
Which was more real, what Peter Nilson's body
was performing or the way his mind was reacting?
You will note that the pressure on him
comes both from the immediate situation and also
from a deep personal insecurity.

Going to Run All Night

HARRY SYLVESTER

They brought him in before the commanding officer, a lieutenant colonel, and stood him there, almost as though he were a prisoner, a slight, almost little man, whose face, they now remembered, had been curiously harassed and marked by strain even before this campaign, or any campaign, had begun. He noticed himself that they walked on either side of him, as if guarding him, as if, indeed, he were a prisoner or someone valued. And since he could think of nothing he had done or left undone for which they should make him a prisoner, he was driven to the incredible conclusion that finally and at last he had come to be of value.

He looked at the lieutenant colonel, seeing that the officer's face was hardly less, though newly, harassed than his own. All day, in the midst of the danger which constantly encircled them and intermittently killed some of them, the new legend of the lieutenant colonel's irascibility had grown, so that now, standing before the man, the corporal could wonder that he was not ripped up and down with words as scores of men had been that day.

From ALL YOUR IDOLS by Harry Sylvester. Copyright 1948 by Harry Sylvester. Reprinted by permission of Holt, Rinehart and Winston, Inc.

The lieutenant colonel looked at him, blinking and staring at the same time, as though making some kind of adjustment, as if from rage to a kind of calm. Which it was, perhaps, for to Nilson's amazement, he said rather mildly, "They tell me that you used to be a runner, Corporal?"

"Why, yes," Nilson said. "Yes, sir, I mean."

"You used to run distances? I mean road races and such."

"Yes, sir."

"Ever run in Marathon races or anything like that?"

"Yes, sir," the corporal said, though he was thinking: There is nothing "like" the Marathon. Just the figures alone mean something that no other race means: 26 miles, 385 yards. "I ran seventh one year in the Boston Marathon."[1] Right after he had said it, he could see that the lieutenant colonel was not impressed, that he did not know that running seventh in the Boston Marathon was not the same as running seventh in just another foot race.

"Well," the officer said, as though making the best of a bad bargain, rubbing his eyes tiredly and slowly with the heels of his hands. "Well, as you know, they've sort of got us over a barrel[2] here. The one radio we still have that is working has been damaged so that we cannot vary the wave or frequency enough to keep the enemy from picking it up rather often."

He went on like that, rubbing his eyes, explaining to the corporal as if the corporal were a general—someone who ought to be told of what the situation was. "We think we can break out at dawn, if we can synchronize our attack with some sort of aid coming from our main forces opposite the point of our own attack. Break through the ring," he said

---

1. **marathon**\ˈmă·rə·thŏn\ a long-distance run. The **Boston Marathon,** held yearly on Patriot's Day (April 19, the anniversary of the Battle of Lexington and Concord), is a run from Hopkinton, Massachusetts, to Exeter Street in Boston, a distance of 26 miles, 385 yards.
2. **over a barrel,** in a very difficult or hopeless position.

vaguely. Then: "Look! You think you could run across the hills by dawn and carry them a message?"

Nilson began to think, for some reason, about how his grandmother used to talk so frequently about lightning and how you never knew where or when it was going to strike. It was not fear in him, although for a little while he would think it was fear. He made a silent gasp, so that his mouth was open before he began to speak. He said, "Why, I guess so. I mean, I'm not in very good shape. I—"

"But in no worse shape than anyone else here," the lieutenant colonel said. "And you used to be a runner. How long since you stopped active competition?"

"Oh, I was running all the time. Right up until my induction,[3] and even then, when I was still in the States and could get leave, I was competing some."

The officer nodded. "Well, that's about all. There'll be no written message in case you might be taken. You'll be picked up by one of our own patrols probably. Just tell them that we can't last another day here and that we're going to try to come through at dawn. It's possible they won't believe you. But that's a chance we'll have to take. If they have time, they can send a plane over with a message, to let us know that they understand, although it hasn't been any too healthy here for planes. There won't be much trouble getting you through their lines at night. I'll send a guard with you until you're beyond their lines and then you'll be on your own. Just follow the road. The main idea is to get there before dawn. I figure it's thirty-five or forty miles before they'll pick you up. We won't attack for six hours. You think you could make it in, say, five hours?"

"Why, if I was in shape," Nilson said, "I could, maybe, easy."

"Still," the officer said, "you're the best we have. Good luck."

"Yes, sir," Nilson said, and saluted and turned.

Outside, the two sergeants stood on either side of him, and the tall one said, "Well, what are you gonna need?"

"I dunno," Nilson said, "I guess I won't need anything. Maybe I'll take a canteen, maybe not." He knew that thirst for water and the actual need for water were not necessarily the same thing; he was already weighing, only half-consciously, the weight of the canteen against the necessity for water.

"Well, let's get going, then," the other sergeant said.

The tall sergeant got Nilson a canteen filled with water, and they moved out into the deeper darkness beyond where the tanks and cars stood in a shallow arc like great animals vaguely huddled in the dark.

They were more than halfway across the plain of three or four miles that separated them from the hills that held the enemy, when Nilson said, "Look, this isn't any good for you two, is it? I mean, if they see us, three isn't going to be much better than one?"

"Stop being noble," the tall sergeant said. "Someone's got to show you through the hills."

"I see what you mean," Nilson said.

It was simpler than he had thought it would be. You could neither hear nor see the enemy. They needed no pickets to hear tanks approaching or a plane.

The three moved upward over the dry hills, the soil crumbling under foot as they climbed, so that at the crest, the sergeants were bushed, panting in the heat and the altitude like animals, and even Nilson was sweating. In the moonlight below them and to the west and right, they could see the road.

"I guess this is where we get off," the tall sergeant said. "You better get going."

"All right," Nilson said. "I gotta get ready, though."

He undressed in the cloud-broken dark, until he sat there in his underwear, his socks and

---

3. **induction**\in ˈdək·shən\ formal enrolling into the armed services.

shoes and his dog tag.[4] The other sergeant handed him the canteen.

"I'll take a drink now," Nilson said, "and that'll have to hold me. The canteen's too heavy—"

"You take that canteen," the tall sergeant said. "You're gonna need it."

"Look," Nilson said, then stopped. He saw that they did not know about water and running or any violent exercise. You could be thirsty for an awfully long time without actually needing water, but this was no time to start explaining that to them. "Well," he said, "I'll go along then."

"Good luck," they said. They watched him move, still walking down the slope toward the road a half-mile away. They thought it was because he couldn't run down a slope that steep, but Nilson was walking until the water he had just drunk was out of his stomach and he could be fairly sure he wouldn't get a stitch when he started to run.

Watching him, the tall sergeant said, "You think he's gonna do any good?"

"No, I don't," the other sergeant said. "Even if he gets through their patrols, he'll drop before he gets to our people—or quit and go hide."

"What do you say that for?" the tall sergeant said.

"Because you're probably thinking the same thing I am!"

In the darkness, the tall sergeant nodded. "We both know we could go along, too, now and hide somewhere until this is over, because they're not going to get through tomorrow morning."

"But we go back, instead," the other sergeant said. "And I don't know why."

"I don't know why, either," the tall sergeant said.

Then they both turned and began to go back the way they had come.

Nearing the road, the sense of great adventure that Nilson had begun to know, started to leave him. Not fear but a sense of futility took him; a sense of his own littleness in the night

and the desert that was also the enemy's country. At the edge of the road he paused, although he could not tell exactly why and so attributed it to fear, long the conventional reason for all unknown hesitations or doubts. It was not fear, though, so much as an unwillingness to undergo one more futility.

He had not been a very good runner, and he was now thirty-one. Like most of the young men of the Scandinavian colonies in Brooklyn, he had run more because it was custom—tradition, among their people. He had liked it, too, although after almost fifteen years of little or no glory, he had unconsciously begun to feel that he was too old to keep losing that often, had begun to realize that, after a while, it did something to a man. Not that it was any fault of his; after all, you'd have to be pretty special to run well Saturdays or Sundays or any other day after being on your feet all day as a post-office clerk.

He still hesitated on the edge of the road; there was in his hesitation a quality that was close to sullenness, a vague, an even shadowy resentment against the long years of defeat.

Without quite knowing what the resentment was, he knew it was, if not wrong, at least inappropriate now and here. He sighed and at the edge of the road did a curious little exercise that relatives of his also had done— oh, say, three hundred years before in Norway. He bent over, touching his toes five or six times and each time straightening up and flinging his arms wide. The idea was to open up his lungs quickly and limber the muscles of his chest and arms. Although he was not a very good runner, he knew all about running; he knew a man ran as much with his arms as with his legs.

Then he stepped onto the road and in a reflective gesture pawed at the crude paving as though it were hard-packed cinders, and the heavy G.I.[5] shoes were the short-spiked ones

---

4. **dog tag,** a soldier's identification tag worn around the neck.

5. **G.I.,** government issue, official army uniform or material.

of the distance runner. He felt sheepish, and in the darkness his mouth twisted into a half-grin. Then he began to run.

Almost immediately he felt easier; felt confidence flow through him as though it were his blood; felt that now, at last, he was in his own country, or, perhaps more accurately, in his own medium. For there are mediums of action that vary with the individual; some people feel best moving in an automobile, others on a horse, a few running or flying.

More or less unconsciously, as he ran, he felt with his feet for the part of the tar-and-gravel road that was best suited to him. The road was slightly crowned in the center and in places pocked lightly by machine-gun bullets from the planes that had gone over it. As on most roads, he found that the shoulder was best suited for running. It was softer, the spike-less shoes slipped less on it, and the slightly more resilient quality of it would keep him from having shin-splints[6] tomorrow. He thought with irony—a new emotion for him—that it was of no importance whether he had

the little pains along the shin from bruising or pulling the tendons there that held the muscle to the bone. Certainly he would run no more tomorrow, come what might; indeed, there might not even be a tomorrow.

This started him thinking of what he called fear—because so many things were called fear—but what was really a saturation in himself of having for so many years done things to no purpose. He wondered if this, too, would be to no purpose; if some burial detail, an indefinite number of days from now, would find his shapeless and twisted body some place along this road.

Then came the thought, also new to him, that it would be worse to get to where he was going and not be believed. There was nothing he could think of to do about that though, so he stopped thinking of it. Like most Scandinavians, he was a fatalist, and the war had not helped him to overcome that.

---

6. **shin-splints,** injuries and inflammations of the feet sometimes experienced by distance runners.

He was running faster, now; too fast, he thought. He was breathing rather hard. It was rather early to be breathing so hard; but he knew that would pass soon, and the thing called second wind would come to him. He slackened his pace a little, feeling more, as he did so, the weight of the shoes and trying to reject the thought that was starting to come in him, before it took too much form; trying not to think of it.

He began to think of the enemy and where the enemy might be; all around him, to be sure, but probably not too near the road, because, by night, planes could see a road. Still, there might always be patrols that would know a man running steadily by night was a strange and perhaps a fearful thing. Still, they might never see him; only hear him and the pounding of his feet on the road. So, deviously, his mind came back to the thought he knew he had been trying to avoid, and now he could not avoid it any longer: there was only one thing to do, take the G.I. shoes off and run without them.

He slowed down gradually until he was walking and then he walked perhaps thirty yards before he stopped. Then he sat on the ground and took his shoes off.

When he stood up he hesitated again. Once, he had lost a shoe in a race and had finished the race, but the cinders hadn't been very good for his bare feet.

The road here was bad, but principally what he feared was stepping on one of the scorpions that they saw every day. He wondered if they were out by night—and then he began to run again.

Without knowing it, he moved at times in a kind of stupor. The nights of little or fitful sleep, the days of too little food and water, were beginning to affect him now, and he began to take refuge from exhaustion and pain in something at times close to unconsciousness.

Twice he passed tanks not far from the road, their crews sleeping, he himself not knowing he passed them. Like a dun ghost, he drifted with the short, more or less effortless stride he had developed over the long years of competi-

tion and training. These little spells of semi-consciousness could no longer occur, though; effort was too much to permit them, too sustained and by now even terrible. So that his senses became acute again, his thoughts long-ranging, sharp and filled with color. It was perhaps this return to full and acute consciousness, induced by pain, that saved him.

Some place there was sound and some place a dull shouting. He could not tell for a moment whether they were in his thoughts or in the reality of the night all around him. Then there came the sound now long familiar to him, but still terrible, of an automatic rifle coughing in the night.

The firing came again, a little farther away, but not near him. He neither heard nor felt bullets. With one of those sudden lifts of speed —but unconscious and desperate now—with which a distance runner sometimes tries to break the hearts of his opponents in the middle of the race, Nilson suddenly started to sprint.

The road ran downhill here, and now through the warm, dark night, the little man cut loose, letting his feet shoot out ahead of him, carrying his legs with the curious sort of controlled abandon of the cross-country runner going downhill.

He ran with an almost incredible lack of sound, although he was not aware of this. The shooting and the sound of guns continued behind him. With a faint pleasure, he realized that it must have been his passing that had alarmed the enemy.

There was, then, a sense of other-worldliness about him as he moved in the night. It made him aware of the strangeness of what he was trying to do. He found a new strength in his body; the legs, the rhythmically moving arms recovered the thing of which, in his boyhood, he and the others trying to be runners had made a fetish—the thing called form.

So, going downhill now, the enemy all around him, he experienced a sense of power, almost as though he were invisible, almost as though he were fleeter and stronger than anything that could seek to kill or hinder him.

Sweat bathed him, so that he glistened as though oiled, and there was a slight froth at his lips.

The road leveled under him, ran flat for perhaps a quarter-mile, then began to mount again. He was aware of this change only gradually. The change he was first aware of was in himself, first the mind, then the body. The sense of power or superhuman ability was gone, almost abruptly; then his lungs began to hurt badly, and the cords in his neck. He was, he suddenly realized, nothing special; he was Pete Nilson from Brooklyn, and he was bushed, he was just about done.

He shook his head, not unlike an animal trapped and bewildered. The desire, the need to stop was extraordinarily strong in him. He tried an old trick, for which he had no name: he tried to analyze his pain, knowing that this sometimes made it disappear. There was the pain in the lungs, in the throat, in the muscles of the eyes, but not yet where his arms went into the shoulders, not yet just above the knees where the thigh muscles overlapped.

His stride had shortened—as it must, uphill—his body leaned forward. He had not been above quitting in a few races in his life, when he was hopelessly outdistanced, when he had not been trained right, when he had not had enough rest the previous week to make him strong.

It seemed to him that he had never been so exhausted as now, and his mind sought for excuses to stop. Oddest and first, there came to him the thought that if he only knew how long he had run, he might endure it. Twenty-six miles, 385 yards—that was the distance of the Marathon, and in Boston, in Toronto[7] you always knew to within a few hundred yards how far you had come, how far you had to go. But now, no one knew or had known, not within four or five miles. The enemy was in the hills, and the hills were all around the lieutenant colonel and his men, and beyond the hills that held the enemy were more of your own men, some place. So late, oh, so very late in his life he learned that it is important to all men in their various endurings to see an end, to know a little bit about how far off an end is.

He was closer to being blind than he knew. He had started to deviate from a straight line, veering slightly from side to side. Although he did not know it, he was beyond the enemy, and all he had to combat was himself.

Some sort of anger formed in him: he could not tell its nature or its object. He realized it might even be at himself; then that it was at himself. He must have been crazy, he thought; he supposed that, all his life, his efforts had been directed obscurely and even deviously toward trying to achieve a sense of usefulness, corrupted sometimes into what was often called a sense of glory. And now that he was close to it, he had almost rejected it.

Why the change in him had occurred, the sudden insight, he might never know. He was on top of a hill, though, and looking down into a plain full of great shadows, and there was a paleness in the sky over the shadows. He was on top of this hill, but whether he was running or standing still, he might also never know, for it was just as great an effort to stand as to run.

He began to move downhill again, but still veering from side to side. He sensed, if he did not see, that there were no more hills beyond and he knew that his own people must be somewhere near, perhaps at the bottom of the hill he was now descending.

As he staggered, half-blind in the half-light, to the foot of the hill, he thought of the Athenian runner finishing the first Marathon[8] and as he collapsed, crying, "Rejoice, we conquer!" Nilson realized only now how much that image, those words had been with him, influencing him all his life. They heartened him now, sealed the sense of meaning in him.

---

7. **Toronto** also holds a marathon race.
8. **At Marathon,** some twenty-six miles from Athens, the Greeks defeated the Persians in 490 B.C. According to legend, **Pheidippides**\\'fai ▲dĭ·pĭ 'dēz\\ ran to Athens to bring news of the victory.

A sentry challenged him as the road leveled out into the plains, and Nilson, not knowing the password, figured that this was the place, if there ever was a place, for him to collapse. Pheidippides, finishing the first Marathon, had cried, "Rejoice, we conquer!" but Pete Nilson, thinking this, and finishing his own run, only said in a kind of prayer, "Hey, buddy, don't shoot," and knelt and quietly fell forward in the dust.

He didn't remember exactly what he said to them, but they took him with surprising quickness to another lieutenant colonel. And the miracle was not done yet. He could not believe it then; all the rest of his life, he could hardly believe it. They believed him: they believed him, and some place about him as he sat stupefied on a canvas stool in a tent, he heard all around him, in the first light, the sound of armor beginning to move, the clank and roar of the tanks.

A staff sergeant tried to explain to him. "Look," the sergeant said, "nobody comes down here in the shape you're in to lie to somebody else. You see?" Especially the feet, the sergeant thought.

But all Nilson did was sit on the canvas stool and stare.

"Look," the sergeant said again, "you'll get something big for this. Don't you catch?"

Nilson stared right at him. He was beginning to catch, but it would be a long time, if ever, before he could make anyone understand. The big thing, the most important thing in his life, was that he had come down here, without credentials of any sort, and they had believed him. The citation, the medal, nothing was ever going to mean that much.

"Look," the sergeant said. "They're getting you a doctor. You want anything now, though? Coffee or something?" Don't the guy know about his feet, he thought.

The little froth at his lips still, Nilson shook his head slightly. He looked like a madman, and the sergeant thought that maybe he was mad. But all Nilson was doing was sitting there listening to the roar—the clamor that was the

sound of salvation for a lot of men who couldn't hear it, yet—and thinking that he, Pete Nilson, had actually set it in motion. He didn't want anything right now, only to sit there and listen.

I

THE CONTINUITY OF EXPERIENCE

Through its reference to the Marathon race, this story suggests a continuity of human experience from Greek times down to the present. The exploit of the Greek runner Pheidippides has become a legend of self-sacrificing heroism. Although the present account of Peter Nilson's ordeal is a fictional one, it suggests that the spirit of such heroism survives in our own day. As long as there are wars, pressures will be brought to bear on individual soldiers, offering them the opportunity to respond with courage or with weakness.

II

IMPLICATIONS

A. The outcome of this story is delayed until the last few minutes. The author maintains suspense by raising doubts about Nilson's chances of success. What does each of the following quotations from the story tell you about his chances?

1. " 'Still,' the officer said, 'you're the best we have. Good luck.' "

2. " 'No, I don't,' the other sergeant said. 'Even if he gets through their patrols, he'll drop before he gets to our people—or quit and go hide.' "

3. "Not fear but a sense of futility took him; a sense of his own littleness in the night and the desert that was also the enemy's country."

4. "He wondered if this, too, would be to no purpose; if some burial detail, an indefinite number of days from now, would find his shapeless and twisted body some place along this road."

5. "It seemed to him that he had never been so exhausted as now, and his mind sought for excuses to stop."

6. "Some sort of anger formed in him. . . . He realized it might even be at himself; then that it was at himself. . . . all his life, his efforts had been directed obscurely and even deviously toward trying to achieve a sense of usefulness. . . . And now that he was close to it, he had almost rejected it."

B. Three of the quotations above reveal a struggle in Nilson separate from the physical struggles of his ordeal. Understanding what it is will help you form an opinion about the following statements. Give your reasons for supporting or disagreeing with them.

1. The real pressure that Nilson is fighting against is not physical but mental. It is his sense of continuous failure.

2. A man needs to know how far he has gone and how far he has yet to go in order to endure fatigue.

3. The fact that they believe him when he arrives is more important to Peter than the fact of his having got there at all. Their belief restores to him his self-respect.

4. When a man is under a great strain, his body dominates his mind.

III
TECHNIQUES

Theme

The theme of this story might be stated as a man's response to pressures of personal anxiety under conditions of war. Nowhere in the story is it mentioned where the war is taking place, who the enemy are, or even what war it is. What do you think the author is implying about his theme by omitting these specific details?

Style

Compare the style of writing in "Going to Run All Night" with the style in "The Open Window." Which is more like a newspaper account of the happenings? Without rereading either of the stories, decide which has left a more vivid impression on your mind. What connection is there between the sharpness of impression and the kind of language in the two stories? Try to explain the effect that the style in each had on your response to the story.

Identification

"Going to Run All Night" is the story of an ordeal. Few of its readers ever have or ever will go through a comparable experience, and yet it is almost impossible not to identify with Peter Nilson as he undertakes his task. What reactions did you have to the following elements of his experience, and how did that reaction lead you to identify yourself with him?

1. His immediate willingness to try the run.

2. His fear of failing.

3. His physical suffering.

Most people have a secret desire to perform, just once in their lives, some heroic deed. If you have ever experienced this desire, how do you think it affected your feelings about Peter Nilson?

IV
WORDS

A. Using words figuratively with originality and appropriateness is basic to vocabulary growth. In "The Open Window" a character assumes that "total strangers are *hungry* for details." What does the word *hungry* suggest? Comment on the effectiveness of the following expressions. What associations do the words convey? What figure, if any, is used?

> whirl of apologies; self-possessed young girl of fifteen; danger which intermittently killed some of them; sweat bathed him; road levelled under him; controlled abandon; shook his head not unlike an animal trapped and bewildered.

B. From context determine the meaning of the italicized words:

1. flatter the niece without unduly *discounting* the aunt that was to come.

2. He was preparing to *migrate* to this retreat.

3. It was certainly an unfortunate *coincidence* that he should have paid his visit on this tragic anniversary.

4. He was driven to the *incredible* conclusion that finally and at last he had come to be of value. . . . He ran with an almost *incredible* lack of sound.

5. We can break at dawn, if we can *synchronize* our attack with some sort of aid coming from our main forces.

C. What do the roots in the following pairs of words mean: *progress-succession* ("a succession of total strangers"); *immigrant-migrate* ("to migrate to this rural retreat"); *reduction-introduction* ("letters of introduction"); *geology-apology* ("a whirl of apologies for being late"); *annual-anniversary* ("his visit on this tragic anniversary"); *illusion-delusion* ("the tolerably widespread delusion that total strangers and chance acquaintances are hungry for the least detail of one's ailments"); *elision-collision* ("to avoid imminent collision").

In the reading so far in this section,
the pressures coming to bear on individuals
have been fairly direct and simple. There was
the pressure of great fatigue, the pressure
of suggestion, the pressure to achieve.
However, pressures are often built
out of a complex series of little factors,
as illustrated in the skillfully written essay
that follows. It narrates an actual experience
of the writer, George Orwell,
when he was serving as a police officer
in Burma during his youth.

Shooting an Elephant

G E O R G E   O R W E L L

In Moulmein,[1] in lower Burma, I was hated by large numbers of people—the only time in my life that I have been important enough for this to happen to me. I was subdivisional police officer of the town, and in an aimless, petty kind of way an anti-European feeling was very bitter. No one had the guts to raise a riot, but if a European woman went through the bazaars[2] alone somebody would probably spit betel juice over her dress. As a police officer I was an obvious target and was baited whenever it seemed safe to do so. When a nimble Burman tripped me up on the football[3] field and the referee (another Burman) looked the other way, the crowd yelled with hideous laughter. This happened more than once. In the end the sneering yellow faces of young men that met me everywhere, the insults hooted after me when I was at a safe distance, got badly on my nerves. The young Buddhist priests were the worst of all. There were several thousands of them in the town and none of them seemed to have anything to do except

stand on street corners and jeer at Europeans.

All this was perplexing and upsetting. For at that time I had already made up my mind that imperialism was an evil thing and the sooner I chucked up my job and got out of it the better. Theoretically—and secretly, of course—I was all for the Burmese and all against their oppressors, the British. As for the job I was doing, I hated it more bitterly than I can perhaps make clear. In a job like that you see the dirty work of Empire at close quarters. The wretched prisoners huddling in the stinking cages of the lockups, the gray, cowed faces of the long-term convicts, the scarred buttocks of men who had been flogged with bamboos—all these oppressed me with an intolerable sense of guilt. But I could get nothing into perspective. I was young and ill-educated and I had to think out my problems in the utter silence that is imposed on every Englishman in the East. I did not know that the British Empire is dying, still less did I know that it is a great deal better than the younger empires that are going to supplant it. All I knew was that I was stuck between my hatred of the empire I served and my rage against the evil-spirited little beasts who tried to make my job impossible. With one part of my mind I thought of the British Raj as an unbreakable tyranny, as something clamped down, in *saecula saeculorum*,[4] upon the will of prostrate peoples; with another part I thought that the greatest joy in the world would be to drive a bayonet into a Buddhist priest's guts. Feelings like these are the normal by-product of imperialism; ask any Anglo-Indian[5] official, if you can catch him off duty.

---

1. **Moulmein**\ˈmūl ˈmān\ a coastal city.
2. **bazaar**\bə ˈzar\ an oriental market consisting of many shops and stalls. The **betel**\ˈbē·təl\ **palm,** an Asiatic palm whose leaves and nuts are chewed much as Americans chew gum.
3. **football,** Orwell means the game we usually call "soccer."
4. **Raj**\raj\ rule, domination. **In saecula saeculorum** \ˈsai·kyu·la ˈsai·kyu ˈlō·rəm\ "forever and forever."
5. **Anglo-Indian,** designating or pertaining to an Englishman serving in Indian or adjacent areas.

One day something happened which in a roundabout way was enlightening. It was a tiny incident in itself, but it gave me a better glimpse than I had had before of the real nature of imperialism—the real motives for which despotic governments act. Early one morning the sub-inspector at a police station the other end of the town rang me up on the phone and said that an elephant was ravaging the bazaar. Would I please come and do something about it? I did not know what I could do, but I wanted to see what was happening and I got onto a pony and started out. I took my rifle, an old .44 Winchester and much too small to kill an elephant, but I thought the noise might be useful *in terrorem.*[6] Various Burmans stopped me on the way and told me about the elephant's doings. It was not, of course, a wild elephant, but a tame one which had gone "must."[7] It had been chained up, as tame elephants always are when their attack of "must" is due, but on the previous night it had broken its chain and escaped. Its mahout,[8] the only person who could manage it when it was in that state, had set out in pursuit, but had taken the wrong direction and was now twelve hours' journey away, and in the morning the elephant had suddenly reappeared in the town. The Burmese population had no weapons and were quite helpless against it. It had already destroyed somebody's bamboo hut, killed a cow, and raided some fruit stalls and devoured the stock; also it had met the municipal rubbish van and, when the driver jumped out and took to his heels, had turned the van over and inflicted violences upon it.

The Burmese sub-inspector and some Indian constables were waiting for me in the quarter where the elephant had been seen. It was a very poor quarter, a labyrinth of squalid huts, thatched with palm leaf, winding all over a steep hillside. I remember it was a cloudy, stuffy morning at the beginning of the rains. We began questioning the people where the elephant had gone and, as usual, failed to get any definite information. That is invariably the case in the East; a story always sounds clear enough at a distance, but the nearer you get to the scene of events the vaguer it becomes. Some of the people said that the elephant had gone in one direction, some said that it had gone in another, some professed not even to have heard of any elephant. I had made up my mind that the whole story was a pack of lies, when I heard yells a little distance away. There was a loud, scandalized cry of "Go away, child! Go away this instant!" and an old woman with a switch in her hand came round the corner of a hut, violently shooing away a crowd of naked children. Some more women followed, clicking their tongues and exclaiming; evidently there was something the children ought not to have seen. I rounded the hut and saw a man's dead body sprawling in the mud. He was an Indian, a black Dravidian coolie,[9] almost naked, and he could not have been dead many minutes. The people said that the elephant had come suddenly upon him round the corner of the hut, caught him with its trunk, put its foot on his back, and ground him into the earth. This was the rainy season and the ground was soft, and his face had scored a trench a foot deep and a couple of yards long. He was lying on his belly with his arms crucified and head sharply twisted to one side. His face was coated with mud, the eyes wide open, the teeth bared and grinning with an unendurable agony. (Never tell me, by the way, that the dead look peaceful. Most of the corpses I have seen looked devilish.) The friction of the great beast's foot had stripped the skin from his back as neatly as one skins a rabbit. As soon as I saw the dead man I sent an orderly to a friend's house nearby to borrow an elephant rifle. I had already sent back the pony, not wanting it to go mad with fright and throw me if it smelt the elephant.

---

6. **.44**, a rifle of moderate caliber. **In terrorem**\ĭn tĕ ˈrō·rĕm\ "in case of fright."
7. **must**\mŭst\ frenzied and out of control.
8. **mahout**\ma ˈhaut\ an elephant driver and tender.
9. **Dravidian**\drə ˈvĭ·dē·ən\ the ancient inhabitants of southern India. **coolie**\ˈkū·lē\ a Far Eastern laborer.

In Burma the elephant is a vital factor in the teakwood industry. Here, a mother and a baby and their keeper arrive in the forest for a day's labor.

The orderly came back in a few minutes with a rifle and five cartridges, and meanwhile some Burmans had arrived and told us that the elephant was in the paddy[10] fields below, only a few hundred yards away. As I started forward practically the whole yellow population of the quarter flocked out of the houses and followed me. They had seen the rifle and were all shouting excitedly that I was going to shoot the elephant. They had not shown much interest in the elephant when he was merely ravaging their homes, but it was different now that he was going to be shot. It was a bit of fun to them, as it would be to an English crowd; besides they wanted the meat. It made me vaguely uneasy. I had no intention of shooting

the elephant—I had merely sent for the rifle to defend myself if necessary—and it is always unnerving to have a crowd following you. I marched down the hill, looking and feeling a fool, with the rifle over my shoulder and an ever growing army of people jostling at my heels. At the bottom, when you got away from the huts, there was a metaled road[11] and beyond that a miry waste of paddy fields a thousand yards across, not yet plowed but soggy from the first rains and dotted with coarse grass. The elephant was standing eight yards from

---

10. **paddy**\ˈpă·dē\ rice fields.
11. **metaled road,** one with surfaces reinforced with metal strips or slabs.

the road, his left side toward us. He took not the slightest notice of the crowd's approach. He was tearing up bunches of grass, beating them against his knees to clean them, and stuffing them into his mouth.

I had halted on the road. As soon as I saw the elephant I knew with perfect certainty that I ought not to shoot him. It is a serious matter to shoot a working elephant—it is comparable to destroying a huge and costly piece of machinery—and obviously one ought not to do it if it can possibly be avoided. And at that distance, peacefully eating, the elephant looked no more dangerous than a cow. I thought then and I think now that his attack of "must" was already passing off; in which case he would merely wander harmlessly about until the mahout came back and caught him. Moreover, I did not want in the least to shoot him. I decided that I would watch him a little while to make sure that he did not turn savage again, and then go home.

But at that moment I glanced round at the crowd that had followed me. It was an immense crowd, two thousand at the least and growing every minute. It blocked the road for a long distance on either side. I looked at the sea of yellow faces above the garish clothes—faces all happy and excited over this bit of fun, all certain that the elephant was going to be shot. They were watching me as they would watch a conjurer about to perform a trick. They did not like me, but with the magical rifle in my hand I was momentarily worth watching. And suddenly I realized that I would have to shoot the elephant after all. The people expected it of me and I had got to do it; I could feel their two thousand wills pressing me forward irresistibly. And it was at this moment, as I stood there with the rifle in my hands, that I first grasped the hollowness, the futility of the white man's dominion in the East. Here was I, the white man with his gun, standing in front of the unarmed crowd—seemingly the leading actor of the piece; but in reality I was only an absurd puppet pushed to and fro by the will of those yellow faces behind. I perceived in this moment that when the white man turns tyrant it is his own freedom that he destroys. He becomes a sort of hollow, posing dummy, the conventionalized figure of a sahib.[12] For it is the condition of his rule that he shall spend his life in trying to "impress the natives," and so in every crisis he has got to do what the "natives" expect of him. He wears a mask, and his face grows to fit it. I had got to shoot the elephant. I had committed myself to doing it when I sent for the rifle. A sahib has got to act like a sahib; he has got to appear resolute, to know his own mind and do definite things. To come all that way, rifle in hand, with two thousand people marching at my heels, and then to trail feebly away, having done nothing—no, that was impossible. The crowd would laugh at me. And my whole life, every white man's in the East, was one long struggle not to be laughed at.

But I did not want to shoot the elephant. I watched him beating his bunch of grass against his knees, with that preoccupied grandmotherly air that elephants have. It seemed to me that it would be murder to shoot him. At that age I was not squeamish about killing animals, but I had never shot an elephant and never wanted to. (Somehow it always seems worse to kill a large animal.) Besides, there was the beast's owner to be considered. Alive, the elephant was worth at least a hundred pounds; dead, he would only be worth the value of his tusks, five pounds, possibly. But I had got to act quickly. I turned to the experienced-looking Burmans who had been there when we arrived, and asked them how the elephant had been behaving. They all said the same thing; he took no notice of you if you left him alone, but he might charge if you went too close to him.

It was perfectly clear to me what I ought to do. I ought to walk up to within, say, twenty-five yards of the elephant and test his behavior. If he charged, I could shoot; if he took no notice of me, it would be safe to leave him until

---

12. **sahib**\ˈsä·ĭb\ a European master or gentleman.

the mahout came back. But I also knew that I was going to do no such thing. I was a poor shot with a rifle and the ground was soft mud into which one would sink at every step. If the elephant charged and I missed him, I should have about as much chance as a toad under a steam roller. But even then I was not thinking particularly of my own skin, only of the watchful yellow faces behind. For at that moment, with the crowd watching me, I was not afraid in the ordinary sense, as I would have been if I had been alone. A white man mustn't be frightened in front of "natives"; and so, in general, he isn't frightened. The thought in my mind was that if anything went wrong those two thousand Burmans would see me pursued, caught, trampled on, and reduced to a grinning corpse like that Indian up the hill. And if that happened it was quite probable that some of them would laugh. That would never do. There was only one alternative. I shoved the cartridges into the magazine and lay down on the road to get a better aim.

The crowd grew very still, and a deep, low, happy sigh, as of people who see the theater curtain go up at last, breathed from innumerable throats. They were going to have their bit of fun after all. The rifle was a beautiful German thing with cross-hair sights. I did not know then that in shooting an elephant one would shoot to cut an imaginary bar running from earhole to earhole. I ought, therefore, as the elephant was sideways on, to have aimed straight at his earhole; actually I aimed several inches in front of this, thinking the brain would be further forward.

When I pulled the trigger I did not hear the bang or feel the kick—one never does when a shot goes home—but I heard the devilish roar of glee that went up from the crowd. In that instant, in too short a time, one would have thought, even for the bullet to get there, a mysterious, terrible change had come over the elephant. He neither stirred nor fell, but every line of his body had altered. He looked suddenly stricken, shrunken, immensely old, as though the frightful impact of the bullet had

paralyzed him without knocking him down. At last, after what seemed a long time—it might have been five seconds, I dare say—he sagged flabbily to his knees. His mouth slobbered. An enormous senility seemed to have settled upon him. One could have imagined him thousands of years old. I fired again into the same spot. At the second shot he did not collapse but climbed with desperate slowness to his feet and stood weakly erect, with legs sagging and head drooping. I fired a third time. That was the shot that did for him. You could see the agony of it jolt his whole body and knock the last remnant of strength from his legs. But in falling he seemed for a moment to rise, for as his hind legs collapsed beneath him he seemed to tower upward like a huge rock toppling, his trunk reaching skywards like a tree. He trumpeted for the first and only time. And then down he came, his belly toward me, with a crash that seemed to shake the ground even where I lay.

I got up. The Burmans were already racing past me across the mud. It was obvious that the elephant would never rise again, but he was not dead. He was breathing very rhythmically with long rattling gasps, his great mound of a side painfully rising and falling. His mouth was wide open—I could see far down into caverns of pink throat. I waited a long time for him to die, but his breathing did not weaken. Finally I fired my two remaining shots into the spot where I thought his heart must be. The thick blood welled out of him like red velvet, but still he did not die. His body did not even jerk when the shots hit him, the tortured breathing continued without a pause. He was dying, very slowly and in great agony, but in some world remote from me where not even a bullet could damage him further. I felt that I had got to put an end to that dreadful noise. It seemed dreadful to see the great beast lying there, powerless to move and yet powerless to die, and not even to be able to finish him. I sent back for my small rifle and poured shot after shot into his heart and down his throat. They seemed to make no impression. The tortured gasps continued as steadily as the ticking of a clock.

In the end I could not stand it any longer and went away. I heard later that it took him half an hour to die. Burmans were bringing dahs[13] and baskets even before I left, and I was told they had stripped his body almost to the bones by afternoon.

Afterwards, of course, there were endless discussions about the shooting of the elephant. The owner was furious, but he was only an Indian and could do nothing. Besides, legally I had done the right thing, for a mad elephant has to be killed, like a mad dog, if its owner fails to control it. Among the Europeans, opinion was divided. The older men said I was right, the younger men said it was a shame to shoot an elephant for killing a coolie, because an elephant was worth more than any Coringhee[14] coolie. And afterwards I was very glad that the coolie had been killed; it put me legally in the right and gave me a sufficient pretext for shooting the elephant. I often wondered whether any of the others grasped that I had done it solely to avoid looking a fool.

I
THE PUBLIC AND THE PRIVATE LIFE

In this essay, George Orwell makes clear the conflicts that may confront a man who lives in a world of political and cultural tensions. Orwell is, first of all, a person of strong private principles and sympathies. But he is also a police official whose role is a public one. Furthermore, he is a European among Eastern peoples, a member of a powerful ruling minority. He is one man living several lives. An elephant gone mad suddenly brings his public life into direct conflict with his private one, and he finds that one must yield to the other.

II
IMPLICATIONS

1. To see clearly the conflict forced upon Orwell, define the pressures caused by the following:

---

13. **dahs**\daz\ bowls.
14. **Coringhee**\kō ˈrĭŋ·gē\ Southern Indian.

a. His attitude toward the British Empire.

b. The nature of his relationship with the people of Burma.

c. His feelings about the elephant itself.

2. How do the following quotations show the conflicting pressures of the situation?

a. "I was hated by large numbers of people—the only time in my life that I have been important enough for this to happen to me."

b. "The insults hooted after me when I was at a safe distance got badly on my nerves."

c. "I was stuck between my hatred of the empire I served and my rage against the evil-spirited little beasts who tried to make my job impossible."

d. "I could feel their two thousand wills pressing me forward irresistibly."

e. "And my whole life, every white man's in the East, was one long struggle not to be laughed at."

f. "But I did not want to shoot the elephant."

III
TECHNIQUES

Theme

An essay such as "Shooting an Elephant" is held together by a theme in much the same way that a short story is. The theme is revealed through the crucial events in the experience. Orwell is showing that a man is not always free to choose his course of action. From the essay, outline the specific events which build up to force him to act as he does.

Style

George Orwell was one of the most skillful and respected essayists of recent times. To see one of his stylistic devices, choose from the first two paragraphs half a dozen unexpected phrases like "No one had the guts to . . ." that are almost slang expressions. What qualities does the inclusion of such phrases give to the writing? Does it make it more or less formal? Does it make Orwell's experiences more or less immediate to the reader? Why?

Identification

Because the situation in this essay is a complicated one, and because George Orwell is a complicated person, a reader's feelings about him are likely not to be simple. Briefly list those qualities in his personality that you find admirable. Then list those that you find offensive or unsympathetic. How would you sum up your opinion of him?

There he hung shivering and past knowing
what more he could ever do.

The
Vertical Ladder

WILLIAM SANSOM

As he felt the first watery eggs of sweat
moistening the palms of his hands, as with
every rung higher his body seemed to weigh
more heavily, this young man, Flegg, regretted
in sudden desperation, but still in vain, the
irresponsible events that had thrust him into
his present precarious climb. Here he was, isolated on a vertical iron ladder flat to the side
of a gas tank, and bound now to climb higher
and higher until he reached the vertiginous[1]
skyward summit.

How could he ever have wished this on himself? How easy it had been to laugh away his
cautionary fears on the firm ground! Now he
would give the very hands that clung to the
ladder for a safe conduct to solid earth.

It had been a strong spring day, abruptly as
warm as midsummer. The sun flooded the
parks and streets with sudden heat—Flegg
and his friends had felt stifled in their thick
winter clothes. The green glare of the new
leaves everywhere struck the eye too fiercely,
the air seemed almost sticky from the exhalations of buds and swelling resins. Cold winter
senses were overcome—the girls had complained of headaches, and their thoughts had
grown confused and as uncomfortable as the
wool underneath against their skins. They had
wandered out from the park by a back gate
into an area of back streets.

The houses there were small and old, some
of them already falling into disrepair; short
streets, cobbles,[2] narrow sidewalks, and the
only shops a tobacconist or a desolate drugstore to color the gray—it was the outcrop of
some industrial undertaking beyond. At first
these quiet, almost deserted streets had
seemed more restful than the park; but soon a
dusty air of peeling plaster and powdering
brick, the dark windows and the dry stone
steps, the very dryness altogether, had proved
more wearying than before, so that when suddenly the houses had ended and the ground
had opened to reveal the yards of a disused
gasworks, Flegg and his friends had welcomed
the green of nettles and milkwort that grew
among the scrap iron and broken brick.

They walked out into the wasteland, the
two girls and Flegg and the other two boys,
and stood presently before the old gas tank
itself. Among the ruined sheds this was the
only structure still whole; it still predominated
over the yards, towering high above other
buildings for hundreds of feet around. So
they threw bricks against its rusted sides.

The rust flew off in flakes, and the iron rang
dully. Flegg, who wished to excel in the eyes
of the dark-haired girl, began throwing bricks
higher than the others, at the same time lob-
bing them, to suggest that he knew something
of grenade throwing, claiming for himself
vicariously the glamour of a uniform. He felt
the girl's eyes follow his shoulders; his shoulders broadened. She had black eyes, un-
shadowed beneath short, wide-awake lids, as
bright as a boy's eyes; her lips pouted with
difficulty over a scramble of irregular teeth, so
that it often looked as if she were laughing;
she always frowned, and Flegg liked her earnest, purposeful expression. Altogether she
seemed a wide-awake girl, who would be the
first to appreciate an active sort of man. Now
she frowned and shouted, "Bet you can't climb
as high as you can throw!"

From THE STORIES OF WILLIAM SANSOM by William
Sansom, by permission of Atlantic-Little, Brown and Co.
Copyright © 1960 by William Sansom.

1. **vertiginous**\vər ᵃtĭj·ə·nəs\ causing dizziness.
2. **cobbles**, cobblestones with which the streets were
paved.

Then there began one of those uneasy jokes, innocent at first, that, taken seriously, can accumulate a hysterical volume of spite. Everyone recognizes this underlying unpleasantness—it is plainly felt. But just because of this, the joke must at all costs be pressed forward; one becomes frightened, one laughs all the louder, pressing to drown the embarrassments of danger and guilt.

The third boy shouted instantly, "Course he can't. He can't climb no higher than himself." Flegg turned round, scoffing, so that the girl shouted again, laughing shrilly and pointing upward. Already all five of them felt uneasy. Then in quick succession, all in a few seconds, the third boy repeated, "Course he can't." Flegg said, "Climb to the top of anything." The other boy said, "Climb to the top of my Aunt Fanny." The girl said, "Climb to the top of the gas tank then."

Flegg said, "That's nothing." And the girl, pressing on then as she had to, suddenly introduced the inevitable detail that made these suppositions into fact: "Go on then, climb it. Here—tie my hanky on the top. Tie my flag on the top."

Even then Flegg had a second's chance. It occurred to him instantly that he could laugh it off; but hysterical emphasis now possessed the girl's face—she was dancing up and down and clapping her hands insistently—and this confused Flegg. He began stuttering after the right words. But the words refused to come. At all costs he had to cover his stuttering. So: "Off we go then!" he said. And he turned to the gas tank.

It was not, after all, so very high. It was hardly a full-sized tank, its trellised[3] iron top-rail would have stood level with the roof coping[4] of a five- or six-story tenement. Until then Flegg had seen the gas tank as a rough mass of iron, but now every detail sprang into abrupt definition. He studied it intently, alertly considering its size and every feature of stability: the brown, rusted iron sheeting smeared here and there with red lead; a curious buckling that sometimes deflated its curved bulk,

as though a vacuum were collapsing it from within; the ladders scaling the sides flush with the sheeting; the grid of girders, a complexity of struts,[5] the bolting.

There were two ladders, one Jacob's ladder[6] clamped fast to the side, another that was more of a staircase, zigzagging up the belly of the tank in easy gradients[7] and provided with a safety rail. This must have been erected later as a substitute for the Jacob's ladder, which demanded an unnecessarily stringent climb and was now in fact in disuse, for some twenty feet of its lower rungs had been torn away. However, there was apparently some painting in progress, for a painter's wooden ladder had been propped beneath with its top reaching to the undamaged bottom of the vertical ladder —the ascent was thus serviceable again. Flegg looked quickly at the foot of the wooden ladder—was it well grounded?—and then at its top farther up—was this secure?—and then way to the top, screwing his eyes to note any fault in the iron rungs reaching innumerably and indistinctly to the summit platform.

Flegg, rapidly assessing these structures, never stopped sauntering forward. He was committed, and so while deliberately sauntering to appear thus the more at ease, he knew that he must never hesitate. The two boys and his own girl kept up a chorus of encouraging abuse. "How I climbed Mount Everest," they shouted. "He'll come down quicker'n he went up." "Mind you don't bang your head on a harp, Sir Galahad."[8] But the second girl had remained quiet throughout; she was already frightened, sensing instantly that the guilt for some tragedy was hers alone—although she never had opened her mouth. Now she chewed passionately on gum that kept her jaws firm and circling.

Suddenly the chorus rose shriller. Flegg had

---

3. **trellised**\ˈtrĕl·əst\ having a frame of latticework.
4. **coping**\ˈkō·piŋ\ a finishing cap to a wall.
5. **struts,** bars for bracing.
6. **Jacob's ladder,** a flat ladder with iron rungs.
7. **gradients**\ˈgrād·ē·əntz\ angles of slope.
8. **Sir Galahad,** a knight of King Arthur's Round Table. In this context the name means gentlemanly.

veered slightly toward the safer staircase. His eyes naturally had questioned this along with the rest of the gas tank, and almost unconsciously his footsteps had veered in the direction of his eyes. Then this instinct had emerged into full consciousness: perhaps he could use the staircase—no one actually had mentioned the Jacob's ladder; there might yet be a chance. But the quick eyes behind him had seen, and immediately the chorus rose: "No, you don't!" "Not up those sissy stairs!"

Flegg switched his course by only the fraction that turned him again to the perpendicular ladder. "Who's talking about stairs?" he shouted back.

Behind him they still kept up a din, still kept up to pitch, worrying at him viciously. "Look at him, he doesn't know which way to go—he's like a duck's uncle without an aunt."

So that Flegg realized finally there was no alternative. He had to climb the tank by the vertical ladder. And as soon as this was finally settled, the doubt cleared from his mind. He braced his shoulders and suddenly found himself really making light of the job. "After all," he thought, "it isn't so high. Why should I worry? Hundreds of men climb such ladders every day, no one falls, the ladders are clamped as safe as houses." He began to smile within himself at his earlier perturbations.

Added to this, the girl now ran up to him and handed him her handkerchief. As her black eyes frowned a smile at him, he saw that her expression no longer held its vicious, laughing scorn, but had grown softer, with a look of real encouragement and even admiration. "Here's your flag," she said. And then she even added, "Tell you what—you don't really have to go! I'll believe you!" But this came too late. Flegg had accepted the climb—it was fact, and already he felt something of an exhilarating glow of glory. He took the handkerchief, blew the girl a dramatic kiss, and started up the lowest rungs of the wooden ladder at a run.

This painter's ladder was placed at a comfortable slant. Nevertheless, Flegg had climbed only some ten feet—what might correspond to the top of a first-floor window—when he began to slow up; he stopped running and gripped harder at the rungs above and placed his feet more firmly on the unseen bars below. Although he had not yet measured his distance from the ground, somehow he sensed distinctly that he was already unnaturally high, with nothing but air and a precarious skeleton of wooden bars between him and the receding ground. He felt independent of solid support; yet, according to his eyes, which stared straight forward at the iron sheeting, he might have been still standing on the lowest rungs by the ground. The sensation of height infected him strongly; it had become an urgent necessity to maintain a balance; each muscle of his body became unnaturally alert. This was not an unpleasant feeling; he almost enjoyed a new athletic command of every precarious movement. He climbed then methodically until he reached the ladder top and the first of the perpendicular iron rungs.

Here for a moment Flegg paused. He rested his knees against the last three steps of the safely slanting wooden ladder; he grasped the two side supports of the rusted iron that led so straightly upward. His knees then clung to the motherly wood; his hands felt the iron cold and gritty. The rust powdered off and smeared him with its red, and one large scrap flaked off and fell onto his face as he looked upward. He wanted to brush this away from his eye, but the impulse was, to his surprise, much less powerful than the vicelike will that clutched his hand to the iron support. His hand remained firmly gripping the iron; he had to shake off the rust flake with a jerk of his head. Even then, this sharp movement nearly unbalanced him, and his stomach gulped coldly with sudden shock. He settled his knees more firmly against the wood; and though he forced himself to laugh at this sudden fear, so that in some measure his poise did really return, nevertheless he did not alter the awkward knock-kneed position of his legs patently clinging for safety. With all this, he had scarcely paused. Now he pulled at the stanchions[9] of the iron ladder; they were as firm as if they had been driven into rock.

He looked up, following the dizzying rise of the rungs to the skyline. From this angle, flat against the iron sheeting, the gas tank appeared higher than before. The blue sky seemed to descend and almost touch it. The redness of the rust dissolved into a deepening gray shadow; the distant, curved summit loomed black and high. Although it was immensely stable, as seen in rounded perspective from a few yards away, there against the side it appeared top-heavy, so that this huge segment of sheet iron seemed to have lost the support of its invisible complement behind—the support that was now unseen and therefore unfelt—and Flegg imagined despite himself that the entire erection had become unsteady, that quite possibly the gas tank might suddenly blow over like a gigantic, top-heavy sail. He lowered his eyes quickly and concentrated on the hands gripped on the ladder before him. He began to climb.

From below, there still rose a few cries from the boys. But the girl had stopped shouting— probably she was following Flegg's every step with admiring eyes. He imagined again her frown and her peculiarly pouting mouth, and from this image drew new strength with which he clutched the rungs more eagerly. But now he noticed that the cries had begun to ring with an unpleasant new echo, as though they were already far off. And Flegg could not so easily distinguish their words. Even at this height he seemed to have penetrated into a distinct stratum[10] of separate air, for it was certainly cooler, and for the first time that day he felt the light fanning of a wind.

He looked down. His friends appeared shockingly small. Their bodies had disappeared, and he saw only their upturned faces. He wanted to wave to demonstrate in some way a carefree attitude; but then instantly he felt frustrated as his hands refused to unlock their grip. He turned to the rungs again, with the smile dying on his lips.

He swallowed uneasily and continued to tread slowly upward, hand after hand, foot after foot. He had climbed ten rungs of the iron ladder when his hands first began to feel moist; when suddenly, as though a catastrophe had overtaken him not gradually but in one overpowering second, he realized that he was afraid—incontrovertibly. He could conceal it no longer; he admitted it all over his body. His hands gripped with pitiable eagerness; they were now alert to a point of shivering, as though the nerves inside them had been forced taut for so long that now they had burst beyond their strained tegument.[11] His feet no longer trod firmly on the rungs beneath, but first stepped for their place timorously, then glued themselves to the iron. In this way his body lost much of its poise; these nerves and muscles in his two legs and two arms seemed to work independently, no longer integrated with the rhythm of his body, but moving with the dangerous, the unwilled jerk of crippled limbs.

His body hung slack away from the ladder, with nothing beneath it but a thirty-foot drop to the ground; only his hands and feet were fed with the security of an attachment—most of him lay off the ladder, hanging in space. His arms revolted at the strain of their unfamiliar angle, as though they were flies' feet denying all natural laws. For the first time, as the fear took hold of him, he felt that what he had attempted was impossible. He never could achieve the top. If at this height of only thirty feet—as it were, three stories of a building— he felt afraid, what would he feel at sixty feet? Yet he trod heavily up. He was afraid, but not desperate. He dreaded each step, yet forced himself to believe that at some time it would be over; it could not take long.

A memory crossed his mind. It occurred vividly, then flashed away, for his eyes and mind were continually concentrated on the

---

9. **stanchions**\ˈstăn·chənz\ upright bars of the ladder.
10. **stratum**\ˈstrāt·əm\ a layer.
11. **tegument**\ˈtĕg·yə·mənt\ covering.

rusted iron bars and white knuckles of his hands. But for an instant he remembered waking up long ago in the nursery and seeing that the windows were light, as if they reflected a coldness of moonlight. Only they were not so much lit by light as by a sensation of space. The windows seemed to echo with space. He crawled out of bed and climbed onto a chair that stood below the window. It was as he had thought: outside there was space, nothing else—a limitless area of space. Yet this was not unnatural, for soon his logical eyes supplied for what had at first appeared an impossible infinity the later image of a perfectly reasonable flood. A vast plain of still water continued as far as his eyes could see. The tennis courts and the houses beyond had disappeared; they were quite submerged. Motionless water spread out immeasurably to the distant arched horizon all around. It lapped silently at the sides of the house, and in the light of an unseen moon winked and washed darkly, concealing great beasts of mystery beneath its black, calm surface.

This water attracted him; he wished to jump into it from the window and immerse himself in it and allow his head to sink slowly under. However, he was perched too high. He felt, alone at the window, infinitely high, so that the flood seemed to lie in miniature at a great distance below, as later in life when he was ill he saw the objects of his bedroom grow small and infinitely remote in the fevered reflection behind his eyes. Isolated at the little window, he was frightened by the emptiness surrounding him—only the sky and the water and the marooned stone wall of the house. He was terrified, yet drawn down by dread and desire.

Then a battleship sailed by. He awakened, saved by the appearance of the battleship. And now, on the ladder, he had a sudden hope that something as large and stable would intervene again to help him.

But ten rungs farther up he began to sweat more violently than ever. His hands streamed with wet rust, the flesh inside his thighs blenched. Another flake of rust fell on his fore-

head; this time it stuck in the wetness. He felt physically exhausted. Fear was draining all his strength, and the precarious position of his body demanded an awkward physical effort. From his outstretched arms suspended most of the weight of his body. Each stressed muscle ached. His body weighed more heavily at each step upward; it sagged beneath his arms like a leaden sack. His legs no longer provided their adequate support; it seemed as though they needed every pull of their muscles to force themselves, as independent limbs, close to the ladder. The wind blew faster. It dragged now at his coat, it blew its space about him, it echoed silently a lonely spaciousness. "Don't look down," the blood whispered in his temples. "Don't look down, *don't look down*."

Three quarters up the tank and fifty feet from the ground, Flegg grew desperate. Every other consideration suddenly left him. He wanted only to reach the ground as quickly as possible—only that. Nothing else mattered. He stopped climbing and clung to the ladder panting. Very slowly, lowering his eyes carefully so that he could raise them instantly if he saw too much, he looked down a rung, and another past his armpit, past his waist, and focused on the ground below. He looked quickly up again.

He pressed himself to the ladder. Tears started in his eyes. For a moment they reeled red with giddiness. He closed them, shutting out everything. Then instantly opened them, afraid that something might happen. He must watch his hands, watch the bars, watch the rusted iron sheeting itself; no movement should escape him. The struts might come creaking loose, the whole edifice might sway over. Although a fading reason told him that the gas tank had remained firm for years and was still steady as a cliff, his horrified senses suspected that this was the one moment in the building's life when a wind would blow that was too strong for it, some defective strut would snap, the whole structure would heel over and go crashing to the ground. This image became so clear that he could see the sheets of iron buckling and folding like cloth as the huge weight sank to the earth.

The ground had receded horribly; the drop now appeared terrifying, out of all proportion to this height he had reached. From the ground such a height would have appeared unnoteworthy. But now, looking down, the distance seemed to have doubled. Each object familiar to his everyday eyes—his friends, the lampposts, a brick wall, the sidewalk—all these had grown infinitely small. His senses demanded that these objects should be of a certain accustomed size. Alternatively, the world of chimneys and attic windows and roof copings would grow unpleasantly giant as his sidewalk-bred eyes approached. Even now the iron sheeting that stretched to either side and above and below seemed to have grown; he was lost among such huge, smooth dimensions—grown smaller himself, and clinging now like a child lost on some monstrous desert of red dust.

These unfamiliarities shocked his nerves more than the danger of falling. The sense of isolation was overpowering. All things were suddenly alien. Yet exposed on the iron spaces, with the unending winds blowing round him, among such free things—he felt shut in. Trembling and panting, so that he stifled himself with the shortness of his own breath, he took the first step downward.

A commotion began below. A confusion of cries came drifting up to him. Above all he could hear the single voice of the girl who so far had kept quiet. She was screaming high, a shrill scream that rose in the air incisively, like a gull's shriek. "Put it back, put it back, put it back!" the scream seemed to say. So that Flegg, thinking that these cries were to warn him of some new danger apparent only from the ground, gripped himself onto the ladder and looked down again. He glanced down for only a fraction of a second, but in that time saw enough. He saw that the quiet girl was screaming and pointing to the base of the iron ladder. He saw the others crowding round her, gesticulating. He saw that she really had been

crying, "Put it back!" And he realized now what the words meant. Someone had removed the painter's ladder.

It lay clearly on the ground, outlined like a child's drawing of a ladder. The boys must have seen his first step downward, and then, from fun or from spite, they had removed his only means of retreat. He remembered that from the base of the iron ladder to the ground the drop fell twenty feet. He considered quickly descending and appealing from the bottom of the ladder, but foresaw that for precious minutes they would jeer and argue, refusing to replace the ladder, and he felt then that he never could risk these minutes, unnerved, with his strength failing.

Besides, he already had noticed that the whole group was wandering off. The boys were driving the quiet girl away, now more concerned with her than with Flegg. The quiet girl's sense of guilt had been brought to a head by the removal of the ladder. Now she was hysterically terrified. She was yelling to them to put the ladder back. She—only she, the passive one—sensed the terror that awaited them all. But her screams defeated their own purpose. They had altogether distracted the attention of the others; now it was fun to provoke more screams, to encourage this new distraction—and they forgot about Flegg far up and beyond them. They were wandering away. They were abandoning him, casually unconcerned that he was alone and helpless up in his wide prison of rust. His heart cried out for them to stay. He forgot their scorn in new and terrible torments of self-pity. An uneasy feeling lumped his throat; his eyes smarted with dry tears.

But they were wandering away. There was no retreat. They did not even know he was in difficulties. So Flegg had no option but to climb higher. Desperately he tried to shake off his fear; he actually shook his head. Then he stared hard at the rungs immediately facing his eyes and tried to imagine that he was not high up at all. He lifted himself tentatively by one rung, then by another, and in this way dragged himself higher and higher—until he must have been some ten rungs from the top, over the fifth story of a house, with now perhaps only one more story to climb.. He imagined that he might then be approaching the summit platform, and to measure this last distance he looked up.

He looked up and heaved. He felt for the first time panicked beyond desperation, wildly, violently loose. He almost let go. His senses screamed to let go, yet his hands refused to open. He was stretched on a rack[12] made by these hands that would not unlock their grip and by the panic desire to drop. The nerves left his hands, so that they might have been dried bones of fingers gripped round the rungs—hooks of bone fixed perhaps strongly enough to cling on, or perhaps ready at some moment of pressure to uncurl and straighten to a drop. His insteps pricked with cold cramp. The sweat sickened him. He shivered, grew giddy, and flung himself froglike onto the narrow iron ladder.

The sight of the top of the gas tank had proved more frightful than the appearance of the drop beneath. There lay about it a sense, not of material danger, not of the risk of falling, but of something removed and inhuman—a sense of appalling isolation. It echoed its elemental iron aloofness; a wind blew round it that never had known the warmth of flesh or the softness of green fibers. Its blind eyes were raised above the world. It might have been the eyeless iron vizor[13] of an ancient god. It touched against the sky, having risen in awful perpendicular to this isolation, solitary as the gray gannet cliffs[14] that mark the end of the northern world. It was immeasurably old, outside the connotation of time; it was nothing human, only washed by the high weather, echoing with wind, visited never, and silently alone.

And in this summit Flegg measured clearly the full distance of his climb. This close skyline emphasized the whirling space beneath him. He clearly saw a man fall through this space, spread-eagling, to smash with the sick-

ening force of a locomotive on the stone beneath. The man turned slowly in the air, yet his thoughts raced faster than he fell.

Flegg, clutching his body close to the rust, made small weeping sounds through his mouth. Shivering, shuddering, he began to tread up again, working his knees and elbows outward like a frog so that his stomach could feel the firm rungs. Were they firm? His ears filled with a hot roaring; he hurried himself; he began to scramble, wrenching at his last strength, whispering urgent, meaningless words to himself like the swift whispers that close in on a nightmare. A huge weight pulled at him, dragging him to drop.

He climbed higher. He reached the top rung —and found his face staring still at a wall of red rust. He looked, wild with terror. It was the top rung! The ladder had ended! Yet—no platform. The real top rungs were missing. The platform jutted five impassable feet above. Flegg stared dumbly, circling his head like a lost animal. Then he jammed his legs in the lower rungs and his arms past the elbows to the armpits through the top rungs, and there he hung shivering and past knowing what more he could ever do.

I

CHALLENGED BY FRIENDS

George Orwell was pressured into an action he despised because he had to save face. Flegg finds an innocent game of rock throwing suddenly taking an unexpected turn. He feels that his manhood is being challenged. He too moves into a situation from which his whole being recoils. The reader may have been involved in similar situations himself. Why is it so important to an individual to look good in the eyes of other people that he allows himself to be forced into an unpleasant or

---

12. **rack,** an instrument of torture on which the body was stretched.
13. **vizor** \ˈvaɪ·zər\ the front piece of a helmet.
14. **gannet cliffs,** cliffs inhabited by gannets, large fish-eating birds.

untenable position? Is Sansom saying something about the nature of man, or about the society in which he lives, or both?

II
IMPLICATIONS

How do the following quotations relate to the story and to your own experiences?

1. "Then there began one of those uneasy jokes, innocent at first, that, taken seriously, can accumulate a hysterical volume of spite."

2. "He wanted to brush [the flake] away from his eye, but the impulse was, to his surprise, much less powerful than the vicelike will that clutched his hand to the iron support."

3. "He looked up, following the dizzying rise of the rungs to the skyline. From this angle, flat against the iron sheeting, the gas tank appeared higher than before."

4. "He was afraid, but not desperate. He dreaded each step, yet forced himself to believe that at some time it would be over . . . ."

5. "Fear was draining all his strength . . . ."

6. ". . . his horrified senses suspected that this was the one moment in the building's life when a wind would blow that was too strong for it, some defective strut would snap, the whole structure would heel over and go crashing to the ground."

III
TECHNIQUES

Theme

Most readers live with Flegg as he climbs; some so intensely that they actually have sensations of panic. What were your reactions as you read the story? How would you define the theme? What details from the story support your statement?

Style

This story has a rough, uneven, almost harsh quality that you can perhaps feel by rereading a paragraph from it aloud and then following it with a paragraph from "Shooting an Elephant." In Orwell's story the language flows smoothly and easily. "The Vertical Ladder" has a hard, staccato quality. Is this appropriate to the subject matter? Can you discover particular uses of language that give it this quality?

IV
WORDS

A. Some of Flegg's companions shouted teasingly that he would later write about his conquest of Mount Everest. They called him Sir Galahad. Mount Everest is the highest mountain on Earth and is the ultimate challenge to mountain climbers. In Arthurian legend, Sir Galahad was the pure and noble knight who succeeded in his quest for the Holy Grail. A reference to a place or a thing like Mount Everest or to a person like Sir Galahad with which the reader or listener is presumed to be familiar is called an *allusion*. Allusions have their origins in history, folklore, the Bible, and literature, to name a few sources. Our daily language abounds in these familiar references; for example, "solid as the rock of Gibraltar," "poor as Job," "honest Abe," "the wisdom of Solomon," and "the Midas touch." Other allusions appear in the sentences which follow. Can you identify the source of each?

1. Like the phoenix, he will rise out of the ashes of defeat.

2. Don't be enchanted by her Siren song.

3. That doubting Thomas accepts nothing on faith alone.

4. This project has been his Golgotha.

5. Like Cassius, he has a lean and hungry look.

6. Johnny has a Dr. Jekyll and Mr. Hyde personality.

B. Though in everyday language we do not speak poetry, we do use *metaphors*, which are often used in poetry. When the author of "The Vertical Ladder" refers to "the belly of the tank," he is using a metaphor. Since strictly speaking, an inanimate object cannot have a belly, the author is implying a comparison between the tank and an animal. Through metaphor, *belly* has come to mean an object or a surface rounded or curved like the human stomach or the undersurface of an animal. Elsewhere in the story, the writer mentions "sheet of iron," meaning thin layers of iron. The comparison here is obvious: the layers are thin like sheets. During the winter, we speak of a "sheet of ice." Here are several other common metaphors: *face of a clock, foot of a mountain, legs of a chair, eye of a hurricane,* and *family tree.* Can you think of others?

Most people have something they cherish
above all else: a pet, another person, their job,
a particular ability. James Thurber creates
a quiet little man who cherishes his job,
a man so meek that he seems incapable
of defending himself. But when his position
is threatened, he rises to the challenge.
Suddenly there is an unexpected struggle to see
who will end up sitting in the catbird seat—
who will end up sitting pretty.

The Catbird Seat

JAMES THURBER

Mr. Martin bought the pack of Camels on
Monday night in the most crowded cigar store
on Broadway. It was theater time and seven or
eight men were buying cigarettes. The clerk
didn't even glance at Mr. Martin, who put the
pack in his overcoat pocket and went out. If
any of the staff at F & S had seen him buy the
cigarettes, they would have been astonished,
for it was generally known that Mr. Martin did
not smoke, and never had. No one saw him.

It was just a week to the day since Mr. Martin had decided to rub out Mrs. Ulgine Barrows. The term "rub out" pleased him because
it suggested nothing more than the correction
of an error—in this case an error of Mr. Fitweiler. Mr. Martin had spent each night of the
past week working out his plan and examining
it. As he walked home now he went over it
again. For the hundredth time he resented the
element of imprecision, the margin of guesswork that entered into the business. The project as he had worked it out was casual and
bold, the risks were considerable. Something

might go wrong anywhere along the line. And
therein lay the cunning of his scheme. No one
would ever see in it the cautious, painstaking
hand of Erwin Martin, head of the filing department at F & S, of whom Mr. Fitweiler had
once said, "Man is fallible but Martin isn't."
No one would see his hand, that is, unless it
were caught in the act.

Sitting in his apartment, drinking a glass of
milk, Mr. Martin reviewed his case against
Mrs. Ulgine Barrows, as he had every night for
seven nights. He began at the beginning. Her
quacking voice and braying laugh had first profaned the halls of F & S on March 7, 1941 (Mr.
Martin had a head for dates). Old Roberts, the
personnel chief, had introduced her as the
newly appointed special adviser to the president of the firm, Mr. Fitweiler. The woman
had appalled Mr. Martin instantly, but he
hadn't shown it. He had given her his dry hand,
a look of studious concentration, and a faint
smile. "Well," she had said, looking at the
papers on his desk, "are you lifting the oxcart
out of the ditch?" As Mr. Martin recalled that
moment, over his milk, he squirmed slightly.
He must keep his mind on her crimes as a special adviser, not on her peccadillos as a personality. This he found difficult to do, in spite
of entering an objection and sustaining it. The
faults of the woman as a woman kept chattering on in his mind like an unruly witness. She
had, for almost two years now, baited him. In
the halls, in the elevator, even in his own office, into which she romped now and then like a
circus horse, she was constantly shouting these
silly questions at him. "Are you lifting the oxcart out of the ditch? Are you tearing up the
pea patch? Are you hollering down the rain
barrel? Are you scraping around the bottom
of the pickle barrel? Are you sitting in the catbird seat?"

It was Joey Hart, one of Mr. Martin's two assistants, who had explained what the gibberish
meant. "She must be a Dodger fan," he had
said. "Red Barber announces the Dodger games
over the radio and he uses those expressions

—picked 'em up down South."[1] Joey had gone on to explain one or two. "Tearing up the pea patch" meant going on a rampage; "sitting in the catbird seat" meant sitting pretty, like a batter with three balls and no strikes on him. Mr. Martin dismissed all this with an effort. It had been annoying, it had driven him near to distraction, but he was too solid a man to be moved to murder by anything so childish. It was fortunate, he reflected as he passed on to the important charges against Mrs. Barrows, that he had stood up under it so well. He had maintained always an outward appearance of polite tolerance. "Why, I even believe you like the woman," Miss Paird, his other assistant, had once said to him. He had simply smiled.

A gavel rapped in Mr. Martin's mind and the case proper was resumed. Mrs. Ulgine Barrows stood charged with willful, blatant, and persistent attempts to destroy the efficiency and system of F & S. It was competent, material, and relevant to review her advent and rise to power.[2] Mr. Martin had got the story from Miss Paird, who seemed always able to find things out. According to her, Mrs. Barrows had met Mr. Fitweiler at a party, where she had rescued him from the embraces of a powerfully built drunken man who had mistaken the president of F & S for a famous retired Middle Western football coach. She had led him to a sofa and somehow worked upon him a monstrous magic. The aging gentleman had jumped to the conclusion there and then that this was a woman of singular attainments, equipped to bring out the best in him and in the firm. A week later he had introduced her into F & S as his special adviser. On that day confusion got its foot in the door. After Miss Tyson, Mr. Brundage, and Mr. Bartlett had been fired and Mr. Munson had taken his hat and stalked out, mailing in his resignation later, old Roberts had been emboldened to speak to Mr. Fitweiler. He mentioned that Mr. Munson's department had been "a little disrupted" and hadn't they perhaps better resume the old system there? Mr. Fitweiler had said certainly not. He had the greatest faith in Mrs. Barrows' ideas. "They require a little seasoning, a little seasoning, is all," he had added. Mr. Roberts had given it up. Mr. Martin reviewed in detail all the changes wrought by Mrs. Barrows. She had begun chipping at the cornices of the firm's edifice and now she was swinging at the foundation stones with a pickaxe.

Mr. Martin came now, in his summing up, to the afternoon of Monday, November 2, 1942— just one week ago. On that day, at 3 P.M., Mrs. Barrows had bounced into his office. "Boo!" she had yelled. "Are you scraping around the bottom of the pickle barrel?" Mr. Martin had looked at her from under his green eyeshade, saying nothing. She had begun to wander about the office, taking it in with her great, popping eyes. "Do you really need *all* these filing cabinets?" she had demanded suddenly, Mr. Martin's heart had jumped. "Each of these files," he had said, keeping his voice even, "plays an indispensable part in the system of F & S." She had brayed at him, "Well, don't tear up the pea patch!" and gone to the door. From there she had bawled, "But you sure have got a lot of fine scrap in here!" Mr. Martin could no longer doubt that the finger was on his beloved department.[3] Her pickaxe was on the upswing, poised for the first blow. It had not come yet; he had received no blue memo from the enchanted Mr. Fitweiler bearing nonsensical instructions deriving from the obscene woman. But there was no doubt in Mr. Martin's mind that one would be forthcoming. He must act quickly. Already a precious week had gone by. Mr. Martin stood up in his living room, still holding his milk glass. "Gentlemen of the jury," he said to himself, "I demand the death penalty for this horrible person."

---

1. The reference is to the Brooklyn Dodger team before the organization was moved to Los Angeles. **Red Barber** announced the Brooklyn Dodger games and had a wide following in New York.
2. In using the phrase "**competent, material, and relevant,**" Mr. Martin is using legalistic terminology.
3. **That the finger was on his beloved department,** that the finger of doom or fate, as personified by Mrs. Barrows, was now pointing at his department.

The next day Mr. Martin followed his routine, as usual. He polished his glasses more often and once sharpened an already sharp pencil, but not even Miss Paird noticed. Only once did he catch sight of his victim; she swept past him in the hall with a patronizing "Hi!" At five-thirty he walked home, as usual, and had a glass of milk, as usual. He had never drunk anything stronger in his life—unless you could count ginger ale. The late Sam Schlosser, the S of F & S, had praised Mr. Martin at a staff meeting several years before for his temperate habits. "Our most efficient worker neither drinks nor smokes," he had said. "The results speak for themselves." Mr. Fitweiler had sat by, nodding approval.

Mr. Martin was still thinking about that red-letter day as he walked over to the Schrafft's on Fifth Avenue near Forty-Sixth Street.[4] He got there, as he always did, at eight o'clock. He finished his dinner and the financial page of the *Sun* at a quarter to nine, as he always did. It was his custom after dinner to take a walk. This time he walked down Fifth Avenue at a casual pace. His gloved hands felt moist and warm, his forehead cold. He transferred the Camels from his overcoat to a jacket pocket. He wondered, as he did so, if they did not represent an unnecessary note of strain. Mrs. Barrows smoked only Luckies. It was his idea to puff a few puffs on a Camel (after the rubbing-out), stub it out in the ashtray holding her lipstick-stained Luckies, and thus drag a small red herring across the trail. Perhaps it was not a good idea. It would take time. He might even choke, too loudly.

Mr. Martin had never seen the house on West Twelfth Street where Mrs. Barrows lived, but he had a clear enough picture of it. Fortunately, she had bragged to everybody about her ducky[5] first-floor apartment in the perfectly darling three-story red-brick. There would be no doorman or other attendants; just the tenants of the second and third floors. As he walked along, Mr. Martin realized that he would get there before nine-thirty. He had considered walking north on Fifth Avenue from Schrafft's to a point from which it would take him until ten o'clock to reach the house. At that hour people were less likely to be coming in or going out. But the procedure would have made an awkward loop in the straight thread of his casualness, and he had abandoned it. It was impossible to figure when people would be entering or leaving the house, anyway. There was a great risk at any hour. If he ran into anybody, he would simply have to place the rubbing-out of Ulgine Barrows in the inactive file forever. The same thing would hold true if there were someone in her apartment. In that case he would just say that he had been passing by, recognized her charming house, and thought to drop in.

It was eighteen minutes after nine when Mr. Martin turned into Twelfth Street. A man passed him, and a man and a woman, talking. There was no one within fifty paces when he came to the house, halfway down the block. He was up the steps and in the small vestibule in no time, pressing the bell under the card that said "Mrs. Ulgine Barrows." When the clicking in the lock started,[6] he jumped forward against the door. He got inside fast, closing the door behind him. A bulb in a lantern hung from the hall ceiling on a chain seemed to give a monstrously bright light. There was nobody on the stair, which went up ahead of him along the left wall. A door opened down the hall in the wall on the right. He went toward it swiftly, on tiptoe.

"Well, I'll be, look who's here!" bawled Mrs. Barrows, and her braying laugh rang out like the report of a shotgun. He rushed past her like a football tackle, bumping her. "Hey, quit shoving!" she said, closing the door behind them. They were in her living room,

---

4. **red-letter day,** one marked by great joy and celebration. **Schrafft's**\shräfts\ a New York restaurant chain. Mr. Martin is in midtown Manhattan.
5. **ducky,** women's slang, "very pleasant."
6. When the tenant's bell was pressed from without, he could press a bell in his own apartment that would release a catch on the front door.

which seemed to Mr. Martin to be lighted by a hundred lamps. "What's after you?" she said. "You're as jumpy as a goat." He found he was unable to speak. His heart was wheezing in his throat. "I—yes," he finally brought out. She was jabbering and laughing as she started to help him off with his coat. "No, no," he said. "I'll put it here." He took it off and put it on a chair near the door. "Your hat and gloves, too," she said. "You're in a lady's house." He put his hat on top of the coat. Mrs. Barrows seemed larger than he had thought. He kept his gloves on. "I was passing by," he said. "I recognized—is there anyone here?" She laughed louder than ever. "No," she said, "we're all alone. You're as white as a sheet, you funny man. Whatever *has* come over you? I'll mix you a toddy."[7] She started toward a door across the room. "Scotch-and-soda be all right? But say, you don't drink, do you?" She turned and gave him her amused look. Mr. Martin pulled himself together. "Scotch-and-soda will be all right," he heard himself say. He could hear her laughing in the kitchen.

Mr. Martin looked quickly around the living room for the weapon. He had counted on finding one there. There were andirons and a poker and something in a corner that looked like an Indian club.[8] None of them would do. It couldn't be that way. He began to pace around. He came to a desk. On it lay a metal paper knife with an ornate handle. Would it be sharp enough? He reached for it and knocked over a small brass jar. Stamps spilled out of it and it fell to the floor with a clatter. "Hey," Mrs. Barrows yelled from the kitchen, "are you tearing up the pea patch?" Mr. Martin gave a strange laugh. Picking up the knife, he tried its point against his left wrist. It was blunt. It wouldn't do.

When Mrs. Barrows reappeared, carrying two highballs, Mr. Martin, standing there with his gloves on, became acutely conscious of the fantasy he had wrought. Cigarettes in his pocket, a drink prepared for him—it was all too grossly improbable. It was more than that; it was impossible. Somewhere in the back of his mind a vague idea stirred, sprouted. "For heaven's sake, take off those gloves," said Mrs. Barrows. "I always wear them in the house," said Mr. Martin. The idea began to bloom, strange and wonderful. She put the glasses on a coffee table in front of a sofa and sat on the sofa. "Come over here, you odd little man," she said. Mr. Martin went over and sat beside her. It was difficult getting a cigarette out of the pack of Camels, but he managed it. She held a match for him, laughing. "Well," she said, handing him his drink, "this is perfectly marvellous. You with a drink and a cigarette."

Mr. Martin puffed, not too awkwardly, and took a gulp of the highball. "I drink and smoke all the time," he said. He clinked his glass against hers. "Here's nuts to that old windbag, Fitweiler," he said, and gulped again. The stuff tasted awful, but he made no grimace. "Really, Mr. Martin," she said, her voice and posture changing, "you are insulting our employer." Mrs. Barrows was now all special adviser to the president. "I am preparing a bomb," said Mr. Martin, "which will blow the old goat higher than heck." He had only had a little of the drink, which was not strong. It couldn't be that. "Do you take dope or something?" Mrs. Barrows asked coldly. "Heroin," said Mr. Martin. "I'll be coked to the gills when I bump that old buzzard off."[9] "Mr. Martin!" she shouted, getting to her feet. "That will be all of that. You must go at once." Mr. Martin took another swallow of his drink. He tapped his cigarette out in the ashtray and put the pack of Camels on the coffee table. Then he got up. She stood glaring at him. He walked over and put on his hat and coat. "Not a word about this," he said, and laid an index finger against his lips. All Mrs. Barrows could bring out was "Really!"

---

7. **toddy**\\▲tŏ·dē\ an alcoholic drink usually made of whiskey and water.
8. **andirons**\ăn ▲dai·rənz\ firedogs or metal objects in fireplaces to insure draft. **Indian club**, a wooden club used in gymnastics and shaped somewhat like a tenpin.
9. **heroin**\hĕ ′rō·ən\ a powerful narcotic drug made from morphine. **coked to the gills**, entirely under the influence of a narcotic.

Mr. Martin put his hand on the doorknob. "I'm sitting in the catbird seat," he said. He stuck his tongue out at her and left. Nobody saw him go.

Mr. Martin got to his apartment, walking, well before eleven. No one saw him go in. He had two glasses of milk after brushing his teeth, and he felt elated. It wasn't tipsiness, because he hadn't been tipsy.[10] Anyway, the walk had worn off all effects of the whiskey. He got in bed and read a magazine for a while. He was asleep before midnight.

Mr. Martin got to the office at eight-thirty the next morning, as usual. At a quarter to nine, Ulgine Barrows, who had never before arrived at work before ten, swept into his office. "I'm reporting to Mr. Fitweiler now!" she shouted, "if he turns you over to the police, it's no more than you deserve!" Mr. Martin gave her a look of shocked surprise. "I beg your pardon?" he said. Mrs. Barrows snorted and bounced out of the room, leaving Miss Paird and Joey Hart staring after her. "What's the matter with that old devil now?" asked Miss Paird. "I have no idea," said Mr. Martin, resuming his work. The other two looked at him and then at each other. Miss Paird got up and went out. She walked slowly past the closed door of Mr. Fitweiler's office. Mrs. Barrows was yelling inside, but she was not braying. Miss Paird could not hear what the woman was saying. She went back to her desk.

Forty-five minutes later, Mrs. Barrows left the president's office and went into her own, shutting the door. It wasn't until half an hour later that Mr. Fitweiler sent for Mr. Martin. The head of the filing department, neat, quiet, attentive, stood in front of the old man's desk. Mr. Fitweiler was pale and nervous. He took his glasses off and twiddled them. He made a small, bruffing sound in his throat. "Martin," he said, "you have been with us more than twenty years." "Twenty-two, sir," said Mr. Martin. "In that time," pursued the president, "your work and your—uh—manner have been exemplary." "I trust so, sir," said Mr. Martin. "I have under-stood, Martin," said Mr. Fitweiler, "that you have never taken a drink or smoked." "That is correct, sir," said Mr. Martin. "Ah, yes." Mr. Fitweiler polished his glasses. "You may de-scribe what you did after leaving the office yesterday, Martin," he said. Mr. Martin al-lowed less than a second for his bewildered pause. "Certainly, sir," he said. "I walked home. Then I went to Schrafft's for dinner. Afterward I walked home again. I went to bed early, sir, and read a magazine for a while. I was asleep before eleven." "Ah, yes," said Mr. Fitweiler again. He was silent for a moment, searching for the proper words to say to the head of the filing department. "Mrs. Barrows," he said finally, "Mrs. Barrows has worked hard, Martin, very hard. It grieves me to report that she has suffered a severe breakdown. It has taken the form of a persecution complex ac-companied by distressing hallucinations." "I am very sorry, sir," said Mr. Martin. "Mrs. Bar-rows is under the delusion," continued Mr. Fit-weiler, "that you visited her last evening and behaved yourself in an—uh—unseemly man-ner." He raised his hand to silence Mr. Martin's little pained outcry. "It is the nature of these psychological diseases," Mr. Fitweiler said, "to fix upon the least likely and most innocent party as the—uh—source of persecution. These mat-ters are not for the lay mind to grasp, Martin. I've just had my psychiatrist, Doctor Fitch, on the phone. He would not, of course, commit himself, but he made enough generalizations to substantiate my suspicions. I suggested to Mrs. Barrows, when she had completed her—uh—story to me this morning, that she visit Doctor Fitch, for I suspected a condition at once. She flew, I regret to say, into a rage, and demanded —uh—requested that I call you on the carpet. You may not know, Martin, but Mrs. Barrows had planned a reorganization of your depart-ment—subject to my approval, of course, sub-ject to my approval. This brought you, rather than anyone else, to her mind—but again that is a phenomenon for Doctor Fitch and not for

10. **tipsy,** informal: drunk.

us. So, Martin, I am afraid Mrs. Barrows' usefulness here is at an end." "I am dreadfully sorry, sir," said Mr. Martin.

It was at this point that the door to the office blew open with the suddenness of a gas-main explosion and Mrs. Barrows catapulted through it. "Is the little rat denying it?" she screamed. "He can't get away with that!" Mr. Martin got up and moved discreetly to a point beside Mr. Fitweiler's chair. "You drank and smoked at my apartment," she bawled at Mr. Martin, "and you know it! You called Mr. Fitweiler an old windbag and said you were going to blow him up when you got coked to the gills on your heroin!" She stopped yelling to catch her breath and a new glint came into her popping eyes. "If you weren't such a drab, ordinary little man," she said, "I'd think you'd planned it all. Sticking your tongue out, saying you were sitting in the catbird seat, because you thought no one would believe me when I told it! Oh my, it's really too perfect!" She brayed loudly and hysterically, and the fury was on her again. She glared at Mr. Fitweiler. "Can't you see how he has tricked us, you old fool? Can't you see his little game?" But Mr. Fitweiler had been surreptitiously pressing all the buttons under the top of his desk and employees of F & S began pouring into the room. "Stockton," said Mr. Fitweiler, "you and Fishbein will take Mrs. Barrows to her home. Mrs. Powell, you will go with them." Stockton, who had played a little football in high school, blocked Mrs. Barrows as she made for Mr. Martin. It took him and Fishbein together to force her out of the door into the hall, crowded with stenographers and office boys. She was still screaming imprecations at Mr. Martin, tangled and contradictory imprecations. The hubbub finally died down the corridor.

"I regret that this has happened," said Mr. Fitweiler. "I shall ask you to dismiss it from your mind, Martin." "Yes, sir," said Mr. Martin, anticipating his chief's "That will be all" by moving to the door. "I will dismiss it." He went out and shut the door, and his step was light and quick in the hall. When he entered his department he had slowed down to his customary gait, and he walked quietly across the room to the W20 file, wearing a look of studious concentration.

I
A MODERN FABLE

David and Goliath, Cinderella and the wicked sisters, the tortoise and the hare—this plot of the unlikely hero winning out over a favored adversary is one of the most cherished in literature. Readers like it because they identify themselves with the underdog and are led to hope that they too can find a secret weapon against the bullies of their own world. Since he has neither the strength to overcome her physically nor the influence to dislodge her through office politics, what could be more ingenious than Mr. Martin's psychological warfare against Mrs. Barrows?

II
IMPLICATIONS

James Thurber had an almost unequaled skill in exposing the absurdities of human conduct without ridiculing them. His eye was sharp but not cruel. One of his favorite themes was the differences among the way people see themselves, the way others see them, and the way they really are.

1. What is the picture that Mr. Martin has of himself? What is the picture that Mrs. Barrows has of herself? What is the picture that each has of the other?

2. What kind of executive does Mr. Fitweiler think he is? What kind would you say he really is?

3. Is Martin's ingenious plan for getting himself into the catbird seat consistent with his character or not? Give reasons for your opinion.

4. No one knows about Martin's success but himself. Does this lead him to take more or less pleasure in it? Why?

III
TECHNIQUES

Theme

Below are some general statements. In your opinion which comes closest to stating the theme of "The Catbird Seat"? Support your choice with reasons.

1. The weak win out in the long run.

2. Appearances are deceptive.

3. There is more than one way to achieve one's ends.

4. Office regimentation makes direct actions difficult.

5. Everyone has a point at which he will turn and fight.

Style

Humor, as you have already learned, is often the result of the unexpected and the incongruous. Below are five quotations from "The Catbird Seat" that are good examples of Thurber's comic style. What element is it in each that makes it humorous? Is it a word or a phrase? Or the general picture it evokes?

1. ". . . Mrs. Barrows had met Mr. Fitweiler at a party, where she had rescued him from the embraces of a powerfully built drunken man who had mistaken the president of F & S for a famous retired Middle Western football coach. She had led him to a sofa and somehow worked upon him a monstrous magic."

2. "She had begun chipping at the cornices of the firm's edifice and now she was swinging at the foundation stones with a pickaxe."

3. "If he ran into anybody, he would simply have to place the rubbing-out of Ulgine Barrows in the inactive file forever."

4. "He clinked his glass against hers. 'Here's nuts to that old windbag, Fitweiler,' he said, and gulped again."

5. "Mr. Fitweiler was pale and nervous. He took his glasses off and twiddled them. He made a small, bruffing sound in his throat."

Identification

To make a person laugh is one of the quickest ways to engage his sympathy. Great comic figures like Charlie Chaplin's little tramp are held in universal affection, and when the comic figure is also an underdog, as Mr. Martin is in this story, the reader's sympathy is almost guaranteed. Yet Mrs. Barrows is also a comic figure; but it could hardly be said that she evokes sympathy. What reasons can you give for this difference? How might they be related to identifying with the two characters?

IV

WORDS

A. 1. Orwell's description of the dying elephant is highly figurative. What vividness does each of the following add beyond the literal statement? Try replacing the figure with a literal statement and see what happens.

> great mound of a side; caverns of pink throat; blood welled out of him like red velvet; gasps continued as steadily as the ticks of a clock.

2. In "The Catbird Seat" James Thurber uses slang in the dialogue and metaphorical expressions which seem slangy. Comment on the effectiveness and appropriateness of the following:

> rushed past like a football tackle; as jumpy as a goat; tearing up the pea patch; sitting in the catbird seat.

B. Determine from context the meaning of the italicized words.

1. clamped down upon the will of *prostrate* peoples.

2. It was a very poor quarter, a *labyrinth* of *squalid* huts, winding all over a steep hillside.

3. that I first grasped the hollowness, the *futility*.

4. an enormous *senility* seemed to have settled upon him. One could have imagined him thousands of years old.

5. he resented the element of *imprecision*, the margin of guesswork.

6. You have been with us more than twenty years . . . your work and your manner have been *exemplary*.

7. he made enough generalizations to *substantiate* my suspicions.

C. 1. Orwell speaks of "some Indian constables." Look up the word *constable*. Is it related to *count* or to *stable*? Orwell writes of a dead man "lying on his belly with arms crucified." The word *crucify* is made up of the root *-cruc-*, meaning "cross," and the root or suffix *-fy*, meaning "make." What is the relationship between *crucify* and *crucial*?

2. In "Trifles" *pneumonia* is mentioned in the first lines of the dialogue. What is the relationship between *pneumonia* and *pneumatic*? There is— rather naturally—mention of the coroner in this story. In earlier times a coroner was the king's officer or official. Is there a relationship between *coroner* and *coronet* and *coronation*?

Jack London saw life as a constant process
of "pursuing and being pursued, of hunting
and being hunted . . . a chaos . . . ruled over
by chance, merciless, planless, endless." He felt
that in living one either exerted pressures
or resisted the pressures exerted on one.
Life was an uninterrupted struggle,
always against the odds, in which the strong
survived and the weak succumbed.

To Build a Fire

JACK LONDON

Day had broken cold and gray, exceedingly
cold and gray, when the man turned aside from
the main Yukon trail and climbed the high
earthbank, where a dim and little-traveled trail
led eastward through the fat spruce timber-
land. It was a steep bank, and he paused for
breath at the top, excusing the act to himself
by looking at his watch. It was nine o'clock.
There was no sun nor hint of sun, though there
was not a cloud in the sky. It was a clear day,
and yet there seemed an intangible pall over
the face of things, a subtle gloom that made the
day dark, and that was due to the absence of
sun. This fact did not worry the man. He was
used to the lack of sun. It had been days since
he had seen the sun, and he knew that a few
more days must pass before that cheerful orb,
due south, would just peep above the sky-line
and dip immediately from view.

The man flung a look back along the way he
had come. The Yukon lay a mile wide and
hidden under three feet of ice. On top of this
ice were as many feet of snow. It was all pure
white, rolling in gentle undulations where the
ice-jams of the freeze-up had formed. North
and south, as far as his eye could see, it was unbroken white, save for a dark hair-line that
curved and twisted from around the spruce-
covered island to the south, and that curved
and twisted away into the north, where it
disappeared behind another spruce-covered
island. This dark hair-line was the trail—the
main trail—that led south five hundred miles
to the Chilkoot Pass, Dyea, and salt water; and
that led north seventy miles to Dawson, and
still on to the north a thousand miles to Nulato,
and finally to St. Michael on Bering Sea, a
thousand miles and half a thousand more.[1]

But all this—the mysterious, far-reaching
hair-line trail, the absence of sun from the sky,
the tremendous cold, and the strangeness and
weirdness of it all—made no impression on the
man. It was not because he was long used to it.
He was a newcomer in the land, a *chechaquo*,[2]
and this was his first winter. The trouble with
him was that he was without imagination. He
was quick and alert in the things of life, but
only in the things, and not in the significances.
Fifty degrees below zero meant eighty-odd
degrees of frost. Such fact impressed him as
being cold and uncomfortable, and that was all.
It did not lead him to meditate upon his frailty
as a creature of temperature, and upon man's
frailty in general, able only to live within certain narrow limits of heat and cold; and from
there on it did not lead him to the conjectural
field of immortality and man's place in the universe. Fifty degrees below zero stood for a bite
of frost that hurt and that must be guarded
against by the use of mittens, ear-flaps, warm
moccasins, and thick socks. Fifty degrees below
zero was to him just precisely fifty degrees
below zero. That there should be anything
more to it than that was a thought that never
entered his head.

---

1. **Chilkoot**\\ˆchĭl ˈkūt\\ **Pass** is in extreme northwestern
British Columbia between Alaska and the Yukon. **Dyea**
\\ˆdai•ā\\ a former Alaska village at which the Chilkoot
Pass Trail started. **Dawson** is west central Yukon Territory. **Nulato**\\nṳ ˆla•tō\\ is in west central Alaska on
the Yukon. **St. Michael** is on the Alaskan coast north
of the mouth of the Yukon.
2. **chechaquo**\\ˈchē ˆcha•kō\\ a newcomer to the Northwest.

Reprinted by permission of Mr. Irving Shepard.

As he turned to go on, he spat speculatively. There was a sharp, explosive crackle that startled him. He spat again. And again, in the air, before it could fall to the snow, the spittle crackled. He knew that at fifty below spittle crackled on the snow, but this spittle had crackled in the air. Undoubtedly it was colder than fifty below—how much colder he did not know. But the temperature did not matter. He was bound for the old claim on the left fork of Henderson Creek, where the boys were already. They had come over across the divide from the Indian Creek country, while he had come the roundabout way to take a look at the possibilities of getting out logs in the spring from the islands in the Yukon. He would be in to camp by six o'clock; a bit after dark, it was true, but the boys would be there, a fire would be going, and a hot supper would be ready. As for lunch, he pressed his hand against the protruding bundle under his jacket. It was also under his shirt, wrapped up in a handkerchief and lying against the naked skin. It was the only way to keep the biscuits from freezing. He smiled agreeably to himself as he thought of those biscuits, each cut open and sopped in bacon grease, and each enclosing a generous slice of fried bacon.

He plunged in among the big spruce trees. The trail was faint. A foot of snow had fallen since the last sled had passed over, and he was glad he was without a sled, traveling light. In fact, he carried nothing but the lunch wrapped in the handkerchief. He was surprised, however, at the cold. It certainly was cold, he concluded, as he rubbed his numb nose and cheek-bones with his mittened hand. He was a warm-whiskered man, but the hair on his face did not protect the high cheek-bones and the eager nose that thrust itself aggressively into the frosty air.

At the man's heels trotted a dog, a big native husky, the proper wolf-dog, gray-coated and without any visible or temperamental difference from its brother, the wild wolf. The animal was depressed by the tremendous cold. It knew that it was no time for traveling. Its in-

stinct told it a truer tale than was told to the man by the man's judgment. In reality, it was not merely colder than fifty below zero; it was colder than sixty below, than seventy below. It was seventy-five below zero. Since the freezing-point is thirty-two above zero, it meant that one hundred and seven degrees of frost obtained. The dog did not know anything about thermometers. Possibly in its brain there was no sharp consciousness of a condition of very cold such as was in the man's brain. But the brute had its instinct. It experienced a vague but menacing apprehension that subdued it and made it slink along at the man's heels, and that made it question eagerly every unwonted movement of the man as if expecting him to go into camp or to seek shelter somewhere and build a fire. The dog had learned fire, and it wanted fire, or else to burrow under the snow and cuddle its warmth away from the air.

The frozen moisture of its breathing had settled on its fur in a fine powder of frost, and especially were its jowls, muzzle, and eyelashes whitened by its crystaled breath. The man's red beard and mustache were likewise frosted, but more solidly, the deposit taking the form of ice and increasing with every warm, moist breath he exhaled. Also, the man was chewing tobacco, and the muzzle of ice held his lips so rigidly that he was unable to clear his chin when he expelled the juice. The result was that a crystal beard of the color and solidity of amber was increasing its length on his chin. If he fell down it would shatter itself, like glass, into brittle fragments. But he did not mind the appendage. It was the penalty all tobacco-chewers paid in that country, and he had been out before in two cold snaps. They had not been so cold as this, he knew, but by the spirit thermometer at Sixty Mile he knew they had been registered at fifty below and at fifty-five.

He held on through the level stretch of woods for several miles, crossed a wide flat of nigger-heads,[3] and dropped down a bank to the frozen bed of a small stream. This was

---

3. **nigger-head**, a clump or mound of plant growth.

Henderson Creek, and he knew he was ten miles from the forks. He looked at his watch. It was ten o'clock. He was making four miles an hour, and he calculated that he would arrive at the forks at half-past twelve. He decided to celebrate that event by eating his lunch there.

The dog dropped in again at his heels, with a tail drooping discouragement, as the man swung along the creek-bed. The furrow of the old sled-trail was plainly visible, but a dozen inches of snow covered the marks of the last runners. In a month no man had come up or down that silent creek. The man held steadily on. He was not much given to thinking, and just then particularly he had nothing to think about save that he would eat lunch at the forks and that at six o'clock he would be in camp with the boys. There was nobody to talk to; and, had there been, speech would have been impossible because of the ice-muzzle on his mouth. So he continued monotonously to chew tobacco and to increase the length of his amber beard.

Once in a while the thought reiterated itself that it was very cold and that he had never experienced such cold. As he walked along he rubbed his cheek-bones and nose with the back of his mittened hand. He did this automatically, now and again changing hands. But rub as he would, the instant he stopped his cheek-bones went numb, and the following instant the end of his nose went numb. He was sure to frost his cheeks; he knew that, and experienced a pang of regret that he had not devised a nose-strap of the sort Bud wore in cold snaps. Such a strap passed across the cheeks, as well, and saved them. But it didn't matter much, after all. What were frosted cheeks? A bit painful, that was all; they were never serious.

Empty as the man's mind was of thoughts, he was keenly observant, and he noticed the changes in the creek, the curves and bends and timber-jams, and always he sharply noted where he placed his feet. Once, coming around a bend, he shied abruptly, like a startled horse, curved away from the place where he had been walking, and retreated several paces back along the trail. The creek he knew was frozen clear to the bottom,—no creek could contain water in that arctic winter,—but he knew also that there were springs that bubbled out from the hillsides and ran along under the snow and on top the ice of the creek. He knew that the coldest snaps never froze these springs, and he knew likewise their danger. They were traps. They hid pools of water under the snow that might be three inches deep, or three feet. Sometimes a skin of ice half an inch thick covered them, and in turn was covered by the snow. Sometimes there were alternate layers of water and ice-skin, so that when one broke through he kept on breaking through for a while, sometimes wetting himself to the waist.

That was why he had shied in such panic. He had felt the give under his feet and heard the crackle of a snow-hidden ice-skin. And to get his feet wet in such a temperature meant trouble and danger. At the very least it meant delay, for he would be forced to stop and build a fire, and under its protection to bare his feet while he dried his socks and moccasins. He stood and studied the creek-bed and its banks, and decided that the flow of water came from the right. He reflected awhile, rubbing his nose and cheeks, then skirted to the left, stepping gingerly and testing the footing for each step. Once clear of the danger, he took a fresh chew of tobacco and swung along at his four-mile gait.

In the course of the next two hours he came upon several similar traps. Usually the snow above the hidden pools had a sunken, candied appearance that advertised the danger. Once again, however, he had a close call; and once, suspecting danger, he compelled the dog to go on in front. The dog did not want to go. It hung back until the man shoved it forward, and then it went quickly across the white, unbroken surface. Suddenly it broke through; floundered to one side, and got away to firmer footing. It had wet its forefeet and legs, and almost immediately the water that clung to it turned to ice. It made quick efforts to lick the ice off its legs, then dropped down in the snow and began to bite out the ice that had formed between the toes. This was a matter of instinct. To permit the ice to remain would mean sore feet. It did not know this. It merely obeyed the mysterious prompting that rose from the deep crypts of its being. But the man knew, having achieved a judgment on the subject, and he removed the mitten from his right hand and helped tear out the ice-particles. He did not expose his fingers more than a minute, and was astonished at the swift numbness that smote them. It certainly was cold. He pulled on the mitten hastily, and beat the hand savagely across his chest.

At twelve o'clock the day was at its brightest. Yet the sun was too far south on its winter journey to clear the horizon. The bulge of the earth intervened between it and Henderson Creek, where the man walked under a clear sky at noon and cast no shadow. At half-past twelve, to the minute, he arrived at the forks of the creek. He was pleased at the speed he had made. If he kept it up, he would certainly be with the boys by six. He unbuttoned his jacket and shirt and drew forth his lunch. The action consumed no more than a quarter of a minute, yet in that brief moment the numbness laid hold of the exposed fingers. He did not put the mitten on, but, instead, struck the fingers a dozen sharp smashes against his leg. Then he sat down on a snow-covered log to eat. The sting that followed upon the striking of his fingers against his leg ceased so quickly that he was startled. He had had no chance to take a bite of biscuit. He struck the fingers repeatedly and returned them to the mitten, baring the other hand for the purpose of eating. He tried to take a mouthful, but the ice-muzzle prevented. He had forgotten to build a fire and thaw out. He chuckled at his foolishness, and as he chuckled he noted the numbness creeping into the exposed fingers. Also, he noted that the stinging which had first come to his toes when he sat down was already passing away. He wondered whether the toes were warm or numb. He moved them inside the moccasins and decided that they were numb.

He pulled the mitten on hurriedly and stood up. He was a bit frightened. He stamped up and down until the stinging returned into the feet. It certainly was cold, was his thought. That man from Sulphur Creek had spoken the truth when telling how cold it sometimes got in the country. And he had laughed at him at the time! That showed one must not be too sure of things. There was no mistake about it, it *was* cold. He strode up and down, stamping his feet and threshing his arms, until reassured by the returning warmth. Then he got out matches and proceeded to make a fire. From the undergrowth, where high water of the previous spring had lodged a supply of seasoned twigs, he got his firewood. Working carefully from a small beginning, he soon had a roaring fire, over which he thawed the ice from his face and in the protection of which he ate his biscuits. For the moment the cold of space was outwitted. The dog took satisfaction in the fire, stretching out close enough for warmth and far enough away to escape being singed.

When the man had finished, he filled his pipe and took his comfortable time over a smoke. Then he pulled on his mittens, settled the earflaps of his cap firmly about his ears, and took the creek trail up the left fork. The dog was disappointed and yearned back toward the fire. This man did not know cold. Possibly all the generations of his ancestry had been ignorant of cold, of real cold, of cold one hundred and seven degrees below freezing-point. But the dog knew; all its ancestry knew, and it had inherited the knowledge. And it knew that it was not good to walk abroad in such fearful cold. It was the time to lie snug in a hole in the snow and wait for a curtain of cloud to be drawn across the face of outer space whence this cold came. On the other hand, there was no keen intimacy between the dog and the man. The one was the toil-slave of the other, and the only caresses it had ever received were the caresses of the whiplash and of harsh and menacing throat-sounds that threatened the whiplash. So the dog made no effort to communicate its apprehension to the man. It was not concerned in the welfare of the man; it was for its own sake that it yearned back toward the fire. But the man whistled, and spoke to it with the sound of whiplashes, and the dog swung in at the man's heels and followed after.

The man took a chew of tobacco and proceeded to start a new amber beard. Also, his moist breath quickly powdered with white his mustache, eyebrows, and lashes. There did not seem to be so many springs on the left fork of the Henderson, and for half an hour the man saw no signs of any. And then it happened. At a place where there were no signs, where the soft, unbroken snow seemed to advertise solidity beneath, the man broke through. It was not deep. He wet himself halfway to the knees before he floundered out to the firm crust.

He was angry, and cursed his luck aloud. He had hoped to get into camp with the boys at six o'clock, and this would delay him an hour, for he would have to build a fire and dry out his foot-gear. This was imperative at that low temperature—he knew that much; and he turned aside to the bank, which he climbed. On top, tangled in the underbrush about the trunks of several small spruce trees, was a high-water deposit of dry fire-wood—sticks and twigs, principally, but also larger portions of seasoned branches and fine, dry, last-year's grasses. He threw down several large pieces on top of the snow. This served for a foundation and prevented the young flame from drowning itself in the snow it otherwise would melt. The flame he got by touching a match to a small shred of birch-bark that he took from his pocket. This burned even more readily than paper. Placing it on the foundation, he fed the young flame with wisps of dry grass and with the tiniest dry twigs.

He worked slowly and carefully, keenly aware of his danger. Gradually, as the flame grew stronger, he increased the size of the twigs with which he fed it. He squatted in the snow, pulling the twigs out from their entanglement in the brush and feeding directly to the flame. He knew there must be no failure. When

it is seventy-five below zero, a man must not fail in his first attempt to build a fire—that is, if his feet are wet. If his feet are dry, and he fails, he can run along the trail for half a mile and restore his circulation. But the circulation of wet and freezing feet cannot be restored by running when it is seventy-five below. No matter how fast he runs, the wet feet will freeze the harder.

All this the man knew. The old-timer on Sulphur Creek had told him about it the previous fall, and now he was appreciating the advice. Already all sensation had gone out of his feet. To build the fire he had been forced to remove his mittens, and the fingers had quickly gone numb. His pace of four miles an hour had kept his heart pumping blood to the surface of his body and to all the extremities. But the instant he stopped, the action of the pump eased down. The cold of space smote the unprotected tip of the planet, and he, being on that unprotected tip, received the full force of the blow. The blood of his body recoiled before it. The blood was alive, like the dog, and like the dog it wanted to hide away and cover itself up from the fearful cold. So long as he walked four miles an hour, he pumped that blood, willy-nilly, to the surface; but now it ebbed away and sank down into the recesses of his body. The extremities were the first to feel its absence. His wet feet froze the faster, and his exposed fingers numbed the faster, though they had not yet begun to freeze. Nose and cheeks were already freezing, while the skin of his body chilled as it lost its blood.

But he was safe. Toes and nose and cheeks would be only touched by the frost, for the fire was beginning to burn with strength. He was feeding it with twigs the size of his finger. In another minute he would be able to feed it with branches the size of his wrist, and then he could remove his wet foot-gear, and, while it dried, he could keep his naked feet warm by the fire, rubbing them at first, of course, with snow. The fire was a success. He was safe. He remembered the advice of the old-timer on Sulphur Creek, and smiled. The old-timer had been very serious in laying down the law that no man must travel alone in the Klondike after fifty below. Well, here he was; he had had the accident; he was alone; and he had saved himself. Those old-timers were rather womanish, some of them, he thought. All a man had to do was to keep his head, and he was all right. Any man who was a man could travel alone. But it was surprising, the rapidity with which his cheeks and nose were freezing. And he had not thought his fingers could go lifeless in so short a time. Lifeless they were, for he could scarcely make them move together to grip a twig, and they seemed remote from his body and from him. When he touched a twig, he had to look and see whether or not he had hold of it. The wires were pretty well down between him and his finger-ends.

All of which counted for little. There was the fire, snapping and crackling and promising life with every dancing flame. He started to untie his moccasins. They were coated with ice; the thick German socks were like sheaths of iron halfway to the knees; and the moccasin strings were like rods of steel all twisted and knotted as by some conflagration. For a moment he tugged with his numb fingers, then, realizing the folly of it, he drew his sheath-knife.

But before he could cut the strings, it happened. It was his own fault or, rather, his mistake. He should not have built the fire under the spruce tree. He should have built it in the open. But it had been easier to pull the twigs from the brush and drop them directly on the fire. Now the tree under which he had done this carried a weight of snow on its boughs. No wind had blown for weeks, and each bough was fully freighted. Each time he had pulled a twig he had communicated a slight agitation to the tree—an imperceptible agitation, so far as he was concerned, but an agitation sufficient to bring about the disaster. High up in the tree one bough capsized its load of snow. This fell on the boughs beneath, capsizing them. This process continued, spreading out and involving the whole tree. It ~~~like an avalanche, and it descended with-

out warning upon the man and the fire, and the fire was blotted out! Where it had burned was a mantel of fresh and disordered snow.

The man was shocked. It was as though he had just heard his own sentence of death. For a moment he sat and stared at the spot where the fire had been. Then he grew very calm. Perhaps the old-timer on Sulphur Creek was right. If he had only had a trail-mate he would have been in no danger now. The trail-mate could have built the fire. Well, it was up to him to build the fire over again, and this second time there must be no failure. Even if he succeeded, he would most likely lose some toes. His feet must be badly frozen by now, and there would be some time before the second fire was ready.

Such were his thoughts, but he did not sit and think them. He was busy all the time they were passing through his mind. He made a new foundation for a fire, this time in the open, where no treacherous tree could blot it out. Next, he gathered dry grasses and tiny twigs from the high-water flotsam. He could not bring his fingers together to pull them out, but he was able to gather them by the handful. In this way he got many rotten twigs and bits of green moss that were undesirable, but it was the best he could do. He worked methodically, even collecting an armful of the larger branches to be used later when the fire gathered strength. And all the while the dog sat and watched him, a certain yearning wistfulness in its eyes, for it looked upon him as the fire-provider, and the fire was slow in coming.

When all was ready, the man reached in his pocket for a second piece of birchbark. He knew the bark was there, and, though he could not feel it with his fingers, he could hear its crisp rustling as he fumbled for it. Try as he would, he could not clutch hold of it. And all the time, in his consciousness, was the knowledge that each instant his feet were freezing. This thought tended to put him in a panic, but he fought against it and kept calm. He pulled on his mittens with his teeth, and threshed his arms back and forth, beating his hands with all his might against his sides. He did this sitting down, and he stood up to do it; and all the while the dog sat in the snow, its wolf-brush of a tail curled around warmly over its forefeet, its sharp wolf-ears pricked forward intently as it watched the man. And the man, as he beat and threshed with his arms and hands, felt a great surge of envy as he regarded the creature that was warm and secure in its natural covering.

After a time he was aware of the first faraway signals of sensation in his beaten fingers. The faint tingling grew stronger till it evolved into a stinging ache that was excruciating, but which the man hailed with satisfaction. He stripped the mitten from his right hand and fetched forth the birchbark. The exposed fingers were quickly going numb again. Next he brought out his bunch of sulphur matches. But the tremendous cold had already driven the life out of his fingers. In his effort to separate one match from the others, the whole bunch fell in the snow. He tried to pick it out of the snow, but failed. The dead fingers could neither touch nor clutch. He was very careful. He drove the thought of his freezing feet, and nose, and cheeks, out of his mind, devoting his whole soul to the matches. He watched, using the sense of vision in place of that of touch, and when he saw his fingers on each side the bunch, he closed them—that is, he willed to close them, for the wires were down, and the fingers did not obey. He pulled the mitten on the right hand, and beat it fiercely against his knee. Then, with both mittened hands, he scooped the bunch of matches, along with much snow, into his lap. Yet he was no better off.

After some manipulation he managed to get the bunch between the heels of his mittened hands. In this fashion he carried it to his mouth. The ice crackled and snapped when by a violent effort he opened his mouth. He drew the lower jaw in, curled the upper lip out of the way, and scraped the bunch with his upper teeth in order to separate a match. He succeeded in getting one, which he dropped on his lap. He was no better off. He could not pick it

up. Then he devised a way. He picked it up in his teeth and scratched it on his leg. Twenty times he scratched before he succeeded in lighting it. As it flamed he held it with his teeth to the birchbark. But the burning brimstone went up his nostrils and into his lungs, causing him to cough spasmodically. The match fell into the snow and went out.

The old-timer on Sulphur Creek was right, he thought in the moment of controlled despair that ensued; after fifty below, a man should travel with a partner. He beat his hands, but failed in exciting any sensation. Suddenly he bared both hands, removing the mittens with his teeth. He caught the whole bunch between the heels of his hands. His arm-muscles not being frozen enabled him to press the hand-heels tightly against the matches. Then he scratched the bunch along his leg. It flared into flame, seventy sulphur matches at once! There was no wind to blow them out. He kept his head to one side to escape the strangling fumes, and held the blazing bunch to the birch-bark. As he so held it, he became aware of sensation in his hand. His flesh was burning. He could smell it. Deep down below the surface he could feel it. The sensation developed into pain that grew acute. And still he endured it, holding the flame of the matches clumsily to the bark that would not light readily because his own burning hands were in the way, absorbing most of the flame.

At last, when he could endure no more, he jerked his hands apart. The blazing matches fell sizzling into the snow, but the birch-bark was alight. He began laying dry grasses and the tiniest twigs on the flame. He could not pick and choose, for he had to lift the fuel between the heels of his hands. Small pieces of rotten wood and green moss clung to the twigs, and he bit them off as well as he could with his teeth. He cherished the flame carefully and awkwardly. It meant life, and it must not perish. The withdrawal of blood from the surface of his body now made him begin to shiver, and he grew more awkward. A large piece of green moss fell squarely on the little

"The sight of the dog put a wild idea into his head."

fire. He tried to poke it out with his fingers, but his shivering frame made him poke too far, and he disrupted the nucleus of the little fire, the burning grasses and tiny twigs separating and scattering. He tried to poke them together again, but in spite of the tenseness of the effort, his shivering got away with him, and the twigs were hopelessly scattered. Each twig gushed a puff of smoke and went out. The fire-provider had failed. As he looked apathetically about him, his eyes chanced on the dog, sitting across the ruins of the fire from him, in the snow, making restless, hunching movements, slightly lifting one forefoot and then the other, shifting its weight back and forth on them with wistful eagerness.

The sight of the dog put a wild idea into his head. He remembered the tale of the man, caught in a blizzard, who killed a steer and ~~~wled inside the carcass, and so was saved.

He would kill the dog and bury his hands in the warm body until the numbness went out of them. Then he could build another fire. He spoke to the dog, calling it to him; but in his voice was a strange note of fear that frightened the animal, who had never known the man to speak in such way before. Something was the matter, and its suspicious nature sensed danger —it knew not what danger, but somewhere, somehow, in its brain arose an apprehension of the man. It flattened its ears down at the sound of the man's voice, and its restless, hunching movements and the liftings and shiftings of its forefeet became more pronounced; but it would not come to the man. He got on his hands and knees and crawled toward the dog. This unusual posture again excited suspicion, and the animal sidled mincingly away.

The man sat up in the snow for a moment and struggled for calmness. Then he pulled on his mittens, by means of his teeth, and got upon his feet. He glanced down at first in order to assure himself that he was really standing up, for the absence of sensation in his feet left him unrelated to the earth. His erect position in itself started to drive the webs of suspicion from the dog's mind; and when he spoke peremptorily, with the sound of whiplashes in his voice, the dog rendered its customary allegiance and came to him. As it came within reaching distance, the man lost his control. His arms flashed out to the dog, and he experienced genuine surprise when he discovered that his hands could not clutch, that there was neither bend nor feeling in the fingers. He had forgotten for the moment that they were frozen and that they were freezing more and more. All this happened quickly, and before the animal could get away, he encircled its body with his arms. He sat down in the snow, and in this fashion held the dog, while it snarled and whined and struggled.

But it was all he could do, hold its body encircled in his arms and sit there. He realized that he could not kill the dog. There was no way to do it. With his helpless hands he could neither draw nor hold his sheath-knife nor throttle the animal. He released it, and it plunged wildly away, with tail between its legs, and still snarling. It halted forty feet away and surveyed him curiously, with ears sharply pricked forward. The man looked down at his hands in order to locate them, and found them hanging on the ends of his arms. It struck him as curious that one should have to use his eyes in order to find out where his hands were. He began threshing his arms back and forth, beating the mittened hands against his sides. He did this for five minutes, violently, and his heart pumped enough blood up to the surface to put a stop to his shivering. But no sensation was aroused in the hands. He had an impression that they hung like weights on the ends of his arms, but when he tried to run the impression down, he could not find it.

A certain fear of death, dull and oppressive, came to him. This fear quickly became poignant as he realized that it was no longer a mere matter of freezing his fingers and toes, or of losing his hands and feet, but that it was a matter of life and death with the chances against him. This threw him into a panic, and he turned and ran up the creek-bed along the old, dim trail. The dog joined in behind and kept up with him. He ran blindly, without intention, in fear such as he had never known in his life. Slowly, as he ploughed and floundered through the snow, he began to see things again,—the banks of the creek, the old timber-jams, the leafless aspens, and the sky. The running made him feel better. He did not shiver. Maybe, if he ran on, his feet would thaw out; and, anyway, if he ran far enough, he would reach camp and the boys. Without doubt he would lose some fingers and toes and some of his face; but the boys would take care of him, and save the rest of him when he got there. And at the same time there was another thought in his mind that said he would never get to the camp and the boys; that it was too many miles away, that the freezing had too great a start on him, and that he would soon be stiff and dead. This thought he kept in the background and refused to consider. Sometimes it pushed itself forward and demanded to be heard, but he thrust it back and strove to think of other things.

It struck him as curious that he could run at all on feet so frozen that he could not feel them when they struck the earth and took the weight of his body. He seemed to himself to skim along above the surface, and to have no connection with the earth. Somewhere he had once seen a winged Mercury, and he wondered if Mercury[4] felt as he felt when skimming over the earth.

His theory of running until he reached camp and the boys had one flaw in it: he lacked the endurance. Several times he stumbled, and finally he tottered, crumpled up, and fell. When he tried to rise, he failed. He must sit and rest, he decided, and next time he would merely walk and keep on going. As he sat and

4. **Mercury**, a Greek and Roman god and messenger for the other gods, was winged.

regained his breath, he noted that he was feeling quite warm and comfortable. He was not shivering, and it even seemed that a warm glow had come to his chest and trunk. And yet, when he touched his nose or cheeks, there was no sensation. Running would not thaw them out. Nor would it thaw out his hands and feet. Then the thought came to him that the frozen portions of his body must be extending. He tried to keep this thought down, to forget it, to think of something else; he was aware of the panicky feeling that it caused, and he was afraid of the panic. But the thought asserted itself, and persisted, until it produced a vision of his body totally frozen. This was too much, and he made another wild run along the trail. Once he slowed down to a walk, but the thought of the freezing extending itself made him run again.

And all the time the dog ran with him, at his heels. When he fell down a second time, it curled its tail over its forefeet and sat in front of him, facing him, curiously eager and intent. The warmth and security of the animal angered him, and he cursed it till it flattened down its ears appeasingly. This time the shivering came more quickly upon the man. He was losing in his battle with the frost. It was creeping into his body from all sides. The thought of it drove him on, but he ran no more than a hundred feet, when he staggered and pitched headlong. It was his last panic. When he had recovered his breath and control, he sat up and entertained in his mind the conception of meeting death with dignity. However, the conception did not come to him in such terms. His idea of it was that he had been making a fool of himself, running around like a chicken with its head cut off—such was the simile that occurred to him. Well, he was bound to freeze anyway, and he might as well take it decently. With this new-found peace of mind came the first glimmerings of drowsiness. A good idea, he thought, to sleep off to death. It was like taking an anesthetic. Freezing was not so bad as people thought. There were lots worse ways to die.

He pictured the boys finding his body next day. Suddenly he found himself with them, coming along the trail and looking for himself. And, still with them, he came around a turn in the trail and found himself lying in the snow. He did not belong with himself any more, for even then he was out of himself, standing with the boys and looking at himself in the snow. It certainly was cold, was his thought. When he got back to the States he could tell the folks what real cold was. He drifted on from this to a vision of the old-timer on Sulphur Creek. He could see him quite clearly, warm and comfortable, and smoking a pipe.

"You were right, old hoss; you were right," the man mumbled to the old-timer of Sulphur Creek.

Then the man drowsed off into what seemed to him the most comfortable and satisfying sleep he had ever known. The dog sat facing him and waiting. The brief day drew to a close in a long, slow twilight. There were no signs of a fire to be made, and, besides, never in the dog's experience had it known a man to sit like that in the snow and make no fire. As the twilight drew on, its eager yearning for the fire mastered it, and with a great lifting and shifting of forefeet, it whined softly, then flattened its ears down in anticipation of being chidden by the man. But the man remained silent. Later, the dog whined loudly. And still later it crept close to the man and caught the scent of death. This made the animal bristle and back away. A little longer it delayed, howling under the stars that leaped and danced and shone brightly in the cold sky. Then it turned and trotted up the trail in the direction of the camp it knew, where were the other food-providers and fire-providers.

I

DANGER AND FEAR

Jack London introduces the reader to the quiet, subtle, indifferent, and yet ever present pressure of nature on man. The sky is gray, the landscape bleak, but this is usual in the Far North. A man and a dog are alone in the vast expanses of snow. This, too, is usual. But it is seventy-five degrees below zero, and this is unusual. It is also extremely dangerous, but the man is unaware of his danger until it is too late. When he does realize it, he begins to feel that he is being hunted down by nature as surely as if he were being tracked by a wolf. But is this feeling accurate, or is it really a sign of his own panic?

II
IMPLICATIONS

A. It could be said that the man's real enemy in this story is his own nature, not the cold. Discuss this proposition in the light of the following quotations. What elements in this character, as revealed by the quotations, help the man to cope with the cold? What elements hinder him? How does the balance of these elements create suspense?

1. "The trouble with him was that he was without imagination. He was quick and alert in the things of life, but only in the things, and not in the significances."

2. "Empty as the man's mind was of thoughts, he was keenly observant, and he noticed the changes in the creek, the curves and bends and timber-jams, and always he sharply noted where he placed his feet."

3. "He had forgotten to build a fire and thaw out. He chuckled at his foolishness. . . ."

4. "This man did not know cold. Possibly all the generations of his ancestry had been ignorant of cold, of real cold. . . ."

5. "He worked slowly and carefully [building the fire], keenly aware of his danger."

B. To what extent do you think the following statements are accurate generalities? Discuss them with reference to your own experience as well as to your understanding of "To Build a Fire."

1. The man in this story dies because of his own weaknesses.

2. Once a man's self-confidence is shaken, it becomes increasingly difficult to act rationally.

3. People are more likely to make mistakes when they are frightened than when they are not.

4. Man is ill-equipped by nature to endure extremes of climate, or even live at all outside of civilization. Whenever he ventures into the wilderness, he must therefore survive by his wits.

III
TECHNIQUES

Theme

If the theme of this story is the disintegration of rationality under the pressure of fear, how does the extreme cold contribute to the theme? How does the man's lack of imagination contribute to it? Where does Jack London show you the man's first sign of fear? What step-by-step incidents reveal its growing power over him?

On what basis could you say that the development of the theme is complex and disguised, or simple and straightforward?

Style and Identification

Jack London's manner of telling this story is matter-of-fact and impersonal almost to the point of seeming heartless. This style, however, is deliberate, and is calculated to evoke certain responses in the reader. Recall your feelings while you were reading the story. Did you care about the man from the beginning? For what reasons did you want him to survive? What was your reaction to his behavior as he grew more and more desperate? How did you feel about his death?

Why does London call the central figure simply "the man"? Why doesn't he describe the man's family, friends, ambitions, etc.? On the other hand, choose several passages and show how he describes the physical setting and action with great detail. Why does London emphasize factual rather than personal details? How does this affect your feelings toward the man? What might your response to the action and the man have been if London had told the story in very emotional prose, full of his own feelings about the situation?

Now briefly discuss the following proposition: In telling a tragic event, the more unemotional the style, the greater the impact on the reader.

Beneath the waters of Lake Geneva,
in the depths of an ancient castle in Switzerland,
lies a dungeon which captured the imagination
of Lord Byron, a poet with a passionate belief
in freedom. Traveling in Switzerland,
he learned that in the sixteenth century
a Swiss patriot had spent four long years
chained to a pillar in that dungeon.
Bryon scratched his name on the column
as if to identify himself with the chained man.
He then wrote his narrative poem
"The Prisoner of Chillon,"
turning that chained man into a moving symbol
of all men's struggles and sacrifices
for freedom. The poem is told by Bonnivard,
the prisoner, as he remembers his experiences
after his release.

The Prisoner of Chillon [1]

I

My hair is gray, but not with years,
  Nor grew it white
  In a single night,
As men's have grown from sudden fears.
My limbs are bow'd, though not with toil,   5
But rusted with a vile repose,
For they have been a dungeon's spoil,
And mine has been the fate of those
To whom the goodly earth and air
Are bann'd, and barr'd—forbidden fare: 10
But this was for my father's faith
I suffer'd chains and courted death;
That father perish'd at the stake
For tenets he would not forsake;
And for the same his lineal race [2]   15
In darkness found a dwelling-place;
We were seven—who now are one,
Six in youth, and one in age,
Finish'd as they had begun,
Proud of Persecution's rage;   20

One in fire, and two in field,
Their belief with blood have seal'd,
Dying as their father died,
For the God their foes denied;
Three were in a dungeon cast,   25
Of whom this wreck is left the last.

II

There are seven pillars of Gothic mould, [3]
In Chillon's dungeons deep and old,
There are seven columns, massy and gray,
Dim with a dull imprison'd ray,   30
A sunbeam which hath lost its way,
And through the crevice and the cleft
Of the thick wall is fallen and left;
Creeping o'er the floor so damp,
Like a marsh's meteor lamp: [4]   35
And in each pillar there is a ring,
And in each ring there is a chain;
That iron is a cankering [5] thing,
For in these limbs its teeth remain,
With marks that will not wear away,   40
Till I have done with this new day,
Which now is painful to these eyes,
Which have not seen the sun so rise
For years—I cannot count them o'er,
I lost their long and heavy score   45
When my last brother droop'd and died,
And I lay living by his side.

III

They chain'd us each to a column stone,
And we were three—yet, each alone;
We could not move a single pace,   50
We could not see each other's face,
But with that pale and livid light
That made us strangers in our sight:
And thus together—yet apart,

1. **Chillon**\shĭ ▲lŏn\. François de Bonnivard\'bō·nē-▲var\ (1496–1570) fell into the hands of his political and religious enemies in 1530 and was confined in Chillon from 1532 to 1536.
2. **his lineal race,** his sons, since they were in a direct line of descent from him.
3. **of Gothic mould,** after the order of Gothic \▲gŏ·thĭk\ construction.
4. **marsh's meteor lamp,** a phosphorescent light in a marsh.
5. **canker**\▲căn·kər\ to eat away or consume as a canker does.

*The Castle of
Chillon near Montreux
on Lake Geneva.*

Fetter'd in hand, but join'd in heart, 55
'Twas still some solace, in the dearth
Of the pure elements of earth,
To hearken to each other's speech,
And each turn comforter to each
With some new hope, or legend old, 60
Or song heroically bold;
But even these at length grew cold.
Our voices took a dreary tone,
An echo of the dungeon stone,
A grating sound—not full and free 65
As they of yore were wont to be;
It might be fancy—but to me
They never sounded like our own.

IV

I was the eldest of the three,
And to uphold and cheer the rest
I ought to do—and did my best— 70
And each did well in his degree.
The youngest, whom my father loved,
Because our mother's brow was given
To him—with eyes as blue as heaven— 75

For him my soul was sorely moved;
And truly might it be distress'd
To see such bird in such a nest;
For he was beautiful as day—
(When day was beautiful to me 80
As to young eagles, being free)—
A polar day,[6] which will not see
A sunset till its summer's gone,
Its sleepless summer of long light,
The snow-clad offspring of the sun: 85
And thus he was as pure and bright,
And in his natural spirit gay,
With tears for nought but others' ills,
And then they flow'd like mountain rills,[7]
Unless he could assuage the woe 90
Which he abhorr'd to view below.

---

6. **polar day,** near the poles of the earth the sun never
sets in summer.
7. **rills,** brooks.

V

The other was as pure of mind,
But form'd to combat with his kind;
Strong in his frame, and of a mood
Which 'gainst the world in war had stood,   95
And perish'd in the foremost rank
With joy:—but not in chains to pine:
His spirit wither'd with their clank,
I saw it silently decline—
And so perchance in sooth[8] did mine: 100
But yet I forced it on to cheer
Those relics of a home so dear.
He was a hunter of the hills,
Had follow'd there the deer and wolf;
To him his dungeon was a gulf,   105
And fetter'd feet the worst of ills.

VI

Lake Leman[9] lies by Chillon's walls,
A thousand feet in depth below
Its massy waters meet and flow;
Thus much the fathom-line was sent   110
From Chillon's snow-white battlement,
Which round about the wave inthralls:
A double dungeon wall and wave
Have made—and like a living grave.
Below the surface of the lake   115
The dark vault lies wherein we lay;
We heard it ripple night and day;
Sounding o'er our heads it knock'd;
And I have felt the winter's spray
Wash through the bars when winds were
  high   120
And wanton in the happy sky;
And then the very rock hath rock'd,
And I have felt it shake, unshock'd,
Because I could have smiled to see
The death that would have set me free.   125

VII

I said my nearer brother pined,
I said his mighty heart declined,
He loathed and put away his food;
It was not that 'twas coarse and rude,
For we were used to hunters' fare,   130
And for the like had little care:
The milk drawn from the mountain goat
Was changed for water from the moat,

Our bread was such as captives' tears
Have moisten'd many a thousand years,   135
Since man first pent[10] his fellow men
Like brutes within an iron den;
But what were these to us or him?
These wasted not his heart or limb;
My brother's soul was of that mould   140
Which in a palace had grown cold,
Had his free breathing been denied
The range of the steep mountain's side;
But why delay the truth?—he died.
I saw, and could not hold his head,   145
Nor reach his dying hand—nor dead,—
Though hard I strove, but strove in vain,
To rend and gnash my bonds in twain.
He died—and they unlock'd his chain,
And scoop'd for him a shallow grave   150
Even from the cold earth of our cave.
I begg'd them, as a boon,[11] to lay
His corse[12] in dust whereon the day
Might shine—it was a foolish thought,
But then within my brain it wrought,   155
That even in death his freeborn breast
In such a dungeon could not rest.
I might have spared my idle prayer—
They coldly laugh'd, and laid him there:
The flat and turfless earth above   160
The being we so much did love;
His empty chain above it leant,
Such murder's fitting monument!

VIII

But he, the favorite and the flower,
Most cherish'd since his natal hour,[13]   165
His mother's image in fair face,
The infant love of all his race,
His martyr'd father's dearest thought,
My latest care, for whom I sought
To hoard my life, that his might be   170
Less wretched now, and one day free;

---

8. **perchance,** archaic: perhaps. **sooth**\sūth\ archaic: truth.
9. **Leman**\ˈlē·mən\ another name for **Geneva**\jə ˈnē-və\ a lake in western Switzerland and southern France.
10. **pent,** penned.
11. **boon**\būn\ an aid, kindness, or favor.
12. **corse**\kōrs\ corpse, body.
13. **natal**\ˈnā·təl\ **hour,** the hour of birth.

He, too, who yet had held untired
A spirit natural or inspired—
He, too, was struck, and day by day
Was wither'd on the stalk away.   175
Oh, God! it is a fearful thing
To see the human soul take wing
In any shape, in any mood:
I've seen it rushing forth in blood,
I've seen it on the breaking ocean   180
Strive with a swoll'n convulsive motion,
I've seen the sick and ghastly bed
Of Sin delirious with its dread;
But these were horrors—this was woe
Unmix'd with such—but sure and slow;   185
He faded, and so calm and meek,
So softly worn, so sweetly weak,
So tearless, yet so tender—kind,
And grieved for those he left behind;
With all the while a cheek whose bloom   190
Was as a mockery of the tomb,
Whose tints as gently sunk away
As a departing rainbow's ray—
An eye of most transparent light,
That almost made the dungeon bright,   195
And not a word of murmur—not
A groan o'er his untimely lot,—
A little talk of better days,
A little hope my own to raise,
For I was sunk in silence—lost   200
In this last loss, of all the most;
And then the sighs he would suppress
Of fainting nature's feebleness,
More slowly drawn, grew less and less:
I listen'd, but I could not hear—   205
I call'd, for I was wild with fear;
I knew't was hopeless, but my dread
Would not be thus admonished;
I call'd, and thought I heard a sound—
I burst my chain with one strong bound,   210
And rush'd to him:—I found him not,
I only stirr'd in this black spot,
I only lived, *I* only drew
The accursed breath of dungeon-dew;
The last—the sole—the dearest link   215
Between me and the eternal brink,[14]
Which bound me to my failing race,
Was broken in this fatal place,

One on the earth, and one beneath—
My brothers—both had ceased to breathe: 220
I took that hand which lay so still,
Alas! my own was full as chill;
I had not strength to stir, or strive,
But felt that I was still alive—
A frantic feeling, when we know   225
That what we love shall ne'er be so.
      I know not why
      I could not die,
I had no earthly hope—but faith,
And that forbade a selfish death.   230

IX

What next befell me then and there
I know not well—I never knew—
First came the loss of light, and air,
And then of darkness too:
I had no thought, no feeling—none;   235
Among the stones I stood a stone,
And was, scarce conscious what I wist,[15]
As shrubless crags within the mist;
For all was blank, and bleak, and gray;
It was not night, it was not day;   240
It was not even the dungeon-light,
So hateful to my heavy sight,
But vacancy absorbing space,
And fixedness—without a place;
There were no stars—no earth—no time—   245
No check—no change—no good—no
      crime—
But silence, and a stirless breath
Which neither was of life nor death;
A sea of stagnant idleness,
Blind, boundless, mute, and motionless!   250

X

A light broke in upon my brain,—
It was the carol of a bird;
It ceased, and then it came again,
The sweetest song ear ever heard,
And mine was thankful till my eyes   255
Ran over with the glad surprise,
And they that moment could not see
I was the mate of misery;

---

14. **eternal brink,** death.
15. **wist**\wĭst\ knew.

But then by dull degrees came back
My senses to their wonted track;   260
I saw the dungeon walls and floor
Close slowly round me as before;
I saw the glimmer of the sun
Creeping as it before had done,
But through the crevice where it came   265
That bird was perch'd, as fond and tame,
And tamer than upon the tree;
A lovely bird, with azure wings,
And song that said a thousand things,
And seem'd to say them all for me!   270
I never saw its like before,
I ne'er shall see its likeness more:
It seem'd like me to want a mate,
But was not half so desolate,
And it was come to love me when   275
None lived to love me so again,
And cheering from my dungeon's brink,
Had brought me back to feel and think.
I know not if it late were free,
Or broke its cage to perch on mine,   280
But knowing well captivity,
Sweet bird! I could not wish for thine!
Or if it were, in winged guise,
A visitant from Paradise;
For—Heaven forgive that thought! the
    while   285
Which made me both to weep and smile—
I sometimes deem'd that it might be
My brother's soul come down to me;
But then at last away it flew,
And then 'twas mortal—well I knew,   290
For he would never thus have flown,
And left me twice so doubly lone,—
Lone—as the corse within its shroud,
Lone—as a solitary cloud,
A single cloud on a sunny day,   295
While all the rest of heaven is clear,
A frown upon the atmosphere,
That hath no business to appear
When skies are blue, and earth is gay.

XI

A kind of change came in my fate,   300
My keepers grew compassionate;
I know not what had made them so,

They were inured to sights of woe,
But so it was:—my broken chain
With links unfasten'd did remain,   305
And it was liberty to stride
Along my cell from side to side,
And up and down, and then athwart,
And tread it over every part;
And round the pillars one by one,   310
Returning where my walk begun,
Avoiding only, as I trod,
My brothers' graves without a sod;
For if I thought with heedless tread
My step profaned their lowly bed,   315
My breath came gaspingly and thick,
And my crush'd heart fell blind and sick.

XII

I made a footing in the wall,
It was not therefrom to escape,
For I had buried one and all   320
Who loved me in a human shape;
And the whole earth would henceforth be
A wider prison unto me:
No child—no sire—no kin had I,
No partner in my misery;   325
I thought of this, and I was glad,
For thought of them had made me mad;
But I was curious to ascend
To my barr'd windows, and to bend
Once more, upon the mountains high,   330
The quiet of a loving eye.

XIII

I saw them—and they were the same,
They were not changed like me in frame;
I saw their thousand years of snow
On high—their wide long lake below,   335
And the blue Rhone[16] in fullest flow;
I heard the torrents leap and gush
O'er channell'd rock and broken bush;
I saw the white-wall'd distant town,
And whiter sails go skimming down;   340
And then there was a little isle,
Which in my very face did smile,
    The only one in view;
A small green isle, it seem'd no more,

---

16. **Rhone**\rōn\ the river which forms Lake Geneva.

*Bonnivard's cell
in the Castle of Chillon.
Parts of the structure
date from the ninth century.*

Scarce broader than my dungeon floor,   345
But in it there were three tall trees,
And o'er it blew the mountain breeze,
And by it there were waters flowing,
And on it there were young flowers
    growing,
    Of gentle breath and hue.   350
The fish swam by the castle wall,
And they seem'd joyous each and all;
The eagle rode the rising blast,
Methought[17] he never flew so fast
As then to me he seem'd to fly;   355
And then new tears came in my eye,
And I felt troubled—and would fain

I had not left my recent chain;
And when I did descend again,
The darkness of my dim abode   360
Fell on me as a heavy load;
It was as in a new-dug grave,
Closing o'er one we sought to save,—
And yet my glance, too much opprest,
Had almost need of such a rest.   365

XIV

It might be months, or years, or days—
I kept no count—I took no note,
I had no hope my eyes to raise,

---

17. **methought**, archaic: it seemed to me.

And clear them of their dreary mote;
At last men came to set me free;   370
I ask'd not why, and reck'd not where;
It was at length the same to me,
Fetter'd or fetterless to be,
I learn'd to love despair.
And thus when they appear'd at last,   375
And all my bonds aside were cast,
These heavy walls to me had grown
A hermitage—and all my own!
And half I felt as they were come
To tear me from a second home: 380
With spiders I had friendship made,
And watch'd them in their sullen trade,
Had seen the mice by moonlight play,
And why should I feel less than they?
We were all inmates of one place,   385
And I, the monarch of each race,
Had power to kill—yet, strange to tell!
In quiet we had learn'd to dwell—
My very chains and I grew friends,
So much a long communion tends   390
To make us what we are:—even I
Regain'd my freedom with a sigh.

GEORGE GORDON, LORD BYRON

I
MANY PRISONS

While Byron's poem is a magnificent story of the effects of imprisonment on the human spirit, it has a wider meaning. Byron saw clearly that any loss of freedom is like a prison that bit by bit breaks the spirit of human beings. The story of Bonnivard's surrender to the pressure of imprisonment is really the story of the way many people surrender to conditions that confine or restrict them. Poverty, fear, segregation, ignorance, political persecution are all prisons, pressures, that may affect the spirit of a man as Bonnivard's was affected.

II
IMPLICATIONS

When the human mind is faced with pressures too great to bear, it finds refuge in many ways. Two of Bonnivard's brothers died. But Byron sug-

gests that Bonnivard's adjustment to the pressures of imprisonment may be a fate more horrible than death. What attitudes of the prisoner toward his imprisonment do the following lines reveal?

1. "That iron is a cankering thing." (l. 38)
2. "Our voices took a dreary tone." (l. 63)
3. ". . . I could have smiled to see
   The death that would have set me free."
   (ll. 124–125)
4. "I had no thought, no feeling—none;
   Among the stones I stood a stone."
   (ll. 235–236)
5. "And when I did descend again,
   The darkness of my dim abode
   Fell on me as a heavy load . . .
   And yet my glance, too much opprest,
   Had almost need of such a rest."
   (ll. 359–365)
6. "I learn'd to love despair." (l. 374)
7. "These heavy walls to me had grown
   A hermitage—and all my own!"
   (ll. 377–378)
8. "My very chains and I grew friends,
   So much a long communion tends
   To make us what we are:—even I
   Regain'd my freedom with a sigh."
   (ll. 389–392)

The last three quotations above show that Bonnivard made a strange adjustment to his imprisonment. In your opinion, was this a tragic adjustment, in which he virtually lost his soul, or a happy one, in which he regained it?

III
TECHNIQUES

In considering the craftsmanship of "The Prisoner of Chillon," do you agree or disagree with the following statements?

1. The narration loses effectiveness through the use of the flashback technique. The poem would have been more moving if written as if Bonnivard were still a prisoner.

2. The episodic quality of the first seven stanzas, in which the narration jumps from subject to subject, develops the reader's interest.

3. The sound of the words often suggests the mood of what is being said.

4. The reader's emotions reach a climax in the story with the death of the second brother.

◆
The concluding lines
of William Henley's famous poem "Invictus"
read, "I am the master of my fate;
I am the captain of my soul."
To what extent each person controls
the course and outcome of his life is a question
that all men ask themselves. What answer
does the following story give?
Is Paul the master of his fate or not?

Paul's Case

WILLA CATHER

It was Paul's afternoon to appear before the faculty of the Pittsburgh High School to account for his various misdemeanors. He had been suspended a week ago, and his father had called at the Principal's office and confessed his perplexity about his son. Paul entered the faculty room suave and smiling. His clothes were a trifle outgrown, and the tan velvet on the collar of his open overcoat was frayed and worn; but for all that there was something of the dandy about him, and he wore an opal pin in his neatly knotted black four-in-hand,[1] and a red carnation in his buttonhole. This latter adornment the faculty somehow felt was not properly significant of the contrite spirit befitting a boy under the ban of suspension.

Paul was tall for his age and very thin, with high, cramped shoulders and a narrow chest. His eyes were remarkable for a certain hysterical brilliancy, and he continually used them in a conscious, theatrical sort of way, peculiarly offensive in a boy. The pupils were abnormally large, as though he were addicted to belladonna,[2] but there was a glassy glitter about them which that drug does not produce.

When questioned by the Principal as to why he was there, Paul stated, politely enough, that he wanted to come back to school. This was a lie, but Paul was quite accustomed to lying; found it, indeed, indispensable for overcoming friction. His teachers were asked to state their respective charges against him, which they did with such a rancor and aggrievedness as evinced that this was not a usual case. Disorder and impertinence were among the offenses named, yet each of his instructors felt that it was scarcely possible to put into words the real cause of the trouble, which lay in a sort of hysterically defiant manner of the boy's; in the contempt which they all knew he felt for them, and which he seemingly made not the least effort to conceal. Once, when he had been making a synopsis of a paragraph at the blackboard, his English teacher had stepped to his side and attempted to guide his hand. Paul had started back with a shudder and thrust his hands violently behind him. The astonished woman could scarcely have been more hurt and embarrassed had he struck at her. The insult was so involuntary and definitely personal as to be unforgettable. In one way and another, he had made all his teachers, men and women alike, conscious of the same feeling of physical aversion. In one class he habitually sat with his hand shading his eyes; in another he always looked out of the window during the recitation; in another he made a running commentary on the lecture, with humorous intent.

His teachers felt this afternoon that his whole attitude was symbolized by his shrug and his flippantly red carnation flower, and they fell upon him without mercy, his English teacher leading the pack. He stood through it smiling, his pale lips parted over his white teeth. (His lips were continually twitching, and he had a habit of raising his eyebrows that was contemptuous and irritating to the last degree.) Older boys than Paul had broken

1. **four-in-hand** necktie, an ordinary necktie that is not a bow tie.
2. **belladonna**\ˌbĕ•lə ˈdŏ•nə\ a poisonous plant, some doses of which dilate the pupils of the eyes.

Reprinted from YOUTH AND THE BRIGHT MEDUSA, by Willa Cather, courtesy of Alfred A. Knopf, Inc.

down and shed tears under that ordeal, but his set smile did not once desert him, and his only sign of discomfort was the nervous trembling of the fingers that toyed with the buttons of his overcoat, and an occasional jerking of the other hand which held his hat. Paul was always smiling, always glancing about him, seeming to feel that people might be watching him and trying to detect something. This conscious expression, since it was as far as possible from boyish mirthfulness, was usually attributed to insolence or "smartness."

As the inquisition proceeded, one of his instructors repeated an impertinent remark of the boy's, and the Principal asked him whether he thought that a courteous speech to make to a woman. Paul shrugged his shoulders slightly and his eyebrows twitched.

"I don't know," he replied. "I didn't mean to be polite or impolite, either. I guess it's a sort of way I have, of saying things regardless."

The Principal asked him whether he didn't think that a way it would be well to get rid of. Paul grinned and said he guessed so. When he was told that he could go, he bowed gracefully and went out. His bow was like a repetition of the scandalous red carnation.

His teachers were in despair, and his drawing-master voiced the feeling of them all when he declared there was something about the boy which none of them understood. He added: "I don't really believe that smile of his comes altogether from insolence; there's something sort of haunted about it. The boy is not strong, for one thing. There is something wrong about the fellow."

The drawing-master had come to realize that, in looking at Paul, one saw only his white teeth and the forced animation of his eyes. One warm afternoon the boy had gone to sleep at his drawing-board, and his master had noted with amazement what a white, blue-veined face it was; drawn and wrinkled like an old man's about the eyes, the lips twitching even in his sleep.

His teachers left the building dissatisfied and unhappy; humiliated to have felt so vin-

dictive toward a mere boy, to have uttered this feeling in cutting terms, and to have set each other on, as it were, in the gruesome game of intemperate reproach. One of them remembered having seen a miserable street cat set at bay by a ring of tormentors.

As for Paul, he ran down the hill whistling the Soldiers' Chorus from *Faust*,[3] looking behind him now and then to see whether some of his teachers were not there to witness his light-heartedness. As it was now late in the afternoon and Paul was on duty that evening as usher at Carnegie Hall,[4] he decided that he would not go home to supper.

When he reached the concert hall, the doors were not yet open. It was chilly outside, and he decided to go up into the picture gallery—always deserted at this hour—where there were some of Raffaelli's[5] gay studies of Paris streets and an airy blue Venetian scene or two that always exhilarated him. He was delighted to find no one in the gallery but the old guard, who sat in the corner, a newspaper on his knee, a black patch over one eye and the other closed. Paul possessed himself of the place and walked confidently up and down, whistling under his breath. After a while he sat down before a blue Rico and lost himself. When he bethought him to look at his watch, it was after seven o'clock, and he rose with a start and ran downstairs, making a face at Augustus Caesar peering out from the east-room, and an evil gesture at the Venus of Milo[6] as he passed her on the stairway.

When Paul reached the ushers' dressing-room, half a dozen boys were there already, and he began excitedly to tumble into his uni-

---

3. **Faust,** an opera by Gounod, of which the soldiers' chorus beginning "Glory and love to the men of old" is well known.

4. **Carnegie\\'kar ▲nä·gē\\ Hall,** a music hall in the Oakland district of Pittsburgh.

5. **Jean Raffaelli\\ra 'fa·ĕ ▲lē** (1850–1924), a French painter.

6. He made a face at the cast of the bust of **Augustus Caesar,** the Roman Emperor (63 B.C.–A.D. 14). The **Venus of Milo\\▲mē·lō** (the Greek island better known as Melos) one of the world's most famous statues. Paul makes his gesture at a copy.

*Jean François Raffaelli's painting
of the Place St. Germain
des Prés, Paris.*

form. It was one of the few that at all approached fitting, and Paul thought it very becoming—though he knew the tight, straight coat accentuated his narrow chest, about which he was exceedingly sensitive. He was always excited while he dressed, twanging all over to the tuning of the strings and the preliminary flourishes of the horns in the music-room; but tonight he seemed quite beside himself, and he teased and plagued the boys until, telling him that he was crazy, they put him down on the floor and sat on him.

Somewhat calmed by his suppression, Paul dashed out to the front of the house to seat the early comers. He was a model usher. Gracious and smiling he ran up and down the aisles. Nothing was too much trouble for him; he carried messages and brought programs as though it were his greatest pleasure in life, and all the people in his section thought him a charming boy, feeling that he remembered and admired them. As the house filled, he grew more and more vivacious and animated, and the color came to his cheeks and lips. It was very much as though this were a great reception and Paul were the host. Just as the musicians came out to take their places, his English teacher arrived with checks for the seats which a prominent manufacturer had taken for the season. She betrayed some embarrassment when she handed Paul the tickets, and a hauteur which subsequently made her feel very foolish. Paul was startled for a moment, and had the feeling of wanting to put her out; what business had she here among all these fine people and gay colors? He looked her over and decided that she was not appropriately dressed and must be a fool to sit downstairs in such togs.[7] The tickets had probably been sent her out of kindness, he reflected, as he put down a seat for her, and she had about as much right to sit there as he had.

When the symphony began, Paul sank into one of the rear seats with a long sigh of relief, and lost himself as he had done before the Rico. It was not that symphonies, as such, meant anything in particular to Paul, but the first sigh of the instruments seemed to free some hilarious spirit within him; something that struggled there like the Genius in the bottle found by the Arab fisherman.[8] He felt a sudden zest of life; the lights danced before his eyes and the concert hall blazed into unimaginable splendor. When the soprano soloist came on, Paul forgot even the nastiness of his teacher's being there, and gave himself up to the peculiar intoxication such personages always had for him. The soloist chanced to be a German woman, by no means in her first youth, and the mother of many children; but she wore a satin gown and a tiara, and she had that indefinable air of achievement, that world-shine upon her, which always blinded Paul to any possible defects.

After a concert was over, Paul was often irritable and wretched until he got to sleep—and tonight he was even more than usually restless. He had the feeling of not being able to let down; of its being impossible to give up

this delicious excitement which was the only thing that could be called living at all. During the last number he withdrew and, after hastily changing his clothes in the dressing-room, slipped out to the side door where the singer's carriage stood. Here he began pacing rapidly up and down the walk, waiting to see her come out.

Over yonder the Schenley,[9] in its vacant stretch, loomed big and square through the fine rain, the windows of its twelve stories glowing like those of a lighted cardboard house under a Christmas tree. All the actors and singers of any importance stayed there when they were in Pittsburgh, and a number of the big manufacturers of the place lived there in the winter. Paul had often hung about the hotel, watching the people go in and out, longing to enter and leave schoolmasters and dull care behind him forever.

At last the singer came out, accompanied by the conductor, who helped her into her carriage and closed the door with a cordial *auf wiedersehen*,[10]—which set Paul to wondering whether she were not an old sweetheart of his. Paul followed the carriage over to the hotel, walking so rapidly as not to be far from the entrance when the singer alighted and disappeared behind the swinging glass doors which were opened by a Negro in a tall hat and a long coat. In the moment that the door was ajar, it seemed to Paul that he, too, entered. He seemed to feel himself go after her up the steps, into the warm, lighted building, into an exotic, a tropical world of shiny, glistening surfaces and basking ease. He reflected upon the mysterious dishes that were brought into the dining-room, the green bottles in buckets of

---

7. **togs**\tŏgz\ informal: clothes.
8. In one of the **Arabian Nights** stories, a fisherman finds a bottle in which a huge and powerful supernatural creature called a jinn or genius has been imprisoned.
9. **Schenley**\ˈshĕn·lē\ a large hotel in the Oakland district of Pittsburgh. The building is now part of the University of Pittsburgh.
10. **auf wiedersehen**\auf 'vē·dər ˈsē·ən\ German: "good-bye, until we meet again."

ice, as he had seen them in the supper party pictures of the Sunday supplement.[11] A quick gust of wind brought the rain down with sudden vehemence, and Paul was startled to find that he was still outside in the slush of the gravel driveway; that his boots were letting in the water and his scanty overcoat was clinging wet about him; that the lights in front of the concert hall were out, and that the rain was driving in sheets between him and the orange glow of the windows above him. There it was, what he wanted—tangibly before him, like the fairy world of a Christmas pantomime; as the rain beat in his face, Paul wondered whether he were destined always to shiver in the black night outside, looking up at it.

He turned and walked reluctantly toward the car tracks. The end had to come sometime; his father in his night-clothes at the top of the stairs, explanations that did not explain, hastily improvised fictions that were forever tripping him up, his upstairs room and its horrible yellow wallpaper, the creaking bureau with the greasy plush collar-box, and over his painted wooden bed the pictures of George Washington and John Calvin, and the framed motto, "Feed My Lambs," which had been worked in red worsted by his mother, whom Paul could not remember.[12]

Half an hour later, Paul alighted from the Negley Avenue car and went slowly down one of the side streets off the main thoroughfare. It was a highly respectable street, where all the houses were exactly alike, and where business men of moderate means begot and reared large families of children, all of whom went to Sabbath-school and learned the shorter catechism, and were interested in arithmetic; all of whom were as exactly alike as their homes, and of a piece with the monotony in which they lived. Paul never went up Cordelia Street without a shudder of loathing. His home was next to the house of the Cumberland minister.[13] He approached it tonight with the nerveless sense of defeat, the hopeless feeling of sinking back forever into ugliness and commonness that he had always had when he came home. The mo-

ment he turned into Cordelia Street he felt the waters close above his head. After each of these orgies of living, he experienced all the physical depression which follows a debauch; the loathing of respectable beds, of common food, of a house permeated by kitchen odors; a shuddering repulsion for the flavorless, colorless mass of every-day existence; a morbid desire for cool things and soft lights and fresh flowers.

The nearer he approached the house, the more absolutely unequal Paul felt to the sight of it all: his ugly sleeping chamber; the cold bathroom with the grimy zinc tub, the cracked mirror, the dripping spigots; his father, at the top of the stairs, his hairy legs sticking out from his nightshirt, his feet thrust into carpet slippers. He was so much later than usual that there would certainly be inquiries and reproaches. Paul stopped short before the door. He felt that he could not be accosted by his father tonight; that he could not toss again on that miserable bed. He would not go in. He would tell his father that he had no car-fare, and it was raining so hard he had gone home with one of the boys and stayed all night.

Meanwhile, he was wet and cold. He went around to the back of the house and tried one of the basement windows, found it open, raised it cautiously, and scrambled down the cellar wall to the floor. There he stood, holding his breath, terrified by the noise he had made; but the floor above him was silent, and there was no creak on the stairs. He found a soapbox, and carried it over to the soft ring of light that streamed from the furnace door, and sat down. He was horribly afraid of rats, so he did not try to sleep, but sat looking distrustfully at the dark, still terrified lest he might have awakened his father. In such reactions, after

---

11. **supplement,** in this sense an additional section of a newspaper devoted to special features.

12. **John Calvin** (1509–1564), a French theologian important in the rise of Protestantism. **worsted** *wus•təd\\ a heavy woolen fabric.

13. The **Cumberland minister** belonged to a revivalist group in the Presbyterian Church.

one of the experiences which made days and nights out of the dreary blanks of the calendar, when his senses were deadened, Paul's head was always singularly clear. Suppose his father had heard him getting in at the window and had come down and shot him for a burglar? Then, again, suppose his father had come down, pistol in hand, and he had cried out in time to save himself, and his father had been horrified to think how nearly he had killed him? Then, again, suppose a day should come when his father would remember that night, and wish there had been no warning cry to stay his hand? With this last supposition Paul entertained himself until daybreak.

The following Sunday was fine; the sodden November chill was broken by the last flash of autumnal summer. In the morning Paul had to go to church and Sabbath-school, as always. On seasonable Sunday afternoons the burghers[14] of Cordelia Street usually sat out on their front "stoops,"[15] and talked to their neighbors on the next stoop, or called to those across the street in neighborly fashion. The men sat placidly on gay cushions placed upon the steps that led down to the sidewalk, while the women, in their Sunday "waists," sat in rockers on the cramped porches, pretending to be greatly at their ease. The children played in the streets; there were so many of them that the place resembled the recreation grounds of a kindergarten. The men on the steps, all in their shirt-sleeves, their vests unbuttoned, sat with their legs well apart, their stomachs comfortably protruding, and talked of the prices of things, or told anecdotes of the sagacity of their various chiefs and overlords. They occasionally looked over the multitude of squabbling children, listened affectionately to their high-pitched, nasal voices, smiling to see their own proclivities reproduced in their offspring, and interspersed their legends of the iron kings[16] with remarks about their sons' progress at school, their grades in arithmetic, and the amounts they had saved in their toy banks.

On this last Sunday of November, Paul sat all the afternoon on the lowest step of his "stoop," staring into the street, while his sisters, in their rockers, were talking to the minister's daughters next door about how many shirt-waists they had made in the last week, and how many waffles someone had eaten at the last church supper. When the weather was warm, and his father was in a particularly jovial frame of mind, the girls made lemonade, which was always brought out in a red-glass pitcher, ornamented with forget-me-nots in blue enamel. This the girls thought very fine, and the neighbors joked about the suspicious color of the pitcher.

Today Paul's father, on the top step, was talking to a young man who shifted a restless baby from knee to knee. He happened to be the young man who was daily held up to Paul as a model, and after whom it was his father's dearest hope that he would pattern. This young man was of a ruddy complexion, with a compressed, red mouth, and faded, near-sighted eyes, over which he wore thick spectacles, with gold bows that curved about his ears. He was clerk to one of the magnates of a great steel corporation, and was looked upon in Cordelia Street as a young man with a future. There was a story that, some five years ago—he was now barely twenty-six—he had been a trifle "dissipated," but in order to curb his appetites and save the loss of time and strength that a sowing of wild oats might have entailed, he had taken his chief's advice, oft reiterated to his employees, and at twenty-one had married the first woman whom he could persuade to share his fortunes. She happened to be an angular schoolmistress, much older than he, who also wore thick glasses, and who had now borne him four children, all near-sighted like herself.

The young man was relating how his chief, now cruising in the Mediterranean, kept in touch with all the details of the business, arranging his office hours on his yacht just as though he were at home, and "knocking off

14. **burgher**\\ˈbər·gər\\ "townsman" or "citizen," but here suggests stodgy middle-class.
15. **stoop,** a dialect word meaning "small front porch."
16. **iron kings,** leaders in the steel industry.

work enough to keep two stenographers busy." His father told, in turn, the plan his corporation was considering, of putting in an electric railway plant at Cairo. Paul snapped his teeth; he had an awful apprehension that they might spoil it all before he got there. Yet he rather liked to hear these legends of the iron kings, that were told and retold on Sundays and holidays; these stories of palaces in Venice, yachts on the Mediterranean, and high play at Monte Carlo[17] appealed to his fancy, and he was interested in the triumphs of cash-boys[18] who had become famous, though he had no mind for the cash-boy stage.

After supper was over, and he had helped to dry the dishes, Paul nervously asked his father whether he could go to George's to get some help in his geometry, and still more nervously asked for car-fare. This latter request he had to repeat, as his father, on principle, did not like to hear requests for money, whether much or little. He asked Paul whether he could not go to some boy who lived nearer, and told him that he ought not to leave his school work until Sunday; but he gave him the dime. He was not a poor man, but he had a worthy ambition to come up in the world. His only reason for allowing Paul to usher was that he thought a boy ought to be earning a little.

Paul bounded upstairs, scrubbed the greasy odor of the dishwater from his hands with the ill-smelling soap he hated, and then shook over his fingers a few drops of violet water from the bottle he kept hidden in his drawer. He left the house with his geometry conspicuously under his arm, and the moment he got out of Cordelia Street and boarded a downtown car, he shook off the lethargy of two deadening days, and began to live again.

The leading juvenile of the permanent stock company which played at one of the downtown theaters was an acquaintance of Paul's, and the boy had been invited to drop in at the Sunday-night rehearsals whenever he could. For more than a year Paul had spent every available moment loitering about Charley Edwards's dressing-room. He had won a place among Edwards's following not only because the young actor, who could not afford to employ a dresser, often found him useful, but because he recognized in Paul something akin to what churchmen term "vocation."

It was at the theater and at Carnegie Hall that Paul really lived; the rest was but a sleep and a forgetting. This was Paul's fairy tale, and it had for him all the allurement of a secret love. The moment he inhaled the gassy, painty, dusty odor behind the scenes, he breathed like a prisoner set free, and felt within him the possibility of doing or saying splendid, brilliant things. The moment the cracked orchestra beat out the overture from *Martha*, or jerked at the serenade from *Rigoletto*,[19] all stupid and ugly things slid from him, and his senses were deliciously, yet delicately fired.

Perhaps it was because, in Paul's world, the natural nearly always wore the guise of ugliness, that a certain element of artificiality seemed to him necessary in beauty. Perhaps it was because his experience of life elsewhere was so full of Sabbath-school picnics, petty economics, wholesome advice as to how to succeed in life, and the unescapable odors of cooking, that he found this existence so alluring, these smartly clad men and women so attractive, that he was so moved by these starry apple orchards that bloomed perennially under the limelight. It would be difficult to put it strongly enough how convincingly the stage entrance of that theater was for Paul the actual portal of Romance. Certainly none of the company ever suspected it, least of all Charley Edwards. It was very like the old stories that used to float about London of fabulously rich Jews, who had subterranean halls, with palms, and fountains, and soft lamps and richly appareled women who never saw the

---

17. **Monte Carlo**\mŏn ᴀtä ᴀkar·lō\ a gambling resort in Monaco on the northern Mediterranean coast.
18. **cash-boy,** an errand boy entrusted with the delivery of cash, as to a bank.
19. **Martha,** an opera written in 1847 by Flotow (1812–1883). **Rigoletto**\'rĭ·gə ᴀlĕ·tō\ an opera (1851) by Verdi (1813–1901).

disenchanting light of London day. So, in the midst of that smoke-palled city, enamored of figures and grimy toil, Paul had his secret temple, his wishing-carpet, his bit of blue-and-white Mediterranean shore bathed in perpetual sunshine.

Several of Paul's teachers had a theory that his imagination had been perverted by garish fiction; but the truth was, he scarcely ever read at all. The books at home were not such as would either tempt or corrupt a youthful mind, and as for reading the novels that some of his friends urged upon him—well, he got what he wanted much more quickly from music; any sort of music, from an orchestra to a barrel-organ. He needed only the spark, the indescribable thrill that made his imagination master of his senses, and he could make plots and pictures enough of his own. It was equally true that he was not stage-struck—not, at any rate, in the usual acceptation of that expression. He had no desire to become an actor, any more than he had to become a musician. He felt no necessity to do any of these things; what he wanted was to see, to be in the atmosphere, float on the wave of it, to be carried out, blue league after league, away from everything.

After a night behind the scenes, Paul found the schoolroom more than ever repulsive; the bare floors and naked walls; the prosy men who never wore frock coats, or violets in their buttonholes; the women with their dull gowns, shrill voices, and pitiful seriousness about prepositions that govern the dative.[20] He could not bear to have the other pupils think, for a moment, that he took these people seriously; he must convey to them that he considered it all trivial, and was there only by way of a joke, anyway. He had autographed pictures of all the members of the stock company which he showed his class mates, telling them the most incredible stories of his familiarity with these people, of his acquaintance with the soloists who came to Carnegie Hall, his suppers with them and the flowers he sent them. When these stories lost their effect, and his audience

grew listless, he would bid all the boys good-bye, announcing that he was going to travel for a while; going to Naples, to California, to Egypt. Then next Monday, he would slip back, conscious and nervously smiling; his sister was ill, and he would have to defer his voyage until spring.

Matters went steadily worse with Paul at school. In the itch to let his instructors know how heartily he despised them, and how thoroughly he was appreciated elsewhere, he mentioned once or twice that he had no time to fool with theorems; adding—with a twitch of the eyebrows and a touch of that nervous bravado which so perplexed them—that he was helping the people down at the stock company; they were old friends of his.

The upshot of the matter was that the Principal went to Paul's father, and Paul was taken out of school and put to work. The manager at Carnegie Hall was told to get another usher in his stead; the doorkeeper at the theater was warned not to admit him to the house; and Charley Edwards remorsefully promised the boy's father not to see him again.

The members of the stock company were vastly amused when some of Paul's stories reached them—especially the women. They were hard-working women, most of them supporting indolent husbands or brothers, and they laughed rather bitterly at having stirred the boy to such fervid and florid inventions. They agreed with the faculty and with his father, that Paul's was a bad case.

The east-bound train was ploughing through a January snowstorm; the dull dawn was beginning to show gray when the engine whistled a mile out of Newark.[21] Paul started up from

---

20. Just as the nominative and objective are "cases" in English grammar, Latin grammar has a *dative* case. It is sometimes preceded by certain prepositions, and Paul's Latin teacher is evidently very intent on such matters.
21. **Newark**\ˈnū·ərk\ a large city in northern New Jersey on the main line of the Pennsylvania Railroad, on which Paul is traveling.

the seat where he had lain curled in uneasy slumber, rubbed the breath-misted window glass with his hand, and peered out. The snow was whirling in curling eddies above the white bottom lands, and the drifts lay already deep in the fields and along the fences, while here and there the tall dead grass and dried weed stalks protruded black above it. Lights shone from the scattered houses, and a gang of laborers who stood beside the track waved their lanterns.

Paul had slept very little, and he felt grimy and uncomfortable. He had made the all-night journey in a day coach because he was afraid if he took a Pullman[22] he might be seen by some Pittsburgh business man who had noticed him in Denny & Carson's office. When the whistle woke him, he clutched quickly at his breast pocket, glancing about him with an uncertain smile. But the little, clay-bespattered Italians were still sleeping, the slatternly women across the aisle were in open-mouth oblivion, and even the crumby, crying babies were for the time stilled. Paul settled back to struggle with his impatience as best he could.

When he arrived at the Jersey City station, he hurried through his breakfast, manifestly ill at ease and keeping a sharp eye about him. After he reached the Twenty-third Street station, he consulted a cabman, and had himself driven to a men's furnishing establishment which was just opening for the day. He spent upward of two hours there, buying with endless reconsidering and great care. His new street suit he put on in the fitting-room; the frock coat and dress clothes he had bundled into the cab with his new shirts. Then he drove to a hatter's and a shoe house. His next errand was at Tiffany's,[23] where he selected silver-mounted brushes and a scarf-pin. He would not wait to have his silver marked, he said. Lastly, he stopped at a trunk shop on Broadway, and had his purchases packed into various traveling-bags.

It was a little after one o'clock when he drove up to the Waldorf,[24] and after settling with the cabman, went into the office. He registered from Washington; said his mother and father had been abroad, and that he had come down to await the arrival of their steamer. He told his story plausibly and had no trouble, since he offered to pay for them in advance, in engaging his rooms; a sleeping-room, sitting-room, and bath.

Not once, but a hundred times Paul had planned this entry into New York. He had gone over every detail of it with Charley Edwards, and in his scrapbook at home there were pages of description about New York hotels, cut from the Sunday papers.

When he was shown to his sitting-room on the eighth floor, he saw at a glance that everything was as it should be; there was but one detail in his mental picture that the place did not realize, so he rang for the bell-boy and sent him down for flowers. He moved about nervously until the boy returned, putting away his new linen and fingering it delightedly as he did so. When the flowers came, he put them hastily into water, and then tumbled into a hot bath. Presently he came out of his white bathroom, resplendent in his new silk underwear, and playing with the tassels of his red robe. The snow was whirling so fiercely outside his windows that he could scarcely see across the street; but within, the air was deliciously soft and fragrant. He put the violets and jonquils on the taboret beside the couch, and threw himself down with a long sigh, covering himself with a Roman blanket. He was thoroughly tired; he had been in such haste, he had stood up to such a strain, covered so much ground in the last twenty-four hours, that he wanted to think how it had all come about. Lulled by the sound of the wind, the warm air, and the cool fragrance of the flowers, he sank into deep, drowsy retrospection.

---

22. **Pullman**\ˈpu̇l·mən\ a railroad car with sleeping berths.
23. **Tiffany's**\ˈtĭ·fə·nēz\ a well-known New York jewelry store.
24. The **Waldorf**\ˈwȯl ˈdȯrf\ an important New York hotel.

*The main entrance of the Waldorf Hotel
as it appeared in 1893.*

It had been wonderfully simple; when they had shut him out of the theater and concert hall, when they had taken away his bone, the whole thing was virtually determined. The rest was a mere matter of opportunity. The only thing that at all surprised him was his own courage—for he realized well enough that he had always been tormented by fear, a sort of apprehensive dread which, of late years, as the meshes of the lies he had told closed about him, had been pulling the muscles of his body tighter and tighter. Until now, he could not remember a time when he had not been dreading something. Even when he was a little boy, it was always there—behind him, or before, or on either side. There had always been the shadowed corner, the dark place into which he dared not look, but from which something seemed always to be watching him—and Paul had done things that were not pretty to watch, he knew.

But now he had a curious sense of relief, as

though he had at last thrown down the gauntlet[25] to the thing in the corner.

Yet it was but a day since he had been sulking in the traces;[26] but yesterday afternoon that he had been sent to the bank with Denny & Carson's deposit, as usual—but this time he was instructed to leave the book to be balanced. There was above two thousand dollars in checks, and nearly a thousand in the banknotes which he had taken from the book and quietly transferred to his pocket. At the bank he had made out a new deposit slip. His nerves had been steady enough to permit his returning to the office, where he had finished his work and asked for a full day's holiday tomorrow, Saturday, giving a perfectly reasonable pretext. The bank book, he knew, would not be returned before Monday or Tuesday, and his father would be out of town for the next week. From the time he slipped the banknotes into his pocket until he boarded the night train for New York, he had not known a moment's hesitation.

How astonishingly easy it had all been; here he was, the thing done; and this time there would be no awakening, no figure at the top of the stairs. He watched the snowflakes whirling by his window until he fell asleep.

When he awoke, it was four o'clock in the afternoon. He bounded up with a start; one of his precious days gone already! He spent nearly an hour in dressing, watching every stage of his toilet carefully in the mirror. Everything was quite perfect; he was exactly the kind of boy he had always wanted to be.

When he went downstairs, Paul took a carriage and drove up Fifth Avenue toward the Park.[27] The snow had somewhat abated; carriages and tradesmen's wagons were hurrying soundlessly to and fro in the winter twilight; boys in woolen mufflers were shoveling off the doorsteps; the avenue stages made fine spots of color against the white street. Here and there on the corners whole flower gardens blooming behind glass windows, against which the snowflakes stuck and melted; violets, roses, carnations, lilies-of-the-valleys—some-

how vastly more lovely and alluring that they blossomed thus unnaturally in the snow. The Park itself was a wonderful stage winter-piece.

When he returned, the pause of the twilight had ceased, and the tune of the streets had changed. The snow was falling faster, lights streamed from the hotels that reared their many stories fearlessly up into the storm, defying the raging Atlantic winds. A long, black stream of carriages poured down the avenue, intersected here and there by other streams, tending horizontally. There were a score of cabs about the entrance of his hotel, and his driver had to wait. Boys in livery were running in and out of the awning stretched across the sidewalk, up and down the red velvet carpet laid from the door to the street. Above, about, within it all, was the rumble and roar, the hurry and toss of thousands of human beings as hot for pleasure as himself, and on every side of him towered the glaring affirmation of the omnipotence of wealth.

The boy set his teeth and drew his shoulders together in a spasm of realization; the plot of all dramas, the text of all romances, the nerve-stuff of all sensations was whirling about him like the snowflakes. He burnt like a fagot in a tempest.

When Paul came down to dinner, the music of the orchestra floated up the elevator shaft to greet him. As he stepped into the thronged corridor, he sank back into one of the chairs against the wall to get his breath. The lights, the chatter, the perfumes, the bewildering medley of color—he had, for a moment, the feeling of not being able to stand it. But only for a moment; these were his own people, he told himself. He went slowly about the corridors, through the writing-rooms, smoking-rooms, reception-rooms, as though he were exploring the chambers of an enchanted palace, built and peopled for him alone.

---

25. To throw down the **gauntlet** (\ˈgɔnt·lət\ an old word meaning "glove"), to issue a final challenge.
26. He had been acting as a restless horse which might sulk in its harness.
27. **Park,** Central Park.

When he reached the dining-room he sat down at a table near a window. The flowers, the white linen, the many-colored wine-glasses, the gay toilets of the women, the low popping of corks, the undulating repetitions of "The Blue Danube"[28] from the orchestra, all flooded Paul's dream with bewildering radiance. When the roseate tinge of his champagne was added —that cold, precious, bubbling stuff that creamed and foamed in his glass—Paul wondered that there were honest men in the world at all. This was what all the world was fighting for, he reflected; this was what all the struggle was about. He doubted the reality of his past. Had he ever known a place called Cordelia Street, a place where fagged looking business men boarded the early car? Mere rivets in a machine they seemed to Paul—sickening men, with combings of children's hair always hanging to their coats, and the smell of cooking in their clothes. Cordelia Street—Ah, that belonged to another time and country! Had he not always been thus, had he not sat here night after night, from as far back as he could remember, looking pensively over just such shimmering textures, and slowly twirling the stem of a glass like this one between his thumb and middle finger? He rather thought he had.

He was not in the least abashed or lonely. He had no especial desire to meet or to know any of these people; all he demanded was the right to look on and conjecture, to watch the pageant. The mere stage properties were all he contended for. Nor was he lonely later in the evening, in his loge[29] at the Opera. He was entirely rid of his nervous misgivings, of his forced aggressiveness, of the imperative desire to show himself different from his surroundings. He felt now that his surroundings explained him. Nobody questioned the purple;[30] he had only to wear it passively. He had only to glance down at his dress coat to reassure himself that here it would be impossible for anyone to humiliate him.

He found it hard to leave his beautiful sitting-room to go to bed that night, and sat long watching the raging storm from his turret window. When he went to sleep, it was with the lights turned on in his bedroom; partly because of his old timidity, and partly so that, if he should wake in the night, there would be no wretched moment of doubt, no horrible suspicion of yellow wallpaper, or of Washington and Calvin above his bed.

On Sunday morning the city was practically snowbound. Paul breakfasted late, and in the afternoon he fell in with a wild San Francisco boy, a freshman at Yale, who said he had run down for a "little flyer"[31] over Sunday. The young man offered to show Paul the night side of the town, and the two boys went off together after dinner, not returning to the hotel until seven o'clock the next morning. They had started out in the confiding warmth of a champagne friendship, but their parting in the elevator was singularly cool. The freshman pulled himself together to make his train, and Paul went to bed. He awoke at two o'clock in the afternoon, very thirsty and dizzy, and rang for ice-water, coffee, and the Pittsburgh papers.

On the part of the hotel management, Paul excited no suspicion. There was this to be said for him, that he wore his spoils with dignity and in no way made himself conspicuous. His chief greediness lay in his ears and eyes, and his excesses were not offensive ones. His dearest pleasures were the gray winter twilights in his sitting-room; his quiet enjoyment of his flowers, his clothes, his wide divan, his cigarette, and his sense of power. He could not remember a time when he had felt so at peace with himself. The mere release from the necessity of petty lying, lying every day and every day, restored his self-respect. He had never lied for pleasure, even at school; but to make himself noticed and admired, to assert his difference from other Cordelia Street boys; and he felt a good deal

---

28. **The Blue Danube,** a famous waltz by Johann Strauss the younger (1825–1899).
29. **loge**\lōzh\ a booth or box at the theater.
30. **Purple** is associated with kings, Roman Caesars, and aristocrats. The author means that no one questioned Paul's right to the way he was living.
31. **little flyer,** a little weekend vacation trip.

*"Peacock Alley" in the old Waldorf-Astoria Hotel.
The picture was taken shortly after the turn
of the century.*

more manly, more honest, even, now that he had no need for boastful pretensions, now that he could, as his actor friends used to say, "dress the part." It was characteristic that remorse did not occur to him. His golden days went by without a shadow, and he made each as perfect as he could.

On the eighth day after his arrival in New York, he found the whole affair exploited in the Pittsburgh papers, exploited with a wealth of detail which indicated that local news of a sensational nature was at a low ebb. The firm of Denny & Carson announced that the boy's father had refunded the full amount of his theft, and that they had no intention of prosecuting. The Cumberland minister had been interviewed, and expressed his hope of yet reclaiming the motherless lad, and Paul's Sabbath-school teacher declared that she would spare no effort to that end. The rumor had reached Pittsburgh that the boy had been seen in a New York hotel, and his father had gone East to find him and bring him home.

Paul had just come in to dress for dinner; he sank into a chair, weak in the knees, and clasped his head in his hands. It was to be worse than jail, even; the tepid waters of Cordelia Street were to close over him finally and forever. The gray monotony stretched before him in hopeless, unrelieved years; Sabbath-school, Young People's Meeting, the yellow-papered room, the damp dish-towels; it all rushed back upon him with sickening vividness. He had the old feeling that the orchestra had suddenly stopped, the sinking sensation that the play was over. The sweat broke out on his face, and he sprang to his feet, looked about him with his white, conscious smile, and winked at himself in the mirror. With something of the childish belief in miracles with which he had so often gone to class, all his lessons unlearned, Paul dressed and dashed whistling down the corridor to the elevator.

He had no sooner entered the dining-room and caught the measure of the music than his remembrance was lightened by his old elastic power of claiming the moment, mounting with it, and finding it all sufficient. The glare and glitter about him, the mere scenic accessories had again, and for the last time, their old potency. He would show himself that he was game, he would finish the thing splendidly. He doubted, more than ever, the existence of Cordelia Street, and for the first time he drank his wine recklessly. Was he not, after all, one of these fortunate beings: Was he not still himself, and in his own place? He drummed a nervous accompaniment to the music and looked about him, telling himself over and over that it had paid.

He reflected drowsily, to the swell of the violin and the chill sweetness of his wine, that he might have done it more wisely. He might have caught an outbound steamer and been well out of their clutches before now. But the other side of the world had seemed too far away and too uncertain then; he could not have waited for it; his need had been too sharp. If he had to choose over again, he would do the same thing tomorrow. He looked affectionately about the dining-room, now gilded with a soft mist. Ah, it had paid indeed!

Paul was awakened next morning by a painful throbbing in his head and feet. He had thrown himself across the bed without undressing, and had slept with his shoes on. His limbs and hands were lead heavy, and his tongue and throat were parched. There came upon him one of those fateful attacks of clear-headedness that never occurred except when he was physically exhausted and his nerves hung loose. He lay still and closed his eyes and let the tide of realities wash over him.

His father was in New York; "stopping at some joint or other," he told himself. The memory of successive summers on the front stoop fell upon him like a weight of black water. He had not a hundred dollars left; and he knew now, more than ever, that money was everything, the wall that stood between all he loathed and all he wanted. The thing was winding itself up; he had thought of that on his first glorious day in New York, and had even provided a way to snap the thread. It lay on his dressing-table now; he had got it out last night when he came blindly up from dinner—but the shiny metal hurt his eyes, and he disliked the look of it, anyway.

He rose and moved about with a painful effort, succumbing now and again to attacks of nausea. It was the old depression exaggerated; all the world had become Cordelia Street. Yet somehow he was not afraid of anything, was absolutely calm; perhaps because he had looked into the dark corner at last, and knew. It was bad enough, what he saw there; but somehow not so bad as his long fear of it had been. He saw everything clearly now. He had a feeling that he had made the best of it, that he had lived the sort of life he was meant to live, and for half an hour he sat staring at the revolver. But he told himself that was not the way, so he went downstairs and took a cab to the ferry.

When Paul arrived at Newark, he got off the train and took another cab, directing the driver to follow the Pennsylvania tracks out of the town. The snow lay heavy on the roadways and had drifted deep in the open fields. Only here and there the dead grass or dried weed stalks projected, singularly black, above it. Once well into the country, Paul dismissed the carriage and walked, floundering along the tracks, his mind a medley of irrelevant things. He seemed to hold in his brain an actual picture of everything he had seen that morning. He remembered every feature of both his drivers, the toothless old woman from whom he had bought the red flowers in his coat, the agent from whom he had got his ticket, and all of his fellow-passengers on the ferry. His mind, unable to cope with vital matters near at hand, worked feverishly and deftly at sorting and grouping these images. They made for him a part of the ugliness of the world, of the ache in his head, and the bitter burning on his tongue. He stooped and put a handful of snow into his mouth as he walked, but that, too, seemed hot. When he reached a little hillside, where the tracks ran through a cut some twenty feet below him, he stopped and sat down.

The carnations in his coat were drooping with the cold, he noticed; all their red glory over. It occurred to him that all the flowers he had seen in the show windows that first night must have gone the same way, long before this. It was only one splendid breath they had, in spite of their brave mockery at the winter outside the glass. It was a losing game in the end, it seemed, this revolt against the homilies by which the world is run. Paul took one of the blossoms carefully from his coat and scooped a little hole in the snow, where he covered it up. Then he dozed awhile, from his weak condition, seeming insensible to the cold.

The sound of an approaching train woke him, and he started to his feet, remembering only his resolution, and afraid lest he should be too late. He stood watching the approaching locomotive, his teeth chattering, his lips drawn away from them in a frightened smile; once or twice he glanced nervously sidewise, as though he were being watched. When the right moment came, he jumped. As he fell, the folly of his haste occurred to him with merciless clearness, the vastness of what he had left undone.

There flashed through his brain clearer than ever before, the blue of Adriatic[32] water, the yellow of Algerian sands. He felt something strike his chest—his body was being thrown swiftly through the air, on and on, immeasurably far and fast, while his limbs gently relaxed. Then, because the picture-making mechanism was crushed, the disturbing visions flashed into black, and Paul dropped back into the immense design of things.

I
DREAMS AND REALITY

The title "Paul's Case" suggests that this story bears a resemblance to the case history of a psychologist or a social worker. There is an irony in this suggestion. Such case histories are completely objective records of the behavior and attitudes of abnormal personalities; the psychologist never indulges his own feelings about the subject. To those who pass judgment on him—his teacher, his father, even his schoolmates—Paul is, indeed, a bad "case," a thoroughly abnormal boy. But Willa Cather makes us see deeper than that. She makes us recognize the poignantly normal quality in Paul's desires and his disgust with his dreary life. But his dreams of escape to an exotic life hold him so hypnotized that he fails to see that they are only dreams. Believing them to be the only "real" things in his life, he fails to deal with the hard and sometimes brutal facts of everyday reality. By doing so, he dooms himself to a desperate awakening and a tragic end.

II
IMPLICATIONS

Consider the following questions. In your discussion of them, put yourself as much as you can in Paul's place. Do not be deceived by the attitudes of the other characters toward him.

1. What aspects of Paul's character are revealed in the following scenes in the story?
   a. Paul at the teachers' meeting.
   b. Paul at the concert hall.

---

32. **Adriatic**\ˈā·drē ˈa·tĭk\ the sea between Italy and Yugoslavia.

c. Paul at home with his family.

d. Paul in New York.

e. Paul waiting for the train.

2. What are the elements in Paul's environment that put pressure on him? What are the elements in his own personality? How does each kind of pressure increase the other?

3. Could Paul have acted differently from the way he did? Discuss whether or not it was weakness in him to give way to his fantasies?

III
TECHNIQUES

Theme

Which of the following possibilities do you think most clearly states the theme of this story? Give the reason for your choice, citing incidents in the story as evidence. If you think none of them fit the story, what others would you suggest?

1. The disintegration of a person's mind obsessed with fantasies.

2. The destruction of a sensitive person by a drab, insensitive society.

3. The dangers of choosing the wrong dreams to live by.

4. The hunger of the human heart for a way of life that fulfills its desires.

Style

"Paul's Case" is clearly a complex story. Apart from describing a large number of settings and presenting a large number of minor characters from various walks of life, it examines its central character in great depth and detail. In order to contain these complexities and give them adequate expression, the style of writing is necessarily complex too. Choose a typical passage of several sentences and examine it from the point of view of style. Are the sentences long or short, simple or compound? How are the long and short ones mixed together? Are the pictures created by the author vivid, unusual, ordinary, detailed, general? Are the words used common conversational ones? Uncommon "literary" ones?

Identification

How completely did you identify yourself with Paul while you were reading this story? Name some aspects of his personality which you consider yourself to possess also. Name some which

you do not share. What do you think the author intended you to feel about Paul? How does she show her own feelings?

IV
WORDS

A. From context determine what the italicized words mean. Then check the meaning of each in your dictionary.

1. The Yukon was all pure white, rolling in gentle *undulations*.

2. The wolf-dog experienced a vague but *menacing* apprehension that subdued it and that made it question eagerly every *unwonted* movement of the man.

3. The result was that a crystal beard was increasing its length on his chin. But he did not mind the *appendage*.

4. Once in a while the thought *reiterated* itself that it was very cold.

5. A certain fear of death, dull and oppressive, came to him. This fear quickly became *poignant*.

6. Father perished at the stake for *tenets* he would not forsake.

7. The woe which he *abhorred* to view below.

8. His teachers were asked to state their *respective* charges against him.

9. He made a running *commentary* on the lecture.

10. This conscious expression was usually attributed to *insolence* or "smartness."

B. 1. London mentions "a subtle gloom" in his first paragraph. The word *subtle* is an interesting illustration of semantic change; it is composed of two elements, the prefix *sub-*, meaning "under," and what is left of the Latin word *tilis*, meaning "woven." Check the root of the word *temperature*. How has its meaning changed? The chief character in "To Build a Fire" suffers "a stinging ache that was excruciating." What is the root in *excruciate*, and what is the modern meaning of the word?

2. Find the root in the word *carnation* ("a red carnation in his buttonhole") in "Paul's Case," and be prepared to tell why the flower is so called. The drug *belladonna* ("as though he were addicted to belladonna") is colorfully named; what do the parts of this word mean? How is intoxication ("the peculiar intoxication such personages always had for him") related to *toxic, toxin,* and *toxicology*?

The moment is intense. The first sentences
picture a man on a bridge. He is
about to be hanged. How does such
pressure affect the mind of the victim?

An Occurrence
at
Owl Creek Bridge

AMBROSE BIERCE

1

A man stood upon a railroad bridge in northern Alabama, looking down into the swift water twenty feet below. The man's hands were behind his back, the wrists bound with a cord. A rope loosely encircled his neck. It was attached to a stout cross-timber above his head, and the slack fell to the level of his knees. Some loose boards laid upon the sleepers[1] supporting the metals of the railway supplied a footing for him and his executioners —two private soldiers of the Federal army, directed by a sergeant who in civil life may have been a deputy sheriff. At a short remove upon the same temporary platform was an officer in the uniform of his rank, armed. He was a captain. A sentinel at each end of the bridge stood with his rifle in the position known as "support," that is to say, vertical in front of the left shoulder, the hammer resting on the forearm thrown straight across the chest—a formal and unnatural position, enforcing an erect carriage of the body. It did not appear to be the duty of these two men to know what was occurring at the center of the bridge; they merely blockaded the two ends of the foot plank which traversed it.

Beyond one of the sentinels, nobody was in sight; the railroad ran straight away into a forest for a hundred yards, then, curving, was lost to view. Doubtless there was an outpost farther along. The other bank of the stream was open ground—a gentle acclivity topped with a stockade of vertical tree trunks, loopholed for rifles, with a single embrasure through which protruded the muzzle of a brass cannon commanding the bridge. Midway of the slope between bridge and fort were the spectators—a single company of infantry in line, at "parade rest," the butts of the rifles on the ground, the barrels inclining slightly backward against the right shoulder, the hands crossed upon the stock. A lieutenant stood at the right of the line, the point of his sword upon the ground, his left hand resting upon his right. Excepting the group of four at the center of the bridge, not a man moved. The company faced the bridge, staring stonily, motionless. The sentinels, facing the banks of the stream, might have been statues to adorn the bridge. The captain stood with folded arms, silent, observing the work of his subordinates, but making no sign. Death is a dignitary who when he comes announced is to be received with formal manifestations of respect, even by those most familiar with him. In the code of military etiquette silence and fixity are forms of deference.

The man who was engaged in being hanged was apparently about thirty-five years of age. He was a civilian, if one might judge from his habit, which was that of a planter. His features were good—a straight nose, firm mouth, broad forehead, from which his long, dark hair was combed straight back, falling behind his ears to the collar of his well-fitting frock coat. He wore a mustache and pointed beard, but no whiskers; his eyes were large and dark gray, and had a kindly expression which one would hardly have expected in one whose

reprinted from THE COLLECTED WRITINGS OF AMBROSE BIERCE, Citadel Press, Inc., New York, N.Y.

1. **sleepers,** timbers to keep rails in place.

neck was in the hemp.[2] Evidently this was no vulgar assassin. The liberal military code makes provision for hanging many kinds of persons, and gentlemen are not excluded.

The preparations being complete, the two private soldiers stepped aside and each drew away the plank upon which he had been standing. The sergeant turned to the captain, saluted, and placed himself immediately behind that officer, who in turn moved apart one pace. These movements left the condemned man and the sergeant standing on the two ends of the same plank, which spanned three of the crossties of the bridge. The end upon which the civilian stood almost, but not quite, reached a fourth. This plank had been held in place by the weight of the captain; it was now held by that of the sergeant. At a signal from the former, the latter would step aside, the plank would tilt, and the condemned man go down between two ties. The arrangement commended itself to his judgment as simple and effective. His face had not been covered nor his eyes bandaged. He looked a moment at his "unsteadfast footing," then let his gaze wander to the swirling water of the stream racing madly beneath his feet. A piece of dancing driftwood caught his attention and his eyes followed it down the current. How slowly it appeared to move! What a sluggish stream!

He closed his eyes in order to fix his last thoughts upon his wife and children. The water, touched to gold by the early sun, the brooding mists under the banks at some distance down the stream, the fort, the soldiers, the piece of drift—all had distracted him. And now he became conscious of a new disturbance. Striking through the thought of his dear ones was a sound which he could neither ignore nor understand, a sharp, distinct, metallic percussion like the stroke of a blacksmith's hammer upon the anvil; it had the same ringing quality. He wondered what it was, and whether immeasurably distant or near by—it seemed both. Its recurrence was regular, but as slow as the tolling of a death knell. He awaited each stroke with impatience and—he knew not why—apprehension. The intervals of silence grew progressively longer; the delays became maddening. With their greater infrequency the sounds increased in strength and sharpness. They hurt his ear like the thrust of a knife; he feared he would shriek. What he heard was the ticking of his watch.

He unclosed his eyes and saw again the water below him. "If I could free my hands," he thought, "I might throw off the noose and spring into the stream. By diving I could evade the bullets and, swimming vigorously, reach the bank, take to the woods, and get away home. My home, thank God, is as yet outside their lines; my wife and little ones are still beyond the invader's farthest advance."

As these thoughts, which have here to be set down in words, were flashed into the doomed man's brain rather than evolved from it, the captain nodded to the sergeant. The sergeant stepped aside.

2

Peyton Farquhar was a well-to-do planter of an old and highly respected Alabama family. Being a slave owner and like other slave owners a politician, he was naturally an original secessionist and ardently devoted to the Southern cause. Circumstances of an imperious nature, which it is unnecessary to relate here, had prevented him from taking service with the gallant army which had fought the disastrous campaigns ending with the fall of Corinth, and he chafed under the inglorious restraint, longing for the release of his energies, the larger life of the soldier, the opportunity for distinction. That opportunity, he felt, would come, as it comes to all in war time. Meanwhile he did what he could. No service was too humble for him to perform in aid of the South, no adventure too perilous for him to undertake if consistent with the character of a civilian who was at heart a soldier, and who in good faith and without too

---

2. **hemp,** rope; the noose.

much qualification assented to at least a part of the frankly villainous dictum[3] that all is fair in love and war.

One evening while Farquhar and his wife were sitting on a rustic bench near the entrance to his grounds, a gray-clad soldier rode up to the gate and asked for a drink of water. Mrs. Farquhar was only too happy to serve him with her own white hands. While she was fetching the water her husband approached the dusty horseman and inquired eagerly for news from the front.

"The Yanks are repairing the railroads," said the man, "and are getting ready for another advance. They have reached the Owl Creek bridge, put it in order, and built a stockade on the north bank. The commandant has issued an order, which is posted everywhere, declaring that any civilian caught interfering with the railroad, its bridges, tunnels, or trains will be summarily hanged. I saw the order."

"How far is it to the Owl Creek bridge?" Farquhar asked.

"About thirty miles."

"Is there no force on this side the creek?"

"Only a picket post half a mile out, on the railroad, and a single sentinel at this end of the bridge."

"Suppose a man—a civilian and student of hanging—should elude the picket post and perhaps get the better of the sentinel," said Farquhar, smiling, "what could he accomplish?"

The soldier reflected. "I was there a month ago," he replied. "I observed that the flood of last winter had lodged a great quantity of driftwood against the wooden pier at this end of the bridge. It is now dry and would burn like tow."

The lady had now brought the water, which the soldier drank. He thanked her ceremoniously, bowed to her husband, and rode away. An hour later, after nightfall, he repassed the plantation, going northward in the direction from which he had come. He was a Federal scout.

3

As Peyton Farquhar fell straight downward through the bridge he lost consciousness and was as one already dead. From this state he was awakened—ages later, it seemed to him—by the pain of a sharp pressure upon his throat, followed by a sense of suffocation. Keen, poignant agonies seemed to shoot from his neck downward through every fiber of his body and limbs. These pains appeared to flash along well-defined lines of ramification and to beat with an inconceivably rapid periodicity. They seemed like streams of pulsating fire heating him to an intolerable temperature. As to his head, he was conscious of nothing but a feeling of fullness—of congestion. These sensations were unaccompanied by thought. The intellectual part of his nature was already effaced; he had power only to feel, and feeling was torment. He was conscious of motion. Encompassed in a luminous cloud, of which he was now merely the fiery heart, without material substance, he swung through unthinkable arcs of oscillation,[4] like a vast pendulum. Then all at once, with terrible suddenness, the light about him shot upward with the noise of a loud plash; a frightful roaring was in his ears, and all was cold and dark. The power of thought was restored; he knew that the rope had broken and he had fallen into the stream. There was no additional strangulation; the noose about his neck was already suffocating him and kept the water from his lungs. To die of hanging at the bottom of a river!—the idea seemed to him ludicrous. He opened his eyes in the darkness and saw above him a gleam of light, but how distant, how inaccessible! He was still sinking, for the light became fainter and fainter until it was a mere glimmer. Then it began to grow and brighten, and he knew that he was rising toward the surface—knew it with reluctance, for he was now very comfortable. "To be hanged and

---

3. **dictum,** pronouncement.
4. **oscillation**\'äs·ə ˈlā·shən\   swinging   back   and forth.

drowned," he thought, "that is not so bad; but I do not wish to be shot. No; I will not be shot; that is not fair."

He was not conscious of an effort, but a sharp pain in his wrist apprised him that he was trying to free his hands. He gave the struggle his attention, as an idler might observe the feat of a juggler, without interest in the outcome. What splendid effort!—what magnificent, what superhuman strength! Ah, that was a fine endeavor! Bravo! The cord fell away; his arms parted and floated upward, the hands dimly seen on each side in the growing light. He watched them with a new interest as first one and then the other pounced upon the noose at his neck. They tore it away and thrust it fiercely aside, its undulations resembling those of a water snake. "Put it back, put it back!" He thought he shouted these words to his hands, for the undoing of the noose had been succeeded by the direst pang that he had yet experienced. His neck ached horribly; his brain was on fire; his heart, which had been fluttering faintly, gave a great leap, trying to force itself out at his mouth. His whole body was racked and wrenched with an insupportable anguish! But his disobedient hands gave no heed to the command. They beat the water vigorously with quick, downward strokes, forcing him to the surface. He felt his head emerge; his eyes were blinded by the sunlight; his chest expanded convulsively, and with a supreme and crowning agony his lungs engulfed a great draught of air, which instantly he expelled in a shriek!

He was now in full possession of his physical senses. They were, indeed, preternaturally keen and alert. Something in the awful disturbance of his organic system had so exalted and refined them that they made record of things never before perceived. He felt the ripples upon his face and heard their separate sounds as they struck. He looked at the forest on the bank of the stream, saw the individual trees, the leaves and the veining of each leaf—saw the very insects upon them: the locusts, the brilliant-bodied flies, the gray spiders stretching their webs from twig to twig. He noted the prismatic colors in all the dewdrops upon a million blades of grass. The humming of the gnats that danced above the eddies of the stream, the beating of the dragonflies' wings, the strokes of the water spiders' legs, like oars which had lifted their boat—all these made audible music. A fish slid along beneath his eyes and he heard the rush of its body parting the water.

He had come to the surface facing down the stream; in a moment the visible world seemed to wheel slowly round, himself the pivotal point, and he saw the bridge, the fort, the soldiers upon the bridge, the captain, the sergeant, the two privates, his executioners. They were in silhouette against the blue sky. They shouted and gesticulated, pointing at him. The captain had drawn his pistol, but did not fire; the others were unarmed. Their movements were grotesque and horrible, their forms gigantic.

Suddenly he heard a sharp report and something struck the water smartly within a few inches of his head, spattering his face with spray. He heard a second report, and saw one of the sentinels with his rifle at his shoulder, a light cloud of blue smoke rising from the muzzle. The man in the water saw the eye of the man on the bridge gazing into his own through the sights of the rifle. He observed that it was a gray eye and remembered having read that gray eyes were keenest, and that all famous marksmen had them. Nevertheless, this one had missed.

A counterswirl had caught Farquhar and turned him half round; he was again looking into the forest on the bank opposite the fort. The sound of a clear, high voice in a monotonous singsong now rang out behind him and came across the water with a distinctness that pierced and subdued all other sounds, even the beating of the ripples in his ears. Although no soldier, he had frequented camps enough to know the dread significance of that deliberate, drawling, aspirated chant; the lieutenant on shore was taking a part in the morning's work.

How coldly and pitilessly—with what an even, calm intonation, presaging and enforcing tranquillity in the men—with what accurately measured intervals fell those cruel words:

"Attention, company! . . . Shoulder arms! . . . Ready! . . . Aim! . . . Fire!"

Farquhar dived—dived as deeply as he could. The water roared in his ears like the voice of Niagara, yet he heard the dulled thunder of the volley and, rising again toward the surface, met shining bits of metal, singularly flattened, oscillating slowly downward. Some of them touched him on the face and hands, then fell away, continuing their descent. One lodged between his collar and neck; it was uncomfortably warm and he snatched it out.

As he rose to the surface, gasping for breath, he saw that he had been a long time under water; he was perceptibly farther downstream—nearer to safety. The soldiers had almost finished reloading; the metal ramrods flashed all at once in the sunshine as they were drawn from the barrels, turned in the air, and thrust into their sockets. The two sentinels fired again, independently and ineffectually.

The hunted man saw all this over his shoulder; he was now swimming vigorously with the current. His brain was as energetic as his arms and legs; he thought with the rapidity of lightning.

"The officer," he reasoned, "will not make that martinet's error a second time. It is as easy to dodge a volley as a single shot. He has probably already given the command to fire at will. God help me, I cannot dodge them all!"

An appalling plash within two yards of him was followed by a loud, rushing sound, *diminuendo*,[5] which seemed to travel back through the air to the fort and died in an explosion which stirred the very river to its deeps! A rising sheet of water, which curved over him, fell down upon him, blinded him, strangled him! The cannon had taken a hand in the game. As he shook his head free from the commotion of the smitten water, he heard the deflected shot humming through the air ahead, and in an instant it was cracking and smashing the branches in the forest beyond.

"They will not do that again," he thought; "the next time they will use a charge of grape. I must keep my eye upon the gun; the smoke will apprise me—the report arrives too late; it lags behind the missile. That is a good gun."

Suddenly he felt himself whirled round and round—spinning like a top. The water, the banks, the forests, the now distant bridge, fort, and men—all were commingled and blurred. Objects were represented by their colors only; circular horizontal streaks of color—that was all he saw. He had been caught in a vortex and was being whirled on with a velocity of advance and gyration which made him giddy and sick. In a few moments he was flung upon the gravel at the foot of the left bank of the stream—the southern bank—and behind a projecting point which concealed him from his enemies. The sudden arrest of his motion, the abrasion of one of his hands on the gravel, restored him, and he wept with delight. He dug his fingers into the sand, threw it over himself in handfuls, and audibly blessed it. It looked like diamonds, rubies, emeralds; he could think of nothing beautiful which it did not resemble. The trees upon the bank were giant garden plants; he noted a definite order in their arrangement, inhaled the fragrance of their blooms. A strange, roseate light shone through the spaces among their trunks and the wind made in their branches the music of aeolian harps. He had no wish to perfect his escape—was content to remain in that enchanting spot until retaken.

A whiz and rattle of grapeshot among the branches high above his head roused him from his dream. The baffled cannoneer had fired him a random farewell. He sprang to his feet, rushed up the sloping bank, and plunged into the forest.

All that day he traveled, laying his course by the rounding sun. The forest seemed interminable; nowhere did he discover a break in

---

5. **diminuendo**\də ˈmĭn•yə ◂wĕn•dō\ diminishing.

it, not even a woodman's road. He had not known that he lived in so wild a region. There was something uncanny in the revelation.

By nightfall he was fatigued, footsore, famishing. The thought of his wife and children urged him on. At last he found a road which led him in what he knew to be the right direction. It was as wide and straight as a city street, yet it seemed untraveled. No fields bordered it, no dwelling anywhere. Not so much as the barking of a dog suggested human habitation. The black bodies of the trees formed a straight wall on both sides, terminating on the horizon in a point, like a diagram in a lesson in perspective. Overhead, as he looked up through this rift in the wood, shone great golden stars looking unfamiliar and grouped in strange constellations. He was sure they were arranged in some order which had a secret and malign significance. The wood on either side was full of singular noises, among which—once, twice, and again—he distinctly heard whispers in an unknown tongue.

His neck was in pain and lifting his hand to it he found it horribly swollen. He knew that it had a circle of black where the rope had bruised it. His eyes felt congested; he could no longer close them. His tongue was swollen with thirst; he relieved its fever by thrusting it forward from between his teeth into the cold air. How softly the turf had carpeted the untraveled avenue—he could no longer feel the roadway beneath his feet!

Doubtless, despite his suffering, he had fallen asleep while walking, for now he sees another scene—perhaps he has merely recovered from a delirium. He stands at the gate of his own home. All is as he left it, and all bright and beautiful in the morning sunshine. He must have traveled the entire night. As he pushes open the gate and passes up the wide white walk, he sees a flutter of female garments; his wife, looking fresh and cool and sweet, steps down from the veranda to meet him. At the bottom of the steps she stands waiting, with a smile of ineffable joy, an attitude of matchless grace and dignity. Ah, how beautiful she is! He springs forward with extended arms. As he is about to clasp her, he feels a stunning blow upon the back of the neck; a blinding white light blazes all about him with a sound like the shock of a cannon—then all is darkness and silence!

Peyton Farquhar was dead; his body, with a broken neck, swung gently from side to side beneath the timbers of the Owl Creek bridge.

I

THE PRESSURE OF CRISIS

People report that in moments of extreme crisis a person's whole life flashes before his eyes. Psychologists estimate that the mind works about ten times as rapidly as the voice can speak. Therefore, we can think a great deal more rapidly, even mentally putting the ideas into words, than we can possibly express out loud. This story is built upon that premise. Notice how the story is structured in three sections: the first is the actual hanging, the second backs up and tells us how Farquhar got himself into the situation, and the third deals with his imaginary escape. Through this structure the reader is led by his emotions to believe that Farquhar's escape is real. Then the last paragraph hits with a sudden, unexpected force.

II

IMPLICATIONS

Consider the following statements. From what you learned through reading the story and from your own experiences, do you agree or disagree?

1. The reader hopes that Farquhar escapes.

2. As Farquhar waits, the ticking of his watch sounds like a loud bell in the distance. There are several instances in the story of intensified sensory reactions. In times of great stress, one's sensory responses are heightened.

3. Since the escape happens only in Farquhar's mind, it is not reasonable that he would imagine himself experiencing such ordeals as being shot at in the water or having his tongue swell from thirst.

4. There are clues in the description of the escape tipping off the reader that Farquhar is not experiencing reality.

5. What a person experiences in his mind (his imagining) has as much reality as what happens to him physically.

III
TECHNIQUES

Theme

The theme of the story is fairly obvious. Are you more concerned with the external events or with the internal reactions? What, then, does Bierce seem to be exploring?

Style

When a person has read a good deal of literature, he comes to recognize that styles of writing are related to the historical period in which a work was written as well as to the peculiarities of the individual writer. Shakespeare's language does not sound like present-day English. Hemingway would not have written as he did if he had lived in the eighteenth century. Bierce first published this story in 1881. Reread sentence three of Part 2. It begins, "Circumstances of an imperious nature . . . ." What are the details of phrasing or of the arrangement of words which make this sentence different from the way a contemporary author would write it? If you cannot pick out specific details, try to rewrite the sentence as a writer might do it today.

IV
WORDS

A. Military titles such as those used in "An Occurrence at Owl Creek Bridge" have come into the language from a variety of sources. A *private* is "deprived" of status or rank. This title is derived from the Latin word *privare*, meaning "to deprive." It is related—and you can easily see the resemblance—to *privation*, which means "a lack of what is needed for existence." A *captain* is the "head" of his troop, battery, or company. This title comes from *caput*, meaning in Latin "head." Based on the same Latin word are *capital*, the "head" city of a state or a country, and *decapitate*, which means the severing of the head from the body as was done by the infamous French guillo-

tine. Another military title, *lieutenant*, has its origin in two French words, *lieu*, "place," and *tenant*, "holding." A lieutenant, then, is "holding" the "place" of another, probably that of a higher officer who is relieved of the duties the lieutenant performs. *Lieutenant* has obvious kinship with the common phrase *in lieu of*, meaning "in place of." It is also related to *tenant*, the name given a person who "holds" or rents an apartment or house. Using your dictionary, see whether you can determine the source of these military titles: *major, sergeant, colonel, general, corporal,* and *admiral*.

B. In the story, the bridge crosses over a fairly shallow body of water called a *creek*. In Louisiana, a similar body of water is called a *bayou*. In still other parts of the country, it is referred to as *stream, brook, fork, burn, gulf, rivulet, riverlet,* and *branch*. Another word in the story, *veranda*, also has a different name in other sections of the country. A veranda is the extended platform, usually roofed, at the entrance to a building. Among its other names are *porch, portico, gallery,* and *piazza*. Another example of vocabulary difference is reflected in the various names given to what some speakers call *eaves troughs: gutters, canals, spouts, water troughs,* and *spouting*. When you travel from one part of the country to another, you will discover that vocabulary is often one aspect of regional differences. What other names, if any, do you know for each of the following: *cottage cheese, string beans, faucet, paper bag, shed, weather boards, seesaw, peanuts, sofa,* and *window shades?*

C. While awaiting execution, Peyton Farquhar hears the *recurrence* of "a sharp, distinct, metallic percussion." The word *recurrence* shares a common Latin root, -*curr*-, with the word *occurrence* in the title of the story. The root means "to run." A *recurrence* of anything is a repetition or "rerunning" of it. An *occurrence* is the taking place of an action or an event; for it to come about, some movement or "running" is necessary. Also based on -*curr*- is the word *current*, referring to the swiftest "running" part of a stream, river, or other body of water. Keeping the meaning of -*curr*- and its variant, *curs*, in mind, try to answer the following questions: Would a good doctor be likely to give an ill patient a cursory examination? What is a cursive style of writing? In what sense was John the Baptist a precursor of Christ? What is an excursion?

You are sixty-one years old, living comfortably, or so you think, a life of quiet contentment. Can it be that even so, you are under pressures from your subconscious which cause you to lose your grip on reality?

Miriam

T R U M A N   C A P O T E

For several years Mrs. H. T. Miller had lived alone in a pleasant apartment (two rooms with kitchenette) in a remodeled brownstone[1] near the East River. She was a widow; Mr. H. T. Miller had left a reasonable amount of insurance. Her interests were narrow, she had no friends to speak of, and she rarely journeyed farther than the corner grocery. The other people in the house never seemed to notice her: her clothes were matter of fact, her hair iron-gray, clipped, and casually waved; she did not use cosmetics, her features were plain and inconspicuous, and on her last birthday she was sixty-one. Her activities were seldom spontaneous: she kept the two rooms immaculate, smoked an occasional cigarette, prepared her own meals, and tended a canary.

Then she met Miriam. It was snowing that night. Mrs. Miller had finished drying the supper dishes and was thumbing through an afternoon paper when she saw an advertisement of a picture playing at a neighborhood theater. The title sounded good, so she struggled into her beaver coat, laced her galoshes, and left the apartment, leaving one light burning in the foyer—she found nothing more disturbing than a sensation of darkness.

The snow was fine, falling gently, not yet making an impression on the pavement. The wind from the river cut only at street crossings. Mrs. Miller hurried, her head bowed, oblivious as a mole burrowing a blind path. She stopped at a drugstore and bought a package of peppermints.

A long line stretched in front of the box office; she took her place at the end. There would be (a tired voice groaned) a short wait for all seats. Mrs. Miller rummaged in her leather handbag till she collected exactly the correct change for admission. The line seemed to be taking its own time and, looking around for some distraction, she suddenly became conscious of a little girl standing under the edge of the marquee.

Her hair was the longest and strangest Mrs. Miller had ever seen: absolutely silver-white, like an albino's. It flowed waist-length in smooth, loose lines. She was thin and fragilely constructed. There was a simple, special elegance in the way she stood with her thumbs in the pockets of a tailored plum velvet coat.

Mrs. Miller felt oddly excited, and when the little girl glanced toward her, she smiled warmly. The little girl walked over and said, "Would you care to do me a favor?"

"I'd be glad to, if I can," said Mrs. Miller.

"Oh, it's quite easy. I merely want you to buy a ticket for me; they won't let me in otherwise. Here, I have the money." And gracefully she handed Mrs. Miller two dimes and a nickel.

They went into the theater together. An usherette directed them to a lounge; in twenty minutes the picture would be over.

"I feel just like a genuine criminal," said Mrs. Miller gaily, as she sat down. "I mean that sort of thing's against the law, isn't it? I do hope I haven't done the wrong thing. Your mother knows where you are, dear? I mean she does, doesn't she?"

The little girl said nothing. She unbuttoned

1. **brownstone,** a house faced with reddish-brown standstone, once very popular.

her coat and folded it across her lap. Her dress underneath was prim and dark blue. A gold chain dangled about her neck and her fingers, sensitive and musical-looking, toyed with it. Examining her more attentively, Mrs. Miller decided the truly distinctive feature was not her hair, but her eyes; they were hazel, steady, lacking any childlike quality whatsoever and, because of their size, seemed to consume her small face.

Mrs. Miller offered a peppermint. "What's your name, dear?"

"Miriam," she said, as though, in some curious way, it were information already familiar.

"Why, isn't that funny? My name's Miriam too. And it's not a terribly common name either. Now, don't tell me your last name's Miller!"

"Just Miriam."

"But isn't that funny?"

"Moderately," said Miriam, and rolled the peppermint on her tongue.

Mrs. Miller flushed and shifted uncomfortably. "You have such a large vocabulary for such a little girl."

"Do I?"

"Well, yes," said Mrs. Miller, hastily changing the topic to: "Do you like the movies?"

"I really wouldn't know," said Miriam. "I've never been before."

Women began filling the lounge; the rumble of the newsreel bombs exploded in the distance. Mrs. Miller rose, tucking her purse under her arm. "I guess I'd better be running now if I want to get a seat," she said. "It was nice to have met you."

Miriam nodded ever so slightly.

It snowed all week. Wheels and footsteps moved soundlessly on the street, as if the business of living continued secretly behind a pale but impenetrable curtain. In the falling quiet there was no sky or earth, only snow lifting in the wind, frosting the window glass, chilling the rooms, deadening and hushing the city. At all hours it was necessary to keep a lamp lighted, and Mrs. Miller lost track of the days:

Friday was no different from Saturday and on Sunday she went to the grocery: closed, of course.

That evening she scrambled eggs and fixed a bowl of tomato soup. Then, after putting on a flannel robe and cold-creaming her face, she propped herself up in bed with a hot-water bottle under her feet. She was reading the *Times* when the doorbell rang. At first she thought it must be a mistake and whoever it was would go away. But it rang and rang and settled to a persistent buzz. She looked at the clock: a little after eleven; it did not seem possible, she was always asleep by ten.

Climbing out of bed, she trotted barefoot across the living room. "I'm coming; please be patient." The latch was caught; she turned it this way and that way and the bell never paused an instant. "Stop it!" she cried. The bolt gave way and she opened the door an inch. "What in heaven's name?"

"Hello," said Miriam.

"Oh . . . why, hello," said Mrs. Miller, stepping hesitantly into the hall. "You're that little girl."

"I thought you'd never answer, but I kept my finger on the button; I knew you were home. Aren't you glad to see me?"

Mrs. Miller did not know what to say. Miriam, she saw, wore the same plum velvet coat and now she had also a beret to match; her white hair was braided in two shining plaits and looped at the ends with enormous white ribbons.

"Since I've waited so long, you could at least let me in," she said.

"It's awfully late."

Miriam regarded her blankly. "What difference does that make? Let me in. It's cold out here and I have on a silk dress." Then, with a gentle gesture, she urged Mrs. Miller aside and passed into the apartment.

She dropped her coat and beret on a chair. She was indeed wearing a silk dress. White silk. White silk in February. The skirt was beautifully pleated and the sleeves long; it made a faint rustle as she strolled about the room. "I like your place," she said. "I like the rug; blue's my favorite color." She touched a paper rose in a vase on the coffee table. "Imitation," she commented wanly. "How sad. Aren't imitations sad?" She seated herself on the sofa, daintily spreading her skirt.

"What do you want?" asked Mrs. Miller.

"Sit down," said Miriam. "It makes me nervous to see people stand."

Mrs. Miller sank to a hassock. "What do you want?" she repeated.

"You know, I don't think you're glad I came."

For a second time Mrs. Miller was without an answer; her hand motioned vaguely. Miriam giggled and pressed back on a mound of chintz pillows. Mrs. Miller observed that the girl was less pale than she remembered; her cheeks were flushed.

"How did you know where I lived?"

Miriam frowned. "That's no question at all. What's your name? What's mine?"

"But I'm not listed in the phone book."

"Oh, let's talk about something else."

Mrs. Miller said, "Your mother must be insane to let a child like you wander around at all hours of the night . . . and in such ridiculous clothes. She must be out of her mind."

Miriam got up and moved to a corner where a covered bird cage hung from a ceiling chain. She peeked beneath the cover. "It's a canary," she said. "Would you mind if I woke him? I'd like to hear him sing."

"Leave Tommy alone," said Mrs. Miller anxiously. "Don't you dare wake him."

"Certainly," said Miriam. "But I don't see why I can't hear him sing." And then, "Have you anything to eat? I'm starving! Even milk and a jam sandwich would be fine."

"Look," said Mrs. Miller, arising from the hassock, "look, if I make some nice sandwiches will you be a good child and run along home? It's past midnight, I'm sure."

"It's snowing," reproached Miriam. "And cold and dark."

"Well, you shouldn't have come here to begin with," said Mrs. Miller, struggling to control her voice. "I can't help the weather. If you want anything to eat you'll have to promise to leave."

Miriam brushed a braid against her cheek. Her eyes were thoughtful, as if weighing the proposition. She turned toward the bird cage. "Very well," she said, "I promise."

How old is she? Ten? Eleven? Mrs. Miller, in the kitchen, unsealed a jar of strawberry preserves and cut four slices of bread. She poured a glass of milk and paused to light a cigarette. *And why has she come?* Her hand shook as she held the match, fascinated, till it burned her finger. The canary was singing— singing as he did in the morning and at no other time. "Miriam," she called, "Miriam, I told you not to disturb Tommy." There was no answer. She called again; all she heard was the canary. She inhaled the cigarette and discovered she had lighted the cork-tip end and . . . oh, really, she mustn't lose her temper.

She carried the food in on a tray and set it on the coffee table. She saw first that the bird cage still wore its night cover. And Tommy was singing. It gave her a queer sensation. And no one was in the room. Mrs. Miller went through an alcove leading to her bedroom; at the door she caught her breath.

"What are you doing?" she asked.

Miriam glanced up, and in her eyes there was a look that was not ordinary. She was standing by the bureau, a jewel case opened before her. For a minute she studied Mrs. Miller, forcing their eyes to meet, and she smiled. "There's nothing good here," she said. "But I like this." Her hand held a cameo brooch. "It's charming."

"Suppose—perhaps you'd better put it back," said Mrs. Miller, feeling suddenly the need of some support. She leaned against the doorframe; her head was unbearably heavy; a pressure weighted the rhythm of her heartbeat. The light seemed to flutter defectively. "Please, child—a gift from my husband . . . ."

"But it's beautiful and I want it," said Miriam. *"Give it to me."*

As she stood, striving to shape a sentence

which would somehow save the brooch, it came to Mrs. Miller there was no one to whom she might turn; she was alone; a fact that had not been among her thoughts for a long time. Its sheer emphasis was stunning. But here in her own room in the hushed snow city were evidences she could not ignore or, she knew with startling clarity, resist.

Miriam ate ravenously, and when the sandwiches and milk were gone, her fingers made cobweb movements over the plate, gathering crumbs. The cameo gleamed on her blouse, the blond profile like a trick reflection of its wearer. "That was very nice," she sighed, "though now an almond cake or a cherry would be ideal. Sweets are lovely, don't you think?"

Mrs. Miller was perched precariously on the hassock, smoking a cigarette. Her hair net had slipped lopsided and loose strands straggled down her face. Her eyes were stupidly concentrated on nothing, and her cheeks were mottled in red patches, as though a fierce slap had left permanent marks.

"Is there a candy . . . a cake?"

Mrs. Miller tapped ash on the rug. Her head swayed slightly as she tried to focus her eyes. "You promised to leave if I made the sandwiches," she said.

"Dear me, did I?"

"It was a promise and I'm tired and I don't feel well at all."

"Mustn't fret," said Miriam. "I'm only teasing."

She picked up her coat, slung it over her arm, and arranged her beret in front of a mirror. Presently she bent close to Mrs. Miller and whispered, "Kiss me good night."

"Please . . . I'd rather not," said Mrs. Miller.

Miriam lifted a shoulder, arched an eyebrow. "As you like," she said, and went directly to the coffee table, seized the vase containing the paper roses, carried it to where the hard surface of the floor lay bare, and hurled it downward. Glass sprayed in all directions and she stamped her foot on the bouquet.

Then slowly she walked to the door, but before closing it she looked back at Mrs. Miller with a slyly innocent curiosity.

Mrs. Miller spent the next day in bed, rising once to feed the canary and drink a cup of tea; she took her temperature and had none, yet her dreams were feverishly agitated; their unbalanced mood lingered even as she lay staring wide-eyed at the ceiling. One dream threaded through the others like an elusively mysterious theme in a complicated symphony, and the scenes it depicted were sharply outlined, as though sketched by a hand of gifted intensity: a small girl, wearing a bridal gown and a wreath of leaves, led a gray procession down a mountain path, and among them there was unusual silence till a woman at the rear asked, "Where is she taking us?" "No one knows," said an old man marching in front. "But isn't she pretty?" volunteered a third voice. "Isn't she like a frost flower—so shining and white?"

Tuesday morning she woke up feeling better; harsh slats of sunlight, slanting through Venetian blinds, shed a disrupting light on her unwholesome fancies. She opened the window to discover a thawed, mild-as-spring day; a sweep of clean new clouds crumpled against a vastly blue, out-of-season sky; and across the low line of rooftops she could see the river and smoke curving from tugboat stacks in a warm wind. A great silver truck plowed the snow-banked street, its machine sound humming on the air.

After straightening the apartment, she went to the grocer's, cashed a check, and continued to Schrafft's, where she ate breakfast and chatted happily with the waitress. Oh, it was a wonderful day . . . more like a holiday . . . and it would be so foolish to go home.

She boarded a Lexington Avenue bus and rode up to Eighty-sixth Street; it was here that she had decided to do a little shopping.

She had no idea what she wanted or needed, but she idled along, intent only upon the passers-by, brisk and preoccupied, who gave her a disturbing sense of separateness.

It was while waiting at the corner of Third Avenue that she saw the man: an old man, bowlegged and stooped under an armload of bulging packages; he wore a shabby brown coat and a checkered cap. Suddenly she realized they were exchanging a smile; there was nothing friendly about this smile, it was merely two cold flickers of recognition. But she was certain she had never seen him before.

He was standing next to an el[2] pillar, and as she crossed the street he turned and followed. He kept quite close; from the corner of her eye she watched his reflection wavering on the shopwindows.

Then in the middle of the block she stopped and faced him. He stopped also and cocked his head, grinning. But what could she say? Do? Here, in broad daylight, on Eighty-sixth Street? It was useless and, despising her own helplessness, she quickened her steps.

Now Second Avenue is a dismal street, made from scraps and ends; part cobblestone, part asphalt, part cement; and its atmosphere of desertion is permanent. Mrs. Miller walked five blocks without meeting anyone, and all the while the steady crunch of his footfalls in the snow stayed near. And when she came to a florist's shop, the sound was still with her. She hurried inside and watched through the glass door as the old man passed; he kept his eyes straight ahead and didn't slow his pace, but he did one strange, telling thing: he tipped his cap.

"Six white ones, did you say?" asked the florist. "Yes," she told him, "white roses."

From there she went to a glassware store and selected a vase, presumably a replacement for the one Miriam had broken, though the price was intolerable and the vase itself (she thought) grotesquely vulgar. But a series of unaccountable purchases had begun, as if by prearranged plan—a plan of which she had not the least knowledge or control.

She bought a bag of glazed cherries, and at a place called the Knickerbocker Bakery she paid forty cents for six almond cakes.

Within the last hour the weather had turned cold again; like blurred lenses, winter clouds cast a shade over the sun, and the skeleton of an early dusk colored the sky; a damp mist mixed with the wind and the voices of a few children who romped high on mountains of gutter snow seemed lonely and cheerless. Soon the first flake fell, and when Mrs. Miller reached the brownstone house, snow was falling in a swift screen and foot tracks vanished as they were printed.

The white roses were arranged decoratively in the vase. The glazed cherries shone on a ceramic plate. The almond cakes, dusted with sugar, awaited a hand. The canary fluttered on its swing and picked at a bar of seed.

At precisely five the doorbell rang. Mrs. Miller *knew* who it was. The hem of her house coat trailed as she crossed the floor. "Is that you?" she called.

"Naturally," said Miriam, the word resounding shrilly from the hall. "Open this door."

"Go away," said Mrs. Miller.

"Please hurry—I have a heavy package."

"Go away," said Mrs. Miller. She returned to the living room, lighted a cigarette, sat down and calmly listened to the buzzer; on and on and on. "You might as well leave. I have no intention of letting you in."

Shortly the bell stopped. For possibly ten minutes Mrs. Miller did not move. Then, hearing no sound, she concluded Miriam had gone. She tiptoed to the door and opened it a sliver; Miriam was half reclining atop a cardboard box with a beautiful French doll cradled in her arms.

"Really, I thought you were never coming," she said peevishly. "Here, help me get this in, it's awfully heavy."

It was not spell-like compulsion that Mrs. Miller felt, but rather a curious passivity; she brought in the box, Miriam the doll. Miriam curled up on the sofa, not troubling to remove her coat or beret, and watched disinterestedly as Mrs. Miller dropped the box and stood trembling, trying to catch her breath.

---

2. **el**, elevated railway.

"Thank you," she said. In the daylight she looked pinched and drawn, her hair less luminous. The French doll she was loving wore an exquisite powdered wig and its idiot glass eyes sought solace in Miriam's. "I have a surprise," she continued. "Look into my box."

Kneeling, Mrs. Miller parted the flaps and lifted out another doll; then a blue dress which she recalled as the one Miriam had worn that first night at the theater; and of the remainder she said, "It's all clothes. Why?"

"Because I've come to live with you," said Miriam, twisting a cherry stem. "Wasn't it nice of you to buy me the cherries——"

"But you can't! For God's sake go away—go away and leave me alone!"

"——and the roses and the almond cakes? How really wonderfully generous. You know, these cherries are delicious. The last place I lived was with an old man; he was terribly poor and we never had good things to eat. But I think I'll be happy here." She paused to snuggle her doll closer. "Now, if you'll just show me where to put my things . . . ."

Mrs. Miller's face dissolved into a mask of ugly red lines; she began to cry, and it was an unnatural, tearless sort of weeping, as though, not having wept for a long time, she had forgotten how. Carefully she edged backward till she touched the door.

She fumbled through the hall and down the stairs to a landing below. She pounded frantically on the door of the first apartment she came to; a short, redheaded man answered and she pushed past him. "Say, what is this?" he said. "Anything wrong, lover?" asked a young woman who appeared from the kitchen, drying her hands. And it was to her that Mrs. Miller turned.

"Listen," she cried, "I'm ashamed behaving this way, but—well, I'm Mrs. H. T. Miller and I live upstairs and"—she pressed her hands over her face—"it sounds so absurd . . . ."

The woman guided her to a chair, while the man excitedly rattled pocket change. "Yeah?"

"I live upstairs and there's a little girl visiting me, and I suppose that I'm afraid of her. She won't leave and I can't make her and—she's going to do something terrible. She's already stolen my cameo, but she's about to do something worse—something terrible!"

The man asked, "Is she a relative, huh?"

Mrs. Miller shook her head. "I don't know who she is. Her name's Miriam, but I don't know for certain who she is."

"You gotta calm down, honey," said the woman, stroking Mrs. Miller's arm. "Harry here'll tend to this kid. Go on, lover." And Mrs. Miller said, "The door's open—5A."

After the man left, the woman brought a towel and bathed Mrs. Miller's face. "You're very kind," Mrs. Miller said. "I'm sorry to act like such a fool, only this wicked child . . . ."

"Sure, honey," consoled the woman. "Now, you better take it easy."

Mrs. Miller rested her head in the crook of her arm; she was quiet enough to be asleep. The woman turned a radio dial; a piano and a husky voice filled the silence and the woman, tapping her foot, kept excellent time. "Maybe we oughta go up too," she said.

"I don't want to see her again. I don't want to be anywhere near her."

"Uh huh, but what you shoulda done, you shoulda called a cop."

Presently they heard the man on the stairs. He strode into the room frowning and scratching the back of his neck. "Nobody there," he said, honestly embarrassed. "She musta beat it."

"Harry, you're a jerk," announced the woman. "We been sitting here the whole time and we woulda seen . . ." She stopped abruptly, for the man's glance was sharp.

"I looked all over," he said, "and there just ain't nobody there. Nobody, understand?"

"Tell me," said Mrs. Miller, rising, "tell me, did you see a large box? Or a doll?"

"No, ma'am, I didn't."

And the woman, as if delivering a verdict, said, "Well, for cryinoutloud . . . ."

Mrs. Miller entered her apartment softly; she walked to the center of the room and stood quite still. No, in a sense it had not changed: the roses, the cakes, and the cherries were in place. But this was an empty room, emptier than if the furnishings and familiars were not present, lifeless and petrified as a funeral parlor. The sofa loomed before her with a new strangeness: its vacancy had a meaning that would have been less penetrating and terrible had Miriam been curled on it. She gazed fixedly at the space where she remembered setting the box and for a moment the hassock spun desperately. And she looked through the window; surely the river was real, surely snow was falling. But then one could not be certain witness to anything: Miriam, so vividly *there* . . . and yet, where was she? Where, where?

As though moving in a dream, she sank to a chair. The room was losing shape; it was dark and getting darker and there was nothing to be done about it: she could not lift her hand to light a lamp.

Suddenly, closing her eyes, she felt an upward surge, like a diver emerging from some deeper, greener depth. In times of terror or immense distress there are moments when the mind waits, as though for a revelation, while a skein of calm is woven over thought; it is like sleep, or a supernatural trance; and during this lull one is aware of a force of quiet reasoning: well, what if she had never really known a girl named Miriam? That she had been foolishly frightened on the street? In the end, like everything else, it was of no importance. For the only thing she had lost to Miriam was her identity, but now she knew she had found again the person who lived in this room, who cooked her own meals, who owned a canary, who was someone she could trust and believe in: Mrs. H. T. Miller.

Listening in contentment, she became aware of a double sound: a bureau drawer opening and closing; she seemed to hear it long after completion—opening and closing. Then gradually the harshness of it was replaced by the murmur of a silk dress and this, delicately faint, was moving nearer and swelling in intensity till the walls trembled with the vibration and the room was caving under a wave of whispers. Mrs. Miller stiffened and opened her eyes to a dull, direct stare.

"Hello," said Miriam.

I

A QUIET DESPERATION

Everyone experiences times when things that are real seem to take on an unreal quality: the ordinary is extraordinary; the known is unknown. This distortion of the familiar may take place in a heavy fog that changes our perspective or during a heat wave accompanied by an oppressive wind that brings on irrational emotions. In times of illness, pain and fever may distort a room or make faces strangely weird. Capote's story has this same quality. Notice that it takes place during a prolonged snowstorm when the life of the city has momentarily stopped. The reader slowly comes to feel the strangely disoriented feelings that Mrs. Miller herself is experiencing, which produce a kind of quiet desperation.

II

IMPLICATIONS

A. The following statements were generated by the story you have read. They are not necessarily right or wrong. What do your own experiences lead you to believe is the truth about these implications?

1. Loneliness is a terrible pressure. Mrs. Miller only imagines Miriam.

2. Miriam is trying to take over Mrs. Miller's personality.

3. In legend, the Snow Queen is often portrayed as Death. Many details in the story tie Miriam to this legend.

4. Mrs. Miller's strange passivity when Miriam arrives to stay is a stage of dying.

5. Mrs. Miller is trying to withstand two pressures at one time: that of her moral obligation to help a child and her feeling that she is being used.

B. Discuss the following quotations. How valid are the ideas presented? What do they imply about life?

1. " 'Imitation,' she commented wanly. 'How sad. Aren't imitations sad?' "

2. "But a series of unaccountable purchases had begun, as if by prearranged plan—a plan of which she had not the least knowledge or control."

3. "In the end, like everything else, it was of no importance. For the only thing she had lost to Miriam was her identity. . . ."

III

TECHNIQUES

Theme

What happens to Mrs. Miller's personality as the story progresses? Considering this, how would you express the theme?

Style

How does the language reflect Mrs. Miller's personality? How does this style contrast with the events?

IV

WORDS

A. Words often spring from seemingly unlikely backgrounds. It appears improbable, for example, that Mrs. Miller's canary could be related to the canine (dog) family. Yet, in an etymological sense, it is. (*Etymology* is the study of the origin and development of words.) The canary is a native of the Canary Islands from which it gets its name. When the Romans landed on the islands, they were astonished to find many huge dogs. They were so impressed by these wild animals that they named the islands *"Canariae Insulae,"* that is, "The Canary Islands," meaning "The Isles of Dogs." *Canariae* is derived from *canis,* "dog." The little bird was later named after the islands.

B. The English lexical (word) stockpile has been greatly enriched, as you have seen elsewhere in this book, by borrowings from French. The following words from "Miriam" are all French contributions: *beret, bouquet, alcove, marquee, foyer,* and *bureau.* A dictionary ordinarily indicates, usually within brackets, the derivation of a word. If the word originated from French, the abbreviation, when used, is *F.* When *O* or *M* precedes the *F,* it means Old French or Middle French. Frequently, a French loan-word is traceable to yet another language. *Alcove,* for example, goes back to Spanish *alcoba,* from Arabic *al-qubbah,* "the vault." Using a dictionary, look up the meaning as well as the background of each of these words borrowed from French: *sacrament, vestige, chaperone, brochure, encore, liaison, melee, rapport, surveillance,* and *protégé.*

PEOPLE
UNDER
PRESSURE

People under pressure is a major theme
in modern art and literature. Fortunately,
many of the modern statements on this theme
seem to spring from a humanitarian urgency
to discover trouble and bring help.
However, man's long history of torture
and deliberate cruelty reminds us that this theme
is an ancient one and our preoccupation
with it springs from a dark well.

MIGRATION
William Gropper
Oliver B. James Collection of American Art,
Arizona State University, Tempe

Nature has many ways of putting
men under pressure. A dust-bowl
family has been forced to move on
in search of greener pastures.

TORNADO OVER KANSAS
John Steuart Curry

Astorm funnel threatens a Kansas farm family
in the action-filled painting
by the contemporary painter Curry.
Luckier than some, these people are able to respond
to the pressure by evacuating to a storm cellar.

The pressures that war imposes upon people
are all too well known. This sketch
of the occupants of an invasion craft
points out the pressures of waiting
to be landed in battle.

FRAIL CRAFT
Lieut. Mitchell Jamieson, USNR

The atmosphere
of death hangs
over the blue
painting of tragedy.
The pressure of loss
and its damage
to the spirit
are movingly
recorded.

THE TRAGEDY
Pablo Picasso
National Gallery of Art,
Washington, D.C.,
Chester Dale Collection

Confinement, real or imagined, is one of mankind's most destructive pressures. The unhappy circle of defeated men revolving within the high confining prison walls is Van Gogh's stirring statement of this bitter pressure.

TERROR IN BROOKLYN
Louis Guglielmi
*1941, Oil, Collection
of the Whitney Museum of
American Art, New York*

The terrified women in Guglielmi's painting are trapped
in a confining glass, and the horrors that they fear are indicated
by the painter's symbols. You must decide
whether the threats are real or imagined.

The Biblical hero Samson,
like all epic heroes,
often found himself
under great pressure.
Here, blinded,
he is tied to a mill wheel
and tormented by slave drivers.
This painting is an early work
of the modern French painter
Rouault whose later style
was much less detailed
than what you see.

SAMSON AT THE MILLSTONE
Georges Rouault
Los Angeles County Museum of Art,
Museum Purchase with De Sylva Funds

THE PIT AND THE PENDULUM
Alphonse Legros
Philadelphia Museum of Art

In his etching
for Edgar Allan Poe's story
of the same name,
Legros depicts
the unendurable pressures
on the prisoner in the
rat-infested pit waiting for
the descending blade swinging
closer on the pendulum.

> He would have liked a few more minutes in which to turn things around in his head. As it was, with Jennie chiding him about being afraid, he had to keep going.

A Summer Tragedy

ARNA BONTEMPS

Old Jeff Patton, the black share farmer, fumbled with his bow tie. His fingers trembled and the high, stiff collar pinched his throat. A fellow loses his hand for such vanities after thirty or forty years of simple life. Once a year, or maybe twice if there's a wedding among his kinfolks, he may spruce up; but generally fancy clothes do nothing but adorn the wall of the big room and feed the moths. That had been Jeff Patton's experience. He had not worn his stiff-bosomed shirt more than a dozen times in all his married life. His swallow-tailed coat lay on the bed beside him, freshly brushed and pressed, but it was as full of holes as the overalls in which he worked on weekdays. The moths had used it badly. Jeff twisted his mouth into a hideous toothless grimace as he contended with the obstinate bow. He stamped his good foot and decided to give up the struggle.

"Jennie," he called.

"What's that, Jeff?" His wife's shrunken voice came out of the adjoining room like an echo. It was hardly bigger than a whisper.

"I reckon you'll have to he'p me wid this heah bow tie, baby," he said meekly. "Dog if I can hitch it up."

Her answer was not strong enough to reach him, but presently the old woman came to the door, feeling her way with a stick. She had a wasted, dead-leaf appearance. Her body, as scrawny and gnarled as a string bean, seemed less than nothing in the ocean of frayed and faded petticoats that surrounded her. These hung an inch or two above the tops of her heavy unlaced shoes and showed little grotesque piles where the stockings had fallen down from her negligible legs.

"You oughta could do a heap mo' wid a thing like that'n me—beingst as you got yo' good sight."

"Looks like I oughta could," he admitted. "But my fingers is gone democrat on me. I get all mixed up in the looking glass an' can't tell wicha way to twist the devilish thing."

Jennie sat on the side of the bed, and old Jeff Patton got down on one knee while she tied the bow knot. It was a slow and painful ordeal for each of them in this position. Jeff's bones cracked, his knee ached, and it was only after a half dozen attempts that Jennie worked a semblance of a bow into the tie.

"I got to dress maself now," the old woman whispered. "These is ma old shoes an' stockings, and I ain't so much as unwrapped ma dress."

"Well, don't worry 'bout me no mo', baby," Jeff said. "That 'bout finishes me. All I gotta do now is slip on that old coat 'n ves' an' I'll be fixed to leave."

Jennie disappeared again through the dim passage into the shed room. Being blind was no handicap to her in that black hole. Jeff heard the cane placed against the wall beside the door and knew that his wife was on easy ground. He put on his coat, took a battered top hat from the bed post, and hobbled to the front door. He was ready to travel. As soon as Jennie could get on her Sunday shoes and her old black silk dress, they would start.

Outside the tiny log house, the day was warm and mellow with sunshine. A host of wasps were humming with busy excitement in the trunk of a dead sycamore. Gray squirrels were searching through the grass for hickory nuts, and blue jays were in the trees, hopping from branch to branch. Pine woods stretched away to the left like a black sea. Among them were scattered scores of log houses like Jeff's, houses of black share farmers. Cows and pigs wandered freely among the trees. There was no danger of loss. Each farmer knew his own stock and knew his neighbor's as well as he knew his neighbor's children.

Down the slope to the right were the cultivated acres on which the colored folks worked. They extended to the river, more than two miles away, and they were today green with the unmade cotton crop. A tiny thread of a road, which passed directly in front of Jeff's place, ran through these green fields like a pencil mark.

Jeff, standing outside the door, with his absurd hat in his left hand, surveyed the wide scene tenderly. He had been forty-five years on these acres. He loved them with the unexplained affection that others have for the countries to which they belong.

The sun was hot on his head, his collar still pinched his throat, and the Sunday clothes were intolerably hot. Jeff transferred the hat to his right hand and began fanning with it. Suddenly the whisper that was Jennie's voice came out of the shed room.

"You can bring the car round front whilst you's waitin'," it said feebly. There was a tired pause; then it added, "I'll soon be fixed to go."

"A'right, baby," Jeff answered. "I'll get it in a minute."

But he didn't move. A thought struck him that made his mouth fall open. The mention of the car brought to his mind, with new intensity, the trip he and Jennie were about to take. Fear came into his eyes; excitement took his breath. Lord, Jesus!

"Jeff . . . . O Jeff," the old woman's whisper called.

He awakened with a jolt. "Hunh, baby?"

"What you doin'?"

"Nuthin. Jes studyin'. I jes been turnin' things round 'n round in ma mind."

"You could be gettin' the car," she said.

"Oh yes, right away, baby."

He started round to the shed, limping heavily on his bad leg. There were three frizzly chickens in the yard. All his other chickens had been killed or stolen recently. But the frizzly chickens had been saved somehow. That was fortunate indeed, for these curious creatures had a way of devouring "poison"[1] from the yard and in that way protecting against conjure[2] and black luck and spells. But even the frizzly chickens seemed now to be in a stupor. Jeff thought they had some ailment; he expected all three of them to die shortly.

The shed in which the old T-model Ford stood was only a grass roof held up by four corner poles. It had been built by tremulous hands at a time when the little rattletrap car had been regarded as a peculiar treasure. And, miraculously, despite wind and downpour, it still stood.

Jeff adjusted the crank and put his weight upon it. The engine came to life with a sputter and bang that rattled the old car from radiator to tail light. Jeff hopped into the seat and put his foot on the accelerator. The sputtering and banging increased. The rattling became more violent. That was good. It was good banging, good sputtering and rattling, and it meant that the aged car was still in running condition. She could be depended on for this trip.

Again Jeff's thought halted as if paralyzed. The suggestion of the trip fell into the machinery of his mind like a wrench. He felt dazed and weak. He swung the car out into the yard, made a half turn, and drove around to the front door. When he took his hands off the wheel, he noticed that he was trembling violently. He cut off the motor and climbed to the ground to wait for Jennie.

A few minutes later she was at the window, her voice rattling against the pane like a broken shutter.

"I'm ready, Jeff."

---

1. **poison,** something left in the yard to cast spells on the occupants of the house.
2. **conjure\\ˈkən·jər** harmful magic or spells.

He did not answer, but limped into the house and took her by the arm. He led her slowly through the big room, down the step, and across the yard.

"You reckon I'd oughta lock the do'?" he asked softly.

They stopped and Jennie weighed the question. Finally she shook her head.

"Ne' mind the do'," she said. "I don't see no cause to lock up things."

"You right," Jeff agreed. "No cause to lock up."

Jeff opened the door and helped his wife into the car. A quick shudder passed over him. Jesus! Again he trembled.

"How come you shaking so?" Jennie whispered.

"I don't know," he said.

"You mus' be scairt, Jeff."

"No, baby, I ain't scairt."

He slammed the door after her and went around to crank up again. The motor started easily. Jeff wished that it had not been so responsive. He would have liked a few more minutes in which to turn things around in his head. As it was, with Jennie chiding him about being afraid, he had to keep going. He swung the car into the little pencil-mark road and started off toward the river, driving very slowly, very cautiously.

Chugging across the green countryside, the small battered Ford seemed tiny indeed. Jeff felt a familiar excitement, a thrill, as they came down the first slope to the immense levels on which the cotton was growing. He could not help reflecting that the crops were good. He knew what that meant, too; he had made forty-five of them with his own hands. It was true that he had worn out nearly a dozen mules, but that was the fault of old man Stevenson, the owner of the land. Major Stevenson had the odd notion that one mule was all a share farmer needed to work a thirty-acre plot. It was an expensive notion, the way it killed mules from overwork, but the old man held to it. Jeff thought it killed a good many share farmers as well as mules, but he had no sympathy for them. He had always been strong, and he had been taught to have no patience with weakness in men. Women or children might be tolerated if they were puny, but a weak man was a curse. Of course, his own children—

Jeff's thought halted there. He and Jennie never mentioned their dead children any more. And naturally, he did not wish to dwell upon them in his mind. Before he knew it, some remark would slip out of his mouth and that would make Jennie feel blue. Perhaps she would cry. A woman like Jennie could not easily throw off the grief that comes from losing five grown children within two years. Even Jeff was still staggered by the blow. His memory had not been much good recently. He frequently talked to himself. And, although he had kept it a secret, he knew that his courage had left him. He was terrified by the least unfamiliar sound at night. He was reluctant to venture far from home in the daytime. And that habit of trembling when he felt fearful was now far beyond his control. Sometimes he became afraid and trembled without knowing what had frightened him. The feeling would just come over him like a chill.

The car rattled slowly over the dusty road. Jennie sat erect and silent with a little absurd hat pinned to her hair. Her useless eyes seemed very large, very white in their deep sockets. Suddenly Jeff heard her voice, and he inclined his head to catch the words.

"Is we passed Delia Moore's house yet?" she asked.

"Not yet," he said.

"You must be drivin' mighty slow, Jeff."

"We just as well take our time, baby."

There was a pause. A little puff of steam was coming out of the radiator of the car. Heat wavered above the hood. Delia Moore's house was nearly half a mile away. After a moment Jennie spoke again.

"You ain't really scairt, is you, Jeff?"

"Nah, baby, I ain't scairt."

"You know how we agreed—we gotta keep on goin'."

Jewels of perspiration appeared on Jeff's forehead. His eyes rounded, blinked, became fixed on the road.

"I don't know," he said with a shiver, "I reckon it's the only thing to do."

"Hm."

A flock of guinea fowls, pecking in the road, were scattered by the passing car. Some of them took to their wings; others hid under bushes. A blue jay, swaying on a leafy twig, was annoying a roadside squirrel. Jeff held an even speed till he came near Delia's place. Then he slowed down noticeably.

Delia's house was really no house at all, but an abandoned store building converted into a dwelling. It sat near a crossroads, beneath a single black cedar tree. There Delia, a cattish old creature of Jennie's age, lived alone. She had been there more years than anybody could remember, and long ago had won the disfavor of such women as Jennie. For in her young days Delia had been gayer, yellower, and saucier than seemed proper in those parts. Her ways with menfolks had been dark and suspicious. And the fact that she had had as many husbands as children did not help her reputation.

"Yonder's old Delia," Jeff said as they passed.

"What she doin'?"

"Jes sittin' in the do'," he said.

"She see us?"

"Hm," Jeff said. "Musta did."

That relieved Jennie. It strengthened her to know that her old enemy had seen her pass in her best clothes. That would give the old she-devil something to chew her gums and fret about, Jennie thought. Wouldn't she have a fit if she didn't find out? Old evil Delia! This would be just the thing for her. It would pay her back for being so evil. It would also pay her, Jennie thought, for the way she used to grin at Jeff—long ago, when her teeth were good.

The road became smooth and red,[3] and Jeff could tell by the smell of the air that they were nearing the river. He could see the rise where the road turned and ran along parallel to the

---

3. **red**, the color of a clay road.

stream. The car chugged on monotonously. After a long silent spell, Jennie leaned against Jeff and spoke.

"How many bale o' cotton you think we got standin'?" she said.

Jeff wrinkled his forehead as he calculated.

"'Bout twenty-five, I reckon."

"How many you make las' year?"

"Twenty-eight," he said. "How come you ask that?"

"I's jes thinkin'," Jennie said quietly.

"It don't make a speck o' difference though," Jeff reflected. "If we get much or if we get little, we still gonna be in debt to old man Stevenson when he gets through counting up agin us. It's took us a long time to learn that."

Jennie was not listening to these words. She had fallen into a trance-like meditation. Her lips twitched. She chewed her gums and rubbed her gnarled hands nervously. Suddenly, she leaned forward, buried her face in the nervous hands, and burst into tears. She cried aloud in a dry, cracked voice that suggested the rattle of fodder on dead stalks. She cried aloud like a child, for she had never learned to suppress a genuine sob. Her slight old frame shook heavily and seemed hardly able to sustain such violent grief.

"What's the matter, baby?" Jeff asked awkwardly. "Why you cryin' like all that?"

"I's jes thinkin'," she said.

"So you the one what's scairt now, hunh?"

"I ain't scairt, Jeff. I's jes thinkin' 'bout leavin' eve'thing like this—eve'thing we been used to. It's right sad-like."

Jeff did not answer, and presently Jennie buried her face again and cried.

The sun was almost overhead. It beat down furiously on the dusty wagon-path road, on the parched roadside grass and the tiny battered car. Jeff's hands, gripping the wheel, became wet with perspiration; his forehead sparkled. Jeff's lips parted. His mouth shaped a hideous grimace. His face suggested the face of a man being burned. But the torture passed and his expression softened again.

"You mustn't cry, baby," he said to his wife.

"We gotta be strong. We can't break down."

Jennie waited a few seconds, then said, "You reckon we oughta do it, Jeff? You reckon we oughta go 'head an' do it, really?"

Jeff's voice choked; his eyes blurred. He was terrified to hear Jennie say the thing that had been in his mind all morning. She had egged him on when he had wanted more than anything in the world to wait, to reconsider, to think things over a little longer. Now she was getting cold feet. Actually, there was no need of thinking the question through again. It would only end in making the same painful decision once more. Jeff knew that. There was no need of fooling around longer.

"We jes as well to do like we planned," he said. "They ain't nothin' else for us now—it's the bes' thing."

Jeff thought of the handicaps, the near impossibility, of making another crop with his leg bothering him more and more each week. Then there was always the chance that he would have another stroke, like the one that had made him lame. Another one might kill him. The least it could do would be to leave him helpless. Jeff gasped—Lord, Jesus! He could not bear to think of being helpless, like a baby, on Jennie's hands. Frail, blind Jennie.

The little pounding motor of the car worked harder and harder. The puff of steam from the cracked radiator became larger. Jeff realized that they were climbing a little rise. A moment later the road turned abruptly, and he looked down upon the face of the river.

"Jeff."

"Hunh?"

"Is that the water I hear?"

"Hm. Tha's it."

"Well, which way you goin' now?"

"Down this-a way," he said. "The road runs 'long 'side o' the water a lil piece."

She waited a while calmly. Then she said, "Drive faster."

"A'right, baby," Jeff said.

The water roared in the bed of the river. It was fifty or sixty feet below the level of the road. Between the road and the water there was a long smooth slope, sharply inclined. The slope was dry, the clay hardened by prolonged summer heat. The water below, roaring in a narrow channel, was noisy and wild.

"Jeff."

"Hunh?"

"How far you goin'?"

"Jes a lil piece down the road."

"You ain't scairt, is you, Jeff?"

"Nah, baby," he said trembling. "I ain't scairt."

"Remember how we planned it, Jeff. We gotta do it like we said. Brave-like."

"Hm."

Jeff's brain darkened. Things suddenly seemed unreal, like figures in a dream. Thoughts swam in his mind foolishly, hysterically, like little blind fish in a pool within a dense cave. They rushed again. Jeff soon became dizzy. He shuddered violently and turned to his wife.

"Jennie, I can't do it. I can't." His voice broke pitifully.

She did not appear to be listening. All the grief had gone from her face. She sat erect, her unseeing eyes wide open, strained and frightful. Her glossy black skin had become dull. She seemed as thin, as sharp and bony, as a starved bird. Now, having suffered and endured the sadness of tearing herself away from beloved things, she showed no anguish. She was absorbed with her own thoughts, and she didn't even hear Jeff's voice shouting in her ear.

Jeff said nothing more. For an instant there was light in his cavernous brain. The great chamber was, for less than a second, peopled by characters he knew and loved. They were simple, healthy creatures, and they behaved in a manner that he could understand. They had quality. But since he had already taken leave of them long ago, the remembrance did not break his heart again. Young Jeff Patton was among them, the Jeff Patton of fifty years ago who went down to New Orleans with a crowd of country boys to the Mardi Gras[4] doings. The gay young crowd, boys with candy-striped shirts and rouged brown girls in noisy silks, was like a picture in his head. Yet it did not make him sad. On that very trip Slim Burns had killed Joe Beasley—the crowd had been broken up. Since then Jeff Patton's world had been the Greenbriar Plantation. If there had been other Mardi Gras carnivals, he had not heard of them. Since then there had been no time; the years had fallen on him like waves. Now he was old, worn out. Another paralytic stroke (like the one he had already suffered) would put him on his back for keeps. In that condition, with a frail blind woman to look after him, he would be worse off than if he were dead.

Suddenly Jeff's hands became steady. He actually felt brave. He slowed down the motor of the car and carefully pulled off the road. Below, the water of the stream boomed, a soft thunder in the deep channel. Jeff ran the car onto the clay slope, pointed it directly toward the stream, and put his foot heavily on the accelerator. The little car leaped furiously down the steep incline toward the water. The movement was nearly as swift and direct as a fall. The two old black folks, sitting quietly side by side, showed no excitement. In another instant the car hit the water and dropped immediately out of sight.

A little later it lodged in the mud of a shallow place. One wheel of the crushed and upturned little Ford became visible above the rushing water.

I

THE END OF THE ROPE

What do people do when they come to the end of their rope? The old couple in this story, having reached this point in their lives, obviously must have talked things over before reaching a decision. They approach their last day almost as if it were

---

4. **Mardi Gras**\\'mär·dē ᴬgra\\ a carnival period celebrated before Lent, especially in New Orleans.

a holiday. They put on their best clothes, set their house in order, and climb into their old car. There is something almost creative about the way they have chosen to take their own lives. The very intensity of the story is heightened because these are simple people, acting with great dignity from some inner sense of destiny.

II
IMPLICATIONS

What does the story indicate about the following statements? Do you have any facts to support your opinion?

1. It takes great courage to commit suicide.

2. The way the two old people end their lives says a great deal about the kind of people they have been.

3. The reader is caught by surprise at the very end when he realizes that Jeff and Jennie are commiting suicide.

III
TECHNIQUES

Theme

List the pressures accumulating on Jeff and Jennie. Are there other alternatives open to them? What is the real "tragedy" of the story? How would you state the theme?

Style

The story has great pathos which grows steadily throughout the tale. Yet there is no use of emotional language. Actions and words are quiet and simple. What everyday activities do the couple perform that give a quality of simple dignity to their behavior?

IV
WORDS

A. To make his characters believable, Arna Bontemps has Jennie and Jeff Patton speak the variety of American English that poor share-farmers in real life might use. Their language pattern, with its own rules of pronunciation, vocabulary, and grammar, is called a *dialect*. Language scholars regard all dialects as being equal rather than one being superior or inferior to another. Each variety of American English, they maintain, serves its speakers equally well. However, they

do acknowledge that, for one reason or another, a speaker of one dialect may wish to learn another one for use in different situations. In "A Summer Tragedy" the writer has faithfully reproduced the dialectal features common to speakers like the Pattons. Examples are: pronunciation—*scairt* (scared) and *do'* (door); vocabulary—*reckon* (suppose) and *poison* (evil substance); and grammar—*I'se* (I am) and *What she doin'?* (What is she doing?). What other identifying features can you find?

B. At one point in the story, Jennie is described as being "as scrawny and gnarled as a string bean." At another point, she is pictured as being "as thin, as sharp and bony, as a starved bird." In yet another place, her "shrunken" voice is said to sound "like an echo." By comparing Jennie's body to a string bean and to a starved bird and her voice to an echo, Arna Bontemps is attempting to sensitize the reader to the corrosive effects of poverty. Comparisons like the examples above, in which *like* or *as* are used, are called similes. The purpose of a simile is to paint a vivid picture in the reader's mind. The success of this figure of speech depends largely upon how striking and how original the comparison is. Note how these similes sparkle: "eyes like burning anthracite, "small and deadly as an asp," and "as ever-present as sin." On a scale of *poor to excellent*, how would you rate each of the following similes: "as fierce as a tigress protecting her young," "as spry and mean as a woodchuck," "like a gazelle, the picture of fluid motion," "tough as tungsten," and "as calm as the eye of a hurricane"?

C. Making use of context clues, try to determine the meaning of the italicized word in each of the following sentences from "A Summer Tragedy":

1. "Jeff twisted his mouth into a hideous toothless *grimace* as he contended with the obstinate bow."

2. "But even the frizzly chickens seemed now to be in a *stupor*. Jeff thought they had some ailment . . . ."

3. "As it was, with Jennie *chiding* him about being afraid, he had to keep going."

4. "The car chugged on *monotonously*."

5. "Her slight old frame shook heavily and seemed hardly able to *sustain* such violent grief."

SUMMING UP

People under Pressure

This group of selections has been focused on the effects that various kinds of pressure can create in the lives of human beings. Some individuals respond to pressure with an angry surge of resistance. Others quietly pit their ingenuity against the force. And some give way until their spirits are destroyed. Continuing pressure distorts, compresses, and shifts the focus of a person's life. It changes the pattern, but whether the change is for the better or worse depends on the individual's character and his strength. Though pressures vary in kind and in degree, every man must face them, for they are as natural to living as the air he breathes. It is the response to those pressures that determines what a man may be.

It is also natural that writers should frequently choose the theme of people under pressure as the subject matter of their writing. Pressure provides a natural kind of conflict, and by dealing with men's reactions to it, the writer is able to explore and evolve new understandings of life.

IMPLICATIONS

Recall the selections you have just read, and use illustrations from them to support your evaluation of each of the following statements. Wherever possible, make comparisons between the stories and your own experience.

1. The way a person reacts to pressure reveals his personality.

2. Pressure on an individual tends to distort his normal reactions.

3. External pressures often bring out submerged internal ones.

4. Internal pressures are more devastating than external pressures.

5. People often put one another under pressure without intending to do so.

6. A crushing pressure builds up from inconsequential things, none of which are very important in themselves.

TECHNIQUES

Theme

Think back on the selections and decide what particular pressure or pressures were brought to bear on the principal character in each selection. Make a list of these pressures, and using it as a reference, consider the following questions.

1. Which story did you like best? Did this selection have only one pressure or more than one?

2. Do you feel a story which piles many pressures on an individual makes a more telling impression than one with a single pressure?

3. There were two humorous stories in this group, "The Open Window" and "The Catbird Seat." Do you think this theme is a good one for a humorous treatment?

Style

Style reflects the personality of a writer as well as giving a piece of writing a distinctive quality. From the way he writes, as much as from what he writes about, you often learn a great deal about an author: whether he sees life as tragic or comic or neither; whether he is compassionate, emotional, reserved, intellectual, detached, involved, angry, or calm. In a few sentences, describe the personality of two of the following authors as you feel it must have been from reading their works. How are they different? What have they in common?

1. Saki
2. James Thurber
3. Jack London
4. Willa Cather
5. George Orwell

Identification

You have met a wide variety of characters in the preceding selections. To which central characters did you feel yourself most drawn?

Which of the following reasons helped you identify with them:

1. Did they have character traits similar to your friends'? to your own?

2. Were they involved in actions you have never had but frequently wanted to experience?

3. Did they have feelings you have known yourself?

4. Were they confronted by problems similar to ones you have faced?

Introduction to The Pearl

Some years ago while traveling in Mexico, John Steinbeck came across a moving story about an Indian boy who found and attempted to sell a wondrous pearl. The story of the boy's subsequent suffering and loss of the pearl so haunted Steinbeck that in *Sea of Cortez* he wrote:

> This seems to be a true story, but it is so much like a parable that it almost can't be. This Indian boy is too heroic, too wise. He knows too much and acts on his knowledge. In every way he goes contrary to human direction. The story is probably true, but we can't believe it; it is far too reasonable to be true.

In *The Pearl*, he has recast this "true" story and enlarged its meaning. The Indian boy has become Kino, the fisherman, and Kino has a young wife, Juana, and first baby, Coyotito. Through this young family Steinbeck ponders many of the questions which trouble all men. In exploring Kino's and Juana's reactions to the terrible pressures of poverty and ignorance, wealth and power, ambition and hope, love and hate, he leads the reader in a parable-like way to search beyond the apparently simple action of the story to the lessons it embodies. To do this Steinbeck says of *The Pearl*, "I tried to write it as folklore, to give it that set-aside, raised-up feeling that all folk stories have."

One of the chief means Steinbeck uses to give Kino's story that "raised-up feeling" is to present the characters, events, and objects in the story in such a way that they become symbols of timeless truths about God, man, and the world. We feel the power of the "boundless" sea and the "eternal" mountains. We sense a certain universal fear in the shadows of night. When we know that Kino is named after a great seventeenth-century missionary-explorer, we have a sense of man's heroic effort to overcome nature. When we consider that the name *Juana* simply means "woman," we sense that her fate belongs in some way to all women.

But most symbolic of all is the pearl itself, especially when we recall its long history in literature and symbolism. In the Bible it is most often a symbol of earthly riches—riches that can be either good or bad. As good, the pearl is a symbol of physical beauty and goodness through which man is able, in a small way, to value spiritual truths; as bad, the pearl represents the wealth and worldly pleasures which lead man to destruction. But on two significant occasions the pearl represents spiritual truths. Jesus uses the pearl to symbolize the word of God, heavenly wisdom. "Do not throw your pearls before swine, lest they trample them underfoot and turn to attack you" (Matthew 7:6). Later (Matthew 13:45–46), Jesus uses the pearl to represent both the kingdom of heaven and the committed soul which sells all and dedicates all of its talents and energies to one end—acquiring a share in the kingdom. "Again, the kingdom of heaven is like a merchant in search of fine pearls, who, finding one pearl of great value, went and sold all that he had and bought it."

In the rich symbolism of the Middle Ages the pearl represents integrity and purity. In a very famous and beautiful fifteenth-century poem entitled "The Pearl," an unknown poet laments the loss of his girl child "who lived upon the earth two years." To the poet, the pearl becomes both the symbol of his little daughter's innocence and the daughter herself, for she had been his riches, his most valued possession. To Kino and to Juana, too, their pearl becomes a symbol . . . one that takes on new dimensions and new meanings as the story unfolds.

Steinbeck also uses a simple, subdued, straightforward style to give *The Pearl* the flavor of a folk story or parable. His sentences are plain and uncomplicated. His words are common and even folksy. Scenes are drawn with cameralike clarity and objectivity. The story moves directly from one incident to another. In stark simplicity Steinbeck records the internal and external pressures which beset man in search of his soul.

THE PEARL

JOHN STEINBECK

In the town they tell the story of the great pearl—how it was found and how it was lost again. They tell of Kino, the fisherman, and of his wife, Juana, and of the baby, Coyotito.[1] And because the story has been told so often, it has taken root in every man's mind. And, as with all retold tales that are in people's hearts, there are only good and bad things and black and white things and good and evil things and no in-between anywhere.

"If this story is a parable, perhaps everyone takes his own meaning from it and reads his own life into it. In any case, they say in the town that . . ."

1

Kino awakened in the near dark. The stars still shone, and the day had drawn only a pale wash of light in the lower sky to the east. The roosters had been crowing for some time, and the early pigs were already beginning their ceaseless turning of twigs and bits of wood to see whether anything to eat had been overlooked. Outside the brush house in the tuna clump, a covey[2] of little birds chittered and flurried with their wings.

Kino's eyes opened, and he looked first at the lightening square which was the door, and then he looked at the hanging box where Coyotito slept. And last he turned his head to Juana, his wife, who lay beside him on the mat, her blue head shawl over her nose and over her breasts and around the small of her back.

Juana's eyes were open too. Kino could never remember seeing them closed when he awakened. Her dark eyes made little reflected stars. She was looking at him as she was always looking at him when he awakened.

Kino heard the little splash of morning waves on the beach. It was very good—Kino closed his eyes again to listen to his music. Perhaps he alone did this, and perhaps all of his people did it. His people had once been great makers of songs so that everything they saw or thought or did or heard became a song. That was very long ago. The songs remained; Kino knew them, but no new songs were added. That does not mean that there were no personal songs. In Kino's head there was a song now, clear and soft; and if he had been able to speak it, he would have called it the Song of the Family.

His blanket was over his nose to protect him from the dank air. His eyes flicked to a rustle beside him. It was Juana arising, almost soundlessly. On her hard bare feet she went to the hanging box where Coyotito slept, and she leaned over and said a little reassuring word. Coyotito looked up for a moment and closed his eyes and slept again. Juana went to the fire pit and uncovered a coal and fanned it alive while she broke little pieces of brush over it.

Now Kino got up and wrapped his blanket about his head and nose and shoulders. He slipped his feet into his sandals and went outside to watch the dawn.

Outside the door he squatted down and gathered the blanket ends about his knees. He saw the specks of Gulf clouds flame high in the air. And a goat came near and sniffed at him and stared with its cold, yellow eyes. Behind him Juana's fire leaped into flame and threw spears of light through the chinks of the brush-house wall and threw a wavering square of light out the door. A late moth blustered in to

---

1. **Kino**\ˈkē·nō\. **Juana**\ˈhwä·nä\. **Coyotito**\kȯi·ō ˈtē·tō\.
2. **tuna**\ˈtü·nə\ a common tropical prickly pear. **covey** \ˈkə·vē\a group of young birds.

The poverty of Kino and Juana is reflected in this scene taken from a motion picture of The Pearl.

find the fire. The Song of the Family came now from behind Kino. And the rhythm of the family song was the grinding stone where Juana worked the corn for the morning cakes.

The dawn came quickly now, a wash, a glow, a lightness, and then an explosion of fire as the sun arose out of the Gulf. Kino looked down to cover his eyes from the glare. He could hear the pat of the corncakes in the house and the rich smell of them on the cooking plate. The ants were busy on the ground, big black ones with shiny bodies, and little dusty, quick ants. Kino watched with the detachment of God while a dusty ant frantically tried to es-

cape the sand trap an ant lion[3] had dug for him. A thin, timid dog came close and, at a soft word from Kino, curled up, arranged its tail neatly over its feet, and laid its chin delicately on the pile. It was a black dog with yellow-gold spots where its eyebrows should have been. It was a morning like other mornings and yet perfect among mornings.

Kino heard the creak of the rope when Juana took Coyotito out of his hanging box and cleaned him and hammocked him in her shawl, in a loop that placed him close to her breast. Kino could see these things without looking at

_____

3. **ant lion,** an insect the larva of which traps ants in pits.

them. Juana sang softly an ancient song that had only three notes and yet endless variety of interval. And this was part of the family song too. It was all part. Sometimes it rose to an aching chord that caught the throat, saying this is safety, this is warmth, this is the *Whole*.

Across the brush fence were other brush houses, and the smoke came from them too, and the sound of breakfast; but those were other songs, their pigs were other pigs, their wives were not Juana. Kino was young and strong, and his black hair hung over his brown forehead. His eyes were warm and fierce and bright, and his mustache was thin and coarse. He lowered his blanket from his nose now; for the dark poisonous air was gone, and the yellow sunlight fell on the house. Near the brush fence, two roosters bowed and feinted at each other with squared wings and neck feathers ruffed out. It would be a clumsy fight. They were not game chickens. Kino watched them for a moment, and then his eyes went up to a flight of wild doves twinkling inland to the hills. The world was awake now, and Kino arose and went into his brush house.

As he came through the door, Juana stood up from the glowing fire pit. She put Coyotito back in his hanging box, and then she combed her black hair and braided it in two braids and tied the ends with thin green ribbon. Kino squatted by the fire pit and rolled a hot corncake and dipped it in sauce and ate it. And he drank a little pulque,[4] and that was breakfast. That was the only breakfast he had ever known, outside of feast days and one incredible fiesta on cookies that had nearly killed him. When Kino had finished, Juana came back to the fire and ate her breakfast. They had spoken once, but there is not need for speech if it is only a habit anyway. Kino sighed with satisfaction— and that was conversation.

The sun was warming the brush house, breaking through its crevices in long streaks. And one of the streaks fell on the hanging box where Coyotito lay and on the ropes that held it.

It was a tiny movement that drew their eyes to the hanging box. Kino and Juana froze in their positions. Down the rope that hung the baby's box from the roof support, a scorpion moved slowly. His stinging tail was straight out behind him, but he could whip it up in a flash of time.

Kino's breath whistled in his nostrils, and he opened his mouth to stop it. And then the startled look was gone from him and the rigidity from his body. In his mind a new song had come, the Song of Evil, the music of the enemy, of any foe of the family, a savage, secret, dangerous melody; and underneath, the Song of the Family cried plaintively.

The scorpion moved delicately down the rope toward the box. Under her breath Juana repeated an ancient magic to guard against such evil, and on top of that she muttered a Hail Mary[5] between clenched teeth. But Kino was in motion. His body glided quietly across the room, noiselessly and smoothly. His hands were in front of him, palms down; and his eyes were on the scorpion. Beneath it, in the hanging box, Coyotito laughed and reached up his hand toward it. It sensed danger when Kino was almost within reach of it. It stopped; and its tail rose up over its back in little jerks, and the curved thorn on the tail's end glistened.

Kino stood perfectly still. He could hear Juana whispering the old magic again, and he could hear the evil music of the enemy. He could not move until the scorpion moved, and it felt for the source of the death that was coming to it. Kino's hand went forward very slowly, very smoothly. The thorned tail jerked upright. And at that moment the laughing Coyotito shook the rope, and the scorpion fell.

Kino's hand leaped to catch it; but it fell past his fingers, fell on the baby's shoulder, landed and struck. Then, snarling, Kino had it, had it in his fingers, rubbing it to a paste in his hands. He threw it down and beat it into the earth floor with his fist, and Coyotito screamed

---

4. **pulque**\ˈpül ˈkā\ a fermented drink made from the juice of the agave plant in Mexico.
5. **Hail Mary,** a brief prayer to the Virgin Mary.

with pain in his box. But Kino beat and stamped the enemy, until it was only a fragment and a moist place in the dirt. His teeth were bared, and fury flared in his eyes, and the Song of the Enemy roared in his ears.

But Juana had the baby in her arms now. She found the puncture with redness starting from it already. She put her lips down over the puncture and sucked hard and spat and sucked again, while Coyotito screamed.

Kino hovered; he was helpless; he was in the way.

The screams of the baby brought the neighbors. Out of their brush houses they poured— Kino's brother Juan Tomás and his fat wife Apolonia and their four children crowded in the door and blocked the entrance, while behind them others tried to look in, and one small boy crawled among legs to have a look. And those in front passed the word back to those behind—"Scorpion. The baby has been stung."

Juana stopped sucking the puncture for a moment. The little hole was slightly enlarged and its edges whitened from the sucking, but the red swelling extended farther around it in a hard lymphatic mound.[6] And all of these people knew about the scorpion. An adult might be very ill from the sting, but a baby could easily die from the poison. First, they knew, would come swelling and fever and tightened throat, and then cramps in the stomach, and then Coyotito might die if enough of the poison had gone in. But the stinging pain of the bite was going away. Coyotito's screams turned to moans.

Kino had wondered often at the iron in his patient, fragile wife. She, who was obedient and respectful and cheerful and patient, she could arch her back in child pain with hardly a cry. She could stand fatigue and hunger almost better than Kino himself. In the canoe she was like a strong man. And now she did a most surprising thing.

"The doctor," she said. "Go to get the doctor."

The word was passed out among the neighbors where they stood close-packed in the little yard behind the brush fence. And they repeated among themselves, "Juana wants the doctor." A wonderful thing, a memorable thing, to want the doctor. To get him would be a remarkable thing. The doctor never came to the cluster of brush houses. Why should he, when he had more than he could do to take care of the rich people who lived in the stone and plaster houses of the town.

"He would not come," the people in the yard said.

"He would not come," the people in the door said, and the thought got into Kino.

"The doctor would not come," Kino said to Juana.

She looked up at him, her eyes as cold as the eyes of a lioness. This was Juana's first baby —this was nearly everything there was in Juana's world. And Kino saw her determination, and the music of the family sounded in his head with a steely tone.

"Then we will go to him," Juana said, and with one hand she arranged her dark blue shawl over her head and made of one end of it a sling to hold the moaning baby and made of the other end of it a shade over his eyes to protect him from the light. The people in the door pushed against those behind to let her through. Kino followed her. They went out of the gate to the rutted path and the neighbors followed them.

The thing had become a neighborhood affair. They made a quick soft-footed procession into the center of the town, first Juana and Kino, and behind them Juan Tomás and Apolonia, her big stomach jiggling with the strenuous pace, then all the neighbors with the children trotting on the flanks. And the yellow sun threw their black shadows ahead of them so that they walked on their own shadows.

They came to the place where the brush houses stopped and the city of stone and plaster began, the city of harsh outer walls and inner cool gardens, where a little water played

---

6. **lymphatic mound,** a swelling caused mostly by accumulation of lymph and white corpuscles.

and the bougainvillaea crusted the walls with purple and brick-red and white. They heard from the secret gardens the singing of caged birds and heard the splash of cooling water on hot flagstones.[7] The procession crossed the blinding plaza and passed in front of the church. It had grown now, and on the outskirts the hurrying newcomers were being softly informed how the baby had been stung by a scorpion, how the father and mother were taking it to the doctor.

And the newcomers, particularly the beggars from the front of the church who were great experts in financial analysis, looked quickly at Juana's old blue skirt, saw the tears in her shawl, appraised the green ribbons on her braids, read the age of Kino's blanket and the thousand washings of his clothes, and set them down as poverty people and went along to see what kind of drama might develop. The four beggars in front of the church knew everything in the town. They were students of the expressions of young women as they went into confession, and they saw them as they came out and read the nature of the sin. They knew every little scandal and some very big crimes. They slept at their posts in the shadow of the church so that no one crept in for consolation without their knowledge. And they knew the doctor. They knew his ignorance, his cruelty, his avarice, his appetites, his sins. They knew his clumsy operations and the little brown pennies he gave sparingly for alms. They had seen his corpses go into the church. And, since early Mass was over and business was slow, they followed the procession, these endless searchers after perfect knowledge of their fellow men, to see what the fat, lazy doctor would do about an indigent baby with a scorpion bite.

The scurrying procession came at last to the big gate in the wall of the doctor's house. They could hear the splashing water and the singing of caged birds and the sweep of the long brooms on the flagstones. And they could smell the frying of good bacon from the doctor's house.

Kino hesitated a moment. This doctor was not of his people. This doctor was of a race which for nearly four hundred years had beaten and starved and robbed and despised Kino's race, and frightened it, too, so that the indigene[8] came humbly to the door. And as always when he came near to one of this race, Kino felt weak and afraid and angry at the same time. Rage and terror went together. He could kill the doctor more easily than he could talk to him, for all of the doctor's race spoke to all of Kino's race as though they were simple animals. And as Kino raised his right hand to the iron ring knocker in the gate, rage swelled in him, and the pounding music of the enemy beat in his ears, and his lips drew tight against his teeth—but with his left hand he reached to take off his hat. The iron ring pounded against the gate. Kino took off his hat and stood waiting. Coyotito moaned a little in Juana's arms, and she spoke softly to him. The procession crowded close the better to see and hear.

After a moment the big gate opened a few inches. Kino could see the green coolness of the garden and little splashing fountains through the opening. The man who looked out at him was one of his own race. Kino spoke to him in the old language. "The little one—the first born—has been poisoned by the scorpion," Kino said. "He requires the skill of the healer."

The gate closed a little, and the servant refused to speak in the old language. "A little moment," he said. "I go to inform myself," and he closed the gate and slid the bolt home. The glaring sun threw the bunched shadows of the people blackly on the white wall.

In his chamber the doctor sat up in his high bed. He had on his dressing gown of red watered silk that had come from Paris, a little tight over the chest now if it was buttoned. On his lap was a silver tray with a silver chocolate pot and a tiny cup of eggshell china, so delicate that it looked silly when he lifted it with his big hand, lifted it with the tips of thumb and forefinger and spread the other three fingers

---

7. **flagstone,** a large flat paving stone.
8. **indigene**\ˈǐn·dǐ·jēn\ a native, aborigine.

wide to get them out of the way. His eyes rested in puffy little hammocks of flesh, and his mouth drooped with discontent. He was growing very stout, and his voice was hoarse with the fat that pressed on his throat. Beside him on a table was a small Oriental gong and a bowl of cigarettes. The furnishings of the room were heavy and dark and gloomy. The pictures were religious, even the large tinted photograph of his dead wife, who, if Masses willed and paid for out of her own estate could do it, was in Heaven. The doctor had once for a short time been a part of the great world, and his whole subsequent life was memory and longing for France. "That," he said, "was civilized living"—by which he meant that on a small income he had been able to keep a mistress and eat in restaurants. He poured his second cup of chocolate and crumbled a sweet biscuit in his fingers. The servant from the gate came to the open door and stood waiting to be noticed.

"Yes?" the doctor asked.

"It is a little Indian with a baby. He says a scorpion stung it."

The doctor put his cup down gently before he let his anger rise.

"Have I nothing better to do than cure insect bites for 'little Indians'? I am a doctor, not a veterinary."

"Yes, Patron,"[9] said the servant.

"Has he any money?" the doctor demanded. "No, they never have any money. I, I alone in the world am supposed to work for nothing— and I am tired of it. See if he has any money!"

At the gate the servant opened the door a trifle and looked out at the waiting people. And this time he spoke in the old language.

"Have you money to pay for the treatment?"

Now Kino reached into a secret place somewhere under his blanket. He brought out a paper folded many times. Crease by crease he unfolded it, until at last there came to view eight small, misshapen seed pearls,[10] as ugly and gray as little ulcers, flattened and almost valueless. The servant took the paper and closed the gate again, but this time he was not

gone long. He opened the gate just wide enough to pass the paper back.

"The doctor has gone out," he said. "He was called to a serious case." And he shut the gate quickly out of shame.

And now a wave of shame went over the whole procession. They melted away. The beggars went back to the church steps; the stragglers moved off; and the neighbors departed so that the public shaming of Kino would not be in their eyes.

For a long time Kino stood in front of the gate with Juana beside him. Slowly he put his suppliant hat on his head. Then, without warning, he struck the gate a crushing blow with his fist. He looked down in wonder at his split knuckles and at the blood that flowed down between his fingers.

2

The town lay on a broad estuary, its old yellow plastered buildings hugging the beach. And on the beach the white and blue canoes that came from Nayarit[1] were drawn up, canoes preserved for generations by a hard, shell-like water-proof plaster whose making was a secret of the fishing people. They were high and graceful canoes with curving bow and stern and a braced section midships where a mast could be stepped to carry a small lateen sail.[2]

The beach was yellow sand, but at the water's edge a rubble of shell and algae took its place. Fiddler crabs bubbled and sputtered in their holes in the sand, and in the shallows little lobsters popped in and out of their tiny homes in the rubble and sand. The sea bottom was rich with crawling and swimming and

---

9. **Patron**\English pro. ▲pā•trən\ here means "sir, master, lord."

10. **seed pearl,** a quite small and often irregular pearl.

1. **Nayarit**\▲na•ya•rēt\ a small state in western Mexico northwest of Mexico City.

2. **lateen**\lă ▲tēn\ **sail,** one hung from a long spar attached to a short mast.

growing things. The brown algae waved in the gentle currents, and the green eel grass swayed, and little sea horses clung to its stems. Spotted botete,[3] the poison fish, lay on the bottom in the eel-grass beds; and the bright-colored swimming crabs scampered over them.

On the beach, the hungry dogs and the hungry pigs of the town searched endlessly for any dead fish or sea bird that might have floated in on a rising tide.

Although the morning was young, the hazy mirage was up. The uncertain air that magnified some things and blotted out others hung over the whole Gulf so that all sights were unreal and vision could not be trusted; so that sea and land had the sharp clarities and the vagueness of a dream. Thus it might be that the people of the Gulf trust things of the spirit and things of the imagination, but they do not trust their eyes to show them distance or clear outline or any optical exactness. Across the estuary from the town, one section of mangroves stood clear and telescopically defined, while another mangrove clump was a hazy black-green blob. Part of the far shore disappeared into a shimmer that looked like water. There was no certainty in seeing, no proof that what you saw was there or was not there. And the people of the Gulf expected all places were that way, and it was not strange to them. A copper haze hung over the water, and the hot morning sun beat on it and made it vibrate blindingly.

The brush houses of the fishing people were back from the beach on the right-hand side of the town, and the canoes were drawn up in front of this area.

Kino and Juana came slowly down to the beach and to Kino's canoe, which was the one thing of value he owned in the world. It was very old. Kino's grandfather had brought it from Nayarit; and he had given it to Kino's father, and so it had come to Kino. It was at once property and source of food, for a man with a boat can guarantee a woman that she will eat something. It is the bulwark against starvation. And every year Kino refinished his canoe with the hard, shell-like plaster by the secret method that had also come to him from his father. Now he came to the canoe and touched the bow tenderly as he always did. He laid his diving rock and his basket and the two ropes in the sand by the canoe. And he folded his blanket and laid it in the bow.

Juana laid Coyotito on the blanket, and she placed her shawl over him so that the hot sun could not shine on him. He was quiet now, but the swelling on his shoulder had continued up his neck and under his ear and his face was puffed and feverish. Juana went to the water and waded in. She gathered some brown seaweed and made a flat, damp poultice of it; and this she applied to the baby's swollen shoulder, which was as good a remedy as any and probably better than the doctor could have done. But the remedy lacked his authority because it was simple and didn't cost anything. The stomach cramps had not come to Coyotito. Perhaps Juana had sucked out the poison in time, but she had not sucked out her worry over her first-born. She had not prayed directly for the recovery of the baby—she had prayed that they might find a pearl with which to hire the doctor to cure the baby, for the minds of people are as unsubstantial as the mirage of the Gulf.

Now Kino and Juana slid the canoe down the beach to the water; and when the bow floated, Juana climbed in, while Kino pushed the stern in and waded beside it until it floated lightly and trembled on the little breaking waves. Then, in co-ordination, Juana and Kino drove their double-bladed paddles into the sea; and the canoe creased the water and hissed with speed. The other pearlers were gone out long since. In a few moments Kino could see them clustered in the haze, riding over the oyster bed.

Light filtered down through the water to the bed where the frilly pearl oysters lay fastened to the rubbly bottom, a bottom strewn with shells of broken, opened oysters. This was the

3. botete\\'bō ▲tä·tĕ\.

bed that had raised the King of Spain to be a great power in Europe in past years, had helped to pay for his wars, and had decorated the churches for his soul's sake. The gray oysters with ruffles like skirts on the shells, the barnacle-crusted oysters with little bits of weed clinging to the skirts and small crabs climbing over them. An accident could happen to these oysters; a grain of sand could lie in the folds of muscle and irritate the flesh until, in self-protection, the flesh coated the grain with a layer of smooth cement. But once started, the flesh continued to coat the foreign body until it fell free in some tidal flurry or until the oyster was destroyed. For centuries men had dived down and torn the oysters from the beds and ripped them open, looking for the coated grains of sand. Swarms of fish lived near the bed to live near the oysters thrown back by the searching men and to nibble at the shining inner shells. But the pearls were accidents; and the finding of one was luck, a little pat on the back by God or the gods or both.

Kino had two ropes, one tied to a heavy stone and one to a basket. He stripped off his shirt and trousers and laid his hat in the bottom of the canoe. The water was oily smooth. He took his rock in one hand and his basket in the other, and he slipped feet first over the side, and the rock carried him to the bottom. The bubbles rose behind him until the water cleared and he could see. Above, the surface of the water was an undulating mirror of brightness, and he could see the bottoms of the canoes sticking through it.

Kino moved cautiously so that the water would not be obscured with mud or sand. He hooked his foot in the loop on his rock; and his hands worked quickly, tearing the oysters loose, some singly, other in clusters. He laid them in his basket. In some places the oysters clung to one another so that they came free in lumps.

Now, Kino's people had sung of everything that happened or existed. They had made songs to the fishes, to the sea in anger and to the sea in calm, to the light and the dark and the sun and the moon; and the songs were all in Kino and in his people—every song that had ever been made, even the ones forgotten. And as he filled his basket, the song was in Kino; and the beat of the song was his pounding heart as it ate the oxygen from his held breath; and the melody of the song was the gray-green water and the little scuttling animals and the clouds of fish that flitted by and were gone. But in the song there was a secret little inner song, hardly perceptible, but always there, sweet and secret and clinging, almost hiding in the counter-melody; and this was the Song of the Pearl That Might Be, for every shell thrown in the basket might contain a pearl. Chance was against it, but luck and the gods might be for it. And in the canoe above him, Kino knew that Juana was making the magic of prayer, her face set rigid and her muscles hard to force the luck, to tear the luck out of the god's hands, for she needed the luck for the swollen shoulder of Coyotito. And because the need was great and the desire was great, the little secret melody of the pearl that might be was stronger this morning. Whole phrases of it came clearly and softly into the Song of the Undersea.

Kino, in his pride and youth and strength, could remain down over two minutes without strain, so that he worked deliberately, selecting the largest shells. Because they were disturbed, the oyster shells were tightly closed. A little to his right a hummock of rubbly rock stuck up, covered with young oysters not ready to take. Kino moved next to the hummock; and then, beside it, under a little overhang, he saw a very large oyster lying by itself, not covered with its clinging brothers. The shell was partly open, for the overhang protected this ancient oyster, and in the liplike muscle Kino saw a ghostly gleam, and then the shell closed down. His heart beat out a heavy rhythm, and the melody of the maybe pearl shrilled in his ears. Slowly he forced the oyster loose and held it tightly against his breast. He kicked his foot free from the rock loop, and his body rose to the surface, and his black hair gleamed in the sunlight. He reached over the side of the canoe and laid the oyster in the bottom.

Then Juana steadied the boat while he climbed in. His eyes were shining with excitement, but in decency he pulled up his rock, and then he pulled up his basket of oysters and lifted them in. Juana sensed his excitement, and she pretended to look away. It is not good to want a thing too much. It sometimes drives the luck away. You must want it just enough, and you must be very tactful with God or the gods. But Juana stopped breathing. Very deliberately Kino opened his short, strong knife. He looked speculatively at the basket. Perhaps it would be better to open *the* oyster last. He took a small oyster from the basket, cut the muscle, searched the folds of flesh, and threw it in the water. Then he seemed to see the great oyster for the first time. He squatted in the bottom of the canoe, picked up the shell, and examined it. The flutes were shining black to brown, and only a few small barnacles adhered to the shell. Now Kino was reluctant to open it. What he had seen, he knew, might be a reflection, a piece of flat shell accidentally drifted in, or a complete illusion. In this Gulf of uncertain light there were more illusions than realities.

But Juana's eyes were on him, and she could not wait. She put her hand on Coyotito's covered head. "Open it," she said softly.

Kino deftly slipped his knife into the edge of the shell. Through the knife he could feel the muscle tighten hard. He worked the blade leverwise, and the closing muscle parted, and the shell fell apart. The liplike flesh writhed up and then subsided. Kino lifted the flesh; and there it lay, the great pearl, perfect as the moon. It captured the light and refined it and gave it back in silver incandescence. It was as large as a sea gull's egg. It was the greatest pearl in the world.

Juana caught her breath and moaned a little. And to Kino the secret melody of the maybe pearl broke clear and beautiful, rich and warm and lovely, glowing and gloating and triumphant. In the surface of the great pearl he could see dream forms. He picked the pearl from the dying flesh and held it in his palm, and he turned it over and saw that its curve was perfect. Juana came near to stare at it in his hand, and it was the hand he had smashed against the doctor's gate, and the torn flesh of the knuckles was turned grayish-white by the sea water.

Instinctively Juana went to Coyotito where he lay on his father's blanket. She lifted the poultice of seaweed and looked at the shoulder. "Kino," she cried shrilly.

He looked past his pearl, and he saw that the swelling was going out of the baby's shoulder, the poison was receding from its body. Then Kino's fist closed over the pearl, and his emotion broke over him. He put back his head and howled. His eyes rolled up, and he screamed, and his body was rigid. The men in the other canoes looked up, startled; and then they dug their paddles into the sea and raced toward Kino's canoe.

3

A town is a thing like a colonial animal. A town has a nervous system and a head and shoulders and feet. A town is a thing separate from all other towns, so that there are no two towns alike. And a town has a whole emotion. How news travels through a town is a mystery not easily to be solved. News seems to move faster than small boys can scramble and dart to tell it, faster than women can call it over the fences.

Before Kino and Juana and the other fishers had come to Kino's brush house, the nerves of the town were pulsing and vibrating with the news—Kino found the Pearl of the World. Before panting little boys could strangle out the words, their mothers knew it. The news swept on past the brush houses, and it washed in a foaming wave into the town of stone and plaster. It came to the priest walking in his garden, and it put a thoughtful look in his eyes and a memory of certain repairs necessary to the church. He wondered what the pearl would be worth. And he wondered whether he had baptized Kino's baby, or married him for that matter. The news came to the shopkeepers, and they looked at men's clothes that had not sold so well.

The news came to the doctor where he sat with a woman whose illness was age, though neither she nor the doctor would admit it. And when it was made plain who Kino was, the doctor grew stern and judicious at the same time. "He is a client of mine," the doctor said. "I'm treating his child for a scorpion sting." And the doctor's eyes rolled up a little in their fat hammocks, and he thought of Paris. He remembered the room he had lived in there as a great and luxurious place; and he remembered the hard-faced woman who had lived with him as a beautiful and kind girl, although she had been none of these three. The doctor looked past his aged patient and saw himself sitting in a restaurant in Paris and a waiter was just opening a bottle of wine.

The news came early to the beggars in front of the church, and it made them giggle a little with pleasure, for they knew that there is no almsgiver in the world like a poor man who is suddenly lucky.

Kino had found the Pearl of the World. In the town, in little offices, sat the men who bought pearls from the fishers. They waited in their chairs until the pearls came in, and then they cackled and fought and shouted and threatened until they reached the lowest price the fishermen would stand. But there was a price below which they dared not go, for it had happened that a fisherman in despair had given his pearls to the church. And when the buying was over, these buyers sat alone; and their fingers played restlessly with the pearls; and they wished they owned the pearls. For there were not many buyers really—there was only one, and he kept these agents in separate offices to give a semblance of competition. The news came to these men, and their eyes squinted and their fingertips burned a little, and each one

thought how the patron could not live forever and someone had to take his place. And each one thought how with some capital he could get a new start.

All manner of people grew interested in Kino—people with things to sell and people with favors to ask. Kino had found the Pearl of the World. The essence of pearl mixed with essence of men and a curious, dark residue was precipitated. Every man suddenly became related to Kino's pearl; and Kino's pearl went into the dreams, the speculations, the schemes, the plans, the futures, the wishes, the needs, the lusts, the hungers, of everyone; and only one person stood in the way, and that was Kino; so that he became curiously every man's enemy. The news stirred up something infinitely black and evil in the town; the black distillate was like the scorpion, or like hunger in the smell of food, or like loneliness when love is withheld. The poison sacs of the town began to manufacture venom, and the town swelled and puffed with the pressure of it.

But Kino and Juana did not know these things. Because they were happy and excited, they thought everyone shared their joy. Juan Tomás and Apolonia did, and they were the world too. In the afternoon, when the sun had gone over the mountains of the Peninsula to sink in the outward sea, Kino squatted in his house with Juana beside him. And the brush house was crowded with neighbors. Kino held the great pearl in his hand, and it was warm and alive in his hand. And the music of the pearl had merged with the music of the family, so that one beautified the other. The neighbors looked at the pearl in Kino's hand, and they wondered how such luck could come to any man.

And Juan Tomás, who squatted on Kino's right hand because he was his brother, asked, "What will you do now that you have become a rich man?"

Kino looked into his pearl, and Juana cast her eyelashes down and arranged her shawl to cover her face so that her excitement could not be seen. And in the incandescence of the pearl, the pictures formed of the things Kino's mind had considered in the past and had given up as impossible. In the pearl he saw Juana and Coyotito and himself standing and kneeling at the high altar, and they were being married now that they could pay. He spoke softly, "We will be married—in the church."

In the pearl he saw how they were dressed—Juana in a shawl stiff with newness and a new skirt, and from under the long skirt Kino could see that she wore shoes. It was in the pearl—the picture glowing there. He himself was dressed in new white clothes, and he carried a new hat—not of straw but of fine black felt—and he too wore shoes—not sandals but shoes that laced. But Coyotito—he was the one—he wore a blue sailor suit from the United States and a little yachting cap such as Kino had seen once when a pleasure boat put into the estuary. All of these things Kino saw in the lucent pearl and he said, "We will have new clothes."

And the music of the pearl rose like a chorus of trumpets in his ears.

Then to the lovely gray surface of the pearl came the little things Kino wanted: a harpoon to take the place of one lost a year ago, a new harpoon of iron with a ring in the end of the shaft; and—his mind could hardly make the leap—a rifle—but why not, since he was so rich. And Kino saw Kino in the pearl, Kino holding a Winchester carbine. It was the wildest daydreaming and very pleasant. His lips moved hesitantly over this—"A rifle," he said. "Perhaps a rifle."

It was the rifle that broke down the barriers. This was an impossibility; and if he could think of having a rifle, whole horizons were burst; and he could rush on. For it is said that humans are never satisfied, that you give them one thing and they want something more. And this is said in disparagement, whereas it is one of the greatest talents the species has and one that has made it superior to animals that are satisfied with what they have.

The neighbors, close pressed and silent in the house, nodded their heads at his wild imaginings. And a man in the rear murmured, "A rifle. He will have a rifle."

But the music of the pearl was shrilling with triumph in Kino. Juana looked up, and her eyes were wide at Kino's courage and at his imagination. And electric strength had come to him now the horizons were kicked out. In the pearl he saw Coyotito sitting at a little desk in a school, just as Kino had once seen it through an open door. And Coyotito was dressed in a jacket and he had on a white collar and a broad silken tie. Moreover, Coyotito was writing on a big piece of paper. Kino looked at his neighbors fiercely. "My son will go to school," he said, and the neighbors were hushed. Juana caught her breath sharply. Her eyes were bright as she watched him, and she looked quickly down at Coyotito in her arms to see whether this might be possible.

But Kino's face shone with prophecy. "My son will read and open the books, and my son will write and will know writing. And my son will make numbers, and these things will make us free because he will know—he will know, and through him we will know." And in the pearl Kino saw himself and Juana squatting by the little fire in the brush hut while Coyotito read from a great book. "This is what the pearl will do," said Kino. And he had never said so many words together in his life. And suddenly he was afraid of his talking. His hand closed down over the pearl and cut the light away from it. Kino was afraid as a man is afraid who says, "I will," without knowing.

Now the neighbors knew they had witnessed a great marvel. They knew that time would now date from Kino's pearl and that they would discuss this moment for many years to come. If these things came to pass, they would recount how Kino looked and what he said and how his eyes shone; and they would say, "He was a man transfigured. Some power was given to him, and there it started. You see what a great man he has become, starting from that moment. And I myself saw it."

And if Kino's planning came to nothing, those same neighbors would say, "There it

581

started. A foolish madness came over him so that he spoke foolish words. God keep us from such things. Yes, God punished Kino because he rebelled against the way things are. You see what has become of him. And I myself saw the moment when his reason left him."

Kino looked down at his closed hand, and the knuckles were scabbed over and tight where he had struck the gate.

Now the dusk was coming. And Juana looped her shawl under the baby so that he hung against her hip, and she went to the fire hole and dug a coal from the ashes and broke a few twigs over it and fanned a flame alive. The little flames danced on the faces of the neighbors. They knew they should go to their own dinners, but they were reluctant to leave.

The dark was almost in, and Juana's fire threw shadows on the brush walls when the whisper came in, passed from mouth to mouth. "The Father is coming—the priest is coming." The men uncovered their heads and stepped back from the door, and the women gathered their shawls about their faces and cast down their eyes. Kino and Juan Tomás, his brother, stood up. The priest came in—a graying, aging man with an old skin and a young sharp eye. Children he considered these people, and he treated them like children.

"Kino," he said softly, "thou art named after a great man—and a great Father of the Church." He made it sound like a benediction. "Thy namesake tamed the desert and sweetened the minds of thy people, didst thou know that? It is in the books."

Kino looked quickly down at Coyotito's head, where he hung on Juana's hip. Someday, his mind said, that boy would know what things were in the books and what things were not. The music had gone out of Kino's head; but now, thinly, slowly, the melody of the morning, the music of evil, of the enemy sounded; but it was faint and weak. And Kino looked at his neighbors to see who might have brought this song in.

But the priest was speaking again. "It has come to me that thou hast found a great fortune, a great pearl."

Kino opened his hand and held it out, and the priest gasped a little at the size and beauty of the pearl. And then he said, "I hope thou wilt remember to give thanks, my son, to Him who has given thee this treasure and to pray for guidance in the future."

Kino nodded dumbly, and it was Juana who spoke softly. "We will, Father. And we will be married now. Kino has said so." She looked at the neighbors for confirmation, and they nodded their heads solemnly.

The priest said, "It is pleasant to see that your first thoughts are good thoughts. God bless you, my children." He turned and left quietly, and the people let him through.

But Kino's hand had closed tightly on the pearl again; and he was glancing about suspiciously; for the evil song was in his ears, shrilling against the music of the pearl.

The neighbors slipped away to go to their houses, and Juana squatted by the fire and set her clay pot of boiled beans over the little flame. Kino stepped to the doorway and looked out. As always, he could smell the smoke from many fires, and he could see the hazy stars and feel the damp of the night air so that he covered his nose from it. The thin dog came to him and threshed itself in greeting like a wind-blown flag, and Kino looked down at it and didn't see it. He had broken through the horizons into a cold and lonely outside. He felt alone and unprotected, and scraping crickets and shrilling tree frogs and croaking toads seemed to be carrying the melody of evil. Kino shivered a little and drew his blanket more tightly against his nose. He carried the pearl still in his hand, tightly closed in his palm, and it was warm and smooth against his skin.

Behind him he heard Juana patting the cakes before she put them down on the clay cooking sheet. Kino felt all the warmth and security of his family behind him, and the Song of the Family came from behind him like the purring of a kitten. But now, by saying what his future was going to be like, he had created it. A plan is a real thing, and things projected are experienced. A plan, once made and visualized, becomes a reality along with other realities—never to be destroyed but easily to be attacked. Thus Kino's future was real; but having set it up, other forces were set up to destroy it; and this he knew, so that he had to prepare to meet the attack. And this Kino knew also—that the gods do not love men's plans and the gods do not love success unless it comes by accident. He knew that the gods take their revenge on a man if he be successful through his own efforts. Consequently Kino was afraid of plans; but having made one, he could never destroy it. And to meet the attack, Kino was already making a hard skin for himself against the world. His eyes and his mind probed for danger before it appeared.

Standing in the door, he saw two men approach; and one of them carried a lantern which lighted the ground and the legs of the men. They turned in through the opening of Kino's brush fence and came to his door. And Kino saw that one was the doctor and the other the servant who had opened the gate in the morning. The split knuckles on Kino's right hand burned when he saw who they were.

The doctor said, "I was not in when you came this morning. But now, at the first chance, I have come to see the baby."

Kino stood in the door, filling it, and hatred raged and flamed in back of his eyes, and fear too; for the hundreds of years of subjugation were cut deep in him.

"The baby is nearly well now," he said curtly.

The doctor smiled, but his eyes in their little lymph-lined hammocks did not smile.

He said, "Sometimes, my friend, the scorpion sting has a curious effect. There will be apparent improvement, and then without warning—pouf!" He pursed his lips and made a little explosion to show how quick it could be, and he shifted his small black doctor's bag about so that the light of the lamp fell upon it, for he knew that Kino's race love the tools of any craft and trust them. "Sometimes," the doctor went on in a liquid tone, "sometimes there will

be a withered leg or a blind eye or a crumpled back. Oh, I know the sting of the scorpion, my friend; and I can cure it."

Kino felt the rage and hatred melting toward fear. He did not know, and perhaps this doctor did. And he could not take the chance of putting his certain ignorance against this man's possible knowledge. He was trapped as his people were always trapped, and would be until, as he had said, they could be sure that the things in the books were really in the books. He could not take a chance—not with the life or with the straightness of Coyotito. He stood aside and let the doctor and his man enter the brush hut.

Juana stood up from the fire and backed away as he entered, and she covered the baby's face with the fringe of her shawl. And when the doctor went to her and held out his hand, she clutched the baby tight and looked at Kino where he stood with the fire shadows leaping on his face.

Kino nodded, and only then did she let the doctor take the baby.

"Hold the light," the doctor said, and when the servant held the lantern high, the doctor looked for a moment at the wound on the baby's shoulder. He was thoughtful for a moment, and then he rolled back the baby's eyelid and looked at the eyeball. He nodded his head while Coyotito struggled against him.

"It is as I thought," he said. "The poison has gone inward, and it will strike soon. Come look!" He held the eyelid down. "See—it is blue. And Kino, looking anxiously, saw that indeed it was a little blue. And he didn't know whether or not it was always a little blue. But the trap was set. He couldn't take the chance.

The doctor's eyes watered in their little hammocks. "I will give him something to try to turn the poison aside," he said. And he handed the baby to Kino.

Then from his bag he took a little bottle of white powder and a capsule of gelatine. He filled the capsule with the powder and closed it, and then around the first capsule he fitted a second capsule and closed it. Then he worked very deftly. He took the baby and pinched its lower lip until it opened its mouth. His fat fingers placed the capsule far back on the baby's tongue, back of the point where he could spit it out, and then from the floor he picked up the little pitcher of pulque and gave Coyotito a drink, and it was done. He looked again at the baby's eyeball and he pursed his lips and seemed to think.

At last he handed the baby back to Juana, and he turned to Kino. "I think the poison will attack within the hour," he said. "The medicine may save the baby from hurt, but I will come back in an hour. Perhaps I am in time to save him." He took a deep breath and went out of the hut, and his servant followed him with the lantern.

Now Juana had the baby under her shawl, and she stared at it with anxiety and fear. Kino came to her, and he lifted the shawl and stared at the baby. He moved his hand to look under the eyelid, and only then saw that the pearl was still in his hand. Then he went to a box by the wall, and from it he brought a piece of rag. He wrapped the pearl in the rag, then went to the corner of the brush house and dug a little hole with his fingers in the dirt floor, and he put the pearl in the hole and covered it up and concealed the place. And then he went to the fire where Juana was squatting, watching the baby's face.

The doctor, back in his house, settled into his chair and looked at his watch. His people brought him a little supper of chocolate and sweet cakes and fruit, and he stared at the food discontentedly.

In the houses of the neighbors, the subject that would lead all conversations for a long time to come was aired for the first time to see how it would go. The neighbors showed one another with their thumbs how big the pearl was, and they made little caressing gestures to show how lovely it was. From now on they would watch Kino and Juana very closely to see whether riches turned their heads, as riches turn all people's heads. Everyone knew why the doctor had come. He was not good at dis-

sembling, and he was very well understood.

Out in the estuary a tight-woven school of small fishes glittered and broke water to escape a school of great fishes that drove in to eat them. And in the houses the people could hear the swish of the small ones and the bouncing splash of the great ones as the slaughter went on. The dampness arose out of the Gulf and was deposited on bushes and cacti and on little trees in salty drops. And the night mice crept about on the ground, and the little night hawks hunted them silently.

The skinny black puppy with flame spots over his eyes came to Kino's door and looked in. He nearly shook his hind quarters loose when Kino glanced up at him, and he subsided when Kino looked away. The puppy did not enter the house, but he watched with frantic interest while Kino ate his beans from the little pottery dish and wiped it clean with a corncake and ate the cake and washed the whole down with a drink of pulque.

Kino was finished and was rolling a cigarette when Juana spoke sharply. "Kino." He glanced at her and then got up and went quickly to her for he saw fright in her eyes. He stood over her, looking down, but the light was very dim. He kicked a pile of twigs into the fire hole to make a blaze, and then he could see the face of Coyotito. The baby's face was flushed and his throat was working and a little thick drool of saliva issued from his lips. The spasm of the stomach muscles began, and the baby was very sick.

Kino knelt beside his wife. "So the doctor knew," he said; but he said it for himself as well as for his wife; for his mind was hard and suspicious, and he was remembering the white powder. Juana rocked from side to side and moaned out the little Song of the Family as though it could ward off the danger, and the baby vomited and writhed in her arms. Now uncertainty was in Kino, and the music of evil throbbed in his head and nearly drove out Juana's song.

The doctor finished his chocolate and nibbled the little fallen pieces of sweet cake. He brushed his fingers on a napkin, looked at his watch, arose, and took up his little bag.

The news of the baby's illness traveled quickly among the brush houses, for sickness is second only to hunger as the enemy of poor people. And some said softly, "Luck, you see, brings bitter friends." And they nodded and got up to go to Kino's house. The neighbors scuttled with covered noses through the dark until they crowded into Kino's house again. They stood and gazed, and they made little comments on the sadness that this should happen at a time of joy; and they said, "All things are in God's hands." The old women squatted down beside Juana to try to give her aid if they could and comfort if they could not.

Then the doctor hurried in, followed by his man. He scattered the old women like chickens. He took the baby and examined it and felt its head. "The poison it has worked," he said. "I think I can defeat it. I will try my best." He asked for water, and in the cup of it he put three drops of ammonia, and he pried open the baby's mouth and poured it down. The baby spluttered and screeched under the treatment, and Juana watched him with haunted eyes. The doctor spoke a little as he worked. "It is lucky that I know about the poison of the scorpion, otherwise—" and he shrugged to show what could have happened.

But Kino was suspicious, and he could not take his eyes from the doctor's open bag and from the bottle of white powder there. Gradually the spasms subsided, and the baby relaxed under the doctor's hands. And then Coyotito sighed deeply and went to sleep, for he was very tired with vomiting.

The doctor put the baby in Juana's arms. "He will get well now," he said. "I have won the fight." And Juana looked at him with adoration.

The doctor was closing his bag now. He said, "When do you think you can pay this bill?" He said it even kindly.

"When I have sold my pearl, I will pay you," Kino said.

"You have a pearl? A good pearl?" the doctor asked with interest.

And then the chorus of the neighbors broke in. "He has found the Pearl of the World," they cried, and they joined forefinger with thumb to show how great the pearl was.

"Kino will be a rich man," they clamored. "It is a pearl such as one has never seen."

The doctor looked surprised. "I had not heard of it. Do you keep this pearl in a safe place? Perhaps you would like me to put it in my safe?"

Kino's eyes were hooded now, his cheeks were drawn taut. "I have it secure," he said. "Tomorrow I will sell it, and then I will pay you."

The doctor shrugged and his wet eyes never left Kino's eyes. He knew the pearl would be buried in the house, and he thought Kino might look toward the place where it was buried. "It would be a shame to have it stolen before you could sell it," the doctor said, and he saw Kino's eyes flick involuntarily to the floor near the side post of the brush house.

When the doctor had gone and all the neighbors had reluctantly returned to their houses, Kino squatted beside the little glowing coals in the fire hole and listened to the night sound: the soft sweep of the little waves on the shore and the distant barking of dogs, the creeping of the breeze through the brush-house roof and the soft speech of his neighbors in their houses in the village. For these people do not sleep soundly all night; they awaken at intervals and talk a little and then go to sleep again. And after a while, Kino got up and went to the door of his house.

He smelled the breeze and he listened for any foreign sound of secrecy or creeping, and his eyes searched the darkness, for the music of evil was sounding in his head, and he was fierce and afraid. After he had probed the night with his senses, he went to the place by the side post where the pearl was buried; and he dug it up and brought it to his sleeping mat, and under his sleeping mat he dug another little hole in the dirt floor and buried his pearl and covered it up again.

And Juana, sitting by the fire hole, watched him with questioning eyes; and when he had buried his pearl, she asked, "Who do you fear?"

Kino searched for a true answer, and at last he said, "Everyone." And he could feel a shell of hardness drawing over him.

After a while they lay down together on the sleeping mat, and Juana did not put the baby in his box tonight, but cradled him on her arms and covered his face with her head shawl. And the last light went out of the embers in the fire hole.

But Kino's brain burned, even during his sleep, and he dreamed that Coyotito could read, that one of his own people could tell him the truth of things. And in his dream, Coyotito was reading from a book as large as a house with letters as big as dogs, and the words galloped and played on the book. And then darkness spread over the page, and with the darkness came the music of evil again, and Kino stirred in his sleep; and when he stirred, Juana's eyes opened in the darkness. And then Kino awakened with the evil music pulsing in him, and he lay in the darkness with his ears alert.

Then from the corner of the house came a sound so soft that it might have been simply a thought, a little furtive movement, a touch of a foot on earth, the almost inaudible purr of controlled breathing. Kino held his breath to listen, and he knew that whatever dark thing was in his house was holding its breath too, to listen. For a time no sound at all came from the corner of the brush house. Then Kino might have thought he had imagined the sound. But Juana's hand came creeping over to him in warning, and then the sound came again! the whisper of a foot on dry earth and the scratch of fingers in the soil.

And now a wild fear surged in Kino's breast, and on the fear came rage, as it always did. Kino's hand crept into his breast where his knife hung on a string, and then he sprang like an angry cat, leaped striking and spitting for the dark thing he knew was in the corner of the house. He felt cloth, struck at it with his knife

and missed, and struck again and felt the knife go through cloth; and then his head crashed with lightning and exploded with pain. There was a soft scurry in the doorway and running steps for a moment, and then silence.

Kino could feel warm blood running down from his forehead, and he could hear Juana calling to him. "Kino! Kino!" And there was terror in her voice. Then coldness came over him as quickly as the rage had, and he said, "I am all right. The thing has gone."

He groped his way back to the sleeping mat. Already Juana was working at the fire. She uncovered an ember from the ashes and shredded little pieces of cornhusk over it and blew a little flame into the cornhusks so that a tiny light danced through the hut. And then from a secret place Juana brought a little piece of consecrated candle and lighted it at the flame and set it upright on a fireplace stone. She worked quickly, crooning as she moved about. She dipped the end of her head shawl in water and swabbed the blood from Kino's bruised forehead. "It is nothing," Kino said; but his eyes and his voice were hard and cold, and a brooding hate was growing in him.

Now the tension which had been growing in Juana boiled up to the surface, and her lips were thin. "This thing is evil," she cried harshly. "This pearl is like a sin! It will destroy us," and her voice rose shrilly. "Throw it away, Kino. Let us break it between stones. Let us bury it and forget the place. Let us throw it back into the sea. It has brought evil. Kino, my husband, it will destroy us." And in the firelight her lips and her eyes were alive with her fear.

But Kino's face was set, and his mind and his will were set. "This is our one chance," he said. "Our son must go to school. He must break out of the pot that holds us in."

"It will destroy us all," Juana cried. "Even our son."

"Hush," said Kino. "Do not speak any more. In the morning we will sell the pearl, and then the evil will be gone and only the good remain. Now hush, my wife." His dark eyes scowled into the little fire, and for the first time he knew that his knife was still in his hands, and he raised the blade and looked at it and saw a little line of blood on the steel. For a moment he seemed about to wipe the blade on his trousers, but then he plunged the knife into the earth and so cleansed it.

The distant roosters began to crow, and the air changed, and the dawn was coming. The wind of the morning ruffled the water of the estuary and whispered through the mangroves, and the little waves beat on the rubbly beach with an increased tempo. Kino raised the sleeping mat and dug up his pearl and put it in front of him and stared at it.

And the beauty of the pearl, winking and glimmering in the light of the little candle, cozened his brain with its beauty. So lovely it was, so soft; and its own music came from it —its music of promise and delight, its guarantee of the future, of comfort, of security. Its warm lucence promised a poultice against illness and a wall against insult. It closed a door on hunger. And as he stared at it, Kino's eyes softened and his face relaxed. He could see the little image of the consecrated candle reflected in the soft surface of the pearl, and he heard again in his ears the lovely music of the undersea, the tone of the diffused, green light of the sea bottom. Juana, glancing secretly at him, saw him smile. And because they were in some way one thing and one purpose, she smiled with him.

And they began this day with hope.

⟨⟩ 4

It is wonderful the way a little town keeps track of itself and of all its units. If every single man and woman, child and baby, acts and conducts itself in a known pattern and breaks no walls and differs with no one and experiments in no way and is not sick and does not endanger the ease and peace of mind or steady unbroken flow of the town, then that unit can disappear and never be heard of. But let one man step out of the regular thought or the known and trusted pattern, and the nerves of the townspeople ring with nervousness and communication travels over the nerve lines of the town. Then every unit communicates to the whole.

Thus, in La Paz,[1] it was known in the early morning through the whole town that Kino was going to sell his pearl that day. It was known among the neighbors in the brush huts, among the pearl fishermen; it was known among the Chinese grocery-store owners; it was known in the church, for the altar boys whispered about it. Word of it crept in among the nuns; the beggars in front of the church spoke of it, for they would be there to take the tithe[2] of the first fruits of the luck. The little boys knew about it with excitement, but most of all the pearl buyers knew about it; and when the day had come, in the offices of the pearl buyers, each man sat alone with his little black velvet tray; and each man rolled the pearls about with his fingertips and considered his part in the picture.

It was supposed that the pearl buyers were individuals acting alone, bidding against one another for the pearls the fishermen brought in. And once it had been so. But this was a wasteful method, for often, in the excitement of bidding for a fine pearl, too great a price had been paid to the fishermen. This was extravagant and not to be countenanced. Now there was only one pearl buyer with many hands; and the men who sat in their offices and waited for Kino knew what price they would offer, how high they would bid, and what method each one would use. And although these men would not profit beyond their salaries, there was excitement among the pearl buyers; for there was excitement in the hunt; and if it be a man's function to break down a price, then he must take joy and satisfaction in breaking it as far down

---

1. **La Paz**\English pro. la paz\ a Mexican town near the tip of lower California on La Paz Bay in the Gulf of California.
2. **tithe**\taith\ technically a tenth, but loosely any portion given to charity.

as possible. For every man in the world functions to the best of his ability, and no one does less than his best, no matter what he may think about it. Quite apart from any reward they might get, from any word of praise, from any promotion, a pearl buyer was a pearl buyer, and the best and happiest pearl buyer was he who bought for the lowest prices.

The sun was hot yellow that morning, and it drew the moisture from the estuary and from the Gulf and hung it in shimmering scarves in the air, so that the air vibrated and vision was insubstantial. A vision hung in the air to the north of the city—the vision of a mountain that was over two hundred miles away, and the high slopes of this mountain were swaddled with pines, and a great stone peak arose above the timber line.

And the morning of this day the canoes lay lined up on the beach; the fishermen did not go out to dive for pearls, for there would be too much happening, too many things to see when Kino went to sell the great pearl.

In the brush houses by the shore, Kino's neighbors sat long over their breakfasts; and they spoke of what they would do if they had found the pearl. And one man said that he would give it as a present to the Holy Father in Rome. Another said that he would buy Masses for the souls of his family for a thousand years. Another thought he might take the money and distribute it among the poor of La Paz; and a fourth thought of all the good things one could do with the money from the pearl, of all the charities, benefits, of all the rescues one could perform if one had money. All of the neighbors hoped that sudden wealth would not turn Kino's head, would not make a rich man of him, would not graft onto him the evil limbs of greed and hatred and coldness. For Kino was a well-liked man; it would be a shame if the pearl destroyed him. "That good wife Juana," they said, "and the beautiful baby Coyotito, and the others to come. What a pity it would be if the pearl should destroy them all."

For Kino and Juana this was the morning of mornings of their lives, comparable only to the day when the baby was born. This was to be the day from which all other days would take their arrangement. Thus they would say, "It was two years before we sold the pearl," or, "It was six weeks after we sold the pearl." Juana, considering the matter, threw caution to the winds; and she dressed Coyotito in the clothes she had prepared for his baptism, when there would be money for his baptism. And Juana combed and braided her hair and tied the ends with two little bows of red ribbon, and she put on her marriage skirt and waist. The sun was quarter high when they were ready. Kino's ragged white clothes were clean at least, and this was the last day of his raggedness. For tomorrow, or even this afternoon, he would have new clothes.

The neighbors, watching Kino's door through the crevices in their brush houses, were dressed and ready too. There was no self-consciousness about their joining Kino and Juana to go pearl selling. It was expected, it was an historic moment, they would be crazy if they didn't go. It would be almost a sign of unfriendship.

Juana put on her head shawl carefully; and she draped one end under her right elbow and gathered it with her right hand so that a hammock hung under her arm; and in this little hammock she placed Coyotito, propped up against the head shawl so that he could see everything and perhaps remember. Kino put on his large straw hat and felt it with his hand to see that it was properly placed, not on the back or side of his head, like a rash, unmarried, irresponsible man, and not flat as an elder would wear it, but tilted a little forward to show aggressiveness and seriousness and vigor. There is a great deal to be seen in the tilt of a hat on a man. Kino slipped his feet into his sandals and pulled the thongs up over his heels. The great pearl was wrapped in an old soft piece of deerskin and placed in a little leather bag, and the leather bag was in a pocket in Kino's shirt. He folded his blanket carefully and draped it in a narrow strip over his left shoulder, and now they were ready.

Kino stepped with dignity out of the house;

and Juana followed him, carrying Coyotito. And as they marched up the freshet-washed alley toward the town, the neighbors joined them. The houses belched people; the doorways spewed out children. But because of the seriousness of the occasion, only one man walked with Kino, and that was his brother Juan Tomás.

Juan Tomás cautioned his brother. "You must be careful to see they do not cheat you," he said.

And, "Very careful," Kino agreed.

"We do not know what prices are paid in other places," said Juan Tomás. "How can we know what is a fair price, if we do not know what the pearl buyer gets for the pearl in another place."

"That is true," said Kino, "but how can we know? We are here, we are not there."

As they walked up toward the city, the crowd grew behind them; and Juan Tomás, in pure nervousness, went on speaking.

"Before you were born, Kino," he said, "the old ones thought of a way to get more money for their pearls. They thought it would be better if they had an agent who took all the pearls to the capital and sold them there and kept only his share of the profit."

Kino nodded his head. "I know," he said. "It was a good thought."

"And so they got such a man," said Juan Tomás, "and they pooled the pearls, and they started him off. And he was never heard of again, and the pearls were lost. Then they got another man, and they started him off, and he was never heard of again. And so they gave the whole thing up and went back to the old way."

"I know," said Kino. "I have heard our father tell of it. It was a good idea, but it was against religion, and the Father made that very clear. The loss of the pearl was a punishment visited on those who tried to leave their station. And the Father made it clear that each man and woman is like a soldier sent by God to guard some part of the castle of the Universe. And some are in the ramparts and some far deep in the darkness of the walls. But each one must remain faithful to his post and must not go running about, else the castle is in danger from the assaults of Hell."

"I have heard him make that sermon," said Juan Tomás. "He makes it every year."

The brothers, as they walked along, squinted their eyes a little, as they and their grandfathers and their great-grandfathers had done for four hundred years, since first the strangers came with arguments and authority and gunpowder to back up both. And in the four hundred years Kino's people had learned only one defense—a slight slitting of the eyes and a slight tightening of the lips and a retirement. Nothing could break down this wall, and they could remain whole within the wall.

The gathering procession was solemn, for they sensed the importance of this day, and any children who showed a tendency to scuffle, to scream, to cry out, to steal hats and rumple hair, were hissed to silence by their elders. So important was this day that an old man came to see, riding on the stalwart shoulders of his nephew. The procession left the brush huts and entered the stone and plaster city, where the streets were a little wider and there were narrow pavements beside the buildings. And as before, the beggars joined them as they passed the church; the grocers looked out at them as they went by; the little saloons lost their customers, and the owners closed up shop and went along. And the sun beat down on the streets of the city, and even tiny stones threw shadows on the ground.

The news of the approach of the procession ran ahead of it, and in their little dark offices the pearl buyers stiffened and grew alert. They got out papers so that they could be at work when Kino appeared, and they put their pearls in the desks, for it is not good to let an inferior pearl be seen beside a beauty. And word of the loveliness of Kino's pearl had come to them. The pearl buyers' offices were clustered together in one narrow street, and they were barred at the windows, and wooden slats cut out the light so that only a soft gloom entered the offices.

A stout, slow man sat in an office waiting. His face was fatherly and benign, and his eyes twinkled with friendship. He was a caller of good mornings, a ceremonious shaker of hands, a jolly man who knew all jokes and yet who hovered close to sadness, for in the midst of a laugh he could remember the death of your aunt, and his eyes could become wet with sorrow for your loss. This morning he had placed a flower in a vase on his desk, a single scarlet hibiscus,[3] and the vase sat beside the black, velvet-lined pearl tray in front of him. He was shaved close to the blue roots of his beard, and his hands were clean and his nails polished. His door stood open to the morning, and he hummed under his breath while his right hand practiced legerdemain.[4] He rolled a coin back and forth over his knuckles and made it appear and disappear, made it spin and sparkle. The coin winked into sight and as quickly slipped out of sight, and the man did not even watch his own performance. The fingers did it all mechanically, precisely, while the man hummed to himself and peered out the door. Then he heard the tramp of feet of the approaching crowd, and the fingers of his right hand worked faster and faster until, as the figure of Kino filled the doorway, the coin flashed and disappeared.

"Good morning, my friend," the stout man said. "What can I do for you?"

Kino stared into the dimness of the little office, for his eyes were squeezed from the outside glare. But the buyer's eyes had become as steady and cruel and unwinking as a hawk's eyes, while the rest of his face smiled in greeting. And secretly, behind his desk, his right hand practiced with the coin.

"I have a pearl," said Kino. And Juan Tomás stood beside him and snorted a little at the understatement. The neighbors peered around the doorway, and a line of little boys clambered on the window bars and looked through. Several little boys, on their hands and knees, watched the scene around Kino's legs.

"You have a pearl," the dealer said. "Sometimes a man brings in a dozen. Well, let us see your pearl. We will value it and give you the best price." And his fingers worked furiously with the coin.

Now Kino instinctively knew his own dramatic effects. Slowly he brought out the leather bag, slowly took from it the soft and dirty piece of deerskin; and then he let the great pearl roll into the black velvet tray, and instantly his eyes went to the buyer's face. But there was no sign, no movement; the face did not change, but the secret hand behind the desk missed in its precision. The coin stumbled over a knuckle and slipped silently into the dealer's lap. And the fingers behind the desk curled into a fist. When the right hand came out of hiding, the forefinger touched the great pearl, rolled it on the black velvet; thumb and forefinger picked it up and brought it near to the dealer's eyes and twirled it in the air.

Kino held his breath, and the neighbors held their breath, and the whispering went back through the crowd. "He is inspecting it—No price has been mentioned yet—They have not come to a price."

Now the dealer's hand had become a personality. The hand tossed the great pearl back to the tray, the forefinger poked and insulted it, and on the dealer's face there came a sad and contemptuous smile.

"I am sorry, my friend," he said, and his shoulders rose a little to indicate that the misfortune was no fault of his.

"It is a pearl of great value," Kino said.

The dealer's fingers spurned the pearl so that it bounced and rebounded softly from the sides of velvet tray.

"You have heard of fool's gold," the dealer said. "This pearl is like fool's gold. It is too large. Who would buy it? There is no market for such things. It is a curiosity only. I am sorry. You thought it was a thing of value, and it is only a curiosity."

---

3. **hibiscus**\hĭ ▲bĭs·kəs\ a southern shrub or small tree with a large colorful flower.
4. **legerdemain**\▲lĕ·jər·də 'mān\ magic, conjuring, or extreme skill at card tricks.

*"I am cheated," Kino cried fiercely.
"My pearl is not for sale here."*

Now Kino's face was perplexed and worried. "It is the Pearl of the World," he cried. "No one has ever seen such a pearl."

"On the contrary," said the dealer, "it is large and clumsy. As a curiosity it has interest; some museum might perhaps take it to place in a collection of seashells. I can give you, say, a thousand pesos."

Kino's face grew dark and dangerous. "It is worth fifty thousand," he said. "You know it. You want to cheat me."

And the dealer heard a little grumble go through the crowd as they heard his price. And the dealer felt a little tremor of fear.

"Do not blame me," he said quickly. "I am only an appraiser. Ask the others. Go to their offices and show your pearl—or better let them come here, so that you can see there is no collusion. Boy," he called. And when his servant looked through the rear door, "Boy, go to such a one, and such another one and such a third one. Ask them to step in here and do not tell them why. Just say that I will be pleased to see them." And his right hand went behind the desk and pulled another coin from his pocket, and the coin rolled back and forth over his knuckles.

Kino's neighbors whispered together. They had been afraid of something like this. The pearl was large, but it had a strange color.

They had been suspicious of it from the first. And after all, a thousand pesos was not to be thrown away. It was comparative wealth to a man who was not wealthy. And suppose Kino took a thousand pesos. Only yesterday he had nothing.

But Kino had grown tight and hard. He felt the creeping of fate, the circling of wolves, the hover of vultures. He felt the evil coagulating about him, and he was helpless to protect himself. He heard in his ears the evil music. And on the black velvet the great pearl glistened, so that the dealer could not keep his eyes from it.

The crowd in the doorway wavered and broke and let the three pearl dealers through. The crowd was silent now, fearing to miss a word, to fail to see a gesture of an expression. Kino was silent and watchful. He felt a little tugging at his back, and he turned and looked in Juana's eyes; and when he looked away, he had renewed strength.

The dealers did not glance at one another nor at the pearl. The man behind the desk said, "I have put a value on this pearl. The owner here does not think it fair. I will ask you to examine this—this thing and make an offer. Notice," he said to Kino, "I have not mentioned what I have offered."

The first dealer, dry and stringy, seemed now to see the pearl for the first time. He took it up, rolled it quickly between thumb and forefinger, and then cast it contemptuously back into the tray.

"Do not include me in the discussion," he said dryly. "I will make no offer at all. I do not want it. This is not a pearl—it is a monstrosity." His thin lips curled.

Now the second dealer, a little man with a shy soft voice, took up the pearl, and he examined it carefully. He took a glass from his pocket and inspected it under magnification. Then he laughed softly.

"Better pearls are made of paste," he said. "I know these things. This is soft and chalky, it will lose its color and die in a few months. Look—" He offered the glass to Kino, showed

him how to use it; and Kino, who had never seen a pearl's surface magnified, was shocked at the strange-looking surface.

The third dealer took the pearl from Kino's hands. "One of my clients likes such things," he said. "I will offer five hundred pesos, and perhaps I can sell it to my client for six hundred."

Kino reached quickly and snatched the pearl from his hand. He wrapped it in the deerskin and thrust it inside his shirt.

The man behind the desk said, "I'm a fool, I know, but my first offer stands. I still offer one thousand. What are you doing?" he asked, as Kino thrust the pearl out of sight.

"I am cheated," Kino cried fiercely. "My pearl is not for sale here. I will go, perhaps, even to the capital."

Now the dealers glanced quickly at one another. They knew they had played too hard; they knew they would be disciplined for their failure; and the man at the desk said quickly, "I might go to fifteen hundred."

But Kino was pushing his way through the crowd. The hum of talk came to him dimly, his rage blood pounded in his ears, and he burst through and strode away. Juana followed, trotting after him.

When the evening came, the neighbors in the brush houses sat eating their corncakes and beans, and they discussed the great theme of the morning. They did not know; it seemed a fine pearl to them, but they had never seen such a pearl before, and surely the dealers knew more about the value of pearls than they. "And mark this," they said. "Those dealers did not discuss these things. Each of the three knew the pearl was valueless."

"But suppose they had arranged it before?"

"If that is so, then all of us have been cheated all of our lives."

Perhaps, some argued, perhaps it would have been better if Kino took the one thousand five hundred pesos. That is a great deal of money, more than he has ever seen. Maybe Kino is being a pigheaded fool. Suppose he should really go to the capital and find no buyer for his pearl. He would never live that down.

And now, said other fearful ones, now that he had defied them, those buyers will not want to deal with him at all. Maybe Kino has cut off his own head and destroyed himself.

And others said, Kino is a brave man and a fierce man; he is right. From his courage we may all profit. These were proud of Kino.

In his house Kino squatted on his sleeping mat, brooding. He had buried his pearl under a stone of the fire hole in his house, and he stared at the woven tules[5] of his sleeping mat until the crossed design danced in his head. He had lost one world and had not gained another. And Kino was afraid. Never in his life had he been far from home. He was afraid of strangers and of strange places. He was terrified of that monster of strangeness they called the capital. It lay over the water and through the mountains, over a thousand miles; and every strange, terrible mile was frightening. But Kino had lost his old world, and he must clamber on to a new one. For his dream of the future was real and never to be destroyed; and he had said "I will go," and that made a real thing, too. To determine to go and to say it was to be halfway there.

Juana watched him while he buried his pearl, and she watched him while she cleaned Coyotito and nursed him, and Juana made the corncakes for supper.

Juan Tomás came in and squatted down beside Kino and remained silent for a long time, until at last Kino demanded, "What else could I do? They are cheats."

Juan Tomás nodded gravely. He was the elder, and Kino looked to him for wisdom. "It is hard to know," he said. "We do know that we are cheated from birth to the overcharge on our coffins. But we survive. You have defied not the pearl buyers, but the whole structure, the whole way of life; and I am afraid for you."

"What have I to fear but starvation?" Kino asked.

But Juan Tomás shook his head slowly. "That we must all fear. But suppose you are correct—suppose your pearl is of great value—do you think then the game is over?"

"What do you mean?"

"I don't know," said Juan Tomás, "but I am afraid for you. It is new ground you are walking on, you do not know the way."

"I will go. I will go soon," said Kino.

"Yes," Juan Tomás agreed. "That you must do. But I wonder if you will find it any different in the capital. Here, you have friends and me, your brother. There, you will have no one."

"What can I do?" Kino cried. "Some deep outrage is here. My son must have a chance. That is what they are striking at. My friends will protect me."

"Only so long as they are not in danger or discomfort from it," said Juan Tomás. He arose, saying, "Go with God."

And Kino said, "Go with God," and did not even look up; for the words had a strange chill in them.

Long after Juan Tomás had gone, Kino sat brooding on his sleeping mat. A lethargy had settled on him and a little gray hopelessness. Every road seemed blocked against him. In his head he heard only the dark music of the enemy. His senses were burningly alive; but his mind went back to the deep participation with all things, the gift he had from his people. He heard every little sound of the gathering night: the sleepy complaint of settling birds, the love agony of cats, the strike and withdrawal of little waves on the beach, and the simple hiss of distance. And he could smell the sharp odor of exposed kelp from the receding tide. The little flare of the twig fire made the design on his sleeping mat jump before his entranced eyes.

Juana watched him with worry, but she knew him, and she knew she could help him best by being silent and by being near. And as though she too could hear the Song of Evil, she fought it, singing softly the melody of the family, of the safety and warmth and wholeness of the family. She held Coyotito in her arms

---

5. **tule**\ˈtū·lē\ a tropical reed or rush.

and sang the song to him, to keep the evil out; and her voice was brave against the threat of the dark music.

Kino did not move nor ask for his supper. She knew he would ask when he wanted it. His eyes were entranced; and he could sense the wary, watchful evil outside the brush house; he could feel the dark, creeping things waiting for him to go out into the night. It was shadowy and dreadful, and yet it called to him and threatened him and challenged him. His right hand went into his shirt and felt his knife; his eyes were wide; he stood up and walked to the doorway.

Juana willed to stop him; she raised her hand to stop him, and her mouth opened with terror. For a long moment Kino looked out into the darkness, and then he stepped outside. Juana heard the little rush, the grunting struggle, the blow. She froze with terror for a moment, and then her lips drew back from her teeth like a cat's lips. She set Coyotito down on the ground. She seized a stone from the fireplace and rushed outside, but it was over by then. Kino lay on the ground, struggling to rise; and there was no one near him. Only the shadows and the strike and rush of waves and the hiss of distance. But the evil was all about, hidden behind the brush fence, crouched beside the house in the shadow, hovering in the air.

Juana dropped her stone, and she put her arms around Kino and helped him to his feet and supported him into the house. Blood oozed down from his scalp, and there was a long, deep cut in his cheek from ear to chin, a deep, bleeding slash. And Kino was only half conscious. He shook his head from side to side. His shirt was torn open and his clothes half pulled off. Juana sat him down on his sleeping mat, and she wiped the thickening blood from his face with her skirt. She brought him pulque to drink in a little pitcher, and still he shook his head to clear out the darkness.

"Who?" Juana asked.

"I don't know," Kino said. "I didn't see."

Now Juana brought her clay pot of water, and she washed the cut on his face while he stared dazed ahead of him.

"Kino, my husband," she cried, and his eyes stared past her. "Kino, can you hear me?"

"I hear you," he said dully.

"Kino, this pearl is evil. Let us destroy it before it destroys us. Let us crush it between two stones. Let us—let us throw it back in the sea where it belongs. Kino, it is evil; it is evil!"

And as she spoke, the light came back in Kino's eyes so that they glowed fiercely; and his muscles hardened, and his will hardened.

"No," he said. "I will fight this thing. I will win over it. We will have our chance." His fist pounded the sleeping mat. "No one shall take our good fortune from us," he said. His eyes softened then, and he raised a gentle hand to Juana's shoulder. "Believe me," he said. "I am a man." And his face grew crafty.

"In the morning we will take our canoe, and we will go over the sea and over the mountains to the capital, you and I. We will not be cheated. I am a man."

"Kino," she said huskily. "I am afraid. A man can be killed. Let us throw the pearl back into the sea."

"Hush," he said fiercely. "I am a man. Hush." And she was silent, for his voice was command. "Let us sleep a little," he said. "In the first light we will start. You are not afraid to go with me?"

"No, my husband."

His eyes were soft and warm on her then; his hand touched her cheek. "Let us sleep a little," he said.

5

The late moon arose before the first rooster crowed. Kino opened his eyes in the darkness, for he sensed movement near him, but he did not move. Only his eyes searched the darkness; and in the pale light of the moon that crept through the holes in the brush house, Kino saw Juana arise silently from beside him. He saw her move toward the fireplace. So carefully did she work that he heard only the lightest sound when she moved the fireplace stone. And then like a shadow she glided toward the door. She paused for a moment beside the hanging box where Coyotito lay, then for a second she was back in the doorway, and then she was gone.

And rage surged in Kino. He rolled up to his feet and followed her as silently as she had gone, and he could hear her quick footsteps going toward the shore. Quietly he tracked her, and his brain was red with anger. She burst clear of the brush line and stumbled over the little boulders toward the water, and then she heard him coming, and she broke into a run. Her arm was up to throw when he leaped at her and caught her arm and wrenched the pearl from her. He struck her in the face with his clenched fist, and she fell among the boulders, and he kicked her in the side. In the pale light he could see the little waves break over her, and her skirt floated about and clung to her legs as the water receded.

Kino looked down at her, and his teeth were bared. He hissed at her like a snake; and Juana stared at him with wide, unfrightened eyes, like a sheep before the butcher. She knew there was murder in him, and it was all right; she had accepted it, and she would not resist or even protest. And then the rage left him, and a sick disgust took its place. He turned away from her and walked up the beach and through the brush line. His senses were dulled by his emotion.

He heard the rush, got his knife out and lunged at one dark figure and felt his knife go home; and then he was swept to his knees and swept again to the ground. Greedy fingers went through his clothes; frantic fingers searched him; and the pearl, knocked from his hand, lay winking behind a little stone in the pathway. It glinted in the soft moonlight.

Juana dragged herself up from the rocks on the edge of the water. Her face was a dull pain, and her side ached. She steadied herself on her knees for a while, and her wet skirt clung to her. There was no anger in her for Kino. He had said, "I am a man," and that meant certain things to Juana. It meant that he was half insane and half god. It meant that Kino would drive his strength against a mountain and plunge his strength against the sea. Juana, in her woman's soul, knew that the mountain would stand while the man broke himself, that the sea would surge while the man drowned in it. And yet it was the thing that made him a man, half insane and half god; and Juana had need of a man; she could not live without a man. Although she might be puzzled by these differences between man and woman, she knew them and accepted them and needed them. Of course she would follow him; there was no question of that. Sometimes the quality of women, the reason, the caution, the sense of preservation, could cut through Kino's manness and save them all. She climbed painfully to her feet, and she dipped her cupped palms in the little waves and washed her bruised face with the stinging salt water, and then she went creeping up the beach after Kino.

A flight of herring clouds[1] had moved over the sky from the south. The pale moon dipped in and out of the strands of clouds, so that Juana walked in darkness for a moment and in light the next. Her back was bent with pain and her head was low. She went through the line of brush when the moon was covered; and when it looked through, she saw the glimmer of the great pearl in the path behind the rock. She sank to her knees and picked it up, and the moon went into the darkness of the clouds again. Juana remained on her knees while she considered whether to go back to the sea and finish her job; and as she considered, the light came again; and she saw two dark figures lying in the path ahead of her. She leaped forward and saw that one was Kino and the other a stranger, with dark shiny fluid leaking from his throat.

Kino moved sluggishly; arms and legs stirred like those of a crushed bug; and a thick muttering came from his mouth. Now, in an instant, Juana knew that the old life was gone forever.

---

1. **herring clouds**, formations that show a strongly marked streaked effect.

A dead man in the path and Kino's knife, dark-bladed beside him, convinced her. All of the time Juana had been trying to rescue something of the old peace, of the time before the pearl. But now it was gone, and there was no retrieving it. And knowing this, she abandoned the past instantly. There was nothing to do but to save themselves.

Her pain was gone now, her slowness. Quickly she dragged the dead man from the pathway into the shelter of the brush. She went to Kino and sponged his face with her wet skirt. His senses were coming back, and he moaned.

"They have taken the pearl. I have lost it. Now it is over," he said. "The pearl is gone."

Juana quieted him as she would quiet a sick child. "Hush," she said. "Here is your pearl. I found it in the path. Can you hear me now? Here is your pearl. Can you understand? You have killed a man. We must go away. They will come for us; can you understand? We must be gone before the daylight comes."

"I was attacked," Kino said uneasily. "I struck to save my life."

"Do you remember yesterday?" Juana asked. "Do you think that will matter? Do you remember the men of the city? Do you think your explanation will help?"

Kino drew a great breath and fought off his weakness. "No," he said. "You are right." And his will hardened, and he was a man again.

"Go to our house and bring Coyotito," he said, "and bring all the corn we have. I will drag the canoe into the water, and we will go."

He took his knife and left her. He stumbled toward the beach, and he came to his canoe. And when the light broke through again, he saw that a great hole had been knocked in the bottom. And a searing rage came to him and gave him strength. Now the darkness was closing in on his family; now the evil music filled the night, hung over the mangroves, skirled in the wave beat. The canoe of his grandfather, plastered over and over, and a splintered hole broken in it. This was an evil beyond thinking. The killing of a man was not so evil as the kill-ing of a boat. For a boat does not have sons, and a boat cannot protect itself, and a wounded boat does not heal. There was sorrow in Kino's rage, but this last thing had tightened him beyond breaking. He was an animal now, for hiding, for attacking; and he lived only to preserve himself and his family. He was not conscious of the pain in his head. He leaped up the beach, through the brush line toward his brush house; and it did not occur to him to take one of the canoes of his neighbors. Never once did the thought enter his head, any more than he could have conceived breaking a boat.

The roosters were crowing, and the dawn was not far off. Smoke of the first fires seeped out through the walls of the brush houses, and the first smell of cooking corncakes was in the air. Already the dawn birds were scampering in the bushes. The weak moon was losing its light, and the clouds thickened and curdled to the southward. The wind blew freshly into the estuary, a nervous, restless wind with the smell of storm on its breath; and there was change and uneasiness in the air.

Kino, hurrying toward his house, felt a surge of exhilaration. Now he was not confused, for there was only one thing to do, and Kino's hand went first to the great pearl in his shirt and then to his knife hanging under his shirt.

He saw a little glow ahead of him, and then without interval a tall flame leaped up in the dark with a crackling roar, and a tall edifice of fire lighted the pathway. Kino broke into a run; it was his brush house, he knew. And he knew that these houses could burn down in a very few moments. And as he ran, a scuttling figure ran toward him—Juana, with Coyotito in her arms and Kino's shoulder blanket clutched in her hand. The baby moaned with fright, and Juana's eyes were wide and terrified. Kino could see the house was gone, and he did not question Juana. He knew; but she said, "It was torn up and the floor dug—even the baby's box turned out; and as I looked, they put the fire to the outside."

The fierce light of the burning house lighted Kino's face strongly. "Who?" he demanded.

"I don't know," she said. "The dark ones."

The neighbors were tumbling from their houses now, and they watched the falling sparks and stamped them out to save their own houses. Suddenly Kino was afraid. The light made him afraid. He remembered the man lying dead in the brush beside the path, and he took Juana by the arm and drew her into the shadow of a house away from the light, for light was danger to him. For a moment he considered, and then he worked among the shadows until he came to the house of Juan Tomás, his brother; and he slipped into the doorway and drew Juana after him. Outside, he could hear the squeal of children and the shouts of the neighbors, for his friends thought he might be inside the burning house.

The house of Juan Tomás was almost exactly like Kino's house; nearly all the brush houses were alike, and all leaked light and air; so that Juana and Kino, sitting in the corner of the brother's house, could see the leaping flames through the wall. They saw the flames tall and furious; they saw the roof fall and watched the fire die down as quickly as a twig fire dies. They heard the cries of warning of their friends, and the shrill, keening cry of Apolonia, wife of Juan Tomás. She, being the nearest woman relative, raised a formal lament for the dead of the family.

Apolonia realized that she was wearing her second-best head shawl, and she rushed to her house to get her fine new one. As she rummaged in a box by the wall, Kino's voice said quietly, "Apolonia, do not cry out. We are not hurt."

"How do you come here?" she demanded.

"Do not question," he said. "Go now to Juan Tomás and bring him here and tell no one else. This is important to us, Apolonia."

She paused, her hands helpless in front of her; and then, "Yes, my brother-in-law," she said.

In a few moments Juan Tomás came back with her. He lighted a candle and came to them where they crouched in a corner, and he said, "Apolonia, see to the door, and do not let any-

one enter." He was older, Juan Tomás, and he assumed the authority. "Now, my brother," he said.

"I was attacked in the dark," said Kino. "And in the fight I have killed a man."

"Who?" asked Juan Tomás quickly.

"I do not know. It is all darkness—all darkness and shape of darkness."

"It is the pearl," said Juan Tomás. "There is a devil in this pearl. You should have sold it and passed on the devil. Perhaps you can still sell it and buy peace for yourself."

And Kino said, "Oh, my brother, an insult has been put on me that is deeper than my life. For on the beach my canoe is broken, my house is burned, and in the brush a dead man lies. Every escape is cut off. You must hide us, my brother."

And Kino, looking closely, saw deep worry come into his brother's eyes; and he forestalled him in a possible refusal. "Not for long," he said quickly. "Only until a day has passed and the new night has come. Then we will go."

"I will hide you," said Juan Tomás.

"I do not want to bring danger to you," Kino said. "I know I am like a leprosy. I will go tonight, and then you will be safe."

"I will protect you," said Juan Tomás, and he called, "Apolonia, close up the door. Do not even whisper that Kino is here."

They sat silently all day in the darkness of the house, and they could hear the neighbors speaking of them. Through the walls of the house, they could watch their neighbors raking the ashes to find the bones. Crouching in the house of Juan Tomás, they heard the shock go into their neighbors' minds at the news of the broken boat. Juan Tomás went out among the neighbors to divert their suspicions, and he gave them theories and ideas of what had happened to Kino and to Juana and to the baby. To one he said, "I think they have gone south along the coast to escape the evil that was on them." And to another, "Kino would never leave the sea. Perhaps he found another boat." And he said, "Apolonia is ill with grief."

And in that day the wind rose up to beat the Gulf and tore the kelps[2] and weeds that lined the shore, and the wind cried through the brush houses, and no boat was safe on the water. Then Juan Tomás told among the neighbors, "Kino is gone. If he went to the sea, he is drowned by now." And after each trip among the neighbors Juan Tomás came back with something borrowed. He brought a little woven straw bag of red beans and a gourd full of rice. He borrowed a cup of dried peppers and a block of salt, and he brought in a long working knife, eighteen inches long and heavy, as a small ax, a tool, and a weapon. And when Kino saw this knife his eyes lighted up; and he fondled the blade, and his thumb tested the edge.

The wind screamed over the Gulf and turned the water white, and the mangroves plunged like frightened cattle, and a fine sandy dust arose from the land and hung in a stifling cloud over the sea. The wind drove off the clouds and skimmed the sky clean and drifted the sand of the country like snow.

Then Juan Tomás, when the evening approached, talked long with his brother. "Where will you go?"

"To the north," said Kino. "I have heard that there are cities in the north."

"Avoid the shore," said Juan Tomás. "They are making a party to search the shore. The men in the city will look for you. Do you still have the pearl?"

"I have it," said Kino. "And I will keep it. I might have given it as a gift, but now it is my misfortune and my life, and I will keep it." His eyes were hard and cruel and bitter.

Coyotito whimpered, and Juana muttered little magics over him to make him silent.

"The wind is good," said Juan Tomás. "There will be no tracks."

They left quietly in the dark before the moon had risen. The family stood formally in the house of Juan Tomás. Juana carried Coyotito on her back, covered and held in by her head shawl; and the baby slept, cheek turned sideways against her shoulder. The head shawl covered the baby, and one end of it came across Juana's nose to protect her from the evil night air. Juan Tomás embraced his brother with the double embrace and kissed him on both cheeks. "Go with God," he said, and it was like a death. "You will not give up the pearl?"

"This pearl has become my soul," said Kino. "If I give it up, I shall lose my soul. Go thou also with God."

⟨⟩ 6

The wind blew fierce and strong; and it pelted them with bits of sticks, sand, and little rocks. Juana and Kino gathered their clothing tighter about them and covered their noses and went out into the world. The sky was brushed clean by the wind, and the stars were cold in a black sky. The two walked carefully, and they avoided the center of town where some sleeper in a doorway might see them pass. For the town closed itself in against the night, and anyone who moved about in the darkness would be noticeable. Kino threaded his way around the edge of the city and turned north, north by the stars, and found the rutted sandy road that led through the brushy country toward Loreto where the miraculous Virgin has her station.[1]

Kino could feel the blown sand against his ankles, and he was glad, for he knew there would be no tracks. The little light from the stars made out for him the narrow road through the brushy country. And Kino could hear the pad of Juana's feet behind him. He went quickly and quietly, and Juana trotted behind him to keep up.

Some ancient thing stirred in Kino. Through his fear of dark and the devils that haunt the night, there came a rush of exhilaration; some animal thing was moving in him so that he was cautious and wary and dangerous; some an-

---

2. **kelp**\kĕlp\ seaweed.

1. **Loreto**\lō ▲rä·tō\. **station,** established place for religious observance.

cient thing out of the past of his people was alive in him. The wind was at his back, and the stars guided him. The wind cried and whisked in the brush; and the family went on monotonously, hour after hour. They passed no one and saw no one. At last, to their right, the waning moon arose; and when it came up, the wind died down; and the land was still.

Now they could see the little road ahead of them, deep-cut with sand-drifted wheel tracks. With the wind gone there would be footprints, but they were a good distance from the town, and perhaps their tracks might not be noticed.

"Come," he said. "We will go into the mountains. Maybe we can lose them in the mountains."

Kino walked carefully in a wheel rut, and Juana followed in his path. One big cart, going to the town in the morning, could wipe out every trace of their passage.

All night they walked and never changed their pace. Once Coyotito awakened, and Juana shifted him in front of her and soothed him until he went to sleep again. And the evils of the night were about them. The coyotes cried and laughed in the brush, and the owls screeched and hissed over their heads. And once some large animal lumbered away, crackling the undergrowth as it went. And Kino gripped the handle of the big working knife and took a sense of protection from it.

The music of the pearl was triumphant in Kino's head, and the quiet melody of the family underlay it, and they wove themselves into the soft padding of sandaled feet in the dusk. All night they walked, and in the first dawn Kino searched the roadside for a covert to lie in during the day. He found his place near to the road, a little clearing where deer might have lain; and it was curtained thickly with the dry, brittle trees that lined the road. And when Juana had seated herself and had settled to nurse the baby, Kino went back to the road. He broke a branch and carefully swept the footprints where they had turned from the roadway. And then, in the first light, he heard the creak of a wagon; and he crouched beside the road and watched a heavy two-wheeled cart go by, drawn by slouching oxen. And when it had passed out of sight, he went back to the roadway and looked at the rut and found that the footprints were gone. And again he swept out his traces and went back to Juana.

She gave him the soft corncakes Apolonia had packed for them, and after a while she slept a little. But Kino sat on the ground and stared at the earth in front of him. He watched the ants moving, a little column of them near to his foot, and he put his foot in their path. Then the column climbed over his instep and continued on its way, and Kino left his foot there and watched them move over it.

The sun arose hotly. They were not near the Gulf now; and the air was dry and hot, so that the brush cricked[2] with heat, and a good resinous[3] smell came from it. And when Juana awakened, when the sun was high, Kino told her things she knew already.

"Beware of that kind of tree there," he said, pointing. "Do not touch it, for if you do and then touch your eyes, it will blind you. And beware of the tree that bleeds. See, that one over there. For if you break it, the red blood will flow from it; and it is evil luck." And she nodded and smiled a little at him, for she knew these things.

"Will they follow us?" she asked. "Do you think they will try to find us?"

"They will try," said Kino. "Whoever finds us will take the pearl. Oh, they will try."

And Juana said, "Perhaps the dealers were right and the pearl has no value. Perhaps this has all been an illusion."

Kino reached into his clothes and brought out the pearl. He let the sun play on it until it burned in his eyes. "No," he said, "they would not have tried to steal it if it had been valueless."

"Do you know who attacked you? Was it the dealers?"

"I do not know," he said. "I didn't see them."

He looked into his pearl to find his vision.

"When we sell it at last, I will have a rifle," he said; and he looked into the shining surface for his rifle, but he saw only a huddled dark body on the ground with shining blood dripping from its throat. And he said quickly, "We will be married in a great church." And in the pearl he saw Juana with her beaten face, crawling home through the night. "Our son must learn to read," he said frantically. And there in the pearl Coyotito's face, thick and feverish from the medicine.

And Kino thrust the pearl back into his clothing, and the music of the pearl had become sinister in his ears, and it was interwoven with the music of evil.

The hot sun beat on the earth, so that Kino and Juana moved into the lacy shade of the brush; and small, gray birds scampered on the ground in the shade. In the heat of the day, Kino relaxed and covered his eyes with his hat and wrapped his blanket about his face to keep the flies off; and he slept.

But Juana did not sleep. She sat quiet as a stone, and her face was quiet. Her mouth was

---

2. **crick**\krĭk\ to turn or twist.
3. **resinous**\ˈrĕ•zĭ•nəs\ of or pertaining to resin, an insoluble thick plant substance like pine tar.

still swollen where Kino had struck her, and big flies buzzed around the cut on her chin. But she sat as still as a sentinel; and when Coyotito awakened, she placed him on the ground in front of her and watched him wave his arms and kick his feet; and he smiled and gurgled at her, until she smiled too. She picked up a little twig from the ground and tickled him, and she gave him water from the gourd she carried in her bundle.

Kino stirred in a dream, and he cried out in a guttural voice, and his hand moved in symbolic fighting. And then he moaned and sat up suddenly, his eyes wide and his nostrils flaring. He listened and heard only the cricking heat and the hiss of distance.

"What is it?" Juana asked.

"Hush," he said.

"You were dreaming."

"Perhaps." But he was restless; and when she gave him a corncake from her store, he paused in his chewing to listen. He was uneasy and nervous; he glanced over his shoulder; he lifted the big knife and felt its edge. When Coyotito gurgled on the ground, Kino said, "Keep him quiet."

"What is the matter?" Juana asked.

"I don't know."

He listened again, an animal light in his eyes. He stood up then, silently; and crouched low, he threaded his way through the brush toward the road. But he did not step into the road; he crept into the cover of a thorny tree and peered out along the way he had come.

And then he saw them moving along. His body stiffened, and he drew down his head and peeked out from under a fallen branch. In the distance he could see three figures, two on foot and one on horseback. But he knew what they were, and a chill of fear went through him. Even in the distance he could see the two on foot moving slowly along, bent low to the ground. Here, one would pause and look at the earth, while the other joined him. They were the trackers; they could follow the trail of a bighorn sheep in the stone mountains. They were as sensitive as hounds. Here, he and

Juana might have stepped out of the wheel rut; and these people from the inland, these hunters, could follow, could read a broken straw or a little tumbled pile of dust. Behind them, on a horse, was a dark man, his nose covered with a blanket; and across his saddle a rifle gleamed in the sun.

Kino lay as rigid as the tree limb. He barely breathed, and his eyes went to the place where he had swept out the track. Even the sweeping might be a message to the trackers. He knew these inland hunters. In a country where there is little game, they managed to live because of their ability to hunt; and they were hunting him. They scuttled over the ground like animals and found a sign and crouched over it while the horseman waited.

The trackers whined a little, like excited dogs on a warming trail. Kino slowly drew his big knife to his hand and made it ready. He knew what he must do. If the trackers found the swept place, he must leap for the horseman, kill him quickly, and take the rifle. That was his only chance in the world. And as the three drew nearer on the road, Kino dug little pits with his sandaled toes, so that he could leap without warning, so that his feet would not slip. He had only a little vision under the fallen limb.

Now Juana, back in her hidden place, heard the pad of the horse's hoofs; and Coyotito gurgled. She took him up quickly and put him under her shawl and gave him her breast, and he was silent.

When the trackers came near, Kino could see only their legs and only the legs of the horse from under the fallen branch. He saw the dark, horny feet of the men and their ragged white clothes, and he heard the creak of leather of the saddle and the clink of spurs. The trackers stopped at the swept place and studied it, and the horseman stopped. The horse flung his head up against the bit, and the bit-roller[4] clicked under his tongue, and the

---

4. **bit-roller,** the roller or round bar to which the bit of a horse's bridle is attached.

horse snorted. Then the dark trackers turned and studied the horse and watched his ears.

Kino was not breathing, but his back arched a little, and the muscles of his arms and legs stood out with tension, and a line of sweat formed on his upper lip. For a long moment the trackers bent over the road; and then they moved on slowly, studying the ground ahead of them; and the horseman moved after them. The trackers scuttled along, stopping, looking, and hurrying on. They would be back, Kino knew. They would be circling and searching, peeping, stooping; and they would come back sooner or later to his covered track.

He slid backward and did not bother to cover his tracks. He could not; too many little signs were there, too many broken twigs and scuffed places and displaced stones. And there was a panic in Kino now, a panic of flight. The trackers would find his trail; he knew it. There was no escape, except in flight. He edged away from the road and went quickly and silently to the hidden place where Juana was. She looked up at him in question.

"Trackers," he said. "Come!"

And then a helplessness and a hopelessness swept over him, and his face went black, and his eyes were sad. "Perhaps I should let them take me."

Instantly Juana was on her feet, and her hand lay on his arm. "You have the pearl," she cried hoarsely. "Do you think they would take you back alive to say they had stolen it?"

His hand strayed limply to the place where the pearl was hidden under his clothes. "They will find it," he said weakly.

"Come," she said. "Come!"

And when he did not respond, "Do you think they would let me live? Do you think they would let the little one here live?"

Her goading struck into his brain; his lips snarled and his eyes were fierce again. "Come," he said. "We will go into the mountains. Maybe we can lose them in the mountains."

Frantically he gathered the gourds and the little bags that were their property. Kino carried a bundle in his left hand, but the big knife swung free in his right hand. He parted the brush for Juana; and they hurried to the west, toward the high stone mountains. They trotted quickly through the tangle of the undergrowth. This was panic flight. Kino did not try to conceal his passages; he trotted, kicking the stones, knocking the telltale leaves from the little trees. The high sun streamed down on the dry, creaking earth, so that even vegetation ticked in protest. But ahead were the naked granite mountains, rising out of erosion rubble and standing monolithic against the sky. And Kino ran for the high place, as nearly all animals do when they are pursued.

This land was waterless, furred with the cacti which could store water and with the great-rooted brush, which could reach deep into the earth for a little moisture and get along on very little. And underfoot was not soil but broken rock, split into small cubes, great slabs, but none of it water-rounded. Little tufts of sad, dry grass grew between the stones, grass that had sprouted with one single rain and headed, dropped its seed, and died. Horned toads watched the family go by and turned their little pivoting dragon heads. And now and then a great jackrabbit, disturbed in his shade, bumped away and hid behind the nearest rock. The singing heat lay over this desert country, and ahead the stone mountains looked cool and welcoming.

And Kino fled. He knew what would happen. A little way along the road the trackers would become aware that they had missed the path, and they would come back, searching and judging; and in a little while they would find the place where Kino and Juana had rested. From there it would be easy for them—these little stones, the fallen leaves and the whipped branches, the scuffed places where a foot had slipped. Kino could see them in his mind, slipping along the track, whining a little with eagerness, and behind them, dark and half disinterested, the horseman with the rifle. His work would come last, for he would not take them back. Oh, the music of evil sang loud in Kino's head now; it sang with the whine of heat and with the dry ringing of snake rattles. It was not large and overwhelming now, but secret and poisonous; and the pounding of his heart gave it undertone and rhythm.

The way began to rise; and as it did, the rocks grew larger. But now Kino had put a little distance between his family and the trackers. Now, on the first rise, he rested. He climbed a great boulder and looked back over the shimmering country, but he could not see his enemies, not even the tall horseman riding through the brush. Juana had squatted in the shade of the boulder. She raised her bottle of water to Coyotito's lips; his little dried tongue sucked greedily at it. She looked up at Kino when he came back; she saw him examine her ankles, cut and scratched from the stones and brush; and she covered them quickly with her skirt. Then she handed the bottle to him, but he shook his head. Her eyes were bright in her tired face. Kino moistened his cracked lips with his tongue.

"Juana," he said, "I will go on, and you will hide. I will lead them into the mountains, and when they have gone past, you will go north to Loreto or to Santa Rosalia.[5] Then, if I can escape them, I will come to you. It is the only safe way."

She looked full into his eyes for a moment. "No," she said. "We go with you."

"I can go faster alone," he said harshly. "You will put the little one in more danger if you go with me."

"No," said Juana.

"You must. It is the wise thing, and it is my wish," he said.

"No," said Juana.

He looked then for weakness in her face, for fear or irresolution; and there was none. Her eyes were very bright. He shrugged his shoulders helplessly then, but he had taken strength from her. When they moved on, it was no longer panic flight.

The country, as it rose toward the mountains, changed rapidly. Now there were long outcroppings of granite with deep crevices between, and Kino walked on bare unmarkable stone when he could and leaped from ledge to ledge. He knew that wherever the trackers lost his path they must circle and lose time before they found it again. And so he did not go straight for the mountains any more; he moved in zigzags, and sometimes he cut back to the south and left a sign and then went toward the mountains over bare stone again. And the path rose steeply now, so that he panted a little as he went.

The sun moved downward toward the bare stone teeth of the mountains, and Kino set his direction for a dark and shadowy cleft in the range. If there were any water at all, it would be there where he could see, even in the distance, a hint of foliage. And if there were any passage through the smooth stone range, it would be by this same deep cleft. It had its danger, for the trackers would think of it too, but the empty water bottle did not let that consideration enter. And as the sun lowered, Kino and Juana struggled wearily up the steep slope toward the cleft.

High in the gray stone mountains, under a frowning peak, a little spring bubbled out of a rupture in the stone. It was fed by shade-preserved snow in the summer, and now and then it died completely, and bare rocks and dry algae were on its bottom. But nearly always it gushed out, cold and clean and lovely. In the times when the quick rains fell, it might become a freshet and send its column of white water crashing down the mountain cleft, but nearly always it was a lean little spring. It bubbled out into a pool and then fell a hundred feet to another pool, and this one, overflowing, dropped again, so that it continued, down and down, until it came to the rubble of the upland; and there it disappeared altogether. There wasn't much left of it then anyway; for every time it fell over an escarpment,[6] the thirsty air drank it; and it splashed from the pools to the dry vegetation. The animals

---

5. **Santa Rosalia**\\ˈsan·ta ˈrō ˈza·lē·a\\ a town on the west coast of lower California. Other places in the story have been on the east coast.
6. **escarpment**\ĕ ˈskarp·mĭnt\ a long sheer cliff.

from miles around came to drink from the little pools; and the wild sheep and the deer, the pumas and raccoons, and the mice—all came to drink. And the birds which spent the day in the brushland came at night to the little pools, that were like steps in the mountain cleft. Beside this tiny stream, wherever enough earth collected for roothold, colonies of plants grew, wild grape and little palms, maidenhair fern, hibiscus, and tall pampas[7] grass with feathery rods raised above the spike leaves. And in the pool lived frogs and waterskaters,[8] and waterworms crawled on the bottom of the pool. Everything that loved water came to these few shallow places. The cats took their prey there and strewed feathers and lapped water through their bloody teeth. The little pools were places of life because of the water, and places of killing because of the water, too.

The lowest step, where the stream collected before it tumbled down a hundred feet and disappeared into the rubbly desert, was a little platform of stone and sand. Only a pencil of water fell into the pool, but it was enough to keep the pool full and to keep the ferns green in the underhang of the cliff, and wild grape climbed the stone mountain, and all manner of little plants found comfort here. The freshets had made a small sandy beach through which the pool flowed, and bright green watercress grew in the damp sand. The beach was cut and scarred and padded by the feet of animals that had come to drink and to hunt.

The sun had passed over the stone mountains when Kino and Juana struggled up the steep, broken slope and came at last to the water. From this step they could look out over the sunbeaten desert to the blue Gulf in the distance. They came utterly weary to the pool, and Juana slumped to her knees and first washed Coyotito's face and then filled her bottle and gave him a drink. And the baby was weary and petulant, and he cried softly until Juana gave him her breast, and then he gurgled and clucked against her. Kino drank long and thirstily at the pool. For a moment, then, he

stretched out beside the water and relaxed all his muscles and watched Juana feeding the baby, and then he got to his feet and went to the edge of the step where the water slipped over, and he searched the distance carefully. His eyes set on a point and he became rigid. Far down the slope he could see the two trackers; they were little more than dots or scurrying ants and behind them a larger ant.

Juana had turned to look at him, and she saw his back stiffen.

"How far?" she asked quietly.

"They will be here by evening," said Kino. He looked up the long, steep chimney of the cleft where the water came down. "We must go west," he said, and his eyes searched the stone shoulder behind the cleft. And thirty feet up on the gray shoulder he saw a series of little erosion caves. He slipped off his sandals and clambered up to them, gripping the bare stone with his toes, and he looked into the shallow caves. They were only a few feet deep, wind-hollowed scoops, but they sloped slightly downward and back. Kino crawled into the largest one and lay down and knew that he could not be seen from the outside. Quickly he went back to Juana.

"You must go up there. Perhaps they will not find us there," he said.

Without question she filled her water bottle to the top, and then Kino helped her up to the shallow cave and brought up the packages of food and passed them to her. And Juana sat in the cave entrance and watched him. She saw that he did not try to erase their tracks in the sand. Instead, he climbed up the brush cliff beside the water, clawing and tearing at the ferns and wild grape as he went. And when he had climbed a hundred feet to the next bench, he came down again. He looked carefully at the smooth rock shoulder toward the cave to see that there was no trace of passage,

---

7. pampas\ˈpăm·pəs\ grass, a South and Central American grass that grows in tall stalks from thick clumps.

8. waterskater, an insect that skims on the surface of the water.

and last he climbed up and crept into the cave beside Juana.

"When they go up," he said, "we will slip away, down to the lowlands again. I am afraid only that the baby may cry. You must see that he does not cry."

"He will not cry," she said, and she raised the baby's face to her own and looked into his eyes, and he stared solemnly back at her.

"He knows," said Juana.

Now Kino lay in the cave entrance, his chin braced on his crossed arms, and he watched the blue shadow of the mountain move out across the brushy desert below until it reached the Gulf, and the long twilight of the shadow was over the land.

The trackers were long in coming, as though they had trouble with the trail Kino had left. It was dusk when they came at last to the little pool. And all three were on foot now, for a horse could not climb the last steep slope. From above they were thin figures in the evening. The two trackers scurried about on the little beach, and they saw Kino's progress up the cliff before they drank. The man with the rifle sat down and rested himself, and the trackers squatted near him, and in the evening the points of their cigarettes glowed and receded. And then Kino could see that they were eating, and the soft murmur of their voices came to him.

Then darkness fell, deep and black in the mountain cleft. The animals that used the pool came near and smelled men there and drifted away again into the darkness.

He heard a murmur behind him. Juana was whispering, "Coyotito." She was begging him to be quiet. Kino heard the baby whimper, and he knew from the muffled sounds that Juana had covered his head with her shawl.

Down on the beach a match flared; and in its momentary light Kino saw that two of the men were sleeping, curled up like dogs, while the third watched; and he saw the glint of the rifle in the match light. And then the match died, but it left a picture on Kino's eyes. He could see it, just how each man was, two sleep-ing curled and the third squatting in the sand with the rifle between his knees.

Kino moved silently back into the cave. Juana's eyes were two sparks reflecting a low star. Kino crawled quietly close to her, and he put his lips near to her cheek.

"There is a way," he said.

"But they will kill you."

"If I get first to the one with the rifle," Kino said, "I must get to him first, then I will be all right. Two are sleeping."

Her hand crept out from under her shawl and gripped his arm. "They will see your white clothes in the starlight."

"No," he said. "And I must go before moon-rise."

He searched for a soft word and then gave it up. "If they kill me," he said, "lie quietly. And when they are gone away, go to Loreto."

Her hand shook a little, holding his wrist.

"There is no choice," he said. "It is the only way. They will find us in the morning."

Her voice trembled a little. "Go with God," she said.

He peered closely at her, and he could see her large eyes. His hand fumbled out and found the baby, and for a moment his palm lay on Coyotito's head. And then Kino raised his hand and touched Juana's cheek, and she held her breath.

Against the sky in the cave entrance Juana could see that Kino was taking off his white clothes; for dirty and ragged though they were, they would show up against the dark night. His own brown skin was a better protection for him. And then she saw how he hooked his amulet[9] neck-string about the horn handle of his great knife, so that it hung down in front of him and left both hands free. He did not come back to her. For a moment his body was black in the cave entrance, crouched and silent; and then he was gone.

Juana moved to the entrance and looked out. She peered like an owl from the hole in the mountain; and the baby slept under the

---

9. **amulet**\ˈăm•yu̇ ˈlĕt\ a charm, a magic ornament.

blanket on her back, his face turned sideways against her neck and shoulder. She could feel his warm breath against her skin; and Juana whispered her combination of prayer and magic, her Hail Marys and her ancient intercession, against the black, unhuman things.

The night seemed a little less dark when she looked out; and to the east there was a lightening in the sky, down near the horizon where the moon would show. And, looking down, she could see the cigarette of the man on watch.

Kino edged like a slow lizard down the smooth rock shoulder. He had turned his neckstring so that the great knife hung down from his back and could not clash against the stone. His spread fingers gripped the mountain, and his bare toes found support through contact, and even his chest lay against the stone, so that he would not slip. For any sound, a rolling pebble or a sigh, a little slip of flesh on rock, would rouse the watchers below. Any sound that was not germane to the night would make them alert. But the night was not silent: the little tree frogs that lived near the stream twittered like birds, and the high metallic ringing of the cicadas[10] filled the mountain cleft. And Kino's own music was in his head, the music of the enemy, low and pulsing, nearly asleep. But the Song of the Family had become as fierce and sharp and feline as the snarl of a female puma. The family song was alive now and driving him down on the dark enemy. The harsh cicada seemed to take up its melody, and the twittering tree frogs called little phrases of it.

And Kino crept silently as a shadow down the smooth mountain face. One bare foot moved a few inches, and the toes touched the stone and gripped, and the other foot a few inches, and then the palm of one hand a little downward, and then the other hand, until the whole body, without seeming to move, had moved. Kino's mouth was open so that even his breath would make no sound, for he knew that he was not invisible. If the watcher, sensing movement, looked at the dark place against the stone which was his body, he could see

him. Kino must move so slowly he would not draw the watcher's eyes. It took him a long time to reach the bottom and to crouch behind a little dwarf palm. His heart thundered in his chest, and his hands and face were wet with sweat. He crouched and took slow long breaths to calm himself.

Only twenty feet separated him from the enemy now, and he tried to remember the ground between. Was there any stone which might trip him in his rush? He kneaded his legs against cramp and found that his muscles were jerking after their long tension. And then he looked apprehensively to the east. The moon would rise in a few moments now, and he must attack before it rose. He could see the outline of the watcher, but the sleeping men were below his vision. It was the watcher Kino must find—must find quickly and without hesitation. Silently he drew the amulet string over his shoulder and loosened the loop from the horn handle of his great knife.

He was too late; for as he rose from his crouch, the silver edge of the moon slipped above the eastern horizon; and Kino sank back behind his bush.

It was an old and ragged moon, but it threw hard light and hard shadow into the mountain cleft, and now Kino could see the seated figure of the watcher on the little beach beside the pool. The watcher gazed full at the moon, and then he lighted another cigarette, and the match illumined his dark face for a moment. There could be no waiting now; when the watcher turned his head, Kino must leap. His legs were as tight as wound springs.

And then from above came a little murmuring cry. The watcher turned his head to listen, and then he stood up, and one of the sleepers stirred on the ground and awakened and asked quietly, "What is it?"

"I don't know," said the watcher. "It sounded like a cry, almost like a human—like a baby."

The man who had been sleeping said, "You

---

10. **cicada**\sĭ ˄kā·də\ an insect with a stout body and wide wings whose vibrations make a distinctive sound.

can't tell. Some coyote bitch with a litter. I've heard a coyote pup cry like a baby."

The sweat rolled in drops down Kino's forehead and fell into his eyes and burned them. The little cry came again, and the watcher looked up the side of the hill to the dark cave.

"Coyote maybe," he said, and Kino heard the harsh click as he cocked the rifle.

"If it's a coyote, this will stop it," the watcher said as he raised the gun.

Kino was in mid-leap when the gun crashed, and the barrel-flash made a picture on his eyes. The great knife swung and crunched hollowly. It bit through neck and deep into chest, and Kino was a terrible machine now. He grasped the rifle even as he wrenched free his knife. His strength and his movement and his speed were a machine. He whirled and struck the head of the seated man like a melon. The third man scrabbled away like a crab, slipped into the pool; and then he began to climb frantically, to climb up the cliff where the water penciled down. His hands and feet threshed in the tangle of the wild grapevine, and he whimpered and gibbered as he tried to get up. But Kino had become as cold and deadly as steel. Deliberately he threw the lever of the rifle, and then he raised the gun and aimed deliberately and fired. He saw his enemy tumble backward into the pool, and Kino strode to the water. In the moonlight he could see the frantic frightened eyes, and Kino aimed and fired between the eyes.

And then Kino stood uncertainly. Something was wrong; some signal was trying to get through to his brain. Tree frogs and cicadas were silent now. And then Kino's brain cleared from its red concentration, and he knew the sound—the keening,[11] moaning, rising hysterical cry from the little cave in the side of the stone mountain, the cry of death.

Everyone in La Paz remembers the return of the family; there may be some old ones who saw it, but those whose fathers and whose grandfathers told it to them remember it never-

theless. It is an event that happened to everyone.

It was late in the golden afternoon when the first little boys ran hysterically in the town and spread the word that Kino and Juana were coming back. And everyone hurried to see them. The sun was settling toward the western mountains, and the shadows on the ground were long. And perhaps that was what left the deep impression on those who saw them.

The two came from the rutted country road into the city, and they were not walking in single file, Kino ahead and Juana behind, as usual, but side by side. The sun was behind them, and their long shadows stalked ahead, and they seemed to carry two towers of darkness with them. Kino had a rifle across his arm, and Juana carried her shawl like a sack over her shoulder. And in it was a small, limp, heavy bundle. The shawl was crusted with dried blood, and the bundle swayed a little as she walked. Her face was hard and lined and leathery with fatigue and with the tightness with which she fought fatigue. And her wide eyes stared inward on herself. She was as remote and as removed as Heaven. Kino's lips were thin and his jaws tight, and the people say that he carried fear with him, that he was as dangerous as a rising storm. The people say that the two seemed to be removed from human experience, that they had gone through pain and had come out on the other side, that there was almost a magical protection about them. And those people who had rushed to see them crowded back and let them pass and did not speak to them.

Kino and Juana walked through the city as though it were not there. Their eyes glanced neither right nor left nor up nor down, but stared only straight ahead. Their legs moved a little jerkily, like well-made wooden dolls, and they carried pillars of black fear about them. And as they walked through the stone and plaster city, brokers peered at them from barred windows, and servants put one eye to a

---

11. **keen,** to lament a death with loud outcry.

slitted gate, and mothers turned the faces of their youngest children inward against their skirts. Kino and Juana strode side by side through the stone and plaster city and down among the brush houses, and the neighbors stood back and let them pass. Juan Tomás raised his hand in greeting and did not say the greeting and left his hand in the air for a moment uncertainly.

In Kino's ears the Song of the Family was as fierce as a cry. He was immune and terrible, and his song had become a battle cry. They trudged past the burned square where their house had been without even looking at it. They cleared the brush that edged the beach and picked their way down the shore toward the water. And they did not look toward Kino's broken canoe.

And when they came to the water's edge, they stopped and stared out over the Gulf. And then Kino laid the rifle down, and he dug among his clothes, and then he held the great pearl in his hand. He looked into its surface, and it was gray and ulcerous. Evil faces peered from it into his eyes, and he saw the light of burning. And in the surface of the pearl he saw the frantic eyes of the man in the pool. And in the surface of the pearl he saw Coyotito lying in the little cave with the top of his head shot away. And the pearl was ugly; it was gray, like a malignant growth. And Kino heard the music of the pearl, distorted and insane. Kino's hand shook a little, and he turned slowly to Juana and held the pearl out to her. She stood beside him, still holding her dead bundle over her shoulder. She looked at the pearl in his hand for a moment, and then she looked into Kino's eyes and said softly, "No, you."

And Kino drew back his arm and flung the pearl with all his might. Kino and Juana watched it go, winking and glimmering under the setting sun. They saw the little splash in the distance, and they stood side by side watching the place for a long time.

And the pearl settled into the lovely green water and dropped toward the bottom. The waving branches of the algae called to it and

beckoned to it. The lights on its surface were green and lovely. It settled down to the sand bottom among the fernlike plants. Above, the surface of the water was a green mirror. And the pearl lay on the floor of the sea. A crab scampering over the bottom raised a little cloud of sand; and when it settled, the pearl was gone.

And the music of the pearl drifted to a whisper and disappeared.

I

THE MEANING OF LIFE

Steinbeck has cast the story in the form of a folk legend, but the reader quickly realizes that though the story is seemingly following this simple pattern, it is far more complicated in all its elements than the usual folk story. Steinbeck presents the reader with two people and their child, but they are involved in events and a situation that is intended to demonstrate the complicated relationship of man and his society. The language is carefully controlled and detailed by the writer . . . it appears simple but is really a triumph of artistry. What the writer is saying about life escapes a simple formula . . . it is no mere moral lesson . . . it is a delicate judgment on man, far-reaching and intricate. To help you isolate the complex parts of the story, carefully think through the following considerations.

II

IMPLICATIONS

A. Consider the implications of the following quotations in relationship to: (1) plot development, (2) revelation of character, (3) theme, (4) life in general.

1. "Perhaps he alone did this [activities in getting up in the morning], and perhaps all of his people did it."

2. "They had spoken once, but there is not need for speech if it is only a habit anyway. Kino sighed with satisfaction—and that was conversation."

3. "But the remedy lacked his authority [that of the doctor] because it was simple and didn't cost anything."

4. "It is not good to want a thing too much. It sometimes drives the luck away."

5. "For it is said that humans are never satisfied, that you give them one thing and they want something more. And this is said in disparagement, whereas it is one of the greatest talents the species has and one that has made it superior to animals that are satisfied with what they have."

6. "A plan, once made and visualized, becomes a reality along with other realities—never to be destroyed but easily to be attacked."

7. " 'Luck, you see, brings bitter friends.' "

8. "But let one man step out of the regular thought or the known and trusted pattern, and the nerves of the townspeople ring with nervousness. . . ."

9. "He had said, 'I am a man,' and that meant certain things to Juana. It meant that he was half insane and half god."

10. "The killing of a man was not so evil as the killing of a boat."

11. " 'This pearl has become my soul. . . . If I give up I shall lose my soul.' "

12. "The people say that the two seemed to be removed from human experience, that they had gone through pain and had come out on the other side, that there was almost a magical protection about them."

B. Examine the following statements. Are they true? untrue? partly true? Assemble evidence from the story to support your opinion.

1. The pressures in this story were twofold: the inner pressure of Kino's dream and the external pressures of greedy men.

2. No one knows of what he is capable until put under great pressures.

3. The Pearl of the World is basically an evil thing.

4. In the world that Steinbeck pictures there was absolutely no hope of Kino's dream becoming a reality.

5. There is something of greatness in every human being, no matter how stupid, uneducated, or poverty-stricken he may be.

6. When Kino kills the thief, the reader knows that the story must end tragically.

7. To accept one's lot in life is a more admirable human trait than the desire to change it.

8. The desires of men and those of women tend to be quite different.

III
TECHNIQUES

Theme

The theme of *The Pearl,* like that of the other selections in this section, is the impact of pressures, both external and internal. But more specifically, Steinbeck is concerned with the effect these pressures have on man's search for his soul. This theme is embedded in the entire fabric of the story. Consider the following.

1. What is the sequence of pressures that come to bear on Kino? How is each a natural outgrowth of the one that comes before?

2. Throughout the story Steinbeck mentions certain things again and again, and with each recurrence they gather additional meaning. Where and how are the following used? How is each related to Kino's search?

   a. The various songs . . . of the family . . . of the pearl . . . of evil

   b. Kino's injured hand

   c. Kino's boat

   d. Coyotito

3. Reread the last three paragraphs of the story. What is Kino admitting to Juana when he offers her the pearl? What does her refusal mean to Kino? Amid the pressures of shifting personal values and the confused forces of a mad society, what is the value that yet endures?

Style

Steinbeck has given *The Pearl* the flavor of a folk story by using a simple, straightforward pattern of sentences. For example, how many sentences in the first four paragraphs of Chapter 1 are simple sentences? How many are compound sentences with short clauses joined by *and?* How many clauses follow the most common English word order of subject-predicate-(complement)? In general, are these first paragraphs characteristic of the rest of the story?

Steinbeck also develops the folklike flavor by rendering the scenes, actions, and emotions of the story objectively, like a camera. He paints La Paz and the mountains as they are without interjecting his personal feelings about them. Nor does he describe the characters' emotions directly. How do the various songs reveal Kino's emotions? How are others' emotions revealed? For instance, how can you tell that the first pearl buyer in Chapter 4 is nervous? Does Steinbeck say so?

Identification

With which character did you identify yourself most strongly? How did Steinbeck win your sympathy for Kino and Juana? Which pressures suffered by Kino and Juana are shared, in your opinion, by all human beings?

IV

WORDS

A. The force of a narrative depends upon the impressions formed through words. To recreate an experience a writer may use figurative or concrete representations. What do the phrases and clauses below suggest?

> a late moth blustered in to find the fire; his mouth drooped with discontent; electric strength; flames danced on the faces of the neighbors; inaudible purr of controlled breathing; hissed to silence; coin stumbled over a knuckle; he felt the evil coagulating about him; senses were burningly alive; the bare stone teeth of the mountains.

B. From context determine the meaning of the italicized words.

1. A *covey* of little birds chittered and flurried with their wings.

2. The surface of the water was an *undulating* mirror of brightness.

3. What he had seen might be a reflection, a piece of flat shell accidentally drifted in, or a complete *illusion*.

4. She looked at the neighbors for *confirmation* and they nodded their heads solemnly.

5. The hundreds of years of *subjugation* were cut deep in him.

6. High slopes of the mountain were *swaddled* with pines.

7. Gradually the spasms *subsided* and the baby relaxed.

C. 1. Steinbeck tells us that Kino was attentive to inner music of various kinds. What does the root of the word *music* mean? Is it related to the word *museum*?

2. When the baby is bitten by the scorpion, Juana tries to find the puncture. What does the root of *puncture* mean? Is it related to *punctuate*, *punctilious*, *pungent*?

3. The appetites of the doctor were known to the people. Is the word *appetite* related to the word *petition*? In what way has the word *appetite* undergone specialization?

4. The pearl "captured the light and refined it and gave it back in silver incandescence." The root in *incandescence* is -*cand*-, meaning "white, glowing." Does the same root appear in the word *candidate*?

5. The root of *patron* ("each one thought how the patron could not live forever") is -*patr*-, originally meaning "father." How are *patron* and *patronize* related to this same root? What has happened to these words? What words in English illustrate the form -*pater*- with its original meaning?

6. What are the roots in the following words and what do they mean: *explosion* ("an explosion of fire"); *detachment* ("the detachment of God"); *incredible* ("one incredible fiesta on cookies"); *fragment* ("a fragment and a moist place in the dirt"); *subsequent* ("his whole subsequent life was memory and longing for France"); *magnified* ("the uncertain air that magnified some things"); *undulating* ("an undulating mirror of brightness"); *subsided* ("the flesh writhed up and then subsided"); *semblance* ("a semblance of competition"); *rebelled* ("he rebelled against the way things are"); *consecrated* ("a little piece of consecrated candle")?

BIOGRAPHICAL NOTES

Saki

Saki (1870–1916) was the pseudonym for Hector Hugo Munro, who delighted in spoofing British Victorian society. Born in Burma of British parents, he was educated in England by two strict aunts. Later he returned to Burma to serve with the military police. But seven fevers in 13 months forced his return to Britain. In London he discovered he could earn a living by writing. His first popular successes were political satires for the *Westminster Gazette*. Later he wrote short stories satirizing British society and, especially, aunts. He was killed by a sniper's bullet in France during World War I.

Harry Sylvester

Harry Sylvester (1908–   ) was born in Brooklyn and attended Notre Dame University, graduating in 1930. He sold his first short story when he was a senior at Notre Dame, and within 10 years had published more than 100, mainly sports stories in various magazines such as *Colliers, Scribners, Story,* and *Pictorial Review.* He has had some of his works reprinted in England and Scandinavia, showing the universal appeal of a good sports story. *A Boxer Old* was published in the *O. Henry Memorial Award Prize Stories* of 1934. At different times he worked for both the *New York Evening Post* and the *New York Herald Tribune,* and in 1943 published his first novel, *Dearly Beloved,* set in a small southern town.

George Orwell

George Orwell (1903–1950) was the pen name of Eric Blair, a tall, gentle Englishman who wrote in bitter, satiric fashion of the things he hated: Communists, leftists, intellectuals, cruelty in life. Born in Burma, he was educated at Eton and later served in the Indian Imperial Police in Burma. He is unusual among writers in that he deliberately lived under the social conditions he wrote about. He fought in the Spanish Civil War and acquired an undying hatred of Communism which inspired *Animal Farm* and *Nineteen Eighty-Four.* Orwell once said that the subject matter of most books could be summarized in a single word, *decency.* He felt that men must act decently toward themselves and toward their fellow men if liberty and justice are to be achieved.

William Sansom

William Sansom (1912–   ), British novelist and short story writer, reports of his beginnings: "I was born, and soon began writing. The pattern is familiar. The worried baby, the shy child, schooldays spent avoiding the ball, the first rungs of the commercial ladder—indeed, in a bank—and then the revolt that ended not in a garret but an advertising agency." World War II extracted him from advertising, and during the blitz of London he learned to write seriously. Instead of trying to write what he imagined people wanted, Sansom wrote what he himself really thought. And suddenly he was published. Eudora Welty says: "He makes you see, hear, taste, touch, and smell to his order—Mr. Sansom's descriptive power is a steady fireworks."

James Thurber

James Thurber (1894–1961) is considered by many as the best American humorist since Mark Twain. His books are illustrated with his own drawings of shapeless but determined women; droopy-eared, sad dogs; and worried-looking men. Many of his prose sketches concern the same kind of characters: little people unable to cope with their world. His fables are a blend of nonsense and fact, showing how well Thurber knew people and their foibles. His last years were a struggle against blindness.

Jack London

Jack London (1876–1916) was an American novelist and short-story writer who used many of his own adventures as the basis for his work. Although he attended the University of California for one year, his real education came from his experiences as a longshoreman, sailor, gold hunter in the Klondike, and as a war correspondent during the Russo-Japanese War. Although physically he appeared as a rough character, he was unusually sensitive, especially to social injustices. Some feel his careless, rough life was an outward expression of his revolt against society. Unfortunately, his health was damaged by his way of life and he died a relatively young man. In 16 years he wrote some 50 books, the first of which, *The Son of the Wolf,* was published in 1900. His best known books are *Call of the Wild* (1903), *The Sea Wolf* (1904), and *White Fang* (1906).

George Gordon, Lord Byron

George Gordon, Lord Byron (1788–1824) was such a dominant personality in the early nineteenth century that the period is often characterized as "Byronic." He was a man of contradictions: an aristocrat who made fun of his own class; physically handicapped by a clubfoot, yet an athlete; an irresistible lover who attracted women, yet rejected them; a remarkable genius, overrated in his own time and underrated for years following. His poetry has lived because of his ability to describe nature, to ridicule sham, and to capture strong human emotions. His love of liberty is reflected in his poems, "Childe Harold" and "The Prisoner of Chillon." He died on a trip to Greece where he had gone to help the Greeks gain their independence. Ironically, he did not die on the battlefield but from pneumonia contracted during a ride in the rain.

Willa Cather

Willa Cather (1873–1947), born in Winchester, Virginia, moved at age nine with her family to the Nebraska village of Red Cloud. Her friends and neighbors were the immigrants from Europe: Swedes, Bohemians, Russians, and Germans whom she came to know, understand, and respect. Her well-known novels, such as *O Pioneers* and *My Ántonia,* were built on the theme of the pioneers' spirit and courage. Her next group of books depicted the struggle of a talent to emerge from the restricting and stifling prairie life: *Song of the Lark, Youth and the Bright Medusa,* and *Lucy Gayheart.* In her mature years, she again turned to the pioneer spirit, but this time it was the spirit in an earlier pioneer age: *Death Comes for the Archbishop, Shadows on the Rock.* Her stories are honest and direct. They detail the successful conquest of physical and material hardships by people of spirit and determination.

Ambrose Bierce

Ambrose Bierce (1842–1914?), born in Ohio, fought in the Civil War and then moved west to become a successful journalist in San Francisco. He also lived several years in England and there published three books. In California he was the dominant literary figure in the 1890s, but a series of unhappy personal experiences made him an increasingly bitter man. Primarily a short story writer, his best collections are *Tales of Soldiers and Civilians* and *Can Such Things Be?* both published in the nineties. In 1913 he went to Mexico to join the civil war there and disappeared.

Truman Capote

Truman Capote (1924–   ) was born in New Orleans to parents of long Southern lineage. He attended six different schools in five different parts of the country. Dropping out of school at seventeen, he worked briefly as a protégé of a fortune-teller and then for *The New Yorker* in various departments. Beginning to write early, Capote won his first prize at the age of eight for a short story. As an adult he has won two O'Henry short story awards. Though he claims writing is an exceedingly slow process for him, Capote insists that nothing else appeals to him. In 1966 he became one of the most-discussed authors in the country when his book *In Cold Blood* was published. Capote claimed that it was a new kind of literature, a nonfiction novel. It was later made into a movie.

Arna Bontemps

Arna Bontemps (1902–   ) was reared in California, graduating in 1923 from Pacific Union College. The following year he headed for Harlem, abandoning his plan to be a doctor for the challenge and excitement of writing. He won several poetry prizes while teaching in private schools. In the 1930s, while teaching in Alabama and Chicago, Bontemps found time to write three novels and two children's books. After studying at both Columbia University and the University of Chicago, Bontemps became Head Librarian at Fisk University, a position he held for twenty-two years. But he never gave up his own writing or the anthologizing of other black writers' works. His forty-five years of writing, teaching, and inspiring black writers has made him one of the best-known contributors to the field of black literature.

John Steinbeck

John Steinbeck (1902–   ) is an American fiction writer whose book *Grapes of Wrath,* a story of the dispossessed Oklahoma farmers and their trek to California, has been called the "Uncle Tom" of the migrant workers. Born in California, Steinbeck went intermittently to Stanford University, but never achieved his degree. He had published several books before his story *The Red Pony,* published in the *North American Review,* attracted an interested group of readers. His first real success was *Tortilla Flat,* which was followed by *Of Mice and Men. Grapes of Wrath,* for which Steinbeck was awarded the Pulitzer Prize, was both attacked and praised. Lewis Gannett, a critic, wrote that there was something Emersonian about the book, because it was Emerson who wrote that "in the mud and scum of things there always, always, something sings." "Steinbeck," says Gannet, "almost alone among all the modern writers who write of mud and scum, invariably hears, and communicates, the song." In 1962, Steinbeck received the Nobel Prize for Literature.

We Real Cool

We real cool. We
Left school. We

Lurk late. We
Strike straight. We

Sing sin. We
Thin gin. We

Jazz June. We
die soon.

GWENDOLYN BROOKS

Gwendolyn Brooks' poem hits hard with the unexpectedness of the last line. Life (or death) has a way of striking back at us no matter how self-confident we may be. This is life's irony.

Just to be alive is to be subject to life's ironies. Whether rich or poor, ambitious or lazy, talented or not talented, a person cannot escape the strange incongruities that arise at times between what he expects and what actually happens. These are life's ironies: a person extends himself to catch an earlier flight and rides to sudden death in a crash; a health faddist insists on jogging two miles a day and drops dead of a heart attack after a workout; a contractor cuts back a hill to build his garage and loses it in a landslide.

Ironies that arise in life are not all generated by the same forces. Sometimes nature triggers the unexpected; sometimes society forces the surprise; and sometimes something within a person springs the ironic trap.

Writers have always turned to life's ironies as a rich theme for their storytelling. Usually, such writing leaves an indelible impression on the reader, hitting him with all the force of a blow to the stomach. At times, the reader, upon finishing such a story, may want to argue that such a thing could not happen . . . wishes it hadn't happened . . . is emotionally shaken by its unexpected ending. And yet, as the reader thinks about the selection he is often aware that the outcome, though unexpected, is peculiarly right, peculiarly just. Because of this emotional impact, stories centering on life's ironies are long remembered.

The arrogance and pride of the wealthy is satirized in this deeply ironical painting by Georges Rouault. The Society Lady Fancies She Has a Reserved Seat in Heaven. *Collection, The Museum of Modern Art, New York. Gift of the artist.*

Life may startle us by the ironic
twist of permitting us to achieve a desired
goal but demanding an unexpected
forfeit in return.

The Wrath
of the Raped

MacKINLAY KANTOR

I arranged to spend the weekend with Aunt
Thesnelda in Eagle Falls—to eat the bacon
gravy and plum preserves which were always
on her table, to sleep in the too-short walnut
bed where I had slept so many times before,
to stroll with her around the tiny garden, and
hear lamentations concerning the elm which
shaded her nasturtium plot, and the dog from
next door who carried on sundry excavations
amid her moss-roses.

All of these events took place according to
schedule, and as I hadn't intended driving on
until Tuesday morning, I took a solitary jaunt
in my car on Monday afternoon, driving over
forgotten hill roads along the Eagle River.

The hill roads were not as forgotten as I
had thought. I remembered them as cart
paths, clustered with brier bushes and crab
trees, where the grass switched high enough
between the wheel ruts to kiss a wagon axle.
Now one of the lanes had been made into a
primary road, with embankments chopped
away, raw culverts lifting their concrete ridges
on either side. Taut fences of rustproof wire
stretched beside the fields, and several times I

caught a sparkling flash from the roadside
which could mean only one thing—an empty
bottle. A new race had inhabited the valley of
the Eagle, and I felt my kinship dwindling.

But when I had parked the car near the old
Burgess farm, and wandered down across the
hill pasture, something of ancient lure and
contentment sang in my ears again. This was
the same field—the creek had cut a little
deeper, roadside trees had been chopped
down—but undeniably it was the same field.
Scrub red cattle grazing near the river cottonwoods were doubtless the legitimate descendants of the cows that wandered there so long
before. And overhead was the same sky,
washed to a porcelain blue and filmed with
puffing clouds that broke from the prairie beyond the river.

One stubborn smokestack emerged from
green haze at an upper bend of the river.
There had been no smokestack there twenty
years before, but I felt that no one should be-
grudge Eagle Falls whatever bustling institution was giving birth to that thin strand of
black smoke.

Once along the river, I wandered in a daze.
A fallen cottonwood, holding a dry drift of
polished sticks, should have been there. I
should have observed a gaping hole in the
high bank opposite the first bend, and there
should have been a muskrat rippling doggedly
among the quiet shadows . . . . Drift, hole and
muskrat—all were gone. The bank had caved
alarmingly, and the huge pink boulder which
used to bulge in the center of the narrows was
high and dry on the opposite shore. Even the
river had moved itself during twenty years.

I strolled north through the thin fringe of
undergrowth; a distant crow squawled peevishly, and I smiled as I remembered how
Georgie Terrell and I had lain in wait for
hours, concealed near a bait of corn and hoping with futile confidence to club marauding
crows.

Georgie Terrell, I recalled, had been able
to stay under water longer than anyone else.
He could plunge from an arching elm branch,

and go down, down in the glassy greenness, until only bubbles broke the sheer surface and you'd think he was gone for good . . . . Sadly enough, this accomplishment had availed him little when the *Tuscania* rolled beneath wintry waters. The Irish Sea was not like Howard's Hole on the Eagle River.

Somewhere in the woods ahead of me I heard a shrill wavering cry that brought a sudden ripple under my skin. It might have been the naked ghost of Georgie Terrell, calling to me that the water was over his head and hand . . . . And then I smiled ruefully, and with sudden thanksgiving. Georgie's name was on a bronze tablet in the courthouse, but still there were boys to splash the dim waters of Howard's Hole, and scramble up the bank in wet pink skins.

Little boys. Noisy boys. I could hear them now, singing and whooping, talking with the blasphemous assurance of boys who are alone.

"Duck him, Gorsey!" one of them was yelling, and "Sit on him, Skeet!" shrilled another.

Their damp bedlam was suddenly stilled when I came out on the bank above their heads. Yes, the boys were still swimming in Howard's Hole. The broad pool had shrunk to a narrow ribbon, and areas of greasy mud clotted along the opposite shore, but the same trees still swung above the dark mirror. Somehow the mirror did not seem so freshly green as I remembered it.

The boys watched me; four of them, their slick wet heads bobbing quietly on the surface.

"How's the water?" I asked.

"All right." They watched me with suspicion; they seemed to feel that I might interfere with their splashing riot. I could not help knowing that they wished I hadn't come.

But I clung fiercely to those vestiges of a quiet past which were lifting in my mind. "How deep?"

To my surprise, one of the boys suddenly emerged from the water to a point at his nipples, and remained mutely standing for my delectation.[1]

"Do you mean to tell me that it's only rib deep in there?"

They stared, wide-eyed. "Why, this is pretty deep, ain't it?" one of them asked cautiously. "Last summer it was only up to my belly, sometimes."

I sat down stupidly on the bank. "It's tough, to see that," I told them. "When I used to go swimming here it was always over my head and hand, in the deep hole."

It was a fairy story to them. "Gosh!" they exploded. "When was that?"

"Oh, twenty years ago," I had to tell them in confusion. "Don't mind me, boys. Go ahead and swim. I'm just going to sit here and smoke awhile."

They began to move about, cautiously and reluctantly, but gaining in freedom as they observed that my thoughts were evidently far removed from them. Before long they were tumbling about—swimming a few strokes, dog-paddling, wrestling in the water like a troop of maudlin puppies.

I bit down fiercely on my pipe, but was unable to see where I could have improved matters. The river was there; the farmers owned the land; if they wanted to cut down trees until the banks caved, if they wanted to drain their corn-bottom silt into the stream and clog the channel, there was little I could do about it.

One of the boys stepped on a piece of glass and came clambering up the bank to examine his wound. It was not a bad cut, and he sat there hugging his glistening knees while we talked together.

"What's that stuff on your shoulder?" I asked curiously.

He turned, and with a careless gesture brushed off a string of matted filth. "It's in the water. See, there's some more just going by." He pointed to another putrescent[2] object slowly turning in the sluggish current.

---

1. **delectation**\ˈdē ˈlěk ˄tā·shən\ pleasure, enjoyment.
2. **putrescent**\pyū ˄trěs·ənt\ decomposing, rotting.

I sniffed. There was a sickening odor. "Where does it come from?"

"Rendering plant.[3] It's up the river a ways."

"And is this stuff in the river all the time?"

"Sure." He looked at me indignantly. "Wasn't there any rendering plant when you lived here?"

"No," I replied fervently. "I don't see how you can swim in that filth. I don't think you ought to."

"Where'd we swim, then?" he countered belligerently.

That was right. "Nowhere, I guess," I admitted.

He forgave me kindly. "Aw, we don't mind it so much. It isn't real bad unless you get it in your mouth . . . . We can all swim fine."

"Can you?"—absently.

"Sure. Gorsey"—he pointed to a yellow head between two brown ones in the water—"he can swim better'n any of the other guys. He can stay under water the longest, too."

So Georgie Terrell's laurels were endangered by the advance of a new champion. "What's his name?"

"Gorsey. Joe Gorse. He can swim good!"

My companion began to pull on his shirt. I put my pipe in my pocket, called a goodbye to the swimmers, and picked my way through the undergrowth back to the open pasture. I broke off a maple sprout and flicked my leg as I walked . . . . Once in a while I forgot myself and became an unconscious masochist;[4] the skin was black and blue when I removed my clothes that night.

Two weeks in Omaha, Sioux Falls, Minneapolis, and Mason City. Two weeks of customers and order-blanks and restaurant fare. Then I swung back to Eagle Falls for another night at Aunt Thesnelda's before I returned to the main office in Chicago. But misfortune lay in wait for me.

Aunt Nelda has no garage, or need for one, unless it would be as quarters for her tomcat, and who ever kept a tomcat in a garage? . . . I parked my car in front of the old house that night, and long before morning some son of Satan, driving without lights, smashed into the front of it. Dawn showed a shattered wheel, a bent axle and a twisted radiator. Also a great deal of broken glass which proved that the malefactor had not escaped undamaged.

There was nothing for it but to leave the car in a local garage for repairs, and take the afternoon train to Chicago.

Thirty seconds after I had seated myself in the observation car of the Limited, a fat, beaming-eyed gentleman puffed into a chair beside me. He was the only other parlor-car passenger from Eagle Falls.

"Going far?" he inquired.

"Chicago."

"Waterloo's my home," he offered expansively. "Name's Madger. Julius R. Madger."

Wearily enough, I told him my name. I had hoped for a drowsy afternoon, filled with relaxation from the strain of driving, but this was not to be.

He spouted effusively as the train sped across the bridge and up the long grade.

"Eagle Falls . . . nice little burg . . . good, live town. Things going good, now."

"They are?"

"Sure. Banking slump hit them rather hard but they're making things hum again. Not your home, huh?"

"I've been visiting a relative," I said.

"Oh, I see. Don't know many people there, huh? Know Gorse?"

Gorse, Gorse. The name lodged in my mind . . . . Then I remembered: the boy, the golden-head, the contender for George Terrell's forgotten honors. "I met a boy—" I began, but he was already giving me the history of the Gorse fortunes.

". . . Didn't do so well at Waterloo. Came out there from Chicago; used to be with a soap company; company went broke and he was out. Tried one thing and then another.

---

3. **rendering plant,** a plant treating dead animals so as to convert them into industrial oils and fats and fertilizers.

4. **masochist**\\ˈmăs•ə•kəst\\ a person who takes delight in hurting himself.

618

Finally his wife's old man died and that gave him a little capital."

He waggled his cigar with emphatic punctuation.

"Now, here's the point I'd like to bring out. My friend Gorse took advantage of an opportunity which no one else had touched. He went to Eagle Falls and established his business. Virgin territory. Chance for anybody with the guts to do it." He chuckled suddenly. "That was a pun, by golly—guts!"

"What was it?" I asked.

"Dead animals! Dead animals, that people burn or bury or drag away to let them rot. Always wasted before. You wouldn't think of that, see?"

I agreed. "No, I wouldn't."

"Well, that's the kind of a fellow Gorse is. He's got a man-size plant there at Eagle Falls, now. A lot of employees. Drive around in trucks —cover more than a thousand square miles of territory. Dead cows, pigs, horses, sheep—even down to dogs and cats. No, sir, Gorse doesn't miss an opportunity. Even a dog or cat's got a little grease in it."

He rumbled at his own humor.

"Where is this plant—on the river?" I was beginning to remember an odor; the sight of floating scum; the black smokestack that reared itself above the river trees . . . .

"Yes, sir, on the river, mile and a half below town. That way the smell (it's rather a smelly process, see?) doesn't bother folks. Oh, a few of 'em kick now and then. But Gorse can tell 'em to go to hell if they don't like it. He's got a legitimate business, and he's making a darn good thing out of it."

I asked, automatically and not because of any interest: "I suppose you've been over to Eagle Falls to see your friend Gorse?"

"Sure. Didn't I tell you?" His face was suddenly very sober. "Tough on Gorse—awful tough on him. I've been back there to a funeral. His kid died. His boy."

"Died?" was all I could say.

"Yes. Died on Tuesday night. It was his only son, too. Gorse had the best doctors in the State, but no use. The kid died of a—a— what you call it—Mastoid infection, I think. Infection in his ear. It was a funny thing; nobody could figure out how he ever got it."

I
THE PROPHECY OF LITERATURE

"The Wrath of the Raped" was first published in 1929. Yet it probably has a greater impact and meaning for today's reader than it did when it was written because the prophecies in the story have proved increasingly true. Note the number of details throughout the selection that indicate that man is destroying the very environment that nurtures him. In addition to the obvious detail that the rendering plant is dumping raw sewage into the stream, the narrator notes that the stream bed has moved and is narrower than it used to be, the topsoil has silted into the pool lowering the water's depth, the very water has changed color, the muskrats and their dam have vanished, and the stream has cut deeper into the earth. A smokestack pours black waste into the formerly clear sky. Empty bottles litter the roadside. All of these details are startling to the reader when he realizes that this is a description written forty years ago. Ironically, even the attitudes of the people are unchanged and very familiar.

II
IMPLICATIONS

Opinions may be based on both the materials given in the stories and on students' own experiences. There is no clear-cut right or wrong answer.

1. Owners of a piece of property should be able to do anything they want with it.

2. The good the plant does for the people in the town makes up for the pollution it causes.

3. There are two ironic happenings in the story: (1) Joe Gorse dies from the pollution caused by his father's plant and (2) Joe Gorse's father is unaware that he has caused his son's death. The first is more ironic than the second.

III
TECHNIQUES

As you read stories centering on life's ironies, your attention will be directed to two more qualities that enhance the impact of a piece of literature. These are atmosphere and suspense.

Atmosphere

The atmosphere is the prevailing mood a story creates in the reader's mind. If it is well done, it establishes certain expectations about the story: that it will be down-to-earth or lighthearted or somber or melancholy. Atmosphere might be likened to color tonality. Some stories seem to be bright yellow and orange; some ooze mysterious deep red or purple; others seem dark brown or drab gray.

In "The Wrath of the Raped" the story centers on a man's return to the small Iowa town he had known as a boy. He feels a kind of despair at the passing of the good things he had known and the devastating changes man is inflicting on his environment. Even the conversation with the stranger on the train is written so that the reader feels the narrator's disgust at the sentiments being expressed. The single effect is that of overwhelming despair and disgust.

Suspense

Suspense is one of the most common ways of holding the reader's interest. His curiosity is aroused by a problem, a situation, or a question. But the writer, instead of satisfying the reader's curiosity, holds back the answer. He may, instead, elaborate the problem by adding complications, by taking characters through a sequence of trials and failures, or he may extend the waiting by philosophical reflections on the situation. Suspense is usually the ingredient that makes a plot "go."

In "The Wrath of the Raped" the suspense is unusual. The reader is not involved with the narrator, nor is there any specific problem set forth. The details do not take on real significance until the very end of the story. The reader's curiosity is tantalized by the sheer puzzle about where the story is going. It is a little like the game children play in which a person must tell a story about a group of unrelated items: a snake, a handkerchief, a pizza, and a chess set. So in this story you assemble a group of seemingly unrelated pieces: a traveling salesman revisiting his childhood town, a group of boys in a swimming hole, a rendering plant, an accidentally damaged car, a ride on a train. . . . The reader keeps wondering—well, what is this all about?

IV

WORDS

A. As you have learned elsewhere in this book, words are often traceable to proper names. Refering to some youngsters swimming in Howard's Hole, the narrator in "The Wrath of the Raped" speaks of their "damp bedlam." The word *bedlam* is actually a dialectal pronunciation of the word *Bethlehem.* In the dialect of London in the thirteenth century, the last word in the name St. Mary's of Bethlehem was pronounced *bedlam.* In the fifteenth century, St. Mary's, a priory, was converted into an insane asylum. In time, *bedlam* became associated with the uproar and confusion common in such an institution. As used in the story, *bedlam* refers to the noisy, unrestrained fun the boys were having in their swimming hole. Like *bedlam,* the word *maudlin* is derived from a proper name, in this case, Mary Magdalene. In the Bible, Mary Magdalene is the sinner from whom Christ cast out seven devils. In classical art, she is portrayed quite often as a weeping, repentant figure. Thus, anyone, who is given to weeping, especially an overly sentimental person, is said to be *maudlin.* Comparing the water to tears, the narrator says that the boys were "dog-paddling, wrestling in the water like a troop of maudlin puppies." From what proper names are these words derived: *dunce, shrapnel, hooligan, limerick, academy, maverick, mausoleum, cologne, braille,* and *cardigan?*

B. Many an American place name has its origin in an Indian language. For instance, *Sioux Falls, Omaha,* and *Minneapolis,* all of which are mentioned in "The Wrath of the Raped," originated in an American Indian language. *Sioux Falls* (in South Dakota) is derived from *Sioux,* which is traceable to a Chippewa Indian word meaning "little snake." The Sioux peoples were North American Indians who formerly occupied parts of the Great Plains in the Dakotas, Minnesota, and Nebraska. *Minneapolis* (Minnesota) is obviously related to *Minnesota,* which in the Dakotan language is *minisota,* "clear water." The last part, *polis,* is Greek for "city." From Dhegiha, a Siouan language, comes *umāhā,* "upstream," or *Omaha* (Nebraska). Using your dictionary, try to find out the Indian language and the original meaning behind each of these place names: *Nebraska, Wichita, Milwaukee, South Dakota, Mississippi, Delaware,* and *Connecticut.*

Inspired by an actual event, Hawthorne weaves a story of contrasts—contrasts between the inner security and the outer forces of nature, between the dreams of simple people and the dreams of a worldly visitor—all of which suddenly become highly ironic.

The Ambitious Guest

NATHANIEL HAWTHORNE

One September night a family had gathered round their hearth, and piled it high with the driftwood of mountain streams, the dry cones of the pine, and the splintered ruins of great trees that had come crashing down the precipice. Up the chimney roared the fire, and brightened the room with its broad blaze. The faces of the father and mother had a sober gladness; the children laughed; the eldest daughter was the image of Happiness at seventeen; and the aged grandmother, who sat knitting in the warmest place, was the image of Happiness grown old. They had found the "herb, heart's-ease," in the bleakest spot of all New England. This family were situated in the Notch of the White Hills, where the wind was sharp throughout the year, and pitilessly cold in the winter,—giving their cottage all its fresh inclemency before it descended on the valley of the Saco. They dwelt in a cold spot and a dangerous one; for a mountain towered above their heads, so steep, that the stones would often rumble down its sides and startle them at midnight.

The daughter had just uttered some simple jest that filled them all with mirth, when the wind came through the Notch[1] and seemed to pause before their cottage—rattling the door, with a sound of wailing and lamentation, be-fore it passed into the valley. For a moment it saddened them, though there was nothing unusual in the tones. But the family were glad again when they perceived that the latch was lifted by some traveller, whose footsteps had been unheard amid the dreary blast which heralded his approach, and wailed as he was entering, and went moaning away from the door.

Though they dwelt in such a solitude, these people held daily converse with the world. The romantic pass of the Notch is a great artery, through which the life-blood of internal commerce is continually throbbing between Maine, on one side, and the Green Mountains and the shores of the St. Lawrence, on the other. The stage-coach always drew up before the door of the cottage. The wayfarer, with no companion but his staff, paused here to exchange a word, that the sense of loneliness might not utterly overcome him ere he could pass through the cleft of the mountain, or reach the first house in the valley. And here the teamster, on his way to Portland market, would put up for the night; and, if a bachelor, might sit an hour beyond the usual bedtime, and steal a kiss from the mountain maid at parting. It was one of those primitive taverns where the traveller pays only for food and lodging, but meets with a homely kindness beyond all price. When the footsteps were heard, therefore, between the outer door and the inner one, the whole family rose up, grandmother, children, and all, as if about to welcome some one who belonged to them, and whose fate was linked with theirs.

The door was opened by a young man. His face at first wore the melancholy expression, almost despondency, of one who travels a wild and bleak road, at nightfall and alone, but soon brightened up when he saw the kindly warmth of his reception. He felt his heart spring forward to meet them all, from the old woman, who wiped a chair with her apron, to the little child that held out its arms to him. One glance

---

1. **the Notch,** a deep, narrow mountain pass in northern New Hampshire.

and smile placed the stranger on a footing of innocent familiarity with the eldest daughter.

"Ah, this fire is the right thing!" cried he; "especially when there is such a pleasant circle round it. I am quite benumbed; for the Notch is just like the pipe of a great pair of bellows; it has blown a terrible blast in my face all the way from Bartlett."

"Then you are going towards Vermont?" said the master of the house, as he helped to take a light knapsack off the young man's shoulders.

"Yes; to Burlington, and far enough beyond," replied he. "I meant to have been at Ethan Crawford's to-night; but a pedestrian lingers along such a road as this. It is no matter; for, when I saw this good fire, and all your cheerful faces, I felt as if you had kindled it on purpose for me, and were waiting my arrival. So I shall sit down among you, and make myself at home."

The frank-hearted stranger had just drawn his chair to the fire when something like a heavy footstep was heard without, rushing down the steep side of the mountain, as with long and rapid strides, and taking such a leap in passing the cottage as to strike the opposite precipice. The family held their breath, because they knew the sound, and their guest held his by instinct.

"The old mountain has thrown a stone at us, for fear we should forget him," said the landlord, recovering himself. "He sometimes nods his head and threatens to come down; but we are old neighbors, and agree together pretty well upon the whole. Besides we have a sure place of refuge hard by if he should be coming in good earnest."

Let us now suppose the stranger to have finished his supper of bear's meat; and, by his natural felicity[2] of manner, to have placed himself on a footing of kindness with the whole family, so that they talked as freely together as if he belonged to their mountain brood. He was of a proud, yet gentle spirit—haughty and reserved among the rich and great; but ever ready to stoop his head to the lowly cottage door, and be like a brother or a son at the poor

man's fireside. In the household of the Notch he found warmth and simplicity of feeling, the pervading intelligence of New England, and a poetry of native growth, which they had gathered when they little thought of it from the mountain peaks and chasms, and at the very threshold of their romantic and dangerous abode. He had travelled far and alone; his whole life, indeed, had been a solitary path; for, with the lofty caution of his nature, he had kept himself apart from those who might otherwise have been his companions. The family, too, though so kind and hospitable, had that consciousness of unity among themselves, and separation from the world at large, which, in every domestic circle, should still keep a holy place where no stranger may intrude. But this evening a prophetic sympathy impelled the refined and educated youth to pour out his heart before the simple mountaineers, and constrained them to answer him with the same free confidence. And thus it should have been. Is not the kindred of a common fate a closer tie than that of birth?

The secret of the young man's character was a high and abstracted ambition. He could have borne to live an undistinguished life, but not to be forgotten in the grave. Yearning desire had been transformed to hope; and hope, long cherished, had become like certainty, that, obscurely as he journeyed now, a glory was to beam on all his pathway,—though not, perhaps, while he was treading it. But when posterity should gaze back into the gloom of what was now the present, they would trace the brightness of his footsteps, brightening as meaner glories faded, and confess that a gifted one had passed from his cradle to his tomb with none to recognize him.

"As yet," cried the stranger—his cheek glowing and his eyes flashing with enthusiasm—"as yet, I have done nothing. Were I to vanish from the earth to-morrow, none would know so much of me as you: that a nameless youth

---

2. felicity\fə ⁴lĭ·sə·tē\ happiness; here, charm of manner.

came up at nightfall from the valley of the Saco, and opened his heart to you in the evening, and passed through the Notch by sunrise, and was seen no more. Not a soul would ask, 'Who was he? Whither did the wanderer go?' But I cannot die till I have achieved my destiny. Then, let Death come! I shall have built my monument!"

There was a continual flow of natural emotion, gushing forth amid abstracted reverie, which enabled the family to understand this young man's sentiments, though so foreign from their own. With quick sensibility of the ludicrous, he blushed at the ardor into which he had been betrayed.

"You laugh at me," said he, taking the eldest daughter's hand, and laughing himself. "You think my ambition as nonsensical as if I were to freeze myself to death on the top of Mount Washington, only that people might spy at me from the country round about. And, truly, that would be a noble pedestal for a man's statue!"

"It is better to sit here by this fire," answered the girl, blushing, "and be comfortable and contented, though nobody thinks about us."

"I suppose," said her father, after a fit of musing, "there is something natural in what the young man says; and if my mind had been turned that way, I might have felt just the same. It is strange, wife, how his talk has set my head running on things that are pretty certain never to come to pass."

"Perhaps they may," observed the wife. "Is the man thinking what he will do when he is a widower?"

"No, no!" cried he, repelling the idea with reproachful kindness. "When I think of your death, Esther, I think of mine, too. But I was wishing we had a good farm in Bartlett, or Bethlehem, or Littleton, or some other township round the White Mountains; but not where they could tumble on our heads. I should want to stand well with my neighbors and be called Squire,[3] and sent to General Court for a term or two; for a plain, honest man may do as much good there as a lawyer. And when I

The Maine Central Railroad crosses Willey Brook in a picturesque section of Crawford Notch, N.H. This notch, one of four in the White Mountains, is believed to be the one Hawthorne had in mind when he wrote "The Ambitious Guest."

should be grown quite an old man, and you an old woman, so as not to be long apart, I might die happy enough in my bed, and leave you all crying around me. A slate gravestone would suit me as well as a marble one—with just my name and age, and a verse of a hymn, and something to let people know that I lived an honest man and died a Christian."

"There now!" exclaimed the stranger; "it is our nature to desire a monument, be it slate or

---

3. **Squire**\skwair\ *U.S.* a title used in certain small towns and country districts and applied to a justice of the peace, a local judge, or other local dignitary.

marble, or a pillar of granite, or a glorious memory in the universal heart of man."

"We're in a strange way, to-night," said the wife, with tears in her eyes. "They say it's a sign of something, when folks' minds go a wandering so. Hark to the children!"

They listened accordingly. The younger children had been put to bed in another room, but with an open door between, so that they could be heard talking busily among themselves. One and all seemed to have caught the infection from the fireside circle, and were outvying[4] each other in wild wishes, and childish projects of what they would do when they came to be men and women. At length a little boy, instead of addressing his brothers and sisters, called out to his mother.

"I'll tell you what I wish, mother," cried he. "I want you and father and grandma'm, and all of us, and the stranger too, to start right away, and go and take a drink out of the basin of the Flume!"

Nobody could help laughing at the child's notion of leaving a warm bed, and dragging them from a cheerful fire, to visit the basin of the Flume,—a brook, which tumbles over the precipice, deep within the Notch. The boy had hardly spoken when a wagon rattled along the road, and stopped a moment before the door. It appeared to contain two or three men, who were cheering their hearts with the rough chorus of a song, which resounded, in broken notes, between the cliffs, while the singers hesitated whether to continue their journey or put up here for the night."

"Father," said the girl, "they are calling you by name."

But the good man doubted whether they had really called him, and was unwilling to show himself too solicitous of gain by inviting people to patronize his house. He therefore did not hurry to the door; and the lash being soon applied, the travellers plunged into the Notch, still singing and laughing, though their music and mirth came back drearily from the heart of the mountain.

"There, mother!" cried the boy, again. "They'd have given us a ride to the Flume."

Again they laughed at the child's pertinacious[5] fancy for a night ramble. But it happened that a light cloud passed over the daughter's spirit; she looked gravely into the fire, and drew a breath that was almost a sigh. It forced its way, in spite of a little struggle to repress it. Then starting and blushing, she looked quickly round the circle, as if they had caught a glimpse into her bosom. The stranger asked what she had been thinking of.

"Nothing," answered she, with a downcast smile. "Only I felt lonesome just then."

"Oh, I have always had a gift of feeling what is in other people's hearts," said he, half seriously. "Shall I tell the secrets of yours? For I know what to think when a young girl shivers by a warm hearth, and complains of lonesomeness at her mother's side. Shall I put these feelings into words?"

"They would not be a girl's feelings any longer if they could be put into words," replied the mountain nymph, laughing, but avoiding his eye.

All this was said apart. Perhaps a germ of love was springing in their hearts, so pure that it might blossom in Paradise, since it could not be matured on earth; for women worship such gentle dignity as his; and the proud, contemplative, yet kindly soul is oftenest captivated by simplicity like hers. But while they spoke softly, and he was watching the happy sadness, the lightsome shadows, the shy yearnings of a maiden's nature, the wind through the Notch took a deeper and drearier sound. It seemed, as the fanciful stranger said, like the choral strain of the spirits of the blast, who in old Indian times had their dwelling among these mountains, and made their heights and recesses a sacred region. There was a wail along the road, as if a funeral were passing. To chase away the gloom, the family threw pine

---

4. **outvying**\aᴜt ▴vai·ĭŋ\ outdoing each other, competing.
5. **pertinacious**\pər·tən ▴ā·shəs\ stubborn, obstinate.

branches on their fire, till the dry leaves crackled and the flame arose, discovering once again a scene of peace and humble happiness. The light hovered about them fondly, and caressed them all. There were the little faces of the children, peeping from their bed apart, and here the father's frame of strength, the mother's subdued and careful mien,[6] the high-browed youth, the budding girl, and the good old grandam, still knitting in the warmest place. The aged woman looked up from her task, and, with fingers ever busy, was the next to speak.

"Old folks have their notions," said she, "as well as young ones. You've been wishing and planning; and letting your heads run on one thing and another, till you've set my mind a wandering too. Now what should an old woman wish for, when she can go but a step or two before she comes to her grave? Children, it will haunt me night and day till I tell you."

"What is it, mother?" cried the husband and wife at once.

Then the old woman, with an air of mystery which drew a circle closer round the fire, informed them that she had provided her grave-clothes some years before,—a nice linen shroud, a cap with a muslin ruff, and everything of a finer sort than she had worn since her wedding day. But this evening an old superstition had strangely recurred to her. It used to be said, in her younger days, that if anything were amiss with a corpse, if only the ruff were not smooth, or the cap did not set right, the corpse in the coffin and beneath the clods would strive to put up its cold hands and arrange it. The bare thought made her nervous.

"Don't talk so, grandmother!" said the girl, shuddering.

"Now,"—continued the old woman, with singular earnestness, yet smiling strangely at her own folly,—"I want one of you, my children—when your mother is dressed and in the coffin—I want one of you to hold a looking-glass over my face. Who knows but I may take a glimpse at myself, and see whether all's right?"

"Old and young, we dream of graves and monuments," murmured the stranger youth. "I wonder how mariners feel when the ship is sinking, and they, unknown and undistinguished, are to be buried together in the ocean —that wide and nameless sepulchre?"

For a moment, the old woman's ghastly conception so engrossed the minds of her hearers that a sound abroad in the night, rising like the roar of a blast, had grown broad, deep, and terrible, before the fated group were conscious of it. The house and all within it trembled; the foundations of the earth seemed to be shaken, as if this awful sound were the peal of the last trump.[7] Young and old exchanged one wild glance, and remained an instant, pale, affrighted, without utterance, or power to move. Then the same shriek burst simultaneously from all their lips.

"The Slide! The Slide!"

The simplest words must intimate, but not portray,[8] the unutterable horror of the catastrophe. The victims rushed from their cottage, and sought refuge in what they deemed a safer spot—where, in contemplation of such an emergency, a sort of barrier had been reared. Alas! they had quitted their security, and fled right into the pathway of destruction. Down came the whole side of the mountain, in a cataract of ruin. Just before it reached the house, the stream broke into two branches—shivered not a window there, but overwhelmed the whole vicinity, blocked up the road, and annihilated everything in its dreadful course. Long ere the thunder of the great Slide had ceased to roar among the mountains, the mortal agony had been endured, and the victims were at peace. Their bodies were never found.

The next morning, the light smoke was seen stealing from the cottage chimney up the

---

6. mien\mēn\ air or bearing.
7. **the last trump,** the last trumpet. See Revelation 8:6, "And the seven angels which had the seven trumpets prepared themselves to sound."
8. **intimate**\ˈĭn·tə ˈmāt\, **but not portray,** suggest but not describe.

mountain side. Within, the fire was yet smouldering on the hearth, and the chairs in a circle round it, as if the inhabitants had but gone forth to view the devastation of the Slide, and would shortly return, to thank Heaven for their miraculous escape. All had left separate tokens, by which those who had known the family were made to shed a tear for each. Who has not heard their name? The story has been told far and wide, and will forever be a legend of these mountains. Poets have sung their fate.

There were circumstances which led some to suppose that a stranger had been received into the cottage on this awful night, and had shared the catastrophe of all its inmates. Others denied that there were sufficient grounds for such a conjecture. Woe for the high-souled youth, with his dream of Earthly Immortality! His name and person utterly unknown; his history, his way of life, his plans, a mystery never to be solved, his death and his existence equally a doubt! Whose was the agony of that death moment?

I
WHOSE WAS THE AGONY OF THAT DEATH MOMENT?

Thus ends Hawthorne's story, underlining the terrible irony of the guest's fate: he who wanted nothing more from life than to be remembered is irrevocably forgotten, and those who were content to be forgotten are immortalized forever in legend. There is an added note of irony to the story: if the people had stayed in the cottage, they would have been spared; in attempting to save themselves, they rushed to their destruction.

II
IMPLICATIONS

Consider these statements from the story. Why have they become ironic at the story's end? Do they also expand to say something about life itself?

1. "They had found the 'herb, heart's-ease,' in the bleakest spot of all New England."

2. "Is not the kindred of a common fate a closer tie than that of birth?"

3. " ' . . . it is our nature to desire a monument, be it slate or marble, or a pillar of granite, or a glorious memory in the universal heart of man.' "

4. "Alas! they had quitted their security, and fled right into the pathway of destruction."

5. "The story has been told far and wide, and will forever be a legend of these mountains."

III
TECHNIQUES

Atmosphere

List the things you saw, the sounds you heard, and the feelings you had as you read the story. Can you find a word or two to express the atmosphere that Hawthorne created?

Suspense

What hints does Hawthorne give the reader that this night is not quite usual . . . that a mysterious force seems to be working?

IV
WORDS

From the number of words of Latin derivation you have studied so far, it should be clear that Latin has contributed significantly to the vocabulary of English. "The Ambitious Guest" has many words of Latin origin; for example, *lamentation, solitude, transformed, precipice,* and *felicity.* The infusion of Latin into English began in the middle of the first century with the conquest of Britain by the Romans, who remained there until A.D. 410. Even after the departure of the Romans, Latin words still flowed into English and were in varying degrees anglicized; that is, made into English-sounding words. During the Old English period (449–1100), *alter, demon, martyr, rule,* and *port* (which are not long and unfamiliar) came into English. Borrowed from Latin during the Middle English period (1100–1500) were such words as *subpoena, library, medicine, client,* and *recipe.* The great influx of Latin words, however, occurred during the Modern period (after 1500) when such words as *abdomen, urban, penetrate, lapse,* and *notorious* entered English.

How frustrating must it be for a
brilliant man to find his complicated
thoughts bottled up inside him because he
cannot use his native language
nor conquer a new one.

The
German Refugee

BERNARD MALAMUD

1

Oskar Gassner sits in his cotton-mesh undershirt and summer bathrobe at the window of his stuffy, hot, dark hotel room on West Tenth Street while I cautiously knock. Outside, across the sky, a late-June green twilight fades in darkness. The refugee fumbles for the light and stares at me, hiding despair but not pain.

I was in those days a poor student and would brashly attempt to teach anybody anything for a buck an hour, although I have since learned better. Mostly I gave English lessons to recently-arrived refugees. The college sent me. I had acquired a little experience. Already a few of my students were trying their broken English, theirs and mine, in the American market place. I was then just twenty, on my way into my senior year in college, a skinny, life-hungry kid, eating himself waiting for the next world war to start. It was a rotten cheat. Here I was palpitating to get going, and across the ocean Adolph Hitler, in black boots and a square mustache, was tearing up and spitting out all the flowers. Will I ever forget what went on with Danzig[1] that summer?

Times were still hard from the Depression but anyway I made a little living from the poor refugees. They were all over uptown Broadway in 1939. I had four I tutored—Karl Otto Alp, the former film star; Wolfgang Novak, once a brilliant economist; Friedrich Wilhelm Wolff, who had taught medieval history at Heidelberg;[2] and after the night I met him in his disordered cheap hotel room, Oskar Gassner, the Berlin critic and journalist, at one time on the *Acht Uhr Abenblatt*.[3] They were accomplished men. I had my nerve associating with them, but that's what a world crisis does for people, they get educated.

Oskar was maybe fifty, his thick hair turning gray. He had a big face and heavy hands. His shoulders sagged. His eyes, too, were heavy, a clouded blue; and as he stared at me after I had identified myself, doubt spread in them like underwater currents. It was as if, on seeing me, he had again been defeated. I had to wait until he came to. I stayed at the door in silence. In such cases I would rather be elsewhere but I had to make a living. Finally he opened the door and I entered. Rather, he released it and I was in. "Bitte,"[4] he offered me a seat and didn't know where to sit himself. He would attempt to say something and then stop, as though it could not possibly be said. The room was cluttered with clothing, boxes of books he had managed to get out of Germany, and some paintings. Oskar sat on a box and attempted to fan himself with his meaty hand. "Zis heat," he muttered, forcing his mind to the deed. "Impozzible. I do not know such heat." It was bad enough for me but terrible for him. He had difficulty breathing. He tried to speak, lifted a hand, and let it drop like a dead duck. He breathed as though he were fighting a battle; and maybe he won because after ten minutes we sat and slowly talked.

Like most educated Germans Oskar had at

1. **Danzig,** the Polish city invaded by Hitler in 1939.
2. **Heidelberg,** a German university.
3. **Acht Uhr Abenblatt,** *The Eight O'Clock Evening News,* a German newspaper.
4. **Bitte,** please.

one time studied English. Although he was certain he couldn't say a word he managed to put together a fairly decent, if sometimes comical, English sentence. He misplaced consonants, mixed up nouns and verbs, and mangled idioms, yet we were able at once to communicate. We conversed in English, with an occasional assist by me in pidgin-German or Yiddish, what he called "Jiddish." He had been to America before, last year for a short visit. He had come a month before Kristallnacht, when the Nazis shattered the Jewish store windows and burnt all the synagogues, to see if he could find a job for himself; he had no relatives in America and getting a job would permit him quickly to enter the country. He had been promised something, not in journalism, but with the help of a foundation, as a lecturer. Then he returned to Berlin, and after a frightening delay of six months was permitted to emigrate. He had sold whatever he could, managed to get some paintings, gifts of Bauhaus[5] friends, and some boxes of books

out by bribing two Dutch border guards; he had said goodbye to his wife and left the accursed country. He gazed at me with cloudy eyes. "We parted amicably," he said in German, "my wife was gentile. Her mother was an appalling anti-Semite. They returned to live in Stettin." I asked no questions. Gentile is gentile, Germany is Germany.

His new job was in the Institute for Public Studies, in New York. He was to give a lecture a week in the fall term, and during the next spring, a course, in English translation, in "The Literature of the Weimar Republic."[6] He had never taught before and was afraid to. He was in that way to be introduced to the public, but the thought of giving the lecture in English just about paralyzed him. He didn't see how he could do it. "How is it pozzible? I cannot say two words. I cannot pronounziate. I will make a fool of myself." His melan-

5. **Bauhaus,** a school of design in the city of Weimar.
6. **Weimar Republic,** the German republic (1919–1933) established at Weimar.

choly deepened. Already in the two months since his arrival, and a round of diminishingly expensive hotel rooms, he had had two English tutors, and I was the third. The others had given him up, he said, because his progress was so poor, and he thought he also depressed them. He asked me whether I felt I could do something for him, or should he go to a speech specialist, someone, say, who charged five dollars an hour, and beg his assistance? "You could try him," I said, "and then come back to me." In those days I figured what I knew, I knew. At that he managed a smile. Still, I wanted him to make up his mind, or it would be no confidence down the line. He said, after a while, he would stay with me. If he went to the five-dollar professor it might help his tongue but not his stomach. He would have no money left to eat with. The Institute paid him in advance for the summer but it was only three hundred dollars and all he had.

He looked at me dully. "Ich weiss nicht wie ich weiter machen soll."[7]

I figured it was time to move past the first step. Either we did that quickly or it would be like drilling rock for a long time.

"Let's stand at the mirror," I said.

He rose with a sigh and stood there beside me, I thin, elongated, red-headed, praying for success, his and mine; Oskar, uneasy, fearful, finding it hard to face either of us in the faded round glass above his dresser.

"Please," I said to him, "could you say 'right'?"

"Ghight," he gargled.

"No—right. You put your tongue here." I showed him where as he tensely watched the mirror. I tensely watched him. "The tip of it curls behind the ridge on top, like this."

He placed his tongue where I showed him.

"Please," I said, "now say right."

Oskar's tongue fluttered. "Rright."

"That's good. Now say 'treasure'—that's harder."

"Tgheasure."

"The tongue goes up in front, not in the back of the mouth. Look."

He tried, his brow wet, eyes straining, "Trreasure."

"That's it."

"A miracle," Oskar murmured.

I said if he had done that he could do the rest.

We went for a bus ride up Fifth Avenue and then walked for a while around Central Park Lake. He had put on his German hat, with its hatband bow at the back, a broad-lapeled wool suit, a necktie twice as wide as the one I was wearing, and walked with a small-footed waddle. The night wasn't bad, it had got a bit cooler. There were a few large stars in the sky and they made me sad.

"Do you sink I will succezz?"

"Why not?" I asked.

Later he bought me a bottle of beer.

2

To many of these people, articulate as they were, the great loss was the loss of language— that they could not say what was in them to say. You have some subtle thought and it comes out like a piece of broken bottle. They could, of course, manage to communicate but just to communicate was frustrating. As Karl Otto Alp, the ex-film star who became a buyer for Macy's,[8] put it years later, "I felt like a child, or worse, often like a moron. I am left with myself unexpressed. What I know, indeed, what I am, becomes to me a burden. My tongue hangs useless." The same with Oskar it figures. There was a terrible sense of useless tongue, and I think the reason for his trouble with his other tutors was that to keep from drowning in things unsaid he wanted to swallow the ocean in a gulp: Today he would learn English and tomorrow wow them with an impeccable Fourth of July speech, followed by a successful lecture at the Institute for Public Studies.

We performed our lessons slowly, step by

---

7. "I don't know how I can go on."
8. **Macy's,** a New York department store.

step, everything in its place. After Oskar moved to a two-room apartment in a house on West 85th Street, near the Drive,[9] we met three times a week at four-thirty, worked an hour and a half, then, since it was too hot to cook, had supper at the 72nd Street Automat[10] and conversed on my time. The lessons we divided into three parts: diction exercises and reading aloud; then grammar, because Oskar felt the necessity of it, and composition correction; with conversation, as I said, thrown in at supper. So far as I could see, he was coming along. None of these exercises was giving him as much trouble as they apparently had in the past. He seemed to be learning and his mood lightened. There were moments of elation as he heard his accent flying off. For instance when sink became think. He stopped calling himself "hopelezz," and I became his "bezt teacher," a little joke I liked.

Neither of us said much about the lecture he had to give early in October, and I kept my fingers crossed. It was somehow to come out of what we were doing daily, I think I felt, but exactly how, I had no idea; and to tell the truth, though I didn't say so to Oskar, the lecture frightened me. That and the ten more to follow during the fall term. Later, when I learned that he had been attempting with the help of the dictionary, to write in English and had produced "a complete disahster," I suggested maybe he ought to stick to German and we could afterwards both try to put it into passable English. I was cheating when I said that because my German is meager, enough to read simple stuff but certainly not good enough for serious translation; anyway, the idea was to get Oskar into production and worry about translating later. He sweated with it, from enervating[11] morning to exhausted night, but no matter what language he tried, though he had been a professional writer for a generation and knew his subject cold, the lecture refused to move past page one.

It was a sticky, hot July and the heat didn't help at all.

3

I had met Oskar at the end of June and by the seventeenth of July we were no longer doing lessons. They had foundered on the "impozzible" lecture. He had worked on it each day in frenzy and growing despair. After writing more than a hundred opening pages he furiously flung his pen against the wall, shouting he could no longer write in that filthy tongue. He cursed the German language. He hated the country and the people. After that what was bad became worse. When he gave up attempting to write the lecture, he stopped making progress in English. He seemed to forget what he already knew. His tongue thickened and the accent returned in all its fruitiness. The little he had to say was in handcuffed and tortured English. The only German I heard him speak was in a whisper to himself. I doubt he knew he was talking it. That ended our formal work together, though I did drop in every other day or so to sit with him. For hours he sat motionless in a large green velours armchair, hot enough to broil in, and through tall windows stared at the colorless sky above 85th Street, with a wet depressed eye.

Then once he said to me, "If I do not this legture prepare, I will take my life."

"Let's begin, Oskar," I said. "You dictate and I'll write. The ideas count, not the spelling."

He didn't answer so I stopped talking.

He had plunged into an involved melancholy. We sat for hours, often in profound silence. This was alarming to me, though I had already had some experience with such depression. Wolfgang Novak, the economist, though English came more easily to him, was another. His problems arose mainly, I think, from physical illness. And he felt a greater

---

9. **Drive,** Riverside Drive, an avenue running along the Hudson River.
10. **Automat,** a chain of inexpensive restaurants in New York.
11. **enervating**\ˈĕn·ər 'vāt·iŋ\ lessening vitality and strength.

sense of the lost country than Oskar. Sometimes in the early evening I persuaded Oskar to come with me for a short walk on the Drive. The tail end of sunsets over the Palisades[12] seemed to appeal to him. At least he looked. He would put on full regalia—hat, suit coat, tie, no matter how hot or what I suggested—and we went slowly down the stairs, I wondering whether he would ever make it to the bottom. He seemed to me always suspended between two floors.

We walked slowly uptown, stopping to sit on a bench and watch night rise above the Hudson. When we returned to his room, if I sensed he had loosened up a bit, we listened to music on the radio; but if I tried to sneak in a news broadcast, he said to me, "Please, I can not more stand of world misery." I shut off the radio. He was right, it was a time of no good news. I squeezed my brain. What could I sell him? Was it good news to be alive? Who could argue the point? Sometimes I read aloud to him—I remember he liked the first part of *Life on the Mississippi*.[13] We still went to the Automat once or twice a week, he perhaps out of habit, because he didn't feel like going anywhere—I to get him out of his room. Oskar ate little, he toyed with a spoon. His dull eyes looked as though they had been squirted with a dark dye.

Once after a momentary cooling rainstorm we sat on newspapers on a wet bench overlooking the river and Oskar at last began to talk. In tormented English he conveyed his intense and everlasting hatred of the Nazis for destroying his career, uprooting his life after half a century, and flinging him like a piece of bleeding meat to the hawks. He cursed them thickly, the German nation, an inhuman, conscienceless, merciless people. "They are pigs mazquerading as peacogs," he said. "I feel certain that my wife, in her heart, was a Jew hater." It was a terrible bitterness, an eloquence almost without vocabulary. He became silent again. I hoped to hear more about his wife but decided not to ask.

Afterwards in the dark Oskar confessed that he had attempted suicide during his first week in America. He was living, at the end of May, in a small hotel, and had one night filled himself with barbiturates; but his phone had fallen off the table and the hotel operator had sent up the elevator boy who found him unconscious and called the police. He was revived in the hospital.

"I did not mean to do it," he said, "it was a mistage."

"Don't ever think of it again," I said, "it's total defeat."

"I don't," he said wearily, "because it is so arduouz[14] to come back to life."

"Please, for any reason whatever."

Afterwards when we were walking, he surprised me by saying, "Maybe we ought to try now the legture onze more."

We trudged back to the house and he sat at his hot desk, I trying to read as he slowly began to reconstruct the first page of his lecture. He wrote, of course, in German.

4

He got nowhere. We were back to nothing, to sitting in silence in the heat. Sometimes, after a few minutes, I had to take off before his mood overcame mine. One afternoon I came unwillingly up the stairs—there were times I felt momentary surges of irritation with him—and was frightened to find Oskar's door ajar. When I knocked no one answered. As I stood there, chilled down the spine, I realized I was thinking about the possibility of his attempting suicide again. "Oskar?" I went into the apartment, looked into both rooms and the bathroom, but he wasn't there. I thought he might have drifted out to get something from a store and took the opportunity to look quickly around. There was noth-

---

12. **Palisades**, the line of cliffs extending along the west bank of the lower Hudson River.
13. **Life on the Mississippi**, a book by Mark Twain.
14. Oskar means **arduous**\ˈärj·ə·wəs\ difficult; marked by great effort.

ing startling in the medicine chest, no pills but aspirin, no iodine. Thinking, for some reason, of a gun, I searched his desk drawer. In it I found a thin-paper airmail letter from Germany. Even if I had wanted to, I couldn't read the handwriting, but as I held it in my hand I did make out a sentence: "Ich bin dir siebenundzwanzig Jahre treu gewesen."[15] There was no gun in the drawer. I shut it and stopped looking. It had occurred to me if you want to kill yourself all you need is a straight pin. When Oskar returned he said he had been sitting in the public library, unable to read.

Now we are once more enacting the changeless scene, curtain rising on two speechless characters in a furnished apartment, I, in a straightback chair, Oskar in the velours armchair that smothered rather than supported him, his flesh gray, the big gray face, unfocused, sagging. I reached over to switch on the radio but he barely looked at me in a way that begged no. I then got up to leave but Oskar, clearing his throat, thickly asked me to stay. I stayed, thinking, was there more to this than I could see into? His problems, of course, were real enough, but could there be something more than a refugee's displacement, alienation, financial insecurity, being in a strange land without friends or a speakable tongue? My speculation was the old one; not all drown in this ocean, why does he? After a while I shaped the thought and asked him, was there something below the surface, invisible? I was full of this thing from college, and wondered if there mightn't be some unknown quantity in his depression that a psychiatrist maybe might help him with, enough to get him started on his lecture.

He meditated on this and after a few minutes haltingly said he had been psychoanalyzed in Vienna as a young man. "Just the jusual drek,"[16] he said, "fears and fantazies that afterwaards no longer bothered me."

"They don't now?"

"Not."

"You've written many articles and lectures before," I said. "What I can't understand, though I know how hard the situation is, is why you can never get past page one."

He half lifted his hand. "It is a paralyzis of my will. The whole legture is clear in my mind but the minute I write down a single word— or in English or in German—I have a terrible fear I will not be able to write the negst. As though someone has thrown a stone at a window and the whole house—the whole idea, zmashes. This repeats, until I am dezperate."

He said the fear grew as he worked that he would die before he completed the lecture, or if not that, he would write it so disgracefully he would wish for death. The fear immobilized him.

"I have lozt faith. I do not—not longer possezz my former value of myself. In my life there has been too much illusion."

I tried to believe what I was saying: "Have confidence, the feeling will pass."

"Confidenze I have not. For this and alzo whatever elze I have lozt I thank the Nazis."

5

It was by then mid-August and things were growing steadily worse wherever one looked. The Poles were mobilizing for war. Oskar hardly moved. I was full of worries though I pretended calm weather.

He sat in his massive armchair with sick eyes, breathing like a wounded animal.

"Who can write aboud Walt Whitman in such terrible times?"

"Why don't you change the subject?"

"It mages no differenze what is the subject. It is all uzelezz."

I came every day, as a friend, neglecting my other students and therefore my livelihood. I had a panicky feeling that if things went on as they were going they would end in Oskar's suicide; and I felt a frenzied desire to prevent that. What's more, I was sometimes afraid I was myself becoming melancholy, a

---

15. "I have been faithful to you for twenty-seven years."

16. **drek,** trash; junk.

new talent, call it, of taking less pleasure in my little pleasures. And the heat continued, oppressive, relentless. We thought of escape into the country but neither of us had the money. One day I bought Oskar a second-hand fan—wondering why we hadn't thought of that before—and he sat in the breeze for hours each day, until after a week, shortly after the Soviet-Nazi nonaggression pact was signed, the motor gave out. He could not sleep at night and sat at his desk with a wet towel on his head, still attempting to write his lecture. He wrote reams on a treadmill, it came out nothing. When he slept out of exhaustion he had fantastic frightening dreams of the Nazis inflicting tortures on him, sometimes forcing him to look upon the corpses of those they had slain. In one dream he told me about, he had gone back to Germany to visit his wife. She wasn't home and he had been directed to a cemetery. There, though the tombstone read another name, her blood seeped out of the earth above her shallow grave. He groaned aloud at the memory.

Afterwards he told me something about her. They had met as students, lived together, and were married at twenty-three. It wasn't a very happy marriage. She had turned into a sickly woman, physically unable to have children. "Something was wrong with her interior structure."

Though I asked no questions, Oskar said, "I offered her to come with me here but she refused this."

"For what reason?"

"She did not think I wished her to come."

"Did you?" I asked.

"Not," he said.

He explained he had lived with her for almost twenty-seven years under difficult circumstances. She had been ambivalent about their Jewish friends and his relatives, though outwardly she seemed not a prejudiced person. But her mother was always a violent anti-Semite.

"I have nothing to blame myself," Oskar said.

He took to his bed. I took to the New York Public Library. I read some of the German poets he was trying to write about, in English translation. Then I read *Leaves of Grass* and wrote down what I thought one or two of them had got from Whitman. One day, towards the end of August, I brought Oskar what I had written. It was in good part guessing but my idea wasn't to write the lecture for him. He lay on his back, motionless, and listened utterly sadly to what I had written. Then he said, no, it wasn't the love of death they had got from Whitman—that ran through German poetry—but it was most of all his feeling for Brudermensch,[17] his humanity.

"But this does not grow long on German earth," he said, "and is soon deztroyed."

I said I was sorry I had got it wrong, but he thanked me anyway.

I left, defeated, and as I was going down the stairs, heard the sound of someone sobbing. I will quit this, I thought, it has gotten to be too much for me. I can't drown with him.

I stayed home the next day, tasting a new kind of private misery too old for somebody my age, but that same night Oskar called me on the phone, blessing me wildly for having read those notes to him. He had got up to write me a letter to say what I had missed, and it ended by his having written half the lecture. He had slept all day and tonight intended to finish it up.

"I thank you," he said, "for much, alzo including your faith in me."

"Thank God," I said, not telling him I had just about lost it.

6

Oskar completed his lecture—wrote and rewrote it—during the first week in September. The Nazis had invaded Poland, and though we were greatly troubled, there was some sense of release; maybe the brave Poles would beat them. It took another week to translate

---

17. **Brudermensch,** literally, brother-men.

the lecture, but here we had the assistance of Friedrich Wilhelm Wolff, the historian, a gentle, erudite man, who liked translating and promised his help with future lectures. We then had about two weeks to work on Oskar's delivery. The weather had changed, and so, slowly, had he. He had awakened from defeat, battered, after a wearying battle. He had lost close to twenty pounds. His complexion was still gray; when I looked at his face I expected to see scars, but it had lost its flabby unfocused quality. His blue eyes had returned to life and he walked with quick steps, as though to pick up a few for all the steps he hadn't taken during those long hot days he had lain torpid in his room.

We went back to our former routine, meeting three late afternoons a week for diction, grammar, and the other exercises. I taught him the phonetic alphabet and transcribed long lists of words he was mispronouncing. He worked many hours trying to fit each sound into place, holding half a matchstick between his teeth to keep his jaws apart as he exercised his tongue. All this can be a dreadfully boring business unless you think you have a future. Looking at him I realized what's meant when somebody is called "another man."

The lecture, which I now knew by heart, went off well. The director of the Institute had invited a number of prominent people. Oskar was the first refugee they had employed and there was a move to make the public cognizant of what was then a new ingredient in American life. Two reporters had come with a lady photographer. The auditorium of the Institute was crowded. I sat in the last row, promising to put up my hand if he couldn't be heard, but it wasn't necessary. Oskar, in a blue suit, his hair cut, was of course nervous, but you couldn't see it unless you studied him. When he stepped up to the lectern, spread out his manuscript, and spoke his first English sentence in public, my heart hesitated; only he and I, of everybody there, had any idea of the anguish he had been through. His enunciation wasn't at all bad—a

few s's for th's, and he once said bag for back, but otherwise he did all right. He read poetry well—in both languages—and though Walt Whitman, in his mouth, sounded a little as though he had come to the shores of Long Island as a German immigrant, still the poetry read as poetry:

> "And I know the spirit of God is the brother of my own,
> And that all the men ever born are also my brothers, and the women my sisters and lovers,
> And that the kelson[18] of creation is love . . ."

Oskar read it as though he believed it. Warsaw had fallen but the verses were somehow protective. I sat back conscious of two things: how easy it is to hide the deepest wounds; and the pride I felt in the job I had done.

7

Two days later I came up the stairs into Oskar's apartment to find a crowd there. The refugee, his face beet-red, lips bluish, a trace of froth in the corners of his mouth, lay on the floor in his limp pajamas, two firemen on their knees, working over him with an inhalator. The windows were open and the air stank.

A policeman asked me who I was and I couldn't answer.

"No, oh no."

I said no but it was unchangeably yes. He had taken his life—gas—I hadn't even thought of the stove in the kitchen.

"Why?" I asked myself. "Why did he do it?" Maybe it was the fate of Poland on top of everything else, but the only answer anyone could come up with was Oskar's scribbled note that he wasn't well, and had left Martin Goldberg all his possessions. I am Martin Goldberg.

---

18. **kelson**\ˈkĕl·sən\ the structure that stiffens and strengthens the keel of a boat; hence, the foundation of the world, the strength that holds it together.

I was sick for a week, had no desire either to inherit or investigate, but I thought I ought to look through his things before the court impounded them, so I spent a morning sitting in the depths of Oskar's armchair, trying to read his correspondence. I had found in the top drawer a thin packet of letters from his wife and an airmail letter of recent date from his anti-Semitic mother-in-law.

She writes in a tight script it takes me hours to decipher, that her daughter, after Oskar abandons her, against her own mother's fervent pleas and anguish, is converted to Judaism by a vengeful rabbi. One night the Brown Shirts appear, and though the mother wildly waves her bronze crucifix in their faces, they drag Frau Gassner, together with the other Jews, out of the apartment house, and transport them in lorries[19] to a small border town in conquered Poland. There, it is rumored, she is shot in the head and topples into an open tank ditch, with the naked Jewish men, their wives and children, some Polish soldiers, and a handful of gypsies.

I
THE FINAL IRONY

Oskar's bitterness toward the Nazis for uprooting him, destroying his career, and tossing him away is deep and fierce. But even deeper is his anger toward his wife of twenty-seven years with whom he had shared not the happiest of marriages. He felt cheated.

The news that his wife had become a Jew after he left and had been executed in Poland is the final irony for this man. Imagine Oskar's horror when he realizes that for twenty-seven years he had misunderstood the feelings of the person closest to him. He had cheated himself.

II
IMPLICATIONS

A. Discuss the meaning of the following quotations from the story.

1. ". . . that's what a world crisis does for people, they get educated."

2. "To many of these people, articulate as they were, the great loss was the loss of language—that they could not say what was in them to say."

3. ". . . how easy it is to hide the deepest wounds."

B. How do you feel about the ideas suggested in the following statements.

1. The irony in this selection is double-pronged: Martin Goldberg does not really understand Oskar; Oskar never understood his wife.

2. When things begin going wrong in one area of a person's life, they tend to go wrong in other areas as well.

3. No one can ever really know another person.

III
TECHNIQUES

Atmosphere

1. What was your mood when you finished reading "The German Refugee"?

2. Give four or five details in the story that contributed to this feeling.

3. How does Section 7 affect your final reaction to the story?

Suspense

By informing the reader early in the story of the deadline that Oskar must meet, a question is immediately raised—will Oskar learn to speak English well enough to give the lecture? Now quickly skim through the story and see at which point you have a glimmering that Oskar can succeed?

Why does Section 7 come as a surprise? Does this add to or detract from the impact?

---

19. **lorries**\\ˈlȯ·rēz\\ motor trucks.

One of life's little ironies
is having a newfound enthusiasm
lead one into a trap.

Suppressed Desires

SUSAN GLASPELL

Characters

(in order of appearance)

HENRIETTA BREWSTER
STEPHEN BREWSTER
MABEL

SCENE I

A studio apartment in an upper story, *Washington Square South. Through an immense north window in the back wall appear tree tops and the upper part of the Washington Arch. Beyond it you look up Fifth Avenue. Near the window is a big table, loaded at one end with serious-looking books and austere scientific periodicals. At the other end are architect's drawings, blue prints, dividing compasses, square, ruler, etc. At the left is a door leuding to the rest of the apartment; at the right the outer door. A breakfast table is set for three, but only two are seated at it—*HENRIETTA *and* STEPHEN BREWSTER. *As the curtains withdraw,* STEVE *pushes back his coffee cup and sits dejected.*

Reprinted by permission of DODD, MEAD & COMPANY from PLAYS by Susan Glaspell. Copyright 1920 by Dodd, Mead & Company, Inc. Copyright renewed 1948 by Susan Glaspell.

HENRIETTA. It isn't the coffee, Steve dear. There's nothing the matter with the coffee. There's something the matter with *you*.

STEVE. (*Doggedly.*) There may be something the matter with my stomach.

HENRIETTA. (*Scornfully.*) Your stomach! The trouble is not with your stomach but in your subconscious mind.

STEVE. Subconscious piffle! (*Takes morning paper and tries to read.*)

HENRIETTA. Steve, you never used to be so disagreeable. You certainly have got some sort of a complex.[1] You're all inhibited.[2] You're no longer open to new ideas. You won't listen to a word about psychoanalysis.[3]

STEVE. A word! I've listened to volumes!

HENRIETTA. You've ceased to be creative in architecture—your work isn't going well. You're not sleeping well——

STEVE. How can I sleep, Henrietta, when you're always waking me up to find out what I'm dreaming?

HENRIETTA. But dreams are so important, Steve. If you'd tell yours to Dr. Russell he'd find out exactly what's wrong with you.

STEVE. There's nothing wrong with me.

HENRIETTA. You don't even talk as well as you used to.

STEVE. Talk? I can't say a thing without you looking at me in that dark fashion you have when you're on the trail of a complex.

HENRIETTA. This very irritability indicates that you're suffering from some suppressed desire.

STEVE. I'm suffering from a suppressed desire for a little peace.

HENRIETTA. Dr. Russell is doing simply wonderful things with nervous cases. Won't you go to him, Steve?

1. **complex**\ˈkäm ˈplĕks\ desires and memories suppressed (that is, prevented from becoming conscious) that affect one's personality and behavior.
2. **inhibited**\'in ˈhĭb·ə·təd\ prevented by some inner hindrance from free activity, expression, or functioning.
3. **psychoanalysis**\ˈsai·kə·wə ˈnăl·ə·səs\ a method of treating emotional disorders by bringing repressed desires to consciousness.

STEVE. (*Slamming down his newspaper.*) No, Henrietta, I won't!

HENRIETTA. But Stephen——!

STEVE. Tst! I hear Mabel coming. Let's not be at each other's throats the first day of her visit.

(*He take out cigarettes.* MABEL *comes in from door left, the side opposite* STEVE, *so that he is facing her. She is wearing a rather fussy negligee in contrast to* HENRI-ETTA, *who wears "radical" clothes.* MABEL *is what is called plump.*)

MABEL. Good morning.

HENRIETTA. Oh, here you are, little sister.

STEVE. Good morning, Mabel.

(MABEL *nods to him and turns, her face lighting up, to* HENRIETTA.)

HENRIETTA. (*Giving* MABEL *a hug as she leans against her.*) It's so good to have you here. I was going to let you sleep, thinking you'd be tired after the long trip. Sit down. There'll be fresh toast in a minute and (*Rising.*) will you have——

MABEL. Oh, I ought to have told you, Henrietta. Don't get anything for me. I'm not eating breakfast.

HENRIETTA. (*At first in mere surprise.*) Not eating breakfast? (*She sits down, then leans toward* MABEL *who is seated now, and scrutinizes her.*)

STEVE. (*Half to himself.*) The psychoanalytical look!

HENRIETTA. Mabel, why are you not eating breakfast?

MABEL. (*A little startled.*) Why, no particular reason. I just don't care much for breakfast, and they say it keeps down—(*A hand on her hip—the gesture of one who is reducing.*) that is, it's a good thing to go without it.

HENRIETTA. Don't you sleep well? Did you sleep well last night?

MABEL. Oh, yes, I slept all right. Yes, I slept fine last night, only (*Laughing.*) I did have the funniest dream!

STEVE. S-h! S-t!

HENRIETTA. (*Moving closer.*) And what did you dream, Mabel?

STEVE. Look-a-here, Mabel, I feel it's my duty to put you on. Don't tell Henrietta your dreams. If you do she'll find out that you have an underground desire to kill your father and marry your mother——

HENRIETTA. Don't be absurd, Stephen Brewster. (*Sweetly to* MABEL.) What was your dream, dear?

MABEL. (*Laughing.*) Well, I dreamed I was a hen.

HENRIETTA. A hen?

MABEL. Yes; and I was pushing along through a crowd as fast as I could, but being a hen I couldn't walk very fast—it was like having a tight skirt, you know; and there was some sort of creature in a blue cap—you know how mixed up dreams are—and it kept shouting after me, "Step, Hen! Step, Hen!" until I got all excited and just couldn't move at all.

HENRIETTA. (*Resting chin in palm and peering.*) You say you became much excited?

MABEL. (*Laughing.*) Oh, yes; I was in a terrible state.

HENRIETTA. (*Leaning back, murmurs.*) This is significant.

STEVE. She dreams she's a hen. She is told to step lively. She becomes violently agitated. What can it mean?

HENRIETTA. (*Turning impatiently from him.*) Mabel, do you know anything about psychoanalysis?

MABEL. (*Feebly.*) Oh—not much. No—I—(*Brightening.*) It's something about the war, isn't it?

STEVE. Not that kind of war.

MABEL. (*Abashed.*) I thought it might be the name of a new explosive.

STEVE. It *is*.

MABEL. (*Apologetically to* HENRIETTA, *who is frowning.*) You see, Henrietta, I—we do not live in touch with intellectual things, as you do. Bob being a dentist—somehow our friends—

STEVE. (*Softly.*) Oh, to be a dentist! (*Goes to window and stands looking out.*)

HENRIETTA. Don't you see anything more of that editorial writer—what was his name?

MABEL. Lyman Eggleston?

HENRIETTA. Yes, Eggleston. He was in touch with things. Don't you see him?

MABEL. Yes, I see him once in a while. Bob doesn't like him very well.

HENRIETTA. Your husband does not like Lyman Eggleston? (*Mysteriously.*) Mabel, are you perfectly happy with your husband?

STEVE. (*Sharply.*) Oh, come now, Henrietta— that's going a little strong!

HENRIETTA. Are you perfectly happy with him, Mabel?

(STEVE *goes to work-table.*)

MABEL. Why—yes—I guess so. Why—of course I am!

HENRIETTA. Are you happy? Or do you only think you are? Or do you only think you *ought* to be?

MABEL. Why, Henrietta, I don't know what you mean!

STEVE. (*Seizes stack of books and magazines and dumps them on the breakfast table.*) This is what she means, Mabel. Psychoanalysis. My work-table groans with it. Books by Freud, the new Messiah; books by Jung,[4] the new St. Paul; the *Psychoanalytical Review*—back numbers two-fifty per.

MABEL. But what's it all about?

STEVE. All about your sub-un-non-conscious mind and desires you know not of. They may be doing you a great deal of harm. You may go crazy with them. Oh, yes! People are doing it right and left. Your dreaming you're a hen—(*Shakes his head darkly.*)

HENRIETTA. Any fool can ridicule anything.

MABEL. (*Hastily, to avert a quarrel.*) But what do you say it is, Henrietta?

STEVE. (*Looking at his watch.*) Oh, if Henrietta's going to start that! (*During* HENRI-ETTA's *next speech settles himself at work-table and sharpens a lead pencil.*)

HENRIETTA. It's like this, Mabel. You want something. You think you can't have it. You think it's wrong. So you try to think you don't want it. Your mind protects you— avoids pain—by refusing to think the forbidden thing. But it's there just the same. It stays there shut up in your unconscious mind, and it festers.

STEVE. Sort of an ingrowing mental toenail.

HENRIETTA. Precisely. The forbidden impulse is there full of energy which has simply got to do something. It breaks into your consciousness in disguise, masks itself in dreams, makes all sorts of trouble. In extreme cases it drives you insane.

MABEL. (*With a gesture of horror.*) Oh!

HENRIETTA. (*Reassuring.*) But psychoanalysis has found out how to save us from that. It brings into consciousness the suppressed desire that was making all the trouble. Psychoanalysis is simply the latest scientific method of preventing and curing insanity.

STEVE. (*From his table.*) It is also the latest scientific method of separating families.

HENRIETTA. (*Mildly.*) Families that ought to be separated.

STEVE. The Dwights, for instance. You must have met them, Mabel, when you were here before. Helen was living, apparently, in peace and happiness with good old Joe. Well—she went to this psychoanalyzer—she was "psyched," and biff!—bang!—home she comes with an unsuppressed desire to leave her husband. (*He starts work, drawing lines on a drawing board with a T-square.*)

MABEL. How terrible! Yes, I remember Helen Dwight. But—but did she have such a desire?

STEVE. First she'd known of it.

MABEL. And she *left* him?

HENRIETTA. (*Coolly.*) Yes, she did.

MABEL. Wasn't he good to her?

---

4. **Freud**\froid\, **Jung**\yuŋ\ important pioneers in the psychoanalytical field.

HENRIETTA. Why, yes, good enough.

MABEL. Wasn't he kind to her?

HENRIETTA. Oh, yes—kind to her.

MABEL. She left her good, kind husband——!

HENRIETTA. Oh, Mabel! "Left her good, kind husband!" How naïve—forgive me, dear, but how bourgeois[5] you are! She came to know herself. And she had the courage!

MABEL. I may be very naïve and—bourgeois— but I don't see the good of a new science that breaks up homes.

(STEVE *applauds.*)

STEVE. In enlightening Mabel, we mustn't neglect to mention the case of Art Holden's private secretary, Mary Snow, who has just been informed of her suppressed desire for her employer.

MABEL. Why, I think it is terrible, Henrietta! It would be better if we didn't know such things about ourselves.

HENRIETTA. No, Mabel, that is the old way.

MABEL. But—but her employer? Is he married?

STEVE. (*Grunts.*) Wife and four children.

MABEL. Well, then, what good does it do the girl to be told she has a desire for him? There's nothing can be done about it.

HENRIETTA. Old institutions will have to be re-shaped so that something can be done in such cases. It happens, Mabel, that this suppressed desire was on the point of landing Mary Snow in the insane asylum. Are you so tight-minded that you'd rather have her in the insane asylum than break the conventions?

MABEL. But—but have people always had these awful suppressed desires?

HENRIETTA. Always.

STEVE. But they've just been discovered.

HENRIETTA. The harm they do has just been discovered. And free, sane people must face the fact that they have to be dealt with.

MABEL. (*Stoutly.*) I don't believe they have them in Chicago.

HENRIETTA. (*Business of giving* MABEL *up.*) People "have them" wherever the living Libido—the center of the soul's energy—is in conflict with petrified moral codes. That means everywhere in civilization. Psycho-analysis——

STEVE. Good grief! I've got the roof in the cellar!

HENRIETTA. The roof in the cellar!

STEVE. (*Holding plan at arm's length.*) That's what psychoanalysis does!

HENRIETTA. That's what psychoanalysis could *un*-do. Is it any wonder I'm concerned about Steve? He dreamed the other night that the walls of his room melted away and he found himself alone in a forest. Don't you see how significant it is for an architect to have *walls* slip away from him? It symbolizes his loss of grip in his work. There's some suppressed desire——

STEVE. (*Hurling his ruined plan viciously to the floor.*) Suppressed!

MABEL. (*Looking at* STEVE, *who is tearing his hair.*) Don't you think it would be a good thing, Henrietta, if we went somewhere else?

(*They rise and begin to pick up the dishes.* MABEL *drops a plate which breaks.* HENRIETTA *draws up short and looks at her—the psychoanalytic look.*)

I'm sorry, Henrietta. One of the Spode plates, too. (*Surprised and resentful as* HENRIETTA *continues to peer at her.*) Don't take it so to heart, Henrietta.

HENRIETTA. I can't help taking it to heart.

MABEL. I'll get you another. (*Pause. More sharply as* HENRIETTA *does not answer.*) I said I'll get you another plate, Henrietta.

HENRIETTA. It's not the plate.

MABEL. For heaven's sake, what is it then?

HENRIETTA. It's the significant little false movement that made you drop it.

MABEL. Well, I suppose everyone makes a false movement once in a while.

HENRIETTA. Yes, Mabel, but these false movements all mean something.

---

5. **bourgeois**\ˈburzh 'wä\ middle-class; ordinary; not intellectual.

MABEL. (*About to cry.*) I don't think that's very nice! It was just because I happened to think of that Mabel Snow you were talking about——

HENRIETTA. *Mabel* Snow!

MABEL. Snow—Snow—well, what was her name, then?

HENRIETTA. Her name is Mary. You substituted *your own* name for hers.

MABEL. Well, *Mary* Snow, then; *Mary* Snow. I never heard her name but once. I don't see anything to make such a fuss about.

HENRIETTA. (*Gently.*) Mabel dear—mistakes like that in names—

MABEL. (*Desperately.*) They don't mean something, too, do they?

HENRIETTA. (*Gently.*) I am sorry, dear, but they do.

MABEL. But I'm always doing that!

HENRIETTA. (*After a start of horror.*) My poor little sister, tell me about it.

MABEL. About what?

HENRIETTA. About your not being happy. About your longing for another sort of life.

MABEL. But I *don't*.

HENRIETTA. Ah, I understand these things, dear. You feel Bob is limiting you to a life in which you do not feel free——

MABEL. Henrietta! When did I ever say such a thing?

HENRIETTA. You said you are not in touch with things intellectual. You showed your feeling that it is Bob's profession—that has engendered a resentment which has colored your whole life with him.

MABEL. Why—Henri*etta*!

HENRIETTA. Don't be afraid of me, little sister. There's nothing can shock me or turn me from you. I am not like that. I wanted you to come for this visit because I had a feeling that you needed more from life than you were getting. No one of these things I have seen would excite my suspicion. It's the combination. You don't eat breakfast. (*Enumerating on her fingers.*) You make false moves; you substitute your own name for

the name of another *whose love is misdirected.* You're nervous; you *look* queer; in your eyes there's a frightened look that is most unlike you. And this dream. A *hen.* Come with me this afternoon to Dr. Russell! Your whole life may be at stake, Mabel.

MABEL. (*Gasping.*) Henrietta, I—you—you always were the smartest in the family, and all that, but—this is terrible! I don't think we *ought* to think such things. (*Brightening.*) Why, I'll tell you why I dreamed I was a hen. It was because last night, telling about that time in Chicago, you said I was as mad as a wet hen.

HENRIETTA. (*Superior.*) Did you dream you were a *wet* hen?

MABEL. (*Forced to admit it.*) No.

HENRIETTA. No. You dreamed you were a *dry* hen. And why, being a hen, were you urged to step?

MABEL. Maybe it's because when I am getting on a street car it always irritates me to have them call "Step lively."

HENRIETTA. No, Mabel, that is only a child's view of it—if you will forgive me. You see merely the elements used in the dream. You do not see into the dream; you do not see its meaning. This dream of the hen——

STEVE. Hen—hen—wet hen—dry hen—mad hen! (*Jumps up in a rage.*) Let me out of this!

HENRIETTA. (*Hastily picking up dishes, speaks soothingly.*) Just a minute, dear, and we'll have things so you can work in quiet. Mabel and I are going to sit in my room. (*She goes out left, carrying dishes.*)

STEVE. (*Seizing hat and coat from an alcove near the outside door.*) I'm going to be psychoanalyzed. I'm going now! I'm going straight to that infallible doctor of hers— that priest of this new religion. If he's got honesty enough to tell Henrietta there's nothing the matter with my unconscious mind, perhaps I can be let alone about it, and then I *will* be all right. (*From the door in a loud voice.*) Don't tell Henrietta I'm going. It might take weeks, and I couldn't stand all the talk. (*He hurries out.*)

HENRIETTA. (*Returning.*) Where's Steve? Gone? (*With a hopeless gesture.*) You see how impatient he is—how unlike himself! I tell you, Mabel, I'm nearly distracted about Steve.

MABEL. I think he's a little distracted, too.

HENRIETTA. Well, if he's gone—you might as well stay here. I have a committee meeting at the bookshop, and will have to leave you to yourself for an hour or two. (*As she puts her hat on, taking it from the alcove where* STEVE *found his, her eye, lighting up almost carnivorously, falls on an enormous volume on the floor beside the work-table. The book has been half hidden by the wastebasket. She picks it up and carries it around the table toward* MABEL.) Here, dear, is one of the simplest statements of psychoanalysis. You just read this and then we can talk more intelligently.

(MABEL *takes volume and staggers back under its weight to chair rear center,* HENRIETTA *goes to outer door, stops and asks abruptly.*)

How old is Lyman Eggleston?

MABEL. (*Promptly.*) He isn't forty yet. Why, what made you ask that, Henrietta? (*As she turns her head to look at* HENRIETTA *her hands move toward the upper corners of the book balanced on her knees.*)

HENRIETTA. Oh, nothing. Au revoir.

(*She goes out.* MABEL *stares at the ceiling. The book slides to the floor. She starts; looks at the book, then at the broken plate on the table.*)

MABEL. The plate! The book! (*She lifts her eyes, leans forward, elbow on knee, chin on knuckles and plaintively queries.*) Am I unhappy?

(*Curtain.*)

SCENE II

Two weeks later. The stage is as in Scene I, except that the breakfast table has been removed. During the first few minutes the dusk of a winter afternoon deepens. Out of the darkness spring rows of double street-lights almost meeting in the distance. HENRIETTA *is at the psychoanalytical end of* STEVE's *work-table, surrounded by open books and periodicals, writing.* STEVE *enters briskly.*

STEVE. What are you doing, my dear?

HENRIETTA. My paper for the Liberal Club.

STEVE. Your paper on——?

HENRIETTA. On a subject which does not have your sympathy.

STEVE. Oh, I'm not sure I'm wholly out of sympathy with psychoanalysis, Henrietta. You worked it so hard. I couldn't even take a bath without its meaning something.

HENRIETTA. (*Loftily.*) I talked it because I knew you needed it.

STEVE. You haven't said much about it these last two weeks. Uh—your faith in it hasn't weakened any?

HENRIETTA. Weakened? It's grown stronger with each new thing I've come to know. And Mabel. She is with Dr. Russell now. Dr. Russell is wonderful! From what Mabel tells me I believe his analysis is going to prove that I was right. Today I discovered a remarkable confirmation of my theory in the hen-dream.

STEVE. What is your theory?

HENRIETTA. Well, you know about Lyman Eggleston. I've wondered about him. I've never seen him, but I know he's less bourgeois than Mabel's other friends—more intellectual—and she doesn't see much of him because Bob doesn't like him.

STEVE. But what's the confirmation?

HENRIETTA. Today I noticed the first syllable of his name.

STEVE. Ly?

HENRIETTA. No—egg.

STEVE. Egg?

HENRIETTA. (*Patiently.*) Mabel dreamed she was a *hen*. (STEVE *laughs*.) You wouldn't laugh if you knew how important names are in interpreting dreams. Freud is full of just such cases in which a whole hidden complex is revealed by a single significant syllable—like this egg.

STEVE. Doesn't the traditional relation of hen and egg suggest rather a maternal feeling?

HENRIETTA. There is something maternal in Mabel's love, of course, but that's only one element.

STEVE. Well, suppose Mabel hasn't a suppressed desire to be this gentleman's mother, but his beloved. What's to be done about it? What about Bob? Don't you think it's going to be a little rough on him?

HENRIETTA. That can't be helped. Bob, like everyone else, must face the facts of life. If Dr. Russell should arrive independently at this same interpretation I shall not hesitate to advise Mabel to leave her present husband.

STEVE. Um—hum! (*The lights go up on Fifth Avenue.* STEVE *goes to the window and looks out.*) How long is it we've lived here, Henrietta?

HENRIETTA. Why, this is the third year, Steve.

STEVE. I—we—one would miss this view if one went away, wouldn't one?

HENRIETTA. How strangely you speak! Oh, Stephen, I *wish* you'd go to Dr. Russell. Don't think my fears have abated because I've been able to restrain myself. I had to on account of Mabel. But now, dear—won't you go?

STEVE. I—(*He breaks off, turns on the light, then comes and sits beside* HENRIETTA.) How long have we been married, Henrietta?

HENRIETTA. Stephen, I don't understand you! You *must* go to Dr. Russell.

STEVE. I have gone.

HENRIETTA. You—what?

STEVE. (*Jauntily.*) Yes, Henrietta, I've been psyched.

HENRIETTA. You went to Dr. Russell?

STEVE. The same.

HENRIETTA. And what did he say?

STEVE. He said—I—I was a little surprised by what he said, Henrietta.

HENRIETTA. (*Breathlessly.*) Of course—one can so seldom anticipate. But tell me—your dream, Stephen? It means——?

STEVE. It means—I was considerably surprised by what it means.

HENRIETTA. *Don't* be so exasperating!

STEVE. It means—you really want to know, Henrietta?

HENRIETTA. Stephen, you'll drive me mad!

STEVE. He said—of course he may be wrong in what he said.

HENRIETTA. He *isn't* wrong. *Tell* me!

STEVE. He said my dream of the walls receding and leaving me alone in a forest indicates a suppressed desire——

HENRIETTA. Yes—yes!

STEVE. To be freed from——

HENRIETTA. Yes—freed from——?

STEVE. Marriage.

HENRIETTA. (*Crumples. Stares.*) Marriage!

STEVE. He—he may be mistaken, you know.

HENRIETTA. *May* be mistaken?

STEVE. I—well, of course, I hadn't taken any stock in it myself. It was only your great confidence——

HENRIETTA. Stephen, are you telling me that Dr. Russell—Dr. A. E. Russell—told you this?

(STEVE *nods.*)

Told you you have a suppressed desire to separate from *me?*

STEVE. That's what he said.

HENRIETTA. Did he know who you were?

STEVE. Yes.

HENRIETTA. That you were married to me?

STEVE. Yes, he knew that.

HENRIETTA. And he told you to leave me?

STEVE. It seems he must be wrong, Henrietta.

HENRIETTA. (*Rising.*) And I've sent him more patients—! (*Catches herself and resumes coldly.*) What reason did he give for this analysis?

STEVE. He says the confining walls are a symbol of my feeling about marriage and that their fading away is a wish-fulfillment.

HENRIETTA. (*Gulping.*) Well, is it? Do you want our marriage to end?

STEVE. It was a great surprise to me that I did. You see I hadn't known what was in my unconscious mind.

HENRIETTA. (*Flaming.*) What did you tell Dr. Russell about me to make him think you weren't happy?

STEVE. I never told him a thing, Henrietta. He got it all from his confounded clever inferences. I—I tried to refute them, but he said that was only part of my self-protective lying.

HENRIETTA. And that's why you were so—happy—when you came in just now!

STEVE. Why, Henrietta, how can you say such a thing? I was *sad*. Didn't I speak sadly of—of the view? Didn't I ask how long we had been married?

HENRIETTA. (*Rising.*) Stephen Brewster, have you no sense of the seriousness of this? Dr. Russell doesn't know what our marriage has been. You do. You should have laughed him down! Confined—in life with me? Did you tell him that I *believe* in freedom?

STEVE. I very emphatically told him that his results were a great surprise to me.

HENRIETTA. But you accepted them.

STEVE. Oh, not at all. I merely couldn't refute his arguments. I'm not a psychologist. I came home to talk it over with you. You being a disciple of psychoanalysis——

HENRIETTA. If you are going, I wish you would go tonight!

STEVE. Oh, my dear! I—surely I couldn't do that! Think of my feelings. And my laundry hasn't come home.

HENRIETTA. I ask you to go tonight. Some women would falter at this, Steve, but I am not such a woman. I leave you free. I do not repudiate psychoanalysis; I say again that it has done great things. It has also made mistakes, of course. But since you accept this analysis—(*She sits down and pretends to begin work.*) I have to finish this paper. I wish you would leave me.

STEVE. (*Scratches his head, goes to the inner door.*) I'm sorry, Henrietta, about my unconscious mind.

(*Alone,* HENRIETTA's *face betrays her outraged state of mind—disconcerted, resentful, trying to pull herself together. She attains an air of bravely bearing an outrageous thing. The outer door opens and* MABEL *enters in great excitement.*)

MABEL. (*Breathless.*) Henrietta, I'm so glad you're here. And alone? (*Looks toward the inner door.*) Are you alone, Henrietta?

HENRIETTA. (*With reproving dignity.*) Very much so.

MABEL. (*Rushing to her.*) Henrietta, he's found it!

HENRIETTA. (*Aloof.*) Who has found what?

MABEL. Who has found what? Dr. Russell has found my suppressed desire!

HENRIETTA. That is interesting.

MABEL. He finished with me today—he got hold of my complex—in the most amazing way! But, oh, Henrietta—it is so terrible!

HENRIETTA. Do calm yourself, Mabel. Surely there's no occasion for all this agitation.

MABEL. But there is! And when you think of the lives that are affected—the readjustments that must be made in order to bring the suppressed desire out of me and save me from the insane asylum——!

HENRIETTA. The insane asylum!

MABEL. You said that's where these complexes brought people!

HENRIETTA. What did the doctor tell you, Mabel?

MABEL. Oh, I don't know how I can tell you—it is so awful—so unbelievable.

HENRIETTA. I rather have my hand in at hearing the unbelievable.

MABEL. Henrietta, who would ever have thought it? How can it be true? But the doctor is perfectly certain that I have a suppressed desire for——(*Looks at* HENRIETTA, *is unable to continue.*)

HENRIETTA. Oh, go on, Mabel. I'm not unprepared for what you have to say.

MABEL. Not unprepared? You mean you have suspected it?

HENRIETTA. From the first. It's been my theory all along.

MABEL. But, Henrietta, I didn't know myself that I had this secret desire for Stephen.

HENRIETTA. (*Jumps up.*) Stephen!

MABEL. My brother-in-law! My own sister's husband!

HENRIETTA. *You* have a suppressed desire for *Stephen!*

MABEL. Oh, Henrietta, aren't these unconscious selves terrible? They seem so unlike *us!*

HENRIETTA. What insane thing are you driving at?

MABEL. (*Blubbering.*) Henrietta, don't you use that word to me. I don't *want* to go to the insane asylum.

HENRIETTA. What did Dr. Russell say?

MABEL. Well, you see—oh, it's the strangest thing! But you know the voice in my dream that called "Step, Hen!" Dr. Russell found out today that when I was a little girl I had a story-book in words of one syllable and I read the name Stephen wrong. I used to read it S-t-e-p, step, h-e-n, hen. (*Dramatically.*) Step Hen is Stephen.

(*Enter* STEPHEN, *his head bent over a time-table.*)

Stephen is Step Hen!

STEVE. I? Step Hen?

MABEL. (*Triumphantly.*) S-t-e-p, step, H-e-n, hen, Stephen!

HENRIETTA. (*Exploding.*) Well, what if Stephen is Step Hen? (*Scornfully.*) Step Hen! Step Hen! For that ridiculous coincidence——

MABEL. Coincidence! But it's childish to look at the mere elements of a dream. You have to look *into* it—you have to see what it *means!*

HENRIETTA. On account of that trivial, meaningless play on syllables—on that flimsy basis—you are ready—— (*Wails.*) O-h!

STEVE. What on earth's the matter? What has happened? Suppose I *am* Step Hen? What about it? What does it mean?

MABEL. (*Crying.*) It means—that I—have a suppressed desire for *you!*

STEVE. For me! The deuce you have! (*Feebly.*) What—er—makes you think so?

MABEL. Dr. Russell has worked it out scientifically.

HENRIETTA. Yes. Through the amazing discovery that Step Hen equals Stephen!

MABEL. (*Tearfully.*) Oh, that isn't all—that isn't near all. Henrietta won't give me a chance to tell it. She'd rather I'd go to the insane asylum than be unconventional.

HENRIETTA. We'll all go there if you can't control yourself. We are still waiting for some rational report.

MABEL. (*Drying her eyes.*) Oh, there's such a lot about names. (*With some pride.*) I don't see how I ever did it. It all works in together. I dreamed I was a hen because that's the first syllable of *Hen*rietta's name, and when I dreamed I was a hen, I was putting myself in Henrietta's place.

HENRIETTA. With Stephen?

MABEL. With Stephen.

HENRIETTA. (*Outraged.*) Oh!

(*Turns in rage upon* STEPHEN, *who is fanning himself with the time-table.*)

What are you doing with that time-table?

STEVE. Why—I thought—you were so keen to have me go tonight—I thought I'd just take a run up to Canada, and join Billy—a little shooting—but——

MABEL. But there's more about the names.

HENRIETTA. Mabel, have you thought of Bob—dear old Bob—your good, kind husband?

MABEL. Oh, Henrietta, "my good, kind husband!"

HENRIETTA. Think of him, Mabel, out there alone in Chicago, working his head off, fixing people's *teeth*—for you!

MABEL. Yes, but think of the living Libido—in conflict with petrified moral codes! And thing of the perfectly wonderful way the names all prove it. Dr. Russell said he's never seen anything more convincing. Just look at Stephen's last name—Brewster. I dream I'm a hen, and the name Brewster—you have to say its first letter by itself—and then the hen, that's me, she says to him: "Stephen, Be Rooster!"

(HENRIETTA *and* STEPHEN *collapse into the nearest chairs.*)

MABEL. I think it's perfectly wonderful! Why, if it wasn't for psychoanalysis you'd never find out how wonderful your own mind is!

STEVE. (*Begins to chuckle.*) Be Rooster! Stephen, Be Rooster!

HENRIETTA. You think it's funny, do you?

STEVE. Well, what's to be done about it? Does Mabel have to go away with me?

HENRIETTA. Do you want Mabel to go away with you?

STEVE. Well, but Mabel herself—her complex, her suppressed desire——!

HENRIETTA. (*Going to her.*) Mabel, are you going to insist on going away with Stephen?

MABEL. I'd rather go with Stephen than go to the insane asylum!

HENRIETTA. For heaven's sake, Mabel, drop that insane asylum! If you *did* have a suppressed desire for Stephen hidden away in you—God knows it isn't hidden now. Dr. Russell has brought it into your consciousness—with a vengeance. That's all that's necessary to break up a complex. Psychoanalysis doesn't say you have to *gratify* every suppressed desire.

STEVE. (*Softly.*) Unless it's for Lyman Eggleston.

HENRIETTA. (*Turning on him.*) Well, if it comes to that, Stephen Brewster, I'd like to know why that interpretation of mine isn't as good as this one? Step, Hen!

STEVE. But Be Rooster! (*He pauses, chuckling to himself.*) Step-Hen Be rooster. And *Henrietta.* Pshaw, my dear, Doc Russell's got you beat a mile! (*He turns away and chuckles.*) Be rooster!

MABEL. What has Lyman Eggleston got to do with it?

STEVE. According to Henrietta, you, the hen, have a suppressed desire for *Eggleston,* the egg.

MABEL. Henrietta, I think that's indecent of you! He is bald as an egg and little and fat—the idea of you thinking such a thing of me!

HENRIETTA. Well, Bob isn't little and bald and fat! Why don't you stick to your own husband? (*To* STEPHEN.) What if Dr. Russell's interpretation has got mine "beat a mile"? (*Resentful look at him.*) It would only mean that Mabel doesn't want Eggleston and does want you. Does that mean she has to have you?

MABEL. But you said Mabel Snow——

HENRIETTA. *Mary* Snow! You're not as much like her as you think—substituting your name for hers! The cases are entirely different. Oh, I wouldn't have *believed* this of you, Mabel. (*Beginning to cry.*) I brought you here for a pleasant visit—thought you needed brightening *up*—wanted to be *nice* to you—and now you—my husband—you insist—— (*In fumbling her way to her chair she brushes to the floor some sheets from the psychoanalytical table.*)

STEVE. (*With solicitude.*) Careful, dear. Your paper on psychoanalysis! (*Gathers up sheets and offers them to her.*)

HENRIETTA. I don't want my paper on psychoanalysis! I'm sick of psychoanalysis!

STEVE. (*Eagerly.*) Do you mean that, Henrietta?

HENRIETTA. Why shouldn't I mean it? Look at all I've done for psychoanalysis—and— (*Raising a tear-stained face.*) What has psychoanalysis done for me?

STEVE. Do you mean, Henrietta, that you're going to stop *talking* psychoanalysis?

HENRIETTA. Why shouldn't I stop talking it? Haven't I seen what it does to people? Mabel has gone crazy about psychoanalysis!

(*At the word "crazy" with a moan* MABEL *sinks to chair and buries her face in her hands.*)

STEVE. (*Solemnly.*) Do you swear never to wake me up in the night to find out what I'm dreaming?

HENRIETTA. Dream what you please—I don't care what you're dreaming.

STEVE. Will you clear off my work-table so the Journal of Morbid Psychology doesn't stare me in the face when I'm trying to plan a house?

HENRIETTA. (*Pushing a stack of periodicals off the table.*) I'll *burn* the Journal of Morbid Psychology!

STEVE. My dear Henrietta, if you're going to separate from psychoanalysis, there's no reason why I should separate from *you*.

(*They embrace ardently.* MABEL *lifts her head and looks at them woefully.*)

MABEL. (*Jumping up and going toward them.*) But what about me? What am I to do with my suppressed desire?

STEVE. (*With one arm still around* HENRIETTA, *gives* MABEL *a brotherly hug.*) Mabel, you just keep right on suppressing it!

(*Curtain*)

I
TABLES TURNED

From Henrietta's opening comment in the play, we do not really like her. Why? She is intellectually alive; she is interested in her sister and her husband; she is efficient in running her house. All of these are admirable traits and yet there is something about Henrietta that makes us delight in seeing her put down. The play is built on this expectancy of the audience, and amusement is created by the ironic way in which the tables are turned. What is there in human beings that makes them enjoy seeing the "tables turned" on the Henriettas of the world?

II
IMPLICATIONS

Consider the following statements. Do you agree or disagree with them?

1. Henrietta will probably move on to a new enthusiasm now that this one has been abandoned.

2. The Henriettas of the world tend to make us feel inferior.

3. Stephen is secretly amused by Henrietta's passions. This is part of what he finds attractive in her.

4. People are better off just bumbling along rather than dissecting their every thought and dream for some hidden subconscious source.

5. It's a good thing for people to have enthusiasms for new ideas and discoveries.

6. If Stephen had been the one enthusiastic about psychoanalysis, the audience reaction would have been different.

III
TECHNIQUES

Atmosphere

The atmosphere of the play is light and breezy, thus giving the audience a clue that nothing grimly serious will happen. How do the following elements contribute to this atmosphere?

1. The time of day the play begins.

2. The arrangement of the equipment on the work table.

3. The opening conversation between Henrietta and Stephen.

4. Mabel's dream.

5. Mabel's definition of psychoanalysis as "something about a war . . . a new explosive."

Suspense

Two beautiful examples of suspense occur in Scene II when both Stephen and Mabel tell what the analyst has said. Reread this section of the play. Notice the point at which they start to tell what happened to them and how long it takes them to get the actual information said. What do they say that teases the audience's expectations and heightens the curiosity?

"Each year in the past," says the chairman
of the Board of Directors as he opens
the annual meeting, "Mr. Kovac has been the
object of a cruel and criminal action
by the members of this Board. Each year
in the past, it has been our decision
to repeat this crime." Now the group
once again must face the decision.

The
Cold, Cold Box

HOWARD FAST

As always, the annual meeting of the Board of Directors convened at nine o'clock in the morning, on the 10th of December. Nine o'clock in the morning was a sensible and reasonable hour to begin a day's work, and long ago, the 10th of December had been chosen as a guarantee against the seduction of words.[1] Every one of the directors would have to be home for the Christmas holiday—or its equivalent—and therefore the agenda was timed for precisely two weeks and not an hour more.

In the beginning, this had caused many late sessions, sometimes two or three days when the directors met the clock round, with no break for sleep or rest. But in time, as things fell into the proper place and orderly management replaced improvisation, each day's meeting was able to adjourn by four o'clock in the afternoon—and there were even years when the general meeting finished its work a day or two early.

By now, the meeting of the Board of Directors was very matter-of-fact and routine. The big clock on the wall of the charming and spacious meeting room was just sounding nine, its voice low and musical, as the last of the directors found their seats. They nodded pleasantly to each other, and if they were seated close to old friends, they exchanged greetings. They were completely relaxed, neither tense nor uneasy at the thought of the long meeting that lay ahead of them.

There were exactly three hundred of these directors, and they sat in a comfortable circle of many tiers of seats—in a room not unlike a small amphitheatre. Two aisles cut through to a center circle or stage about twenty feet in diameter, and there a podium was placed which allowed the speaker to turn in any direction as he spoke. Since the number of three hundred was an arbitrary one, agreed upon after a good deal of trial and error, and maintained as an excellent working size, half the seats in the meeting room were always empty. There was some talk now and then of redesigning the meeting room, but nobody ever got down to doing it and by now the empty seats were a normal part of the decor.

The membership of the Board was about equally divided between men and women. No one could serve under the age of thirty, but retirement was a matter of personal decision, and a reasonable number of members were over seventy. Two-thirds of them were in their fifties. Since the Board was responsible for an international management, it was only natural that all nations and races should be represented, black men and white men and brown men and yellow men—and all the shadings and gradations in between. Like the United Nations—they were too modest to make such a comparison themselves—they had a number of official languages and a system of simultaneous translation; but as with the United Nations, English was most frequently used.

As a matter of fact, the Chairman of the Board, who had been born in Indochina,

1. **seduction of words**\sə ˈdək·shən\ the temptation to talk too long.

opened this meeting in English, which he spoke very well and with ease, and after he had welcomed them and announced the total attendance—all members present—he said, "At the beginning of our annual meeting—and this is an established procedure, I may say— we deal with a moral and legal point, the question of Mr. Steve Kovac. We undertake this before the reading of the agenda, for we have felt that the question of Mr. Kovac is not a matter of agenda or business, but of conscience. Of our conscience, I must add, and not without humility; for Mr. Kovac is the only secret of this meeting. All else that the Board discusses, votes upon and decides or rejects will be made public, as you know. But of Mr. Steve Kovac, the world knows nothing; and each year in the past, our decision has been that the world should continue to know nothing about Mr. Kovac. Each year in the past, Mr. Kovac has been the object of a cruel and criminal action by the members of this Board. Each year in the past, it has been our decision to repeat this crime."

To these words, most of the members of the Board did not react at all—but here and there young men and women showed their surprise, bewilderment and unease, either by the expression on their faces or by low protestations of disbelief. The members of the Board were not insensitive people.

"This year, as in the past, we make this question of Mr. Kovac our first piece of business—because we cannot go on to our other business until it is decided. As in the past, we will decide whether to engage in a criminal conspiracy or not."

A young woman, a new member of the Board, her face flushed and angry, rose and asked the Chairman if he would yield for a question. He replied that he would.

"Am I to understand that you are serious, Mr. Chairman, or is this some sophomoric prank for the edification of new members?"

"This Board is not used to such descriptive terms as sophomoric, as you should know, Mrs. Ramu," he answer mildly. "I am quite serious."

The young woman sat down. She bit her lower lip and stared at her lap. A young man arose.

"Yes, Mr. Steffanson?" the Chairman said pleasantly.

The young man sat down again. The older members were gravely attentive, thoughtful without impatience.

"I do not intend to choke off any discussion, and I will gladly yield to any questions," said the Chairman, "but perhaps a little more about this troublesome matter first. There are two reasons why we consider this problem each year. Firstly, because the kind of crime we have committed in the past is hardly anything to which we should grow indifferent; we need to be reminded; premeditated crime is a deadly threat to basic decency, and God help us if we should ever become complacent! Secondly, each year, there are new members on this Board, and it is necessary that they should hear all the facts in the case of Mr. Kovac. This year, we have seven new members. I address myself to them, but not only to them; I include all of my fellow members of this Board."

"Steve Kovac," the Chairman of the Board began, "was born in Pittsburgh in the year 1913. He was one of eleven children, four of whom survived to adulthood. This was not too unusual in those days of poverty, ignorance and primitive medicine.

"John Kovac, Steve Kovac's father, was a steelworker. When Steve Kovac was six years old, there was a long strike—an attempt on the part of the steelworkers to increase their wages. I am sure you are all familiar with the method of the strike, and therefore I will not elaborate.

"During this strike, Steve Kovac's mother died; a year later, John Kovac fell into a vat of molten steel. The mother died of tuberculosis, a disease then incurable. The father's body was dissolved in the molten steel. I mention these things in terms of their very deep and lasting effect on the mind and character of Steve

Kovac. Orphaned at the age of seven, he grew up like an animal in the jungle. Placed in a county home for orphan children, he was marked as a bad and intractable boy, beaten daily, deprived of food, punished in every way the ignorance and insensitivity of the authorities could devise. After two years of this, he ran away.

"This is a very brief background to the childhood of a most remarkable man, a man of brilliance, character and determination, a man of high inventive genius and grim determination. Unfortunately, the mind and personality of this man had been scarred and traumatized[2] beyond redemption. A psychiatric analysis of this process has been prepared, and each of you will find a copy in your portfolio. It also itemizes the trials and suffering of Steve Kovac between the ages of nine and twenty—the years during which he fought to survive and to grow to adulthood.

"It also gives a great many details of this time of his life—details I cannot go into. You must understand that while the question before us is related to this background, there are many other features I will deal with."

At this point, the Chairman of the Board paused to take a drink of water and to glance through his notes. The younger members of the Board glanced hurriedly at the psychiatric report; the older members remained contemplative, absorbed in their own thoughts. As many times as they had been through this, somehow it was never dull.

"At the age of twenty," the Chairman resumed, "Steve Kovac was working in a steel mill outside of Pittsburgh. He was friendly then with a man named Emery. This man, Emery, was alone, without family or means of support. A former coal miner, he suffered from a disease of the lungs, common to his trade. All he had in the world was a five-thousand-dollar insurance policy. Steve Kovac agreed to support him, and in return he made Kovac the

days, insurance polices were frequently the only means by which a family could survive the death of the breadwinner.

"Four months later, Emery died. Years afterward, it was rumored that Kovac had hastened his death, but there is no evidence for the rumor. The five thousand dollars became the basis for Steve Kovac's subsequent fortune. Twenty-five years later, the net worth of Steve Kovac was almost three billion dollars. As an individual, he was possibly the wealthiest man in the United States of America. He was a tycoon in the steel and aluminum industries, and he controlled chemical plants, copper mines, railroads, oil refineries and dozens of associated industries. He was then forty-six years old. The year was 1959.

"The story of his climb to power and wealth is unique for the generations he lived through. He was a strong, powerful, handsome man— tortured within himself, driven by an insatiable lust to avenge himself, and his father and mother too, for the poverty and suffering of his childhood. Given the traumatic factors of his childhood, his craving for power turned psychopathic and paranoid,[3] and he built this structure of power securely in his own hands. He owned newspapers as well as airlines, television stations and publishing houses, and much more than he owned, he controlled. Thereby, he was able to keep himself out of the public eye. In any year of the fifties, you can find no more than an occasional passing reference to him in the press.

"How an individual achieved this in a time of the public corporation and the 'corporation man' is a singular tale of drive and ambition. Steve Kovac was ambitious, ruthless, merciless and utterly without compassion or pity. His policy was to destroy what stood in his way, if he could; if he could not, he bent to his will in one way or another. He wrecked lives and

---

2. **traumatized**\ˈtrau·mə ˈtaizd\ wounded in spirit.
3. **psychopathic**\ˈsai·kə ˈpăth·ĭk\ mentally ill or unstable, **paranoid**\ˈpar·ə ˈnoid\ characterized by suspiciousness, feelings of persecution, and belief in one's

fortunes. He framed and entrapped his competitors; he used violence when he had to—when he could not buy or bribe what he wanted. He corrupted individuals and bribed parliaments and bought governments. He erected a structure of power and wealth and control that reached out to every corner of the globe.

"And then, in his forty-sixth year, at the height of his wealth and power, he discovered that he had cancer."

The Chairman of the Board paused to allow the impact of the words to settle and tell. He took another drink of water. He rearranged the papers in front of him.

"At this time," he said, "I propose to read to you a short extract from the diary of Dr. Jacob Frederick. I think that most of you are familiar with the work of Dr. Frederick. In any case, you know that he was elected a member of our Board. Naturally, that was a long time ago. I need only mention that Dr. Frederick was one of the many wise and patient pioneers in the work of cancer research—not only a great physician, but a great scientist. The first entry I propose to read is dated January 12, 1959."

"I had an unusual visitor today," the Chairman of the Board read, "Steve Kovac, the industrial tycoon. I had heard rumors to the effect of the wealth and power of this man. In himself, he is a striking individual, tall, muscular, handsome with a broad strong face and a great mane of prematurely white hair. He has blue eyes, a ruddy complexion and appears to be in the prime of life and health. Of course, he is not. I examined him thoroughly. There is no hope for the man.

" 'Doctor,' he said to me, 'I want the truth. I know it already. You are not the first physician I have seen. But I also want it from you, plainly and bluntly.'

"I would have told him in any case. He is not the kind of a man you can lie to easily. 'Very well,' I said to him, 'you have cancer.

There is no cure for your cancer. You are going to die.'

" 'How long?'

" 'We can't say. Perhaps a year.'

" 'And if I undergo operative procedure?'

" 'That could prolong your life—perhaps a year or two longer if the operation is successful. But it will mean pain and incapacity.'

" 'And there is no cure?' His surface was calm, his voice controlled; he must have labored for years to achieve that kind of surface calm and control; but underneath, I could see a very frightened and desperate man.

" 'None as yet.'

" 'And the quacks and diet men and the rest—they promise cures.'

" 'It's easy to promise,' I said. 'But there isn't any cure.'

" 'Doc,' he said to me, 'I don't want to die and I don't intend to die. I have worked twenty-five years to be where I am now. The tree is planted. I'm going to eat the fruit. I am young and strong—and the best years of my life are ahead of me.'

"When Kovac talked like that, he was convincing, even to me. It is his quality, not simply to demand of life, but to take. He denies the inevitable. But the fact remained.

" 'I can't help you, Mr. Kovac,' I told him.

" 'But you're going to help me,' he said calmly. 'I came to you because you know more about cancer than any man in the world. Or so I am told.'

" 'You have been misinformed,' I said shortly. 'No one man knows more than anyone else. Such knowledge and work is a collective thing.'

" 'I believe in men, not mobs. I believe in you. Therefore, I am ready to pay you a fee of one million dollars if you can make it possible for me to beat this thing and live a full lifespan.' He then reached into his coat for his wallet and took out a certified check for one million dollars. 'It is yours—if I live.'

"I told him to return the following day—that is, tomorrow. And now I have been sitting here for hours, thinking of what one million dollars would mean to my work, my hopes—indeed, through them, to all people. I have been thinking with desperation and with small result. Only one thought occurs to me. It is fantastic, but then Steve Kovac is a fantastic man."

Again, the Chairman of the Board paused and looked inquiringly at some of the younger members. They had been listening with what appeared to be hypnotic concentration. There were no questions and no comments.

"Then I will continue with the diary of Dr. Frederick," the Chairman nodded.

"*January 13.* Steve Kovac returned at 2:00, as we had arranged. He greeted me with a confident smile.

"'Doc, if you are ready to sell, I am ready to buy.'

"'And you really believe that you can buy life?'

"'I can buy anything. It's a question of price.'

"'Can you buy the future?' I asked him. 'Because that is where the cure for cancer lies. Do you want to buy it?'

"'I'll buy it because you have decided to sell,' he said flatly. 'I know with whom I am dealing. Make your offer, Dr. Frederick.'

"I made it, as fantastic as it was. I told him about my experiments with the effect of intense cold upon cancer cells. I explained that though, as yet, the experiments had not produced any cure, I had made enormous strides in the intense and speedy application of extreme cold—or, to put it more scientifically, my success in removing heat from living objects. I detailed my experiments—how I had begun with frogs and snakes, freezing them, and then removing the cold and resuming the life process at a later date, how I had experimented with mice, cats, dogs—and most recently, monkeys.

"He followed me and anticipated me. 'How do you restore life?' he wanted to know.

"'I don't restore it. The life never dies. In the absence of heat, what might be called the ripening or aging process of life is suspended, but the life remains. Time and motion are closely related; and under intense cold, motion slows and theoretically could cease—all motion, even within the atomic structure. When the motion ceases, time ceases.'

"'Is it painful?'

"'As far as I know, it isn't. The transition is too quick.'

"'I would like to see an experiment myself.'

"I told him that I had in my laboratory a spider monkey that had been frozen seven weeks ago. My assistants could attest to that. He went into the laboratory with me and watched me as we successfully restored the monkey. Seemingly, it was none the worse.

"'And the mind?' he asked me.

"I shrugged. 'I don't know. I have never attempted it with a human being.'

"'But you think it would work?'

"'I am almost certain that it would work. I would need better and larger equipment. With some money to spend, I can improve the process—well, considerably.'

"He nodded and took the certified check out of his wallet. 'Here is your retainer—apart from what you have to spend. Buy whatever you need, and charge it to me. Spend whatever you have to spend and buy the best. No ceiling, no limit. And when I wake up, after a cure has been discovered, there will be a second million to add to your fee. I am not a generous man, but neither am I niggardly when I buy what I want. When will you be ready, Doctor?'

"'Considering the prognosis[4] of your disease,' I said, 'we should not delay more than five weeks. I will be ready then. Will you?'

"Steve Kovac nodded. 'I will be ready. There are a good many technical and legal details to work out. I have many and large interests, as you may know, and this is a journey of uncertain duration. I will also take care of your own legal responsibilities.'

---

4. **prognosis**\prŏg▲nō·səs\ prospect for recovery.

"Then he left, and it was done—possibly the strangest agreement ever entered into by a doctor and his patient. I try to think only of one thing—that I now have a million dollars to put into my work and research."

The Chairman of the Board wore pince-nez,[5] and now he paused to wipe them. He cleared his throat, rearranged the papers on the lectern once again, and explained, "You see, the plan was a simple one and a sensible one, too. Since Mr. Kovac's condition could not be cured, here was a means of preserving his life and arresting the disease until science had found a cure. Timidity was never one of Mr. Kovac's qualities. He analyzed the situation, faced it and accepted the only possible escape offered to him. So he went about placing his affairs in such order as to guarantee the success and prosperity of his enterprises while he slept—and also their return to his bidding and ownership when he awoke.

"In brief, he formed a single holding company for all of his many interests. He gathered together a Board of Directors to manage that holding company in his absence, making himself president in absentia,[6] with a substitute Chairman to preside while he was gone. He made a set of qualifying bylaws, that no Chairman could hold office for more than two years, that the Board was to be enlarged each year and a number of other details, each of them aimed at the single goal of retaining all power for himself. And because he was not dead, but merely absent, he created a unique situation, one unprecedented in all the history of finance.

"This holding company was exempted from all the traditional brakes and tolls placed upon previous companies through the mechanism of death. Until Mr. Kovac returned, the holding company was immortal. Naturally, Dr. Frederick was placed upon the Board of Directors. In other words," the Chairman of the Board concluded, "that is how this Board of Directors came into being."

He allowed himself his first smile then. "Are there any questions at this point?" he asked mildly.

A new member from Japan rose and wanted to know why, if this was the case, the whole world should be taught otherwise?

"We thought it best," said the Chairman. "Just as we, on this Board, have great powers for progress and construction, so do we have no inconsiderable powers of concealment and alternation. The people of the United States and the United Kingdom might have accepted the knowledge that Steve Kovac brought this Board of Directors into being, but certainly in the Soviet Union and China, such knowledge might have been most disconcerting and destructive. Remember that once we had established an open trade area in the Soviet Union and had brought three of her leading government people onto our Board of Directors, our situation changed radically. We were enabled then, through a seizure of all fuel supplies on earth, to prevent the imminent outbreak of World War III.

"At that point, neither the extent of our holdings nor the amount of our profits could be further concealed. I say we," the Chairman deferred modestly, "but of course, it was our predecessors who faced these problems. Our cash balance was larger than that of the United States Treasury, our industrial potential greater than that of any major power. Believe me, without planned intent or purpose, this Board of Directors suddenly found itself the dominant force on earth. At that point, it became desperately necessary for us to explain ourselves, who we were and what we represented."

A new member from Australia rose and asked, "How long was that, Mr. Chairman, if I may inquire, after the visit of Mr. Kovac to Dr. Frederick?"

The Chairman nodded. "It was the year

---

5. **pince-nez**\pă(n) ▲snā\ eyeglasses pinched to the nose by a spring.
6. **in absentia,** in his absence.

Dr. Frederick died—twenty-two years after the treatment began. By then, five types of cancer had already surrendered their secrets to science. But there was not yet any cure for Mr. Kovac's disease."

"And all the time, the treatment had remained secret?"

"All the time," the Chairman nodded.

"You see," he went on, "at that time, the Board felt that the peoples of earth had reached a moment of crisis and decision. A moment, I say, for the power was only momentarily in the hands of this Board. We had no armies, navies or air-fleets—all we had were a major portion of the tools of production. We knew we had not prevented war but simply staved it off. This was a Board of Directors for management, not for power, and any day the installations and plants we owned and controlled could have been torn from our grasp. That was when our very thoughtful and wise predecessors decided to embark on a vast, global propaganda campaign to convince the world that we represented a secret parliament of the wisest and best forces of mankind—that we were in effect a Board of Directors for the complex of mankind.

"And in this we succeeded, for the television stations, the newspapers, the radio networks, the film industry and the theatre—all these were ours. And in that brief, fortunate moment, we launched our attack. We used the weapons of Steve Kovac—let us be honest and admit that. We acted as he would have acted, but out of different motives entirely.

"We bought and bribed and framed. We infiltrated the parliaments of all mankind. We bought the military commanders. We dissolved the armies and navies in the name of super-weapons, and then we destroyed the super-weapons in the name of mankind. Where leaders could not be bought or bribed, we brought them into our Board. And above all, we bought control—control of every manufacturing, farming or mining unit of any consequence upon the face of the earth.

"It took the Board of Directors twenty-nine years more to accomplish this; and at the end of that twenty-nine years, our earth was a single complex of production for use and happiness—and if I may say so, for mankind. A semblance of national structure remained, but it was even then as ritualistic and limited as any commonwealth among the old states of the United States. Wars, armies, navies, atom bombs—all of these were only ugly memories. The era of reason and sanity began, the era of production for use and life under the single legal code of man. Thus, we have become creatures of law, equal under the law, and abiding by the law. This Board of Directors was never a government, nor is it now. It is what it purports to be, a group management for the holding company. Only today, the holding company and the means of mankind are inseparable. Thereby, our very great responsibility, which of course you understand . . . ."

The Chairman of the Board wiped his face and took a few more sips of water. A new member from the United States rose and said, "But, Mr. Chairman, the cure for all types of cancer was discovered sixty-two years ago."

"So it was," the Chairman agreed.

"Then, Steve Kovac—" The new member paused. She was a beautiful, sensitive woman in her middle thirties, a physicist of note and also an accomplished musician.

"You see, my dear," the Chairman said, lapsing into a most informal mode of address, pardonable only because of his years and dignity, "it faced us. When we make a law for mankind and submit to it, we must honor it. Sixty-two years ago, Steve Kovac owned the world and all its wealth and industry, a dictator beyond the dream of any dictator, a tyrant above all tyrants, a king and emperor to dwarf all other kings and emperors—"

As he spoke, two of the older members left the meeting room. Minutes later, they returned, wheeling into the room and up to the podium a rectangular object, five feet high,

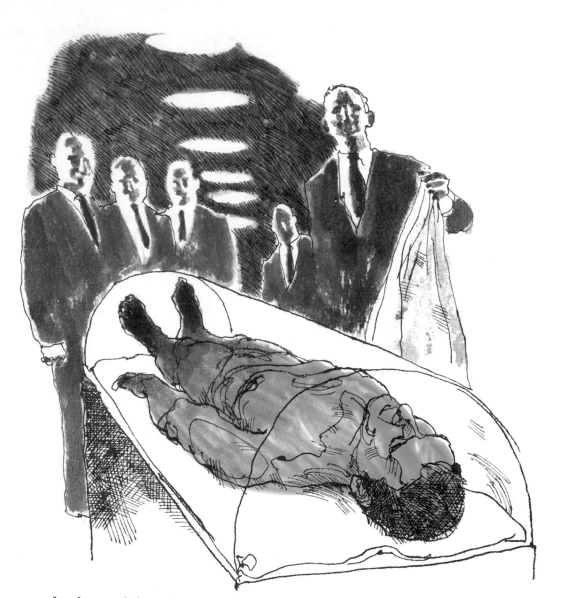

seven feet long and three feet wide, the whole of it covered with a white cloth. They left it there and returned to their seats.

"—yes, and he owned the world. Think of it—for the first time in history, a just peace governed the nations of mankind. Cities were being rebuilt, deserts turned into gardens, jungles cleared, poverty and crime a thing of the past. Man was standing erect, flexing his muscles, reaching out to the planets and the stars—and all of this belonged to a single savage, merciless, despotic paranoid, Steve

654

Kovac. Then, as now, my dear associates, this Board of Directors was faced with the problem of the man to whom we owed our existence, the man who all unwittingly unified mankind and ushered in the new age of man —yes, the man who gave us the right and authority to hold and manage, the man whose property we manage. Then as now, we were faced with Steve Kovac!"

Almost theatrical in his conclusion and gestures, the Chairman stepped down from the podium and with one motion swept the cloth aside. The entire Board fixed their eyes on the cabinet where, under a glass cover, in a cold beyond all concept of cold, a man lay sleeping in what was neither life nor death, but a subjective pause[7] in the passage of time. He was a handsome man, big and broad, ruddy of face and with a fine mane of white hair. He seemed to sleep lightly, expectantly, confidently—as if he were dreaming hungrily but pleasantly of what he would awaken to.

"Steve Kovac," the Chairman said. "So he sleeps, from year to year, no difference, no changes. So he appeared to our predecessors sixty-two years ago, when they first had the means to cure him and the obligation to awaken him. They committed the first of sixty-two crimes; they took no action in the face of a promise, a duty, a legality and an almost sacred obligation. Can we understand them? Can we forgive them? Can we forgive the Board of Directors that voted this same decision again and again? Above all, can we forgive ourselves if we stain our honor, break the law, and ignore our own inheritance of an obligation?

"I am not here to argue the question. It is never argued. The facts are presented, and then we vote. Therefore, will all those in favor of awakening Mr Kovac raise their right hands?"

The Chairman waited. Long moments became minutes, but no hands were raised. The two older members covered the cold, cold box and wheeled it out. The Chairman of the Board took a sip of water and announced, "We will now have the reading of the agenda."

I
THE ULTIMATE IRONY—
A MAN'S MASTERPIECE DESTROYS HIM

Steve Kovac, in making his decision to be frozen so that he can await a cure for his particular type of cancer, never dreams that the corporation he created to handle his affairs while he is absent will one day own the world. Nor does he dream that his Board of Directors, having produced a prosperous and peaceful society where men live together in harmony, cannot justify reactivating him, even though legally he owns it all. Thus, Steve Kovac is the victim of the masterpiece he created.

II
IMPLICATIONS

In your opinion, considering both the selection and your experiences, are the following statements right, wrong, or somewhere in between?

1. The Board of Directors should have eliminated Steve Kovac long ago, since reactivating him could destroy the new order.

2. The Chairman claims that the peoples of the world have now become creatures of law, yet the society had been founded on illegal actions. Ultimately, right cannot exist founded on a wrong.

3. The irony in this story is that the peoples of the world are ignorant of Steve Kovac's part in creating the peaceful new order.

III
TECHNIQUES

Atmosphere

The atmosphere of the story is one of quiet, matter-of-fact dignity. How does this contrast with the content of the story itself?

Suspense

The reader is startled by the opening words of the Chairman, who speaks of Mr. Steve Kovac about whom the world knows nothing. One wonders why. And what is the crime committed against him each year? The Board members are obviously going to vote on the question again. How will the vote go this time? All these questions tease the reader's curiosity and lead him to continue reading in order to find the answers.

When the chairman's final word of explanation is given and the vote called for, what was your reaction? Did you want it to be for restoring the man or for letting him sleep? How then did you react to the Board's vote?

---

7. **subjective pause,** a pause in all mental and sensory functions.

LIFE'S IRONIES

The public world provides for an endless harvest of ironic circumstances in which pretense and dishonesty hide under a mask of smiling virtue. The political cartoonist loves to show the wolf grinning under its lambskin costume.

FOR DISCOVERING THE MOTION OF THE EARTH
Francisco Goya

SHADOWS
Grandville

..... Vous avez la parole, expliquez-vous; vous êtes libre !

"YOU HAVE THE FLOOR, EXPLAIN YOURSELF"
Honoré Daumier
Courtesy Museum of Fine Arts, Boston, Babcock Bequest

The earliest of this gallery of political cartoons is *For Discovering the Motion of the Earth,* one of a series by the remarkable Spaniard Goya, whose artistic influence extends from his day to ours. The series arouses outrage over man's inhumanity to man, specifically, the Inquisition's treatment of Galileo.

Shadows, 1830, is a grim observation of the character of France's ministers of state during an autocratic rule. With fiendish shadows, Grandville states his case satirically.

The artist Daumier was a crusading cartoonist, and the cartoon *"You have the floor, explain yourself,"* was part of his attack on the questionable legality of a trial of rebels in 1835. Censorship of the press halted his cartoons later that year.

BREADLINE—NO ONE HAS STARVED
Reginald Marsh

México se transforma en una gran ciudad. . . .

MEXICO TRANSFORMS ITSELF INTO A GREAT CITY
Alfredo Zalce
The Metropolitan Museum of Art
Whittelsey Fund, 1946

Marsh's *Breadline—No One Has Starved*, winding endlessly, speaks of hopelessness during the Great Depression and "too little, too late" methods of dealing with social crises.

The pillaged, starving inner city overwhelms the signs of progress in *Mexico Transforms Itself Into a Great City*. Zalce's comment could apply to many cities in the world today.

The startling symbolism of *The Cog*, 1905, protests the destruction of man in favor of machinery.

THE COG   *Franz Kupka*

ORDER REIGNS
IN WARSAW
Grandville

Until very recently, continuous strife raged among the land-hungry European states.
In 1830, Poland attempted to overthow Russian invaders, but the revolt was squelched.
Order Reigns in Warsaw, 1831, pictures the return to "normal" and angrily depicts the bloody
price. Thomas Nast's *Military Glory*, 1870, is a similar protest. Ironically, Nast created
the first drawing of the fat and jolly Santa Claus that children still enjoy today.

Death's donkey chase after victory by the American, Boardman Robinson, reflects anti-war
convictions during World War I.

The cartoonist has a rare knack for pinpointing the heart of the matter. His work is worth
examining not only for deftness of line but also for insight into basic issues.

MILITARY GLORY
Thomas Nast

VICTORY, 1916
Boardman Robinson
Reproduced from The Masses, *Oct. 1916*
Columbia University Library, New York

661

This piece of raw irony under the
Chicago El shows a society doing
what it bitterly condemns others for doing
in the rest of the world.

Prelude

ALBERT HALPER

I was coming home from school, carrying
my books by a strap, when I passed Gavin's
poolroom and saw the big guys hanging
around. They were standing in front near the
windows, looking across the street. Gavin's has
a kind of thick window curtain up to eye
level, so all I saw was their heads. The guys
were looking at Mrs. Oliver, who lately has
started to get talked about. Standing in her
window across the street, Mrs. Oliver was
doing her nails. Her nice red hair was hanging
loose down her back. She certainly is a nice-
looking woman. She comes to my father's
newspaper stand on the corner and buys five
or six movie magazines a week, also the afternoon papers. Once she felt me under the chin,
and laughed. My father laughed, too, stamping about in his old worn leather jacket to
keep warm. My old man stamps a lot because
he has leg pains and he's always complaining
about a heavy cold in his head.

When I passed the poolroom one or two
guys came out. "Hey, Ike, how's your good-
looking sister?" they called, but I didn't turn
around. The guys are eighteen or nineteen and
haven't ever had a job in their life. "What they
need is work," my father is always saying
when they bother him too much. "They're not
bad; they get that way because there's nothing
to do," and he tries to explain the meanness

of their ways. But I can't see it like my father.
I hate those fellas and I hope every one of
them dies under a truck. Every time I come
home from school past Lake Street they jab
me, and every time my sister Syl comes along
they say things. So when one of them, Fred
Gooley, calls, "Hey, Ike, how's your sister?"
I don't answer. Besides, Ike isn't my name
anyway. It's Harry.

I passed along the sidewalk, keeping close
to the curb. Someone threw half an apple but
it went over my head. When I went a little
farther someone threw a stone. It hit me in
the back of the leg and stung me but it didn't
hurt much. I kept a little toward the middle
of the sidewalk because I saw a woman coming the other way and I knew they wouldn't
throw.

When I reached the corner under the Elevated two big news trucks were standing with
their motors going, giving my father the latest
editions. The drivers threw the papers onto
the sidewalk with a nice easy roll so the
papers wouldn't get hurt. The papers are
bound with that heavy yellow cord which my
father saves and sells to the junkyard when he
fills up a bag. "All right, Silverstein," a driver
called out. "We'll give you a five-star[1] at six,"
and both trucks drove off.

The drivers are nice fellas and when they
take back the old papers they like to kid my
old man. They say, "Hey, you old banker,
when are you gonna retire?" or, "Let's roll
him, boys, he's got bags of gold in his socks."
Of course they know my old man isn't wealthy
and that the bags in the inside of the newsstand hold only copper pennies. But they like
to kid him and they know he likes it. Sometimes the guys from Gavin's pitch in, but the
truck drivers would flatten them if they ever
got rough with my old man.

I came up to the newsstand and put my
school books inside. "Well, Pa," I said, "you
can go to Florida now." So my Pa went to
"Florida," that is, a chair near the radiator

1. **five-star,** a late edition of the newspaper.

that Nick Pappas lets him use in his restaurant. He has to use Nick's place because our own flat is too far away, almost a quarter-mile off.

While my father was in Nick's place another truck came to a stop. They dropped off a big load of early sport editions and yelled, "Hey, there, Harry, how's the old man?" I checked off the papers, yelling back, "He's okay, he's in Nick's." Then the truck drove away and the two helpers waved.

I stood around, putting the papers on the stand and making a few sales. The first ten minutes after coming home from school and taking care of the newsstand always excites me. Maybe it's the traffic. The trucks and cars pound along like anything and of course there's the Elevated right up above you which thunders to beat the band. We have our newsstand right up against a big El post and the stand is a kind of cabin which you enter from the side. But we hardly use it, only in the late morning and around two P.M., when business isn't very rushing. Customers like to see you stand outside over the papers ready for business and not hidden inside where they can't get a look at you at all. Besides, you have to poke your head out and stretch your arm to get the pennies, and kids can swipe magazines from the sides, if you don't watch. So we most always stand outside the newsstand, my father, and me, and my sister. Anyhow, I like it. I like everything about selling papers for my father. The fresh air gets me and I like to talk to customers and see the rush when people are let out from work. And the way the news trucks bring all the new editions so we can see the latest headlines, like a bank got held up on the South Side on Sixty-third Street, or the Cubs are winning their tenth straight and have a good chance to cop the pennant, is exciting.

The only thing I don't like is those guys from Gavin's. But since my father went to the police station to complain they don't come around so often. My father went to the station a month ago and said the gang was bothering him, and Mr. Fenway, he's the desk sergeant there, said, "Don't worry any more about it, Mr. Silverstein, we'll take care of it. You're a respectable citizen and taxpayer and you're entitled to protection. We'll take care of it." And the next day they sent over a patrolman who stood around almost two hours. The gang from Gavin's saw him and started to go away, but the cop hollered, "Now listen, don't bother this old fella. If you bother him any I'll have to run some of you in."

And then one of the guys recognized that the cop was Butch, Fred Gooley's cousin. "Listen who's talkin'," he yells back. "Hey, Fred, they got your cousin Butch takin' care of the Yid." They said a lot of other things until the cop got mad and started after them. They ran faster than lightning, separating into alleys. The cop came back empty-handed and said to my father, "It'll blow over, Mr. Silverstein; they won't give you any more trouble." Then he went up the street, turning into Steuben's bar.

Well, all this happened three or four weeks ago and so far the gang has let us alone. They stopped pulling my sixteen-year-old sister by her sweater and when they pass the stand going home to supper all they give us is dirty looks. During the last three or four days, however, they passed by and kinda muttered, calling my father a communist banker and me and my sister reds. My father says they really don't mean it, it's the hard times and bad feelings, and they got to put the blame on somebody, so they put the blame on us. It's certain speeches on the radio and the pieces in some of the papers, my father told us. "Something is happening to some of the people and we got to watch our step," he says.

I am standing there hearing the traffic and thinking it over when my little fat old man comes out from Nick's looking like he liked the warm air in Nick's place. My old man's cheeks looked rosy, but his cheeks are that way from high blood pressure and not from good health. "Well, colonel," he says smiling, "I am back on the job." So we stand around, the two of us, taking care of the trade. I hand out change snappy and say thank you after each sale. My old man starts to stamp around in a little while and, though he says nothing, I know he's got pains in his legs again. I look at the weather forecast in all the papers and some of them say flurries of snow and the rest of them say just snow. "Well, Pa," I tell my old man, "maybe I can go skating tomorrow if it gets cold again."

Then I see my sister coming from high school carrying her briefcase and heading this way. Why the heck doesn't she cross over so she won't have to pass the poolroom, I say to myself; why don't she walk on the other side of the street? But that's not like Sylvia; she's a girl with a hot temper, and when she thinks she is right you can't tell her a thing. I knew she wouldn't cross the street and then cross back, because according to her, why, that's giving in. That's telling those hoodlums that you're afraid of their guts. So she doesn't cross over but walks straight on. When she comes by the pool hall two guys come out and say something to her. She just holds herself tight and goes right on past them both. When she finally comes up she gives me a poke in the side. "Hello, you mickey mouse, what mark did you get in your algebra exam?" I told her I got A, but the truth is I got a C.

"I'll check up on you later," she says to me. "Pa, if he's lying to us we'll fine him ten years!"

My father started to smile and said, "No, Harry is a good boy, two years is enough."

So we stand around kidding and pretty soon, because the wind is coming so sharp up the street, my old man has to "go to Florida" for a while once more. He went into Nick's for some "sunshine," he said, but me and Syl could tell he had the pains again. Anyway, when he was gone we didn't say anything for a while. Then Hartman's furniture factory, which lately has been checking out early, let out and we were busy making sales to the men. They came up the sidewalk, a couple of hundred, all anxious to get home, so we had

to work snappy. But Syl is a fast worker, faster than me, and we took care of the rush all right. Then we stood waiting for the next rush from the Hillman's cocoa factory up the block to start.

We were standing around when something hit me in the head, a half of a rotten apple. It hurt a little. I turned quick but didn't see anybody, but Syl started yelling. She was pointing to a big El post across the street behind which a guy was hiding.

"Come on, show your face," my sister was saying. "Come on, you hero, show your yellow face!" But the guy sneaked away, keeping the post between. Syl turned to me and her face was boiling. "The rats! It's not enough with all the trouble over in Europe; they have to start it here."

Just then our old man came out of Nick's and when he saw Syl's face he asked what was the matter.

"Nothing," she says. "Nothing, I'm just thinking."

But my old man saw the half of a rotten apple on the sidewalk, and at first he didn't say anything but I could see he was worried. "We just have to stand it," he said, like he was speaking to himself, "we just have to stand it. If we give up the newsstand where else can we go?"

"Why do we have to stand it?" I exploded, almost yelling. "Why do we—"

But Mrs. Oliver just then came up to the stand, so I had to wait on her. Besides, she's a good customer and there's more profit on two or three magazines than from a dozen papers.

"I'll have a copy of *Film Fan,* a copy of *Breezy Stories,* and a copy of *Movie Stars on Parade,*" she says. I go and reach for the copies.

"Harry is a nice boy," Mrs. Oliver told my father, patting my arm. "I'm very fond of him."

"Yes, he's not bad," my father answered smiling. "Only he has a hot temper once in a while."

But who wouldn't have one, that's what I

wanted to say! Who wouldn't? Here we stand around minding our own business and the guys won't let us alone. I tell you sometimes it almost drives me crazy. We don't hurt anybody and we're trying to make a living, but they're always picking on us and won't let us alone. It's been going on for a couple of years now, and though my old man says it'll pass with the hard times, I know he's worried because he doesn't believe what he says. He reads the papers as soon as he gets them from the delivery trucks and lately the news about Europe is all headlines and I can see that it makes him sick. My old man has a soft heart and every time he sees in the papers that something bad in Europe has happened again he seems to grow older and he stands near the papers kind of small and all alone. I tell you, sometimes it almost drives me crazy. My old man should be down in Florida, where he can get healthy, not in Nick Pappas' "Florida," but down in real Florida where you have to go by train. That's where he should be. Then maybe his legs would be all right and he wouldn't have that funny color in his cheeks. Since our mother died last year it seems the doctor's treatments don't make him any better, and he has to skip a treatment once in a while because he says it costs too much. But when he stands there with a customer chuckling you think he's healthy and hasn't got any worries and you feel maybe he has a couple thousand in the bank.

And another thing, what did he mean when he said something two days ago when the fellas from Gavin's passed by and threw a stone at the stand? What did he mean, that's what I want to know. Gooley had a paper rolled up with some headlines about Europe on it and he wiggled it at us and my father looked scared. When they were gone my father said something to me, which I been thinking and thinking about. My Pa said we got to watch our step extra careful now because there's no other place besides this country where we can go. We've always been picked on, he said, but we're up against the

last wall now, he told me, and we got to be calm because if they start going after us here there's no other place where we can go. I been thinking and thinking about that, especially the part about the wall. When he said that, his voice sounded funny and I felt like our newsstand was a kind of island and if that went we'd be under the waves.

"Harry, what are you thinking of?" Mrs. Oliver asked me. "Don't I get any change?" She was laughing.

And then I came down from the clouds and found she had given me two quarters. I gave her a nickel change. She laughed again. "When he looks moody and kind of sore like that, Mr. Silverstein, I think he's cute."

My old man crinkled up his eyes and smiled. "Who can say, Mrs. Oliver. He should only grow up to be a nice young man and a good citizen and a credit to his country. That's all I want."

"I'm sure Harry will," Mrs. Oliver answered, then talked to Syl a while and admired Syl's new sweater and was about to go away. But another half of a rotten apple came over and splashed against the stand. Some of it splashed against my old man's coat sleeve. Mrs. Oliver turned around and got mad.

"Now you boys leave Mr. Silverstein alone! You've been pestering him long enough! He's a good American citizen who doesn't hurt anybody! You leave him alone!"

"Yah!" yelled Gooley, who ducked behind an El post with two other guys. "Yah! Sez you!"

"You leave him alone!" hollered Mrs. Oliver.

"Aw, go peddle your papers," Gooley answered. "Go run up a rope."

"Don't pay any attention to them," Syl told Mrs. Oliver. "They think they're heroes, but to most people they're just yellow rats."

I could tell by my old man's eyes that he was nervous and wanted to smooth things over, but Syl didn't give him a chance. When she gets started and knows she's in the right not even the Governor of the State could make her keep quiet.

"Don't pay any attention to them," she said in a cutting voice while my old man looked anxious. "When men hide behind Elevated posts and throw rotten apples at women you know they're not men but just things that wear pants. In Europe they put brown shirts on them and call them saviors of civilization. Here they haven't got the shirts yet and hang around poolrooms."

Every word cut like a knife and the guys ducked away. If I or my father would have said it we would have been nailed with some rotten fruit, but the way Syl has of getting back at those guys makes them feel like yellow dogs. I guess that's why they respect her even though they hate her, and I guess that's why Gooley and one or two of his friends are always trying to get next to her and date her up.

Mrs. Oliver took Syl's side and was about to say something more when Hillman's cocoa factory up the block let out and the men started coming up the street. The 4:45 rush was on and we didn't have time for anything, so Mrs. Oliver left, saying she'd be back when the blue-streak edition of the *News* would arrive. Me and Syl were busy handing out the papers and making change and our Pa helped us while the men took their papers and hurried for the El. It started to get darker and colder and the traffic grew heavier along the street.

Then the *Times* truck, which was a little late, roared up and dropped a load we were waiting for. I cut the strings and stacked the papers and when my father came over and read the first page he suddenly looked scared. In his eyes there was that hunted look I had noticed a couple of days ago. I started to look at the first page of the paper while my old man didn't say a word. Nick came to the window and lit his new neon light and waved to us. Then the light started flashing on and off, flashing on the new headlines. It was all about Austria and how people were fleeing toward the borders and trying to get out of the country before it was too late. My old man grew

sick and looked kind of funny and just stood there. Sylvia, who is active in the high-school social science club, began to read the *Times* out loud and started analyzing the news to us; but our Pa didn't need her analysis and kept standing there kind of small with that hunted look on his face. He looked sick all right. It almost drove me crazy.

"For Pete's sake," I yelled at Syl. "Shut up, shut up!"

Then she saw our Pa's face, looked at me, and didn't say anything more.

In a little while it was after five and Syl had to go home and make supper. "I'll be back in an hour," she told me. "Then Pa can go home and rest a bit and me and you can take care of the stand." I said all right.

After she was gone it seemed kind of lonesome. I couldn't stop thinking about what my father had said about this being our last wall. It got me feeling funny and I didn't want to read the papers any more. I stood there feeling queer, like me and my old man were standing on a little island and the waves were coming up. There was still a lot of traffic and a few people came up for papers, but from my old man's face I could tell he felt the same as me.

But pretty soon some more editions began coming and we had to check and stack them up. More men came out from factories on Walnut Street and we were busy making sales. It got colder than ever and my old man began to stamp again. "Go into Nick's, Pa," I told him. "I can handle it out here." But he wouldn't do it because just then another factory let out and we were swamped for a while. "Hi, there, Silverstein," some of the men called to him, "what's the latest news, you king of the press?" They took the papers, kidding him, and hurried up the stairs to the Elevated, reading all about Austria and going home to eat. My father kept staring at the headlines and couldn't take his eyes off the print where it said that soldiers were pouring across the border and mobs were robbing people they hated and spitting on them and making them go down on their hands and knees to scrub the streets. My old man's eyes grew small, like he had the toothache and he shook his head like he was sick. "Pa, go into Nick's," I told him. He just stood there, sick over what he read.

Then the guys from Gavin's poolroom began passing the stand on their way home to supper after a day of just killing time. At first they looked as if they wouldn't bother us. One or two of them said something mean to us, but my old man and me didn't answer. If you don't answer hoodlums, my father once told me, sometimes they let you alone.

But then it started. The guys who passed by came back and one of them said: "Let's have a little fun with the Yids." That's how it began. A couple of them took some magazines from the rack and said they wanted to buy a copy and started reading.

In a flash I realized it was all planned out. My father looked kind of worried but stood quiet. There were about eight or nine of them, all big boys around eighteen and nineteen, and for the first time I got scared. It was just after six o'clock and they had picked a time when the newspaper trucks had delivered the five-star and when all the factories had let out their help and there weren't many people about. Finally one of them smiled at Gooley and said, "Well, this physical culture magazine is mighty instructive, but don't you think we ought to have some of the exercises demonstrated?" Gooley said, "Sure, why not?"

So the first fella pointed to some pictures in the magazine and wanted me to squat on the sidewalk and do the first exercise. I wouldn't do it. My father put his hand on the fella's arm and said, "Please, please." But the guy pushed my father's hand away.

"We're interested in your son, not you. Go on, squat."

"I won't," I told him.

"Go on," he said. "Do the first exercise so that the boys can learn how to keep fit."

"I won't," I said.

"Go on," he said, "do it."

"I won't."

Then he came over to me smiling, but his face looked nasty. "Do it. Do it if you know what's good for you."

"Please, boys," said my Pa. "Please go home and eat and don't make trouble. I don't want to have to call a policeman—"

But before I knew it someone got behind me and tripped me so that I fell on one knee. Then another of them pushed me, trying to make me squat. I shoved someone and then someone hit me, and then I heard someone trying to make them stop. While they held me down on the sidewalk I wiggled and looked up. Mrs. Oliver, who had come for the blue-flash edition, was bawling them out.

"You let him alone! You tramps, you hoodlums, you let him alone!" She came over and tried to help me, but they pushed her away. Then Mrs. Oliver began to yell as two guys twisted my arm and told me to squat.

By this time a few people were passing and Mrs. Oliver called at them to interfere. But the gang were big fellows and there were eight or nine of them, and the people were afraid.

Then while they had me down on the sidewalk Syl came running up the street. When she saw what was happening she began kicking them and yelling and trying to make them let me up. But they didn't pay any attention to her.

"Please," my Pa kept saying. "Please let him up; he didn't hurt you. I don't want to have to call the police—"

Then Syl turned to the people who were watching and yelled at them. "Why don't you help us? What are you standing there for?" But none of them moved. Then Syl began to scream:

"Listen, why don't you help us? Why don't you make them stop picking on us? We're human beings the same as you!"

But the people just stood there afraid to do a thing. Then while a few guys held me, Gooley and about four others went for the stand, turning it over and mussing and stamping on all the newspapers they could find. Syl started to scratch them, so they hit her, then

I broke away to help her, and then they started socking me too. My father tried to reach me, but three guys kept him away. Four guys got me down and started kicking me and all the time my father was begging them to let me up and Syl was screaming at the people to help. And while I was down, my face was squeezed against some papers on the sidewalk telling about Austria and I guess I went nuts while they kept hitting me, and I kept seeing the headlines against my nose.

Then someone yelled, "Jiggers, the cops!" and they got off of me right away. Nick had looked out the window and had called the station, and the guys let me up and beat it away fast.

But when the cops came it was too late; the stand was a wreck. The newspapers and magazines were all over the sidewalk and the rack that holds the *Argosy* and *Western Aces* was all twisted up. My Pa, who looked sicker than ever, stood there crying and pretty soon I began to bawl. People were standing looking at us like we were some kind of fish, and I just couldn't help it, I started to bawl.

Then the cops came through the crowd and began asking questions right and left. In the end they wanted to take us to the station to enter a complaint, but Syl wouldn't go. She looked at the crowd watching and she said, "What's the use? All those people standing around and none of them would help!" They were standing all the way to the second El post, and when the cops asked for witnesses none of them except Mrs. Oliver offered to give their names. Then Syl looked at Pa and me and saw our faces and turned to the crowd and began to scream.

"In another few years, you wait! Some of you are working people and they'll be marching through the streets and going after you too! They pick on us Jews because we're weak and haven't any country; but after they get us down they'll go after you! And it'll be your fault; you're all cowards, you're afraid to fight back!"

"Listen," one of the cops told my sister, "are you coming to the station or not? We can't hang around here all evening."

Then Syl broke down and began to bawl as hard as me. "Oh, leave us alone," she told them and began wailing her heart out. "Leave us alone. What good would it do?"

By this time the crowd was bigger, so the cops started telling people to break it up and move on. Nick came out and took my father by the arm into the lunchroom for a drink of hot tea. The people went away slowly and then, as the crowd began to dwindle, it started to snow. When she saw that, Syl started bawling harder than ever and turned her face to me. But I was down on my hands and knees with Mrs. Oliver, trying to save some of the magazines. There was no use going after the newspapers, which were smeared up, torn, and dirty from the gang's feet. But I thought I could save a few, so I picked a couple of them up.

"Oh, leave them be," Syl wept at me. "Leave them be, leave them be!"

I

THE IRONY OF FRANTIC DESPERATION

Syl and Harry, born and brought up in the United States, are confident that the persecution of the Jews taking place in Nazi Germany can never happen in America. Mr. Silverstein's long experience has not offered him much hope, yet he continues to feel that the United States is the last country open to Jews. Each approaches the tormenting poolroom gang in his own way: Syl defies them; Harry avoids them; Mr. Silverstein treats them as mischievous boys. When the gang attacks, life underlines the irony for all three family members, for none of their attitudes produces the hoped-for result. As their livelihood is destroyed, people stand around and stare; the only person who attempts to help is a woman little respected in the neighborhood.

II

IMPLICATIONS

Following are a group of quotations from the story. Consider the persons who are speaking.

What do their words say about them? How would you feel and talk in similar situations? Is there an ironic element in the remark?

1. "What they need is work . . . . They're [the gang] not bad; they get that way because there's nothing to do." (Mr. Silverstein)

2. "I knew she [Sylvia] wouldn't cross the street and then cross back, because according to her, why, that's giving in. That's telling those hoodlums that you're afraid of their guts." (Harry)

3. "We've always been picked on, he said, but we're up against the last wall now, he told me, and we got to be calm because if they start going after us here there's no other place where we can go." (Mr. Silverstein)

4. " 'We just have to stand it,' he said . . . 'we just have to stand it.' " " 'Why do we have to stand it?' I exploded." (Harry)

5. "Don't pay any attention to them," Syl [said]. "They think they're heroes, but to most people they're just yellow rats." (Sylvia)

6. ". . . Why don't you help us? Why don't you make them stop picking on us? We're human beings the same as you!" (Sylvia)

7. "Oh, leave us alone [to the police] . . . . Leave us alone. What good would it do?" (Sylvia)

III
TECHNIQUES

Atmosphere

The mood of this selection is one of desperation and despair. What details of setting contribute to the dark, dreary atmosphere?

Suspense

What are the brief actions before the final confrontation between the boys and the Silversteins?

Did the boys' attack come as a surprise or did you expect it? How did this add to the suspense?

After five years of rebellion against England, Ireland was offered dominion status. De Valera's Republicans refused to sign the treaty, holding out for complete independence. But other Sinn Fein leaders did sign, and the Irish Free State became official in 1922, setting off guerrilla warfare between the dissident Republicans and the Free Staters. The next story is set in the Ireland of the 1920s when civil war enveloped the small country.

The Sniper

LIAM O'FLAHERTY

The long June twilight faded into night. Dublin lay enveloped in darkness, but for the dim light of the moon, that shone through fleecy clouds, casting a pale light as of approaching dawn over the streets and the dark waters of the Liffey. Around the beleaguered Four Courts the heavy guns roared. Here and there through the city, machine guns and rifles broke the silence of the night, spasmodically, like dogs barking on lone farms. Republicans and Free Staters were waging civil war.

On a roof-top near O'Connell Bridge, a Republican sniper lay watching. Beside him lay his rifle and over his shoulders were slung a pair of field-glasses. His face was the face of a student—thin and ascetic,[1] but his eyes had the cold gleam of the fanatic. They were deep and thoughtful, the eyes of a man who is used to looking at death.

He was eating a sandwich hungrily. He had eaten nothing since morning. He had been

---

1. **ascetic**\ə ˈsĕt·ĭk\ as if practicing strict self-denial.

From SPRING SOWING by Liam O'Flaherty. Reprinted by permission of Harcourt Brace Jovanovich, Inc.

too excited to eat. He finished the sandwich, and taking a flask of whiskey from his pocket, he took a short draught.[2] Then he returned the flask to his pocket. He paused for a moment, considering whether he should risk a smoke. It was dangerous. The flash might be seen in the darkness and there were enemies watching. He decided to take the risk. Placing a cigarette between his lips, he struck a match, inhaled the smoke hurriedly and put out the light. Almost immediately, a bullet flattened itself against the parapet of the roof. The sniper took another whiff and put out the cigarette. Then he swore softly and crawled away to the left.

Cautiously he raised himself and peered over the parapet. There was a flash and a bullet whizzed over his head. He dropped immediately. He had seen the flash. It came from the opposite side of the street.

He rolled over the roof to a chimney stack in the rear, and slowly drew himself up behind it, until his eyes were level with the top of the parapet. There was nothing to be seen —just the dim outline of the opposite housetop against the blue sky. His enemy was under cover.

Just then an armoured car came across the bridge and advanced slowly up the street. It stopped on the opposite side of the street fifty yards ahead. The sniper could hear the dull panting of the motor. His heart beat faster. It was an enemy car. He wanted to fire, but he knew it was useless. His bullets would never pierce the steel that covered the grey monster.

Then round the corner of a side street came an old woman, her head covered by a tattered shawl. She began to talk to the man in the turret of the car. She was pointing to the roof where the sniper lay. An informer.

The turret opened. A man's head and shoulders appeared, looking towards the sniper. The sniper raised his rifle and fired. The head fell heavily on the turret wall. The woman darted toward the side street. The sniper fired again. The woman whirled round and fell with a shriek into the gutter.

Suddenly from the opposite roof a shot rang out and the sniper dropped his rifle with a curse. The rifle clattered to the roof. The sniper thought the noise would wake the dead. He stopped to pick the rifle up. He couldn't lift it. His fore-arm was dead.

Dropping flat on to the roof, he crawled back to the parapet. With his left hand he felt the injured right fore-arm. The blood was oozing through the sleeve of his coat. There was no pain—just a deadened sensation, as if the arm had been cut off.

Quickly he drew his knife from his pocket, opened it on the breastwork of the parapet and ripped open the sleeve. There was a small hole where the bullet had entered. On the other side there was no hole. The bullet had lodged in the bone. It must have fractured it. He bent the arm below the wound. The arm bent back easily. He ground his teeth to overcome the pain.

Then, taking out his field dressing, he ripped open the packet with his knife. He broke the neck of the iodine bottle and let the bitter fluid drip into the wound. A paroxysm of pain swept through him. He placed the cotton wadding over the wound and wrapped the dressing over it. He tied the end with his teeth.

Then he lay still against the parapet, and closing his eyes, he made an effort of will to overcome the pain.

In the street beneath all was still. The armoured car had retired speedily over the bridge, with the machine gunner's head hanging lifeless over the turret. The woman's corpse lay still in the gutter.

The sniper lay for a long time nursing his wounded arm and planning escape. Morning must not find him wounded on the roof. The enemy on the opposite roof covered his escape. He must kill that enemy and he could not use his rifle. He had only a revolver to do it. Then he thought of a plan.

Taking off his cap, he placed it over the muzzle of his rifle. Then he pushed the rifle

_____
2. **draught**\drăft\ British spelling of draft.

slowly upwards over the parapet, until the cap was visible from the opposite side of the street. Almost immediately there was a report, and a bullet pierced the centre of the cap. The sniper slanted the rifle forward. The cap slipped down into the street. Then, catching the rifle in the middle, the sniper dropped his left hand over the roof and let it hang, lifelessly. After a few moments he let the rifle drop to the street. Then he sank to the roof, dragging his hand with him.

Crawling quickly to the left, he peered up at the corner of the roof. His ruse had succeeded. The other sniper, seeing the cap and rifle fall, thought that he had killed his man. He was now standing before a row of chimney pots, looking across, with his head clearly silhouetted against the western sky.

The Republican sniper smiled and lifted his revolver above the edge of the parapet. The distance was about fifty yards—a hard shot in the dim light, and his right arm was paining him like a thousand devils. He took a steady aim. His hand trembled with eagerness. Pressing his lips together, he took a deep breath through his nostrils and fired. He was almost deafened with the report and his arm shook with the recoil.

Then, when the smoke cleared, he peered across and uttered a cry of joy. His enemy had been hit. He was reeling over the parapet in his death agony. He struggled to keep his feet, but he was slowly falling forward, as if in a dream. The rifle fell from his grasp, hit the parapet, fell over, bounded off the pole of a barber's shop beneath and then cluttered on to the pavement.

Then the dying man on the roof crumpled up and fell forward. The body turned over and over in space and hit the ground with a dull thud. Then it lay still.

The sniper looked at his enemy falling and he shuddered. The lust of battle died in him. He became bitten by remorse. The sweat stood out in beads on his forehead. Weakened by his wound and the long summer day of fasting and watching on the roof, he revolted from the sight of the shattered mass of his dead enemy. His teeth chattered. He began to gibber to himself, cursing the war, cursing himself, cursing everybody.

He looked at the smoking revolver in his hand and with an oath he hurled it to the roof at his feet. The revolver went off with the concussion, and the bullet whizzed past the sniper's head. He was frightened back to his senses by the shock. His nerves steadied. The cloud of fear scattered from his mind and he laughed.

Taking the whiskey flask from his pocket, he emptied it at a draught. He felt reckless under the influence of the spirits. He decided to leave the roof and look for his company commander to report. Everywhere around was quiet. There was not much danger in going through the streets. He picked up his revolver and put it in his pocket. Then he crawled down through the sky-light to the house underneath.

When the sniper reached the laneway on the street level, he felt a sudden curiosity as to the identity of the enemy sniper whom he had killed. He decided that he was a good shot whoever he was. He wondered if he knew him. Perhaps he had been in his own company before the split in the army. He decided to risk going over to have a look at him. He peered around the corner into O'Connell Street. In the upper part of the street there was heavy firing, but around here all was quiet.

The sniper darted across the street. A machine gun tore up the ground around him with a hail of bullets, but he escaped. He threw himself face downwards beside the corpse. The machine gun stopped.

Then the sniper turned over the dead body and looked into his brother's face.

TRAGIC IRONY

The two opponents are evenly matched, but the writer centers his attention on the one he calls "the sniper." The man's calculating brutality is vividly demonstrated by his almost mechanical killing of the gunner in the armored car and the old woman informer. After the sniper is wounded, the duel between him and his opponent is intensified. To survive, the wounded man executes a plan which deceives his enemy, whom he kills. Only then does the sniper feel remorse. But how much deeper must this remorse be when he turns over the body of the dead man and sees his brother's face. Again, Fate gives a tragic ironic twist to an encounter.

II

IMPLICATIONS

What is your reaction to the following statements? Use the selection and your own experiences to form your opinion.

1. If both snipers had known who their enemy was, they could not have shot at each other.

2. It is worse to kill one's brother than to kill an unknown person.

3. In this story, people are only enemies to be slain.

III

TECHNIQUES

Atmosphere

Reread the first three paragraphs. What kind of sentences are used: simple or complex? long or short? direct or involved? What atmosphere or expectancy is created by these sentence patterns?

Suspense

There are five vivid actions described in the story. How does each add to the story's suspense?

IV

WORDS

A. Some words sound very much like the sounds they name. The bullet that "whizzed" over the sniper's head made a hissing sound. When you say the word *whizzed,* you can hear a similar sound. Another word that imitates the sound it names is *thud.* The pronunciation of this word comes fairly close to the dull, heavy sound to which it refers. No doubt, this sound is permanently etched in the sniper's mind, for his brother's body "hit the ground with a thud." Words such as *whizzed* and *thud* are called *onomatopoetic* words. Other words in this category are: *buzz, rattle, crunch, meow, hiss, crackle, roar, clank, zoom,* and *crack.* Can you think of others?

B. At one point in the story, the sniper "struck a match, inhaled the smoke hurriedly and *put out* the light." At another point, having dropped it a few minutes earlier, he "stopped to *pick* the rifle *up.*" In the two quotations just given, the words *put* and *out* as well as *pick* and *up* are so closely related that they function as one word. In other words, they form a verb-adverb combination that serves the same purpose as a single verb. *Put out* means "to extinguish," and *pick up* means "to lift." The use of *out* or *up* with a verb does not always result in a verb-adverb unit, however. For example, in the sentence "John put out the cat," the word *out* functions in its normal way, telling the reader where John put the cat. By contrast, *out* in the first quotation above does not tell where the light is. Two-word verbs like *put out* and *pick up* abound in English; for example, *check up, fill in, set up, slow down,* and *hand out.* Can you add others? Here are some to get you started: *pick up, speed up,* and *check out.*

Do people really know themselves? One of the tricks life plays on human beings is confronting them with situations which reveal them not to be the people they thought they were. Decide for yourself if the outcome of the duel in this story is peculiarly appropriate.

The Pistol Shot

ALEXANDER PUSHKIN

"We fired at each other."—*Bariatynski*
"I vowed to kill him, according to the code of dueling, and I still have my shot to fire."—*A Night on Guard*

1

We were in camp in the village of ——. Everyone knows the life of an officer of the line: in the morning, drill and horseback exercise; then comes dinner with the colonel of the regiment, or else at the Jewish restaurant; and at night drinks and cards. At ——, there were no entertainments of any kind, for no one had a marriageable daughter to bring out. We spent our time in each other's quarters, and at our evening gatherings there were uniforms only.

However, there was one man in our set who was not a soldier. He must have been about thirty-five and consequently we looked upon him as quite old. His experience had great weight with us, and besides his reserve, his grand air and sarcastic manner made a deep impression on us young men. There seemed to be something mysterious about his life. He looked like a Russian, though he bore a foreign name. In days gone by he had been in a regiment of Hussars[1] where he was quite prominent at one time; but suddenly he had sent in his resignation, no one knew why, and had retired to this poor out-of-the-way village, where he fared very badly, while at the same time spending much money. He always wore a shabby overcoat and still he kept open house where every officer was made welcome. To tell the truth, his dinners generally consisted of two or three simple dishes prepared by his servant, an old discharged soldier, but the champagne always flowed. No one knew anything of his circumstances or his means, and no one dared ask him any questions on the subject. There were plenty of books in his house—mostly military—and a few novels. He lent them willingly and never asked for them again; on the other hand, he never returned those he borrowed. His one pastime was pistol shooting. The walls of his room were riddled with bullets, giving it the appearance of a honeycomb. A rich collection of pistols was the only luxury to be seen in the miserable house he occupied. The accuracy of his aim was remarkable, and if he had taken a bet that he could shoot the pompon on a helmet, not one of us would have hesitated to put the helmet on. Sometimes we talked of dueling, but Silvio (I will give him that name) never opened his lips on the subject. If someone asked him had he ever fought a duel, he answered shortly that he had, and that was all; he never entered into any particulars and it was evident that he disliked being asked such questions. We surmised that the death of one of his victims had left a blight on his life. Never for a minute would any of us have thought that he could have been guilty of faintheartedness. There are some people whose very appearance precludes such an idea.

One day eight or ten of our officers were dining at Silvio's. We drank as much as usual, that is, excessively. When dinner was over, we begged of our host to take the bank in a game of faro. After refusing to do so, for he seldom played, he finally called for cards and

1. **Hussars**\ˈhə ˈzŏrz\ members of a European light cavalry unit.

laying fifty ducats on the table before him, he sat down and shuffled. We formed in a circle about him and the game began. When playing, Silvio never uttered a word, neither objecting nor explaining. If a player made a mistake, he paid out exactly the amount due him or else credited it to himself. We were all familiar with his manner of playing and always let him have his own way. But on the day I speak of, there was with us an officer newly arrived who, through absentmindedness, doubled his stakes on a certain card. Silvio took the chalk and marked down what was due him. The officer, convinced that there was a mistake, made some objections. Silvio, still mute, went on dealing as if he had not heard. The officer, out of patience by this time, took the brush and wiped off the figures. Silvio picked up the chalk and wrote them down again. At this, the officer, excited by the wine, by the play and the laughter of his comrades, and thinking he had been insulted, took up a brass candlestick and hurled it at Silvio, who by bending aside, averted the blow. Great was the uproar! Silvio rose, pale with rage, and with eyes blazing:

"My dear sir," he said, "you will please leave this room, and be thankful that this has happened in my house."

Not one of us doubted the outcome of this fray, and we all looked upon our new comrade as a dead man. The officer went out saying he was ready to meet the banker just as soon as it was convenient. The game proceeded a few minutes longer, but it was evident that the master of the house was not paying much attention to what was going on; we all left, one by one, and returned to our quarters discussing the while the vacancy in our ranks which was sure to take place.

Next morning, while at riding exercise, we all wondered if the poor lieutenant were dead or alive, when, to our surprise, he appeared among us. We plied him with questions and he answered that he had had no challenge from Silvio, which caused us all much surprise. We called on Silvio and found him in

his yard, firing bullet after bullet at an ace nailed to the door. He received us in his usual manner, never mentioning the scene of the night before. Three days went by and the lieutenant was still alive. We kept saying to each other: "Will Silvio not fight?" amazed at such a thing. But Silvio did not fight. He simply gave a very lame explanation and that was all that was said.

This forbearance on his part did him much harm among us young men. A want of courage is never quite forgiven by youth, for to him fearlessness is the greatest quality one can possess and it excuses many faults. Still, after a while, all this was forgotten and by degrees Silvio regained his old ascendency over us.

I, alone, could never feel the same toward him. Being of a romantic turn of mind, I had loved this man, whose life was an enigma to us all, more than anyone else, and I had made him, in my thoughts, the hero of some mysterious drama. And he liked me, of this I felt sure, for when we were alone, dropping his sharp and sarcastic speeches, he would converse on all sorts of subjects, and unbend to me in a fascinating manner. Ever since that unlucky evening I speak of, the fact that he had been insulted and had not wiped out the offense in blood worried me to such an extent that I never could feel at ease with him as in the days gone by. I even avoided looking at him, and Silvio was too clever and quick not to notice and guess at the reason. He seemed to me to feel it deeply. On two occasions, I thought I detected a wish on his part to explain matters, but I avoided him and he did not follow me. After that I never saw him except when others were present, and we never again resumed our intimate talks.

Those happy mortals who live in cities, where there is so much to see and do, can never imagine how important certain small happenings can become in an out-of-the-way village or town. One of these is the arrival of the mail. Tuesdays and Fridays, the offices of our regiment were besieged with men. One expected money, another a letter, and again others looked for newspapers. As a rule, everything was opened and read on the spot; news was given and the improvised post office was full of animation. Silvio's letters were addressed in care of our regiment and he called for them with us. One day a letter was handed to him, the seal of which he broke hurriedly. While reading it his eyes flashed with excitement. None of the officers but myself noticed this, as they were all busy reading their own letters.

"Gentlemen," said Silvio, "business compels me to leave town immediately. I must go tonight. I hope none of you will refuse to dine with me for the last time. I will expect you," said he, turning to me pointedly. "I hope you will not disappoint me."

After saying which he went away in great haste, and we all retired to our own quarters, agreeing to meet at his house later.

I arrived at Silvio's at the hour he had named and found almost the whole regiment there. Everything he possessed was packed and the bare walls riddled with bullets stared back at us. We sat down to dinner and our host was in such a jovial mood that before long we were all in the greatest of spirits. Corks flew about; the froth rose in our glasses, which we refilled as rapidly as they emptied. We all felt great affection for our host and wished him a pleasant journey with joy and prosperity at the end of it. It was very late when we got up from the table and while we were all picking out our caps in the hall, Silvio took me by the hand and detained me as I was about to leave.

"I must speak to you," he said in a low tone.

So I remained after the others went away and, seated facing each other, we smoked our pipes in silence for a while. Silvio seemed worried, and there was no trace of the feverish gaiety he had displayed in the earlier part of the evening. This dreadful pallor, the brilliancy of his eyes, and the long puffs of smoke he blew from his mouth, gave him the appearance of a fiend. After a few minutes he broke the silence.

"It may be," he said, "that we will never see each other again; before we part, I wish to explain certain things to you. You have noticed, perhaps, that I attach very little importance to the average man's opinion, but I like you and I feel I cannot leave without seeing you think better of me than you do."

He stopped to shake the ashes out of his pipe. I remained silent and avoided looking at him.

"It may have seemed strange to you," he continued, "that I did not ask any satisfaction from that drunkard, that young fool R——. You will admit that, having the choice of weapons, he was at my mercy and that there was not much chance of his killing me. I might call it generosity on my part, but I will not lie about it. If I could have given R—— a good lesson, without in any way risking my life, he would not have been rid of me so easily."

I looked at Silvio in the greatest surprise. Such an admission from him was astounding. He went on:

"As it is, unhappily, I have no right to risk my life. Six years ago, I received a blow and the man who struck me is still alive."

This excited my curiosity to an unusual degree.

"You did not meet him?" I asked. "Surely some extraordinary circumstance must have prevented your doing so?"

"I did meet him," answered Silvio, "and here you see the result of our encounter."

He rose and drew from a box near him a cap of red cloth with a gilt braid and tassel such as Frenchmen call *bonnet de police*.[2] He put it on his head and I saw that a bullet had pierced it about an inch above the forehead.

"You know," said Silvio, "that I was in the Hussars of——, and you also know what kind of a disposition I have: I like to rule everyone. Well, in my youth, it was positively a passion with me. In my day, brawlers were in fashion and I was the foremost brawler of the regiment. To get drunk was then considered a

---

2. **bonnet de police**\bɔ ˈnĕ•də•pɔ ▴lēs\

thing to be proud of; I could outdrink the famous B——, celebrated in song by D. D——. Every day brought its duel, and every day saw me either the principal actor in one or else taking the part of a second. My comrades looked up to me, and our superior officers, who were constantly being transferred, considered me a plague of which they could not be rid.

"As for me, I kept on quietly (or rather riotously) in my glorious career, when one day there was transferred to our regiment a young fellow who was very wealthy and of good family. I will not name him to you, but never have I met a fellow with such unheard-of luck. Imagine having youth, a fine figure, no end of spirits, a daring which was utterly indifferent to danger, a great name, and unlimited means to do with as he liked, and you may have a faint idea of the impression he created among us. My power was gone in an instant. At first, dazzled by my reputation, he tried to make friends with me; but I received his advances very coldly, seeing which, he quietly dropped me without showing any annoyance whatever. I took such a dislike to him, when I saw his popularity in the regiment and his success with the ladies, that I was driven almost to despair. I tried to pick a quarrel with him, but to my sarcastic remarks he answered with caustic and unexpected wit that had the merit besides of being more cheerful than mine. He was always in jest, while I was in dead earnest. Finally one night, while at a ball in a Polish house, seeing how much the ladies admired him, especially our hostess with whom I had been very friendly, I whispered in his ear some insulting remark which I have long since forgotten. He turned around and struck me. We grasped our swords, some of the ladies fainted, and a few officers parted us. We went out immediately to fight it out right then and there.

"The three witnesses and myself reached the meeting place, and I awaited the coming of my adversary with no ordinary impatience. The sun rose, and its intense heat was being felt more and more every minute when I finally saw him coming in the distance. He was on foot and in his shirt-sleeves, carrying his uniform over his arm—he was attended by only one witness. I went forward to meet him, and I noticed that his cap, which he carried in his hand, was full of cherries. Our witnesses placed us twelve paces from each other. It was my privilege to shoot first, but what with passion and hatred blinding me I feared my aim would be poor, and to gain time to steady my hand, I offered to let him fire first. He refused to do so, and it was then agreed we would leave it to chance. Luck was, as usual, with this spoilt child of fortune. He fired and pierced my cap. It was now my turn, and I felt he was at my mercy. I looked at him with eagerness, hoping to find him at least a little uneasy. Not at all, for there he stood, within range of my pistol, coolly picking the ripest cherries out of his cap and blowing the pits in my direction where they fell at my feet.

"'What will I gain,' thought I, 'by taking his life, when he thinks so little of it?'

"A diabolical thought crossed my mind. I unloaded a pistol.

"'It seems,' I said, 'that you care very little whether you die or not at the present moment. You seem more anxious to breakfast instead. It will be as you please. I have no wish to disturb you.'

"'You will be kind enough to attend to your own business,' answered he, 'and to please fire, . . . but after all you may do as you like. You can always fire your shot when and where you like. I will always be at your call.'

"I went away with my witnesses to whom I said that I did not care to shoot just then, and the thing ended there.

"I sent in my resignation and retired to this out-of-the-way village. From that day to this, I have thought of nothing but revenge. And now, the time has come . . .!"

Silvio drew from his pocket the letter received that morning. Someone, his lawyer it seemed, had written from Moscow that *the person in question* was soon to be married to a young and pretty girl.

"You can guess, I have no doubt," said Silvio, "who is *the person in question*. I am leaving for Moscow and we will see if he will look at death in the midst of bridal festivities with as much coolness as he did when facing it with a pound of cherries in his cap!"

After saying these words he rose and, throwing his cap viciously on the floor, he walked back and forth the length of the room like a caged tiger. I had listened to him without saying a word, stirred by very contradictory feelings.

A servant entered saying the carriage was at the door. Silvio grasped my hand, which he shook with all his might. He entered a small open carriage where were two boxes already, one containing his pistols and the other his luggage. We said good-bye once more, and he was driven away.

2

Years went by, when family matters compelled me to live in an obscure village in the district of ——. While looking after my interests, I often sighed for the enjoyable life I had led until then. The long solitary evenings of winter and spring were the hardest to bear. I could not become reconciled to their lonesomeness. Until the dinner hour I managed somehow to kill time by chatting with the starosty (Polish landowner) visiting my workmen, and watching the new buildings being erected. But as soon as night came I was at a loss to know what to do. I knew by heart the few books I had found in the ancient bookcases and in the garret. All the stories known to my old housekeeper, Kirilovna, I had asked her to tell me over and over again, and the songs of the peasants saddened me. I drank everything at hand, soft drinks and others, until my head ached. I will even admit that at one time I thought I should become a drunkard from sheer desperation, the worst kind of drunkard, of which this district offered me a good many examples.

My nearest neighbors consisted of two or three of these confirmed inebriates, whose conversations were forever interspersed with sighs and hiccoughs, so that even complete solitude was to be preferred to their society. I finally got into the habit of dining as late as possible and retiring as early as I could afterward, and in that way I solved the problem of shortening the evenings and lengthening the days.

About four versts[3] from my house was a beautiful property belonging to the Countess B——. It was occupied by her steward, the Countess herself never having lived in the place but a month at a time, and that in the first year of her marriage.

One day, in the second year of this lonely existence of mine, I heard that the Countess and her husband were to occupy their residence during the summer months. In the early part of June, they arrived with all their household.

The coming of a rich neighbor is always an event in the life of country people. The owners of property and their servants also speak of it two months before they arrive, and it is still a topic of interest three years after they have left. For my part, the fact that a young and pretty woman would live so near upset me very much. I was dying to see her, and the first Sunday after they were settled, I walked over after dinner to pay my respects to the lady and introduce myself as her nearest neighbor and her devoted slave.

A footman led me to the Count's library and left to announce me. This library was large and magnificently furnished. Against the walls were shelves filled with books, and on each one was a figure in bronze; above a marble mantelpiece stood a large mirror. The floor was covered with green cloth over which were thrown rich Persian rugs. Unused as I was in my hovel to any kind of luxury, it was so long since I had seen anything like this display of wealth that I actually felt timid and experienced inward tremblings while waiting for the Count, such as a country solicitor might feel when asking an audience of a minister. The door opened and a young man, about thirty-two years of age, entered. He greeted me in a most cordial and charming manner. I tried to appear at ease and was just going to make the usual commonplace remarks about being delighted at having such neighbors when he forestalled me by saying how welcome I was.

We sat down and his manner was so cordial that it soon dispelled my unusual timidity. I was just beginning to feel like my old self again when the Countess appeared in the doorway, and once more I grew desperately shy. She was a beauty. The Count introduced me and the more I tried to be natural and quite at ease, the more I looked awkward and embarrassed. My hosts, in order to give me time to recover from my bashfulness, chatted

---

3. **versts**\vərsts\ four versts equal about two and two-thirds miles.

together, as if to show that they considered me an old acquaintance already and one to be treated as such, so that while walking about the library I looked at the books and pictures. As far as pictures are concerned, I am no connoisseur, but there was one there that attracted my attention. It represented a Swiss scene, and the beauty of the landscape did not attract me quite as much as did the fact that the canvas was pierced by two bullets evidently fired one on the other.

"That is a pretty good shot!" I cried, turning toward the Count.

"Yes," said he "and rather a peculiar one. Are you a pistol shot?" he added.

"Why, yes, a fairly good one," I answered, delighted to have a chance to speak of something with which I was familiar. "I think I could hit a card at thirty paces, with my own pistols of course."

"Really?" said the Countess, seemingly much interested. "And you, my dear," this to her husband, "could you hit a card at thirty paces?"

"I don't know about that," answered the Count, "I was a pretty good shot in my day, but it must be four years now since I used a pistol."

"In that case, sir," I continued, "I'll bet you anything that even at twenty paces you could not hit a card; because to excel at pistol shooting one requires constant practice. I know this from experience. At home, I was considered one of the best shots in the regiment, but it happened once that I was a month without using a pistol, mine being at the gunsmith's. We were called to the shooting gallery one day, and what do you think happened to me, sir? I missed a bottle standing twenty-five paces away, four times in succession. There was with us at the time a major of cavalry, a good fellow, who was forever joking: 'Faith, my friend,' he said to me, 'this is too much moderation. You have too great a respect for the bottle.' Believe me, sir, one must practice all the time. Otherwise, one gets rusty. The best marksman I ever knew practiced every day, firing at least three shots before his dinner; he would no more have missed them than he would have omitted his cognac before dinner."

Both the Count and his wife seemed pleased to listen to me.

"And how did he shoot?" asked the Count.

"How? Let me tell you. He would see a fly on the wall. . . . You laugh? Madam——, I swear to you this is true. 'Eh! Kouska! a pistol!' Kouska would bring one loaded. Crack! there lay the fly flattened against the wall."

"What consummate skill!" cried the Count, "and what was this man's name?"

"Silvio, sir."

"Silvio!" cried the Count, starting to his feet. "You have known Silvio?"

"Have I known him? Well, rather. We were the greatest of friends; he was like one of us in the regiment. But it is five years now since I heard of him. And you also knew him?"

"Yes, I knew him well. Did he ever tell you a peculiar thing which happened to him once?"

"How he received a slap in the face, one evening, from a cad?"

"And did he tell you the name of this cad?"

"No, sir, he did not. Ah!" I cried, guessing at the truth. "Forgive me, sir, I did not know. Can it be you?"

"Yes, it was I," answered the Count, in an embarrassed manner, "and that picture with a hole in it is a souvenir of our last interview."

"For God's sake, my dear," said the Countess, "don't speak of it—the thought of it terrifies me to this day."

"No," said the Count. "I feel I ought to tell this gentleman. He knows how I offended his friend and it is only fair that he should learn how he revenged himself."

The Count drew an armchair for me to sit in, and I listened with the greatest interest to the following story:

"Five years ago we were married. We spent the first month of our honeymoon here in this house, and to it clings the memory of the happiest days of my life, coupled with one of the most painful experiences I have ever had.

"One evening, we had both gone out horseback riding. My wife's horse became very restless and she was so frightened that she begged me to lead him to the stables and she would walk back by herself. On reaching the house, I found a traveling coach at the door and was told that a man was waiting in the library. He had refused to give his name, saying he wished to see me on business. I came into this room and in the half light I saw a man with a beard standing before the mantelpiece, still in his dusty traveling clothes. I drew nearer to him, trying to place him in my memory.

" 'You do not remember me, Count?' said he, in a voice that shook.

" 'Silvio!' I cried.

"And to be candid with you, I felt as if my hair were standing on end.

" 'Exactly,' he continued, 'and it is my turn to shoot. I have come to fire. Are you ready?'

"I saw a pistol sticking out of his left pocket. I measured twelve paces and stood there in that corner, begging him to be quick about it, as my wife would return in a few moments. He said he wanted a light first, and I rang for candles.

"I closed the door after giving orders not to admit anyone, and once more I told him to proceed. He raised his pistol and took aim . . . . I was counting the seconds . . . . I was thinking of her . . . . All this lasted a full minute and suddenly Silvio lowered his weapon.

" 'I am very sorry,' he said, 'but my pistol is not loaded with cherry pits . . . and bullets are hard . . . . After all, come to think of it, this does not look much like a duel. It is more like a murder. I am not in the habit of firing on an unarmed man. Let us begin all over again. Let us draw lots to see who will shoot first.'

"My head was in whirl, and it turned out that I refused at first. Finally, we loaded our pistols and we put two papers in the very cap I had once perforated with a bullet. I took one of the papers and as luck would have it, I drew number one.

" 'You are devilish lucky, Count!' said he, with a smile I will never forget.

"I cannot to this day understand it, but he finally compelled me to fire, . . . and my bullet hit that picture there."

The Count pointed to the landscape with the hole in it. His face was crimson. There was the Countess as white as a sheet, and as for me I barely suppressed a cry.

"I fired at him," continued the Count, "and thank God, I missed him.

"Then Silvio—at that moment he was positively hideous—stood back and took aim. Just then, the door opened. My wife came in and seeing us facing each other, threw herself in my arms. Her presence gave me back my courage.

" 'My dear,' I said, 'do you not see that we are only jesting? How frightened you are! Go now, get a glass of water and come back to us. I will then introduce my old friend and comrade to you.'

"But my wife knew better than to believe my words.

" 'Tell me, is what my husband says true?' she asked of the terrible Silvio. 'Is it true that this is only a jest?'

" 'He is always jesting, Madam,' replied Silvio. 'Once upon a time he gave me a slap, in jest; again, in jest, he pierced my cap with a bullet; and a few minutes ago, still jesting, he just missed me. Now it is my turn to laugh a little.'

"Saying which, he took aim once more, with my wife looking on. She fell on her knees at his feet.

" 'Get up, Marsha!' I cried enraged. 'Are you not ashamed of yourself? And you, sir, do you wish to drive this poor woman crazy? Will you please fire, yes or no?'

" 'I will not,' answered Silvio, 'I am satisfied. I saw you falter. You were pale with fright, and that is all I hoped to see. I compelled you to fire on me and I know you will never forget me. I leave you to your conscience.'

"He walked toward the door and turning round, he glanced at the picture with the bullet hole and without aiming at all, he fired, and doubled my shot. Then he went out. My wife fainted—none of the servants dared stop him, and the doors opened before him in great haste. On the porch he called for his carriage, and he was already some distance when I recovered from my bewilderment."

The Count stopped.

It was thus I heard the end of a story, the beginning of which interested me much. I have never seen Silvio. It was said that at the time of the insurrection of Alexander Ypsilanti,[4] he was at the head of a regiment of rebels and that he was killed when their army was routed at Skouliani.

I
PATTERNS OF IRONY

"The Pistol Shot" is a story that is told in three parts. The first part centers around the narrator, who reveals his experiences with a mysterious officer. The second part centers around the mysterious officer and his part in an unusual duel. And the final part centers around the opponent in the duel, who relates the outcome of the duel. Thus the plot is put together like a kind of jigsaw puzzle. Each piece adds to the suspense, rising in intensity toward the final element of irony. Can you locate ironic incidents in each section of the story?

II
IMPLICATIONS

How do you react to the following statements? Some are taken from the story itself; others are suggested by the story.

1. Lack of courage is the last thing to be forgiven by young people.

2. We generally dislike a person like the Count, who is described as having all the good things: youth, intelligence, good looks, boundless gaiety, courage, a great name, and money. It seems unfair that one person should have so much.

3. It is infuriating when a person refuses to react to our taunts, as does the Count in the cherry eating incident.

4. In the long run, the Count shows more courage than Silvio.

III
TECHNIQUES

Atmosphere

The atmosphere of the story is created by the narrator, an observer, who is not really a participant in the central plot of Silvio and the Count. You probably formed some sort of impression of the narrator. What details do you know about his age, his level of education, his life style? What tonality or atmosphere do these details give to the story?

Suspense

1. What is the first incident in the story in which you, the reader, anticipate some immediate reaction? How is the reaction withheld?

2. Where do you find out the central problem of the story and anticipate a climax? How is the story structured so that your curiosity is not immediately satisfied? Suppose you had followed the narrator directly to the Count's house and had been told in usual chronological order the events as they happened: why wouldn't the story have had the same impact?

---

4. **Ypsilanti**\ˈip·sə ᵃlant·ē\ a Greek who was a general in the Russian army. He led his forces in a revolt against the Turks in 1821. The revolt to free Greece from Turkey was unsuccessful.

The power of one's mind can sometimes be stronger than the reality outside it. A pale blue hotel whipped by a wintery blizzard seems a snug and cozy haven to a group of travelers— until the fears of one guest set off a chain of reactions.

The Blue Hotel

STEPHEN CRANE

1

The Palace Hotel at Fort Romper was painted a light blue, a shade that is on the legs of a kind of heron, causing the bird to declare its position against any background. The Palace Hotel, then, was always screaming and howling in a way that made the dazzling winter landscape of Nebraska seem only a gray swampish hush. It stood alone on the prairie, and when the snow was falling the town two hundred yards away was not visible. But when the traveler alighted at the railway station he was obliged to pass the Palace Hotel before he could come upon the company of low clapboard houses which composed Fort Romper, and it was not to be thought that any traveler could pass the Palace Hotel without looking at it. Pat Scully, the proprietor, had proved himself a master of strategy when he chose his paints. It is true that on clear days, when the great transcontinental expresses, long lines of swaying Pullmans, swept through Fort Romper, passengers were overcome at the sight, and the cult that knows the brown-reds and the subdivisions of the dark greens of the East expressed shame, pity, horror, in a laugh. But to the citizens of this prairie town and to the people who would naturally stop there, Pat Scully had performed a feat. With this opu-lence and splendor, these creeds, classes, ego-tisms, that streamed through Romper on the rails day after day, they had no color in common.

As if the displayed delights of such a blue hotel were not sufficiently enticing, it was Scully's habit to go every morning and evening to meet the leisurely trains that stopped at Romper and work his seductions upon any man that he might see wavering, gripsack in hand.

One morning, when a snow-crusted engine dragged its long string of freight cars and its one passenger coach to the station, Scully per-formed the marvel of catching three men. One was a shaky and quick-eyed Swede, with a great shining cheap valise; one was a tall bronzed cowboy, who was on his way to a ranch near the Dakota line; one was a little silent man from the East, who didn't look it, and didn't announce it. Scully practically made them prisoners. He was so nimble and merry and kindly that each probably felt it would be the height of brutality to try to escape. They trudged off over the creaking board sidewalks in the wake of the eager little Irishman. He wore a heavy fur cap squeezed tightly down on his head. It caused his two red ears to stick out stiffly, as if they were made of tin.

At last, Scully, elaborately, with boisterous hospitality, conducted them through the por-tals of the blue hotel. The room which they entered was small. It seemed to be merely a proper temple for an enormous stove, which, in the center, was humming with godlike violence. At various points on its surface the iron had become luminous and glowed yellow from the heat. Beside the stove Scully's son Johnnie was playing High-Five with an old farmer who had whiskers both gray and sandy. They were quarreling. Frequently the old farmer turned his face toward a box of saw-dust—colored brown from tobacco juice—that was behind the stove, and spat with an air of great impatience and irritation. With a loud flourish of words Scully destroyed the game of cards, and bustled his son upstairs with part of the baggage of the new guests. He himself conducted them to three basins of the coldest water in the world. The cowboy and the Easterner burnished themselves fiery red with this water, until it seemed to be some kind of metal polish. The Swede, however, merely dipped his fingers gingerly and with trepidation. It was notable that throughout this series of small ceremonies the three travelers were made to feel that Scully was very benevolent. He was conferring great favors upon them. He handed the towel from one to another with an air of philanthropic impulse.

Afterward they went to the first room, and, sitting about the stove, listened to Scully's officious clamor at his daughters, who were preparing the midday meal. They reflected in the silence of experienced men who tread carefully amid new people. Nevertheless, the old farmer, stationary, invincible in his chair near the warmest part of the stove, turned his face from the sawdust box frequently and addressed a glowing commonplace to the strangers. Usually he was answered in short but adequate sentences by either the cowboy or the Easterner. The Swede said nothing. He seemed to be occupied in making furtive estimates of each man in the room. One might have thought that he had the sense of silly suspicion which comes to guilt. He resembled a badly frightened man.

Later, at dinner, he spoke a little, addressing his conversation entirely to Scully. He volunteered that he had come from New York, where for ten years he had worked as a tailor. These facts seemed to strike Scully as fascinating, and afterward he volunteered that he had lived at Romper for fourteen years. The Swede asked about the crops and the price of labor. He seemed barely to listen to Scully's extended replies. His eyes continued to rove from man to man.

Finally, with a laugh and a wink, he said that some of these Western communities were very dangerous; and after his statement he straightened his legs under the table, tilted his head, and laughed again, loudly. It was plain that the demonstration had no meaning to the others. They looked at him wondering and in silence.

2

As the men trooped heavily back into the front room, the two little windows presented views of a turmoiling sea of snow. The huge arms of the wind were making attempts—mighty, circular, futile—to embrace the flakes as they sped. A gatepost like a still man with a blanched face stood aghast amid this profligate fury. In a hearty voice Scully announced the presence of a blizzard. The guests of the blue hotel, lighting their pipes, assented with grunts of lazy masculine contentment. No island of the sea could be exempt in the degree of this little room with its humming stove. Johnnie, son of Scully, in a tone which defined his opinion of his ability as a card player, challenged the old farmer of both gray and sandy whiskers to a game of High-Five. The farmer agreed with a contemptuous and bitter scoff. They sat close to the stove, and squared their knees under a wide board. The cowboy and the Easterner watched the game with interest. The Swede remained near the window, aloof, but with a countenance that showed signs of an inexplicable excitement.

The play of Johnnie and the graybeard was suddenly ended by another quarrel. The old man arose while casting a look of heated scorn at his adversary. He slowly buttoned his coat, and then stalked with fabulous dignity from the room. In the discreet silence of all other men the Swede laughed. His laughter rang somehow childish. Men by this time had begun to look at him askance, as if they wished to inquire what ailed him.

A new game was formed jocosely. The cowboy volunteered to become the partner of Johnnie, and they all then turned to ask the Swede to throw in his lot with the little Easterner. He asked some questions about the game, and, learning that it wore many names, and that he had played it when it was under an alias, he accepted the invitation. He strode toward the men nervously, as if he expected to be assaulted. Finally, seated, he gazed from face to face and laughed shrilly. This laugh was so strange that the Easterner looked up quickly, the cowboy sat intent and with his mouth open, and Johnnie paused, holding the cards with still fingers.

Afterward there was a short silence. Then Johnnie said, "Well, let's get at it. Come on now!" They pulled their chairs forward until their knees were bunched under the board. They began to play, and their interest in the game caused the others to forget the manner of the Swede.

The cowboy was a board-whacker. Each time that he held superior cards he whanged them, one by one, with exceeding force, down upon the improvised table, and took the tricks with a glowing air of prowess and pride that sent thrills of indignation into the hearts of his opponents. A game with a board-whacker in it is sure to become intense. The countenances of the Easterner and the Swede were miserable whenever the cowboy thundered down his aces and kings, while Johnnie, his eyes gleaming with joy, chuckled and chuckled.

Because of the absorbing play none considered the strange ways of the Swede. They paid strict heed to the game. Finally, during a lull caused by a new deal, the Swede suddenly addressed Johnnie: "I suppose there have been a good many men killed in this room." The jaws of the others dropped and they looked at him.

"What are you talking about?" said Johnnie.

The Swede laughed again his blatant laugh, full of a kind of false courage and defiance. "Oh, you know what I mean all right," he answered.

"I'm a liar if I do!" Johnnie protested. The card game was halted, and the men stared at the Swede. Johnnie evidently felt that as the son of the proprietor he should make a direct inquiry. "Now, what might you be drivin' at, mister?" he asked. The Swede winked at him.

It was a wink full of cunning. His fingers shook on the edge of the board. "Oh, maybe you think I have been to nowheres. Maybe you think I'm a tenderfoot?"

"I don't know nothin' about you," answered Johnnie, "and I don't give a damn where you've been. All I got to say is that I don't know what you're driving at. There hain't never been nobody killed in this room."

The cowboy, who had been steadily gazing at the Swede, then spoke: "What's wrong with you, mister?"

Apparently it seemed to the Swede that he was formidably menaced. He shivered and turned white near the corners of his mouth. He sent an appealing glance in the direction of the little Easterner. During these moments he did not forget to wear his air of advanced pot-valor.[1] "They say they don't know what I mean," he remarked mockingly to the Easterner.

The latter answered after prolonged and cautious reflection. "I don't understand you," he said, impassively.

The Swede made a movement then which announced that he thought he had encountered treachery from the only quarter where he had expected sympathy, if not help. "Oh, I see you are all against me. I see—"

The cowboy was in a state of deep stupefaction. "Say," he cried, as he tumbled the deck violently down upon the board, "say, what are you gittin' at, hey?"

The Swede sprang up with the celerity of a man escaping from a snake on the floor. "I don't want to fight!" he shouted. "I don't want to fight!"

The cowboy stretched his long legs indolently and deliberately. His hands were in his pockets. He spat into the sawdust box. "Well, who thought you did?" he inquired.

The Swede backed rapidly toward a corner of the room. His hands were out protectingly in front of his chest, but he was making an

---

1. **pot-valor**\ˆpat 'val·ər\ a boldness resulting from alcoholic consumption.

obvious struggle to control his fright. "Gentlemen," he quavered, "I suppose I am going to be killed before I can leave this house! I suppose I am going to be killed before I can leave this house!" In his eyes was the dying-swan look. Through the windows could be seen the snow turning blue in the shadow of dusk. The wind tore at the house, and some loose thing beat regularly against the clapboards like a spirit tapping.

A door opened, and Scully himself entered. He paused in surprise as he noted the tragic attitude of the Swede. Then he said, "What's the matter here?"

The Swede answered him swiftly and eagerly: "These men are going to kill me."

"Kill you!" ejaculated Scully. "Kill you! What are you talkin'?"

The Swede made the gesture of a martyr.

Scully wheeled sternly upon his son. "What is this, Johnnie?"

The lad had grown sullen. "Darned if I know," he answered. "I can't make no sense to it." He began to shuffle the cards, fluttering them together with an angry snap. "He says a good many men have been killed in this room, or something like that. And he says he's goin' to be killed here too. I don't know what ails him. He's crazy, I shouldn't wonder."

Sully then looked for explanation to the cowboy, but the cowboy simply shrugged his shoulders.

"Kill you?" said Scully again to the Swede. "Kill you? Man, you're off your nut."

"Oh, I know," burst out the Swede. "I know what will happen. Yes, I'm crazy—yes. Yes, of course, I'm crazy—yes. But I know one thing —" There was a sort of sweat of misery and terror upon his face. "I know I won't get out of here alive."

The cowboy drew a deep breath, as if his mind was passing into the last stages of dissolution. "Well, I'm doggoned," he whispered to himself.

Scully wheeled suddenly and faced his son. "You've been troublin' this man!"

Johnnie's voice was loud with its burden of grievance. "Why, good Gawd, I ain't done nothin' to 'im."

The Swede broke in. "Gentlemen, do not disturb yourselves. I will leave this house. I will go away, because"—he accused them dramatically with his glance—"because I do not want to be killed."

Scully was furious with his son. "Will you tell me what is the matter, you young divil? What's the matter, anyhow? Speak out!"

"Blame it!" cried Johnnie in despair, "don't I tell you I don't know? He—he says we want to kill him, and that's all I know. I can't tell what ails him."

The Swede continued to repeat: "Never mind, Mr. Scully; never mind. I will leave this house. I will go away, because I do not wish to be killed. Yes, of course, I am crazy—yes. But I know one thing! I will go away. I will leave this house. Never mind, Mr. Scully; never mind. I will go away."

"You will not go 'way," said Scully. "You will not go 'way until I hear the reason of this business. If anybody has troubled you I will take care of him. This is my house. You are under my roof, and I will not allow any peaceable man to be troubled here." He cast a terrible eye upon Johnnie, the cowboy, and the Easterner.

"Never mind, Mr. Scully; never mind. I will go away. I do not wish to be killed." The Swede moved toward the door which opened upon the stairs. It was evidently his intention to go at once for his baggage.

"No, no," shouted Scully peremptorily; but the white-faced man slid by him and disappeared. "Now," said Scully severely, "what does this mane?"

Johnnie and the cowboy cried together: "Why, we didn't do nothin' to 'im!"

Scully's eyes were cold. "No," he said, "you didn't?"

Johnnie swore a deep oath. "Why, this is the wildest loon I ever see. We didn't do nothin' at all. We were just sittin' here playin' cards, and he——"

The father suddenly spoke to the Easterner.

"Mr. Blanc," he asked, "what has these boys been doin'?"

The Easterner reflected again. "I didn't see anything wrong at all," he said at last, slowly.

Scully began to howl. "But what does it mane?" He stared ferociously at his son. "I have a mind to lather you for this, me boy."

Johnnie was frantic. "Well, what have I done?" he bawled at his father.

3

"I think you are tongue-tied," said Scully finally to his son, the cowboy, and the Easterner; and at the end of this scornful sentence he left the room.

Upstairs the Swede was swiftly fastening the straps of his great valise. Once his back happened to be half turned toward the door, and, hearing a noise there, he wheeled and sprang up, uttering a loud cry. Scully's wrinkled visage showed grimly in the light of the small lamp he carried. This yellow effulgence, streaming upward, colored only his prominent features, and left his eyes, for instance, in mysterious shadow. He resembled a murderer.

"Man! man!" he exclaimed, "have you gone daffy?"

"Oh, no! Oh, no!" rejoined the other. "There are people in this world who know pretty nearly as much as you do—understand?"

For a moment they stood gazing at each other. Upon the Swede's deathly pale cheeks were two spots brightly crimson and sharply edged, as if they had been carefully painted. Scully placed the light on the table and sat himself on the edge of the bed. He spoke ruminatively. "By cracky, I never heard of such a thing in my life. It's a complete muddle. I can't, for the soul of me, think how you ever got this idea into your head." Presently he lifted his eyes and asked: "And did you sure think they were going to kill you?"

The Swede scanned the old man as if he wished to see into his mind. "I did," he said at last. He obviously suspected that this answer might precipitate an outbreak. As he pulled on a strap his whole arm shook, the elbow wavering like a bit of paper.

Scully banged his hand impressively on the footboard of the bed. "Why, man, we're goin' to have a line of ilictric streetcars in this town next spring."

"'A line of electric streetcars,'" repeated the Swede, stupidly.

"And," said Scully, "there's a new railroad goin' to be built down from Broken Arm to here. Not to mintion the four churches and the smashin' big brick schoolhouse. Then there's the big factory, too. Why, in two years Romper'll be a met-tro-*pol*-is."

Having finished the preparation of his baggage, the Swede straightened himself. "Mr. Scully," he said, with sudden hardihood, "how much do I owe you?"

"You don't owe me anythin'," said the old man, angrily.

"Yes, I do," retorted the Swede. He took seventy-five cents from his pocket and tendered it to Scully; but the latter snapped his fingers in disdainful refusal. However, it happened that they both stood gazing in a strange fashion at three silver pieces on the Swede's open palm.

"I'll not take your money," said Scully at last. "Not after what's been goin' on here." Then a plan seemed to strike him. "Here," he cried, picking up his lamp and moving toward the door. "Here! Come with me a minute."

"No," said the Swede, in overwhelming alarm.

"Yes," urged the old man. "Come on! I want you to come and see a picter—just across the hall—in my room."

The Swede must have concluded that his hour was come. His jaw dropped and his teeth showed like a dead man's. He ultimately followed Scully across the corridor, but he had the step of one hung in chains.

Scully flashed the light high on the wall of his own chamber. There was revealed a ridiculous photograph of a little girl. She was leaning against a balustrade of gorgeous dec-oration, and the formidable bang to her hair was prominent. The figure was as graceful as an upright sledstake, and, withal, it was of the hue of lead. "There," said Scully, tenderly, "that's the picter of my little girl that died. Her name was Carrie. She had the purtiest hair you ever saw! I was that fond of her, she—"

Turning then, he saw that the Swede was not contemplating the picture at all, but, instead, was keeping keen watch on the gloom in the rear.

"Look, man!" cried Scully, heartily. "That's the picter of my little gal that died. Her name was Carrie. And then here's the picter of my oldest boy, Michael. He's a lawyer in Lincoln, an' doin' well. I gave that boy a grand eddication, and I'm glad for it now. He's a fine boy. Look at 'im now. Ain't he bold as blazes, him there in Lincoln, an honored an' respicted gintleman! An honored and respicted gintleman," concluded Scully with a flourish. And, so saying, he smote the Swede jovially on the back.

The Swede faintly smiled.

"Now," said the old man, "there's only one more thing." He dropped suddenly to the floor and thrust his head beneath the bed. The Swede could hear his muffled voice. "I'd keep it under me piller if it wasn't for that boy Johnnie. Then there's the old woman— Where is it now? I never put it twice in the same place. Ah, now come out with you!"

Presently he backed clumsily from under the bed, dragging with him an old coat rolled into a bundle. "I've fetched him," he muttered. Kneeling on the floor, he unrolled the coat and extracted from its heart a large yellow-brown whiskey bottle.

His first maneuver was to hold the bottle up to the light. Reassured, apparently, that nobody had been tampering with it, he thrust it with a generous movement toward the Swede.

The weak-kneed Swede was about to eagerly clutch this element of strength, but he suddenly jerked his hand away and cast a look of horror upon Scully.

"Drink," said the old man affectionately. He had risen to his feet, and now stood facing the Swede.

There was a silence. Then again Scully said: "Drink!"

The Swede laughed wildly. He grabbed the bottle, put it to his mouth; and as his lips curled absurdly around the opening and his throat worked, he kept his glance, burning with hatred, upon the old man's face.

4

After the departure of Scully the three men, with the cardboard still upon their knees, preserved for a long time an astounded silence. Then Johnnie said: "That's the doddangedest Swede I ever see."

"He ain't no Swede," said the cowboy, scornfully.

"Well, what is he then?" cried Johnnie. "What is he then?"

"It's my opinion," replied the cowboy deliberately, "he's some kind of a Dutchman." It was a venerable custom of the country to entitle as Swedes all light-haired men who spoke with a heavy tongue. In consequence the idea of the cowboy was not without its daring. "Yes, sir," he repeated. "It's my opinion this feller is some kind of a Dutchman."

"Well, he says he's a Swede, anyhow," muttered Johnnie, sulkily. He turned to the Easterner: "What do you think, Mr. Blanc?"

"Oh, I don't know," replied the Easterner.

"Well, what do you think makes him act that way?" asked the cowboy.

"Why, he's frightened." The Easterner knocked his pipe against a rim of the stove. "He's clear frightened out of his boots."

"What at?" cried Johnnie and the cowboy together.

The Eastern reflected over his answer.

"What at?" cried the others again.

"Oh, I don't know, but it seems to me this man has been reading dime novels, and he thinks he's right out in the middle of it—the shootin' and stabbin' and all."

"But," said the cowboy, deeply scandalized, "this ain't Wyoming, ner none of them places. This is Nebrasker."

"Yes," added Johnnie, "an' why don't he wait till he gits *out West?*"

The traveled Easterner laughed. "It isn't different there even—not in these days. But he thinks he's right in the middle of hell."

Johnnie and the cowboy mused long.

"It's awful funny," remarked Johnnie at last.

"Yes," said the cowboy. "This is a queer game. I hope we don't git snowed in, because then we'd have to stand this here man bein' around with us all the time. That wouldn't be no good."

"I wish pop would throw him out," said Johnnie.

Presently they heard a loud stamping on the stairs, accompanied by ringing jokes in the voice of old Scully, and laughter, evidently from the Swede. The men around the stove stared vacantly at each other. "Gosh!" said the cowboy. The door flew open, and old Scully, flushed and anecdotal, came into the room. He was jabbering at the Swede, who followed him, laughing bravely. It was the entry of two roisterers from a banquet hall.

"Come now," said Scully sharply to the three seated men, "move up and give us a chance at the stove." The cowboy and the Easterner obediently sidled their chairs to make room for the newcomers. Johnnie, however, simply arranged himself in a more indolent attitude, and then remained motionless. "Come! Git over, there," said Scully.

"Plenty of room on the other side of the stove," said Johnnie.

"Do you think we want to sit in the draught?" roared the father.

But the Swede here interposed with a grandeur of confidence. "No, no. Let the boy sit where he likes," he cried in a bullying voice to the father.

"All right! All right!" said Scully, deferentially. The cowboy and the Easterner exchanged glances of wonder.

The five chairs were formed in a crescent about one side of the stove. The Swede began to talk; he talked arrogantly, profanely, angrily. Johnnie, the cowboy, and the Easterner maintained a morose silence, while old Scully appeared to be receptive and eager, breaking in constantly with sympathetic ejaculations.

Finally the Swede announced that he was thirsty. He moved in his chair, and said that he would go for a drink of water.

"I'll git it for you," cried Scully at once.

"No," said the Swede, contemptuously. "I'll get it for myself." He arose and stalked with the air of an owner off into the executive parts of the hotel.

As soon as the Swede was out of hearing Scully sprang to his feet and whispered intensely to the others: "Upstairs he thought I was tryin' to poison 'im."

"Say," said Johnnie, "this makes me sick. Why don't you throw 'im out in the snow?"

"Why, he's all right now," declared Scully. "It was only that he was from the East, and he thought this was a tough place. That's all. He's all right now."

The cowboy looked with admiration upon the Easterner. "You were straight," he said. "You were on to that there Dutchman."

"Well," said Johnnie to his father, "he may be all right now, but I don't see it. Other time he was scared, but now he's too fresh."

Scully's speech was always a combination of Irish brogue and idiom, Western twang and idiom, and scraps of curiously formal diction taken from the story-books and newspapers. He now hurled a strange mass of language at the head of his son. "What do I keep? What do I keep? What do I keep?" he demanded, in a voice of thunder. He slapped his knee impressively, to indicate that he himself was going to make reply, and that all should heed. "I keep a hotel," he shouted. "A hotel, do you mind? A guest under my roof has sacred privileges. He is to be intimidated by none. Not one word shall he hear that would prijudice him in favor of goin' away. I'll not have it. There's no place in this here town where they can say they iver took in a guest of mine because he was afraid to stay here." He wheeled suddenly upon the cowboy and the Easterner. "Am I right?"

"Yes, Mr. Scully," said the cowboy, "I think you're right."

"Yes, Mr. Scully," said the Easterner, "I think you're right."

5

At six-o'clock supper, the Swede fizzed like a fire-wheel. He sometimes seemed on the point of bursting into riotous song, and in all his madness he was encouraged by old Scully. The Easterner was encased in reserve; the cowboy sat in wide-mouthed amazement, forgetting to eat, while Johnnie wrathily demolished great plates of food. The daughters of the house, when they were obliged to replenish the biscuits, approached as warily as Indians, and, having succeeded in their purpose, fled with ill-concealed trepidation. The Swede domineered the whole feast, and he gave it the appearance of a cruel bacchanal. He seemed to have grown suddenly taller; he gazed, brutally disdainful, into every face. His voice rang through the room. Once when he jabbed out harpoon-fashion with his fork to pinion a biscuit, the weapon nearly impaled the hand of the Easterner, which had been stretched quietly out for the same biscuit.

After supper, as the men filed toward the other room, the Swede smote Scully ruthlessly on the shoulder. "Well, old boy, that was a good, square meal." Johnnie looked hopefully at his father; he knew that shoulder was tender from an old fall; and, indeed, it appeared for a moment as if Scully was going to flame out over the matter, but in the end he smiled a sickly smile and remained silent. The others understood from his manner that he was admitting his responsibility for the Swede's new viewpoint.

Johnnie, however, addressed his parent in an aside. "Why don't you license somebody to kick you downstairs?" Scully scowled darkly by way of reply.

When they were gathered about the stove, the Swede insisted on another game of High-Five. Scully gently deprecated the plan at first, but the Swede turned a wolfish glare upon him. The old man subsided, and the Swede canvassed the others. In his tone there was always a great threat. The cowboy and the Easterner both remarked indifferently that they would play. Scully said that he would presently have to go to meet the 6:58 train, and so the Swede turned menacingly upon Johnnie. For a moment their glances crossed like blades, and then Johnnie smiled and said, "Yes, I'll play."

They formed a square, with the little board on their knees. The Easterner and the Swede were again partners. As the play went on, it was noticeable that the cowboy was not board-whacking as usual. Meanwhile, Scully, near the lamp, had put on his spectacles and, with an appearance curiously like an old priest, was reading a newspaper. In time he went out to meet the 6:58 train, and, despite his precautions, a gust of polar wind whirled into the room as he opened the door. Besides scattering the cards, it chilled the players to the marrow. The Swede cursed frightfully. When Scully returned, his entrance disturbed a cozy and friendly scene. The Swede again cursed. But presently they were once more intent, their heads bent forward and their hands moving swiftly. The Swede had adopted the fashion of board-whacking.

Scully took up his paper and for a long time remained immersed in matters which were extraordinarily remote from him. The lamp burned badly, and once he stopped to adjust the wick. The newspaper, as he turned from page to page, rustled with a slow and comfortable sound. Then suddenly he heard three terrible words: "You are cheatin'!"

Such scenes often prove that there can be little of dramatic import in environment. Any room can present a tragic front; any room can be comic. This little den was now hideous as a torture chamber. The new faces of the men themselves had changed it upon the instant.

The Swede held a huge fist in front of Johnnie's face while the latter looked steadily over it into the blazing orbs of his accuser. The Easterner had grown pallid; the cowboy's jaw had dropped in that expression of bovine amazement which was one of his important mannerisms. After the three words, the first sound in the room was made by Scully's paper as it floated forgotten to his feet. His spectacles had also fallen from his nose, but by a clutch he had saved them in air. His hand, grasping the spectacles, now remained poised awkwardly and near his shoulder. He stared at the card-players.

Probably the silence was while a second elapsed. Then, if the floor had been suddenly twitched out from under the men they could not have moved quicker. The five had projected themselves headlong toward a common point. It happened that Johnnie, in rising to hurl himself upon the Swede, had stumbled slightly because of his curiously instinctive care for the cards and the board. The loss of the moment allowed time for the arrival of Scully, and also allowed the cowboy time to give the Swede a great push which sent him staggering back. The men found tongue together, and hoarse shouts of rage, appeal, or fear burst from every throat. The cowboy pushed and jostled feverishly at the Swede, and the Easterner and Scully clung wildly to Johnnie; but through the smoky air, above the swaying bodies of the peace-compellers, the eyes of the two warriors ever sought each other in glances of challenge that were at once hot and steely.

Of course the board had been overturned, and now the whole company of cards was scattered over the floor, where the boots of the men trampled the fat and painted kings and queens as they gazed with their silly eyes at the war that was waging above them.

Scully's voice was dominating the yells. "Stop now! Stop, I say! Stop, now—"

Johnnie, as he struggled to burst through the rank formed by Scully and the Easterner, was crying, "Well, he says I cheated! He says

I cheated! I won't allow no man to say I cheated! If he says I cheated, he's a ——!"

The cowboy was telling the Swede, "Quit, now! Quit, d'ye hear—"

The screams of the Swede never ceased: "He did cheat! I saw him! I saw him—"

As for the Easterner, he was importuning in a voice that was not heeded: "Wait a moment, can't you? Oh, wait a moment. What's the good of a fight over a game of cards? Wait a moment—"

In this tumult no complete sentences were clear. "Cheat"— "Quit"— "He says"—these fragments pierced the uproar and rang out sharply. It was remarkable that, whereas Scully undoubtedly made the most noise, he was the least heard of any of the riotous band.

Then suddenly there was a great cessation. It was as if each man had paused for breath; and although the room was still lighted with the anger of men, it could be seen that there was no danger of immediate conflict, and at once Johnnie, shouldering his way forward, almost succeeded in confronting the Swede. "What did you say I cheated for? What did you say I cheated for? I don't cheat, and I won't let no man say I do!"

The Swede said, "I saw you! I saw you!"

"Well," cried Johnnie, "I'll fight any man what says I cheat!"

"No, you won't," said the cowboy. "Not here."

"Ah, be still, can't you?" said Scully, coming between them.

The quiet was sufficient to allow the Easterner's voice to be heard. He was repeating, "Oh, wait a moment, can't you? What's the good of a fight over a game of cards? Wait a moment!"

Johnnie, his red face appearing above his father's shoulder, hailed the Swede again. "Did you say I cheated?"

The Swede showed his teeth. "Yes."

"Then," said Johnnie, "we must fight."

"Yes, fight," roared the Swede. He was like a demoniac. "Yes, fight! I'll show you what kind of a man I am! I'll show you who you want to fight! Maybe you think I can't fight! Maybe you think I can't! I'll show you, you skin, you card-sharp! Yes, you cheated! You cheated! You cheated!"

"Well, let's go at it, then, mister," said Johnnie, coolly.

The cowboy's brow was beaded with sweat from his efforts in intercepting all sort of raids. He turned in despair to Scully. "What are you goin' to do now?"

A change had come over the Celtic[2] visage of the old man. He now seemed all eagerness; his eyes glowed.

"We'll let them fight," he answered, stalwartly. "I can't put up with it any longer. I've stood this damned Swede till I'm sick. We'll let them fight."

6

The men prepared to go out-of-doors. The Easterner was so nervous that he had great difficulty in getting his arms into the sleeves of his new leather coat. As the cowboy drew his fur cap down over his ears his hands trembled. In fact, Johnnie and old Scully were the only ones who displayed no agitation. These preliminaries were conducted without words.

Scully threw open the door. "Well, come on," he said. Instantly a terrific wind caused the flame of the lamp to struggle at its wick, while a puff of black smoke sprang from the chimney-top. The stove was in mid-current of the blast, and its voice swelled to equal the roar of the storm. Some of the scarred and bedabbled cards were caught up from the floor and dashed helplessly against the farther wall. The men lowered their heads and plunged into the tempest as into a sea.

No snow was falling, but great whirls and clouds of flakes, swept up from the ground by the frantic winds, were streaming southward with the speed of bullets. The covered land was blue with the sheen of an unearthly satin, and there was no other hue save where, at the low black railway station—which seemed incredibly distant—one light gleamed like a tiny jewel. As the men floundered into a thigh-deep drift, it was known that the Swede was bawling out something. Scully went to him, put a hand on his shoulder, and projected an ear. "What's that you say?" he shouted.

"I say," bawled the Swede again, "I won't stand much show against this gang. I know you'll all pitch on me."

Scully smote him reproachfully on the arm. "Tut, man!" he yelled. The wind tore the words from Scully's lips and scattered them far alee.

"You are all a gang of—" boomed the Swede, but the storm also seized the remainder of this sentence.

Immediately turning their backs upon the wind, the men had swung around a corner to the sheltered side of the hotel. It was the function of the little house to preserve here, amid this great devastation of snow, an irregular V-shape of heavily encrusted grass, which crackled beneath the feet. One could imagine the great drifts piled against the windward side. When the party reached the comparative peace of this spot it was found that the Swede was still bellowing.

"Oh, I know what kind of a thing this is! I know you'll all pitch on me. I can't lick you all!"

Scully turned upon him panther-fashion. "You'll not have to whip all of us. You'll have to whip my son Johnnie. An' the man what troubles you durin' that time will have me to dale with."

The arrangements were swiftly made. The two men faced each other, obedient to the harsh commands of Scully, whose face, in the subtly luminous gloom, could be seen set in the austere impersonal lines that are pictured on the countenances of the Roman veterans. The Easterner's teeth were chattering, and he was hopping up and down like a mechanical toy. The cowboy stood rock-like.

The contestants had not stripped off any

---

2. **Celtic**\ˈsel·tĭk\ a member of the early Indo-European people found chiefly in the British Isles.

clothing. Each was in his ordinary attire. Their fists were up, and they eyed each other in a calm that had the elements of leonine cruelty in it.

During this pause, the Easterner's mind, like a film, took lasting impressions of three men—the iron-nerved master of the ceremony; the Swede, pale, motionless, terrible; and Johnnie, serene yet ferocious, brutish yet heroic. The entire prelude had in it a tragedy greater than the tragedy of action, and this aspect was accentuated by the long, mellow cry of the blizzard, as it sped the tumbling and wailing flakes into the black abyss of the south.

"Now!" said Scully.

The two combatants leaped forward and crashed together like bullocks. There was heard the cushioned sound of blows, and of a curse squeezing out from between the tight teeth of one.

As for the spectators, the Easterner's pent-up breath exploded from him with a pop of relief, absolute relief from the tension of the preliminaries. The cowboy bounded into the air with a yowl. Scully was immovable as from supreme amazement and fear at the fury of the fight which he himself had permitted and arranged.

For a time the encounter in the darkness was such a perplexity of flying arms that it presented no more detail than would a swiftly revolving wheel. Occasionally a face, as if illumined by a flash of light, would shine out, ghastly and marked with pink spots. A moment later, the men might have been known as shadows, if it were not for the involuntary utterance of oaths that came from them in whispers.

Suddenly a holocaust of warlike desire caught the cowboy, and he bolted forward with the speed of a bronco. "Go it, Johnnie! go it! Kill him! Kill him!"

Scully confronted him. "Kape back," he said; and by his glance the cowboy could tell that this man was Johnnie's father.

To the Easterner there was a monotony of unchangeable fighting that was an abomination. This confused mingling was eternal to his sense, which was concentrated in a longing for the end, the priceless end. Once the fighters lurched near him, and as he scrambled hastily backward he heard them breathe like men on the rack.

"Kill him, Johnnie! Kill him! Kill him! Kill him!" The cowboy's face was contorted like one of those agony masks in museums.

"Keep still," said Scully, icily.

Then there was a sudden loud grunt, incomplete, cut short, and Johnnie's body swung away from the Swede and fell with sickening heaviness to the grass. The cowboy was barely in time to prevent the mad Swede from flinging himself upon his prone adversary. "No, you don't," said the cowboy, interposing an arm. "Wait a second."

Scully was at his son's side. "Johnnie! Johnnie, me boy!" His voice had a quality of melancholy tenderness. "Johnnie! Can you go on with it?" He looked anxiously down into the bloody, pulpy face of his son.

There was a moment of silence, and then Johnnie answered in his ordinary voice, "Yes, I—it—yes."

Assisted by his father he struggled to his feet. "Wait a bit now till you git your wind," said the old man.

A few paces away the cowboy was lecturing the Swede. "No, you don't! Wait a second!"

The Easterner was plucking at Scully's sleeve. "Oh, this is enough," he pleaded. "This is enough! Let it go as it stands. This is enough!"

"Bill," said Scully, "git out of the road." The cowboy stepped aside. "Now." The combatants were actuated by a new caution as they advanced toward collision. They glared at each other, and then the Swede aimed a lightning blow that carried with it his entire weight. Johnnie was evidently half stupid from weakness, but he miraculously dodged, and his fist sent the overbalanced Swede sprawling.

The cowboy, Scully, and the Easterner burst into a cheer that was like a chorus of triumphant soldiery, but before its conclusion the Swede had scuffled agilely to his feet and come in berserk abandon at his foe. There was another perplexity of flying arms, and Johnnie's body again swung away and fell, even as a bundle might fall from a roof. The Swede instantly staggered to a little wind-waved tree and leaned upon it, breathing like an engine, while his savage and flame-lit eyes roamed from face to face as the men bent over Johnnie. There was a splendor of isolation in his situation at this time which the Easterner felt once when, lifting his eyes from the man on the ground, he beheld that mysterious and lonely figure, waiting.

"Are you any good yet, Johnnie?" asked Scully in a broken voice.

The son gasped and opened his eyes languidly. After a moment he answered, "No—I ain't—any good—any—more." Then, from shame and bodily ill, he began to weep, the tears furrowing down through the bloodstains on his face. "He was too—too—too heavy for me."

Scully straightened and addressed the waiting figure. "Stranger," he said, evenly, "it's all up with our side." Then his voice changed into that vibrant huskiness which is commonly the tone of the most simple and deadly announcements. "Johnnie is whipped."

Without replying, the victor moved off on the route to the front door of the hotel.

The cowboy was formulating new and unspellable blasphemies. The Easterner was startled to find that they were out in a wind that seemed to come direct from the shadowed arctic floes. He heard again the wail of the snow as it was flung to its grave in the south. He knew now that all this time the cold had been sinking into him deeper and deeper, and he wondered that he had not perished. He felt indifferent to the condition of the vanquished man.

"Johnnie, can you walk?" asked Scully.

"Did I hurt—hurt him any?" asked the son.

"Can you walk, boy? Can you walk?"

Johnnie's voice was suddenly strong. There was a robust impatience in it. "I asked you whether I hurt him any!"

"Yes, yes, Johnnie," answered the cowboy, consolingly; "he's hurt a good deal."

They raised him from the ground, and as soon as he was on his feet he went tottering off, rebuffing all attempts at assistance. When the party rounded the corner they were fairly blinded by the pelting of the snow. It burned their faces like fire. The cowboy carried Johnnie through the drift to the door. As they entered, some cards again rose from the floor and beat against the wall.

The Easterner rushed to the stove. He was so profoundly chilled that he almost dared to embrace the glowing iron. The Swede was not in the room. Johnnie sank into a chair and, folding his arms on his knees, buried his face in them. Scully, warming one foot and then the other at a rim of the stove, muttered to himself with Celtic mournfulness. The cowboy had removed his fur cap, and with a dazed and rueful air he was running one hand through his tousled locks. From overhead they could hear the creaking of boards, as the Swede tramped here and there in his room.

The sad quiet was broken by the sudden flinging open of a door that led toward the kitchen. It was instantly followed by an inrush of women. They precipitated themselves upon Johnnie amid a chorus of lamentation. Before they carried their prey off to the kitchen, there to be bathed and harangued with that mixture of sympathy and abuse which is a feat of their sex, the mother straightened herself and fixed old Scully with an eye of stern reproach. "Shame be upon you, Patrick Scully!" she cried. "Your own son, too. Shame be upon you!"

"There, now! Be quiet, now!" said the old man, weakly.

"Shame be upon you, Patrick Scully!" The girls, rallying to this slogan, sniffed disdainfully in the direction of those trembling accomplices, the cowboy and the Easterner. Presently they bore Johnnie away, and left the three men to dismal reflection.

7

"I'd like to fight this here Dutchman myself," said the cowboy, breaking a long silence.

Scully wagged his head sadly. "No, that wouldn't do. It wouldn't be right. It wouldn't be right."

"Well, why wouldn't it?" argued the cowboy. "I don't see no harm in it."

"No," answered Scully, with mournful heroism. "It wouldn't be right. It was Johnnie's fight, and now we mustn't whip the man just because he whipped Johnnie."

"Yes, that's true enough," said the cowboy; "but—he better not get fresh with me, because I couldn't stand no more of it."

"You'll not say a word to him," commanded Scully, and even then they heard the tread of the Swede on the stairs. His entrance was made theatric. He swept the door back with a bang and swaggered to the middle of the room. No one looked at him. "Well," he cried, insolently, at Scully, "I s'pose you'll tell me now how much I owe you?"

The old man remained stolid. "You don't owe me nothin'."

"Huh!" said the Swede, "huh! Don't owe 'im nothin'."

The cowboy addressed the Swede. "Stranger, I don't see how you come to be so gay around here."

Old Scully was instantly alert. "Stop!" he shouted, holding his hand forth, fingers upward. "Bill, you shut up!"

The cowboy spat carelessly into the sawdust box. "I didn't say a word, did I?" he asked.

"Mr. Scully," called the Swede, "how much do I owe you?" It was seen that he was attired for departure, and that he had his valise in his hand.

"You don't owe me nothin'," repeated Scully in the same imperturbable way.

"Huh!" said the Swede. "I guess you're right. I guess if it was any way at all, you'd owe me somethin'. That's what I guess." He turned to the cowboy. "'Kill him! Kill him! Kill him!'" he mimicked, and then guffawed victoriously.

"'Kill him!'" He was convulsed with ironical humor.

But he might have been jeering the dead. The three men were immovable and silent, staring with glassy eyes at the stove.

The Swede opened the door and passed into the storm, giving one derisive glance backward at the still group.

As soon as the door was closed, Scully and the cowboy leaped to their feet and began to curse. They trampled to and fro, waving their arms and smashing into the air with their fists. "Oh, but that was a hard minute!" wailed Scully. "That was a hard minute! Him there leerin' and scoffin'! One bang at his nose was worth forty dollars to me that minute! How did you stand it, Bill?"

"How did I stand it?" cried the cowboy in a quivering voice. "How did I stand it? Oh!"

The old man burst into sudden brogue. "I'd loike to take that Swade," he wailed, "and hould 'im down on a shtone flure and bate 'im to a jelly wid a shtick!"

The cowboy groaned in sympathy. "I'd like to git him by the neck and ha-ammer him"— he brought his hand down on a chair with a noise like a pistol-shot—"hammer that there Dutchman until he couldn't tell himself from a dead coyote!"

"I'd bate 'im until he—"

"I'd show *him* some things—"

And then together they raised a yearning, fanatic cry—"Oh-o-oh! if we only could—"

"Yes!"

"Yes!"

"And then I'd—"

"O-o-oh!"

8

The Swede, tightly gripping his valise, tacked across the face of the storm as if he carried sails. He was following a line of little naked, gasping trees which, he knew, must mark the way of the road. His face, fresh from the pounding of Johnnie's fists, felt more pleasure than pain in the wind and the driving snow. A number of square shapes loomed upon him finally, and he knew them as the houses of the main body of the town. He found a street and made travel along it, leaning heavily upon the wind whenever, at a corner, a terrific blast caught him.

He might have been in a deserted village. We picture the world as thick with conquering and elate humanity, but here, with the bugles of the tempest pealing, it was hard to imagine a peopled earth. One viewed the existence of man then as a marvel, and conceded a glamor of wonder to these lice which were caused to cling to a whirling, fire-smitten, ice-locked, disease-stricken, space-lost bulb. The conceit of man was explained by this storm to be the very engine of life. One was a coxcomb not to die in it. However, the Swede found a saloon.

In front of it an indomitable red light was burning, and the snowflakes were made blood-color as they flew through the circumscribed territory of the lamp's shining. The Swede pushed open the door of the saloon and entered. A sanded expanse was before him, and at the end of it four men sat about a table drinking. Down one side of the room extended a radiant bar, and its guardian was leaning upon his elbows listening to the talk of the men at the table. The Swede dropped his valise upon the floor and, smiling fraternally upon the barkeeper, said, "Gimme some whiskey, will you?" The man placed a bottle, a whiskey glass, and a glass of ice-thick water upon the bar. The Swede poured himself an abnormal portion of whiskey and drank it in three gulps. "Pretty bad night," remarked the bartender, indifferently. He was making the pretension of blindness which is usually a distinction of his class; but it could have been seen that he was furtively studying the half-erased bloodstains on the face of the Swede. "Bad night," he said again.

"Oh, it's good enough for me," replied the Swede, hardily, as he poured himself some more whiskey. The barkeeper took his coin and maneuvered it through its reception by the highly nickeled cash-machine. A bell rang; a card labeled "20 cts." had appeared.

"No," continued the Swede, "this isn't too bad weather. It's good enough for me."

"So?" murmured the barkeeper, languidly.

The copious drams made the Swede's eyes swim, and he breathed a trifle heavier. "Yes, I like this weather. I like it. It suits me." It was apparently his design to impart a deep significance to these words.

"So?" murmured the bartender again. He turned to gaze dreamily at the scroll-like birds and bird-like scrolls which had been drawn with soap upon the mirrors in back of the bar.

"Well, I guess I'll take another drink," said the Swede, presently. "Have something?"

"No, thanks; I'm not drinkin'," answered the bartender. Afterward he asked, "How did you hurt your face?"

The Swede immediately began to boast loudly. "Why, in a fight. I thumped the soul out of a man down here at Scully's hotel."

The interest of the four men at the table was at last aroused.

"Who was it?" said one.

"Johnnie Scully," blustered the Swede. "Son of the man what runs it. He will be pretty near dead for some weeks, I can tell you. I made a nice thing of him, I did. He couldn't get up. They carried him in the house. Have a drink?"

Instantly the men in some subtle way encased themselves in reserve. "No, thanks," said one. The group was of curious formation. Two were prominent local businessmen; one was the district attorney; and one was a professional gambler of the kind known as "square." But a scrutiny of the group would not have enabled an observer to pick the gambler from the men of more reputable pursuits. He was, in fact, a man so delicate in manner, when among people of fair class, and so judicious in his choice of victims, that in the strictly masculine part of the town's life he had come to be explicitly trusted and admired. People called him a thoroughbred. The fear and contempt with which his craft was regarded were undoubtedly the reason why his quiet dignity shone conspicuous above the quiet dignity of men who might be merely hatters, billiard-markers, or grocery clerks. Beyond an occasional unwary traveler who came by rail, this gambler was supposed to prey solely upon reckless and senile farmers, who, when flush with good crops, drove into town in all the pride and confidence of an absolutely invulnerable stupidity. Hearing at times in circuitous fashion of the despoilment of such a farmer, the important men of Romper invariably laughed in contempt of the victim, and if they thought of the wolf at all, it was with a kind of pride at the knowledge that he would never dare think of attacking their wisdom and courage. Besides, it was popular that this gambler had a real wife and two real children in a neat cottage in a suburb, where he led an exemplary home life; and when any one even suggested a discrepancy in his character, the crowd immediately vociferated descriptions of this virtuous family circle. Then men who led exemplary home lives, and men who did not lead exemplary home lives, all subsided in a bunch, remarking that there was nothing more to be said.

However, when a restriction was placed upon him—as, for instance, when a strong clique of members of the new Pollywog Club refused to permit him, even as a spectator, to appear in the rooms of the organization—the candor and gentleness with which he accepted the judgment disarmed many of his foes and made his friends more desperately partisan. He invariably distinguished between himself and a respectable Romper man so quickly and frankly that his manner actually appeared to be a continual broadcast compliment.

And one must not forget to declare the fundamental fact of his entire position in Romper. It is irrefutable that in all affairs outside his business, in all matters that occur eternally and commonly between man and man, this thieving card-player was so generous, so just, so moral, that, in a contest, he could have put to flight the consciences of nine tenths of the citizens of Romper.

And so it happened that he was seated in this saloon with the two prominent local merchants and the district attorney.

The Swede continued to drink raw whiskey, meanwhile babbling at the barkeeper and trying to induce him to indulge in potations. "Come on. Have a drink. Come on. What—no? Well, have a little one, then. By gawd, I've whipped a man tonight, and I want to celebrate. I whipped him good, too. Gentlemen," the Swede cried to the men at the table, "have a drink?"

"Ssh!" said the barkeeper.

The group at the table, although furtively attentive, had been pretending to be deep in talk, but now a man lifted his eyes toward the Swede and said, shortly, "Thanks. We don't want any more."

At this reply the Swede ruffled out his chest like a rooster. "Well," he exploded, "it seems I can't get anybody to drink with me in this town. Seems so, don't it? Well!"

"Ssh!" said the barkeeper.

"Say," snarled the Swede, "don't you try to shut me up. I won't have it. I'm a gentleman, and I want people to drink with me. And I want 'em to drink with me now. *Now*—do you understand?" He rapped the bar with his knuckles.

Years of experience had calloused the bartender. He merely grew sulky. "I hear you," he answered.

"Well," cried the Swede, "listen hard then. See those men over there? Well, they're going to drink with me, and don't you forget it. Now you watch."

"Hi!" yelled the barkeeper, "this won't do!"

"Why won't it?" demanded the Swede. He stalked over to the table, and by chance laid his hand upon the shoulder of the gambler. "How about this?" he asked wrathfully. "I asked you to drink with me."

The gambler simply twisted his head and spoke over his shoulder. "My friend, I don't know you."

"Oh, come on," answered the Swede, "and have a drink."

"Now, my boy," advised the gambler, kindly, "take your hand off my shoulder and go 'way and mind your own business." He was a little, slim man, and it seemed strange to hear him use this tone of heroic patronage to the burly Swede. The other men at the table said nothing.

"What! You won't drink with me, you little dude? I'll make you, then! I'll make you!" The Swede had grasped the gambler frenziedly at the throat, and was dragging him from his chair. The other men sprang up. The barkeeper dashed around the corner of his bar. There was a great tumult, and then was seen a long blade in the hand of the gambler. It shot forward, and a human body, this citadel of virtue, wisdom, power, was pierced as easily as if it had been a melon. The Swede fell with a cry of supreme astonishment.

The prominent merchants and the district attorney must have at once tumbled out of the place backward. The bartender found himself hanging limply to the arm of a chair and gazing into the eyes of a murderer.

"Henry," said the latter, as he wiped his knife on one of the towels that hung beneath the bar rail, "you tell 'em where to find me. I'll be home, waiting for 'em." Then he vanished. A moment afterward the barkeeper was in the street dinning through the storm for help and, moreover, companionship.

The corpse of the Swede, alone in the saloon, had its eyes fixed upon a dreadful legend that dwelt atop of the cash-machine: "This registers the amount of your purchase."

9

Months later, the cowboy was frying pork over the stove of a little ranch near the Dakota line, when there was a quick thud of hoofs outside, and presently the Easterner entered with the letters and the papers.

"Well," said the Easterner at once, "the chap that killed the Swede has got three years. Wasn't much, was it?"

"He has? Three years?" The cowboy poised his pan of pork, while he ruminated upon the news. "Three years. That ain't much."

"No. It was a light sentence," replied the Easterner as he unbuckled his spurs. "Seems there was a good deal of sympathy for him in Romper."

"If the bartender had been any good," observed the cowboy, thoughtfully, "he would have gone in and cracked that there Dutchman on the head with a bottle in the beginnin' of it and stopped all this here murderin'."

"Yes, a thousand things might have happened," said the Easterner, tartly.

The cowboy returned his pan of pork to the fire, but his philosophy continued. "It's funny, ain't it? If he hadn't said Johnnie was cheatin' he'd be alive this minute. He was an awful fool. Game played for fun, too. Not for money. I believe he was crazy."

"I feel sorry for that gambler," said the Easterner.

"Oh, so do I," said the cowboy. "He don't deserve none of it for killin' who he did."

"The Swede might not have been killed if everything had been square."

"Might not have been killed?" exclaimed the cowboy. "Everythin' square? Why, when he said that Johnnie was cheatin' and acted like such a fool? And then in the saloon he fairly walked up to git hurt?" With these arguments the cowboy browbeat the Easterner and reduced him to rage.

"You're a fool!" cried the Easterner, viciously. "You're a bigger fool than the Swede by a million majority. Now let me tell you one thing. Let me tell you something. Listen! Johnnie *was* cheating!"

" 'Johnnie,' " said the cowboy, blankly. There was a minute of silence, and then he said, robustly, "Why, no. The game was only for fun."

"Fun or not," said the Easterner, "Johnnie was cheating. I saw him. I know it. I saw him. And I refused to stand up and be a man. I let the Swede fight it out alone. And you—you were simply puffing around the place and wanting to fight. And then old Scully himself!

We are all in it! This poor gambler isn't even a noun. He is kind of an adverb. Every sin is the result of a collaboration. We, five of us, have collaborated in the murder of this Swede. Usually there are from a dozen to forty women really involved in every murder, but in this case it seems to be only five men—you, I, Johnnie, old Scully; and that fool of an unfortunate gambler came merely as a culmination, the apex of a human movement, and gets all the punishment."

The cowboy, injured and rebellious, cried out blindly into this fog of mysterious theory: "Well, I didn't do anythin', did I?"

I
THE IRONY IN FEAR

The story examines the ironic effects of fear on an individual. Very early, the reader recognizes the Swede is obviously a frightened man. His fears breed dark emotions, venom, distrust, and hatred, which in turn trigger hostility in all the people he meets. Though the Cowboy and Johnny think the Swede is crazy, they hanker to fight him; the Easterner knows that the Swede's accusation is true but feels such resentment toward the Swede that he will not stand up for him; Scully, usually an expert at conciliation, can hardly resist attacking the Swede physically. It is ironic that when the Swede thinks he is safe from being killed, when he tries to celebrate his victory over the "enemy," he meets the very fate he thought he had escaped.

II
IMPLICATIONS

What does the story have to say about the validity of the following statements. How do your own experiences lead you to react?

1. Fear springs from ignorance.

2. Often the very thing we fear we may bring to pass by our actions.

3. Nothing is so much to be feared as fear itself.

4. Perhaps the most ironic aspect of the story is the Swede's coming to the West when he is so deathly afraid of it.

5. The best way to get over a fear is to face it.

6. The Swede's death could be attributed to everyone he met that last day.

III
TECHNIQUES

Atmosphere

1. Atmosphere often creates dominant color images for the reader. What colors come to mind for this story?

2. What sounds do you remember hearing in the story? What is their effect on the mood?

3. How do the conversations affect the atmosphere?

Suspense

How is suspense created by the following incidents in the story?

1. The Swede's remark, "I suppose there have been a good many men killed in this room."

2. Scully's giving the Swede whiskey.

3. Scully's excusing himself from the card game to go meet the train.

4. The Swede's winning the fight.

SUMMING UP

Life's Ironies

Like brief encounters, life's ironies hold a peculiar fascination for people. Do they result from sheer accident or are they evidence that our lives are controlled by something outside ourselves? Since the individual who experiences irony receives the opposite of his expectations, one may sense the operation of a malicious, insensitive force. And yet, after further thought, one sees that the character's fate is singularly appropriate. A young stranger who stumbles into a mountain inn and reveals that more than anything else he wants to be remembered is buried by an avalanche and no one even knows he is among the dead. A soldier carefully sets a trap to kill an unknown enemy only to find out later that he has killed his own brother. A young man tutors a distinguished scholar all summer and succeeds in teaching him English, but his efforts are negated when the old man commits suicide after his first lecture.

Because human beings are fascinated with people and their actions which produce irony, irony is a natural source for storytellers. As you have seen, the ironic story is one in which the impact is saved until the very end. Suddenly everything that has gone before is seen in a new light. This adds to the emotional shock. The pollution of a stream by a rendering plant becomes a deeply personal matter, not just a part of a larger problem. A woman's passion for "movements" is revealed for what it is, a passing fancy. The new world order of peace, progress, and harmonious living is the unwitting gift of a ruthless man who spawned the organization for his own interests. Therefore, in the stories in LIFE'S IRONIES, it is the "afterburn" that provides the real thrust.

IMPLICATIONS

1. In the stories you have read, irony springs from a number of different kinds of situations and operates in various ways.

a. In which stories does the irony seem to be almost a payment for a character's faults?

b. In which stories does the irony develop because of social problems?

c. In which stories does the irony seem to result from sheer accident?

d. In which stories does nature contribute to the ironic fate?

2. The statements that follow are designed to help you sum up your new and old ideas about life's ironies. Use the selections as well as your own experiences to support your opinions.

a. Ironic twists are always unexpected, but not all unexpected events are ironic.

b. The possibility of ironic results makes human endeavors seem useless.

c. Everyone experiences ironic twists fairly frequently.

d. It takes a sensitive person to perceive the irony in a situation.

TECHNIQUES

Atmosphere

1. Is the atmosphere more often created by the tone and rhythm of language or by the choice of details? Use selections to support your contention.

2. If the atmosphere is at variance with the content of the story, what is the effect?

3. Once established, should the atmosphere be consistent throughout a story?

4. Turn to the Table of Contents for this unit. As you look at the title of each selection, try to pin down in one or two words the mood you felt after you had finished the story.

Suspense

1. In which of the selections is there a deliberate slowing down of answers to the questions in the reader's mind in order to create suspense?

2. Can a good story be told and still have little suspense?

3. Which of the stories in this unit best held your attention? How did the author create his suspense?

4. Give titles of stories either in comic strips or in other reading which depend entirely on suspense. How do they rate in literary quality?

Introduction to The Man That Corrupted Hadleyburg

Samuel Clemens, better known as Mark Twain, is one of the most important writers America has produced. This in itself is somewhat ironic, for Clemens became a writer almost accidentally. He had grown up in a harum-scarum way in the river town of Hannibal, Missouri. He tried a number of vocations: typesetter, river boat pilot, Confederate soldier, miner. But in 1862, when a particularly bad spell of weather confined him to his cabin in the Nevada mountains, he sent off some humorous pieces to the newspaper in Virginia City. Later when his finances were at low ebb, this same paper offered him a position as a feature writer, and he accepted. Through this experience he discovered his ability with words and found his true vocation as a spinner of tales.

It is also ironic that most people think of Twain only as a humorist. There is no doubt that he could see the amusing twist in a situation. And he developed a great reputation as a lecturer because of his ability to keep people laughing. But looking at the comic in human life led him toward a basically pessimistic view of mankind. For humor often depicts the inconsistencies, the pretensions, and the weaknesses of people.

Ultimately Twain came to feel that human beings are rascals. Nevertheless, he found them to be interesting rascals. Toward the end of his life, his stories dwelt more and more on the inconsistencies of man's behavior. One of the finest of these stories is "The Man That Corrupted Hadleyburg." Someone has said that here Twain is like a puppet master making people dance at the ends of their strings. But he is not vicious. He is more amused and pitying than vindictive as he systematically shows people as they really are.

THE MAN THAT CORRUPTED HADLEYBURG

MARK TWAIN

1

It was many years ago. Hadleyburg was the most honest and upright town in all the region round about. It had kept that reputation unsmirched during three generations, and was prouder of it than any other of its possessions. It was so proud of it, and so anxious to insure its perpetuation, that it began to teach the principles of honest dealing to its babies in the cradle, and made the like teachings the staple of their culture thenceforward through all the years devoted to their education. Also, throughout the formative years temptations were kept out of the way of the young people, so that their honesty could have every chance to harden and solidify, and become a part of their very bone. The neighboring towns were jealous of this honorable supremacy, and affected to sneer at Hadleyburg's pride in it and call it vanity; but all the same they were obliged to acknowledge that Hadleyburg was in reality an incorruptible town; and if pressed they would also acknowledge that the mere fact that a young man hailed from Hadleyburg was all the recommendation he needed when he went forth from his natal town to seek for responsible employment.

But at last, in the drift of time, Hadleyburg had the ill luck to offend a passing stranger— possibly without knowing it, certainly without caring, for Hadleyburg was sufficient unto itself, and cared not a rap for strangers or their opinions. Still, it would have been well to make an exception in this one's case, for he was a bitter man and revengeful. All through his wanderings during a whole year he kept his injury in mind, and gave all his leisure moments to trying to invent a compensating satisfaction for it. He contrived many plans, and all of them were good, but none of them was quite sweeping enough; the poorest of them would hurt a great many individuals, but what he wanted was a plan which would comprehend the entire town, and not let so much as one person escape unhurt. At last he had a fortunate idea, and when it fell into his brain it lit up his whole head with an evil joy. He began to form a plan at once, saying to himself, "That is the thing to do—I will corrupt the town."

Six months later he went to Hadleyburg, and arrived in a buggy at the house of the old cashier of the bank about ten at night. He got a sack out of the buggy, shouldered it, and staggered with it through the cottage yard, and knocked at the door. A woman's voice said "Come in," and he entered, and set his sack behind the stove in the parlor, saying politely to the old lady who sat reading the *Missionary Herald* by the lamp:

"Pray keep your seat, madam, I will not disturb you. There—now it is pretty well concealed; one would hardly know it was there. Can I see your husband a moment, madam?"

No, he was gone to Brixton, and might not return before morning.

"Very well, madam, it is no matter. I merely wanted to leave that sack in his care, to be delivered to the rightful owner when he shall be found. I am a stranger; he does not know me; I am merely passing through the town tonight to discharge a matter which has been long in my mind. My errand is now completed, and I go pleased and a little proud, and you will never see me again. There is a paper attached to the sack which will explain everything. Good night, madam."

The old lady was afraid of the mysterious big stranger, and was glad to see him go. But her curiosity was roused, and she went straight to the sack and brought away the paper. It began as follows:

"TO BE PUBLISHED: *or, the right man sought out by private inquiry—either will answer. This sack contains gold coin weighing a hundred and sixty pounds four ounces—*"

"Mercy on us, and the door not locked!"

Mrs. Richards flew to it all in a tremble and locked it, then pulled down the window shades and stood frightened, worried, and wondering if there was anything else she could do toward making herself and the money more safe. She listened awhile for burglars, then surrendered to curiosity and went back to the lamp and finished reading the paper:

"*I am a foreigner, and am presently going back to my own country, to remain there permanently. I am grateful to America for what I have received at her hands during my long stay under her flag; and to one of her citizens—a citizen of Hadleyburg—I am especially grateful for a great kindness done me a year or two ago. Two great kindnesses, in fact. I will explain. I was a gambler. I say I WAS. I was a ruined gambler. I arrived in this village at night, hungry and without a penny. I asked for help—in the dark; I was ashamed to beg in the light. I begged of the right man. He gave me twenty dollars—that is to say, he gave me life, as I considered it. He also gave me fortune; for out of that money I have made myself rich at the gaming table. And finally, a remark which he made to me has remained with me to this day, and has at last conquered me; and in conquering has saved the remnant of my morals: I shall gamble no more. Now I have no idea who that man was, but I want him found, and I want him to have this money, to give away, throw away, or keep, as he pleases. It is merely my way of testifying my gratitude to him. If I could stay, I would find him myself; but no matter, he will be found. This is an honest town, an incorruptible town, and I know I can trust it without fear.*

This man can be identified by the remark which he made to me; I feel persuaded that he will remember it.

"*And now my plan is this: If you prefer to conduct the inquiry privately, do so. Tell the contents of this present writing to any one who is likely to be the right man. If he shall answer, 'I am the man; the remark I made was so-and-so,' apply the test—to wit: open the sack, and in it you will find a sealed envelope containing that remark. If the remark mentioned by the candidate tallies with it, give him the money, and ask no further questions, for he is certainly the right man.*

"*But if you shall prefer a public inquiry, then publish this present writing in the local paper—with these instructions added, to wit: Thirty days from now, let the candidate appear at the town hall at eight in the evening (Friday), and hand his remark, in a sealed envelope, to the Rev. Mr. Burgess (if he will be kind enough to act); and let Mr. Burgess there and then destroy the seals of the sack, open it, and see if the remark is correct; if correct, let the money be delivered, with my sincere gratitude, to my benefactor thus identified.*"

Mrs. Richards sat down, gently quivering with excitement, and was soon lost in thinkings—after this pattern: "What a strange thing it is! . . . And what a fortune for that kind man who set his bread afloat upon the waters! . . . If it had only been my husband that did it—for we are so poor, so old and poor! . . ." Then, with a sigh—"But it was not my Edward; no, it was not he that gave a stranger twenty dollars. It is a pity, too; I see it now . . . ." Then, with a shudder—"But it is *gambler's* money! the wages of sin: we couldn't take it; we couldn't touch it. I don't like to be near it; it seems a defilement." She moved to a farther chair. . . . "I wish Edward would come, and take it to the bank; a burglar might come at any moment; it is dreadful to be here all alone with it."

At eleven Mr. Richards arrived, and while his wife was saying, "I am *so* glad you've come!" he was saying, "I'm so tired—tired clear out; it is dreadful to be poor, and have to make these dismal journeys at my time of life. Always at the grind, grind, grind, on a salary—another man's slave, and he sitting at home in his slippers, rich and comfortable."

"I am so sorry for you, Edward, you know that; but be comforted: we have our livelihood; we have our good name——"

"Yes, Mary, and that is everything. Don't mind my talk—it's just a moment's irritation and doesn't mean anything. Kiss me—there, it's all gone now, and I am not complaining any more. What have you been getting? What's in the sack?"

Then his wife told him the great secret. It dazed him for a moment; then he said:

"It weighs a hundred and sixty pounds? Why, Mary, It's forty thousand dollars—think of it—a whole fortune! Not ten men in this village are worth that much. Give me the paper."

He skimmed through it and said:

"Isn't it an adventure! Why, it's a romance; it's like the impossible things one reads about in books, and never sees in life." He was well stirred up now; cheerful, even gleeful. He tapped his old wife on the cheek, and said, humorously, "Why, we're rich, Mary, rich; all we've got to do is to bury the money and burn the papers. If the gambler ever comes to inquire, we'll merely look coldly upon him and say: 'What is this nonsense you are talking? We have never heard of you and your sack of gold before'; and then he would look foolish, and——"

"And in the meantime, while you are running on with your jokes, the money is still here, and it is fast getting along toward burglar-time."

"True. Very well, what shall we do—make the inquiry private? No, not that: it would spoil the romance. The public method is better. Think what a noise it will make! And it will make all the other towns jealous; for no stranger would trust such a thing to any town but Hadleyburg, and they know it. It's a great card for us. I must get to the printing office now, or I shall be too late."

"But stop—stop—don't leave me here alone with it, Edward!"

But he was gone. For only a little while, however. Not far from his own house he met the editor-proprietor of the paper, and gave him the document, and said, "Here is a good thing for you, Cox—put it in."

"It may be too late, Mr. Richards, but I'll see."

At home again he and his wife sat down to talk the charming mystery over; they were in no condition for sleep. The first question was, Who could the citizen have been who gave the stranger the twenty dollars? It seemed a simple one; both answered it in the same breath—

"Barclay Goodson."

"Yes," said Richards, "he could have done it, and it would have been like him, but there's not another in the town."

"Everybody will grant that, Edward—grant it privately, anyway. For six months, now, the village has been its own proper self once more —honest, narrow, self-righteous, and stingy."

"It is what he always called it, to the day of his death—said it right out publicly, too."

"Yes, and he was hated for it."

"Oh, of course; but he didn't care. I reckon he was the best-hated man among us, except the Reverend Burgess."

"Well, Burgess deserves it—he will never get another congregation here. Mean as the town is, it knows how to estimate *him*. Edward, doesn't it seem odd that the stranger should appoint Burgess to deliver the money?"

"Well, yes—it does. That is—that is——"

"Why so much *that-is*-ing? Would *you* select him?"

"Mary, maybe the stranger knows him better than this village does."

"Much *that* would help Burgess!"

The husband seemed perplexed for an answer; the wife kept a steady eye upon him, and waited. Finally Richards said, with the hesitancy of one who is making a statement which is likely to encounter doubt.

"Mary, Burgess is not a bad man."

His wife was certainly surprised.

"Nonsense!" she exclaimed.

"He is not a bad man. I know. The whole of his unpopularity had its foundation in that one thing—the thing that made so much noise."

"That 'one thing,' indeed! As if that 'one thing' wasn't enough, all by itself."

"Plenty. Plenty. Only he wasn't guilty of it."

"How you talk! Not guilty of it! Everybody knows he *was* guilty."

"Mary, I give you my word—he was innocent."

"I can't believe it, and I don't. How do you know?"

"It is a confession. I am ashamed, but I will make it. I was the only man who knew he was innocent. I could have saved him, and—and —well, you know how the town was wrought up—I hadn't the pluck to do it. It would have turned everybody against me. I felt mean, ever so mean; but I didn't dare; I hadn't the manliness to face that."

Mary looked troubled, and for a while was silent. Then she said, stammeringly:

"I—I don't think it would have done for you to—to— One mustn't—er—public opinion —one has to be so careful—so—" It was a difficult road, and she got mired; but after a little she got started again. "It was a great pity, but— Why, we couldn't afford it, Edward—we couldn't indeed. Oh, I wouldn't have had you do it for anything!"

"It would have lost us the good will of so many people, Mary; and then—and then——"

"What troubles me now is, what *he* thinks of us, Edward."

"He? *He* doesn't suspect that I could have saved him."

"Oh," exclaimed the wife, in a tone of relief, "I am glad of that. As long as he doesn't know that you could have saved him, he—he—well, that makes it a great deal better. Why, I might have known he didn't know, because he is

703

always trying to be friendly with us, as little encouragement as we give him. More than once people have twitted me with it. There's the Wilsons, and the Wilcoxes, and the Harknesses, they take a mean pleasure in saying, '*Your friend* Burgess,' because they know it pesters me. I wish he wouldn't persist in liking us so; I can't think why he keeps it up."

"I can explain it. It's another confession. When the thing was new and hot, and the town made a plan to ride him on a rail, my conscience hurt me so that I couldn't stand it, and I went privately and gave him notice, and he got out of the town and stayed out till it was safe to come back."

"Edward! If the town had found it out—"

"*Don't!* It scares me yet, to think of it. I repented of it the minute it was done; and I was even afraid to tell you, lest your face might betray it to somebody. I didn't sleep any that night, for worrying. But after a few days I saw that no one was going to suspect me, and after that I got to feeling glad I did it. And I feel glad yet, Mary—glad through and through."

"So do I, now, for it would have been a dreadful way to treat him. Yes, I'm glad; for really you did owe him that, you know. But, Edward, suppose it should come out yet, some day!"

"It won't."

"Why?"

"Because everybody thinks it was Goodson."

"Of course they would!"

"Certainly. And of course *he* didn't care. They persuaded poor old Sawlsberry to go and charge it on him, and he went blustering over there and did it. Goodson looked him over, like as if he was hunting for a place on him that he could despise the most, then says, 'So you are the Committee of Inquiry, are you?' Sawlsberry said that was about what he was. 'Hm. Do they require particulars, or do you reckon a kind of a *general* answer will do?' 'If they require particulars, I will come back, Mr. Goodson; I will take the general answer first.' 'Very well, then, tell them to get lost—

I reckon that's general enough. And I'll give you some advice, Sawlsberry; when you come back for the particulars, fetch a basket to carry the relics of yourself home in.' "

"Just like Goodson; it's got all the marks. He had only one vanity: he thought he could give advice better than any other person."

"It settled the business, and saved us, Mary. The subject was dropped."

"Bless you, I'm not doubting *that*."

Then they took up the gold-sack mystery again, with strong interest. Soon the conversation began to suffer breaks—interruptions caused by absorbed thinkings. The breaks grew more and more frequent. At last Richards lost himself wholly in thought. He sat long, gazing vacantly at the floor, and by and by he began to punctuate his thoughts with little nervous movements of his hands that seemed to indicate vexation. Meantime his wife too had relapsed into a thoughtful silence, and her movements were beginning to show a troubled discomfort. Finally Richards got up and strode aimlessly about the room, plowing his hands through his hair, much as a somnambulist[1] might do who was having a bad dream. Then he seemed to arrive at a definite purpose; and without a word he put on his hat and passed quickly out of the house. His wife sat brooding, with a drawn face, and did not seem to be aware that she was alone. Now and then she murmured, "Lead us not into t— . . . but —but—we are so poor, so poor! . . . Lead us not into . . . . Ah, who would be hurt by it?— and no one would ever know . . . . Lead us . . . ." The voice died out in mumblings. After a little she glanced up and muttered in a half-frightened, half-glad way—

"He is gone! But, oh dear, he may be too late—too late . . . . Maybe not—maybe there is still time." She rose and stood thinking, nervously clasping and unclasping her hands. A slight shudder shook her frame, and she said, out of a dry throat, "God forgive me— it's awful to think such things—but . . . Lord,

---

1. **somnambulist**\sŏm ˈnam·byə ˈlĭst\ sleepwalker.

how we are made—how strangely we are made!"

She turned the light low, and slipped stealthily over and kneeled down by the sack and felt of its ridgy sides with her hands, and fondled them lovingly; and there was a gloating light in her poor old eyes. She fell into fits of absence; and came half out of them at times to mutter, "If we had only waited!—oh, if we had only waited a little, and not been in such a hurry!"

Meantime Cox had gone home from his office and told his wife all about the strange thing that had happened, and they had talked it over eagerly, and guessed that the late Goodson was the only man in the town who could have helped a suffering stranger with so noble a sum as twenty dollars. Then there was a pause, and the two became thoughtful and silent. And by and by nervous and fidgety. At last the wife said, as if to herself,

"Nobody knows this secret but the Richardses . . . and us . . . nobody."

The husband came out of his thinkings with a slight start, and gazed wistfully at his wife, whose face was become very pale; then he hesitatingly rose, and glanced furtively at his hat, then at his wife—a sort of mute inquiry. Mrs. Cox swallowed once or twice, with her hand at her throat, then in place of speech she nodded her head. In a moment she was alone, and mumbling to herself.

And now Richards and Cox were hurrying through the deserted street, from opposite directions. They met, panting, at the foot of the printing-office stairs; by the night-light there they read each other's face. Cox whispered,

"Nobody knows about this but us?"

The whispered answer was,

"Not a soul—on honor, not a soul!"

"If it isn't too late to—"

The men were starting upstairs; at this moment they were overtaken by a boy, and Cox asked,

"Is that you, Johnny?"

"Yes, sir."

"You needn't ship the early mail—nor *any* mail; wait till I tell you."

"It's already gone, sir."

"*Gone?*" It had the sound of an unspeakable disappointment in it.

"Yes, sir. Timetable for Brixton and all the towns beyond changed today, sir—had to get the papers in twenty minutes earlier than common. I had to rush; if I had been two minutes later—"

The men turned and walked slowly away, not waiting to hear the rest. Neither of them spoke during ten minutes; then Cox said, in a vexed tone,

"What possessed you to be in such a hurry, I can't make out."

The answer was humble enough:

"I see it now, but somehow I never thought, you know, until it was too late. But the next time—"

"Next time be hanged! It won't come in a thousand years."

Then the friends separated without a good-night, and dragged themselves home with the gait of mortally stricken men. At their homes their wives sprang up with an eager "Well?"—then saw the answer with their eyes and sank down sorrowing, without waiting for it to come in words. In both houses a discussion followed of a heated sort—a new thing; there had been discussions before, but not heated ones, not ungentle ones. The discussions tonight were a sort of seeming plagiarisms of each other. Mrs. Richards said,

"If you had only waited, Edward—if you had only stopped to think; but no, you must run straight to the printing office and spread it all over the world."

"It *said* publish it."

"That is nothing; it also said do it privately, if you liked. There, now—is that true, or not?"

"Why, yes—yes, it is true; but when I thought what a stir it would make, and what a compliment it was to Hadleyburg that a stranger should trust it so——"

"Oh, certainly, I know all that; but if you had only stopped to think, you would have seen that you *couldn't* find the right man, because he is in his grave, and hasn't left chick nor child nor relation behind him; and as long as the money went to somebody that awfully needed it, and nobody would be hurt by it, and—and—"

She broke down, crying. Her husband tried to think of some comforting thing to say, and presently came out with this:

"But after all, Mary, it must be for the best —it *must* be; we know that. And we must remember that it was so ordered—"

"Ordered! Oh, everthing's *ordered*, when a person has to find some way out when he has been stupid. Just the same, it was *ordered* that the money should come to us in this special way, and it was you that must take it on yourself to go meddling with the designs of Providence—and who gave you the right? It was wicked, that is what it was—just blasphemous presumption, and no more becoming to a meek and humble professor of——"

"But, Mary, you know how we have been trained all our lives long, like the whole village, till it is absolutely second nature to us to stop not a single moment to think when there's an honest thing to be done——"

"Oh, I know it, I know it—it's been one everlasting training and training and training in honesty—honesty shielded, from the very cradle, against every possible temptation, and so it's *artificial* honesty, and weak as water when temptation comes, as we have seen this night. God knows I never had shade nor shadow of a doubt of my petrified and indestructible honesty until now—and now, under the very first big and real temptation, I—Edward, it is my belief that this town's honesty is as rotten as mine is; as rotten as yours is. It is a mean town, a hard, stingy town, and hasn't a virtue in the world but this honesty it is so celebrated for and so conceited about; and so help me, I do believe that if ever the day comes that its honesty falls under great temptation, its grand reputation will go to ruin like a house of cards. There, now, I've made confession, and I feel better;

I am a humbug, and I've been one all my life, without knowing it. Let no man call me honest again—I will not have it."

"I—well, Mary, I feel a good deal as you do; I certainly do. It seems strange, too, so strange. I never could have believed it— never."

A long silence followed; both were sunk in thought. At last the wife looked up and said,

"I know what you are thinking, Edward."

Richards had the embarrassed look of a person who is caught.

"I am ashamed to confess it, Mary, but——"

"It's no matter, Edward, I was thinking the same question myself."

"I hope so. State it."

"You were thinking, if a body could only guess out *what the remark was* that Goodson made to the stranger."

"It's perfectly true. I feel guilty and ashamed. And you?"

"I'm past it. Let us make a pallet here; we've got to stand watch till the bank vault opens in the morning and admits the sack . . . . Oh, dear, oh, dear—if we hadn't made the mistake!"

The pallet was made, and Mary said:

"The open sesame—what could it have been? I do wonder what that remark could have been? But come; we will go to bed now."

"And sleep?"

"No, think."

"Yes, think."

By this time the Coxes too had completed their spat and their reconciliation, and were turning in—to think, to think, and toss, and fret, and worry over what the remark could possibly have been which Goodson made to the stranded derelict; that golden remark; that remark worth forty thousand dollars, cash.

The reason that the village telegraph office was open later than usual that night was this: The foreman of Cox's paper was the local representative of the Associated Press. One might say its honorary representative, for it wasn't four times a year that he could furnish thirty words that would be accepted. But this

706

time it was different. His dispatch stating what he had caught got an instant answer:

"Send the whole thing—all the details— twelve hundred words."

A colossal order! The foreman filled the bill; and he was the proudest man in the state. By breakfast time the next morning the name of Hadleyburg the Incorruptible was on every lip in America, from Montreal to the Gulf, from the glaciers of Alaska to the orange groves of Florida; and millions and millions of people were discussing the stranger and his money sack, and wondering if the right man would be found, and hoping some more news about the matter would come soon—right away.

2

Hadleyburg village woke up world-celebrated—astonished—happy—vain. Vain beyond imagination. Its nineteen principal citizens and their wives went about shaking hands with each other, and beaming, and smiling, and congratulating, and saying *this* thing adds a new word to the dictionary— *Hadleyburg*, synonym for *incorruptible*—des- tined to live in dictionaries forever! And the minor and unimportant citizens and their wives went around acting in much the same way. Everybody ran to the bank to see the gold sack; and before noon grieved and envious crowds began to flock in from Brixton and all neighboring towns; and that afternoon and next day reporters began to arrive from everywhere to verify the sack and its history and write the whole thing up anew, and make dashing freehand pictures of the sack, and of Richards' house, and the bank, and the Presbyterian church, and the Baptist church, and the public square, and the town hall where the test would be applied and the money delivered; and portraits of the Richardses, and Pinkerton the banker, and Cox, and the foreman, and Reverend Burgess, and the postmaster—and even of Jack Halliday, who was the loafing, good-natured, no-account, irreverent fisherman, hunter, boys' friend, stray-dogs' friend, typical "Sam Lawson"[2] of the town. The little, mean, smirking, oily Pinkerton showed the sack to all comers, and rubbed his sleek palms together pleasantly, and enlarged upon the town's fine old reputation for honesty and upon this wonderful endorsement of it, and hoped and believed that the example would now spread far and wide over the American world, and be epoch-making in the matter of moral regeneration. And so on, and so on.

By the end of a week things had quieted down again; the wild intoxication of pride and joy had sobered to a soft, sweet, silent delight—a sort of deep, nameless, unutterable content. All faces bore a look of peaceful, holy happiness.

Then a change came. It was a gradual change: so gradual that its beginnings were hardly noticed; maybe were not noticed at all, except by Jack Halliday, who always noticed everything; and always made fun of it, too, no

---

2. **Sam Lawson,** a shiftless, amusing Yankee who tells the stories related in Harriet Beecher Stowe's *Old Town Folks.*

matter what it was. He began to throw out chafing remarks about people not looking quite so happy as they did a day or two ago; and next he claimed that the new aspect was deepening to positive sadness; next, that it was taking on a sick look; and finally he said that he could rob the meanest man in town of a cent out of the bottom of his breeches pocket and not disturb his reverie.

At this stage—or at about this stage—a saying like this was dropped at bedtime—with a sigh, usually—by the head of each of the nineteen principal households: "Ah, what *could* have been the remark that Goodson made?"

And straightway—with a shudder—came this, from the man's wife:

"Oh, *don't!* What horrible thing are you mulling in your mind? Put it away from you!"

But that question was wrung from those men again the next night—and got the same retort. But weaker.

And the third night the men uttered the question yet again—with anguish, and absently. This time—and the following night—the wives fidgeted feebly, and tried to say something. But didn't.

And the night after that they found their tongues and responded—longingly,

"Oh, if we *could* only guess!"

Halliday's comments grew daily more and more sparklingly disagreeable and disparaging. He went diligently about, laughing at the town, individually and in mass. But his laugh was the only one left in the village: it fell upon a hollow and mournful vacancy and emptiness. Not even a smile was findable anywhere. Halliday carried a cigar box around on a tripod, playing that it was a camera, and halted all passers and aimed the thing and said, "Ready!—now look pleasant, please," but not even this capital joke could surprise the dreary faces into any softening.

So three weeks passed—one week was left. It was Saturday evening—after supper. Instead of the aforetime Saturday-evening flutter and bustle and shopping and larking, the streets were empty and desolate. Richards and his old wife sat apart in their little parlor—miserable and thinking. This was become their evening habit now: the lifelong habit which had preceded it, of reading, knitting, and contented chat, or receiving or paying neighborly calls, was dead and gone and forgotten, ages ago—two or three weeks ago; nobody talked now, nobody read, nobody visited—the whole village sat at home, sighing, worrying, silent. Trying to guess out that remark.

The postman left a letter. Richards glanced listlessly at the superscription and the postmark—unfamiliar, both—and tossed the letter on the table and resumed his might-have-beens and his hopeless dull miseries where he had left them off. Two or three hours later his wife got wearily up and was going away to bed without a good-night—custom now—but she stopped near the letter and eyed it awhile with a dead interest, then broke it open, and began to skim it over. Richards, sitting there with his chair tilted back against the wall and his chin between his knees, heard something fall. It was his wife. He sprang to her side, but she cried out:

"Leave me alone; I am too happy. Read the letter—read it!"

He did. He devoured it, his brain reeling. The letter was from a distant state, and it said:

"*I am a stranger to you, but no matter: I have something to tell you. I have just arrived home from Mexico, and learned about that episode. Of course you do not know who made that remark, but I know, and I am the only person living who does know. It was* GOODSON. *I knew him well, many years ago. I passed through your village that very night, and was his guest till the midnight train came along. I overheard him make that remark to the stranger in the dark—it was in Hale Alley. He and I talked of it the rest of the way home, and while smoking in his house. He mentioned many of your villagers in the course of his talk—most of them in a very uncompli-*

mentary way, but two or three favorably; among these latter yourself. I say 'favorably'—nothing stronger. I remember his saying he did not actually LIKE any person in the town—not one; but that you—I THINK he said you—am almost sure—had done him a very great service once, possibly without knowing the full value of it, and he wished he had a fortune, he would leave it to you when he died, and a curse apiece for the rest of the citizens. Now, then, if it was you that did him that service, you are his legitimate heir, and entitled to the sack of gold. I know that I can trust to your honor and honesty, for in a citizen of Hadleyburg these virtues are an unfailing inheritance, and so I am going to reveal to you the remark, well satisfied that if you are not the right man you will seek and find the right one and see that poor Goodson's debt of gratitude for the service referred to is paid. This is the remark: 'YOU ARE FAR FROM BEING A BAD MAN: GO, AND REFORM.'

HOWARD L. STEPHENSON."

"Oh, Edward, the money is ours, and I am so grateful, *oh,* so grateful—kiss me, dear, it's forever since we kissed—and we needed it so—the money—and now you are free of Pinkerton and his bank, and nobody's slave any more; it seems to me I could fly for joy."

It was a happy half-hour that the couple spent there on the settee caressing each other; it was the old days come again—days that had begun with their courtship and lasted without a break till the stranger brought the deadly money. By and by the wife said:

"Oh, Edward, how lucky it was you did him that grand service, poor Goodson! I never liked him, but I love him now. And it was fine and beautiful of you never to mention it or brag about it." Then, with a touch of reproach, "But you ought to have told *me,* Edward, you ought to have told your wife, you know."

"Well, I—er—well, Mary, you see—"

"Now stop hemming and hawing, and tell me about it, Edward. I always loved you, and

now I'm proud of you. Everybody believes there was only one good generous soul in this village, and now it turns out that you—Edward, why don't you tell me?"

"Well—er—er—Why, Mary, I can't!"

"You *can't*? *Why* can't you?"

"You see, he—well, he—he made me promise I wouldn't."

The wife looked him over, and said, very slowly,

"Made—you—promise? Edward, what do you tell me that for?"

"Mary, do you think I would lie?"

She was troubled and silent for a moment, then she laid her hand within his and said:

"No . . . no. We have wandered far enough from our bearings—God spare us that! In all your life you have never uttered a lie. But now—now that the foundations of things seem to be crumbling from under us, we—we—" She lost her voice for a moment, then said, brokenly, "Lead us not into temptation . . . . I think you made the promise, Edward. Let it rest so. Let us keep away from that ground. Now—that is all gone by; let us be happy again; it is no time for clouds."

Edward found it something of an effort to comply, for his mind kept wandering—trying to remember what the service was that he had done Goodson.

The couple lay awake the most of the night, Mary happy and busy, Edward busy but not so happy. Mary was planning what she would do with the money. Edward was trying to recall that service. At first his conscience was sore on account of the lie he had told Mary—if it was a lie. After much reflection—suppose it *was* a lie? What then? Was it such a great matter? Aren't we always *acting* lies? Then why not *tell* them? Look at Mary—look what she had done. While he was hurrying off on his honest errand, what was she doing? Lamenting because the papers hadn't been destroyed and the money kept! Is theft better than lying?

That point lost its sting—the lie dropped into the background and left comfort behind it. The next point came to the front: *Had* he rendered that service? Well, here was Goodson's own evidence as reported in Stephenson's letter; there could be no better evidence than that—it was even *proof* that he had rendered it. Of course. So that point was settled . . . . No, not quite. He recalled with a wince that this unknown Mr. Stephenson was just a trifle unsure as to whether the performer of it was Richards or some other—and, oh dear, he had put Richards on his honor! He must himself decide whither that money must go—and Mr. Stephenson was not doubting that if he was the wrong man he would go honorably and find the right one. Oh, it was odious to put a man in such a situation—ah, why couldn't Stephenson have left out that doubt! What did he want to intrude that for?

Further reflection. How did it happen that *Richards'* name remained in Stephenson's mind as indicating the right man, and not some other man's name? That looked good. Yes, that looked very good. In fact, it went on looking better and better, straight along—until by and by it grew into positive *proof*. And then Richards put the matter at once out of his mind, for he had a private instinct that a proof once established is better left so.

He was feeling reasonably comfortable now, but there was still one other detail that kept pushing itself on his notice: of course he had done that service—that was settled; but what *was* that service? He must recall it—he would not go to sleep till he had recalled it; it would make his peace of mind perfect. And so he thought and thought. He thought of a dozen things—possible services, even probable services—but none of them seemed adequate, none of them seemed large enough, none of them seemed worth the money—worth the fortune Goodson had wished he could leave in his will. And besides, he couldn't remember having done them, anyway. Now, then—now, then—what *kind* of a service would it be that would make a man so inordinately grateful? Ah—the saving of his soul! That must be it. Yes, he could remember, now, how he once

set himself the task of converting Goodson, and labored at it as much as—he was going to say three months; but upon closer examination it shrunk to a month, then to a week, then to a day, then to nothing. Yes, he remembered now, and with unwelcome vividness, that Goodson had told him to go to thunder and mind his own business—*he* wasn't hankering to follow Hadleyburg to heaven!

So that solution was a failure—he hadn't saved Goodson's soul. Richards was discouraged. Then after a little came another idea: had he saved Goodson's property? No, that wouldn't do—he hadn't any. His life? That is it! Of course. Why, he might have thought of it before. This time he was on the right track, sure. His imagination-mill was hard at work in a minute, now.

Thereafter during a stretch of two exhausting hours he was busy saving Goodson's life. He saved it in all kinds of difficult and perilous ways. In every case he got it saved satisfactorily up to a certain point; then, just as he was beginning to get well persuaded that it had really happened, a troublesome detail would turn up which made the whole thing impossible. As in the matter of drowning, for instance. In that case he had swum out and tugged Goodson ashore in an unconscious state with a great crowd looking on and applauding, but when he had got it all thought out and was just beginning to remember all about it, a whole swarm of disqualifying details arrived on the ground: the town would have known of the circumstance, Mary would have known of it, it would glare like a limelight in his own memory instead of being an inconspicuous service which he had possibly rendered "without knowing its full value." And at this point he remembered that he couldn't swim, anyway.

Ah—*there* was a point which he had been overlooking from the start: it had to be a service which he had rendered "possibly without knowing the full value of it." Why, really, that ought to be an easy hunt—much easier than those others. And sure enough, by and by he found it. Goodson, years and years ago, came near marrying a very sweet and pretty girl, named Nancy Hewitt, but in some way or other the match had been broken off; the girl died, Goodson remained a bachelor, and by and by became a soured one and a frank despiser of the human species. Soon after the girl's death the village found out, or thought it had found out, that she carried a spoonful of bad blood in her veins. Richards worked at these details a good while, and in the end he thought he remembered things concerning them which must have gotten mislaid in his memory through long neglect. He seemed dimly to remember that it was *he* that found out about the bad blood; that it was he that told the village; that the village told Goodson where they got it; that he thus saved Goodson from marrying the tainted girl; that he had done him this great service "without knowing the full value of it," in fact without knowing that he *was* doing it; but that Goodson knew the value of it, and what a narrow escape he had had, and so went to his grave grateful to his benefactor and wishing he had a fortune to leave him. It was all clear and simple now, and the more he went over it the more luminous and certain it grew; and at last, when he nestled to sleep satisfied and happy, he remembered the whole thing just as if it had been yesterday. In fact, he dimly remembered Goodson's *telling* him his gratitude once. Meantime Mary had spent six thousand dollars on a new house for herself and a pair of slippers for her pastor, and then had fallen peacefully to rest.

That same Saturday evening the postman had delivered a letter to each of the other principal citizens—nineteen letters in all. No two of the envelopes were alike, and no two of the superscriptions were in the same hand, but the letters inside were just like each other in every detail but one. They were exact copies of the letter received by Richards—handwriting and all—and were all signed by Stephenson, but in place of Richards' name each receiver's own name appeared.

All night long eighteen principal citizens did what their caste-brother Richards was doing at the same time—they put in their energies trying to remember what notable service it was that they had unconsciously done Barclay Goodson. In no case was it a holiday job; still they succeeded.

And while they were at this work, which was difficult, their wives put in the night spending the money, which was easy. During that one night the nineteen wives spent an average of seven thousand dollars each out of the forty thousand in the sack—a hundred and thirty-three thousand altogether.

Next day there was a surprise for Jack Halliday. He noticed that the faces of the nineteen chief citizens and their wives bore that expression of peaceful and holy happiness again. He could not understand it, neither was he able to invent any remarks about it that could damage it or disturb it. And so it was his turn to be dissatisfied with life. His private guesses at the reasons for the happiness failed in all instances, upon examination. When he met Mrs. Wilcox and noticed the placid ecstasy in her face, he said to himself, "Her cat has had kittens"—and went and asked the cook: it was not so; the cook had detected the happiness, but did not know the cause. When Halliday found the duplicate ecstasy in the face of "Shadbelly" Billson (village nickname), he was sure some neighbor of Billson's had broken his leg, but inquiry showed that this had not happened. The subdued ecstasy in Gregory Yates's face could mean but one thing—he was a mother-in-law short: it was another mistake. "And Pinkerton—Pinkerton—he has collected ten cents that he thought he was going to lose." And so on, and so on. In some cases the guesses had to remain in doubt, in the others they proved distinct errors. In the end Halliday said to himself, "Anyway it foots up that there's nineteen Hadleyburg families temporarily in heaven: I don't know how it happened; I only know Providence is off duty today."

An architect and builder from the next state

had lately ventured to set up a small business in this unpromising village, and his sign had now been hanging out a week. Not a customer yet; he was a discouraged man, and sorry he had come. But his weather changed suddenly now. First one and then another chief citizen's wife said to him privately:

"Come to my house Monday week—but say nothing about it for the present. We think of building."

He got eleven invitations that day. That night he wrote his daughter and broke off her match with her student. He said she could marry a mile higher than that.

Pinkerton the banker and two or three other well-to-do men planned countryseats—but waited. That kind don't count their chickens until they are hatched.

The Wilsons devised a grand new thing—a fancy-dress ball. They made no actual promises, but told all their acquaintanceship in confidence that they were thinking the matter over and thought they should give it—"and if we do, you will be invited, of course." People were surprised, and said, one to another, "Why, they are crazy, those poor Wilsons, they can't afford it." Several among the nineteen said privately to their husbands, "It is a good idea: we will keep still till their cheap thing is over, then *we* will give one that will make it sick."

The days drifted along, and the bill of future squanderings rose higher and higher, wilder and wilder, more and more foolish and reckless. It began to look as if every member of the nineteen would not only spend his whole forty thousand dollars before receiving-day, but be actually in debt by the time he got the money. In some cases light-headed people did not stop with planning to spend, they really spent—on credit. They bought land, mortgages, farms, speculative stock, fine clothes, horses, and various other things, paid down the bonus, and made themselves liable for the rest—at ten days. Presently the sober second thought came, and Halliday noticed that a ghastly anxiety was beginning to show

up in a good many faces. Again he was puzzled, and didn't know what to make of it. "The Wilcox kittens aren't dead, for they weren't born; nobody's broken a leg; there's no shrinkage in mother-in-laws; *nothing* has happened—it is an unsolvable mystery."

There was another puzzled man, too—the Rev. Mr. Burgess. For days, wherever he went, people seemed to follow him or to be watching out for him; and if he ever found himself in a retired spot, a member of the nineteen would be sure to appear, thrust an envelope privately into his hand, whisper "To be opened at the town hall Friday evening," then vanish away like a guilty thing. He was expecting that there might be one claimant for the sack —doubtful, however, Goodson being dead— but it never occurred to him that all this crowd might be claimants. When the great Friday came at last, he found that he had nineteen envelopes.

DISCUSSION FOR UNDERSTANDING

1. What do you find out about Jack Halliday?

2. How would you describe the town's mood the first week? the next two weeks? the last week?

3. In the second letter, the writer leaves a doubt that he is addressing the right person. How does this affect Richards?

4. What possible service does Richards imagine he did for Goodson and then discard? What is the service he decides he must have performed?

5. Who else receives a letter similar to Richards'?

3

The town hall had never looked finer. The platform at the end of it was backed by a showy draping of flags; at intervals along the walls were festoons of flags; the gallery fronts were clothed in flags; the supporting columns were swathed in flags; all this was to impress the stranger, for he would be there in considerable force, and in a large degree he would be connected with the press. The house was full. The 412 fixed seats were occupied; also the 68 extra chairs which had been packed into the aisles; the steps of the platform were occupied; some distinguished strangers were given seats on the platform; at the horseshoe of tables which fenced the front and sides of the platform sat a strong force of special correspondents who had come from everywhere. It was the best dressed house the town had ever produced. There were some tolerably expensive toilets there, and in several cases the ladies who wore them had the look of being unfamiliar with that kind of clothes. At least the town thought they had that look, but the notion could have arisen from the town's knowledge of the fact that these ladies had never inhabited such clothes before.

The gold sack stood on a little table at the front of the platform where all the house could see it. The bulk of the house gazed at it with a burning interest, a mouth-watering interest, a wistful and pathetic interest; a minority of nineteen couples gazed at it tenderly, lovingly, proprietarily, and the male half of this minority kept saying over to themselves the moving little impromptu speeches of thankfulness for the audience's applause and congratulations which they were presently going to get up and deliver. Every now and then one of these got a piece of paper out of his vest pocket and privately glanced at it to refresh his memory.

Of course there was a buzz of conversation going on—there always is; but at last when the Rev. Mr. Burgess rose and laid his hand on the sack he could hear his microbes gnaw, the place was so still. He related the curious history of the sack, then went on to speak in warm terms of Hadleyburg's old and well-earned reputation for spotless honesty, and of the town's just pride in this reputation. He said that this reputation was a treasure of priceless value; that under Providence its value had now become inestimably enhanced, for the recent episode had spread this fame far and wide, and thus had focused the eyes of the American world upon this village, and made its name for all time, as he hoped and believed, a synonym for commercial incorruptibility. [*Applause.*] "And who is to be the guardian of this noble treasure—the community as a whole? No! The responsibility is individual, not communal. From this day forth each and every one of you is in his own person its special guardian, and individually responsible that no harm shall come to it. Do you—does each of you—accept this great trust? [*Tumultuous assent.*] Then all is well. Transmit it to your children and to your children's children. Today your purity is beyond reproach—see to it that it shall remain so. Today there is not a person in your community who could be beguiled to touch a penny not his own—see to it that you abide in this grace. ["*We will! We will!*"] This is not the place to make comparisons between ourselves and other communities—some of them ungracious toward us; they have their ways, we have ours; let us be content. [*Applause.*] I am done. Under my hand, my friends, rests a stranger's eloquent recognition of what we are; through him the world will always henceforth know what we are. We do not know who he is, but in your name I utter your gratitude, and ask you to raise your voices in endorsement."

The house rose in a body and made the walls quake with the thunders of its thankfulness for the space of a long minute. Then it sat down, and Mr. Burgess took an envelope out of his pocket. The house held its breath while he slit the envelope open and took from it a slip of paper. He read its contents—slowly and impressively—the audience listening with tranced attention to the magic document, each of whose words stood for an ingot of gold:

"'*The remark which I made to the distressed stranger was this: "You are very far from being a bad man: go, and reform."*'" Then he continued:

"We shall know in a moment now whether the remark here quoted corresponds with the one concealed in the sack; and if that shall prove to be so—and it undoubtedly will—

this sack of gold belongs to a fellow citizen who will henceforth stand before the nation as the symbol of the special virtue which has made our town famous throughout the land—Mr. Billson!"

The house had gotten itself all ready to burst into the proper tornado of applause; but instead of doing it, it seemed stricken with a paralysis; there was a deep hush for a moment or two, then a wave of whispered murmurs swept the place—of about this tenor: "*Billson!* oh, come, this is *too* thin! Twenty dollars to a stranger—or *anybody—Billson!* tell it to the marines!" And now at this point the house caught its breath all of a sudden in a new access of astonishment, for it discovered that whereas in one part of the hall Deacon Billson was standing up with his head meekly bowed, in another part of it Lawyer Wilson was doing the same. There was a wondering silence now for awhile.

Everybody was puzzled, and nineteen couples were surprised and indignant.

Billson and Wilson turned and stared at each other. Billson asked, bitingly,

"Why do *you* rise, Mr. Wilson?"

"Because I have a right to. Perhaps you will be good enough to explain to the house why *you* rise?"

"With great pleasure. Because I wrote that paper."

"It is an impudent falsity! I wrote it myself."

It was Burgess's turn to be paralyzed. He stood looking vacantly at first one of the men and then the other, and did not seem to know what to do. The house was stupefied. Lawyer Wilson spoke up, now, and said,

"I ask the Chair to read the name signed to that paper."

That brought the Chair to itself, and it read out the name,

"'John Wharton *Billson.*'"

"There!" shouted Billson, "what have you got to say for yourself, now? And what kind of apology are you going to make to me and to this insulted house for the imposture which you have attempted to play here?"

714

"No apologies are due, sir; and as for the rest of it, I publicly charge you with pilfering my note from Mr. Burgess and substituting a copy of it signed with your own name. There is no other way by which you could have gotten hold of the test-remark; I alone, of living men, possessed the secret of its wording."

There was likely to be a scandalous state of things if this went on; everybody noticed with distress that the shorthand scribes were scribbling like mad; many people were crying "Chair, Chair! Order! Order!" Burgess rapped with his gavel, and said:

"Let us not forget the proprieties due. There has evidently been a mistake somewhere, but surely that is all. If Mr. Wilson gave me an envelope—and I remember now that he did—I still have it."

He took one out of his pocket, opened it, glanced at it, looked surprised and worried, and stood silent a few moments. Then he waved his hand in a wandering and mechanical way, and made an effort or two to say something, then gave it up, despondently. Several voices cried out:

"Read it! Read it! What is it?"

So he began in a dazed and sleepwalker fashion:

"'*The remark which I made to the unhappy stranger was this:* "You are far from being a bad man.* [The house gazed at him, marveling.] *Go, and reform.*"' [*Murmurs:* "Amazing! What can this mean?"] This one," said the Chair, "is signed Thurlow G. Wilson."

"There!" cried Wilson, "I reckon that settles it! I knew perfectly well my note was purloined."

"Purloined!" retorted Billson. "I'll let you know that neither you nor any man of your kidney must venture to—"

The Chair. "Order, gentlemen, order! Take your seats, both of you, please."

They obeyed, shaking their heads and grumbling angrily. The house was profoundly puzzled; it did not know what to do with this curious emergency. Presently Thompson got up. Thompson was the hatter. He would have liked to be a Nineteener; but such was not for him: his stock of hats was not considerable enough for the position. He said:

"Mr. Chairman, if I may be permitted to make a suggestion, can both of these gentlemen be right? I put it to you, sir, can both have happened to say the very same words to the stranger? It seems to me——"

The tanner got up and interrupted him. The tanner was a disgruntled man; he believed himself entitled to be a Nineteener, but he couldn't get recognition. It made him a little unpleasant in his ways and speech. Said he:

"Sho, *that's* not the point? *That* could happen—twice in a hundred years—but not the other thing. *Neither* of them gave the twenty dollars!"

[*A ripple of applause.*]

Billson. "I did!"

Wilson. "I did!"

Then each accused the other of pilfering.

The Chair. "Order! Sit down, if you please —both of you. Neither of the notes has been out of my possession at any moment."

A Voice. "Good—that settles *that!*"

The Tanner. "Mr. Chairman, one thing is now plain: one of these men has been eavesdropping under the other one's bed, and filching family secrets. If it is not unparliamentary to suggest it, I will remark that both are equal to it. [*The Chair.* "Order Order!"] I withdraw the remark, sir, and will confine myself to suggesting that *if* one of them has overheard the other reveal the test-remark to his wife, we shall catch him now."

A Voice. "How?"

The Tanner. "Easily. The two have not quoted the remark in exactly the same words. You would have noticed that, if there hadn't been a considerable stretch of time and an exciting quarrel inserted between the two readings."

A Voice. "Name the difference."

The Tanner. "The word *very* is in Billson's note, and not in the other."

Many Voices. "That's so—he's right!"

The Tanner. "And so, if the Chair will ex-amine the test-remark in the sack, we shall know which of these two frauds—[*The Chair.* "Order!"]—which of these two adventures— [*The Chair.* "Order! Order!"]—which of these two gentlemen—[*Laughter and applause.*]— is entitled to wear the belt as being the first dishonest blatherskite ever bred in this town— which he has dishonored, and which will be a sultry place for him from now out!" [*Vigorous applause.*]

Many Voices. "Open it!—open the sack!"

Mr. Burgess made a slit in the sack, slid his hand in and brought out an envelope. In it were a couple of folded notes. He said:

"One of these is marked, 'Not to be examined until all written communications which have been addressed to the Chair—if any— shall have been read.' The other is marked 'The Test.' Allow me. It is worded—to wit:

"'I do not require that the first half of the remark which was made to me by my benefactor shall be quoted with exactness, for it was not striking, and could be forgotten; but its closing fifteen words are quite striking, and I think easily rememberable; unless *these* shall be accurately reproduced, let the applicant be regarded as an impostor. My benefactor began by saying he seldom gave advice to anyone, but that it always bore the hallmark of high value when he did give it. Then he said this— and it has never faded from my memory: "*You are far from being a bad man—*"'"

Fifty Voices. "That settles it—the money's Wilson's! Wilson! Wilson! Speech! Speech!"

People jumped up and crowded around Wilson, wringing his hand and congratulating fervently—meantime the Chair was hammering with the gavel and shouting:

"Order, gentlemen! Order! Order! Let me finish reading, please." When quiet was restored, the reading was resumed—as follows:

"'"*Go, and reform—or, mark my words— some day, for your sins, you will die and go to hell or Hadleyburg—*TRY AND MAKE IT THE FORMER.*"'"

A ghastly silence followed. First an angry cloud began to settle darkly upon the faces of the citizenship; after a pause the cloud began to rise, and a tickled expression tried to take its place; tried so hard that it was only kept under with great and painful difficulty; the reporters, the Brixtonites, and other strangers bent their heads down and shielded their faces with their hands, and managed to hold in by main strength and heroic courtesy. At this most inopportune time burst upon the stillness the roar of a solitary voice—Jack Halliday's:

"That's got the hallmark on it!"

Then the house let go, strangers and all. Even Mr. Burgess's gravity broke down presently; then the audience considered itself officially absolved from all restraint, and it made the most of its privilege. It was a good long laugh, and a tempestuously wholehearted one, but it ceased at last—long enough for Mr. Burgess to try to resume, and for the people to get their eyes partially wiped; then it broke out again; and afterward yet again; then at last Burgess was able to get out these serious words:

"It is useless to try to disguise the fact—we find ourselves in the presence of a matter of grave import. It involves the honor of your town, it strikes at the town's good name. The difference of a single word between the test-remarks offered by Mr. Wilson and Mr. Billson was itself a serious thing, since it indicated that one or the other of these gentlemen had committed a theft—"

The two men were sitting limp, nerveless, crushed; but at these words both were electrified into movement, and started to get up—

"Sit down!" said the Chair, sharply, and they obeyed. "That, as I have said, was a serious thing. And it was—but for only one of them. But the matter has become graver; for the honor of *both* is now in formidable peril. Shall I go even further, and say in inextricable peril? *Both* left out the crucial fifteen words." He paused. During several moments he allowed the pervading stillness to gather and deepen its impressive effects, then added: "There would seem to be but one way whereby this could happen. I ask these gentlemen—

Was there *collusion?—agreement?"*

A low murmur sifted through the house; its import was, "He's got them both."

Billson was not used to emergencies; he sat in a helpless collapse. But Wilson was a lawyer. He struggled to his feet, pale and worried, and said:

"I ask the indulgence of the house while I explain this most painful matter. I am sorry to say what I am about to say, since it must inflict irreparable injury upon Mr. Billson, whom I have always esteemed and respected until now, and in whose invulnerability to temptation I entirely believed—as did you all. But for the preservation of my own honor I must speak—and with frankness, I confess with shame—and I now beseech your pardon for it—that I said to the ruined stranger all of the words contained in the test-remark, including the disparaging fifteen. [*Sensation.*] When the late publication was made I recalled them, and I resolved to claim the sack of coin, for by every right I was entitled to it. Now I will ask you to consider this point, and weigh it well: that stranger's gratitude to me that night knew no bounds; he said himself that he could find no words for it that were adequate, and that if he should ever be able he would repay me a thousandfold. Now, then, I ask you this: Could I expect—could I believe—could I even remotely imagine—that, feeling as he did, he would do so ungrateful a thing as to add those quite unnecessary fifteen words to his test?— set a trap for me?—expose me as a slander of my own town before my own people assembled in a public hall? It was preposterous; it was impossible. His test would contain only the kindly opening clause of my remark. Of that I had no shadow of doubt. You would have thought as I did. You would not have expected a base betrayal from one whom you had befriended and against whom you had commited no offense. And so, with perfect confidence, perfect trust, I wrote on a piece of paper the opening words—ending with 'Go, and reform'—and signed it. When I was about to put it in an envelope I was called into my back office, and without thinking I left the paper lying open on my desk." He stopped, turned his head slowly toward Billson, waited a moment, then added: "I ask you to note this: when I returned, a little later, Mr. Billson was retiring by my street door." [*Sensation.*]

In a moment Billson was on his feet and shouting:

"It's a lie! It's an infamous lie!"

The Chair. "Be seated, sir! Mr. Wilson has the floor."

Billson's friends pulled him into his seat and quieted him, and Wilson went on:

"Those are the simple facts. My note was now lying in a different place on the table from where I had left it. I noticed that, but attached no importance to it, thinking a draft had blown it there. That Mr. Billson would read a private paper was a thing which could not occur to me; he was an honorable man, and he would be above that. If you will allow me to say it, I think his extra word '*very*' stands explained: it is attributable to a defect of memory. I was the only man in the world who could furnish here any detail of the test-remark—by *honorable* means. I have finished."

There is nothing in the world like a persuasive speech to fuddle the mental apparatus and upset the convictions and debauch the emotions of an audience not practiced in the tricks and delusions of oratory. Wilson sat down victorious. The house submerged him in tides of approving applause; friends swarmed to him and shook him by the hand and congratulated him, and Billson was shouted down and not allowed to say a word. The Chair hammered and hammered with its gavel, and kept shouting.

"But let us proceed, gentlemen, let us proceed!"

At last there was a measurable degree of quiet, and the hatter said:

"But what is there to proceed with, sir, but to deliver the money?"

Voices. "That's it! That's it! Come forward, Wilson!"

The Hatter. "I move three cheers for Mr. Wilson, Symbol of the special virtue which ——"

The cheers burst forth before he could finish; and in the midst of them—and in the midst of the clamor of the gavel also—some enthusiasts mounted Wilson on a big friend's shoulder and were going to fetch him in triumph to the platform. The Chair's voice now rose above the noise—

"Order! To your places! You forget that there is still a document to be read." When quiet had been restored he took up the document, and was going to read it, but laid it down again, saying "I forgot; this is not to be read until all written communications received by me have first been read." He took an envelope out of his pocket, removed its enclosure, glanced at it—seemed astonished—held it out and gazed at it—stared at it.

Twenty or thirty voices cried out:

"What is it? Read it! Read it!"

And he did—slowly, and wondering:

" 'The remark which I made to the stranger —[*Voices.* "Hello! how's this?"]—was this: "You are far from being a bad man. [*Voices.* "Great Scott!"] Go, and reform." ' [*Voice.* "Oh, saw my leg off!"] Signed by Mr. Pinkerton the banker."

The pandemonium of delight which turned itself loose now was of a sort to make the judicious weep. Those whose withers were unwrung laughed till the tears ran down; the reporters, in throes of laughter, set down disordered pothooks which would never in the world be decipherable; and a sleeping dog jumped up, scared out of its wits, and barked itself crazy at the turmoil. All manner of cries were scattered through the din: "We're getting rich—*two* Symbols of Incorruptibility!—without counting Billson!" "*Three!*—count Shadbelly in—we can't have too many!" "All right—Billson's elected!" "Alas, poor Wilson—victim of *two* thieves!"

A Powerful Voice. "Silence! The Chair's fished up something more out of its pocket."

Voices. "Hurrah! Is it something fresh? Read it! read! read!"

The Chair [*reading*]. " 'The remark which I made,' etc.: 'You are far from being a bad man. Go,' etc. Signed, 'Gregory Yates.' "

Tornado of Voices. "Four Symbols!" " 'Rah for Yates!" "Fish again!"

The house was in roaring humor now, and ready to get all the fun out of the occasion that might be in it. Several Nineteeners, looking pale and distressed, got up and began to work their way toward the aisles, but a score of shouts went up:

"The doors, the doors—close the doors; no Incorruptible shall leave this place! Sit down, everybody!"

The mandate was obeyed.

"Fish again! Read! read!"

The Chair fished again, and once more the familiar words began to fall from its lips—

" 'You are far from being a bad man——' "

"Name! name! What's his name?"

" 'L. Ingoldsby Sargent.' "

"Five elected! Pile up the Symbols! Go on, go on!"

" 'You are far from being a bad—' "

"Name! name!"

" 'Nicholas Whitworth.' "

"Hooray! hooray! it's a symbolical day!"

Somebody wailed in, and began to sing this rhyme (leaving out "it's") to the lovely "Mikado" tune of "When a man's afraid, a beautiful maid—"; the audience joined in, with joy; then, just in time, somebody contributed another line—

"And don't you this forget—"

The house roared it out. A third line was at once furnished—

"Corruptibles far from Hadleyburg are—"

The house roared that one, too. As the last note died, Jack Halliday's voice rose high and clear, freighted with a final line—

"But the Symbols are here, you bet!"

That was sung, with booming enthusiasm. Then the happy house started in at the beginning and sang the four lines through twice, with immense swing and dash, and finished up with a crashing three-times-three and a tiger for "Hadleyburg the Incorruptible and all Symbols of it which we shall find worthy to receive the hallmark tonight."

Then the shoutings at the Chair began again, all over the place:

"Go on! go on! Read! read some more! Read all you've got!"

"That's it—go on! We are winning eternal celebrity!"

A dozen men got up now and began to protest. They said that this farce was the work of some abandoned joker, and was an insult to the whole community. Without a doubt these signatures were all forgeries—

"Sit down! sit down! Shut up! You are confessing. We'll find *your* names in the lot."

"Mr. Chairman, how many of those envelopes have you got?"

The Chair counted.

"Together with those that have been already examined, there are nineteen."

A storm of derisive applause broke out.

"Perhaps they all contain the secret. I move that you open them all and read every signature that is attached to a note of that sort— and read also the first eight words of the note."

"Second the motion!"

It was put and carried—uproariously. Then poor old Richards got up, and his wife rose and stood at his side. Her head was bent down, so that none might see that she was crying. Her husband gave her his arm, and so supporting her, he began to speak in a quavering voice:

"My friends, you have known us two—Mary and me—all our lives, and I think you have liked us and respected us——"

The Chair interrupted him:

"Allow me. It is quite true—that which you are saying, Mr. Richards: this town *does* know you two; it *does* like you; it *does* respect you; more—it honors you and *loves* you——"

Halliday's voice rang out:

"That's the hallmarked truth, too! If the

Chair is right, let the house speak up and say it. Rise! Now, then—hip! hip! hip!—all together!"

The house rose in mass, faced toward the old couple eagerly, filled the air with a snow-storm of waving handkerchiefs, and delivered the cheers with all its affectionate heart.

The Chair then continued:

"What I was going to say is this: We know your good heart, Mr. Richards, but this is not a time for the exercise of charity toward offenders. [*Shouts of "Right! right!"*] I see your generous purpose in your face, but I cannot allow you to plead for these men——"

"But I was going to——"

"Please take your seat, Mr. Richards. We must examine the rest of these notes—simple fairness to the men who have already been exposed requires this. As soon as that has been done—I give you my word for this—you shall be heard."

Many Voices. "Right!—the Chair is right—no interruption can be permitted at this stage! Go on!—the names! the names!—according to the terms of the motion!"

The old couple sat reluctantly down, and the husband whispered to the wife, "It is piti-fully hard to have to wait; the shame will be greater than ever when they find we were only going to plead for *ourselves.*"

Straightway the jollity broke loose again with the reading of the names.

" 'You are far from being a bad man—' Signature, 'Robert J. Titmarsh.'

" 'You are far from being a bad man—' Signature, 'Eliphalet Weeks.'

" 'You are far from being a bad man—' Signature, 'Oscar B. Wilder.' "

At this point the house lit upon the idea of taking the eight words out of the Chairman's hands. He was not unthankful for that. Thenceforward he held up each note in its turn, and waited. The house droned out the eight words in a massed and measured and musical deep volume of sound (with a dar-ingly close resemblance to a well-known church chant)—" 'You are f-a-r from being a

b-a-a-a-d man.' " Then the Chair said, "Signa-ture. 'Archibald Wilcox.' " And so on, and so on, name after name, and everybody had an increasingly and gloriously good time except the wretched Nineteen. Now and then, when a particularly shining name was called, the house made the Chair wait while it chanted the whole of the test-remark from the begin-ning to the closing words, "And go to hell or Hadleyburg—try and make it the for-or-m-e-r!" and in these special cases they added a grand and agonized and imposing "A-a-a-a-*men!*"

The list dwindled, dwindled, dwindled, poor old Richards keeping tally of the count, wincing when a name resembling his own was pronounced, and waiting in miserable suspense for the time to come when it would be his humiliating privilege to rise with Mary and finish his plea, which he was intending to word thus: ". . . for until now we have never done any wrong thing, but have gone our humble way unreproached. We are very poor, we are old, and have no chick nor child to help us; we were sorely tempted, and we fell. It was my purpose when I got up before to make a confession and beg that my name might not be read out in this public place, for it seemed to us that we could not bear it; but I was prevented. It was just; it was our place to suffer with the rest. It has been hard for us. It is the first time we have ever heard our name fall from anyone's lips—sullied. Be merciful—for the sake of the better days; make our shame as light to bear as in your charity you can." At this point in his reverie Mary nudged him, perceiving that his mind was absent. The house was chanting, "You are f-a-r," etc.

"Be ready," Mary whispered. "Your name comes now; he has read eighteen."

The chant ended.

"Next! next! next!" came volleying from all over the house.

Burgess put his hand into his pocket. The old couple, trembling, began to rise. Burgess fumbled a moment, then said,

"I find I have read them all."

Faint with joy and surprise, the couple sank into their seats, and Mary whispered,

"Oh, bless God, we are saved!—he has lost ours—I wouldn't give this for a hundred of those sacks!"

The house burst out with its "Mikado" travesty, and sang it three times with ever-increasing enthusiasm, rising to its feet when it reached for the third time the closing line—

"But the Symbols are here, you bet!"

and finishing up with cheers and a tiger for "Hadleyburg purity and our eighteen immortal representatives of it."

Then Wingate, the saddler, got up and proposed cheers "for the cleanest man in town, the one solitary citizen in it who didn't try to steal that money—Edward Richards."

They were given with great and moving heartiness; then somebody proposed that Richards be elected sole guardian and Symbol of the now Sacred Hadleyburg Tradition, with power and right to stand up and look the whole sarcastic world in the face.

Passed, by acclamation; then they sang the "Mikado" again, and ended it with,

"And there's *one* Symbol left, you bet!"

There was a pause; then—

A Voice. "Now, then, who's to get the sack?"

The Tanner [*with bitter sarcasm*]. "That's easy. The money has to be divided among the eighteen Incorruptibles. They gave the suffering stranger twenty dollars apiece—and that remark—each in his turn—it took twenty-two minutes for the procession to move past. Staked the stranger—total contribution, $360. All they want is just the loan back—and interest—forty thousand dollars altogether."

Many Voices [*derisively*]. "That's it! Divvy! Divvy! Be kind to the poor—don't keep them waiting!"

The Chair. "Order! I now offer the stranger's remaining document. It says: 'If no claimant shall appear [*grand chorus of groans*], I desire that you open the sack and count out the money to the principal citizens of your town, they to take it in trust [*cries of "Oh! Oh! Oh!"*], and use it in such ways as to them shall seem best for the propagation and preservation of your community's noble reputation for incorruptible honesty [*more cries*]—a reputation to which their names and their efforts will add a new and far-reaching luster.' [*Enthusiastic outburst of sarcastic applause.*] That seems to be all. No—here is a postscript:

"'P. S.—CITIZENS OF HADLEYBURG: There *is* no test-remark—nobody made one. [*Great sensation.*] There wasn't any pauper stranger, nor any twenty-dollar contribution, nor any accompanying benediction and compliment—these are all inventions. [*General buzz and hum of astonishment and delight.*] Allow me to tell my story—it will take but a word or two. I passed through your town at a certain time, and received a deep offense which I had not earned. Any other man would have been content to kill one or two of you and call it square, but to me that would have been a trivial revenge, and inadequate; for the dead do not *suffer*. Besides, I could not kill you all —and, anyway, mad as I am, even that would not have satisfied me. I wanted to damage every man in the place, and every woman— and not in their bodies or in their estate, but in their vanity—the place where feeble and foolish people are most vulnerable. So I disguised myself and came back and studied you. You were easy game. You had an old and lofty reputation for honesty, and naturally you were proud of it—it was your treasure of treasures, the very apple of your eye. As soon as I found out that you carefully and vigilantly kept yourselves and your children *out of temptation,* I knew how to proceed. Why, you simple creatures, the weakest of all weak things is a virtue which has not been tested in the fire. I laid a plan, and gathered a list of names. My project was to corrupt Hadleyburg the Incorruptible. My idea was to make liars and thieves of nearly half a hundred smirchless men and women who had never in their lives uttered a lie or stolen a penny. I was afraid of Goodson. He was neither born nor reared in Hadleyburg. I was afraid that if I started to operate my scheme by getting my letter laid before you, you would say to yourselves, "Goodson is the only man among us who would give away twenty dollars to a poor devil"—and then you might not bite at my bait. But Heaven took Goodson; then I knew I was safe, and I set my trap and baited it. It may be that I shall not catch all the men to whom I mailed the pretended test secret, but I shall catch the most of them, if I know Hadleyburg nature. [*Voices.* "Right—he got every last one of them."] I believe they will even steal ostensible *gamble*-money, rather than miss, poor, tempted, and mistrained fellows. I am hoping to eternally and everlastingly squelch your vanity and give Hadleyburg a new renown—one that will *stick*—and spread far. If I have succeeded, open the sack and summon the Committee on Propagation and Preservation of the Hadleyburg Reputation.'"

A Cyclone of Voices. "Open it! Open it! The Eighteen to the front! Committee on Propagation of the Tradition! Forward—the Incorruptibles!"

The Chair ripped the sack wide, and gathered up a handful of bright, broad, yellow coins, shook them together, then examined them—

"Friends, they are only gilded disks of lead!"

There was a crashing outbreak of delight over this news, and when the noise had subsided, the tanner called out:

"By right of apparent seniority in this business, Mr. Wilson is Chairman of the Committee on Propagation of the Tradition. I suggest that he step forward on behalf of his pals, and receive in trust the money."

A Hundred Voices. "Wilson! Wilson! Wilson! Speech! Speech!"

Wilson [*in a voice trembling with anger*]. "You will allow me to say, and without apologies for my language, *damn* the money!"

A Voice. "Oh, and him a Baptist!"

A Voice. "Seventeen Symbols left! Step up, gentlemen, and assume your trust!"

There was a pause—no response.

The Saddler. "Mr. Chairman, we've got *one* clean man left, anyway, out of the late aristocracy; and he needs money, and deserves it. I move that you appoint Jack Halliday to get up there and auction off that sack of gilt twenty-dollar pieces, and give the result to the right man—the man who Hadleyburg delights to honor—Edward Richards."

This was received with great enthusiasm, the dog taking a hand again; the saddler started the bids at a dollar, the Brixton folk and Barnum's representative fought hard for it, the people cheered every jump that the bids made, the excitement climbed moment by moment higher and higher, the bidders got on their mettle and grew steadily more and more daring, more and more determined, the jumps went from a dollar up to five, then to ten, then to twenty, then fifty, then to a hundred, then—

At the beginning of the auction Richards whispered in distress to his wife: "Oh, Mary, can we allow it? It—it—you see, it is an honor-reward, a testimonial to purity of character, and—and—can we allow it? Hadn't I better get up and—Oh, Mary, what ought we to do?—what do you think we—[*Halliday's voice.* "Fifteen I'm bid!—fifteen for the sack—twenty!—ah, thanks!—thirty—thanks again! Thirty, thirty, thirty!—do I hear forty?—forty it is! Keep the ball rolling, gentlemen, keep it rolling!—fifty!—thanks, noble Roman! going at fifty, fifty, fifty!—seventy!—ninety!—splendid!—a hundred!—pile it up, pile it up!—hundred and twenty—forty!—just in time!—hundred and fifty!—TWO hundred!—superb! Do I hear two h—thanks!—two hundred and fifty!—"*]

"It is another temptation, Edward—I'm all in a tremble—but, oh, we've escaped *one* temptation, and that ought to warn us to—["*Six did I hear?—thanks!—six fifty, six f—SEVEN hundred!*"] And yet Edward, when you think—nobody susp—["*Eight hundred dollars!—hurrah!—make it nine!—Mr. Parsons, did I*"] *hear you say—thanks—nine!—this noble sack of virgin lead going at only nine hundred dollars, gilding and all—come! do I hear—a thousand!—gratefully yours!—did some one say eleven?—a sack which is going to be the most celebrated in the whole Uni—*"] Oh, Edward" [beginning to sob], "we are *so* poor!—but—but—do as you think best—do as you think best."

Edward fell—that is, he sat still; sat with a conscience which was not satisfied, but which was overpowered by circumstances.

Meantime a stranger, who looked like an amateur detective gotten up as an impossible English earl, had been watching the evening's proceedings with manifest interest, and with a contented expression in his face; and he had been privately commenting to himself. He was now soliloquizing somewhat like this: "None of the Eighteen are bidding; that is not satisfactory; I must change that—the dramatic unities require it; they must buy the sack they tried to steal; they must pay a heavy price, too—some of them are rich. And another thing, when I make a mistake in Hadleyburg nature the man that puts that error upon me is entitled to a high honorarium, and someone must pay it. This poor old Richards has brought my judgment to shame; he is an honest man:—I don't understand it, but I acknowledge it. Yes, he saw my deuces *and* with a straight flush, and by rights the pot is his. And it shall be a jackpot, too, if I can manage it. He disappointed me, but let that pass."

He was watching the bidding. At a thousand, the market broke; the prices tumbled swiftly. He waited—and still watched. One competitor dropped out; then another, and another. He put in a bid or two, now. When the bids had sunk to ten dollars, he added a five; someone raised him a three; he waited a moment, then flung in a fifty-dollar jump, and the sack was his—at $1,282. The house broke out in cheers—then stopped; for he was on his feet, and had lifted his hand. He began to speak.

"I desire to say a word, and ask a favor. I am a speculator in rarities, and I have dealings with persons interested in numismatics[3] all over the world. I can make a profit on this purchase, just as it stands; but there is a way, if I can get your approval, whereby I can make every one of these leaden twenty-dollar pieces worth its face in gold, and perhaps more. Grant me that approval, and I will give part of my gains to your Mr. Richards, whose invulnerable probity you have so justly and cordially recognized tonight; his share shall be ten thousand dollars, and I will hand him the money tomorrow. [*Great applause from the house.* But the "invulnerable probity" made the Richardses blush prettily; however, it went for modesty, and did no harm.] If you will pass my proposition by a good majority—I would like a two-thirds vote—I will regard that as the town's consent, and that is all I ask. Rarities are always helped by any device which will rouse curiosity and compel remark. Now if I may have your permission to stamp upon the faces of each of these ostensible coins the names of the eighteen gentlemen who—"

Nine-tenths of the audience were on their feet in a moment—dog and all—and the proposition was carried with a whirlwind of approving applause and laughter.

They sat down, and all the Symbols except "Dr." Clay Harkness got up, violently protesting against the proposed outrage, and threatning to—

"I beg you not to threaten me," said the stranger, calmly. "I know my legal rights, and am not accustomed to being frightened at bluster." [*Applause.*] He sat down. "Dr." Harkness saw an opportunity here. He was one of the two very rich men of the place, and Pinkerton was the other. Harkness was proprietor of a mint; that is to say, a popular patent medicine. He was running for the Legislature on one ticket, and Pinkerton on

3. **numismatics**\\'n(y)ū•məz ▲mat•ĭks\\ the study or collection of coins, tokens, medals, or similar objects.

the other. It was a close race and a hot one, and getting hotter every day. Both had strong appetites for money; each had bought a great tract of land, with a purpose; there was going to be a new railway, and each wanted to be in the Legislature and help locate the route to his own advantage; a single vote might make the decision, and with it two or three fortunes. The stake was large, and Harkness was a daring speculator. He was sitting close to the stranger. He leaned over while one or another of the other Symbols was entertaining the house with protests and appeals, and asked, in a whisper,

"What is your price for the sack?"

"Forty thousand dollars."

"I'll give you twenty."

"No."

"Say thirty."

"The price is forty thousand dollars; not a penny less."

"All right, I'll give it. I will come to the hotel at ten in the morning. I don't want it known; will see you privately."

"Very good." Then the stranger got up and said to the house:

"I find it late. The speeches of these gentlemen are not without merit, not without interest, not without grace; yet if I may be excused I will take my leave. I thank you for the great favor which you have shown me in granting my petition. I ask the Chair to keep the sack for me until tomorrow, and to hand these three five-hundred-dollar notes to Mr. Richards." They were passed up to the Chair. "At nine I will call for the sack, and at eleven will deliver the rest of the ten thousand to Mr. Richards in person, at his home. Good night."

Then he slipped out, and left the audience making a vast noise, which was composed of a mixture of cheers, the "Mikado" song, dog-disapproval, and the chant, "You are f-a-r from being a b-a-a-d man—a-a-a-a-men!"

DISCUSSION FOR UNDERSTANDING

1. How do the hatter and tanner differ in their reaction to Billson's and Wilson's claims to the money?

2. What is surprising about the test-statement in the bag?

3. How do Billson and Wilson each answer the charge of Burgess that there must have been collusion?

4. How does the crowd react to the news that more than two are claiming the money?

5. What is ironic about Richards' attempt to confess at the meeting?

6. What is done with the sack of gilded disks of lead?

7. What is the new test now made of Richards' honesty? How does his wife react? What does he do?

8. What happens in the bidding? Who gets the sack? What is the result of his proposition to the crowd?

✿ 4

At home the Richardses had to endure congratulations and compliments until midnight. Then they were left to themselves. They looked a little sad, and they sat silent and thinking. Finally Mary sighed and said,

"Do you think we are to blame, Edward—*much* to blame?" and her eyes wandered to the accusing triplet of big bank notes lying on the table, where the congratulators had been gloating over them and reverently fingering them. Edward did not answer at once; then he brought out a sigh and said, hesitatingly:

"We—we couldn't help it, Mary. It—well, it was ordered. *All* things are."

Mary glanced up and looked at him steadily, but he didn't return the look. Presently she said:

"I thought congratulations and praises always tasted good. But—it seems to me, now —Edward?"

"Well?"

"Are you going to stay in the bank?"

"N-no."

"Resign?"

"In the morning—by note."

"It does seem best."

Richards bowed his head in his hands and muttered:

"Before, I was not afraid to let oceans of people's money pour through my hands, but—Mary, I am so tired, so tired—"

"We will go to bed."

At nine in the morning the stranger called for the sack and took it to the hotel in a cab. At ten Harkness had a talk with him privately. The stranger asked for and got five checks on a metropolitan bank—drawn to "Bearer"—four for $1,500 each, and one for $34,000. He put one of the former in his pocketbook, and the remainder, representing $38,500, he put in an envelope, and with these he added a note, which he wrote after Harkness was gone. At eleven he called at the Richards house and knocked. Mrs. Richards peeped through the shutters, then went and received the envelope, and the stranger disappeared without a word. She came back flushed and a little unsteady on her legs, and gasped out:

"I am sure I recognized him! Last night it seemed to me that maybe I had seen him somewhere before."

"He is the man that brought the sack here?"

"I am almost sure of it."

"Then he is the ostensible Stephenson, too, and sold every important citizen in this town with his bogus secret. Now if he has sent checks instead of money, we are sold, too, after we thought we had escaped. I was beginning to feel fairly comfortable once more, after my night's rest, but the look of that envelope makes me sick. It isn't fat enough; $8,500 in even the largest bank notes makes more bulk than that."

"Edward, why do you object to checks?"

"Checks signed by Stephenson! I am resigned to take the $8,500 if it could come in bank notes—for it does seem that it was so ordered, Mary—but I have never had much courage, and I have not the pluck to try to market a check signed with that disastrous name. It would be a trap. That man tried to catch me; we escaped somehow or other; and now he is trying a new way. If it is checks—"

"Oh, Edward, it is *too* bad!" and she held up the checks and began to cry.

"Put them in the fire! quick! we mustn't be tempted. It is a trick to make the world laugh at *us*, along with the rest, and—Give them to *me*, since you can't do it!" He snatched them and tried to hold his grip till he could get to the stove; but he was human, he was a cashier, and he stopped a moment to make sure of the signature. Then he came near to fainting.

"Fan me, Mary, fan me! They are the same as gold!"

"Oh, how lovely, Edward! Why?"

"Signed by Harkness. What can the mystery of that be, Mary?"

"Edward, do you think—"

"Look here—look at this! Fifteen—fifteen—fifteen—thirty-four. Thirty-eight thousand five hundred! Mary, the sack isn't worth twelve dollars, and Harkness—apparently—has paid about par for it."

"And does it all come to us, do you think—instead of the ten thousand?"

"Why, it looks like it. And the checks are made to 'Bearer,' too."

"Is that good, Edward? What is it for?"

"A hint to collect them at some distant bank, I reckon. Perhaps Harkness doesn't want the matter known. What is that—a note?"

"Yes. It was with the checks."

It was in the "Stephenson" handwriting, but there was no signature. It said:

"*I am a disappointed man. Your honesty is beyond the reach of temptation. I had a different idea about it, but I wronged you in that, and I beg pardon, and do it sincerely. I honor you—and that is sincere too. This town is not worthy to kiss the hem of your garment. Dear sir, I made a square bet with myself that there were nineteen debauchable men in your self-righteous community. I have lost. Take the whole pot, you are entitled to it.*"

Richards drew a deep sigh, and said:

"It seems written with fire—it burns so. Mary—I am miserable again."

"I, too. Ah, dear, I wish—"

"To think, Mary—he *believes* in me."

"Oh, don't, Edward—I can't bear it."

"If those beautiful words were deserved, Mary—and God knows I believed I deserved them once—I think I could give the forty thousand dollars for them. And I would put that paper away, as representing more than gold and jewels, and keep it always. But now—We could not live in the shadow of its accusing presence, Mary."

He put it in the fire.

A messenger arrived and delivered an envelope.

Richards took from it a note and read it; it was from Burgess.

"You saved me, in a difficult time. I saved you last night. It was at cost of a lie, but I made the sacrifice freely, and out of a grateful heart. None in this village knows so well as I know how brave and good and noble you are. At bottom you cannot respect me, knowing as you do of that matter of which I am accused, and by the general voice condemned; but I beg that you will at least believe that I am a grateful man; it will help me to bear my burden.

[Signed]   BURGESS"

"Saved, once more. And on such terms!" He put the note in the fire. "I—I wish I were dead, Mary, I wish I were out of it all."

"Oh, these are bitter, bitter days, Edward. The stabs, through their very generosity, are so deep—and they come so fast!"

Three days before the election each of two thousand voters suddenly found himself in possession of a prized memento—one of the renowned bogus double-eagles. Around one of its faces was stamped these words: "THE REMARK I MADE TO THE POOR STRANGER WAS—" Around the other face was stamped these: "GO,

AND REFORM. [SIGNED] PINKERTON." Thus the entire remaining refuse of the renowned joke was emptied upon a single head, and with calamitous effect. It revived the recent vast laugh and concentrated it upon Pinkerton; and Harkness's election was a walkover.

Within twenty-four hours after the Richardses had received their checks their consciences were quieting down, discouraged; the old couple were learning to reconcile themselves to the sin which they had committed. But they were to learn, now, that a sin takes on new and real terrors when there seems a chance that it is going to be found out. This gives it a fresh and most substantial and important aspect. At church the morning sermon was of the usual pattern; it was the same old things said in the same old way; they had heard them a thousand times and found them innocuous, next to meaningless, and easy to sleep under; but now it was different: the sermon seemed to bristle with accusations; it seemed aimed straight and specially at people who were concealing deadly sins. After church they got away from the mob of congratulators as soon as they could, and hurried homeward, chilled to the bone at they did not know what—vague, shadowy, indefinite fears. And by chance they caught a glimpse of Mr. Burgess as he turned a corner. He paid no attention to their nod of recognition! He hadn't seen it; but they did not know that. What could his conduct mean? It might mean—it might mean—oh, a dozen dreadful things. Was it possible that he knew that Richards could have cleared him of guilt in that bygone time, and had been silently waiting for a chance to even up accounts? At home, in their distress they got to imagining that their servant might have been in the next room listening when Richards revealed the secret to his wife that he knew of Burgess's innocence; next, Richards began to imagine that he had heard the swish of a gown in there at that time; next, he was sure he *had* heard it. They would call Sarah in, on a pretext, and watch her face: if she had been betraying them to Mr. Burgess, it would show

725

in her manner. They asked her some questions —questions which were so random and incoherent and seemingly purposeless that the girl felt sure that the old people's minds had been affected by their sudden good fortune; the sharp and watchful gaze which they bent upon her frightened her, and that completed the business. She blushed, she became nervous and confused, and to the old people these were plain signs of guilt—guilt of some fearful sort or other—without doubt she was a spy and a traitor. When they were alone again they began to piece many unrelated things together and get horrible results out of the combination. When things had got about to the worst, Richards was delivered of a sudden gasp, and his wife asked,

"Oh, what is it?—what is it?"

"The note—Burgess's note! Its language was sarcastic, I see it now." He quoted: "'At bottom you cannot respect me, *knowing*, as you do, of *that matter* of which I am accused'—oh, it is perfectly plain, now, God help me! He knows that I know! You see the ingenuity of the phrasing. It was a trap—and like a fool, I walked into it. And Mary—?"

"Oh, it is dreadful—I know what you are going to say—he didn't return your transcript of the pretended test-remark."

"No—kept it to destroy us with. Mary, he has exposed us to some already. I know it—I know it well. I saw it in a dozen faces after church. Ah, he wouldn't answer our nod of recognition—*he* knew what he had been doing!"

In the night the doctor was called. The news went around in the morning that the old couple were rather seriously ill—prostrated by the exhausting excitement growing out of their great windfall, the congratulations, and the late hours, the doctor said. The town was sincerely distressed; for these old people were about all it had left to be proud of, now.

Two days later the news was worse. The old couple were delirious, and were doing strange things. By witness of the nurses, Richards had exhibited checks—for $8,500? No—for an amazing sum—$38,500! What could be the explanation of this gigantic piece of luck?

The following day the nurses had more news—and wonderful. They had concluded to hide the checks, lest harm come to them; but when they searched they were gone from under the patient's pillow—vanished away. The patient said:

"Let the pillow alone; what do you want?"

"We thought it best that the checks—"

"You will never see them again—they are destroyed. They came from Satan. I saw the hell-brand on them, and I knew they were sent to betray me to sin." Then he fell to gabbling strange and dreadful things which were not clearly understandable, and which the doctor admonished them to keep to themselves.

Richards was right; the checks were never seen again.

A nurse must have talked in her sleep, for within two days the forbidden gabblings were the property of the town; and they were of a surprising sort. They seemed to indicate that Richards had been a claimant for the sack himself, and that Burgess had concealed that fact and then maliciously betrayed it.

Burgess was taxed with this and stoutly denied it. And he said it was not fair to attach weight to the chatter of a sick old man who was out of his mind. Still, suspicion was in the air, and there was much talk.

After a day or two it was reported that Mrs. Richards' delirious deliveries were getting to be duplicates of her husband's. Suspicion flamed up into conviction, now, and the town's pride in the purity of its one undiscredited important citizen began to dim down and flicker toward extinction.

Six days passed, then came more news. The old couple were dying. Richards' mind cleared in his latest hour, and he sent for Burgess. Burgess said:

"Let the room be cleared. I think he wishes to say something in privacy."

"No!" said Richards: "I want witnesses. I want you all to hear my confession, so that I may die a man, and not a dog. I was clean—artificially—like the rest; and like the rest I fell when temptation came. I signed a lie, and claimed the miserable sack. Mr. Burgess remembered that I had done him a service, and in gratitude (and ignorance) he suppressed my claim and saved me. You know the thing that was charged against Burgess years ago. My testimony, and mine alone, could have cleared him, and I was a coward, and left him to suffer disgrace——"

"No—no—Mr. Richards, you——"

"My servant betrayed my secret to him——"

"No one has betrayed anything to me——"

—"And then he did a natural and justifiable thing; he repented of the saving kindness which he had done me, and he *exposed* me—as I deserved——"

"Never!—I make oath——"

"Out of my heart I forgive him."

Burgess's impassioned protestations fell upon deaf ears; the dying man passed away without knowing that once more he had done poor Burgess a wrong. The old wife died that night.

The last of the sacred Nineteen had fallen a prey to the fiendish sack; the town was stripped of the last rag of its ancient glory. Its mourning was not showing, but it was deep.

By act of the Legislature—upon prayer and petition—Hadleyburg was allowed to change its name to (never mind what—I will not give it away), and leave one word out of the motto that for many generations had graced the town's official seal.

It is an honest town once more, and the man will have to rise early that catches it napping again.

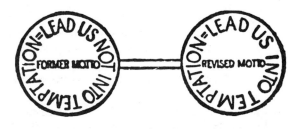

DISCUSSION FOR UNDERSTANDING

1. What is ironic about the effect of the congratulations and praise on the Richardses?

2. How much does Stephenson give the Richardses? Why does he say he has done this?

3. What is the course of the Richardses' reactions to Burgess' note?

4. What is ironic about the Richardses' delirious babblings?

5. What is the final indignity dealt Burgess?

6. What is your reaction to the town's new motto?

I

LEAD US INTO TEMPTATION

This new motto of the town amuses the reader. For he has secretly enjoyed watching as the foremost citizens of Hadleyburg are publicly stripped of their pretensions. Somehow, whenever an individual, a community, or an organization proclaims its virtues to the world, one is suspicious, probably because each of us knows his or her own weaknesses and frailties and doubts that others are really so different. As the story unfolds, there is the added delight of following the characters' thoughts as greed overcomes honesty. Most of us, at some time or other, have used similar flimsy excuses to rationalize a wrong act and we understand and sympathize when we see others act in the same way.

But the story involves more than watching people trapped by their own weaknesses. For what happens to Edward and Mary Richards adds a new dimension. Though they too are guilty, the reader gradually comes to sympathize with them. They seem "more honest" in their dishonesty. Mary even calls herself a humbug. And when Edward's effort to confess at the meeting is turned into a vote of approval by the crowd, the fearsome guilt that results seems almost an unfair burden. What begins as a romp, a gigantic practical joke, becomes tragic with the death of the old couple.

A. React to the following statements:

1. Mrs. Richards says, ". . . it's been one ever-lasting training and training and training in honesty—honesty shielded, from the very cradle, against every possible temptation, and so it's *artificial* honesty . . . ." Mrs. Richards uses the word *training* rather than the word *education*. There is a difference between *training* and *education*.

2. The town is described as being "honest, narrow, self-righteous, and stingy." These attributes are usually found together.

3. There is a difference between calling a person a *rascal* and calling him *wicked*. Try to define the difference. Then decide: Are the characters in this story more rascally than wicked or the other way around?

4. The last sentence of the story: "It is an honest town once more, and the man will have to rise early that catches it napping again" is ironic in its meaning.

B. This is a story of values, and so, as such stories often do, it treats both the vices and the virtues of men. Such qualities have been thought about by man since the time that ideas could be expressed in words. A group of quotations, some by famous individuals, some anonymous, but all dealing with concepts such as guilt, honesty, and temptation follows. Think back to Twain's story. Does it support or negate each quotation?

1. There are several good protections against temptations, but the surest is cowardice. (Mark Twain)

2. What we should really beg of our neighbors is: "Forgive us our virtues." (Nietzsche)

3. Many a person cannot follow the straight and narrow path without becoming straight-laced and narrow-minded.

4. Conscience is the still, small voice which you never hear until you're caught doing something wrong.

5. It is as proper to be proud of ourselves as it is improper to proclaim it to the world. (La Rochefoucauld)

6. Silence is not always golden; sometimes it's guilt.

Atmosphere

One critic has said of Mark Twain: "Whatever his contempt for a thing, he was always amused by it." Consider how you might show amused contempt for a regulation that seems out of date, a car that turns out to be a "lemon," or an elite clique in school. Do you find that to achieve this effect you end with something not unlike the atmosphere Twain creates in this story? Is the contempt or the amusement greater?

Suspense

Suspense can be created by the action or plot, or it can be created through the development of the characters. Our curiosity can be aroused by our eagerness to find out what is going to happen, or it can be stimulated by our need to know how the people are going to react. Do you think it is predominantly one or the other in this story or is it both?

BIOGRAPHICAL NOTES

Gwendolyn Brooks

Gwendolyn Brooks (1917–   ) grew up in Chicago. She began writing poems at seven and had her first poem published at thirteen. Between her graduation from Wilson Junior College in 1936 and her marriage to Henry L. Blakely in 1939, she did newspaper, magazine, and general office work. From the time of her marriage she considered herself a housewife and mother first and a writer only in her spare time. But some of her best poetry was written after she was married. *A Street in Bronzeville* (1945) and *Annie Allen* (1949) received high critical praise and her efforts were capped in 1950 by winning the Pulitzer Prize for poetry. From 1945 to 1968 she wrote five books of verse, one novel, and a children's book, *The Bean Eaters*. Lately she has added teaching in college to her other activities. Her advice to writers: "Live richly with eyes open and heart, too."

MacKinlay Kantor

MacKinlay Kantor (1904–   ) was born in Webster City, Iowa, and grew up under the shadow of his father's escapades as an international confidence man. Determined to show everybody that he could succeed in spite of his father's reputation, he started out upon graduation from high school working on a newspaper, then plunged into free-lance writing. His first novel was published when he was twenty-four, but success did not come until 1934 with the publication of an epic novel centered on the Battle of Gettysburg. By 1967 he had published 36 books, one of which, *Andersonville*, won him the Pulitzer Prize.

Nathaniel Hawthorne

Son of a New England sea captain, Nathaniel Hawthorne (1804–1864) was born in New Salem, Massachusetts. When he was four, his father died and his mother became a recluse even from her children. Little effort was made to give Hawthorne an early education, but during his lonely childhood he developed a taste for reading. At his uncle's expense he attended Bowdoin College. After graduating he returned to Salem and secluded himself in his mother's house; for the next twelve years he worked at becoming a writer. In 1837 he published his first collection of tales and sketches, *Twice-Told Tales*. In 1842 he married Sophia Peabody and moved for a while to the Old Manse at Concord where they were often visited by Thoreau, Emerson, Bronson Alcott, and Margaret Fuller. Here Hawthorne wrote a second collection of stories, *Mosses from an Old Manse*; but his income was still so small that he took a job as surveyor for the Customs House in Salem. Dismissed after three years for political reasons, he devoted full time to writing, and in seven months created his masterpiece, *The Scarlet Letter*. This success was followed shortly by two more novels, *The House of the Seven Gables* and *The Blithedale Romance*. When Franklin Pierce became President of the United States, he sent Hawthorne, a college chum, to Liverpool as consul. He remained abroad until 1860.

Bernard Malamud

Bernard Malamud (1914–   ) received his B.A. from the City College of New York and an M.A. from Columbia University. For nine years he taught English in New York evening high schools, but in 1949 he went to Oregon State University, where he taught until 1961. Two of his books, *The Magic Barrel* (1959) and *The Fixer* (1967), won National Book Awards. In talking about his ideas, Malamud has said: "The good man, the man capable of love, is inevitably the sufferer, the sacrifice, the saint." He feels the future of the novel lies in the sphere of "the more than realistic" and that as a writer: " . . . you either go in honest, or you sink." "Art must interpret or it is mindless. Mindlessness is not mystery. It is the absence of mystery." And he suggests keeping the reader surprised. It is this uncertainty which produces drama.

Susan Glaspell

Susan Glaspell (1882–1948) was born in Davenport, Iowa, and graduated from Drake University in 1899. She immediately went to work for two Des Moines newspapers as a legislative reporter. After her marriage in 1919, she moved to Provincetown, Massachusetts, where she was a pioneer contributor to the success of the Wharf Theater, from which the famous Provincetown Players later developed. She wrote novels, short fiction, a biography, and, of course, a series of plays both short and long. In her novels she showed an almost unearthly sensitivity to those little moments of joy that relieve the drabness of life. Her plays, too, are built on the little happenings in people's lives. In 1931 she won a Pulitzer Prize for her play, *Alison's House*, supposedly suggested by the life of Emily Dickinson.

Howard Fast

Howard Fast (1914–   ), a novelist, short story writer, editor, and lecturer, attended the National Academy of Design for a short time after graduating from high school. Working at several odd jobs and as a page in the New York Public Library to support himself, he published his first novel when he was eighteen. "In the years since," he has said, "I have lectured, preached, exhorted, and agitated on platforms, in the classroom, on radio and television more times than I care to recall." Commenting on *April Morning*, considered by many a teen-age classic, Fast said: "*April Morning* is as good a book as I have ever written, as nearly perfect a book as I could hope to write." He indicates that the writer owes nothing to his material or to the public. "His only obligation is to the truth." His thinking on this point is similar to that of Bernard Malamud.

Albert Halper

Albert Halper (1904–   ) was born in Chicago and educated at Northwestern University, attending classes there in 1924–1925. His short stories and articles have appeared in *The New Yorker, Harpers,* and *The Atlantic.* He has also written novels and plays.

Liam O'Flaherty

Liam O'Flaherty (1897–   ), an Irish novelist born in the Aran Islands, was educated by the Holy Ghost Fathers as a postulant for the priesthood. After studying in Dublin at Holy Cross College he gave up the idea of taking religious orders and entered the University College of Dublin. Soon after, he joined the Irish Guard and was shell-shocked in France during World War I. After his recovery, he worked his way almost around the world. Returning to Ireland in 1922, he headed a group of unemployed workers who seized a public building in Dublin. After this action, the government drove him out of the country. At this point he began writing, publishing two novels, *Thy Neighbor's Wife* and *The Black Soul,* and a collection of short stories, *Spring Sowing,* from which the selection in this unit was taken. In 1925 his novel, *The Informer,* took the world by storm. O'Flaherty's main concern in his writing is with the perpetual struggle of the mass of humanity for bread, freedom, and civilization.

Alexander Pushkin

Alexander Sergeevich Pushkin (1799–1837) was born in Moscow of a noble but poor family. He had Negro blood; his mother's grandfather was Abraham Hannibal, son of an Abyssinian prince, who was bought as a slave at the age of eight and became a favorite of Peter the Great of Russia. Alexander was educated at a school later renamed for him. He graduated at the age of seventeen and entered the civil service, but spent much time among the gay social circles of St. Petersburg. His first volume of poetry in 1820 brought him celebrity. Soon after, he was banished by the Czar to southern Russia because of his outspoken poems in praise of political liberty, but he continued to hold government positions until 1824, when he settled on his father's estate and devoted himself to writing.

Stephen Crane

For a biography of Stephen Crane, see page 307.

Mark Twain

Mark Twain (1835–1910) was born Samuel Langhorne Clemens in Florida, Missouri, but lived as a child in Hannibal, Missouri, on the Mississippi River. He took the pen name, Mark Twain, from the call of the pilots on the river steamers. This call indicated that the water was 12 feet deep, a safe depth for a steamer. Leaving school when he was 12, he served as a printer's apprentice, a riverboat pilot, a Confederate soldier, a prospector, and a reporter. After a junket to Hawaii, he hit the lecture trail and became famous as a platform speaker. In 1869 *Innocents Abroad* established him as an American humorist, but it was *Tom Sawyer* and *The Adventures of Huckleberry Finn,* both set in his hometown, that made his reputation as one of the greatest of American writers. Financial disaster and personal unhappiness marred his last years. Only his daughter, Clara, survived Twain, who died as he had prophesied he would—when Halley's comet returned in 1910.

Glossary

This glossary contains difficult words which are not in the vocabularies of average tenth-grade students. The definitions apply to the uses of the words in this text. For more complete study of the range of meanings for these words, the student must consult his dictionary. Many other specific and uncommon terms have been footnoted with the selections.

Pronunciation Guide

A key to the pronunciation symbols is given at the bottom of every other page. By consulting the most recent dictionaries, the student may notice that the symbols here represent a series of compromises between current scholarly interpretations of sounds and less precise symbols which continue to have wide acceptance. A few minutes' study of the pronunciation key before using this glossary will make it possible for the student to use the pronunciation transcriptions with the greatest ease and efficiency.

The same key is used for pronunciations given here and in the footnotes. Foreign terms and names are transcribed so as to be acceptable in standard American speech rather than precise in terms of their original languages.

Accent marks precede the stressed syllables. The mark ▲ indicates the heaviest stress and the mark ' indicates intermediate stress.

Abbreviations indicate parts of speech and special spellings. The following are used:

n.	noun
v.	verb
adj.	adjective
adv.	adverb
pl.	plural

abash\ə ▲băsh\ v. To make bashful, cause to lose confidence or composure.

abate\ə ▲bāt\ v. To die down, subside, diminish.

ab·er·ra·tion\ 'ăb·ə ▲rā·shən\ n. Departure from the normal or natural way or manner.

ab·hor\əb ▲hōr\ v., -red, -ring. To hate, abominate.

ab·ject\▲ăb 'jĕkt\ adj. Hopeless, dispirited, downcast.

ab·ne·ga·tion\'ăb·nə ▲gā·shən\ n. Self-denial, rejection of egoism.

ab·sorp·tion\əb ▲sōrp·shən\ n. Complete occupation of one's mind and thoughts with one thing, ignoring all others.

ac·cen·tu·ate\ăk ▲sĕn·chu 'āt\ v. To emphasize, stress.

ac·cep·ta·tion\'ăk·sĕp ▲tā·shən\ n. Meaning or interpretation commonly connected with a word.

ac·ces·si·ble\ək ▲sĕ·sĭ·bəl\ adj. Capable of being reached, possible or convenient to come to.

ac·cliv·i·ty\ə ▲klĭv·ət·ē\ n. A slope that ascends.

ac·cord\ə ▲kō(ə)rd\ v. To grant, allow as proper.

ac·cost\ə ▲kŏst\ v. To stop and speak to by way of challenge or inquiry.

ac·qui·si·tion\'ăk·wə ▲zĭsh·ən\ n. Something acquired or gained. (Also v. The act of acquiring or gaining.)

ad·a·mant\▲ă·də·mənt\ adj. Absolutely resolute and not to be deterred by any argument or appeal.

ad·dict\ə ▲dĭkt\ v. To bring about habitual compulsive use. (Also n. \▲ă·dĭkt\)

adieu\ə ▲dū\ n. Good-bye, farewell.

ad·ja·cent\ə ▲jā·sənt\ adj. Touching along one side, neighboring, nearby.

ad·ju·tant\▲a·jə·tənt\ n. A minor military or police officer.

ad·mon·ish\ăd ▲mŏ·nĭsh\ v. To warn, reprimand.

ad·o·les·cence\'ă·də ▲lĕ·səns\ n. Youth, the period between boyhood or girlhood and maturity.

ad·o·ra·tion\'ă·də ▲rā·shən\ n. Love, great respect, veneration.

ad·vent\▲ăd 'vĕnt\ n. Coming, arrival.

af·fa·ble\▲ă·fə·bəl\ adj. Good natured, politely friendly.

af·fir·ma·tion\'ă·fər ▲mā·shən\ n. Assertion, confirming statement.

ag·gres·sive\ə ▲grĕ·sĭv\ adj. 1. Showing fight or determination. 2. Bold, confident, and forward; not at all shy or afraid. (Adv. -ly, n. -ness)

aghast\ə ▲găst\ adj. Extremely afraid, stunned with fear.

agil·i·ty\ə ▲jĭ·lĭ·tē\ n. Nimbleness, spryness.

ag·o·nize\▲ă·gə 'naiz\ v. To cause agony or great pain.

ague\āg *or* ▲ā 'gyū\ n. Sickness, fever.

ail·ment\▲āl·mənt\ n. Illness, malady.

airy\▲ă·rē\ adj. Carefree, nonchalant. (Adv. -ily)

al·che·mist\▲ăl·kə·mĭst\ n. The medieval forerunner of the modern chemist, one who tried to find ways of changing other substances into gold.

al·ga\▲ăl·gə\ n., pl. -ae. A small sea plant giving the effect of scum in the water.

al·le·giance\ə ▲lē·jəns\ n. Loyalty.

al·ler·gy\▲ă·lər·jē\ n., pl. -ies. A physical condition in which certain substances or situations, normally harmless, are very irritating.

al·lure\ə ▲lūr\ v. To attract, charm, enchant. (Also n.)

ă bad, ā bake, a father, ĕ sell, ē equal, ai mile, ĭ sit, ŏ cot, ō note, ɔ law, ū boom, ʊ wood, yū you, yʊ fury, aʊ cow, ɔi boy. The schwa is used for both stressed and unstressed sounds: ə mud, word, even; ch chase, itch; sh shell, wish; th path, thin; th the, either; ŋ wing; w wet, wheat; zh pleasure.

alms·giv·er\\▲amz 'gĭ·vər\ n. One who gives alms; especially, one who gives money to beggars.

al·tim·e·ter\ăl ▲tĭ·mə·tər\ n. A device for measuring altitude.

am·ber\▲ăm·bər\ n. A dark-orange fossil resin.

am·big·u·ous\ăm ▲bĭg·yū·əs\ adj. Subject to more than one meaning or interpretation.

am·bi·va·lent\ăm ▲bĭv·ə·lənt\ adj. Simultaneously attracted toward and turned against an object, person, or action.

am·ble\▲ăm·bəl\ v. To walk slowly, saunter, stroll.

am·bus·cade\▲ăm·bəs 'kād\ n. Ambush. (Also v.)

amend\ə ▲mĕnd\ v. To correct, adjust.

ame·ni·ty\ə ▲mē·nĭ·tē or ə ▲mĕ·nĭ·tē\ n., pl. -ies. Civilized and pleasant comfort.

ami·a·ble\▲ā·mē·ə·bəl\ adj. Showing pleasing friendliness. (Adv. -ly)

am·i·ca·ble\▲ăm·ĭ·kə·bəl\ adj. Characterized by friendship and goodwill.

amiss\ə ▲mĭs\ adj. Wrong, bad. (Also adv.)

am·phi·the·ater\▲ăm·fĭ 'thē·ə·tər\ n. A natural outdoor theater with rising rows of seats (as on a hillside).

am·pu·tate\▲ăm·pyu 'tat\ v. To cut off surgically.

anal·o·gy\ə ▲nă·lə·jē\ n., pl. -ies. A sustained similarity discovered between seemingly unlike things or conditions, a comparison or resemblance sustained between unlike things.

an·es·thet·ic\'ă·nĕs ▲thĕ·tĭk\ n. A drug that eliminates pain.

an·guish\▲ăŋ·gwĭsh\ n. Pain and extreme distress, discomfort, sorrow.

an·gu·lar\▲aŋ·gyu·lər\ adj. 1. Showing distinct angles, as a rectangle, pentagon, or other straight-line figure. 2. Thin, bony, and unattractive.

an·i·mate\▲ă·nĭ·mət\ adj. Alive, having life. (Also v. \▲ə·nĭ·māt\ To inspire, give zest or enthusiasm to.)

an·i·ma·tion\'ă·nĭ ▲mā·shən\ n. High-spirited activity, liveliness, vivacity.

an·ni·hi·la·tion\ə ▲nai·hĭ 'lā·shən\ n. Complete destruction, reduction to nothingness.

an·ti·quat·ed\▲ăn·tĭ 'kwā·təd\ adj. Very old and very much out of date.

an·tiq·ui·ty\ăn ▲tĭ·kwĭ·tē\ n. 1. Very old times. 2. An old object.

ap·a·thet·ic\'ă·pə ▲thĕ·tĭk\ adj. Showing apathy, marked by dull lack of feeling. (Adv. -ally)

a·pex\▲ā 'pĕks\ n. The highest point of something.

apol·o·get·ic\ə 'pŏ·lə 'jĕ·tĭk\ adj. As though expressing an apology, not expressed with full confidence.

ap·pal\ə ▲pɔl\ v., -led, -ling. To shock with dislike or fear, stun with fear.

ap·par·el\ə ▲pă·rəl\ n. Clothing.

ap·pa·ri·tion\'ă·pə ▲rĭ·shən\ n. Phantasm, ghost.

ap·pease\ə ▲pēz\ v. To calm, placate, seek to dispel anger or dislike. (Adv. -ingly)

ap·pen·dage\ə ▲pĕn·dĭj\ n. A limb or similar feature of the body.

ap·per·tain\'ă·pər ▲tān\ v. To pertain, be connected or related to.

ap·praise\ə ▲prāz\ v. To note and estimate the value or status of.

ap·pre·hen·sion\'ă·prē ▲hĕn·shən\ n. Fear, misgiving, worry, foreboding about the future.

aprise\ə ▲praiz\ v. To give notice, inform.

ap·ti·tude\▲ăp·tĭ 'tūd\ n. Natural inclination or bent.

aq·ui·line\▲ă·kwĭ 'lain\ adj. Prominent and suggesting an eagle's beak.

arc\ark\ n. A section of a circle.

arch·an·gel\▲ark 'ān·jəl\ n. An angel of high rank in the heavenly order.

ar·dent\▲ar·dənt\ adj. With much feeling, passionate.

ar·ma·da\ar ▲ma·də\ n. A fleet, especially of armed sailing vessels.

ar·mi·stice\▲ar·mĭ·stĭs\ n. A period in which warfare is halted by mutual agreement between the warring powers.

ar·rears\ə ▲rērz\ n. *plural*. Indebtedness on overdue payments.

ar·tic·u·late\ar ▲tĭk·yə·lət\ adj. Able to speak. (Also v. \ar ▲tĭk·yə·lat\ To give clear and effective utterance to.)

as·cen·sion\ə ▲sĕn·shən\ n. Ascent, rise.

as·pi·ra·tion\'ăs·pə ▲rā·shən\ n. Eventual hope or ambition, a goal that one cherishes.

as·sail\ə ▲sāl\ v. To attack violently.

as·sid·u·ous\ə ▲sĭ·dyu·əs\ adj. With careful and persistent attention. (Adv. -ly)

as·suage\ə ▲swaj\ v. To soothe, comfort, relieve from pain.

as·sump·tion\ə ▲səm·shən\ n. 1. Something assumed, believed, or presumed. 2. The act of taking a command, office, or privilege.

as·ter·oid\▲ăs·tə ▲rɔid\ n. A small starlike body or planet fragment.

asth·ma\▲ăz·mə\ n. A disease marked by great difficulty in breathing.

as·tro·nau·tics\'ăs·trə ▲nɔ·tĭks\ n. The study of space navigation.

as·tron·o·mer\ə ▲strŏ·nə·mər\ n. An expert at or student of the stars.

as·tute\əs ▲tūt\ adj. Shrewd, wise, perceptive. (Adv. -ly)

asy·lum\ə ▲sai·ləm\ n. A place of security, refuge.

athwart\ə ▲thwɔrt\ adv. Across diagonally.

atro·cious\ə ▲tro·shəs\ adj. Awful, shocking.

at·tire\ə ▲tair\ n. Garments. (Also v.)

at·tri·bute\ə ▲trĭ 'byūt\ v. 1. To accredit, acknowledge as source or author, report as from or of. 2. To explain, assign as a cause or origin. (Also n. \▲ă·trĭ 'byūt\ Characteristic, accomplishment.)

au·dac·i·ty\ə ▲dă·sĭ·tē\ n. Daring bravery against superior odds.

au·di·ble\▲ɔ·dĭ·bəl\ adj. Capable of being heard.

aug·ment\'ɔg ▲mĕnt\ v. To add to or increase, increase in force or power.

aus·tere\ɔ ▲stĭr\ adj. Severe, stern, strict.

au·then·tic\ɔ ▲thĕn·tĭk\ adj. Real, genuine, without any suggestion of being imitation.

au·to·mat·ic·i·ty\'ɔ·tə·mə ▲tĭ·sĭ·tē\ n. Automatic operation or nature.

av·a·rice\▲ă·və·rəs\ n. Greed for wealth or possessions.

aver·sion\ə ▲vər·zhən\ n. Dislike, hatred, loathing.

avert\ə ▲vərt\ v. To turn down, aside, or away.

azure\▲ă·zhər\ adj. Clear sky-blue.

bac·cha·nal\'băk·ə nǎl\ n. Any drunken or riotous celebration.

bait\bāt\ v. To tease, heckle, haze, mistreat.

bale·ful\bāl·fəl\ adj. Ominous, menacing, sinister.

balm\bam *or* balm\ n. Soothing ointment, comfort from pain or sorrow.

bal·sa\bȯl·sə\ n. A tropical tree whose wood is quite light and easy to carve.

bap·tism\băp·tĭzm\ n. Initiation.

bar·bi·tu·rate\bar bĭch·ər·ĭt\ n. Any of a group of barbituric acid derivatives used as sedatives.

bask\băsk\ v. To recline at rest.

bat·tle·ment\bă·təl·mənt\ n. A fortified protruding section on top of a walk, superimposed defensive wall at the top of a building.

beach·comb·er\bēch 'kō·mər\ n. One who spends much time loafing on a beach.

be·fud·dle\bē fə·dəl\ v. To confuse, becloud.

beg·gar·ly\bě·gər·lē\ adj. Mean, trivial.

be·hold·en\bē hōl·dən\ adj. Obliged, indebted.

bel·lig·er·ent\bə lĭj·(ə)rənt\ adj. Inclined to or showing a tendency to fight, quarrelsome. (Adv. -ly)

bel·low\bě·lō\ v. To yell very loud. (Also n.)

bene·dic·tion\'bě·nə dĭk·shən\ n. Blessing.

be·nev·o·lent\bə ně·və·lənt\ adj. Well-wishing, kindly, and gentle. (Adv. -ly)

be·nign\bə nain\ adj. Kindly, well-wishing, and charitable.

be·queath\bē· kwēth\ v. To leave a legacy in one's will.

be·rate\bē rāt\ v. To scold, rebuke forcefully.

be·seech\bē sēch\ irreg. v., besought. To beg, implore.

bes·tial\běst·chəl\ adj. Beastlike, inhuman.

bil·let\bĭ·lət\ n. Quarters, a temporary place to stay.

bland\blănd\ adj. Soft, mild, very easy to eat and digest.

blas·phe·mous\blăs·fə·məs\ adj. Irreverent, profane statements about God.

bla·tant\blā·tənt\ adj. Loudly and coarsely demonstrative.

bleak\blēk\ adj. Dark and cheerless.

blench\blěnch\ v. To draw back from lack of courage, flinch.

blithe\blaith\ adj. Very happy, carefree. (Adv. -ly)

bloat·ed\blō·təd\ adj. Abnormally swollen.

bond·age\bŏn·dəj\ n. Complete subjection to another, servitude, slavery.

bond·man\bŏnd·mən\ n. Slave, unfree man.

bour·geois\burzh 'wa\ adj. Middle-class.

bra·va·do\brə va·dō\ n. An extreme show of rash daring.

bray\brā\ v. To make the loud sound of a mule.

bra·zen\brā·zən\ v. To act with self-confident and defiant insolence.

bris·tle\brĭ·səl\ v. To threaten.

bro·ker\brō·kər\ n. Dealer, one who buys and sells.

brusque\brəsk\ adj. So brief, quick, and firm as to approach rudeness.

buf·fet\bə·fət\ n. A heavy blow. (Also v. To hit, strike, beat against.)

bul·wark\bul·wərk\ n. Defense; fortification, especially of earth; rampart.

bur·ble\bər·bəl\ v. To speak in a rapid, enthusiastic, and not very sensible way.

bur·ly\bər·lē\ adj. Large, strong, and brawny.

bur·nish\bər·nĭsh\ v. To polish brightly, give a pleasing metallic lustre to. (Also v.)

but·tocks\bə·təks\ n. *plural*. The lower part of the back, the part on which one sits.

cab·a·lis·tic\'kă·bə lĭs·tĭk\ adj. Suggesting some secret rite or ritual. (Adv. -ally)

ca·dence\kā·dəns\ n. A regular sequence of sound, often a falling one; a measured rhythm.

cal·o·rie\kă·lə·rē\ n. A unit of food value expressed in terms of heat and energy production.

can·o·py\kă·nə·pē\ n., pl. -ies. The hinged covering fitted over the cockpit of a plane.

ca·pit·u·la·tion\kə 'pĭ·chə lā·shən\ n. Yielding, surrender.

ca·price\kə prēs\ n. Whim, unguided chance inclination.

cap·sule\kăp·səl\ n. A medicine-containing shell that dissolves readily.

cap·tion\kăp·shən\ n. A heading, title. (Also v.)

car·bine\kar·bain\ n. A light and short rifle.

car·di·nal\kar·dĭ·nəl\ adj. Main, major.

ca·reer\kə rēr\ v. To run or dash along madly.

car·il·lon\kă·rĭ 'lŏn\ n. A set of bells on which tunes can be played.

car·niv·o·rous\'kar nĭ·və·rəs\ adj. Flesh-eating, existing on a diet of flesh alone.

car·ol\kă·rəl\ n. A joyful song. (Also v.)

case·ment\kās·mənt\ n. A window mounted on hinges at the side.

caste\kăst\ n. An inflexible and changeless social class based on birth.

cat·a·clys·mic\'kă·tə klĭz·mĭk\ adj. Momentous, having overwhelming and disastrous results.

cat·a·pult\kă·tə 'pəlt\ v. To shoot forward as though hurled by a catapult. (Also n.)

ca·tas·tro·phe\kə tăs·trə 'fē\ n. Calamity, great misfortune.

cat·e·chism\kă·tə 'kĭzm\ n. A list of questions and answers setting forth elementary religious beliefs.

ca·thar·sis\kə thar·səs\ n. A cleansing of the emotions through the arts or other means that bring about release from tension.

caul·dron\kȯl·drən\ n. A large kettle for boiling or stewing.

ce·ler·i·ty\sə lěr·ə·tē\ n. Swiftness, quickness, speed.

ce·les·tial\sə lěs·chəl\ adj. Pertaining to the heavens or skies (often as viewed by a pilot).

ă b*a*d, ā b*a*ke, a f*a*ther, ě s*e*ll, ē *e*qual, ai m*i*le, ĭ s*i*t, ŏ c*o*t, ō n*o*te, ɔ l*a*w, ū b*oo*m, ʊ w*oo*d, yū *you*, yʊ f*u*ry, aʊ c*ow*, ɔi b*oy*. The schwa is used for both stressed and unstressed sounds: ə m*u*d, w*o*rd, ev*e*n; ch *ch*ase, i*tch*; sh *sh*ell, wi*sh*; th p*a*th, *thi*n; th *the*, ei*ther*; ŋ wi*ng*; w *w*et, *wh*eat; zh plea*s*ure.

cer·e·mo·ni·ous\'sā·rə ▲mō·nē·əs\ adj. 1. Showing ceremony, marked by slow orderly arrangements. 2. Engaging in much ceremony or stiff formal politeness. (Adv. -ly)

ces·sa·tion\sĕ ▲sā·shən\ n. Stopping, ceasing.

champ\chămp\ v. To make biting or chewing motions.

cha·os\▲kā 'ōs\ n. A complete confusion of things jumbled together in disorder, disturbed utter confusion and disorder.

chas·ten\▲chā·sən\ v. To subdue by rebuke or punishment.

chas·tise·ment\'chăs ▲taiz·mənt\ n. Humbling punishment.

chide\chaid\ v., -ed *or* chid *or* chidden. To scold, rebuke.

chip·per\▲chĭ·pər\ adj. Healthy, active, happy.

cho·ler·ic\▲kŏ·lə·rĭk\ adj. Ill-tempered, angry, quick to take offense.

chord\kōrd\ n. A harmonious combination of tones.

chron·ic\▲krŏ·nĭk\ adj. Ever-present, always continuing.

chron·i·cle\▲krŏ·nĭ·kəl\ n. A history; record, especially a daily record. (Also v.)

cir·cum·scribe\▲sər·kəm 'skraib\ v. To encircle narrowly, be confined to a limited area.

ci·ta·tion\sai ▲tā·shən\ n. A written official notice of special merit or distinction, a formal statement of praise.

clam·or\▲klă·mər\ n. Noise, uproar, commotion. (Also v. To speak out noisily, continuously, and incoherently.)

cli·ent\▲klai·ənt\ n. One who uses another's services or buys another's wares.

clin·i·cal\▲klĭ·nĭ·kəl\ adj. As though produced by a scientific clinic, most exact.

clois·tered\▲klɔis·tərd\ adj. Closed, sealed off, secluded from life around.

co·ag·u·late\kō ▲ă·gyʊ 'lāt\ v. To thicken and congeal as from a liquid to a semisolid state.

cog·i·ta·tion\'kŏ·jĭ ▲tā·shən\ n. Thought, consideration, reflection.

cog·ni·zant\▲kɔg·nə·zənt\ adj. Aware, knowing.

col·lu·sion\kə ▲lū·zhən\ n. Unethical cooperation, secret deceitful working together.

comb·er\▲kō·mər\ n. A long or high wave.

com·mis·er·ate\kə ▲mĭ·zə 'rāt\ v. To extend sympathy to, condole with.

com·mo·di·ous\kə ▲mō·dē·əs\ adj. Spacious, roomy, able to accommodate much or many.

com·mon\▲kŏ·mən\ n. Land to be used by all people of a community for grazing their animals.

com·pact\▲kŏm·păkt\ n. Accord, agreement.

com·pas·sion·ate\kəm ▲pă·shə·nət\ adj. Sympathetic, merciful.

cam·pat·i·ble\kəm ▲pă·tĭ·bəl\ adj. In accordance, fitting in well.

com·pen·sate\▲kŏm·pən 'sāt\ v. To make up for, make amends for.

com·pla·cent\kəm ▲plās·ənt\ adj. Satisfied; especially, self-satisfied.

com·plex\▲kŏm·plĕks\ n. An abnormally compulsive series of notions.

com·pli·ance\kəm ▲plai·əns\ n. Accord, inclination to fit in with.

com·pre·hend\'kŏm·prē ▲hĕnd\ v. To understand.

com·pre·hen·sive\'kŏm·prē ▲hĕn·sĭv\ adj. Inclusive, all-embracing.

com·punc·tion\kəm ▲pəŋ(k)·shən\ n. Anxiety arising from guilt, an uneasy twinge.

com·pute\kəm ▲pyūt\ v. To reckon, calculate.

con·cep·tion\kən ▲sĕp·shən\ n. Idea, notion.

con·cise\kən ▲sais\ adj. Sharp and dexterous without waste motion.

con·clu·sive\kən ▲klū·sĭv\ adj. Marked by (or as if by) a final decision shutting off discussion.

con·fi·den·tial\'kŏn·fĭ ▲dĕn·shəl\ adj. In confidence or secrecy, not to be told to another. (Adv. -ly)

con·fir·ma·tion\'kŏn·fər ▲mā·shən\ n. Agreement, supporting statement, claim.

con·fla·gra·tion\'kăn·flə ▲grā·shən\ n. A great or very destructive fire, a very hot fire.

con·found\kən ▲faund\ v. To confuse, bewilder.

con·front\kən ▲frənt\ v. To oppose and challenge.

con·i·cal\▲kan·ĭ·kəl\ adj. Like a cone in shape.

con·jec·ture\kən ▲jĕk·chər\ v. To make guesses, speculate. (Also n.)

con·joint\kən ▲jɔint\ adj. Together, joined, occurring at the same time or place.

con·junc·tion\kən ▲jəŋ·shən\ n. Joining, juncture.

con·se·crate\▲kŏn·sə 'krāt\ v. To bless, sanctify, treat as holy.

con·sen·sus\kən ▲sĕn·səs\ n. Generality, majority expression or opinion.

con·sign\kən ▲sain\ v. To deliver, assign.

con·sole\kən ▲sōl\ v. To comfort, sympathize with.

con·spic·u·ous\kən ▲spĭk·yū·əs\ adj. Very noticeable, demanding attention, hard or impossible to overlook. (Adv. -ly)

con·ster·na·tion\'kŏn·stər ▲nā·shən\ n. Amazed and agitated dismay, panic.

con·sti·tute\▲kŏn·stĭ 'tūt\ v. To make up, compose.

con·sti·tu·tion·al\'kŏn·stĭ ▲tu·shə·nəl\ n. A short walk taken for health's sake.

con·strue\kən ▲strū\ v. To explain, interpret, understand.

con·sum·mate\kəan ▲səm·ət\ adj. Complete in every detail, of highest excellence.

con·ta·gious\kən ▲tā·jəs\ adj. Readily communicable, spreading readily from one person to another.

con·tam·i·nate\kən ▲tă·mĭ 'nāt\ v. To make unclean, infect, sully, defile with impurity.

con·tem·plate\▲kŏn·tĕm 'plāt\ v. To look at or think about thoughtfully.

con·temp·tu·ous\kən ▲tĕm·chu·əs\ adj. Showing contempt and mocking scorn.

con·tort\kən ▲tōrt\ v. To twist or writhe out of a normal position or appearance.

con·trite\kən ▲trait\ adj. Regretful or sorrowful for one's misconduct or offenses.

con·triv·er\kən ▲trai·vər\ n. One who plans and schemes.

con·ven·tion·al·ize\kən ▲vĕn·shə·nə 'laiz\ v. To make or form according to certain conventions or conventional notions.

con·verge\kən ᐱvərj\ v. To come together and join.

con·vulse\kən ᐱvəls\ v. To be agitated, shaken.

con·vul·sive\kən ᐱvəl·sĭv\ adj. Marked by strong physical agitation or wild motion.

cor·don\ᐱkōr·dən\ v. To isolate and treat as a closed-off area.

cor·nice\ᐱkōr·nĭs\ n. An overhanging structure projecting from the top of a building or wall.

cor·ol·lary\ᐱkō·rə 'lä·rē\ n., pl. -ies. An accompanying effect, a necessarily connected or related notion.

cor·o·net\ᐱkō·rə 'nĕt\ n. A small or plain crown showing a rank below a king's.

cor·po·ral\ᐱkōr·pə·rəl\ adj. Bodily, physical.

cor·rode\kə ᐱrōd\ v. To eat away as in the action of an acid.

cor·rup·tive\kə ᐱrəp·tĭv\ adj. Bringing about corruption and infection.

cos·mic\ᐱkŏz·mĭk\ adj. Pertaining to the whole world, solar system, or universe; hence, extremely important.

cos·mol·o·gy\kŏz ᐱmŏ·lə·jē\ n., pl. -ies. A conception or scheme of the relationships of the heavenly bodies.

cote\kōt\ n. A bird house or shelter.

coun·te·nance\ᐱkaʊn·tə·nəns\ v. To tolerate or sanction. (Also n. Facial appearance.)

court\kōrt\ v. To seek, ask for.

co·vert\ᐱkə·vərt\ n. A concealed or secret place, a hiding place that an animal might use. (Also adj.)

cov·et·ous\ᐱkə·və·təs\ adj. Greedy, grasping.

cow·er\ᐱkaʊ·ər\ v. To flinch down as in fear or fright.

coz·en\ᐱkə·zən\ v. To deceive, beguile, ensnare.

cra·ni·um\ᐱkrā·nē·əm\ n. Skull.

cre·den·tial\krĕ ᐱdĕn·shəl\ n. A certification or official document to back up a person's claims.

cre·ma·tion\ᐱkrĕ ᐱmā·shən\ n. Disposal of dead bodies by reducing to ashes through fire.

cren·el·late or **cren·el·ate**\ᐱkrĕ·nə 'lāt\ v. To furnish with protective or defensive ramparts on the top of the walls of.

crev·ice\ᐱkrĕ·vĭs\ n. A split, chink.

crit·i·cal\ᐱkrĭ·tĭ·kəl\ adj. Criticizing, evaluating, expressing criticism.

cru·ci·ble\ᐱkrū·sĭ·bəl\ n. A vessel for melting down solid substances.

cru·ci·fy\ᐱkrū·sĭ 'faɪ\ v., -ies, -ied. To torture or kill by nailing or binding the hands and feet to a cross with the arms outstretched to the sides.

crypt\krĭpt\ n. Innermost secret recess.

crys·tal\ᐱkrĭs·təl\ v. To form into crystals, turn to crystals. (Also n.)

cull\kəl\ v. To pick, choose.

cul·mi·nate\ᐱkəl·mĭ 'nāt\ v. To attain to a climax, reach to a height or an outcome.

cum·ber\ᐱkəm·bər\ v. To harass, trouble.

cu·mu·lus\ᐱkyū·myʊ·ləs\ n., pl. -i. A cloud formation suggesting heaping or piling up.

cur·dle\ᐱkər·dəl\ v. To thicken or congeal as milk does when it sours.

curt\kərt\ adj. So brief and sparing of words as to be rude and demanding. (Adv. -ly)

cur·tail\kər ᐱtāl\ v. To cut down, diminish.

cyn·ic\ᐱsĭ·nĭk\ n. One given to suspecting evil whenever possible, one suspicious of good motives.

dam\dăm\ n. Mother (especially as used of an animal).

dan·dy\ᐱdăn·dē\ n., pl. -ies. A stylishly dressed person.

dank\dăŋk\ adj. Damp and chill.

daunt\dɔnt\ v. To cause fear or loss of resolution.

dearth\ᐱdərth\ n. Scarcity.

de·bauch\dē ᐱbɔch\ n. An intemperate indulgence in sensual pleasure.

de·bris\də ᐱbrē\ n. Rock fragments.

dec·a·dence\ᐱdĕ·kə·dəns\ n. Decay, deterioration, loss of strength and virtue.

de·ci·sive\dē ᐱsaɪ·sĭv\ adj. Having a definitive result, finally deciding a conflict or question.

de·fer\də ᐱfər\ v., -red, -ring. To postpone.

def·er·ence\ᐱdĕf·ə·rən(t)s\ n. Courteous and respectful regard for another.

deft\dĕft\ adj. Showing graceful or clever skill in handling.

de·hy·drate\ᐱdē ᐱhaɪ·drāt\ v. To remove water or liquid from.

de·lib·er·ate\də ᐱlĭ·bə·rət\ adj. Marked by slow cautious motion. (Adv. -ly)

de·lir·i·ous\də ᐱlē·rē·əs\ adj. Suffering from loss of sense and rationality and experiencing delusions; out of one's mind, as with fever or madness.

del·uge\ᐱdĕl 'yūj\ n. Flood. (Also v.)

de·lu·sion\dē ᐱlū·zhən\ n. A mistaken or totally false notion or belief.

de·luxe\də ᐱlʊks\ adj. Luxurious, elegant.

de·mur\də ᐱmər\ v., -red, -ring. To hesitate and withhold assent or agreement.

de·mure\də ᐱmyūr\ adj. Modest, quiet, and prim.

de·plete\dē ᐱplēt\ v. To diminish by using up.

de·plor·a·ble\dĭ ᐱplōr·ə·bəl\ adj. Strongly regretted, considered unfortunate or wretched.

de·port\dē ᐱpōrt\ v. To send out of a country, exile.

de·pre·cate\ᐱdĕ·prə 'kāt\ v. To suggest lack of worth or significance.

de·pres·sur·ize\dē ᐱprĕ·shə 'raɪz\ v. To reverse pressurizing devices.

der·e·lict\ᐱdĕ·rə 'lĭkt\ n. Something left abandoned and purposeless, a now meaningless relic of past life.

der·e·lic·tion\'dĕ·rə 'lĭk·shən\ n. Neglect or omission of duty.

de·ri·sion\də ᐱrĭ·zhən\ n. Mocking ridicule.

de·rog·a·to·ry\dĭ ᐱrag·ə·tōr·ē\ adj. Expressive of a low opinion.

des·o·late\ᐱdĕ·sə·lət\ adj. Lonely, forlorn, and hopeless. (Also v.)

ă bad, ā bake, a father, ĕ sell, ē equal, aɪ mile, ĭ sit, ŏ cot, ō note, ɔ law, ū boom, ʊ wood, yū you, yʊ fury, aʊ cow, ɔɪ boy. The schwa is used for both stressed and unstressed sounds: ə mud, word, even; ch chase, itch; sh shell, wish; th path, thin; th̲ the, either; ŋ wing; w wet, wheat; zh pleasure.

de·spon·dent\dĭ ▲spon·dənt\ adj. Disheartened, dejected.

des·pot·ic\dĕs ▲pŏ·tĭk\ adj. Oppressive, tyrannical.

des·ti·ny\▲dĕs·tĭ·nē\ n., pl. -ies. Fate, that which is planned by a supernatural power.

de·tach·ment\dĭ ▲tăch·mənt\ n. Aloofness, indifference.

de·vi·ate\▲dē·vē·āt\ v. To twist or bend away from a straightforward course.

de·vi·ous\▲dē·vē·əs\ adj. Roundabout, indirect, not straightforward. (Adv. -ly)

de·vise\də ▲vaiz\ v. To think of, find, invent.

de·void\də ▲void\ adj. Lacking, missing, without.

de·vout\də ▲vaut\ adj. Reverent, showing marked solemnity.

di·a·bol·i·cal\▲dī·ə 'bŏl·ĭ·kəl\ adj. Extremely wicked, fiendishly cruel.

di·aph·a·nous\▲dai ▲ă·fə·nəs\ adj. Sheer, light, and virtually transparent.

dif·fuse\dĭ ▲fyūz\ v. To spread out (or through) softly and evenly.

di·lap·i·dat·ed\dĭ ▲lă·pĭ 'dā·təd\ adj. Thoroughly worn out; thin, torn, and frayed.

di·late\▲dai ▲lāt\ v. To widen, expand, swell abnormally.

dil·i·gent\▲dĭ·lĭ·jənt\ adj. Marked by steady, careful, conscientious work. (Adv. -ly)

di·min·u·tive\dĭ ▲mĭn·yu·tĭv\ adj. Very small, tiny.

dis·cern\dĭ ▲sərn\ v. To perceive, comprehend.

dis·ci·plin·ary\▲dĭ·sĭ·plĭ 'nă·rē\ adj. Of the nature of discipline, applying discipline for some error or omission.

dis·com·fit\dĭs ▲kəm·fĭt\ n. *archaic.* Discomfort, concern.

dis·con·cert\'dĭs·kən ▲sərt\ v. To throw into confusion, disturb the composure of, embarrass.

dis·con·so·late\dĭs ▲kŏn·sə·lət\ adj. Cheerless and discouraged.

dis·course\▲dĭs 'kōrs\ n. Conversation.

dis·creet\dĭs ▲krēt\ adj. 1. With an eye to safety, calculated to protect oneself. 2. Showing restraint and careful moderation. 3. Quiet, well-trained, and maintaining suitable reserve in speech.

dis·dain\dĭz ▲dān\ n. Lofty and haughty scorn and disapproval. (Also v. To shun or scorn, let alone as through pride or taste.)

dis·em·bar·rass\'dĭ·səm ▲bă·rəs\ v. To rid, eliminate.

dis·en·chant·ing\'dĭ·sən ▲chăn·tĭŋ\ adj. Dispelling any enchantment, charm, or appeal.

dis·en·gage\'dĭs·ən ▲gāj\ v. To free from encumbrance, take out or away.

di·shev·eled\dĭ ▲shĕ·vəld\ adj. Wrinkled, mussed up.

dis·par·age·ment\dĭs ▲pă·rəj·mənt\ n. Belittling, lowering of reputation or worth.

dis·pense\dĭs ▲pĕns\ v. To do without.

dis·sem·ble\dĭ ▲sĕm·bəl\ v. To pretend, conceal one's true thoughts or motives.

dis·si·pat·ed\▲dĭ·sĭ 'pā·təd\ adj. Given to drinking and other sensual pleasures.

dis·so·lu·tion\'dĭ·sə ▲lū·shən\ n. Destruction by breaking up into component parts.

dis·til·late\▲dĭs·tĭ 'lāt\ n. A product of distilling, a condensed essence.

dis·tort\dĭs ▲tōrt\ v. To twist or wrench from normal (often grotesquely).

dis·trac·tion\dĭs ▲trăk·shən\ n. Madness, inability to focus one's mind or think rationally.

di·ur·nal\'dai ▲ər·nəl\ adj. Daily.

di·vers\▲dai·vərz\ adj. Various.

di·vert\dĭ ▲vərt\ v. To turn aside, deflect, turn to another course.

di·vine\dĭ ▲vain\ v. To foretell, record and estimate accurately.

di·vin·i·ty\dĭ ▲vĭ·nĭ·tē\ n., pl. -ies. God, deity.

di·vulge\dĭ ▲vəlj\ v. To give out, tell.

dog·ged\▲dŏ·gəd\ adj. Resolute, stubborn, determined not to yield. (Adv. -ly)

do·mi·cile\▲dō·mĭ 'sail\ v. To house, quarter. (Also n.)

dom·i·nate\▲dō·mĭ 'nāt\ v. To possess a commanding or superior position.

do·min·ion\də ▲mĭn·yən\ n. Governmental control, rulership.

dooms·day\▲dūmz 'dā\ n. Judgment Day.

dor·sal\▲dōr·səl\ adj. Joined to or projecting from the back.

dow·er\daur\ n. Gift; especially, a dowry (a gift to the husband from the bride's family at marriage).

dreg\drĕg\ n. Waste remnant left in a container.

dross\drŏs\ n. Scum, waste, impurity.

du·bi·ous\▲dū·bē·əs\ adj. Showing worry or suspicion, doubtful.

dun\dən\ adj. Dark gray.

du·pli·cate\▲dū·plĭ·kət\ n. An exact copy. (Also v.)

ea·sel\▲ē·zəl\ n. A support for an artist's canvas while he is painting.

ec·sta·sy\▲ĕk·stə·sē\ n., pl. -ies. Extreme joy or happiness.

ed·i·fi·ca·tion\'ĕd·ə·fə ▲kā·shən\ n. Act or process of instructing or improving.

ed·i·fice\▲ĕ·də·fĭs\ n. Building, construction.

ef·face\ə ▲fās\ v. To wipe out, erase.

ef·fu·sion\ə ▲fyū·zhən\ n. Noisy, showy display of emotion.

ef·fu·sive\ĭ ▲fyū·sĭv\ adj. Excessively demonstrative, gushing. (Adv. -ly)

ego·ism\▲ē·gō·ĭzm\ n. An inclination to think too much of oneself, to be too self-centered or self-interested.

elat·ed\ē ▲lā·təd\ adj. Extremely joyful and triumphant.

el·e·gant\▲ĕ·lə·gənt\ adj. 1. With meticulous fineness. 2. Very attractive and appetizing.

el·o·quent\▲ĕ·lə·kwənt\ adj. Smooth-spoken and glib; speaking easily, fluently, and persuasively; showing well and clearly.

e·lude\ĭ ▲lūd\ v. To avoid adroitly, escape the notice of.

elu·sive\ē ▲lū·sĭv\ adj. 1. Hard to settle or fix in place. 2. Constantly going away or disappearing. 3. Hard to catch or place in a difficult position.

em·a·na·tion\'ĕ·mə ▲nā·shən\ n. An intangible flowing or issuing outward.

eman·ci·pate\ē ▲măn·sĭ 'pāt\ v. To free, release from the supervision of.

em·bold·en\ĕm ▲bōl·dən\ v. To give courage, brace up, inspire.

em·bra·sure\ĭm ▲brā·zhər\ n. Wall opening with sides flaring outward in order to allow greater angles when firing weapons.

em·u·late\▲ĕm·yu 'lāt\ v. To imitate, attempt to be like.

en·am·ored or en·am·oured\ĕ ▲nă·mərd\ adj. In love, loving, entranced.

en·com·pass\ĕn ▲kəm·pəs\ v. To surround completely.

en·gen·der\ĕn ▲jĕn·dər\ v. To give birth to.

en·hance\ĕn ▲hăns\ v. To augment, increase.

en masse\ĕn ▲măs\ adv. In one group or body.

en·sue\ĕn ▲sū\ v. To follow next, happen in order.

en·tail\ĕn ▲tāl\ v. To involve or include necessarily.

en·thrall or en·thral\ĕn ▲thrəl\ v. To please, delight, and entrance; command blended joy and interest.

en·trails\▲ĕn·trəlz\ n. *plural.* Intestines, along with adjacent inner organs.

en·trance\ĕn ▲trăns\ v. To enchant, delight, charm, enrapture.

en·ven·om\ĕn ▲vĕ·nəm\ v. To poison.

en·vis·age\ĕn ▲vĭz·əj\ v. To picture in one's mind, visualize, imagine.

e·pit·o·me\ĭ ▲pĭt·ə·mē\ n. Embodiment or ideal expression of.

er·rat·ic\ə ▲ră·tĭk\ adj. Unpredictable, uneven, variable, inconsistent.

erup·tion\ə ▲rəp·shən\ n. A violent breaking out.

es·sence\▲ĕ·səns\ n. Real inner nature or significance, genuine inner individualizing quality.

es·trange\ĕ ▲strānj\ v. To make unfamiliar, strange, hostile.

es·tu·ary\▲ĕs·chu 'ā·rē\ n., pl. -ies. A river mouth area where river current and ocean tides meet.

ether\▲ē·thər\ n. Upper air, the part of the air that transmits radio waves.

evince\ē ▲vĭns\ v. To show, demonstrate.

evo·lu·tion\'ĕ·və ▲lū·shən\ n. The process of evolving, of progressing from one stage to another.

ex·alt·ed\ĕg ▲zəl·təd\ adj. Raised, elevated.

ex·cru·ci·ating\ĕks ▲krū·shē 'ā·tĭŋ\ adj. Extremely painful.

ex·em·pla·ry\ĕg ▲zĕm·plə·rē\ adj. Faultless, perfect, fit to serve as an example.

ex·hil·a·rate\ĕg ▲zĭ·lə 'rāt\ v. To inspire with extreme joy or happiness.

ex·or·cist\ĕk ▲sōr·sĭst\ n. One who exorcises or commands and drives out devils and evil spirits.

ex·ot·ic\ĕg ▲zŏ·tĭk\ adj. Far-off, strange, romantic, and interesting.

ex·pan·sive\ĕks ▲păn·sĭv\ adj. 1. Swelling, expanding, tending to grow and become stronger. 2. Extrovertive; outgoing; given to conversation, gaiety, and companionship.

ex·ploit\ĕks ▲plɔit\ v. To make use of, take advantage of, utilize.

ex·pound\ĕks ▲paund\ v. To explain, lecture on and clarify some detail.

ex·punge\ĭk ▲spənj\ v. To obliterate, erase.

ex·qui·site\▲ĕks·kwĭ·zĭt\ adj. Beautiful, compelling wonder and admiration for superb craftsmanship and delicate perfection; showing finest, most delicate performance.

ex·trav·a·gant\ĕks ▲tră·və·gənt\ adj. Elaborate, excessive.

ex·u·ber·ant\ĕk ▲sū·bə·rənt\ adj. Gaily happy.

ex·ul·tant\ĕg ▲zəl·tənt\ adj. Feeling wild joy and triumphant happiness.

fab·u·lous\▲fă·byu·ləs\ adj. As though in or from a fable or myth, incredible, extreme. (Adv. -ly)

fa·ce·tious\fə ▲sē·shəs\ adj. Humorous, light, completely lacking in seriousness. (Adv. -ly)

fa·cil·i·tate\fə ▲sĭl·ə 'tāt\ v. To make a procedure easier and faster to perform.

fac·tion\▲făk·shən\ n. A group linked together for some political purpose.

fag·ot or fag·got\▲fă·gət\ n. A torch, a stick or bundle to be burned for light, a bundle of firewood.

fal·li·ble\▲fă·lĭ·bəl\ adj. Likely to make mistakes.

fa·tal·ist\▲fă·tə·lĭst\ n. One inclined to accept without protest what fate brings.

feint\fānt\ v. To fake, pretend to make an aggressive gesture.

fe·line\▲fē 'lain\ adj. Catlike, of or pertaining to the cat family.

fer·ment\fər ▲mĕnt\ v. To seethe, bubble. (Also n.)

fer·vid\▲fər·vĭd\ adj. Marked by strong feeling or enthusiastic expression.

fer·vor\▲fər·vər\ n. Ardent or intense feeling.

fe·tish\▲fē·tĭsh\ n. A thing or characteristic to be highly valued (perhaps without logical reasons).

fet·ter\▲fĕ·tər\ n. Chain.

fi·del·ity\fə ▲dĕ·lĭ·tē\ n. Faithfulness.

fid·gety\▲fĭ·jə·tē\ adj. Nervous, edgy.

fi·es·ta\'fē ▲ĕs·tə\ n. A celebration and feast (especially in a Latin American country).

fin·icky\▲fĭ·nĭ·kē\ adj. Fussy about details.

fir·ma·ment\▲fər·mə·mənt\ n. The heavens, especially as viewed as background for the stars.

fit·ful\▲fĭt·fəl\ adj. Erratic, marked by stops and starts.

flax·en\▲flăk·sən\ adj. Of the color of flax, blonde, yellowish.

flip·pant\▲flĭ·pənt\ adj. Disrespectfully humorous in a situation calling for sober obedience.

flor·id\▲flŏ·rĭd\ adj. Flowery, elaborate, ornate.

flot·sam\▲flŏt·səm\ n. Material floating around in a sea, lake, or river.

flu·ent\▲flū·ənt\ adj. Marked by ready, easy, and graceful motion.

fol·ly\▲fŏ·lē\ n., pl. -ies. An act of foolishness, instance of stupidity or lack of wisdom.

fon·dle\▲fŏn·dəl\ v. To caress, handle affectionately.

ă bad, ā bake, a father, ĕ sell, ē equal, ai mile, ĭ sit, ŏ cot, ō note, ɔ law, ū boom, ʊ wood, yū you, yʊ fury, au cow, ɔi boy. The schwa is used for both stressed and unstressed sounds: ə mud, word, even; ch chase, itch; sh shell, wish; th path, thin; th the, either; ŋ wing; w wet, wheat; zh pleasure.

for·ay*fō 'rā\ n. A raid, sally, expedition.

fore·bod·ing\fər *bō·dĭŋ\ n. Anxious worry; a vague intuitive feeling of coming disappointment, difficulty, evil, or tragedy.

fore·land*fōr·lănd\ n. A cape, promontory.

fore·stall\fər *stal\ v. To anticipate, prevent possible opposition by using prior measures.

for·mu·late*fōr·myu 'lāt\ v. To put into a customary form, especially to find conventional wording for.

for·sak·en\fər *sā·kən\ adj. Abandoned, left alone.

for·ti·fy*fōr·tĭ 'fai\ v., -ies, -ied. To prepare with additional calories and other food values.

for·ti·tude*fōr·tĭ 'tūd\ n. Blended bravery and resolution.

fort·night*fōrt 'nait\ n. A two-week period.

for·tu·itous\fōr *tū·ĭ·təs\ adj. Accidental, chance.

foun·der*faun·dər\ v. To fail utterly, break down.

found·ling*faund·lĭŋ\ n. Baby or child abandoned to be found (as at an orphanage or church door).

frail·ty*frā·əl·tē\ n., pl. -ies. Weakness, delicateness, lack of real endurance.

fraught\frɔt\ adj. Freighted, packed.

fresh·et*frĕ·shət\ n. A stream in flood, the overflow of a stream caused by melting snow.

fur·tive*fər·tĭv\ adj. As though done or made by a thief; with stealthy, quiet concealment.

fu·tile*fyū·tĭl\ adj. Useless, vain, ineffectual, serving no purpose.

gab·ar·dine*gă·bər 'dēn\ n. A firm, hard-finished, durable, ribbed fabric.

gad\găd\ v. To stroll and mill about.

gait\gāt\ n. Way of walking.

gal·lant·ry*gă·lən·trē\ n., pl. -ies. Chivalrous courtesy, showy courtesy to ladies.

gar·gan·tu·an\'gar *găn·chu·ən\ adj. Huge, immense.

gar·ish*gă·rĭsh\ adj. Brightly or outlandishly colorful, marked by tasteless or untrue flashiness.

gar·land*găr·lənd\ n. A wreath or other similar flower arrangement.

gar·ner*găr·nər\ v. To gather, harvest. (Also n. A granary, storehouse.)

gauche\gōsh\ adj. Crude, awkward, unsophisticated.

gaudy*gɔ·dē\ adj. Marked by overly bright color or ornament.

gaunt\gɔnt\ adj. Very thin and worn (as from hunger or illness).

ge·nial*jē·nē·əl\ adj. Friendly, companionable, pleasant.

ger·mane\jər *mān\ adj. Suitable, appropriate, relevant.

ges·tic·u·late\jĕs *tĭk·yu 'lāt\ v. To motion with the hands to express or emphasize meaning, make demonstrative gestures with hands and facial features.

ges·ture*jĕs·chər\ n. A motion, as with hands or facial features; communicate. (Also v.)

ghast·ly*găst·lē\ adj. Frightful, terrible, deathly.

ghoul·ish*gū·lĭsh\ adj. Like a ghoul (a person given to robbing graves).

gib·ber·ish*jĭ·bə·rĭsh\ n. Nonsense.

gid·dy*gĭ·dē\ adj. Dizzy. (Adv. -ily)

gist\jĭst\ n. Meaning, significance separated out from items unimportant or nonessential.

glean\glēn\ v. To gather or harvest the fruits or products of.

glob·al*glō·bəl\ adj. Pertaining to or affecting the whole earth.

gnash\năsh\ v. To grind the teeth together.

goad\gōd\ v. To urge; spur on, as with a sharp pointed stick. (Also n.)

gran·deur*grăn·dyūr\ n. Grandness, splendid or impressive majesty.

grat·i·fy*grăt·ə·fai\ v. To give or be a source of pleasure or satisfaction to, confer a favor on.

grat·i·tude*gră·tĭ 'tūd\ n. Gratefulness, extreme sense of thankfulness.

gri·mace*grĭ·məs\ v. To contort one's face, make odd facial expressions. (Also n.)

gris·ly*grĭz·lē\ adj. Fearful, dreadful.

gross·ly*grɔs·lē\ adv. Utterly, obviously.

grue·some*grū·səm\ adj. Frightful, grisly. (Adv. -ly)

guile\gail\ n. Deception, fraud, dishonesty.

guise\gaiz\ n. Aspect, semblance, appearance.

gut·tur·al*gə·tə·rəl\ adj. Thick, harsh, throaty.

gy·ra·tion\jai *rā·shən\ n. A revolving around a point, spiral motion.

hab·i·tat*hă·bĭ 'tăt\ n. Dwelling area, place in which one lives.

ha·bit·u·ate\hə *bĭ·chu 'āt\ v. To accustom, make used to.

hag·gard*hă·gərd\ adj. Wan, thin, and wasted (as by hunger or disease).

hal·lo\hă *lō\ v. To call, shout.

hal·loo\hă *lū\ n. A shout, loud call. (Also v.)

hand·i·work*hăn·di·wərk\ n. Craftsmanship.

ha·rass\hə *răs\ v. To worry, oppress, wear down.

har·lot*har·lət\ n. Mistress, prostitute.

har·row·ing*hă·rə·wĭŋ\ adj. Trying, disturbing.

haunt\hɔnt\ v. To visit continually as a ghost does. (Also n. Place, locale.)

hau·teur\hō *tyər\ n. Lofty and chilling pride and haughtiness, aloof extreme pride and disdain.

her·ald*hĕ·rəld\ n. A messenger.

her·mit·age*hər·mĭ·təj\ n. A hermit's quarters, a place where one lives alone.

hes·i·tant*hĕ·zĭ·tənt\ adj. Hesitating, uncertain.

hid·eous*hĭ·dē·əs\ adj. Most ugly and loathsome.

hil·lock*hĭ·lək\ n. A little hill.

hind\haind\ n. Deer.

hom·i·ly*hŏ·mĭ·lē\ n., pl. -ies. A sermon, a moralistic lesson or preaching.

hulk\həlk\ n. 1. A large, awkward, looming form. 2. The frame of an abandoned boat or ship.

hu·mane\hyū *mān\ adj. Merciful and kindly, not cruel or oppressive.

id·i·o·mat·ic\'ĭd·ē·ə *măt·ĭk\ adj. Characteristic of and natural to a given language.

id·io·syn·cra·sy\'ĭ·dē·ō *sĭŋ·krə·sē\ n. pl. -ies. Peculiarity, individual and unusual mannerism or trait.

ig·no·ble\ĭg *nō·bəl\ adj. Low, mean. (Adv. -ly)

il·lu·mine\ĭ *lū·mĭn\ v. To light up, illuminate.

il·lu·sion\ĭ ▲lū·zhən\ n. A false appearance; a false semblance of reality; an ill-based or false vision, perception, notion, or belief.

im·men·si·ty\ĭ ▲měn·sĭ·tē\ n. Enormity, hugeness.

im·merse\ĭ ▲mərs\ v. To dip, submerge.

im·mi·nent\ ▲ĭ·mĭ·nənt\ adj. About to happen, very likely to happen.

im·mo·bile\ĭ ▲mō·bĭl\ adj. Unable to move.

im·mune\ĭ ▲myūn\ adj. Not receptive or responsive, detached and safe from.

im·pal·pa·ble\ĭm ▲păl·pə·bəl\ adj. Incapable or practically incapable of being touched or otherwise sensed.

im·pas·sive\ĭm ▲păs·ĭv\ adj. Showing no emotion, expressionless.

im·pec·ca·ble\'ĭm ▲pěk·ə·bəl\ adj. Flawless.

im·per·a·tive\ĭm ▲pā·rə·tĭv\ adj. 1. Absolutely necessary. 2. Commanding, not to be denied or withstood.

im·per·cep·ti·ble\'ĭm·pər ▲sěp·tĭ·bəl\ adj. Impossible or very difficult to perceive, incapable or barely capable of being perceived. (Adv. -ly)

im·pe·ri·al·ism\ĭm ▲pē·rē·ə 'lĭzm\ n. The policy, procedure, or tendency of the worlds' great powers to bring other areas under their control and dominate and subjugate them.

im·pe·ri·ous\ĭm ▲pē·rē·əs\ adj. Lordly, with haughty command, with command as by an emperor.

im·per·ish·able\ĭm ▲pě·rĭsh·ə·bəl\ adj. Undying, lasting forever.

im·per·ti·nence\ĭm ▲pər·tĭ·nəns\ n. Impudence, lack of obedience, insolence.

im·per·turb·able\'ĭm·pər ▲tər·bə·bəl\ adj. Incapable of being agitated, ruffled, or concerned; calm and composed.

im·plic·it·ly\ĭm ▲plĭs·ət·lē\ adv. 1. Unquestioningly. 2. In a manner unexpressed but implied.

im·po·tence\ ▲ĭm·pə·təns\ n. Powerlessness, utter lack of strength and force.

im·pre·ca·tion\'ĭm·prē ▲kā·shən\ n. An oath, curse.

im·pre·ci·sion\'ĭm·prē ▲sĭ·zhən\ n. Inexactness, uncertainty.

im·preg·na·tion\ĭm·prĕg ▲nā·shən\ n. The act of filling, spreading through, or permeating a substance.

im·pro·vise\ ▲ĭm·prə 'vaiz\ v. To make up at the moment, make up or contrive out of whatever is available, fabricate.

im·pul·sive\ĭm ▲pəl·sĭv\ adj. Acting quickly without measured thought.

in·ad·ver·tent\'ĭn·əd ▲vər·tənt\ adj. Accidental, usually through lack of observation or notice. (Adv. -ly)

inane\ĭ ▲nān\ adj. Empty of meaning or point. (Adv. -ly)

in·an·i·mate\ĭn ▲ă·nĭ·mət\ adj. Lifeless.

in·ar·tic·u·late\ĭn·ar ▲tĭk·yu·lət\ adj. 1. Unable to speak coherently because of extreme emotion. 2. Spoken without clear adequate division between words and hence hard to understand.

in·au·di·ble\ĭn ▲ɔ·dĭ·bəl\ adj. Impossible to hear.

in·can·des·cence\ĭn·kən ▲dě·səns\ n. 1. Brilliant whiteness. 2. Beautiful shining brilliance.

in·car·nate\ĭn ▲kar·nət\ adj. In the flesh, bodily, not existing as a detached spirit.

in·cense\ĭn ▲sĕns\ v. To irritate, anger.

in·ci·sion\ĭn ▲sĭ·zhən\ n. A cutting in or into, as in surgery; a slit.

in·co·her·ent\ĭn·kō ▲hě·rənt\ adj. Without coherence, not logically or clearly thought out or expressed. (Adv. -ly)

in·con·gru·ous\ĭn ▲kŏŋ·gru·əs\ adj. Strikingly out of place, quite discordant with the surroundings.

in·con·se·quent\ĭn ▲kŏn·sə·kwənt\ adj. Unimportant, not worth paying attention to.

in·cred·i·ble\ĭn ▲krě·dĭ·bəl\ adj. Unbelievable.

in·cre·du·li·ty\ĭn·krě ▲dū·lĭ·tē\ n. Disbelief, disinclination or disability to believe or accept.

in·de·fin·able\ĭn·də ▲fai·nə·bəl\ adj. Defying definition, description, or explanation.

in·dif·fer·ent\ĭn ▲dĭ·fə·rənt\ adj. Neither good nor bad, decidely not superior.

in·di·gent\ ▲ĭn·dĭ·jənt\ adj. Quite poor and needy.

in·dis·pens·able\ĭn·dĭs ▲pĕn·sə·bəl\ adj. Completely necessary, impossible to dispense with.

in·do·lent\ ▲ĭn·də·lənt\ adj. Disinclined to any activity; inert, lazy, and inactive.

in·duct\ĭn ▲dəkt\ v. To install, initiate formally, make part of.

in·due\ĭn ▲dū\ v. To imbue, tinge, or color throughout.

in·dulge\ĭn ▲dəlj\ v. To give free rein or play to, permit free range to.

in·ed·i·ble\ĭn ▲ě·dĭ·bəl\ adj. Uneatable, incapable of being digested.

in·ef·fa·ble\ĭn ▲ě·fə·bəl\ adj. Indescribable; not to be narrated, described, or explained in ordinary ways.

in·ef·fec·tu·al\ĭn·ə ▲fĕk·ehəl\ adj. Ineffective; unavailing, weak, and forceless; futile and vain.

in·ert\ĭ ▲nərt\ adj. Unmoving, motionless.

in·ev·i·ta·ble\ĭn ▲ěv·ət·ə·bəl\ adj. Impossible to avoid, bound to come.

in·ex·o·ra·ble\ĭn ▲ěk·sə·rə·bəl\ adj. 1. Unbending, not to be moved or touched by any plea. 2. Unavoidable, inevitably continuing or operating.

in·ex·press·ible\ĭn·əks ▲prě·sĭ·bəl\ adj. Defying expression, incapable of being expressed.

in·ex·tri·ca·ble\ĭn ▲ěk·strĭ·kə·bəl\ adj. Incapable of being disentangled.

in·fal·li·ble\ĭn ▲fă·lĭ·bəl\ adj. Perfect, never showing failure or mistake.

in·fer·ence\ ▲ĭn·f(ə)r·ən(t)s\ n. A conclusion, guess, or surmise drawn from facts; an outcome of thought.

in·fer·nal\ĭn ▲fər·nəl\ adj. Hellishly unpleasant, hellish, damnable, awful.

ă b*a*d, ā b*a*ke, a f*a*ther, ĕ s*e*ll, ē *e*qual, ai m*i*le, ĭ s*i*t, ŏ c*o*t, ō n*o*te, ɔ l*a*w, ū b*oo*m, ʊ w*oo*d, yū *you*, yʊ f*u*ry, aʊ c*ow*, ɔi b*oy*. The schwa is used for both stressed and unstressed sounds: ə m*u*d, w*o*rd, ev*e*n; ch ch*a*se, it*ch*; sh sh*e*ll, wi*sh*; th p*a*th, *th*in; th *the*, ei*th*er; ŋ wi*ng*; w *w*et, *wh*eat; zh plea*s*ure.

in·fer·no\ĭn ⁀fər·nō\ n. Hell or a similar subterranean region.

in·fi·nite\ˈĭn·fĭ·nĭt\ adj. Endless, measureless, unceasing. (Adv. -ly)

in·fin·i·tes·i·mal\ĭn ˈfĭ·nĭ ⁀tĕ·zĭ·məl\ adj. Very tiny.

in·fir·mi·ty\ĭn ⁀fər·mĭ·tē\ n., pl. -ies. Illness, sickness, or weakness.

in·fuse\ĭn ⁀fyūz\ v. To instill, mix in.

in·ge·nious\ĭn ⁀jē·nē·əs\ adj. Clever, able to improvise crafty plans or devices.

in·hib·it\ĭn ⁀hĭb·ət\ v. To hold in check, to repress.

in·i·ti·a·tive\ĭn ⁀ĭsh·ət·ĭv\ n. Energy or aptitude displayed in setting up action, enterprise.

in·noc·u·ous\ĭ ⁀nŏ·kyu·əs\ adj. Innocent, harmless, and seemingly unimportant.

in·no·va·tor\ⁱĭ·nə ⁀vā·tər\ n. One who introduces or practices something new.

in·nu·mer·a·ble\ĭ ⁀nū·mə·rə·bəl\ adj. Numberless.

im·pec·ca·ble\ĭm ⁀pĕk·ə bəl\ adj. Without fault, blemish, or flaw.

in·qui·si·tion\ĭn·kwĭ ⁀zĭ·shən\ n. A prying, sustained series of questions; a series of searching and embarrassing questions to ferret out misconduct.

in·quis·i·tive\ĭn ⁀kwĭ·zĭ·tĭv\ adj. Curious, questioning, investigative.

in·sa·tia·ble\ĭn ⁀sā·shə·bəl\ adj. Incapable of being satisfied.

in·sid·i·ous\ĭn ⁀sĭ·dē·əs\ adj. Not easily perceived or recognized and likely to mislead, endanger, or entrap. (Adv. -ly)

in·so·lence\ⁱĭn·sə·ləns\ n. Impudent disregard of or opposition to authority.

in·sou·ci·ance\ĭn ⁀sū·sē·əns\ n. Carefree nonchalance.

in·sti·ga·tion\ˈĭn·stĭ ⁀gā·shən\ n. Incitement, encouragement to action.

in·suf·fer·able\ĭn ⁀sə·fər·ə·bəl\ adj. Most unpleasant and difficult to be with.

in·sur·rec·tion\ˈĭn·sə ⁀rĕk·shən\ n. Rebellion, revolt.

in·tact\ĭn ⁀tăkt\ adj. Whole, entire, undamaged.

in·tan·gi·ble\ĭn ⁀tăn·jĭ·bəl\ adj. Impossible or hard to perceive clearly or to analyze. (Adv. -ly)

in·tem·per·ate\ĭn ⁀tĕm·pə·rət\ adj. Immoderate, extreme.

in·ter·cede\ĭn ˈtər ⁀sēd\ v. To plead in another's behalf.

in·ter·ces·sion\ˈĭn·tər ⁀sĕ·shən\ n. A prayer to a superior power to intercede and protect.

in·ter·dict\ˈĭn·tər ˈdĭkt\ n. A strict legal prohibition or ban.

in·ter·im\ˈĭn·tə·rĭm\ n. Intervening space or time.

in·ter·mi·na·ble\ĭn ⁀tər·mĭ·nə·bəl\ adj. Endless, unceasing, lasting forever or as if forever. (Adv. -ly)

in·ter·mit·tent\ˈĭn·tər ⁀mĭ·tənt\ adj. Not continuous, occurring or operating at intervals from time to time, starting and stopping.

in·ter·pose\ĭn·tər ⁀pōz\ v. To place or come between.

in·ter·sperse\ˈĭn·tər ⁀spərs\ v. To intermix, insert into at intervals from time to time, scatter about here and there.

in·ti·mate\ˈĭn·tĭ·mət\ adj. Near, very close, marked by close and understanding relationship. (Adv. -ly, v. \ⁱĭn·tĭ ⁀māt\ To hint, suggest.)

in·tol·er·a·ble\ĭn ⁀tŏ·lə·rə·bəl\ adj. Very hard to tolerate or put up with.

in·tri·cate\ⁱĭn·trĭ·kət\ adj. Complicated, delicate, having many interrelations and interconnections.

in·trude\ĭn ⁀trūd\ v. To thrust or press forward or inward without invitation or welcome.

in·tu·ition\ˈĭn·tū ⁀ĭ·shən\ n. A sense of inner perception and quick understanding.

in·ure\ĭn ⁀yūr\ v. To accustom.

in·vin·ci·ble\ĭn ⁀vĭn(t)·sə·bəl\ adj. Unconquerable.

in·vi·o·la·ble\ĭn ⁀vai·əl·ə·bəl\ adj. Not to be violated, interrupted, or profaned; to be treated as sacred; kept from violation; of a secret, never told or divulged.

in·voice\ⁱĭn·vɔis\ n. An itemized statement of goods sold or consigned.

iras·ci·bil·i·ty\ĭ ˈră·sĭ ⁀bĭ·lĭ·tē\ n. Bad temper, anger.

ir·i·des·cent\ˈĭ·rĭ ⁀dĕ·sənt\ adj. Showing a sheen of many colors with a rainbowlike effect.

iron·c\ai ⁀rŏ·nĭk\ adj. Pertaining to or showing a situation opposed to what would be expected from forethought, plans, or probabilities.

ir·ra·di·ate\ĭr ⁀ād·ē·āt\ v. To cast rays of light upon, enlighten, shine.

ir·re·deem·a·ble\ˈĭ·rə ⁀dēm·ə·bəl\ adj. Impossible to redeem, bring back, or compensate for.

ir·rel·e·vant\ĭ ⁀rĕ·lə·vənt\ adj. Unrelated, immaterial.

ir·res·o·lu·tion\ĭ ˈrĕ·zə ⁀lū·shən\ n. Uncertainty, doubt, indecision.

ir·re·vo·ca·ble\ĭ ⁀rĕ·və·kə·bəl\ adj. Impossible to revoke, take back, change, or alter.

item·ize\ⁱai·tə ˈmaiz\ v. To list or record mentioning each individual item.

jab·ber\ⁱjă·bər\ v. To speak excitedly and incoherently.

ja·ded\ⁱjā·dĭd\ adj. Tired, made spiritless by fatigue.

jaun·ty\ⁱjɔn·tē\ adj. Happy, lighthearted, and carefree; good-humored, gay, and self-confident. (Adv. -ily)

jet·ti·son\ⁱjĕ·tĭ·sən\ v. To throw out, pour out, or otherwise get rid of.

jounce\jauns\ v. To pitch or sway as in a rough ride.

jowls\jaulz\ n. *plural.* The slack flesh around the lower jaw or neck.

ju·bi·la·tion\ˈjū·bĭ ⁀lā·shən\ n. Extreme demonstrative joy, celebration of extreme joy and happiness.

ju·di·cious\jū ⁀dĭ·shəs\ adj. Marked by careful judgment, attempting to judge and calculate.

ju·ve·nile\ⁱjū·və·nĭl\ n. An actor or actress who plays children's or adolescents' parts.

ka·lei·do·scope\kə ⁀lai·də ˈskōp\ n. A device in which bits of colored stone produce innumerable colorful patterns.

kin·dred\ⁱkĭn·drəd\ adj. Similar; having the same inclinations, ideas, or emotions.

lab·y·rinth\ⁱlă·bĭ ˈrĭnth\ n. A confusing maze or tangle.

la·con·ic\lə ⁀kŏ·nĭk\ adj. Speaking little, using as few words as possible.

lag·gard\ˈlă·gərd\ n. One who lags behind, slowpoke, loiterer.

la·goon\lə ˈgūn\ n. A section of quiet water ringed about by a coral reef or similar formation.

lam·en·ta·tion\ˈlăm·ən ˈtā·shən\ n. Act of expressing sorrow or regret for, mourning for.

lan·guid\ˈlăŋ·gwĭd\ adj. Marked by very little energy or force. (Adv. -ly)

lan·guor\ˈlăŋ·gər\ n. Tired drowsiness and disinclination to activity.

lar·va\ˈlar·və\ n., pl. -ae. An immature form of an insect.

las·si·tude\ˈlă·sĭ ˈtūd\ n. Tiredness (often during convalescence) and disinclination to move or act.

lath\lăth\ n. A narrow strip of wood used in building a wall.

lave\lāv\ v. To wash, bathe.

lay\lā\ n. A poem, song, story. (Also adj. Untrained, inexperienced, uneducated in a particular area.)

lay·man\ˈlā·mən\ n., pl. -men. A person not trained in or familiar with some profession.

league\lēg\ n. Any of various units of distance from about 2.4 to 4.6 statute miles.

leav·en\ˈlĕ·vən\ v. To cause dough to rise by using a fermenting substance like yeast.

leg·a·cy\ˈlĕ·gə·sē\ n., pl. -ies. What is willed to a survivor.

leg·en·dary\ˈlĕ·jən ˈdā·rē\ adj. Known in a legend, fictitious, mythical.

leth·ar·gy\ˈlĕ·thər·jē\ n. A sense of tired, sleepy, and listless inactivity; disinclination or inability to move or act.

levy\ˈlĕ·vē\ v. To enlist troops for army service (usually by drafting).

li·ai·son\ˈlē ˈā·zŏn\ n. Communication, contact.

lin·tel\ˈlĭn·təl\ n. Threshold.

liq·ui·date\ˈlĭ·kwĭ ˈdāt\ v. To get rid of, end, engage in self-destruction.

list·less\ˈlĭst·ləs\ adj. Inattentive, indifferent, and bored.

lit·a·ny\ˈlĭ·tə·nē\ n., pl. -ies. A long prayer with invocations and responses.

lit·ter\ˈlĭ·tər\ v. To give birth (used of animals).

liv·ery\ˈlĭ·və·rē\ n., pl. -ies. The sort of uniform worn by a driver, coachman, doorman, or the like.

liv·id\ˈlĭ·vĭd\ adj. Unwholesomely pale.

loath\lōth\ adj. Unwilling, reluctant.

lo·cust\ˈlō·kəst\ n. A tall spiny tree with very hard wood and twisted seed pods.

lo·gis·ti·cal\ˈlō ˈjĭs·tĭ·kəl\ adj. Involving the problem of supplies and materials, conditioned by supplies and material.

lope\lōp\ n. A running stride marked by strong steps.

lu·cent\ˈlū·sənt\ adj. Clear and gleaming.

lu·cre\ˈlū·kər\ n. Money, profit in money.

lu·di·crous\ˈlū·dĭ·krəs\ adj. Ridiculous, laughable.

lum·ber\ˈləm·bər\ v. To walk or lurch along heavily or clumsily.

lus·ter\ˈləs·tər\ n. Gleaming brightness.

lux·u·ri·ous\lək ˈshu·rē·əs\ adj. With full enjoyment and relaxation. (Adv. -ly)

lym·phat·ic\lĭm ˈfă·tĭk\ adj. Pertaining to lymph (the bodily fluid containing white blood cells).

ma·ca·bre\mə ˈka·bər\ adj. Grim, ghastly, suggestive of death.

mace\mās\ n. A heavy club or staff carried as a symbol of authority.

mael·strom\ˈmāl·strəm\ n. A whirlpool, eddy.

mag·a·zine\ˈmă·gə ˈzēn\ n. A gun chamber designed to hold cartridges to be fed into the firing mechanism.

mag·na·nim·i·ty\ˈmăg·nə ˈnĭ·mĭ·tē\ n. Great soul or spirit showing extreme generosity.

mag·nate\ˈmăg·nət\ n. A man of great wealth and financial power.

male·dic·tion\ˈmă·lə ˈdĭk·shən\ n. A curse, imprecation.

mal·e·fac·tor\ˈmăl·ə·făk·tər\ n. One who commits an offence against the law, evildoer.

mal·ice\ˈmă·lĭs\ n. Ill-will, hatred.

ma·lign\mə ˈlain\ adj. Evil in nature or effect, injurious.

ma·lig·nant\mə ˈlĭg·nənt\ adj. Utterly evil in nature or effect, producing evil and death.

ma·ni·a\ˈmā·nĭ·ə\ n. An extremely intense desire for something, excessive enthusiasm for something.

man·i·fest\ˈmă·nĭ·fĕst\ adj. Clear, obvious, plain. (Adv. -ly)

man·i·fes·ta·tion\ˈmăn·ə·fə ˈstā·shən\ n. Demonstration or showing of.

ma·nip·u·late\mə ˈnĭ·pyə ˈlāt\ v. To operate or manage skillfully with the hands.

man·tle\ˈmăn·təel\ v. To coat, cloak.

mar·a·thon\ˈmă·rə ˈthŏn\ n. Any activity that is sustained over a remarkably long period.

ma·raud\mə ˈrɔd\ v. To raid, harry, pillage.

mar·i·time\ˈmă·rĭ ˈtaim\ adj. Marine, oceanic.

ma·roon\mə ˈrūn\ v. To leave, abandon, cause abandonment.

mar·ti·net\ˈmar·tə ˈnĕt\ n. A strict disciplinarian.

mas·sive\ˈmă·sĭv\ adj. Extreme and severe.

mas·ti·cate\ˈmăs·tĭ ˈkăt\ v. To chew and intermix with saliva.

maud·lin\ˈmɔd·lən\ adj. Over-sentimental, drunk enough to be emotionally silly, fuddled.

max·im\ˈmăk·sĭm\ n. A proverbial rule or principle.

med·i·tate\ˈmĕ·dĭ ˈtāt\ v. To think and consider, especially quietly and for a long time.

med·ley\ˈmĕd·lē\ n. Miscellany, mixture.

mel·an·choly\ˈmĕ·lən ˈkŏ·lē\ adj. Sad, pensively plaintive.

ă bad, ā bake, a father, ĕ sell, ē equal, ai mile, ĭ sit, ŏ cot, ō note, ɔ law, ū boom, ʊ wood, yū you, yʊ fury, aʊ cow, ɔi boy. The schwa is used for both stressed and unstressed sounds: ə mud, word, even; ch chase, itch; sh shell, wish; th path, thin; th the, either; ŋ wing; w wet, wheat; zh pleasure.

men·ace\ˈmĕ·nəs\ v. To threaten. (Also n. A threat.)

me·nial\ˈmēn·yəl\ n. A servant, especially one serving in a very low capacity.

mer·ce·nary\ˈmər·sə ˈnā·rē\ adj. Motivated only or mainly by money and not by emotions.

mer·cu·ri·al\mər ˈkyu·rē·əl\ adj. Showing very quick changes in mood, often volatile and demonstrative.

me·tic·u·lous\mə ˈtĭk·yu·ləs\ adj. Most careful, neat, precise, and exact; marked by extreme care about details. (Adv. -ly)

met·tle\ˈmĕ·təl\ n. Marked force, strength, and worth; resolution, bravery.

mi·cro·wave\ˈmai·krō ˈwāv\ n. A short electromagnetic wave.

mid·dy\ˈmĭ·dē\ n., pl. -ies. A loose-fitting informal blouse with a collar like a sailor's.

mi·gra·tion\ˈmai ˈgrā·shən\ n. Moving or changing habitation, especially by many people to new lands.

min·i·mum\ˈmĭ·nĭ·məm\ n. Least possible point or degree.

mi·rage\mĭ ˈrazh\ n. A false vision, an illusion.

mis·con·strue\mĭs·kən ˈstrū\ v. To misinterpret, misunderstand.

mis·de·mean·or\mĭs·də ˈmē·nər\ n. An instance of misconduct calling for punishment but less serious than a crime.

mo·bile\ˈmō·bĭl\ adj. Suggesting or expressing motion and freedom to move.

mock·ery\ˈmŏ·kə·rē\ n., pl. -ies. 1. Ridicule and scorn; mocking and defying; a thing, gesture, or statement that mocks. 2. An imitation or substitute ridiculously inadequate.

mo·men·tous\mō ˈmĕn·təs\ adj. Of greatest importance and significance.

mo·men·tum\mō ˈmĕn·təm\ n. Impetus, the force that keeps a moving body in motion.

mo·nas·tic\mə ˈnăs·tĭk\ adj. Characteristic of monks and their self-denying way of life.

mon·grel\ˈməŋ·grəl\ n. A crossbred cur.

mon·i·tor\ˈmŏ·nĭ·tər\ n. One who constantly observes, checks, and records.

mo·no·lith·ic\ˈmŏ·nə ˈlĭ·thĭk\ adj. Huge, tall, and made (or as though made) of one single stone.

mono·tone\ˈmŏ·nə ˈtōn\ n. A single tone or sound endlessly repeated.

mo·not·o·nous\mə ˈnŏ·tə·nəs\ adj. Entirely without variation, boresomely changeless. (Adv. -ly)

mope\mōp\ v. To brood in solitude.

mor·bid\ˈmŏr·bĭd\ adj. Unwholesome, unhealthy, abnormal.

mo·rose\mə ˈrōs\ adj. Gloomy, ill-tempered, sullen.

mor·ti·fy\ˈmŏr·tĭ ˈfai\ v., -ies, -ied. 1. To kill, bring near to death. 2. To shame and embarrass.

mote\mōt\ n. A particle in the eye that interferes with vision.

mul·ish\ˈmyū·lĭsh\ adj. Stubborn, contrary. (Also n. -ness)

mute\myūt\ v. To still, decrease very much in volume or intensity.

my·o·pic\ˈmai ˈŏp·ək\ adj. Nearsighted.

mys·tic\ˈmĭs·tĭk\ n. One who gains perception or knowledge without direct uses of senses and rationality, one whose knowledge or beliefs come from intuition and insight rather than rational factual observation.

mys·ti·fy\ˈmĭs·tĭ ˈfai\ v., -ies, -ied. To puzzle, perplex.

name·sake\ˈnām ˈsāk\ n. A person or figure for whom one is named.

nau·sea\ˈnɔ·zē·ə\ n. Sickness at the stomach, tendency to vomit.

neg·li·gence\ˈnĕg·lĭ·jəns\ n. Neglect.

neg·li·gi·ble\ˈnĕg·lĭ·jĭ·bəl\ adj. So trivial as to be neglected or overlooked completely.

neu·ro·sis\nū ˈrō·səs\ n. A nervous or emotional disorder.

neu·rot·ic\nū ˈrō·tĭk\ adj. Suffering from or pertaining to a functional nervous disorder.

nil\nĭl\ adj. Zero, nonexistent.

noc·tur·nal\ˈnŏk ˈtər·nəl\ adj. Occurring at night, nightly.

nod·ule\ˈnŏ·jəl\ n. A small rounded particle, a bit.

no·mad\ˈnō·măd\ n. A wanderer, especially one of a people without a fixed permanent place of residence.

non·sen·si·cal\nŏn ˈsĕn·sĭ·kəl\ adj. Stupid, ridiculous, composed only of nonsense.

nos·tal·gia\nə ˈstăl·jə\ n. A yearning for something familiar in the past, especially for a home that one has left; a pleasure at such yearning and recollection.

no·ta·tion\ˈnō ˈtā·shən\ n. A note, memorandum.

nov·ice\ˈnŏ·vĭs\ n. A person (especially a woman) in the first stages of becoming a member of a convent or other religious establishment.

nu·cle·us\ˈnū·klē·əs\ n., pl. -ei or -es. Center, core.

nug·get\ˈnə·gət\ n. A little lump (often of gold or other precious mineral).

obliv·i·on\əb ˈlĭ·vē·ən\ n. Forgetfulness in sleep.

obliv·i·ous\əb ˈlĭ·vē·əs\ adj. Entirely unobservant and unaware, not perceiving or noticing, forgetful.

ob·scene\əb ˈsēn\ adj. Vile, loathsome.

ob·scu·ri·ty\əb ˈsku·rĭ·tē\ n. Darkness, blackness.

ob·ses·sion\əb ˈsĕ·shən\ n. An idea or thought (often false) that completely dominates the mind to the exclusion of all else.

ob·sti·nate\ˈŏb·stĭ·nət\ adj. Stubbornly determined not to yield or concede; persistent, determined, and impossible to change.

ocean·og·ra·phy\ˈō·shə ˈnŏg·rə·fē\ n. The science or study of the ocean.

oc·tave\ˈŏk·təv\ n. One group of eight (as of eight colors) set in order within a number of other groups.

o·di·ous\ˈō·dĭ·əs\ adj. Deserving of or exciting hatred, hateful, detestable.

of·fal\ˈɔ·fəl\ n. Trash, rubbish, garbage.

omen\ˈō·mən\ n. A sign or indication of future developments.

om·i·nous\ˈŏ·mĭ·nəs\ adj. Sinister, suggesting or threatening evil developments to come.

om·nip·o·tence\ŏm ˈnĭ·pə təns\ n. Unlimited power.

om·ni·pres·ent\ˈŏm·nĭ ˈprĕ·zənt\ adj. Always present.

on·slaught\ˈŏn ˈslɔt\ n. Fierce or determined attack.

op·ti·cal\ˈŏp·tĭ·kəl\ adj. Pertaining to the eyes or vision.

orb\ōrb\ n. *poetic.* The sun.

or·ches·tra·tion\ˈōr·kəˈstrā·shən\ n. An arranging and combining for best artistic or forceful effect.

or·dain\ȯrˈdān\ v. To establish and follow strictly (as a religious usage).

or·deal\ȯrˈdēl\ n. A period of severe trouble, distress, trial, worry, pain, or danger.

or·gy\ˈȯr·jē\ n., pl. -ies. An excessive indulgence in any pleasure.

or·nate\ȯrˈnāt\ adj. Elaborately decorated.

os·se·ous\ˈŏ·sē·əs\ adj. Composed of bone, like bone.

os·ten·si·ble\ə ˈstĕn·sĭ·bəl\ adj. Seeming, apparent. (Adv. -ly)

os·ten·ta·tious\ˈŏs·tən ˈtā·shəs\ adj. Showy, accomplished or done in such a way as to demand attention.

over·ture\ˈō·vər·chʊr\ n. An instrumental introduction or prelude to an opera.

over·wrought\ˈō·vər ˈrȯt\ adj. Agitated and unnerved.

pag·eant\ˈpă·jənt\ n. A procession of colorfully costumed romantic figures.

pal·ate\ˈpă·lət\ n. Technically, the roof of the mouth; loosely, those parts of the mouth containing the taste buds.

pal·ette\ˈpă·lət\ n. A thin board with a thumb hole on which an artist mixes paints.

pall\pȯl\ n. Something that covers or conceals, often producing an effect of gloom.

pal·lor\ˈpă·lər\ n. Paleness, lack of color.

pal·pi·tate\ˈpăl·pə·tāt\ v. To beat rapidly and strongly, throb.

pal·ter\ˈpȯl·tər\ v. To be insincere, treacherous, cowardly.

pal·try\ˈpȯl·trē\ adj. Puny, weak, slight. (Also n. -ness)

pan·de·mo·ni·um\ˈpăn·dəˈmō·nē·əm\ n. Extreme confused noise preventing rational speech or thought.

pan·to·mime\ˈpăn·tə ˈmaim\ n. 1. Expression of meaning or emotion by gesture alone and entirely without use of words, a series of gestures communicating meaning without words. 2. A dramatic production in which words are not used but gestures and actions express the message involved.

par·a·ble\ˈpă·rə·bəl\ n. A story with a moral or lesson.

par·a·gon\ˈpă·rə·gən\ n. A pattern of excellence, a model of superlative characteristics.

par·a·mount\ˈpăr·maʊnt\ adj. Superior to all others.

para·noia\ˈpă·rə ˈnȯi·ə\ n. A form of madness featuring delusions that one is being persecuted.

par·a·site\ˈpă·rə ˈsait\ n. An animal or fish that depends on another and clings to that creature.

parch·ment\ˈparch·mənt\ n. A document on parchment.

pa·ro·chi·al\pəˈrō·kē·əl\ adj. Pertaining to or restricted to a very small area; narrow, provincial, local.

par·ry\ˈpă·rē\ v., -ies, -ied. To turn aside or withstand, as an onset, attack, rebuke, or question.

par·ti·san\ˈpar·tə·zən\ n. A staunch supporter of a cause or a party.

pas·sive\ˈpă·sĭv\ adj. Without necessary force or action. (Adv. -ly)

pas·to·ral\ˈpăs·tə·rəl\ adj. Of or pertaining to a pastor, churchly, religious.

pa·tent·ly\ˈpăt·ənt·lē\ adv. Obviously, openly.

pa·thos\ˈpā ˈthōs\ n. 1. Deep and genuine feeling for the sad or tragic. 2. Sadness or sorrow that calls forth pity or sympathy.

pa·tron\ˈpā·trən\ n. A wealthy or influential person in control of some enterprise.

pa·tron·age\ˈpā·trə·nəj\ n. Financial assistance, especially given grudgingly and with condescension.

pa·tron·ize\ˈpā·trə ˈnaiz\ v. To condescend, act in a lofty or haughty way toward.

paunchy\ˈpȯn·chē\ adj. Having a noticeable paunch, stout.

pa·vil·ion\pə ˈvĭl·yən\ n. A large spacious tent.

pec·ca·dil·lo\ˈpĕ·kə ˈdĭ·lō\ n. A minor and readily forgivable transgression, sin, or omission.

pee·vish\ˈpē·vĭsh\ adj. Fretful, complaining.

pen·sive\ˈpĕn·sĭv\ adj. Thoughtful, contemplative.

per·cep·ti·ble\pər ˈsĕp·tĭ·bəl\ adj. Capable of being perceived.

pe·remp·to·ry\pəˈrĕm·tə·rē\ adj. Commandingly, with sharp and postive orders. (Adv. -ily)

pe·ren·ni·al\pə ˈrĕ·nē·əl\ adj. Year after year, not dying yearly.

per·me·ate\ˈpər·mē ˈāt\ v. To seep, spread, or diffuse through thoroughly.

per·pen·dic·u·lar\ˈpər·pən ˈdĭk·yə·lər\ adj. Straight up and down.

per·plex\pər ˈplĕks\ v. To puzzle, confuse.

per·sist\pər ˈsĭst\ v. To continue despite causes for stopping.

per·son·age\ˈpər·sə·nəj\ n. An important personality.

per·son·i·fy\pər ˈsə·nĭ ˈfai\ v., -ies, -ied. To typify or represent by a particular person.

per·son·nel\ˈpər·sə ˈnĕl\ n. The sum total of persons employed by a company or engaged in an enterprise.

per·ti·nent\ˈpər·tĭ·nənt\ adj. Relevant, having a connection.

per·tur·ba·tion\ˈpərt·ər ˈbā·shən\ n. Confusion, disturbance of the mind.

per·vade\pər ˈvād\ v. To become diffused through every part.

per·vert\ˈpər ˈvərt\ v. To turn from the normal, usual, or true.

pe·ti·tion\pə ˈtĭ·shən\ n. Prayer, what is asked or sought for.

pet·ri·fy\ˈpĕt·rĭ ˈfai\ v., -ies, -ied. To turn (usually

ă b*a*d, ā b*a*ke, a f*a*ther, ĕ s*e*ll, ē *e*qual, ai m*i*le, ĭ s*i*t, ŏ c*o*t, ō n*o*te, ɔ l*a*w, ū b*oo*m, ʊ w*oo*d, yū *you*, yʊ f*u*ry, aʊ c*o*w, ɔi b*o*y. The schwa is used for both stressed and unstressed sounds: ə m*u*d, w*o*rd, ev*e*n; ch *cha*se, it*ch*; sh *sh*ell, wi*sh*; th pa*th*, *th*in; th *th*e, ei*th*er; ŋ wi*ng*; w *w*et, *wh*eat; zh plea*s*ure.

from wood or other vegetable matter) to stone.

pet·tish\\ˈpĕ·tĭsh\\ adj. Mildly contradictory and fretful.

pet·ty\\ˈpĕ·tē\\ adj. Attaching undue significance to very minor matters.

pet·u·lant\\ˈpĕ·chə·lənt\\ adj. Fretful; inclined to cry, whimper, or protest.

phe·nom·e·non\\fə ˈnŏ·mə·nŏn\\ n., pl. -a. A set of circumstances, a happening.

phil·an·throp·ic\\ˈfĭl·ən ˈthrŏp·ĭk\\ adj. Deeds that reflect love of mankind, benevolent.

phos·pho·res·cence\\ˈfŏs·fə ˈrĕ·səns\\ n. Glowing light, often luminous light without heat, light without heat that comes from forms of marine life.

pick·et\\ˈpĭ·kət\\ n. A guard or sentinel stationed far outside a main base or encampment. (Also v. To attach an animal to a stake with a rope or chain.)

pine\\pain\\ v. To regret in futile sorrow and helplessness.

pi·ous\\ˈpai·əs\\ adj. Showing religious devoutness.

pi·rat·i·cal\\pə ˈră·tĭ·kəl\\ adj. Of or pertaining to pirates.

pit·e·ous\\ˈpĭ·tē·əs\\ adj. Arousing pity. (Adv. -ly)

piv·ot\\ˈpĭ·vət\\ v. To turn the body or head without moving the feet.

plac·id\\ˈplă·sĭd\\ adj. Entirely calm and peaceful, at peace and free from concern.

pla·gia·rism\\ˈplă·jĭ·ə ˈrĭz·əm\\ n. Copying or imitating the language, ideas, and thoughts of another author and passing off the same as one's original work.

plain·tive\\ˈplān·tĭv\\ adj. Sad, mournful, lamenting, marked by sad complaint.

plait\\plat\\ v. To interweave.

plat·i·tude\\ˈplăt·ə ˈtūd\\ n. A flat, dull, or commonplace remark.

plau·si·ble\\ˈplɔ·zĭ·bəl\\ adj. Readily believable, without cause for disbelief. (Adv. -ly)

pla·za\\ˈplă·zə\\ n. A central open square (particularly in an Italian, Spanish, or Latin American town).

pleas·ant·ry\\ˈplĕ·zən·trē\\ n., pl. ies. An amiable or good-natured conversational touch, an unimportant conversational bit intended to be pleasing.

plumb\\pləm\\ n. A vertical position.

plu·ral·i·ty\\plu ˈră·lĭ·tē\\ n., pl. -ies. Manifold nature, multiplicity, great number.

plush\\pləsh\\ n. A fabric like velvet.

poach·er\\ˈpō·chər\\ n. A trespasser who hunts or traps in areas forbidden to him.

poi·gnant\\ˈpɔin·yənt\\ adj. Marked by keen feeling, especially by sadness or pity.

pom·mel\\ˈpəm·əl\\ v. To beat.

pon·der·ous\\ˈpŏn·də·rəs\\ adj. Large, heavy, and awkward.

pon·iard\\ˈpŏn·yərd\\ n. A dagger.

por·tend\\ˈpŏr ˈtĕnd\\ v. To indicate for the future.

por·tent\\ˈpŏr·tĕnt\\ n. A sign or omen of evil to come, the feeling brought about by a threatening sign.

port·fo·lio\\ˈpŏrt ˈfō·lē·ō\\ n. A case or folder for carrying drawings, paintings, or papers.

port·ly\\ˈpŏrt·lē\\ adj. Stout.

por·tray·al\\pər ˈtrā·əl\\ n. A depiction, picturing, description.

pos·sessed\\pə ˈzĕst\\ adj. Obsessed, dominated.

post·hu·mous\\ˈpŏs·chu·məs\\ adj. After one's death.

pos·ture\\ˈpŏs·chər\\ n. Bodily pose or set.

po·ten·cy\\ˈpō·tən·sē\\ n., pl. -ies. Force, effectiveness.

po·ten·ti·al·i·ty\\pə ˈtĕn·chē ˈă·lĭ·tē\\ n., pl. -ies. Possibility, ability to occur.

poul·tice\\ˈpōl·tĭs\\ n. A soft dressing or similar mass applied to a sore or injury.

pre·car·i·ous\\prē ˈkă·rē·əs\\ adj. Dangerous, risky, insecure, likely to lead to a fall or other injury.

pre·cau·tion\\ˈprē ˈkɔ·shən\\ n. An advance safety measure, a cautious measure taken in advance.

pre·ced·ence\\prĭ ˈsē·dəns\\ n. The right to come before in rank or order.

pre·cept\\prē ˈsĕpt\\ n. A command or principle intended as a general rule of behavior.

pre·cinct\\prē ˈsĭŋkt\\ n. Area, space enclosed or included.

pre·cip·i·tate\\prē ˈsĭ·pĭ ˈtāt\\ v. To separate and fall or sink out.

pre·cip·i·tous\\prē ˈsĭ·pĭ·təs\\ adj. Most steep and sheer.

pre·ci·sion\\prē ˈsĭ·zhən\\ n. Exact careful and methodical motion.

pred·a·to·ry\\ˈprĕ·də ˈtō·rē\\ adj. Preying on others, living by killing others.

pre·dic·a·ment\\prē ˈdĭ·kə·mənt\\ n. Difficult or dangerous situation, plight.

pre·dom·i·nate\\prē ˈdŏm·ə·nāt\\ v. To stand out.

prej·u·dice\\ˈprĕ·jə·dĭs\\ n. Unreasonable disliking, liking not based on facts.

prem·is·es\\ˈprĕ·mĭ·səs\\ n. *plural.* A property, especially a house, its adhering buildings, and its land.

pre·oc·cu·pied\\prē ˈŏk·yu ˈpaid\\ adj. Abstracted, intent on only one thing so that others are not noticed.

pre·pos·ter·ous\\prē ˈpŏs·tə·rəs\\ adj. Absurd, ridiculous.

pre·sage\\prə ˈsaj\\ v. To foretell, predict.

pre·ten·sion\\prē ˈtĕn·shən\\ n. A vain or showy pretending at being more than one is.

pre·ter·na·tu·ral\\ˈprē·tər ˈnăch·ə·rəl\\ adj. Beyond what is natural. (Adv. -ly)

pre·text\\prē ˈtĕkst\\ n. A fictitious or made-up reason.

prev·a·lence\\ˈprĕ·və·ləns\\ n. Commonness, frequency.

prim\\prĭm\\ adj. Neat, quiet, and polite.

pri·mal\\ˈprai·məl\\ adj. Going back to the original or primitive, showing primitive simplicity.

pri·me·val\\prai ˈmē·vəl\\ adj. Most primitive, earliest and quite without invention or culture.

pro·ba·tion\\prō ˈbā·shən\\ n. A testing period before fully joining or becoming a member.

probe\\prōb\\ v. To examine deeply and carefully.

pro·claim\\prō ˈklām\\ v. To announce openly and publicly.

pro·cliv·i·ty\\prə ˈklĭ·vĭ·tē\\ n., pl. -ies. Mental or tempermental liking or inclination.

pro·di·gious\\prə ˈdĭ·jəs\\ adj. Of the nature of a prodigy, uncommonly great, huge and remarkable.

pro·fane\\prō ˈfān\\ v. To desecrate, treat with disrespect what should be regarded as sacred.

pro·fess\\prə ˈfĕs\\ v. To declare by words or conduct (often without full honesty).

pro·jec·tile\\prə ˈjĕk·tĭl\\ n. An object (especially a weapon) that is shot or hurled.

pro·lon·ga·tion\'prō 'lŏŋ ᐧgä·shən\ n. Something that lengthens.

pro·pel·lant\prə ᐧpĕ·lənt\ n. Fuel used in high-speed aircraft.

pros·trate\ᐧprŏs·trāt\ adj. Prone on the ground as a defenseless support; powerless, weak, and unable to assert independence.

prosy\ᐧprō·zē\ adj. Dull, commonplace, trite, and unimaginative.

pro·trude\prə ᐧtrūd\ v. To stick or jut up or out.

prov·en·der\ᐧprŏ·vən·dər\ n. Food (often for animals), supplies.

pro·vi·sion·al\prə ᐧvĭ·zhə·nəl\ adj. By way of temporary decision or for temporary expediency. (Adv. -ly)

pro·voc·a·tive\prə ᐧvŏ·kə·tĭv\ adj. Stimulating, arousing new thoughts and discussions.

prow·ess\ᐧprau·ĭs\ n. Valor, bravery, daring, and skill.

prox·im·i·ty\prŏk ᐧsĭ·mĭ·tē\ n. Nearness, closeness, adjacency.

pru·dent\ᐧprū·dənt\ adj. Wise, showing forethought and care.

psy·chi·a·trist\'sai ᐧkai·ə·trĭst\ n. A doctor who treats mental patients.

psy·chol·o·gy\sai 'kŏl·ə·jē\ n. 1. The science of mind and behavior. 2. The mental behavior and characteristics of an individual or group.

pug·nac·i·ty\pəg ᐧnă·sĭ·tē\ n. Aggressiveness, quarrelsomeness, tendency to fight.

puis·sant\ᐧpwĭ·sənt\ adj. Powerful.

pul·sa·tion\pəl ᐧsā·shən\ n. Regular throbbing, like the beating of a heart.

pul·ver·ize\ᐧpəl·və 'raiz\ v. To reduce to dust, demolish as by grinding or breaking.

pun·gent\ᐧpən·jənt\ adj. Showing a sharp stinging or biting taste or smell.

pur·ga·to·ry\ᐧpər·gə 'tŏ·rē\ n., pl. -ies. A division of the afterlife in which souls are purged of their sins before rising to heaven.

pyre\pair\ n. Fire; often, a funeral or cremation fire.

quartz\kwartz\ n. A mineral commonly found in crystals or crystalline masses.

quer·u·lous\ᐧkwĕr·yə·ləs\ adj. Fretful, whining, always complaining. (Adv. -ly)

quin·tes·sence\kwĭn ᐧtĕ·səns\ n. Completely pure essence, most genuine nature.

quip\kwĭp\ n. Jest, witticism.

quiz·zi·cal\ᐧkwĭ·zĭ·kəl\ adj. Questioning, uncertain, speculative.

rai·ment\ᐧrā·mənt\ n. Clothing, garment.

ram·i·fi·ca·tion\'răm·ə·fə ᐧkā·shən\ n. A branching out, outgrowth.

ram·part\ᐧrăm·pərt\ n. A defensive wall, an outer fortification, an embankment or parapet likely to be attacked.

ram·shack·le\ᐧrăm 'shă·kəl\ adj. Most carelessly and haphazardly made and ready to collapse.

ran·cor or **ran·cour**\ᐧrăŋ·kər\ n. Ill will, malice, bitterness.

ran·kle\ᐧrăŋ·kəl\ v. 1. To irritate, vex, serve as a cause of soreness. 2. To feel bitter, show irritation or anger.

rasp\răsp\ v. To grate or scrape with or as with a file.

rau·cous\ᐧrɔ·kəs\ adj. Rough, harsh, and crude.

rav·age\ᐧră·vəj\ v. To lay waste to, destroy and ruin.

re·cep·ta·cle\rə ᐧsĕp·tə·kəl\ n. A container, vessel.

re·cip·ro·cal\rə ᐧsĭp·rə·kəl\ adj. Working or acting with equal motion and return.

re·coil\rē ᐧkɔil\ v. To pull or spring back.

re·con·noi·ter\'rĕ·kə ᐧnɔi·tər\ v. To scout, venture out or forward and observe.

rec·ti·fy\ᐧrĕk·tĭ·fai\ v., -ies, -ied. To remedy, correct.

rec·ti·tude\ᐧrĕk·tə·tūd\ n. Moral integrity, correctness of judgment or procedure, righteousness.

re·doubt·able\rə ᐧdau·tə·bəl\ adj. Formidable and dangerous to oppose.

re·dress\rē ᐧdrĕs\ n. Remedy, correction, compensation. (Also v. To remedy, compensate.)

re·flex\ᐧrē·flĕks\ n. Reaction to a stimulus accomplished without thought or analysis.

re·fute\rĭ·fyūt\ v. To overthrow by argument, evidence, or proof; show to be false or wrong.

re·it·er·ate\'rē ᐧĭ·tə 'rāt\ v. To repeat (often emphatically).

rel·e·vant\ᐧrĕ·lə·vənt\ adj. Suitable, related, appropriate.

rel·ish\ᐧrĕ·lĭsh\ n. Pleasure and appreciation, especially in eating.

re·luc·tant\rē ᐧlək·tənt\ adj. Showing unwillingness or aversion. (Adv. -ly)

re·mon·strate\rē ᐧmŏn·strāt\ v. To argue against with reasoning and pleading.

re·morse·ful\rē ᐧmŏrs·fəl\ adj. Showing genuine regret and contriteness.

rend\rĕnd\ v. to tear, tear apart.

re·nun·ci·a·tion\rē 'nən·sē ᐧā·shən\ n. Denial; especially, self-denial.

re·pel·lent\rə ᐧpĕ·lənt\ adj. Repulsive, loathsome.

re·plen·ish\rē ᐧplĕ·nĭsh\ v. To resupply, stock up.

re·ple·tion\rə ᐧplē·shən\ n. Complete fullness and entire satisfaction of all desire to eat.

re·pose\rē ᐧpōz\ n. Rest, inactivity.

re·prieve\rē ᐧprēv\ n. A delay in punishment; specifically, a postponement of a death sentence.

rep·ri·mand\ᐧrĕp·rĭ·mănd\ v. To scold, rebuke.

re·proach·ful\rē ᐧprōch·fəl\ adj. Expressing reproach or hurt rebuke to another.

re·pu·di·ate\rĭ ᐧpyūd·ē 'āt\ v. To refuse to have anything to do with, refuse to accept, reject as untrue or unjust.

re·pug·nant\rĭ ᐧpəg·nənt\ adj. Exciting distaste, strong dislike, or antagonism.

ă b*a*d, ā b*a*ke, a f*a*ther, ě s*e*ll, ē *e*qual, ai m*i*le, ĭ s*i*t, ŏ c*o*t, ō n*o*te, ɔ l*a*w, ū b*oo*m, ʊ w*oo*d, yū *you*, yʊ f*u*ry, au c*ow*, ɔi b*oy*. The schwa is used for both stressed and unstressed sounds: ə m*u*d, w*o*rd, ev*e*n; ch ch*a*se, *i*tch; sh sh*e*ll, w*i*sh; th p*a*th, th*i*n; th *the*, ei*the*r; ŋ wi*ng*; w w*e*t, *wh*eat; zh plea*s*ure.

re·pul·sion\rə ˈpəl·shən\ n. Aversion, repugnance.

re·pute\rē ˈpyūt\ v. To consider or think of as.

re·sent·ment\rə ˈzĕnt·mənt\ n. A feeling of irritated displeasure and bitterness as for some injury or slight.

res·i·due\ˈrĕz·ĭ ˈdū\ n. Remainder, substance falling from or filtered from a solution.

res·ig·na·tion\ˈrĕ·zĭg ˈnā·shən\ n. Inclination to accept fate without protest, struggle, or regret.

re·signed\rē ˈzaind\ adj. Without emotion and with acceptance as of something inevitable.

re·sil·ient\rə ˈzĭl·yənt\ adj. Springy.

re·sound·ing\rə ˈzaund·ĭŋ\ adj. Seemingly of major importance and promising much.

re·spec·tive\rē ˈspĕk·tĭv\ adj. Different, individual, each for each.

res·pite\ˈrĕs·pət\ n. A temporary interval of rest or relief.

res·tive\ˈrĕ·stĭv\ adj. Moving uneasily, fidgety.

retch\rĕch\ v. To gag, vomit.

ret·i·cent\ˈrĕt·ə·sənt\ adj. Inclined to be silent or secretive, uncommunicative.

re·trieve\rē ˈtrēv\ v. To find and bring back again, restore.

re·tro·spec·tion\ˈrē·trə ˈspĕk·shən\ n. Recollection, remembrance.

rev·eil·le\ˈrĕ·və ˈlĭ\ n. A bugle call to wake up and get up.

rev·el\ˈrĕ·vəl\ v. To exult, take great joy.

rev·e·la·tion\ˈrĕ·və ˈlā·shən\ n. Some enlightening or revealing fact.

re·ver·ber·ate\rē ˈvər·bə ˈrāt\ v. To reecho, resound back and forth.

rhet·o·ric\ˈrĕ·tə·rĭk\ n. The study of the principles of effective composition.

rhyth·mic\ˈrĭth·mĭk\ adj. Showing rhythm, graceful regularity, and coordination of motion.

ric·o·chet\ˈrĭ·kə ˈshā\ v. To rebound from surface to surface.

rift\rĭft\ n. A clear space between clouds.

ri·gid·i·ty\rĭ ˈjĭ·dĭ·tē\ n. Stiffness, unbendingness.

rig·or·ous\ˈrĭ·gə·rəs\ adj. Strict and demanding.

rite\rait\ n. A ritual or ceremony, a form prescribed by etiquette.

rit·u·al\ˈrĭ·chəl\ n. An act customarily performed through or as though through religious reasons.

rive\raiv\ v. To split, rend.

ro·bot\ˈrō·bət\ n. A mechanical man, an automaton.

ro·bust\ˈrō ˈbəst\ adj. Strong, sturdy, and healthy. (Also n. -ness)

ro·manc·er\rō ˈmăn·sər\ n. One who daydreams and makes up stories.

ro·se·ate\ˈrō·zē·ət\ adj. Like or suggestive of roses.

rote\rōt\ n. Memory; especially, memory not accompanied by thoughts or evaluations.

rout\raut\ n. A group or crowd; especially, a mixed, disorderly, noisy crowd.

rub·ble\ˈrə·bəl\ n. Broken rock and stone, a fragment of broken stone.

rue·ful\ˈrū·fəl\ adj. Sorrowful, sad. (Adv. -ly)

ru·mi·nate\ˈrū·mĭ ˈnāt\ v. To think over slowly and repeatedly.

run·nel\ˈrə·nəl\ n. A brook, small stream.

rup·ture\ˈrəp·chər\ n. A break, split.

rus·tic\ˈrəs·tĭk\ adj. Rural, countrified.

ruth·less\ˈrūth·ləs\ adj. Merciless.

sac\săk\ n. A pouch; often, the pouch containing the poison of a poisonous snake.

sa·gac·i·ty\sə ˈgă·sĭ·tē\ n. Wisdom, shrewdness.

sa·lient\ˈsā·lyĕnt\ adj. Conspicuous.

sa·line\ˈsā ˈlĭn\ adj. Salt, salty.

sal·low\ˈsă·lō\ adj. Unwholesomely colorless and pale, gray.

sal·vage\ˈsăl·vəj\ n. The action of saving anything of value from a wrecked or disabled ship.

sanc·ti·fy\ˈsăŋk·tĭ ˈfai\ v., -ies, -ied. To bless, hallow.

sanc·tu·ary\ˈsăŋ·chu ˈā·rē\ n., pl. -ies. A place of refuge in which one may be secure, a place of known certain safety.

sar·don·ic\sar ˈdan·ĭk\ adj. Bitter, mocking.

sa·ti·e·ty\sə ˈtai·ə·tē\ n. A feeling of overfullness from eating too much.

sat·u·rate\ˈsă·chə ˈrāt\ v. To soak, wet completely.

saun·ter\ˈson·tər\ v. To stroll along slowly and unconcernedly.

sa·vor\ˈsā·vər\ n. Taste; especially, a distinctive taste to be relished.

scape·grace\ˈskāp ˈgrās\ n. Rascal, imp.

scin·til·late\ˈsĭnt·əl ˈāt\ v. To sparkle, throw off quick flashes like sparks.

score\skōr\ v. To dig, grave, cut.

scourge\skərj or skōrj\ v. To whip severely as in punishment, compel as by whipping.

scrab·ble\ˈskră·bəl\ v. To crawl as rapidly as possible.

scru·pu·lous\ˈskrū·pyə·ləs\ adj. Strictly honest, upright, and careful. (Adv. -ly)

scru·ti·nize\ˈskrū·tĭ ˈnaiz\ v. To examine closely, minutely, and searchingly.

scut·tle\ˈskə·təl\ v. 1. To sink by opening holes in the hull. 2. To run rapidly but awkwardly, run hastily. 3. To run or scurry, as a small animal or as a crab.

se·date\sə ˈdāt\ adj. Marked by slow, serious, or sober dignity. (Adv. -ly)

sed·u·lous\ˈsĕ·jə·ləs\ adj. Constantly showing painstaking care and industry. (Adv. -ly)

sem·blance\ˈsĕm·bləns\ n. Resemblance, appearance.

sen·a·to·ri·al\ˈsĕ·nə ˈtō·rē·əl\ adj. Pertaining to or intended for a senator.

se·nil·i·ty\sə ˈnĭ·lĭ·tē\ n. Weakened old age without good control of mind or body.

sen·su·ous\ˈsĕn·shu·əs\ adj. Having a pleasing appeal to the senses.

sen·ti·men·tal·i·ty\ˈsĕn·tĭ ˈmĕn ˈtă·lĭ·tē\ n. Artificially played-up feeling, emotion for emotion's sake.

se·quence\ˈsē·kwĕns\ n. Succession in order.

se·quin\ˈsē·kwĭn\ n. A colorful thin metal plate used as a dress adornment.

ser·e·nade\ˈsĕ·rə ˈnād\ n. A musical compliment to a woman (usually to be performed outdoors at night).

ser·vile\ˈsər·vĭl\ adj. Menial, befitting a slave or servant of the lowest sort. (Adv. -ly)

set·tee\sĕ ˈtē\ n. A straight seat with a back for two or three persons.

sev·er\ˈsĕ·vər\ v. To cut.

shack·le\ˈshă·kəl\ n. Chain.

sheen\shēn\ n. Gleam, colorful reflection.

shy\shai\ v., -ies, -ied. To rear back, retreat abruptly.

si·dle\ˈsai·dəl\ v. To proceed sideways.

sim·i·le\ˈsĭ·mĭ 'lē\ n. Comparison; technically, a comparison worded with *like* or *as*.

sin·ewy\ˈsĭn·yu·wē\ adj. Wiry and strong.

sin·is·ter\ˈsĭ·nĭs·tər\ adj. Ominous; threatening, promising, or suggesting extreme evil.

sire\sair\ n. Father.

slan·der\ˈslan·dər\ n. A malicious, false, defamatory statement.

slat·tern·ly\ˈslă·tərn·lē\ adj. Quite untidy and careless about one's appearance, dirty and disorderly.

sod·den\ˈsŏ·dən\ adj. Rain-soaked.

so·journ\ˈsō·jərn\ n. Stay.

so·lace\ˈsō·ləs\ n. Consolation and comfort, comfort and soothing of embarrassment or grief.

sole\sōl\ adj. Solitary, alone.

so·lic·i·tude\sə ˈlĭ·sĭ·tūd\ n. Anxious care and concern.

sol·i·tude\ˈsŏ·lĭ 'tūd\ n. Condition of being alone without necessarily being lonesome.

som·ber\ˈsŏm·bər\ adj. Dark, colorless, and gloomy; dark, gloomy, and reproachful.

som·bre·ro\səm ˈbrĕ·rō\ n. A large straw hat with a wide curving brim (worn in Mexico).

som·nam·bu·list\səm ˈnăm·byu·lĭst\ n. A person who walks in his sleep.

som·no·lence\ˈsŏm·nə·ləns\ n. Sleepiness, lethargy.

son·ics\ˈsŏ·nĭks\ n. The study or the manipulation of sounds.

sooth\sūth\ n. *archaic.* Truth.

soph·o·mor·ic\ˈsof·ə ˈmor·ĭk\ adj. Suggestive of the traditional sophomore, as in intellectual pretensions and self-assurance.

spare\spăr\ adj. Thin, lanky.

spas·mod·ic\ˈspăz ˈmŏ·dĭk\ adj. Marked by spasms, by uneven convulsive fits. (Adv. -ally)

spe·cif·ic\spə ˈsĭ·fĭk\ adj. Definite; not vague, general, or uncertain.

spec·ter\ˈspĕk·tər\ n. A grim supernatural repulsive or deathly figure.

spec·trum\ˈspĕk·trəm\ n. A range of all the colors in order, the orderly arrangement of colors.

spec·u·late\ˈspĕk·yu 'lāt\ v. To guess, conjecture.

spec·u·la·tion\ˈspĕk·yu ˈlā·shən\ n. A surmise, guess.

spi·ral\ˈspai·rəl\ v. To go up or down in a twisting course.

spoor\spūr *or* spōr\ n. The track of an animal.

squal·id\ˈskwa·lĭd\ adj. Very dirty, mean, and sordid.

squan·der\ˈskwan·dər\ v. To waste, dissipate, throw away.

squea·mish\ˈskwē·mĭsh\ adj. Particular and fussy, given to nice objections and scruples.

stag·nant\ˈstăg·nənt\ adj. Motionless and fostering decay or rot.

staid\stād\ adj. Sober, quiet, and dignified.

stalk\stɔk\ v. To stride angrily.

stal·wart\ˈstɔl·wərt\ adj. Strong and robust.

stam·i·na\ˈstă·mĭ·nə\ n. Strength, energy, vitality.

stanch\stɔnch *or* stanch\ v. To stop or abate the flow of.

stan·chion\stăn·shən\ n. An upright pole, post, or support.

state·ly\ˈstāt·lē\ adj. Orderly, dignified, and impressive.

stat·u·ary\ˈstă·chu·wĕ·rē\ n. Statues (collectively).

stave\stāv\ v. Repel, fend off.

stealth\stĕlth\ n. Cautious, quiet, fearful conduct like a thief's.

steep\stēp\ v. To saturate in, instill with.

stew·ard\ˈstū·ərd\ n. An officer in charge of meals and food supplies on a ship.

sti·fle\ˈstai·fəl\ v. To suffocate, deprive of, or cut the supply of breathable air.

sti·let·to\stĭ ˈlĕ·tō\ n. A short dagger.

stole\stōl\ n. A fur (or cloth) neck or shoulder piece.

stol·id\ˈstŏ·lĭd\ adj. Expressionless and unemotional.

stra·te·gic\strə ˈtē·jĭk\ adj. Affording best use of resources and forces in combat or war.

stra·tum\ˈstrā·təm\ n., pl. -a. Layer.

stretch·er\ˈstrĕ·chər\ n. A device on which an artist's canvas can be stretched.

stu·pe·fy\ˈstū·pə 'fai\ v., -ies, -ied. To cause to lose one's senses or one's ability to think or perceive cleary; shock or stun so that talk and thought are impossible.

stu·por\ˈstū·pər\ n. 1. Loss of one's senses and feeling, daze. 2. Deep unconsciousness, as from drugs or injury.

suave\swav\ adj. Smooth, urbane, and unruffled.

sub·ju·ga·tion\ˈsəb·jə ˈgā·shən\ n. A state of affairs in which one is controlled or dominated by another.

sub·junc·tive\səb ˈjən·tĭv\ n. A verb form used to express uncertainty or condition contrary to fact.

sub·lime\ˈsə ˈblaim\ adj. Wonderful, lofty, and exalted.

sub·side\səb ˈsaid\ v. To recede, diminish, grow less.

sub·sist\səb ˈsĭst\ v. To exist, continue to live.

sub·stan·ti·ate\səb ˈstăn·chē·āt\ v. To verify, confirm.

sub·ter·fuge\ˈsəb·tər·fyūj\ n. A deception by a stratagem or ruse.

sub·ter·ra·nean\ˈsəb·tə ˈrā·nē·ən\ adj. Underground.

suc·ces·sive\sək ˈsĕ·sĭv\ adj. Succeeding or following in order or sequence.

suc·cor\ˈsə·kər\ n. Aid or assistance from another.

suc·cumb\sə ˈkəm\ v. To give way, yield.

suf·fer·ance\ˈsə·fə·rəns\ n. Suffering.

suf·fice\sə ˈfais\ v. To be enough or adequate.

suf·fo·cate\ˈsə·fə 'kāt\ v. To stifle, die from lack of air.

sul·len\ˈsə·lən\ adj. Quiet, grim, gloomy, and lonesome.

su·perb\sū ˈpərb\ adj. Wonderful, excellent.

ă b*a*d, ā b*a*ke, a f*a*ther, ĕ s*e*ll, ē *e*qual, ai m*i*le, ĭ s*i*t, ŏ c*o*t, ō n*o*te, ɔ l*aw*, ū b*oo*m, ʊ w*oo*d, yū *you*, yʊ f*u*ry, aʊ c*ow*, ɔi b*oy*. The schwa is used for both stressed and unstressed sounds: ə m*u*d, w*o*rd, *e*ven; ch *ch*ase, it*ch*; sh *sh*ell, wi*sh*; th p*a*th, *th*in; th *th*e, ei*th*er; ŋ wi*ng*; w *w*et, *wh*eat; zh plea*s*ure.

su·per·cil·ious\'sū·pər ▲sĭ·lē·əs\ adj. Proud, haughty, and aloof.

su·per·fi·cial\'sū·pər ▲fĭ·shəl\ adj. On the surface, not deep or dangerous.

sup·plant\sə ▲plănt\ v. To take the place of.

sup·pli·ant\'sə·plē·ənt\ adj. In a begging or beseeching manner.

sup·po·si·tion\'sə·pə ▲zĭ·shən\ n. That which is supposed, idea, notion.

sur·plus\'sər·pləs\ adj. Extra, additional.

ser·rep·ti·tious\sə·rəp ▲tĭ·shəs\ adj. Secret, covert, stealthy, and quick; so as not to be noticed.

sur·veil·lance\sər ▲vā·ləns\ n. Vigilant watch; observation to prevent danger, crime, or escape.

sus·tain\sə ▲stān\ v. To maintain, keep on, support.

sus·te·nance\'səs·tə·nəns\ n. Food, nourishment necessary to life, provision, material to eat.

swad·dle\'swa·dəl\ v. To cover over as with a protective blanket of cloth.

swank\swănk\ adj. Luxurious and upper-class, showing prestige values.

swarthy\'swar·thē\ adj. Dark complexioned.

swath\swath or swoth\ n. A row like that made by a mower in long grass.

sym·bol·ic\sĭm ▲bŏ·lĭk\ adj. Imaginary, figurative.

sym·bol·ize\'sĭm·bə 'līz\ v. To typify, express.

syn·chro·nize\'sĭn·krə 'nīz\ v. To time so as to occur exactly when something else does.

syn·op·sis\sə ▲nŏp·sĭs\ n., pl. -es. Résumé, shortened version.

tac·it\'tă·sĭt\ adj. Unstated and undeclared, but accepted and understood.

tac·i·tur·ni·ty\'tăs·ə·tər·nət·ē\ n. State of being disinclined to talk, be silent.

tack\tăk\ v. To proceed in a diagonal course.

tan·gen·tial\tăn ▲jĕn·chəl\ adj. Following a tangent, a diverging curving or diagonal course. (Adv. -ly)

tan·gi·ble\'tăŋ·jĭ·bəl\ adj. Readily perceptible by the senses, especially, easily touched or felt. (Adv. -ly)

tan·trum\'tăn·trəm\ n. A childish display of wild ungoverned temper.

ta·per\'ta·pər\ n. Candle.

tar·ry\'tă·rē\ v. To delay, linger.

taut\tot\ adj. Tight, with the skin stretched close.

tech·no·log·i·cal\'tĕk·nə ▲lŏ·jĭ·kəl\ adj. Pertaining to applied technical knowledge.

teem\tēm\ v. To be full, replete, packed.

tele·path·ic\'tĕ·lə ▲pă·thĭk\ adj. Of or pertaining to communication without visible or other explicable procedures.

tele·vise\'tĕ·lə 'vaiz\ v. To communicate with by a telephone with an additional visual feature.

tem·per·a·men·tal\'tĕm·pə·rə ▲mĕn·təl\ adj. 1. Pertaining to disposition, attitude, or personality. 2. Showing individual temperament, such as whims, odd desires, or fickle changes of mind. (Adv. -ly)

tem·per·ate\'tĕm·pə·rət\ adj. Showing no excesses.

ten·dril\'tĕn·drĭl\ n. A slender and sensitive shoot or leaf growing out from a plant.

te·net\'tĕ·nət\ n. Belief, idea, ideal.

ten·or\'tĕ·nər\ n. Gist, meaning, significance.

ten·sion\'tĕn·shən\ n. Nervous strain and anxiety, an inner feeling of nervous discomfort.

ten·ta·cle\'tĕn·tə·kəl\ n. A long flexible member like the arm of an octopus.

ten·ta·tive\'tĕn·tə·tĭv\ adj. 1. Doubtfully slow and experimental. 2. Hesitant and uncertain. (Adv. -ly)

ten·u·ous\'tĕn·yu·əs\ adj. 1. Very thin, easily interrupted or broken. 2. Thin and airy, not concentrated or firm.

tep·id\'tĕ·pĭd\ adj. Lukewarm.

ter·res·tri·al\tə ▲rĕs·trē·əl\ adj. Earthly, of the earth in contrast to planets and stars.

terse\tərs\ adj. Brief, expressed without wasting words.

teth·er\'tĕth·ər\ v. To restrain or bind an animal with or as with a halter, rope, or chain.

texture\'tĕks·chər\ n. Composition of woven cloth.

the·o·rem\'thē·ə·rəm\ n. A mathematical formula or proposition.

the·o·ret·i·cal\'thē·ə ▲rĕ·tĭ·kəl\ adj. Based on more or less abstract and detached thought rather than on realities.

thew\thū\ n. Muscle, sinew.

thread·bare\'thrĕd 'bār\ adj. Shabby and practically worn out.

thresh·old\'thrĕ·shəld\ n. Door sill.

throt·tle\'thrŏ·təl\ v. To choke.

ti·ara\tē ▲a·rə\ n. A jeweled band across the forehead.

tim·o·rous\'tĭ·mə·rəs\ adj. Shy, diffident, and afraid. (Also n. -ness)

to·ga\'tō·gə\ n. The Roman citizen's loose gownlike outer garment.

tol·er·a·bly\'tŏ·lə·rə·blē\ adv. Rather, generally, more-or-less, reasonably.

tol·er·ance\'tŏ·lə·rəns\ n. Kindly acceptance of another, despite his faults or despite one's differences with him.

tor·e·ador\'tŏ·rē·ə 'dŏr\ n. A bullfighter.

tor·pid\'tŏr·pĭd\ adj. Sluggish, inactive, lethargic.

tor·por\'tŏr·pər\ n. Sleepy or lethargic inactivity.

tor·so\'tŏr·sō\ n. Trunk, body.

tor·tu·ous\'tŏr·chu·əs\ adj. Winding, twisting.

tran·quil\'trăn·kwĭl\ adj. Entirely peaceful and unworried; calm, peaceful, and quiet. (Adv. -ly)

trans·ac·tion\'trăns ▲ăk·shən\ n. Sale, purchase.

tran·scen·dent\'trăn ▲sĕn·dənt\ adj. Superlative, surpassing anything comparable.

trans·fig·ure\'trăns ▲fĭg·yər\ v. To beautify and illuminate, as by a god's action.

tran·sient\'trăn·shənt\ adj. Temporary, short-lived, not permanent or lasting.

tran·si·to·ry\'trăn(t)s·ə ▲tŏr·ē\ adj. Of brief duration, temporary.

trans·par·en·cy\'trăns ▲pā·rən·sē\ n. The quality of permitting seeing through.

trans·port\'trăns 'pŏrt\ n. Extreme joy.

tra·vail\'trə 'vāl\ n. Labor performed with some difficulty and struggle.

trav·el·ogue\'tră·və 'lŏg\ n. A movie showing travels in a strange land.

tra·verse\trə ▲vərs\ n. A gap or passage affording a safe crossing.

trem·or\'trĕ·mər\ n. A quiver, tremble, or shiver.

trem·u·lous\▲trĕm·yʊ·ləs\ adj. Fluttering in an erratic course like that of a butterfly's.
trep·i·da·tion\'trĕp·ə ▲dā·shən\ n. Tremulous alarm or agitation.
triv·i·al·i·ty\'trĭ·vē ▲ă·lĭ·tē\ n., pl. -ies. 1. Unimportance, lack of significance. 2. Something utterly unimportant or minor.
truss\trəs\ v. To tie, bind, confine.
tu·mult\▲tū·məlt\ n. Noisy confused uproar.
tur·bu·lence\▲tər·byʊ·ləns\ n. Agitated commotion, swift uneven confused motion.
tur·gid\▲tər·jĭd\ adj. Cloudy and murky.
tur·moil\▲tər 'mɔil\ n. Confused turbulent agitation.

ul·cer\▲əl·sər\ n. A festering sore.
ul·te·ri·or\əl ▲tē·rē·ər\ adj. Extending further or deeper than appears at first.
ul·ti·mate\▲əl·tĭ·mət\ adj. 1. Final, last in a series or sequence. 2. Last and most extreme.
um·ber\▲əm·bər\ n. A brownish painting pigment.
um·bil·i·cal\əm ▲bĭ·lĭ·kəl\ adj. Pertaining to the cord that binds an unborn child to its mother.
un·abashed\'ən·ə ▲băsht\ adj. Not embarrassed, confused, or checked.
un·as·sail·able\'ən·ə ▲sā·lə·bəl\ adj. Incapable of being attacked or defeated.
un·can·ny\ən ▲kă·nē\ adj. Weird or supernatural, not to be readily understood or appreciated, strange.
un·com·pre·hend·ing\ən 'kŏm·prə ▲hĕnd·ĭŋ\ adj. Not understanding. (Adv. -ly)
un·de·fin·able\ən·də ▲fai·nə·bəl\ adj. Impossible or difficult to define and analyze.
un·der·ling\▲ən·dər 'liŋ\ n. Inferior, follower, one who takes orders from another.
un·du·la·tion\'ən·də ▲lā·shən\ n. 1. A land contour giving a wavy, up-and-down effect. 2. Arrangement in waves, wavy effect.
un·en·cum·bered\'ən·ən ▲kəm·bərd\ adj. Free of hindrances, weights, and inconveniences.
uni·son\yū·nĭ·sən\ n. Concord, exact agreement in content and time, uniformity.
un·per·turbed\ən·pər ▲tərbd\ adj. Calm, not agitated or concerned.
un·prec·e·dent·ed\ən ▲prĕ·sə 'dĕnt·əd\ adj. Not having happened or been experienced before.
un·seem·ly\ən ▲sēm·lē\ adj. Improper, discourteous, ungentlemanly.
un·so·lic·it·ed\ən·sə ▲lĭ·sĭ·təd\ adj. Unsought, not actively looked for.
un·sub·stan·tial\ən·səb ▲stăn·chəl\ adj. Unreal, nonexistent.
un·time·ly\ən ▲taim·lē\ adj. Extremely unfortunate, touched too young or too soon by death or disaster.
un·wont·ed\ən ▲wɔnt·əd\ adj. Unaccustomed, unusual.
up·surg·ing\əp ▲sərj·ĭŋ\ adj. Rapidly rising.
ur·chin\▲ər·chĭn\ n. A street child, typically one noisy and dirty.
ur·gen·cy\▲ər·jən·sē\ n. An insistent force.
ur·gent\▲ər·jənt\ adj. 1. Important and demanding attention, very important and necessary to prevent failure or catastrophe. 2. Expressing a pressing appeal as though dealing with a most serious or important matter. (Adv. -ly)
ut·ter·most\▲ə·tər 'mōst\ adj. Latest, last.

vac·u·ous\▲văk·yʊ·əs\ adj. Inane, empty of sense or significance.
vag·a·bond\▲vă·gə 'bŏnd\ n. Tramp, wanderer, vagrant.
va·grant\▲vā·grənt\ adj. Homeless, wandering.
vale\vāl\ n. Valley.
val·id\▲vă·lĭd\ adj. Worthwhile, true and important.
va·lid·i·ty\və ▲lĭ·dĭ·tē\ n. Value, worth.
vari·ance\▲vă·rē·əns\ n. Opposition, dissension, disagreement.
var·ie·gat·ed\▲vă·rē·ə 'gāt·əd\ adj. Varied, interspersed with contrasting elements.
vaunt\vɔnt\ v. To brag or boast. (Also n. Brag or boast of triumph.)
ve·he·mence\▲vē·ə·məns\ n. Notable force or intensity.
ve·loc·i·ty\və ▲lŏ·sĭ·tē\ n. Speed, rapidity.
ven·er·a·ble\▲vĕn·ər·ə·bəl\ adj. Calling forth respect through age, character, and attainments; impressive by reason of age.
ven·om\▲vĕ·nəm\ n. Poison.
ver·dict\▲vər·dĭkt\ n. Statement of decision.
ver·dure\▲vər·dər\ n. The greenness of plant growth.
ver·i·ta·ble\▲vĕ·rĭ·tə·bəl\ adj. True, real, genuine. (Adv. -ly)
ver·ti·go\▲vər·tĭ 'gō\ n. Dizziness, usually accompanied by faintness.
ves·tige\▲vĕs·tĭj\ n. A trace or visible sign left by something vanished or lost, a minute remaining amount.
vest·ment\▲vĕst·mənt\ n. Garment, clothing.
vet·er·i·nary\▲vĕ·tə·rĭ 'nā·rē\ n., pl. -ies. A veterinarian, a doctor who treats the ailments of animals.
vi·brant\▲vai·brənt\ adj. Pulsating with life, vigor, or activity.
vi·brate\▲vai·brāt\ v. To swing to and fro or back and forth regularly.
vile\vail\ adj. Loathsome, mean.
vin·dic·tive\vĭn ▲dĭk·tĭv\ adj. Vengeful and savagely determined to hurt or wound.
vir·ile\▲vĕ·rĭl\ adj. Showing manly force and strength.
vir·tu·al·ly\▲vər·chə·lē\ adv. Practically.
vir·tu·ous\▲vər·chʊ·əs\ adj. With show of prim virtue and morality. (Adv. -ly)
vis·cous\▲vĭs·kəs\ adj. Thick and sticky.
vis·i·tant\▲vĭ·zĭ·tənt\ n. Visitor.
vis·ta\▲vĭs·tə\ n. View; vision, especially of large scope or pleasing nature.
vi·su·al·ize\▲vĭ·zhə 'laiz\ v. To form a mental picture of.

ă b*a*d, ā b*a*ke, a f*a*ther, ĕ s*e*ll, ē *e*qual, ai m*i*le, ĭ s*i*t, ŏ c*o*t, ō n*o*te, ɔ l*aw*, ū b*oo*m, ʊ w*oo*d, yū *you*, yʊ f*u*ry, aʊ c*ow*, ɔi b*oy*. The schwa is used for both stressed and unstressed sounds: ə m*u*d, w*o*rd, ev*e*n; ch *ch*ase, it*ch*; sh *sh*ell, wi*sh*; th pa*th*, *th*in; th *th*e, ei*th*er; ŋ wi*ng*; w *w*et, *wh*eat; zh plea*s*ure.

vi·tal·i·ty\vai ⁴tă·lĭ·tē\ n. 1. Active liveliness. 2. Stamina and vigor to endure.

vit·ri·fy\⁴vĭ·trĭ 'faі\ v., -ies, -ied. To turn to glass or a glasslike substance.

vi·va·cious\vĭ ⁴vā·shəs\ adj. Lively and spirited.

viv·id\⁴vĭ·vĭd\ adj. Bright, colorful, showing high intensity.

vo·ca·tion\vō ⁴kā·shən\ n. Calling, profession.

vol·a·tile\⁴vŏ·lə·tĭl\ adj. Readily vaporizing or changing from liquid to gas.

vol·u·ble\⁴vŏl·yu·bəl\ adj. Talkative, constantly chattering and never silent.

vo·ra·cious\və ⁴rā·shəs\ adj. Showing extreme hunger and haste and greed in eating.

vouch·safe\'vauch ⁴sāf\ v. To grant and guarantee.

vul·gar\⁴vəl·gər\ adj. Common, crude.

wad·dle\⁴wa·dəl\ n. An ungainly walk like that of a duck.

wake\wāk\ n. Literally, a trail of wave and foam after a boat or ship; loosely, a trail or track.

wan\wan\ adj. Lacking in normal expression and interest. (Adv. -ly)

wane\wān\ v. To lessen or diminish, as in size or aspect, as a waning moon; dwindle, die out.

wan·ton\⁴wan·tən\ v. To play sportively.

wary\⁴wā·rē\ adj. Cautious and very watchful for possible danger, suspicious.

wat·tle\⁴wa·təl\ n. *usually plural.* A construction employing twigs or reeds sometimes daubed with mud.

way·lay\'wā 'lā\ v., waylaid. To stop after lying in wait for.

way·ward\⁴wā·wərd\ adj. Marked by unpredictable originality or difference.

wench\wĕnch\ n. A low coarse woman or girl.

whelp\wĕlp\ v. To give birth (usually used of dogs and other animals).

where·abouts\⁴wā·rə 'bauts\ n. *plural.* Location.

whet\wĕt\ v. To incite.

wile\waіl\ n. Treacherous or hypocritical action or suggestion.

wil·ly-nil·ly\'wĭ·lē- 'nĭ·lē\ adv. Whether desired or not, regardless of a person's wishes.

wist·ful·ness\⁴wĭst·fəl·nəs\ n. Yearning desire.

wor·sted\⁴wu·stəd\ n. A heavy wool cloth.

writhe\raіth\ v. To twist or contort one's body violently as in pain or distress.

wry\raі\ adj. Sarcastic, ironic. (Adv. -ly)

yon\yŏn\ adj. Yonder.

Literary Terms Index

alliteration 282
allusion 497
anapest 256
assonance 282
atmosphere 620, 626, 635, 646, 655, 669, 672, 681, 698, 699, 728
blank verse 385
characterization 140, 150, 156, 169, 181, 188, 243
climax 28, 36, 51, 63, 65, 127
conflict 27, 36, 51, 63, 65, 127
consonance 282
dactyl 256
dialect 568
dialogue 504
diction 291
dimeter 256
end-rhyme 282
essay 9, 65
etymology 555
exposition 27, 36, 51, 63, 65, 127
feminine rhyme 256
flashback 522
foot 256
hexameter 256
humor 188
iambic foot 256
iambic pentameter 385
identification 475, 483, 489, 504, 515, 538, 569, 609
idiomatic compound 325
idiomatic expression 51
imagery 291
informal essay 9
irony 324, 344, 347, 354, 358, 370, 371, 465
lyric poetry 248, 300
masculine rhyme 256
metaphor 276, 497
metonymy 304
monometer 256
narrative 610
onomatopoeia 672
organization 324, 344, 347, 355, 358, 370, 371, 465
parable 1, 2, 130
pentameter 256
personal narrative 4
personification 303
plot 140, 150, 156, 169, 181, 188, 244
poetry 39, 65
prose 39
pyrrhic 256

rhyme 39
rhythm 255, 334
root 28, 358, 483, 504, 610
short story 27
simile 263
slang 504
spondee 256
stanza 37, 282
structure 282
style 475, 483, 489, 497, 504, 515, 538, 546, 555, 568, 569, 609
suspense 620, 626, 635, 646, 655, 669, 672, 681, 698, 699, 728
symbol 151, 181, 244, 570
synecdoche 304
tetrameter 256
theme 276, 475, 483, 489, 497, 503, 515, 538, 546, 555, 568, 569, 609
tone 290
trimeter 256
trochee 256

Literary Types Index

Dramas

Diary of Anne Frank, The, 189
Julius Caesar, 382
Suppressed Desires, 636

Essays and Personal Accounts

Project of Arriving at Moral Perfection, 348
Shooting an Elephant, 484
Stopover in Querétaro, 4

Novellas

His Enemy, His Friend, 66
Man That Corrupted Hadleyburg, The, 700
Pearl, The, 570

Parables

Parable of the Good Samaritan, The, 1

Parable of the Prodigal Son, The, 130

Poetry—Lyric

After Great Pain a Formal Feeling Comes, 281
Afternoon on a Hill, 293
Alarm Clock, The, 39
As I Grew Older, 331
Black Panther, The, 270
Boots, 469
Break, Break, Break, 289
Channing Way I, 38
Corner, 40
Country Night, 258
Daybreak in Alabama, 328
Death Is a Beautiful Car Parked Only, 254
Dirge, A, 282
Does It Matter, 272
Dream Deferred, 333
Dream Keeper, The, 329
Dream Variation, 327
Dreams, 329
Eldorado, 255
Faces, 43
Fast Run in the Junkyard, 300
For Everything There Is a Season, 247
Good Humor Man, 296
Hate, 272·
Heart, The, 276
Highway: Michigan, 253
Home Thoughts from Abroad, 286
House Fear, 259
House on the Hill, The, 284
I, Too, 330
In a Glass of Cider, 313
in Just-spring, 294
Inland, 286
Lady, The, 259
Let America Be America Again, 332
Man He Killed, The, 37
Miracles, 297
Mood, 271
Music I Heard, 279
My Lost Youth, 287
My November Guest, 278
Noise of Waters, The, 279
Oft-Repeated Dream, The, 259
Panther Possible, The, 261
Pied Beauty, 298
Poison Tree, A, 275
Precious Words, 299
Reveille, 292
Ride a Wild Horse, 252
Sea Fever, 252
Silver, 293
Smells, 298
Sonnet CVI, 299

Souvenir de Londres, 170
Spring, 251
Suicide Pond, 262
Sympathy, 250
Those Winter Sundays, 290
Travel, 251
Traveler's Curse After Misdirection, The, 271
Vagabond Song, A, 296
Velvet Shoes, 294
Warning, The, 260
Waves Against a Dog, 274
We Real Cool, 613
West Wind, The, 285
When I Have Fears That I May Cease to Be, 260
Whipping, The, 171
White House, The, 273
Widow, The, 280
Wild Blackberries, 295
Without a Cloak, 275
Woodspurge, The, 281
Youth, 329

Poetry—Narrative

Prisoner of Chillon, The, 516

Short Stories

Ambassador, The, 157
Ambitious Guest, The, 621
Blue Hotel, The, 682
Catbird Seat, The, 498
Cold, Cold Box, The, 647
Enemy, The, 52
Feels Like Spring, 345
German Refugee, The, 627
Going to Run All Night, 476
Grains of Paradise, The, 16
Mammon and the Archer, 152
Mateo Falcone, 29
Miriam, 547
Occurrence at Owl Creek Bridge, An, 539
One Ordinary Day, With Peanuts, 44
Open Window, The, 472
Paul's Case, 523
Pistol Shot, The, 673
Prelude, 662
Rocking-Horse Winner, The, 141
Scars of Honor, 335
Silent Snow, Secret Snow, 359
Sniper, The, 669
Stone Boy, The, 133
Story of the Good Little Boy, The, 355
Summer Tragedy, A, 562
To Build a Fire, 505
Veldt, The, 172
Vertical Ladder, The, 490

Wooing of Ariadne, The, 316
Wrath of the Raped, The, 616

Fine Art Index

Altdorfer, Albrecht, The Battle of Issus, 375
Beckmann, Max, Family Picture, 184
Bellows, George, Dempsey and Firpo, 12
Burchfield, Charles, An April Mood, 268
Chapin, James, Ruby Green Singing, 269
Cole, Thomas, The Architect's Dream, 314
Curry, John Steuart, Tornado over Kansas, 557
Daumier, Honoré, "You have the floor, explain yourself," 657
d'Harnoncourt, René, The Inn, 22
Dossi, Dosso, The Combat Between Roland and Rodomonte, 10
Egg, Augustus
    Past and Present No. 2, 186
    Past and Present No. 3, 266
El Greco, St. Martin and the Beggar, 11
Gauguin, Paul, The Big Tree, 187
Goya, Francisco
    The Folly of Fear, 265
    For Discovering the Motion of the Earth, 656
Grandville
    Order Reigns in Warsaw, 660
    Shadows, 656
Greenwood, John, Sea Captains Carousing in Surinam, 14
Gropper, William, Migration, 556
Gros, Jean Baron, Bataille d'Eylau, 381
Guglielmi, Louis, Terror in Brooklyn, 560
Homer, Winslow
    Eight Bells, x
    The Gulf Stream, 470
    Prisoners from the Front, 12
Hopper, Edward, Night Hawks, 15
Jamieson, Lieut. Mitchell, USNR, Frail Craft, 557

Koerner, Henry, My Parents, 182
Kupka, Franz, The Cog, 659
Legros, Alphonse, The Pit and the Pendulum, 561
LeNain, Louis, Peasants Interior, 183
Marsh, Reginald, Breadline—No One Has Starved, 658
Matisse, Henri, Woman Before an Aquarium, 267
Munch, Edward
    The Cry, 249
    The Sick Child, 184
Nast, Thomas, Military Glory, 661
Picasso, Pablo
    Family of Saltimbanques, 185
    The Tragedy, 558
Raffaelli, Jean François, Place St. Germain des Prés, Paris, 525
Rembrandt Van Rijn
    Return of the Prodigal Son, 131
    Samson Threatens His Father-in-law, 186
Remington, Frederic, Fight for the Waterhole, 14
Reni, Guido, David with the Head of Goliath, 10
Robinson, Boardman, Victory, 1916, 661
Rouault, Georges
    Samson at the Millstone, 561
    The Society Lady Fancies She Has a Reserved Seat in Heaven, 615
Rubens, Peter Paul, The Death of Maxentius, 376
Sharrer, Honoré, In the Parlor, 183
Tiepolo, Giovanni Domenico, Hannibal With the Head of His Brother Hasdrubal, 377
Tooker, George, The Subway, 266
Van Gogh, Vincent
    Courtyard of a Prison, 559
    Despair, 264
    The Good Samaritan, 2
Vickrey, Robert, Hopscotch, 265
Wyeth, Andrew, Chambered Nautilus, 269
Williamson, Stanford W., They Are All Gone Away, 284
Zalce, Alfredo, Mexico Transforms Itself Into a Great City, 658

Unknown artists
    Alexander the Great, 374
    Marc Antony, 385
    Marcus Brutus, 385
    Julius Caesar, 383

Octavius (Augustus) Caesar,
  462
Cortés, 13
The Crowning of Charle-
  magne, 379
Montezuma, 13
Pompey, 382

General Index

After Great Pain a Formal Feeling
  Comes, 281
Afternoon on a Hill, 293
Aiken, Conrad, 279, 308, 359
Alarm Clock, The, 39
Ambassador, The, 157
Ambitious Guest, The, 621
As I Grew Older, 331

Barney, William D., 261
Baybars, Taner, 274, 307
Beim, Jerrold, 4, 128
Berriault, Gina, 133, 245
Bierce, Ambrose, 539, 612
Black Panther, The, 270
Blake, William, 275, 307
Blue Hotel, The, 682
Bontemps, Arna, 562, 612
Boots, 469
Bradbury, Ray, 172, 246
Brautigan, Richard, 254, 305
Break, Break, Break, 289
Brooks, Gwendolyn, 613, 728
Browning, Robert, 286, 309
Buck, Pearl, 52, 129
Byron, Lord, 516, 611

Capote, Truman, 547, 612
Carman, Bliss, 296, 311
Catbird Seat, The, 498
Cather, Willa, 523, 612
Channing Way I, 38
Coatsworth, Elizabeth, 259, 305
Cold, Cold Box, The, 647
Corner, 40
Country Night, 258
Crane, Stephen, 276, 307, 682
Crapsey, Adelaide, 260, 306
Cullen, Countée, 271, 306
cummings, e.e., 294, 311

Daybreak in Alabama, 328

de la Mare, Walter, 293, 310
Death Is a Beautiful Car Parked
  Only, 254
Diary of Anne Frank, The, 189
Dickinson, Emily, 281, 299, 308
Dirge, A, 282
Does It Matter, 272
Dream Deferred, 333
Dream Keeper, The, 329
Dream Variation, 327
Dreams, 329
Dunbar, Paul Laurence, 250, 304

Eldorado, 255
Enemy, The, 52
Evans, Mari, 39, 129

Faces, 43
Fast, Howard, 647, 729
Fast Run in the Junkyard, 300
Feels Like Spring, 345
For Everything There Is a Season,
  247
Franklin, Benjamin, 348, 372
Frost, Robert, 259, 278, 305, 313

German Refugee, The, 627
Glaspell, Susan, 636, 729
Going to Run All Night, 476
Good Humor Man, 296
Goodrich, Frances, 189
Grains of Paradise, The, 16
Graves, Robert, 271, 306

Hackett, Albert, 189
Halper, Albert, 662, 730
Hardy, Thomas, 37, 128
Hate, 272
Hawthorne, Nathaniel, 621, 729
Hayden, Robert, 171, 245, 290
Heart, The, 276
Henry, O., 152, 245
Highway: Michigan, 253
His Enemy, His Friend, 66
Home Thoughts from Abroad, 286
Hopkins, Gerard Manley, 298, 311
House Fear, 259
House on the Hill, The, 284
Housman, A. E., 292, 310
Hovey, Richard, 251, 304
Hughes, Langston, 326-333, 372

I, Too, 330
In a Glass of Cider, 313
in Just-spring, 294
Inland, 286

Jackson, Shirley, 44, 129
Johnson, Dorothy, 335, 372
Joyce, James, 279, 308
Julius Caesar, 382

Kahn, Hannah, 252, 304

Kantor, MacKinlay, 616, 729
Kaplan, Milton, 345
Keats, John, 260, 306
Kipling, Rudyard, 469

Lady, The, 259
Lawrence, D. H., 141, 245
Let America Be America Again,
  332
London, Jack, 505, 611
Longfellow, Henry Wadsworth,
  287, 309

Malamud, Bernard, 627, 729
Mammon and the Archer, 152
Man He Killed, The, 37
Man That Corrupted Hadleyburg,
  The, 700
Masefield, John, 252, 285, 304
Mateo Falcone, 29
McConnel, Frances, 295, 311
McGinley, Phyllis, 275, 296, 307
McKay, Claude, 273, 307
McKuen, Rod, 38, 128
McLaughlin, Kathy, 262
Mérimée, Prosper, 29, 128
Millay, Edna St. Vincent, 251, 286,
  293, 304
Miracles, 297
Miriam, 547
Mood, 271
Morley, Chistopher, 298, 312
Music I Heard, 279
My Lost Youth, 287
My November Guest, 278

Newhouse, Edward, 157, 245
Nichols, Jeannette, 300
Noise of Waters, The, 279

Occurrence at Owl Creek Bridge,
  An, 539
O'Flaherty, Liam, 669, 730
Oft-Repeated Dream, The, 259
One Ordinary Day, With Peanuts,
  44
Open Window, The, 472
Orwell, George, 484, 611

Panther Possible, The, 261
Parable of the Good Samaritan,
  The, 1
Parable of the Prodigal Son, The,
  130
Paul's Case, 523
Pearl, The, 570
Petrakis, Harry Mark, 316, 371
Pied Beauty, 298
Pistol Shot, The, 673
Poe, Edgar Allan, 255, 305
Poison Tree, A, 275
Pomeroy, Ralph, 40, 129
Precious Words, 299

Prelude, 662
Prisoner of Chillon, The, 516
Project of Arriving at Moral Perfection, 348
Pushkin, Alexander, 673, 730

Reveille, 292
Ride a Wild Horse, 252
Robinson, E. A., 284, 309
Robinson, Selma, 258, 305
Rocking-Horse Winner, The, 141
Roethke, Theodore, 253, 305
Rossetti, Dante Gabriel, 281, 308

Saki, 472, 610
Sansom, William, 490, 611
Sassoon, Siegfried, 272, 306
Scars of Honor, 335
Sea Fever, 252
Shakespeare, William, 299, 382, 467
Shelley, Percy Bysshe, 282, 309
Shooting an Elephant, 484
Silent Snow, Secret Snow, 359
Silver, 293
Smells, 298
Sniper, The, 669
Sonnet CVI, 299
Souvenir de Londres, 170
Spender, Stephen, 170, 245
Spring, 251
Steinbeck, John, 570, 612
Stephens, James, 272, 306
Stone Boy, The, 133
Stopover in Querétaro, 4
Story of the Good Little Boy, The, 355
Street, James, 16, 128
Suicide Pond, 262
Summer Tragedy, A, 562
Suppressed Desires, 636
Sylvester, Harry, 476, 611
Sympathy, 250

Teasdale, Sara, 43, 129
Tennyson, Alfred, Lord, 289, 310
Those Winter Sundays, 290
Thurber, James, 498, 611
To Build a Fire, 505
Travel, 251
Traveler's Curse After Misdirection, The, 271
Tunis, John, 66, 129
Twain, Mark, 355, 372, 700, 730

Vagabond Song, A, 296
Veldt, The, 172
Velvet Shoes, 294
Vertical Ladder, The, 490

Warning, The, 260
Waves Against a Dog, 274
We Real Cool, 613

West Wind, The, 285
Wheelock, John Hall, 270, 306
When I Have Fears That I May Cease to Be, 260
Whipping, The, 171
White House, The, 273
Whitman, Walt, 297, 311
Widow, The, 280
Wild Blackberries, 295
Williams, Miller, 280, 308
Without a Cloak, 275
Woodspurge, The, 281
Wooing of Ariadne, The, 316
Wrath of the Raped, The, 616
Wylie, Elinor, 294, 310

Youth, 329

Illustration Sources

Acknowledgment is gratefully made to the following museums, galleries, collectors, libraries, photo collections, etc., for their gracious and generous assistance, making possible the reproduction of the art and documentary material for this text.

Key for positions: T (top), L (left), C (center), R (right), B (bottom), and any combination of these, such as TRC (top right center).

Addison Gallery of American Art, Phillips Academy, Andover, Massachusetts: x
Alinari Collection: 382, 383, 385, 462
Archives Photographiques, Paris: 374
Arizona State University: 536
Art Institute of Chicago: 15, Friends of American Art Collection; 187, Gift of Kate L. Brewster; 267, Helen Birch Bartlett Memorial Collection
Art Reference: 2, 264, Kröller Müller Museum, Otterlo; 13L & 13R, Museo de America, Madrid; 184B, National Gallery, Oslo; 186B, Staatliche Museum, Berlin; 375, Alte Pinakothek, Munich; 376T, courtesy of the trustees of the Wallace Collection; 377, Kunsthistorisches Museum, Vienna
Bibliotheque Nationale, Paris: 656B, 660
Brown Brothers: 376BL, 376BR
Columbia University Library, New York: 661B, reproduced from The Masses Oct. 1916
d'Harnoncourt, Mrs. Sara: 22
Dick Smith: 362
Editorial Projects, Inc. 659, from Les Temps Nouveaux. Reprinted from The Indignant Eye by Ralph E. Shikes. Published by Beacon Press, 1969
Fred Fehl: 197, 201, 231, 237, 240
Collection of Mr. & Mrs. Lawrence Fleischman: 265B
Folger Library, model by John Cranford Adams and Irwin Smith: 466
French Government Tourist Office: 30
Illustrations by Hal Frenck: 6, 45, 69, 110, 317, 323, 474, 479, 540, 548, 553, 564, 628, 654, 676
George Eastman House: 154, from the collection of Dr. G. L. Howe, Rochester
Giraudon, Paris: 183T, 379, 381, 559
Graphic Presentation Services, Inc.: 67
The Hackley Art Gallery: 557
I.B.M. Art Collection: 599
Henry Koener: 182
Los Angeles County Museum of Art: 561T
Magnum Photos, Inc.: 326
Metropolitan Museum of Art: 12T, Mrs. Frank B. Porter, 1922; 525, Wolfe Fund, 1908; 470, Wolfe Fund, 1906; 658B, Whittelsey Fund, 1946
Collection of Mr. & Mrs. Robert Montgomery: 269
Museo del Prado, Madrid: 656TR
Museum of Fine Arts, Boston: 657
Museum of Fine Arts, Houston: 14T, Hogg Brothers Collection
Museum of Modern Art: 184T, 615
Museum of Modern Art Film Library: 572, 591
National Gallery of Art, Washington, D.C.: 131, 185, 558, Chester Dale Collection; 249, 265T, Rosenwald Collection; 11, Widener Collection
Netherlands Information Service: 190, 191, 192

2 3 4 5 6 7 8 9 10 KPKP 82 81 80 79 78 77 76 75 74 73